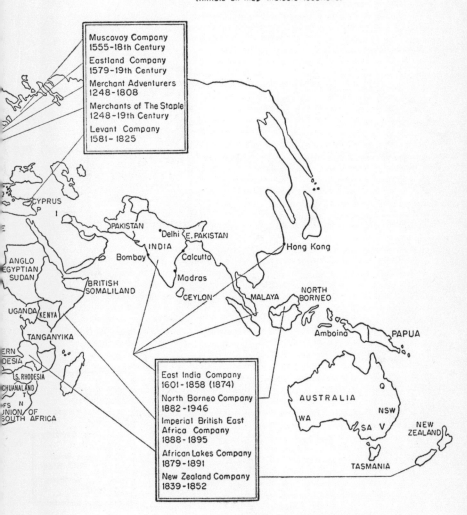

LOSSES, DATES OF AQUISITION AND LOSS

Normandy, 1066-1216, 1415-1436
Aquitaine, 1054-1453
Calais, 1347-1558
Palestine, 1917-1948
United States of America, 1607-1783
Corsica, 1795-1797
Hanover, 1714-1837

Egypt, 1914-1922 (1936)
Iraq, 1917-1932
Burma, 1826-1947
Minorca, 1708-1757, 1762-1783
Eire, 1170-1949
Ionian Islands, 1815-1867

(Initials on map indicate locations)

Muscovoy Company
1555-18th Century

Eastland Company
1579-19th Century

Merchant Adventurers
1248-1808

Merchants of The Staple
1248-19th Century

Levant Company
1581-1825

CYPRUS
P

PAKISTAN

•Delhi E. PAKISTAN

INDIA

Bombay   Calcutta

ANGLO
EGYPTIAN
SUDAN

BRITISH
SOMALILAND   Madras

CEYLON   MALAYA

NORTH
BORNEO

Hong Kong

Amboina   PAPUA

UGANDA KENYA

TANGANYIKA

ERN
DESIA

S. RHODESIA

CHUANALAND   T

FS   N

UNION OF
SOUTH AFRICA

East India Company
1601-1858 (1874)

North Borneo Company
1882-1946

Imperial British East
Africa Company
1888-1895

African Lakes Company
1879-1891

New Zealand Company
1839-1852

AUSTRALIA

WA

Q

NSW

SA V

TASMANIA

NEW
ZEALAND

PROVINCES OF SOUTH AFRICA

C - Cape
T - Transvaal

OFS - Orange Free State
N - Natal

STATES OF AUSTRALIA

WA - Western Australia
SA - South Australia
V - Victoria

NSW - New South Wales
Q - Queensland

McGRAW-HILL SERIES IN HISTORY

BRITAIN, HER PEOPLES
AND THE COMMONWEALTH

McGRAW-HILL SERIES IN HISTORY

BRITAIN, HER PEOPLES
AND THE COMMONWEALTH

ROBERT B. ECKLES

Associate Professor of History
Purdue University

RICHARD W. HALE, Jr.

Curator of Canadian History and Literature
Harvard College Library

NEW YORK   TORONTO   LONDON

McGRAW-HILL BOOK COMPANY, INC.

1954

PREFACE

In writing this history the authors try to tell what has happened to the British in such a way that students in the United States will have some of their questions answered about this remarkable and great people. This book is concerned with problems of political, imperial and colonial, economic, and foreign-relations history, as well as social history. Emphasis has been given the social, economic, imperial, and foreign-affairs stories of the last two hundred and fifty years. It is hoped that a better understanding of modern Britain will come from reading this book.

This book may better serve its purpose if attention is called to certain features of its structure and method. In order to gain flexibility, a general introduction precedes all the parts except the first and last. Not only can the reader begin the book at any one of the parts, but Chapter 17 has been so written as to provide a starting point as well. This allows courses to use the common beginnings of 1688 (Chapter 17), 1782, and 1832, as well as that of 1704 (Part II), which has been suggested as a new teaching device. Since all the parts except the first and last are treated topically, a wide choice of teaching emphases should be possible. In the use of detail, this has been the rule followed: Where information is readily available, conciseness has been the aim, together with the sort of explanation that may help the novice in English history. Where information is less readily available, supporting evidence is provided; hence the greater detail on economics, social history, foreign affairs, and the Empire and Commonwealth. It is hoped that this structure and method will make this volume easy to integrate into courses, and valuable as background reading for English literature.

It is appropriate to thank some of those who have read and given assistance in criticizing the manuscript. Professors C. H. McIlwain and David Owen of Harvard have been most helpful in their criticisms. For reading segments of the book and offering suggestions, appreciation is given to Professor Robert Moody of Boston University and Professor J. A. Estey of Purdue University. Professor Thomas H. Smith of Purdue

University has been more than generous in allowing the authors to make use of statistics and information contained in his dissertation for the doctor's degree. Lastly, the authors feel a deep sense of appreciation for the past help and instruction of their teacher in modern British history, the late Professor Wilbur C. Abbott of Harvard University. If this book satisfies the standard that he set for his students, then they are content.

The authors are indebted to Mrs. Harold E. Witig, Mrs. Warren Williams, Mrs. Joseph Alexander, and Mrs. David Kraus for their patient willingness to help in the preparation of this manuscript, and to David Kraus and Theodore M. Brown for drafting the end-paper map and that on page 4.

Textbooks are inevitably built upon the work of other historians; for example, in this book the quotations on pages 97 and 184, taken respectively from the *Calendar of State Papers, Spanish,* and the *Dropmere Papers,* but brought to the authors' attention by A. L. Rowse's *England of Elizabeth* and G. M. Trevelyan's *Blenheim.* Public documents too numerous to mention have also provided information. While the authors believe that some of their interpretations are original and some are original interpretations of the interpretations of others, they have attempted to indicate the sources they have used within limitations of space, in text or bibliography.

In addition, specific acknowledgments for permission to use or quote copyright material are due the following publishers: Henry Holt and Company, Inc., pages 193, 194, 263, 374, 375, 379, 380, 381, 386, 505, 506, 659, 660, from *An Economic History of England,* by Frederick C. Dietz (1940). Yale University Press, on pages 354, 502, and 504, from *Europe, the World's Banker,* by Herbert Feis (1930). Gerald Duckworth & Co., Ltd., London, on pages 270, 378, 379, 380, 394, 395, 500, 502, 503, 504, 652, 653, 654, 656, 657, from *A Hundred Years of Economic Development in Great Britain,* by G. P. Jones and A. G. Pool. Houghton Mifflin Company, on page 380, from *An Introduction to the Industrial History of England,* by A. P. Usher (1920). Cassell & Co., Ltd., London, and Houghton Mifflin Company, on page 744, from *Hinge of Fate,* by Sir Winston Churchill (1950). New York *World Telegram and Sun,* on pages 669, 670, and 763, from the *World Almanac* for 1952 (1951). Cambridge University Press, on pages 377, 381, 386, 387, 494, 495, 497, 500, 505, 513, from *An Economic History of Modern Britain,* by Sir John Clapham (3 vols., 1930–1938). Methuen & Co., Ltd., London, on pages 640, 641, 642, 643, 645, 646, 647, 648, 649, 650, and tables on pages 644, 650, and 651, from *An Economic Geography of Great Britain,* by Wilfred Smith (1949). Routledge and Kegan Paul, Ltd., London, on pages 257, 259, 262, and 378, from the *Dictionary of Statistics* (4th rev. ed.), by Michael G. Mulhall (1898); and on page 502, from Webb's *Supplement* (1911). Oxford University Press, on page 269, from *Early Victorian England,* G. M. Young (Ed.) (1934); on page 267, from *The Age of Reform, 1815–1870,* by Sir Ernest Woodward (1938); on pages 507 and 508, from *England, 1870–1914,* by R. C. K. Ensor (1938); on pages 622 and 623, from *Consequences of the War to Great Britain,* by Francis W. Hirst (1934); on pages 167 and 459, from *Dictionary of National Biography* (articles James Francis Edward Stuart and Bentinck, Lord William Cavendish). Longmans, Green & Co., Inc., London, on page 294, from *A History of England in the Eighteenth Century,* by W. E. H. Lecky (1887); on page 367, from *English Farming Past and Present,* by R. E. Prothero (Lord Ernle) (1912); Columbia University Press, on page 277, from *Victorian Prelude,* by M. J. Quinlan (1941). Encyclopaedia Britannica, on page 257, from Vol. XXI of the 11th Edition and from Vol. XIV of the 14th Edition. University of California Press, on page 748, from *Crisis in Britain,* by Robert A. Brady (1950). University of Chicago Press, on page 260, from the *Journal of Modern History,* Vol. XIX, No. 2 (1949). Macmillan & Co., Ltd., London, on page 660, from *National Income and Outlay,* by Colin Clark (1951). Macmillan & Co., Ltd., London, and St. Martin's Press, New York, on pages 317 and 705, from *Life of Lord Lloyd,* by Colin Forbes Adam (1948). Hutchinson & Co., Ltd., London, on pages 622 and 730, from *Arthur James Balfour,* by Blanche E. C. Dugdale (1936).

Also Thomas H. Smith for the use of certain tables and information found in Chapter 44 and taken from his unpublished thesis for the University of Wisconsin, *Economic Recovery in the United States and Great Britain during the 1930's.* McGraw-Hill Book Company, Inc., New York, for material and statistics used in Chapter 50, from *Europe from 1914 to the Present,* by Victor L. Albjerg and Marguerite H. Albjerg (1951). Jonathan Cape, Ltd., and Houghton Mifflin Company, for the transcription by the author of Sloan manuscript 2497, fol. 47, and its ascription to the elder Sir Richard Grenville, on page 122, from *Sir Richard Grenville of the Revenge,* by A. L. Rowse (1937). British Library of Information for the map on page 376 and for the use of their Commonwealth map as a basis for the end-paper map.

In division of the labor of writing, Mr. Hale prepared the introductory chapters and those on imperial and foreign-policy history. Mr. Eckles is responsible for the general plan of the book and the chapters on political, social, and economic history. For the opinions and points of view as well as the errors the authors are jointly responsible.

Robert B. Eckles
Richard W. Hale, Jr.

CONTENTS

PART III

The Transition to the Middle Class, 1783–1832

PART IV

The Age of Free Trade, 1832–1870

PART V

The Transition to Collectivism, 1870–1914

1

THE BACKGROUND OF ENGLISH HISTORY

Where should English history start? Such a question can lead into arguments over the meaning of "history." Perhaps, therefore, it had better be rephrased. Of three frequently employed definitions of the starting point of history—the first written record, the first arrival of the present inhabitants, the first known event that has directly influenced the life of the present inhabitants—which will be most useful for the modern reader? The answer seems clear. To choose the first written record leads to a dispute as to which written record is the first—that of the Roman invader Julius Caesar, 55 B.C.; that of the Greek explorer Pytheas, about 325 B.C.; or conjectural earlier references to the British Isles that are now lost, but whose existence is inferred. To choose the arrival of the Angles, Saxons, and Jutes leads to fascinating but complex decisions about the validity of apparently conflicting evidence—whether to trust on certain points the chronicles of monks, the late records of Roman occupation, or the findings of archaeologists. Such matters should be dealt with at length or not at all. Furthermore, when considering such matters, one must sooner or later come back to the geography and the mineral wealth of England. Therefore, the third choice will be made, and this history will start with the geological events that gave England her natural resources and a commanding strategic position.

Without any attempt at geological dating, the first event, then, in English history would seem to be whatever caused tin and iron, copper and zinc, to enter the subsoil of the future British Isles, perhaps when the earth was still a molten mass. Another event would be the crumbling of rocks into fertile soil, from which would grow crops and grass for grazing. Yet a third event would be when, after a period of tropical climate, masses of vegetation were crushed under newly formed mountains to make coal. Thus it was that the British Isles obtained the raw materials needed for their future—copper and tin to smelt together in the

1

Bronze Age, iron to be smelted either by charcoal or coal into steel, wheat which until about 1750 Britain exported to Europe.

Sometime after these events there occurred what must be considered the greatest event in English history. What are now the North Sea and the English Channel sank, and Great Britain became an island. In soil, in natural resources such as tin, iron, and coal, France, north of the Loire, and England, south of the Pennines, remained much the same. Indeed, the science of geology was founded by men who compared layers of rock around Paris and around London and found them to be identical. But twenty-one miles of salt water have made a great difference between the histories of the two countries. Above all other things, England's insularity has controlled her destiny.

Consequently, by 20,000 B.C. or so, the prominent physical features of Great Britain had become much what they are now, except for swamp drainage, forest clearance, and the silting up of some harbors on the south coast. The island Pytheas and Caesar came to is much the same as the island Napoleon and Hitler did not come to. Its history, from Pytheas to Hitler, has turned on certain geographical facts. If one made a high-altitude flight over Great Britain that covered the three corners— Goodwin Sands at the southeast, Lands End at the southwest, John o' Groat's House at the north—one would see some history-making places, which embody those geographical facts: the famous "White Cliffs of Dover," the estuaries of the Thames and the Solent, the Downs, the Midland Plain that runs from the Bristol Channel to the Wash, the Eastern Plain, the Fens, the Breckland of East Anglia, the Cambrian Mountains of Wales, the Pennine Hills which are the "backbone of England," the Cheviot Hills, and the Lowlands and Highlands of Scotland. A mention of some events suggested by an aerial view of these places may serve to show certain constant factors in English history.

One look at the "White Cliffs of Dover" and the steep zigzag path the train takes climbing up from the seaport at their foot will explain why Caesar failed to make a landing there and why Dover is a port for passengers and not for freight. The similar cliffs at Cape Gris-Nez, in France, are equally unscalable and run on to the south, as the Canadians found to their cost at Dieppe in 1942. That is why both King Edward I of England and Field Marshal Montgomery had to capture Calais from the land side. The height of these two sets of cliffs, for military purposes, really makes England and France far more than twenty-one miles apart —or did, till Blériot flew the Channel in 1909. The invasion routes and freight traffic routes are longer and go from the estuaries of the Seine and Schelde to the Solent (or Pevensey) and the Thames. The southern route took Caesar and William the Conqueror into England, Henry V and Eisenhower into France. The northern one took the men back from

Dunkirk and afforded supplies both to Winston Churchill's ancestor, John, Duke of Marlborough, and to General Eisenhower, once he had reached Belgium.

The Solent and Southampton Water (its continuation inland behind the Isle of Wight) have replaced the old ports of South England for two reasons. One is that the mouths of the old ports have been filled up by the action of the tides in the English Channel. What were once open harbors and large bays are now narrow inlets to tidal flats. To this there is one exception; the British Navy has kept Portsmouth clear, to be a naval base. The other reason is the increase in size of ships. Even had they not filled up, the old ports could not have held liners like the *Queen Mary*, which can come up Southampton Water.

But the Solent cannot handle traffic; it is a sort of special side door to England. The real way in, the way Göring's bombers went night after night in the Battle of Britain, is up the Thames estuary. There, past the naval bases of Sheerness on the north and Chatham on the south, past the pilot town of Gravesend, in peacetime and even in wartime, ships flow steadily up to the London docks. This is the greatest transshipping area in the world because so many vessels are going to and from London that it is quicker to send goods there, to be put on an outgoing vessel almost at once, than to wait for some vessel to turn up that may be going directly to the destination to which one is sending. Just above the docks London Bridge stands, where a bridge has always stood since the first one was built, the lowest point at which one can cross over the Thames. Being the head of navigation and river crossing has made London what it is—the largest city in the world and, for many years, the banking and business center of the world as well.

South of the Thames Valley are the Downs; north of it, the Chiltern and Cotswold Hills. They are sheep-raising country, though Kent, as such, is a garden spot, where hops are raised and made ready to brew into English beer and ale. But the aviator will not see vineyards, however keen-sighted he may be, for Great Britain is the same latitude as Labrador, and grapes cannot grow there. That is why England has to import its wine. On the other hand, the way the Gulf Stream crosses the Atlantic to skirt the island allows most of the crops to flourish there that can be found in France. On these hills, especially those of Sussex and Buckinghamshire, grew the oaks that made the "wooden walls" of Nelson's navy. North of these hills is a great plain, probably looking from the air pretty much the same all the way across England. From the east, this is entered not so much by a river valley as by a swamp, a broad estuary called the Wash. The land at the end of the Wash is so like Holland that the "riding" of Lincolnshire that covers most of it is called "Holland."

However, if an aviator would not tell you that there were differences

A. Caesar's Landing, 55 B.C.   B. Caesar's Landing, 54 B.C.   C. Goodwin Sands

1. Stamford Bridge, 1066	9. Marston Moor, 1644
2. Hastings, 1066	10. Naseby, 1645
3. Evesham, 1264	11. Dunbar, 1650
4. Lewes, 1265	12. Worcester, 1651
5. Stirling Bridge, 1297	13. Boyne, 1690
6. Bannockburn, 1314	14. Aughrim, 1691
7. Bosworth, 1485	15. Sheriffmuir, 1715
8. Edge Hill, 1642	16. Culloden, 1746

in the eastern plain, a farmer would. The Breckland of East Anglia, where Norfolk, Suffolk, and Essex jut out between the Thames and the Wash, is still waste, though now marked up with concrete runways and the airfields from which the B-17's by day and the Lancasters by night bombed Germany. Even the edges of this land were waste, more or less, until certain English landlords, such as Jethro Tull, Coke of Norfolk, and "Turnip" Townshend, in the eighteenth century, discovered how to get crops from them by new methods which constituted an "agricultural revolution" and freed men from the land to work in industry in the cities. On the other hand, the plains of Lincolnshire, Leicestershire, Northamptonshire, and Warwickshire are extremely fertile. These are called "the Shires" as against the "Home Counties" around London. Here are the typical English farmers, still regular John Bulls. Here are the famous packs of foxhounds, whose masters are considered more important, by some people, than the Prime Minister. It is from this region that there still come the "country gentlemen" who continue to play so large a part in ruling a now predominantly industrial country.

What has been described so far is agricultural south England, not the mountainous west and north. The sort of dagger that points out southwest into the Atlantic is Cornwall, where are the tin mines whose wealth first brought traders to England. Across the Bristol Channel are the higher mountains of Wales, the Cambrian Mountains, of which Snowdon is the highest in the British Isles. It was from the ports of Devon and from Bristol that adventurers in the reign of Elizabeth I set out to the Americas —the explorers John and Sebastian Cabot, the sea dogs Sir Francis Drake and Sir John Hawkins, and the empire builders Walter Raleigh and Humphrey Gilbert. Cornwall, and especially Wales, have been the sanctuaries where the natives of England took refuge from partial conquests, whether by Roman or by Saxon. From Cornwall, Brittany was founded; and Cornish was a separate language up until it died out around 1800. Welsh is still a separate language, in spite of all the coal mined and shipped out from Cardiff, which might have opened the country. But Wales is apart from England. Its mountains have remained an effective barrier to penetration. Armies of conquest have entered by the north and south coasts, but only with difficulty. New cultures, similarly, have entered Wales slowly. The range of hills that has made English history is the Pennines. These run south from the Scottish border, to give England a sort of backbone. At their south end, near Birmingham, are the coal and iron deposits, close together, which made Birmingham the steel center of the world in its day. Farther north is the hilly county of Yorkshire, famous for its woolen mills, with its capital, York (Eboracum in Roman times), once the capital of England and still the seat of England's second archbishopric. This lies east of the Pennines. West of them is Lancashire.

Until less than two hundred years ago this was a country district. In 1745, when "Bonnie Prince Charlie" marched down from Scotland, his followers composed a song about their welcome at the pleasant green town of Manchester. By 1850, Manchester was black with factory smoke, so black it is an English national joke that the sun never shines there. Manchester had become the cotton center of the world and the seat of a political program of free trade and world industrialization called Manchesterism, which largely guided English policy for many years thereafter. The Pennine Hills did this, along with Indian cotton fiber, and later American cotton. To spin cotton thread, intense moisture is needed to make the fibers hold together at the crucial moment when they are being twisted. Modern factories have special rooms filled with steamy air to carry out this process. In Manchester, such rooms are not needed. The Pennine Hills condense the west winds from the Irish Sea into all the fog and moisture for which one can ask.

North of the Pennines, running east and west, are the Cheviot Hills, above the Tweed River. (It is noticeable how many names of woolen cloths come from English places.) These make the real division between England and Scotland. To get around those hills are two narrow invasion routes, the eastern blocked by the Scottish fortress of Dunbar and the English one of Durham, and the western blocked by the English fortress of Carlisle. Because the invasion routes have been so narrow, and because the Lowlands of Scotland are not rich, it has never been worth the time of the English to conquer Scotland, considering how hard the Scots made it for them. The same effort applied elsewhere got far more results. At the end, Scotland may be said to have conquered England when James VI of Scotland inherited the throne and became James I (of Bible fame) of England.

In the narrow plain of the Lowlands, the kings of Scotland could have their chief power and from there try to control the turbulent lords of the borders and the wild tribes of the Highlands. For the Highland line cuts across Scotland from southwest and Argyll, where the Campbell clan lives, to the Frasers of the northeast. It is a line so marked that one can sit on the actual edge of the Highlands and look at the Lowlands at one's feet. In front are plains where a farmer can make a living. Behind are hills most suitable for deer hunting, where, until after 1745, clans lived almost the same life as barbaric tribes of Afghanistan or Nepal. In these hills, titles are not feudal, but tribal. The Duke of Argyll is spoken of as MacCalein Mor (the Big Man). There the British Army raises what are almost family regiments, like the Cameron or Argyll and Sutherland Highlanders, and landowners are spoken of by the names of their properties. Yet wild as these hills are, they have provided their share of notable men, such as Prime Minister Ramsay MacDonald. The chief sign of the out-of-the-wayness of the Highlands is that there some of the inhabitants today speak a language older than Welsh, the Gaelic.

But the Highlands and Wales are not the only sanctuaries in the British Isles. "John Bull's Other Island," Ireland—or, as the Irish now call three-quarters of it, Eire—is equally a sanctuary. In politics, language, and religion, Ireland is the opposite of England. For that there is a good geographical reason. Ireland is one step beyond England, the natural place to find those driven out of England. Yet the island has scanty natural resources, except a fertile soil, and slight natural barriers. Ireland has no fuel for manufacturing, since peat is not a good substitute for coal. That is why she is trying so hard to develop the waterpower on the Shannon River. She does have a fertile soil, which is why she ate so well during World War II. As she has no high mountains but is a plain surrounded by a ring of low hills, invasion is easy. That is why her independence has been hard to win and is, therefore, very precious to her. But above all, Ireland is cut off from Europe by Great Britain. That is why her policies have had to fit England's or go against them. Ireland is automatically tied in with England, whether or not it pleases either.

The main facts of England's geography can be stated thus: England has one natural external military barrier, the Channel, which keeps her independent. She has no internal barrier, a fact which keeps her unified. She has had many products which have at different times had different uses—tin from Cornwall, the cereal crops of the great Central Plain, iron, wool, coal, and, because of a climate very favorable for spinning cotton cloth, though the raw cotton had to come from India or the United States, a textile industry. England has also had to deal with three large-scale "sanctuaries"—Wales, Scotland, and Ireland—where defeated peoples could support themselves. In one way, Scotland has a sanctuary within a sanctuary, since Scotland is barred off from England and the Highlands are barred off from the Lowlands.

Since natural resources matter little without men to use them, let us turn to the different strains of men that moved into Britain, one after another. It now seems clear that when the Celtic peoples moved into Europe, two waves entered the British Isles. One, which spoke Gaelic, was driven by its successors, who spoke Brythonic, into the sanctuaries, that is, Scotland and Ireland, where Gaelic is still spoken. Both were users of bronze and therefore miners of tin, but they were different in burial customs, shape of the head, and other matters which have left clues for archaeologists. The great stone altars of Stonehenge, near Salisbury, were probably their work. It is these Gaels and Britons who were described by the earliest explorers from the Mediterranean, such as Pytheas. After them, about 200 B.C., came a third wave, some users of iron, who have been identified with the tribe of Belgae, from modern

Belgium. As these men began to take over the island, another invader came to England, Gaius Julius Caesar, Roman proconsul in Gaul.

Caesar was an imperialist, like many a leader of the future British Empire. He followed the policy that John Lawrence and John Nicholson were to make so effective in India at the time of the Mutiny, that of going so far with a small force that everyone thought it invincible. Caesar's method of defending his province in South Gaul was to attack the Belgae in the north, and to go further and chastise the Belgae in Britain for aiding their mainland cousins. Since he wrote of his exploits as a sort of political campaign document, written history came with him to England in 55 B.C.

In actual fact, Caesar's landings did not do him much credit. His first attempt in 55 B.C. was made under the cliffs of Dover. That was repelled by a body of British cavalry, who rode along the tops of the cliffs and came down to fight him at each beach. However, as he moved north, he found it possible to get ashore at the Isle of Thanet. There, he defeated his immediate opponents and reembarked, having taught the Belgae that if they attacked him, he would attack back. His worst foe was the tide in the English Channel, which nearly swept his ships away. Being accustomed to the Mediterranean, he had not pulled them high enough on the beach. In 54 B.C., he came again. This time, he landed south of the cliff barrier, just about where William the Conqueror did later on, and followed a version of the latter's route from Pevensey and Hastings in Sussex to cross the Thames west of London. Caesar then attacked and burned the chief British city where Colchester now is. The kings of the British tribes paid him tribute as long as he stayed on the island, and even after stopping payment, they remained in awe of Rome. Caesar had accomplished something by his raid. He had stopped British meddling in the Romanized province of Gaul, and he had made the British look to Rome for ideas.

That last fact the archaeologists know, for they have found British coins made in copy of Roman ones and have fairly good grounds for believing that a British king made a bridge with Roman methods on the site of the present London Bridge, thus starting London's rise as a combined seaport and river crossing.

Rome left Britain alone for nearly a century after Caesar's raid. Then, in A.D. 43, the Emperor Claudius sent over his general Plautius, who rapidly conquered the main part of the island and the Cornish tin mines and went on to Wales to reduce one refuge of potential rebels. A colony of native priests, or Druids, on the island of Anglesey on the northwest corner of Wales, was wiped out. Roman cruelty caused a revolt led by a queen, whom poets call Boadicea, historians Boudicca, who is sometimes romantically thought of as the first British patriot. This revolt, in A.D. 60, was put down with bloody thoroughness and mass executions.

Then the Roman generals turned to the northern refuge of the British and Picts, or "Painted People," modern Scotland. We know most of the feats of one general, Agricola, since his son-in-law, the historian Tacitus, wrote a biography of him. Even discounting Tacitus's praise, it is likely that Agricola's victory, Mons Graupius, in A.D. 84, finished the Roman conquest. What made that conquest secure was the work of the Emperor Hadrian, who sealed off the Picts of Scotland by building his famous wall. This boundary marker ran from Carlisle along the Cheviot Hills to the Tyne River, and then along its north bank to the North Sea. For a time, when Antoninus Pius was emperor, the Romans tried to hold a shorter line farther north between the Firths of Forth and Clyde, but this was given up. Order was maintained by three legions, one at Chester (note the present pronunciation of the Roman *castra* or camp) to overawe Wales, one at Carlisle to overawe Scotland and garrison the wall, and one at York, the Roman capital, as a strategic reserve. These dispositions gave Roman Britain three hundred years of peace and prosperity.

The Romans brought certain valuable things to Britain. First of all, they brought their roads, which ran straight across the country and were smooth and well surfaced. These roads were much better than any built till very modern times, as is shown by the fact that a message sent from York to Rome in those days went faster than the one sent in 1834 from London to Rome to summon Sir Robert Peel to be Prime Minister. Next, the Romans built cities, as they did wherever they went. Most of the cities built in Britain were military centers, at least at first. That can be told from their names, such as Chester, Lancaster, Doncaster, Dorchester, Cirencester, Colchester, and Chichester. Thirdly, they brought in improved knowledge of the arts and crafts, raising the civilization of the native Britons. But Rome brought Britain very little that was lasting, except roads. At that, Fosse Way (the road from Exeter to Lincoln) is now utterly abandoned. The Great West Road to Exeter, the Great North Road to York, Watling Street to Chester, though still the sites of main traffic arteries out of London, are now completely rebuilt. Cities have Roman names, but nothing else Roman about them. Arts and crafts have left the Romans far behind. For Rome did not bring into Britain what she brought into Gaul—a Roman population. Though much land was cleared for the Roman villas, her agricultural methods did not stay. Indeed, only the conversion of great numbers of the British to Christianity, with which the name of the Roman martyr, St. Alban, has connection, left an important mark on Britain.

However, from A.D. 60 to 360, Britain had peace and importance. From 287 to 293, she was the site of a small naval empire, set up and for a while maintained by sea power by the rebel Carausius. In 306, York was the starting place for the campaign by which Constantine made himself emperor. As late as 350, new villas were being built in Britain, when the rest of the empire had begun to grow poor and collapse.

This prosperity rested on the security given by the three legions permanently stationed in Britain. After 360, that security grew less. The usual strategic reserve stationed at York had to be moved south and stationed on the coast of Essex, to repel the Saxons who were raiding from across the North Sea. A special official, the Count of the Saxon Shore, was appointed to command the region of danger from the Wash to the Solent. Year by year, his task grew more difficult. The Britons realized this, and from 382 on they moved across the Channel to the peninsula then known as Armorica, in such numbers that they changed its name to Brittany. Finally, in 407, the legions were withdrawn, either in whole or in part, to fight in a civil war and to repel the Visigothic invasion of Italy. Then, from the early fifth century, the story of Roman Britain becomes hazy. Written records are scarce and increasingly confusing, since the invading Anglo-Saxons could not write (except by the cumbersome and little used runic alphabet), and all that can be done is to try to piece together the gossip about England that was written down in histories by monks on the Continent and official records of the later Roman Empire. The travels of the religious philosopher Pelagius and the writings of Fastidius prove that Britain could produce men who could challenge St. Augustine and write graceful and serious essays "On the Christian Life." St. Patrick, the son of a Christian landed gentleman, was a product of this Roman British culture. But it is evident that under pressure of both Saxon and Celtic raids not only the high standards represented by these men were lost, but also the government of the Roman province was changed into little principalities or districts, increasingly subject to the whims of Celtic warrior chieftains.

Between monkish gossip and archaeology, scholars have worked out a reconstruction of events of these dark years which seems to confirm three popular legends—that of St. Germanus; that of Vortigern, Hengist, and Horsa; and above all that of King Arthur. Up to the year 451, Roman Gaul was so hard pressed by fear of invasion by Attila the Hun that it could spare no troops. But from Gaul came unexpected aid for Britain in the person of the ex-soldier missionary, St. Germanus. In 447, just by persuading the Britons to ambush an attack by the Picts, St. Germanus won a bloodless victory, the shout of "Hallelujah!" when they rushed to charge being enough to scare their enemies away. But this was not enough to get defense, and, so the Anglo-Saxon Chronicles tell us, King Vortigern summoned in two leaders of the Jutes, Hengist and Horsa, to defend Kent against other invaders, only to have them take over Kent themselves and kill him. But then, after Attila the Hun had been decisively defeated at Châlons in 451, help could be sent to Britain from Gaul. It would seem reasonable to believe that to help the local Roman resistance leader, Ambrosius Aurelianus, came armored cavalry raised and led by one Arthur, perhaps in Latin named Artorius. This cavalry, in twelve battles all over the island, swept the invaders back to the sea, and remained a legend to the Britons. Archaeology, with its insistence that the Angles and Saxons and Jutes took a long time to advance inland and that at first they marched by the uplands and avoided the towns, gives support to this suggestion. It further explains how a mounted warrior in armor could become the national hero of the Britons and eventually, in the guise of a medieval knight, become the subject of a cycle of legends.

But what is important, whether or not this trio of theories is correct, is that pagan Angles, Saxons, and Jutes moved into Britain between 446 and some date near 500, and in a slow but steady conquest so changed the population of the southern half of the island that it got the name of England. In doing this, though it is believed that they did not wipe out the Britons but absorbed them, they made their language the dominant language and their customs the dominant customs. Therefore, it is when these new invaders took over most of the island of Great Britain from the Firth of Forth to the Tamar, or from the edge of the Highlands to the boundary of Cornwall, that a new era in English history really begins, just as a new era in American history begins when the whites from Europe took over the red man's continent. Or, if one prefers the second starting point mentioned at the beginning of this chapter, one may say that what has hitherto been recounted is but background and that what is to come is the truly English part of the history of the British Isles.

2

ANGLO-SAXON ENGLAND

England became England rather than Britain when the English peoples crossed the North Sea and took over the island. This was part of the general "wandering of the peoples" that occurred when the borders of the Roman Empire were forced and barbarians swarmed in, first to rob and then to conquer. Basically, the movement of the English was no different from the movements of the Goths, the Vandals, the Lombards, and the Franks. Like those tribes, the English moved from a homeland outside the Empire into a new home inside it. Originally, they were three different nations living in the vicinity of the North Sea, the Jutes, the Saxons, and the Angles, who chose Britain as the province they would raid. The Jutes, who settled in Kent and the Isle of Wight, came in small numbers. It was once thought that enough stayed behind to give the Jutland peninsula its name. Now they are believed to have come from elsewhere. Many more Saxons came. They settled Essex and all of England south and west of the Thames except Kent and the Isle of Wight. But of these, too, enough were left behind to give a place its name, this time Saxony, at the head of the Elbe River. But the Angles, who settled all England north of the Thames, except Essex, came in such numbers as to leave bare the peninsula of Angeln in Schleswig-Holstein, between the Schleswig and Flensburg fiords. Therefore it was natural for the island to get a new name from its chief conquerors and have its southern part known as England.

In many ways the barbarian invasion of Britain resembled the other barbarian invasions of the crumbling Roman Empire. The invaders knew little or nothing of Roman culture and came for plunder. They robbed and sacked the cities and then tended to settle down in the countryside outside. But the Angles, Saxons, and Jutes went further in the course of destruction than most of the barbarians on the continent of Europe. They did not stop short after a while and begin to take on the customs of the people they had conquered. They kept themselves very much apart. In one hundred and fifty years they absorbed the native British or hustled them into Cornwall, Wales, and Strathclyde (northwest England and southwest Scotland), treating them as foreigners in their own land. Hence comes

12

the name Welsh for the descendants of the native Britons; it is the same word as the German *wälsch* (foreign). During this century and a half the invaders pushed inland from southern, southeastern, and eastern shores and using the marshes and rivers of the Wash ultimately gained control of the upper Thames Valley. Very little is known of the actual dates, battles, and methods of conquest. The Britons resisted so stubbornly that even in King Alfred's days Cornwall had not been made Saxon. A few British probably were held as slaves, but how few is shown by the almost complete absence of words of British origin in modern English. Undoubtedly some intermarriage took place between conquerors and conquered, but that, too, has left little trace. Most of the heritage of the past—religion, cities, laws, the arts and crafts, and Latin language—were rooted out by the Anglo-Saxons, leaving only a few vestiges such as the sturdily built roads and the use of mills to grind flour.

However, to replace what they had destroyed, the Anglo-Saxons brought with them certain very important institutions, notably a social and military organization, a governmental system, and an agricultural system. The first two, greatly modified, may be said still to be in use in England; the last flourished till about one hundred and fifty years ago, and until recently was to be found at Laxton, in Nottinghamshire. The social and military system consisted then of four, now of three, classes. At the top was the king of each tribe of Angles, Saxons, or Jutes, if one man may be considered a class. Next to him in rank came the king's fighting men or nobles. These formed a sort of officer group. Then came the free men, the churls. At the bottom were the thralls; that is, slaves taken in battle, though the Anglo-Saxons tended to dislike slavery and had on the whole little of it. This social system was at the same time a military system. All the Anglo-Saxons needed to do to start an amphibious invasion was to get into their boats, put their wives and children in a fleet to follow, and start off. Automatically, the king of the tribe was the leader of the expedition; equally automatically the nobles took command under him of various ships at sea and of sections of the army when it landed. The churls followed without question those they thought their natural leaders. So it was that the "long ships" of the Anglo-Saxons—vessels like our lifeboats, to judge from one dug up in Flensburg fiord—carried parts of two nations and all of a third across the North Sea and landed them on the beaches of the Firth of Forth around to Portsmouth. Indeed, some seem to have circled the island and landed on the west coast, at the Bristol Channel and the mouths of the Dee and the Mersey. Thus came to the island a new way of life.

From the moment these invaders had cleared the Romans and British out of their way they resumed the sort of farming life they had followed in their native homes. They had been used, so far as we can tell from fragmentary records and arguments by analogy with other tribes, to sharing cattle, tools, and even land. The acre we use today is not really a square area in terms of feet, yards, or rods, because its original purpose was to mark out the oblong of land each man might have as his own and plow with the community plow. Since it is easier to plow oblong fields, an acre, or a day's work in plowing, is forty rods by four rods. The typical field used by Anglo-Saxon villagers might be as large as sixteen or twenty acres, providing plots forty rods by four for sixteen or twenty families. Each plot would be divided from its neighbor by a large furrow, called a headland. This system of large fields is called the "open-field" system as opposed to the relatively smaller "enclosed" field of some one to four acres such as is nowadays customary in England. As the constant cultivation of any one field year after year would exhaust it, villages of the Anglo-Saxons usually had two, three, or more of these open fields, which were cultivated in turn. The commonest sequence of crops was the three-field one, of winter wheat sowed in the winter and reaped in the spring, spring wheat sowed in the spring and reaped in the autumn, and then a year lying fallow. As can be seen, this brought in two crops in the same year and then gave the land a year and a half of rest.

In the earlier centuries such a sharing of the strips on the big open fields was not the only system of sharing the Anglo-Saxons used. The plows and horses to drag the plows were often shared. The land, or common, on which cattle were pastured was shared in common. One or two villagers drove the hogs out to eat acorns in the forest and then drove them back. One flour mill, the use of which they had learned from the Romanized Britons, served the whole village; one baking oven might serve the village as well. All these cooperative enterprises were jointly managed. Some historians believe that villagers met together in a courtyard, in the village or "tun" (town) court to discuss the management of village or tun affairs. Evidence for the existence of these village courts or "folcgemots" is scarce until the records of King Alfred's reign. Only when the function of hundred courts in Anglo-Saxon times is studied do we find a satisfactory account of local government and a court system.

With more definiteness it can be said that by the eleventh century the territorial division was the "hundred," based on a unit of 100 "hides," and that each hundred had its local court and administrative organization. The size of the hundred varied with variations in the definition of a hide —in Mercia about one hundred and twenty acres, in Wessex about sixty. This variation in turn reflected the way settlement and division of land had taken place in each kingdom.

In judicial matters the Anglo-Saxons, like their descendants in the Kentucky hills, often resorted to the blood feud, an eye for an eye, a tooth for a tooth, which vengeance was duly avenged in turn. But they were a fair-minded people and felt that there were times when vengeance might be given up and the damage done paid for. When questions like that arose, a larger group would meet. The smallest governmental unit above the village or tun was also a military one, the hundred. Its nature is shown by the fact that later Danish invaders called a similar institution a wapentake. Here minor disputes could be ironed out. For larger issues, the unit seems to have been the original tribe, in an area called a shire, the court probably being presided over by the king. By the time of written records, most kingdoms were larger than a shire, but the king's agent or reeve presided over the shire court. That is why he was called a shire-reeve, or sheriff. In these hundred and shire courts the freemen of the hundred or shire talked over the situation and, if blame could be fixed, awarded damages according to a fixed scale, the amount depending on the injury done and the rank of the injured man. If he were alive he got the damages. If he were dead—and that mattered less in a world where fighting was the chief pleasure—payment was made to his family. The oldest Anglo-Saxon laws we possess are lists of payments for theft and personal injury. In Wessex 120 shillings were awarded if a Welshman were killed, 200 if the Welshman happened to be a king's messenger. A churl was worth a Welsh royal messenger, 200 shillings, but an earl cost either 600 or 1,200 shillings depending on whether or not he was in the King's personal service. The theft of cattle, as in other parts of the world at the same stage of civilization, was about as serious as murder, and required similar payments. It should be noted that these were not government prosecutions but private damage suits. It should also be noted that there was no jury trial, not even a sifting of evidence. If enough reliable people swore that a man was innocent, he was innocent. In theory, the gods would not permit the innocent to suffer or a false oath be sworn. If enough reliable people swore he was guilty, he was guilty. It was one's duty to support one's kindred by such oaths, just as it was one's duty to avenge one's kindred by carrying on the blood feud. (The technical name for this is compurgation.) In such rough and ready ways of finding the truth and assessing the compensation, there was only one government prosecution—and even that was really a family affair, since it was the kindred that took arms together—prosecution for evading the draft or "fyrd." If one did not go out to fight with the rest of the hundred, one paid toward the cost of the expedition so missed. Thus there was a tradition of letting the upper classes lead and rule in war and legal matters and of having at the same time the people, in their courts, the ultimate judges.

It sometimes happened, however, that a case appeared too intricate for the shire courts to handle. Then, and then alone, was government taken out of the hands of the people. In such difficulties a king would summon the wisest men of his kingdom to his "Witan" and acting on their advice issue a "doom" or statement as to what the law was. Note this—it was not thought of as making a law, but as finding out what the already existing law was. Another duty fell on the Witan, that of selecting within the royal family the man best suited to be king when the king died. For it would never do to turn over a man's job to a boy. The Witan thus formed the peak of the social and governmental structure that the Angles, Saxons, and Jutes brought to the island they conquered.

Though from records and inferences much can be said of this structure, little is known of the details of the conquest that brought it. The only writing the invaders knew was the carving of runes on stones to commemorate important events. The victims left some account of what happened. St. Germanus, Bishop of Auxerre in France, told of his visit in 447, and of victories by Christian Britons over Saxon invaders, his personal share in one of which has been recounted. A Welsh monk, Gildas, writing a century later, lamented that the sins and fratricidal quarrels of the British had brought on God's scourge in the Saxons who had then begun to establish themselves in the land. Gildas tells of a see-saw struggle and a victory at Mons Badonicus that reappears in the Arthurian legend. After that comes almost complete silence as the Britons fled into Wales, Strathclyde, and Cornwall or over the sea to Brittany. On the invaders' side our chief record is *The Ecclesiastical History of England,* written many years later by the Venerable Bede, in the monastery of Jarrow. This gives a general picture. At first the English landed in tribes and set up small kingdoms. Such were the two kingdoms of East Anglia, the Northfolk of Norfolk and the Southfolk of Suffolk, who later combined into one. Such, too, were the two kingdoms of Northumbria, Deira and Bernicia. But even at that early stage the English seem to have sometimes recognized one king as overlord or Bretwalda (ruler of Britain) above the other kings. Heading the list of Bretwaldas is Aella, king of the South Saxons, who commanded the first large-scale invasion. Then the little kingdoms gradually grouped into seven somewhat larger ones, called the Heptarchy. Three northern kingdoms were established by the Angles—Northumbria from the Forth to the Humber, Mercia of the great Central Plain, and East Anglia of Norfolk and Suffolk. Note that Angles settled part of present-day Scotland. The Jutes founded only one kingdom, Kent, where Hengist and Horsa had landed. The Saxons founded three kingdoms, east, south, and west—Essex between the Thames and East Anglia, Sussex between the Solent and Kent, and Wessex stretching west from the Solent to the fluctuating border with the Cornishmen.

The Anglo-Saxons were originally pagans, worshipping much the same gods as did the other Northmen—Woden or Odin, Thor, and the rest of the gods of Valhalla. Like the Norse they believed that those dying in battle would feast and fight eternally, while those who died in their beds would abide in cold and snow. Consequently they were eager to fight. Some were so eager they would strip off their armor and fight in shirts, or "sarks," alone, hence the name "baresark" or berserk for a fighting rage in which one does not care what happens. But all that now remains of this religion is the names of some days of the week, such as Woden's and Thor's preserved in Wednesday and Thursday, and the traditional bravery shown by English troops in battle. Three men, Pope Gregory the Great, St. Augustine of Kent, and Archbishop Theodore of Tarsus, brought Christianity to the Saxons, Jutes, and Angles in England. Along with Christianity, Roman or Latin culture returned whence it had been driven by invaders.

There is an often-repeated story of how Gregory the Great became interested in missionary work among the English. According to it, he once went to the slave market as a young man, and there saw beautiful, fair-haired pagan boys. On asking from what people they came he was told, "The Angles." Whereupon he declared they ought not to be Angles but angels, and asked the name of their kingdom. On learning it was Deira he vowed to save them "from wrath"—*de ira* in Latin—and at once set out to find their land. But the people of Rome valued the young priest too much to let him go, sent after him, and forced him to give up his missionary project. It was only years later, when he had become Pope, that in 597 he could send St. Augustine (known as St. Augustine of Kent to distinguish him from the theologian St. Augustine of Hippo) to convert them. St. Augustine went to Canterbury, the capital of Kent, where Queen Bertha was a Christian. With her aid he converted King Ethelbert, his court, and more and more of his people. For this Pope Gregory made him an archbishop, with Canterbury as his see. To this day the Archbishop of Canterbury has remained "Primate of All England."

At this time, England was ripe for conversion, for the pagan religion of the Anglo-Saxons seemed to have lost hold on the people once they had left the shrines of their original homeland. In one case the pagan high priest himself asked the missionary for more information about the new religion. Convinced by what he heard, he then led the party that went to the pagan temple and smashed the idols. Even pagan kings who attacked and defeated Christian ones in the wars between the seven members of the Heptarchy did not persecute missionaries. They merely exiled them, not as Christian priests but as friends of the king they had beaten. Thus within seventy years, by 664, the whole island became Christian. Wales, being settled by the Roman British, was always Christian.

However, in this seventy years of conversion all was not plain sailing. At first things went well. After Kent came Northumbria, at the other end of the English settlement. There Bishop Paulinus, through the aid of Ethelbert's daughter, the reigning queen, persuaded King Edwin to be a Christian. Thus was founded England's second archbishopric, at the Northumbrian capital of York. Edwin was an important convert because he ruled over a wide area as far as the Firth of Forth where he had built a great fortress, Edwin's Borough, now spelled Edinburgh but still pronounced Edinborough. But Edwin's importance won him enemies, notably a remarkable old pagan, Penda, King of Mercia, who took the throne at fifty and reigned till killed in battle past eighty years of age. Penda overthrew Christian Northumbria and twice held down revolts led by the exiled royal family. As it happened that the exiled royal family fled north, among the Picts, this local warfare had religious consequences. When King Oswy did return and finally killed Penda in battle, he brought back to Northumbria in 635 not the Roman type of Christianity but the type he had learned in exile among the Picts. This was the type which St. Columba had brought to Scotland from Ireland and which, before him, St. Patrick had taught to the Irish. There were differences in the Irish and Roman way of doing things. For one example, the Irish monks tonsured their heads by cutting a strip from back to front while the Roman monks tonsured their heads by cutting a circle off the top. At the Northumbrian court, because calendars differed, King Oswy would be celebrating the Easter feast while his wife, who followed the Roman rite, was still fasting in Lent.

These differences had grown up during the long period in which the Anglo-Saxon conquest of Britain had separated the Christians in Wales and their converts in Ireland from Rome. During that time Christianity and consequent Latin and Greek culture had reached Ireland. Oppression of the remaining British Christians in Wales had accomplished, as is so often the case, a revival. A Briton, St. Patrick, had brought this new leaven into Ireland, and in Ireland a flourishing culture had risen. But this was not a Latin culture; it was an Irish culture using Latin as its intellectual vehicle and inspiration. On the basis of the information St. Patrick and his fellow missionaries had brought into Ireland, the Irish had improvised their own system. As they lived in tribes, bishops and their dioceses were on a tribal basis, not a territorial. Where ritual had not been recorded, or where a difference of interpretation was possible, such differences in tonsures, calendars, and the like took place. But these differences were a sign not of decay but of vigorous life, for the monastic movement had reached Great Britain and Ireland at almost exactly the moment Hengist and Horsa had. Groups of monks, following the rule laid down by St. Benedict, inspired each other with devotion to the Christian religion and with interest in culture. Monasteries multiplied in Ireland especially, bringing the ideals of St. Benedict to the edges of the Atlantic Ocean. In and out of these monasteries Greek was studied, beautiful manuscripts were penned, fine artistic work was done, especially by goldsmiths. Nor did Ireland keep her culture and her religion to herself. Missionaries who spread both went all over Europe. In particular, one nobleman, St. Columba, went north from Ireland over the "Giant's Causeway" to the bleak little island of Iona off Scotland, there to found a monastery. From there he converted the Picts and so Oswy.

When Oswy became aware of the extent of the conflict between the methods of Ireland and Rome, he decided to clear matters up by sending to Canterbury for advice. In 664, representatives of the Roman and Irish rites discussed, at Whitby in Yorkshire, their differences. The discussion was a genuine attempt to arrive at the truth, the clinching argument being an appeal to the Bible text, "Thou art Peter and on this rock I will build my church." Since St. Peter was the founder of the papacy, this was taken to mean that Rome was right. Therefore, after the Synod of Whitby, the Irish rite was gradually supplanted by that of Rome, as news of the decision spread.

It was now up to the Church of England to try to match the Church of Ireland in saintliness and learning. Fortunately at this moment it obtained just the leader it needed. In 668 when an English Archbishop of Canterbury died in Rome just after he had been consecrated there, the Pope replaced him with an aged Greek, Theodore of Tarsus. This sixty-six-year-old man served actively in England until his death at eighty-eight and accomplished two important things: he organized the Church, and he gave it learning. When he landed, the Church of England, like that of Ireland, was largely on a tribal basis, with one bishop for each kingdom, and priests who traveled as missionaries instead of staying in one spot. When he died, dioceses were no longer the same as kingdoms, but smaller—which took bishops out of struggles between kingdoms—and each large village had its priest who was now settled in one parish.

For learning Theodore of Tarsus did much. The English, like the Irish, found a thrill in the new arts of reading and writing. They penned fine manuscripts, not only copying old writings but composing new ones. Furthermore, like the Irish they wrote not only in Latin and Greek but in their own language as well. And, like the Irish, they kept their own national spirit when they wrote. With the Anglo-Saxons this came out in the soldierly way they looked at life. When the monk Caedmon retold much of the Bible in Anglo-Saxon poetry, he used the same alliterative style and the same meter as did the author of the epic *Beowulf*, the story the Angles had told in their old home in Angeln and Christianized and written down in their new home in England. He showed, too, the same attitude of valiant facing of life that is to be found in the story of the king who dove under water to fight the dragon that every night had carried off a warrior from his feasting hall. This note of courage is to be found all through Anglo-Saxon literature, as in what the poet Cynewulf wrote about

Elene (St. Helena, the supposedly British-born mother of the Emperor Constantine of York) or in the *Dream of the Rood* (the dream which the rood, or cross, had about Christ when He was crucified on it). The scholarship of these newly cultured Anglo-Saxons, too, was high. The *Ecclesiastical History* of the Venerable Bede, written at the monastery of Jarrow, has been mentioned as our best source for this period. When the Emperor Charlemagne tried to revive learning in France, he sent for Alcuin of York to teach and conduct his palace school. When missionary endeavors entered Germany, it was an Englishman, St. Boniface, who led in the conversion there. Theodore of Tarsus brought England into the main current of European life by making it a center from which culture spread to the rest of Europe.

But in spite of this learning, this period was not a peaceful age from the late seventh to the late eighth century in English history. It was merely one in which there were no outside invasions. Kings raided each other just as they had before they became Christian. If they "got religion" and turned monk, they merely handed their thrones to equally bellicose successors. Strict inheritance could not be followed in these days of the Heptarchy, for no kingdom of the seven could be entrusted to an heir who was not of fighting age. One of the chief questions Witans had to settle was who, on the death of a king, was the fittest in a royal family to take over his throne. This practice, in a sense, made the English kingdoms partially elective. Gradually, however, England settled down, as first one kingdom and then another took the leadership. First Northumbria held the position of leader, in the days of Edwin. Then, in the struggles of Penda with his successors, Mercia assumed it. After Penda came the Christian Offa, who fought the Welsh, drove them farther into Wales, and built an earthen wall, "Offa's Dike," west of the Severn, that the Welsh should cross at their peril. Later Wessex, under Egbert, took over the leadership. He had the advantage, like Oswy, of an educative period of exile—in his case, at the court of Charlemagne. It is possible to place the period of these Bretwaldaships with the Northumbrian supremacy in the seventh century, the Mercian in the eighth century, and that of Wessex in the ninth.

In Egbert's time the period of no outside invasions came to an end. Indeed, as one looks at this whole period from 300 to 1100, outside invasions all over Europe are the rule. Such a general view should be taken right here because it will be an aid in linking up events. From 300, in the period when the Roman Empire broke up, to the First Crusade of 1096, the Germanic and other tribes outside the Roman Empire were constantly on the march. They both invaded the Empire and then, when they got inside the Empire, moved about conquering and being conquered. Gradually, as the culture of Rome—its language, its customs, and its methods of government and warfare—was adopted by the invaders, those invaders struck back and brought north again law, order, and forms of civilization. So it was that Irish culture went into Scotland, even to bringing a tribe, the Scots, into that country to give it a new name. So it was that St. Boniface brought to Saxony the new religion that had come to the Saxons across the sea in England. So it was that when the Franks, under the family of which the great Charlemagne was the most famous member, restored the idea of the Roman Empire in 800, they carried back into Germany in a counterinvasion the culture that they had adopted. So it would be later on that the Normans, originally overseas invaders who had landed in the Seine valley, would conquer England, Sicily, Jerusalem, and Constantinople. All these countermovements of ex-barbarians fit into much the same pattern as the original barbarian invasions. Indeed, the Crusades can be fitted into the same pattern of large-scale long-distance movements of warriors. From such a point of view it is perfectly natural that sooner or later more overseas invaders would come to England. The only questions really at issue would be which invaders would come, when, and why.

The particular invaders who came to England can usefully be called Northmen, because that will serve as a reminder that they were of the same stock as the Normans who eventually conquered England in 1066, as well as of the original Angles, Saxons, and Jutes. That was why the newcomers, if ever they settled down, found it easy to amalgamate with the English. They came from the present Norway, Sweden, and Denmark although because the majority were Danes they were sometimes spoken of as Danes. They were men of the fiords, or viks, and called themselves "Vikings." They used the same sort of long ships as had the Jutes, Angles, and Saxons years before, the same sort that Eric the Red would use to discover Greenland and his son Lief the Lucky to discover America. The first raids appear to have taken place in either 787 or 793, depending on how one interprets an old manuscript. They were caused by the pressure Charlemagne was putting on the Saxons and through the Saxons on the Danes, in his efforts to conquer and Christianize them. They grew in intensity and changed in method as English resistance grew feebler. In consequence, for the two and a half centuries from 787 to 1066, the central facts in English history are the raids of the Northmen—and the countermeasures of the English—till at last the Normans take over. For indeed it is not far wrong to think of the Norman Conquest of 1066 as a successful raid by Northmen who had adopted Roman culture.

The period of intense raiding began in the reigns of Egbert and his son Ethelwulf of Wessex. It came to a climax in the years that Egbert's four grandsons one after another held the throne of the last unconquered Saxon kingdom, Wessex, and for what it was worth, the Bretwaldaship, from 858 to 900. During those years the raids stopped being sporadic and became permanent. It is recorded that either in 851 or 855 the "army" of the Danes gave up going home for the winter and stayed in England in order to start ravaging the moment camp could be broken in the spring. In 857 the invaders were "a-horsed," that is, they turned themselves into mounted infantry, the better to plunder. In 867 they took York and set up a kingdom of their own. By 871, after both London and Canterbury had been sacked, only Wessex was left in any way free from the Danes, and it fell under the rule of a boy king, Alfred, whose elder brother, Ethelred, had just died after he and Alfred had won the battle of Ashdown in Surrey.

Alfred is the first English king to earn the title of "the Great," and the one most to deserve it. He was that rare combination, a man great in war and in peace, in adversity and in success. At the start of his reign, defeat at the battle of Wilton put him in such desperate straits that he had to levy a special tax, the Danegeld. This tax, which his predecessors had instituted, was as its name implies, money wherewith to buy off the Danes. The existence of the tax shows that England was on a money economy. The use Alfred made of the time it brought him, to create a navy, shows that he understood the strategy of England's defense. But though this navy fulfilled its purpose of holding off small raids, the revival of English strength brought its dangers. The Vikings called off their raids on the Seine and concentrated on trying to crush England. For a time it looked as if they had succeeded. Alfred was so routed and chased that in 878 he was driven to take refuge in the marshes of Athelney. There he lost his crown jewels, which were later dug up after the marshes had been drained in 1693. Legend has it that Alfred was driven to travel alone, unknown to his subjects. The story is often told of how a housewife sheltered him, and discovered it was the King only when he was so inattentive, brooding over England's woes, as to let the cakes burn in the oven. But from this low point his fortunes rose. In that same year he called out the fyrd, or fighting men subject to draft, of the county of Wiltshire and with them defeated the Danish King Guthrum at Ethandune. After that, at the Pact of Chippenham or Peace of Wedmore (historians use both titles), Guthrum accepted baptism and divided England with Alfred, using Watling Street from London to Chester as the boundary. South and west was English; north and east was Danish and therefore called the Danelaw, since Danish custom was used there along with English law in courts. The victory of Ethandune was celebrated by cutting away the turf from the chalk of the South Downs to form a great white horse, which is still kept bare of grass as a landmark for the traveler from Southampton to London. This peace with Guthrum lasted throughout Alfred's reign, with one lapse in 896, during which London seems to have been recaptured by the English.

Once Alfred had peace, he used it. He kept up the navy he had founded. Alfred also reformed the army. He divided the fyrd so that half the men subject to draft would come out at one time, leaving the other half at home. This prevented denuding any region of defenders, wearing out troops by long campaigns, and losing crops for want of men to cultivate and harvest them. Those at home could keep on with the protection against small raids and could build forts and bridges. These three duties, military service, fort building, and bridge building, were named in Anglo-Saxon "fyrdfare," "burghbot," and "bricbot." These Saxon words, not in themselves worth remembering, have been written down because they lead to another reform of Alfred's. He learned from the Danes the value of fortified towns, such as London and York, as bases. He built a circle of town forts around Wessex that checked the Danes even if they did not seal them out of the kingdom. Either in his reign or in that of his successor, Edward the Elder, a list called the Burghal Hidage was compiled of the burghs of South England which suggests that Alfred had refounded some of the cities that the Saxons, Angles, and Jutes had sacked when they landed. Alfred also took over the Danish idea of mounted infantry and gave the rank of thane (sometimes spelled thegn) to anyone who could pay for horse and armor and could prove himself worthy. Three generations of thanehood made the honor hereditary and thus allowed churls to become noble. Men who maintained ships in seacoast towns that could fight with the navy were also granted the rank of thane. From Alfred's time to the Norman Conquest the tendency was to "ennoble" those who could bear the responsibility and cost of defense and administration. To such men were granted not only titles of nobility but also increasingly large areas of land. Thus was a custom gradually established that looked after the legal interests of free cotters and farmers and their dependents. Thanes would support them in hundred and shire courts, as well as lead them in the fyrd. This hierarchy based on a mutual exchange of service and responsibility was part of the evolutionary development that later became a full-grown feudal system under the Normans.

Alfred naturally turned his attention to the court system. He continued the arrangements of his predecessors by which bishops sat with sheriffs in the shire courts, for that brought in the aid of educated men. He also continued the system of trial by ordeal rather than compurgation. That is, he did as had preceding kings—he had the bishop ask the defendant to swear an oath on a relic or a Bible, in the belief that God would punish perjury. As defendants shared this belief, the system was often an effective way of getting at the truth.

Then, too, Alfred had the laws written down as fully as possible, since the disturbances of his reign prevented calling together experienced men. To a certain extent he chose among laws of different kingdoms what his

Witan and he thought best. In theory, he followed the customary belief that laws are already in existence, a sort of property from time immemorial, and that all one does is find out from some old man or from any old records what they are. But in fact, because he had begun to pick and choose, he was making law rather than "discovering" it.

Alfred's reforms did not stop with military and legal matters. Since he felt that the ability to read and write had caused his success, he founded schools and enforced attendance. More than that, he saw to it that there were books in English. He personally translated Bede's *Ecclesiastical History*, Boethius' *Consolations of Philosophy*, Orosius' *History*, and Pope Gregory's *Pastoral Care*. And in order to make a record of contemporary events and otherwise bring books up to date, he added as he translated. For example, since his sea captain Othere had discovered the way around Norway to the White Sea we now know as the Murmansk route, he added that information to Orosius. He also caused to be compiled every year the Anglo-Saxon Chronicle.

In evaluating Alfred's doings, however, it should be remembered that he had had to leave the Danes in their kingdom at York. It was his son, Edward the Elder, and his favorite grandson, Athelstan, who conquered Danelaw and forced Danes, Welsh, Picts, and a new set of Irish invaders in North Britain, the Scots, to acknowledge the House of Wessex as overlord. It is only with the final recapture of York in 954 that it is technically possible to speak of a true king of England rather than a king in the Heptarchy who is also Bretwalda. These successes of the House of Wessex against the Northmen gained England a period of peace and, in consequence, harmed France. Now, instead of Charlemagne's victories in Germany causing raids on England, English victories caused raids on France. When a burst of Viking raids was caused by the way Harold Haarfager, the first true king of Norway, drove out all who would not obey him, the Seine valley suffered. Among the Viking exiles was a gigantic man, too tall to be able to ride a horse when he and his followers were "a-horsed." This got him the name of Rolf the Ganger, or Walker. He and his Northmen founded a sort of Danelaw in France where, under the gallicized name of Rollo, he became the first Duke of Normandy in 911. Of his descendant, William the Conqueror, England would see much at a later date.

Again, in default of serious invasion, England saw a troubled peace. Raids continued, and the kings as of old fought off the raids, as the Anglo-Saxon Chronicle records from year to year. Once the monks who compiled that sometimes dull narrative could not contain themselves and burst into epic poetry, telling of the battle of Brunanburh in the same vigorous alliterative verse in which an earlier generation had recounted the deeds of King Beowulf. But, as the same Chronicle relates, Danes, Welsh, and Scots acknowledged the king of England, even to having eight of their kings in 973 row King Edgar up and down the river Dee. Peace, in this case, brought inevitable changes and end to some of the culture of Alfred and Theodore of Tarsus. A sign of this was that St. Dunstan, Edgar's Archbishop of Canterbury, had to try to drive from the monasteries men who had fled there for protection but who would not live up to the monastic rule of celibacy, and that he met with only partial success. Dunstan's difficulty was created largely by the destruction by the Danes of churches and monasteries in the eastern and northern section of England. But once the Danes had settled down, they adopted Christianity and, like their great leader, Guthrum, lived contentedly in the bosom of holy church. In the tenth century many of the ruined monasteries were rebuilt and reoccupied, while learning and literature revived. Credit for this, along with St. Dunstan, goes to Bishop Ethelwold and Bishop Oswald of Wessex. The former of these compiled the *Regularis concordia,* a code for the discipline and governance of monks and the arrangement in general of church services. Such men as the learned Aelfric wrote in English and encouraged others to do the same. Thus the tenth century in England was a time of revival and reorganization in the Church. Contact with continental thought and religious developments was enthusiastic. As the eleventh century was about to dawn, England appeared to Rome as one of the most devout and most Christian nations in western Europe.

As was probably inevitable, Viking raids began again. The defeated parties in the civil wars then going on in Scandinavia took to raiding England to support themselves in exile, till they were strong enough to go back. It was on such a raid that the men of London fought the Danes on the beach called the Strand and buried them in the then new church of St. Clement Danes. No Alfred arose to command England's defense, and such a leader was badly needed, for the thanes of England were in constant strife with one another, and the English military system could not function unless given unifying leadership. The king who had to meet the problem became a byword for unwisdom, being known as Ethelred the Unready, or Redeless (without good advice). He bought off raids by Danegeld, but built no navy in the time so bought. Finally the Danish leader, Sweyn Forkbeard, copied the old system of wintering in England, and in 1014 drove Ethelred across the Channel to Normandy, where his wife's family took him in. Sweyn was then accepted as King. However, he died in the moment of victory and the English rose to fight for their independence under the leadership of the Atheling (Prince) Edmund, called Edmund Ironside from his strength in battle. Edmund Ironside, despite the handicap of his father's return from exile, fought on even terms and obtained much the draw Alfred had. But Ironside died, and Sweyn's son, Canute (which purists now spell Cnut), became king.

Canute was a wise king who successfully ruled not only England but also Denmark, Norway, and Sweden. He recognized that his English subjects were more advanced and brought Englishmen to Scandinavia as bishops and administrators. He also allied himself to his English subjects by marrying Ethelred's widow, Emma of Normandy. Behind him he left a legend of wit in the face of flattery. When his courtiers told him that all obeyed him, he merely put his chair at low-water mark and sat there, telling the tide not to come in. The courtiers, who were forced to be with him, soon got the idea. He was a religious man, like many a Norseman of those days, and ended his life on a pilgrimage to the Holy Land after richly endowing a church in Rome on the way.

Canute's sons were not up to him in ability. Nor did his consolidation of the kingdoms of the north survive him, for he left England to his elder son, Harold Harefoot, and Denmark to his younger, Hardicanute. The two brothers not unnaturally quarreled, but England was spared invasion for Harold Harefoot died before Hardicanute could cross the North Sea. As for Hardicanute, all that is remembered of him is that "he died in his drink," as the Anglo-Saxon Chronicle bitterly put it. He stood up to offer a toast, keeled over, and died. Quickly the Witan summoned from Normandy Edward the Confessor, the highly religious son of Ethelred the Unready, and England settled down to a period of nominal peace.

But this peace was more apparent than real. There was much disorder in the land, the heritage of the Danish raids. The small cultivator, especially, was under increasing pressure. He found duties pulling him, too often, three ways—the care of his lot of land, fyrd service, attendance in court were mutually incompatible. Men therefore tended to seek protection from those more powerful than they. This tendency had been at work for some time. As early as Alfred's reign, as has been recorded, every man had been ordered to have a lord to vouch for him in court trials. From vague beginnings the tendency grew more definite—as the late F. W. Maitland has said, the tendency in the evolution of institutions is from the vague to the definite. Free villagers and even free villages submitted to some powerful person living nearby, making an arrangement whereby they secured protection in return for special services. Such services were the free cultivation of certain strips of land in the communal fields, fixed proportions of grain ground in the communal mill, or of loaves baked in the communal ovens. Such leaders might be warriors—they might also be monasteries. As can be seen, a new and more specialized way of life is evolving in England to supplant the fairly free cooperation of the Anglo-Saxons.

Authorities differ as to the name to give, at this stage, to this new way of life. The most recent attitude is not to call it feudalism, since feudal agreements concern, strictly speaking, the tenure of land, and many of the surviving records appear to be direct agreements for protection that do not involve land tenure. But what is significant is not the degree but the direction of the change, the fact that England was moving toward feudalism.

3

THE NORMAN CONQUEST

It has been suggested that the Anglo-Saxon period of English history ended and the Norman one began when Edward the Confessor, King Ethelred's son, succeeded his half brother, Hardicanute, in 1042. Edward had been educated in Normandy, where he had spent most of his life in exile, and brought over with him Norman ideas and Norman friends. Already, many ties bound Normandy and England together. The ruling families were closely connected, since Ethelred's Queen Emma, who later married Canute and was the mother of Hardicanute, was of the Norman house. Many of the nobles, too, were related, for the combined forces of Danish and Norwegian Vikings who had indiscriminately raided England and France had equally indiscriminately settled in what might be called the two Danelaws of England and France. In both Normandy and England, similar economic and political forces were at work causing similar results. In an age of invasion and civil war, the free villages in both regions were putting themselves under lords to gain protection, and various lords were obtaining special governing privileges by royal or ducal charters. These steps toward feudalism, however, were occurring faster in Normandy. Authorities disagree as to which, the English or the Normans, were the more advanced. Some point to the superior literacy of the Anglo-Saxons and to the general diffusion of a high standard of living in their population. Others point to the administrative skill of the Normans and the leadership in the revival of church discipline that centered in the Norman monastery of Bec. This fact is a further sign of how comparable the two peoples were. Looked at in this way, it seems that England might well have become a feudal country, in the stream of European culture, by force of example, as Scotland later did, without any Norman Conquest. In that case, all Edward did was to speed up the process with his Norman favorites and his many grants of charters.

However, there was a center of resistance to Norman influence in the persons of a father and son, Earl Godwin of Wessex and his son and heir, Earl Harold. Edward might be easygoing and let the earls who managed several shires at once really rule the kingdom, he might bring in Norman bishops and knights, but whatever of importance was done found Earl Godwin taking the leading part. Godwin's importance had begun about 1018 when King Canute, who had to be in Denmark much of the time, gave up the custom of Egbert's descendants of ruling Wessex directly, and made Godwin Earl of Wessex to rule for him. This importance was increased by two marriages—that of Godwin to Canute's cousin and that of Edward the Confessor to Godwin's daughter Edith—which made the new family doubly royal. Only once was there an attempt to rid England of Godwin and Harold. This was on the complaint of Robert of Jumièges, the Norman whose election as Archbishop of Canterbury Edward had procured. When he asserted, in 1051, that Godwin had not properly punished the citizens of Dover who had vexed him, Godwin was maneuvered into the position of seeming to disobey the King and, therefore, was outlawed and exiled, along with Harold. The next year, father and son returned; and it was the Archbishop who left, being replaced in office by an Anglo-Saxon, Stigand, Bishop of Winchester. After this triumph, Godwin died, but his name is still remembered by English sailors who call the great sandbank off Dover "Goodwin Sands," *i.e.*, Godwin's Sands. Harold of Wessex then took his father's place as leader of the King's advisers, as commander of the expeditions against the Welsh, which won the first new land for the English since Offa's day, and generally as the first man in the realm and heir apparent. He behaved as such, surrounded himself with a bodyguard of "Housecarls," infantrymen armed with the big battle axes used by the Northmen. Such a bodyguard the Emperor of Byzantium had at Constantinople, his famous Varangian Guard. As long as Harold lived, England was going to be an Anglo-Saxon, one might almost say a Scandinavian, country of self-government—a population of farmers and sailors, a navy, all under a king who would lead in war and judge appeals in his Witan but not interfere too much. It was as such a king that the Witan welcomed Harold on January 6, 1066, the day after Edward the Confessor died.

However, though England wanted Harold, there were others who wanted England. One was Harold Haardraade, King of Norway, who once had commanded the Varangian Guard at Constantinople, and who wanted to carry on the old raiding tradition of Guthrum and Sweyn and conquer England. His plan was to ally himself with Harold of England's worthless younger brother, Tostig, whom Harold of England had forced Edward the Confessor to exile. Another claimant was the King of Denmark, by virtue of his inheritance from Canute. He, fortunately, only threatened. But the most important of all was William, Duke of Normandy, who had a claim compounded of many elements, chief of them being a promise from Edward the Confessor, a promise extorted from Harold when the Saxon was shipwrecked on Norman shores, a request from the Pope to avenge Robert of Jumièges, and above all, his own personal ability. That last was the clinching argument, for whoever wanted to take England would have to fight.

The force of Normandy and its duke were remarkable. The Normans kept the fierce fighting spirit of the band of men who, under their first duke, Rolf the Ganger to the Northmen, Rollo to the French, had conquered the duchy in 911. In the course of years, they had added to it education, cunning, a knowledge of mounted fighting wherewith to conquer new lands, and a rare skill in governing the lands they had thus conquered. In the eleventh century, the Normans were to take over the kingdoms of Sicily and Jerusalem; and in the early thirteenth, they were to cap this by taking over the Eastern Empire. But remarkable as they were, they were not as remarkable as their ruling family. Twice young boys, Richard the Fearless and then William, had ruled at the ages, respectively, of ten and eight, and had fought off invasions of nearby nobles and the king of France to keep their duchy. William, the younger of the two, had furthermore had to overcome a stigma against his inheritance. His father, Robert the Devil, had gone off to the Holy Land on a pilgrimage from which he never returned, without ever having bothered to marry William's mother by a Christian marriage but only by the old Viking custom of jumping across a fire together. Nor did William's mother bring him the prestige of nobility, being the daughter of a tanner of Falaise. William overcame all these obstacles and ruled Normandy well. He realized that feudalism might get out of hand unless the man at the top asserted his authority. While he might quibble over points of feudal law with his sovereign, the King of France, and might indulge in the feudal right of private war with his neighbors, such as the Count of Anjou, he did this to augment his authority. He let no one take the liberties with him that he took with others, but enforced his feudal rights to the limit. If he could get the Normans to follow him, Harold of England would be in great danger.

William had a claim that the Middle Ages would think better of than we do. When Harold had been shipwrecked in Normandy, William had forced him to swear an oath of fealty and, unknown to Harold, had put the bones of a saint under the box at which the oath was taken. To the Middle Ages, the sanctity of the bones more than counterbalanced the compulsion of the oath and justified an attempt to secure the English throne. More than that, William's expedition had the Pope's blessing, for it would right the wrong done by the deposition of Robert of Jumièges as Archbishop. Even at that, the Norman nobles did not consider it their feudal duty to help William invade England, and they told him so when the matter was talked over at what was then called a "parliament"— though the word had a very different meaning from the one it has today. Therefore, to recruit an army, William offered to grant manors in England to all who should support him. This move was successful, not only in Normandy but throughout France. Many Norman nobles, who had as his vassals refused to support him, joined him as partners in loot, but the army of invasion was more French than Norman. At the same time, the Pope sent William a banner and sword and blessed his invasion, because Stigand, in the Pope's eyes an improperly chosen archbishop, would be replaced by one pleasing to Rome. William's force thus became an army of God. If only the Channel could be crossed, it was highly likely that this army would introduce feudalism into England with a vengeance.

Of course, there was that "if" of crossing the Channel. Naturally enough, Harold of England had a fleet ready and the Kentish fyrd out to deal with any who might slip past his fleet. As long as that fleet kept the Channel, England was safe. But William, who had been delayed in getting recruits, was able to wait till the fleet had been so storm-tossed it had to go to London for repairs, and only then set sail. Here, another claimant unintentionally came to William's aid. At this moment, Harold Haardraade of Norway and Tostig Godwinson landed in Yorkshire and overcame the local fyrd at the battle of Fulford. Like a whirlwind, Harold Godwinson rushed north with the Housecarls, calling out the fyrd of Lincolnshire as he went. The invaders tried to bargain for terms with him. Harold of England gave them an offer—to his brother, Tostig, if he returned to his allegiance, one-third of England; to Harold of Norway, "seven feet of ground [for a grave], or as much more as he needs as he is taller than most men." The terms were rejected, but at the ensuing battle of Stamford Bridge, Harold Haardraade and Tostig Godwinson both got their seven feet of English ground, and Harold of England and his Housecarls marched in exhausted triumph into recaptured York. There they met the news that William of Normandy had landed at Pevensey in Sussex. Leaving the fyrd behind, the King and the Housecarls took horse in the old Viking way and hastened south to fight another battle.

The battle of Hastings, October 14, 1066, was a test of two different tactics and a symbolic struggle to the death between two different ways of life. On the field of Senlac (hence another name for the battle) stood the Anglo-Saxons, cleverly placed so that the invaders could attack only from the front, where from behind the traditional shield wall of the Northmen their battle axes could do their deadly work, as of old. In the valley below were the mounted knights and supporting archers, representing the new methods of French feudal warfare. Above the English flew the old flag of the Golden Dragon of Wessex that Alfred had carried; in front of the French rode the famous minstrel Taillefer, tossing his sword in the air and chanting the feudal song of Roland of France. Both sides were risking all. If the shield wall of the Housecarls and the fyrd of Kent should break, England was lost. If it did not break, the motley force of invaders would finally be driven in rout to their ships. All day long the battle raged. At one moment, rumor that William had been killed forced him to ride bareheaded along the ranks to rally his followers. At another moment, a feigned retreat enticed the fyrd to break ranks to pursue, only to be cut to pieces by the mounted knights in the valley below. Yet, after that, the Housecarls still stood impregnable on the hill, and still their axes swung and fell to repel every charge. Then, as evening came on, William ordered his archers to fire in the air, so that their arrows would drop down above the shields. One such arrow struck Harold in the eye. He stood in the ranks, leaning in agony on his ax, till a last charge broke the shield wall. Then the Housecarls died, true to tradition, with their master; and England was William's for the taking. The next day, William could found Battle Abbey in honor of the victory, mark on its walls the names of the nobles who had fought with him, send Harold's flag to the Pope in answer for his blessing, and march on London.

England did not yield at once to William. It really took him twenty years to finish the job. First, the Witan tried to set up as king Edgar the Atheling, the grandson of Edmund Ironside. But as William circled around London, laying waste to the countryside, the Witan changed its mind, and chose William king. He was crowned on Christmas Day, 1066, in Westminster Abbey, which Edward the Confessor had built, and which from that day to this has seen all England's coronations. After that, William was the acknowledged ruler of England, those who opposed him rebels or invaders. Sporadic resistance did remain, with which the new king dealt by cleverness, speed, terror, and cavalry. He would allow Saxon leaders who might be dangerous in combination to hold their offices if they paid him for the privilege, and thus he prevented their uniting against him. Then he would deal separately with individuals who seemed disloyal, replacing them with French or Normans who had no local roots and therefore were compelled to stand by the Conquest. Yorkshire particularly learned the cost of disobedience, when it welcomed a raid by the Danish claimant as a sign for revolt, from the speed with which William reached the scene of trouble, the harshness with which he harried the countryside and put down opposition, and the effectiveness with which his cavalry scattered Saxon and Danish foot soldiers. It is true that it took many years to rout the legendary Hereward the Wake from his fastness in the Fenland. It is true that as late as the fourteenth century Saxon exiles were to be found at Constantinople, still speaking their native language, still wielding battle axes, and glad to use them on Normans. But the death of Harold, the wiping out of the Housecarls, and the acknowledgment by the Witan, followed up as they were by William's energetic enforcement of his authority, made him the accepted king of England very quickly considering the previous condition of the country and the slowness of communications of those days. Because he got into the saddle so quickly, he could spend most of his reign giving his new country new institutions.

The outstanding change William made in England was not the introduction of feudalism—that had already occurred—but making it universal. This had to take place. It was the condition on which he recruited the army that won Hastings—that its leaders should get feudal grants as a reward. What William did that makes him most important in the evolution of England was not merely spreading feudalism throughout the land, but also amalgamating it with existing English institutions in such a way as to prevent many of the evil consequences that usually appeared when a European country became feudalized. To understand what William accomplished and how he accomplished it, therefore, it is necessary both to have a general idea of what European feudalism of the time was like and to note the checks he placed on it in England.

The basic idea of feudalism is simple. What can be confusing about it is the special verbiage that has gone along with it. Feudalism can be described as a society linked from top to bottom by mutual agreements of loyalty and service from the inferior in exchange for protection from the superior, running from the cultivator of the soil at the bottom to the sovereign at the very top. It falls, at least in its European form, into two halves—a largely economic relationship between the cultivator of the soil and the man or institution affording him direct protection, and a largely military and political relationship between the "lord of the manor" and the hierarchy that stretched above him to the king. Sometimes the two sets of relationships are called manorialism and feudalism; at other times, they are called economic and political feudalism. Either set of names is suitable, as long as the distinction is kept clearly in mind. Here, to save adjectives, the words "manorialism" and "feudalism" will be used.

When manorialism and feudalism originated, various words were used by lawyers to describe members of various classes, and the relationships each had to another. Later on, a sort of standard vocabulary was rather arbitrarily imposed. So much is this true that once the Professor of Law at Cambridge University, to drive home a point, told his class that feudalism was introduced into England in the early seventeenth century by the lawyer Sir Henry Spelman. Again, as a matter of convenience, that vocabulary will be used. It affords a good general description, inaccurate as it is in many special instances. Here, in brief, is what lawyers of later generations thought the organization of feudalism was, from the serf on the manor up to the king on his throne.

In the eyes of the law, no man could be without a lord. The average cultivator of the soil lived in a village attached to a manor house. In his manor court were handled the agricultural questions of which strip of land should be cultivated by whom, under the supervision of the steward of the manor. This has already been described in considering the town courts of the Anglo-Saxon village. Such a cultivator of the soil "went with the land." He could not leave his manor, nor could he be sold away from his manor as could a slave. He could be punished in the manor court for leaving; and by a payment in the manor court, he might buy the right to leave. If his son left, or if his daughter married someone on another manor, he must pay a fine. When he died, his lord took his "best beast," be it cow, horse, or pig, as a sort of inheritance tax called a "heriot." Such a person was called a "serf" or "villein." From the lord of the manor, he got military protection and enforcement of the decrees of the manor court. In return for this, he paid with the produce of his labor. This sort of thing varied immensely with local conditions called the "custom of the manor." Sometimes he cultivated strips in the open field reserved to the lord of the manor. At other times, he cultivated what was called the "home farm" or demesne of the manor. He had to give so many days a week of work, called "week work." In addition, he had to give extra labor in harvest, called "boon work." Furthermore, he often had to use the grist mill and ovens provided by his lord, paying for this with a fixed percentage of the flour and loaves there ground or baked. In actual practice, therefore, a manor could be largely self-governing, as far as detail and routine went, and as long as the supervision by the steward (or bailiff) secured for the lord of the manor an income on which to live. In return for this supply of board, lodging, and labor, the lord of the manor provided the mounted man or men and supporting foot soldiers who gave such protection from outside danger as the serf got.

The next stage in the feudal scale was the lord of the manor. His relationship with the serf has been described. To him his soldiers owed homage. This word, derived from the French *homme* and Latin *homo* for man, meant that these were his men, primarily loyal to him. Strict feudal law seems often to have drawn a distinction between fealty, or personal loyalty, and homage, or loyalty in exchange for grant of property. But the distinction in practice tended to be blurred. For a general understanding of feudalism, the two words may be considered the same. But since no one except the king could be without a lord, the lord of the manor owed duties and services to those above him. (The word "lord," as here used, means merely feudal superior.) These duties and services fell into two general groups, military and court service. Military service was usually bringing an agreed-upon number of horsemen and foot soldiers for a period of forty days under the command of the superior, either a more important noble or the king. Here, as will be seen from the use of the word "noble," comes the question of a superior governing class, as opposed to the ignoble vulgar below. Service for such a period afforded a highly practical means of resisting raids over the Scotch and Welsh borders, meeting raids from turbulent neighbors, and stopping a cross-Channel invasion. It did not afford a good means of besieging a castle which could hold out against blockade for more than forty days, and it did not afford a good means of making a large-scale expedition. By the time the siege or the expedition was beginning to make progress, it was time for the army to go home. As for "court service," that was a very practical duty in days when few could read and write. The more men came to advise the king, or the other feudal superior, the more chance there was that some man's memory would supply the essential information needed to decide a case. Court service, moreover, had another side to it. If angry nobles and their retainers, as their oath required, came to "advise" the king, the advice might be unpalatable but so presented that the king dared not decline it. Such was the advice that William got from his Parliament or Great Council when he tried to convince the Norman nobles it was their duty to help him invade England. Down through the centuries, kings of England would get similar forceful "advice" from their nobility. This system, on the continent of Europe, ran steadily up the scale, there being a regular hierarchy of nobles—barons at the bottom level, viscounts between the barons and the county units, counts (corresponding to English earls) over the counties into which about the time of Charlemagne France had been divided, marquises over the special border regions of danger called "marches," and dukes above them, with the king at the top. Thus, in France, at that time, because of the constant breaks in this theoretical chain of command, the king had little more real authority than had the Bretwalda in the days when England was in fact divided into kingdoms. Eventually, England would have all these titles, calling earls' wives countesses, but at first she had only barons and earls.

Such was the theoretical, but on the whole generally valid, reconstruction made later of the feudal system on the continent of Europe. Any close inspection would riddle this with exceptions. Towns, monasteries, and bishoprics, because of requirements of defense, were partially integrated into this system, and because of the peculiar requirements of their nature were partially excluded. All sorts of special arrangements existed as to types of service and limitations on service. Names which implied one sort of agreement in one district implied another in another. Cross agreements, by which a noble might owe fealty to one superior for one "fief," and to another for another, caused endless confusion and were used to justify "private war" such as the many wars William himself had conducted as Duke of Normandy. But though the existence of those complications should be mentioned here, essentially this was the way feudal society was organized. Serfs lived on the land in manors. They owed service to their lords, and got protection from the lords. At a higher level, all the country was organized in manors, or, more strictly speaking, fiefs. A fief was property for which fealty was given to a feudal superior. Fief, fee, feud— the words are basically the same—thus became the basic land unit in society. In England, the usual unit of measurement was called a "knight's fee," and manors were rated according to the number of knights they could supply the king. The lords of these units owed court and military service to some superior in return for protection. Sometimes, it was directly to the king. At other times, it was through a longer chain of command. With this general picture of feudalism in mind, it will now be possible to turn to the special form of feudalism William set up in England.

The first thing to be noted about this system is how easily it could be adapted to the existing conditions in England. Each village, with its town court, was a ready-made manor, needing only the addition of a manor house, a lord to live there and give protection, and a steward, a bailiff, or —to use the Anglo-Saxon name already in existence—a reeve to take care of detail for him. Some manors had already sprung into existence before the Conquest. As for the ideas of military and court service, the English had already performed such duties. They had come out to resist invasion in the fyrd, thanes had mounted service resembling that of Norman-French knights, the Housecarls had served the king as did those special retainers who had sworn personal fealty to him. As for the idea of court service, the Angles, Saxons, and Jutes had long been accustomed to meet in shire, hundred, and the Witan to consult as to the meaning of the law. England was ripe for feudalism. Consequently, though it was unpleasant to have Normans and not Saxons introduce many of its features, the actual introduction was accepted. It was an evolution, not a radical change.

The second thing to be noted about this system is that it depended on the loyalty of the nobles. Nobles, on the whole, were loyal. The culture in which they lived stressed the performance of duty. From that age to this survives the dictum "noblesse oblige," the idea that the French-speaking nobility had duties because of their nobility. Our very word for the code of ethics of the feudal nobility, "chivalry," comes from the French word "cheval," or horse, and thereby shows its origin. Chivalry is the duty of protection that the French-speaking mounted man owes to his inferiors, cost him what it may to grant that protection. But this code of ethics, like all such ideals, was not lived up to in practice. And it had inherent in it a great danger. Once the chain of command was broken, the very virtue of loyalty might turn against the king. Unless an overriding oath of "liege homage" were exacted and enforced, if a great noble rebelled against the king, his loyal retainers would fight for him against the king. William well knew that—had he not often called out his vassals (a vassal is the feudal inferior) to fight for him against his lord, the king of France? As king of England, he saw to it that none of his vassals acted to him as he had to his own lord. A pretext he used for this was the assertion that he was preserving the "good laws" of King Edward the Confessor.

One device he used that historians think was arrived at accidentally. He allowed few vassals to hold manors as compact groups. In very few shires, and these mostly border ones, did one Norman lord hold under him enough manors so that his vassals could form a little army. Most men who held several manors would hold one, say, in Kent, another in Gloucestershire, and a third in Yorkshire. Probably this came about because at first Saxons had not been disturbed far from the point of landing, and their lands were confiscated and regranted only when they caused trouble. But intentional or not, it effectually broke up potential foci of rebellion.

Two other devices William found at his hand. One was the system of hundred and shire courts. Here was a court system under royal supervision. He kept it so and added to its powers. Much private war was stopped by ordering that disputes between lords, freemen, or serfs of different manors be tried in these courts. (Note that both freemen and serfs might be tenants on manors. This will help explain the word "freeman" when it appears in Magna Carta, 1215.) This order did not preserve the hundred courts, since most hundreds got swallowed up in manors or groups of manors, but it did preserve the shire system. The shire courts changed in character, since they became gatherings of minor nobles and a few freemen, rather than of all the freemen. The sheriff, under William's eagle eye, became what his Anglo-Saxon name of shire-reeve implied—a man who was the king's reeve or agent and watched out for his interests. Otherwise, at least at the end of his reign, the king quickly got a new sheriff. Since William wanted peace and prosperity in England, the English who had been conquered soon discovered that they could rely on him. Therefore, William found he could preserve yet another Anglo-Saxon institution, the fyrd. In case of revolt, he could trust the fyrd to fight for him against rebels. The shire courts and the fyrd were important institutions to preserve, for from them arose parliamentary elections and national military service. Yet another Anglo-Saxon institution, the Witan, William transformed rather than preserved. As the Anglo-Saxon kings had done, he summoned Saxon lords to council. But, following the methods of the dukes of Normandy, he also summoned to council the chief administrative officers whom he had brought over with him, the Justiciar or chief justice and the Treasurer being the most important of these. For this body, so reconstituted, the names Magnum Concilium and Curia Regis came to be used in England as they had been in Normandy. So, with the reign of William, the word "Witan" disappears from history, to be replaced by Magnum Concilium.

William also found the Church useful for keeping England in hand. Here, his ally was Cardinal Hildebrand, later Pope Gregory VII, who was introducing reforms throughout Europe, among both the monastic or regular clergy and the ordinary or secular clergy. (Priests who are monks are called regular because they obey a *regula* [rule]; other priests are called secular because they are not kept inside monastery walls, but go out into the *seculum* [world].) In 1070, legates sent by the Pope deposed Stigand and made Lanfranc, a former Cluniac monk, Archbishop of Canterbury. Cluniac monasteries (Cluny in Burgundy was the center of the reform movement) were encouraged in England. Tactfully, William withdrew the rule Alfred had made of trying clerical cases in shire courts; and the bishops took the hint and stopped attending those courts. But William carefully protected himself against trouble with the church by devices later spoken of as the "Anglican Liberties." No baron or other noble might be excommunicated without his permission, or any papal bull published in England, or any papal legate enter the kingdom without it. He insisted on retaining the ancestral customs of England, and especially on the control of high ecclesiastical appointment. This is called "lay," *i.e.*, nonclerical, investiture. Like many customs of the time, it made practical sense. Take, for example, the bishopric of Durham. This controlled many manors, their revenues supporting the expense of the bishop. The knights on those manors attended the bishop's court (which was better run because he was an educated man) and owed him military service. Therefore, the Bishop of Durham was perhaps the chief official who protected the Scottish border. Quite rightly, therefore, the king demanded and got a share in appointing a man who in fact would be a judge and a border general.

Still another method of maintaining royal power was keeping the treasury full. Feudalism helped here. There were certain fees that vassals owed their lords. As final, or liege, lord, the king got most benefit by these fees. There was wardship, that is, control of a fief while the heir was a minor or an unmarried woman. There was relief, a fee paid for confirming an inheritor in his estates. Whole estates of one or more manors might come back into a lord's hands through escheat, that is, death without heirs, or through forfeiture, which is conviction of failure to carry out feudal duties. Then regularly the lord got from his vassals three "aids" or payments to meet the expense of special crises. One, help with ransom, did not benefit the lord, but his captor. The other two, the knighting of the eldest son and the consequent festivities, and the marriage of the eldest daughter and the consequent dowry, could be managed to produce income. But William did not rely upon purely feudal means of raising money. Finding that Danegeld was paid in England, he kept on collecting it, Danes or no Danes.

Of all these financial measures we know much, for in 1086, William decided to have written down, in what is called Domesday Book, a list of all the manors of England, of how much they had produced in soldiers and money in Edward the Confessor's time, and how much they produced in 1086. The records of four shires are missing, and of all the boroughs, but there is enough to tell us what feudalism was like under William, including how much he had devastated the country to scare it into submission.

To complete this picture of the changes in English government, two more points should be mentioned. Boroughs remained, with at times new charters, for which, presumably, they had paid well. Furthermore, William loved hunting. They said of him: "He loved the tall deer like their father." From Normandy, he introduced the idea of royal forests, where the king alone could hunt and where special laws were in force to keep the game for him. The most famous of these forests is what is still called New Forest, in Hampshire, on the west shore of the Solent and Southampton Water, opposite the Isle of Wight.

To sum up, then, the changes William made in England, the great one was making feudalism universal. Manors replaced the old village communities, often though not always over the same areas. Feudal military service brought mounted men to the king's army, a knight for each knight's fee, the knights serving under the lord to whom they were vassals if they did not hold directly from the king. However, for infantry, William kept the Anglo-Saxon fyrd. For feudal court service, the manor court superseded the old town courts for regulating agricultural affairs and minor land disputes. The manor courts also tried local cases, largely, though not entirely, superseding the old hundred courts. The king's court, or Magnum Concilium, of his tenants in chief, that is, of the lords who held directly from him, plus special advisers, replaced the Witan of special advisers alone. This made little difference, since William had a will of his own and was fully able to reject advice he did not want. Later on, in future reigns, this feudalizing of the Witan (or replacing it with a feudal council, since there is debate exactly which occurred) would matter much when great nobles forced their advice on the king. But William hung on to the shire courts and the appointment of sheriffs, who now acted as judges as well as administrators. The royal income was of manors the king himself held (this is important later), of feudal dues, and of the Danegeld. Boroughs remained; forest laws were introduced. As for the reform movement in the church, William welcomed it but insisted on the royal control of appointments and of the pope's exercise of authority in England.

Purposely omitted from this list is an event at the end of William's reign, the Oath of Salisbury Plain of 1086. When, twenty years too late, the King of Denmark threatened to invade England to enforce his claim to the throne, William summoned an army and made it swear fealty to him, overriding that owed to any immediate feudal superior. If, which is disputed, he also made knights throughout England swear this oath, then he also introduced the principle that no feudal obligation can force a man to fight against the king, a principle he had flouted himself in Normandy. The King of Denmark died, invasion did not come, and the Oath of Salisbury Plain remains a debatable point.

The next year, 1087, William died in Normandy, and by his will upset much of the good he had done. For he divided his lands and wealth among his three sons. To his eldest, Robert, who was the feudal equivalent of a playboy, he left Normandy. To his second son, William, nicknamed Rufus for his red complexion, he left England. To his third and cleverest son, Henry, called Beauclerc because he had the clerkly ability of reading and writing, he left money. The sons promptly quarreled, causing just the sort of anarchy William had devoted his life to stopping. Robert of Normandy and William Rufus unsuccessfully invaded each other's lands, while nobles who held manors on both sides of the Channel tried to play one brother against the other. Matters were cleared up for a while by the First Crusade. Robert went off to try to rescue the Holy Sepulchre from the Saracens, a truce was patched up, and William turned to ruling England, taking a mortgage on Normandy for the money Robert needed for going on the Crusade. In this period, William Rufus conquered from the Scots Cumberland and Westmorland. Rufus was capricious and harsh, not consistently strong like his father. The English tolerated him, as the lesser evil to turbulent barons; the nobility hated him. But the feeling toward him is shown by the fact that his subjects used to hide when he came by. One day, in the year 1100, when Red William was riding in the New Forest, an arrow struck him dead. Whether this was intentional or not, whether it was shot by a resentful subject or a fellow hunter, is unknown. At any rate, there was little regret. His brother Henry, who was of the hunting party, rushed off to Winchester, seized the royal treasure, and three days later was crowned king in Westminster Abbey. Just too late, a month after that, Robert returned to Normandy from his Crusade. Again brothers quarreled across the Channel. Robert's invasion was warded off by Henry's trickery; Henry's counterinvasion of Normandy succeeded. At the battle of Tinchebray, 1106, Normandy and England were reunited. In a sense, this battle avenged Hastings, for Henry brought with him as infantry the Anglo-Saxon fyrd, thus gaining the affection of his English subjects. Robert, captured after the battle, was kept in honorable, but strict, confinement till his death, at Cardiff Castle, in 1134.

Besides his victory at Tinchebray, Henry did two things of real importance at the start of his reign. First of all, he issued a Charter of Liberties, in which he promised to uphold the "good laws of King Edward the Confessor"—whatever they were—and not to exceed his rights. Though he later broke practically all his specific promises, at least he set a precedent for the idea that the king had to keep the law. Secondly, he married an English queen. This was Maud, or Matilda, the daughter of St. Margaret, the Queen of Scotland and niece of that Edgar the Atheling whom the Witan had tried to elect as king in 1066. Thus, he saw to it that his children would have an English claim to the throne. His reign was a quiet one, because he saw to it that it was quiet. For this, people called him "the Lion of Justice."

As far as can be discovered, Henry I gave England her first effective central administration. The two Williams had ruled largely by personal intervention. Henry went further, making a machinery of government that could do routine work for him. Here emerges more clearly the Magnum Concilium that has replaced the Witan. In practice, though not in law, an inner committee took shape, that came to be known as the Curia Regis, or King's Council. Its functions were both those of a court and those of an administrative body. Three high officials always belonged to this inner council, the Justiciar, the Treasurer, and the Chancellor. The Justiciar was a kind of vice-king running the country when, as often happened, Henry was away in Normandy, and was also a chief justice, as his title indicated. The Treasurer took care of the payments from the treasury. The Chancellor kept the Great Seal of the kingdom and authenticated all important documents and charters. Furthermore, records exist of an accounting, and therefore a tax-collecting, body, the Exchequer. It got this name from the sort of checkerboard on which sums of money were physically laid out and on which notched tally sticks were compared to keep the royal accounts straight. When possible, money, rather than goods, was taken in payments; and coins were examined to see if they met proper standards of weight and fineness. Nor did this administration merely stay at the royal court. Itinerant justices were sometimes sent out to check up on the shire courts and make sure the sheriffs were doing their jobs properly.

Here, it should be noted, is a pattern that will be followed in the evolution of English democratic government, in the evolution of Canadian democratic government, and in the general evolution of self-government in the British Empire. From the Magnum Concilium of nobles and administrators mixed will grow the idea of a legislative Parliament in which administrators are members. From the Curia Regis—the Magnum Concilium members serving in another capacity, at first—will grow the Privy Council, now the supreme court of the Empire, and the Cabinet, now the chief executive body of the kingdom. From the Treasury and the Exchequer will grow a vast civil service. From the travels of the itinerant justices will grow a great system of national law courts. Overseas, by a similar evolution, in which the governor takes the place of the king, similar institutions will grow. Councils that originally help in administration will separate into legislatures and Cabinets that will still remain linked, since all Cabinet members will be members of the legislatures. Much will happen before this evolution reaches its end. But if this pattern of the expansion of the council is kept clearly in mind, the story of that evolution will come into focus, as one sees that pattern repeat itself again and again.

Why, it may be asked, if Henry's reign was so significant, is all this superstructure of results prefaced with the qualification "as far as can be discovered"? The answer is simple: our records are fragmentary. On Henry's death in 1135, England fell into anarchy. Just enough manuscript material has survived the consequent destruction of the civil wars to allow what has been here set down to be considered as a strong probability. It is known that certain of the famous reforms of the next Henry, 1154 to 1189, were based on precedents of his grandfather's reign. It is those precedents that are described, along with their possible ultimate consequences. In between took place the stormy period known as the reign of Stephen and Matilda, that was long to serve to the English subjects and Franco-Norman nobility alike as a horrible example of misrule. For Henry I died without a male heir, his only son William having been drowned in the Channel in the sinking of the "White Ship." Two claimants contested the throne, his nephew, Count Stephen of Blois, and his daughter, the "Empress" Matilda. Matilda was the widow of the Emperor Henry of the Holy Roman Empire, and the wife by a second marriage of Count Geoffrey Plantagenet of Anjou. Neither Stephen, who first seized the throne, nor Matilda, who afterward invaded England, could secure control. The more turbulent nobles took the opportunity to ravage and to gain power by switching from side to side. Disorder was so great that, when Stephen's son died, it was agreed that Matilda's son, Henry Plantagenet, should succeed to the throne and try to control it.

In the three-quarters of a century from 1066 to 1135, three kings greatly changed England. Feudalism became universal after the Norman conquest, with the feudal rulers of a different culture and speech from the inhabitants of their manors. To this day, the English language shows that distinction. We use the Anglo-Saxon word "cow" for the animal the Saxon tended on the farm, the French word "beef" (from *boeuf*) for the food served on the Norman-French lord's table. But the Norman kings, William the Conqueror, William Rufus, and Henry Beauclerc, did more than give England her present aristocracy. They unconsciously started a constitutional evolution. For the first two reigned as kings directly, but the third reigned as well through his council. As this vague beginning takes more and more definite form, there will appear over the centuries a regular pattern by which power goes from the king to the people. First will be the power of the king alone. Then will come the "King in Council." As popular elements enter the council to talk things over, Parliament—an old word, now with a new meaning—will come into existence and the king will rule in Parliament, till today Parliament and council are responsible to the people. Similarly, there will be a parallel evolution overseas, from governors ruling alone, to a "governor in council," a local parliament, and the council becoming responsible not to the governor but to the parliament. All this evolution began by making the kingship a powerful permanent center of government. It was just because England had a strong monarchy, the Belgian historian Esmein says, that she could early have popular safeguards against strong government.

4

HENRY II AND THE COMMON LAW

The importance of what happened in Henry II's reign can be seen by comparing the reigns before and after it. Under Stephen and Matilda England fell into anarchy. But though Richard I spent less than one year of his eleven-year reign in England, the government of the kingdom on the whole improved in those years. What had happened in between was that Henry II had permanently established the English judicial system.

It is a great help to a reformer to have been preceded by an object lesson, and just before Henry came to the throne the years 1135 to 1154 had shown England what was wrong with feudalism. The great lords had played Stephen and Matilda off against each other, had built castles that could laugh at a forty-day feudal siege, and had even gone so far as to use their powers in the Magnum Concilium to force decisions there against the king's will. During this time they oppressed the common people horribly. The chronicles kept in the monasteries tell of what went on, in no unmeasured terms—of kidnaping, extortion, murder, and rape. The situation was so bad that public opinion crystallized, and all concerned were willing to accept Matilda's son as Stephen's heir, if so doing might lead to improvement. That was why Stephen, in 1153, signed the Treaty of Wallingford with Henry FitzEmpress; *i.e.*, son of the former Empress Matilda, which made Henry's accession to the throne uncontested.

Henry FitzEmpress brought much with him to the rule of England. He was the undisputed ruler of Normandy. This had been won for him by his father, Count Geoffrey Plantagenet (*i.e.*, planter of the broom plant or *planta genista* in Latin) of Anjou. The Angevins, hereditary enemies of the Normans, had taken pleasure in thus conquering the future king's duchy for him. Furthermore, Henry ruled, in addition, the County of Maine. Above all, just before he became king of England, Henry had married Eleanor, Duchess of Aquitaine, the divorced wife of King Louis VII of France. That extended his French dominions from the Channel to the Pyrenees, making him, the vassal for them to Louis, much more powerful than his liege lord. From these duchies and counties the new king could draw not only troops and revenues but also experience, and could transplant administrative methods of Anjou and Normandy to England. Last but not least, Henry had the personal qualities needed to be a great king. He had a good mind, immense energy, and a violent temper, which in those days was an asset as well as a liability. His good mind led him to understand fine points of law and know in time when he was beaten. His immense energy allowed his traveling over all his dominions and keeping in touch with what went on. That energy might manifest itself in a passion for hunting, and a passion for having his chaplains rattle off the Mass at top speed to let him out of church quickly, but it also got things done. As for his temper, it was no bad thing to be feared, if he were to be a good king.

The means by which Henry accomplished his reforms was to decide what change was needed, to summon a meeting of the Magnum Concilium and then to announce that it had advised him (which might in part be true) to change the laws of England in some respect or other. Thus the history of his reign is largely of the assizes or sittings of the Magnum Concilium, at which these changes were made.

Henry's first action was to announce that all the charters Stephen had granted were invalid. That ended the hopes of the powerful nobles of keeping what they had extorted from the king during the troublous years from 1135 to 1154. Then he finished what Stephen had started doing; that is, pulling down the "unlicensed castles." This required using some permanent troops, for which his growing revenues paid. Next he refurbished the machinery of government his grandfather Henry I had founded. The judicial members of the Curia Regis followed him about on his travels and saw to it that all his dominions were well governed. The departments of the Exchequer that hoarded bullion, smelted it, and kept permanent records remained at Westminster. The itinerant justices, whom Henry I had sent out, once more went out to check up on the sheriffs, especially after an "Inquest of Sheriffs" had shown what reforms were needed. These justices increased the flow of business to the courts by issuing written orders, called writs to this day, by which plaintiffs could order defendants to come in to trial or face the King's displeasure. These writs, however, also protected the defendants, for only those issues were tried that were specified in the writs. A new cause of complaint could be brought to trial only by persuading the court that there was justification for issuing a different writ.

The full establishment of itinerant royal courts is really the work of Henry II. He saw to it that the justices got the reverence due the King. To this day the judges on circuit receive royal honors even to the point that when at dinner the King's health is drunk they remain seated. It might be possible for a great noble to intimidate a sheriff, who was a resident all the year round of the county (or shire—the words are the same in meaning). But a royal judge, under the King's personal protection, who, moreover, would probably not return the next year, could not be frightened in the same way, and any attempt at illicit pressure would call forth the King's famous Angevin temper. These justices, furthermore, had been given a new method of trial. In Normandy it had long been the custom to settle cases by taking some twelve men, forcing them to swear a terrifying oath, and then asking them to tell the truth about the matter at issue. From these sworn men, "hommes jurés" in French, evolved our grand and petit juries, whose names show their Norman-French origin. Today, in America, a grand jury decides whether or not to prosecute, a petit jury whether or not a man is guilty, or whether or not the facts in a dispute are properly stated. The judge's job, today, is to preside over the management of the trial. Early juries were far different, simply a group of witnesses forced to tell the truth and speak for their whole district.[1] Just the same, they gave a far better brand of justice than was to be obtained either in feudal courts or in the shire courts. Consequently, because it was known that when itinerant justices took over a shire court justice would be done, plaintiffs preferred to bring their cases to them. And, because the fines and fees in court made a profit, the improvement of justice led to an improvement of the royal income.

Gradually, there was specialization into three general types of cases. Some were suits between the King and his subjects over taxes and other payments made across the checkerboard used for accounting; these were the future Exchequer cases. Some were disputed between the King and his subjects over law; these were the future King's Bench cases. Some were disputes between one subject and another; these were the future Common Pleas cases. But the specialization, though emerging, was not complete. The same justices sometimes tried the different sorts of cases, and it is not yet entirely correct to say that the three separate royal courts at Westminster—Exchequer, King's Bench, and Common Pleas—had come into existence. However, a great step toward this separation had been taken when the royal Exchequer was moved from Winchester to Westminster, where a true capital of England was growing up, hard by Edward the Confessor's "Abbey of St. Peter" (the correct name of Westminster Abbey).

From the Magnum Concilium as the effective body of chosen nobles and clerks developed the Courts and the national administrative offices. One should not for a moment lose sight of the fact that it was the pressure of business upon the King that prevented him from carrying out all the functions of collecting revenue and acting as judge. The several courts, of

---

[1] By a similar system of community responsibility, called frankpledge, small local groups were held accountable for each other's good behavior and annually checked on by a View of Frankpledge.

which the Exchequer is the best example, became permanent and of great importance in the administration of law and of government because of the king's delegation of power to those who had the obligation of serving and of advising in the Magnum Concilium. It was the supremacy of royal power that in this period allowed for the development of the legal system and later the establishment and use of the "High Court of Parliament."

Therefore, the next reforms of Henry's reign were discoveries of new pretexts for bringing cases into the royal courts. One such device was the idea of the "King's peace." This was not a novel idea; it was to be found all over Europe. It was not even a novel idea in England, for in Canute's laws is to be found mention of hamesucken, the crime of breaking the King's peace. But under Henry the application of the idea grew apace. As will be remembered, English law had been a matter of damage suits. The King now discovered damages he had been suffering. A crime on the King's highway personally affronted him. The breaking into a house, since homes were under his protection, was also an affront to him. Therefore, he sued the accused. That is why criminal cases in England are in the form of *Rex* (or King) *v. So-and-so,* and in America, where the states and the Federal government are the King's successors in rights, in the form of *State v. So-and-so* or *United States v. So-and-so.* In property cases, too, the King took a hand. As all lands, in feudal theory, are basically the King's, trespass concerns his rights and should be tried in his courts. Naturally, everyone who could have a royal trial wanted one. Royal justice was more impartial and fairer than any known before. Therefore, the King's judges issued written orders, or writs, permitting such trials. When some new situation arose, a new sort of writ was issued. Cases poured in on the royal courts. Although Henry traveled with his court all over England, there was so much to be done that he left a court permanently behind him at Westminster. That began evolving into three courts—King's Bench for criminal cases of *Rex v. So-and-so,* Common Pleas for civil cases, and Exchequer for tax cases and royal revenue of all sorts that were settled across the checkerboard of the royal accounts. More than that, itinerant justices were gradually allowed to add civil cases to the criminal ones they tried on circuit. To give speedier justice, they issued writs taking cognizance of civil suits unless—as rarely if ever happened—those suits came to trial in Westminster earlier. Such was the origin of nisi prius jurisdiction, those being the Latin words for "unless earlier" at the head of the writ.

In the handling of this flood of new business the King's judges naturally had to be consistent. As they rode different circuits, they tried to apply the same principles all over England. Furthermore, as they had a new slant on the cases they tried, they really originated the law they applied.

This was not intentional. They did not mean to make changes, but they made them, just the same. For example, if they had an inheritance case in Kent (which would come under their jurisdiction under the new principle that they would protect the heir against trespassers), they would enforce the peculiar custom of "gavelkind" by which, in Kent, under certain circumstances the youngest son rather than the oldest son got the property. But the news would go all over England that if a lord tried to drive a vassal off land, the vassal could get redress by getting a writ (called Novel Disseisin) for a trial in the King's court. As this new principle was common to all England, it and similar new principles were called Common Law. Common Law, therefore, is judge-made law. It comes from the application of a known principle to a new set of circumstances. In the process often the principle is so stretched as to become a new one, but in theory, at least, the judge is just trying to be reasonable and consistent.

This evolution of a court system involved some basic decisions. If names and dates are wanted, it was the Assizes of Clarendon of 1166 and of Northampton of 1176 that created the effectiveness of the judicial system. These were not the only legislative actions of Henry's reign. He also reconstituted what should now be called the militia rather than the fyrd, and he straightened out the forest laws. The first was done by the Assize of Arms of 1183. This stated the duty of every man, according to his means, to bear arms at the king's order. That put into effect the idea latent in the Oath of Salisbury Plain, that in case of conflict between king and noble, all must support the king. It made that duty explicit; if a man had such and such property, he must provide such and such arms, be he noble, free, or serf. At the Assize of Woodstock, 1184, Henry fixed the rules that protected for him his favorite sport. So it was that by the end of Henry's reign, the general rights and duties of Englishmen were clear, and it was also clear what happened if those rights were infringed or those duties not performed.

But along with these successes Henry had two great failures—the Church and his family, the former coming first. Ten years after he came to the throne, he tackled the problem of the abuse of the special privileges of the clergy. Over the course of years, more and more people had claimed exemption from the ordinary law courts because of some connection with the Church. It got so that every rascal who could read and write, or who could even recite a particular verse from the Bible (John 1:1), claimed "benefit of clergy." As this secured trial before a lenient court that did not use a death sentence, the particular verse which saved one from hanging became known as the "neck verse." Henry, therefore, dug up the idea William the Conqueror had had, of the "ancient liberties" of the Church of England, and had them set down in the Constitutions of Clarendon, 1164 (not to be confused with the assize of the same name two years later).

Slipped into this list of ancient customs was the extension of an agreement about the forest laws. This provided that whenever a cleric had been convicted in a church court he might be retried—and more severely punished—in a royal court, and that to make sure of the second trial clerics so accused might be taken into the custody of the royal courts. Henry proposed to extend this agreement to bring all cases into royal courts for a second trial. Here the King ran up against unexpected opposition. He thought he had the Church of England under good control. He had just succeeded in having consecrated as Archbishop of Canterbury one Thomas Becket, a former official of his. He had not taken Becket's priesthood seriously. Indeed, Becket had been one of those "quasi" clerics against whom the Constitutions of Clarendon were to be directed, one who had taken the most minor orders of priesthood to get legal status and had stopped there. When Becket had become archbishop, it had been necessary to raise him through the degrees of priesthood the day before his consecration. To Henry's surprise, Becket refused to accept the Constitutions, for he considered the King's reforms as tearing down canon law and the clergy's privileges. Six years of struggle ensued, during which Henry tried to enforce the Constitutions in violation of old customs, and Becket used his authority against them. Finally, in 1170, Henry in rage asked: "Who will rid me of this troublous priest?" Four knights took him at his word. They sought out the Archbishop and slew him in the aisle of his own cathedral. At once a popular outcry arose, so great that three years later the Pope canonized Becket as a saint and martyr. Here Henry knew when he was beaten. He might, and did, dicker with the Pope as to the terms of his surrender, and try to save what he could of the Constitutions of Clarendon. But surrender he must, and the sight was seen of the King of England trudging barefoot, with bleeding feet, three miles to the altar of Canterbury, to atone for his sin. It was to the tomb of St. Thomas that the poet Chaucer sent his pilgrims on their travels.

Here it might be well to stop a moment and remember the place of the church in the Middle Ages. In those days everyone (except the Jewish moneylenders who were eventually expelled from England) belonged to one truly Catholic and all-embracing church. This was a sacramental church. Its doctrine was that the way to salvation was through the seven sacraments—baptism, confirmation, penance, ordination, marriage, the Eucharist or Communion or the Mass (to give that sacrament the three names it has under three aspects), and extreme unction, all of which required a priest unless under exceptional circumstances. No wonder that excommunication, or the denial of the sacraments to one man, and interdict, or denial of the sacraments (except baptism and extreme unction) to whole nations or groups, were powerful political weapons. They were not easy to misuse, for priests might and did refuse to use them when they thought the order to do so unjustified. But if public opinion supported the Church, no matter how powerful and determined a king might be, the two working together could bring him to his knees.

Henry's other trouble was his sons and his wife. He spoiled them and could not control them. To his eldest son, Henry, whom he had crowned in boyhood to ensure a safe succession to the throne, he gave Normandy. Then the two kings fought till young Henry died. To Richard, his second and oldest surviving son, he gave Anjou and Aquitaine. Richard he fought, before and after the death of the "Young King." To Geoffrey he gave Brittany, which he secured for him by a judicious marriage. With him he fought, too, till Geoffrey died. John, his youngest and favorite son, long lacked land, hence his nickname of "Lackland." At last to John he gave Ireland, when his vassal Strongbow conquered it for him, under a claim created by the only English Pope, Adrian IV. John repaid his father with revolt, news of which saddened Henry on his deathbed. And through all this Eleanor, Henry's queen, egged her sons on. She, like her husband, had a temper and an unbending will. The reason all this happened was that, though Henry was uncontested King of England, in France he was only the greatest feudal lord, and as such subject to feudal revolt.

At Henry's death, the Third Crusade was starting. Henry himself had been swept up in the enthusiasm for rescuing the Holy Sepulchre from Saladin, and had collected money for an expedition to Palestine by the Saladin Tithe, just before he died, in 1187. His son, Richard, took over the throne, all claims in France, and the duty of going on Crusade. Richard's reign is a curious interlude in English history, because he mattered so little at home, so much abroad. In world history, Richard is the able general who almost but not quite restored Christian rule in Jerusalem. In Arabic legend he is El Melik Ric, the antagonist whose feats of valor bring out the greater valor of the hero Saladin who defeated him. In romance he is the knight errant whose deeds catch men's imagination across the centuries. In French history he is the rebellious vassal who till his death challenged the great King Philip Augustus. But in English history, Richard is an absentee in whose name the kingdom was well ruled by Hubert Walter. For in 1187 Richard set out on the Third Crusade, along with Philip Augustus of France and a motley army from all over Europe. He reached Palestine, saved the fortress of Acre by a daring landing (Acre will reappear in English history), and tried—and failed—to weld the army into a unit that would recapture Jerusalem. In the process he became adored by the rank and file of that army and hated by its leaders. On his return home he was jailed by one of the leaders, the Archduke of Austria, and held incommunicado till his minstrel, Blondel, discovered his whereabouts. Blondel sang one of Richard's favorite tunes outside the prison and heard Richard answer. Then he went back to England to get the necessary ransom. Money had to be raised from Scotland to Gascony, through all the lands of the Plantagenet inheritance. Charters were sold and rights relinquished on all sides. Here it was that the City of London got many of its treasured privileges. On release, Richard spent the rest of his life in France, flouting his liege lord there, Philip Augustus, by constant revolt. A sample of his actions was the building of Chateau Gaillard, the Saucy Fortress, as an insult, in land Philip claimed he had no right to. Finally Richard, in need of money, besieged a vassal who had dug up a treasure, and was killed by a chance arrow. Yet for all this waywardness, Richard in many ways benefited England. His people obeyed his ministers —who would rebel against the first soldier of Europe? He chose good ministers. He gave charters—to get money for his crusade, his ransom, and his wars with Philip. He let the shires elect "coroners" to decide what cases were and were not royal, thus checking overexpansion of the royal courts at the right moment. Therefore, setting aside his not inconsiderable contributions to romance and historical novels, what Richard did was to prove that the governmental structure built by Henry II had been built to last, that the work of his terrible-tempered, energetic father had made English justice a permanent, reliable thing.

5

MAGNA CARTA AND PARLIAMENT

Since 1066 England had had three outstanding rulers—William the Conqueror, Henry I (Beauclerc) and Henry II (FitzEmpress, the first Plantagenet)—as well as two effective ones—William II (Rufus) and Richard I (the Lion-hearted)—as against only one bad reign, that of Stephen and Matilda. This tended to make the central government almost too strong. But then, from 1199 to 1273, England was blessed by the ultimately beneficial rule of two of her worst kings, John and Henry III. Their faults led to the issuing and reissuing of Magna Carta, which ultimately came to be considered the basic law of the land, and to the establishment of Parliament as a working institution. (For this latter Simon de Montfort deserves his share of credit, as well.) Then, after these two reigns, a strong king, Edward I, was able to combine the work of Henry II and of De Montfort and give English government the framework it has today, of executive rule by the King in Council, legislative rule by the King in Parliament, and judicial rule by the King's judges, a system of interlocking rather than of balanced powers.

Henry II had been a powerful king because his government was, on the whole, trusted. Cases were brought to his royal courts rather than to feudal courts because the royal courts—whether assizes with the itinerant justices on circuit or "sedentary" courts at Westminster—gave better justice. In questions of how much relief to pay for an inheritance, or what were legitimate expenses of wardship to pay a guardian, the nobles themselves preferred the decisions of the King's judges. This situation continued during the absentee rule of Richard. But on Richard's death, matters rapidly deteriorated. First of all, there was a disputed succession. In strict law, at least as interpreted later on, the next king should have been Arthur of Brittany, the son of Richard's next brother, Geoffrey. But he was a minor, and the need of an adult king was strongly felt. That made it possible for the youngest brother, John Lackland, to take the throne in England, resting his title on the choice of the people. That did not give John the French fiefs, Normandy, Maine, Brittany, Anjou, and Aquitaine. A civil war, therefore, broke out between John and his nephew. It was quickly ended, for Arthur was captured and soon died— murdered, it is generally believed, by his uncle. John thus obtained an opportunity of showing himself an effective ruler of the whole Angevin inheritance.

But John soon got himself into difficulties. He threw over his fiancée and married a young noblewoman, despite the fact that she too was already engaged to be married. This was not merely personally dishonest; it also raised questions of feudal law, since two dowries had been pledged. As such a case required trial in the court of a feudal superior, King Philip Augustus of France, who had been trying in vain to oust Richard from Normandy and Aquitaine, summoned John to his court. John, not unnaturally, refused to attend, whereupon Philip's court declared John's French fiefs forfeit. Naturally, it took hard fighting to get them; but it was this decision against John that lost him the loyalty of many supporters in France and so made Philip's success possible. By the end of John's reign, all that was left to the English royal house outside the British Isles was the Channel Islands—a part of Normandy the French could not reach—and Aquitaine. This loss eventually benefited England, for it ended the habit the early English kings had of living outside their kingdom, and ended it at just about the moment when such living outside stopped being an education and would have become absenteeism.

But that benefit was not at first realized. For to get money to fight Philip, John turned his royal powers into abuses. He exacted the utmost limit of relief and wardship. He would call out his feudal inferiors for military service, then commute that service for "scutage" or shield money, and then call them out again for more scutage. This transformed into an imposition what had been a sensible arrangement of Henry II's for hiring soldiers on a permanent basis instead of vexing his vassals with a limited forty-day service. Then, John used the soldiers so hired to extort more money. Particularly in the north, this roused the nobility against him. To cap this, John made an enemy of the Church. It had been the custom of the king to exact a sort of relief from each diocese, on the death of a bishop, of the first year's revenues. It had also been customary for the king to take over the feudal administration of a diocese, including its revenues, till another bishop was chosen. John used the death of the Archbishop of Canterbury as a means of exacting money. When, in 1205, the clergy of the cathedral elected a new archbishop, John refused to confirm their candidate, and forced them to elect a man subservient to him. (In theory, to this day, bishops are elected in the Church of England, but the election has become a form of accepting a royal nominee.) Pope Innocent III, perhaps the most powerful pope who ever lived, now took a hand. He sent for a deputation of the clergy and ordered them to hold an election in Rome in his presence. Naturally enough, at that election there was chosen neither the original candidate, nor John's nominee, but Innocent's nominee, Stephen Langton, who fortunately was the best choice.

It took from 1205 to 1215, a decade of misrule and extortion, to bring John to terms, even though he had against him both the Church and his barons. John succeeded in holding out so long because he was able to keep his treasury full and thus hire soldiers. He was able also to win the support of southern towns and those who felt oppressed by the high-handed barons. Not only did he use the revenues of the archbishopric of Canterbury, he also took over other bishoprics when their holders protested against his misdoing. John used torture freely in forcing obedience. One chronicler tells a grim story of how he starved a priest to death, refining the torture by putting him in a room so shaped that he could neither sit nor stand nor lie down, and making him wear a crushingly heavy miter. Against John, Innocent III used the then powerful weapons of the papacy —excommunication, interdict, and finally, deposition from the throne. It took a long time for them to take effect, but at last John, warned by the loss of his French possessions, reversed his stand. He accepted Stephen Langton as Archbishop of Canterbury, and even went so far as to acknowledge he had been deposed and to surrender England as a fief to the Pope, receiving it back again as the Pope's vassal. The respite he secured from his difficulties he then used to invade France, in collaboration with the Emperor Otto of Germany. But Philip Augustus defeated Otto in 1214 at the Battle of Bouvines and thus ended John's hope of getting back his lost provinces. Then, the next year, John had to face the opposition of his barons.

This opposition was all the more serious because John had not succeeded in deceiving Stephen Langton by his submission to the Pope. In spite of Innocent's instructions to the contrary, Langton supported the nobles who had taken up arms in rebellion. More than that, he gave them a practical program. He reminded them of the Charter of Liberties, which Henry I had issued, and suggested their getting a similar charter from John. At Bury St. Edmunds, a meeting of the barons adopted this suggestion. Then the barons joined forces with the Archbishop and the citizens of London; and all three—barons, Archbishop, citizens—met John on the field of Runnymede, near the royal castle of Windsor, on June 15, 1215. There they made him seal Magna Carta, the Great Charter.

Magna Carta was written by barons for barons. Basically, its purpose was to protect nobles against undue feudal exactions. It sets limits to reliefs, aids, wardships, and other feudal customs which might be used to exact money, such as castle-guard. It remedies many specific wrongs to persons, such as the King of Scotland and Llewellyn, a prince of Wales. But—and this is its great significance—it then goes further. Article I gives its freedoms "to all freemen . . . forever." [1] Article 12 prohibits "scutage

---

[1] "Freeman" might mean a suitor in a court; and a man who held by villein tenure in one place might hold by free tenure elsewhere, or might, though a villein, sue in

or aid" being levied except by the "common counsel of our kingdom."
Article 39 promises that arrest and similar processes shall take place only
"by the judgement of [one's] peers or by the law of the land." Article 40
pledges: "To no one will we sell, to no one will we deny, or delay, right
or justice." Just what those articles then meant is arguable, when most of
the population of England were villeins and serfs, not freemen. Did the
"common counsel of our kingdom" mean a sort of parliament? Did trial
by one's peers mean jury trial, or only the right of nobles to be tried
by nobles? That second right is still in existence, and in the 1930's was
used by a peer, who had a bad traffic accident, to get a lighter sentence.
Just what was meant by the "law of the land"—or "due process of law,"
to give the words a twist later generations employed—has been the matter of many a legal dispute. Did "the law of the land" mean what we now
mean by "due process of law"? Or did it mean merely the revival of old
feudal rights the Plantagenet kings had been trying to put down? Or did
it mean the local custom of the shire and manorial courts? The answer
seems to be that Magna Carta was intended for one group and not for
all Englishmen, but it had aspects which made it valuable to all Englishmen. It was expandable, so that later on its supposed provisions could be
applied to all Englishmen when all Englishmen were free. Furthermore,
it had some teeth. By Article 61, a committee of barons was set up, with
power to wage war on John if he broke his promises. Though this committee was never formally constituted, and though the clause was not
repeated in reissues of the charter, the idea may have provided precedent
for future control of the king by his subjects and future armed resistance
to the king to enforce such control. John's son, Henry, certainly was put by
force under such control.

Such a civil war soon broke out, for John, promising to go on a crusade,
secured from Innocent release from the promises of Magna Carta. Not
only did some of the barons take up arms against John, they also invited
Prince Louis of France to come over and be king. On the other hand,
John found support among those barons and townsmen who disliked the
northern barons and their plundering mercenaries. In the height of the
campaign, John got drenched crossing the marshy estuary of the Wash,
grossly overate of peaches and cider, and died October 16, 1216. That
at once changed matters. Now that John's infant son, Henry, would be
king, under a regency, no one wanted Prince Louis of France as regent.
For, fortunately, there was a man who was preeminently fitted to be
regent, William Marshal, Earl of Pembroke. He was the finest knight
in the land, already a figure of legend for his deeds in the wars of Henry

---

a court. That, and similar complications, make a definition of a freeman a difficult
thing.

II and his sons and for what he had accomplished in the Holy Land. He was also too old to be personally ambitious. An epic poem, the *Histoire de Guillaume le Maréchal,* calls him over eighty; more likely he was only over sixty, though that was a great age in itself in those unhealthy and warlike times. Above all, everyone trusted him; he was almost the only person whom both John and the barons trusted. Marshal understood the defense of England. Not only did he drive Louis's army into a corner; he had the Justiciar, Hubert de Burgh, gain command of the seas and prevent reinforcements from coming from France. By a naval battle of Dover in 1217, England gained peace, to be ruled under Magna Carta by its regent or his successors, till the ten-year-old Henry III should come of age. Ever since Magna Carta, the king, in theory at least, has had to keep the law. That this should be so the barons of England saw to, by having Henry, or his regent acting for him, confirm Magna Carta several times. Consequently the version that today has force of law is not that of 1215, nor that of 1217, but that of 1225, which does not contain the enforcement clause.

It was one thing to say that the king had to keep the law; it was another matter to make him do it. When Henry III came of age, he showed faults different from his father's, but almost as serious. He had foreign favorites; he was too obedient to the pope. First of all, he let his tutor, Bishop Peter des Roches, from Poitou, fill offices with Poitevins. Then he let his Savoyard wife, Eleanor of Provence, fill offices with Savoyards. Being deeply religious, and an admirer of England's last religious king, Edward the Confessor, he named his eldest son Edward, and tore down the Confessor's favorite church, Westminster Abbey, to rebuild it more splendidly, as it now stands. He took seriously the idea that England was a fief of the papacy and he a vassal of the pope with duties to his lord, and spent money in the wars between the popes and the Holy Roman Emperor. He even went so far as to let his brother Richard be elected an opposition Emperor, and his son Edmund an opposition King of Sicily. In the eyes of his barons, he was guilty of throwing away his fortune and that of his kingdom in these foreign wars.

All this took money and tempted to violations of feudal laws to get money. Consequently, groups of nobles rose up and secured reissuance of Magna Carta, such meetings of nobles securing from about 1240 the name of Parliaments. Finally, in 1258, at the so-called "Mad Parliament of Oxford," control of the government was taken from Henry and given to a committee of fifteen nobles. They ousted Henry's favorites and put in their own. After five years of this, Henry felt strong enough to make a demand for arbitration. The question was put into the hands of King Louis of France (St. Louis, the son of the Prince Louis above), whom the whole of Europe considered the model of justice. St. Louis decided in favor of his fellow king, in 1264, in the Mise of Amiens. This the barons would not tolerate, and they revolted under the leadership of Earl Simon de Montfort. De Montfort, at Lewes in Sussex, with the aid of the citizens of London, defeated Henry. Then he called a Parliament. To this not only came the greater nobles, but also representatives of the lesser nobility and the cities and boroughs. Following a precedent of 1213, when John had tried to get advice and help from the lesser nobility, De Montfort had the freemen meeting in shire courts send up two knights from each shire. In certain borough courts, the burgesses of the borough also elected two of their number to represent them. By thus broadening the base of his movement, De Montfort changed his revolt from a feudal opposition to the king into a transfer of governing power to representatives of the free people of England. Then he and other nobles ruled as had been suggested at Oxford, responsible to this larger group. In theory, the king ruled because everything was done in his name, but the barons secured the right to advise and counsel the king.

Probably this early experiment of an executive responsible to Parliament would have broken down if it had lasted long. The problems Earl Simon would have had to meet took centuries for later generations of Englishmen to solve, under better conditions. But the experiment was cut short in a year. Henry III's son, Edward, gathered troops, marched against Earl Simon, and killed him at the battle of Evesham, 1265. But the one year's work between Lewes and Evesham was never to be undone. For Edward, who in effect ruled for his father for the rest of the reign, had two abilities his father lacked. He could learn from experience, and he could keep his promises. He saw that laws once established had to be kept, and that the way to rule well was to have public opinion on the king's side. As a result, though Earl Simon died, his ideas lived, and were applied by the man who had beaten him.

At the moment of Henry's death, Edward was in the Holy Land on a crusade. It took him two years to make his way back to England, but so firmly was he in the saddle that there was no question about his accession. On his return, he at once settled to work, so catching the imagination of his subjects and of posterity that he gained not one but three nicknames— Longshanks, for his long legs; Malleus Scotorum, or Hammer of the Scots, for what he did to the Scots; and the English Justinian, for his legal reforms.

Three sets of records that come from his reign tell what he meant to English law. These are the Year Books, the Parliament Rolls, and the Statute Rolls. The Year Books, which begin in 1272, tell of decisions in individual cases. They serve to remind us that the English court system took definitely, in Edward's reign, the form that had been evolving since Henry II or Henry I. To this day, in the many volumes of law reports, similar records of precedent-setting decisions are the basis in practice of the workings of the legal systems of the Commonwealth of Nations and of the United States. But Edward did not merely encourage judges to do their job well. He went beyond that, as is indicated by the Parliament Rolls and by the Statute Rolls. From the Parliament Rolls can be learned how the King, who sometimes sat among his judges, called for wide counsel in difficult cases, by a writ *De veniendo ad parliamentum* (of coming to talk things over). This was his highest court. Here one can see the word "parliament" taking on a new meaning. In 1066, when the Norman barons had refused to join in William's invasion as a feudal duty, it had meant just "talking things over." Now the word had come to mean a supreme court. Such a meaning, in France, became applied to the regional supreme courts, or "parlements," that spring up at about this time. Since the English had become accustomed to think of communities, be they shires or boroughs, being represented much as a district was represented by a jury in those days, it was natural, at times, for knights from the shires, burgesses from the boroughs, to be summoned by such a writ. But Edward did not stop here. At his Parliaments, he, at times, promulgated clarifications or improvements in the law, much as had Henry II with his assizes. All the general statements of one parliamentary session were written on a single roll of manuscript, known as a statute. Hence, when later generations realized that clarification of the law had turned into making new law, it became customary to speak of all the law of one session as chapters of a statute, and to call the final passage of a law its enrollment. Later generations, likewise, when they printed the statutes from the Statute Roll, realized that earlier documents not on the Statute Roll were in fact statutes. That is why in the printed laws of England, Magna Carta is the first statute.

Thus, as we covered much of Henry II's reign by telling of the assizes, so can much of Edward I's reign be covered by telling of the statutes. The first such great action by Edward dealt with the feudal courts. On his return to his kingdom, he had his judges issue a writ of quo warranto (by what warrant) to inquire the justification for the existence of feudal courts. Most nobles obeyed this writ, and either proved their right to hold such courts or desisted from holding them, though in one famous case John de Warenne answered the writ by showing his sword and was questioned no further. The information supplied in response to the writ was duly recorded on the Hundred Rolls. Since to know who sued in what court and why, in feudal times, formed a census, the Hundred Rolls tell us of Edward's England much what Domesday Book tells us of the Conqueror's England. Then, six years later, Edward promulgated in Parliament the Statute of Gloucester, which abolished all feudal courts that did not have charters or that did not go back beyond the first day of Richard I's reign.

Since "justice means fee," that is, since a court system more than paid its way, this increased Edward I's revenues.

Even before Edward had finished his work on feudal courts, he went to work on the royal courts. His three Statutes of Westminster, 1275, 1285, 1290, settled the royal courts and the shire courts. Thenceforth, King's Bench, Common Pleas, and Exchequer had definite form, in law as well as in fact, and definite procedure. In these statutes, there were also important clauses regulating land tenure. In Westminster II was a clause or law, *De donis conditionalibus* (of conditional grants), to quote its first words which are used as its name. This established entail, the holding of land in a family so that it must pass from father to son and cannot be sold without the consent of the heirs. This kept big estates together, since only one heir could inherit under entail, and also protected such estates from being seized for debt. For naturally, the heirs would not let the land be taken away from them. In Westminster III was a clause, *Quia Emptores* (since they are buyers), which forbade subinfeudation. Until then, if a lord sold land, the purchaser became his vassal. Such transactions caused the growth of feudal armies, since most land transfers implied military service. But after *Quia Emptores,* sales of land made the purchaser the vassal not of the seller but of the king.

It was not only the court system that Edward regulated. By the Statute of Acton Burnell or of Merchants, in 1283, he made it possible to collect debts in royal courts and so much improved the transaction of business. By the Statute of Mortmain, in 1279, he forbade the giving of land to the church without permission. Mortmain means "dead hand," and he feared that whatever passed into the dead hand of the church would never get out again. By the Statute of Winchester, of 1285, he recodified the Assize of Arms, established the duty of all to be ready to fight for the king, and set up in every parish an officer, the constable, whose duty it would be to see to it all had the necessary weapons. But as the constable was the one person in each parish who had to have a weapon, it was natural for him to be given powers of entering and arresting. He would be sure to be able to carry out court orders. Thus it is that the title constable for a policeman, and the whole law of arrest, is based on the Statute of Winchester. In fifteen years, from 1275 to 1290, as covered by the Statutes of Westminster and the others here mentioned, the law of England had been made clear. Though much of this was building on previous work, now for the first time England knew that to find out rights and duties all that was needed was to go to the statute rolls and see what the King had promised. He was known for his motto, *Pactum Serva* (I keep my troth), and those written royal promises would be far different from the deceptions of his grandfather, John.

Just how these early statutes were agreed upon is not clear. They were issued in the King's name, as are all statutes in England to this day. They were issued not as acts of the King in Council but as decisions of the King after consultation with a larger group. The size of the group and its composition varied. About one time in nine, knights from the shires and burgesses from the boroughs were present, especially at the more important meetings such as the passing of the Statutes of Westminster and Acton Burnell. This was done to get information from the knights and burgesses and also to disarm opposition. It could be asserted that because the representatives of the shires and boroughs had thus been consulted, everyone in the shire or borough had been committed to agreement. Then when lords, knights, and burgesses went back home, they spread news of the new laws to the people in general. In Edward's case, however, opposition eventually arose. He did not become the Hammer of the Scots without spending money. To get more, he started levying import and export taxes, especially on wool. Matters came to a head in the years from 1295 to 1297.

In 1295, Edward had taken great pains to gather a Parliament, such great pains that some scholars have called this the Model Parliament, though others have pointed out that its model was not entirely followed. To it came not only the great nobles but two knights from each shire, two burgesses from some boroughs, and representatives of the parish clergy. Then the next year, Edward, when fighting in Flanders and needing money, made his celebrated "evil taking" or Maltôte of Wool, a form of customs duty, on which he collected 40s. a sack. Such a taking of property without legal right caused an uproar, and Edward had to back down. At Ghent, November 5, 1297, he issued the Confirmation of the Charters. This was more than just confirming Magna Carta, for it stated that the King would not make any grant of the right to levy a tax once a precedent for levying it again without another grant. Enrolled with the Confirmation of the Charters is a document which historians now consider only to have been a petition, but which has been treated as if it were a law with binding force. This was the so-called statute *De tallagio non concedendo* (of tallage that ought not to be granted) which ran: "No tallage or aid shall henceforth be imposed or levied by us or by our heirs in our kingdom except by the will and common assent of the archbishops, bishops, and other prelates, and of the earls, barons, knights, burgesses, and other freemen in our kingdom."

As *De Tallagio* suggests, the English Parliament in those days did not have a separate organization but met, as far as can be told, as a single body. Gradually, however, it divided into four bodies after a preliminary joint session. The great nobles sat in the House of Lords; the lesser nobles and burgesses, who were present as representatives of shires or boroughs, sat in the House of Commons, and the clergy had a curious arrangement.

As holders of feudal privileges, the archbishops and bishops sat in the House of Lords. Similarly, representatives of the lower clergy appeared at meetings of the House of Commons, but refused to sit. Then the archdioceses of Canterbury and York each had their own Parliaments, or Convocations, that legislated for them on church affairs. After 1343, the situation began to become clear. Parliament in England was a body of two houses, both of which gave assent to legislation when called upon, according to certain precedents. The clergy were bound by its decisions, but in each archdiocese they had their own legislative body, Convocation. By means of Parliament, English laws and taxes were made by the consent of representatives summoned by the king.

In order to understand the growth and development of Parliament, emphasis should not be placed upon the right of the people to be represented in the Middle Ages. All authority and power, of whatever nature, came directly from the power vested in the king. Parliament could be summoned only when he wished and could be dissolved or prorogued at his personal pleasure. When there was a weak king, men sought to govern England by controlling the important offices of the state, such as the Lord Chancellor, the Lord Chamberlain, and the office of Marshal. In one of the Scots wars of Edward II, the entire management of finances as well as nearly all the campaign was carried on through the office of the Privy Seal. Parliament was an efficient instrument in the hands of the monarchs or those who acted in the king's name because of three functions that it performed better than other institutions. First, Parliament became a final resort to which men came carrying the records of their county courts and appealing to the king to make improvements in national policy. The members of Parliament, particularly the House of Commons, whether knights of the shires or burgesses, were, therefore, official representatives of their communities. They could be asked to speak for their communities. Until the late fourteenth century, and beyond into the sixteenth, it was customary for the king to tell the Commons what he desired them to do and for them to agree and bind their communities to accept.

A second function of Parliament, and one that it retains to this day, was that of acting as a court. Later King Henry VIII said that nowhere could he enjoy as great a power or as much majesty as when he sat in his "High Court of Parliament." Best of all, Edward I, Simon de Montfort, and others, who had great political skill, could make use of members of Parliament not only to represent their communities but to carry information concerning the king's desires and to give the king and his ministers a feeling of what Englishmen were thinking. In the Middle Ages, no better way of expressing public opinion could have been found than that of summoning the representatives of the burgesses and the shires to meet once or twice a year with the king. The growth of parliamentary powers, then, came from the fact of royal supremacy and the position of the crown in the English constitution, rather than from the existence of representative and democratic principles in the constitution of the Middle Ages.

At the end of the reign of Edward I, that is, July 7, 1307, England had gone far from the days of Harold Godwinson, two hundred and fifty years and a few months before, and yet had preserved much that was characteristic of Anglo-Saxon popular government. Before turning to the conquests of Edward—which are a separate subject—it is worth while to review the changes which had occurred.

Harold Godwinson's England was an England turning gradually into a feudal state. In war, the country had a small navy (when the king was wise enough to have one), a tiny standing army (the Housecarls) of mounted infantry, and a backbone of militia (the fyrd) for defense. Setting aside the feudalism and manorialism that was creeping in, the court system included all freemen from the town courts which managed the village communities through the hundred and shire courts. Only the last court of appeal, the Witan (which also elected the king in case of emergency), was restricted in membership. The only government officer was the sheriff, the king's representative in the shires. The Church, though obedient to the pope, was largely native, locally controlled, and nationalist. Then 20,000 Norman and French knights and men at arms and a line of energetic kings changed all that.

First of all, England became feudal, but feudal with a difference. Feudalism is the granting of land in exchange for military and court service. By the time Edward was through with English feudalism, it was just the system of granting land and no more. Technically, this is not correct. Military service lasted legally until 1660. One feudal court system, that of the Duchy of Lancaster, is still in nominal existence, though as the monarch is now also Duke of Lancaster, it is in fact a royal court system. But actually, after Edward I's reign, feudalism of the kind that caused the revolts of William of Normandy against the King of France and the English civil war of Stephen and Matilda was dying out. It existed in any vigor only on the Welsh and Scottish borders, where it had special justification. Under *Quia Emptores*, the tendency was for more and more individuals to hold land directly from the king. Such holding differs in fact little, if at all, from ownership such as is common in America.

But though feudalism became transformed into ordinary ownership, its companion, manorialism, remained. The old village communities, now reorganized as manors, had lords over them, and consisted of serfs and villeins rather than freemen. There was an upper class that spoke French and a lower class that spoke English, though fusion was beginning—Edward I could at least swear in English. From the effects of entail, caused by *De Donis,* big estates, large-scale farming, and class distinctions were encouraged.

England was now a country of good, certain law. Henry I's itinerant justices made the assizes held in the shires trustworthy. From the time of Henry II, Common Law had developed with its principles to guide future decisions. By the three Statutes of Westminster, the specialization of the courts at Westminster into King's Bench for crime, Common Pleas for civil cases, and Exchequer for finance had been made definite. Juries bring a popular element into the courts and give surer justice. Indeed, in the reigns of Henry III and Edward, a new profession, that of lawyer, comes into existence. Educated men are to be found who are not clerics, who get their learning in the Inns of Court, the Inner and Middle Temple, Gray's Inn, and Lincoln's Inn, where to this day England's lawyers are trained.

In war, the feudal knight still holds the field, though Edward has begun to change that, too; but now he is hired with shield money and with funds secured at times when the royal treasury was low by the consent of Parliament, for nothing more than the usual feudal dues could be taken without such consent. Here, with the mention of Parliament, comes the key to English history. As indicated above, it is very easy to overestimate Parliament's importance at this time. When an English king is strong, Parliament is just the body that accepts his decisions and colors them into seeming to be the decision of the whole nation. When a king is weak, Parliament is the body which, led perhaps by some Stephen Langton or Simon de Montfort, appears to justify the powerful nobles' refusal to let the king go further. But Parliament has a hidden strength. Even if it is just a cloak for other forces as yet, its true power can grow, for it now has the basis of its eventual strength. Constitutional principles exist. The king is under the law—so say the Charter of Liberties of Henry I and Magna Carta. Laws now are declared in Parliament—so say the precedents of the statutes of Edward I. Parliament represents all free men who have rights in shire or borough courts—so says the organization of Parliament. Above all, there is an idea abroad that what touches all should be decided by representatives properly empowered and consulted—so say the Confirmation of the Charters and the petition accepted as law, *De Tallagio.* Because of these principles, there is a great future before Parliament.

Here, with the reign of Edward, English history enters a new stage, indeed is already partly in it, as is shown in the events of Edward's Scots and Welsh wars and in his struggle with the papacy, of which more later. For not only did Edward finish the work of those who went before him, but he started new work for others to finish. In that new stage, England's basic laws did not change from the great statutes of the 1200's; Edward had founded them too securely. But the outlook on life of England changed greatly. England got a new language, the fusion of Anglo-Saxon and Norman French. It got a new economic life, with the growth of exports and manufactures. It had a stirring military history that inspired it with a national spirit. Finally, it either altered its religion or did not, depending on what one reads into history.

6

THE BRITISH ISLES
IN THE THIRTEENTH CENTURY

Edward I's reign was not only the culmination of the work of his Norman and Angevin predecessors; it was the beginning of a new stage in English history in which England expanded over the rest of the British Isles and back again into France. To understand that expansion, it is necessary to consider certain changes in England and what had happened in the rest of the Isles.

The change in England was both cultural and economic, for changes in one such field often mean changes in the other. The economic changes can be seen in the key events of the reigns of Henry III and Edward. Since towns grew, they had to be consulted in great decisions. That was why Simon de Montfort summoned burgesses to his Parliament. Since the trade of England was now important, it was worth the king's while to have business cases tried in the royal courts. That explains the enactment of the Statute of Merchants. Since England's chief export was wool, the Maltôte of Wool was promptly met by a demand for the Confirmation of the Charters. Otherwise, the rising middle class would have been completely at the king's mercy.

As towns and trade, chiefly in wool, grew, merchants and manufacturers organized and town governments grew stronger. Merchants in various towns organized into merchant guilds, which controlled fairs and markets and otherwise protected trade. Craft guilds regulated the manufactures of most materials. They supervised the training system by which apprentices learning their trade served a term under masters. Then, when the apprentices, now become journeymen, had traveled about and learned still more, the guilds examined the "masterpieces" they offered to prove themselves capable of teaching others. Such craft guilds differed from trade unions in including employers as well as employees, and in regulating prices and training as well as wages. Such self-government in industry naturally led to political self-government. Often, this was a direct step— to this day, the City of London, *i.e.*, London as it was in the Middle Ages, is ruled by the City Companies, the Mercers, Stationers, and the like, who are guilds of a different form. Such self-government was also found in overseas trade with the formation of two trading companies, the Merchants of the Staple, who sold wool, and the Merchant Adventurers, who sold cloth and brought back wines and other continental products.

With this growth of self-government in town life came a change in the ways of doing business. The manorial system had been an exchange of food and services; town life was based on money, which consequently, whether as loans or taxes, played a larger part in the life of England. In the days of Henry II, John, and Henry III, when the Church had strict laws against usury or taking interest, there was comparatively little need to borrow money; and the Jews, exempt from Church laws, were the only money-lenders. In Edward's reign, matters changed. A loophole was found in the laws against usury by claiming that interest on a loan might be charged when there was a chance of losing what had been lent. Italian money-lenders, largely from Lombardy, moved into England to finance English business, giving their name to Lombard Street, the present Wall Street of England; and the sincerely religious Edward, now able to get money from other sources, in 1290 expelled the Jews from England, not to return till brought back by the equally religious Oliver Cromwell.

In this description of the rise of towns, it must be remembered that England remained a predominantly agricultural country. Until 1750, she grew so much food that she exported it; and her chief export was a raw material, wool, procured from her own fields and hills. What has been recorded here are only the first steps toward England's later commercial and industrial greatness.

Cultural changes came with the economic ones. Foremost was the founding of England's two ancient universities, Oxford and Cambridge. Students from Paris in Henry II's reign founded Oxford, and students from Oxford founded Cambridge in John's reign. In early times, these universities were purely examining bodies, just like the guilds. Masters of arts examined the apprentices, or scholars, to let them become bachelors or journeymen, and again examined the bachelors to see if they might become masters and teach. It was only later that residential colleges—Merton, Balliol, and University at Oxford; Peterhouse at Cambridge—were founded, in which students had to live as well as study.

Secondary education in the thirteenth century was in the hands of the local clergy. Not until the fourteenth century was the first great "public school," Winchester, founded by William of Wykeham.

The cultural change in England went deeper than education. A national literature sprang up. There was still a division between the noble, who spoke French, the language of the victors at Hastings, and the villein, who spoke Saxon, the language of the defeated. But noble and villein were sharing pride in their nation. In the noble's hall, minstrels were no longer singing, as had Taillefer at Hastings, of the Frenchman Roland, but of

Ed. I combined the work of Wm II + Simon
de Montfort + gave the Eng Govt
the framework it has to-day:

1) Executive ruled by the King in Council
2. Legislative ,, ,, ,, ,, in Parliament
3 Judicial ruled by the King's judges
   a system of interlocking rather than
   of balanced powers.

June 15, 1215
The Magna Carta was written by the Barons for

protect nobles against undue fiscal extortion

It put limits to relief abbeys wardships

& other feudal customs which ought be more

to speak money   Article I   to all freedom ...?

freemen.   Article 12   Prohibits outright a aid levy

levied except by the Common council of our

Kingdom   Article 39   arrests shall take place

only by the judgment a by the law of the land

Article 40   To noone will we sell deny or delay

the right of justice

the Briton Arthur. Among the English, a new narrative poem was circulating, *Brut*, written in the same alliterative meter as the Anglo-Saxon epic *Beowulf* and telling of British history from the days of an imaginary Brut, who had led Trojans with Aeneas into Italy, and thence to Britain, thus giving the island its name, down through Ambrosius and Arthur and beyond. All this was to lead to a mingling of the races and greater advances in culture.

A sign of England's potentialities in culture was the career of Friar Bacon, or Roger Bacon, whose scientific discoveries, among them the compass and gunpowder, had to be kept in code, lest his contemporaries accuse him of witchcraft.

This rich country, with a pride in itself, naturally expanded. It took over Wales, and tried to take over Scotland. It even showed some energy and success in meddling in Ireland. For a while, England in the Middle Ages was an "imperialist" nation, and here, therefore, should be set down some account of the countries it attacked.

Wales had been a problem to England both before and after the Norman conquest. In early times, the Angles had sporadically pressed into Wales. Offa had built his dike to keep the Welsh in check and set a boundary. Edgar had had Welsh kings row him on the Dee; Harold Godwinson, when Earl of Wessex, had conquered some more border land. After the Conquest, this piecemeal penetration had continued. Henry II's settlement of Flemish mercenaries in Pembrokeshire had gained that southwest corner of the peninsula the name "little England beyond Wales." Marcher lords took over all South Wales, knowing that whatever they conquered would be granted them as manors fairly free of supervision. Only in John's reign did the Welsh make organized resistance, when Llewellyn the Great joined the barons against John, and in a clause of Magna Carta, redeemed his son who had been held as a hostage. Llewellyn the Great, and after him his sons, by clever diplomacy and some fighting, kept Wales semi-independent as against the weak Henry III. But with Edward I it was another story. He could not tolerate even a semi-independent vassal, and he marched against Llewellyn's grandson, Llewellyn ap (*i.e.*, son of) Griffith.

There were two invasions, 1277 to 1278 and 1282 to 1284, which coincided with Edward's issuing statutes at Gloucester and Acton Burnell on the way to war. When the work was done, Wales was securely under English lords. There is a legend that the Welsh, when finally conquered, begged Edward for a prince who would, as they put it, speak neither French nor English; and that at Caernarvon Castle, Edward fulfilled that promise to the letter. For he made Prince of Wales his newborn son, Edward, who could speak no languages at all, let alone French or English. Ever since then, the heir to the throne has been created Prince of Wales, when in the direct line. (It is a sign of how thoroughly the Saxons conquered Cornwall that though the eldest son of the ruler of England has to be created Prince of Wales, he is Duke of Cornwall from birth and passes that title, and the attendant revenues, on to his eldest son when he is born.)

From Edward's time on, Wales was subject to England, but Welshmen were without the rights of Englishmen. South Wales was feudal; North Wales was "the Principality," and governed by the Statute of Wales (1284) which sent royal judges through it. Wales only became "shireland" with rights of representation in Parliament, and other rights of Magna Carta, when a Welsh royal family, the Tudors, ascended the throne. Consequently, the Welsh, from having been set aside so long, have a strong national feeling, even though loyal to England; and many speak their own language.

Having conquered Wales, which was always technically tributary to England, Edward turned to Scotland. There he had an unusual chance to intervene. From the days of Edward the Elder, the Bretwaldaship of England had, according to English theory, included an overlordship over Scotland. This the Scots, of course, hotly denied. They claimed that the only English rights came from the ransom paid for King William the Lion of Scotland, which rights Richard the Lion-hearted of England had sold back again to get money for going on the Third Crusade and for his ransom to Austria. However, when John de Baliol and Robert Bruce the Elder (to distinguish him from his grandson, the great Robert Bruce) disputed the succession to the Scottish throne, they brought their case to Edward's court. Edward awarded the throne to De Baliol and then proceeded to make full use of the overlordship so conceded. But Scotland proved harder than Wales to handle.

When Scotland was last mentioned, it was really Pictland, full of Gaelic tribes organized on the clan system. In it, every man was equal, but all looked up, in the old patriarchal way, to the head of the clan who would have some special title. To this day, Clan Campbell looks up to its head, the Duke of Argyll, and speaks of him by the special name, MacCalein Mor. Clan Mackintosh calls its head The Mackintosh of Mackintosh. Over this disorganized set of tribes one royal family gradually gained sway, partly by conquest and partly by marriage, consent, and consequent inheritance. There is no need to tell in detail how Fergus, the king of Dalriada in Ulster, led his Scots out of Ireland into the present Scotland by way of the "Giant's Causeway," or of the struggle for the throne between King Macbeth and his successor, later King Malcolm III. What matters is the continuity of the royal house since first it brought to Scotland the famous Stone of Scone, allegedly the stone on which Jacob rested his head when he saw his vision of the angels ascending and descending the ladder. The historically important stage in Scotland's history comes when Malcolm III married St. Margaret, the sister of Edgar the Atheling, just after the Norman Conquest. This meant that English exiles took over the Scottish royal court, and that a Northumbrian dialect of English became the language of the Lowlands of Scotland. (It is only in the last two hundred and fifty years that Gaelic was replaced by English as the main language in the Highlands, and Gaelic is still spoken there.)

The English exiles in Scotland were soon followed by Norman-French knights. These men took over the headship of many clans—Campbell, for instance, is Campobello, the Latin or Norman-French for Fairfield. When they so took over, they changed, in the Lowlands, the clan system to the feudal-manorial one. Many nobles held fiefs in both Scotland and England; indeed, the King of Scotland was for many years Earl of Huntingdon. Consequently, the Scots were pulled two ways. The kings were always fighting clans in the Highlands and trying to civilize them. Long after England had forgotten Viking raids, they were still fighting the Norse of the Isles, the last battle being Alexander III's victory of Largs, in 1263, over Haakon of Norway, after which he was acknowledged as Lord of the Isles, that is, of Man, the Hebrides, and the Shetlands. To the south, whenever the English were having baronial civil wars, the Scots intervened, just like any other rebellious vassals. During nominal peace, border lords crossed the hills in cattle-lifting forays. That was why King David, Matilda's uncle by her father's marriage with his sister, joined in the wars of Stephen and Matilda, and was defeated by the Bishop of Durham at the Battle of the Standard. That was why William the Lion raided England, when Henry II's sons were rebelling against him, and so got captured. This rule succeeded because father passed on to son, without difficulty, the effective control of Scotland.

In 1286, this peaceful succession to the throne ended. One night, as Alexander III rode home by the edge of a cliff, his horse stumbled and fell. That left no direct heir except a granddaughter in Norway, Margaret the Maid of Norway. She died on her way home, and left the throne open to thirteen competitors, of whom Edward chose John de Baliol. Edward and De Baliol did not get on. Perhaps Edward was morose. His beloved queen, Eleanor of Castile, had died. In his grief, he carried her home to burial in Westminster Abbey, and erected a cross wherever her bier rested. One such cross is still widely known, Chère Reine, or Dear Queen, Charing Cross, near the present-day Charing Cross railway station. De Baliol irritated Edward further by allying himself with the French, an alliance that lasted long after his time, and led to Scots Guards for the King of France and French words still in use in Scotland. Therefore, in 1295, Edward declared Scotland forfeited to him, and in 1296, enforced his overlordship over the Norman knights of Scotland by a victory at Dunbar. De Baliol submitted; theoretically, all was over.

On the contrary, the struggle had just begun. Something remarkable happened in Scotland. A national spirit was aroused in the common people, and under the guidance of two great heroes, "The Wallace" and "The Bruce," they accomplished what the nobles had failed to do—they won Scotland's independence. Sir William Wallace, a simple knight, became regent, and pinned his faith, militarily speaking, on a new device, infantry formed in a hedge of spears called the schiltron. With the schiltron, he trapped a British army at Stirling Bridge, where the main road across the Forth goes to the Highlands. However, Edward also knew of new weapons. The Welsh had taught him the use of the long bow, which, when properly drawn, could drive a "cloth-yard" arrow through the thigh of an armored knight and pin him in his armor to the horse he was riding. At Falkirk, these cloth-yard arrows, shot by men who knew the knack of "bending the bow" that extra two inches that gave it full force, shattered the schiltron and let the English knights charge home. It took time for Edward to reap the fruits of this victory, for it was at this time that Parliament was checking his expenditures. But with the Norman-Scots nobles, like Robert Bruce, the claimant's grandson, coming over to him, the end seemed in sight. In 1305, Wallace was taken by what the Scots considered treachery and was executed for what the English considered treason. He suffered the harsh execution of a traitor in those days —hanging, drawing (i.e., either disemboweling while semiconscious or dragging bound on a sledge, or both), and quartering. As a warning to others, his body was sent about the kingdom and his head placed on London Bridge. And as for the Stone of Scone, it was put under the king's throne in Westminster Abbey, where it has remained till today, except for a few weeks in 1950 when Scottish nationalists took it and then returned it.

Still the Scottish people refused to give up; and now the nation found its greatest leader. In a feud with the Comyn family, Robert Bruce slew the "Red Comyn" at the altar of Dumfries church. Having thus combined sacrilege with murder and become an outlaw to Church and state, with nothing to lose, he reasserted his claims to the Scottish throne. He succeeded in persuading the Countess of Buchan to crown him at Old Scone, her brother, the head of Clan MacDuff, to whom the duty belonged, having refused. The English easily defeated his tiny army and drove him into the hills and, at one time, even to the ancestral home of the Scots, Ireland. The tale of his wanderings and struggles is part of Scotland's national heritage.

Bruce gathered around himself followers whose deeds, too, have become legendary. One was the founder of a great noble house, the Good

Lord James Douglas to the Scots, the Black Douglas to the English. When he recaptured his own castle, he burned it, saying, "I had rather hear the lark sing than the mouse squeak," for he knew safety was in the hills, not behind walls. At length, Edward had to march to suppress this revolt himself. But he never reached Scotland, dying on the border at Burgh on Sands. He ordered his weakling son, Edward II, to continue and carry his bones to the battle; but after a perfunctory invasion, Edward went home. At last, only the key to Scotland, Stirling Castle above Stirling Bridge, remained in English hands, and it had been forced to promise surrender unless Edward II came by a certain day.

It was on that very day that the dilatory Edward appeared. Bruce was ready for the combination of knights and archers. Pits in a marsh ambushed the knights, his own scanty cavalry by a daring attack cut the bowmen to pieces, and at the crisis of the battle, the sight of his camp followers coming over a hill scared Edward who fled, disorganizing his own army. Scotland was freed at last by this battle of Bannockburn, June 24, 1314.

Bannockburn has a twofold importance. It gave Scotland an independence she still holds by. Though today the two nations are united into Great Britain (1707), yet Scots, not English, law runs in Scotland. Much of the great part played in the history of the world by men of Scots blood comes from the independence of spirit given them as a heritage from this struggle for freedom. But Bannockburn also taught the English new tactics, or rather confirmed them in those that won at Falkirk. Those methods were used on the battlefields of France—Crécy, Poitiers, Agincourt.

Ireland comes into this story very differently. To take the end first, Edward Bruce saw his brother start from nothing and win a kingdom, and he tried to copy him. From Man, Edward Bruce moved on to Ireland where he, too, like his brother, was crowned king. But unlike his brother, he did not make his claim good. At Dundalk, 1317, by the banks of the Castletown, the Norman knights of Ireland won a pyrrhic victory in which they defeated and killed him, at irreplaceable losses to themselves. This battle, Dundalk, like Clontarf in 1014, was most costly to Ireland. To tell, however, what these two meant is to go back over all Irish history.

The parallel between Ireland and Scotland in those first years may serve to bring out the essential differences in the later fates of the two countries. Ireland, like Scotland, was a country of Gaelic clans into which Norman-French knights brought a semblance of English feudalism. But in Scotland feudalism, and comparative progress, won the day; in Ireland there was a disastrous compromise between the two, which made the clan system of agriculture a cause of trouble till 1906 and prevented Ireland from either joining England or getting free.

Irish legendary history begins with four races—the Fomorians, the Firbolgs, the Danaans, and the Milesians or Scots, the last being the present-day Irish who allegedly came from Spain, bringing with them the Stone of Scone. These Milesians, when the rest of the world came into contact with them, were in a state of high barbarism, like the Homeric Greeks. Their early epics, however, differ from the Iliad and the Odyssey in telling, not of piracy on the seas, but of cattle lifting. The Ulster Cycle, telling of Conn of the Hundred Battles and Deirdre of the Sorrows, is still extant in the original Erse. So are many other legends of the pagan Irish, written down just after the conversion of the Irish to Christianity, and consequent enthusiasm for learning. In this period, Ireland was the intellectual leader of western Europe; she converted Scotland and some of England and Germany, and she reinvigorated the church in France. Thus, between early epic poetry and early Christian leadership, the Irish have a great deal to be proud of. It is that pride that today makes an important basis for Irish national feeling. (Otherwise, why would an English-speaking nation put its street signs in Erse?)

However, Ireland did not have Scotland's luck with a royal family. Instead of one good one, it had four quarreling ones of the four kingdoms, Ulster, Munster, Leinster, and Connaught, plus a fifth at first—Meath. The king of Meath was supposedly High King, reigning in Tara, of whose halls good Irishmen will boast. When the Norse came, the kingdoms quarreled; and the Danes could settle in Dublin, Cork, Waterford, and Limerick, and rob the rich monasteries while the five kings fought. At last, King Brian Boru of Leinster defeated the other kings and could meet and crush the Danes. But at Clontarf, where he did this, he, his son, and his grandson, all men tried in battle, were killed. Ireland, therefore, did not have the luck England had where Wessex, the only kingdom left, had the father (Alfred), son (Edward the Elder), and grandson (Athelstan) to reconquer the country. Ireland remained in anarchy.

To this anarchical island in 1169 came Richard Strongbow, Earl of Clare, to try his hand at carving out manors for himself. He alleged an invitation from King Dermot MacMurrough, but soon his overlord at home, Henry II, turned up with a gift of Ireland from Pope Adrian IV, who, as Nicholas Breakspear, was the only Englishman to become pope. On the basis of this, Norman knights, as in Scotland, headed clans, with a slight connection with the king. But just as these men were beginning to start the feudal system, the battle of Dundalk killed them off; and instead of their making Ireland English, the Irish made them Irish. This fact finally was recognized by building around Dublin a palisade or pale. Inside the "Pale," there were English laws; outside, by the Statute of Kilkenny, only the "Five Bloods" of Norman descent had English rights. So, though Ireland developed a Parliament (as did Scotland), she never became a medieval country so like England as to be able to join her. That split in Ireland has made her "England's great failure." For Ireland's national pride has never been brought to an alliance with England. Twice, in 1782 and in 1914, great Irishmen nearly solved the problem, only to have the work bungled. Because Clontarf and Dundalk put a handicap on Ireland, she has been always confused, misunderstood, and misunderstanding, and on bad terms with England.

Subsequent Irish history has been a series of unsolved problems. Since she was a split nation, the Reformation reached only the English part of her people. That made her enter religious wars with England and Scotland, and build up two centuries of hatred. Then, when she sought freedom, at the time of American and French Revolutions, she was given, instead, an inadequate union with England. This, because of a broken promise of religious toleration, led to disunion and a struggle for freedom so bitter that when it was won Ireland stayed neutral in World War II. Therefore, if one keeps in mind what Clontarf and Dundalk meant to Ireland, one can realize how it was that the land problem and what might be called a clan attitude toward life served to complicate the religious and nationalist problems that arose in the sixteenth and eighteenth centuries in Ireland.

Here, then, was the situation of the British Isles at the beginning of Edward II's reign. England was an expanding country. She had a sound legal system, unified law, and a Parliament of potentially great power. She also had a new national culture, national pride, and newly learned tactics that would make her the master of France. Pushed forward by this pride, she conquered Wales, to be subject till the time of the Tudors. Scotland she failed to conquer and, in so failing, gave the gift of a similar and perhaps greater national pride. Ireland's resources were at this time destroyed, to leave her outside for over two hundred years, stalemated between feudalism and the clan. Consequently, England's natural outlet was expansion toward the Continent, where her kings were dukes of Aquitaine and her traders sold wool in Flanders.

7

THE HUNDRED YEARS' WAR
AND THE WARS OF THE ROSES

With the reign of Edward I, English history ended one stage. The law courts and the existence of Parliament were settled permanently. A new stage began, in which England grew richer, expanded over the rest of the British Isles, and invaded France. In this stage, Parliament stopped developing rapidly, and instead moved forward by steps that seemed accidental. Foreign wars and the strengthening of Parliament's methods of work went hand in hand until a civil war broke out, at the end of which England was ruled by a family of Welsh kings who believed in both absolute rule and cooperation with Parliament.

An example of the slow accretion of power to Parliament occurred at the end of Edward I's reign. In 1296 the Pope tried to assert the independence of the clergy from lay control by forbidding the clergy to pay any taxes. Edward replied by "outlawing" the clergy and thus depriving them of the benefit of English law. This soon brought about a compromise, by which the clergy gave a "free gift" of tax money to the king. In doing this, Edward, the last crusading king of England, was taking less drastic action than his neighbor, the king of France. For Philip the Fair went so far as to kidnap the Pope and bring him to Avignon, on the border of France. There the papacy was turned from an international force into an adjunct to the French government. The splendid days when great popes made kings do right were over, for a time. In England, the indirect result was, however, not religious but a change in the composition of Parliament. "Convocation," the assembly of the clergy, had started to develop into a third House of Parliament. This refusal to pay taxes took Convocation out of Parliament. In France, the equivalent of Parliament, the Estates General, had three houses, two of which, nobles and clergy, fought the third, which corresponded to the English Commons. In England, where the clergy did not thus separate itself, bishops and mitered abbots, who were also feudal lords, sat in the House of Lords, and Lords and Commons learned to work together.

Edward II was a worthless king. During most of his reign, the country suffered either under his own misrule or under the misrule of barons, known collectively as the Lords Ordainers. It was in such an interval of restoration of royal power that he lost the battle of Bannockburn. During this alternation of evils, an important constitutional principle was strengthened. The law has always been that "the king can do no wrong," which means that the king cannot be tried in the courts to which he gives authority. That makes practical common sense, as can be seen if one imagines what would happen if he could be so tried. But as the king obviously can do wrong, and has done so, some method must be found to curb him. That method was to hold an official responsible for obeying an order from the king that involved breaking a law. Edward II caused this doctrine to be pushed on further. Sometimes the Lords Ordainers would have their nominees given the chief offices of state, like the treasureship and the chancellorship. Then Edward would issue orders through minor officials, such as the Lord Privy Seal (who held the king's private, as opposed to the official, seal) or the king's personal secretary. These men were then held responsible for their actions, even though they said they were merely obeying the king's orders. Eventually, there would arise out of these squabbles a delimitation of the powers of the various central administrative departments and a means by which Parliament, in the eighteenth century, could gain control of those departments. For once all actions had to be done by specific officials, control of the appointment and dismissal of those officials meant control of the executive.

Edward II also contributed another precedent to the English constitution. He finally became so bad that he was deposed. The deposers were little better than the king. His French queen, Isabella, had been deservedly exiled from England to France, and then deservedly exiled from her own brother's court in France. With nowhere to go, she had utilized the hatred felt for Edward's favorites, Piers Gaveston and the Despenser family, to overthrow her husband and replace him with their son, Edward III. Shortly after this, Edward II was murdered in an upper room in Berkeley Castle; and England found that by good fortune the young Edward III was a good king, who would not let his mother interfere.

Edward III is famous chiefly for his war with France. In great measure it sprang out of the wool trade. His allies in Flanders, then a county of France, begged his help, and pointed out that if he helped them revolt against the King of France, their legal position was bad, but that if he claimed to be King of France, their legal position was good. Although Edward had acknowledged Philip VI of France as his overlord for Aquitaine, he now claimed that he should not have done so. His mother, Isabella, had been the sister of Philip V; Philip VI was only a cousin. This succession of Philip VI has been justified in France by an appeal to the law of the Salian or Salic Franks, under which no woman could inherit. It was asserted that since the Franks had conquered France, their law governed the inheritance of the French throne. Therefore, a great deal of quibbling went on about the Salic law, to justify an English invasion of France, the reason for which was partly economic, a desire to put the wool merchants in Flanders under English protection. The war was marked by two great victories on land, and one on sea.

The sea victory of Sluis—really a sort of land battle of armed men on ships, with no maneuvering of the ships—in 1339, two years after the war broke out, gave England command of the sea and let her put armies ashore wherever she chose. For some time these landings were unsuccessful raids, but in 1346 Edward III and his army got into an apparent trap at Crécy, in Normandy. The French knights made the mistake of charging the English bowmen, who were guarded by dismounted English knights. This in effect formed a Scottish schiltron and also prevented the tactics Bruce had used at Bannockburn, of riding down the archers. The fighting was so fierce that three times those with Edward advised him to send aid to his son, also named Edward, the famous Black Prince (so called from the color of his armor). But the King refused, saying he would send no aid not asked for, and was justified. His son won great renown, the French recoiled and were driven back in slaughter, and the way was open for Edward to besiege Calais, the key to the Channel. This he did and, when Calais proved stubborn, ordered the six chief burghers to come to him with the keys of the city and halters around their necks. What restrained him from using those halters to hang them was the petition of his queen, Phillippa of Hainaut, made in public on her knees. (Note that a royal marriage had reinforced the alliance of England with Flanders.) The French tried to counter Edward's invasion by persuading their allies, the Scots, to attack England, but at Neville's Cross, in that same summer of 1346, David Bruce was defeated and taken prisoner, which ensured peace with Scotland. Ten years later, the Black Prince, at Poitiers, in northern Aquitaine, again defeated the French. There he killed the King of Bohemia and took prisoner the King of France. Ever since, Princes of Wales have carried the crest of Bohemia—three feathers, and the motto *Ich Dien* (I serve). By the Treaty of Brétigny, 1360, it seemed as if England had the better part of France under control, even though the claim to rule France was temporarily set aside.

However, the most important event of Edward's reign was perhaps not a war, but a disease, the Black Death of 1349, a variant of the bubonic plague, which killed off a very large proportion of the population of England. Manors were denuded of serfs, and the remaining ones could no longer be tied down to the land. However, the lords, burgesses, and knights of the shire tried to do the impossible. In 1351, they passed an act, the Statute of Laborers, forbidding high wages or serfs leaving their manors. The enforcement of this was handed over to a recently created set of local royal judges, the Justices of the Peace and of Laborers. The upshot was that the act was not enforced, but the new judges gained greatly in power. Since these justices were first underpaid, then unpaid, only country gentlemen would take the post. Consequently, the bench of justices of the peace became much the same group that as knights of the shire sat in Parliament. To the present day, petty cases in England are tried not in feudal courts, not in the sheriff's courts in shire or hundred, but in the courts of Petty and Quarter Sessions; *i.e.*, interim and trimonthly meetings of the justices of the peace. Like *De Donis,* the Statute of Laborers made England an aristocratic country.

Edward III's reign also had its constitutional changes, as had his father's. In 1369, the English were ill advised enough to renew the war with France. The Black Prince's troops had been exhausted by an intervention in Spain; and a great French leader, Bertrand du Guesclin, had become High Constable of France. He knew how to defeat the English by guerrilla methods and won back from them castle after castle in Aquitaine, while the peasants suffered at the hands of both armies. In England, Edward III grew senile, and control was taken over by his fourth son, John of Gaunt, Duke of Lancaster. The misrule of John of Gaunt led to a popular movement of protest, which culminated in the election of the so-called "Good Parliament" under the sponsorship of the Black Prince, who came back from Aquitaine to take charge. The Commons of the Good Parliament, acting as a sort of indicting or grand jury, accused venal officials, and had the Magnum Concilium, or the House of Lords, try them. This process of "impeachment" provided a method of getting rid of criminal officials. At the time, it did little more, for the Black Prince died, leaving a son to be heir to the throne, Richard of Bordeaux; and John of Gaunt resumed control of England. A Parliament, whose membership he packed, quickly undid the reforms of the Good Parliament. However, a precedent was left by which the representatives of the people could prosecute important offenders in government. Impeachment has remained and is today to be found in the Federal constitution and all the state constitutions of the United States, as an emergency safeguard of liberty.

Edward III was perhaps not a great man, though in the prime of his life he was a great soldier and a gallant knight. But to the tradition of England he means much. Since he fought the French with a line of battle in which king, lords, and commons—or commander, knights, and bowmen—all stood together in the same ranks, he built up the idea that all were Englishmen together. He established high standards of chivalry. His rebuke to jests about the Countess of Salisbury when she dropped her garter in public, *"Honi soit qui mal y pense"* (shame to him who sees evil in it), became the motto for England's noblest order of chivalry, the Order of the Garter, one now reserved for distinguished statesmen and foreign monarchs. The deeds of Edward have been entertainingly written up by a Fleming, Jean Froissart, in his *Chronicles*. They tell of the national glory that gave England a national spirit, such a spirit as Bannockburn, The Bruce, and The Wallace gave to Scotland, and the legends of early days gave to Ireland. That national spirit was Edward's great contribution to England.

During Edward's reign were passed, in 1351, the Statutes of Provisors and Praemunire. These were directed against the French-controlled papacy at Avignon. The first stated that no appointments could be made in advance to an ecclesiastical post. Popes had had a custom of "providing" or so appointing in advance foreigners with English jobs. The second forebade appealing ecclesiastical cases outside the kingdom without the king's consent. The acts were at first merely bargaining devices kings used to allow the "provision" of foreigners with English posts, or appeals to Rome from York and Canterbury, for suitable fees. But later, in the Reformation, these laws would be played up.

In a time of national advance, literature usually advances too. Some poetry was of the old style, the alliterative meter of *Beowulf*. Such a poem was *Piers* (*i.e.*, Peter) *Plowman*, a very noble religious allegory. Some was in a new type of verse. Geoffrey Chaucer, an English professional diplomat, traveled in France and Italy and there learned how to rhyme and use new meters. His greatest work, the *Canterbury Tales*, contains living characters—the Knight, the Squire, the Nun Prioress, the Wife of Bath, the Shipman—and can be read with pleasure today when one has learned the archaic English. For in Edward III's reign, English at last became a real language. In it, a priest, John Wyclif of Balliol College, Oxford, and later of Lutterworth, wrote a translation of the Bible. He had begun by demanding religious reform, which was badly needed in that era of corruption. When church authorities had ordered him to stop, he had begun to challenge their authority and to encourage others to challenge it. He turned to the Bible to see what authority he should obey and came to the conclusion that each individual's conscience, guided by the Bible, was the final authority and that the doctrine of transubstantiation, which is a basic Catholic dogma, was wrong. This his "poor priests" preached throughout England to followers called Lollards. For political reasons, John of Gaunt protected him, and despite persecution, Wyclif died still Rector of Lutterworth. When Edward III's grandson and successor, Richard II, married a Bohemian queen, Wyclif's ideas were carried to Bohemia and became the cause of the Hussite movement there. Consequently, many think Wyclif "the morning star of the Reformation" even though his ideas were driven underground by persecution, especially by the statute *De heretico comburendo* (literally, concerning the heretic who ought to be burned).

This new national pride went with great distress which the young King Richard II had to face. The Black Death seems to have reduced the population of England by three-eighths, and to have killed off 1,500,000 out of an estimated 4,000,000. Oppressed under the Statute of Laborers, the peasants of south England, in 1381, rose in revolt under one Wat Tyler. The revolt was against a poll tax which had been levied to pay for the unsuccessful war in France against Du Guesclin, but it quickly became a demand for all sorts of economic changes. A priest, John Ball, went about asking, "When Adam delved and Eve span, who then was the gentleman?" The rebels entered London; and Richard, not yet old enough to rule himself, bravely went to them and told them he was their king and would see to redress of their grievances. When Tyler insulted him, the Lord Mayor of London struck Tyler dead. That valiant behavior persuaded the rebels to disperse. Though Richard's promises were not carried out by those in power, when he came to the throne he ruled well, at first.

However, the death of Richard's beloved queen, Anne of Bohemia, seems to have soured him. He suddenly turned tyrant. He gave up ruling with Parliament and persuaded a packed Parliament to declare that his ordinances had the force of statutes. To get money, he suddenly exiled his cousin, Henry Bolingbroke, Duke of Lancaster, who, as John of Gaunt's son, had vast estates. Those estates Richard then confiscated. Then he made the error of going to Ireland. When he was in Ireland, in 1399, Henry Bolingbroke landed at Ravenspur in Yorkshire, and so roused the country that when Richard came back from Ireland and landed at Bristol, the country was against the King. Under compulsion, Richard then called a Parliament, which, by a legal fiction, put Henry Bolingbroke on the throne as Henry IV. The fiction was that Bolingbroke's ancestor, Thomas of Lancaster, had been the elder and not the younger brother of Edward I, thus giving Henry a better claim to the throne than Richard. But this could not disguise the vital fact that Parliament had ousted one king in an emergency and chosen another. In 1689, this would provide a vital precedent.

Henry's reign was largely an attempt to stay on the throne. He had to fight Richard's former friends, during which struggle he seems to have had Richard murdered. He had to fight the last of the feudal lords, the Percies of Northumberland and Owen Glendower of Wales. In each struggle, he succeeded. He had a Scottish war, which he ended by the fortunate capture of the Scottish king's son on his way to France. With the future James I as a hostage, England was free from Scotch wars. He persecuted the

Lollards and passed *De heretico comburendo*. Above all, he regretted the promises and gifts he had made when he took the throne, for Parliament would not give him the money needed to make them good. It set up a doctrine, "No supply without redress of grievance." Until Henry gave assent to the laws it wanted passed, he got no money. So his fourteen-year reign went, 1399 to 1413.

His son, Henry V, Henry of Monmouth, had a cure for this discontent. He said he would "fill foolish heads with foreign wars." He got England so interested in the invasion of France it forgot its worries. And at Agincourt, he again proved that English bowmen could defeat French knights. There, another trapped English army showed that it could outfight a vast number of French. Henry V, in five years' further fighting, forced the French to give him in marriage Catherine, the daughter of the mad King Charles VI of France, and to declare him "Heir of France," inheritor of that kingdom when his father-in-law should die. But overwork and exhaustion killed him first, in 1422; and the two thrones came in that year to a boy less than two years old, Henry of Windsor.

The reign of the young king began well. His uncles were worthy brothers of that great general, Henry V, and extended England's rule still further into France, for the dukes of Burgundy had a quarrel with Charles VI and refused to help him fight for his throne. Suddenly, when the hopes of France were at such a low ebb that the English dared break a truce and attack the city of Orleans, Joan of Arc came to the rescue of France. This simple peasant girl believed she had the direct command of God to save Orleans and have Charles VII crowned King of France in Rheims Cathedral. This she did, giving new spirit to the French troops, and after that it little mattered that the English captured Joan of Arc and burned her at the stake. When the feud in France between the Burgundians and the supporters of Charles VII (called Armagnacs) was finally healed, England was gradually ejected from France.

Just at this stage of the game, Henry VI came of age, took control, and married. He let his favorites rule England, in particular the Beaufort family. These were illegitimate descendants of John of Gaunt whom Richard II had legitimatized, this action being confirmed by Parliament under Henry IV. The importance of this was that, with Henry VI and his uncles apparently childless, the Beauforts were the next heirs to the throne. They, being in power and about to reign, were blamed for the conditions then existing in England. For gangsterism, as we would now call it, became the rule. In name, the laws of England were enforced, but juries were packed, courts were intimidated, and the men who as justices of the peace were supposed to keep the peace and issue warrants of arrest to the constables were at the head of the disorder. Kidnaping, carrying off heiresses, armed seizure of property, later defended by trumped-up excuses and exonerated by venal courts, were all the order of the day. Such things had gone on since the beginning of the French wars, in Edward III's time, when returned soldiers had acted as private armies to wealthy men; but now there was no strong king to stamp them down. A new sort of feudalism arose, with troops wearing the "livery" of some great noble and "maintained" by him. For example, the followers of Richard Neville, Earl of Warwick, could be told by their wearing his badge, a "white bear and ragged staff," and red jackets. If a courtroom were filled by men so dressed, Lord Warwick's enemies had no hope of justice. And if some adherent of Warwick's got into trouble, he could count on great efforts being made to get him off, whether by a "hung jury," one of whose members had been bribed to hold out against the unanimous vote necessary for conviction, by intimidation of witnesses, or by even more drastic methods.

This situation became so bad that in 1450 one Jack Cade led a revolt in Kent that came near to taking over England. Though this got rid of the Beauforts, it did not otherwise improve the situation. For Henry, always easily influenced and weak-minded, finally went partially mad. Here, his marriage made trouble. His wife, strong-minded, able Margaret of Anjou, and his cousin, Richard, Duke of York, contested to see who would be regent. As long as Richard, except for the questionable Beaufort claim, was next heir to the throne, matters could be adjusted. But when Margaret had a child and tried to get the regency, trouble inevitably came. The gangster fights, which had had as their prizes rich estates, now moved up a notch—the prize was the whole kingdom. Nobles picked sides, according to legend, in one famous dispute which broke out in a garden, plucking a white rose if they stood for York, a red rose if they stood for Lancaster. So the Wars of the Roses started. Beginning over the regency, they moved up to concern themselves with the succession to the throne.

These wars concerned themselves with a matter of genealogy. For Richard of York, though in the male line he was a direct descendant of Edward III's sixth son, was in the female line a descendant of Edward III's second son. At first, he took over merely as Protector in 1455, two years after the loss of Bordeaux had ended all hopes of conquering France and detached Aquitaine at last from England. But when he was ousted in 1459 and returned in 1460, he took the decisive step of claiming to be king by asserting a right to the royal palace at Westminster. This claim the House of Lords could not quite stand, and it compromised by calling him direct heir ahead of Henry VI's son. However, when York was killed on a trip to his native country, his son, Edward, Earl of March, the so-called "Fortunate Earl," had himself crowned king; with the aid of Richard Neville, Earl of Warwick, the so-called "kingmaker," he won the battle of Towton against the supporters of Lancaster and in 1461 reigned as Edward IV.

In the history of England, Edward IV resembles Henry I, in that what he started a successor brought to full fruition. Edward saw two things— that England's wealth in the future lay in trade overseas and that the cure for the troubles of the times lay in a strong monarchy. He, therefore, made friends with the Londoners; he invested his own money in mercantile ventures; he built royal ships which could both trade and fight; and he fought a naval war with the Hanseatic League of the cities of Germany. To make the monarchy strong, he filled his treasury. He "borrowed" money from rich merchants and never repaid them; he accepted "benevolences," that is, "free gifts" of doubtful freedom; and he persuaded Parliament to override the spirit of *De Tallagio* by granting him the proceeds of the customs duties, not for a year, but for his whole reign. He got popular support by marrying an Englishwoman, Elizabeth Woodville, thus being the last king married outside of royalty till the future George VI married Lady Elizabeth Bowes-Lyon. To control disorder, he did two things. He made his Parliaments pass statutes against the crimes of livery and maintenance; that is, against uniforming and supplying private armies. Then, he used the fact that his Privy Council was technically just as much a royal court as the courts of King's Bench and Common Pleas to try cases of offenders who could laugh at the usual royal courts. In the Privy Council, there was no set of Common Law safeguards for the defendant and, therefore, no red tape to prevent conviction on technicalities.

Of course, with the Yorkists in control, the House of Lancaster tried to foment rebellion. In 1470, the Lancastrians got Warwick on their side and ousted Edward; but the next year, he came back and made short shrift of both Warwick and the Lancastrian royal family. The Prince of Wales was killed, allegedly in Edward's tent, after the final battle of Tewkesbury, and shortly after that, poor mad old Henry VI, the founder of Eton, died in the Tower of London. Edward even went so far, in protecting his claim to the throne, as to kill his own brother, the Duke of Clarence. This was done in 1478 by an act of attainder; that is, a legal putting to death by act of Parliament. Legend has it Clarence was offered his choice of deaths and preferred to be drowned in a butt of his favorite wine, Malmsey. It should be noted that, as Edward claimed to be king by right divine and inheritance, he ignored Parliament as much as possible. It was the House of Lancaster, which had gained the throne by act of Parliament in 1399, that had to stick by Parliament. However, Edward made a mistake in the brother he killed. His hunchbacked brother, Richard, Duke of Gloucester, was also faithless. When Edward died, leaving two sons, the young Edward V and a Richard of York, Richard of Gloucester took the regency and they died in the Tower.

Richard was unpopular; and one of the last remaining Beauforts, Henry Tudor, Earl of Richmond, in 1485 came over from Brittany and landed in Wales. As a Welshman, the descendant of Owen Tudor, the second husband of Henry V's queen, Catherine of France, Henry Tudor was popular in Wales and could raise an army. At Bosworth Field, he met and killed Richard III. He ended the strife of York and Lancaster by marrying Elizabeth of York, Edward IV's daughter, and so combining the claims of both families. With him, a new era dawned.

8

THE EARLY TUDORS

After the Battle of Bosworth, the crown of England was found lying under a hawthorn bush and put on the head of Henry Tudor, Earl of Richmond. Thus the founder of the Tudor dynasty was faced with a great opportunity. For in England, as was also true all over Europe, men were turning away from feudalism and becoming willing to follow a strong and clever king. Great nobles had ceased to be a protection to their vassals and serfs, and instead had become a burden to those under them. As towns grew in size and importance, the businessmen of the new middle class wanted a strong central government that would make it safe to trade. Furthermore, the middle class was growing conscious of its power, because the invention of printing had made ideas circulate much faster than in the days of written books, though still slowly as compared with our days of rotary presses and plentiful pulp paper. When William Caxton, in 1476, set up his press in London, he brought to England a new social force of great potential power. Thus, the time was ripe for a new kind of monarch.

Consequently, all over Europe kings were allying themselves with the middle classes, battering down the nobles' castles with the newly developed cannon, and setting themselves up as absolute rulers backed by strong armies and ruthless officials. The surprising thing about Henry VII is that while he got as much power, and more, as did the powerful kings of the Continent, such as Louis XI and Charles VIII of France, or Ferdinand and Isabella of Spain, he used no trains of cannon, had only a tiny standing army, and engaged in comparatively little legal persecution. Instead, he took the people into his confidence and persuaded them to do his work for him—without, be it noticed, ever giving up claims to royal power the equal of those enforced on the Continent. With Parliament, the justices of the peace, and the Curia Regis, now known by its modern name of the Privy Council, he got nearly absolute power and at the same time the trust, not the hatred, of his subjects. Thus, the new English dynasty prepared for a future that would see Henry VII's descendants remain on the throne of England when the other new dynasties of the age—those of Suleiman the Magnificent in Turkey, of the Hapsburgs in Spain and Austria, of the junior branch of Valois in France—would lose their thrones because of the very policies that, in this period, had given them power.

When news came to London that Henry had defeated and killed Richard, a massacre of all Yorkists was expected. But, on the contrary, Henry was cleverly lenient. He issued pardons; he called Parliament to confirm his title to the crown; at the request of both houses of Parliament, he carried through his promise to marry Elizabeth of York. These well-timed delays built up a feeling that he ought to be king, not merely that he was king by conquest, by act of Parliament, or by marriage with Elizabeth. Henry made good use of this growing feeling of confidence in him to ward off rebellion. For though there were no legitimate closely related Yorkist claimants to the throne, impostors sprang up, claiming to be the little Duke of York, Edward V's brother, who had, with the young king, been murdered in the Tower by Richard III. One impostor, Lambert Simnel, Henry captured and ridiculed by making him a scullion in the royal kitchen. Another, Perkin Warbeck, took five years to capture, owing to the protection given him by the Irish, the Burgundians, and the Scotch. When the facts proved that Ireland was the center of Yorkist resistance, Henry took firm action there. He sent over as Lord Deputy Sir Edward Poynings who, in 1495, forced the Irish Parliament to pass what has since been known as Poynings's Law, or the Statutes of Drogheda. These made all English laws then in existence valid in Ireland and, even more important, gave the Council in England power to veto laws of the Irish Parliament and even to pass on the introduction of bills into the Irish Parliament. There was also a Cornish revolt. But each time Henry cleverly let his people do the work for him. The Cornish, for instance, he let march all the way to London. Then he called out the London militia, that is, the then equivalent of the "fyrd," and surrounded the rebels on Blackheath, just outside London. Having surrounded them, he let the rank and file go home and executed only the ringleaders. Consequently, the Londoners went home thinking what brave patriotic soldiers they had been; the Cornishmen went home thinking how wrong it had been to revolt against such a good king, and how foolish they had been to march so far. As for Henry, he had to pay very little to put down the revolt and, therefore, did not have to raise taxes. This was the essence of Henry's methods—he got his people to do the work of governing for him, and thus he kept taxes down and the people content.

Naturally, Henry had to use some force to keep on the throne. He was the first English king to keep a standing army, unless Harold's Housecarls be considered that. But he kept just a few soldiers to protect his person and his chief prison. Henry also kept a few stern judges. He followed Edward IV (who had used many of the same methods) in remembering that while King's Bench and Common Pleas were courts established by the Statute of Westminster, the king could still in theory act as judge or assign judicial duties to those around him. This he did, with a vengeance. To his Privy Councillors he assigned the trial of cases where he thought the Common Law Courts would be slow, uncertain, or, above all, subject to intimidation. For the Common Law Courts had, in the course of years, become encumbered by a system of red tape which delayed their action, and which sometimes let the obviously guilty escape. Also, during the Wars of the Roses, the judges on circuit, sitting in assizes in the various counties, had either been intimidated themselves or seen juries intimidated. Consequently, the chief laws enforced by the Privy Council were those against livery and maintenance, that is, against powerful nobles' supporting a private army or giving it "livery," or uniforms.

The methods of the Privy Council in getting at the facts were very direct; indeed, torture, which was "unknown to the Common Law" though usual enough in Europe, was at times employed when it was vital to get at facts to prevent rebellion, or in some similar emergency. The methods of interrogation of the Privy Council are remembered to this day, for the special committee of the Privy Council sat in a chamber with a star on the ceiling. Thence comes the phrase "Star Chamber procedure."

Even though this was an age of force, Henry was careful how he used extreme methods. For example, where Edward IV had set up Star Chamber by a royal order, Henry got Parliament to pass an act authorizing what it did. Thus, the function of Parliament began to change. Often before his time, it had been a body that made legal the actions of powerful subjects. Now, it became the means by which the king got the leaders of his people to share responsibility with him. In a sense, his title to the throne came by act of Parliament; and, until 1498, he frequently called it into session. Thereafter, since his treasury was full, he summoned it only once again before his death. But in the early years of his reign, he laid a groundwork on which subsequent Tudors built, so that Englishmen grew to feel they ought to have a share in making the nation's policy.

Henry also knew that a king who had to borrow money was at the mercy of those who lent it to him, and he resorted to many devices to keep his financial independence. In the course of his tortuous diplomacy, he often threatened to go to war with France. Somehow, after Parliament had patriotically voted heavy taxes, he never did go to war but kept the money just the same. His courts fined heavily. This not only brought in revenue but had the added advantage of weakening powerful nobles. Henry, himself, was rather ungenerous about this. Once he visited the Earl of Oxford and was received with great state by servants in splendid uniforms. At the end of the visit, the King thanked the Earl—and told him to see the Chancellor of the Exchequer about the size of the fine for violating the Statute of Livery. His minister, Bishop (later Cardinal) Morton, had a way of assessing ability to pay. If a man seemed to live expensively, he must be rich and could pay well. But if he lived penuriously, he was caught on the other prong of "Morton's Fork," for then he must have saved much and could pay well. Extortionate as some thought Morton to be, two other officials, Empson and Dudley, went further. Henry, himself, rather justly earned a reputation for stinginess. Consequently, England under Henry could always buy what was needed, even if only £5 was paid to John Cabot for the discovery of Newfoundland with its immense wealth of fisheries and its claim to the continent of North America.

The key to Henry's rule, however, was his good and cheap local government. European monarchs sent out a swarm of paid officials to superintend the feudal nobles. Henry made the English equivalent of the minor nobles, the country gentlemen, work for him and not against him. More and more power was given to justices of the peace. They issued warrants for arrest to the constables, then went and tried the men they had arrested. They ordered parish vestries to do public works, such as road repairs. When a legal case was too knotty to solve, they would turn it over to the judges at assizes, but generally speaking, four or five men —or, in a big county, ten or fifteen—ran the county, asking no pay but only the privilege of serving. But these men never got out of control. The local militia, also unpaid, was securely in Henry's hands, under the command of a new official, the Lord Lieutenant (pronounced Lord Lefttenant), who was the chief landowner in the county whom Henry could trust, and whom he kept trustworthy by being able to dismiss him. The justices of the peace were also usually under the control of the Lord Lieutenant, for, with rare exceptions, he also held the office of Custos Rotulorum, or custodian of the rolls of justices. (The fact that there could be a Custos Rotulorum who was not Lord Lieutenant allowed a double check in doubtful districts and made a man twice as loyal by giving him two offices to lose.) A justice of the peace did not get the post as a right; he earned it by being loyal and efficient. Justices were appointed on the recommendation of the Custos Rotulorum, and then checked on by the Privy Council. With Star Chamber back of them to keep them on the right track and to support them in need, the justices of the peace gave England remarkably good government without any burden of taxes.

In foreign affairs, Henry had two main purposes. He saw that France, Spain, and Austria were growing into powerful nations. He saw that the "Low Countries," that is, the modern Belgium and Holland, were the best markets for English goods and also that they were in danger of falling under the control of either Spain, which was being joined to Austria by a series of marriages in the Hapsburg family, or France. He therefore intervened in the diplomacy of Europe to help whichever side was the weaker and to get special rights in Flanders. Three of Henry's actions in foreign affairs deserve attention. First of all, by his in-and-out intervention in the so-called Wars of Brittany (1485 to 1499), Henry laid a foundation for later "balance-of-power" diplomacy. This was not a new idea, nor was it fully carried out. But it was a significant change to see England giving up France as an hereditary enemy and altering her alliance as the situation altered. Secondly, by the *Magnus Intercursus* of 1496, he revived the old policy of using the royal power to help English trade—in this case, by getting free-trade rights in Flanders. Thirdly, by marrying his son Arthur to a Spanish Princess, Catherine of Aragon, he linked his newly founded dynasty with the leading dynasty of Europe, the Hapsburgs, at the moment that the Hapsburgs were taking over Spain by a marriage with Catherine's sister.

Henry VII did very little outwardly to change the English constitution —he was too clever for that. But he breathed new life into its old forms. He gave England a strong government, by the powers inherent in the Privy Council, and thus gave her internal peace that brought with it prosperity. An outward sign of this internal peace is the change of the typical nobleman's residence from the walled castle to the Tudor country house. An economic sign is the steady growth of a class of "new men," the founders of most of England's present-day old nobility. The families of Russell, Spencer, and even Cavendish date back into this period and are significantly different from the now extinct Bohuns and Veres. The many-sided man of the Renaissance is beginning to take the place of the feudal warrior of the Middle Ages. It was the royal favor shown to such men as these that in effect was Henry VII's contribution to the constitution. He enlisted the country gentlemen on the king's side by giving the most loyal ones power in local government, as justices of the peace. He gave these same men, too, a feeling of participation in central government by working so much through Parliament. It was good psychology to make great claims as to the king's rights, because, though Henry never acted on them too often, their assertion persuaded men to believe them.

It should also be remembered that Henry had yet another claim on his subjects' gratitude. Through his marriage with Elizabeth of York, he gave them a well-founded hope that they would not again see wars over the succession like the Wars of the Roses. As long as his heirs lived, other claimants would fall into the background. That was why there was so much concern later over the succession of his four children—Arthur, Prince of Wales, who died young, but left a troublesome widow, Catherine of Aragon; Henry, later Henry VIII; Margaret, Queen of James IV of Scotland; and Mary, for a short time Queen of France and long Duchess of Suffolk.

The years from 1485 to 1509 had given England a new generation which had forgotten the Wars of the Roses and Richard III's tyranny. That generation remembered Henry VII's stinginess and the extortions of Empson and Dudley. Therefore, Henry VIII got some cheap popularity by maintaining a gay court—paid for by Henry VII's savings—and by executing Empson and Dudley. Then he apparently turned over the management of his kingdom to Cardinal Wolsey, the Archbishop of York, while he enjoyed himself. Wolsey ran English diplomacy well, on the same balance-of-power lines as had Henry VII. Trouble was shaping up between France under Francis I and the combination of Spain, Austria, and the "Low Countries" under Charles I of Spain, who became Emperor Charles V of Germany. The pretext of the wars was usually feudal claims to parts of Italy, but war between the two expanding nations was nearly inevitable for their interests were bound to clash. Furthermore, Charles inherited the Low Countries from the House of Burgundy, which had an hereditary feud with its relatives, the French royal family. Wolsey had more grandiose ways of conducting diplomacy than had Henry VII. He actually went to war, by short invasions of France, one of which was known as the "Battle of the Spurs" because a French force ran away from the English so fast. This invasion had an effect on Scotland. Naturally, the French urged the Scots to attack England; and James IV, though he was Henry VIII's brother-in-law, obeyed the request of the Queen of France—"to march three miles on English land, and strike three strokes with Scottish brand" (or sword). This caused the Battle of Flodden, in which the Earl of Surrey outmaneuvered James IV and smashed the two flank columns of the Scottish army. Then the old Scottish schiltron stood firm, while the English closed in, both sides fighting at close quarters because both had the long bow. The deadly English bill, an ax with a curved edge, hewed away at the Scotch spearman until "all the flowers of the forest," the best border fighters in Scotland, lay dead by their king. Till another generation of them grew up, Scotland had not the manpower to invade England again. This defeat in 1515 and the French defeat of Pavia in 1525 put the Spaniards on top and naturally turned England against Spain. For, as the weakest of three parties, she had to help the next weaker against the strongest, to keep her own independence. Wolsey had been clever before in balancing powers. For example, there was the famous "Field of the Cloth of Gold," a diplomatic conference on the coast of France, of great splendor, the upshot of which was that all three nations agreed not to keep their agreements with each other. But now, a crisis arose that was too much for him—England's need for an heir to the throne.

As part of Henry VII's diplomatic maneuvers, his elder son Arthur had been married to Catherine, younger daughter of Ferdinand and Isabella of Spain, and thus aunt of Charles V of the Empire. This had been a nominal marriage, for Arthur had died young. To keep the diplomatic bargain, Henry had then been married to his brother's widow. As the Church then considered a sister-in-law as close as a sister, a special dispensation from the Pope had been secured to validate the marriage. However, Catherine was older than her husband, Henry VIII, and had only one surviving child, the Princess Mary. About 1529, Henry realized two things. One was that he had grown very fond of a lady at his court, Anne Boleyn; the other, that if a queen should sit on England's throne, the danger of civil war would be serious. England's only experiment with a queen, Matilda, had been unsuccessful. Furthermore, if the Princess Mary died without heirs, there would be a struggle between the children of his elder sister, Queen Margaret of Scotland, and those of his younger sister, Duchess Mary of Suffolk. Henry, who believed in witches and the visible powers of evil, began to wonder if the dispensation allowing him to marry Catherine had been legal. If it were not, perhaps that explained why so many of Catherine's children were born dead or died after birth. Therefore, he instructed Wolsey to arrange with the Pope to have his marriage annulled, that is, to declare that it had not been legal in the first place.

At this point, the Pope, who had just seen Charles V's army capture Rome, found himself in a difficult position. He temporized; and Henry got rid of Wolsey, whom he summoned, in 1530, to answer charges of violating the Statute of Praemunire. The Cardinal Archbishop died on the journey to London, thus avoiding final disgrace. Henry then settled down to get his own way.

Henry VIII, like his father, knew how to make his subjects participate in his decisions. He called a Parliament to vote new laws. First of all, he collected large fines from the clergy for violating the Statute of Praemunire. In actual fact, Henry had encouraged appeals to Rome, but that did not deter him from punishing what he had permitted. He needed the money. Then, step by step, Henry put pressure on the Church. In 1532, he took away from the Pope the annates, or first year's revenues of each new bishop, which formed an important part of the finances of the papacy. He also induced the universities of Oxford and Cambridge to declare his marriage invalid. In 1533, he had the Act of Appeals passed, after the Pope had refused to try the marriage question in England, by which Act no ecclesiastical case could be appealed to a court outside England. Then, using that Act, he ordered his new Archbishop of Canterbury, Thomas Cranmer, to conduct a divorce trial. Thus, according to English law, Catherine ceased to be Queen, though Catholics considered this annulment invalid. Henry promptly married Anne Boleyn; and in that same year, the Princess Elizabeth was born. Now England had a different heir to the throne, for in strict logic, the Princess Mary was no longer able to inherit.

In 1534, the Act of Appeals was followed by the Act of Supremacy, which declared Henry to be the Protector and Supreme Head of the Church and Clergy of England. When Sir Thomas More and Bishop John Fisher refused to take the oath of supremacy required by this law, Henry had them executed. Then he turned round and had Anne Boleyn executed, marrying in her place Jane Seymour. Jane Seymour had one advantage over Anne Boleyn; no one could contest the legality of her marriage to Henry. Anne Boleyn was dead on Tower Hill, Catherine of Aragon had conveniently died. Consequently, everyone would admit that Jane Seymour's child, Edward, was the legitimate heir to the throne. But Jane died; and Henry had to continue his search for a wife who could bear another male heir. In the meantime, he had Parliament pass a law enabling him to bequeath the throne of England by his will.

Since the so-called "Long Parliament of the Reformation" (1529 to 1536) remained so long in session, Henry unwittingly trained his subjects in self-government at the national level. His successors would find Parliament a very different body from what it had been in the past. Henry continued to be personally powerful. He still ruled through Council, even going so far as to set up much needed branches of the Council in Wales and the North, to deal with local disorders. But he became also "King in Parliament" as much as "King in Council," to use the phrases of constitutional historians.

During this time, Henry was going badly into debt. He was highly extravagant. Costs were rising, for the flood of Spanish gold now pouring in from Mexico and Peru was creating an inflation. Henry, therefore, was impelled to find yet further means of raising money. He was well aware of irregularities in certain monasteries. As "Supreme Head of the Church," he had first some, then all, of the monasteries investigated. As a result of the investigations, he had them dissolved and took over their property. In the North of England this caused trouble, for there monasteries and nunneries were popular. There, they were missionary enterprises which furnished training in the arts of peace to an unruly region, which taught new agricultural methods, and which gave care to the poor. In 1537, the lawyer Robert Aske led an armed movement of protest called the "Pilgrimage of Grace." This carefully organized rising overpowered the local militia. But, by first bargaining to gain time, then striking with a small regular force sent from London, the Duke of Norfolk was able to put down the Pilgrimage and capture Aske, whom Henry promptly had executed.

However, in the south of England, where Henry's government was seated, there was apparently little, if any, resistance to the closing of the monasteries. There has been much argument as to how far this dissolution was justified and to what extent Thomas Cromwell (the great-uncle of a more famous Oliver) painted conditions as worse than they were for propaganda purposes. There has also been much argument about how Henry used the proceeds of seizing the monasteries—to what extent he used them to pay legitimate debts, and to what extent he gave the properties to favorite courtiers. It is also true that certain famous colleges, such as Trinity College, Cambridge, and Jesus College, Cambridge, were founded from the revenues of monasteries which were turned directly over to education. All these points have been heatedly argued because they afford talking points on the great question of the legality of Henry's divorce and of the consequent separation from Rome. However, the one fact that remains clear is that by the dissolution of the monasteries, and the transfer of them to Henry's debtors and friends, a new landed gentry was founded. England's upper class was no longer feudal nobles, but "new men," whose minds would be turned to the future, not the past.

For, by the reign of Henry VIII, the Renaissance was beginning to come to England. Sir Thomas More, the Chancellor later executed for refusing to admit the divorce, was the author of *Utopia*, that description of a perfect country somewhere else, which has been the byword for impossible perfection. John Colet, the Dean of St. Paul's Cathedral, preached on the New Testament in Greek, and founded a school, St. Paul's, to encourage classical studies. Erasmus, the great scholar of the day, spent the last years of his life at Queen's College, Cambridge, which had been founded by Henry VIII's grandmother, Lady Margaret Beaufort. The Italian Polydore Vergil taught the English to study their own history. After two generations had had the benefit of this culture, the result was to be the great flowering of English literature at the end of Elizabeth's reign.

After the Pilgrimage of Grace had been put down and the monasteries had been dissolved, Henry's titanic energy ceased. He still sought for an heir, and he married three more wives. First was the Princess Anne of Cleves, whom he married by proxy, and divorced on sight when she had come over from Germany, calling her "the Flanders Mare" for her size and ugliness. There was a flighty girl at the court, Catherine Howard, executed for her flightiness. Finally, there was a kindly older woman, Catherine Parr, who nursed him through his last illness. (These wives and their fates may be remembered by a jingle—divorced, beheaded, died, divorced, beheaded, survived.) But there were no more children; and Henry was forced to meet the threat of civil war over the succession by naming in his will Edward, Mary, and Elizabeth, in that order, to succeed him, just as if all had been legitimate.

As Henry's reign is looked back upon, three accomplishments stand out as primarily his: starting the separation from Rome, joining Wales to England, and founding the Royal Navy on a permanent basis. Religiously, the "Henrician" Church was much what it had always been, except for the vital matter of church government. Henry was no Protestant in doctrine; indeed, the Pope had given him the title of Defender of the Faith for an attack he had written against Martin Luther. (Rulers of England to this day bear that title, though now the faith that they defend is different.) A sign of Henry's religious beliefs is the Six Articles which he had Parliament enact. Men called them "the whip with six strings" for it courted a death penalty to deny transubstantiation, the value of auricular confession, or the value of private masses, or to attack vows of chastity, the celibacy of the clergy, or the reservation of the wine for the clergy in the Eucharist. These are Catholic doctrines which Henry protected. But, on the other hand, Henry invited private judgment on religious matters by translating the Bible into English and by depriving the papacy of jurisdiction. These are Protestant tendencies, which, if allowed to grow, might prevent future reunion with Rome and cause irrevocable separation. Especially would this be true when the King had sold to private individuals the monastic lands he had confiscated, thereby creating an economic interest in a Protestant future for England.

Though religious matters filled the center of the stage in Henry's reign, they should not obscure what he did for Wales and the Navy. The Welsh Act of Union of 1536 and subsequent acts accomplished three things. The special position of the Marcher lordships was ended. Wales gained representation in Parliament. The seven already created Welsh counties, together with five new ones that had been created out of the Marcher lordships, were assimilated to the English judicial system. When Wales thus became "shireland" occurred one of those important events that escape notice because they are so successful. Before this, Wales had been the home of revolt and disorder; after it, Wales became not less Welsh and yet completely part of the English nation—one of those rare cases where one may truly say that men were loyal to two nationalities. The rarity of this shows what had been accomplished.

As for the Navy, Henry VIII was not the first king to build a navy—many did that before him—but he was the first to keep one constantly in existence and to use it for naval purposes only and not for trade as well. Furthermore, he introduced "broadside firing." His ships could carry many guns pointing to the side, instead of a few pointing ahead and astern. This fire power could—and in later years did—crush larger ships not so well armed. He was the "Father of the British Navy" and as such deserves a share of the credit for its future deeds.

What, then, can one say that the two Henry Tudors accomplished between 1485 and 1547—from Bosworth to Henry VIII's death? In an age when modern nations were being born, they gave England her national state, with these two significant peculiarities: unpaid national service by the rising class of the landed gentry, and a national church.

9

THE REFORMATION
IN THE BRITISH ISLES

The achievement of the first two Tudors was to establish for a long time the balance of the constitution. Their government by executive council forms an essential link between the Curia Regis and the modern Cabinet. The two medieval institutions through which they brought the landed gentry into partnership with them in government—Parliament and the bench of justices of the peace—remained much the same till the Reform Bills and Local Government Acts of William IV and Victoria three centuries later. It was great statecraft to take Council, Parliament, and the "commission of the peace" and draw out of these institutions such lasting power and strength with surprisingly little formal change. But in religious matters it was different. It was not the first two Tudors but the last three who made the present-day Church of England. The reaction against both Edward VI's Protestantism and Mary I's Catholicism made Elizabeth I's Anglican Compromise stick.

To say this may seem a contradiction of the last few pages. But is it? Did Henry VIII, from 1534 to 1547, in the name of some rather shadowy Anglican Liberties allegedly inherited from William the Conqueror and Edward III, do significantly more than Frenchmen had done—or would do between, say, 1438 and 1750—in the name of much more genuine Gallican Liberties? Here there is no need to go into the details of the claims to church self-government made in France from at least the Pragmatic Sanction of Bourges of 1438 up to the Jansenist controversies of Louis XV's reign. What is important is that claims to self-government were made over a long period of time without diverging far from the doctrine of the Church of Rome. There might be schism—that is, administrative separation; rarely did matters go far over the line to heresy, that is, doctrinal separation. Furthermore, in France at least, the Jansenist controversy ended in reunion. This parallel, both in the respects in which it fits and in those in which it does not fit, may serve to throw light in the course of events from 1547 to 1559, from the death of Henry VIII to the passage and enforcement of the Elizabethan Acts of Supremacy and Uniformity.

Since the new King, Edward VI, was a ten-year-old boy, power naturally fell into the hands of the Council, and particularly of the King's uncle, who speedily made himself Duke of Somerset and Lord Protector. Here the weakness of the above parallel stands out. Somerset had Protestant opinions, and used his position to push them forward by state action. Archbishop Cranmer translated the Sarum Rite—that is, the Latin services customary in England, which always had differed from those on the Continent—with additions into what is known as the First or 1549 Prayer Book of Edward VI. In place of the Six Articles set up by act of Parliament, Forty-two Articles—more Protestant ones—were set up, also by act of Parliament. After the prohibition of Masses for the dead it became plausible to seize the "chantries" or endowments that subsidized chanting such Masses. In theory, such chantry funds as were used for education were kept for educational purposes; hence many a "King Edward VI Grammar School" throughout England. In fact, the government seized what it could and sold it to pay debts or reward favorites. Later on, in 1552, just before Edward died, a Second Prayer Book was issued, with definitely Protestant doctrines as to the Communion service. Here, clearly, may be seen how Henry VIII's claim of local control over the Church could and did lead to doctrinal divergence from Rome.

During Edward's short six-year reign social change went on apace, with serious political repercussions. This was a period in which the wool trade grew and the new owners of lands enclosed the "open fields" when they could, to turn from agriculture to grazing. Somerset was a kindly man who felt sympathy with those suffering from enclosure. As a result, when Ket's Rising in Norfolk was put down by John Dudley, Earl of Warwick, it became possible for Warwick to drive Somerset from power, have Somerset executed, and seize control of the government.

Just then (1552) Edward died, and Warwick, now self-promoted to being Duke of Northumberland, tried to make his daughter-in-law queen instead of Mary. The justification of this move was a will Edward was induced to draw up, to supersede his father's will. Thus the charming, honest, and retiring Lady Jane Grey suddenly found herself proclaimed Queen of England. Northumberland soon learned his mistake. Lady Jane, in her short reign, showed him she was a Tudor and would take orders from no one. Mary Tudor, at Framlingham in Suffolk, ignored Northumberland's illegal actions and started for London, calling out the militia as she went. All England rallied to her; even Northumberland had to go over to her side in hopes of leniency. Mary did not spare him, but treated the unfortunate Lady Jane well. Lady Jane had to go to the Tower, but was let live till Sir Thomas Wyatt's Protestant rebellion. Then, for the safety of the nation, Lady Jane was tried for treason and executed.

On her accession to the throne, Mary Tudor found herself in the curious position, for a devout Catholic, of being Supreme Head of the Church. This was easy to rectify, for Parliament was willing enough to repeal the religious laws of Edward VI's reign, go back to the old Latin service, and let the Bishops run the church. It did not take long to enact the necessary changes, except for the matter of papal supremacy. Here should be noted an aspect of Mary's reign sometimes forgotten—that she had to work through Parliament and that, from the very nature of the policy she wished carried out, Parliament was an obstacle to her. Only reluctantly and partially would the ruling classes go along with her in her great aim in life, the restoration of her mother's religion. They would take back the old services, but they kept the monastic lands. They would let the old bishops run the church, but for a long time they refused to allow the pope to resume jurisdiction in England. They wanted an heir to the throne, but they distrusted Mary's choice of Philip II of Spain for a husband. It took two of the six years of her reign—and, during those two years, government pressure at elections and the creation of new boroughs—to get consent to formal reunion with Rome and the Spanish marriage. But one thing Mary could not do—get back the monastic lands. On the advice of her cousin, Reginald Cardinal Pole, she left them in their owners' hands, for it was clear that to return them to the monks and nuns would merely force powerful men to adopt Protestantism for mercenary reasons. Then she allied herself with her mother's nation, Spain, the defender of Catholicism, by marrying Philip II. Neither her marriage policy nor her religious policy were successful. The former might have worked if Philip had in any way understood the English, and if she had had children. But Philip so estranged the English that Parliament granted him the title but not the power of King. He treated his adoring wife with a rudeness that gained him enemies, and he involved England in a war with France that had as its sole result the loss of Calais.

Then Mary took the step that probably did the most to make England Protestant. She revived the statute *De heretico comburendo,* which Somerset had had repealed. She felt that it was vital to save men's souls and that the harsh death of a few might save the souls of a nation. Therefore she started the fires of Smithfield, to sear Protestantism out of England. The burnings, which started with that of John Rogers, were perhaps the greatest single influence in making England Protestant. The divines who had wrangled and misbehaved in Edward's reign, when they were on top, now shared the greatest dignity and courage. When the two bishops, Latimer and Ridley, were burned at the stake, Hugh Latimer, the famous outspoken preacher, turned to his fellow sufferer and said, "By the grace of God, Master Ridley, we have this day lighted a candle that England shall never see put out." When Thomas Cranmer, Henry's Archbishop, the divorcer of Mary's mother Catherine and the composer of the Book of Common Prayer, met his fate he was likewise noble. This man had been a timeserver. He had recanted. But he plucked up courage, withdrew his recantation of Protestantism, and insisted on being burned. Then, when he went to the stake, he held his right hand into the fire that all watchers might see that the hand that signed the recantation was burned first. Such stories as these caught the imagination of the English, some of whom had grown to love the Bible and services in their own language. In Foxe's *Book of Martyrs* these tales were spread abroad, for later generations to read, in a book which next to the newly Englished Bible became the most widely read book in England. Thus Mary's honest, un-Tudor driving failed and led to the result she least wanted.

Mary, like Edward, was sickly, and soon it was realized she could not live long. She died, in 1558, hoping against hope for a child, and broken-hearted because the French Duke of Guise had captured Calais. That final discouragement speeded her death, for on her deathbed she said they would find "Calais written on her heart."

Under Henry VIII's will Elizabeth was supposed to follow her sister. For a moment there was a chance that another desperate attempt, like Northumberland's proclamation of Lady Jane Grey, might cheat her of the throne. But Elizabeth like Mary showed her bravery, England rallied to her, and she became unquestioned Queen, but Queen in a curious position. Would she follow her half-brother's religion or her half-sister's? Would she side with France or with Spain in the dynastic wars then raging? Would she marry and have children? If not, would her successors be chosen from the descendants of the Scottish royal house, or the native house of Suffolk? All these questions mattered much to England and to Europe, and Elizabeth cleverly traded on that fact. By postponing the answers, some of them till the moment of her death, she won England time to grow strong and secure. She succeeded in this through the aid of her wise advisers, Nicholas Bacon and especially William Cecil, in spite of the dangers of revolt in a country that had seen the Pilgrimage of Grace, Ket's Rebellion, and Wyatt's Rebellion and had no standing army but only militia to keep order.

All eyes turned to Elizabeth to see what she would do. Did she accept or reject a part of a service, did she smile or frown on a bishop? Such details as these were sent back to Paris, Madrid, or Venice—our chief sources of knowledge—by ambassadors. Two sentences written by the Spanish ambassador seem to tell the story of these days: "She is very much wedded to the people and thinks as they do," and, a week later: "She seems to me incomparably more feared than her sister and gives her orders and has her way as absolutely as her father did." Thus that otherwise bamboozled nobleman summed up the essence of Tudor rule, by which the great Tudors got enthusiastic obedience because they knew the right orders to give, and Elizabeth got her way by letting others get their way, too, at the same time.

A fine example of this Tudor statecraft she exhibited in the winter of 1558–1559, when she put the onus of key decisions on others, who might be trusted to decide as she wished. When Parliament met, in composition not far from Mary's last Parliament, a rather Protestant bill was submitted that Commons liked and Lords rejected. Then, as a compromise, two separate acts were passed through both houses, despite the Catholic bishops in the upper House. One, the Act of Supremacy, made the Church of England again independent of Rome, but gave Elizabeth the less provocative title of Supreme Governor rather than Supreme Head. The other, the Act of Uniformity, was the key act. It did three things. It revived Edward VI's Second Prayer Book but added words that might allow taking the Communion service in a Catholic as well as in a Protestant sense. It set up a scale of fines—small ones, the kind that can be enforced because they are not too dramatically large—for nonattendance at church. It set up a controlling body, soon to be called the Court of High Commission, to exact obedience to the Acts of Uniformity and Supremacy. What is significant about this compromise is that it worked and lasted. There is a tendency to speak of the Henrician Church, the Edwardian Church, even at times the Marian, but of the Elizabethan Settlement. The facts of history will show why this is done.

For in 1559 Elizabeth, working through Parliament and High Commission, did settle a great deal. The bishops were her greatest trouble. Of all those in office at the time, only one appears to have taken the oath of supremacy. Even he did not share in the consecration of Reginald Pole's successor as Archbishop of Canterbury. (It is little remembered how lucky Elizabeth was that Pole, made Cranmer's successor at Canterbury, died the same day as Mary.) But bishops of Edward VI's reign had come back from exile; four of them passed on—in Anglican eyes, at least—the apostolic succession to Matthew Parker. Thus the old forms, Englished by Cranmer, continue in the Church of England to this day, with a claim to coming in a direct line from St. Augustine of Kent.

The parish clergy were another matter. Where Mary had had to exile two thousand, Elizabeth's High Commission had to deprive only two hundred. The laity, too, attended the Church services. Because old forms and vestments and an English translation of old rites were used, there was a period of ten years, 1559 to 1569, during which Catholics could excuse themselves for attending Anglican services. Then the enactment by Parliament of the Thirty-nine Articles made the Church of England definitely Protestant. Yet, since the rites had been Englished, since ambiguous English words covered key points—notably in the administration of the Communion and in the use of the word minister for the word priest—extreme

Protestants could attend the same services. For each side might hope that the compromise would resolve itself in a move in their direction. With the more extreme Protestants the compromise lasted longer, till the Prayer Book revision of 1662, at the time of the Restoration of Charles II. As a result, there grew to eventual power in the Church of England an Anglican party, which believed that the Church of England had not changed in 1559 in anything but outward form and return to old principles. This party of which Jewel, Lancelot Andrewes, and above all Hooker, author of the Ecclesiastical Polity, were the early intellectual leaders, marks the continuity of the High Church party of the Church of England of today with the pre-Reformation past. Because of the probably intentional vagueness of the Elizabethan Settlement, such a center party had its chance to take root and grow.

The reader will note that this account is historical, not theological. What matters here is not who was right, but why certain arguments could prove acceptable. Speaking historically, then, this Reformation settlement in England may be roughly summed up in two sentences: "Henry VIII started the Church of England, Elizabeth founded it," and "The Elizabethan Compromise established a Church of England that was national, continuous, and inclusive." The purpose of the first sentence is to point out that though the Reformation in England stems from Henry's divorce of Catherine of Aragon, yet the Henrician Church was reunited to Rome. It is the Elizabethan Church that is still separate. The purpose of the second sentence is to point out the characteristics of the Church during Elizabeth's reign. It was national; that is, under government control. It could claim to be continuous; that is, it was staffed by the old clergy and used forms that had been used in the past. Above all, it contained for a long time the greater part of the population. In the crucial years when men and women unconsciously made up their minds it was the easy and natural thing to go to the church to which one had always gone, and become loyal to its new form. Thus, in an age of religious civil war, when from the Mediterranean to the Baltic there was strife and disunity, England saw a remarkable degree of peace and unity. Indeed, when religion became a party question, it became possible for Elizabeth to call patriotism to her aid to back Protestantism.

Here, perhaps, is the proper place to make yet one more point. England became in these years a politically Protestant country. This took place for many reasons. Foxe's Book of Martyrs reminded men and women and above all children of the Marian persecutions. These memories were reinforced by sad tales brought from Holland and France, and by seamen who had suffered in Spanish galleys and seen their friends burned by the Inquisition in Spanish autos-da-fé. Whatever the religious inclinations of the country at Elizabeth's accession, about which there is ardent dispute, and however long there was a Catholic group of numerical significance, by the seventeenth century England was a Protestant power. This tendency became heightened by the Bull of Deposition of 1570. Once the Pope had told Catholics that Elizabeth was not Queen, once Catholics had in consequence begun to plot to drive her from the throne, a weapon was put into Elizabeth's hands. Especially after the Ridolfi Plot of 1569 and the Norfolk Plot of 1570 her government could rest all its prosecutions against active Catholics on the ground of treason. When agents and priests from overseas were brought to trial, they were asked "the bloody question"—whether it was the duty of Catholics to fight against the Queen. When they answered "Yes," as after 1570 they must, it was for that answer they were condemned, not for any theological matter. In consequence, while Mary Tudor, in her short reign, burnt fifty a year for religion, Elizabeth, in her long reign, executed only four a year, chiefly for treason, and yet was far more successful than her sister in uniting the people of England in one church.

A consequence of this policy of toleration of loyal, quiet Catholics was that the Catholic group in England split in two. One part of it would pay fines for nonattendance at church, if required to, and protest its loyalty. The other would plot against the Queen, and when caught pay the penalties of treason. Most of these plots had as their aim supplanting Elizabeth by her cousin, Mary, Queen of Scots. This danger to England was tied in with that of a Scottish invasion. A pro-French Scotland would mean trouble in wars with France; a Catholic Scotland would mean trouble in war with Spain. Therefore the position of Mary Stuart, Queen of Scotland and in turn Dauphiness, Queen, and Queen Dowager of France, in relation to her Protestant nobles was crucial to Elizabeth. Here she could not temporize but must act. But before telling of Mary, Queen of Scots, something must be said of Scotland itself.

Scotland was a peculiar country. As has been said, it was half feudal, half clan, and held together only by the royal house. The clansmen in the Highlands fought constantly, sometimes for the sheer love of war. Highland clans could be kept behind the Highland line by the Norman Scots nobles, but the Norman Scots nobles had the same thirst for war. The most warlike of all were the Black Douglases whose great battle with the Percies of Northumberland is told in the ballads of "Otterburn" and "Chevy Chase." These nobles were a constant thorn in the side of the new royal house of Stuart. For with the death of David Bruce in 1571 the direct line of the great Bruce had ended, and the throne had gone to the descendants of Marjorie Bruce and Walter the Steward. A glance at the record of the first five Jameses of the Stuart line will show what Scotland went through.

The first two Stuart kings, Robert II and Robert III, died in peace.

But James I as a young boy, when on his way to France, was captured, and lived a prisoner in England till he grew up. Then, married to Lady Joan Beaufort he returned to Scotland where he ruled so well and so strongly that at Perth a group of conspirators trapped him, unguarded. To gain him time for hiding, Lady Catherine Douglas put her arm through the hasps of the door, in place of the bar which the conspirators had had taken away, and held it there till her arm was broken. But the bravery of "Katy-Bar-the-Door," as Scottish legend called her, was of no avail. James came out of his place of hiding too soon and was cut down. Though Joan took stern vengeance, Scotland lost a great and able man in the prime of life and began a series of reigns by children which were to keep her in disorder. James II had trouble with the house of Douglas. The child King's guardians invited the Earl of Douglas to dinner, then had him served with a black bull's head, the sign of an execution, and killed him in the King's presence. This was the ill-famed "Black Dinner." James II, when still young, besieged the border castle of Roxburgh and was killed by the explosion of a cannon made of rods of iron welded together imperfectly. James III was such a weak king that he drove his nobles to revolt. They met to concert measures, and came to an apparently perfect plan, if only someone dared carry it out. One old lord compared the plan to that of the mice to put a bell on the cat, whereat Lord Archibald Douglas said, "I will bell the cat," and led a revolt in which the future James IV shared which defeated James III. The King was murdered, as he fled from the battlefield, by a man pretending to be a priest. In remorse, ever after, James IV wore a hair shirt next his skin to remind him he had caused his father's death. That hair shirt identified his body when it was found on the field of Flodden. His successor, James V, followed the same policies. He was loved in his land, through which he used to wander in disguise, but he too invaded England and died too young of a broken heart at the news of his army's defeat at Solway Moss. As he lay dying, news was brought him of the birth of a daughter, Mary Stuart, his sole heir. The thought came to him of how the first Stuart had gained the throne by marriage with Marjorie Bruce, and he said: "It came with a lass, it will go with a lass." Then for safety's sake, the tiny Queen was sent to France while her mother, Mary of Guise, ruled Scotland as regent.

These tales of revolt, border wars, and tragic struggling singlehanded to keep order can be extended by many more to be found in old ballads and Sir Walter Scott's *Tales of a Grandfather*, as well as in history books. All would serve to show that though Scotland had a Parliament, actual power was divided between king and nobles, not king and Parliament, and that an absolute monarch would do the land good.

However, the Reformation changed all this. In Scotland, the Regent was on the side of the Roman Catholic Church, since it stood for law and order, whereas the nobles wanted the wealth of the monasteries and bishoprics. Allied with the nobles was a new democratic, or rather republican, movement in the church. For the Reformation was coming to Scotland from Geneva, whence John Knox was importing John Calvin's ideas. According to those ideas, the Kirk—to use the name that the Church in Scotland has since then employed—would be a federation of congregations, supervised by a General Assembly. Each congregation would choose its own minister from those qualified. The General Assembly, elected by the congregations, would determine qualifications, largely under the guidance of the clergy and the elders or presbyters of each congregation; hence comes the name of Presbyterianism for the Scottish religion. In the disorders of the times, a religious line-up emerged. Protestant "Lords of the Congregation" joined with the General Assembly in trying to force Protestantism on the Regent. Here Elizabeth saw her chance. She apparently wavered—almost never did she act without a smoke screen of apparent irresolution—but sent a fleet and an army to Scotland to support Knox and the Lords of the Congregation. Admiral Winter had instructions to interfere but if questioned to say he had done so on his own responsibility. There was no questioning, for he captured Leith with ease and, at the sudden death of the Regent, put John Knox in effective power in Scotland. It has been said of this English army that went with Winter that it won the greatest victory ever won by an English army in Scotland— it conquered its own desire for plunder and left the country with the gratitude of the people. From then on the Scottish Presbyterians would work with Elizabeth, and she need no longer fear pro-French or pro-Spanish invasion while they were in power.

It was after this capture of Leith that the Queen of Scotland returned to her native land. She had been brought up in the gay court of Queen Catherine de Médicis, as the daughter-in-law of King Henry II of France, and later as the queen of his eldest son, Francis II. With her husband's death, she and her few court ladies were suddenly plunged into the severe life of Edinburgh, where her religion was looked on as wicked and foreign. Shortly after her return home in 1561 she was married to her first cousin, Henry Stewart, Lord Darnley. The feuds that had been usual under her ancestors continued to go on. In the course of one a quarrel broke out in the royal household, and Darnley had David Rizzio, Queen Mary's secretary, murdered in her presence. This seems to have been the breaking point for her. Shortly after that an heir was born, who would become James VI of Scotland and later on James I of England. Soon after that Darnley fell ill. He went to a house outside Edinburgh, Kirk in the Field, to recuperate. When the Queen was away from it, Kirk in the Field blew up in a gunpowder explosion. James Hepburn, Earl of Bothwell, was accused of this murder, but stood public trial—Mary riding into Edinburgh

with him to it—in a court packed with his retainers, and no one dared
bring an indictment against him. Civil war soon broke out over the fact
that the Catholic Queen married Bothwell, who had been divorced from
a previous wife, by a Protestant ceremony. Mary was captured at Car-
berry Hill. Bothwell was driven out of Scotland to Denmark, and ended
his days in jail for the desertion there of a wife no one had known of.
Mary did escape from her captors, but only after abdicating in favor of
James, and after another defeat, at Langside, fled to her cousin the Queen
of England. Elizabeth promptly put her under what is now called "protective custody" and steadily refused to see her.

There is much discussion whether Mary was implicated in the murder
of Darnley. At the time of her imprisonment the famous Casket Letters
got into circulation. These were alleged copies of letters captured from
one of Bothwell's servants. If they are genuine they completely convict
her, but the question is, which are genuine, which forgeries? Thus it was
that the most romantic member of the Stuart family, the beautiful girl
who left the gay court of France to try to keep the throne to which she
was born, came to England to be a prisoner the rest of her life.

Thus the Scottish Reformation ended with an almost republican form
of church government, the Church in part guiding the state during the
young King's minority, and the Queen in exile, far more important as a
threat to the English throne and to England's peace than to her native
Scotland.

As for Ireland, the course of the Reformation there was far different,
because it became tied in with Ireland's other problems. In brief, the
history of Ireland in this period of the growth of absolutism in Europe
and of the Reformation was a contradiction of what happened in England
and Scotland. When the central governments grew stronger in both
halves of Great Britain, decentralization remained the keynote in Ireland. While the Reformation took over Scotland and England, the Counter
Reformation took over Ireland. It is hard to go beyond these generalizations without getting deep into the disorganization that overwhelmed the
land in those years. But without tracing the struggles of viceroys with
Irish chieftains and Anglo-Irish nobles, and without tracing the contests
of Reformers and Counterreformers, it is possible at least to characterize
the type of change that took place at different periods.

In Henry's VII's reign, the significant thing was that Ireland, as has
been pointed out, was a Yorkist center. Henry VII bided his time, then
sent over Sir Edward Poynings, who in 1495 secured the passage of the
celebrated Poynings's Law or Statutes of Drogheda, which subordinated
the Irish Parliament to the English Council. But Poynings could not
make the Irish taxes pay the cost of an efficient government. Therefore
Henry fell back on the policy of letting Irish government rest in the hands

of the Irish chieftains and the hibernicized Anglo-Irish nobility, as long
as they acted through the forms customary in England, of rule by Parliament and Council. So Ireland drifted, through the rule of Henry VIII and
even Edward VI. On the surface, Henry's nominal changes were accepted. He gave up the title of Lord of Ireland and assumed that of King
of Ireland. He and Edward in name changed the Church to a Church of
Ireland, eventually with a similar Prayer Book. A few administrators, a
few reforming bishops and other clergy were sent over from England.
But Ireland remained surprisingly untouched by all this. Several bishops
whom the supposedly Protestant Edwardian Church kept in office remained all the time in full communion with Rome. Though Anglo-Normans
and Irish leaders were given earldoms they still behaved like clan chieftains. From time to time some chieftain—a Fitzgerald of Kildare, an
O'Neill of Ulster—would go too far and be called a rebel. If he were
caught, he would be executed for treason; if he retired safely to a wilderness fastness, he would eventually be pardoned and restored to title and
office on the condition that he kept up the pretense of ruling through the
King's laws. Even in the more significant—for Ireland—religious changes
of Philip and Mary and of Elizabeth, Ireland seemed—for Ireland—
quiescent. The acts of the English Parliament, after a due interval, would
be transmitted to Dublin by the English Council and there passed into
law by the Irish Parliament.

For, after all, it was just the few counties of the "English Pale" that
took this at all seriously. That is why there is such importance in the fact
that Philip and Mary put into effect the policy of "planting." When they
turned the counties of Leix and Offaly, by settlement by English Catholics,
into Kings County and Queens County, they made the first frontal attack
on the old Irish land system. Here began, outside the Pale, the struggle
between the old relationship of chief and clan and the new relationship
of landlord and tenant that was to cut across Irish politics till the twentieth
century.

Then, with the bull of deposition of Elizabeth, came the Counter Reformation and the sudden eruption of a new Irish problem, superimposed
on the earlier problem of disorganization. Few in Ireland were Reformers;
most of those few had come over from England. The common people in
Ireland, who spoke Erse, found no attraction in the unfamiliar words of
the Irish Book of Common Prayer and were fond of the Latin services
that they knew. To them came emissaries from Rome and Spain, especially Jesuit missionaries, telling them that Elizabeth was an usurper.
This was news that was eagerly listened to. Those who in past years had
been accustomed to revolt anyway now had a sound justification. Now
one "Earl" and now another revolted, to meet death or high office as the
vagaries of Irish politics turned for or against him. In her turn, Elizabeth

tried the method that had worked in Scotland; she sent over an army. But this failed. Fear struck the English, for in 1579 His Holiness the Pope sent his army to liberate Ireland. At Smerwick Elizabeth's captains surrounded it. The degree of their fear of Ireland as an enemy base is shown by the bitter way they interpreted unconditional surrender as justifying killing all prisoners. After that Elizabeth tried to follow the precedent of Philip and Mary and "plant" the land by bringing settlers to southern Ireland from southern England. This largely failed, for two reasons. First of all, it cost too much to settle in Ireland. Those who thought to get landed estates cheap lost their capital and then cut their losses by abandoning their estates. Secondly, those who did stay became hibernicized, took Irish tenants because they were all it was possible to get, and took over the customs of their tenants.

Attempt after attempt was made, with new armies and new grants of land, to bring Ireland to heel. Even the Earl of Essex was to fail and come home to treason and execution. At last there appears on the scene one of the few Englishmen who understood how to rule Ireland, Lord Mountjoy. Mountjoy struck at the heart of the problem, the still independent status of the clan leaders. Then the "Flight of the Earls" took place, as he ravaged the O'Neills out of Ulster to Spain. Deprived of leadership and a rallying point, Irish discontent simmered down, and it became possible for English landlords and with them English institutions and the English language to strike root over the island, beyond the Pale.

Here begins the story of that puzzling group, the Anglo-Irish "Garrison," English in tongue and loyalty, Irish in sympathy and thought. These men were both Protestant and Catholic, for though most were new planters some were of the older Anglo-Irish stock and speedily the two groups intermarried. In part, but not completely, they took the place of the clan chieftains. They kept in spirit though not in law, the old ideas of land tenure, shuffling their tenants around to fit their ideas of the tenants' needs rather than granting permanent leases. They formed an aristocracy both like and unlike the English landed gentry. In times of quiet all went well; when stress came, as it came too often, Protestantism meant loyalty to the King, Catholicism meant revolt, revolt meant reconquest, and a new set of "planters." So, as wave after wave of English upper-class settlement came in, the "Garrison" evolved its special attitude toward life. Its members kept a watchful and suspicious eye on the very tenants with whom they were on terms of warm friendship. A curious relationship of mutual confidence and mutual distrust grew up, comprehensible in full only by Irishmen.

Here the story has moved ahead of itself. It will take generations to reach the fine flower of the "Garrison culture," the mellowed golden age of the "Protestant Ascendancy" at the end of the eighteenth century. Then the Union of 1801, the Famine of 1846, and the Troubles of 1921 will end this gallant race, who neither succeeded nor failed in the duty Elizabeth laid on them, of ruling the land she herself could not rule. But Irish history will turn on the struggles of this garrison of alien religion torn between loyalty to the Crown and sympathy for its tenants.

Perhaps the course of the Reformation in the British Isles may be summed up thus: In England it brought peace through the Elizabethan Compromise, which established a Church obedient to the Crown, continuous with the past, and for a time largely inclusive of the population. In Scotland it brought peace through Protestant religious self-government. But in Ireland it brought bitter civil war, and the creation of a long-standing problem of keeping a population submissive to an alien ruling class of a different religion. Therefore the Reformation was to have three separate results: it was to keep Ireland in turmoil, it was to give Scotland peace internally, and at last peace with a politically Protestant England; in England it was to lead to national unity and peace because the Elizabethan Compromise would free England from civil war in an age of religious civil wars.

10

THE ELIZABETHAN ERA

The last chapter ended by pointing out that, whatever the Reformation did for Ireland it brought peace within England, and on England's border with Scotland. What sort of peace was this? Did it bring prosperity and progress? These are the questions that this chapter will try to answer. One answer can be given immediately—it was a peace of partial isolation and of patriotic self-government. External enemies were kept away by the English Channel and by peace on the Scottish border. Faithfully—and inexpensively—the gentry kept order in the land, through their functions as justices of the peace. Internal enemies were kept down by the relationship that grew up between Elizabeth and her people. Wedded to them, thinking as they did, consequently having her way as absolutely as her father did—again, this time indirectly, the Spanish ambassador is quoted—she got their loyalty. So high was this loyalty that she even was able to use it as a counterbalance to the claims of religion. As the previous chapter also pointed out, she answered the Catholic claim that she should be deposed as an heretic by calling on all her subjects to support her against treason. Thus many native Catholics were kept quiet, foreign agents were driven underground, and an internal as well as an external peace was won that gave England a chance to develop.

Heavy taxation might have blocked this development. But Elizabeth shrewdly knew that her subjects would do anything for her but give her money. She tried, except in emergencies, to "live of her own" from royal estates and the traditional parliamentary grant of the customs for life. By sales of capital, by some sequestrations of property of the disloyal, and by a deft parsimony, she kept from asking for taxes, except in circumstances under which Parliament could be expected to vote money cheerfully. More than that, by good management, Gresham, of Gresham's law fame, got her cheap loans in the world money market. By equally good management, Lord Treasurer the Marquis of Winchester not only husbanded the royal finances, but also recoined the currency that Henry VIII had debased. Here was a positive impetus to commerce and industry.

Nobly commerce and industry took advantage of it. Indeed, some authorities hold that this period saw an industrial revolution. New skills were utilized. Miners and smelters came from Germany and elsewhere. Glass, iron, steel, copper, became native manufactures. By a process later lost and then rediscovered, coal was used for smelting as well as for fuel; coal mines brought new wealth. Each new skill brought another new skill after it. The textile trades advanced. Even a curious fiber named cotton, brought from India and the Mediterranean, found, in northern England, a few weavers who made their living turning it into cloth. Their native town of Manchester, someday, was to have a phenomenal rise. In themselves, each of these additions to England's productivity was small, but their action was cumulative. Wealth begets wealth. Suddenly, at the end of Elizabeth's reign, and even more in that of her successor, James, the process was to pick up speed and have social repercussions. A higher standard of living was to reach the whole island. Again, by modern or absolute standards, the change would be trivial, but by the standards of the time, it would be very great. A new class was to come to power—or rather a class which had existed for a long time, and had always been a recruiting ground for a new elite, was to recruit faster and more effectively. Where one or two merchants rose to wealth and in a generation or two joined the aristocracy, more were to rise, and they were to join the aristocracy more quickly. The degree of fluidity of English society was to change.

Therefore, in a time of such social change, it was no accident that Elizabeth's reign opened with a law of apprenticeship (1563) and closed with one of poor relief (1601). As employment opened out, the guilds could not be trusted to be the training institutions; supervision of training had to be handed over to those maids of all work, the justices of the peace, in 1563. A new urban life was evolving. Yet, on the other hand, changes of employment can mean loss of employment. Elizabethan England had a social conscience. The men who founded grammar schools— Harrow, Rugby, and many other schools date from gifts of these days— had a humanitarian concern in advance of their ancestors and of their continental contemporaries, however heartless some of their sports may seem today. Just what caused the poor-relief problem of Elizabethan England remains arguable. Was it the abolition of the monasteries that threw a burden of the poor on the state, or was it the new social conscience of Protestantism that caused a recognition of the duty of relieving the poor? Did enclosure cause a surplus population, or did it cause the wealth that allowed setting up a higher standard of living? There is truth on both sides of these questions; the difficult thing is to decide how much. But they all form part of the same picture of social change, made possible by years of peace, and reflecting a change in the national spirit.

With this background in mind, let us turn to the events of the years 1570 to 1603.

By 1570, Queen Elizabeth had succeeded in shelving the religious question in such a way that time would finish solving it for her. In this, she was aided by the action of the Pope in declaring her deposed. This rallied patriotic feeling to her side, just as a similar threat of deposition made Henry of Bourbon, King of Navarre, the Protestant leader in France, all the more popular. But by 1570, the "Wars of Religion" had begun, in which Elizabeth's ex-brother-in-law, Philip of Spain, tried to reimpose Catholicism on Europe and at the same time strengthen Spain. In these wars, Protestantism and national spirit allied against Philip under two great but very different leaders, the Dutchman William of Orange-Nassau and the Frenchman Henry of Navarre. These men fought Elizabeth's battles for her until she was strong enough to aid them. It was by a shrewd policy of letting others gain time for her that Elizabeth transformed England from a minor nation to the ruler of the seas, and gave her the national pride that made the Elizabethan era outstanding in England's literary, cultural, and even spiritual history. The word "spiritual" is here used because the Elizabethan age is the one Englishmen look back to for guidance perhaps more than any other.

Properly to judge Elizabeth's foreign policy, it is necessary to understand what she was up against, and what was going on across the Channel in Holland and Belgium, and in France. In Holland and Belgium, then joined as the Netherlands, Philip was trying to enforce Catholicism and at the same time levy heavy taxes, in opposition to the local parliament, the States General. Sporadic revolts broke out, led by the Dutch prince, William of Orange. His raids were uniformly unsuccessful, but his determination and wisdom made him the rallying point for resistance. William had important virtues: he was tolerant in an age of intolerance, accessible to all in an age of haughtiness among rulers, and honest in an age of diplomatic trickery. Almost automatically leadership fell into his hands. Rebellious nobles, who proudly called themselves "beggars" because of a sneer made by one of Philip's governors-general; stolid Dutch and Flemish burghers, who were appalled at high taxes and willing to fight them to the death; daring semipirates, who called themselves the "Sea Beggars"—all put themselves under his command. Slyly, Elizabeth sympathized with them and gave them advice, encouragement, and very little concrete help. If they kept Philip busy, he would leave her alone; and what England needed, desperately, was to be left alone. She had to build up peace at home; she had to keep taxes low; and she could not afford to fight.

In France, the situation was different. There, there were three parties.

In the middle were the young kings of France—Francis II, who married Mary, Queen of Scots, and died young, and his two brothers, Charles IX and Henry III. They ruled in name; in fact, their clever mother, Catherine de Médicis, ran France, though she had to do it indirectly. On the one side was a strong Catholic party, organized in the Catholic League, usually called "the League." At the head of this were the Dukes of Lorraine, of the powerful house of Guise, to which belonged Mary, Queen of Scots' mother and the duke who took Calais. This party was supported by the citizens of Paris. On the other side were the Huguenots, the Protestant group, chiefly nobles and citizens of certain cities, notably La Rochelle, who looked forward to the day when the Valois kings would die without heirs and the Protestant King of Navarre would inherit the throne. Catherine de Médicis played a game of balancing these two against each other. Here too, Elizabeth offered advice and let the Huguenots do her work for her. She was aided by the fact that she had built up a splendid diplomatic and intelligence service, whose records are still in existence. Her intelligence service had already, under Sir Francis Walsingham, nipped in the bud two plots against her, the Norfolk plot of 1569, and the Ridolfi plot of 1570.

Elizabeth had a further set of troubles. Her own seamen were getting her into difficulties with Philip. They wanted their share of American trade; and when Philip tried to keep them out of the West Indies, they went there anyway and bluffed it out. Notable among these traders was one John Hawkins, from Devonshire, then the seafaring county of England. Hawkins was engaged in the slave trade. A pious and noble bishop, Bartolomé de Las Casas, had persuaded the Spanish government that the only way to convert the Indians was to stop using them as labor in the gold mines and sugar plantations, and to import Negroes from Africa in their place. That served two purposes. It saved the lives of the Indians, who could not stand mine and plantation work as the Negroes could; and it allowed the conversion of the Negroes to Christianity. Thus, with the best of intentions, the infamous slave trade began. Hawkins would buy slaves in Africa and then, on reaching the Spanish Main and Mexico, would pretend to have been driven off his course by a storm. Conniving Spanish officials would let him enter ports usually restricted to the ships of the Spanish trading monopoly, where he would sell his slaves. Pretty soon this trick was discovered, and Hawkins had to try another. He pretended to capture a South American city and then force the inhabitants to trade with him. However, in 1568, at San Juan d'Ulloa, in Mexico, the local authorities double-crossed him. When his ships were in the harbor, the Spanish counterattacked and sank or captured all but two. Then they burned the crews as heretics. Hawkins and his young cousin, Francis Drake, barely escaped. Thereafter, Drake, white-hot with indignation, declared a sort of private war against Spain. With this Elizabeth sympathized, for one of the lost ships, the *Jesus,* had been her own property, rented to Hawkins, though that fact she naturally covered up.

Drake, in the eventful year 1572, even went so far as to land in Panama, at Nombre de Dios Bay, to cross the isthmus, make an unsuccessful attack on the city of Panama, and then successfully capture the gold sent from Peru. This venture filled him with a desire to sail the "South Sea," as the Pacific was then called from being south of Panama, where unarmed Spanish galleons carried untold treasure. His raids, and those of others, such as John Oxenham, who built a ship in the Pacific but was captured and killed, gave Elizabeth much difficulty but also took money away from Philip and thus weakened him in his struggle in the Netherlands. Therefore, Elizabeth spent much time stalling Philip when he demanded redress. She also made counterdemands, once blandly seizing the money he had sent to pay his army in the Netherlands, when the ship carrying it entered an English harbor.

Few diplomats could have kept their country out of war under conditions like this. Militantly Protestant elements in England wanted to aid their coreligionists fighting for their lives. Philip was constantly on the edge of declaring war. But through it all, Elizabeth kept an uneasy peace and surmounted crisis after crisis. The year 1572 was, in some ways, her worst. Philip put such pressure on her that she had to expel the Dutch Sea Beggars from England. She survived that, thanks to them, for they captured the seaport of The Brill in Holland and kept it, as the first independent part of that country. From then on, William of Orange had an impregnable base from which he could draw to himself the rest of Holland. Then, in that same year, 1572, Catherine de Médicis, also under great pressure, decided to wipe out the Huguenots. She arranged a marriage between her daughter, Marguerite de Valois, and Henry of Navarre, and invited all the Huguenot nobles to the celebration, including their leader, Admiral de Coligny. The night before the wedding, bands of armed men, aided by the citizens of Paris, killed every Huguenot they could find. (Mr. Secretary Walsingham saw this, and became, therefore, the advocate, on his return to London, of a militantly Protestant foreign policy.) The King of Navarre saved his life by changing his religion for a while, and the Huguenot party was weakened. Yet Elizabeth neither intervened nor gave up hope; she saw the Huguenot party revive and saw Henry of Navarre rejoin it and fight a series of petty civil wars that kept France weak. They also weakened Spain, for Philip was tempted to interfere and waste his strength.

Elizabeth survived many other crises. Another sharp one came in 1576, when Drake carried out his cherished project and brought an English ship into the Pacific. His voyage is a tradition in England, and rightly so.

He overcame all sorts of obstacles. Five vessels started with him, but dissension broke out. It was necessary to deal sternly with a potential mutiny —and to execute one of his closest friends, Christopher Doughty. Only one ship succeeded in entering the Pacific, but on that ship the morale was high. Drake insisted that "the gentlemen must pull and haul with the mariners, and the mariners must pull and haul with the gentlemen." With this often-quoted saying, he founded the comradeship which is the basis of English naval discipline. As he had expected, there were wonderful prizes to be taken from the unsuspecting, unarmed Spaniards. The capture of the great *Cacafuego* and of the Manila Galleon made him and his crew unbelievably wealthy. However, he ran the danger John Oxenham had had to face, that of being trapped on the way back. First, he tried to go around America to the north by the long-believed-in Northwest Passage. But after having nearly reached San Francisco, he changed his mind and went home by the Cape of Good Hope, becoming the second man to sail around the world. On his return, Queen Elizabeth knighted him on his ship, the *Golden Hind*, took her share of the booty in return for what she had lent him, and then soothed Philip of Spain by officially rebuking him.

Elizabeth survived other crises. She seems to have done this and to have stayed at peace because she realized that Spain really had the best army in Europe. The sturdy Spanish infantrymen, armed with long pikes and supported by musketmen, fought much as had the English bowmen with the dismounted knights holding off cavalry charges. They were the successful veterans of many a battle. Only one set of troops were better than they—the superb Italian professional soldiers commanded by Alexander, Duke of Parma, who were also in Philip's service. No matter how brave they were, no untrained English could fight such an army, and Elizabeth could not afford to set up and train an army. Until Elizabeth could see her way clear ahead, she was going to wait.

But she was not going to waste time. She was willing to send some money to the Dutch. She was very willing to let English volunteers, paid for by the Dutch, gain military experience. She was reluctantly willing to let the Earl of Leicester command the Dutch armies. By such means, she both prepared against the future and weakened Philip of Spain.

At last her chance came. Henry III, the last king of the Valois line, finally plucked up courage to resist the Catholic League, which had ousted him from Paris. He summoned Henri le Balafré, the young Duke of Guise, to Amboise Castle, and there had him murdered. Then Henry III joined forces with Henry of Navarre to regain effective control of his kingdom. Now came a time when Elizabeth could take a decisive step. Her intelligence service, which until then had kept Mary Stuart closely watched, began to let her correspond in what she thought safety with the outside and soon had evidence which would allow a treason trial. In 1587, the same year as the murder of Guise, Mary was executed. That gave Philip a free hand. Now he would not, by invading England, put a member of the Guise family on its throne, who would take the side of France against Spain. He therefore declared war, but England was ready.

England had something of an army, for Leicester and others had learned their trade in Holland. This fact gave the English people confidence, and her troops mustered in front of the Queen at Tilbury, confident they could repel Alexander of Parma and his veterans if ever they landed. Better than that, England had naval forces. Elizabeth had put John Hawkins in charge of shipbuilding, and had in her Royal Navy a nucleus of low, fast, broadside-firing ships of the type Henry VIII had originated. In time of crisis, if there were a Spanish fleet in the Channel, to that Royal Navy could be added about three times as many privately owned ships. These privateers would be smaller vessels, less under discipline, but would be superbly fought in defense of homeland and religion and in hopes of booty. England also had a naval policy, for which Drake was to be thanked. He wanted to "singe the King of Spain's beard"—to attack the Spanish fleet, the so-called Invincible Armada, before it started, right in its home ports. This Elizabeth let him do. His small squadron caught parts of it separated from the rest and broke up its preparations, even sailing into Cadiz harbor to do this. That delayed the Armada's sailing a whole year.

The next year Elizabeth seems to have felt that Spanish preparations had been so far advanced that it was too risky to send an English squadron out to Spain. The Spaniards might slip by and find England unprotected. As a result, the Spaniards surprised the English in Plymouth harbor. The story is still told of Drake's calmness when told the Spaniards were in sight. He was playing bowls and went on with the game, saying, "We have time to finish the game and beat the Spaniards too." He was right. Medina-Sidonia, the nobleman whom Philip had forced to take the command in spite of his utter inexperience, failed to seize his chance, and the nimble, heavily gunned English ships shattered the hulls of the Spaniards by low, accurate fire at ranges the Spaniards could not use. A dejected Spanish fleet took refuge at Calais. Lord Howard of Effingham, the English Admiral, sent in fireships, which drove the Spaniards into the North Sea, and the English attacked again, off Gravelines. By that time, the English had run out of gunpowder, for no naval battle had ever before been fought on such a scale, and not enough had been provided. The Spaniards were even less well supplied. But here the weather took a hand and ended the fighting. A fierce storm drove the Spaniards farther north, and the few who got back to Spain, after rounding Scotland, brought Philip the news that he could never conquer England. In pride, the English took to saying: "God's winds arose, and His enemies were scattered."

It took some time for the English to realize how great their success had been. At first, they thought that they had merely opened the way for raids to the West Indies, such as Drake had originally carried on, or perhaps a chance to capture the "Plate" or treasure fleet as it carried gold to Spain. One factor in this belief was the way the Spanish army still ruled the land. It intervened in the war in France, and at last forced Henry of Navarre to become Catholic. In 1589, he had become King of France at the murder of Henry III, but found that Paris would not accept him, that he could not capture Paris, and that the Spanish army could always take time off from its endless fighting in Holland to bring supplies to Paris and so prevent its being starved into surrender. Finally, Henry said, "Paris is worth a Mass," and became a Catholic again after protecting the Huguenots by his Edict of Nantes, which gave them their religion and the right to hold certain forts as a safeguard.

As long as the English just raided, they did little to harm Spain. The nearest they ever came to taking the Plate fleet was in 1591 when Lord Thomas Howard almost surprised it at the Azores but was in turn almost surprised by the Spanish covering squadron. This was the occasion when Sir Richard Grenville refused to give way to Spaniards, tried to sail through them, and with one ship, the *Revenge*, fought fifty-three for two days and a night, till his crew forced him to surrender. In 1595, Drake himself died in the West Indies and was buried at sea, as a sailor should be. In 1596, the true idea of naval strategy was remembered, and an English fleet took Cadiz under partially carried out orders to destroy the Spanish fleet in its home ports. That ended the naval war, and though it technically went on until the end of Elizabeth's reign, it continued because England seemed better off at war than at peace. Her privateers were free to seek plunder wherever they chose, and they did so.

As can be seen, England had evolved a special military policy, what Captain Liddell Hart has called the "English way of war." It consists of two things: first getting the enemy fleet out of the way; then, landing a small but highly effective army at a key point, while using allies or a fifth column or an underground to keep the enemy busy.

This military policy has always gone with the diplomatic policy needed to get allies, or an underground movement, the so-called balance-of-power policy, which goes back to Henry VII and Cardinal Wolsey. England's great commanders—Cromwell, Blake, Marlborough, the elder Pitt, Nelson, Wellington, Fisher, Wavell, have all understood England's way of war. When her diplomats have understood the ideas of balance of power, they have made the task of the commanders easy. That was the secret of success of as diverse men as William Cecil, Lord Burleigh, King William III, the elder Pitt, Lord Castlereagh, Lord Salisbury, Sir Edward Grey, and Winston Churchill. Elizabeth's reign is important, therefore, not only for the way she made England Protestant without civil war and the way she defeated Spain, but also for the model military and diplomatic policy she worked out.

It should not be thought that all went smoothly, even after the defeat of the Armada. England, a land that had seen much turbulence in the not-too-distant past and that had no standing army, was always on the edge of disorder. Men always sensed the possibility of some kind of change. As late as 1600 there came the dramatic episode of Essex's rebellion. The Earl of Essex, stepson of the Earl of Leicester and one of the Queen's chief favorites at the end of her life, after a career of military achievement at sea and in France, failed like many another in Ireland, and, like many another of Elizabeth's courtiers, went to the Tower for his failure. In that age of vigorous men, vigorous measures were needed. Essex wildly believed that some sort of revolt might get him some sort of power. It is a sign of the times that he could attempt this with three hundred followers, and that the Bishop of London should command the hurriedly gathered forces that put down the revolt. For this, Essex was tried and executed in short order.

For the peace Elizabeth gave was a peace in which men could be free to use their energy. She got Englishmen a chance to get things done. By keeping them from useless wars, she enabled a generation to grow up who made England great. A glance at what some Elizabethans did may show what this generation was like.

Take, first of all, the commander of her guard. Such a man naturally had to be an accomplished soldier, with the reputation of being the best soldier in England. This he gained in Ireland, and he won the post of commander of the guard by the manner in which he brought back dispatches and reported on what was going on. Thus Sir Walter Raleigh rose from being a penniless Devonshire gentleman to the first rank in the kingdom and was rewarded with "monopolies," for the thrifty queen had realized that exclusive rights to buy or sell cost her nothing and benefited the recipient. He was a good poet; one of his verses, "The Shepherdess's Reply to her Lover," poking fun at Christopher Marlowe, is in the *Oxford Book of English Verse*. He was a pioneer of the British Empire. He brought the potato to Ireland, he introduced tobacco into England (as witness the story of his servant pouring water on him when he smoked, thinking him afire), and he named Virginia. His ideas, spread abroad by the writings of Richard Hakluyt, did much to make England a great colonial power. He also had the gift of catching men's imagination; it was he who at Cadiz answered a salvo of cannon balls with a bugle call and so sailed on, ignoring a Spanish fort that should have sunk his ship.

Raleigh was merely one of many soldiers. Perhaps the best was Sir Francis Vere, who fought in the pay of the Dutch and trained many another Englishman, among them Myles Standish. His regiment, the Buffs, or East Kent Regiment, is the oldest still serving in the British army, though it did not rejoin the British service from the Dutch until after other regiments had been organized in England. Another splendid soldier was Sir Philip Sidney, known for his death on the battlefield of Zutphen, when he gave a dying soldier water, saying, "Thy need is greater than mine." Such were the men who passed on the spirit of Crécy and Agincourt to the present time.

Elizabeth's England also saw one of the great scientists of all time, who was also Lord Chancellor and a great author. This was Francis Bacon, who took the title of Lord Verulam, but who is so widely known as Lord Bacon that no one bothers to be accurate about his title. His *Novum organum* forms a landmark in modern thinking about science. The scientific impulse he gave to his Cambridge college, Trinity, has made it a world center of physics, whence came Newton and, in the present age, more Nobel Prize winners than from any other institution. Yet all that did not stop him from being a great judge and the author of excellent essays.

Besides soldiers and a great scientist, England had its religious leaders. These were either quiet or rebellious, because of Elizabeth's policies, but not to be ignored. Such was Bernard Gilpin, who preached to the North of England and brought religion to the wild border country. Such, in a different way, was Robert Browne, who got himself ousted from England, Holland, and Scotland for the enthusiasm with which he preached that it was wrong to ordain priests, thus founding Congregationalism.

Elizabethan England also had its businessmen. Good examples are the Thomas Smiths or Smythes, father and son. The elder, who was a Smythe, began as a haberdasher, went on to marry the daughter of a Muscovy merchant, and wound up "farming" the customs. That meant that he paid a fixed sum, collected all the customs dues, and kept what was left over. This arrangement, periodically renewed, both increased the royal revenues markedly and made "Customer Smythe" wealthy. His son, Thomas, a Smith, founded the East India Company, went to Russia to negotiate in person with the Czar for concessions, and founded the Virginia Company, in all these riskings of capital making far more than he lost. Such men provided the economic foundation for this age.

England also had its entertainment industry, three or four playhouses in London and Southwark, each under the patronage of the Queen or of some great lord. The idea of writing plays started at the universities, where students transformed the "mysteries" and "moralities" given by the Church in the Middle Ages into plays more like those they read in Latin and Greek. When university men introduced this idea into London, it caught on, and to the original university playwrights, like Marlowe and Johnson, were added others, like William Shakespeare, who had merely attended a local "grammar school" to learn "little Latin and less Greek." In these made-over inn yards, audiences of erudite courtiers mixed with anyone off the streets of London, the companies of actors gave unconscious propaganda of how great England was, just as the movies today proclaim America's importance, not always well, to the world.

Nor should this picture of Elizabethan society confine itself to the capital. One should remember that out in the country the English country gentlemen, in their jobs as justices of the peace, kept up the Tudor tradition of self-government and, under a new piece of legislation, the Poor Law, saw to it that the unemployed got work. This interest in helping others on was another new thing in the age.

To sum it up, what then was an Elizabethan, that Englishmen today should look back on him and admire him so? He was a man who was interested in life and who was full of vigor in what he did. He was not bound by conventions. In science or in travel or business, he was willing to try something new. He even liked new things for their newness, as witness the number of new words Shakespeare introduced into the language. Often he was religious, always he was wholehearted. Certainly he was a man of the Renaissance, which really flowered in England at this time.

And how was it that the Elizabethans got their chance to do what they did? The answer is that they got it from the leadership of their Queen. She knew how to get others to do things, and she knew how to let them do things. She kept England at peace. She fostered its Church and its stage, its Navy and its civil service, including diplomacy and intelligence. She spared its treasury, selling her own possessions or cadging off her subjects' generosity rather than asking Parliament for taxes she would not get. She always knew what was impossible. When Parliament got tired of her granting new monopolies to courtiers for whom she had no money, she abolished monopolies at once and, in telling Parliament this, spoke so eloquently that what had been started as a protest against her turned into a demonstration of loyalty. She had the gift of handling people; it was amazing what certain diplomats stood from her. In part, she accomplished this by pleading a woman's right to change her mind, but largely it was that she won men's devotion. Once she ordered a man's hand struck off for writing a pamphlet about her foreign policy. When this was done, in public, he waved the stump in the air, to lead cheers for the Queen. A country whose ruler inspired such support could accomplish almost anything—and did.

But the question remained, could anyone but a genius run England as had the Tudors? They could enforce autocratic government without any military backing because of their gift for handling people. When Elizabeth died, could her successor, James of Scotland, do as well?

11

ENGLAND OVERSEAS

The British Empire, as we now know it, came into existence in the Tudor period rather than the Stuart. The fact that England's first lasting colony, Virginia, was established only in 1607, in the reign of James I, should not blind us to the other fact that for over a century before the way had been prepared for this to happen. It is in that period of preparation that is to be found the explanation why the British Empire is so unimperial an institution and why when other colonial empires have fallen by the wayside, it has instead evolved into the Commonwealth of Nations. For in the Tudor and Stuart Periods the British overseas Empire was not merely a copy of its contemporaries, the Portuguese, Spanish, Dutch, and French overseas empires. Besides its important resemblances to them it had essential differences, which gave it its unusual survival power.

All the colonial empires of the sixteenth and seventeenth centuries had much in common. To cross the seas needed leadership, pilotage, and a supply of trained seamen. These factors are to be found in the history of each empire. Portuguese leaders in the eastern seas, such as Camoens wrote about in his epic the *Lusiad*, the Spanish conquistadors of America, the Elizabethan sea dogs all had much the same characteristics. At first Italian pilots, then native sons guided the ocean crossings. Spain's Columbus, England's Cabots, France's Verrazano showed the way, to be followed by Magellan, Jacques Cartier, Willoughby, Frobisher, Hudson, and Abel Tasman, among others, when the new nations of the West learned the navigational skills that had originated in the Mediterranean. In each country certain districts furnished the majority of the seamen—the Gallicians and Biscayans in Spain, the Bretons in France, the men of Devon and Londoners in England. Then when these European nations came to organize the trade with the lands they had discovered, they almost all did what their medieval ancestors had done; they set up trading companies. Such were the Spanish companies based on Cadiz, the Dutch East and West India Companies, the French Compagnie des Indies Orientales and Compagnie de la Nouvelle France, as well as the many English companies, Russia, Levant, East India, and African, to name but a few. Likewise, when it came a matter of parceling out overseas lands and trying to get settlers there, if settlement were needed, another medieval device was used, that of the royal grant. Such were the grants that made Columbus, in Spanish eyes, Admiral of the Ocean Sea; created the French seigneuries in Canada; gave tracts of land to the Dutch patroons in New York; and established English proprietorships in the Barbados, Maryland, Pennsylvania, New Jersey, Maine, and the Carolinas. In using such methods, therefore, the English were not original; they merely applied known methods in a new situation.

But in two important respects, England was original. She had a special problem, that of surplus population; she had a special method, that of local self-government. Both were factors in the growth of England overseas. Her surplus population was of two kinds, economic and religious. The economically surplus population was not created by enclosure alone. That, it is true, did create a body of "sturdy beggars" who badly frightened the rulers of England by Ket's Rebellion of 1549 and who finally caused the passage of the Poor Law of 1601, designed to give them support and get them to work. But more than that, England, as an expanding economy, bred venturesome men, willing to take a chance, because they saw a profit. Such a man was Courteen who took over Barbados from its proprietor and blandly ran it for ten years, at a good profit. While fear of the "sturdy beggars" led to plans for settlement, businessmen made the settlements. Then, too, there were those who might be called religiously surplus, those who wanted to be loyal to England but to worship God in a way forbidden by English laws. This was a problem almost purely English. Tolerant Holland had no such religious surplus. Intolerant Spain and Portugal for different reasons were without such a surplus. France, in the Huguenots, did have such a surplus, but got rid of it, not by emigration but by the Edict of Nantes. Only before that edict of partial toleration or after its revocation does one find Frenchmen moving overseas. Therefore except for Spain, whence came a large migration to South America, England, and England alone, could provide a relatively large body of men willing and even eager to make new homes overseas. Furthermore, England had a different slant on governmental control. Monarchical France, Spain, and Portugal, even to a large degree republican Holland, believed in central control at home and likewise abroad. In contrast Tudor England was ruled at home by the man on the spot, a justice of the peace, a borough councilor, a parish vestryman, or a member of Parliament, and it was natural for the English to carry these institutions overseas with them. So while other colonial empires were garrisons and trading posts, dependent on the government at home, or at best on the "company" at home, the English colonial Empire consisted both of trading posts and of little Englands that governed themselves.

The first step in creating the British Empire, naturally, was one of exploration and staking out a claim. The voyages of the Cabots, father and son, in 1497 and later, discovered the Grand Banks and Newfoundland.

They had surprisingly little effect at first, perhaps because of the secretiveness of Sebastian Cabot, who tried to sell his piloting knowledge to the highest bidder. But they did have two lasting results. They gave England a claim to the lands north of Mexico, for a Queen or a King to grant as she or he chose. They did provide for the West Country sailors a fishing ground more fruitful than the banks off Iceland, where mariners could learn their trade. Therefore fishing fleets regularly crossed the water, caught cod, dried their catch ashore, and returned, thus making it natural to think of crossing the Atlantic for other purposes.

The next step was the attempt made at the end of Edward VI's reign to find a Northeast Passage to China. In this attempt Sir Hugh Willoughby died, frozen to death off Lapland, but he and his associate Richard Chancellor had opened again the Murmansk route, and Chancellor had done more. He had landed at Archangel and gone overland to Moscow, there to get from the Czar of Russia a monopoly of trade. Chancellor, on his return, got from the new Queen, Mary, a charter for the Russia Company, which proceeded to develop this trade. Here was the beginning of a series of companies, by which Elizabeth, in particular, got private citizens to put up the capital wherewith to make the building of an empire pay for itself. This was the application to changed conditions of the medieval methods of overseas self-government by merchants who were supposed to make their own arrangements with local authorities, at their own cost and responsibility. Such, since 1266, had been the organization of the wool merchants as the "Merchants of the Staple" to sell England's staple product at whatever market town—eventually Calais—was chosen as a concentration point. Such, since either 1216, 1296, or 1407, as one chooses to read records, had been the organization of the Merchant Adventurers, who took cloth abroad and brought back wine or other continental products, using as trading posts whatever areas had been granted them overseas, just as the Hansa merchants had used the Steelyard outside London. The name applied to these trading posts was "factory," a word which recurs with that special meaning right into the nineteenth century, for it was not until 1808 that the last English factory in Europe, that of the Merchant Adventurers at Hamburg, was closed by French soldiers. In sequence after the Russia Company came others: the Eastland Company, trading to the Baltic; the Greenland Company, consisting of those members of the Russia Company who made whaling voyages; the Levant Company, for the trade that needed convoy to the Eastern Mediterranean; the African Company, that later took the name the "Company of Adventurers Trading to Gynney and Bynney," trading to Guinea and the Bight of Benin; and above all, the East India Company. It was through these companies that English merchants exploited the riches of the new found worlds of the East. As Lord Bacon wrote, it was natural for the English to trade in companies.

These companies were of two sorts, "regulated" and "joint stock." The first were associations of merchants who made regulations for the conduct of convoys, the management of overseas markets and factories, the keeping of agreements with local authorities, and the payment of dues for joint expenses. For example, the Levant Company long paid the expenses of the English ambassador to Constantinople. "Joint stock" companies were companies where the members jointly put up the stock in trade and jointly shared in the profits, if any, of ships and cargoes. Sometimes profits were jointly shared at the end of the voyage; gradually it became customary to keep capital permanently invested and set off the profit to be divided among the shareholders, calling it by the Latin word *dividendum* (to be divided). Such overseas trading ventures, it will be noted, were really colonies of exploitation, where Englishmen lived temporarily in "factories" to get wealth and return home with it. Two of them, however, the East India Company and the African Company, deserve special mention, for out of them grew the Indian Empire, that is now the Dominion of Pakistan and the Republic of India, and the present English possessions in West Africa.

The East India Company began with speculative voyages around the Cape of Good Hope, that brought back silks, tea, and spices. Finally, in 1600, a permanent charter was granted to form the East India Company. In the years between 1600 and 1640, this company lost the direct spice trade to Dutch competition and secured a direct cloth trade and an indirect tea and spice trade by forming permanent factories in India. The reason it lost the direct spice trade was that in 1621, after sharp practices and hard blows on both sides, the Dutch literally killed off competition by the Massacre of Amboina, in which the English factory on the spice island of Celebes was wiped out. But in India the Mogul Emperor granted privileges at Surat and other ports where silk, native cotton cloth (hence the trade names for madras shirtings and calico cloth), and transshipped tea and spice could be obtained, amid intrigues with the agents of the East India Companies of other nations. So the East India Company had its ups and downs, sometimes making no profit at all, sometimes declaring a 50 per cent dividend, but averaging 6 per cent per annum. It established itself more and more firmly in its factories, remaining, as long as the Mogul Empire was strong, just a national trading monopoly, but being potentially more if ever that Indian Empire should fall apart.

The East India Company was not the only one to establish such factories outside Europe with such potentialities. Just as cotton, silk, tea, and spice attracted businessmen to India, so gold and slaves attracted them to West Africa. There too, on what are still spoken of as the Gold and Slave Coasts, were factory-forts under a company with a monopoly largely similar. Great wealth was not won here. Indeed the African companies

had a habit of going bankrupt and then changing their names on reorganization. But the trade persisted and had before it a future of expansion.

It is important to remember that Englishmen thought of overseas ventures in terms of trade and companies, in order to put in their right perspec-
tive the earliest attempts at settlement. For yet another conception of what
could be gained across the ocean was working in the minds of some men.
Could not Englishmen be planted across the ocean much as Mary, Elizabeth, and James had planted them in Ireland, there to settle down? Could
they not grow such crops as tobacco, or perhaps sassafras, for shipment to
England and sale there? Richard Hakluyt, the geographer, wrote a "Discourse of Western Planting," the manuscript of which he showed to Queen
Elizabeth in the 1580's—though it was not published till 1877, and then
by the Maine Historical Society—in which he argued that surplus population that was a burden at home could be a profit overseas. Three gentlemen
of Devon, among others, took up this idea of transatlantic settlement, the
half-brothers Humphrey Gilbert and Walter Raleigh, and their cousin,
Richard Grenville. In fact, no colony that they planted lasted. Gilbert's
attempts to settle in Newfoundland, on a patent Elizabeth gave him in
1577, ended in his drowning off the Azores, his memorable last words
being, "We are as near to God by sea as by land." Then, as he turned back
to reading his Bible, his tiny ship was swallowed by the sea. His half-
brother, Sir Walter Raleigh, took up the work. In flattery to his mistress,
the Virgin Queen, he named the land she had granted him Virginia. Twice
he tried to found a colony there. Once, just as Richard Grenville was about
to bring it supplies, Francis Drake, who was passing by, picked up the
colonists and took them home. Raleigh tried again, on Roanoke Island,
North Carolina. High hopes were held of success, for was it not there that
the governor's daughter had a child, Virginia Dare, the first English child
born in America? But the Armada prevented supplies being sent out, and
when at last relief came all that was found was the mysterious message,
to this day challenging solution—"Gone to Cro[atan]."

But though Raleigh and his associates failed to make a colony, they
made a tradition. In Richard Hakluyt's *Principal Voyages of the English
Nation*, in Samuel Purchas's continuation of it, *Purchas, His Pilgrimes*, the
English people could read the glories of overseas ventures. Years before,
when Richard Grenville's grandfather had been Marshal of Calais, he had
written these lines, "In Praise of Seafaring Men in Hopes of Good Fortune."

> Who seeks the way to win renown,
> Or flies with wings of high desire,
> Who seeks to wear the laurel crown,
> Or hath the mind that would aspire,
> Tell him his native soil eschew,
> Tell him go range and seek anew.

Something of that spirit caught the minds of Englishmen. It was that, among other motives, that kept them trying to found a colony in Virginia.

After 1600, initiative largely passed from the men of Devon to Londoners, and the institution used to effect settlement changed from royal grant to chartered company. As all Americans know, two Virginia companies were founded by a joint charter and went through three charterings. One, called the London Company from its base, claimed the southern part of the Atlantic Coast; the other, called the Plymouth Company from its base, controlled the northern part of the coast. The London Company, during its sixteen years of effective colonizing, from 1607 to 1623, kept continuous settlement at Jamestown and thus in those years founded a transatlantic England. There is no need here to recite again the well-known obstacles the first Virginians met. The deeds of Captain John Smith in collecting food and restoring morale are too well known for that, even though a suspicion is now abroad that much fiction was mixed in with fact and that the Captain never was rescued by the Indian Princess Pocahontas but copied that story from one told by a Spanish adventurer in Alabama. There may be some value in stressing how John Rolfe—who really did marry Pocahontas—started the profitable cultivation of tobacco, and by what a narrow margin the colony was saved in 1609, when Sir Thomas Dale sailed into Chesapeake Bay to find Jamestown being abandoned in despair. But from the point of view of the Empire what matters is that somehow the settlers stuck it out, and more than that, planted English institutions in Virginia. In 1619—remembered also because that year a shipload of slaves landed at Jamestown, along with a shipload of "respectable maidens"—the Virginia Company instructed its governor to summon a House of Burgesses to pass local legislation. Choosing a former member of the English Parliament, John Pory, as its speaker, this body began the series of local overseas legislatures which to this day forms an essential part of the conception of the British Empire. A little later, Virginia was divided into counties, where justices held Quarter Sessions, holding petty sessions in "hundreds" just as they would have at home in England. Thus Devonshire—records and the local types of architecture suggest that Devonshire gave the pattern to Virginia—was brought overseas, to develop in its own way.

That these institutions had taken root was recognized by the home government. When, in 1623/24, jurisdiction was taken from the Virginia Company by the crown, the House of Burgesses and the county rule by justices of the peace was left untouched. What the British Colonial Office to this day calls the "Old Constitution" type of colony thus evolved. It had "representative government," that is, the legislature made laws but did not control administration. That function was reserved to the governor and Council appointed by the King, acting either through a special committee of his Privy Council, or later through a special American Secretary of State. It will be noticed how closely this resembles the constitution of the states of the United States, except that the governor of a state is elected. It should also be noted that the existence of these assemblies elected by the people of a colony implied that they had a natural right to govern themselves, similar to the natural right to govern themselves that Englishmen have unhistorically but effectively deduced from Magna Carta. So it was that the tobacco planters of Virginia settled down to life in hundred and county, under justices of the peace in Petty and Quarter Sessions, with life in the Old Dominion remarkably resembling county life in the Old Country. When the shire courts met and the freemen in open county court watched the justices transact county business as, at times, was done in England, a great tradition implanted itself, to last till Carter Glass's revision of the Virginia Constitution in 1902. When the county courts, sitting as courts of election, saw the freemen elect burgesses to represent them at the capital, Virginia became the home of English rights. This lesson a certain justice of the peace named Washington was to teach King George of England, just as King Charles was to learn similar lessons from justices of the peace named Hampden, Pym, and Cromwell. The American Revolution had much in common with the English Revolution of the 1640's.

Though Virginia was the first of these "Old Constitution" colonies, she was not the only one. In these same years, Bermuda and the Barbados were to travel the same constitutional road, with local variations. The Bermuda or Somers Islands Company was founded in 1616, its Parliament first met in 1621, its charter was not revoked till 1683, but the course of evolution was the same as in Virginia. Today Bermuda can boast that it has the oldest parliament in the British Empire. The course of events in Barbados varies, because there a proprietorship, of the Lord Proprietor of the Caribees, comes into the picture, in rivalry with the illegal but successful taking over of the island by the London merchant Courteen. Lord Carlisle found the island, which was off the beaten track of West Indies voyages, planted it, and then had to drive off Courteen, who took out ten years' profits. But by 1639 Lord Carlisle's heirs had to grant an assembly. Here the sugar planters of the West Indies were following the tobacco planters of Virginia.

While Virginia was thus confirming her self-government, experiments in religious settlement were taking place to the north of her and were giving new patterns to overseas England.[1] The story of the founding of Plymouth is well known, of how religious fugitives from Scrooby, Lincolnshire, joined to themselves fur traders as well as coreligionists and landed in 1620 from the *Mayflower,* to govern themselves religiously and politically until 1683. From the Empire point of view what is significant about

---

[1] Details of how the Plymouth Company faded away into the Council of New England are spared the reader as complex and unimportant.

them is not that they drew up aboard ship the so-called Mayflower Compact for self-government, the philosophical suggestiveness of which was not understood till John Quincy Adams drew attention to it in 1802, but that they proved it was possible to live in New England. Their success drew followers and caused in that way the unusual experiment of the Massachusetts Bay Company. Again, only the outline of well-known events need be repeated, of how property rights in New England between the Charles and Merrimac Rivers were acquired by certain men resisting Charles I's religious policy, of how they formed a Massachusetts Bay Company to hold and govern that land, of how at Cambridge certain members of that company formed a compact to emigrate, bringing their charter with them, and of how that company eventually caused the migration of over 20,000 to New England in twelve years, a prodigious number in those days of difficult travel. What is here important to the story of the Empire is what those migrants did to the company that brought them over. For they forced the tight oligarchy that at one time had dropped to seven men to admit the leading inhabitants to company membership, as "freemen." They forced the Governor and Company of the Massachusetts Bay to hold regular meetings at which a House of Deputies representing each town sat concurrently with the House of Magistrates. They forced the recognition of each religious parish—they had sometimes migrated as whole parishes, bringing along their favorite Puritan clergyman—as a political entity, under the name of town, which could choose its own officials, the chosen men or "selectmen," and conduct its own affairs in town meetings. They caused the division of this new land into counties like the shires of England whence they had come, to be ruled by justices in Quarter Sessions and judged by judges riding circuit and holding assizes. When their theocratically minded rulers tried to give them laws out of the Bible, they turned about and secured the enactment of a "Body of Liberties" that were the recognized liberties of Englishmen. This movement spread beyond the bounds of the Massachusetts Bay grant. By 1640, clusters of settlers, with different religious ideas, were centered at New Haven, at Hartford on the Connecticut River, on Rhode Island, and with the apostle of religious liberty, Roger Williams, at Providence Plantations. All were governed in much the same way, in town, county, and in colony, with the last under an elected governor.

For here the company structure of Massachusetts had evolved unexpectedly. Since a comparatively large number of inhabitants became voting members of the company, what had been a business corporation became a self-governing unit, with some at least of the people electing the chief executive. Then, when others copied facts of the situation, not the theory, they set up an elected executive, along with an elected legislature.

To look at all this again from the Empire point of view, what is significant is that in ten years six tiny republics grew up in New England—like Virginia in that English self-government had taken transatlantic roots, unlike Virginia in two significant ways. First of all, the executive, instead of being appointed by the King, was elected by the people. Secondly, the parish or town, rather than the county, became the key unit of local self-government, and the type of parish taken from England was the "open vestry" to use a technical term, the parish where almost all decisions were made by almost all the people. Here came to flower a democracy of a vigor only rarely to be found in the mother country, that eventually would make Empire history. Again, English and American Revolutions will show a parallel. For these new towns, of Suffolk and Middlesex and Essex in New England, would in 1775 show a resistance to King George equal to that shown to King Charles in 1642 by Suffolk and Middlesex and Essex in Old England.

Yet one more colony of settlement should be mentioned, also north of Virginia, the proprietorship of Maryland. Here again is a sign that the more things outwardly changed, the more the essence of these Stuart colonies remained the same. The fact that the proprietor, George Calvert, Lord Baltimore, was a Catholic, did mean that this was the only colony, unless in tolerant Rhode Island, where it was not illegal to be a Catholic. Just the same, Catholics were a minority, and eventually the Church of England came to be the established church, as was the case in Bermuda, Barbados, and Virginia. All these overseas Englands were English counties transplanted but remarkably little changed.

To sum up the Empire as it was by 1640, it had four aspects worth considering. First there were the old trading companies, to be remembered as prototypes of later evolution. With the loss of Calais, the Merchants of the Staple sank into unimportance, but there still remained the Merchant Adventurers, the Eastland, Russia, and Levant Companies. Then there was the individualistic fishing on the Grand Banks and the shores of Newfoundland. Thirdly, there were the exploiting companies with their factories in India and Africa, little different from the trading companies of Europe in organization but vitally different in potentialities. These provided the greater part of England's overseas wealth. But England's overseas population was not there but in the string of colonies from Barbados to beyond Cape Ann. Here were counties and colonial assemblies where justices of the peace ruled like their English counterparts at home. Here were self-governing congregations that were carving out for themselves in secular matters a tradition of democracy like that of the Scottish Kirk in religious matters. In a century and a half these habits and traditions would blaze out into revolt. For it is this tradition of an overseas right to self-government that has made the British Empire so different from other overseas empires.

12

KING VERSUS COUNTRY GENTLEMEN

About the time of James I a new rank in society came to prominence. Generally speaking, until then three sorts of people had occupied the center of the stage in English history—kings and their officials, nobles, and priests—though there had been a few others standing in the wings. Then, first with the appearance of the "new men" of the Renaissance, increasingly in Elizabeth's reign, and markedly in James's reign a new group became important. It consisted in part of the lower nobility, in part of the upper middle class, and provided such men as the great lawyer Sir Edward Coke and the great parliamentary leaders Thomas Wentworth, Sir John Eliot, John Hampden, and John Pym, to make English history in this period.

This rise of the middle class was not unique in England. At this time all over Europe men from the lower nobility and upper middle class were rising to power and importance. What was almost unique in England was the way these men fought their way to the top. In Europe, generally, the old nobility blocked their climb and the kings aided it. As a result, in Europe, the power of the kings was supported by these newcomers. Kings needed strength to defend their countries, to keep internal order, and to replace local feudal laws by a uniform code of law. As the middle classes also sought these ends, they turned against the nobles and not unwillingly paid the taxes that made the kings powerful. Similarly, for the same practical reasons, they were willing to accept the theory of "divine right of kings." That doctrine, for example, would allow a Frenchman who was a Catholic to support the then Protestant Henry of Navarre against the Catholic League and thus put on the throne the man best fitted to fill it.

But in England these reasons for supporting the king and his "prerogative" hardly existed. In Wales and the North of England, where there was some disorder, "prerogative courts," the Councils of Wales and the North, did have justification. But otherwise these arguments fell flat. England could very well defend herself with her Navy. The country gentlemen kept order perfectly well themselves acting as justices of the peace with constables, or as lord lieutenants and deputy lieutenants if the militia had to be called out. It could not be claimed that a uniform set of laws had to be instituted all over the kingdom, for in England the Common Law had existed since Henry II's reign and, when necessary, had been amended by parliamentary statutes without any exercise of royal prerogative. Furthermore, in England the lesser nobility and the merchants were allies. The law of entail saw to that, by turning younger sons out to earn their living in London while the eldest son kept the family home going. It also brought the merchants into the ranks of the country gentlemen by providing safe investments. Where better could one put money than in an entailed estate which would go to one's heirs even if one went bankrupt? Therefore, while in Europe the rising middle class sided with the king against nobles and accepted the theory of the divine right of kings, in England the rising middle class sided with nobles and Parliament against the king, by accepting the idea of parliamentary limitations on the king.

The Tudors, being English themselves, understood how to handle this situation. Queen Mary did have to get her Counter Reformation step by step. Queen Elizabeth did have some trouble with the country gentlemen and merchants who made up her Parliaments, but she got her way so successfully that it is only recently that historians have dug up her squabbles with them and realized that what came to a head in James's reign had begun in hers. James, on the other hand, was brought up in Scotland under far different conditions. In Scotland there was some danger of invasion, much disorder, and much local law. For example, up until 1746 there were still feudal jurisdictions in Scotland such as Edward I had restricted by the Statute of Gloucester. Consequently James found the doctrine of divine right of kings a help in ruling Scotland and brought the doctrine with him to England at a time when Parliament was about to rise in power. In religious matters, too, James had ideas that fitted Scotland better than they did England. In Scotland he had been ordered around by the General Assembly of the Church, and had succeeded in curbing that assembly by the "Black Acts" of 1584, which allowed him to control the Kirk by means of bishops. Therefore, he came to England believing that Presbyterianism was dangerous and that the bishops should be given more power, at a time when an influential group of English clergy felt that the bishops had too much power. Thus James was almost certain to clash with his new subjects, when he became king of England in 1603. The clash would not be eased by his doctrinaire, dogmatic behavior, which had caused his fellow king, Henry IV of France, to dub him "the wisest fool in Christendom." Thus the story of James's twenty-two-year reign, from 1603 to 1625, is one of applying Scotch policies in England with failure in religious matters, modified success in Irish matters, and a breakdown in finance and diplomacy.

James seems not to have understood the tolerance by means of comprehension that was the basis of the Elizabethan religious settlement. On arriving in England he did try to make easier the situation of those who wished to "purify" the Church of England, by summoning the Hampton Court Conference of 1604. This secured one great result, the issuance of the King James or Authorized Version of the Bible, to combat the version that the English Catholics were issuing at Rheims and Douai, the so-called Douai Version. But when James was asked to make changes in the service he shouted out that men must conform or he would harry them out of the land, and stated as his policy: "No bishop, no king." Thereafter James gave up hopes of comprehension and turned to the court of High Commission to strengthen the authority of the bishops. Already the Puritans had been dabbling in parliamentary politics in hopes of getting control of the church through control of legislation. Now they worked still harder for this. Thus James created for himself unnecessary political opposition.

Nor did James succeed with the English Catholics. In Scotland he had gotten useful support by patronizing the Catholics. He tried the same tack in England, by negotiating with the papacy to formalize the unspoken agreement by which loyal Catholics would not be persecuted if they stayed quiet. This seems to have encouraged the extremists. On November 5, 1605, underneath the House of Lords, ready to blow it up together with the King and the Commons at the opening of Parliament, was found one Guy Fawkes, a flaming torch, and many barrels of gunpowder. As a result the anti-Catholic laws were enforced still more strictly, and England got a national holiday. Those who quietly practiced the "Old Religion" did draw nearer the King, but the militantly Protestant element grew suspicious, and unlike the case in Scotland, James lost more than he gained. For this would be a line-up of forces that would remain constant until 1688, when it would drive James's grandson from the throne.

But though what are here for convenience called Scottish methods— perhaps they should better be called Stuart methods—were less effective in matters of religion in England, in matters of government in Ireland they worked well. At one and the same time James seems to have accomplished two things: he lightened the burdens of his Catholic subjects in Ireland, and he provided himself with a Protestant garrison. He did the first by allowing the Irish Parliament to function more effectively than in the past by allowing to sit in it Catholic peers and Catholic members from Catholic-controlled boroughs. This formed a safety valve and lessened opposition. Meanwhile he "planted" the North of Ireland far more effectively than Elizabeth had planted the South of Ireland. Elizabeth had found that while it was possible to get an Englishman to take over an estate in Ireland because it might make him rich, it was not so easy to get an Englishman to leave home to take the same kind of a job on an Irish farm or in an Irish village. Thus her plantations had failed from want of a Protestant lower class. But James found a solution to this problem; he made it so uncomfortable for ardent Presbyterians in Scotland that they were glad to move to Ireland. James gave them the lands in Ulster that had been left vacant when the O'Neills had been driven out. He borrowed enough money to keep an army there for three years, paying for that money not interest but the grant of an hereditary knighthood called a baronetcy. Thereafter the Scots-Irish, as they are called, took very good care of themselves. Thus James got a truly Protestant population in one quarter of Ireland—with results seen today in the separation of Eire from Northern Ireland.

In matters of finance James had his troubles. Elizabeth had managed to "live of her own"—*i.e.*, to pay her regular expenses from royal income-producing properties and from the grant of the customs duties for her life. Parliament had voted her extra monies for emergencies, and parsimony and a small amount of borrowing had kept her solvent. But with James it was different. He was extravagant and kept an expensive court, in a time of rising costs. Somehow, he had to get more money. For some years he tried to make a deal with Parliament that would secure him a larger income in return for concessions. But King and Parliament could not come to terms. In 1614 the Parliament of that year was sent home without passing a single measure and therefore got the name of the "Addled Parliament" for being like an egg that would not hatch. Then he turned to ruling without Parliament and sought to increase his income by stretching the royal powers. There were enough debatable points, such as whether the customs duties could be varied, to afford very real opportunities. But to do this, James had to go against not only the traditional claims of Parliament that it voted taxes, but also the lawyers and judges. Consequently James began a running battle with the judge Sir Edward Coke, first trying to influence him by promoting him to a higher court, then dismissing him from office. If ever an emergency came, these actions would bring to the forefront constitutional issues that the Tudors had sedulously avoided. Foreign affairs might well bring up an emergency where Parliament would have to be asked to levy taxes and would answer by discussing the basis of the British constitution.

Foreign affairs did bring such an emergency. James had long been disgracefully weak in this field. He probably had been wise to make peace with Spain, on his accession to the English throne. Little was gained any longer by being at war, and much damage was done to English trade. But he steadily lost England prestige by the personal ascendancy he allowed the Spanish ambassador to obtain over him and by his failure to take a firm stand. He also lost by a habit of meddling in German politics—as by marrying his beautiful daughter Elizabeth, called the Queen of Hearts, to the Elector Palatine—and then withdrawing. Typical of his methods was his treatment of Sir Walter Raleigh. Since James needed money, he released Raleigh from the Tower and let him sail to South America to seek gold, after giving him instructions not to attack the Spaniards. When Raleigh did what Drake or Hawkins would have done—attacked the Spaniards when he had failed to find gold—James did what Elizabeth would not have done—he had Raleigh executed. Finally, in 1618, after this constant loss of prestige, the emergency did come. His son-in-law, the Elector Palatine, started the Thirty Years' War (1618 to 1648) by trying to seize Bohemia. The Austrians ejected him so quickly as to earn him the nickname of the "Winter King" and then started a war of conquest. Protestant principalities fell one after the other before the march of the Austrian armies. English public opinion became aroused. Would James intervene to save his son-in-law and the Protestant religion? This seemed to James a chance to summon a Parliament that would vote money both for his son-in-law's needs and for his own. But the Parliament that met in 1621 thought differently. Under Coke's leadership it followed the old rule of "No supply without redress of grievance" and challenged some of James's methods of raising funds.

The points on which issue was joined were whether James had had a right to sell various licenses and to raise the customs duties. When James started to protect the men who had done this, Parliament thumbed over its old records and discovered that in the reigns of Edward III, Richard II, and Henry IV it had impeached those who had violated the law. It promptly impeached first the men who had been extorting money for licenses and then Lord Chancellor Bacon, who had advised the King in his extensions of his prerogative. It is true that James could have stopped these impeachments by dissolving Parliament, but then he would not have been voted money, and the next Parliament he called would have been more intractable and less likely to vote money. But when Parliament began arguing with the King about its privileges, he did dissolve it.

James next tried to act as peacemaker and persuade the Austrian Hapsburgs to evacuate his son-in-law's territories, which they had just conquered. His method of doing this was to propose a match between his son Charles and a Spanish Hapsburg. This move gained him only the suspicions of his subjects and the contempt of the Spaniards. Then the marriage fell through and James realized, too late, that if his son-in-law were to be saved troops must be sent. But a new Parliament in 1625 refused to vote him enough money. A tiny force of volunteers went to Germany, only to suffer shameful defeat. Then James died that same year.

When James was succeeded by his son Charles, the situation between king and Parliament grew worse. James had had experience and some diplomatic ability. He knew what was impossible. Charles did not. First Charles married the sister of the King of France, thus acquiring a Catholic consort. Then he tried to gain popularity and aid the Protestant cause by interfering on the Huguenot side in a civil war that had broken out in

France. Thus he antagonized his Catholic brother-in-law instead of attacking England's real enemies, the Hapsburg powers of Spain and Austria. Charles gave the command to his intimate friend, the Duke of Buckingham, who was unsuccessful; then the King was unwise enough to demand money from Parliament to retrieve the Duke's failures. Parliament, angry over the still unsettled constitutional problems, refused him an emergency grant. It went further. To keep him under control it did not give him the customs duties for life, as had been customary since the reign of Edward IV, but restricted the grant to one year. Indignant, Charles dissolved Parliament and used what money he had in further failures in France. Then he called another Parliament, to try again for money, only to find this one in a still more truculent mood. By now Parliament knew what it wanted. During the long years it had been in existence it had learned how to protect itself from the king. For once the Charters had been confirmed by Edward I, the kings of England had tried to find ways around Parliament's power of the purse, by intimidating or otherwise influencing Parliament, and Parliament had blocked those devices. Old-fashioned English history books are full of discussions of minor events in the Middle Ages by which some one or another parliamentary privilege was established. But there is no need here to go into the origins of all the special rights of Parliament in this way; all that matters is to know what those rights were.

First of all, there was freedom of debate. Members of Parliament early saw that they could not get at the truth of what was told them and vote laws and appropriations properly unless things could be fully talked over. Therefore they secured the right that no member be called to account for what he said in Parliament. Along with this privilege of talking as one pleased was the parallel one of having the opinions of Parliament as a body expressed by a neutral person speaking for it, the Speaker, who was not to be punished for giving the thoughts of others. Control of its membership was another vital privilege of Parliament. Had the king been able to decide contested elections, Parliament would soon have lost its independence as would also have been true could he have expelled members. Furthermore, unless Parliament could enforce its orders, it could have gotten no results. Therefore it had obtained the right to imprison. That was vital if it wanted to find out the truth. Those called to its "bar" must answer at their peril.

The Stuart kings, in order to raise money without going to Parliament for new taxes, tried to discover new sources of revenue. James, for example, frankly sold titles. An earldom was worth so much, and so on. He even went further and created a new title of hereditary knighthood, the baronetcy. Baronets were to rank between barons and knights. In theory, the money they paid for their titles was to go to colonize Ulster and Nova Scotia and then be repaid. But later on, in practice it went to the king and was not repaid. Charles, whose hands were tied by the refusal of tunnage and poundage (the old name for customs) for life, went even further and used "forced loans." His hope was that if he won a victory, a grateful Parliament would vote the money to repay the loans. He won no such victory but disgrace in his struggles for the Huguenots, and Parliament met in January, 1628, in no mood to tolerate either his inefficient ministers or the sale of titles, forced loans, and methods used to force loans, such as quartering soldiers in the houses of recalcitrant men or their imprisonment without explanation. Nor would it stand for the collection of tunnage and poundage after the year had expired.

However, Parliament was still mindful of the prestige and importance of a king. Therefore, Parliament approached Charles with the utmost politeness. It merely petitioned him to state that certain things had always been the rights of Englishmen. Charles grudgingly consented to confirm the Petition of Right. Its terms were these. First of all it confirmed the principles of *De Tallagio*. No taxes should be levied save by act of Parliament. To make sure that no "accidental" gifts would be forced from the people, three methods of so forcing "gifts" were prohibited: arbitrary arrest, quartering troops in private homes, and the proclamation of martial law.

This measure satisfied Parliament. It reassured such men as Sir Edward Coke, the great lawyer, that the old laws of England would continue in force. It gave some ease to such leaders of the country gentlemen as John Pym and his cousin Oliver Cromwell that Parliament could control the King, or at least check him. And it reassured a Yorkshire gentleman of great ability, Thomas Wentworth, that the King would soon surround himself with efficient advisers. But Charles quickly dispelled the confidence felt by all but Wentworth. Wentworth's distrust was not of the King but of his ministers, and when the Duke of Buckingham was killed in August, 1628, Wentworth took service under the King. Charles showed that he could not keep his word. He collected tunnage and poundage illegally and had the face to summon Parliament and ask for more money, after having broken the Petition of Right he had so solemnly signed. At the same time, Charles roused suspicions of his religious policy. The actions of the Court of High Commission in enforcing religious ceremonies seemed to some to imply that the King was favoring the Catholics. Yet nothing was being done about the way the Austrians were conquering Protestant Germany. Feelings grew tense. Charles at last realized that he could get nothing out of Parliament and sent to the House of Commons a message ordering them to come to the Lords to hear the formal adjournment of the session. In that way he hoped to stop Parliament from going further. But as the messenger of the House of Lords, Black Rod, was knocking at the door of Commons, Sir John Eliot rose and moved that it was treasonable to change the religion of England or pay tunnage and poundage without act of Parliament. To pass such a measure before Commons were adjourned, it was necessary for four members to hold the Speaker in his chair. Then Parliament was adjourned, and with immunity over, Sir John Eliot went to the Tower of London.

For eleven years Charles ruled England without Parliament. During these years, fortunately, others did England's work for her in Europe. The Swedish hero-king, Gustavus Adolphus, first conquered the shores of the Baltic and then brought his hard-fighting "Blue Boys" into Germany. Some of these highly trained cavalrymen were English Protestants; many more were Scotsmen who had gone abroad as mercenaries—such men as Generals Alexander and David Leslie. Others like Sir Ralph Hopton, who had carried Charles's sister out of Bohemia on the pillion of his saddle, learned the art of war while England was at peace. Gustavus himself, riding at the head of his troopers, the first in modern times to charge at the trot and not the walk and to use pistols, freed northern Germany of the Austrians but died in the moment of victory at Lützen. Then the French took up England's work and checked the advance of the Hapsburgs of Spain and Austria. Thus it was that powers stayed balanced.

Meanwhile, Charles looked for money. As has been explained, he saved by not having any foreign policy. He saved expenses in Ireland by sending Wentworth there. That efficient man, whose motto was the single word "Thorough," called the Irish Parliament, got its cooperation, and made the Irish government pay its way, instead of being a drain on the King's resources. But still Charles could not "live of his own," that is, could not manage on the revenues that were uncontestably his. So he continued to collect tunnage and poundage against the vote of Commons. He also found new sources of supply which technically did not violate the law. As the grant of monopolies to individuals had been prohibited, he set up corporations to handle them. He remembered the Assize of Arms of Henry II, and ordered all of a certain wealth to become knights, which cost money, or pay a fine. This was called "distraint of knighthood." He remembered that royal forests of William the Conqueror's time had wider boundaries in the past, and punished with fines those who had unwittingly broken the forest laws. His foremost reliance, however, was on ship-money. Traditionally, the Cinque Ports, the seacoast towns of Kent and Sussex, had held their charters by virtue of providing a fleet in the Channel or money with which the King could provide a fleet. Such was the fleet that had won at Sluis. Charles enforced his calls for ship-money in peace as well as in war, took money and not ships, and tried to make all England pay ship-money. Here he met his most important resistance. A Buckinghamshire squire, John Hampden, refused to pay the 10s. for which he was assessed. So momentous was this case that the Exchequer, King's Bench, and Common Pleas were combined to hear it. By a vote of only seven to five, John Hampden was condemned to pay. Since the King appointed and removed the judges, it was clear that Hampden had won the moral victory. The people of England had been reminded by the lawyers of Magna Carta and *De Tallagio*. Those laws, forgotten for many years and now misinterpreted out of their old feudal meanings, were making the English stand up for what they thought were their rights.

In the meantime Charles succeeded in rousing more opposition on religious grounds. He acquired an Archbishop of Canterbury who entirely believed in the Stuart religious policies. William Laud really wanted to enforce the Act of Uniformity to the utmost and to make all the clergy think alike and perform the services in the same way. It is now recognized that Laud did much good in stopping laxities and in making the churchgoers of England familiar with the beauties of the Book of Common Prayer. But at the time he was cordially hated for the savage sentences the Court of High Commission handed out. Nor were Charles and Laud content to struggle with the movement in England that wanted to "purify" the Church and make it more Presbyterian. In 1637 they started to bring English liturgical forms and English vestments to Scotland, thus attacking Presbyterianism in its home in the British Isles.

Charles little realized what he had done in striking at the religion of the Scots. When the new Prayer Book was introduced in Edinburgh, an angry woman threw the stool on which she was sitting the length of the cathedral, to stop the service. Scotland rose in anger. Almost everyone signed the National Covenant, swearing to resist the innovation to the death. Charles had no army in England with which to fight, no money with which to pay soldiers. A few troops whom he gathered together and led to Scotland melted away face to face with Alexander Leslie's veterans of the war in Germany. All Charles could do was send for the man who had run Ireland with a Parliament, Thomas Wentworth.

13

THE CIVIL WARS

Thomas Wentworth, who in 1640 was made Earl of Strafford, was a great man who did not have a chance. In Ireland he proved how great he could be. In England he proved that no one could succeed with Charles I as master. From 1633 to 1640 he had governed Ireland as a Tudor would have and had got the same sort of results the Tudors got. He summoned the Irish Parliament, told it what he wanted, and persuaded it to vote the funds and legislation for which he had asked. This was not as great an achievement as similar management of the English Parliament would have been, for the Irish Parliament was not as powerful a body. It lacked the tradition of independence, its members were subject to pressure, and it was subject to control from England under the terms of Poynings's Law. But Wentworth's success came not from abusing his strength but from using it wisely. He knew that more could be done by fairness and efficiency than by threats. Because he gave the Irish, both Catholic and Protestant, better government than they had had for a long time, they were glad to let him have autocratic powers and new taxes. Because he trusted them, they trusted him, and in Ireland he could live up to his one-word motto—"Thorough."

When, in 1639, Charles got into trouble with the Scots, he turned to Wentworth for his advice. Wentworth suggested doing in England what he himself had done in Ireland, that is, calling Parliament and working with it. Charles made him, that January, Earl of Strafford and sent him back to Ireland. The plan seems to have been that an Irish army would come to the aid of the English army and that the two armies would then bring the Scots to terms. Meanwhile, Parliament would be called in England. The plan worked in Ireland, where Strafford—as Wentworth should now be called—got the votes of money he hoped for. But in England the plan did not work. Parliament, meeting in April, 1640, told Charles that there would be no supply without redress of grievance and that there were plenty of grievances. Quickly Charles, in May, dissolved Parliament, which gave it the name of the Short Parliament. Then, though without funds, he tried to gather an army. The undisciplined men so collected were routed by the Scots, who this time did not stop at the border but invaded England. They marched to Durham and forced Charles to sign a treaty promising to pay the expenses of the troops until he should give them satisfaction. This forced Charles to summon a Parliament and to keep it in session till he got funds, no matter what concessions it forced from him. Thus was elected the famous Long Parliament, which lasted till 1653, 1659, or even 1660, depending on which of its three dissolutions one considers the significant one.

Even more than the Short Parliament, the Long Parliament was ready for Charles. John Pym, perhaps the greatest leader Parliament has ever had, had toured the counties of England with his cousin, John Hampden, the hero of the ship-money case. In counties, where votes were freer and more open than in many boroughs, and at the ancient shire courts, public opinion was formed. Pym and Hampden saw that men they wanted were chosen to enter the Commons, in spite of royal counterpressure. The Long Parliament went right to work. It saw that Charles had been using three weapons against Parliament: the King's power of dissolution, Strafford's administrative ability, and the King's control of the prerogative courts, whereby he could legalize evasions of the Petition of Right. Since it had Charles in a position where he had to make concessions to get funds, it took measures to get rid of all three. It asked of him a pledge never given since—that the Parliament could not be dissolved without its own consent. Specific bills were introduced prohibiting ship-money, monopolies, distraint of knighthood, and the use of the forest laws. Similarly, specific bills were introduced to abolish High Commission, Star Chamber, and the Councils of Wales and the North. Strafford was impeached. But still Charles did not give in. He would not give assent to make the bills law. He would not pledge not to send Parliament home before it had finished its reforms. Worst of all, when Strafford appeared at the bar of the House of Lords to defend himself against Pym and the other managers sent up by the Commons, it soon appeared that he had broken no law. He had broken no Irish law, for whenever he had wanted legal powers he had obtained them from the Irish Parliament. He argued that he had broken no English law. The specific charge against him was that the elder Sir Harry Vane had heard Strafford at a meeting of the King's Council urge that the Irish army be used in "another kingdom." Was that other kingdom England or Scotland? Strafford was claiming it was Scotland, and appeared to be winning the Lords to his side. What would happen if the impeachment failed and "Black Tom Tyrant," as his enemies called him, went free?

For Charles, men were beginning to realize, had a peculiar ethical code. As a private individual he was the soul of honor. He raised high the level of behavior at the royal court. He showed the greatest dignity in personal danger. Later his noble death on the scaffold would do more than any other single event to enshrine the kingship in the hearts of the English people. But in public affairs he followed his father's teachings. He felt that it was justifiable to practice "kingcraft," that a king's first duty was to be powerful to benefit his country, and that any action of a king might be justified by the end in view. Would such a man, even though he was hinting he would promise never to employ Strafford again, keep such a promise? Would not Charles turn right around, after getting the funds needed to pay the Scots, and put Strafford back into office? Would the King ever give assent to the essential bills the House of Commons wanted passed into law?

Therefore, the hotter heads in Parliament thought that England's liberties would not be safe with Strafford alive. As the Puritan Earl of Essex put it, "Stone dead hath no fellow." Impeachment was dropped and a bill of attainder, or putting to death by act of Parliament, was hurried through both houses. Rumors of an army plot sped about London heightening the excitement. The night the bill was presented to Charles for his signature a mob surrounded Whitehall Palace and clamored for Strafford's death. The heavy stone building shook as the mob surged around it, and all night long the nobles of the court stood on the stairways with swords drawn, ready to fight if the mob broke in. At that the King's nerve gave way, and despite his promise that Strafford should not "suffer in person, life, or fortune," on May 10, 1641, he assented to the attainder and, at the same time, to the law that the Long Parliament might not be dissolved without its own consent. Two days later Strafford went to the scaffold. Then, from June to August, royal assent was wrung to the other constitutional measures.

By the execution of Strafford and the passage of acts forbidding methods of personal government, England's liberties were secured and the rise of the King's prerogative was checked. But there remained one more problem to face, the position of the bishops in the state. Here Parliament was not certain what it wanted. There were those who accepted the ideas of the Puritan "Root and Branch Petition" of December, 1640, and were willing to get rid of the bishops "root and branch." The two Puritan leaders in Parliament—John Pym, the chunky, shaggy leader of men who had already gained the name "King Pym" from the way he had mastered his fellows in the House of Commons by his wisdom and debating ability, and John Hampden, of ship-money fame—pressed for some such solution. But there were others, devoted to the Book of Common Prayer, who wanted to keep the good of Laud's reforms. Of these the leaders were Edward Hyde, a wise and steady lawyer, and Lucius Cary, Viscount Falkland, a Scots nobleman eligible to sit in the English Commons because he was a "postnatus," that is, had been born after James had ascended the English throne. During the spring and summer these two men, who had been the allies of Pym and Hampden in their other measures, differed from them increasingly. Gradually the differences ceased to be arguments between political allies over the best means of attaining the same ends and became arguments between something like two political parties. Pym and Hampden took to sitting on the Speaker's left, which has since then become traditionally the "Opposition" side of the House of Commons. Eventually Falkland accepted the office of Secretary of State from Charles. Even before that both men acted as the King's spokesmen. These two sat on the Speaker's right, which has since then been the "Government" side.

During the summer of 1641 the Long Parliament debated various means of curbing the bishops. The House of Commons met regularly in the forenoon, about ten, and sat straight through the day. Pym had general control of what went on, and always around the dinner hour—men then ate their principal meal at noon—could rely on his supporters' staying away from their meals to give him their votes. But day by day, whenever he and Hyde clashed, he saw men change their voting habits. In those days votes were counted by one side leaving the House while "tellers" counted those who went out and those who stayed in. Gradually the numbers on each side grew more equal after each "division." Then two issues came to a climax, the Bishops' Exclusion Bill and the Irish Rebellion. In October, 1641, when Parliament reassembled after a short vacation, a bill was introduced to exclude the bishops from the House of Lords and from civil office. At the same time dire news came from Ireland. Revolt had broken out. Stories, now known to have been exaggerated, told of slaughter of Protestants by Catholics. What would Parliament do? Could Charles be trusted with an army?

Pym, along with the Bishops' Bill, introduced the Grand Remonstrance. This was to remind Charles of all he had left undone and to recommend that he appoint as his ministers—who would have to take some sort of responsibility for their actions—men Parliament could trust. For what would happen if Charles sent an army to Ireland and then brought it back to England to rule by force? Just the same, this proposal seemed to many to be going too far. This was claiming executive control by Parliament. It was contrary to the usual conception of the King as the chief executive and Parliament as only the lawmaking and sometimes judicial body. Furthermore, would the attack on the bishops stop with exclusion? There had been a Root and Branch Petition to get rid of them and a Root and Branch Bill to carry out the petition and alter the Prayer Book. There were those who felt—to use Falkland's phrase, "When it is not necessary to change, it is necessary not to change." All the length of a November day the Grand Remonstrance was debated, and on into the night. Candles were called for, a sight Parliament had rarely seen in the less partisan past. Toward two in the morning, tempers flared up, hands went to sword hilts. Some onlookers thought that only Hampden's coolness and personal ascendance prevented bloodshed. (Since then it has been a rule that swords cannot be worn in Commons, and to this day in the lobbies outside are hooks on which to hang one's sword.) At the end only eleven votes carried the Grand Remonstrance, so narrow was the margin. As the members went home in the early morning, Oliver Cromwell told Falkland that, had the vote gone the other way, he "would have sold all he had and never have seen England any more." Presumably he would have joined his fellow Puritans in Massachusetts. Later Hyde wrote, "Thus near was the Kingdom to its deliverance."

Here was Charles's chance for a compromise. Falkland and Hyde might well have won some waverers over and gained him back effective control of government. With incredible foolishness Charles threw this chance away. He did sign the Bishops' Exclusion Bill—repealed in 1662—but then he turned to force. First he tried to impeach Pym and four other members of Commons, something no king had ever done. When this was blocked, Charles first "gave the word of a King" he would do the Commons no violence and the next day marched into the House at the head of a file of soldiers. Fortunately Pym's intelligence service worked well and the "Five Members" were at the moment safe in the City of London, where legally the King could not go without permission and where the London "trainbands," or militia, were ready to back up any denial of that permission. Charles asked the Speaker where the members were. To him the Speaker replied, "Sire, I have neither eyes to see nor voice to speak, save as this House shall command." Charles said, "I see the birds have flown," and went out, foiled, hearing shouts of "Privilege," the usual warning when the rights of the House were in danger. The next day, Charles was refused admission to the City of London (Parliament sits in Westminster) and left Whitehall, which he never saw again till the day of his death. This attack on Commons made war inevitable.

It should be noted that though the occasion of this war was a constitutional issue between King and Parliament, a basic motive of the war was religion. The King's supporters feared for the Established Church they loved. The Parliamentarians dreaded a continuation of what they considered Laud's oppression of their consciences and were ready to fight their earthly sovereign in the name of their heavenly one.

No one wanted to fight, but no one wanted to take any chances. Parliament rapidly saw to it that all military supplies were guarded, and as best it could took control of the Army and Navy. The attitude of Parliament and those on its side may well be illustrated by the actions of Sir John Hotham at Hull. When Charles appeared at the gates of that seaport, demanding it be surrendered to him, Sir John spoke to him from the walls, kneeling as befitted a subject in the presence of his king. But he refused to disobey the Parliament's orders, and he kept his cannon loaded and aimed at those next the King. But it was not everyone who was on Parliament's side. Later, when war actually broke out, at one battle a group of fox hunters rode across the battlefield, between the armies, and refused to join either side. Many in England did not care which won. Then there were others who felt the urge of loyalty too strongly. Such a one was Sir Edmund Verney, who had voted with Pym but carried the King's standard in the first battle and won his wish of dying on it. Still others there were who naturally joined the King, for they disliked what Parliament stood for. These last, especially Queen Henrietta Maria, urged Charles to fight. In August, 1642, war did come, when Charles raised his standard at Nottingham. Perhaps prophetically, the flagstaff broke, and his flag fell to the ground.

At the outset Parliament was the better prepared. Lord Warwick secured the loyalty of the Navy, and the very ships built by Charles's ship-money were the cause of his defeat. For usually if a beaten Parliamentary army could get to the seacoast it could escape and fight again, and it could always get supplies by sea, but Charles could get no help from Europe. Parliament also had the money and soon was levying taxes far heavier than any it had objected to when Charles benefited from them. Therefore, Lord Essex thought he had an easy job when he marched out of London to disperse those around the King and bring His Majesty back to Westminster. But he was in error. Charles had a great advantage. On his side were many of the country nobles, especially the Catholics. These men, accustomed to riding, were natural cavalrymen. To command them he also had, in the person of his nephew, Prince Rupert of the Rhine, the son of the Elector Palatine, a great cavalry leader. So Charles's army grew, as noble after noble sold his silver plate—as did Oxford, and as Cambridge tried to do—to raise money and enlist troops of cavalry and companies of infantry. Essex, in want of supplies, had to return to London. At Edge Hill, in the Midlands, Charles and Rupert caught him. Rupert's cavalry swept most of the Parliamentary cavalry off the field, but then chased far away, in search of plunder. Meanwhile, the "trainbands" of the City of London stood firm and with the aid of two regiments of horse drove Charles's infantry back, killing Sir Edmund Verney and nearly taking his flag. Honors were even, and the stout pikemen under Sergeant-Major-General Skippon could march safely back to London.

Edge Hill set the pattern for the war that year and the next. Rupert's cavalry could defeat anything it met, as it charged in Swedish style at the trot, fired its pistols, and then a second time charged home. But whenever London itself was in danger, the trainbands would leave their jobs and march where they chose. For their strong formation, like the old Scottish schiltron, now reinforced by muskets instead of bows, could hold off cavalry. However, as time went on, more and more Royalist or Cavalier armies advanced toward London. Sir Ralph Hopton took over Cornwall and gradually recruited enough men to take Bristol with Rupert's help and advance nearer and nearer London through Devon and Dorsetshire. In the north the Marquis of Newcastle raised his famous Whitecoats, infantry the equal of the trainbands, who disdained the red uniforms many others wore, swearing they would dye their uniforms red in Puritan blood. For a while Lord Fairfax and his son Sir Thomas Fairfax held Newcastle off, from bases in the wool towns of Yorkshire and in the spinning towns of Lancashire, that were hotbeds of Puritanism and Parliamentary supporters. But it was hard for them to keep in touch with the other strong point of Roundheads, as the Parliamentary men were called from their custom of cutting their hair short. It was a long way to Lincolnshire and Cambridgeshire, where Oliver Cromwell was training cavalry to fight as well as Rupert's. Therefore during 1643 it looked as if Charles would gradually win.

What Parliament badly needed was troops of the same quality as Rupert's cavalry. It was perfectly possible to find such men, if one tried. John Hampden proved this, for a detachment he gathered met a greater number of Rupert's cavalry on a raid, at Chalgrove, and outfought them, till they were wiped out and Hampden mortally wounded. But isolated regiments were not enough; what was needed was a whole army. Pym, who was a realist, knew where to get one. Though he was dying of cancer, he pulled himself together long enough to get the men who could do the job. He sent to Scotland for help and persuaded Parliament to pay the price Scotland demanded for her veterans of the Swedish wars. That price was making England Presbyterian. A group of Scottish and English divines met at Westminster, and drew up a creed, the Westminster Confession, designed to bind both national churches. To this day it is the creed of the Church of Scotland. A Solemn League and Covenant (note it is a league of two nations, not a National Covenant like that of 1638) was sworn to by both sides, and Scottish troops were sent south. Pym died before the League was implemented, but he had saved Parliament.

In 1644 the fruits of Pym's treaty with Scotland were gathered. The strategic key to the north was York. To relieve its Royalist garrison came Rupert from the south, the Marquis of Newcastle from the north. To cover the siege Alexander Leslie, Lord Leven, brought his Scots to join Oliver Cromwell from the south. Outside York, at Marston Moor, the two armies met. At last Rupert's cavalry met their match. Cromwell's men, because of Scottish support in a crucial moment, were able to withstand Rupert's charge, rally, charge back, and not only sweep Rupert's men from the field but also ride down the Marquis of Newcastle's Whitecoats. This was a feat of discipline, for on the other wing of the battle the Cavaliers had swept all before them. Rupert left the field, declaring the "Ironsides" could not be broken. Thus their greatest opponent gave the Puritan cavalry their famous nickname; thus Cromwell proved himself the master trainer of troops on either side. For he had a clear idea of the sort of men he wanted to recruit: "Men who had the fear of God before them and made some conscience of what they did." In an age of a stratified society he chose men purely for merit and devotion to the cause. He paid them well, kept them under strict discipline, and treated them with respect. As a result he got soldiers who had their heart in their cause and who were willing to take responsibility. His men proved themselves invincible, never losing a battle till they were disbanded.

However, not all the armies of the Parliament were like the Ironsides. Shortly after Marston Moor, Lord Essex wandered—that best describes his methods—into Cornwall after Sir Ralph Hopton, and was trapped at Lostwithiel. He surrendered and was allowed to ship his troops home— or rather Skippon was allowed to do it, after Essex had broken out and escaped with a few cavalrymen. The Scots, too, were drawn home. For in an almost miraculous campaign, James Graham, Marquis of Montrose, raised the Highlands for King Charles, defeating armies larger than his own. That meant Leven's veterans could not be spared for England. It was clear that if Parliament were to win without the Scots it must have a new army and new generals.

A new army Parliament got. Cromwell's ideas were adopted. Good pay was offered, and good service was demanded. All troops raised under the new standards of recruiting, many of them picked veterans and some of them ex-Royalists, were called the New Model. These soon became the sole Parliamentary army. The question of new generals was settled by an ingenious compromise, known as the "Self-denying Ordinance." All the members of Parliament who had commands resigned in a bloc. Then those who were good were reappointed. Thus Essex was replaced by Sir Thomas Fairfax, who had supreme command as general. He had as his lieutenant, and cavalry commander, Cromwell. In charge of the infantry was Philip Skippon, the chief drillmaster, or sergeant-major-general, a title soon shortened to major-general. Thus it was that our military titles began, with the grades of general, lieutenant general, and major general. By midsummer 1645, the New Model army was ready to take the field. North England had been cleared of Royalists, and pressure was being put on the King's temporary capital, Oxford. Now, to finish the job, South England had to be conquered. In 1645 came the final struggle between Roundhead and Cavalier, at the battle of Naseby. Again one wing overwhelmed its opponents; again the Cavaliers charged too far, while Cromwell's men turned at command, rode down the enemy center, and won the day. Thus the Ironsides routed the King's forces in the south, leaving

Charles without any large body of troops with which to carry on. For in Scotland the diversion made by Montrose was coming to an end. Montrose's luck had turned, a clan quarrel had caused his men to desert, and at Philiphaugh David Leslie had at last defeated him. Worse still, right after Naseby, Charles's secret papers were captured, and it became known that he was inviting Spain and France to intervene and treating with the Irish rebels. Not only had Charles lost the war, he had lost public opinion. The fighting stopped in May, 1646, when Charles surrendered to the Scots.

The situation at the end of the First Civil War was well summed up by the last Royalist commander to surrender. He told his captors: "You have now done your work, and may go to play, unless you fall out among yourselves." For fall out among themselves the victors did. During the years 1646 and 1647, the Scots, Parliament, and the Army could not agree on a settlement. The Scots soon withdrew from the picture, after turning Charles over to Parliament in exchange for their arrears of pay. Charles started to bargain with Parliament, since none of its actions would be fully legal till he gave his assent. He had another card to play as well, a religious one. Parliament, having signed the Solemn League and Covenant, was trying to make England Presbyterian. It had ousted nearly 2,000 clergymen who had refused to sign the Covenant. Consequently, those who remained faithful to the suppressed Book of Common Prayer tended to support the King. As long as they could be held down by force, this did not matter. But the fact of this growing support for Charles made the Army more and more important if the Presbyterians in Parliament were to have their way. Here Parliament made its great mistake of mishandling the Army.

Now that peace had come, fewer troops were needed. Parliament tried to disband regiments first and pay them afterwards. Parliament also tried to tell the soldiers what their religion should be. The combination was too much. Though the pay of the New Model had been far better than in the past, it was still not out of arrears, and the soldiers feared with much justification that if they did not get paid when they had arms in their hands they would never be paid. Furthermore, the New Model was being increasingly permeated with the religious ideas of the Independents and with the political ideas that were natural concomitants of those religious ideas. The phrase "freedom of conscience" goes far to sum up those ideas, if the word conscience is stressed equally with freedom. They respected only those who acted from a sense of divinely inspired duty, but they were willing to give very great freedom to those who they felt were so acting. This may explain the otherwise curious combination of tyranny over conduct and toleration for ideas that characterized them in the days of their power.

For when the Parliament failed to reach terms with Charles, but offered to demobilize half the Army and send the other half to put down the Irish revolt, which was still simmering for want of troops there, the soldiers mutinied. In this they had the full though reluctant support of their officers. Committees of soldiers, called Agitators, presented their claims and were very willing to tell Parliament how to mind its own business, thinking with much justice they could do better. Cromwell and other officers tried to restrain them but also gave good but unpalatable advice. The answer was for Parliament to order the Army to disband or go to Ireland. At that point the Army acted. Cornet Joyce rode to Charles's prison and carried him off for safe keeping. His answer to the King's request for a warrant of arrest was to point to his troop of horse. Then the Army marched on London.

Even this did not get results. Charles escaped to the Isle of Wight and made an agreement with some Scots to come to his aid. In January, 1648, there broke out concerted risings all over England, known as the Second Civil War. It was no use to attack the New Model, especially as its members were now thoroughly enraged. Speedily they drove the Royalists into fortresses, notably Colchester in Essex and Pontefract in Wales, and by starvation and bombardment took those fortresses. Their feelings were shown by the treatment of prisoners. The New Model gave no quarter to those who had promised not again to take up arms. Then, the King's few Scots allies were routed by Cromwell at Preston, and the angry Army was in control again, the victor in the Second Civil War.

The Army now returned to its negotiations with Parliament, for it wanted peace and legality. But still the members of Parliament did not realize that the way to demobilize the Army was to give it pay. They temporized; the Army lost its patience. On December 6, 1648, Colonel Pride stood at the door of the House of Commons, admitting only those the Army thought fit and excluding the rest. "Pride's Purge" left behind what was derisively called the "Rump," or sitting part, a name used to this day for an illegal minority of a legislature that remains in session after the majority has gone. This small body consisted of those in agreement with the Army, and it did what the Army wanted. Above all, the Army wanted to punish "Charles Stuart, the man of blood," as they called the King, for the harm he had done the country. So the Rump voted it treason for a king to fight Parliament, and when the Lords, now down to a dozen members, objected, it abolished the House of Lords. Then the Rump set up a court, under John Bradshaw, that tried Charles in Westminster Hall. Naturally, considering its composition, the court found Charles guilty. On January 30, 1649, Charles I stepped from the Banqueting Hall at Whitehall to the scaffold. Thus the Civil Wars ended with the victor neither King nor Parliament, but the Army.

14

COMMONWEALTH, PROTECTORATE, AND RESTORATION

When Charles I was executed, England automatically became a republic. Ever since then there has been ardent dispute as to whether his execution was justified. Here two things should be considered—Charles's record as a king, and what right John Bradshaw's court had to try him. Charles's record as a king was extremely bad. At the start he had bungled foreign affairs, failing to intervene successfully in the Thirty Years' War where both his family and England's religion were involved. Instead he worsened the plight of the Huguenots in France. His good faith was nil; he had twisted his way around the Petition of Right and levied money most "unconstitutionally." He had not even spent his ill-gotten ship-money successfully. His navy did cut down piracy but was forced to tolerate insults. In 1639 a Dutch fleet under Tromp had attacked and defeated a Spanish fleet in English waters off the coast of Kent, the Battle of the Downs, while the English admiral had had to watch impotently a violation of England's sovereignty. Charles, it was believed, had tried to use an Irish army against some of his subjects and had, in the case of the Five Members, attacked the precious privileges of both Commons and the City of London. As documents seized at the end of the First Civil War had shown, he had been negotiating with various foreign powers behind the backs and against the interests of his own supporters. He even went to the point of "selling out" his loyal viceroy in Ireland, Lord Ormonde, who was miraculously keeping most of that island on his side in the English Civil War. If Strafford deserved execution, Charles, who had betrayed Strafford, certainly did, too.

But there is a second question. What right had John Bradshaw and his "High Court of Justice" to try the King, who "can do no wrong," and lay violent hands on "the Lord's Anointed"? This action could be excused only if the Commons, which had already abolished the Lords and the kingship, really represented the people. But they did not. They had been elected in 1640. In 1642 all the opposition members had gone over to the King at his capital at Oxford. Since then Pride's Purge had made Parliament a fragment of its former self, the Rump. The incompetence of Parliament to try

Charles was so obvious that there was a great change of feeling toward him. The Rump could stay in power only by relying on the Army. Therefore, in fact, England was ruled by those army officers who as members of the Rump retained a power of passing laws, and who as members of the newly set up Council of State enforced the laws they had just passed. England therefore went under a dictatorship of a small body of men. Eventually, as was not unnatural, that group shrank to one man—Oliver Cromwell.

There are two sorts of dictators—those who mean well and those who do not. Fortunately for England, her new dictators meant well. They believed in fair play. When one unusual soldier, Colonel John Lilburne, called "Freeborn John," challenged their powers, they gave him not one but repeated fair trials and were perfectly willing to have the courts let him off. They were men who had wanted freedom of religion from Laud, and they were willing to grant freedom of religion to all except those who used the Book of Common Prayer and were therefore automatic royalists, and those who were Roman Catholics and so might be agents of a foreign government. To show their real belief in toleration, they negotiated with the Pope to see if Catholics might be allowed to have their services after taking an oath not to mix religion with politics. However, they were believers in strict conduct, and willingly enforced laws against sports on Sunday, games such as bearbaiting, and stage plays. Consequently, under their rule England experienced a dictatorship under the best possible conditions, and obtained from that experience a lasting feeling about dictators, however honest they might be.

With this preliminary explanation, it may be possible to understand just what happened between the execution of Charles I and the return of his son, Charles II. The first problem was to use the Army in 1649 for the purpose for which it had been raised in 1642—restoring order to Ireland. This the Army did, in a way that has made the worst curse an Irishman can give "The curse of Cromwell be on you." In 1649 Cromwell did his job very thoroughly. He struck hard. Men still argue whether his putting the garrison of Drogheda to the sword was justified. It caused others to surrender, but roused undying hatred. When he and his veterans had conquered Ireland, the island was parceled out among them, land being given in place of back pay. The necessary land was taken from Catholics and from those who had supported Charles I. For the dispossessed the alternative was "Hell or Connaught," Connaught being the most barren and westernmost of the four "kingdoms" of Ireland. Thus by 1650 Ireland was under control.

From Ireland Cromwell was brought back by the news that Scotland had again taken a hand in the game. Charles I's son, now claiming to be Charles II, was at his father's tricks of turning one kingdom against another. First he had sent Montrose to try again to conquer Scotland by raising the clans. Then when Montrose had been captured and executed, he turned around and made terms with the Presbyterians in power. Montrose's bones were hanging from the gibbet in Edinburgh as Charles entered as nominal king, the real ruler being the General Assembly. Here came a test of two great veteran armies, the Scots of the Swedish wars and the New Model of Cromwell. At first it looked as if the Scots were better, for David Leslie trapped Cromwell at Dunbar where he seemed to have no way of escape but the sea. To Cromwell were sent insulting demands for surrender, to which he sent his famous reply—"I beseech you, in the bowels of Christ, think it possible you may be mistaken." Such an answer was typical of the way the Independents patiently tried to be reasonable when dealing with fellow Puritans. But the Scots would not listen to reason, and the clergy ordered Leslie to attack. By the end of the day, September 3, 1650, the Scots were in full flight, not to stop till they had crossed the Firth of Forth where they were seemingly safe from further attack. Stirling Bridge was thought impregnable, and it was notorious that amphibious operations were the most risky sort. To Cromwell's veterans this was just a challenge, and they crossed the Firth of Forth to force an issue. Charles II, who by this time was very sick of his advisers, took the bold stroke of invading England. Cromwell pursued him, and at Worcester, after a daring march across the Pennine Hills, a small army of Ironsides cut in half a larger Scottish army and annihilated both halves. The Worcester fight, September 3, 1651, ended any possible question of the second Charles Stuart ruling against the wishes of the Long Parliament and its army. Charles II was lucky to escape through the loyalty of the common people of England to their king. One night he had to spend in an oak tree listening to Cromwell's troopers riding below him. On another occasion, which had important later results, a Catholic priest, John Huddleston, saved his life. Finally Charles II got away to live in exile in France and Holland. For whatever the people might think, after Dunbar and Worcester the Rump and the Army ruled all three kingdoms. Even the Scottish General Assembly could not stand against them and was abolished in 1653.

Therefore, part of the next stage of England's history became a struggle between Army and Rump. The Army was an unusual body. As it consisted of the men who had been most ready to fight Charles I, its members naturally were not fond of Laud's Church of England. Its chief interest was ability. Among its troopers were worldly men. Such a one was the former Royalist George Monck, who had been taken prisoner and, after switching sides, had risen to the top. But most often these men cared much about their religion. They argued much, and they came to believe that the truest religion was to be found when each man was free to follow his own conscience. These Independents, as they were called, guided the thinking of the Army and brought to their way of mind their general, Oliver Cromwell, who became a Republican, but more conservatively so than his men.

Cromwell is a man much misunderstood. He honestly did not want power, and just as honestly he did not want to leave a job undone. He had a saying—"He goes furthest who knows not where he is going." As a result he seemed a hypocrite, for he was always "wrestling with his conscience," was always seeming to hold back, and was always the man to take the bold, harsh course. But the answer to that apparent inconsistency is that people followed him in his strong measures just because they knew that he felt that they were used only in an emergency. People followed him because they trusted him, and as will be seen, he led England over a long road before he was through.

In the years from 1650 to 1660 four important things happened in or to England. She regained her station among the powers of Europe; she experimented, unsuccessfully, with her government; she demonstrated her naval strength to the world; and then she called back her king. The dates for these four somewhat overlap, but they can be best understood by treating them separately.

When England cut off Charles I's head, she made herself an outlaw among nations. Even republican Holland showed no sympathy, and two English ambassadors, in Holland and in Spain, were assassinated without the governments of those countries making any effort to bring the offenders to justice. Prince Rupert by this time had seized a few ships which had mutinied against Parliament in the Second Civil War, and he was engaged in a cross between a naval war and a high grade of piracy, in which he was given assistance by Holland and Portugal. After him the Council of State of the Commonwealth sent its "generals-at-sea," of whom the most famous was Robert Blake, who, though he was a soldier who some think never was at sea till he commanded a squadron, became as an admiral the equal of Drake and Nelson. He blockaded Rupert in Lisbon harbor with such effect that soon the Spanish government found itself, as an enemy of Portugal, giving recognition to the "regicide" English Commonwealth through the person of its admiral. Here Blake started the tradition that an English admiral can and should take part in diplomacy. Other nations also found that it was wise to recognize the Commonwealth. When the French tried to withhold recognition, Blake's fleet blocked the supplies they were sending to Dunkirk, then under siege by the Spaniards in the Netherlands. The loss of Dunkirk secured French recognition of the Commonwealth.

But the key question was Holland. Holland and England had been spoiling for a fight for some years. England had some scores to settle. In 1621, at Amboina in the East Indies, a British "factory" or trading post on the Island of Celebes had been wiped out by the Dutch. That is why the British East India Company confined its attentions to India and did not extend its operations to the East Indies. For this massacre no apology or retribution had been made. There was also that matter of the sinking by the Dutch of a Spanish fleet in English territorial waters, in 1639. Therefore in 1651 the English Parliament enacted the Navigation Laws, directed at the Dutch. These stated that no non-European goods should be imported into England except in English ships or ships of the producing nation. The same requirement held for England's colonies. As Dutch carrying trade made the wealth of Holland, this meant war. This, from 1652 to 1654, was perhaps the first great purely naval war. In it the "generals-at-sea," particularly Blake and Monck, fought the great Dutch leader, Maarten Tromp. Legend says that once Tromp sailed the Channel with a broom at his masthead, boasting he had swept the English from the sea, but at the end Tromp was killed in one last desperate battle, and the Dutch were so crushed they had to yield. For the Zuider Zee had become a "forest of masts," so many ships were tied up at anchor. They could not trade, and had to accept England's terms. Thus England, though isolated, became respected.

By now a change had come in the English government. The Army was full of men with democratic ideals. Students of English history can find the roots of all sorts of modern political philosophies in the soldiers' writings of the times. On the extreme edge, for example, were the "Diggers" who claimed that private property had begun in England with the Norman Conquest, that the execution of Charles had ended private property along with the kingship, and that they should put communism into practice by taking over some "common" land and digging gardens. More important were the "Levelers," who recognized all men as equal and demanded manhood suffrage and annual Parliaments—like the Chartists of Victoria's reign. With such ideas fermenting in it, there is no wonder the Army continued to urge that the Rump dissolve and allow a genuine Parliament to be elected. But after Charles's death, as before, the Rump clung to power. Even when it at last set a date for dissolution, it turned around and tried to keep power for itself by providing that its members need not be reelected. Even more, it tried to provide that its members could keep anyone they chose out of the new Parliament. When Cromwell heard this, he exploded with wrath, sent for soldiers, drove out the members, and locked the door. As he did this, he picked up the Speaker's mace, the symbol of the authority of Commons, and said: "Take this bauble away." Thus, on April 20, 1653, England found herself a military dictatorship with no ruler but the Lord General.

Cromwell did not want to be a dictator. He wanted a Parliament but thought that universal suffrage tended to anarchy. As the best way of getting a good Parliament, he had the Independent ministers of England nominate members. This body got the nickname Barebones Parliament from the name of one of its members, Praise-God Barebones. Its members got so tangled in theory in their debates they could achieve no practical results, except, fortunately, that of agreeing to dissolve and go home. Cromwell had to try again. There was issued a written constitution, the Instrument of Government, under which Cromwell took oath as Lord Protector and by which one Parliament represented England, Scotland, and Ireland. This Parliament worked so ill that Cromwell dissolved it the moment its five-month session under the Instrument had ended. In 1655 he tried to give England good rule by setting eleven major generals to rule eleven districts. This remedy was worse than the disease. Yet another Parliament, to vote war funds, tried to solve the constitutional question by offering Cromwell a Humble Petition and Advice to become king, with a House of Lords. Cromwell wavered, but at the last moment refused. The reason, it seems, was that he felt that would be betraying his fellow soldiers. So the Humble Petition was rewritten, and in 1657 England had the equivalent of a House of Lords and a king, in the form of "another House" and a Lord Protector with the power to appoint a successor. But the Houses quarreled, and Cromwell again dissolved Parliament, early in 1658. England's experiments with written constitutions had failed.

However, Cromwell was not pinched for money, as the Stuarts had been. The heavy war taxes levied by the Long Parliament were still in effect, and the condemnation of the property of Royalists—or, as the Puritans called them, Malignants—brought in much money. That money was spent at once, for Cromwell was building up a powerful navy for Blake to use. Already by messages he had secured the cooperation of New England, and by force of arms he had made Virginia and Barbados obey the Commonwealth. Now he had a "Western Design." By this Penn's fleet struck at the West Indies and, though it failed at Santo Domingo, in 1655 took Jamaica. To the Mediterranean he sent Blake, for one of England's greatest naval campaigns from 1654 to 1657.

Here is what Blake accomplished: By his mere presence he forced the Duke of Savoy to stop persecuting the Vaudois Protestants, thus backing up the messages and sonnet, "Avenge, O Lord, thy slaughtered saints," of Cromwell's Latin Secretary, John Milton. By bombarding Tunis he forced better behavior to England by the Barbary pirates. By staying at sea throughout the winter in a blockade of Cadiz he brought Spain to terms and showed that England was mistress of all European seas except the Black Sea and perhaps the Baltic. As part of this same blockade he took part of the Spanish Plate fleet. Then to everyone's surprise he led his ships against the land forts of Teneriffe. Normally ships cannot fight forts; his did. There was another admiral who later tried to attack the forts of Teneriffe and failed—that was where Nelson lost his arm. Because of this Nelson himself said he could not compare himself with Blake, an admission which was not all modesty. For of Britain's three greatest admirals, Drake, Blake, and Nelson, perhaps Blake's achievements were the most significant, for he was the first admiral to secure and use the command of the sea outside English waters.

Cromwell had an important land campaign. He lent his redcoats to Cardinal Mazarin of France. At the battle of the Dunes in Belgium they swept off the field all the opposing troops except the redcoats of Charles II's personal Guards, demonstrating thus the high quality of the English Army. For reward Cromwell received Dunkirk, which Mazarin had taken from the Spaniards. England's fleets also intervened in the Baltic, to protect English trade there. Cromwell and Blake, rather than Queen Elizabeth and Drake, really made England mistress of the seas.

But this whole structure of British power rested on two things—the personality of Oliver Cromwell, and the amount of money which could be secured by confiscating the estates of Cavaliers. It was true that in the intervals in which Cromwell and his Parliaments cooperated, good legislation was passed, but Cromwell's government was not particularly acceptable to the English, especially when he had divided England into districts, under the control of major generals. These Puritan officers were liberal enough about ideas. Their only religious persecutions were undertaken for political reasons. Catholics were persecuted because they still refused to obey heretical governments even in nonreligious matters, or so it was believed by the English. Here Cromwell's government tried to arrange for toleration, but unfortunately failed. The reading of the Book of Common Prayer was illegal, since by it Charles II was king, though most Englishmen clung to it and preferred it. But in moral matters the Puritans were illiberal, and enforced their strict ideas with military might. No plays were given, no games were played on Sunday. Even Englishmen would not tolerate this, though the English Sunday is a legacy of Puritan times.

Soon there came a chance to change. Oliver Cromwell died, on his lucky day, September 3, 1658. In his place was put, as Lord Protector, his son Richard. But the Army would not listen to Richard, Army and Parliament quarreled, and out went the Lord Protector, with the nickname "Tumbledown Dick." Then the Army ousted Parliament. Soon, though England was still ruled by the Council of State, it seemed as if the Councilors would be at each other's throats—even with the best of intentions—and so would the troops under them. At this stage the major general in Scotland, George Monck, began to act. His orders were not to cross from Scotland into England. Therefore he massed his troops at the border, camping near a brook called Cold Stream. There he watched things getting worse. Finally he disobeyed his orders, and marched on London. No one knew just what he would do; everyone knew that he had a plan, and that his soldiers would obey him, whereas the soldiers of the other major generals would not fight against their fellow Englishmen. Monck let drop some hints as he marched south. One was to get a legal Parliament. The Rump met again. Another, made when he reached London, was to readmit the excluded members. Pride's Purge was reversed. Then Monck advised the calling of a real Parliament. In 1659 the Long Parliament at last dissolved itself, and called for the election of a new Convention Parliament.[1] It had to be a Convention Parliament since no king had summoned it, and no true Parliament could exist without the king's summons. Then it became clear what Monck had been driving at. Englishmen had begun to realize that no government could exist without a head, even a figurehead. The phrase was going the rounds that what was needed was "government by a single person, whether it be Richard, George, or Charles." Richard Cromwell was useless; he had been tried and had failed. George Monck had no intention of making himself king. That was not what the English wanted. He was being trusted and obeyed because it was felt he was being patriotic, not selfish. Charles II, in exile in Holland—where his widowed sister, Mary, Princess of Orange, was giving him shelter—was the logical choice for a single person to hold England together, if he had learned the lessons his father would not learn. At the strategic moment, Charles issued the Declaration of Breda to prove that he had, and Parliament summoned him back.

The Declaration of Breda, then, is a key document in English history, for it contains the requirements necessary to keep England a kingdom. In it Charles promised (1) to govern with Parliament, (2) to pardon everyone whom Parliament did not except from pardon, (3) to let all legitimate purchasers of estates hold them, and (4) to give as much toleration as Parliament would allow. And on May 29, 1660, Charles was restored, in what lawyers solemnly called the eleventh year of his reign.

Charles soon saw to it that he was securely on the throne. He did not make the mistake the Long Parliament had made in 1646. He paid off the soldiers quickly and sent them home on the whole satisfied. Then he let Parliament take the responsibility for what came next. The bodies of Pym, Cromwell, and Blake were torn out of their graves in Westminster Abbey and thrown with the bodies of murderers. An Act of Indemnity and Oblivion covered all manifestations of revenge, but was so managed that the returning Cavaliers who had been in exile and who looked for rewards for themselves and proscription for their enemies called it "indemnity for

[1] In 1660, just to make sure, an act of Parliament was passed dissolving the Long Parliament.

the King's enemies and oblivion for the King's friends." Then Charles quietly got rid of the Parliament that had brought him back, and got one even more favorable to him. In January, 1661, there was a revolt by Fifth Monarchy men, Puritans who believed that the Fifth Kingdom foretold by the Bible, the Kingdom of Jesus Christ, was at hand and that it was their duty to seize power by force. The last remaining troops of the New Model, Monck's men who had camped at the Coldstream, put down the revolt and in the ensuing excitement Charles called an election for a new Parliament. The result was the devotedly Royalist Cavalier Parliament. Of it Charles said that he now had a Parliament so to his liking he would never let it go. In fact, this Parliament lasted longer—in actual power, though not in technical existence—than the Long Parliament: 1660 to 1678 as against 1640 to 1653, with legal existence to 1659 or perhaps 1660.

Charles's new Parliament gave him the legislation he wanted. The Fifth Monarchy scare justified two regiments of Guards. One, the Grenadiers, were those who had guarded him in exile; the others, the Coldstreams, were the men who had put down the revolt. (There is a rivalry in age. The Grenadiers in the days of numbers were the First Guards; the Coldstreams never took a number, but the motto, *Secundus Nulli.*) But the chief legislation that was passed was that to keep the Puritans down. Since Edward Hyde, who was made Earl of Clarendon, was the Lord Chancellor and chief royal adviser at this time, this legislation is collectively known as the Clarendon Code. It was enacted in the years from 1661 to 1665. By the Corporation Act of 1661, no city or borough government post could be held by one not a member of the Church of England, who had taken the Communion and abjured the Covenant. That ousted the extreme Presbyterian and Independent group of the Puritans from their strongholds. The Act of Uniformity of 1662 required the acceptance of a revised Prayer Book. By the revision later made, doubtful points were interpreted in a "High Church" direction. In particular the formulas of administration of Communion and ordination of the clergy were so changed that mild Puritans could no longer stay within the Church of England. There was an attempt at bringing in some of those, but the only fruit of this attempt, it may be said, was the addition to the Prayer Book of the General Thanksgiving, written by one of the Presbyterian negotiators. Thus an important part of the Elizabethan Compromise was abandoned. Until 1662, Puritans were those who wished to purify the Church of England from within. Now the word changed meaning and became applied, as it now is, to those whose behavior is as strict as was that of the ill-famed but well-meaning major generals. Meanwhile new words—Nonconformist and Dissenter—came into use, to describe those who would not conform to the services of the Church of England and who dissented from some of its doctrines.

To deal with them two more laws were passed. By the Conventicle Act of 1664 religious meetings could not be held in towns or within five miles of an incorporated town. That meant that no Protestant service other than that of the Church of England could legally be held where Puritans were most common. It was, in effect, the end of the Breda promise of toleration. Then this was clinched by a Five Mile Act of 1665, prohibiting Dissenting clergymen from living within five miles of a town.

What then were the results of this period of the Commonwealth and the Protectorate, when the Restoration had done its work? It may be said that England had a far stronger Parliament, a permanent army, a sound naval organization, and a less inclusive but deeper rooted Church. But if one tries to call these, in a sense, the victors in the long run by the Civil War, then what of the vanquished, the Puritans? It must not be forgotten what Puritanism did. It was the Puritans who were in the front line of the struggle against James I and Charles I. It was their ethical ideas which gave courage to the Parliamentary side, their men who did the hardest fighting. It was also the ethical standards of the Puritan army, or rather the Independent army, that made it so liberal in its administration, in some matters, when it had power, and that caused it to lay down its arms so quietly when Charles came back. A sign of the ethical superiority of the Puritans lies in the English literature of this time. The two greatest writers of the age were members of the Puritan party. One was Cromwell's Latin Secretary, John Milton, the author of *Paradise Lost*. The other was a private in Fairfax's army, John Bunyan, the author of *Pilgrim's Progress*. No other English writing of any length of that period can compare with what those two wrote, even if some Cavaliers wrote nobly of their loyalty—such as Sir Richard Lovelace's *To Lucasta on Going to the Wars* or *To Althea from Prison;* or Montrose's immortal lines, written the night before his execution—"He either fears his fate too much, or deserves it not at all, who will not put it to the touch, to win or lose it all." That literary comparison may sum up the merits of the two sides.

15

CHARLES II

Perhaps the best way to describe the government of England in the 1660's would be to say that men succeeded for a while in turning the clock back to the summer of 1641. King, Parliament, and local authorities all worked with the legislation that the Long Parliament had then passed and Charles I had then signed. In effect this went back to the Tudor rule by the country gentry without the Tudor control of the country gentry by means of the Privy Council. Since in 1641 all "courts unknown to the Common Law" had been abolished, the country gentlemen really ruled England in local matters. With no Star Chamber to supervise them, the justices of the peace—who were all country gentlemen in the shires—had things their own way. Difficult cases did go to the judges at assizes, but all simple cases were handled at Petty and Quarter Sessions. As the justices in Petty and Quarter Sessions supervised the parish vestries, they also controlled public works and poor relief. And whenever serious trouble broke out, the same men, holding the different offices of Lord Lieutenant and Deputy Lieutenant, supervised the militia. In Church affairs, matters were much the same. Since High Commission had been abolished, the justices of the peace were the enforcing authorities behind the Clarendon Code of the Corporation Act, the Act of Uniformity, the Five Mile Act, and the Conventicle Act. In a different sense the country gentlemen also controlled the Church. In England the appointment to each parish is called its "advowson." Advowsons were owned by many people, but these were usually country gentlemen who saw to it their parishes had the kind of parsons they wanted. Later on, when the revenues of the Church of England rose, squires often appointed their own sons as parsons. Thus the policy of the Declaration of Breda really made England more of an aristocracy than ever. Even in lawmaking the country gentlemen reigned supreme, for they made up the majority of the House of Commons and all of the House of Lords. Furthermore, it became harder to enter that aristocracy. The "social mobility" of Tudor and early Stuart times ended sharply.

However, the country gentlemen did not have it all their own way. Some boroughs were "counties in themselves." Such, above all, was London, whose sheriff was also the sheriff of Middlesex and was not a royal appointee. Other boroughs had special rights and courts of their own, more or less independent of Quarter Sessions. All boroughs sent members to Parliament, and while they might and usually did send country gentlemen, they sent country gentlemen who knew what businessmen wanted. More and more England was becoming a trading nation, whose businessmen were alive to the importance of foreign affairs, and those country gentlemen who wanted to succeed in politics had to understand foreign affairs.

This smooth acceptance of the early work of the Long Parliament was possible because, as the laws of England stood, there had never been a Commonwealth. Charles II's reign technically began on January 30, 1649, and acts of the first year of his reign were dated the eleventh year. Only those laws to which Charles I had given his assent were considered legal. Theoretically the king's powers remained just as they had been when Charles I had gone to Nottingham to raise his standard. Even the idea of the king's prerogative remained. Furthermore, even though Charles II had lost much power through the early legislation of the Long Parliament, he had equally gained by the revulsion of feeling over his father's execution. Some of the clergy of the Church of England were speaking of Charles I as "Blessed Charles the Martyr." Many were teaching a doctrine that the king must be obeyed, no matter what he did, and succeeded in drumming that idea into the heads of their congregations. Here was a chance for a diplomatic king to increase his power. Across the Channel, Charles II's first cousin, Louis XIV of France, was strengthening the monarchy by similar steps. When he had come to the throne, Cardinal Mazarin, his regent, had been faced with a civil war, the Fronde, which was put down only with difficulty. But Louis built up a superb army, took all the reins into his own hand, and became an almost absolute monarch by a clever twisting of the laws of France. Could Charles II do somewhat the same, under not too dissimilar circumstances?

His subjects found Charles a very different man from his shy, correct father. The second Charles was a gay soul. He was the founder of English horse racing. Indeed his courtiers nicknamed him "Old Rowley" after his famous racehorse. He spent much time at Newmarket Heath, which even today is a famous racing center. He was a sportsman, one of the first to shoot birds flying with a shotgun, no easy task in those days of uncertain flintlock guns. He was an ardent player of the difficult game of tennis—not the lawn tennis of today, but royal or court tennis which is played in a stone courtyard with balls bouncing off the walls as well as coming across the net. It was Charles who praised the climate of England, from a sportsman's point of view, as the only one in the world in which one can be out of doors every day of the year. The life of Charles's court at Whitehall was gay and "fast," but at the same time gentlemanly in outward form. As the court was the center of English society then in a way it has never been since, the King could wield great indirect influence, and thus could get things done without appearing to compel. Charles could use this opportunity. He had very great charm. He understood how to handle Englishmen, and knew just how far he could go. As a result, before he died he came near to being as powerful as ever Henry VIII was.

He was able to accomplish this because, theoretically, the king had the complete executive power in the country even though his ministers could be held responsible for illegal actions. Therefore, were he astute, he had at his command all the powers of the Treasury which pays all bills, the Exchequer which passes on taxes, the secretaryship of state which issues government orders, the Horse Guards which used to be the commander in chief's office, the Admiralty, and the lord-chancellorship which technically issued the commissions of justices of the peace and all charters and such important permanent documents. Although in 1641 there was a division of the powers between the king as executive and Parliament as legislative, which was supreme was still to be decided.

Charles almost at once found himself in debt. This was not entirely his fault. Cromwell had run up big bills for the Navy and had run out of Cavaliers whose estates he could confiscate. It is known how hard Charles worked for the Navy; the Secretary of the Admiralty, Samuel Pepys, left a confidential diary in code, and the code has been deciphered. In that diary, among fascinatingly frank personal records, are found examples of Charles's work, and that of his brother, James, Duke of York, the Lord High Admiral of the early years of the reign. But Charles knew that Parliament did not like to spend money, especially when the Protestantism of the court was suspect, and he tried to find sources of money outside. Since he owned a French fort, Dunkirk, he sold it. He married a Portuguese wife and with her got Bombay, which he sold to the East India Company; some cash; and Tangier, where he kept some regular soldiers out of the view of England. Tangier, however, proved a drain on his resources, and finally had to be given up. His Queen, too, failed in her essential duty and did not give him an heir. This was not Charles's fault, for he had already founded several illegitimate families. One son, James Stuart, he made the Duke of Monmouth; others he made Dukes of St. Albans and Grafton. But the English people felt they had been somehow defrauded. On the door of Edward Hyde, now Lord Chancellor Clarendon, was posted this rhyme: "This year were three wonders seen, Dunkirk, Tangier, and a barren Queen." For no one wanted the bitter, tactless James, Duke of York, to inherit the throne, as he would if Charles had no legitimate children. Charles knew England, for all the protestations of loyalty he heard, would throw him out if ever he violated its liberties openly, and his first aim was to die King of England, even if he could not fulfill his second aim, to become king in fact as well as in name. Charles had a third aim, of making England Catholic if he could, but this he kept secret until his deathbed, except from his cousin Louis and a few trusted intimates.

With England in an apparently precarious state when, to quote Pepys's *Diary*, men were "thinking on Brave Oliver and the deeds he did," the Dutch thought they saw their chance to force revision of the Navigation Act which the Cavalier Parliament had reenacted. In 1665 they declared war and fought a series of epic naval battles. But George Monck, now Duke of Albemarle, James, Duke of York, and even old Prince Rupert put to sea and so harried the Dutch as to cripple their trade. Holland sued for peace, for she now began to realize her greatest danger was a French invasion by land once Louis had finished conquering Alsace-Lorraine. England promptly agreed and disbanded her Navy. She had been struck hard; the Great Fire of 1665 had swept London, and the Great Plague had decimated the population. The Dutch seized the chance to show they were still fighting by entering the Medway and burning English naval vessels tied up at the naval base of Chatham. The memory of the Dutch in the Medway was a bitter lesson of unpreparedness to England, and was no easier to bear because Charles that very night was giving an extremely gay party during which he and his current favorite, Lady Castlemaine, chased a moth around the dinner table to the pleasure of their guests.

However, Charles found a way out of his troubles. He laid the blame on his Lord Chancellor, Edward Hyde, Lord Clarendon, and let Parliament impeach him. In 1667 Clarendon went into exile in France, and there wrote the *Memoirs of the Rebellion* which provide an eyewitness account of the Civil War. It was a sad fall for one whose daughter Anne had married James of York and whose granddaughters, Mary and Anne, were to inherit the throne. Out of the fall came an important increase in the power of Parliament. Charles let Parliament dictate how he spent the money it granted him. From then on, that has remained an essential principle in the English so-called constitution, and it is to be found in our Federal constitution in the clause "No money shall be drawn from the Treasury but in consequence of appropriations made by law."

Having slid out of this difficulty by securing someone else to take the blame, Charles went on to find others to be scapegoats. A principle gradually grew up that the king should take advice only from important people to whom he had given the title Privy Councilor, which bears with it the title Right Honorable and gives the right of access to the king's presence. In particular he gave control over foreign affairs to a group of five men —Lord Clifford (a Catholic), Lord Arlington (also a Catholic), the Duke of Buckingham, Anthony Ashley Cooper, and the Scottish Duke of

Lauderdale. The word cabal had already been applied to a small group of plotters and was found to fit this group well, since the initials of their names made up the word. These five took action against the threat of French control of Europe, and the diplomat Sir William Temple made a Triple Alliance (1668) with Holland and Sweden, the two other Protestant powers. This satisfied Parliament, and all seemed well.

But Charles had not the slightest intention of letting Parliament run his foreign policy for him. He meant to be king indeed, and needed for rule only a source of money independent of Parliament. This he found in his cousin Louis. For Louis had become with advancing age more and more religious and had finally married as his second wife a converted Huguenot, Madame de Maintenon. He started a campaign of driving the Huguenots out of France. This naturally disturbed the English who had sentimental ties with the Huguenots. Louis naturally shared Charles's desire to make England Catholic. Charles and Louis made an agreement. All that the English people knew of the meeting at which this was settled was that the King's sister Henrietta, who had married Louis's brother Philippe, Duke of Orleans, came to Dover to see her brother Charles. But the pair secretively made long-range plans for the future of England. When "Minette" and Charles parted, an annual subsidy was agreed upon and one of her ladies in waiting, Louise de Kéroualle, had been installed as King's favorite and message carrier. (Her son by Charles was made Duke of Richmond and was Charles James Fox's grandfather.) Thus by the Treaty of Dover of 1670 Charles got everything he wanted—help in becoming King by a subsidy independent of Parliament, and help in making England Catholic.

For this, naturally, a return had to be made. This took the form of help for France against her rival in religion and trade, Holland. In 1672 Louis made a surprise attack and nearly overran Holland. The situation was so critical that the Dutch revolted against their own government, killed the key leaders, and installed as Stadtholder the twenty-two-year-old William of Orange, the great-grandson of the first William of Orange, and son of Charles's sister Mary, who was thus a potential heir to the English throne. His heroic resistance stemmed the tide and saved Holland. For Holland had had to fight alone. Sweden had been bought off, as had England. Indeed Charles seized the opportunity to advance his program of strengthening his power. Two days before the war broke out he used the royal pardoning power to let out of jail not merely individual offenders but by a Declaration of Indulgence all, whether Puritan or Catholic, who had broken a religious law. Then he declared war against Holland. But England's heart was not in the war. She lost New York, which she had taken in the Second Dutch War, and which Charles had given to his brother James, to get it back only at peace. Furthermore, Parliament feared that Charles had been too lenient to Catholics, and so it passed the Test Act. This required every officeholder—not merely those holding borough offices—to submit a certificate that he had attended a Church of England Communion service. A Dissenter could probably comply with this requirement, for most Dissenters accepted the Church of England Communion. But no Catholic could, for to do that would be to deny the Mass. To the surprise of many, James, Duke of York, thereupon resigned the office of Lord High Admiral and thus avowed himself a Catholic. Pressure was so great that Charles finally switched sides, and England actually ended the war fighting with Holland against France. True to his policy of making others take the blame, Charles put the Cabal out of power and replaced it by the Earl of Danby. He also talked Louis into continuing the subsidy. But Charles had learned his lesson. No longer did the Catholics receive open favor. Not again did he try the device of a blanket pardon. For the events of the Third Dutch War were showing that Charles was losing his hold on the Cavalier Parliament and had better do something about it.

Charles had done well in managing Parliament. He could make friends easily, and he did so with the leading lords and commoners. Where personal charm was not enough, a little judicious patronage helped. Jobs that paid well were handed out to members of both houses but were promptly lost if they voted wrong. Thus he built up a "court party" which persuaded Parliament in most cases to do as he wanted. Charles also did well in running his other two kingdoms, Scotland and Ireland. In Scotland no Stuart king ever had real trouble, except when the nobles used physical force against them. Therefore the Stuarts, once they lived outside Scotland, were able to rule strongly. Charles let the Duke of Lauderdale and others rule Scotland for him and reinstalled bishops in the Presbyterian Church to prevent any religious challenge to his authority. Only the more extreme Presbyterians, such as the Cameronians, resisted. These took to the hills of Western Scotland, fought guerrilla action, demanded to be allowed to meet and hear their own preachers, and were harried by John Graham, later Viscount Dundee, in what Scots still speak of as "the Killing Time." These bitter Presbyterians gained the name of Whiggamores, or Whigs for short, and were the only ones to resist Charles's carefully moderate but power-absorbing policy. In Ireland, Lord Ormonde, that tough old Cavalier, still ruled, and still somehow held the balance even between Catholic and Protestant. He made it possible for Cromwell's soldiers, who had been paid in land, to live with the native Irish, and successfully followed Strafford's policy of acting through the Irish Parliament with the check of Poynings's Law, which required final English ratification. To Ormonde, who had been made a duke—a cheap reward—there was only one armed opposition, that of Irish Catholic guerrillas in the bogs, the so-called Tories. By their existence, these men kept alive memories of the massacres of Protestants in 1642. Thus Charles, without a standing army except for the Guards and the regiments at Tangier, had real control over all three kingdoms, more than either of his Stuart predecessors.

However, this position rested wholly on Charles's control of Parliament. If some new Pym arose and took it from him, all the King's plans of becoming absolute and gradually introducing Catholicism would fall to the ground. A new Pym arose in the person of Anthony Ashley Cooper, whom the King had made Earl of Shaftesbury. England was growing uneasy about her king. It was becoming obvious that something was wrong in the way Charles was running the country. He might be the same gay blade—gambling, racing, shooting, playing tennis, joking with his courtiers, laughing with his actress favorite Nell Gwynn as well as with Louise de Kéroualle—but it was being noticed that he was doing nothing about what was going on across the water where Louis was absorbing more and more land and was consolidating his power and his nation's wealth through the able efforts of his minister, Colbert. French trade was challenging English; the French navy was growing apace. Huguenots were being persecuted and fleeing to Holland and England. Yet in England no such measures were being taken with the Queen, James, Duke of York, and his new Catholic Duchess and somehow the King was richer than he ought to have been according to the sums voted to him. Here was material for an able agitator who could arouse Parliament against the King. All that was needed was a dramatic incident to focus men's attention, something like the stories of massacres in Ireland that had triggered off the Grand Remonstrance, the incident of the Five Members, and thus the Civil War.

That incident came in the murder of the man who was unofficial chief of police and head of the secret service, Sir Edmund Berry Godfrey. It had long been recognized that the job of justice of the peace in Westminster was a full-time one. In the area around the Houses of Parliament and Whitehall Palace it was not enough to rely on different country gentlemen to meet different crises by summoning their servants to be constables. Some one man should assume the duty of protecting King and Parliament and either arresting political prisoners or tactfully letting them get away. He should have permanent constables and be ready to act at a moment's notice. So the custom grew up of giving a pension to one justice called the Court Justice, and expecting him to earn his pension by acting as chief of police. He usually had his headquarters in New Scotland Yard; in modern times the London police force has evolved out of this informal arrangement. In 1678 Sir Edmund Berry Godfrey was Court Justice. He began investigating suspicious behavior on the part of friends of the Duke of York and thereafter was found with his head bashed in. An arrant impostor, Titus Oates, came forward and swore he had seen the murder. On his testimony the Duke of York's secretary was arrested and found to have papers describing a plot to make England Catholic and let in the French. At once the hunt was on. Anyone Oates accused was as good as dead. When in the court room he croaked "Tory" at a reluctant witness, the jury no more believed that witness than it would have a real Tory from the Irish bogs.

Here was Shaftesbury's chance. He took it. He found that Danby—to whom England owes much since he had married James's daughter, Mary, to William of Orange—was implicated in the subsidy payments from France and had him impeached. Fortunately for Danby, Lords quarreled with Commons over whether a peer could be impeached when Lords had already jailed him, and Danby escaped on that technicality. It was believed that Sir Edmund Godfrey could have saved his life had he carried a flail to defend himself, and Shaftesbury used that belief as a pretext for organizing a gang of "brisk boys" armed with "Protestant flails." These were useful for terrorizing his opponents. He also organized the "Green Ribbon Club" of rich merchants and his political supporters, who got him money for electioneering. Such forces he used to back a political program. James, Duke of York, was to be excluded from the throne and in his place would be put—legitimatized by act of Parliament—the popular and Protestant Duke of Monmouth. Thus Shaftesbury founded perhaps the first true political party in English history, one with vote-getting election machinery as well as followers in Parliament.

Election machinery was needed. For Charles, when he saw that he had lost control of the Cavalier Parliament, promptly dissolved it, even though its successor was filled with Shaftesbury's followers, whom men nicknamed Whigs after the Scotch Whiggamores. This Parliament of 1679–1680 was deadlocked. Shaftesbury controlled the Commons; Charles controlled the Lords, but only by a thin margin. This Parliament passed only one important measure, and that for a joke. Shaftesbury knew that the clause in the Petition of Right promising no arbitrary arrest was useless unless there was punishment for those refusing to bring a prisoner to court when a writ of habeas corpus was issued. Therefore a bill full of stringent punishments was passed in Commons. In Lords it apparently was also passed, since as a joke the Whigs counted a very fat lord as ten. Charles signed the bill, anyway. It was a popular measure, and as long as he appointed the judges he knew he could find a way around it. This Parliament he dissolved, but the next one, of 1680, was as Whiggish. However, this new Parliament failed in its main work, the Exclusion Bill to keep James of York from the throne. This was due to a great leader in the Lords, George Savile, Marquis of Halifax, who openly took credit for being willing to change sides. He said he did it as a sailor would throw his weight against the movement of the ship, to "trim" it level. He joined the unpopular side and blocked Exclusion. He also showed that Oates was an impostor. At this Charles dissolved Parliament once more. The next Parliament, that of 1681, he summoned to meet at Oxford, where the "brisk boys" could not swing their flails. When it had lost its energy, he dissolved it too, by a sudden surprise. It had long been his custom to listen to debates in the Lords, where no rule excluded him. One day he appeared followed by a second sedan chair. As crude jokes were being made as to which mistress had followed him, he took out his special robes and dissolved Parliament.

Then he struck, and struck hard. Shaftesbury he drove into exile. He revived Edward I's writ of quo warranto, for the purpose of attacking not feudal courts but borough and other charters. By reissuing charters he made the boroughs "Tory" and so any future Parliament Tory. Fortified by loyal support in key positions and by Louis's subsidy, Charles could now rule as he chose, so long as he remained in the good graces of the now dominant Tory party. But since the party was more Anglican than he liked, he still lacked complete freedom of action.

16

THE GLORIOUS REVOLUTION

At the end of his reign, Charles II had secured administrative control of England, but so cleverly had he proceeded that the English hardly realized it. He had ended the independence of the boroughs by using the writ of quo warranto. Thus he had temporarily closed London as a Whig and opposition center, for with a Tory sheriff and a Tory Lord Mayor, the city was run as the Tories chose—which meant that London juries would convict those that Charles wanted convicted. If Charles had to take the advice of those on his Privy Council, that mattered not, for the Privy Council contained enough for his own supporters to advise him as he wanted to be advised. In fact, thanks to Louis's subsidy, he no longer needed to call Parliament, but if he had had to, the Tory-managed boroughs would have given him a Parliament he could have coaxed into doing as he chose. Had Charles had a legitimate heir who approached him in the same ability, the liberties of England would have been in great danger.

The extent of Charles's control was shown by what he did when a revolt threatened. A group of Whig extremists hatched a wild plot to capture him as he rode back from Newmarket to Westminster. They took over a house (still standing) on the Great North Road, the Rye House, whence they could sally forth to the attack. Being extremists, they talked too much, and the plot was discovered. Charles seized the chance to use this discovery for the Tories as Shaftesbury had used the "Popish Plot" for the Whigs. In particular, on very flimsy evidence, he had tried and executed the Earl of Bedford's son, William, Lord Russell, and a stern ex-Puritan, Algernon Sidney, both of whom were merely outspoken believers in the right of Parliament to give orders to the King. These men were railroaded, with the result that so often takes place in England after an unjust trial; they became martyrs. Men remembered how Rachel, Lady Russell, sat by her husband, taking notes of evidence to aid him in his hopeless defense, and they remembered the courage both men showed at their execution. Soon men were speaking again, as had the Parliamentarians of the 1640's, of "the Good Cause," and describing it as the cause for which "Hampden died in the field, Sidney and Russell on the scaffold." However, despite this discontent, when Charles died in 1685, he handed over to his brother James more real power, perhaps, than any of the previous Stuart sovereigns had possessed.

Charles's death was dramatic. First of all, Bright's disease was then unknown, and consequently it was believed he had been poisoned. Then, on his deathbed, Charles at last acknowledged his Catholicism. He sent for Father Huddleston, the priest who had sheltered him after Worcester, and from him received Extreme Unction. Thus he passed on to James the idea that England had a Catholic king and that James was merely succeeding another Catholic.

James should have had an easy time. The "high" members of the Church of England were preaching the new doctrine of nonresistance. They said it was wrong to resist a king; it had been sinful to resist Charles I, and it would be sinful to resist any king, were he as wicked as Nero. England was in a mood to make much from James, as long as he did not go too far. Charles had found ways around the letter of the law that the English would accept. All James had to do was to continue in those ways.

But James had no discretion. He started off his reign by technically violating the Petition of Right. He ordered tunnage and poundage collected even before a new Parliament could vote them to him. Tunnage and poundage were so voted, at once, but he had started with an unnecessary black mark against him. Then his nephew, James, Duke of Monmouth, made a wild try at invading England. With a very few followers he landed at Lyme Regis, in Dorsetshire, and tried to collect an army. The peasants came out for "King Monmouth," but the country gentlemen saw the attempt was hopeless, and did not support him. James sent down his guards, and at Sedgemoor the brave peasants almost succeeded in defeating the royal troops by a night attack, but were prevented in large part by General John Churchill, the second in command. Then Monmouth was captured and executed. This victory James misused. Some of the abuse of it was not his fault. A cavalry regiment just back from Tangier, and nicknamed Kirke's Lambs because they were anything but lambs, used on Englishmen methods more fitted for Moorish tribes. Then James sent down his Chief Justice, Judge Jeffreys, who was suffering from gallstones and in a vicious temper, to hold a special assize. This gained the name "the Bloody Assizes" from his vindictive handling of the prisoners in the dock and his savage sentences after he had browbeaten juries into convicting.

James now decided to make sure of his control of England. He brought all the troops he could find—30,000 in all, a vast army for those days—to Hounslow Heath, for the express purpose of overawing London. To officer this army, James called on Catholics, in spite of the Test Act. He merely granted them pardons in advance for such violations and, in the case of one officer whom somebody did prosecute, got his judges, whom he could dismiss, to declare that such a pardon held good. After that he even sent to Ireland to get some of the original Tories to fill the ranks of his army. No wonder the English thought their religion in danger, especially as at this moment Louis XIV revoked the Edict of Nantes and exiled the Huguenots. James then decided to revive the now illegal Court of High Commission, to which he assigned the duty of legalizing the appointment of Roman Catholic priests to positions in the Church of England. Having put this strain on the doctrine of nonresistance, he went further. He revived Charles's unsuccessful idea of a declaration of indulgence for all who violated the religious laws and ordered the clergy of the Church of England to read his declaration to their congregations. When seven bishops respectfully called on him and told him their objections, he had them tried for libel, being confident that a hand-picked jury would convict. Whig lawyers saved the "Seven Bishops" by pointing out that a libel must be published and that reading a statement in a private room is not publication.

Even before the trial of the Seven Bishops, matters had come to a head. It had been possible for the Protestant English to endure James's Catholic reign as an uncomfortable interlude, knowing he would be succeeded by his ardently Protestant daughter, Mary, the wife of William of Orange. But, twenty days before the trial, James's second wife gave birth to a son. This put a different complexion on matters, for should James be succeeded by an heir whom he had had brought up as a Catholic, England's religion would be lost. Already a rumor was sweeping England that the Queen had not had a child, but that a baby had been smuggled into the palace in a warming pan. Credence was somewhat possible, for James had had the foolishness to have only Catholics and courtiers as official witnesses to the birth. The fact was that, as the *Dictionary of National Biography* puts it, "The nation was prepared to disbelieve almost any evidence," as to the child's royal birth. With the nation in such a mood, the night the Seven Bishops were acquitted seven leaders, four Whigs and three Tories, headed by the Tory Danby, sent a letter to William, asking him to bring over an army to protect their liberties and promising him support if he did so. One of them, Admiral Russell, himself carried the treasonable document to William, to prove to William he would not meet with the reception which Monmouth had been given.

Such an expedition would be highly risky. Louis, who suspected it from the obvious preparations William had to make, was certain that if the attempt were made England would be torn by civil war. Therefore, fortunately for William, the French army was sent into the Rhineland, where it became so involved it could not make a counterinvasion of Holland. Despite the odds against him, William did make the attempt. Taking with him the English regiments in Dutch service and Dutch and Danish veterans, he set sail. James's navy pretended to come out to intercept William but purposely went down an estuary of the Thames where the tide held it back till too late. A strong east wind blocked William's original plan of landing in Yorkshire but earned from grateful Englishmen, after the event, the name "the Protestant wind." For it helped prevent James's fleet from getting to sea, hurried William along till he reached Torbay in Devonshire, and then veered, allowing him to land, on November 5, the anniversary of the day the Gunpowder Plot had been discovered.

England was ready to rise to join William, and the fact that he had landed in a distant part of the country made it possible for the news of his coming to spread and the people to take action before any fighting could take place. Perhaps that saved England from the civil war Louis had expected. As in 1641, news from Ireland was stirring up the English, with rumors of an invasion army about to come over. Richard Talbot, Earl of Tyrconnel, had replaced the old Duke of Ormonde and was putting Protestants down and Catholics up. About this Thomas Wharton (later Lord Wharton) had written a doggerel song, "Lilliburlero," telling of James's plot with Talbot. The words of the song have largely been forgotten, but its catchy tune carried them all over England while they were still topical. Wharton later claimed that he had "whistled a king out of three kingdoms." Certainly, whether the song was cause or effect, it became a symbol of the united English resistance, that spread so fast that James lost England without striking a serious blow. For it did no good to send troops to attack William. Only one skirmish is recorded. In it, Irish troops of James's were beaten by native Englishmen under William. Then as English advance guards met the English regiments of the Dutch army, they went over and joined them. Probably John Churchill saw to it that only troops that would go over went to the front. Later James's younger daughter, Anne, along with Sarah Churchill, fled to join William and her sister Mary. James did try to call out the militia, but the lord lieutenants, almost to a man, were already assembling volunteers to fight for William, not James. What rallied Englishmen to William was his policy and his promise. It could be seen on the banner William had borne in front of him, pledging he would maintain the Protestant religion and the liberties of Parliament. At Westminster pressure was put on James, and the idea was allowed to slip into his head that England could not do without a king. James fell into this trap, threw the Great Seal into the Thames (whence it was later fished up), and tried to leave England. This saved William much trouble, for had James stayed to face the music, he could have made the same sort of trouble that so exasperated Parliament when Charles I was its prisoner. William was aware of this and, when James was captured by some fishermen, sent him under guard of Dutch troops to the seacoast, whence James escaped with such ease that a less flustered man might have seen a trap. By the end of 1688 England was without a king.

Under English law there could be no government without a king, and no one wanted to be outside the law. The experience of Cromwell's rule made all agree to that. Therefore it became necessary to find a legal loophole. For advice William called together the surviving members of the last fairly elected Parliament, that which Charles had dissolved at Oxford in 1681. Its members, not unexpectedly, advised him to follow the precedent of 1660 and summon a Convention, which was done using the election lists as they were before quo warranto had put the boroughs under royal control. Then William sat back, as Monck had in 1660, and waited for the inevitable to happen. He, along with Halifax, saw how things would have to turn out. The rest spent a month getting to the same point. Some wanted William to take over as regent for his uncle James. But this would no more have worked than it did when Richard of York took over as regent for Henry VI; sooner or later there would have been an attempt to end the regency. Some wanted William elected king, just as he had been elected Stadtholder in Holland. But that would not have worked, for one great party, the Tories, centered its whole belief on loyalty to the throne, and was engaged in this revolution only because it loved the Church of England more than it loved one particular Stuart. Some wanted to replace James by his daughter Mary. But that would have been a clumsy way of putting William in power, which he rejected, saying he would not be "gentleman usher" to his wife. As men began to see that none of these plans would work, Halifax was able to get attention to his plan. It would be declared that the throne was vacant and that James had abdicated. A formula was worked out to this effect that was not strictly logical but that had the great advantage that both Whigs and Tories were willing to subscribe to it. Then the vacancy would be filled by offering the crown to William and Mary.

William and Mary were to rule jointly, with William having sole power when he was in England. That would prevent a conflict of orders. If Mary died before William, he would continue King but could be succeeded only by Mary's children. Children by any second wife would have to yield to Mary's sister Anne and any children she might have. Thus it was that Halifax followed the precedent of 1399, and rearranged the succession to the throne within the royal family.

However, William and Mary did not succeed to the throne at once. First, the Convention presented to them a Declaration of Rights which listed all the things James had done wrong. He had levied money without Parliament's consent, he had set up a prerogative court, he had used the pardoning power to dispense with the laws, he had tampered with juries, he had asked undue bail, and above all, he had tried to subvert England's religion and had kept a standing army without the consent of Parliament.

Only when the Prince and Princess of Orange should acknowledge that these acts violated the rights of Englishmen would they be asked to accept the crown. England was determined that in the future those who should reign over her should know the limits of their powers.

Thus it was that with the Glorious Revolution one era in England's constitutional history ended and another began.

17

TRANSITION: THE REVOLUTION SETTLEMENT

On February 13, 1689, a great historic drama was enacted in the Banqueting Hall of Whitehall Palace. There, in the room from which Charles I had stepped to his execution, his grandson and his granddaughter, the Prince and Princess of Orange, were proffered the Declaration of Rights. This document, drawn up by the Lords and Commons of the Convention, listed certain "undoubted rights and liberties" of England. Only after the recital of these did the Marquis of Halifax step forward to voice the Convention's resolve that "William and Mary, prince and princess of Orange, be and be declared king and queen of England, France, and Ireland and the dominions thereunto belonging." Then William, speaking for himself and his wife, "did accept the crown and royal dignity" and stated that he and his wife "were pleased that the said lords spiritual and temporal, being the two houses of parliament, should continue to sit." There is no need here to go into the constitutional arguments about the validity of this offer, acceptance, and transformation of a Convention into a Parliament. As has been well and succinctly stated by F. W. Maitland in his *Constitutional History of England,* this was unconstitutional and revolutionary, no matter how peaceably it was done. Nor is it necessary to go into the arguments that led Tories for one set of reasons, Whigs for another, to agree on the legal fiction that James II had abdicated the throne on December 11, 1688, and that after two months' interregnum a new reign had begun. These were special pleadings of the sort that make it easier to give up old established ideas. What matters is that the Lords and Commons of the Convention spoke for almost all the people of England in stating what henceforth would be the new relationship with the king or queen. The monarchy would still be hereditary, but it would be a limited monarchy. Consequently later generations have considered that with that new reign there also began a new era in history and have found it hard to remember that William, Mary, and their successor Anne belonged to the Stuart dynasty along with the Jameses and the Charleses.

For thus, at the end of the seventeenth century, the landed gentry, in alliance with the merchant class, won from a new set of Stuarts the rights for which they had been struggling against the earlier Stuarts. Henceforth the position of Parliament as against the Crown was made impregnable. It was now impossible to rule against Parliament or without Parliament, for the "undoubted rights and liberties" of the Declaration of Rights were those protections from the Crown recent experience had shown to be needful. Parliament consisted of the hereditary lords, who owned landed estates; the knights of the shires, who owned landed estates; and the burgesses of the boroughs and citizens of the cities, who either owned landed estates or were merchants. The benefits of the Declaration of Rights therefore gave power to the landowning class and the merchant class. Furthermore, local government in the counties was in the hands of the justices of the peace, who were landed gentry. In the boroughs and cities it rested in the hands of the chartered municipal corporations, composed of merchants. Again the pattern is followed. In this sense, there truly was a Revolution Settlement. The Convention that had assembled to take control in an emergency had settled the struggle for power of the Crown and the ruling class. When a change would come, it would come when a new ruling class would arise, at the time of the Reform Bill of 1832.

However, settling one problem often creates another. A new relationship had to be worked out between the king on the one hand and Parliament and those whom Parliament represented on the other. The key to this new relationship was that the new king was also the Stadtholder of Holland and that Holland and England were engaged in a struggle for survival against France. If Louis won the war then about to resume its course as the campaigning months began, the Protestant religion and the mercantile wealth of both Holland and England would be destroyed. Thus King William was indispensable to his English Parliament; his English Parliament was indispensable to Stadtholder William of Holland. King and Parliament were forced to cooperate, because they shared a common aim, even though they at times differed strongly as to the right way to attain that aim. In eight years of war, four of uneasy peace, and a winter of resumed war, this partnership would achieve results that certainly neither foresaw at the start. For out of the informal working arrangements that William and Parliament worked out there evolved a large part of Britain's "unwritten constitution." Temporary expedients became more and more permanent, until later generations considered them conventions of the constitution. For though at the start William was "a real working, governing king—a king with a policy," as Maitland puts it in his *Constitutional History*, Parliament insisted on sharing the making and administering of policy. And, to get what he wanted in the struggle with Louis, William was increasingly compelled to allow Parliament to take such a share.

The Declaration of Rights did not settle merely the way that England should be ruled, it also settled the religious question. By its terms, the

Protestant Stuarts should reign. During his life William would be king, to be followed by any children he and Mary might have. Then would come Anne and her children, and only after that any children William might have by a second marriage. As long as Anne had a living child, William, Duke of Gloucester, this ensured England a Protestant Stuart dynasty. Later on, in December, 1689, when the Declaration of Rights was reenacted into law as the Bill of Rights, clauses were added forbidding a Catholic or the husband or wife of a Catholic from holding the throne, thus making the Protestant religion doubly secure. But this did not settle what kind of Protestantism England would have. Would the Church of England continue to oppress a Nonconformist minority? Would that minority be "comprehended" into the Church of England? Or would the Clarendon Code be relaxed, as a reward for the loyalty the Nonconformists had shown in time of crisis? As in 1662, comprehension was tried, and failed of passage. Instead by the Act of Toleration the Clarendon Code was not repealed but by-passed. It was enacted that any who accepted thirty-five of the Thirty-nine Articles of belief of the Church of England by either an oath or a declaration—which thus included Quakers—would be freed from its restrictions. Only Roman Catholics and Unitarians and a few extreme Protestants would in any way remain oppressed. Thus the Revolution Settlement protected the religious causes for which the Revolution had been made.

It is sometimes thought that freedom of the press was part of the Revolution Settlement. This is not correct, except in so far as it was in the spirit of the times and was secured during this reign. In 1693, when the Licensing Act was about to expire, the censor was tricked into allowing the publication of a pamphlet asserting William of Orange had conquered England. This made the licensing of books so ridiculous that the Licensing Act was continued for only two years and then allowed to expire.

Scotland and Ireland, too, had their Revolutions of 1688/89, but they were less glorious and did not lead to final settlements. When news came to Scotland of William's landing, the course of events in the larger kingdom was with some differences followed in the smaller. Popular excitement drove James's officials from power or caused them to turn to William. A Convention was called. Its Scottish members had none of the reluctance about getting rid of a king that had been shown by the law-abiding English. Enough Stuarts had been driven out or kidnaped to make the Scots willing to do it again. James was declared to have "forefaulted" the crown, which was offered along with a Claim of Right to William and Mary. Naturally, William accepted, but only after he had checked carefully as to what was meant by the "extirpation of heresy" in its phrasing. For he feared, and feared rightly, that the Scotch Presbyterians would now persecute the Scotch Episcopalians in revenge for the persecution that they had suffered under Charles II and James II. Out of this came a religious settlement of sorts, whereby first of all bishops were abolished and then, the next year, the General Assembly of the Kirk was revived. However, in the homeland of the Stuarts, there were men who would fight to keep James on the throne. John Graham, Viscount Dundee, who had persecuted the Presbyterians during the "Killing Time," took the field. Like his illustrious namesake, James Graham, Marquis of Montrose, he raised the Highland clans for James. In July, 1689, he routed the Lowland troops at Killiecrankie but died in the hour of victory. Thereafter, resistance fell apart. In 1691 it was possible to disarm the clans. In 1692, by a shabby plot, the Macdonalds of Glencoe were massacred for failure to comply with the letter of the disarmament proclamation. So the Revolution came to Scotland, restoring her General Assembly, giving her Parliament a freedom it had never had before, but leaving disaffected clans in the Highlands as material for a revolt for James. Hereafter Scotland ruled herself more than ever before in her history. She even tried for a colonial empire, adventuring her hard-won savings in the Darien adventures of 1695. This attempt to gain a colony in Central America roused the jealousy of the English, who would not give it protection or support, and ended in disaster and bankruptcy. It left behind it a double legacy—anger at England for leaving the Scots in the lurch, determination that somehow Scotland would gain a share of England's overseas wealth. The first emotion hindered the Union of England and Scotland, the second eventually helped bring it about. Of this a later chapter will tell.

In Ireland what broke out was not a Glorious Revolution but a counter-revolution. There the news of James's flight and William's taking over was received with pleasure, but for a different reason. The Catholic Irish realized that if they stuck by James when the English ousted him they could become independent of England and masters of their own island. The Lord Deputy, Richard Talbot, Earl of Tyrconnel, promptly sent for French troops and for James, called a Parliament, and invaded Ulster, the Protestant stronghold. Protestants were harshly driven out, till only two places remained to them, a guerrilla base at Enniskillen and the besieged seaport of Londonderry. There, when the commander fled, the apprentice boys and other untrained citizens put up a marvelous resistance, even though supply by sea was cut off by an iron chain across Lough Foyle. Their motto—"No Surrender"—is an Ulster rallying cry to this day. The question was, could the Garrison Irish hold out against the returned James and his Irish and French troops till help came? Then, with that help, could they reconquer Ireland, at their Parliament repeal the pro-Catholic measures James's Parliament had passed, and restore the "Protestant Ascendancy"? This they did do, though the doing took three years and was disgraced by a broken promise. In July, 1689, the siege of Derry was raised by a naval expedition. The next year, William himself came over, and at the Battle of the Boyne defeated James. As the great Irish leader Patrick Sarsfield marched his men away while James fled, the retreating Irish shouted to the victors, with much justification: "Change kings and we'll fight you again." Even after that the Catholic Irish still held out. When besieged in Limerick, they fought off the siege. It was not until after the battle of Aughrim in 1692 and a second siege of Limerick that they surrendered on terms. Officers were allowed to leave Ireland if they wished. They did so, en masse. This took away from Ireland its native aristocracy, who went on to rule other lands. Such men were Prime Minister Taaffe of Austria, President MacMahon of France. The Irish at home spoke of them, poetically, as the Wild Geese who had flown across the sea and never acknowledged the supplanting English aristocracy as genuine. As for those who stayed behind, mostly enlisted men, William's general offered them peaceful occupation of their lands and their religion, subject to the consent of the English Parliament. But Parliament was not as generous as the general, nor as wise. The terms were violated, Penal Laws against the Catholics were piled up. Therefore the native Irish, who might have accepted a tolerant, just conquest, were oppressed for a century, rose to win a brief freedom, from 1783 to 1800, and then, after a century and a quarter of further struggle, won it definitely in 1921.

Here, therefore, is the situation that faced the Dutch king of England at the beginning of his reign, after he had supplanted his uncle and father-in-law, James II. He had restricted power in England and Scotland, having started off by a promise never to rule without or against Parliament. His kingdom of Ireland he held in subjection. In all three kingdoms, he must fear an attempt by "Jacobites" (*i.e.*, followers of James, in Latin *Jacobus*) to overthrow him. His Stadtholderate of Holland was at war with the French. His chief asset was that his English Parliament had asked him to declare war on France. Now, under war conditions—each summer campaigning on the military battlefields, each winter campaigning on parliamentary battlefields—he must make his English kingship work to save both England and his native Holland.

It will prove simpler to speak of the war front first and then of the home front, taking each story separately up to the peace of Ryswick of 1697. Holland had not entered unprepared the war that broke out in 1688. Already in 1686 there had been formed the League of Augsburg, comprising Sweden, Spain, the Empire, and some German states, for mutual protection against France. With this grouping William was in close touch and in May and September, 1689, respectively as Stadtholder of Holland and as King of England, he joined forces with the League by the Grand Alliance, having secured by September a Secretary of State in England who would take the responsibility of signing the alliance. This combination of powers grew wider and wider, till even the Pope came to its support. This was no small feat for the "Governor" of the Church of England when engaged in a war with His Most Christian Majesty of France. This fact may serve to show the spirit with which William handled the traditional "balance-of-power" policy. He, who had spent his whole adult life trying to stop Louis from conquering Holland, realized that the only way to stop one strong nation from conquering many weak states is to band those small states together, and that the only way to do that is to gain their trust. He therefore preached and practiced the doctrine of tolerance and fairness he believed in. When that could not persuade, judicious gifts of money could. Thus the instruments of William's policy were an Army, a Navy, and wealth, along with the attraction of the policy itself.

This policy of balance of power, of banding the many weak against the few strong and of appealing to principle to unite the weak, is the policy of a naval power. Under William, the British Navy grew more effective. Already, since Blake's time it had learned how to keep the seas the year round, winter and summer. In Charles II's reign Mr. Secretary Pepys and Lord High Admiral the Duke of York had preserved the standards of organization begun by Blake and the other generals-at-sea. But one thing was lacking still, an integrated officer corps. The generals-at-sea had been what their name implied, land officers in charge of ships. They knew strategy, but not sailing. Often George Monck had ordered, in his excitement, "Right wheel" instead of "Port your helm." On the other hand, the ordinary sea captains, the "tarpaulins" as they were called from their canvas sea clothes, who could give the right orders, did not understand military affairs. It was necessary to do for the Navy what the Long Parliament had done for the Army when it brought in professional standards with its "New Model." George Savile, Marquis of Halifax, saw this and in 1694 proposed a remedy in his pamphlet, A New Model at Sea. His ideas were taken up. Previously begun reforms were completed. No commissions were granted in the Navy except to "passed midshipmen," that is, to young men who had spent an apprenticeship at sea, neither among the sailors in the forecastle nor among the officers in the afterguard but amidships, learning from both, and who had then passed an examination in navigation. Thus future naval officers were recruited from the upper middle class and from the younger sons of country gentlemen. They were "bred to the sea" but also were educated in the principles of war. Because the English officer corps thus became as good ship handlers as the Dutch, as good sea soldiers as the French, the British Navy became increasingly dominant, and after 1692 may be said to have given William effective though not complete command of the sea.

Likewise during this period the British Army really took shape. The battle flags of the famous English regiments show that their oldest honors usually go back to this time, with such names as Neerwinden, Steenkerke, and Namur. For William and his Parliaments early realized that sending a few English soldiers as a reinforcement gave more courage to an ally than many times their cost in gold. Therefore, William coaxed from Parliament, year by year, consent to keeping more and more troops. After the custom of the times he would offer some distinguished soldier a fixed sum if he raised one or more battalions for a regiment, giving him and his officers commissions if the ranks were full. It was profitable and honorable to be colonel of a regiment; indeed, William fixed a scale for the purchase of commissions in regiments which hung on to plague the British Army till 1872. Within limits each regiment was run as its colonel chose. This saved trouble and allowed the building up of pride in the unit. Just as our Seventh Cavalry marches to the tune of "Garryowen" because Custer liked it, many British regiments have some peculiarity they keep up: a special badge, a custom going back to a famous battle, special privileges that keep the men keen. Morale in the British Army early reached a very high point. It became a tradition for officers who had any money at all to spend it for the benefit of "the regiment," so that then as now English aristocrats willingly served in the army at a serious financial loss. The standards of technical skill were perhaps not as high as in the Navy; the Navy has usually been the more intelligent service, the Army the more aristocratic. But the standard of courage was very high. One English general, Lord Cutts, won the name of the "Salamander" because like that legendary animal he seemed to love to be in fire.

The actual fighting of the war of the League of Augsburg was not spectacular. At sea there was a dangerous moment, when in 1690 a combined Anglo-Dutch fleet, at Beachy Head, engaged the French against the will of its commander, because of stringent orders. This defeat, which took place the day before the Battle of the Boyne, gave the French temporary command of the sea, which they failed to use properly. Then, in 1692, command of the sea was won back at La Hogue. Though it was never complete, as in the sad moment when the Levant convoy was captured in 1695, thereafter William could move troops and supplies to the continent with confidence and need fear no invasion of Ireland. On land, after Ireland had been secured, the war consisted of maneuvers and sieges in Belgium, which was then the Spanish Netherlands. Usually William wisely refrained from meeting Louis's superb army in the open field, but marched back and forth from city to city, building forts and bringing in supplies. In this war of fortresses at first Louis's marshals won some of the races and captured key points. Then William by sheer organizing power got into the field earlier each year, thus got the initiative, and by the courage of his British infantry began recapturing what had been lost.

Finally he recaptured the key city of Namur, and took prisoner one of the legendary marshals of France. That finally convinced Louis that he could not win and that all the war would do would be to exhaust France's strength. Then William was able to negotiate peace, by the Treaty of Ryswick in 1697.

All this had been accomplished not only because England could provide a Navy and an Army for the League of Augsburg, but because she had growing wealth. The national debt, the Bank of England, and recoinage all played their part. In 1692 it became clear that taxes were not raising enough money. Charles Montagu, therefore, proposed that annuities guaranteed by the assignment of taxes be sold to the public. Thus he raised a loan of a million pounds. Two years later, in 1694, he raised £1,200,000 by persuading Parliament to take up the idea of the Scotsman, William Paterson, and to incorporate the subscribers as the Governor and Company of the Bank of England. The bank could issue notes to be used as money and agreed to act as receiver and payer of monies for the government. In 1696, Montagu went further, and called in all the coins then current for reissue. During this period, in order to meet the needs of the nation for means of exchange, he issued the first government short-term loans, called Exchequer Bills. These were largely war measures, for they brought money into the Exchequer or made dealing with money easier. But in the long run they created wealth. Government bonds, which soon followed the annuities, became a form of transferable wealth that allowed larger-scale capital transactions and so fostered the growth of the London money market. The Bank of England became a bank for London bankers. Thus the war pushed forward the replacement of Amsterdam by London as the chief money market of Europe. England came out of the war economically stronger than she went in and therefore that much more powerful in world affairs.

So far there have been related affairs on the war front and those home-front developments that had bearing on the war front. Now let us turn to the political and constitutional events of this reign. This was a period when King and Parliament learned how to bargain with each other. At times reasoning obtained agreement between them; at times it did not. Each side had weapons it could use. The King's were the veto, dissolution, and patronage; Parliament's were refusal of supply and the passage of annual legislation. Parliament got its innings in first, when in the spring of 1689 it established three principles. As has been said, it made clear to William that if he wanted support for a war he had better not use the royal power to declare war without a previous vote from Parliament. Then it gave him the revenues he needed for the conduct of the government not for life, as in the past, but for four years. Then trouble in disbanding James's troops revealed to Parliament perhaps its most powerful weapon against the crown. The troops that had been loyal to James were being shipped over to the Low Countries, when mutiny broke out at Ipswich. Hurriedly, an act was passed allowing courts-martial to punish mutiny, sedition, and desertion. But the act was to expire on November 10, 1689, for there was no intention of going back on the Declaration of Rights. Here was, in embryo, the device of the annually expiring law. Every year thereafter a Mutiny Act was passed, but William had to bargain for it, and the act strictly limited the size of the army. Indeed, there were times in his reign and Anne's when for a short period there was no Mutiny Act. Thus Parliament found that its lawmaking power enabled it to control the King. To law after law were added similar restrictions. Finally, in the 1880's, long after the need of such devices had ended, an Expiring Laws Continuance Act was passed, to allow the repassage of such acts without the labor of going over them each year clause by clause. This sort of thing made William walk warily and make sure that he had Englishmen help share the responsibility of his actions, as when he secured a Secretary of State who would sign the Grand Alliance for him. But in the winter of 1689–1690 William had his innings, too.

For the tolerant William wanted to get rid of any punishment for the past before the Revolution. His first Parliament was Whiggish and looked forward to proscribing Tories. He therefore dissolved it, called an election in the spring of 1690, and used all the power of the crown to aid the Tories. In many a borough a few government officials held the balance of power either directly or by control—in days of open voting that was easier—of the votes of others. For example, the "tidewaiters" or customs officials of Dover made so large a part of that borough's electorate that the Lord Treasurer used merely to send Dover a message whom to elect. By the use of Treasury boroughs and Treasury influence in boroughs, besides making appeals to key men, William put the Tories in power and got through a decent act of amnesty. Then when in 1693 the Tories began being a nuisance in the way they blocked his war effort, he turned his favor to the Whigs, and began giving Whig members of Parliament jobs. Thus the idea of a two-party system of government began to grow up. It was aided by the passage of the Triennial Act of 1694, which required a new Parliament to be elected every three years.

Thus during William's reign—Mary died in 1694, which left the throne to William with her sister Anne as heiress—the English people got plenty of practice in politics and electioneering. Gradually the idea sank into the minds of the English that a political defeat could be taken in a sporting way, since there would always be another election soon. With this rising spirit of fair play some old methods fell into disuse. Impeachment with all its red tape and pompousness was largely abandoned when it was found that "refusing supplies" would secure the dismissal of an official far more quickly. The savage acts of attainder were given up completely. In 1696 there was an attempt to murder William as he crossed a ford near Windsor Castle. Besides those obviously guilty, one Sir John Fenwick seemed, as in so many spy cases, to be implicated but not in a way that could be proved in a court of law. In anger the Whigs attainted him, only to realize later on that he was no more than a sympathizer with James II. Never since then has Parliament used an act of attainder.

On the king's side, the veto became disused. William found that it irritated individuals to have him refuse assent to measures. Since his reign it was used once by Anne, and never again. But though it irritated some to have him give posts to members of Lords and Commons, William persisted in doing this. This caused the constant introduction of "place bills." These were intended to forbid any member of the House of Commons from holding any other office. Somehow, they never got passed. Once Lords threw out what Commons accepted, once Commons threw out what Lords accepted, and twice William used his power of veto. For many officeholders wanted not to lose the jobs they held, and some others vaguely saw that if Parliament were to control the king it would be wise for members of Parliament to help run the government. Finally, in 1700, it became necessary to meet a constitutional crisis. The Princess Anne's son, William, Duke of Gloucester, had died. With the deaths of William and Anne, the Protestant Stuart line would become extinct, with one exception. In Hanover there lived the first cousin of Charles II and James II, the Electress Sophia. It would be therefore necessary to settle the succession to the throne.

There was some desire to bring James II back. English believers in nonresistance refused to take an oath to William and Mary. Four of the Seven Bishops thus became "nonjurors," and vacated their sees rather than give up allegiance to the king who had oppressed them. There were those, mainly country squires, who, when they drank the king's health passed their wine glass over a water glass, thus drinking to "the King over the Water." In exile with the Court at Saint-Germain were valiant fighting men. Such were the noble Patrick Sarsfield, Earl of Lucan by James's creation, and the Scots and Irish regiments of the French army. But this was a small, though dangerous, minority. Much of the Jacobitism of the times was a form of insurance and counterespionage. Many an English statesman was in deceptive correspondence with James II. John Churchill, Earl of Marlborough, for example, when he was temporarily out of William's favor in 1694 sent to James a warning of an English attack on Brest, knowing that James already knew about it. William well understood this sort of thing and seems to have taken some effort not to know, officially, of this kind of correspondence. In sum, there was a genuine, though slight, possibility that the exiled Stuarts would return, and precautions had to be taken against some moment of confusion about the succession that might make such a return practical politics.

At this time there was much dissatisfaction with the Dutch friends whom William had brought over with him. Already, at the Peace of Ryswick, William had been compelled to send his Dutch guards home. Shortly thereafter Parliament had taken back from his Dutch favorites grants of land in Ireland. While Anne, the granddaughter of Edward Hyde, Earl of Clarendon, was thoroughly English in her sentiments, would Sophia or Sophia's German children be the same? Therefore the Act of Settlement of 1701 had tacked on to it two important constitutional clauses. When the House of Hanover should reign, judges would become undismissible, except upon an address of both houses of Parliament. William had been making undismissible appointments but would not give up the right of making dismissible ones. Then, on that far-off day, no member of the House of Commons might have a government post or pension.

With the Act of Settlement the constitutional evolution of this reign ended. But the struggle with Louis of France did not. Louis had been held in check because four large states—Spain, Austria, Holland, and England—had formed a league against him. A key to this League was Spain, which then held the Spanish Netherlands (Belgium), Milan, Naples, Sicily, and a vast overseas empire. But the King of Spain was about to die leaving no children and a disputed inheritance. Either a French or an Austrian prince would take over. This would incur two dangers: either France would become preponderant, or Austria would encircle France. During the four years of peace, 1697 to 1701, William tried to avoid these dangers by partition treaties. One attempt at finding a neutral heir broke down when the Electoral Prince of Bavaria died in 1699. A second partition treaty arranged for Archduke Charles of Austria to be king, with compensation for the French in Italy. But when Charles II of Spain died, he left his entire possessions to Louis's grandson. Louis accepted this, and William's troubles began again. Had Louis been diplomatic, Philip's inheritance might have gone off peaceably. But when French troops took over the Spanish Netherlands and Louis chose that moment, at James II's death, to proclaim his son King of England, both Holland and England were ready to fight and let the Stadtholder-King declare war.

But William never campaigned in this war. He was by now a weary man. A fall from his horse led indirectly to his death from pneumonia, and it was his heiress, Anne Stuart, in whose reign was fought the last and greatest war with Louis XIV of France. Gleefully the Jacobites toasted the "little gentleman in black velvet," the mole over whose hill William's horse had stumbled, who had thus brought down their greatest enemy. They were right in thus praising the mole, for William's reign had shut the door on the past for which they stood. But had it opened the door for the future? Here is a question that must be answered if that reign is to be properly assessed.

In the field of foreign affairs, this reign may be considered the first time for many centuries that England had a truly powerful force behind a clear-cut policy. Without going back to Henry V and the battle of Agincourt, the two high points of England's foreign policy previously had been first Elizabeth I's reign and then Cromwell and the Protectorate. From 1559 to 1601 Elizabeth had had an effective policy and force so inadequate she had to use privateers to augment her navy. From 1653 to 1659 Cromwell had had a powerful navy and an efficient army but had been isolated in foreign affairs. Under William, England had both power and policy. Here was clearly a change for the better. Yet not a complete change; France was still the preponderant nation in Europe.

In the field of economics, England gained financial strength. Her national debt became a sound investment; she had a central bank that strengthened the London money market. In 1698 a rudimentary London Stock Exchange was opened. Here again a new era seemed to open.

In the field of constitutional affairs, however, matters were different. What is typical of England today is the fusion of executive and legislative. The Crown is a symbol that holds together what is now called not the British Empire but the Commonwealth of Nations. In place of the King as executive are the Prime Minister and the Cabinet, who are members of one or the other house of Parliament. Today England has what is called "responsible" government, as opposed to the American system of the separation of the powers, often called in contrast "representative" government. In William's reign, England was governed much more as the United States is today. In fact, the structure of our Federal and state constitutions is modeled on England in the 1690's. Bills of Rights, "place bill" prohibitions on members of the legislature having executive posts, independence of the judiciary, prohibitions on acts of attainder, independence of the executive—all these are today distinctively American. The important difference, it would seem, between England at the end of the seventeenth century and America today is that representative government is rigidly written into our constitutions, whereas in England a loophole was left by which representative government evolved into responsible government.

This raises a question that may throw light on this and subsequent periods of British history. If, for the purposes of discussion, the modern period of British history begins when England both evolves responsible government and supplants France as the major European power, when did that modern period begin? Various dates are given for this. Sometimes the premiership of Robert Walpole, dated either 1721 or 1730, is chosen, since he is often considered England's first Prime Minister. Again, the premiership of the younger William Pitt, beginning in 1783, is chosen, since he wielded greater power, and since the Industrial Revolution was then gaining great momentum. Sometimes the year 1815, the end of the Napoleonic Wars, is chosen, for then the last great French effort at European ascendance was ended. Again, 1832, the year of the passage of the Reform Bill, can be considered the beginning of modern British history, for then the industrial and commercial middle classes got control of Parliament. Naturally, choice among these is largely a matter of definition of the word modern. But if the above definition is used, can it not be argued that modern British history began, not at these dates, not at 1688, but at 1704?

For while the Glorious Revolution meant a break with the past, it did not point toward the future. But in 1704 four things happened. By the battle of Blenheim, England permanently checked Louis's threat of dominance in Europe. By the seizure of Gibraltar she gained control of the mouth of the Mediterranean. By the naval battle of Malaga she gained full control of the sea. Above all, by these successes and the popular support that they gained, the group of politicians led by Lord Godolphin and the Duke of Marlborough held together a majority in Parliament that allowed them to take over practical executive control from Queen Anne. Let us therefore see whether the year of Blenheim can be considered a key year. For whether the answer be "Yes" or "No," the inquiry affords an opportunity for a general view of English history.

INTRODUCTION

At the end of the last chapter, it was suggested that the summer of 1704 formed a significant turning point in English history, perhaps even more significant than those usually emphasized. Here is an attempt to show the reader the situation as it was at the time, for him to judge its significance.

In the summer of 1704, the rulers of England had "put it to the touch, to win or lose it all." Her Army had been sent to disappear into the heart of Germany, there to fight against superior numbers. If it lost, French troops might soon be camped on the shores of the English Channel. Her Navy had similarly been sent out of sight, into the Mediterranean, to face the superior French Grand Fleet at Toulon. Should it fail to win against odds, those same French troops might cross the Channel. No wonder a heated English House of Commons was only prevented by adjournment from making it impossible for Lord Treasurer Godolphin to carry on the nation's business. No wonder a Scottish Parliament, which had not adjourned, forced through an Act of Security that would allow it to choose whomsoever it would as ruler of Scotland, when Queen Anne should die. No wonder that, in distant India, Governor Thomas Pitt wrote back: "I like not the appearance of public affairs at home and abroad. God send a miracle to save Old England." For the nation's future depended on what news came from the Army and Navy.

On August 10, 1704, a tired colonel rode into London, bearing with him as written credentials merely a note scribbled on the back of a tavern bill. Pausing only to show it to a lady of the Queen's court, he pushed on to give his oral report to the Queen at Windsor. But that note was enough to cause the cannon at the Tower of London to boom and the Londoners to go wild with joy. As hastily printed copies of it circulated through the streets, all might read what Captain General the Duke of Marlborough had told his wife. The French commander was a prisoner in his coach; the victory of Blenheim had put a check to Louis XIV's dream of European conquest. A month later, Admiral Sir George Rooke cast anchor at

Saint Helens with more news. He could tell how the door to the Mediterranean had been seized by the capture of the Rock of Gibraltar and how it had been slammed shut by the battle of Malaga. It had been a near thing on those distant fields of war. Perhaps only two men in all the army would have dared attack across the marshes at Blenheim; fortunately, those two had been the joint commanders, John Churchill, Duke of Marlborough, and Prince Eugene of Savoy. As for Rooke, he had had to burst his way from Malaga back to Gibraltar through fog and the French fleet, when some of his ships had hardly a round of shot left in their lockers. Narrow though the margin had been, the miracle had come. Old England had been saved; and Thomas Pitt's grandson and his great-grandson, both named William Pitt, would lead to an age of glory and achievement not England alone, but England and Scotland united into Great Britain.

While a single thread—the element of time—connects these events with each other, separate threads connect each of these events with different phases of the history of the eighteenth century. Gibraltar and Malaga ushered in an age of English command of the sea that won a world-wide empire. Blenheim struck France from the first place in Europe and made England her equal, if not her superior, thus changing English foreign policy. In the political field, the news of these two victories and the reception of that news set in motion a train of cause and effect that led to a long period of Whig ascendancy. In the constitutional field, it was this same reassurance that made possible union with Scotland. Furthermore, the changed political situation of the Godolphin Ministry had constitutional results, since Cabinet government in Great Britain evolved out of that Ministry's success in securing support in Parliament. Then, as one digs deeper, the Blenheim campaign points up a fundamental truth about the development of England in these years. That campaign was won, among other reasons, simply and prosaically because Marlborough's men had new shoes and ample rations. This happened because Mr. Davenant, the Treasurer of the Army, had been able to buy the food and shoes on the spot. He had been so able because Lord Treasurer Lord Godolphin had the money to give him, money that Parliament had voted from England's growing wealth. Trade and manufacture underlay England's statesmanship and strength. If this vignette of a dramatic moment in history brings out that truth, then it will have served its purpose and may be set aside while this chapter goes on to consider how the economic, constitutional, political, foreign-affairs, and imperial parts of English history fit together.

It should here be noted that from now on this book will follow this general pattern. For each period of English history, a chapter of general introduction will be followed by chapters on the economic background, on constitutional evolution, on politics, on foreign affairs, and on the Empire or, as it later became, the Commonwealth. It is believed that this treatment follows a logical sequence and will give order and meaning to the apparently complex events that will be dealt with. Now to return to the generalizations here broken off by generalizations as to the value of generalization.

It should not be imagined that this progress was undisturbed or even. Though the victories of Blenheim and Malaga did put England in the first rank of European powers and make her perhaps the greatest imperial power, she met defeats, like Fontenoy, on land. Even after she had, by the Treaty of Paris at the end of the Seven Years' War (1756 to 1763), become the leading world empire, with more territory, wealth, and industry than anyone had dreamed of, she met bitter defeat in the War of the American Revolution. Then, by another Treaty of Paris, that of 1783, she had to acknowledge the independence of thirteen of her twenty transatlantic colonies and lose yet others of those colonies to France and Spain.

In the years from 1704 to 1783, England—or Great Britain, as she had become after the union with Scotland in 1707—had made herself so wealthy and so powerful that loss of the American colonies merely opened a new chapter in the story of a people's rise to greatness. It was in these years that England laid the foundations for her paramount position in the world of the nineteenth century.

In order to sustain defeat, England had to acquire material wealth and prosperity and new skills by which to add to this wealth steadily in decade after decade. England could do this because of her institutions and the great vigor of her sons. With the economic development, known generally as the Industrial Revolution, an Agricultural Revolution went hand in hand. As forests were cut down and the wood used to make charcoal for blast furnaces became scarce, the English before this period had turned increasingly to the use of coal for all sorts of industrial purposes. Fortunately, coal, and the iron that coal smelted, were found in sufficient quantities and in close proximity so that ironmasters and miners could work side by side to expand the production of iron, one of the essential commodities for the needs of a new industrial society. Copper and tin, also mined in England, were available when needed. A population that grew from about four million at the turn of the century to about eight million, including the Scots in 1783, naturally increased the demand for heavy capital goods. The demand for woolen goods, cotton, and pottery also stepped up industrial production. With a growing population in the colonies, with new markets in India and the Mediterranean area, England, in 1783, was not only meeting the ever-increasing demands of her people at home but also satisfying the hunger for woven cloth of the Hindus, Americans, and Europeans.

Toward the end of this period, inventions by Arkwright, Hargreaves, and Crompton made possible the mechanical spinning of thread; Kay's flying shuttle of 1733 vastly speeded up the weaving of thread into cloth. When Watt had perfected condensers for steam engines, it would be possible to have a power-driven textile industry. In other industries, as well as in textiles, after 1750, the trend was to assemble machines in factories. Although old practices such as domestic weaving were kept up till such inventions as Cartwright's power loom should be made effective, the handwriting on the wall, foretelling the victory of the factory system, was there for all to read. As factories and mines turned out even more goods, workers flowed into the mills and mines in great numbers. The privates in the ranks of the industrial army came from the farms and villages. Often they were unwilling recruits, for the Agricultural Revolution had decreased the standard of living of thousands in England by forcing them from their ancestral occupations. New root crops, better methods of planting and reaping, and the development of livestock breeds for meat production required large farms. Those with the capital to undertake these new methods saw to it that the common land, which as open fields under strip cultivation had supported large numbers of small farmers, should be "enclosed" by acts of Parliament. These pieces of class legislation made it profitable for the English gentry to operate on a large scale, while many a small farmer was forced to the wall.

These tendencies had two divergent results. On the one hand, an industrial proletariat grew up in the towns, that heavily taxed the primitive sanitation of those days. This illiterate, underfed, and demoralized population would create social problems the solution of which would challenge succeeding generations. On the other hand, it was the production of iron and cloth, the expansion of exports and imports, the growing of so much grain that the English people changed their staple bread from rye to wheat that gave England the economic strength to win the Seven Years' War and stand the shock of losing most of her colonies.

A major cause for the industrial and agricultural rise of England was her constitution and government. Unlike many countries on the Continent, the central government in London did not attempt too close a regulation of industry. Though laws were on the books to protect domestic markets from foreign competition, within England there were no tariff barriers; and no man was prevented by law from engaging in ordinary trade or business. Initiative and enterprise were given the right of way. The Bank of England supported credit in London, and local banks developed in the provincial centers of trade and industry, particularly in the Midlands and in the North. Thus, the lifeblood of capitalistic endeavor —money—was made available for the new industries.

The laws of England operated in favor of those individuals who had the initiative and energy to develop business enterprise. One of the most important aspects of English life was that men of all opinions could trade and produce to their hearts' content, without interference from the state. The political restrictions on Dissenters and Catholics did not extend to the commercial sphere. Also important was the fact that from 1714 to 1739 there was no major war to drain resources or to call for heroic efforts on the part of the nation.

Within this period, there were three political subperiods, 1704 to 1714, 1714 to 1761, and 1761 to 1783. In the first subperiod, there was violent alternation between Whig and Tory in Parliament and a parallel violent alternation between Whig and Tory in the Privy Council of the Queen and in the Queen's personal circle. It is highly significant what varied political allies Marlborough and Godolphin had to call to their aid—first moderate Tories, then the Whig Junto—and what court allies they had to do their work with the Queen. It is highly significant that the change in Parliament, when Tories finally ousted the Whigs and with them Marlborough and Godolphin, coincided with the court change by which Abigail Hill broke up the friendship between Queen Anne and Sarah Churchill. This atmosphere of struggle explains the drama of Queen Anne's death day, when two dukes strode uninvited into the Privy Council meeting and forced the dying Queen to put the Lord Treasurer's white staff into the hands of yet a third duke. Then comes a sharp change in political history, when, for all practical purposes, one political party rules England. In it, there is intrigue; in it, constitutional conventions are quietly built up and strengthened. But the drama played on the political stage is quieter, except for occasional moments of crisis. The long political masteries of Sir Robert Walpole, often considered England's first Prime Minister, of Henry Pelham, and of the Duke of Newcastle—this last in alliance with the elder William Pitt—reduce the amount of significant political history.

In the period 1761 to 1782, a new alignment appears. King George III, from a sense of duty, takes more and more interest in the politics of England. Whoever may be the Prime Minister, he is the central figure. Indeed, it might well be said that at the end he was the true Prime Minister. Because he is so much the central figure, political history takes a special color, until the royal power is checked by the second Rockingham Ministry. Then, when the prime-ministership ascribed to Walpole is re-created and strengthened by the accession to power of the younger William Pitt, yet another period of political and constitutional history begins, to be dealt with in another section of this book.

Constitutionally it was during these years that Sir Robert Walpole worked out the Cabinet system and made the House of Commons the principal instrument of government in the Empire. The power of the

Crown remained great and in principle unchanged, but the practice was so altered that Parliament attained even greater powers and occupied an even greater position in the constitution in 1782 than in 1704.

Of equal importance with the development of the Cabinet system is the way in which England was governed locally. Contrary to what was taking place on the Continent at this time, the central government exercised very little control over local government. The work of the Tudors had been well and thoroughly done. Justices of the peace continued, as they did into the nineteenth century, as unpaid servants of society. Through the lord lieutenants and assizes, the central administration and the central court system dealt occasionally with local government, but for the large part that sturdy and vigorous body of men, the English country gentry, filled the needs of county and local administration. The boroughs under their charters were governed much as they had been under the Tudors. Although by the end of the period the necessity for more efficient local administration was felt on all sides, still the country gentlemen gave England a good government and one well suited for a nation relying upon agriculture for its chief support. One reason for this was that the country gentry, after the turmoil and stress of the seventeenth century, did not press to the limit religious restrictions upon Dissenters, Roman Catholics, or Jews.

These years between 1704 and 1783 were distinguished not only by the development of that great reform movement within the Church of England, led by John Wesley, but also by a broad tolerance called at the time "latitudinarianism." This meant that the individual enjoyed, in spite of restricting legislation, a right to worship as he chose. The legal measures against Roman Catholics and Dissenters were rarely enforced. Religious persecution, except for one or two moments, was a thing of the past. The result was an unusual domestic tranquillity throughout the period. What the Church of England lost in vigor was probably more than made up by the development of a community spirit from this religious tolerance.

While England was enjoying peace and internal security at home, her expansion overseas led to the loss of one empire, and the belated acceptance of constitutional concepts that would allow, in the twentieth century, the creation of the Commonwealth of Nations. Ireland gained a freedom she was unable to use and keep, and therefore lost, after a quarter of a century.

The opportunity for expansion and her peculiar colonial system of government left England in 1763 with a string of wealthy, vigorous trading and planting colonies that extended from Barbados to Hudson's Bay. The errors of George III's government, and the rise of an American nationality, brought about the American Revolution and its accompanying international war. The Revolution not only gave the United States their independence; it caused Great Britain to renounce for the West Indies and for Ireland the claims that had driven the Americans to revolt. The war, though it led to defeat and gave France and Spain revenge for past defeats, did not lead to loss of the command of the sea. In the East, at the same time, the British East India Company acted as a pioneer of Empire. From a monopolistic trading company it became the paramount European political power in India during the Seven Years' War. If any one man was responsible for this success, it was Robert Clive. Later, Warren Hastings saved India for Great Britain during the American Revolutionary War. What held together the British Empire in the latter portion of this period was the British Navy that, in spite of neglect in times of peace, was always sufficiently well led and well supplied to win the last battle with the French and other naval powers. An over-all view of the growth of Britain between 1704 and 1783 gives one the picture of a people whose vast and unflagging energies were channeled from domestic revolution and turmoil into the more lucrative and peaceful channels of trade, industrial revolution, agricultural development, and material wealth. These energies poured forth in expanding and acquiring overseas possessions and trade, and in making England the leading Western imperial power of the eighteenth century. Successful government at home, toleration of religion of the average man, opportunities to make and invest money safely, combined with the energy and vigor of a hardy, seafaring people, made up the strength and character of the Empire that in 1783 stood upon the threshold of a new era of perils and victories.

18

ECONOMIC HISTORY

1704–1783

A quiet revolution in the economic life of Great Britain and her empire began in the years between 1704 and 1783. In the seventeenth century the use of coal, the technique of experimentation in applied science, and the application of capital to industrial development had inaugurated what has been called the Industrial Revolution. Interest in improved methods of farming led to equally vital changes in agriculture. The rapid expansion in production of both manufactured goods and agricultural products was speeded up and encouraged by the equally profitable increase in trade with the colonies and nations overseas. Africa, the Americas, and Asia were offering more and more opportunities for exchange of goods and services.

As this period opened, the predominant economic philosophy was that of mercantilism and protection. England feared competition with other nations in her overseas and domestic trade, and she defended herself by the Navigation Laws. Vested interests such as the ancient wool trade were protected against low prices and foreign competition. Agriculture, the chief occupation of the majority, was fenced around with tariffs and prohibitory regulations to meet underproduction and export bounties to meet overproduction. Even the fact that the American colonists suffered in their purses from protection and trade restrictions had little effect on the government's thinking. Though mercantilist laws helped push the Americans to rebellion, George III's administration continued to hold to the belief that goods could be manufactured only in the mother country and that providing her with raw materials should be the only economic activity of the colonials. But this was nothing unusual. All European states in the eighteenth century applied the principles of protection or mercantilism to their economic organization.

It should be noted that protection did not prevent the economic revolution of the eighteenth century. Vital and far-reaching changes did occur under the mercantilist system of regulation. Farming methods were improved; the factory system was introduced. It is useless to say that free trade would have speeded up these changes or that protective regulations necessarily held them back. The general direction taken by the change was toward industrialization. But throughout these years, and this point should be emphasized, the predominant way of life in Great Britain was agricultural.

Starting in these years even the appearance of the English countryside was radically changed by enclosures. Special acts of Parliament enabled landlords to purchase and fence in much ancient common land. Fences and hedgerows marking out pasture lands or tillage cut up the twenty- to forty-acre or larger fields that had been known as champaign or champion. In another place the social and economic consequences of the enclosure movement will be described. Here it should be noted that it was the spread of this movement that made the Agricultural Revolution possible.

Factory and mill building either created new towns or built up old ones. Wedgwood's kilns at "Etruria" made, in effect, a town where none had been before. Manchester, a village in 1704, by the end of our period was a good-sized town as the result of the new mills. In like case was the town of Birmingham. Both these were prototypes of the average industrial city of the early nineteenth century. Already slum dwellings in blocks were being put up as near the factories as possible. But growing pains in industrial communities were just beginning by 1783. How the new mill towns reached maturity, and in what condition, can best be told in that section devoted to the economic and social life of the nineteenth century. A more thorough account of the Industrial and Agricultural Revolutions is postponed to the next section of this book, to allow considering these revolutions when they took effect on the life of England. Generally speaking, in this chapter we are concerned with origins; in the later one, with results.

One of the causes for the flowering of the Industrial Revolution was the increase in population that occurred between 1704 and 1783. Not until the first decade of the nineteenth century were reasonably accurate population statistics available. It has been estimated, however, that the population in England and Wales increased from about 5,835,000 in 1700 to about 6,012,000 in 1740 and to about 7,580,000 by 1780. When the population increase occurred in urban and industrial areas, more people demanded more goods, and also better communications to make those goods more available. As a result, in the course of the eighteenth century 1,100 turnpike trusts were created by local worthies who had secured permission to build roads and charge tolls to users. The trusts and the technical advance in road building by the end of the century made it possible for stagecoaches to travel from Edinburgh to London in about forty hours. There were few major centers of population in Great Britain that did not have regular coach service connected ultimately with London. Travel was easier, and the carrying of mail was more rapid. For transportation of goods, canals were dug which made far cheaper the carrying of coal, iron, and other bulk commodities from port to factory and from mine to mill. In 1759 the Duke of Bridgewater decided to dig a canal that would make easier the rapid carriage of coal to smelter. When the canal was completed in 1761 its utility became evident at once, and the Duke employed James Brindley to extend it to Liverpool and Manchester. Before the end of the century the central industrial areas, the woolen-producing areas of Yorkshire, and the cotton towns of Lancashire were in touch with each other by water.

Since this was an age of individual initiative and enterprise, the canals were often constructed according to the fancies of each small corporation. Thus the weight of the goods that could be carried by each barge was determined by the width of the narrowest waterway. However, by the end of this period the expense of building them was more than repaid from profits, and those carrying bulk traffic to and from the mills and the mines were in the end serving the great ports from which the ships of Great Britain sailed to the rest of the world.

According to the best figures we possess, in 1702 the port of London cleared about 839 ships; in the year 1794 it cleared 2,219 ships. Liverpool, Bristol, Glasgow, and Edinburgh were ports from which the cotton cloth, iron tools, and wool cloth were carried to Ireland, India, the Mediterranean, and American ports. The British West Indies in the eighteenth century had as their basic export sugar, which in bulk or in the form of rum became one of the staple articles of trade of Great Britain. The triangular trade involving British-manufactured goods, slaves, and American colonial products brought wealth and prosperity in Great Britain and increased by more thousands the population of America and the British West Indies.

This maritime growth transformed England's world position. At the beginning of the eighteenth century England and Holland were comparable as carriers of the world's goods. By the end of the century, the relationship was different. Though England never had a monopoly, she was now predominant on the seas. Similarly, London took over the financial leadership from Amsterdam. The mark of this was when Dutch capital deserted England when Holland entered the war of the American Revolution. At that time Englishmen bought up the two-fifths of the national debt the Dutch threw on the market. Thus, when America was winning her political independence, England in a sense won a financial independence. As London became more of a financial leader, her business institutions strengthened. Long years of experience taught the discount houses and the insurance brokers how to do their work. Of this there is a significant proof, in the way Lord Mansfield and his special juries created the Law Merchant. Sitting at the Guildhall to try civil cases, this great Scotsman led his juries of businessmen to guide him as to the customs of business procedure, which he codified in a series of practical decisions.

The British East India Company in these years joined in sending bulk raw cotton and cotton cloth for processing and dyeing to Great Britain. Here is a good example of how the supplying of a product from overseas builds a new industry. Manufactured cotton cloth was highly desirable for its use in women's dresses. Particularly fancied by the ladies of Great Britain was the finespun calico. When the demand exceeded the supply, men in England turned to the problem of spinning and weaving the cotton cloth, and by the end of the century inventive genius and determination had supplied the answer to cheap bulk home production of a former imported luxury product. From these rude beginnings in Lancashire the great and powerful textile industry grew until by the end of this period it became a lusty elder child of the Industrial Revolution.

In both agriculture and industrial change, it was the genius of the men adventuring with experiments that made possible the over-all and general use of new methods and products. Indeed the beginning of the Agricultural and Industrial Revolutions in this period might almost be described in a series of biographies. Jethro Tull developed a ploughing and hoeing machine that after 1702 made it possible to plant and cultivate turnips and similar root crops. So successful were Tull's methods that Lord Townshend, Sir Robert Walpole's brother-in-law, when forced to retire from politics, showed the farmers of England how to use Tull's methods to put weight on their livestock and to enrich their soil. Robert Bakewell during these years studied the art of livestock breeding and developed certain breeds of sheep, especially the "Leicesters," better suited to the climate and to the market demands for better wool and more meat. Perhaps the most outstanding of these new farmers was Thomas Coke, later the Earl of Leicester, who in the 1770's grew wheat on his farms in Norfolk where none had been grown before. He set Great Britain an example of how to grow crops and till the soil in the most scientific manner. Agricultural societies were founded that published the results of experimentation. Arthur Young, traveler and author, told all the world how the Agricultural Revolution was making farming better and increasing the products of the soil to feed the rapidly growing public.

On the industrial side the same story of individual enterprise and experimentation can be told. Almost everyone is familiar with the growth and development of the steam engine in the eighteenth century. It is well known how Thomas Newcomen in 1711 made changes in the steam engine which allowed it to be applied to pumping out flooded mines. His engine was modified, adapted, and changed but was used mainly for pumping work until James Watt secured, in 1769, a patent for a steam engine with improved condensation of steam back to water. After even more experimentation, which allowed using the engine to drive a shaft, Watt installed a successful commercial steam engine in 1788 and thereby showed that industry could now easily use steam in place of water power. The capital that Watt used and many of the improvements made on his patent were furnished by his partner, Matthew Boulton. In the art of casting iron one has but to remember the developments in smelting and making molds of sand of the Darby family at Colbrookdale. In Scotland a group of financiers founded the Carron Iron Works which soon became famous throughout the world because of the quality of an internationally used iron gun, the carronade. In the field of pottery, the factory system and mass-production methods were successfully applied by Josiah Wedgwood, who thus founded Etruria, a town which from 1769 to the present has produced earthenware and pottery of outstanding utility and beauty. Another pioneer in manufacturing was Hargreaves, whose spinning-jenny patent in 1770 helped solve the problem of producing cotton yarn. In the next year, 1771, Arkwright introduced his water frame which employed rollers instead of spindles and successfully applied outside power to machines inside a mill. Samuel Crompton's mule, a hybrid of these two, after 1779 made possible the production of yarn and cloth in great quantities. The men who developed these machines all seem to have had one quality in common, the ability to give practical form to ideas. Some of them, like Crompton, worked at night in home workshops. Others, like Arkwright, took someone else's ideas and made them work. Still others, like Watt, were in touch with the experimental science of the day, either directly or by one or two removes through more philosophically minded associates. It was with this pragmatically creative gift that they were about to change the face of England and relieve men of the burden of laboring with their hands. But in order to accomplish these miracles the lifeblood of industry—capital—had to be found, and to be found in sufficient quantity.

Two types of funds are usually required for business: permanently invested capital, and either "working capital" or in place of it commercial credit. Permanently invested capital was not too easy to get. The South Sea Bubble of 1720–1721 made men fearsome of speculation, as they saw the savings of thousands wiped away in an uncontrolled stock-market crash. However, the South Sea Bubble showed not only the desire for speculation, which in this case was deplorable, but also a sound instinct for profit making. Wiser men than those who had thus lost their money did lend to turnpike trusts, canal corporations, and inventors like Watt. Existing capital in this manner moved out of land and government stock into industry. Often, however, businesses started on a small, even a tiny, scale and ploughed back profits with startling results. Samuel Walker built a furnace in 1741, as a means of part-time employment, which mush-roomed into Samuel Walker and Co., in 1812 worth £299,015. However, once a business had started, either from investment or from savings, it could use the ever-growing machinery of commercial credit. Funds could be secured from local banks, which in turn could draw upon rich seaport banks and the discount houses and banks of London. Back of all this, in support, was the Bank of England, which by the discount and rediscount of notes established the money market. London was not only the principal seaport of the realm; it was also the financial and investment center of the empire. From here were made loans for factory building in the North and for merchants in the West Indian and African trade. To London banking houses were sent bills for discount from all over Britain and Ireland. Thus, when it was needed, the capital that came from profits made on farms, through trade, and from industry, was available in ever-increasing amounts. A second necessity for the Industrial and Agricultural Revolutions was therefore present in ample supply. Beside men to invent and lead, England had astute investors to supply money.

Thus, in the years 1704 to 1783, the base was laid on which a towering economic structure could be built. At the time men merely saw that England was prosperous. Later generations, benefited by hindsight, have realized something of what had been going on. Raw materials, capital, new methods, and personal enterprise were combined in an atmosphere of free institutions. In agriculture England's food supply, her stock of capital available for productive investment, and her labor supply were all increased at the same time, by the enclosure movement. For by enclosure more food was produced by fewer men, and the wealth thus created was ploughed back into land or industry. In communications the turnpike and the canal reduced costs of shipping or traveling, made new methods of production economically possible by making raw materials available, and again created capital that might be reinvested. In business the Law Merchant, the London finance markets, the London insurance market grew and thus facilitated enterprise. In industry, new methods made possible power driven mass production, for the first time in the world's history. Thus it might be said that England began the eighteenth century as one of several maritime nations and ended it as *the* manufacturing nation as well as *the* maritime nation.

19

CONSTITUTIONAL HISTORY

1704–1783

In 1752 William Blackstone started giving his lectures at Oxford on the laws of England. As so often happens with professors' lectures, a book was based on them—the great *Commentaries on the Laws of England.* Blackstone's purpose was to describe what the laws were and how they affected the lives of the people. The conclusion he came to was that the British nation owed much of its greatness to the institutions by which it was governed. Because of them, he thought, it was blessed with more freedom, more security, more wealth, more ease, and more privileges than any other nation. Compared with a German or a Frenchman even the humblest of Britons had better protection from arbitrary arrest, fine, or impressment into the armed services. He was, in theory at least, represented in Parliament; he might even have the right to vote. He could not be deprived of liberty or property without a hearing in court. Nor was Blackstone alone in holding such beliefs. Foreigners of proven wit and discernment agreed with him. The Frenchmen Montesquieu and Voltaire —Montesquieu in his *Spirit of the Laws,* Voltaire in his *History of England*—praised the constitution of England as a safeguard of human rights and liberties. Especially did they praise what Blackstone had emphasized, the system of checks and balances among executive crown, legislative Parliament, and judiciary. The question is, were these thinkers right?

The idea of checks and balances appealed to the Frenchmen because they had reason to fear a strong and dictatorial government. In contrast to the apparently overpowering position of the king in France, they liked what they saw in England. There, it seemed, that the Revolution of 1688/89 had shown that a bad king could be held in check by Parliament and the courts. The life-tenure judiciary, in turn, could not overcheck since judges might be removed by an address of both houses to the king. Since Parliament and king shared in making the laws, each was protected against the other. Yet, on the other hand, present-day English constitutional theory disagrees with these conclusions and assumes the "omnicompetence" of Parliament. To resolve this difference, it is necessary to examine the powers of the Crown, of Parliament, and of the courts as they were in the years from 1704 to 1783.

As for the position of the Crown, the Revolution of 1689 had settled two arguments about it. The monarch must be a Protestant. James II, and after him his son and his grandson, were kept from the throne by their religion, for the British were not to be moved from their dislike of Popery. Then the monarch, in the long run, must yield to the desires of the people as expressed through Parliament. Since 1689 no monarch has pushed his rights to the point of open quarrel with Parliament once Parliament has taken a stand and stuck to it. When the Convention of 1689 transferred the throne from the Catholic James to the Protestants William and Mary, it was settled that Parliament rather than the Crown made the final decisions on matters of grave national interest. The Revolution checked and in due course buried the idea that the monarch ruled by divine right.

On the other hand, the legal rights of the Crown remained and gave the king or queen great power. The theory of the constitution as to administration was clear. The king was the executive head of the nation. He gave public office and honors. Laws required his signature for validity. National administrative actions were done in his name. The Army, the Navy, the civil service, even the clergy swore an oath to him. The Government was his Government. But all this was theory, and gradually, though outside observers such as the Frenchmen above quoted did not recognize it, practice diverged from theory. Some royal powers lapsed, though technically still in existence; new institutions were created, though technically they did not exist. Thus the "conventions of the constitution" silently changed, and England was transformed from a nation with representative government to one which had what Canadian statesmen later named responsible government, where a Cabinet, not the monarch, held the executive power.

Some readers to whom these terms are unfamiliar may ask what are "conventions of the constitution," "responsible government," and a "Cabinet." Here are brief answers. Much of the British constitution is unwritten, a matter of custom rather than of formally enacted law. For example, the royal power of veto has never been given up, but today it would be unthinkable for Queen Elizabeth II to veto a law, though William III did so several times. Many changes besides the abeyance of the veto have come about in this way, as will be seen. As for responsible government, that is a government in which the chief executive officers hold office at the will of the legislature. As for the Cabinet, it is the group of high officers of state who jointly control administration, jointly decide policy, and stand or fall by their ability to keep with them a majority in Parliament. Let this suffice for the moment, while we turn to the way that newly formed "conventions of the constitution" grew up, whereby a small group of leaders in the Houses of Lords and Commons became a Cabinet and took over the executive power.

One of the things that the eighteenth century decided was that the king must rule through his ministers. The king might, and did, choose who those ministers might be. In the eighteenth century this power was more than the tactful advice now sometimes used; it was one almost of veto. George II kept the Elder Pitt out of office till he was forced upon him. George III, George IV, and—in one case, it appears—Victoria "blacklisted" men they did not want to hold office. George III and even William IV dismissed a whole Cabinet. But though the king could propose, Parliament disposed. If Parliament wanted a man in office, into office he went.

The reason that Parliament thus gained the whip hand was that its approval was essential to the conduct of business. It was true that nominally the monarch paid directly for the chief departments, Exchequer, Treasury, Secretaryships of State, as well as the judges, the Army, the Navy, and the royal Household. But the money for these came from Parliament. Indeed, it really came from one house of Parliament, for Commons had long since successfully asserted that it alone could originate "money bills" and that the Lords might not amend such bills. Furthermore, not only the Mutiny Act but many another "annually expiring law" was essential to the conduct of government. A mere threat not to renew such laws was enough to bring the monarch to heel.

A much-quoted example of this is the so-called "Long Administration" of 1746. George II, in that year, balked when told that it was necessary to have William Pitt the Elder in office. Promptly the ministry resigned, and after two days' attempt at creating a new administration—hence the derisive name—George II gave in. Pitt got office, though not the one to which he had aspired. This was one of many precedents which built up a constitutional convention that the king must take the actions recommended by his Cabinet if he could not find another Cabinet to take its place.

This episode deserves careful attention, because it shows not only how present-day constitutional conventions grew up, but also what power the Crown still possessed. George II did not knuckle under completely; he bargained, and bargained with some success, so that Pitt had to be Vice Treasurer of Ireland instead of Secretary at War. That may make clear why George III, in the years from 1760 up to 1809, was able to take active part in Cabinet making and, from 1760 to 1782, in details of administration. A king could and did make deals with factions in Parliament; George III could even build up his own faction in Parliament, the so-called "King's Friends." It happened that for different reasons, largely Anne's health and the preoccupation of George I and George II with Hanover, George

III was the only monarch of this period who actively used the royal powers. For it should be thoroughly realized that in the eighteenth century the ideas of "Cabinet responsibility," of the requirement that the king should obey his "constitutional advisers," were innovations. In the following political chapter will be recounted the steps by which this came about. Here it will suffice to point to four stages in this evolution.

First of all, during Anne's reign, key government actions were taken by a group of Privy Councilors who met in her cabinet or business room, and told her the policy they thought it wisest to adopt. Hence, to this day members of the Cabinet are made members of the Privy Council. Next, in the reign of George I and of his successor, Sir Robert Walpole established in fact but not in law the convention that the First Lord of the Treasury was the "prime" or chief minister, who communicated the decisions of the Cabinet to the king. After his fall from power, in the years from 1742 to 1760, this convention was strengthened. Then, in the years from 1760 to 1782, the new king, George III, made such use of his then undoubted legal rights as to discredit them from his failure in the American Revolution. Consequently, when a constitutional struggle arose in the late 1770's, to culminate in Dunning's Resolution of 1780, what had been innovations approached being conventions. The words of that resolution, "The power of the crown has increased, is increasing, and should be diminished," became a sort of rallying cry to justify parliamentary control of the executive. Thus it was that these years, during which men praised the balance of the constitution, saw the beginning of the end of that balance. By 1782 it was decided that Parliament would take the major part in constituting the true executive, the Cabinet, even though the king remained a partner in the work. Just after our period ends, in 1784, another constitutional struggle would make the electorate, by its decision in a general election to Parliament, supreme over both king and Parliament if the two should fall out. Thus England, during the eighteenth century, would gain responsible government, with the ultimate responsibility going through Parliament to the people.

Just what had happened would not be realized for some time. The office of Prime Minister would not get legal recognition till 1905. The Cabinet would long be described as a "body unknown to the law." But eighteenth-century innovation and practice would make the basis of nineteenth-century convention and theory.

In this description of how the power of the Crown diminished, there is implicit a description of how the power of Parliament correspondingly increased. Since Commons paid the bills, it became the supreme body in the land, especially as it was, from regular reelection, responsive to the will of the people. Lords lost in importance, though individual lords, from their control of groups in Commons, remained key political figures. Add to this the fact that the great Speaker, Arthur Onslow, in his long tenure of office from 1728 to 1761, taught Commons dignity and gave his successors an example of impartiality, and one has the story of constitutional change in Parliament.

In the eighteenth century, the House of Lords and the House of Commons worked together to provide the nation with a stable government. As the century progressed, the political parties developed new characteristics. Instead of having different long-term purposes, they came to share long-term purposes and to differ about the means by which those purposes should be achieved. Those who were in the Government had definite policies; and those who were not in the Government had other policies for doing the same thing. Those in the Opposition, with the exception of a constantly diminishing handful of Jacobites, were never in favor of violent overthrow of the constitution or the use of force to gain place and power. Thus the Whigs and Tories built up a party system that fought with words and political maneuvers rather than arms or mobs. After 1770, the Tories replaced the Whigs as the dominant party and were, with only occasional interruptions, to remain in power till 1830.

As for the courts, after 1714, that is, once the Act of Settlement of 1701 gave life tenure to the judges, all that need be said is that England had great judges, chief among them Mansfield and Camden. In a series of great decisions Lord Mansfield created the Law Merchant, that body of customary law which henceforth formed the basis for business transactions. In a great decision in the Somersett case he decided that residence in Great Britain automatically gave freedom to slaves. In another decision growing out of the Wilkes arrest and the North Briton affair, Camden ruled that general warrants, i.e., warrants that did not specify a particular person, were illegal. Such decisions justified the claim that the British constitution guaranteed personal liberty.

All this may be considered a positive advance constitutionally. As eighteenth-century theory gave way to eighteenth-century practice a machinery of government evolved that facilitated England's becoming a democracy in the nineteenth and twentieth centuries. But in one way England grew less democratic. In local government, more and more power fell into the hands of the justices of the peace. The country gentlemen who held that office were honorable men, who did their duty according to their lights. However, the tendency was for them to use their supervisory power over parish vestries to destroy initiative in those below them. It would take time before the common man in England regained the power and habit of self-government he had enjoyed in the seventeenth century. Thus as the evolution in method in national affairs may serve to explain why England in the nineteenth century moved so comparatively smoothly

into more democratic ways, the retrogression in method in local government may serve to explain why it took until 1928 for England to gain
full universal suffrage.

Just the same, though Blackstone may have been wrong about checks
and balances, he was right about one thing. The British constitution,
whether the practical one or the theoretical, did preserve liberty.

20

POLITICS AND SOCIETY

1704–1783

No one in 1704 could have anticipated the domestic tranquillity that England enjoyed during the eighteenth century. Men looked forward to political alarms and excursions such as had, since 1689, filled England with strife and turmoil. But aside from the years between 1701 and 1714 the eighteenth century was politically rather peaceful. Indeed from 1714 to 1760 there was for all practical purposes only one party, and it was not until after the personal intervention in politics of George III that Whigs and Tories once more engaged in full-scale battle in Parliament and on the hustings.

This unexpected turn of political life after 1714 was due as much to the personalities of those who shaped the policies of the country as it was to the winding up of the War of the Spanish Succession by the Treaty of Utrecht. During these eight decades of the eighteenth century, leadership, or its absence, was the decisive factor in determining what policies government would follow. In 1704 this was particularly the case because of the personalities and ideals of Queen Anne and her advisers.

Queen Anne, at her accession, was a sick and retiring woman, who had no wish to take an active part in government. But though she turned over to others the management of affairs, she kept in her own hands the choice of those who would so manage affairs. She was stubborn and devoted to her personal prejudices like all the Stuart rulers. But since she was devoted to certain of her personal clique, she could be dominated by them. This gave England a queen who listened to backstairs intrigue and determined policy at times on the basis of personal whim. On the other hand, she had an instinct for the feelings of the English people. In religion her ardent attachment to the Established Church represented the attitude of a cross section of her subjects. For she never pressed her religion into extreme politics, as did the true "high fliers," the extreme Tory High-churchmen. Instead, she showed truly royal generosity. In 1704 she turned over to the "Governors of Queen Anne's Bounty" the first fruits and tenths which Henry VIII had seized in 1533. This the Governors have used to this day, according to her desires, to increase the income of the poorest clergy. In politics Queen Anne had either the good sense or the good fortune to change from the Tory side to the Whig side and back again at the same time as her people did. When Whigs were needed in office to push the war against France, she put Whigs in office and ousted Tories to make room for them. When Tories were needed in office to make a sensible peace, she ousted Whigs and put in Tories. Finally, when the Protestant succession became endangered, her last political action was to give office to the neutral statesman who best could bring George I to his new throne.

Queen Anne wanted to have her ministers and her household officials Tories, for the Tory party by tradition and belief supported the Established Church and the authority of the monarch. At her accession in 1702 the Tories did have control of the House of Commons, and also held the chief offices of state. The chief official of the Ministry, the Lord Treasurer, was Lord Godolphin. Since he controlled all payments, he could make his wishes obeyed, as long as he fulfilled two conditions: that he secure votes of money from Parliament, and that he keep the confidence of the Queen and keep himself in office. Godolphin was noted as a financier as well as a breeder of race horses and a patron of cockfights and the gaming table. He was an ally of the Duke and Duchess of Marlborough, John and Sarah Churchill. The Duchess of Marlborough, as Queen Anne's confidante and the chief lady of her household, dominated her. Thus, any government who had the Duchess of Marlborough on their side could be sure of Queen Anne's approval if not affection.

This meant that whenever the Duke of Marlborough supported a policy it would receive favorable consideration. For the future of England this was perhaps fortunate because Marlborough, while nominally a Tory, became convinced that the only way to preserve England and save Europe from French domination was to follow the Whig foreign policy—to fight on the Continent with the Austrians and Dutch as allies, and to defeat the combination of France and Spain. From 1702 to 1711, when he was dismissed from his offices, Marlborough was able to lead the armies to those victories whose names remain glorious on British banners to this day. At Ramillies, Blenheim, Oudenarde, and the Ne Plus Ultra Lines he ended Louis XIV's hopes of continental supremacy.

The special position of the Marlboroughs at the court had the further effect of bringing the executive government into line with the legislature. In those days the executive government was in theory the whole Privy Council; in fact it was the group of chief officers of state who met with the Queen in her business room, or cabinet. Until 1710 two men, Lord Treasurer Lord Godolphin and Captain General the Duke of Marlborough, constantly held office, with such ascendancy that men called them the "prime" or chief ministers. Other officers of state were changed with the changes in the political picture, largely by the blandishments of Sarah Churchill. If Tories were needed in office to get Tory votes in Commons, Anne was persuaded to put them in. If Whigs were needed to deal with the Whig majority in Lords, Anne was persuaded to oust Tories and replace them with Whigs. Thus was built up a group of politicians—more and more called the Cabinet—who held office as long as they secured, at one and the same time, the votes of both Houses of Parliament and the favor of the monarch.

The basic problem before the Godolphin-Marlborough Cabinet—the name that will henceforth be used for it in this book—was how to get the Whig lords to help them without alienating the moderate prowar Tories in the House of Commons. The Whigs in the House of Lords were led by a group of remarkable politicians called the Junto. Among these were Lord Somers, Lord Sunderland, and Lord Wharton. Three political events served to bring these men onto the side of the "prime ministers." These were the Aylesbury petition, the Occasional Conformity bill, and the Regency Act. The Aylesbury petition was a dispute over which body, the House of Commons or the law courts, protected a voter's right to vote. In the election of 1702 a man named Ashby had been deprived of his right to vote simply because he was a Whig. Whig lords paid for an appeal, ultimately, to the supreme law court, the House of Lords. This raised a question of privilege, for the House of Commons claimed exclusive jurisdiction over its membership, whereas the House of Lords said that the right to vote was a property right. As Ashby had been discriminated against, though the case was never settled, it made good Whig propaganda. The Occasional Conformity bill was an attempt by the "highflying" Tories to punish those Dissenters who occasionally but irregularly attended Church of England services in order to obtain political privileges. A notorious case was a Lord Mayor of London who had been stupid enough to attend a Dissenting chapel in full regalia. Attempts to punish them served also as good Whig propaganda. To top this, the highflying Tories insulted Anne by trying to invite her heiress, the Electress Sophia, to come to England. This the Whigs deftly countered by the Regency Act, which set up arrangements, later most valuable, for the emergency of the Queen's death with her successor in Germany.

One clause in the Regency Act had such great subsequent constitutional importance that it was later spoken of as "the Act of Queen Anne." It by-passed the clause in the Act of Settlement intended to prevent executive officials from sitting in the House of Commons after Queen Anne's death. The "acceptance of an office of profit under the Crown" would still "vacate a seat." Hence came the method long used to resign from the House of Commons, that of accepting the nominal office of "Steward of the Chiltern Hundreds." But the holders of certain policy-making offices were made reeligible. As such posts were offered to men sure of reelection, this ended the separation of the powers and made possible the fusing of legislature and executive in the Cabinet system.

When combined with enthusiasm over the victory of Blenheim, the political result of these things was to ensure a Whig majority at the election of 1705. At the same time there was an administrative change. Queen Anne was induced to dismiss highfliers from her Cabinet and replace them with prowar Tories. Here came forward two men, Robert Harley, later Earl of Oxford, and Henry St. John, later Viscount Bolingbroke. Harley was a deft party manager who had once been a Dissenter and who instinctively understood the sentiments of the mercantile classes and could win their support. St. John was an adventurous man of fashion and literary light, a cynic about religion who yet allied himself with the High-Church movement. He was also highly able; as Secretary at War (note the curious title for the business head of military affairs) he did much to help win the Blenheim campaign. Thus the change in the executive paralleled the change in the House of Commons.

This Whiggish House of Commons faced and overcame the great problem of Scotland in 1707 by putting through the Act of Union. In retrospect it appears little short of a miracle that the English and Scots ever agreed to make a new country known as Great Britain, with a common flag that combined the crosses of St. Andrew and St. George. For ever since James I had united the crowns of England and Scotland a century earlier, the English and the Scotch had agreed upon one thing— to despise each other.

Yet the English urgently wanted the Scots to join them. Then clans of the Highlands, little more civilized than many savage Indian tribes in the North American colonies, might cease to be a recruiting ground for Jacobite sympathizers. Under a union the Scots would be more content to accept direction and leadership from the stronger partner in the south and less likely to revolt or choose another king should a non-Stuart Protestant succeed Queen Anne. Likewise the Scots wanted union. The very Act of Security that the Scots Parliament had passed in 1704 to separate Scotland from England at Anne's death had laid down a condition for union. If Scotland could share England's overseas trade she would deign to share the same government. This was too much for the English to swallow. They pointed out to the Scots that they were fortunate in being treated as English subjects when in England, and replied to the Act of Security by an Alien Act, saying that if the Scots did not join England in a union, they would lose their present privileges of being treated as Englishmen once they crossed the border.

This pair of threats brought both sides to terms. The Scots said that they would negotiate for a union; the English, that the offer of negotiation was justification for the repeal of the Alien Act. Now there remained two more obstacles: the emotions left over from Darien failure, and the special position of the Church of Scotland. The Darien failure the Scots blamed on the British, and most Scots loved the Kirk and feared English interference with it. That lesson Charles I had learned to his cost, in 1638 and 1640. If a majority in the Scots Parliament could be induced to feel that Darien was no longer a sore spot and that the Kirk was safe, union might be possible.

Union was possible. It took two years of negotiation to reach a simple agreement. Darien's sting was mollified by the English Government's paying to the last shilling the value of the subscriptions to stock in the Darien Company, as well as some other outstanding local debts. The bitter feeling that Scotsmen had died and potential overseas wealth had been lost because the English navy had not protected the Darien settlement against Spanish attacks was thus partially assuaged. The special position of the Kirk was enshrined in the Church Security Act that was made part of the Treaty of Union. (Queen Elizabeth II, consequently, is technically an Anglican south of the Tweed, a Presbyterian north of it.) Then it was agreed that no legal changes be made in Scotland. The old laws would remain. For example, Advocates and Writers to the Signet would practice in the Courts of Inner and Outer Session, in contrast to English barristers and solicitors in the courts of King's Bench, Common Pleas, and Exchequer. But a joint Parliament of Great Britain would make laws for the whole island for the future. To this Parliament's House of Commons forty-five Scots would be elected by the constituencies that had elected to the Scottish Estates. To this Parliament's House of Lords the many Scots peers would elect, for each Parliament, sixteen of their number. So, on May 1, 1707, England and Scotland were merged into Great Britain.

Now Great Britain settled down to winning the war. Here the war party got above itself. In the enthusiasm over Marlborough's victories and in a belief that Philip could be driven from Spain, Louis XIV's offers of peace were rejected. At the same time an even more Whiggish House of Commons was elected in 1708, under the Triennial Act requiring elections every three years. Pressure was put on Queen Anne to dismiss all Tories. Out went even Harley and St. John. But this had repercussions. Anne grew vexed with the dominating Sarah. Harley established back-stairs contact with the Queen through Mrs. Abigail Hill Masham, a lady of the Court who was his cousin. Then in 1709 the battle of Malplaquet shocked England by its long casualty lists for little apparent value. Because of this and other matters, the wheel of fortune turned full circle in the next year.

In February and March, 1710, Dr. Henry Sacheverell was impeached for a sermon in which he attacked both Lord Godolphin and the Glorious Revolution. Parliament being Whig, Sacheverell was convicted. But the result benefited the Tories. From top to bottom England changed its mind. The common people mobbed the Nonconformists and condemned the war. The privileged electorate, roused by Jonathan Swift's pamphlets, prepared to vote Tory. Her Majesty quarreled irrevocably with Sarah Churchill and dismissed from office, one by one, those whom Sarah had induced her to put in. In their stead went those whose names Abigail Hill Masham suggested, notably Harley and St. John.

Then came the election, with heated canvassing on both sides. In the battle of the pamphlets carried on by the Whigs Addison and Steele and the Tory Swift, the Tories won the advantage. They pointed out, in Swift's *Conduct of the Allies*, that the original aims of the war had been won and that the Whigs were uselessly continuing it. They roused the country squires to the heavy land tax, which was paying for the war while Whig merchants grew rich. They raised the cry of "the Church in danger" over an Alien Protection Act which naturalized foreign Protestants who would swell the number of Dissenters. This sort of argument was clinched by the Whig refusal of a suitable and honorable settlement with France at the negotiations carried on at Gertruydenberg in July, 1710.

The election returned a Tory House of Commons. Now the problem before the Tory leaders Harley and St. John was similar to that which had faced Marlborough and Godolphin in 1704. Could they gain control of the House of Lords, which was still a Whig stronghold? Foolishly, first Harley and then St. John left the Commons, taking the titles of Oxford and Bolingbroke, by which we shall in future know them. They should have learned their lesson in the troubles Harley had steering his budget through Commons and in the success he had in gaining support when he chartered the South Sea Company to hold the monopoly of trade with South America after the war had been won. But all that these two did to make the Commons safe for Tories was unjustly to impeach a rising young Whig, Robert Walpole, for indirectly benefiting from contracts when he was Secretary at War.

In the House of Lords the battle was protracted. Gradually the Tories drew even. They were able to put through at last the Occasional Conformity Bill. But the margin was too narrow for safety. Therefore Harley-Oxford set a constitutional procedent. On New Year's Day Her Majesty, in what is now customary "New Year's Honors," created twelve peers whose votes would make the House of Lords safely Tory. In future the Whigs in 1832, the Liberals in 1911, would copy this device, when again Lords and Commons became deadlocked. With this strength peace was made at Utrecht in 1713.

Then the Tories sought to entrench themselves in power. To keep Whig merchants out of the House of Commons they passed a law requiring that every member possess landed property worth £300 a year. To prevent a future generation of Dissenters from growing up they passed the Schism Act that required that after August 1, 1714, all teachers be members of the Church of England. Should these laws not be repealed or evaded, Whiggery and Dissent would wither away. Yet this Tory control of Britain rested on one thing, the favor of Queen Anne.

When, in the summer of 1714, it became clear that Anne would die in weeks or days, many Tories became alarmed. They feared that on the accession of the Elector of Hanover—his mother the Electress had predeceased Queen Anne by a matter of months—the Whigs would hold royal favor. Then their accomplishments would be reversed. Some, too, hankered to see a Stuart somehow back on the throne. Besides the Jacobites who would accept James III either as a Catholic or if he changed religion —which he refused to do, though pressed to—there were Tories like Bolingbroke who were ready to play a deep game and, by pretending to favor James, to force the future George I to confirm them in power as a means of gaining the English throne. As part of this, Bolingbroke drove Oxford from office as Lord Treasurer on July 27, 1714. This gave Bolingbroke only three days to consolidate his power, so ill was Anne. But the danger to the Protestant succession was real. What would happen if a Bolingbroke-dominated Privy Council, technically the chief executive organ of the realm, should disregard the Act of Settlement and bring over the Pretender? On July 30 took place one of the dramatic moments of English history. That morning two dukes, Somerset, the "Proud Duke," and Argyll, the Scottish soldier who had won the honorable name of "Red John of the Battles," entered Kensington Palace where the Council was meeting, though they had had no summons. They proposed that the Duke of Shrewsbury be made Lord Treasurer. This was a shrewd stroke, for Shrewsbury was one of the few who were neutral between Whig and Tory, and yet he was a last survivor of those intrepid seven who had invited William of Orange in 1688. Then they went into the Queen's room, where the Duchess of Somerset was in attendance as Lady of the Bedchamber. Her Majesty put into Shrewsbury's hand the white staff of the lord-treasurership, and he came out, to preside at the Council and there to give those orders that would make easy the accession of George I. Thus, by this rather British *coup d'état*, the Hanoverian succession was secured.

The failure of the Tory ministers to act on behalf of the Pretender in August, 1714, did not end the Jacobite threat. Bolingbroke fled to France, openly joined the court of the Pretender, and there plotted an uprising. In 1715 the Highland Earl of Mar and the Earls of Derwentwater and Nithsdale led a forlorn hope on behalf of the Pretender. The forces of the Crown easily defeated the Jacobite English at Preston and the Scots at Sheriffmuir. The rising was finally put down in February, 1716.

Two acts were an indirect result of the "Fifteen," as the Scots call it. The Riot Act of 1715 allowed force to be used against an assembly of twelve or more whom a magistrate had ordered to disperse, with due formality. (Hence the phrase "reading the Riot Act" to connote the warning of severe consequences.) The Septennial Act of 1716 extended the three-year term of the House of Commons to seven. This put more power in the politicians' hands, taking it from the electorate. It also froze in power and office the Whig leaders whom George I had appointed on his landing.

For now British history has new dramatis personae. Anne and Godolphin are dead, Marlborough has retired, Oxford and Bolingbroke are permanently disgraced, though Bolingbroke does have before him a long life as an anti-Whig political theorist. Even Shrewsbury disappears, for one of the first of George I's actions on landing is to "break the white staff," on which Shrewsbury goes into retirement. In these men's stead come the new King, George I, and new Whig leaders, notably James, Earl Stanhope, Charles, Viscount Townshend, John, Earl Carteret, and Robert Walpole.

George I, founder of the Hanoverian dynasty, has been severely criticized. He was gross in his habits. He was unforgiving and cruel, as is shown by his imprisonment of his wife Dorothea after he divorced her. He was jealous of his place and power, as is shown by his unfeeling treatment of his son, the future George II. In a society that judged a man by his choice of mistresses, his were known by the unlovely names of "the Elephant" and "the Bean Pole." Consequently, George was thoroughly disliked by most Englishmen, who were prepared to dislike any foreigner who would be made their king. William III, before him, had received the same treatment with less justification.

What is overlooked is that George I had more ability than he is usually credited with. He had been a first-rate general in the Imperial Army. He had distinguished himself as an enlightened, sensible, and even likable master of Hanover. In diplomatic dealings with Hanover's neighbors in Germany, he had shown skill and insight. He made a very wise, though negative, decision—one that should have made his contemporaries and historians respect him as a man of intelligence, and one upon which the future peace and domestic tranquillity of Great Britain depended. In effect, he handed over domestic administration to the Whig leaders in Parliament as being men better qualified than he to manage it.

At first George ruled through Stanhope, a first-rate diplomat, who agreed with him on foreign affairs. He led the House of Commons; Lord Townshend, the House of Lords. George also showed favor to Carteret, an expert in the Baltic problems in which, as Elector of Hanover, he was really more interested than British affairs. But the two men fell out, and George I gradually learned a basic fact about English politics. If he turned control of British affairs over to a member of the House of Lords, that lord would have to rely on a commoner to run the more important house. Therefore it was better to deal directly with a member of Commons. He also learned that it was better to deal with one man than with many. If he set one man to watch another—as he had tried with Stanhope and Townshend—both eventually knew of it, quarreled, and failed to govern well. An example of this second point was the quarrel between Stanhope on one side and Townshend and his brother-in-law, Robert Walpole, on the other, which led to the dismissal of the latter two. An example of the first point was the eventual fall of Stanhope. Stanhope had guided policy well and gotten rid of the Schism and Occasional Conformity Acts. But in 1717 he had left Commons for Lords and shortly thereafter took his first defeat from Walpole. This was over the peerage bill, an attempt to freeze the membership of that house as it was after George I had re-created a Whig majority. Thanks to Walpole's opposition in Commons, this failed, and the Crown retained the right of creating as many peers as it chose.

But Stanhope was no financier, and a financial crisis, the South Sea Bubble, brought him low. After six years of peace without reduction in the national debt, there arose a demand to cut the interest rate. It was decided to try the method used when the Bank of England had been founded—to raise money by granting special privileges to a corporation. Two corporations bid for the presumed advantages—the South Sea Company that had been founded in 1711 by Harley to benefit from the monopoly of the South American trade, and the Bank of England. Fortunately for England, the South Sea Company bid higher. For men suddenly went mad buying stocks—any stocks—to sell again as the stock market rose. Inevitably, the crash came, and it was the South Sea Company rather than the Bank that crashed as well. It brought down with it the Stanhope Ministry, for revelations that certain politicians had been bribed by shares of South Sea stock and that others had fanned the speculation for their own gain discredited those in office. So violent were the attacks that they lost Stanhope political support, and an insult in the House of Lords brought on a stroke of which he died in a few hours. The King had to find another politician to manage Parliament for him.

He made the obvious choice of Robert Walpole. Walpole had purchased shares in the South Sea Company and had sold them at the right moment. Furthermore, fortunately for his reputation, he had not been in the Ministry. This combination of financial insight and virtue was irresistible. For the next twenty-one years Walpole was First Lord of the Treasury and as such first minister of the Crown. He is usually considered to have been the first Prime Minister, in the modern sense of the term, though sometimes that honor is given to the younger William Pitt.

Walpole realized that the House of Commons was the center of political power. To show that he was a House of Commons man, he refused a peerage, though he accepted knighthood in 1725 and the Order of the Garter in 1726. He had high attainments in three fields of politics. He was a splendid manager of men, who could gauge correctly what each man wanted and how best to win his support, his friendship, his affection. He was sure and sound in his financial proposals. He could choose the right policy for the time. His motto *Quieta Non Movere* (freely translated as "Let Sleeping Dogs Lie") gave Great Britain peace and a chance for the economic growth previously described. Walpole knew how to handle the two kings he dealt with. He gained the confidence of George I because he had straightened out the South Sea Bubble and because under him administration ran smoothly. Thus from 1721 to George's death in 1727, Walpole held the whip hand, though the King tended to play Lord Carteret and Lord Townshend against him. When George II came to the throne there was a moment when Walpole was out of favor, for regularly in the Hanoverian period the Prince of Wales led the opposition to the King and the King's ministers. But Walpole soon got back to favor by showing George II that he, and he alone, could secure from the House of Commons the vote of a larger Civil List, or payment for the King's Household. Then Walpole struck a firm alliance with Queen Caroline, who well knew how to manage her blustering, vain, but essentially sensible little husband.

Walpole knew how to handle the House of Commons. He played the political game according to the rules of the time harder and better than his opponents. To his discredit is the fact that he could not abide men of mark associated with him. William Pulteney he drove into opposition. Pulteney's abilities were wasted in trying to concert measures with Bolingbroke, who had been allowed to return from exile but had been denied his seat in the House of Lords. Bolingbroke wrote great literature—the newspaper the *Craftsman*, the essay *A Patriot King*—but his words did Walpole no harm. As for Walpole's brother-in-law, Lord Townshend, the Prime Minister drove him from office in 1731. When the speeches of the young William Pitt disturbed Walpole, Walpole said, "We must muzzle this terrible Cornet of Horse," and took his cavalry commission away from him. This had repercussions; soon an act was passed forbidding the canceling of military and naval commissions except by court-martial. To Walpole's discredit, too, in modern eyes was his frank purchase of votes and support. From the £100,000 per annum that he in effect gave to George II to keep himself in office, down to the minor offices and even cash that he and his henchmen paid for votes, Walpole made a business of being Prime Minister. Recently a revealing account book has turned up, and we know just who got what for certain years. But if Walpole made a business of politics, he made a sound one. He ran Great Britain as it should be run. Most of his political support came because the House of Commons trusted him. Few statesmen can stand comparison with him in English history. Perhaps only "King" Pym in the 1640's and Althorp in the 1830's had that same mastery over the House. The red-faced squire, reading letters from his gamekeeper at the table of the House of Commons, instinctively knew what his fellow squires felt.

Furthermore, Walpole was a great House of Commons man because, in times of peace, he had an instinct for what the English wanted. He knew what could not be done. Only once did he guess wrong. When, in 1733, he tried to reduce smuggling and raise more revenue by levying excise taxes on tobacco and spirits, he ran into the solid British instinct that an Englishman's home is his castle, not to be entered by any exciseman. The opposition took the chance of raising a storm. To this storm, he yielded. The Excise was dropped. But woe betide those who had deserted him politically. Sharp and sudden was their punishment, by loss of office or pension.

As this shows, Walpole added to his intuitive understanding of the English an experienced understanding of how to manage elections. The old days when the Crown could get a majority in Parliament by creating new boroughs had ended in the reign of Charles II, with the Newark case. But now the ministers of the Crown could influence elections, as long as no popular movement swung the voters' minds. These were times of party peace, when the House of Commons was Whig, except for a few lingering Jacobites led by Squire Shippen and a few Tories who had survived the debacle of their party. Therefore Walpole set to work to entrench himself in power, not by measures that would rouse resentment, as the Tories had, but by quietly controlling those who could control votes.

In those days of public polling of votes this was not hard. In the county elections of England, there was a comparatively large electorate of all the freeholders. But it was customary to vote almost automatically for the leading man of the county, to show respect and trust. This was the good side of county elections. The bad side was that many freeholders also held land as tenants, and landlords used threats of eviction to win votes. Thus in many of the fifty-two counties of England and Wales if Walpole could influence a few leaders he could get elected the men he wanted. In Scotland this was easier, because the county franchise was closely restricted.

But county seats made up only a fraction of the House of Commons.

English counties had only 80 members out of 558. Most members of the House of Commons came from the boroughs. Almost every borough differed in some respect from every other borough in the way in which its representatives were chosen for the House of Commons. Some boroughs had ceased to exist altogether as towns. The owners of the land upon which they had stood would pitch tents on the townsite or row out to a rock where the town had once stood and there with two or three tenants elect members of the House of Commons. Such a borough was called a "close" or "nomination" borough because the electoral rolls were closed and one man could nominate its member or members. Many towns were represented by members chosen by the aldermen. In a few boroughs the right to vote was determined by the ownership and occupancy of houses or land within narrow ancient boundaries. Then a town of 5,000 or 6,000 persons might have only a dozen voters. Such boroughs often got the name of "rotten" boroughs since corrupt influences could win elections in them. In many boroughs the number of voters was so large that no single individual could influence the outcome of the election by using threats of eviction. Often the franchise then belonged to those individuals who owned a hearth upon which a pot could be boiled for cooking purposes, who were called "pot-wallopers." Also, in many instances property in the town would be owned by three or four members of opposing political parties. These two types would be called "open" boroughs.

It was this borough electorate which had to be influenced to keep Walpole in power. From the past many a story has come down about the means of persuasion then used, to gain crucial votes. Then as now, votes were won by blandishments and flattery, and election addresses praised the trueborn Englishman—or Scotsman, or Welshman, or for the Dublin Parliament, Irishman. Votes were won by "treating," when public houses were opened at the expense of a candidate, and the true Briton, who could exercise the right of franchise, was not infrequently a drunk Briton for weeks on end. Votes were won by direct bribes; often there was a customary charge for votes, and in many a small borough the voters reaped a golden harvest at election time. In such a borough the election costs could be determined almost to the last penny by multiplying the number of voters by a fixed sum per head. Votes were won by less direct bribes, of places in the public service for the voter or his family or friends. Thus were managed the Crown or Treasury boroughs, where promises of tidewater places in the revenue collection or jobs in a dockyard enabled the government to nominate members at a price.

It is true that often elections were not opposed. In 1784, a year of ardent political struggle, three-quarters of the seats in the House of Commons were won by uncontested elections. The reason for this was simple. Why, if a candidate sees he will lose anyway, should he incur the expense of a contest? But the winner still had to make sure of his seat by payments and treating, for fear of the last-moment appearance of opposition, and to make sure of support for the future. Consequently, many, if not most, seats in the House of Commons were a form of negotiable property that could be bought and sold. An adequate sum would either defeat opposition or pay the necessary expenses of keeping the electorate loyal. Though this system of election seems theoretically indefensible, in practice it did not work badly. Counties and some open boroughs sent up honestly elected members. Corruption to a certain extent canceled out, since there was either a two-party system or factions working against each other, when the members reached Parliament. Above all, this gave the holders of close or nomination and rotten boroughs a chance to send good men into Parliament. Of course this system brought into the House of Commons only the landed gentry and a few rich merchants, but as long as these were responsive to public opinion, as they usually were, the House of Commons to a surprising degree did speak for the nation.

When Queen Caroline died in 1737, Walpole lost a valuable ally at the court. Then came a problem he could not handle, the War of Jenkins's Ear. He saw no reason to go to war because a sea captain claimed his ear had been torn off in a squabble with a Spanish official. But the nation wanted war, and what the nation wanted he gave it, as had been the case with the Excise. He had been a good war administrator in his youth, but he was not a strategist. The failures of the Navy were blamed on him, as Pulteney and Carteret led the political pack against him. The elections of 1741 lost him support. He saw his key supporters, Henry Pelham and the Duke of Newcastle, about to desert him. Therefore, he sensibly handed George II the seals of his office and retired. Then, and only then, he took a peerage, as Earl of Orford. When the next year, Pulteney became Earl of Bath, Orford met him in the House of Lords and said: "Here we are, my Lord, two of the most insignificant men in England." For Walpole truly knew that the House of Commons ruled England, with its money power and its representation of the will of the people.

However, this was a lesson others had yet to learn. For a short while it seemed as if everyone was contented with the new political arrangements. A pleasant nonentity, Lord Wilmington, held Walpole's post of First Lord of the Treasury.[1] As Secretary of State for the Northern

---

[1] Ever since the Duke of Shrewsbury went out of office as Lord Treasurer, the Treasury has been "in commission," that is, managed by a board of "Lords Commissioners." But the head of that board, the First Lord of the Treasury, has been the chief officer of state. From the time of Walpole on, the Prime Minister has been First Lord, with two exceptions. From 1766 to 1768, though Pitt was Prime Minister, the Duke of Grafton was First Lord. On occasions from 1885 to 1902, Lord Salisbury let Lord Iddesleigh, W. H. Smith, and A. J. Balfour be First Lord while he was Foreign Secretary.

Department, Lord Carteret would manage diplomatic affairs in concert with the King. Home affairs would be handled by the Southern Secretary, the Duke of Newcastle, while his brother, Henry Pelham, held the lucrative post of Paymaster of the Forces. When Wilmington died, Pelham moved up to being First Lord of the Treasury and Chancellor of the Exchequer.

Had George II searched the kingdom purposely, he could not have found two brothers apparently less likely to succeed as ministers. Henry Pelham was timid, a man of peace, frightened at making decisions, and diffident to those who argued with him. Yet he possessed one talent: his budgets were sound. Pelham's brother, the Duke of Newcastle, had unusual characteristics. He learned nothing from experience. He was unusually inefficient. He was always in a hurry and never on time. He worked hard but finished few appointed tasks. Even more than his brother, he sought the opinions of others. After being in public life almost forty years, he could not write a note thanking the Mayor of Bristol for a testimonial without asking advice about the phrasing of his reply. Yet he, too, had something that made him powerful. As Henry Pelham learned from Walpole how to draw up a budget, the Duke of Newcastle learned from the master how to give offices, pensions, and places to those who asked. He brought in the necessary majorities in the House of Commons. These two men gave a lesson in politics to Carteret and the King. In 1744, because they did not like the way Carteret was spending English money in Germany, they forced the King to put him out of office. This ended what had been known as the Drunken Administration, so called from Carteret's ability with the bottle, and began the Broadbottomed Administration, so called because the Pelham brothers had brought together such a large foundation of House of Commons voting support on which to build their power. The King bided his time, knuckled under when he had to, and finally gave battle in 1746. He dismissed the Pelhams when they insisted that office be given to William Pitt, and he sent for Pulteney, now Lord Bath, and Carteret. This, in derision, became known as the "Long Administration" because it took only two days for Bath and Carteret to realize what Walpole-Orford had meant with his joke about being the most insignificant men in the kingdom. Members of the House of Lords as such could not command a majority in Commons. Back into office went Henry Pelham and the Duke of Newcastle. Thus it was made clear that the working relationship between Crown and Cabinet created by Walpole still existed, with the Cabinet the master but forced to work with the King.

In 1745 and 1746 came the last Jacobite Rebellion. Charles, the grandson of James II, tried to win for his father, "the Old Pretender," the islands his grandfather had lost. This was, then, the third important Stuart invasion. In 1689 James II had landed in Ireland and spent a year before he was driven out by the battle of the Boyne. His son, "the Old Pretender," had tried to land in 1715 when the Earl of Mar was defeated at Sheriffmuir. Now the Young Pretender took his turn.

The brief success of the Young Pretender was due to the dislike of Highlander for Lowlander and of Scotsman for Englishman, and to the backward social and economic conditions of parts of Highland Scotland. Few of the English who held sentimental memories of the Stuarts were ready to risk life and security for Prince Charles. So the English Tories stayed home when Bonnie Prince Charlie proclaimed "James III" as their rightful king. But Highlanders ever bent on plunder of Lowlanders and clan chieftains who held dear ancestral loyalty to the Stuarts answered the summons. Edinburgh was occupied by the Jacobites, its loyal castle besieged. England was invaded as far as Derby, where Prince Charles's lack of recruits and supplies forced him back into Scotland. At last the Duke of Cumberland destroyed the Jacobite army in 1746 at Culloden Moor. Bonnie Prince Charlie threw himself on the mercy of his Highlanders, who spirited him away from place to place until he could at last sail safely to France.

The "Forty-five," as the Jacobite uprising is called, caused change in Scotland. New roads into the Highlands made policing easier and brought civilization to the clans. Feudal jurisdictions were abolished. Thus Jacobitism was largely stamped out. Eleven years later some of the very clans that had gone out in 1745 for Prince Charles served King George II in battle, becoming some of the finest regiments in the British Army. The Lowlands, henceforth free from Highland depredations, blossomed out into a new era of industrial and farming prosperity. Edinburgh became a center for wits and philosophers, the most renowned of whom was David Hume.

Until the death of Henry Pelham in 1754 only two events of domestic political importance occurred. In 1746 William Pitt, when made Paymaster General, astonished Great Britain by refusing to pocket interest on the deposits in his charge, which was the way, until the "economic reforms" of 1782, that politicians made money out of this office. This act of patriotism gained him a remarkable degree of public confidence. In 1751 there died Frederick, Prince of Wales, known irreverently as "foolish Fred," who had been intriguing against his father, as did all eighteenth-century Princes of Wales. This made heir to the throne his son George, a rather backward thirteen-year-old boy. Indeed perhaps the most significant event of the time was the resignation, in 1751, of John Wesley from his fellowship at Lincoln College, Oxford. This was one of the steps by which, during the 1740's and 1750's, the Methodist movement left the Church of England. Of the place of Methodism in British life a later chapter will tell. Even when Henry Pelham died, all that happened was a shuffle of offices, his brother the Duke of Newcastle becoming Prime Minister. Then war changed matters.

The Seven Years' War opened in 1756. The Duke of Newcastle ran true to form. He was opposed to the war. He mismanaged the preparations and early campaigns in America and on the Continent. His system of alliances collapsed, leaving Hanover open to French troops while the Hanoverian and Hessian soldiers he hired came over to protect England. For once public opinion could not be ignored. His parliamentary followers left him in the lurch, and he had to resign. George II, while disliking the way his hand was forced, gave the administration to the Duke of Devonshire in 1756—Pitt, however, being the real head of the Government. He started to repair the losses and correct the errors made by Newcastle. He sent the German mercenaries home. He called on the English to defend themselves. The nation took him to its heart and gave him the support and approval he needed.

The people might follow Pitt, but the politicians and the courtiers intrigued against him. Newcastle and his followers blocked Pitt's measures in Parliament, the Duke of Cumberland urged the King to dismiss him. This George II did. But no alternative government could be formed. Therefore, for a crucial period Great Britain was leaderless, while public opinion demanded that Pitt come back to office. Showers of complimentary gold snuffboxes—the "rain of gold boxes"—were sent him, and eighteen cities and boroughs elected him an honorary freeman. This forced a compromise whereby Pitt dominated a new administration in which Newcastle was Prime Minister and handled the patronage. This combination of efficiency, popularity, and patronage saved Britain from defeat and won her an empire. Even George II came round to supporting Pitt.

Then the King died, to be succeeded by his grandson, the young George III. The new King electrified the nation by the public statement: "Born and educated in this country I glory in the name of Britain." He started out his reign determined to be a good king, like his remote ancestor, Alfred. Instead of thinking in terms of Hanover, he took part in the conduct of British affairs. He ousted first Pitt, then Newcastle; he raised to power his former tutor, the Earl of Bute, first as Secretary of State, then as Prime Minister. It would have been suicide for the professional Whig politicians who controlled most of the votes in Commons to resist the new King's wishes, and they were tired of seeing Newcastle give out the jobs and Pitt give the orders. But once they had allowed the King his way, they soon taught him lessons in practical politics. Even though he wanted to marry the Lady Sarah Lennox, the niece of the Paymaster of the Forces, Henry Fox, they made him marry a German Princess. Once Bute had bumbled along long enough to have made some mistakes, they forced George not only to dismiss him as First Lord of the Treasury, but to forbid him to come near the royal palace. The lesson of what Sarah Churchill, Abigail Masham, and the Duke of Shrewsbury had done was not lost on English politicians. Direct access to the King, for any reason, has been subject to political control. So Bute left the stage of history, with a bad reputation in England as having taught George III tyranny and in America as having started the oppression that led to the Revolution.

In his stead George Grenville, as the master of the biggest block of votes in Commons, became Prime Minister, but the King now began to get his own personal group of votes in Commons. Some were the remnants of the old Tory party and ex-Jacobites who had been the most popular men in their counties or had had control of "rotten boroughs." These men were overjoyed to see a king who would be King, and they backed George out of loyalty. Thus George III revived the old Tory party of Bolingbroke and gave it new life. He also created in a sense a new party —"the King's Friends," corrupt members of Parliament who voted for him for money or jobs, just as they and their likes had in the past voted for Walpole or Newcastle. Therefore Grenville had to cooperate with George.

Grenville and George III, however, came up against public opinion, which early in the reign should have taught, but did not teach, the pair how strong it was. John Wilkes was publishing a scurrilous paper, the *North Briton,* which was blaming Scots in general and Bute in particular for everything that went wrong. Number 45 of this paper was particularly offensive to the King. Therefore the House of Commons acted against it, using its power of arrest. Wilkes was expelled from Commons; the printers were summoned before the bar of Commons, to explain their actions. This infringement on free speech was all the more serious because the principles of the Petition of Right were violated. As it was not then known who had published the *North Briton,* a general warrant was issued, allowing the arrest of anyone. Partly in joy of attacking authority, partly in defense of Englishmen's rights, Wilkes was defended by the London mob and by certain high-minded Whigs in Parliament. "No. 45" was chalked up all over Westminster, mobs shouted outside Wilkes's jail, and when the slow process of law had been gone through and people could consider the matter less passionately, Chief Justice Pratt handed down a decision that general warrants were contrary to the basic law of England. Wilkes skipped off to France, having gotten out of jail on a technicality, and became the figurehead for resistance to George III.

Grenville had a perfectly sensible idea that the only way to keep the Indians from attacking the frontiersmen in America was to have an English army there. He also had the perfectly sensible idea that Americans should pay for an army that was to protect them. But he did not have the wisdom of Pitt to see that Americans ought to have the same rights as

Englishmen and be able to vote the money and control the army that was to be put on their frontier. Pitt had gotten important sums from Massachusetts, particularly, just by asking and cooperating. Grenville, on the contrary, simply had Parliament extend a stamp tax on certain business documents from England to America, and then he was puzzled by the fact that the American people refused to let the tax be paid. Having roused this hornet's nest in America, Grenville then insulted George by trying to pass a Regency Act, necessary in case the King died suddenly, which omitted the King's mother from the council that would govern in the name of the infant Prince of Wales. The combination of mistakes was too much, and Commons, that is, the Tories, the King's Friends, and the honest Whigs, voted Grenville out. Into power was put the shy Lord Rockingham.

Rockingham was an unusual man. He was so modest he would not speak in Parliament unless urged. He tried not to take responsibility and took it only from a sense of duty. Consequently politicians who would not cooperate with each other cooperated with him. He ran an honest administration, whose results are best described in a short pamphlet written by his private secretary, Edmund Burke, entitled *A Short Account of a Short Administration*. When Rockingham took office the King, as was customary, made a speech to Parliament written for him by his Cabinet, which was, in our phrase, the "platform" of the new Government. Every plank of that platform was put into practice, and every plank was the reform of an abuse. The Stamp Act was repealed, though a Declaratory Act was passed which stated that Parliament had the right to legislate for England's colonies. Until the Statute of Westminster of 1931, the principle of that Act has remained in effect, and the British Empire has been run on the ideas of William Pitt that in an emergency Parliament can run the affairs of the Empire, but that it will intervene only when there is an emergency, and that Englishmen overseas have in general the same liberties and rights of self-government that are possessed by Englishmen in England. Rockingham's administration was too honest to stay in power in those days of "rotten boroughs" and soon was maneuvered out by George III and the professional politicians, that is, the noblemen who owned to all practical purposes about half the seats in Commons.

George III found a masterly way to manage the defeat of Rockingham. He replaced him by Pitt, the Great Commoner, who had been persuaded to go to the Lords as the Earl of Chatham. Chatham, as he must now be called, was very ill of the gout and very deferential to the King. Therefore, George III more and more got control of the Cabinet. Historians argue over just when particular men became Prime Minister at this period. At one time it was Chatham, except that he was at home sick most of the time, almost out of his mind. Later on the Duke of Grafton had the doubtful honor of taking technical responsibility for what went on. When he resigned in disgust, the eldest son of the Earl of Guildford, who held the "courtesy title" of Lord North, was First Lord of the Treasury. Lord North, being a lord in name only, held a seat in Commons and "led the House," that is, made the official announcements and proposed the official business. But as the prime-ministership is the job of telling the King what must be done, there was really no Prime Minister once Chatham had gone into semiretirement. England was run from Windsor Castle by George III, who was his own Prime Minister. He must be held responsible for all the mistakes that were made. When the Chancellor of the Exchequer, Charles Townshend, inspired by champagne, declared that he would make America pay taxes and not mind it, and stirred up another hornet's nest in America over the Townshend duties, George III may not have been at fault for the original proposal. He was at fault for obstinately going on with an attempt to tax America indirectly, since the colonials would not stand for any direct tax like the Stamp Act. He was also responsible for Lord North's hanging on to a tax on tea, when the City of London forced the repeal of the other taxes, just to assert Parliament's authority. Above all, George III was responsible for a direct breach of the Bill of Rights, interference in the Middlesex election.

For in 1768, at the general election that came in the course of the workings of the Septennial Act, John Wilkes came back from France and got himself elected Member of Parliament for the County of Middlesex. Instead of letting him alone, the House of Commons, on instructions from George III, solemnly expelled Wilkes. The flimsy pretext was that he had published an improper poem, an "Essay on Woman." But as the complaint had been made by Lord Sandwich, who had helped print the poem privately and had one of the worst reputations in the country, public opinion felt that it was a thief accusing a thief. Sandwich earned public disgrace, and the post of First Lord of the Admiralty. Middlesex promptly reelected Wilkes, at a riotous election. He was again expelled, and at the third election a Colonel Luttrell, who fought his way with a gang of toughs to the "hustings" and collected their votes, was declared elected. As the House of Commons is judge, and quite rightly so, of its own membership, there was little that could be done about it. George Grenville did something. Just before he died, in 1772, he got Parliament to pass an act regulating investigations into elections and putting such investigations into the hands of a "Select Committee." All England was roused over the Wilkes case. A series of letters, signed "Junius," attacked the Government and were read everywhere. It is not known who wrote them; that was kept secret. But from the fact that when Sir Philip Francis went to India they stopped, and for other reasons, it is believed he wrote them. The House of Commons again made a fool of itself by trying to arrest the printer, until it realized that it had gone too far. The effect, therefore, of the Middlesex election and the *Letters of Junius* was to make England aware that freedom of speech, freedom of election, and freedom from arbitrary arrest were in danger from George III's policy.

Here, then, was how matters stood around 1770. George III, to his credit, was doing his dull best to be a good and real king of England. Because he was honestly trying to be the kind of king the English thought that they wanted, he had much popular support. But he was playing the same kind of dirty politics that Walpole had played. He was obviously buying votes in Parliament, and was then using those purchased votes to have "His Majesty's debts" paid. Parliament was thus voting out of the Treasury the very monies used to bribe it. This sort of thing was shocking to that small but important group of men led by Rockingham and his secretary Burke, who wanted to raise the ethical standards of English politics. George was also blindly and obstinately striking at England's liberties and rights. If in America he wanted taxation without representation, thus violating *De Tallagio* and countless other royal promises, that was almost the only violation of rights he was not committing in England as well. Free speech, free elections, and freedom from arbitrary arrest were in danger in England, and subtly so, since it was the House of Commons, supposedly the guardian of the people's liberties, that was infringing upon them. But as long as George held Commons in his grasp, through his electioneering, bribery, and patronage, the supremacy of Parliament was going to mean the supremacy of the Crown. Only a series of mistakes in a great crisis could save England by giving Commons courage to vote away the control of the King. Fortunately for England, George made those mistakes by causing and losing the American Revolution. How he did that is related elsewhere.

For along with the Revolution in America came a parallel struggle in Great Britain in Parliament and the press. Some Englishmen, like Chatham, sympathized with everything America did except the Declaration of Independence. Chatham, leaning on the arm of his younger son, also William Pitt, went to Lords and told them to make peace with America before it was too late. Then he collapsed and was taken home to die. Others, like Lord Shelburne and later Lord Rockingham, believed that America had better be let go. All agreed that George III was unfair to America and that Sandwich was imperiling the Navy. In Commons Burke told North these home truths in as eloquent words as were ever used there. He was joined, and soon surpassed, by a new recruit, the dissolute and charming Charles James Fox. Fox, originally a supporter of Lord North but independent politically since his doting father had given him a rotten borough, suddenly switched from attacking Wilkes to talking the soundest and most persuasive of sense about America. As time went on, as money and troops were poured into the West Indies without results, "the tongue of Fox rather than the scepter of George III" began to rule England. The most stubborn members of Parliament swerved in their allegiance to bribes and patronage at the cost of the British Empire and England's liberties. In this swerving they were encouraged by a press campaign and by a revival of an old Anglo-Saxon custom. The freeholders of the shires, especially Yorkshire, met to express their opinions on how matters were being conducted, and went directly against George III. This movement might have led to revolution. It did not, because the ruling classes in England showed firmness in keeping order. It did lead, eventually, to "Reform of Parliament" for the demands made by the extremists such as Major Cartwright formed a program put into effect at last by the Reform Bill of 1832.

Finally, in 1780, a distinguished lawyer arose from the benches of Commons to move that "the power of the Crown has increased, is increasing, and ought to be diminished." This vote should have been a body blow to George III but was not. He still had one more weapon in his armory. Against his will—he was a strong Protestant—Parliament had passed an act to remove "Catholic disabilities," that is, to give Catholics rights in law that they now had in practice, such as the right to hold property and to be free from fines for not attending Church of England services. The mad son of a Duke, Lord George Gordon, led the infamous "No Popery" riots of 1780, which George III bravely helped put down at the head of his own Household troops. In the wave of personal popularity and anti-Popery which followed this, George III dissolved Parliament. This secured him, for a while, a Tory House of Commons.

With expert management and some heavy outlay of money Lord North won the election of 1780. In the new House of Commons Lord North had things his own way until the news of the disaster at Yorktown changed the course of events. Though the King set his will to stem the sudden tide of events, Fox led the Whigs against the ministry. Censures against the management of the Navy were carried by majorities of 22 and 19. Then even the King had to concede that Lord North must go. So on March 20, 1782, Lord North resigned and the King sent for Rockingham, who insisted that American independence be the declared policy of his ministry and that Fox be at the newly created Foreign Office. While Shelburne was given the Home and Colonial seal, Edmund Burke, the ablest man on the Whig side, was given the office, out of the Cabinet, of Paymaster of the Forces. The Whigs, knowing well the hostility of the King toward their policies, now faced the tasks of reforming and of ending the war.

The Whigs came out for American independence and "economical reform," or purification of the voting system. In twelve weeks of 1782 the Whigs disenfranchised revenue officers and government contractors, thus eliminating a corrupt electorate that would naturally do the bidding of a royal patron and ministers with power to grant favors. The fund for pensions was limited in order to prevent the King from buying votes. However, Rockingham was ill when he took the seals of office and died in the early summer of 1782. The Whigs wanted the King to appoint the Duke of Portland to head the new ministry. But the King wanted to be rid of Fox and all who were of his stripe. He called on Shelburne to make up a new Cabinet.

Shelburne was able to do this. His Government, in which young William Pitt was Chancellor of the Exchequer, concluded the peace with America. The way in which he made peace brought the resignations of Admiral Keppel, the Duke of Grafton, and Lord Camden. No one trusted him; all abused him for the terms of the treaties. The question of political interest was not whether Shelburne was going out, but who would the King have to take as successor. Soon the political world of Great Britain was rocked to its foundations by the news of a most improbable coalition. Fox and North, who had spent hours abusing each other, announced in February, 1783, that they were ready to assume the responsibilities of a coalition ministry. They would rule Great Britain and force George III to knuckle under. Now uppermost in politics was the issue, what could the King do? The answer he gave introduced a new period in British political history.

21

FOREIGN AFFAIRS

1702–1783

The period from the crisis of Blenheim to the crisis of Yorktown, that is, from the beginning of the War of the Spanish Succession in 1702 to the end of the American Revolution in 1783, may be considered one in which the English public got its education in the handling of foreign affairs. At the beginning of those eighty-odd years what public opinion advocated was usually wrong and the government was justified in going against it. At the end of that period what public opinion advocated was usually right. Stage by stage the judgment of those who could influence diplomacy from the outside improved, whether that influence was exercised by Parliament, by publicists, by the electorate, or by the bond buyer. In the War of the Spanish Succession, Parliament was against the war when it started, was for continuing it when it should have been stopped, and eventually created a situation by which a good peace was shamefully obtained. When that war ended in 1713 and when, after 1714, the Hanoverian kings took over, it may be said that the first two Georges, whatever their faults, were wiser than their Parliaments and their people. Diplomatic successes in the Northern War, against the Spanish revival of Alberoni, and in the tangles of the War of the Austrian Succession were won in spite of, not because of, the intervention of Parliament and the Cabinet. However, at this time there appeared a growing understanding, on the part of the King and of Parliament, of sound measures. Then, about 1750, a dramatic change took place. It was public opinion that forced on George II England's savior, William Pitt the Elder. The diplomatic crash of the war of the American Revolution came because George III failed to listen to public opinion. The remarkably favorable terms of peace that were negotiated at the end of that war, however, were secured by the second Rockingham Ministry, that was forced into office by an aroused public opinion. By then, in the field of foreign affairs, one might feel that the English public had reached adulthood.

The basic problem of the War of the Spanish Succession was the danger that when Charles II of Spain should die without direct heirs either the French Bourbons or the Austrian Hapsburgs would gain the whole Spanish

Empire and by sheer weight of power become the masters of the civilized world. For Spain, then, meant not only Spain proper but Belgium, much of Italy, and Spanish America. If Austria held it, France would be crushed; if France held it, no other state could face her. The task before William of Orange in the last years of his life was to get general consent to a suitable partition. After much endeavor he thought he had succeeded. Even after a neutral heir, a Bavarian prince, had died, he managed, in a second partition treaty, to induce Louis of France to agree to a division by which, while an Austrian prince would rule Spain, the Dauphin of France would rule in Italy. But when Charles II died he left a will forbidding the partition of Spain. It would go to the French Prince Philip intact and, failing him, to the Austrian Archduke Charles.

Louis could either allow Philip to accept the Spanish throne and run the risk of war, or see Spain pass to an Austrian and France become encircled. He chose to let Philip become King of Spain and take the chance of war. Then he brought war closer by sending French troops into Belgium, thus threatening Holland, and by proclaiming "the Old Pretender" King of England when James II died. That move finally roused the English, and what William hoped for happened: Parliament asked him to declare war.

William did not live to conduct this war. This made a great change in the way foreign affairs were managed. The fact that William was both Stadtholder of Holland and King of England automatically unified foreign affairs. Now it would be necessary for some Englishman to learn how to work at one and the same time with the Dutch, with Queen Anne, and with Parliament. Fortunately for England, the man was ready. The Earl of Marlborough, John Churchill, had been groomed by William for that very function, in part because Marlborough's wife, Sarah, had such influence over Anne. Not only did Marlborough have court influence and military experience, he was closely bound by ties of interest and even of family marriage with Lord Godolphin, the Lord Treasurer. Marlborough speedily made his personal ascendancy felt. Soon his Queen made him a duke; soon thereafter he proved he was worthy to carry on William's work. It was difficult to persuade the Dutch, accustomed to fortress warfare, to take chances. It was almost impossible to get sense into the heads of the Austrians. But Marlborough persevered. The story of England's foreign affairs is of how he won diplomatic victories in order to be free to win military ones and how an overelated nation went too far.

In brief, Marlborough won five victories: Blenheim (1704), Ramillies (1706), Oudenarde (1708), Malplaquet (1709), and the turning of the Ne Plus Ultra Lines (1711). In 1704 the Navy won the battle of Malaga and took Gibraltar. On land in Spain, in 1705 Lord Peterborough took Barcelona, in 1707 the battle of Almanza was lost, and in 1710 was lost the battle of Brihuega. In 1711, the Emperor Joseph of Austria died. Each battle had its diplomatic significance, and so did Joseph's death. Blenheim meant that Louis could not conquer Austria, then crush Holland, and bring England to terms. It brought the war back to Belgium. Malaga and Gibraltar gave England the command of the sea and permitted landings in Spain. The capture of Barcelona encouraged the Allies to dream that Philip could be ousted from Spain and replaced by Charles. Ramillies won Belgium back from Louis. Almanza ended any practical possibility of putting Charles on the Spanish throne, but not the hopes of doing so. Oudenarde ended a revival of French strength. Malplaquet, though a victory, was won at such a cost that public opinion in England began turning against the war. Unfortunately the Government was out of touch with public opinion, and at Gertruydenberg in July, 1710, they refused terms better than those later accepted. But the defeat at Brihuega and the death of Joseph ended all hopes of making Charles king of Spain. Spain clearly could not be conquered; to make the Emperor of Austria—as he had become—king of Spain would create a danger of Hapsburg hegemony as serious as the danger of French hegemony against which the whole war was directed. Thus it was that the bloodless turning of the Ne Plus Ultra Lines, Marlborough's finest victory, came too late. An open road to Paris was by then of little if any use.

Once Sir George Rooke won the command of the sea at Malaga, there was surprisingly little naval action in the war. Sir John Leake did superbly in support of the landing at Barcelona and the campaign that followed. Indeed, the whole basis of the Spanish campaign was that England could carry troops unimpeded to Lisbon or Barcelona. In 1709 the British did take Minorca; in 1707 they failed to capture Acadia, in 1710 they succeeded; in 1711 "Jack" Hill, Abigail Hill Masham's brother, bungled an attack on Quebec, which should have succeeded. This summary may serve to show the effectiveness of English command of the sea.

But though this was not, after 1704, a war memorable for sea battles, it was a war of epic land battles. Marlborough won every battle he fought; captured every fortress he besieged; and, more than that, left an imperishable tradition behind him.

This war was fought on a sort of double front, or even a triple one. Marlborough had to win diplomatic and political victories in order to be able to win military ones. There was a time when the Dutch refused to fight, and Marlborough, to rub in the lesson, showed the Dutch generals the French pouring in disorder over a field where half the allied army could have won a glorious victory. Only the fact that he struck up an intimate friendship with Prince Eugene made it possible to get any sense out of the insanely proud Austrians. As for the home political front, first Marlborough got too little support, then too much. It took Blenheim to get adequate votes of supplies. After Blenheim, two offers of peace—one after Oudenarde, with the renunciation by Louis of Philip's claim to Spain—were rejected. For then the Whigs had gone wild over their slogan, "No Peace without Spain." Finally Marlborough lost the political battle when he had won the military one. Just as he had opened the way to Paris, he was dismissed.

Public opinion in England entered foreign affairs by ousting the Whigs from control of Parliament at the same time as Queen Anne was ousting them from office. This Tory public opinion demanded peace, and the Tory leaders gave it what it asked for. Marlborough was dismissed. Britain's allies were deserted. The new Secretary of State, St. John, even went so far as to force those allies to agree to the terms he had dictated by ordering the British troops to cease fighting the French and instead act as their silent partners. The decision to stop trying to keep Philip off the throne was wise, for now Louis offered adequate safeguards that Spain would be kept independent of France. But the means by which it was obtained were shameful, and in his haste St. John threw away some of the fruits of victory.

So England ended the war, having by the Treaty of Utrecht won Acadia in North America, Gibraltar and Minorca as Mediterranean bases, and a right of trade with the Spanish colonies, known as "the assiento." This last will reappear as the basis for the South Sea Company and as the cause of the War of Jenkins's Ear. Above all, England had prestige. So ends the first stage.

The postwar problem was the usual one of keeping the peace. Events can be briefly recounted, for in most cases all that was needed was a word from England and the belief that England meant what she said. Stanhope, as Secretary of State and at the same time a sort of roving ambassador, forced the various signatories to the Treaty of Utrecht to live up to their terms. George I, as Elector of Hanover with interests in the Baltic, persuaded his ministers to intervene to make peace in the Great Northern War, by which Sweden, under Charles XII, was prevented from making the Baltic a Swedish lake. When, in 1718 to 1720, Cardinal Alberoni began a Spanish expansion into Italy and threatened to invade Scotland, one English fleet at Cape Passero isolated the Spanish army in Sicily and forced Spain to terms while another warded off the raid. When Austria tried to found, in what was now the Austrian Netherlands, an East India Company, English pressure in 1731 gave it short shrift. But to do all this took parliamentary support and that was hard to get. Finally, in 1733, when the War of the Polish Succession broke out, Prime Minister Robert Walpole—by this time the premiership existed in fact though not in name—stayed out, with his subsequent boast that in one year 100,000 men were slain, and not one Englishman. But this lost him—among many other things—parliamentary prestige. It became the move of the opposition to call itself patriotic.

When trouble broke out with Spain, the "Patriots" forced Walpole into a war that speedily wound up with England fighting not only against Spain at sea but for Austria and against the French on land. The Silesian War, by which Frederick the Great of Prussia was trying to wrest that province from Austria, spread, and involved Hanover. George I and his favorite Carteret therefore intervened, which at home resulted in the fall of Carteret. It was a curious and complicated struggle, in which the English and French for some time helped their allies but stayed technically at peace until 1745. Gradually the war widened. Especially important was the extension overseas in which the French captured Madras and the Province of Massachusetts captured Louisburg. Finally the war petered out, leaving things as they were.

The terms of the Treaty of Aix-la-Chapelle have been summed up thus: "To Frederick, Silesia; the rest as they were." That, of course, pleased the British East India Company and enraged Massachusetts, which had paid for the Louisburg expedition. However, this was just a dress rehearsal for the Seven Years' War of 1757 to 1763.

Under Newcastle England stumbled along from 1748 to 1756, unprepared for trouble. Then came that diplomatic upheaval known as the Reversal of the Alliances, where England found herself allied with her enemy of seven years before, Prussia, against France, Russia, and Austria, and without the help of Holland. Suddenly England was hit hard on all sides. Her diplomats knew that she was being double-crossed by her old ally Austria, for she was trying to double-cross Austria and line up Prussia and Russia on the same side, but the French and Austrian agents in Russia outwitted her agents. But she did not use this information in time, as Prussia did. Frederick the Great in 1756 invaded Austria before Austria attacked him. The initiative so gained enabled him to hold off the armies of Austria, Russia, and France. But Britain let herself be surprised, all over the world. The fact that Austria, and therefore the Austrian Netherlands, were on France's side forced Holland to be neutral and allowed the French to invade Hanover. In 1757 the Anglo-Hanoverian army under the Duke of Cumberland was surrounded and compelled to surrender by the Convention of Kloster-Zeven. In the Mediterranean, where the British had had complete control, the French captured Minorca, under circumstances which led to the unjust execution of Admiral Byng for "failure to do his utmost in the presence of the enemy." In America, unexpectedly large French forces in the Ohio valley in 1755 captured Major George Washington of the Virginia Militia and set up Fort Duquesne at the forks of the Ohio. Those same forces, in 1756, annihilated General Braddock's force, Washington (now a colonel) having difficulty in bringing off the survivors. In India, Calcutta was taken by an ally of the French, and the captive Englishmen and women were immured in an almost airless cellar—the Black

Hole of Calcutta—where most of them died of suffocation. In a crisis like this, of defeat all over the world, the nation called for Pitt.

Despite political difficulties, and after some false starts not recounted here, Pitt was able to take the right actions. After Kloster-Zeven he supported Frederick of Prussia by an English army under a good Prussian general, Prince Ferdinand of Brunswick. From the Scottish clans which had fought for the Young Pretender in the "Forty-five" and which had since then been forbidden to wear their tartans and bear arms, he raised the tartan-wearing regiments such as the Black Watch and the Argyll and Sutherland Highlanders. To the Admiralty he sent Lord Anson, the circumnavigator. To America he sent Jeffrey Amherst and George, Lord Howe. To India he needed to send no one, for there Robert Clive had already saved the day.

To back up this vast world war, Pitt persuaded the City of London to pour out money like water. For he had taught England a political lesson. He had proved, by the "rain of gold boxes," that public opinion meant pounds, shillings, and pence; votes in Commons; morale in the army; and, because he brought it, efficiency in government. Newcastle himself said, "In the last ten days we have done more business than in the last ten months."

It took two years for Pitt to get the machinery working, and then in the year 1759 Horace Walpole, Robert Walpole's younger son, could truly say, "Every wind brings news of a victory." In Hanover Prince Ferdinand, who was taking French pressure off Frederick the Great, surrounded a French army at Minden. This should have been a victory of annihilation, but some French escaped because Lord George Sackville wilfully disobeyed orders. (For this he was cashiered, amid public disgrace. He will reappear as Lord George Germain, having changed his name under a will.) Because Minden forced the French to put more effort on the land war, less on the sea war, Pitt could say he was conquering Canada on the banks of the Elbe. Conquer Canada he did. British fleets kept the French in port. Admiral Hawke caught one French fleet out in a storm and ran it ashore at Quiberon. In America, though Howe lost his life in a stupid attack on Ticonderoga, and Wolfe his in victory on the Plains of Abraham, they, along with Amherst, built up a tradition of cooperation with "provincial" forces by which Louisburg, Quebec, and Montreal were taken. Washington formed part of the expedition which captured Fort Duquesne and renamed it Pittsburgh. In India Clive avenged the Black Hole of Calcutta by the victory of Plassey and won Bengal. At Wandewash Sir Eyre Coote ended French hopes in India and won Madras for the East India Company to rule. In desperation France turned to Spain for aid. Pitt then planned counterstrokes—attacks on Havana and Manila. But at that moment George II died, and George

III decided to assert his authority by dismissing Pitt. This was done on the pretext that he was preparing for a war with Spain that would not take place. But take place it did, and Pitt's plans had to be carried out. They were, and England got Cuba and the Philippines.

However, George III was able to rule England himself, for reasons already explained, and he promptly threw away Pitt's conquests. He even deserted Frederick, who temporarily lost Berlin to the Russians and escaped final defeat only because of a change of rulers in Russia. Of all that was acquired by this war, England, at the Treaty of Paris, kept Canada, India, Tobago, and Florida. Perhaps it was as well that she got no more, for she failed to handle well this "First Empire" that Pitt had won.

There is an interesting parallel here between Marlborough and Pitt. Each was ousted because of Spain, at the height of his success. For now the pattern has changed. In the War of the Spanish Succession it had been the Queen's favorite, Marlborough, who was right, the publicist Swift who was wrong. Now it had become the reverse: Pitt, the molder of public opinion, was right; Bute, the man who rose by influence and the ways of the court, was wrong. But there is this that stays true of the parallel: Bute, though he gave way to the defeated for the wrong reasons, like Bolingbroke got the better and more permanent peace for it. In each case the English generosity did much to stop bitterness and make the terms palatable.

It is interesting to conjecture why the molders of British public opinion were now wiser. Was it because the "City," that is, the London businessmen, knew more about the world, as they were taking the place of the Dutch as the leading merchants of the world? Or was it perhaps that the eighteenth century was the age of the Grand Tour, when the sort of English nobleman or gentleman who would sit in one house or the other of Parliament had seen the world? For where Stanhope, in the first two decades of the century, was unique in his travels, now the "English milord" was the traveler par excellence.

In the twenty years from 1763 to 1783, England had little foreign policy, for George III was trying to guide the Government and had no time for such matters. Aside from a squabble with Spain over who had claim to the Falkland Islands, England's diplomats met with few problems. Suddenly, in 1778 and 1779, England found France and Spain at war with her, while Holland first recognized the American states and then in 1781 joined in the war.

To American readers there is no use in repeating the military details of our Revolution. What should here be emphasized is the effect on Great Britain of committing her armed forces across the Atlantic and thus making herself vulnerable to European attack. To meet such a strain would require a strong government, public confidence, and a well-thought-out program.

Lord North's Government was ineffective. Two of its members, First Lord of the Admiralty Lord Sandwich and American Secretary Lord George Germain (late Sackville), were despised, the one for his part in the Wilkes case, the other for Minden. The policy with America was to put in command Admiral Richard, Lord Howe, and General Sir William Howe, on the ground that the Americans would be more willing to surrender to the brothers of George, Lord Howe. These men carried on an easygoing campaign that allowed the Americans to recover from defeats. In 1777, thanks to a bungle between the Howes and Germain, Burgoyne's army was captured at Saratoga. Then, despite pleas from Chatham to make some sort of deal with the Americans while there was still time, France entered the war.

For Great Britain the character of the war now changed. It became a sea war for survival, with the odds against her. The combined French and Spanish fleets had command of the Channel, and it was more by enemy ineptness than British ability that invasion was prevented. Gibraltar and Minorca were besieged, and Minorca lost. Britain's blockade policy roused against her the League of Neutrals, of the Scandinavian nations and Prussia. In both the East and West Indies the French had the upper hand. Worst of all, many naval officers refused to serve while Sandwich was First Lord of the Admiralty. For when the Whig Admiral, Lord Keppel, blocked an invasion attempt in 1779 he was rewarded by a loaded political court-martial. Despite the bravery with which Sir Gilbert Elliot held Gibraltar, despite the skill with which Admiral Rodney led the West Indian fleet, it seemed probable that a naval disaster would come.

Meanwhile on the American continent—again well-known facts are passed over—there was a stalemate. The British could win battles but not hold territory. Finally what Captain Knox, U.S.N., has called "the naval genius of George Washington" brought a decision. By hard begging Washington secured three months' loan of the French West Indies fleet during the hurricane season of 1781. When De Grasse cut off Cornwallis from escape by sea, a blow was struck that drove Lord North from power. The surrender of Cornwallis at Yorktown ended George III's personal rule, and the Whigs took over in March, 1782, with a program of retrieving disaster at sea and making peace with America.

That program the new Rockingham Ministry carried out, or had carried out for it. By making Keppel First Lord of the Admiralty, good officers were brought back to service. Among them was that splendid seaman, Richard, Lord Howe, who brought a relief convoy to save hard-pressed Gibraltar. But even before another trustworthy admiral could reach the West Indies, England had, as usual, "won the last battle." On April 12, 1782, at the Battle of the Saints, Admirals Rodney and Hood "broke" De Grasse's line by the first successful use of a new system of tactics, smashed the French fleet, and regained command of the sea.

Now was a chance to get terms. To improve the conduct of diplomacy the Whigs had ended the old system of joint secretaries of state who got into each other's way, abolished the American secretaryship, and separated the functions of the Home and Foreign Secretaries. This did not entirely prevent confusion, since Foreign Secretary Fox was sure America was independent and dealt with him, and Home Secretary Shelburne was equally sure that the United States were still technically British possessions and dealt with him. But as both men stood for the same general political principles as the Americans, they were able to split the Americans from the French and Spaniards by conceding independence. Then Fox was able to get satisfactory terms from the others. All England lost was Tobago and Senegambia to France, Florida and Minorca to Spain. Thus the period ends with the men whom public opinion has put in office showing themselves better commanders in war and negotiators in peace than the King's favorites. For in the eighteenth century the British ruling classes learned the responsibilities a Parliament must bear if it is to control foreign affairs.

22

THE "FIRST BRITISH EMPIRE"

1640–1783

The title of this chapter has been put into quotation marks because it can be argued that the so-called "First British Empire" of the usual textbooks either never existed or was founded after 1750. Before then the overseas possessions of Britain hardly fitted the usual definition of an empire, that is, of one nation ruling another. Either they were "factories" of trading companies, as in Africa, India, and Germany, or they were little British shires and hundreds and parishes transplanted overseas but ruling themselves through miniature parliaments. Only after 1750, that is, after the East India Company began evolving into a governing body, did Englishmen rule other peoples. Yet, on the other hand, in many ways this "First British Empire" had much in common with the usual colonial empire of its times. Therefore the purpose of this chapter will be to examine the validity of this argument. First will be taken up the Newfoundland fisheries and the trading companies to continue what had been previously said about them. Next, though full discussion of the East India Company will be postponed to a later chapter, enough will be told of that Company, Gibraltar, Minorca, Quebec, and Senegambia to show the extent of what might be called "normal" imperialism and the forms it took. Then it will be possible to concentrate on the transatlantic colonies of settlement in the West Indies and North America, where is to be found the key to the peculiar nature of the "First British Empire."

Newfoundland continued to have economic importance. Men from the West Country continued to fish on "the Banks" and dry fish on the island's shores. Gradually, more and more permanent settlements grew up, of Irish and English, which in the nineteenth century would obtain self-government; gradually French influence was weakened.

As for the European trading companies, a sharp blow was given them in the 1690's, when Parliament started to interfere with the granting of charters and attacked monopolies. As a consequence, their economic importance ended with the lapse of most of their special privileges. However, they continued to exist, since the property they possessed still had value.

From 1700 on, they fade from the picture. As for the overseas exploiting companies, they continue important. The Royal African Company, despite bankruptcies and reorganizations, remained in existence because someone had to take care of the forts needed in Guinea and the Bight of Benin, and it kept going through reorganizations because no one wanted to pay for those forts. In 1670 there was founded the Hudson's Bay Company, which is still in profitable existence. In 1711 was founded the South Sea Company, to take advantage of the grant of the assiento, or special trading privilege with the Spanish colonies. Its stock-market adventures have already been recounted. After this inauspicious start, it struggled along through years of deficit until 1807, taking in subscriptions of capital stock and rarely if ever paying out dividends.

During the seventeenth century and early in the eighteenth century the British East India Company remained a business organization. It was successful and expanded. In 1645 it leased a new factory at Madras; in 1662 it bought Bombay from Charles II. Then in 1690 Job Charnock started what proved to be the company's most important base, on the Hooghly River. This was the present-day Calcutta, then named Fort William in honor of the new sovereign, William III. During the parliamentary attack on monopolies of the 1690's, the original East India Company had to struggle against a competitor, the New Company, its struggle being finally ended by merger in 1708. But as the eighteenth century wore on, the situation in India changed. The Mogul Empire began to break down. From its center at Delhi it had never been entirely successful in asserting its authority on the sea coast; now the outlying parts of the Empire began to rebel. All the trading companies, English, French, Dutch, and Danish, had to arm themselves in self-defense. The French East India Company went further. Its leader, Dupleix, trained native troops, gave them French commanders, and joined in the civil wars of the time, for the profit of the company. Naturally, he used the strength of his armies against the British. In 1746, he captured Madras, though it was returned in 1748. Here there arose one of England's greatest empire builders, Robert Clive. In 1751 this civilian took a few soldiers, seized the inland fort of Arcot, and by holding that strategic point against overwhelming odds, forced the eventual raising of a second siege of Madras. Once having started such a career of conquest, it was hard to stop. In 1757, Plassey, in 1760, Wandewash, gave the Company the rule of Bengal and of the Carnatic between Madras and Bengal. Then the Company had to face the problems of transforming itself from a group of traders to a government. In took not only the genius of Clive to establish the government, in the late 1760's, but the genius of Warren Hastings to make that government effective. Of that, however, a later chapter will tell, for it is part of the story of the Second British Empire rather than the First.

The military posts of Gibraltar and Minorca created a special problem. These not only had the strategic importance of commanding the western Mediterranean, they had the constitutional importance of exemplifying the difference between conquered and settled colonies. By a decision of 1608, *Calvin's case,* the courts held that the king could do as he pleased with conquered territories but must acknowledge the rights of Englishmen as such in other territories. A later decision, *Campbell v. Hall* of 1774, held that once the king granted rights to a conquered territory those rights could not be revoked save by an act of Parliament. The natural consequence of these decisions was that the ministers in charge of colonial affairs became very chary of granting any rights at all to conquered territories. Thus there grew up an autocratic form of government, with the only restriction on the governor his responsibility to his superiors at home and at times to a council appointed to advise him on the spot. Before 1783 such governments were rare in the Empire, to be found only in military conquests. The important point about these governments is that they set a pattern of government which in the 1840's would gain the name of Crown colony and which would form the model of the present-day colonial empire of Great Britain.

Two of these colonies, Quebec and Senegambia, added to the Empire in 1763, show a significant aspect. It is in each case an act of Parliament that creates this form of government, in Senegambia in 1765, in Quebec in 1774. Thus Senegambia, which was lost to the French in 1783, affords the precedent for parliamentary encouragement of rule by a governor and council, much like the rule by the king and Curia Regis in the Middle Ages.

But for an understanding of the "First Empire" what matter are the American colonies, those on the mainland and those in the West Indies. It is easy to forget how many were not in the future United States; perhaps a list of them as they were in 1640 and in 1740 may prove instructive. In 1640 there were Nova Scotia (then Scotland's only colony), Maine, New Hampshire, Massachusetts, Plymouth, Rhode Island, Providence Plantations, New Haven, Connecticut, Maryland, Virginia, Bermuda or the Somers Islands, Barbados, Saint Kitts, and perhaps the Mosquito Coast and Belize. In 1740 there were Nova Scotia (lost to France but regained in 1710), New Hampshire, Rhode Island and Providence Plantations, Massachusetts, Connecticut, New York, the two Jerseys as united into New Jersey, Delaware or the South Counties, Pennsylvania, Maryland, Virginia, North Carolina and South Carolina (into which the proprietorship of the Carolinas had been divided), Georgia, the Bahamas, Bermuda, Jamaica, Saint Kitts, Nevis, Barbados, Barbuda, Belize, and perhaps the Mosquito Coast. Scotland had had—and lost—a colony at Darien. As can be seen, the colonies have increased in number, have been concentrated, and are equally divided between the future United States and those that did not revolt.

The increase came partly by settlement, partly by war; the fusions and separations were matters of practical common sense. Jamaica was captured by Cromwell in 1655, and Nova Scotia, or Acadia, was reconquered from the French in 1710. The rest of the expansion came by a steady migration across the Atlantic. Virginia increased in size, and its population oozed over into the Carolinas. Most of the colonies of this period were created by Charles II as a way of paying his debts in American lands. Such were the grant of the Carolinas to six proprietors, that of Pennsylvania and then Delaware to William Penn, and that of New York and also New Jersey to his brother, James, Duke of York. Georgia, founded in the eighteenth century, was a grant to proprietors who had a humanitarian hope of emptying jails into a transatlantic settlement, a project which had just about the success that might have been expected. The charter was surrendered in twenty years. The fusions in New England came about naturally. New Haven and Connecticut were too small for separate existence, and the same was true of Rhode Island and Providence Plantations; both pairs were joined when in 1663 they got royal charters as companies. Likewise, when a charter was issued to the Province of Massachusetts Bay in 1692 to replace the charter of the Massachusetts Bay Company that had been revoked in 1685, fusion with Plymouth and Maine was a simplification. But far more important than the increase in numbers of colonies was their increase in wealth and population. By 1740 there were about 1,000,000 inhabitants in the North American mainland colonies and about 100,000 in the West Indies islands. But the proportion was reversed as to wealth. The first enumeration of colonies in order of commercial importance to England had placed Barbados and Jamaica ahead of Virginia and Maryland and other continental colonies. Sugar and indigo brought more wealth than tobacco or naval stores. England had recovered from the spasm of fear of overpopulation that had fostered "Western Planting" in Tudor and early Stuart times. This should serve to explain the mercantilist policy that the home government adopted toward the colonies.

Up to 1688 and the Glorious Revolution, it was the Crown rather than Parliament that concerned itself with the colonies, except as to the Navigation Acts. Naturally enough, James I and Charles I used the Privy Council to control Englishmen overseas. The Virginia Company's charter was canceled in 1624, and that of Massachusetts Bay was investigated in 1638. Lords Commissioners for Plantations in General were appointed in 1634 and threatened to become powerful but never got the same control as similar committees or councils in France, Spain, and Portugal. For all this centralization was checked by the Civil War, in which the colonies stayed largely neutral. Then in 1650 when the Civil War had ended in the British Isles, the Commonwealth brought the overseas empire to heel. Virginia, for all its calling itself "the Old Dominion" for its loyalty to the king, was forced to submit to threats of force. At Barbados there was actual fighting; there the American Revolution was foreshadowed. For when Sir George Ayscue summoned the island to surrender, on the basis of an act of Parliament, the Assembly of the island replied that it, not Parliament, was the supreme lawmaking body for Barbados. Sir George replied with cannon, and that was that. But here is the very doctrine to be found in the Declaration of Independence, with its reference to Parliament as "a jurisdiction foreign to our constitution and unacknowledged by our laws." Then came the Restoration and the acceptance of Charles II as king.

One legacy the Commonwealth and the Protectorate left to Charles, the policy of mercantilism. The Commonwealth Navigation Act of 1651 was quickly reenacted and strengthened, and a committee of the Privy Council on Trade and Plantations was set up. Then, as Charles and James drew more power into their hands, attempts were made to increase royal authority. In particular, the special status of the "corporate" colonies of Massachusetts, Rhode Island, and Connecticut was attacked. When, in 1684, Charles II got rid of borough charters in England, he similarly got rid of the charters of these three colonies. James went further. New York, when captured from the Dutch in 1666, had been granted to him—indeed, had been named New York after his dukedom. Now he combined it with New England, in one royal government to be known as the Dominion of New England. This overseas Stuart absolutism, however, fell with the Stuart absolutism in England at the landing of William of Orange. When news of that came, Massachusetts revolted, imprisoning Governor Andros as the militia of Middlesex, Essex, and Suffolk marched on Boston, as they would again in 1775. In New York there was fighting and the excesses of Leisler's seizure of power. But all through New England, with the Glorious Revolution in the homeland, its principles were recognized. Rhode Island and Connecticut's charters were revived. Massachusetts got a new charter making its governor a royal official and giving a veto in London on its laws. New York got those same rights, not in the form of a charter but as instructions to the governors. As a result, the Glorious Revolution fixed the pattern throughout the western possessions of England that the "Old Constitution" colonies possess today. Rule in the colony was by an elected assembly and a royal governor who acted through an appointed council. The reference of laws to England for final assent, coupled with the appellate jurisdiction of the Privy Council, had the important result of encouraging the laws of the colonies to tend toward uniformity with each other and to correspond with the basic trends of English law. Imperial affairs, that is, the regulation of trade and foreign affairs, were conducted in London by the Lords of Trade and Plantations, the Secretaries of State, and such relevant departments as found themselves from time to time concerned with transatlantic business.

This system worked well enough if it was not pushed too far and if imagination or restraint, or both, was shown. Up to 1740, the history of English central administration of the colonies is a maze of events that did not happen. Many suggestive ideas got on paper in Whitehall for researchers of future generations to study; at times attempts were even made to put them into effect. But the delays consequent upon sending messages across the Atlantic, and the even greater delays consequent upon the facts of bureaucratic inertia in England, caused those ideas to have only one effect. They created in London a belief that if only someone did act, a strong and efficient government could be set up overseas. As the American Revolution was to show, such a belief could have unfortunate results.

In contrast to what was happening in English offices, in the West Indies and on the American continent institutions and ideas were being created. There is not space here to put down all the history of Jamaica and New York, Tobago and Pennsylvania, Barbados and Massachusetts, Bermuda and Virginia, and the rest of the colonies. But enough should be told to make clear that in these colonies were planted seeds which grew into the present Commonwealth of Nations. Distance from London, the forces of the frontier, and a humanitarian experiment created problems that demanded local solution. Consequently there was a constitutional evolution in which the colonists led and the homeland was offered the choice of following or losing the colonies, as specific examples will show.

The classic early example of the frontier movement is Bacon's Rebellion in Virginia in 1676. Then the men of the inland counties took into their own hands the defense against the Indians, under the leadership of Nathaniel Bacon. This is also an early example of the mistake of checking such action. Because Governor Berkeley blocked Bacon, Bacon and his followers felt forced to revolt. When in due course the revolt was put down, a tradition of resistance had been created. In contrast to this may be put Jamaica. There in the late 1660's, in resistance to Spanish aggression Henry Morgan and other "buccaneers" counterattacked and, in two famous feats of arms and plunder, captured and sacked Panama and Maracaibo. For this Charles II was wise enough to make Morgan a knight and Lieutenant Governor of Jamaica, and he got loyal support in return.

But rarely did British rulers show such practical wisdom. In consequence a constitutional tradition grew up overseas. It is found in the resistance to taxation in Massachusetts, in 1686, when the Rev. John Wise of Ipswich formulated the ringing phrase "no taxation without representation," which the people of Massachusetts put into effect by their own "Glorious Revolution" of 1689. It is found in New York, in 1732 in the Zenger case, when a truculent German printer published annoying truths about the royal governor. Zenger's defense by Andrew Hamilton of Philadelphia made it a principle of Anglo-Saxon law that truth might be a defense against a charge of libel, though it took legislation to complete this development.

Pennsylvania is significant as the first great example of English overseas humanitarianism and also as a living proof that the doctrine of natural rights made practical sense. When, in 1682, William Penn took American lands and jurisdiction from Charles II in exchange for a bad debt, he caught the imagination of the world in a way it is now hard to realize. Here was an attempt to set up a Christian Commonwealth, where not only Quakers but all men might live in peace. A home was given to refugees from religious persecution, so that the Rhineland Protestants fleeing Louis XIV became the ancestors of the Pennsylvania Dutch of today. Indians, too, met with justice. Land was purchased from them, not taken. And these ideas proved themselves in practice. The valley of the Susquehanna filled with homes, prosperity came to those who worked for it. The Quaker ideals of natural rights justified themselves. A challenge to upper-class rule appeared to bear fruit when Benjamin Franklin of Philadelphia became the idol of Paris and when future marshals of Napoleon's armies marched through Pennsylvania as sergeants in French royal regiments. Here, as in other respects, America served as a model for the French Revolution.

As these examples show, here was a problem in statesmanship. These colonies wanted to be loyal to the British Crown, and they would be, if they were sympathetically handled. The trouble was that they usually were not so handled. Then friction came, and men began asking questions about constitutional rights. What happened in Jamaica may throw light on this, for two reasons. First of all, taking a West India island into consideration serves as a reminder of the importance of those islands. Secondly, Jamaica had an especial constitutional problem, which it shared with Tobago; it might be considered a "conquered," rather than a "settled" colony. Whereas, under the doctrine of *Calvin's case* in 1608 Englishmen in a settled colony had automatically the rights of Englishmen, whatever those rights were, Englishmen in a conquered colony had only those rights His Majesty might deign to assign them. The Jamaica Assembly would have none of this. It fought constant battles with the royal governors and in 1679 blandly announced that it had of right all the privileges of the House of Commons. For, it claimed, once the king had promised that an assembly might meet, he could not recall that promise. Later, in a law suit, a resident of Tobago named Campbell secured in 1774 the acknowledgment by the great judge, Lord Mansfield, that such was the law. Then the Jamaica assembly set to work to circumscribe the governor's powers. Potentially, such actions might change the British Empire from a unit into a collection of parliaments held together by a common sovereign.

What, then, do all these things add up to? Virginia, Pennsylvania, Massachusetts, Jamaica, as well as fourteen other colonies, had in them men believing in a doctrine of the rights of Englishmen. More than that, Jamaica had taken a step that Canada would one day follow and had declared that the people of any colony could take over rule just as Parliament had done in England, basing it on this doctrine. Somewhere here the germ of a nation is to be found. It would take mobs and a "tea party," guns and a Congress or two, before the nation would be made. Here is a lesson of these comparatively quiet years. Colonies that governed themselves became nations; the British Empire would continue to exist only if it could incorporate within it such growing nations. And if they were denied the rights of Englishmen, they might go a step further and talk of "natural rights."

In the 1750's something happened to the British Empire. It is an oversimplification to say that that something was William Pitt the Elder. In point of time his access to power was preceded by Robert Clive's defense of Arcot and by Halifax's [1] appointment as President of the Board of Trade. But that simplification may underline the change that occurred. Between 1750 and 1760 imagination and some conscious purpose came to the leadership of imperial affairs, so that what in 1750 had been a collection of colonies and company properties had imbued in it, by 1760, a spirit that made it a conscious Empire. And the tragedy of it is that this empire that was created in a decade was largely thrown away in the two subsequent decades because imagination was lost from the central guidance of the Empire. To continue with this oversimplification, the Empire that Pitt won and made George III lost.

Empire is a tricky word to use, especially when it is preceded by the adjective British. Of course, if one means overseas sovereignty, then England had an Empire long before 1750. But, if one means more than that, if one is thinking of some ideal, some purpose, some uniting spirit, then it is fair to say that what William Pitt symbolized came to fruition in the 1750's. For Pitt had a perhaps illogical but highly practical vision of free self-government across the Atlantic at the same time as joint action by all the King's dominions. This vision was made practical because the time was ripe for it.

[1] The reader should distinguish among George Savile, Marquis of Halifax, 1633 to 1695; Charles Montagu, Earl of Halifax, 1661 to 1715; the above George Montagu Dunk, Earl of Halifax, 1716 to 1771; and the present Edward Frederick Wood, Earl of Halifax, born in 1881. He will, the authors hope, accept their apologetic assurance that all these Halifaxes fill too important niches in the history of England for any one to be left out.

In America a proof of that ripeness was the proposals of the Albany Congress of 1754. That body, though summoned by Lord Halifax to consider Indian problems, went beyond its terms of reference. Under the leadership of Benjamin Franklin the Congress proposed a federal union of the colonies under a royally appointed President General and an elective assembly. This went too far for the colonial assemblies, who rejected it so quickly that no official British rejection was necessary. But significant for the future is that men in America were ready for self-government and imperial cooperation on a large scale.

In India a proof of that ripeness was the sudden expansion of the East India Company's rule, under the leadership of Clive, which should be mentioned here to put it in chronological order, though for topical reasons it is dealt with elsewhere. In Britain, too, the time was ripe for Pitt, when popular opinion called him to power to meet the disasters of the year 1756. An office was waiting for him, the secretaryship of state, the holder of which could issue orders in the king's name wherever the king held sway. Pitt used that dormant power of command to waken the Empire to life. Because he suggested the right measures, he caught men's imagination. His letters to the colonial governments gained willing compliance. It is true he got comparatively small grants of men and money from the colonies, but what he got was freely given.

Elsewhere it is recounted how Pitt's armies and navies made "every wind bring news of victory." Here our theme must be what happened to this spirit of free obedience to central orders, which Pitt had called to life, after George III drove Pitt from office and it fell to other, lesser men to handle the harder questions of peace. For the return to peace brought to the fore certain problems that seem constantly to recur in the history of the British Empire: those of native populations and white settlement; those of imperial troops to keep order and who will pay for them; those of imperial economic cooperation and how it will be guided; and, growing out of these others, those of constitutional relationships within the Empire. It may prove simpler to take each of these problems separately and then to sum up by dealing with the great constitutional problems that arose because the others were mishandled.

When the war ended, there was a tightened enforcement of the Navigation Laws. Authorities dispute whether this was as significant in causing resistance as the American leaders in retrospect asserted. Whether or not it was, out of the discussions of these laws evolved a potential solution to the "constitutional" problem. Some American leaders were willing to admit that the British Parliament had a right to levy on American "external" taxes such as the customs duties which enforced the Navigation Acts. Here was a chance for both sides to make graceful concessions. How it was lost will be told later.

Western lands and relations with the Indians caused further friction and consequent constitutional problems. In London plans were made for dividing up the land; none of these plans came to fruition, but most of them involved violations of early grants to the colonies. Then in 1763 came Pontiac's Conspiracy, the greatest of all the attempts of the red man to drive out the white man. Fortunately for the future United States, the British army defeated it by the skillful generalship of Henry Bouquet at the battle of Bushy Run. But unfortunately for the relations between America and Britain, the Board of Trade in London thereupon issued the Proclamation of 1763, forbidding settlement across the Appalachians, and transferring rule of that area to the military governor of Quebec. It was sensible to have a control of the area where white men and red men might clash, but would-be settlers did not like to be stopped by orders from London. Now arose the further problem of paying for the soldiers who were defending the frontier. To the British it seemed natural for Parliament to levy taxes for this purpose. Did not certain West India islands pay a 4 per cent export tax? Therefore, George Grenville extended across the Atlantic to the North American and West Indian Colonies, the British tax on legal documents, collected by stamps.

At once the British Government ran into a hornet's nest. Already jurists had seriously doubted the rights of the English Government in regard to the colonies across the Atlantic. The Attorney General of Massachusetts, James Otis, had refused to act upon "general warrants," thus preceding the fight made by John Wilkes against them. A local colonial resistance arose that surprised almost everyone with its virulence. "Sons of Liberty" organized and terrorized the men who had accepted posts under the Stamp Act. More than that, the spirit of colonial union, which in 1754 had tended to support the connection with Great Britain, now turned against it. In New York the Stamp Act Congress met to concert measures. The Stamp Act became unenforceable. The Government that proposed it fell, and Shelburne came to office in the first Rockingham Ministry. This repealed the Stamp Act but replaced it by the Declaratory Act of 1766, the basic law of the Empire up until the Colonial Laws Validity Act of 1865 and the Statute of Westminster of 1931. This Act declared that Parliament could legislate for the colonies but normally would not.

At this point there is no need to tell American readers which statesman on which side of the Atlantic wrote which pamphlet or made which speech. What concerns us here is the general course of events and how the story of this internal struggle in the First Empire fits with that of similar struggles in the Second Empire. What is significant is that out of these disputes about western lands, Navigation Laws, and above all taxation there arose a great constitutional dispute. If these problems had been solved, there might have been no raising of "constitutional problems." But they were not solved, and on both sides of the Atlantic men began thinking about principles. By and large, two principles came into conflict. On the one hand it was asserted, by the majority in the British Parliament, that Parliament was the supreme legislature for the Empire, and that to disobey it was disloyalty. On the other hand it was asserted that there were certain basic rights that should not be violated—indeed, truly could not be violated. At first men's arguments on these points were not clear-cut. The Americans and their English friends first spoke of the rights of Englishmen. It was only later, when the Americans were hard pressed in logic, that they turned from legal rights to natural rights as the justification for their resistance. Though many of their English friends here parted company from them, yet those same English friends agreed that many, if not all, the American assertions were sound in English constitutional law. Without going into the details of argument, it seems true that an opportunity for compromise was missed.

Would both sides, could both sides, have come to practical agreement? Perhaps there remained a moment when the old spirit of cooperation might have been revived. There exists, in Pitt's handwriting, a plan for a Cabinet in which there should be a third, or American, Secretary of State. This would be Pitt himself, who would personally solve the problems of the Empire. This is a provoking might-have-been of history, for there is a parallel between 1766 and 1926. Both were years of Empire crisis. In 1926 Arthur James Balfour worked out with General Hertzog of South Africa a formula which kept South Africa loyal to the king. Could Pitt have done the same? After all, what the Americans asked right up to the time of John Dickinson's Olive Branch Petition of 1774 was less than was needed to satisfy Hertzog in 1926. Indeed, yet another parallel exists. What the chief American leaders asked was what was given to Ireland in 1782.

For all the Americans asked was what is now called dominion status. They merely asserted that, though they were subjects of the king, Parliament could not bind them. If their legislatures could settle their problems, they would be loyal to His Majesty and as his subjects would enjoy the rights of Englishmen. That, wrote James Madison many years later, was all that there was to it—though, of course, he did not use the Canadian word "dominion" when he wrote.

Madison seems to have been right—if it is not rather condescending to put it that way. The course of the whole constitutional struggle fits a regular pattern with local variants that has been repeated in Canada, South Africa, Ireland (twice), India, and Egypt. First some sort of seminationalist feeling appears, rather unconsciously. In America it comes from the constant friction between the British official and the local resident. Sometimes it can be overcome—as when George, Lord Howe, and Wolfe got cordial cooperation from colonial troops. Often it cannot. Then measures by the home government irritate the colonists more and more. Such were the Proclamation of 1763, perhaps the revision of the Navigation Acts, and attempts at imperial taxation. Nationalist feeling expresses itself and organizes, as in the outcry against the Stamp Act and the calling of the Stamp Act Congress. The problem of statesmanship is to get that new national feeling on the side of the British Government and not against it.

Unfortunately, though Pitt did come into office, it was not as American Secretary. That office when created in 1768 fell to less able men. Pitt, though Prime Minister, was crippled by gout and by going to the House of Lords as Earl of Chatham. The Cabinet over which he nominally presided and which he seldom attended made the mistake of being too literal-minded. The Chancellor of the Exchequer, Charles Townshend, tried to get American revenue to balance his budget by levying customs duties. Logically, this was in accordance with the distinction Americans were making between internal and external taxation. But the result was merely to rouse resistance once more, and to make Americans reexamine their thinking. Nonimportation agreements were widely signed. Local bodies took high stands. New York and Jamaica both asserted that their assemblies had the rights of the British Parliament. Jamaica might be neglected; an act of Parliament deprived New York of its Assembly. But the nonimportation agreement so affected the London merchants that they forced Parliament to repeal Townshend's taxes, except that on tea. However, with a persistence worthy of a wiser cause, George III caused Parliament, now largely under his direction, to make an issue of principle. A Board of American Customs Commissions was set up in Boston to enforce not only previously accepted customs duties but the Grenville tax on tea.

A lull did come in agitation, except in Virginia, where Patrick Henry in his fight against the "Parson's Cause" was struggling against the endowment of the Church of England, and in Massachusetts. Boston, the seat of Commissioners of Customs, became the seat of trouble. Ships and troops had to be concentrated there. Then came that series of events about which all Americans have studied in school—the Boston Massacre of 1770, the Boston Tea Party of 1774, and the "Intolerable Acts" by which Parliament tried to punish Massachusetts. From the Empire point of view what is significant about them is that out of them grew a body of propaganda which united American and English Whigs in defense of historic English liberties and that out of them also grew the machinery by which American resistance was directed, the Continental Congress.

The sight of Massachusetts being punished by the loss of its liberties and denial of the right to trade through Boston frightened men. Add to this the fact that the Quebec Act, passed at the same time, took western lands away from the other colonies, and suggested that they, too, might feel the retribution of Parliament as had New York and Massachusetts and it is no wonder that, in a surge of sympathy, the Americans united themselves and concerted measures in the First Continental Congress at Philadelphia, in 1774.

Yet still there was hope for peaceable solution. At that Congress Joseph Galloway of Pennsylvania proposed his plan of continental union, which failed of passage by one vote. Such a plan would have settled the whole problem, for this government would have handled all the problems of taxation, defense, and western lands that were causing the trouble. It is true that instead of this the Congress sent to England the inflammatory Suffolk Resolves, sent down from Massachusetts. But wise heads in England could have seized on the opportunity of conciliation. Instead, Chatham's plan of conciliation was rejected.

The English answer was to pour more troops into Boston. Naturally, the reaction was to prepare to resist. The Massachusetts militia was quietly purged of officers and men who might obey royal orders and reorganized to come out at a minute's notice; hence the famous name of "Minutemen." As all know, they did so come out, at Lexington and Concord. Then the siege of Boston turned constitutional protest into an active civil war. Yet even then there were possibilities for statesmanship to heal the breach. When a Second Continental Congress met, another Pennsylvanian, John Dickinson, persuaded that body to send to His Majesty the Olive Branch Petition. Blindly, the King refused to look at it. Chatham (as Pitt now was) and many another Whig sadly told Parliament that coercion was wrong, that Americans were right to defend their rights as Englishmen. But because conciliation failed, new ideas spread abroad in America. A pamphlet, *Common Sense,* got avid attention. And on July 2 and July 4, 1776, the Continental Congress voted the Independence of the Thirteen Colonies and declared the reasons for its action.

With the Declaration of Independence, the American part of the story of the First Empire comes to an end. Once the United Colonies had come to the conclusion that their rights were natural, not just the rights of Englishmen, they were able to bring themselves to renounce allegiance to their sovereign. But the story of the First Empire does not end here. There remains still to be told what may be called a dominion part, an English part, and an Irish part. What is called the dominion part is merely the suggestion of drawing a parallel between the efforts of the thirteen colonies to unite themselves—at Albany, New York, and Philadelphia—with efforts at overseas union elsewhere, such as the Charlottetown and Quebec Conventions of Canada, the two Australian Federal Conventions, and the peripatetic Union Convention of South Africa. In that sense, indeed, the Mount Vernon Conference and the Annapolis and Philadelphia Conventions that finally brought about the federal union of the United States might almost be called part of the history of the British Empire, since they gave the "Fathers of Confederation" in Canada models to follow.

What, however, is more directly to the point is the Renunciation Act of 1778. As Lord North's government began to realize that it could not conquer America, its members bethought themselves, about five or ten years too late, of acceding to American demands. So was passed what became a charter for the West Indies, the Renunciation Act. This pledged. that the British Parliament would never tax for revenue across the Atlantic, and it set up practical rules for preventing any fees or customs duties for the regulation of trade from turning into a tax.

There is yet another commentary on this question of the rights of Englishmen overseas, to be found in the contemporary struggle of the Irish for the rights of Irishmen. Consistently throughout the eighteenth century —indeed, beginning with the Molyneux pamphlets of the 1690's—the Irish had asserted that they had a natural right to independence, that the claims of England as expressed by Poynings's Law were invalid. In 1719 the Irish House of Lords tried to prevent appeals going to the English House of Lords. Though it failed and was met by a Declaratory Act, whose very wording was copied in 1766 for the Declaratory Act of that year relating to America, yet the ideas here raised spread widely. But arguments were of little avail against the facts of English control.

Then, after 1760, matters changed. There was a favorable viceroy, the Lord Halifax we have seen as President of the Board of Trade. Agitation by "patriots" for elections to the Irish Parliament at more frequent intervals than once each reign secured the Octennial Act, which provided for such elections at least once in eight years. It became harder and harder for the viceroys and chief secretaries sent over from England to manage the Irish Parliament as had Strafford in days of old. The speeches of Henry Flood and Henry Grattan were too telling and secured the support of too many independent members. Some sort of crisis might allow the Irish Parliament to break free from the chains of Poynings's Law and become independent of English veto power. That crisis was the War of the American Revolution and, in particular, the exploits of John Paul Jones.

During the later stages of the Revolution, Ireland was denuded of troops to go to the West Indies and America. Then came John Paul Jones's landing at Carrickfergus in 1778. In alarm, regiments of largely Protestant volunteers were raised throughout Ireland under the chief command of the Earl of Charlemont. Here was a situation where the voters in boroughs and counties had arms in their hands and were officered by the members of the Irish Houses of Commons and Lords. The Volunteer Army encamped at Dungannon outside Dublin. Every morning the Convention of the Volunteers met under the presidency of the Earl of Charlemont, who thus won the name of the "Irish Washington." Every afternoon the Parliament at College Green repeated the measures the Convention had voted. All that was asked was the rights of Irishmen to govern themselves without the restrictions of Poynings's Law. That was what the Whigs believed in. When the Rockingham Ministry came into office it repealed Poynings's Law and the act forbidding the Irish Lords to hear appeals. The next year the Fox-North government rephrased that repeal, to give a perpetual pledge that Ireland would be an independent kingdom under the same king as Great Britain, by another Renunciation Act.

What, then, happened to the First Empire? This Irish example suggests that something definitely did happen. The American Revolution won its victories not only on the North American continent but also in the West Indies and in Ireland. By North's Renunciation Act of 1778 a definite policy was set up. It became the intention of the British government never to tax a colony for an imperial revenue. That policy has been followed, by and large, to this day. It also became, under the decision in *Campbell v. Hall*, a rule that once a colony had special rights, those rights, though given by the executive Crown, could be taken away only by a legislative act of Parliament. Furthermore, it became a custom of the constitution that such parliamentary action should be jealously regarded. Bureaucrats in Whitehall were reluctant to ask for such action for fear that Parliament would take the bit between its teeth and change the situation to the benefit not of the bureaucrats but the colonists. This had peculiar results. One solution was to give no rights at all; this was the policy in regard to Canada and Australia. Another was to found colonies with special legislation allowing the executive withdrawal of self-government. This eventually became Empire policy in the British Settlements Act of 1843. But though the principles of the First Empire, as will be told, were evaded, their general tenor remained. It became a basic tenet that an English colony should be self-governing and that any status of tutelage should be but a step toward self-government.

Thus, it would seem that the two Renunciation Acts, the transatlantic one of 1778 and the Irish one of 1783, summed up the character of the First Empire. That Empire had in it, as Professor Gipson has pointed out in his inaugural lecture at Oxford as Harmsworth Professor of American History, the ideas of the present-day Commonwealth of Nations, that a single crown could unite many independent parliaments. Many aspects of the First Empire—chief among these being mercantilism and the then larger claims to power of the Crown—do make it different from the present Commonwealth. But do not the facts bear out this generalization? Or, if they do not entirely, does not this generalization give those facts their truest significance?

Part Three THE TRANSITION TO THE MIDDLE
CLASS 1783–1832

INTRODUCTION

On October 19, 1781, the British soldiers of General Cornwallis marched to the surrender field at Yorktown, Virginia. As the red columns approached the spot where the Americans and French were lined up to receive them, the bands played a new tune, "The World Turned Upside Down." As far as the old British Empire was concerned no tune could have been more appropriate, because both an empire and a system of government had come to an end. The most important colonies of the British Empire were lost, and in consequence George III's personal government was about to fall. In the next year the colonies, now the United States of America, were to draft a treaty of peace with Britain. In 1783 the allies of the Americans, the French, Spanish, and Dutch, were to bring war to a formal conclusion by the Treaty of Paris. At Paris, Great Britain was let off comparatively lightly by these enemies. The French got Tobago and Senegal; the Spaniards, Florida and Minorca. India, Canada, and the West Indies remained British. To contemporaries it appeared that England had suffered a most severe setback. Few realized that the loss of the American colonies might actually make possible the development of Great Britain in the nineteenth century as a great industrial and imperial nation.

But Adam Smith, among others, was bold enough to say that the loss of the colonies would improve rather than hurt the trade and commerce of Great Britain. As time went on, more and more men of influence were converted to his belief that the old system of high protection for Britain's industries had been proven unworkable and that a free exchange of goods and services would bring greater wealth. However, this change would come in the future. At the time most Englishmen were deeply humiliated by the loss of the war and were immediately concerned with the breakdown of the political system that for nearly a decade and a half had been operating under the direction of George III.

The eighteenth-century Empire of Britain had fallen partly because of the colonial administrative policy of the mother country, partly because of the stifling of colonial trade, and partly because of the bad judgment of the individuals whom George III chose to carry out his policies. The loss of the war definitely put an end to the personal government of the King. Political control was returned to the Whigs and Tories. Events soon proved that neither group, however, could long thrive without the sunshine of royal favor and approval.

When Charles James Fox and Lord North formed a Coalition Cabinet, they found out that the King could wreck, if not control, any ministry. Against their India Bill the King threw the entire weight of his personal and constitutional power. Then he replaced them by William Pitt, the second son of the great Earl of Chatham, who thus, in 1784, became the youngest Prime Minister in British history. He was one of the greatest, if not the greatest; fate chose him to pilot the ship of state through the stormy seas of the French Revolutionary Wars. He was equal to the task; the King had used his powers better than he knew when he had asked William Pitt to save him from Fox and North.

William Pitt was a Tory. Except at the end of the period under review, the government of Great Britain was Tory. Addington, Grenville, Perceval, Liverpool, George Canning, Goderich and the Duke of Wellington, the Prime Ministers up to 1830, were Tories. The Duke of Portland was an ex-Whig, but Lord Grey, in 1830, was the first genuine Whig Prime Minister after Pitt. This was a Tory era, because loyalty to the nation in war led to loyalty to the party that led the nation during the war.

Almost a decade of peace and reorganization found Great Britain thriving under the leadership Pitt gave her, from 1783 to the outbreak of the French Revolutionary War in 1792. Only when control of the Channel was threatened did England enter that war. Then, since Fox, the chief Whig, expressed sympathy with the French Republicans, their Rights of Man, and their gospel of liberty, equality, and fraternity, the true Whigs were left in opposition until 1830, the short coalition "Ministry of All the Talents" being but the exception that proves the rule. Credit for final victory belongs to Pitt and his followers, as does blame for defeats and wrong decisions made under the stress of war.

The Tories not only won a great war; at the same time, they helped bring about a new social and economic order without knowing it. For the French Revolution and the Napoleonic Wars changed the face of the world and of Great Britain. On the Continent new nations with new aspirations grew out of the bloodshed that lasted till the battle of Waterloo in 1815. The British played the major role in bringing this about. In Spain and Portugal, in Italy, and in Germany British policies, treasure, and blood created and maintained opposition to French conquests. The Nile, Copenhagen, Trafalgar, and Waterloo were victories that served to one great end—peace. At the Congress of Vienna, where the victors met to create the new world, it was the British whose wisdom caused the drafting of truly lasting terms. Likewise, it was British wisdom that recognized the nature of the new world so created. For this reason Castlereagh and Canning were among the greatest of England's foreign secretaries.

Discovery and recognition of this new way of life was both fast and slow, both complete and incomplete. Because they had lost one Empire in 1783, Britons generally refused to acknowledge the fact that by 1815 they had founded another in Australasia, South Africa, and India, as the wars had confirmed to England control of the sea, the key to such an empire. Demands for materials for the battlefield, demands for income to pay Pitt's income tax and so pay for the battles, made statesmen conscious of the needs of trade and commerce. After the war the security of the sea lanes allowed British merchants to sell British manufactures in the four corners of the earth. Thus, as the Empire became the magnet that attracted migrants, economic power shifted from the farm to the factory, from the squire to the mill owner. It took some time for this truth to achieve political recognition, but it did so when, in 1832, the Reform Bill gave power to the middle classes.

It was hard for the country gentleman to face up to this truth. He knew that he and his kind had led the nation through great peril; he knew that, in days of agricultural prosperity, the land had done its share in paying for the war. It was not clear to him that he could no longer rule alone. Before 1830 some farsighted Tories did dimly recognize this truth. Pitt did, in the measures he sponsored that fostered trade, during the late 1780's. Peel and Huskisson did, in the practical, common-sense measures they sponsored in the late 1810's and early 1820's. For a long time, because the Tories were the party that understood finance, much middle-class opinion gave the Tories support. But many Tories were not farsighted; they did not realize that the weight of money, cotton, and metal gave the middle class overwhelming strength. While the Whigs of this age did not have the financial acumen of their early eighteenth-century predecessors, they still had the traditional Whig alliance with the social and political aims of the middle class. Ideas of *laissez faire*, economic reform, reform of the franchise were among those aims. So were religious tolerance and a hatred of slavery. These were urban ideas, for an urban age, and it was because the Whigs happened to share them that Whigs became the inheritors of political power. For such reasons the old parties of the landed gentry still held sway, because they obeyed the classical politicians' rule of joining those whom one cannot defeat.

Stresses and strains of war raised new problems and accentuated old ones. Naturally enough, new ideas came to men's minds wherewith to meet these problems. Some of the needs of the town were only dimly recognized. Little was done about slums and disease, only slightly more about illiteracy and child labor. But other problems met with more attention. Men thought about how to get more raw materials and adopted Adam Smith's gospel of free trade. Men thought about how to get better administration, and some journeyed to sit at the feet of the political philosopher Jeremy Bentham. There was abroad in the land a belief that men could reform bad government by passing the right kind of laws. Generally, such laws would free men from restraints and let the natural play of common sense solve problems. But at the same time men were wondering what restraints would be the most effective. So it would be that a generation which had planned for liberty laid the foundations for a collective society. But however men thought, with one leading idea the middle classes were more and more being imbued—a belief in the perfectibility of the world.

To give effect to these ideas required struggle. The years from 1815 to 1832 saw riots, one dramatic shedding of blood at "Peterloo," and much invective. Sometimes the riots were hunger riots; at other times they were the consequence of the agitation of new doctrines. But, England being England, the fortunate upshot was that the reform that was demanded noisily was given peacefully. If England had a quiet Glorious Revolution in 1688, she really had another such in 1832. Lists can be given of the outbreaks—the march of the "Blanketeers" of 1816, "Peterloo" in 1818, above all the shameful divorce case of Queen Caroline which had the beneficial effect of allying the aristocratic Whigs with the popular movement. It is a tribute to the political sense of the agitators Cobbett and Hunt and the Whig noble Grey that mutual trust—or, rather, trust on the part of Cobbett and Hunt—bridged a vast social gap. Then when, after the comparative peace of the years from 1822 to 1830, troublous times came again, it was possible for a disciplined agitation to put arguments of force back of Grey's arguments of reason. Thus Grey put through that highly aristocratic revolution, the Great Reform Bill, when an upper-class Cabinet— even the members of the House of Commons in Grey's Cabinet had titles —caused the government of England to become responsive to the will of the people.

Thus the transition during the years from 1783 to 1832 from an agricultural economy to an industrial one was gradual but steady, and the transition from the rule of an established class of landlords to sharing that rule with the newly powerful urban middle class was also gradual but steady. This transition was marked by the rise and spread of ideas—that the franchise should be given to those with a "stake in the country," that freedom of trade caused prosperity, above all the Benthamite idea that the aim of government was "the greatest happiness of the greatest number." It is true that hardships came with these transitions. The change from country to urban living caused the slums that became the "Condition of England"

INTRODUCTION 255

question. But over all, this was an age of progress. In these years men's faith in progress seemed justifiable.

With its changes, good and bad, the Great Britain of 1832 was noticeably different from the Great Britain of 1783. A victory after a generation of war, till then her most costly and bloody war, had left her even more mistress of the seas and the owner of a new Empire. After the American war she had been largely a trading and agricultural country; after the Napoleonic Wars she was primarily the workshop of the world, then its merchant and carrier of goods, and only in third degree an agricultural nation. Becoming an industrial nation required that society and its institutions become adjusted to new conditions and new ideas, and called forth a new set of leaders who would better understand a new age. After 1832 the history of Great Britain is that of the growth and development of an urbanized society. The years from 1783 to 1832 may be thought of as years of painful but successful transition, in which the machine replaced the plough, the factory the farm, while the middle-class businessman joined the squire in the seats of the mighty.

23

ECONOMIC AND SOCIAL HISTORY

1783–1832

The sixteenth and seventeenth centuries were a seedtime in the history of Western culture. Then were sown broadcast ideas of the Renaissance and Reformation, out of which grew our modern world. In more ways than can be considered here these ideas germinated. From these seeds, in the early eighteenth century, strong plants sprouted up in the form of new methods in industry and agriculture. In a previous chapter it has been told how such inventions as Kay's flying shuttle, Hargreave's spinning jenny, and Crompton's mule transformed the manufacture of textiles; how Watt's steam engine made practicable the use of a new form of power; how the work of the Darby family, among others, gave Great Britain more and better iron and steel. Likewise the new techniques of the so-called Agricultural Revolution have been mentioned. With these economic changes, naturally, came corresponding social changes. Then, to continue this horticultural metaphor, in the late eighteenth and early nineteenth centuries these new plants bore abundant fruit. It is of that fruition that this chapter will speak. But this it will do with a changed metaphor. Instead of speaking of the growing plant, it will speak of the turning wheel, by using the phrases Industrial Revolution and Agricultural Revolution.

The Industrial and Agricultural Revolutions may be summed up as the use of machines in turning out goods both to satisfy demands and to create them. For when the ideas of applied mechanics took form in factories, towns, farm machinery, canals, and roads, then new markets were inevitably produced. Both in tempo of production and in bulk of goods produced, the late eighteenth and early nineteenth centuries saw a social and economic turnover. The factory system opened up a new life for the British. It made necessary the adoption of new economic and social policies and resulted in the gradual replacement of the plough by the machine as the implement used by most men in earning a livelihood. Between 1783 and 1832 the history of the Industrial Revolution in Great Britain is that of consolidation and extension. Prosperity and misery naturally accompanied these rapid changes. Men lived less and less in the country and more and more in towns, where were to be found the banks and factories. These years of mechanization were years of urbanization.

One evidence of the effect of the Industrial Revolution on the nation is found in the unprecedented growth of population. At the beginning of the eighteenth century the total population of the United Kingdom was under eight million. In 1780 it had shot up to 12,560,000; in 1801, to 15,717,000; in 1811, to 17,927,000; and in 1831, to 24,133,000. In about fifty years the population had doubled itself. The factory and trading centers of the north and midlands grew dramatically, Glasgow grew from a town of 77,385 in 1801 to 140,043 in 1821. In the same period Liverpool grew from 77,653 to 135,000. Wherever the factory system was developed, as in Birmingham, Sheffield, or Bradford, villages and towns became busy cities in less than two generations. Sometimes cities were the direct result of industrial activities. Etruria in the northern Midlands became after 1769 first a village, then a factory town because pottery of the finest texture and glaze was fired there under the management of Josiah Wedgwood. While towns and villages were becoming factory cities, trade with the world reflected the stimulus of the revolution.

In spite of years of war and partly because of war demands, manufactures and trade showed a surprising increase. Years of blockade and shipping hazards and losses had some effect in holding back trade. Depression following the end of the wars retarded it only temporarily, as the statistics in the accompanying table show. These figures demonstrate the power and vital role of the machine in the new era. As demand and use increased production, more efficient means of transportation naturally were found.

TRADE, 1780–1830
(In pounds sterling)

Year	Imports	Exports	Total
1780	£ 10,800,000	£ 12,600,000	£ 23,400,000
1800	24,100,000	43,200,000	67,300,000
1820	29,700,000	44,200,000	73,900,000
1830	43,200,000	45,800,000	85,100,000

The ancient and sure carriage by coastal sailing vessel was rivaled for the first time by canals, by turnpikes, and finally by railways. The happy combination of trial of new methods, their application, and consequent creation of demand that sums up the story of the Industrial Revolution is found in the canals. It has already been told how James Brindley and the Duke of Bridgewater first connected a coal mine with Manchester by canal and then extended that canal to allow goods to be shipped from Manchester to the sea. By 1777 the Bridgewater experiment had successfully led to the construction of a network of canals across the Pennine range of hills, so that by the Grand Trunk Canal woolens made in Yorkshire could be more easily sent from Liverpool to India and the colonies. Expenses in carrying were slashed, while the safety and comparative speed of delivery were sharply increased. By trunk and branch canals in 1832 goods from London could be exchanged with those of the northern mill towns. Canals provided means of sending in bulk, whether raw material or finished products. With such arteries open for it, it is not surprising that trade increased. Hand in hand with the digging of canals went the construction of efficient all-weather turnpikes. It has also been told how turnpike trusts developed a network of roads, to allow men and messages to travel faster than ever they had since Roman times. Here again, an engineer had to lead the way. Thomas Telford, originally a bridge engineer, showed how to build roads in the most difficult of terrains in Scotland, and John Macadam, who gave his name to the new type of road, developed a construction of crushed stones and fine stones, that, after being rolled and tamped, made possible rapid safe travel by coach.

Coaching inns, regular runs by mail coaches, and swarms of passengers were the products of the new highway construction. An average of eleven miles per hour was maintained in good weather by the fast coaches which ran on schedule from London and provincial towns. Traffic became heavy enough that the tolls on trunk roads brought comfortable profits during the first and second decades of the nineteenth century. Afterward highways were forced into the background by the railroads. Then by the 1850's the trusts gave place to local-government bodies that assumed responsibility for road repair and construction.

By 1832 came another development in the communications revolution, the use of the steam engine. Robert Fulton's experiments on the Hudson River proved practical when the *Savannah* crossed the Atlantic in 1819. On land George Stephenson, backed by the loans of Quaker bankers, successfully applied steam to railway locomotion in the years between 1825 and 1830. Stationary steam engines had been used to pump water from mines, lift heavy loads, and haul cars of coal up steep inclines. Rails had been laid to run cars from mine heads to canals or loading points. Stephenson made possible hauling cars on rails. To do this, iron T rails had to be cast. Construction experiments on roadbeds and rail carriages had to be carried out. The tubular boiler had to be invented. The steam engine did not merely change communications; it also changed manufacturing, as it replaced water as the chief motive power for machines.

Development of a steam-powered economy was particularly easy in Britain. The basic ingredients of iron and coal for making engines and rails were on hand. They were usually found together in industrial areas, of good quality, and with no apparent limit to the amounts that could be cheaply mined. There was present the fortunate combination of demand, invention, engineering genius, and raw materials to make up a thriving and expanding industry. Later on, in connection with the factory system, the implications of this fact will be discussed.

England's tax policy during these years favored industrial expansion. Pitt's remissions of customs duties in the late 1780's made raw materials cheaper. Though there was a wartime income tax, levied from 1797 on, it was immediately repealed when peace came in 1815. Though there was, on the statute books, a system of Navigation Laws potentially crippling to overseas trade, the long period of war from 1793 to 1815 in effect canceled them out. England's command of the seas eventually gave her a monopoly of the carrying trade, though there was competition from the growing American merchant marine and from the merchant marines of such nations as from time to time were able to be neutral in the world struggle. When the war ended and trade revived, a sliding scale of tariffs for imported grain and reciprocal trade treaties carried out Pitt's ideas in part. In the 1820's William Huskisson, at the Board of Trade, did much to remove restrictions on business, whether in the form of nagging rules or in the form of shackling and really unproductive taxation. It is true that war, in 1797, forced England off the gold standard, not to be resumed till 1819. It is true that the national debt ballooned upward from £370 million pounds in 1793 to £900 million in 1816. But the burden was bearable, because those who governed England knew that high taxes often reduced revenue, and because they were judicious in the way they taxed or strained the money market with loans.

The financial structure of Great Britain was also an aid to the Industrial Revolution. Here a widespread system of private banks did much. From these banks came notes to use in regions where metal currency was scarce, commercial credit necessary for day-to-day business transactions, and sometimes construction loans or contact with would-be investors. In London, at least, this credit structure was backed up by the resources of the Bank of England.

The Bank of England had been organized as a joint stock company in 1694. After 1751 it took on the payment and management of the national debt. In the eighteenth century it had come to be the bank of the government. Up to 1826 it was the only incorporated bank allowed to issue notes; after that, it had the monopoly of such issue within sixty-five miles of Threadneedle Street in London. Furthermore, it held the government deposits. Since London, with seventy other important banks, was the financial center of the nation, the Bank's steady and reliable operations gave strength and confidence to all banks. During this time a central clearinghouse evolved, taking formal shape in 1810. Lloyd's, the center of overseas insurance, and the largest of the country's stock exchanges were there, too.

In the years 1783 to 1832 there were, in England and Wales, over 800 private banks. Some were badly managed or, as the crash of 1825 and 1826 showed, speculated too much. Often their managers failed to learn the first lesson of banking—the difference between a note and a mortgage. Yet they were essential to business in the areas they served, for their notes supplied the currency with which to do business. That was why, in 1826, the foundation of provincial joint stock banks was legalized. This added such provincial banks as the well-managed Liverpool and Manchester District Bank to the national credit system.

Money to lend was very seldom in short supply. Great London houses such as those of the Rothschilds and Barings had enough to lend to foreign governments, as in the case of the French loan in 1817. In the early 1820's a speculative lending mania hit British banks and some £21,129,000 was put into South America. Most of the South American loans turned out badly. This was not the case in these years with the millions put in building factories or canals, and in backing new business ventures.

Even sounder and more farsighted than English and Welsh bankers were those of Scotland. The Scottish banking system consisted of joint stock banks, i.e., incorporated banks, with many branches. Most of Scotland's lending was done through four or five banks. Unlike some English banks there was rarely a question of insufficient reserves or threats of closing because of runs for specie or falling off in business. Their stability and excellent management greatly aided the start of the factory system in Scotland.

Important in pushing forward the Industrial Revolution was a new man of industry, the factory manager and owner. For factories by the 1780's were spreading throughout England and changing the face of the land. The matter of names must not confuse us here. Factories, after all, are places where machines are concentrated. Englishmen did call places where spindles were concentrated cotton mills. They did call the concentration of power looms in one spot a cotton shed. But essentially these are factories, and the essence of a factory is that it is a place where machines are brought together and where to those machines are brought workers willing to submit to a discipline which will enable them to produce more efficiently than if they were alone. Furthermore, there must be someone to instill this discipline. If one says that Sir Richard Arkwright was more important for having invented the foreman than for having invented the water frame, the statement would be technically incorrect, on two counts: in 1785, a court gave Kay the credit for the idea of the frame; foremen had been known long before Arkwright's time. But the statement may serve to drive home the importance of what Arkwright achieved in organizing labor so as to gain the maximum productivity. It was that achievement which raised him, literally, from rags to riches and won him his title.

Managers of this type often were intelligent and hardy workmen who by energy, hard work, and ruthlessness got ahead of their fellows. They founded dynasties of middle-class wealth and power. Between 1783 and 1832 the Peels, the Arkwrights, the Darbys, and the Wedgwoods became millionaires and men of stature in the land. The son of the wealthy Robert Peel became a leader of the Conservative party in the 1820's and was later Prime Minister. These men grew up with the business. They knew intimately every phase of the operation. They were too often unsympathetic with their fellow workers. Too often they sacrificed human to financial consideration. They were, however, the men who made the Industrial Revolution a success. They were naturally believers in *laissez faire* in government and business. This attitude guaranteed that they would be ignorant of the social problems created by their factories and policies of management.

One of the reasons for the development of the new type of industrial manager was the fact that the Nonconformists, numerous in the north of England, were traditionally interested in trade and business. Many Nonconformists believed that working very hard, paying debts, saving money, and carefully investing it were acts thoroughly in keeping with God's laws. The business community of England in general knew that the devil lay in wait for those who were idle and poor. Poverty was a sign of sin and sloth. Wealth was a symbol of the industrious and virtuous application of time and energy. The good Christian was he who had employment and saved his money.

The middle-class Nonconformists were not the only ones who were eager to gain wealth through factory operations. The members of the Established Church of England were just as eager to take part in making money as the Nonconformists and for much the same reasons. The Scotch Presbyterian found his Calvinism a help rather than an impediment in his pursuit of honestly earned profits. Work, saving, and shrewdness kept away poverty and the devil from the industrious Scot.

In addition to the factory owner, another member of the industrial family became important, for slightly different reasons. This man was the factory worker, who unlike the owner or manager could not amass wealth and have open to him and his children a place in the governing classes of the nation. While everyone in these years looked to the owner and manager for leadership as a representative in the new age, few thought of the worker who slaved at very low wages from twelve to fourteen hours a day in the owner's factory. The worker's economic and social plight in these years will be discussed later. It should be mentioned here before we consider how the factory where he worked became the center of the industrial town and the smoking symbol of British urbanization.

The factory was built to house machinery, but it raised social problems. In days when the medical profession was only dimly aware of the causes of epidemics of cholera and smallpox, the factory owner could not have known about sanitary engineering, light, heat, or safety devices. Factories were all too often dirty, unlighted, and full of booby traps in the form of unguarded machinery. They were constructed with an eye to machine production and not to the physical needs of men who tended the machines. In many industries proximity to a waterfall, a canal, or a mine determined the factory site. Then workers' homes were built to conform to the factory. The object in view was to have as many workers as possible crowded together as close to the factory as possible. Concern was not shown for how the barracklike dormitories for workers were constructed or whether they were supplied with living comforts.

Only the exceptional mill owner like Robert Owen built with a regard for the worker's health and the development of his character. Growing cities in the industrial areas presented a gray, dirty, and odoriferous façade to the visitor. Rows and rows of houses were joined together with rudimentary paving and sanitation. Factory buildings enclosed by fences were merely more noisy and larger buildings. The Industrial Revolution in this sense was not a pretty or wholesome thing to see and know. Within these towns and factories, however, goods were turned out of such quality and in such profusion from 1783 to 1832 that a nation could live and grow from their sale. Some idea of the increase of the production of textiles in this period may be gained by noting the increased value of the total production, taking into account the unusual rise in prices brought about by the French wars. Also an indication of the growth of the industry will be found in the figures on the increase of the number of pounds produced. During the years from 1781 to 1800, the value of textiles produced in the British Isles was £620,000. In the years from 1801 to 1820, the value had risen to £980,000. In the years from 1781 to 1800, approximately 2,000,000 pounds of cotton goods were manufactured; in the years from 1801 to 1820, 2,500,000 pounds. Woolen goods showed the same type of increase. From 1781 to 1801, 4,100,000 pounds of woolen goods were manufactured; from 1801 to 1820, 4,400,000 pounds.

Textile manufacture was but one of the many industries that flourished. Iron was another. In the business of smelting and making iron goods the demands of war as well as the discovery of new processes gave tremendous encouragement to the growth of the factory system. Ironmasters had experimented with coal, steam, and new types of furnaces and smelters during the eighteenth century. The war years, of course, demanded more cannon than had been made previously.

Initiative of individuals as well as war were contributing factors to the growth of the iron and steel industry and the Industrial Revolution in general. Ironmasters such as the Darby family experimented with the use of coke and sand molds in the process of smelting. In the 1780's the Darby interest owned both mines and smelters, and in the following years this family helped develop new methods, such as puddling and pouring pig iron into ingots.

The immediate effect of the war years upon the demand for iron was so great that while in 1788 only 68,300 tons were produced, 300,000 tons were turned out in 1810. The production of iron increased in 1830 to 680,000 tons. Part of this increase was absorbed in overseas markets. When President Thomas Jefferson imposed the United States embargo on British goods in 1807, over two-fifths of the metal goods of Birmingham were being sent to the United States.

Making possible exports of iron and of textiles was the new use of coal. For centuries London had heated its drafty houses with coal carried by broad-bottomed sailing barges from Newcastle. Men thought of it only as a domestic fuel. Into the seventeenth century wood provided the charcoal necessary to smelt iron. As the forests were cut down and wood became a scarce item, coal was tried and found usable for industrial purposes. Since coal and iron were found in the ground in proximity, this development was almost inevitable. In the form of coke, coal satisfied superbly well the demands for industrial fuel. By 1783 and after, industrial areas of Britain were distinguished by the haze created by coal smoke. Soon coal mining became one of the major industries of the nation.

It should not be thought that in becoming a manufacturing nation Great Britain ceased to be a mercantile one. Because the Napoleonic Wars drove the merchant marines of most other nations from the sea, she obtained a near monopoly of the carrying trade, her nearest rival being the United States. In consequence technical advances were made elsewhere, especially in the United States where was developed not only the steamboat but shipping lines with regular sailing, beginning with the Black Ball Line from New York to Liverpool in 1816.

It is sometimes easy to attribute the entire success of the British to their factories and ships. It is easy to forget that from 1783 to 1832 the basic economic activity of Great Britain was farming and that application of new farming techniques met the pressure of unusual times for agricultural production, in what amounted to an agricultural revolution. Though attraction of labor from the farms to work in the mills altered the living patterns of thousands, agriculture continued throughout the period to be the basic means of livelihood for a majority of the people. Urban areas may have grown in size and wealth, but in 1820 fewer than a dozen towns in Great Britain had a population of over 50,000. In any city, London included, an hour's drive in a carriage from the center of the town would put the traveler in green fields. The country life and its traditional social and economic system continued to supply Britons with both food and ideas of social behavior.

The center and heart of the British rural community was the village, a unit for the most part economically and socially self-sufficient. Its lands produced enough to feed its inhabitants. Its spinning wheels produced the thread which its looms wove into enough cloth to clothe them. The village inn provided them with refreshment; a church, and sometimes as well a Dissenting chapel, took care of their spiritual needs. This was the rock-bottom foundation of British life.

Its economic basis was agricultural methods that went back to the open-field system that the Angles, Jutes, and Saxons had brought with them across the North Sea. The land was tilled in common; its pasturage was grazed in common. In great open fields of twenty to forty acres' extent, furrows or ridges (called headlands), marked out strips which either were annually assigned in rotation to each villager, according to ancient custom, or were more permanently his. Also according to ancient custom, crops were assigned to the fields. Usually two fields would be planted, while one would lie fallow, so that crops were rotated each year that the fields were planted. A field would bear wheat one year, bear rye the next, and the third year lie fallow. The farmer had cows or pigs and horses that grazed with those of his neighbors on the village common, land traditionally free to all to use. The large farmers might work, with help, thirty or forty strips of land. The smaller farmer might cultivate from five to ten strips. Each type of farmer lived in a one- or two-room cottage to which were attached a garden and outbuildings. In the period between 1783 and 1832 this over-all pattern was not followed in every portion of the nation. In southern counties, such as Kent, the open-field system had been replaced by enclosures as was true in small areas throughout the country. Also in some areas fields tilled one year might be allowed to lie fallow so that they might be grazed over by the livestock the next year. But this was the norm to which Englishmen referred in their thinking about rural life.

With practically every rural community of this sort was associated a distinctive hierarchy and an active and persistent way of life. At its base were the agricultural laborers, working for daily wages, with but rarely a chance to rise in the world. Next came the farmers, usually men who leased land, usually employers of the agricultural laborers. At the top came the landlord class, some of them plain squires and some men of titles and vast estates. But all these were bound together in the nexus of their common agricultural interest. For the upper classes were farmers themselves in thought and occupation. They planted crops and rode to hounds as did their tenants, so that every villager knew the squire. They worshipped God in reserved pews in the same church where their tenants sat behind them. Often from the county bench, as justices of the peace, they imposed fines or ordered roads mended. At times of crises, such as were deputy lieutenants commanded the yeomanry, who too often had to back up the unpaid and unwilling village constables in keeping the peace. Thus agricultural laborer, farmer, and landlord looked at most things the same way.

It was this basic similarity of thought that kept rural Britain at peace during the generation of war, from 1793 to 1815, and in the agricultural distress that followed. It took many years of distress to trigger off the "Last Laborers' Revolt" of 1830, and that has now also slipped into oblivion because it was not really a revolt but a mass movement of protest. For even those who had left the village way of life looked back on it nostalgically. The reformer Cobbett was most telling when in his *Rural Rides* he contrasted the countryside, which he loved for what it stood for, with the fast-growing "wens" that were breaking out on the body politic, the cities that somehow seemed to him so un-English. Many an officer in Army or Navy could handle his men the better because he was a gentleman born or perhaps a parson's son, like Nelson, and for that reason instinctively knew what was in their minds. Englishmen accepted this social as well as economic hierarchy as a natural thing. As children they learned in their catechism "to order themselves lowly and reverently to all their betters . . . and to do their duty in that state of life to which it shall please God to call them." In later life they usually followed these injunctions, without giving up a sturdy independence of mind. Thus the village life gave England great social solidarity. But this way of life soon would receive an economic shock.

At the end of the eighteenth century the age-old pattern of open fields, cultivated in strips and interspersed between woodlands and commons, was to be radically changed. As has been described, in the mid-eighteenth century there came innovations in agriculture. Such was the sowing of turnips to fertilize the land and provide winter food for cattle, with which is connected the name of Lord Townshend, "Turnip Townshend." Such were the emphasis on sheep grazing caused by Robert Bakewell's improvements in the breeds of sheep, and the mechanical sowing of seed by drills, advocated by Jethro Tull. The ruling classes of England enthusiastically took up these innovations. Did not King George III himself breed pigs and cattle and write articles for agricultural magazines under the name of "Farmer George"? All these innovations required that the great open fields be broken up and "enclosed" into more manageable fields of some two or three acres. Then seven- and nine-course rotations of crops, as proposed by

Arthur Young and used by Thomas Coke at Holkham, would be feasible. Therefore legally—or illegally—attacks were made on the basis of this rural economy, the sharing in common of field, pasture, and woodland. The name for these attacks is enclosure.

Enclosure was no new thing. Since the fifteenth century landlords and yeomen alike had nibbled away at the common-field system. Sometimes yeomen agreed to split up the fields. This seems to have happened in Kent, when hop cultivation came in. Sometimes landlords seem to have taken their lion's share of this. But agreement, purchase, or inheritance could go only so far. Villagers had vested rights in the common land, of which they could be deprived only by act of Parliament. Therefore, increasingly, applications were made to Parliament for Acts of Enclosure. During the eighteenth century there were over 4,000 such separate acts. These usually went smoothly through a Parliament of landowners. Finally, in 1801, a General Enclosure Act was passed, to facilitate the process of piecemeal legislation.

Enclosure had the effect of making the rich richer, the poor poorer. It struck particularly at the yeoman, the man who had control of enough land to support himself and his family in decent comfort. Either he got a bit more land, and rose to being a large farmer, or he sank to being a property-less hired laborer. To him the loss of common rights, such as to pasture a cow and cut firewood, meant far more than the few shillings of cash he was paid for it under the average enclosure act. The appearance of threshing machines was a severe blow. Many an agricultural laborer had raised himself in life from the high seasonal wages paid a man who had a flail and a threshing floor. That was why threshing machines were a special target for mob violence in riots. Thus enclosure and new methods helped to destroy a class of independent and self-respecting farmers. In the past they had been hailed as the best type of Englishman. Progress, in this instance, was dearly bought because it reduced the prosperity of so many small farmers and workers. The yeomen as a class, however, were not entirely destroyed. A large number of yeomen and small landholders were to be found farming under handicaps in every county well into the nineteenth century. Prosperity withheld from the smaller farmer was not denied to his richer and more scientific neighbor, for under enclosure agricultural production rose markedly.

Throughout the years of war the demand for grain and meat was unusual. High prices prevailed because of the pressure of war and the unusual number of bad harvests. The farmer of means and broad acres greatly prospered. He bought land or enclosed it. His labor was to be had cheaply because his men had to work or starve. The weekly wages he paid his laborers increased on the average of about three shillings from 1783 to 1815, but this increase did not mean that the farm laborer could buy more because of a tremendous increase in the cost of living to all classes. Then with the end of the war came the end of this war-created prosperity for the landlords and the large-scale farmers. Therefore, they turned to the government for help, through strengthening of the tariffs on foodstuffs, known as the Corn Laws. (The English call all food grains "corn.") After 1815, the English rural way of life became closely tied with these Corn Laws. Such laws dated back, in fact, to medieval times, when taxes on imports and bounties on exports had helped keep farm prices up. As long as England grew her own food, which was true up to about 1750, and again as long as war and the consequent reduction of trade with the grain ports of the Baltic and the Black Sea kept grain prices up, the Corn Laws remained secondary in economic importance. But after 1815 world trade reopened and grain poured in. Here came a struggle between the landed gentry and the farmers, demanding protection for agriculture, and the mill owners and mill hands, demanding that the price of food be cut. During these years both sides became dissatisfied. Food prices were kept up, by a Corn Law which set a sliding tariff. They were not kept up enough to preserve many an overextended farmer from ruin, with consequent ruin of landlords from loss of rents. Between 1820 and 1825 wheat prices, measured in shillings for the imperial quarter of eight bushels, fell as low as 46, and never rose above 67, when in the war years they had gone above 80. It was these bad years which bred agricultural distress, and made many, Tory landlords and the Radical Cobbett alike, fear that Old England was going to rack and ruin.

A general idea of the production of agriculture in this period may be obtained by comparing the acreage in England and Wales which was put to various uses in 1808 and 1827. In 1808 arable land in use was estimated at 11,575,000 acres. In 1827 this fell to 11,143,370 acres. In 1808 meadow and grazing lands were estimated at 17,479,000 acres; in 1827 this rose to 17,605,630 acres. Total for both types of land in 1808 was 29,054,000 and in 1827 it was 28,749,000. The above figures show the effect of the enclosure movement in increased pasturage and also a general decline in the number of acres devoted to agricultural activities.

The vast changes caused by the introduction of the factory system and the enclosure of the open fields has been called revolutionary. These two certainly caused a social revolution. They made a few much more wealthy than they had been. That contrast highlighted the poverty of the poor. Those poor, it should be noted, were moved from a way of life which they knew and understood, the common-field rural village, to one they did not understand, of being propertyless wage earners either in the fields or the towns. About the significance of this change, men had many ideas. But on one thing they did agree, that there was a "Condition of England Question." At this point some general thoughts may prove clarifying.

It is easy, by gathering statistics and quoting contemporary opinions, to make out a case against the ruling classes of Britain as socially callous. But before passing judgment certain facts must be kept in mind. First of all, these were new problems they were facing. They had had no experience of the past to guide them. Secondly, when the British middle classes were shown an evil that needed remedying, they were willing to act. The very men who saw nothing wrong in working a nine-year-old child fourteen hours a day in a dark factory regarded the slave trade as a mortal sin and gave generously not only of money but of time to free the slave. Furthermore, what authoritative guidance these men could find told them that the cure was letting things alone. If they read the works of Adam Smith, Thomas Malthus, or David Ricardo, they found piled up arguments to the effect that interference was harmful. They looked around themselves and saw many proofs of the validity of this generalization. Why not believe that it was universally true, and that the ills they did notice were best cured by the efforts of those suffering from those ills? It is only proper to hold the balance scales even. If there were ills created by the Industrial and Agricultural Revolutions, there were also counterbalancing, even overbalancing, benefits. It can be said that the total wealth of the land, even the total wealth per head, was raised. By wealth is here meant much what is meant by the phrase "real wages"—not monetary advantage but being better off, all things considered. Without condoning what then was wrong, this should be kept in mind.

The laboring multitudes were badly off when their lot is compared to that of their grandchildren. When his life is measured against those of his fellow workers in Germany or France, the British laborer, whether in town or country, was fortunately placed. True, in both town and country he was likely to be illiterate. Furthermore, he was usually hungry. Hence, he was willing to riot for bread, for the Whigs, for peace, or for the breaking of machines that he thought kept him unemployed. In the towns he was likely to live more unhealthily than did his poverty-stricken cousin in the country. He was, however, in these years, slowly learning that in his numbers lay his hope for recognition and salvation. In spite of, and because of, his dirty, lowly position, he started out to win practical and economic control over his destinies. With the help and encouragement of many of the middle and upper classes, the worker cut out some of his old vices. During the war years and throughout the years of depression, he became less drunken and more eager to work. He was to be found trying generally to know more and to say more, and in the end he was to succeed partly in making known his opinions.

It is possible also to paint the condition of the masses in too somber colors. If the hovels and gutters had truly been as horrible as royal commissions and reformers described, it is doubtful if anyone living in them could have survived. The high death rate and the unquestioned prevalence of epidemics, however, show that in the towns the shocked humanitarian did not draw too much on his imagination.

Necessity, or the prospect of better housing, food, and perhaps advancement were the reasons why people sought employment in the factories. Both parents and children were put to work. It was discovered that children could more ably than adults carry on certain spinning operations such as tying broken yarns. At once there developed a systematic exploitation of children. Among other things, these were more amenable to a foreman's discipline than were adults. They could be made more easily to work fourteen hours a day with little time off for recreation or food. Their health was undermined in ill-ventilated, ill-heated, and dangerous work places. They and their parents were held to rigid discipline of six long working days a week, with overtime sometimes on Sundays and holidays. In many mills it was customary for the foreman to use the whip to restore the flagging energies of children who were not sufficiently nimble in mending thread or in operating machines.

If children and adults were neglected in matters of health and safety within the factories, they were forced to submit to even worse conditions outside. New mill towns grew without the slightest care for public health or civic planning. Jerry-built slums thrown together by speculators were the order of the day. Families were herded into badly lighted, disease-ridden barracks unsupplied with water or the basic conveniences of life. In Glasgow and Manchester were found dark courts in whose apartments perhaps a dozen people were expected to live in one room. Filth of the household was thrown into the open courtyard below.

In Manchester thousands slept on damp straw in basement rooms which constantly were flooded by frequent rains. Often workers in coal mines spent months underground. In less than a generation the manufacturing towns, like the mines, became the abodes of sickly, malformed, and physically inferior people. It is a sad fact that mentality and the morals of British industrial workers were all too often in keeping with the sordidness of their environment. It is a wonder that so many of them had the strength and courage to struggle at all.

A few statistics, vital and sickening, may give some idea of how town life affected the worker. At the end of this period, 1832, England was swept by a cholera epidemic. In one town, Exeter, 402 persons, or 1.4 per cent of the population, died during the summer's plague because there were no sewer pipes and an inadequate water supply. In the city of Bristol 1,300 of the 3,000 houses had no water supply. In the town of Leeds one street had not, in 1832, been cleaned for fifteen years. In Manchester from 60 to 65 per cent of the children born in the slums of Ancoats died from disease or similar causes before their fifth year. In nearly every town it was common practice to throw refuse on the streets, which were not drained by sewers. Wells were sunk in courtyards or street intersections that caught filth as it drained downward. Typhoid fever was accepted as an inevitable and unavoidable disease.

The need of the workers for better conditions led many to condemn the factory system on humanitarian and moral grounds. Many, including factory owners such as the first Sir Robert Peel, sought to improve the factory system by abolishing some of the most vicious phases in its operation. In 1802 a Health and Morals Act for apprentices in factories was passed by Parliament under Sir Robert Peel's sponsorship providing for the improvement in standards of living for operatives in textile factories. Thus during and after the Napoleonic Wars the condition of the English factory worker was made a political issue.

Richard Oastler at the beginning of the 1830's organized, for purely philanthropic reasons, the Ten Hour movement. This reform demanded a reasonable working day, good working conditions, and fair treatment for workers. As an estate agent he had been thrown in contact with agricultural workers and was shocked by their plight. A visit to Bradford in 1830 showed him the plight of workers in industry, and he began an agitation that spread throughout the industrial areas of Lancashire and Yorkshire. Although he personally did not succeed in winning his own immediate goals, he nevertheless was instrumental in awakening the middle and upper classes to the need for humanitarian reforms in the factory system.

Oastler and his fellow practical philanthropists were savagely attacked by mill owners and theoretical political economists. These said that interference with the operation of the factory system would shorten hours and raise wages and was an attack upon the immutable laws of economics. This honestly held belief, along with plenty of self-interest, explains the strength of opposition to factory reform later on, among members of the political party that called itself Liberal.

The rise and the fall of real wages, here, affected the degree of social discontent. During the generation of the French wars, the twenty-odd years from 1793 to 1815, the average wage increased 20 per cent. But the cost of living, while fluctuating, increased 87 per cent. Not until the depression of 1815 to 1820 had hit industry did the cost of living fall. Thus in the 1820's the worker's penny bought more. Increased demand for food and clothing helped also to stimulate supply. A trend was started in the 1820's that continued long after 1832, the time limit of our present study. Falling prices and steady demand allowed the worker to get more of the goods of farm and factory. His real wages increased about 50 per cent over what they had been during the war period. At first the worker probably felt only slightly the improvement made by a gradual increase in the amount his money could buy. He was more concerned with living from day to day in unpleasant circumstances.

The Industrial and Agricultural Revolutions had an obvious outward effect. The face of Great Britain, especially that of England, Wales, and southern Scotland, was permanently altered between 1783 and 1832. Before this period the factory system had not caused a rebuilding of the towns, nor had the canal creased the landscape. By 1832 industrial areas were wearing what came to be a fixed expression—dank, sooty, and drab.

In the country the enclosures had a somewhat similar affect. As broad expanses of common land became a thing of the past, fences became more noticeable. The grazing herd and the scientifically tended field or pasture replaced the wildness of the common. As people were forced from the villages their cottages naturally fell into disrepair. William Cobbett in his *Rural Rides* ruefully noted the unpleasant aspect of many villages that were falling apart in the 1820's. The local gentry were faced with as severe a social problem in the villages as were city employers.

In consequence, these revolutions did not have an outward effect alone. To the credit of the landlord class, it should be said that the condition of the poor, today called "the underprivileged," was a cause of major concern to contemporaries. Allowing for inexperience, lack of knowledge, and tightly held prejudices, the years from 1783 to 1832 saw both deep concern and reform. The ruling classes were not negligent or witless. They were appalled and genuinely fearful of the hungry mobs whose occasional violence seemed to foreshadow society's downfall. France was a vivid example of what happened when a mob gained the upper hand. Having told of such concern as there was for the urban worker, let us turn to what was done for his rural brother.

In the 1790's war caused bad times. This roused the sympathies of the justices of the peace. After all, they did not pay poor rates—in England such taxes are paid by the tenant, not the landlord. Furthermore, there was a lurking fear of revolt. Therefore, the squires labored and produced one of the worst administrative actions of the times, what later generations have called the "Speenhamland system" of poor relief. In May, 1795, the justices of the peace of Berkshire met at Speenhamland, considered the prevailing distress, decided not to use their age-old power to fix wages, and instead voted to require the parish overseers of the poor to grant relief to anyone with wages below a certain level, even though that person was employed. A scale of payments was set up, which the justices said they would "allow," *i.e.*, require, the overseers to meet. This was done as a form of subsidy of wages, in a summer of fright, when there was fear of a French invasion that might try to stir up an agricultural uprising. But whatever political justification it might have had at the time, it had dire social effects. In county after county benches of justices set up a "scale," only to find that once "allowance" had started it could not be stopped. For farmers soon realized that they could pay substandard wages and rely on the parish authorities to make up the difference. Promptly the wage level dropped, and a larger and larger proportion of laborers were put on relief. For why keep a man on the job when relief was so easy to get? When in some cases three generations of paupers had as their daily employment standing in a gravel pit waiting for the overseer of the poor to assign them to a farmer who might need extra labor, it can be seen why no better system could have been created to brutalize the agricultural workers or to divide England into hostile social classes. No wonder that in the autumn of 1830 South England saw what has been called "the Last Laborers' Revolt." No wonder it was necessary to pass the New Poor Law of 1834, which got the justices of the peace out of the control of relief. Other factors—the fall of prices, the spread of enclosure, bad harvests, postwar depression—caused the terrible poverty of the agricultural worker. But the Speenhamland system of "allowance" certainly aggravated it and probably prevented many agricultural workers from rising above their crippling environment.

Another social problem, that of the Game Laws and of poaching, the landlord class created for themselves. When the landlord thought of his land and its products, he also thought of its game. Protection of birds, fish, and beasts from the surreptitious attacks of poachers had for centuries been a passionate concern of the landlord. Hidden guns and traps with hair triggers and springs were legally set in order to catch and maim the poacher.

The Game Laws forbade anyone's keeping guns and dogs for bird hunting unless he had lands of £100 annual income or leased lands of £150 value per year. No one but the owners of land and their licensed keepers could legally kill the game. Inevitably villagers turned into poachers. A nation with so many smugglers on the coasts naturally had a full quota of poachers. The landlords stubbornly fought for their feudal privileges. In 1818 a committee of the House of Commons suggested a reform, while some landlords in that body got a law passed sentencing poachers to transportation in penal colonies for seven years. Only in 1831 were the Game Laws amended, allowing tenants to be licensed by the owners of their land. Not until a later date, in the 1840's, were these outmoded privileges finally abolished by law. Even then the gentry grumbled and protested at their abolition as they had not done at the First Reform Bill's enactment.

The record of the landlord class as to public order is better. This is especially true when it is remembered what ineffective means it had to use. There were few paid constables. Practically speaking, only the Bow Street Runners in London, the Thames Police, and after 1812, Peel's Peace Preservation Police in Ireland made a full-time job of their work. Reliance for ordinary police duty was placed on the unpaid village constable, chiefly important as a tax collector. In emergency the yeomanry, mounted farmers, were called out by the orders of the justices. Little wonder there were so many emergencies.

Mob violence in Britain in these years was a thing to be feared. As the period opened, men had fresh in their memories the bloody anti-Catholic riots of 1780, when a mad noble, Lord George Gordon, had organized a mob that attacked Catholics and turned to looting and burning. Only the presence of regular troops had secured peace and order. At the end of this period, in the years 1831 and 1832, the homes of Tory statesmen, the Houses of Parliament, and palaces of bishops were stoned or burned by mobs. Between these dates uprisings were frequent and involved considerable loss of life and property. During the French wars coastal towns experienced rioting when Navy press gangs and sailors struggled. Agricultural communities after bad harvests saw food shops pillaged and manor houses raided. Cities witnessed breakage of machines when workers thought they were the causes of unemployment. From 1810 to 1815 farm workers broke machinery for the same reason. These sporadic riots through the manufacturing districts were called "Luddite riots," from the reputation of a Ned Lud of Leicestershire who broke up some stocking frames. These riots were particularly bad in 1811 and 1816. Political issues, too, brought out the mob, as will be recounted elsewhere.

In the opinion of some scholars, violent revolution in these years was avoided because of Wesleyanism. Another opinion holds that popular education and social reform was retarded by Wesleyanism and Nonconformist opposition to state-controlled education. Another view would have it that the churches in England held together a social system that otherwise might have crumbled into chaos. Still another opinion holds that practical political and social reform would have been accomplished but for the opposition of religious institutions. As is so often the case, all the above opinions are true to some degree. Wesleyanism did serve as a school for the working classes in political conduct and organization. The religious and social ideals to which the workers firmly held determined the trend of their political opinions. Especially the churches put the slavery controversy in the forefront. In this way the religious history of this period vitally influenced the "condition of England" question and the progress of the reform movement. A review of Great Britain's religious situation is therefore pertinent.

Most powerful and commanding the largest number of adherents was the Church acknowledged by law, known after 1800 as the United Church of England and Ireland. In 1811, half the population of eleven million in Britain was said to be legally its members; in Ireland only about one person in twenty. With the exception of the northern five or six counties of Ireland, where dissenting Presbyterians were most numerous, the rest of Ireland was overwhelmingly Roman Catholic. Scotland's Established

Church was actively or passively supported by a majority of the people. There were also in England and Wales nearly three million Nonconformists or Dissenters who were members of the Baptist, Independent, Presbyterian, and after 1760, the Wesleyan or Methodist Churches.

The Established Church had a highly privileged position. Its nominal head was the king. Parliament could establish its doctrine and discipline. Its bishops sat in the House of Lords. It received revenues from lands that it possessed outright. Income also came from tithes. These originally had been payments to the Church of one-tenth of the produce of a field or one-tenth of a man's income. Then tithes had often become fixed charges. At the time of the Reformation many such fixed charges had been "impropriated" or made the property of laymen. As a result rural England was pestered by a tangle of lay and clerical claims to portions of the crops. The tangle was worse confounded by the ownership of advowsons. An advowson was the legal right to appoint to a living, subject to confirmation by the bishop of the diocese, the owner of the advowson often, though not always, being the "lay rector" who might or might not collect the "great tithe." These names in themselves may not be self-explanatory, but they should serve to explain how in the English countryside church and state became inextricably mixed.

During the eighteenth century the Established Church was characterized by a general lack of religious enthusiasm on the part of its members both lay and spiritual. Both at the beginning and at the end of the century, outbursts of religious enthusiasm occurred that were reflected in the sending of missionaries to the heathen overseas and in extensive projects for building of churches such as those of Christopher Wren in London. However, only five or six of the fifty churches planned for London in 1713 were actually built, a fact that may serve to measure the religious enthusiasm of the average member of the Established Church.

In the years under review, the clergy of the Established Church were tolerant or latitudinarian. The eighteenth-century clergyman was likely to be lazy. Frequently he was unable to translate either Greek or Latin but was ready, willing, and able to join in a jolly fox hunt or display a shapely calf at the county balls. There were over 11,000 rectories, prebendships, and other offices in the Established Church. Appointment to these offices depended upon the good will of the bishop of the diocese or upon that of the landlord upon whose property the holy edifice was built. Some clergymen received income for the performance of a plurality of religious offices. Often such clergymen employed curates to carry out their duties for them, while the bulk of the income went to the nonfunctioning rector. Such a system was discouraging to those interested in awakening spiritual life.

The general tone of clerical life and learning was set by the two universities in England. Oxford and Cambridge in the eighteenth century afforded sound training in the drinking of port and the turning of Latin phrases. At Cambridge, however, mathematics could be studied for competitive examinations, which served to stimulate intellectual life. These two were the only English universities available for the purposes of taking holy orders. Here theology was almost altogether neglected. The only actual requirements that a parson had to fulfill were to fail to fail a very simple examination in "Divinity," to be willing to swear that he believed the Thirty-nine Articles, and favorably to impress someone who could get him an appointment. Actually the universities were institutions where small numbers of wealthy gentlemen and poor theological students studied quietly in an intelligently torpid atmosphere. This easygoing tolerance was disturbed by the appearance on the scene of John Wesley.

John Wesley was, in the opinion of many, the greatest evangelist of modern times. He started a spiritual revival in Great Britain that affected both the Established Church and the Dissenting sects and reformed the everyday morals of millions of his fellow countrymen. Wesley had started as a clergyman of the Church of England. While at Oxford he had been one of a small group of students who earned the scorn of their fellow students by praying openly and frequently. After a visit to the New World, where he attempted to convert American colonists to a more active love of God, Wesley returned home with the profound conviction that he should personally take religion to the masses. He preached to the poor and underprivileged, who were shunned by both the Established Church and the Nonconformists. With George Whitefield and others like-minded, he stirred up thousands in open-air prayer meetings to walk the Methody Way. He insisted that divine grace could be obtained only through divine guidance. Wesley and his followers exhorted the people to pray loudly in public, to confess their sins publicly, and to conform to a new type of daily living preparing everyone to be ready to meet his Maker face to face. In dealing with the miseries—so vivid and real—created by the Industrial Revolution, Wesley advised the poor not to be misled by political reformers or radical agitators. It was his teaching that kept thousands of workingmen content and loyal and made soldiers fight from a sense of duty.

The Wesleyan teaching of forbearance assisted in holding the economically underprivileged classes to their allegiance to the Crown and within the social pattern of English society. This was accomplished in England at a time when, in France and in other European countries, a world-shaking social revolution was going on. By preaching temperance, Wesley also had a tremendous influence on the social life of the English people. He demanded that each Christian examine his own conscience and that the only spirit moving him come from God and not the grog shop. Distillers in the later years of the eighteenth and the early years of the nineteenth century were as a result unfavorably disposed toward

Methodists. The working class in England became more sober, and hence more industrious and more attentive to political ideals and social obligations.

Not the least of the influences of Methodism on eighteenth- and nineteenth-century Great Britain arises from the model organization of Wesley's church. At the turn of the nineteenth century there were from 200,000 to 250,000 active Methodists. They were organized so thoroughly that no worshipper need go without the benefits or attention of a preacher. A group of worshippers were organized into a class, a number of classes made up a circuit, a number of circuits made up a district, and the districts made up finally what was known as the church connection. This pyramidal organization permitted management from the top in disbursement and collection of funds and provided traveling preachers or circuit riders for every class. When a class was too poor to pay for its preacher, the connection at the top could meet the expense.

The immediate effect of Wesley's conversions had been his own expulsion from the Church of England along with that of clergymen who agreed with his methods and ideas. He then established his own chapels. This naturally did not prevent some of Wesley's followers after his death from forming branches of Wesleyanism and seceding from the mother church as he and his associates had seceded from the Church of England.

During the 1770's and 1780's many sober and enthusiastic members of the Church of England and the Nonconformist sects started to take seriously the task of reviving the devotional life of the English and the Welsh. A renewed interest in spreading the word of God is to be seen in the activities of the Society for the Promotion of Christian Knowledge, which in the fifty years after 1804 published and distributed over twenty million Bibles.

This evangelical movement, for all its preaching of forbearance, did not remain purely theological. It led to humanitarian movements. For example, at the end of the eighteenth century the Quaker Thomas Clarkson and a philanthropic political friend of William Pitt, William Wilberforce, became leaders in an agitation directed against the slave trade. They were so determined in their opposition to the buying and selling of fellow human beings that they were able to convert a sufficiently large proportion of the upper classes to their point of view. In 1807 the slave trade in the British Empire was prohibited by law.

A general reform in social behavior took place within the ranks of the upper classes, who have always in England set the fashionable as well as the moral tone. Departing from the tolerance of the eighteenth century, they ceased to regard drunkenness and promiscuity as minor vices to be displayed publicly. The effect of the evangelical revival upon the manners of the upper class was, therefore, to demand sober conformity in public appearances and some actual observance of a more chaste and religious life. The Established Church, for example, took up the Sunday-school movement that was founded in 1786 by Robert Raikes. The turn of the century saw Anglicans and Nonconformists interested in the improvement of the children who now worked in the factories. On Sunday these children were gathered together and, following Raikes's plan, were taught to read and write and were encouraged to listen to stories from the Gospel and the Old Testament in order that they might improve their spiritual lives.

The reforming zeal was carried further by the educational plans of Bell and Lancaster. Bell introduced, in 1797, a scheme for teaching thousands of illiterates. Lancaster, a year later, adopted Bell's plan and improved upon it. The system that these two advocated was that of teaching a selected group of bright students, called monitors, a well-organized, but specific, lesson immediately preceding the meeting of a large class that might number over a thousand. The monitors then repeated the lesson in the classroom. Children learned by memorizing words and phrases a little at a time. While students of this system were not taught to think or to develop their own critical faculties, they were taught to read and to work simple arithmetic problems. Unfortunately, the Established Church and the Nonconformists quarreled over the teaching methods because Bell was the champion of the Established Church that demanded an over-all supervision of British education. Lancaster became the champion of the Nonconformists' claim that Nonconformists' children should be educated outside the influence of the Established Church.

These years saw the publication of thousands of moral tales giving sober and well-considered advice to the young. One of the most enthusiastic supporters of virtue was Miss Hannah More. She wrote improving stories pointing out the triumph of virtue over vice and advising young people to stay away from strong drink, gambling, and other easily accessible pleasures. The industrious apprentice who attended church was usually rewarded by Miss More with the hand of his employer's daughter and the ownership of his father-in-law's mills. The boisterous and drunken apprentice died a horrible death under conditions described in minute detail.

Between 1790 and 1832 millions of tracts were distributed by church groups advocating abstinence from alcohol. Consumption of spirits greatly declined as a direct result. Religious leaders and moralists were not alone in trying to improve the sad lot of the poor. During these years, politicians, businessmen, and professional people became very much interested in the education of the people. In slum areas of Manchester and London were established day schools through the generous gifts of enthusiastic evangelists who founded these schools and themselves took part in the teaching. The best example of this type of philanthropist was a young man who, in a later period, as the Earl of Shaftsbury headed up many of the evangelical movements in the second quarter of the nineteenth century. This wave of philanthropy helped on the movement to the education of mechanics headed by Whig reformers and enthusiasts such as Henry Brougham.

Brougham and the philanthropist George Birkbeck helped found the Mechanics Institute of London in 1827 with the aid of William Cobbett and Jeremy Bentham. A wave of founding of institutes for mechanics swept over the nation in these years. Debating about reforms, as well as the study of mechanics and the sciences, made up the curriculum. Part of the support given to the middle-class reformers in the 1830's originated in the classes of these institutes. Another notable educational achievement was the foundation in 1828 of the University of London, later to become the first nonsectarian degree-granting university in England. Bentham and Brougham were among its patrons. Indeed, one of the unusual features of this great institution is its custody and careful preservation of Bentham's skeleton. Both as a tribute to Bentham and an acknowledgment of educational philosophy, the university still displays the great man's bones, majestically seated in a chair.

Educational reforms were accompanied by legal reforms. In 1800 the English penal code was as antiquated as it was barbarous. Capital punishment might be imposed for rather minor crimes. Sir Samuel Romilly, a Whig lawyer, tried to arouse the public's interest in criminal-law reform. He advocated reduction of sentences and procedures less dependent upon the personal whims of judges. From 1806 until his death in 1818 he made the revision of the criminal code an issue. Usually he was blocked in his efforts by Lord Eldon, later Tory Lord Chancellor. Finally Robert Peel, when Home Secretary in 1823, carried five bills that removed nearly a hundred felonies from the list of capital offenses. Once reform of the criminal code was started, within a generation the most glaring legal cruelties and anachronisms were removed from the statute books. Romilly's activities in advocating remaking of criminal law in the light of humanitarian ideas were ably seconded from 1812 onward by Sir James Mackintosh, a Scots doctor and political philosopher well acquainted with both Whig and Tory leaders. His popularity in London society as well as in the Commons served well the cause of enlightenment.

There were others who thus pressed for social reform. One such group was the so-called "Clapham Sect," nicknamed for the London suburb where most of its members lived in pleasant proximity to each other. Here they concerted measures against slavery—and also sponsored the Society for the Suppression of Vice. The strict observance of the Sabbath was the chief aim of the Society. Its pamphlets and the actions of its members helped to change the observance of Sunday by the upper middle classes. Members of the Clapham Sect were called the Saints by those who disliked the disturbing effect of their teachings upon a worldly and tolerant society. The Established Church, the growth of evangelical enthusiasts, the appearance of the Wesleyans to lead and agitate for a change in morals—all had a definite and measured result in changing the religious and social habits of a people.

This general reform in morals did not pass over the Nonconformist sects without also leaving its mark on them. The older groups of Nonconformists have been numbered at two million in 1811. They were made up for the most part of Baptists, Presbyterians, and Independents or Congregationalists. Their religious worship and political rights had been strictly confined by Charles II's Clarendon Code. However, during the more tolerant eighteenth century the Nonconformists were loyal followers of the Hanoverian kings. They had joined with the Whigs in opposing High-Church and Roman Catholic influence, but they had offered no opposition to the Established Church or government. In return a broad-minded administration, such as that of Sir Robert Walpole, had allowed Nonconformists to take part in public affairs through the occasional attendance on their part at the ritual of the Established Church. Though they could not use ordinary burying grounds and their marriages were not regarded as strictly legal, they were let alone by the Established Church and the state. For, by the Toleration Act of 1689, their worship in their own chapels was exempt from penalty. But civil rights were another matter and required the annual passing by Parliament of an Indemnity Act. Thus the Government, the Established Church, and the Dissenters reached an understanding. A Committee of Three Denominations met in London during the session of Parliament and was acknowledged as representative of the wishes of the Dissenters.

The Dissenting sects during the eighteenth century had become complacent with the practical toleration granted them. Most Nonconformist congregations were divided into the "church" group which routinely attended prayer meetings and filled the offices and the "congregation" that attended only on Sunday or special days. The evangelical fire and vigor that had distinguished preaching and the actions of Nonconformists in the seventeenth century had almost died out by the dawn of the new century.

Perhaps the notable achievement of the Nonconformists in the eighteenth century lay in the development of a system of elementary and advanced education for their children, who were denied admittance to the schools under the control of the Church of England. Oxford and Cambridge were, of course, not open to Nonconformists. In the North of England and in Welsh towns, some very good Nonconformist academies were functioning where theology and the classics as well as science and mathematics were taught by men of sound training.

The Baptists and Independents were aroused by the challenge of Wesleyan evangelism. During the French wars the Nonconformists copied the Methodists in giving complete allegiance to the crown and government. In each denomination there was started a campaign for a stricter observance of temperance practices. Their activities improved the moral standards of the working class in town and country by persuading workers to save money and not spend it in "horrid" grog shops and to apply their energies to securing better opportunities whenever possible in learning to read and write in Sunday schools or in day schools. These schools gave students an opportunity to learn something about the science of engineering and enough mathematics to assist them practically in the performance and work in the mills. Some went further; the great Dissenting academies at times rivaled Oxford and Cambridge, though that was then not hard to do.

As a result of the Nonconformists' support of the Government, in 1812 an act was passed that lifted the strictest rules of the Clarendon Code. Ministers now were allowed to preach without fear of state interference in their chapels. Marriage by a Nonconformist minister was recognized as legal. The only Nonconformist sect in the period under review that did not increase and multiply in numbers was the Presbyterian. It would seem that Presbyterianism did not flourish in the warmer or more temperate areas of Wales and England. What it lacked in the way of vigor and growth in the South was made up for most amply in Scotland.

Unlike the Nonconformist sects and the Established Church in England and Wales, the Presbyterian or state Church of Scotland lost neither its spiritual vigor nor its membership in the period under review. It was certainly the most vigorous of Scottish national institutions. What self-government was to be found in Scotland was to be found in the government of the Presbyterian Church. The parish was represented by its minister in the Synod, and the Synod sent its representatives to the General Assembly of the Church. In the General Assembly of the Presbyterian Church was to be found the moral and intellectual life of Scotland. It was the Presbyterian Church that saw to it that every Scot got to attend a school—usually a poor, but an effective, one—and learn to read and write. Unlike the universities in England, the Scotch universities were free of intellectual sluggishness and intellectual censorship. However, they were, like so many institutions in Scotland, prevented from reaching full effectiveness because of the lack of funds.

The intellectual and spiritual life of Scotland in the eighteenth century produced such men as Adam Smith and the great skeptic David Hume. In the years between 1783 and 1832 there occurred the founding of the great

Whig magazine, the *Edinburgh Review*. This magazine, under the editorship of such brilliant Scots as Jeffrey, indoctrinated the upper and middle classes of the British Isles with principles of reform and assisted greatly in converting the Whig party to a platform of parliamentary reform.

In Scotland it would only be natural to expect the church to be carried on in the traditions of John Calvin and John Knox and to support the crown against atheist Frenchmen. It was natural to expect that a nation whose people were so devoted to the acquisition of material wealth would not oppose the partnership with England that had proved so lucrative.

When one looks across the Saint George's Channel to Ireland, it is obvious that an entirely different situation existed. Except in the northern counties, the vast majority of the Irish people were Roman Catholic. Protestants in the northern counties, Protestant landlords in the south, a dwindling number of Protestant tenants and townsmen, and the official aristocracy in Dublin and a few other towns were the minority that held this majority in subjection. The Catholic Irishman was made to pay tithes to the state Church and then was asked to contribute voluntarily to support his own bishops and clergymen. The Catholics, too, were denied all political, legal, and social privileges until, in the course of the wars of the American Revolution, the organization of the Irish Volunteers secured a relaxation of these oppressive laws.

At first Irish Protestants, feeling the urge of nationalism, had protested against British political interference and had demanded, and won, concessions from London. Thus in 1771 Catholics were allowed to take the oath of allegiance in a special form. Only in 1778 were Catholics permitted to hold land in Ireland on terms of equality with the English. In 1793 the Irish parliament, representing Protestant Ireland, extended the franchise to Catholics and allowed them to hold commissions in the Irish regiments up to the rank of colonel. Since Ireland had no navy, Irish Catholics were not commissioned in that branch. However, there was no hesitation on the part of His Majesty's Government in impressing and enlisting thousands of Irish Catholics to fight between decks and in the ranks as privates and as common seamen. Indeed, in 1797, during the Mutiny of the Nore, one of the grievances of the sailors was the unfair and discriminating treatment of Catholic sailors by the Protestants in His Majesty's Navy.

As the result of economic, social, and political discomfort, a cruel civil war broke out in 1798. As the outcome of the war, Pitt and the English administration felt that the Irish parliament should be moved from Dublin to Westminster and that Irish noblemen should sit in the House of Lords as Irish representatives were to sit in the House of Commons. The union was completed in 1800.

In order to bring about the union of the British and Irish parliaments, Pitt had to promise political and religious freedom for Irish Catholics. But he could not carry out his pledge, because George III believed that such a concession would be contrary to his coronation oath. Pitt resigned as Prime Minister, and the Irish started an uphill battle for toleration and equality that lasted until 1829.

In Ireland the Catholic clergy had been leaders not only in religion but also in politics. They had depended upon their flocks literally for food and drink. When they spoke, they truly spoke for the Irish people. The story will be told elsewhere of how Daniel O'Connell became the personification of Irish Catholic political persistence and how the Catholics finally secured the right to sit in Parliament in the year 1829. The Irish did not secure the abolition of the established state Church. That was an issue raised during this period that was to be settled later in the new century. It should be observed here, however, that in attaching the religious to the political issue, O'Connell set the pattern for a century struggle between the English-Protestant faction, both in Great Britain and in Ireland, with the Catholic Irish.

Daniel O'Connell once remarked that the English were not anti-Catholic but anti-Irish. There appears to be some foundation for his statement. With the exception of the brief anti-Catholic flare-up of the Gordon riots in 1780, Catholics in England enjoyed practical religious toleration. Most Protestant Englishmen respected the political loyalty of their Catholic neighbors. The laws against Catholic schools remained in England and Scotland, but the worship of Catholics in private chapels was not disturbed. Actually, during the French wars exiled French Catholic clergy were pensioned and given asylum by the British government, and the Catholic school at Douai was temporarily moved to England. Moreover, it should not be forgotten that in 1814 the English had helped restore the pope to his temporal sovereignty. However, the English Catholics gave a general support to the agitation for political equality and religious toleration that was carried through successfully by their Irish coreligionists.

It is apparent in reviewing the religious enthusiasm and the political changes brought about by war, as well as the effect that evangelicalism had on public morals and habits, that British life was greatly changed in the years between 1783 and 1832. The people of Great Britain and Ireland moved from a less tolerant state of mind and sluggish religious observance to a more tolerant attitude. Certainly they acquired a point of view better adjusted to a demand for intellectual and religious understanding and freedom that was to be characteristic of the nineteenth and twentieth centuries.

A great deal has been said about the condition of the poor in town and country. Something should be said about the landed gentry and the middle class in order to fill in our picture of social England from 1783 to 1832. Though in these years the gentry and the landlords as a group made up a comparatively small proportion of the population of England, they formed a well-integrated and socially well-organized class. It was not uncommon for members of the Cabinet to have attended the same public school. Most party leaders were personally acquainted with the leaders of the opposition party. In private life they often met in social ease and equality. The gentry lived on large estates, traveled at home, and when possible traveled abroad extensively. They had town houses in London and, in some cases, in the provincial centers.

During the hunting season, society lived in the saddle. Frequently members postponed attendance at Parliament, even during the most trying times, in order to enjoy horseraces, cockfights, or boxing matches and, of course, to follow the hounds. For those who were of this class or who gained admission to it, as did Edmund Burke, there was freedom of expression of opinion, the like of which was found only in the drawing rooms of prerevolutionary France. Good food and good talk could always be found during week ends in large country houses of the nobility. House parties moved into London during Parliament's sessions. Unofficial party headquarters of both Tory and Whig gentlemen were to be found in such houses as Holland House, the residence of Lord and Lady Holland. In drawing rooms like Lady Holland's, the leading poets, the leading playwrights, the Prime Minister or leader of the Opposition, editors, and authors were to be found giving of their best in mutual exchange of ideas and wit.

The country gentry, in wealth somewhat below that of the leading nobility throughout the period, stayed more or less at home, venturing only occasionally to London. They formed the solid foundation which held together the social structure during the war years and the years of depression immediately following. They attended the hunt balls, tended their fields, and in a patriarchal fashion looked after the welfare of their tenants. It was this group of gentlemen, typical of "Old England," that Cobbett wanted to unite with "hearts of oak," the yeomanry, and remake English society. The country gentleman, possessing broad acres and limited vision, gradually during these years found his social position in the county challenged by the factory owner, who bought acres and established an estate next to him. The middle classes observed the manners and the gracious ease of living of the country gentry. Immediately this group turned its social aspiration to an imitation of this way of life. Sir Robert Peel's father bought an ancient estate, Drayton, where he did his best to identify his interests and those of his family with the country. Sir Robert Peel distinguished himself in the eyes of his neighbors by his enthusiastic pursuit of the fox and his devotion to agricultural engineering. So it was with others of the middle class who attained wealth and prestige.

The social ideas of middle-class England between 1783 and 1832 were identified with those of the landed upper classes. It should not be assumed that this meant that the middle classes were oblivious to their obligations in connection with the poor. Indeed, the ideas of reform were best propagated and most clearly represented in the Whig drawing rooms and in the gathering places of the professions, whether in a country house or a town house, because the more those in authority could listen to and learn about the desires of middle-class men, the more was it possible to spread the ideas of Benthamite reform. When one could meet at the table of a noted lord a reformer such as Sir James Mackintosh, or a man with latest opinions about the tariff, such as William Huskisson, the impression made and the ideas circulated were much more effective than if a mob had stormed the gates of the town. When Wilberforce and the Rev. Sydney Smith could discourse about human rights and problems to a group of gentlemen gathered around the port after dinner, the cause of reform was effectively advanced. Because of this ease of communication, ideas concerning economics, politics, and social trends were circulated easily and in a palatable fashion to those classes whose entrenched privileges were likely to be deeply affected by social and economic change.

While all this was going on, the life of the upper classes was easy and pleasant. The sons of gentlemen, before the days of the French wars, toured the continent. Young blades just out of Oxford were turned into sophisticated young gentlemen by traveling to Italy, France, and the Rhineland. The private morals of many of the nobility would probably not bear close scrutiny by enthusiastic evangelicals, but their wealth afforded them an opportunity to develop a taste in dress and in furnishings that has made the Regency Period a celebrated age in domestic architecture and furniture. During the Napoleonic Wars, many of the ideas of dress and style and general canons of taste became more English than that of the preceding period. This development was due to the lack of communication between France and Great Britain. Sir Walter Scott and Jane Austen published in this period. One must not forget that this was the era of Byron, Wordsworth, Keats, and Shelley. In the theater the great Kean was carrying on the high standard of British acting set by David Garrick and Mrs. Siddons. London was becoming more important as the center of British art, letters, and music. Well-trained choral societies and literary groups were to be found in provincial capitals such as Norwich and Liverpool. But the upper classes were turning more and more in these years to London, its modes and its fashions, for inspiration. Perhaps this reflects the taste for town life of the middle classes who were so largely responsible for building the suburban villas and everywhere putting up the big house on the hill that overlooked the mines and the shops of industrial towns.

One comes away from the study of this period with a feeling that the social patterns of an agricultural society were in the process of cracking, but that the cracks were neither broad enough nor of sufficient length to warrant a feeling that old Britain was no more. The changes in the economic and social life of the rich occurred more rapidly than they had in the years before 1783. Another way of looking at it, of course, is to say that economic and social progress made before 1783 was now showing its real force for the first time. If one observes the constitutional changes that occurred between 1783 and 1832, a clearer picture of the nature and rapidity of movement in the institutions and life of Great Britain is found.

24

CONSTITUTIONAL HISTORY

1783–1832

Frequently, changes occur in the British constitution with the stealth and quiet characteristic of the proverbial soft-footed Arab. Because no violent revolution took place while attention was focused on winning the French Revolutionary and Napoleonic Wars, it is possible to take the superficial view that the only significant changes took place just before this period, with the establishment of Cabinet responsibility; at the beginning of the period, when the office of Prime Minister gained a new importance; and at the end of this period, when the "middling orders of society" entered the seats of the mighty by gaining the parliamentary franchise. But to consider English constitutional development thus would be to ignore, among others, such significant changes as great improvements in financial accountability, the reorganization of the offices of the Secretaries of State, the development of the Board of Trade, the beginning of a new theory of colonial administration, and the union with Ireland. Nor should the evolution of rudimentary democratic local government be passed over.

The starting point from which these changes came was a general agreement on the workings of the unwritten British constitution. After 1782 it was held that policy was made not by the king but by his "constitutional advisers," and that those advisers, *i.e.* the Cabinet, were responsible to Parliament for the advice they gave. Subject to parliamentary ratification the king might change his advisers; he certainly could thrash out with them whether their advice was correct; but in the last resort the responsibility for policy was Parliament's. Historically, this was an innovation. As has been pointed out, George III did nothing "unconstitutional" when in the 1760's and 1770's he guided policy. Much of the obloquy cast upon that monarch is, therefore, misdirected. He should not be blamed for governing improperly but for governing unwisely. However, in subsequent periods it would have been, and was, held wrong for monarchs to do as George III did. Thereafter Cabinet, not king, was the supreme executive as long as it held office.

The two dramatic changes in England's constitution occurred when

William Pitt the Younger became Prime Minister and held his post by an appeal to the electorate in 1784, and when Lord Grey and Lord Althorp put through the Great Reform Bill of 1832. The first change has led some authorities to consider Pitt, rather than Walpole, as the first true Prime Minister. The events of 1784 set a definite precedent. It was not the first time that a king had dissolved a Parliament he did not like and called an election to get a better one. Charles II and William III, among others, had done just that. But this was the first time that a Prime Minister had given the king "constitutional advice" to do so. It set a precedent, to be followed in April, 1831, when William IV specifically announced he had dissolved Parliament to ascertain the will of his people. Later on this precedent, throughout the Empire and Commonwealth, would harden into a constitutional convention that it was the right of the Prime Minister, and the Prime Minister alone, to decide on a dissolution. It is possible to read into the actual events of 1784 more meaning than they had. As with Magna Carta and many another great seminal event in English history, a superstructure of constitutional custom has been built up on a base that turns out hardly to support that superstructure. Perhaps, in strict logic, the dissolution of 1831, with its dramatic dash to the House of Lords by William IV and Lord Grey, is the true setting of the precedent. But, as the reader must be aware after this piling up of argument, somewhere along the line there was an important change in the British constitution. By it, the electorate was made the judge of any deadlock between Cabinet and Parliament.

Again, as so often in the review of English history, one must be cautious about reading into a period a characteristic of one that comes later. From 1784 to 1831 there were no general elections in which the public was asked to decide between a Cabinet and a House of Commons. What happened was that the idea of such an appeal took root.

Naturally, with the electorate made supreme in this way, what happened to it became of supreme importance. The electorate which had judged between Pitt and the House of Commons in 1784 was the electorate of the rotten boroughs. That year it happened to give a decision with which the people agreed. But even then there was distrust of the ability of that electorate to speak for the people of England. As the political chapter will tell, the Reform movement steadily grew. Finally, in 1831, a Cabinet did propose to end the rotten-borough system, and the rotten-borough electorate itself voted itself out of existence. This it did by adding to those already enfranchised the possessors of property of £10 per annum assessed rental value. Then, when in the future English Prime Ministers would dissolve the House of Commons—as in 1834, 1841, 1846, 1852, 1857, 1859, and 1868—the purpose would be to make the middle classes the judge between political parties.

Consequently, it should be here mentioned that the two political parties, Whig and Tory, during these years took on some new characteristics. The Tory "Church and King" party added to its appeal to loyalty, religion, and law and order a claim to superior financial efficiency. The Whig party, as the following political chapter will tell, added also to its platform. It had stood for the rights of Parliament and the subject, for the liberty of the Nonconformist, and for business. Now it lost its tradition of being the businessman's party, but its more ardent members took on a triple program—the abolition of slavery, the reform of Parliament, and "Catholic emancipation." Here were the choices that would be offered, when next a true election was held.

With this rise in the power of Parliament came a corresponding diminishment of the power of the Crown. Perhaps some of this drop was caused by Dunning's resolution of 1780, referred to previously. But more came from three causes—the Regency crisis of 1788, the insanity of George III, and the bad character of George IV. When the Regency crisis of 1788 had ended, there had silently but effectively ended with it any belief that the Tory party would stand for the rights of the king as against the rights of Parliament. Once Tories had voted to limit the royal powers, a precedent had been set that would put king below Parliament. Then George III, from his mental weaknesses, withdrew from his intense preoccupation with politics. When, at long last, in 1811, the Prince of Wales became Prince Regent, he was in no position to wield authority. Men just did not trust him, and for sound reasons. He had royal authority, in law; he did not have the control of men's minds that comes from being respected. In 1801, William Pitt the Younger left office when George III said it was a matter of conscience with him not to let Catholics sit in Parliament. But in 1829, the Duke of Wellington answered a similar statement of George IV by telling the King he had to accept the Cabinet's decision. That contrast may show the silent and great constitutional change which had taken place.

It was not only in Crown and Parliament that the constitution evolved. New methods of administration were tantamount to constitutional change. In the financial field there came the growth of the Consolidated Fund and the decline of the Civil List. These words, in themselves technical, stand for a new and an old way of thinking about payments. The old conception had been that the king had been granted money by Parliament for such expenses as his personal income could not meet. William Pitt found a network of payments of particular taxes to meet particular needs, with the inevitable result that the amount raised was either too little or too much for the amount that was to be spent. Pitt set up the Consolidated Fund as the basic source of money in 1785. He got rid, whenever possible, of assignments of particular taxes. Instead, he had all taxes paid into one

Consolidated Fund, and all payments made out of that Fund. That made it possible to see where the money went. Naturally, a demand arose for seeing where the Civil List expenditures went. Year by year the Civil List was cut down. The "hereditary revenues of the Crown" were transferred by the King to Parliament, in exchange for a fixed grant. At last it was found out who got what from the Civil List, what pensions and sinecures were on it. The "Black Book" made up of those exposures formed potent propaganda for reform. Finally, in 1830, the anachronism of Secretaries of State being paid as if part of the king's Household was ended, and the Civil List became what it should be—the royal Household expenses, plus a device for ensuring the inviolability of judges' salaries. Thus the affairs of the Treasury were put on a business footing, as a business age came into being.

Nor was the growth of efficiency only in the area of finances. In the area of administration there was improvement. The year 1782 had seen the abolition of the American secretaryship of state and of the system of joint secretaries. Thereafter, instead of a Northern and a Southern Secretary, each to get in the other's way, there were a Foreign Secretary, the first being Charles James Fox, and a Home Secretary, the first being Lord Shelburne. Each man set his mark for good on his office. Soon came a third secretaryship of War and Colonies, the efficient Dundas being the first to hold this office. In each case, undersecretaries and permanent clerks improved office routine. Other offices came into existence. One of the feats of the second Rockingham Ministry had been to abolish the old Board of Trade and Plantations with a flourish of rhetorical sneers. But soon Pitt found the need of an advisory body to deal with commercial problems, so the Board of Trade came into existence again. When Huskisson in this period, Gladstone and Joseph Chamberlain in later periods, would hold its presidency, this department would greatly help business. Another office came into existence at this time—the undersecretaryship of state for the colonies. It would not be until Robert Peel held that office in 1811 that Parliament would have in front of it an official responsible for the Empire and the Empire alone. But as England conquered new colonies to replace those lost, the need of this office would appear. During the period under review, war and colonies would be the duty of the Third Secretary of State, the title of this secretaryship witnessing how the colonies were gained. But now there would be a central administration and a policy.

That policy would have constitutional results. The name Crown colony is a creation of the 1840's. But Crown colony government dates from this period. Along with the First Empire that had been largely self-governing, would arise an Empire, as will be told, that was administered from Whitehall. As for Ireland, she would in 1801 merge in a restive union with Great Britain and cease to be a separate kingdom.

To conclude this review, it should be pointed out that there was in this period a sporadic growth of representative local government. As in the past, the county justices of the peace, at Quarter Sessions, were the administrative and even in a sense legislative rulers of the counties. Boroughs were ruled under their out-of-date charters. But here and there a special act of Parliament would set up bodies of commissioners. Sometimes these would be men appointed to do a special job, such as the Commissioners of the New Street, who added to London's beauties the façade of Regent Street. Other boards of commissioners, however, were made elective. Among such bodies, for example, was the Manchester Police Commissioners, which helped the growth of that sprawling village. Then, in 1817, came the Sturges Bourne Vestry Act, which allowed a few parishes which chose to adopt the Act to rule themselves much as does a New England town. Here was a beginning in that training in minor municipal experience which is now so typical of the political life of modern England.

But, again, a word of caution: these were just beginnings. These were the silent changes stealing like Arabs into English constitutional life, unnoticed because they were not yet numerically significant. It would be only when the new Reform Bill electorate took hold that these changes would flower. It was to take the Municipal Corporations Act of 1835 to bring the cities new political life. It was to take the Civil Service Commission of 1852 to create a unified Home Civil Service. It was to take the Durham Report of 1839 and the British Settlements Act of 1843 to create the Second British Empire. The significance of these minor constitutional events was that they are beginnings for the future.

25

POLITICAL HISTORY

1783–1832

In spite of a contemporary tendency to look intensively at other matters, political history remains fundamental for understanding any period. That can be seen in the politics of the years from 1783 to 1832. During that time two leaders, the Younger Pitt and Fox, in person or through their followers dominate the political stage. Pitt's program of efficient finance and resistance to the French Revolution brought his Tories first victory and finally, in 1830, defeat. Fox's triple program of Catholic emancipation, abolition of slavery, and reform of Parliament doomed his Whigs to half a century of exclusion from office and then won that same party overwhelming success. Yet both men represent the aspirations of the middle class; Pitt's policies aided the rise of that class, Fox's were the policies which that class demanded. Nor is this true only in general matters. In details, too, it will be found that the politics of this time reflect and exemplify the rise of the middle class, which culminated in the Reform Bill.

It will be remembered that when Lord North and the "King's Friends" were driven from power in March, 1782, they were replaced by a coalition of the opposition. This coalition was held together by respect for the dying Marquis of Rockingham. Even before Rockingham died, in July of that year, Charles James Fox had quarreled with Lord Shelburne. Forced to choose between the two men, George III, who hated both, chose Shelburne but communicated with the Cabinet through the Lord Chancellor and not the Prime Minister. Such a Government was doomed to fall, even without the added burden of signing an ignominious peace with France, the United States, and England's other enemies. Some respite was won for it by the twenty-one-year-old Chancellor of the Exchequer, the younger William Pitt, and the fact that though Fox and his friends could not stand Shelburne—whom they called "the Jesuit of Berkeley Square"—the only alternative was a coalition with their recent adversary, Lord North. But the coalition was made, and the world saw the sight of Fox and North sitting side by side on the Treasury Bench, as Secretaries of State, while the Duke of Portland served as nominal Prime Minister. For George III was unable to stomach frequent direct relations with Fox.

The Fox-North Cabinet was faced with the Indian problem. As is recounted in a later chapter on the Empire, it was necessary to control the East India Company now that that body had become a government instead of a trading company. The attempt by Lord North's Regulating Act of 1774 to set up a council in India had merely blocked all effective action without creating a responsible political authority. The cure was obvious—to have a single governor-general in India, responsible to the East India Company for business matters, to a Board of Control in Westminster for political matters. But it was equally obvious that this would create a patronage problem. By recent legislation the Whigs had cut off from George III his power of using government appointments to affect elections. But all the good done by this would be undone if ever George III could appoint an official who could wield the vast wealth of the East India Company. Therefore the Fox-North India Bill vested control in a board of commissioners to be named in the bill, in order that men they trusted might control the patronage. Thus the Indian question became a question of who would wield a great vote-getting machine.

The course of the bill was dramatic. Fox and North got it through Commons, despite Pitt's sharp attack and despite the East India Company's lobbying. But the independent members of Commons, unhappy about the coalition of enemies on the Treasury Bench, began to swing away from Fox and North. At this, George III plucked up courage. He set to work assiduously to unseat the ministry, using all the devices that remained to him. Finally, when the bill reached the Lords, Lord Temple, who was Pitt's cousin, stood up and stated that His Majesty would consider as enemies any who voted for the bill introduced by His Majesty's ministers. That worked. The bill was thrown out late in the evening. Before dawn royal messengers had found Fox in a gambling den, routed North from his bed, and had brought back to King George the seals that symbolize the tenure of office. As soon as possible William Pitt was made First Lord of the Treasury and Chancellor of the Exchequer. Thus, as the Whig wits put it, there was "A sight to make surrounding nations stare, A Kingdom entrusted to a schoolboy's care."

At last King George had a Prime Minister whom he did not hate and fear. Yet the situation was not that of 1770, when Lord North had been in office. Pitt was the master, not the servant. He was the one man who could gain back from Fox and North the independent members of the House of Commons. The very measures that the Rockingham Ministry had put through gave Pitt strength. No longer could George III bribe in the old way. Though there was plenty of bribery still, as will be seen, and though patronage was used to back Pitt, the young Prime Minister had to win key votes by reasoned argument. So began an epic parliamentary battle. In December, 1783, and the spring of 1784, Fox and North tried to use their majority in the House of Commons to drive Pitt from office. At the same time, as debate after debate was pressed to a vote, Pitt won over the informed public opinion of the capital. Daily the majorities against him dropped, till at last he won a majority of one vote. Then Pitt went to George III and secured a dissolution of parliament.

The ensuing election is a classic in English history. Legend has it that Pitt's eloquence and reason won the overwhelming support of the English people, who drove from the House of Commons the supporters of Fox and North. By a play upon the title of the then frequently read book about the Marian religious persecutions, *Foxe's Martyrs,* the 160 members of the House of Commons who then lost their seats were spoken of as "Fox's Martyrs." But subsequently the researches of Professor Laprade have thrown cold water on this. It appears that for the last time George III's great political machine swung into action. John Robinson, his political agent, went to work with a vigor shocking even to himself. The King's private funds were poured out in bribes. All the means of pressure still available to him and to Robinson were used with a will. It was the combination of Pitt's leadership and George III's political machine that won the election. Had the common people voted freely, under modern conditions, the result might have been different. Fox himself proved this by holding the borough of Westminster, where there was something close to universal male suffrage.

The consequences of this election on the political history of England were twofold. It was the swan song of the political machine that had created the "King's Friends." Just as 1688 saw the freedom of Parliament from direct attack by the king, 1784 saw the end of indirect attack from the king. A new Tory party came to existence at this time, of peers and businessmen, that could and did hold a majority in the House of Commons practically continuously till 1830. But it held office by virtue of the personal qualities of William Pitt. Right up to 1792 Fox could get temporary majorities against Pitt on selected issues, such as the impeachment of Hastings, the Russian war scare, and the Libel Act. Thus each—Pitt and the new Tory party—was the prisoner of the other. If the Tory backbenchers did not want to abolish the slave trade, the slave trade remained legal, for all that Pitt was against it. But executive control had to rest in Pitt's hands; no one else could stay in office. Therefore the great accomplishments of Pitt's premiership were those things on which he and his followers could agree: the restoration of the crippled finances of Great Britain, and the passage of some sort of measure for governing India.

Pitt's India Bill, when looked at now, seems very little different from the Fox-North proposal, except that political control would be vested in members of the government then in power. The details in which it otherwise differed appear now as alterations made to provide debating points. The great difference was one which no one needed to mention. Now that Pitt was the indispensable Prime Minister, Indian patronage would be honestly handled. It would not go to George III's friends or to the friends of Fox and North. The best man then available, Lord Cornwallis, was sent out to supplant Hastings, and under him an admirable civil service was built up. There would be some inevitable political give and take. The fact that the Scotchman Dundas became "President of the Board of Control" would not be unconnected with the large number of Scots who went to India. But the men who went out would be good men, and India could be left outside the political arena.

To this statement there is one exception. Sir Philip Francis came back from India, burning with a desire to get revenge on Warren Hastings. He persuaded Burke to start impeachment proceedings. Pitt yielded to this flood, Whigs were chosen managers of the impeachment, and from 1787 till the acquittal of 1795 a great deal was said, on both sides. At the end two things stood out. One was that the charges against Hastings were grossly exaggerated. The other was that, though Hastings was a great improvement on his rapacious predecessors in office, there was still room for improvement in the administration in India, and the people of England would not tolerate low standards. This impeachment, therefore, created the tradition that England should be concerned with keeping the behavior of colonial officials up to the highest standards.

The other great problem confronting Pitt was that of finances. The American war had increased the debt from about £976,000 in 1776 to about £250,000,000 in 1783. At the same time bonds had dropped to £55 on a par of £100. Pitt met this crisis in two ways: he raised more revenue, and he made government bonds more valuable. The first he did by the simple method of reducing customs duties. That made smuggling unprofitable, its risks no longer being worth its rewards. It also increased imports, since lowering duties lowered the price of goods as delivered in England. Especially did this help manufactures, since cheaper raw materials meant cheaper manufactured goods, and more sales. Then, from the surplus of 1784, a million pounds were set aside as a sinking fund. This money was used to buy bonds on the open market, and to apply the interest so acquired to redeem the debt. This raised the market value of future bond issues and thus strengthened government credit.

While this was being done, there was agitation in the electorate for three reforms: the removal of religious disabilities, the ending of the shame of the slave trade, and the reform of parliamentary elections. With these ideas William Pitt was in agreement. To the end of his life he was a member of the Whig social club, Brooks's; by family tradition he was a

Whig. But he was not able to get his Cabinet associates to agree with him. Each of these proposals struck at vested interests. The long-standing English hatred of popery, the idea that the King's coronation oath against transubstantiation meant a national policy, the fears of the Established Church—all caused resistance to the removal of disabilities from Catholics and Nonconformists. The "West India Interest" and the merchants of such seaports as Liverpool wanted the slave trade to go on. "Borough mongers" did not want to lose the power and profit given them by control of elections to the House of Commons. As it was on these groups that Pitt depended for his parliamentary majority, he could not make a "Cabinet issue" of his desires for reform.

But though these interests were strong, they were interests of the past. It was the growing liberal belief in religious tolerance, the growing humanitarian hatred of slavery, the growing middle-class discontent with disenfranchisement that supplied support to a reform movement. At first this support went to Pitt, for all knew his desires. In the end of the 1780's there were repeated votes for parliamentary reform. The attractive country squire, Christopher Wyvill, spoke for such reforms with the argument that to give the vote more widely was a conservative measure, going back to the olden days of more extended voting. Later this argument would have great value in weakening resistance to parliamentary reform. The noble William Wilberforce and his supporter, the Quaker Thomas Clarkson, piled up grim evidence before parliamentary committees, from 1788 on, which would recruit new antislavery workers. In 1792, a Catholic relief bill became law, which gave civil rights to Catholics such as Dissenters had enjoyed, including the right to vote in parliamentary elections. But Pitt's failure to do more than speak and cast a personal vote for these measures meant that by lapse they became Whig policies, with the exception that some Tories, especially George Canning, stood also for aiding the Catholics.

In 1787 came the impeachment of Hastings, which has already been described. In 1788 came George III's serious mental illness. At first it was hoped that this was temporary, for the King had earlier had short seizures from which he had recovered. Therefore, by a constitutional expedient the Lord Chancellor affixed the Great Seal to a commission for giving assent to laws, thus allowing the routine of legislation to go on. But the illness kept on, and it became likely that the Prince of Wales would have to be made regent. Had this happened, the influence of the Crown would have been thrown to the Whigs, and Pitt would have been driven from office. Therefore Pitt prepared a regency bill, to put limitations on the powers to be held by the Prince of Wales. A bitter parliamentary fight broke out, in which Pitt, as he put it, "un-Whigged" Fox, by showing how inconsistent it was for a Whig, a supporter of the Glorious Revolution, to assert that Parliament could not control the powers of the Crown. But just as the Irish Whigs had offered the regency to the Prince of Wales, just as Pitt was prepared to retire from English office, George III recovered. The result of this was to demonstrate that now Tories believed that Parliament should control the Crown, to increase Pitt's political prestige, and to make the question of a regency seem also a question of putting the Tories out and the Whigs in.

In the year 1789 the whole picture changed with the onset of the French Revolution. This movement, at first, met with favor in England. The action of the Estates General in forming themselves into a National Assembly and creating a constitutional monarchy seemed a copying of England. English politics went on undisturbed. The general election of 1790 brought into Parliament more supporters of Pitt, but it changed the kind of support he had. Fewer were "King's Friends," men chosen at the orders of John Robinson and Lord Hawkesbury; more were independent Tories, supporting Pitt from their own convictions or the convictions of those who owned the boroughs for which they sat. Pitt was still a prisoner of his majority, still in danger of defeat by Fox on specific matters. Indeed, two such defeats took place, on the Russian Armament and on the Libel Act. Fox's silver tongue persuaded the Parliament to make statute law of the principles of Zenger's case in New York. Thereafter truth would be defense in a libel suit. Likewise, by ridicule Fox defeated a proposal to go to war with Russia because Turkey was being driven out of the Black Sea fortress of Oczacoff.

But in 1792 the French Revolution took an ominous turn. Prussia and Austria went to war with France to restore King Louis XVI's powers; the French Convention deposed Louis, proclaimed a republic, and grew increasingly violent as it preached international revolution. Its insulting diplomats forced England into war more quickly than England would have gone. Its armies and agents threatened to bring revolutionary ideas from France into other countries. Now it became necessary for Englishmen to take a stand one way or another on the principles of the French Revolution.

On the one side was, roughly speaking, a triple combination: sympathizers with the French Revolution; the early group of parliamentary reformers, such as Christopher Wyvill and Major Cartwright; and a small group of aristocratic Whigs in the Friends of the People Society, led by Charles Fox and his young friend Charles Grey. The intellectual leader of this side—or the writer whose ideas were most attacked, which is not always the same—was Thomas Paine. This Northamptonshire stay maker, whose pamphlet *Common Sense* had done so much to persuade the Americans to declare their independence, issued his *Rights of Man* which scared Tories into thinking England would be in danger of rebellion. The

Rights of Man was an answer to the opinions of another friend of the Americans, Edmund Burke, and the latter's *Reflections on the Revolution in France.* For in this, and in his *Letters on a Regicide Peace,* Burke expressed the emotions of the English majority. These were horror at the execution of Louis XVI and his Queen and fear of the excesses of the Revolution. All sorts of people turned against the Revolution. The Methodists stoutly preached against disorder and for obedience to lawful authority. "Church and King" mobs went wild against alleged sympathizers with France; they wrecked, for instance, the laboratory of the great chemist Priestley. The larger part of the Whig party, in 1794, came to Pitt's support; the Duke of Portland, William Windham, and Lord Fitzwilliam entered Pitt's Cabinet. Such were the political battle lines.

The political struggle was fought, largely, in four areas: the courts, the relief rolls, Parliament, and the press. Again it may be said, loosely speaking, that the reformers won the struggle in the courts and lost it elsewhere. The basic charge against the minority was that it was organizing a Corresponding Society that bore ominous resemblance to the Committees of Correspondence of the American Revolution or the network of Jacobin Societies of the French Revolution. Therefore the shoemaker Thomas Hardy and the veteran Major Cartwright were tried for seditious libel, in England. By the genius of the Whig lawyer Erskine, by the common sense of the London jury that heard the case, and by the provisions of Fox's Libel Act, which turned over to the jury the decision as to the truth of the alleged libels, Hardy and Cartwright were freed. The Scottish Reformers Muir and Palmer fared less well in front of Braxfield, and were transported. The immediate effect of these trials was to silence the reform organizations, which dared not go on for fear that next time a jury would not be as sane. But in the long run freedom of speech was thus preserved, and future reformers, such as William Cobbett, would be able to take up the torch from Cartwright, Hardy, and Wyvill.

As has been explained elsewhere, in the year of danger of 1795, the so-called Speenhamland system of relief allowance in aid of substandard wages took the edge off distress and stopped short any danger of internal revolt such as had been such an aid to the French Revolutionary armies elsewhere. The naval mutinies of the Nore and Spithead did not have land counterparts.

In Parliament, the Portlandite Whig defection to Pitt gave him overwhelming majorities, to the point that after 1799 Fox and his friends largely "seceded" from the House of Commons, appearing once a session or so to have their say and then retire.

But the great counterattack was the propaganda campaign of the *Anti-Jacobin.* When, in the Whig defection to the Tories, friend after friend of Fox had "turned his coat," one penniless politician who so changed, George Canning, was so young that the Whigs sneered that a "boy had turned his jacket." Canning and his friends in 1797 issued a paper, the *Anti-Jacobin*, in which humor—especially that of the "needy knife grinder"—struck hard at the French Revolution. Here, rather than in strict laws against "combinations," was the true answer. The *Anti-Jacobin* and such propaganda rallied the nation to war with France, finishing the work of the popular Crown and Anchor Societies.

For Pitt was having plenty of trouble with the war. His new Whig Cabinet members meant votes but not efficiency. The European allies he bought were defeated almost as fast as he sent out subsidies. Even his own re-creation, England's credit, was weakened when it was necessary, in 1797, to go off gold. But gradually Pitt built up a team of younger men. The Scot, Dundas, from the beginning had been his "trouble shooter," handling first India, then the War Office, then the Navy. George Canning's aid has been described. It was enhanced by the independence he won by his marriage to "the rich Miss Scott." Another recruit was Robert Stewart, Viscount Castlereagh, the eldest son of Lord Londonderry. As Chief Secretary for Ireland, as will be recounted, Castlereagh put through the Union, which was thought of as an essential defense measure. Bit by bit, as these men rose higher in office and as others of ability, such as the Commander in Chief, Frederick, Duke of York, found their right niches, things went better.

Thus in this period, after many years of wandering in the wilderness, a new Tory party was born. For from the time in July, 1714, when the Treasurer's white staff was put into the Duke of Shrewsbury's hands, to the time in December, 1783, when "a kingdom was entrusted to a schoolboy's care," no Tory, with the exception of Lord North, had been Prime Minister. And Lord North had started life as a Whig, ruled always in coalition with Whigs, either the Bedford gang or Fox, and ended his life in opposition to Pitt. But now, though from 1794 to 1809 there was always a Whiggish infusion in the Cabinet, the administration was Tory in spirit and the young men who rose came up through the Tory ranks. But the old parliamentary era was not yet dead. In 1801 George III used his royal power of dismissal and told Pitt that his pledge of Catholic membership in Parliament, the so-called Catholic emancipation, as a condition of Union with Ireland would not be honored. Pitt resigned and was replaced by the son of the King's doctor, the Speaker of the House, Henry Addington.

Back England went toward the system of government by coalescing groups. Pitt urged those who followed him to support Addington. But in debates he had to speak the truth, and the truth was that Addington fumbled. The wits put it thus: "As London is to Paddington [a minor suburb], So is Pitt to Addington." As is recounted later, Addington bumbled out of war with France, and back in again. Demand grew to have Pitt at the helm. Was he not, as George Canning had called him, "the pilot that weathered the storm"? Pitt came back, to do his best to build up an alliance against Napoleon. It was crushingly hard work, for the Whigs still were strong, still sniped at him, as in the impeachment of his trusted friend Dundas, now First Lord of the Admiralty Lord Melville, whom they unjustly drove from office. But Pitt bore up. As recounted later, he planned for eventual peace. He gave the direction to strategy which won Trafalgar and thus gained for England a century of uncontested mastery of the seas. Pitt even brought together an alliance of land powers to join him against France. But here he failed. It was the dread news of the Austrian defeat of Austerlitz that broke him at last. The "Austerlitz look" came on his face, and early in 1806 he died.

Thus ended a marvelous career. Single-handed, Pitt had put through the measures that restored England after the War of the American Revolution. As a peace premier he ranks among the highest. As a war premier, serving in a period of defeat, he made many mistakes. But he learned his trade, he taught his successors their trade, and he, as will be recounted, took the great decision that made possible a lasting peace after the war. No wonder George Canning said "My political allegiance is buried in the grave of Mr. Pitt." In war, too, when the evidence is weighed, Pitt was among the greatest.

Pitt was followed as Prime Minister by his cousin, Lord Grenville, and a coalition ministry, called the Ministry of All the Talents, was formed, in which Fox was Foreign Secretary and Leader of the House of Commons. The great achievement of this Ministry was the abolition of the slave trade, a measure that it saw passed through the House of Lords the very day it resigned office. It was a weak government, as coalition governments usually have been, and was held together chiefly by Fox. But Fox died in 1806. Here ended another great career. Fox's private morals do not bear too much inspection. He was a notorious spendthrift and gambler. Even up to the time of the Regency Bill of 1788, his public morals, too, had their weak spots, for he was willing to make shady alliances with North or the Prince of Wales. But at the end of his life he did England great service. Because in a time of fear and confusion he stoutly stood for liberal and democratic principles and the reform of Parliament when others had shown the white feather, he taught some aristocratic Whigs, especially Charles, Earl Grey, to devote themselves to the cause of the people. In consequence in later years he became a sort of patron saint to the Whigs, who remembered his charm and his magnanimity and for their sake forgave him his foibles. Soon after Fox's death the coalition was driven from office by George III. First he refused the ministry permission to introduce in Parliament the Roman Catholic Army and Navy Service Bill, which would have allowed Catholics and Dissenters to hold commissions while fighting Napoleon. Then he demanded that the Ministry promise never to ask for any concessions for Catholics. That was too much for proud men to stomach, and they resigned, their last official act being to see the royal assent given to the abolition of the slave trade. Thus the Whigs went into political darkness that lasted for the party as a whole until 1830. But they went with pride, not with the shame of the Fox-North coalition of 1783 or of the attempt to get power through a regency in 1788. Now they had a triple program: emancipation of Catholics, restriction of slavery, and above all, reform of Parliament. In their place, there came as Tory leader the same Duke of Portland who had been nominal Premier in the Fox-North coalition. This Ministry stumbled along till it fell from the Clark scandal and the Walcheren failure. Miss Clark, the mistress of the Duke of York, was accused of securing promotions in the Army when properly paid. An attack on Walcheren Island near Antwerp was bungled. Indeed, so curiously was it handled that the Secretary of State for War, Lord Castlereagh, was forced to fight a duel with the Secretary of State for Foreign Affairs, George Canning, over the way Canning had secured his dismissal from office. These two affairs were too much for the ministry, and the old Duke resigned just before he died in 1809.

Portland was succeeded by Spencer Perceval. He was a loyal servant of the crown, had a good head for parliamentary business, and was an able, if not a brilliant, debater.

Much foolishness remained in party politics. The Government still saw spies under every bed. When the Whig Sir Francis Burdett supported one John D. Jones, who had been criticizing the House of Commons, he was arrested. Since he was able to arrange that the arrest be made while he was reading Magna Carta to his children, this incident made good propaganda for reform. On the other hand, Whig noblemen spoke praise of "General Bonaparte"—the English stoutly refused to admit the legality of the French Empire—and tried to ridicule the feats of Lord Wellington in Spain. Yet administration went on well. Parliament functioned sensibly. The investigation into the question of gold payment of its Bullion Committee would later make national financial policy. Ships, soldiers, and subsidies were provided to defeat Napoleon. Indeed Perceval succeeded in overcoming the obstacle Pitt had feared, a regency, when George III, in 1811, became unmanageably insane. After some dickering with the Prince of Wales and some talk of bringing into office some, at least, of the Prince's Whig friends, Perceval succeeded in staying in power. But, in 1812, a madman assassinated him and in his place Lord Liverpool took over. Liverpool was the son of Lord Hawkesbury, who had aided John Robinson as party manager for George III. He won the favor of the Prince

Regent by the appointment of the chief of his Whig friends, Lord Moira, as Governor-general of India and thus also kept the Whigs out.

Now began a new era in political life. Pitt and Fox were both off the stage. Pitt's followers were in power. It is true that it was the Liverpool Cabinet that finished the great war, but that was not by new policies but by continuing with old ones. What this Cabinet must be judged by is its peace record. That was mixed. Liverpool was not in himself a great leader, but he was an able chairman. Men who could not work independently with each other could work together under him. He could have such a reactionary as the highly able Lord Chancellor, Lord Eldon, as a colleague, after 1816, of the pro-Catholic Canning. He could keep the bumbling Addington (now Sidmouth) as the co-worker of the clear-cut, vigorous Castlereagh. He could "stand pat" while Sidmouth foolishly aided repression and at the same time let the younger men, such as Peel and Huskisson, at the Home Office, and the Board of trade, make valuable innovations. The history of this period therefore has two aspects, the repression that would cause discontent and lead to the overthrow of the Tories, and the practical reforms that would give the early nineteenth century a belief that the Tory—later Conservative—party was the party of administrative efficiency.

Disorder in England was always just below the surface. Except at Bow Street and a few other metropolitan "police offices" and on the Thames River, there were no full-time paid constables. Order was kept by the individual action of justices of the peace. For minor matters, unpaid village constables were the arresting officers, as they had been since the days of Edward I. For more serious matters, the deputy lieutenants, who were really the leading justices of the peace under another name, would call out the yeomanry, a local volunteer cavalry. Consequently, riots were far too common as the symptom of distress. Toward the end of the war they took place in the Midlands and the Shires, where power looms were broken by a fictional "Ned Lud." (There had been a real Ned Lud to give his name to these "Luddite" riots.) After the war was over, and with it war prosperity, distress in the North led to the march of the "Blanketeers" on London. Fatigue, not the forces of law and order, broke that up. Furthermore this type of distress riot might have political implications. For with peace there arose again agitation for political Reform. Two powerful speakers, "Orator" Hunt and William Cobbett, toured the land. Cobbett's eloquence has come down to later times, in his vigorous *Two Penny Trash*, in his hard-hitting *Register*, and in his nostalgic picture of the countryside that enclosure had ended, his *Rural Rides*. Hunt, contemporaries seem to have thought, was perhaps the more powerful speaker, though his words are now lost. It was he who triggered off the greatest of the riots. At St. Peter's Field in Manchester, those waiting to hear him speak were charged by the yeomanry, who killed eleven and injured many. Promptly the propaganda machine got to work. Just as the Americans got the story of Lexington and Concord to England first, with incalculable effect on their cause, so the story of the massacre at "Peterloo," so called in sneering allusion to Waterloo, was spread by the reformers before official denials could circulate. At once the Tories made it worse, by passing the repressive Six Acts. In fact, most of these acts were a sensible approach to the problem of order. They gave additional protection to civil law officers, thus obviating use of the yeomanry for lesser affairs; they forbade drilling privately, restricted mass public meetings, and controlled the possession and hoarding of arms. Only two might be considered objectionable: the suspension of habeas corpus, soon repealed, and a tax on pamphlets, which lasted till 1861. But the timing, and the two bad ones, made "the Six Acts" a phrase of invective.

In another way 1820 was a turning point in the political history of Great Britain. In this year George III died and was succeeded by the Prince Regent as George IV. It was hoped that a new reign would bring about better conditions. The first disappointment was in George IV himself. In spite of attempts to picture him as a jovial gentleman, he possessed few qualifications to rule a nation recently in economic straits. He was drunken, immoral in his private life, frequently bad mannered, and wholly selfish. His callousness to members of his family and entourage was notorious.

George IV inaugurated his reign with a demand that Queen Caroline's name be dropped from the Prayer Book and that a bill of divorce be brought against her. Since 1806 he had refused to have any dealings whatsoever with her. Caroline, on her part, had lived in Italy and elsewhere on the Continent in exile with a band of retainers of doubtful character. Gossip, never reliable, had it that she had lived in an improper manner with one of her Italian couriers. On the death of George III she decided to return to England and claim the dignity of Queen. The result was scandal of the attempted divorce by act of Parliament. This was seized upon at once by the Whigs who were able to build in the public mind an idea that their policies and the Queen's cause meant liberty and reform. Therefore, what George IV and his Cabinet had hoped would be a quiet divorce suit became a political sideshow. Party fought party on the floor of the House of Lords.

The King lost. The ministers had to withdraw the bill. Caroline also lost favor with the British people at the time of the King's accession and was never crowned as his consort. Fortunately for the Whig cause, Caroline died within a year. George IV had by now lost any popularity he possessed. He had left only the memory of a selfish and stubborn king. Politically important results of the trial were to be found in the showing made by the rejuvenated Whig party. On the other hand, this same Liverpool Ministry had in it men who met the problems of the time. Robert Peel, as yet without a title because his baronet father was still alive, as Chief Secretary of Ireland founded the "Peace Preservation Police"—the "Peelers" as the Irish called them—who later became the Royal Irish Constabulary. Here was one approach to the problem of keeping order, a civilian professional police force. Another was that which Peel took up when he became Home Secretary, in 1822. Long had the Whig lawyers Romilly and Mackintosh spoken against the foolishness of oversevere punishment; long had a crusty Tory majority in Commons voted down their proposals. Now a leader the Tories trusted came forward. Was not Peel the Chief Secretary who in 1812 had blocked Catholic emancipation in the face of three separate resolutions in Commons? That leader they allowed, in five years, to repeal 250 obsolete statutes and make sense out of the outmoded jury law.

In economics, too, the Tories showed ability. In 1819 Peel, for the moment a private member, persuaded the House of Commons to resume "specie payment," on the lines of the Bullion Committee Report of 1810. Thus, after an initial shock, England's position in world trade was made secure. Nor was Peel the only man of practical progress among the Tories. In 1824 there came to the Board of Trade William Huskisson. The Tory stand was for protection. In 1815 the wartime Corn Laws, taxing the import of grain for the benefit of English agriculturalists, were strengthened. But Huskisson turned in the opposite direction. He kept up the work Pitt had done in the 1780's, by improving the Navigation Acts and putting in a sliding scale in the Corn Laws. Nor, indeed, was it just a few Tories who led their obscurantist brethren. When, in 1824, a committee sat on the question of combinations of workingmen, it listened to the arguments of the radical tailor, Francis Place, and the radical member for Northampton, Joseph Hume. Not only were the combinations of businessmen into corporations facilitated, but trade unions, hitherto forbidden by war legislation of 1799 and often disguised as savings associations, were given a legal right to exist.

Thus it can be said that Liverpool's Cabinet had achievements to its credit, even though it stood firm against Reform and Catholic emancipation. The Cabinet, till 1822, was dominated by Robert Stewart, Viscount Castlereagh, who as a courtesy lord was a member of the House of Commons till his father's death in 1821. As Leader of the House, Castlereagh was a sort of deputy premier. Realistic and averse to unnecessary change, he set the tone of politics. In the Cabinet, after 1816 as President of the Board of Control, was his rival, George Canning, chafing for a chance to show his abilities. Finally Canning gave up in disgust and took the post of Governor-general of India. But as he was on the point of sailing came the sudden news that Castlereagh (now Londonderry by his father's death) had committed suicide. Canning rushed back to be Leader of the House and Foreign Secretary. Here, in foreign affairs, came a new era of liberalism in which Canning dramatized policies not too different from Castlereagh's. But at home it remained still, on the surface, much the same Tory political world.

All this, however, turned on the feats by which Liverpool held together his team. In 1827 Liverpool died. Canning, his successor, died soon afterward. George IV now had to find a premier who could either balance factions or make one faction preponderant. An attempt to make the Chancellor of the Exchequer, F. J. Robinson, Prime Minister as Lord Goderich did cause a gain. The often-suggested fusion with Whigs seemed about to take place. But though some Whigs did enter the Goderich Cabinet the fusion was so incomplete that Goderich resigned office without ever meeting Parliament. In his place was put a national hero, the Duke of Wellington.

On paper this looked like a strong government. It held both branches of the Tory party—the Canningites who believed in Catholic emancipation, and the others who did not. Tory confidence should be strong in the Duke and in Peel, both staunch upholders of law and order and the Church. But the Duke could not handle politics. First he lost the Canningites, when two rotten boroughs were disenfranchised and he refused to give the seats to unrepresented Manchester and Birmingham but merely extended the voting area of the old boroughs. Then came the Clare election, at which Daniel O'Connell, though ineligible as a Catholic, was returned at the head of the poll by such an overwhelming majority that it was clear no other man would ever sit for Clare as long as O'Connell chose to run. By this time Commons had taken to passing emancipation bills for Lords to kill. Now a variant appeared. The rising young Whig Lord John Russell got Commons to repeal part of the Test and Corporation Acts. Wellington and Peel had to swallow their ideas or give up office. They swallowed their ideas. First the relevant clauses of the Test and Corporation Acts were repealed. Then Catholics were admitted to both houses of Parliament, with the shabby addition that the Irish voting qualification was raised to disenfranchise many Catholic peasants. When George IV tried to claim that his coronation oath forbade accepting such a law, the Duke of Wellington compelled him to give in.

One effective act, with political implications, was passed at this time, the Metropolitan Police Act. Peel brought to London, that is, to the suburbs around the medieval city limits, his Irish idea of civilian, paid law-enforcement constables. It became an immense success; to this day the Londoner affectionately calls a policeman "Robert," especially on Boat Race Night, in memory of the statesman who created The Force. These tactful men—then usually, now invariably, unarmed—made of London perhaps the most orderly city in the world, and themselves a model to the rest of the world.

But the year 1830 became too much for the Duke. In July, George IV died. As the law then stood, his death automatically brought about a general election to Parliament, which took place in July. By history-making chance, the polling took place just as news came from France that a quiet, middle-class Revolution had taken place. Charles X had been driven out, Louis Phillippe put in, and the monarchy made constitutional, in a way resembling the Glorious Revolution of 1688 in England. Because of this development, many a Whig got into Parliament unexpectedly. Then a revolution broke out in Belgium. Here the Duke seemed to public opinion to favor unduly the reactionary king of Holland. Next, in the autumn, there broke out "the Last Laborer's Revolt." Mobs, breaking threshing machines and maltreating overseers of the poor, circled London in agricultural South England, alleging orders from a mythical "Captain Swing." Riots reminiscent of the Luddite riots threatened in the North. The fear was that "Lud might join Swing." At this point the Wellington-Peel government was challenged in Parliament on extravagance, with the threat of a vote the next day on the need for parliamentary Reform. In the Lords Wellington said: "I never read or heard of any measure up to the present moment which in any degree satisfies my mind that the state of the representation can be improved." When he sat down, he asked a colleague, "I have not said too much, have I?" He had. By those words he had lost office, ended half a century of Tory supremacy, and brought in Reform.

For the Reform period which was now about to open can be understood properly only when account is taken of the theories that had come to fill men's minds and of the men who preached those theories. Steadily there had grown up a new body of opinion, to which such a statement as the Duke's was shocking. It was a variegated body of opinion. In it were as diverse groups as the followers of Cobbett and "Orator" Hunt, the Whig intellectuals of the *Edinburgh Review,* the Benthamites, and the Political Economy Club, not to mention many others who do not fall into these groups. All, however, shared two beliefs: that British institutions were sadly amiss, and that legislation could provide a cure. Therefore they all wanted a Reformed Parliament. Hunt and Cobbett sympathized with the general ideas of the American and French Revolutions. They believed that men had natural rights to a vote and to work for their own advancement. They also had a habit of reading history as they chose and were confident that, at some time in the dim past, free Englishmen had had these rights. That allowed them to claim to be conservative restorers, not revolutionary overturners. Thoughtful Whigs, since 1818, had published the *Edinburgh Review,* under the editorship of Francis Jeffrey. This preached the inevitability of progress and the need of accepting change and seeing it run in the right channels. Allied to the *Review* was Henry Brougham. He had been Queen Caroline's attorney. He had founded a series of "mechanic's institutions" and the Society for the Diffusion of Knowledge. In July, 1830, he had crowned this by standing as an anti-slavery Whig and winning the great Yorkshire seat, the holder of which, since the days of Sir George Savile and William Wilberforce, had spoken for the conscience of England. Such were the leading missionaries of new ideas.

Behind them were the formulators of ideas. High above the rest stood Jeremy Bentham, the prophet of Utilitarianism. An independently wealthy man, a protégé of Lord Shelburne when that able and ill-loved nobleman retired into privacy and the title of Marquis of Lansdowne, Bentham had worked out a philosophy for all problems conceivable to him, based on one simple question: "What is the use of it?" He believed that problems could be solved by a sort of common-sense arithmetic, in which advantages and disadvantages were weighed, according to a table of pleasures and pains. Like many a prophet, he was without honor in his own country. While many Englishmen laughed at his ponderous vocabulary—"postprandial circumgyrations" for an after-dinner walk—Frenchmen translated and published his works and South American republics asked him to write their constitutions. But in the course of a long life he drew to himself a group of ardent disciples, rather reminiscent of the eager young men of the New Deal, who with tremendous industry infiltrated movements, contributed greatly to their success, and then claimed credit for Bentham for what had been done. Some of that credit was deserved. Today words Bentham coined, such as maximize and minimize, are part of our current speech. The government of England today largely resembles the pattern he set up, in his *Fragment on Government*. But overmuch credit is often given to Bentham. Frequently what looks like a following of his ideas is actually a case where other minds independently traveled similar roads to a similar goal. The great municipal reform of 1835, for example, was the work of Joseph Parkes of Birmingham. The great Poor Law reform of 1834 was the work primarily of Nassau W. Senior, and secondarily of Edwin Chadwick. Senior's ideas were drawn from field experience; Chadwick, though he had been Bentham's secretary, stoutly asserted all his life that his contributions to that reform were his independent creation. Bentham's great importance, it would seem, lay in his philosophy of "the greatest happiness of the greatest number," which England adopted with all its democratic implications, rather than in specific proposals, which usually were by-passed.

Therefore one should look at the other formative thinkers, the economists. As early as 1776 the Scottish Professor of Logic at Glasgow, Adam

Smith, published his *Wealth of Nations*. This book, the Younger Pitt confessed to its author, taught him his trade as Chancellor of the Exchequer. Until recent years it has remained a fundamental starting point in economic thinking. In 1798 the Rev. Thomas Malthus published his *Essay on Population*, to be revised and extended in 1804. During the 1800's and 1810's David Ricardo evolved his theories about rent and the labor base of value. By 1821, with appearance on the scene of the elder and younger Mills, James and John Stuart, there was founded the Political Economy Club, an association of businessmen, economic theorists, and statesmen. This became a means of coordinated thinking between these three groups, so that legislation often had a trial run before the Club before being introduced into Parliament. This may serve as a sign of the widespread belief that there were discoverable laws of society and business which intelligent men could apply to their own affairs. It is this belief in the perfectability of society through reason which the Duke of Wellington challenged with his ill-chosen words.

Of course those words were not the basic cause of political change, however well they symbolize Tory blindness to facts. But out of Wellington's resignation, to which they led, came a political revolution. William IV, the new king, an ex-naval officer, had, like those later naval-officer kings, George V and George VI, a real sense of constitutional duty. He sent for the leader of the opposition, Charles, Earl Grey. Grey had been a close personal friend of Charles James Fox. He had stuck by him and stuck by Fox's espousal of the ideal of a right to vote, inherent in those with a stake in the country. In Queen Caroline's divorce Grey had played a straightforward part. He had refused to coalesce with Goderich. As a result, his consistency gained him public confidence, at all levels of society. By his character he was able to gather a team that had real hopes of holding on to office. In the Lords he was supported by William Lamb, Lord Melbourne, who was made Home Secretary. Melbourne, by a combination of firmness and common sense for which he has never been given sufficient credit, put down the "Swing riots" without bloodshed and with some improvement in the condition of the abused laborers. In Commons Grey had two chief lieutenants, the highly respected Lord Althorp and the clever and energetic young Lord John Russell, the brother of the Duke of Bedford. Lord Althorp was in politics as the representative of Northamptonshire only from a stern sense of duty. He so obviously wanted to be relieved of that duty and so obviously was trying merely to do what he believed right, that he soon as Leader of the House of Commons won the confidence of that body as no other man has. The classic story of this is his assuring the House of Commons that he had had the reasons for a measure explained, had been convinced by them, but regretted he had forgotten what they were. That was enough to ensure the acceptance of the measure. "Little Lord John" had been the persuasive Whig who had secured the disenfranchisement of two rotten boroughs, Grampound and Penryn, and the removal of disabilities on Nonconformists. With this group, and others such as the Earl of Durham—"Radical Jack," to the men of his native county of Durham— Grey tried to govern England.

On two points Grey soon failed. Lord Althorp might be the greatest Leader the House of Commons ever had, but he was one of the worst Chancellors of the Exchequer. The Belgian affair went little better with Lord Palmerston as Foreign Secretary than it had with Lord Aberdeen. Thus the one issue on which Grey could hold power was that closest to his heart, his promise to Fox to reform Parliament. Grey had long since gotten over his more democratic ideas of the 1790's. What he now wanted was the kind of uninfluenced voting by property owners that was typical of the elections in the counties. Similar men in the boroughs, he and his friends felt, should be added to the electorate. Seats from tiny boroughs should be transferred to the new cities that were unrepresented. Then England, Scotland, Wales, and Ireland would have the right sort of men choosing members of Parliament. In their opinion these made up the safe and reliable portions of the unenfranchised electorate. The Whigs were never democrats, and after Fox's death they were unsympathetic to proposals for universal manhood suffrage.

A Reform bill, however, could only be carried peacefully by a House of Commons convinced that in killing the old electorate and creating a new one no great changes would result in the order of society or the constitution. Lord Grey and Lord John Russell were the very men to assure all concerned that the Reform, though necessary, would only advance slightly toward democracy and would then come to a stop. This stand won Lord John the nickname "Finality John."

With care a Cabinet committee drafted the famous measure, which, on March 1, 1831, "Little Lord John" Russell presented to the House of Commons and to the world. Though Tories laughed as they were told which seats would be abolished, instantly the nation came to the support of the Grey Government. The issue was the Whigs and Reform or the Tories and civil commotion. It was a triumph of the British constitution that no blood was shed but that crisis after crisis was surmounted. The first crisis came when the crucial vote in the House of Commons went in favor of Reform by one vote, 302 to 301. The second came when the Grey Government was beaten on a proposed amendment, the Chandos Clause, which would allow tenants in the counties the vote and thus preserve the power of great landlords to influence elections. Here William IV stepped in. Because the principle of the bill had been carried by a one-vote margin, he was willing to dissolve Parliament and call a general election. He hurried down to announce the dissolution and say: "I have been induced to resort to this measure for the purpose of ascertaining the sense of my people." King William's people told him their sense quickly enough. Counties and open boroughs that had never gone Whig in generations did so this time. Instead of a majority of 1, the Whigs had a majority of 136.

Now the obstacle was the House of Lords, which in that autumn threw out a second Reform Bill, as passed by Commons. Grey tried again, in 1832, with a third Reform Bill. For a moment King William wavered, when the Lords again blocked this, and planned to dismiss Grey and have Wellington and Peel put through some sort of compromise reform. Here the people made themselves heard. Cobbett issued a war cry: "The Bill, the Whole Bill, Nothing But the Bill." In Birmingham and elsewhere the Political Unions that had been formed by Attwood made ominous plans for drilling, even going so far as to select certain army officers to lead them, if worst came to worst. In London Francis Place not only laid similar plans, but caused a run on the Bank of England with a placard, "To Beat the Duke, Go for Gold." But worst did not come to worst. Peel refused to be so foolish as even to try to pass a Reform Bill. King William was persuaded that he should copy the precedent of 1711 and change the votes in the House of Lords by creating enough new Whig peers to make the difference. The mere announcement that he would do this was enough. The Tory Lords had to pass the bill or see their house turned into a huge and unwieldy half-popular assembly, with a Whig majority. Thus the third version of the Reform Bill finally became law.

The important provisions of the bill were as follows: (1) fifty-six boroughs lost their franchise; (2) thirty-two lost one member; (3) sixty-five seats were given to new boroughs, twenty-two boroughs receiving two members each and twenty-one receiving one member; (4) sixty-five seats were given to English counties, eight seats to Scottish counties and five seats to Irish counties; (5) the franchise was given to (a) all householders in towns who paid £10 annual rent, and (b) all who in the counties held a forty-shilling freehold, or were ten-pound copyholders or fifty-pound leaseholders. Possessors of old borough franchises such as the freedom of the city were allowed to hold their voting rights. The new House of Commons had 658 members.

The middle classes profited most from the new franchise. About 270,000 received the right to vote. This increased the electorate by one-half. Most of the newly enfranchised were residents of towns, and ten-pound householders were able to express the will of their group. The Whigs thus secured the support of the town dwellers. The small towns and middle-sized boroughs in the Midlands and North, as well as the larger towns, were to vote Whig and later on to vote Liberal. The Reform Bill not only put the middle class in government, but it put the party sponsoring middle-class programs, the Whigs, in power, to stay for most of the time until 1874. This Whig era has been called the era of Reform, or the era of middle-class supremacy.

When it was announced that the Reform Bill had become law, the bells were rung and the bonfires were burned everywhere as if a great victory had been won for the people. All sorts of benefits were expected. The new era had dawned, when the middle classes had been admitted to the franchise. Theirs would now be the deciding voice in the government of the empire. Two of the radical and reformers' proposals, universal manhood suffrage and the ballot, were not part of the Reform Bill. The old order had not been changed in many respects, but in one it had been so completely altered that its effect upon the course of history was fundamental. The Reform Bill of 1832 had shown that the people through protests and organization could change the laws in a way to conform to the demands of the moment. For the future it meant that more reform and more changes were possible and inevitable. Thus the gradual democratization of the British franchise was brought about. Thus the government in the course of the next hundred years was to become that of a constitutional democracy responsive to the will of the whole people. The Reform Bill was the first great breach in the wall of political and social privilege. Once breached, the fortification of class and special-interest rule was to prove unable to withstand further attacks.

26

POLITICS, IRELAND

1783–1832

Since Irish history is something about which Irishmen feel passionately even today, they speak of it allusively. In talking of this period they speak of the Parliament on College Green, the Garrison, the Protestant Ascendancy, the Volunteers, Dublin Castle, and the United Men. Their hero is "the Emancipator." Perhaps the simplest way of getting at the heart of the matter would be to explain these allusions.

The "Parliament on College Green" is the Irish Parliament that sat in a building facing Trinity College, Dublin. It was founded, Irishmen then claimed, by King John. It had legislative and, in its House of Lords, judicial, supremacy over Ireland, ever since the Renunciation Act of 1783. For all practical purposes it was much the same sort of Parliament as the English, with the same customs slightly varied; e.g., if one wished to resign, one did not apply for the nominal Stewardship of the Chiltern Hundreds but for the equally nominal Escheatorship of Munster. It had its rotten boroughs, its open boroughs, its honest enough county elections. The "Protestant Ascendancy" and the "Garrison" refer to the fact that the Protestant landlord and middle class were immigrants from England who had come to hold down the Catholic natives and prevent Ireland from being an enemy base. The "Volunteers" were, as an earlier chapter pointed out, really the Protestant electorate that had been given arms during the American Revolution and had used those arms to win Irish Protestant legislative freedom. "Dublin Castle" refers to the two major English-appointed officials who ruled Ireland from that building, the Viceroy and the Chief Secretary. The "United Men" were the idealistic Society of United Irishmen, who believed that Catholic and Protestant could be united, who tried in the early 1790's to achieve this by legal means, and some of whom revolted in the "Ninety-eight" when this failed. The "Emancipator" was Daniel O'Connell, who gained what the Catholics considered the final step in freedom and emancipation, the right to sit in Parliament.

In a previous section of this book, Ireland was treated as part of the overseas Empire, because in the years from 1700 to 1783 she gained more and more the status of part of the self-governing Empire. For the period under review, Irish questions are treated as part of English politics, because in the years from 1783 to 1832 Ireland lost that status and became on January 1, 1801, the first day of the nineteenth century, part of the United Kingdom of Great Britain and Ireland. Irish history in this period can be summed up simply by saying that for twenty-seven years the Protestant upper- and middle-class Irish nationalists tried and failed to rule a legislatively independent Ireland with an executive appointed by and responsible to the English Cabinet. Then, for thirty-two years, a Catholic middle- and lower-class nationalist movement tried and succeeded in winning rights that the Protestant Irish had been more willing to give them than had the Protestant English. But Irish history is not simple, unless it has been oversimplified. For proper understanding one must dig a bit deeper than this set of statements, true though they are as far as they go.

Roughly speaking, Ireland was two nations, one Protestant and one Catholic, which were beginning to merge. The Protestant nation was uppermost. It held the great majority—but significantly not all—of the landlords; it held perhaps the larger part of the urban middle classes when preponderantly Protestant Belfast and Londonderry are balanced against largely Catholic Dublin and preponderantly Catholic Cork; it contained many prosperous farmers in Ulster and some farmers in the rest of Ireland. For all practical purposes there were no lower-class Protestants. The Catholics had a few old nobles, organized quietly in the Catholic Association, and a larger "Squireen" class, from which O'Connell would spring. These classes had saved their property in spite of a bitter penal code for two reasons: the peasantry had been willing to pay double rent—and likewise double tithe—to save their Catholic leaders and their Catholic Church, and Protestant Irishmen had been willing to act as "straw" owners to preserve their neighbors' property. There was a real Catholic urban middle class. The peasantry were Catholic; many still spoke only the native Irish language, though that was dying out.

These two nations had begun to merge, in the atmosphere of liberal nationalism that was sweeping the world in the years between the American and French Revolutions. It has been recounted how the Protestant Garrison secured the legislative independence of Ireland because the Catholic majority backed it up. Then, in part as a reward, in part in accordance with the principles in which the Volunteers believed, the Parliament on College Green had removed most though not all Catholic disabilities. Catholics might hold land. Catholic peasants could vote and could bear arms in the service of the king. Indeed, Catholic gentlefolk were allowed to hold the King of Ireland's commission in his land forces.

One step more and the Catholics would have full emancipation. They were yet barred from seats in Parliament. This, in part, is the reason that the phrase Catholic emancipation meant "the right for Catholics to sit in Parliament."

It might be thought that with the passage of the Renunciatory Act of 1783, Ireland could develop on her own as Canada did when, after 1867, she became a dominion, as twenty-six counties of Ireland have done since in 1921 the Irish Free State gained dominion status. But Ireland did not. The reason for this was simple and painful. Though in 1782 Ireland freed her legislature from English control by the repeal of Poynings's Law, though in 1783 she freed her judiciary from English control by the Renunciatory Act, she did not, even in 1794, free her executive from English control. English Cabinets, responsible to the English Parliament, appointed the Irish Viceroy and the Irish Chief Secretary. In turn these officials "managed" the Irish Parliament. By cash and peerages, offices and pensions, they bought votes. This was easy to do because the Irish Parliament was as sadly in need of reform as the English. A chance to reform the Irish Parliament was lost when in 1783 the Volunteer Convention met again; its resolutions frightened Lord Charlemont, its presiding officer. He therefore quietly dissolved it before it could repeat its earlier pressure on the legal Parliament in College Green. Perhaps he bitterly regretted this, before he died. For the "Irish Washington" lived to 1799 to see his work about to be undone, and Ireland was to be subjected to England once more, legislatively and judicially, as well as in its executive.

The annals of the free Ireland at the end of the eighteenth century are short but not without honor. They turn on two essential problems that Irish statesmen were either unable or unwilling to solve—the eternal imperial problems of trade and defense. Just as free Scotland in the beginning of the eighteenth century had wanted to eat her commercial cake and have it too, free Ireland had the same desires. Just as Scotland had wanted to get protection from the British Navy for trade but not pay for it, so Ireland wanted to have the advantages of free trade but not to pay the price.

For a while Ireland did have her cake and eat it. The economic demands of the Protestant Ascendancy had been that Ireland might sell Irish products freely. When the Volunteers had marched to Dublin, one battery, commanded by Napper Tandy, the darling of the Dublin populace, had carried this placard on a gun: "Free Trade or This." England had granted free trade, and Irish wealth mounted. These are the great days of building in Dublin, when prosperity for a moment looked on the Emerald Isle. This prosperity might have been permanent. The young English premier, William Pitt, was willing to perpetuate free trade by a mutual treaty between King George's two kingdoms in return for support of the Navy. But the Whigs, delighted to defeat Pitt, honest believers in protection, and partisanly suspicious that Ireland's rights would be infringed, got the Irish votes needed to block the proposed treaty. Thus one possibility was lost.

At this point Ireland began to "feel her oats." She enjoyed threatening war with England's oldest ally, Portugal, safe in the knowledge that her bluff would not be called. In 1788 Irish Whigs joyously made the Prince of Wales Regent, thus creating in the Empire a danger of dividing the crown against which the present Commonwealth is carefully guarded by the Statute of Westminster.

In the 1790's this same impulse of nationality—by the laws which seem usually to apply to it—moved in two directions. On the one hand there was the evolutionary movement toward what would now be called "responsible" government. This was what the "United Men" first asked for. Almost was it possible to persuade Pitt that this should be granted and that the Viceroy of Ireland should appoint a cabinet in the same way as did the King of Great Britain. In 1794 the Whig Viceroy Lord Fitzwilliam, appointed when Pitt took Whigs into his English Cabinet, did cross over with this aim in mind. But the wirepullers soon got rid of him. There disappeared an opportunity. On the other hand, nationality worked in the opposite direction. Nationalism seemed about to bridge the gap between Protestant and Catholic and to unite them all as Irishmen. Should not the noble impulse from France be obeyed? Should not Ireland rise to become free—free with England, if England quickly granted rights, but free without England if need be? So it was that Wolfe Tone and the Duke of Leinster's son, Lord Edward Fitzgerald, planned an uprising. The word went about: "The French are on the sea." Though Tone and Lord Edward were taken, the pikemen came out, and died bravely under the harp flag on Vinegar Hill. But it was in vain. The French did not bring enough. Their troops did defeat some militia at the well-named Castlebar Races but then were rounded up. And then came two grim forms of vengeance.

First of all the rebels were hunted down. It shocked good soldiers, like Moore and Cornwallis, to see what was done. For a harsh side of Ireland, the Protestant Ascendancy, here came out. The rise of the lower classes, as seen in the United Irishmen, had roused the fears of the landlord class. Those fears coagulated into revival of the memories of 1688, those bitter memories that still keep Ulster apart from Eire. Orange Lodges, that had not the nobility and tolerance of William of Orange for whom they were named, organized repression and started to beat the Catholic peasantry back to where they had been at the worst period of the eighteenth century. It is memories of this that have caused such hatred of England.

After this grim reprisal, political reprisal came. Pitt decided that an Irish Parliament was as dangerous a luxury when fighting republican France as a Scottish one had been when Queen Anne fought Louis XIV. So he got a union. The Irish Parliament could be bought, if a man dared stand up and lead the buying. Robert Stewart, Viscount Castlereagh, dared to do this. It took peerages. Look at the dating of the existing Irish peerages and see how many were erected in 1799 and 1800. It took bribes, it took a vote to buy boroughs as if they were property, but the job was done. It was done when one more thing was promised—Catholic emancipation, which, as has been said, was the right for Catholics to sit in Parliament. This promise Pitt made. In return, the Catholic hierarchy threw its weight into the scales. The Union, for the new arrangement was so called, and the manner in which it was inaugurated were portents of the trouble that was to come in the nineteenth century from this act. Pitt had pledged his support of Catholic emancipation in return for Catholic support for Union. The Catholic leaders lived up to their part of the bargain, but George III, because of his coronation oath, forbade Pitt to live up to his.

In spite of this, at first the Union appeared acceptable. There were grumblings in Ireland, from lovers of Irish independence, from a mild-mannered Catholic Committee. But the only overt act was Robert Emmet's romantic hopeless revolt of 1803, the last effort of the United Irishmen. To the House of Commons in Westminster went 100 Irish members; to the House of Lords went four bishops and twenty-eight elected lay peers. (Those Irish peers who were not elected to the House of Lords were allowed to sit in Commons for non-Irish seats.) Almost all of these joined in the regular political game as if they were English Whigs and Tories. But under the surface two great problems grew more severe: that of the condition of the people, and that of Catholic disabilities. Population rose with alarming speed; in a generation it increased from one and a half million to four million. As the number of mouths to feed grew faster than the supply of food, living standards dropped. Irish institutions were unsuited to meet such problems. Ireland had no poor relief at all, and Protestant tithes oppressed a Catholic peasantry. Many another ill needed legislative cure. But Irish Catholics, who could best speak for Ireland, could not sit in Parliament. Here is where Daniel O'Connell, the Emancipator, came to give Ireland new hope, first for emancipation and then, perhaps, for repeal of the Union.

O'Connell's early career was a constant battle to earn his living as a lawyer and give heart to movements of protest. From 1808 to 1823 he traveled throughout Ireland building up support. Finally, in 1823, he founded the nationwide Catholic Association, to agitate for emancipation. After a series of legal battles with Dublin Castle, he built up a fund-collecting system popularly called O'Connell's Rent. High and low, rich and poor, all gave. What mattered was not the amount so raised, surprisingly large though it was, but the movement back of the giving. Then, in

1828, he took the final step, of standing for Parliament, at a by-election in County Clare. He won the election overwhelmingly. Though the House of Commons would not seat O'Connell since he was a Catholic, obviously it had become impossible to rule Ireland without emancipation. For it was good fortune for the British government that O'Connell threw all the vast weight of his influence against disorder. Had he not hated revolution with a fervent hatred born of his religion and of education in France during the excesses of the Jacobin period, Ireland would have been aflame with riot and perhaps rebellion. This truth sank into the minds not only of the Cabinet but even of George IV. He gave up his father's claims that the coronation oath forbade the royal assent being given to such a measure, and after the formality of a reelection, Daniel O'Connell sat in the House of Commons. But to prevent O'Connell from sweeping every Irish county seat south of Ulster, the forty-shilling Irish freeholders were disenfranchised.

O'Connell, by his pertinacity, showed the world that Ireland was a nation. More than that, O'Connell changed the character of Irish nationalism. He tied it in with religion. The middle- and upper-class nationalism of the Volunteers of the 1780's and of the United Men of the 1790's had cut across lines of race and creed. This new Irish nationalism would be a nationalism of the Catholic peasant. It would be this nationalism—often led, it is true, by Protestants of the landlord class—that would achieve O'Connell's further aim of repeal of the Union. Therein lies his importance.

27

FOREIGN AFFAIRS

1783–1830

In diplomacy, as well as at bridge, one must hold cards to be able
to make a finesse. That truth was well put in 1935, at a low point in England's foreign affairs, when Lord Lloyd gave Neville Chamberlain this
explanation of what had gone wrong: "Strength comes before policy—
that is what the Cabinet has forgotten." Therefore, to understand England's
foreign policy, whether in the days of Neville Chamberlain or in those of
the Younger Pitt, one must first know her strength. What, then, were the
cards that British diplomats held in 1783? Only by knowing them can one
judge how well those diplomats played their game.

The top cards certainly were the Royal Navy and, paired with it, the
Army. Then, in a different suit but in their ways as important, came England's wealth and her reputation. These, generally speaking, were what
gave English diplomats a voice that had to be heard. Because Pitt understood these cards he could truthfully say at a dire crisis: "England has saved
herself by her exertions and will, I trust, save Europe by her example." Because Castlereagh improved on the lessons his master Pitt taught him, he
was able to complete Pitt's unfinished task and put together the team of
allies that crushed Napoleon. And because Canning knew how to play his
hand when there had been a shuffle and redeal after the Congress of Vienna
he was justified in boasting that he had called a New World into existence
to redress the balance of the Old.

Englishmen have long known how essential to them is their Navy. Since
Queen Elizabeth I's day, the ceremony by which officers and men have
joined the Senior Service has been to have read to them the Articles of War,
including this admonition: "It is the Navy whereon, under the good providence of God, the wealth, power and safety of this country doth chiefly
depend." That Navy, in 1783, was a remarkably successful adaptation of
methods of the past to needs of the present. The system of command by
the Lords of the Admiralty did rest on the fiction that "Lords Commissioners" were filling in for an as-yet-not-appointed Lord High Admiral. In
fact this allowed a Cabinet member, the First Lord of the Admiralty, a

member of the ministry, the Financial Secretary, and a civilian administrator, the Secretary of the Admiralty, to sit with professional sailors, the
"Sea Lords," so as to combine in one body responsibility to Parliament and
professional guidance in professional matters. So effective was this that
when in 1904 the Army command was overhauled the Army Council was
copied from the Lords of the Admiralty.

There was a rigid system of promotion by seniority. When an officer became "posted" to command of an important ship, he held captain's rank
till death. But as there was no obligation to send him to sea, "selection by
nonemployment" or using only the best officers in time of peace allowed
building up a large reserve of experienced commanders on half pay and
quick expansion of the Navy in war. Similarly, promotion to the rank of
admiral went by seniority, but only the capable ones secured command.
The in-service training by which boys entered the Navy as midshipmen,
learned their trade as officers, and then passed a lieutenant's examination
created a supply of trained junior officers. Though British ship design was
poor compared to French, the men of war were sturdy and seaworthy. Built
of British oak, they could stand battering by round shot. With hulls copper-
bottomed in the 1770's and 1780's they could keep the seas for months and
even years without losing too much of their sailing qualities from fouling.
This made possible such long stretches at sea without landing as Nelson's
in the *Victory* of over two years. Recruitment by impressment and treatment of the ordinary seaman were shameful and a weak point of the Navy.
A "hot press" in a seaport town when war broke out swept all and sundry
into the "lower deck," to serve at bad pay and under foul conditions. Discipline was autocratic and kept by harsh flogging. This did cause the great
mutinies of 1797. But the morale of the Navy was so high that once at sea
crews usually shook down and fought like tigers. Certainly impressment
was an effective sea conscription to man the fleet quickly. In command,
supply of vessels, and supply of officers and men the Royal Navy in 1783
was ready for great emergencies.

Furthermore, it had back of it not only a tradition of almost invariable
success nearly two centuries old but new tactical skills. The Navy that
under Drake had defeated the Armada and under Blake had achieved the
impossible time and again had, at the end of the American Revolution,
solved the problem of sailing-ship warfare. At the Battle of the Saints,
which in 1782 had saved England's command of the sea, a century of naval
deadlock had been broken. Until then the concentrated broadside fire of
ships in defensive line of battle had either driven attackers off or forced
them to stultify their attack by forming defensive line as well. At the Saints
it was shown that the new ideas of "breaking the line" were practical. During the 1780's Lord Howe, who had advocated them, and Lord Hood, who
had put them into practice, would teach them to the Navy. After 1783 the

British Navy, instead of merely hustling the enemy fleets back into port and blockading them there—the typical naval action of the eighteenth century—would win battles of annihilation, such as the Nile and Trafalgar.

Thus in 1783 the Royal Navy was ready to do more than ever before. It could give England safety by preventing invasion. It could give her wealth by keeping the sea lanes open. It could add to that wealth by capturing ports and colonies, those captures being also an exercise of power. More than that, it could sweep the enemy from the sea and strike at his homeland by blockade and invasion.

Not only could the Navy do this, it would do it. English strategic doctrine—navally—was far advanced. Generations of seamen and statesmen had seen what the Navy could accomplish. They knew of defeated invasions, of convoys carried through bearing the wealth of the Levant and India, and of what had happened "on 'Change" the dread year in which both Levant and India convoys had been lost. They knew of a long roll of colonies added to the Empire. They had seen one enemy, Holland, brought to her knees by blockade, until the Zuider Zee had become a "forest of masts" of ships daring not sail and the Dutch had had to sue for peace. Ever since Sir Francis Drake had "singed the King of Spain's beard" by a landing in Spain, they had been aware that "the Army was a projectile for the Navy to fire," even though it would be a century and a quarter before Lord Fisher would use these words in the Guildhall of the City of London. If foreign affairs should prove a naval game, the English would know how to play it.

Britain's Army was no such effective world-wide force as her Navy. Its command was diversified between tactical and administrative control by the Commander in Chief at the Horse Guards, strategic control by the Secretary of State for War, munitions control by the Master General of the Ordinance, and supply control by the Secretary at War, of whom only the two secretaries were parliamentary officials. Each regiment was in many matters a law unto itself; usually each regiment was so small as to be of only one battalion. For reasons that had made sense in the reigns of Charles II and William III, officers got promotion by buying their commissions, unless death created a vacancy; hence a favorite army toast of "A bloody war and a sickly season," since only bullets or fever could help poor men of merit to rise in rank. The enlisted men were characterized by the greatest general of the period, Arthur Wellesley, Duke of Wellington, as "the scum of the earth, enlisted for drink." Few sober men, unless desperate, would join an army whose pay was less than what was given men on relief, there to face discipline as in the Navy by flogging of terrible harshness.

The training for war of the troops was highly conservative. When

European armies gave up the line formation for the column, the British declined to follow and stuck to the methods of the past. Yet though the Horse Guards might be considered moss-bound, this Army was surprisingly effective. It had two great advantages, effective fire power and high morale. British battalions could fire by platoons from the famous "thin red line" so crushingly that after 1800 only twice—at Maida in 1806, at Waterloo in 1815—did French infantry get close enough to cross bayonets. British bayonets, bristling from British squares, again and again repulsed the finest cavalry. The independence of each regiment could create an *esprit de corps* that would cheerfully bear indignity and privations. The second part of Wellington's remark is often forgotten, that he said of the men he called "scum of the earth" on enlistment, "It is a wonder we make them the fine fellows they are." When after 1799 Frederick, Duke of York, put vigor into the Commander in Chief's office, the British Army, though comparatively small, became as effective a fighting force as any in the world. It could strike hard when the Navy put it ashore, at Waterloo it could link up with other armies and end Napoleon's career. Its successes from 1808 on were a trump card for diplomats.

Why was it not better used at first? For this, too, there is a reason. Memories of Pride's Purge, Cromwell's Ironsides, the rule by the major generals, and James II's camp at Hounslow Heath to overawe London have caused the British to distrust a large army. Parliament has used the threat of not renewing the Mutiny Act to force the Crown to come to heel. The tendency has been to keep the Guards for show, and some regiments for garrison duty and capturing colonies. Then, when war comes, the same mistake is far too often repeated. A small, valiant, and devoted band is sent overseas to die to buy the time for their compatriots to build up an adequate force.

The Navy and the Army were not the sole cards British diplomats had to play. Britain's greatest strength was economic and in the field of ideas. The trade history of the Napoleonic Wars demonstrates how crushing could be British economic pressure. When Napoleon tried to destroy England's markets by shutting the Continent of Europe to her trade, his "Continental System" recoiled on him. He had sneered at the British as a "nation of shopkeepers." He was to learn what the efforts of thousands of merchants and traders could do to foil his customs officials. Smugglers, sometimes based on nearby islands such as Heligoland, poured goods into Europe. Deft financial devices made trade possible across battle lines. Meanwhile, British blockade cut off overseas imports such as tobacco, sugar, and coffee to such a degree that the European habit of adulterating coffee with chicory probably stems from this period. In time of peace, too, the ability to trade with Britain and to tap the resources of the London money market made Europeans listen to British diplomats.

The reputation of Great Britain, too, was a diplomatic asset. Her French enemy might call her *"perfide Albion,"* but to her friends there was an attraction in examples of British altruism and British consistency. Because the second Rockingham Ministry believed in the political and constitutional principles for which the American Revolution was fought, it gave the United States better terms than France and Spain, the allies of the United States, were prepared to recommend. Because the Liverpool Cabinet had a program for peace laid down in 1805, in 1815 it returned conquered colonies to Holland and even France and spent effort in setting up international restrictions on the slave trade. It is true that such acts of principle and generosity were balanced by others of less noble behavior. It is true that such acts also often paid practical dividends. But the world knew that England stood for an ideal of liberty and honor and made conscious efforts to live up to that idea. The fact that in certain parts of the world the phrase "word of an Englishman" is a very solemn form of promise has not been a disadvantage to England.

Not only did Britain's diplomats have these cards to play, by 1783 long experience had taught them how to play them. They knew that Britain's "wealth, power, and safety" depended on certain special interests. Overseas naval bases and a safe home base were essential for her Navy to be effective. For that reason they used Gibraltar, Corsica, and Malta to command the Mediterranean; Saint Helena, Mauritius, and the Cape of Good Hope to secure the sea route to India; and West Indies bases and Halifax to protect transatlantic trade. In a subsequent period, they would use Singapore and Hong Kong for the China trade. For a similar reason they saw to it that no unfriendly power held the Channel coast from Brest to the Zuider Zee. If that happened, England was soon at war. Her diplomats also knew that it was wise to support the weaker side, instead of "rushing to the aid of the victor," then shift when the weaker became the stronger. This policy of "trimming the ship" combined long-sighted self-interest with a feeling for justice. Both for practical reasons and for idealistic reasons, England, like other sea powers, has been on the side of liberty more often than not. To sum up, then, these have been England's chief aims: security on the Channel coast, a balance among whatever powers needed balancing, the ownership of key ports and forts, and if possible, international justice. Not all her diplomatic leaders have followed these aims; the successful ones have.

When one speaks of England's diplomats this way, one should not merely think of the Secretary of State for Foreign Affairs, the ambassadors, the ministers plenipotentiary, the secretaries of legation, the Foreign Office clerks, and the King's Messengers with their traditional symbol of office of a silver greyhound. Nor should one merely widen this definition to include other foreign-office officials, such as consuls and consul generals. Diplomatic decisions and actions were taken by still others. At the Cabinet level there were the Secretary of State for War, the President of the Board of Trade, the President of the Board of Control (for India), and a most important trio: the First Lord of the Treasury, who usually was Prime Minister and paid out the monies; the Chancellor of the Exchequer, who raised the monies and knew how much the First Lord could pay out; and the First Lord of the Admiralty, whose fleets would back up the words of the Foreign Secretary. At lower levels, the subordinates of these officials, especially admirals and generals, conducted foreign affairs, as at times did even private individuals. Foreign policy, then, was collectively decided. The English have long recognized this truth, and show recognition of it by treating the word "Government" as a plural noun. Official despatches do not say "His Majesty's Government has decided to do so-and-so," as if the Government were a single unit, but "His Majesty's Government have decided to do so-and-so," as if—which is the fact—many minds have come together to agree on the decision. Thus to understand England's foreign policy it is not enough to look at the forces behind it—Navy, Army, wealth, and reputation—or at its aims. One must also realize that that policy was determined not by one man alone, but by many men, working in cooperation. Then it will be possible to assess what parts different men or events played in shaping the policy of His Majesty's Government.

In 1783 His Majesty's Government did not have serious direct problems of foreign policy to face. The Treaty of Paris, signed that year but in fact negotiated in 1782 by Shelburne and Fox, had largely cleared the decks. Then these two men, even though they disliked each other, had contrived to split apart England's enemies, America, France, and Spain and, by making a separate and wisely generous treaty with the United States, had cut down on the concessions it was necessary to give to the others. It was true the England in 1783 was diplomatically isolated and in poor financial condition, but she was free to turn her mind to getting new allies and improving her finances.

In foreign affairs the Pitt ministry did well. In 1786 it negotiated a free-trade treaty with France. Between 1787 and 1789 a joint intervention with Prussia in Holland put back in power the pro-English Orange dynasty and thus made the Channel the more safe. In the Nootka Sound controversy of 1790, Spain was forced to acknowledge English title to the future British Columbia. Only in the attempted intervention in 1791 in favor of Turkey against Russia did the Government meet a check, and that came not from Russia but from the House of Commons, when Fox ridiculed the idea and so stopped the intervention. More important than these things, Pitt restored England's strength. His financial measures brought bonds from 53⅞ to 93. Furthermore, during the so-called Spanish and Russian

Armaments of 1790 and 1791, Lords Hood and Howe got veteran officers back to sea duty and indoctrinated them with the signals that embodied the new tactical ideas. This increase in financial strength and naval efficiency were to make a great difference when the storm of the French Revolution broke on England in 1793, with a declaration of war February 1 by the newly founded French Republic.

At first in 1789 the beginnings of the French Revolution had found English opinion favorable. After all it was flattering to see France, once an absolute monarchy, become like England a constitutional monarchy. But as the Revolution gained in intensity English opinion changed. When in September, 1792, the French monarchy was abolished amid a series of massacres, when immediately thereafter French armies invaded the Austrian Netherlands to counter invasion by Austria and Prussia, Pitt's Cabinet became alarmed. They tried to keep the peace, but the arrogance of the French blocked this probably hopeless attempt. For England must fight sooner or later if an active military power controls the shores of the Channel. Shocked by the execution of Louis XVI, British public opinion was ready to go to war. For such a continental war the English government had a traditional formula. On land England would supply a token force, to prove willingness to help, and would pay the bills for armies of allies. On the sea, English fleets would drive the enemy fleets into their harbors, and so gain command of the sea and all that that entailed in powers of blockade and landing. Overseas England would pick off enemy colonies one by one, thus depriving commerce raiders of bases and adding to the nation's wealth. Elizabeth I, Cromwell, William III, Marlborough, and the Elder Pitt had all used this formula. So the Younger Pitt used it, too. The Lords of the Admiralty summoned trusted post captains to command men-of-war, and the post captains so chosen put their press gangs to work, and then took the fleets to sea. The fleet under Lord Howe was to block the French base of Brest in the Channel, and that under Lord Hood was to block Toulon in the Mediterranean. The Horse Guards, with their usual shortsightedness, merely sent the Duke of York with three battalions of the Guards to Flanders and began the perennial policy of wasting veterans by driblets without training any replacements. Then the Admiralty, the Horse Guards, and the Secretaries of State prepared a larger expeditionary force for the West Indies. Meanwhile, English diplomats in Amsterdam, Berlin, and Vienna haggled over how much per day should be paid for the soldiers England's allies would put into the field against France. Thus was formed the First Coalition against France, with good apparent prospects for success.

The trouble was that this time the formula did not work. On the contrary, the armies of the French revolutionaries did all the conquering there was to be done in Europe, and the West Indies islands did not stay captured as they should have. Allies faded away, were conquered, or switched sides. There were even a series of sad moments when the fleets of France or under French control most emphatically did not stay blockaded, while England's fleets were driven from the Mediterranean and, worse still, crippled by mutiny at home. Here was a storm it took all Pitt's ability to weather, since England's traditional military policy failed to meet the situation, and it was not until three more coalitions had been formed that the danger from France ended.

Many reasons led to this failure of England's traditional policy. In part it came because her allies did not do their share. Prussia and Austria spent energy in partitioning Poland in 1793 and again in 1795 that might have made the difference in France, before the revolutionary armies became properly organized. Some of the Prussian, Austrian, Dutch, and Spanish generals were, let us say, up to British standards of incompetence, high as those were in some brigades and regiments in the Duke of York's expanding army in Flanders. But the chief reason for this failure was not that England and her allies were too weak for a normal continental war, but that this was not a normal continental war. France was a revolutionary nation, using a conscript army, for the first time in modern times. Till she could be met with equal enthusiasm and equal manpower, her armies were unconquerable. Nor was mass warfare France's only new fighting device. On her side, at this time, was a world revolutionary movement. Different though the Jacobin doctrines of individualism and nationalism were from the communist doctrines of today, the behavior of the Jacobin revolutionary movement closely parallels in outward form that of the communist movement. Whenever a French army entered a country, help would come to it from men inspired with revolutionary ideals. Whenever a French army occupied a country, these ideas as brought with the army would win France new friends, who would set up pro-French governments that today we would call satellite states, in many cases to be later absorbed into revolutionary France. Long before General Franco boasted in 1935 of the "fifth column" that would rise within the city of Madrid as his four columns converged on it, the French Republic used fifth-column techniques to open the war for its armies.

On the first of the three general fronts on which the English fought, that is, on land in Europe, the French secured outstanding successes once the momentum of their armies and their revolution built up. The few English veterans covered themselves with glory to no avail, while the mongrel forces of English, Dutch, Prussians and Austrians were driven out of Belgium. Then, too late, the Horse Guards embodied new regiments, gave commissions to any who paid for them, and sent out recruiting sergeants to enlist men in those regiments. This both prevented any replacements filling the ranks of the depleted veteran outfits and made sure that the new regiments had no stiffening of experienced officers or men. Consequently, the French pushed 50,000 English out of Holland even more easily than they had 10,000 out of Belgium. At one dramatic moment French hussars rode up to a Dutch fleet trapped by connivance in the ice, and by capturing it weakened England's naval position the next spring. Meanwhile, on the other frontiers of France an Austrian invasion from Italy, and a Spanish one across the Pyrenees were equally repelled. Thus France became dominant in western Europe.

As for the West Indies front, at first it seemed as if English expeditions could not fail. Despite the ability of the Horse Guards to mismanage, despite the ravages of much fever and a few French bullets, the minor French West Indies islands were taken. But they were hard to hold; the French had abolished slavery in 1791, and their counterexpeditions to the West Indies raised the slaves in revolt. In fighting those revolts England had to pour out streams of blood and treasure, and pour them out away from the center of the war effort, before her hold on the West Indies was solid. However, before condemning this waste as entirely useless it should be realized that it deprived French commerce raiders of bases and gave England a temporary world monopoly of sugar, which latter both in effect blockaded France and provided wealth to pay for the war. Though all this could have been secured without such cost by abolishing slavery, it was secured.

In North America there was no fighting until the War of 1812 broke out, but there was war-inspired diplomacy. Britain and France had to bid against each other to keep the United States neutral. Fortunately the United States refused to honor its alliance with France, and the French minister Genêt's attempt to put political pressure on President Washington backfired. Some outstanding disputes were settled by the Jay Treaty of 1794, under which British garrisons were withdrawn from the Old Northwest and American coastal vessels were allowed to trade with the West Indies. Then French aggression on American shipping led to the short "Quasi War" of 1798 between France and the United States. Thus in the presidencies of Washington and John Adams British diplomacy, aided by French blunders, kept the United States a friendly neutral. But, as can be seen, with the loss of Holland and Belgium, with the West Indies a drain, with America a hesitant neutral, during these years from 1793 to 1795, the "wealth, power and safety" of England did very much depend on the Royal Navy.

The Navy did its job well, taking the initiative from the start. At the outbreak of the war, the veteran admirals Lords Hood and Howe did more than they were told to do. Hood, on finding that a counterrevolution had broken out in Toulon, landed English and Spanish troops and captured the French squadron there. But what he took he could not hold. A

Corsican artillery officer, Napoleon Buonaparte, shelled the allies out of Toulon, being aided by Spanish incompetence so utter as to let the French men-of-war be recaptured without even scuttling them. The Mediterranean fleet now had to search for a new base. That was speedily found. In the fourteen years from 1755 to 1769, the island of Corsica had been independent under General Paoli, who since the French conquest of that last year had been living in London. Promptly he was shipped out to the Mediterranean. Such officers as Captain Horatio Nelson, R.N., and Lieutenant Colonel John Moore of the Fifty-first Infantry were put on shore to help the Paolists capture the forts held by the Revolutionaries. A Corsican government was set up, and, at the invitation of the Corsican people, for a short time King George III held the title of King of Corsica. Using bases on the island the English squadron, often with Captain Nelson commanding detached units, aided the Austrian, Piedmontese, and Neapolitan forces that were still making gestures at invading France across the Alps.

While this was happening, Lord Howe in the years 1793 and 1794 steadily blockaded Brest. This blockade pressed France hard with hunger. The winter of 1793–1794 was a bad one; moreover, people were too busy having a revolution to reap crops properly. It seemed to the French authorities that the stability of their republic depended on the safe arrival of a convoy of food ships from America. Therefore the Brest fleet was sent out to sacrifice itself, if need be, to bring the convoy through. In 1794, on what is still spoken of as "the Glorious First of June" the two fleets met. The new British tactics proved themselves in a smashing victory. Had the attack been pressed home, the French might have been annihilated. It was not, and most of their battered men-of-war got back to safety. After repairs, therefore, the Brest fleet was able to strain British resources just by being a fleet in being. English men-of-war which might have been used elsewhere had to be stationed in the Channel to watch it.

The war now became one of land power against sea power, with French successes making English diplomatic persuasions ineffective. For England defeats on land led to defections of allies, defections of allies led to further defeats, till the First Coalition fell apart, leaving England to fight on alone. First of all Prussia slipped out, because of the conquest of Holland, purchasing neutrality by a promise in the Treaty of Basel that Northern Germany would also stay neutral. This forced George III in his position as Elector of Hanover to stay out of the war that as King of Great Britain, Ireland, and Corsica he was fighting against France. Then conquered Holland not only switched sides but became the Batavian Republic. In 1796 the Spanish monarchy left England and joined France. These two defections added to the French navy many more warships than they had lost at Toulon and on the First of June. Austria and the Italian states of Sardinia-Piedmont and Naples were now all the allies left in the First Coalition.

Perhaps peace might have been obtained at this point had not a military genius appeared on the French side and been sent to the Italian front. This was that Bonaparte—he had dropped his Corsican "u"—who had shelled Hood out of Toulon. He showed what could be accomplished in the face of sea power. He outflanked Nelson's inshore squadron, by a march through Alpine passes, and then split and destroyed the Austrian armies in the Italian plains. He gained support by setting up revolutionary governments in North Italy and finally advanced to a point where he could threaten to invade Austria and thus in the spring of 1797 dictate peace. Meanwhile, since strength breeds strength, he got control of bases near his native Corsica, notably the Island of Elba, making it unsafe for the English fleet to use Corsica. It was obvious that sooner or later his men would make a landing there, rouse the French revolutionaries against the Paolists and give the Mediterranean fleet the same treatment he had at Toulon. When in November, 1796, a bungle of supply had reduced that fleet below a safe minimum, its commander, Sir John Jervis, reluctantly abandoned Corsica and withdrew to the Atlantic. Land power had destroyed Pitt's First Coalition; England's hope now lay in the Royal Navy. And even the Royal Navy was in danger. Its enemies had been augmented by the addition of Spanish and Dutch fleets to the French; its discipline was at perhaps the lowest ebb in all England's history.

Such was the situation when, early in 1797, off Cape Saint Vincent, Sir John Jervis with seventeen vessels met a Spanish squadron of twenty-seven. Saying, "England has need of a victory today," Sir John ordered an attack. By an act of brilliant initiative Captain Horatio Nelson placed his ship into a gap in the Spanish line and enabled Sir John to crush half the Spaniards before the rest could come to their aid. By this battle Jervis reversed the tide of war and earned himself the Earldom of Saint Vincent, the first title ever given for a battle, not an estate.

Throughout the year 1797 England's situation remained crucial. By an unsound policy the Channel fleet spent too much time in Portsmouth Harbor, too little at sea off Brest. Not only was this bad strategy in that it gave the French an opportunity to send out minor expeditions unobserved, but it was bad for morale. In harbor sailors were painfully conscious of the injustice with which they were being treated. Quietly they organized, and suddenly in a respectful but firm manner they struck for higher pay. Striking rather than mutiny seems the better way to describe what happened at Spithead. There were complaints about some officers and ill-treatment of some, but in general the sailors promised to fight the French if they should put to sea and, as at Invergordon in 1931, carried out the customary daily duties. At this crisis of the mutiny at Spithead, "Black Dick" Howe did England his last and perhaps his greatest service. He came down from London where he was handing over after resigning his command, had himself rowed from ship to ship, and by his personal promise of redress got the fleet to sea again.

The mutiny at the Nore, the anchorage of the North Sea fleet, was another matter. It was a revolutionary movement, triggered off by the success of the mutiny at Spithead. The red flag was hoisted with all that that means to sailors, and the mutineers blockaded the Thames till a mixture of force and conciliation persuaded them to return to duty and turn their ringleaders over to punishment. The shame of this mutiny at the Nore is such that the Royal Navy to this day does not sound five bells in the second dog watch, which was the agreed signal for its breaking out. Fortunately for England, neither the French Fleet nor the Dutch came out during the mutinies. Off Brest and off the Dutch base in the Texel a few loyal ships kept watch and by the bluff of their being there kept the enemy fleets from coming out. When, that autumn, the Dutch fleet did come out, off Camperdown shoals Adam Duncan drove half of it ashore. But England was in such straits that she had to go off the gold standard.

Discipline in the Navy did not revive immediately. St. Vincent, even the magnetic Nelson, had to take stern measures. But when St. Vincent was put in command of the Channel fleet the corner was turned. After that the Navy became once more completely reliable. It kept the seas clear and began the grinding economic pressure of blockade. Sea power thus gave back to Britain the strength needed as a basis for policy.

At this point it might be well to review briefly the psychological-warfare aspect of the struggle with France from 1793 to 1798 to bring to mind why the fifth-column side to the French military policy failed in England and Scotland and nearly succeeded in Ireland. As the political chapter has told, the ideals of the French Revolution did appeal to those who wanted Reform of Parliament, though its excesses shocked the majority of Britons. Repression forced the Reformers into silence, though fortunately basic rights were preserved by Erskine's successful defense of Horne Tooke and Cartwright. Counterpropaganda such as Burke's and Canning's writings roused the British against France. Here Methodism played an important part, along with the relief of agricultural distress caused by the Speenhamland system. Basically it may be said that, because the average Briton already enjoyed most of the rights the French were struggling for, he was immune to French propaganda. In Ireland matters were different. There because the United Irishmen had the technical independence of Ireland to defend and make real, the danger was great. Only the British Navy, storms, repressive measures, and finally the Act of Union prevented French aid reaching what up to 1798 was a potential danger spot. After 1798, and especially after the Union in 1801, the crisis was past. From then on Great Britain was more and more united behind the war.

At sea 1798 was also a turning point, for then England took the offensive once more. News came of a French fleet fitting out at Toulon—it was believed, for an attack on Ireland. Nelson, recently promoted because of seniority to the rank of Rear Admiral, was sent into the Mediterranean with a squadron. Nelson immediately showed his greatness. He roused in the officers under his command a spirit of initiative and cooperation that made him speak of them as "a band of brothers." The French fleet for a while eluded him because its destination was Egypt, not Ireland. It captured Malta and landed Bonaparte and an army in Egypt. Nelson finally caught up with it at Abukir Bay near the mouth of the Nile. When the French were discovered, it was nightfall and they were anchored in an apparently impregnable defensive position. But Nelson had taught his officers to achieve what others would not dare attempt. Despite the hazards of a night action they attacked, and before the French ships could raise anchor and flee all but four were sunk or captured. These Nelson indefatigably pursued to Malta and captured when he took that island. The Nile, or Abukir—both names are used—was a victory of complete annihilation, which left a French army stranded in Egypt.

Bonaparte's only way now to conquer Turkey and perhaps India was to escape by land through Palestine and Syria. But the Turkish fort of Saint-Jean-d'Acre blocked him. Commodore Sir Sidney Smith's part of Nelson's squadron captured the siege guns that were going to Acre by water and turned them on the French besiegers, English marines were landed to aid the Turks, and the French were beaten off. Later when Bonaparte in exile reviewed his career and thought how his veterans might have pushed on to India and there swept all before them, he used to say, "I missed my chance at Saint-Jean-d'Acre."

Nelson did not merely keep watch on Bonaparte's army of Egypt. He followed up the victory of the Nile throughout the Mediterranean and began a two-year siege of Malta. His victory and its follow-up gave cards at last to the English diplomats, so that with new strength England could have a policy again. The supply of nations willing to fight victorious France was small. It consisted of Austria, which wanted to regain at least an equivalent of the lost Belgium, the Kingdom of Naples or the Two Sicilies which was ruled by a reactionary relative of the exiled French royal family, and Russia, whose mad Czar, Paul, had been appealed to by the ousted Knights of St. John of Malta to act as Grand Master of their order and recover their island for them. Paul might be insane enough to order an ill-drilled regiment to march to Siberia on the spot, but as hundreds of thousands of men marched at his orders, he was worth humoring.

So it was that in 1799 a Second Coalition was organized and paid for by England. At first it succeeded, as Austrian and Russian armies pressed close to France, recovering much of Italy and southern Germany, and an Anglo-Russian expeditionary force invaded Holland. But then the advance stalled, with the Austrians trying to get the Russians to do all the work. At that moment Bonaparte calmly deserted his army in Egypt, just in time before an expeditionary force from England and another from India converged on it. He landed in France and seized power by a *coup d'état*. Here, with the quarrels among revolutionary leaders and what amounted to purges, can be seen another parallel with the communist Revolution and the struggle for power between Trotsky and Stalin, ending up in the efficient dictatorship of Stalin. Bonaparte made his seizure of power stick by another whirlwind campaign in Italy, which again knocked Austria out of the war. Having done this, he then began turning the tables on the English by intensifying what today would be called economic warfare.

Blockade, interference with trade on the high seas, commerce raiding, the seizure of colonies that had a monopoly of supplies, the closing of straits and other supply routes naturally had long been means of forcing one nation to yield to another's will. England had steadily, through her law courts and especially her admiralty courts, built up a policy that combined full use of her command of the sea with at least an appearance of consistency, so that her court decisions formed a large part of whatever international law existed covering sea trade in wartime. A merchant vessel ordered to stop by an English man-of-war knew pretty much what to expect and could have confidence that if the English man-of-war broke English-made rules he would have redress. But those rules, which every war grew stricter and stricter as loopholes in them were plugged, bore hard on neutrals and especially on the neutral countries bordering on the Baltic Sea. These neutrals, too, had navies. Bonaparte saw his chance. After defeating Austria, war really stopped with Russia, since Russia and France had no common boundary to cross. He persuaded Denmark, Sweden, and Russia, as well as Prussia, to protest and back their protests by sending out their fleets to protect their merchantmen. This brought England into immediate action. What ships could be spared from watching the French fleets were sent to the Baltic under Sir Hyde Parker, with Nelson as second in command. The arithmetic of the situation suggested that England was in dire straits, for there were enough men-of-war in the Baltic first to crush Parker, then to lift the blockade of Brest, give the command of the sea to France, and allow an invasion of England. Moreover, the Danish fleet could quietly wait at Copenhagen safe under the guns of forts till the Swedes and Russians came to join it.

But arithmetic does not win naval battles. "At sea, above all, something must be left to chance," wrote Nelson a few years later. Nelson at Copenhagen saw that some Danish ships were anchored with insufficient protection. He got Parker's consent to attack them, while making a strong feint attack against the ships under the main forts. Firing was very heavy, so heavy that Parker from outside Copenhagen harbor signaled Nelson to retire. On the signal being reported to Nelson, he calmly put his telescope to his blind eye, stated he could not read the signal, and went ahead to pound the Danes into submission. The armed neutrality collapsed, for the same morning of Nelson's victory at Copenhagen, a group of Russian nobles, discontented with Paul's policy, murdered him and put on the throne his son Alexander who reversed his father's policy. This made a deadlock between France and England and gave an apparent opportunity for making peace. For in England, over the crisis of Irish Union and the broken pledge by Pitt that Catholics might sit in the Union parliament, Pitt had resigned and been replaced by a nonentity, Addington. Addington gave terms Pitt never would have given, returning many colonies such as the Cape of Good Hope to the Dutch and Guadeloupe to the French. Bonaparte promptly began a career of expansion, sending armies to San Domingo and forcing Spain to cede to France the Louisiana territory. These actions, incidentally, lost him the friendship of the revolted slaves, who had previously pestered the English, and forced the United States to buy out Louisiana, for, as President Thomas Jefferson put it, if France owned Louisiana "the United States would have to marry themselves to the English fleet and nation." As a further part of his expansion policy, Bonaparte refused to give up a claim to Malta.

During the years 1801 to 1803, Addington bumbled along as Prime Minister, while Pitt's friends chafed at seeing him out of office. At last it was so clear that Bonaparte could not be trusted that England refused to give up Malta without assurances that Bonaparte would not give. His ultimatum was Malta or war, and war it was.

The war of land against sea was renewed. Bonaparte—or, as he should be now called, Napoleon, since he had himself made the Emperor Napoleon in 1804—put at Boulogne the army of England, ready to cross the Channel the moment a chance came. While waiting he drilled and trained the Republican armies into enthusiasm for their leader and purged former republican generals and the Duc d'Enghien, a relative of the exiled royal family. On the other side of the Channel in Kent, preparations were made for the worst. The Duke of York as commander in chief inspired administrative reforms, such as a military school, a staff college, and an improved enlistment policy. Pitt, who soon was made Prime Minister again to "weather the storm," took very seriously his duties in the hitherto sinecure post of Warden of the Cinque Ports, in organizing militia and building fortifications. More important, at Shorncliffe England's best tactician, Sir

John Moore, trained his "Light Division," perhaps the finest body of troops then on the planet, with an emphasis on initiative in the ranks, fire power, and the use of rifles.

But the basic struggle remained at sea. English fleets watched the three bases of Toulon, Cadiz, and Brest, from which covering forces might emerge to convoy the army of England across the Channel. Napoleon made and remade plans by which his admirals might get out of port, rendezvous at sea, and make invasion possible. At last in 1805 the Toulon fleet did slip out. But Nelson pursued it so hotly that all its twistings and turnings were useless, and the moment it met a small British squadron sent to intercept it, it fled into Cadiz harbor, there to be blockaded along with some Spaniards. It looked as if Napoleon were checkmated and would never be able to invade England. This seemed all the more true when Admiral Villeneuve, goaded to desperation by Napoleon's reprimands, put to sea in October, 1805, from Cadiz with the "Combined Fleets." Though the French and Spaniards outnumbered the British, that was no longer considered to matter. So high were England's standards of fighting at sea that Sir Robert Calder, the admiral who had driven the French into Cadiz with an inferior force, was facing a court-martial for not having done more. The English were ready for these odds. Nelson had just distributed to his captains his famous battle order, "the Nelson Touch," which contained the quintessence of Howe's new tactical doctrine. When he met the French he deliberately exposed two lead ships to crushing fire, his own *Victory* naturally being one of the two, in order that two English lines could break the combined fleets into three parts and hope to annihilate two of them. This he came close to doing. He probably would have done it, had he survived to command the pursuit. He died in action, leaving as a legacy an imperishable tradition that is embodied in his last signal to his fleet, the endlessly quoted "England expects every man to do his duty." For in war, as Bonaparte said, the moral is to the physical as two to one, and it was Nelson who made the morale of the British Navy, by his life and his death. Strategically, the Battle of Trafalgar was an anticlimax to the pursuit that drove the Toulon fleet into harbor and prevented the army of England from crossing the Channel. But as a matter of prestige it gave England command of the sea for over a century. When in 1812 single American ships fought it out on even terms with English ships, it astonished the world. In a sense, Trafalgar was even more a battle of annihilation than Abukir Bay, for until 1908 no fleet was built to fight England, and until 1915 no fleet put to sea to fight England. Trafalgar removed all navies, as opposed to commerce raiders, from England's path and allowed her to utilize to the limit her command of the sea.

For a moment after the news of Trafalgar it seemed as if England had won. For with that news, other news reached London; a Third Coalition had been formed. Russia and Austria had come into the field again, and Napoleon's army of England had to march into Germany to meet them. More than that, though it could not be revealed at the time, Pitt had secured general agreement to a practicable peace settlement. It would be a peace in which Russia and Austria would be rewarded for their efforts but in which a liberal constitutional French monarchy would keep for France the blessings of the Revolution before it had become extreme. In that way France would be more likely to accept the terms that would be dictated to her. In this conception Pitt indoctrinated the group of young followers he had gathered around him, notably Robert Stewart, Viscount Castlereagh. No wonder that Pitt at the annual Guildhall Banquet in November told the Lord Mayor of London and other guests, "England has saved' herself by her exertions and will, I trust, save Europe by her example." But he spoke too soon. On December 2, 1805, the lucky day of the Bonapartes, the massed artillery of the French smashed a combined Russian and Austrian army at Austerlitz and drove Austria out of the war. The news broke Pitt's heart. On reaching his home he said, "Roll up the map of Europe; we will not need it these ten years," and in a few weeks died of overwork and dejection.

Pitt was wrong about the map. It proved very useful to his successors sooner than that. His disciples, especially George Canning and Robert Stewart, Viscount Castlereagh, fulfilled his hopes and saved Europe from Napoleon. They knew how to use economic warfare, psychological warfare, and the British Army as a projectile for the Navy to fire. Even those who were not his disciples adopted his policies. In the few months of 1806 when Fox was Foreign Secretary the short-lived Ministry of All the Talents prosecuted the war with vigor.

For a while England's straits grew steadily worse. Napoleon struck down enemies one by one. Prussia fell in 1806, having been bamboozled into neutrality in 1805. Russia could not be conquered by armed force, for Russian numbers brought even the swarms of Napoleon's men to a standstill. But the Czar Alexander could be, and was, charmed and argued into changing sides and adopting Napoleon's Continental System. For now Napoleon, realizing he could not land an army in England, turned to economic warfare. He planned to blockade England by cutting off trade where it started, in European ports. By the Berlin and Milan decrees, of 1806 and 1807, he treated all ships trading with England as English and, as such, as legitimate prizes of war. The English naturally retaliated with similar regulations, the Orders in Council, that made all vessels trading with France or her allies prizes of war. That meant that, though many merchants could and did get much trade done with forged papers, the coast from Trieste to Hamburg, with the exception of Portugal, was potentially blocked to English goods. Then Napoleon planned to plug the gaps. At a meeting on a raft in the Niemen River (hence the story of how the news of the agreement got to Foreign Secretary George Canning from an agent under the raft) Alexander and Napoleon made a supposedly secret agreement to force neutrals to join in the Continental System and, in particular, to put an army on the Danish border. But now England acted with Nelsonic speed. Before that army could reach Copenhagen it had been forestalled by an English expedition, which had calmly ordered the Danes to hand over their fleet and sailed away with it. Napoleon made a similar swoop later on on Portugal and again was forestalled. Sir Sidney Smith, of Saint-Jean-d'Acre fame, persuaded the Portuguese royal family to move across the Atlantic and set up there the Empire of Brazil.

Napoleon now began to show his true colors. In 1808 he persuaded the Russians to take over Finland from Sweden, and the next year he used this fact to persuade the childless King of Sweden to adopt the French Marshal Bernadotte as his heir and the effective ruler of Sweden in order to protect Sweden from Russia. He also got the Austrians to put pressure on Turkey, then the ruler of the Balkan peninsula. It looked as if all Europe except for Sicily was closed to English trade, or as closed as customs officials could make it. But in doing this Napoleon laid himself open to charges of mistreatment of neutrals and his subjects. He became a target for propaganda, largely originating in countries under his control but stirred up from England. There was no widespread policy of psychological warfare, no Ministry of Information to supervise the pamphlets that were circulated, but intentional statements by English leaders were calculated to stir up discontent, and did so. When the first signs of what today would be called a resistance movement sprang up, England took advantage of it. For England was now finding a new ally on the Continent, the forces of Liberal nationalism. There is no need here to list the patriots, soldiers, and philosophers who created those forces. It is important to realize that those forces existed and that in such men as the Baron vom und zum Stein England was at last to find allies who shared her will to fight Napoleon to the bitter end.

The first important active resistance took place in Spain. There Napoleon, by one of the harsh and brutal actions which so aided his enemies in the long run, forced both the king and heir apparent to the Spanish throne to abdicate and replaced them by his brother Joseph. On May 2, 1808, the Dos Mayo, the people of Madrid drove Joseph out, the whole nation revolted, and a new method of warfare was shown the world, the little war, or to use the Spanish name for it, *guerrilla* warfare. Companies, regiments, in one case a whole French army, were destroyed. England seized the opportunity, and an expedition was landed in Portugal under Sir Arthur Wellesley, which cleared the French from that country.

At last England had a military opening and a good general to use it. From then on the whole aspect of England's war effort changed. It took time to settle down to the right man in the right place. Wellesley was superseded by two inefficient generals who bungled the surrender of Lisbon. They were dismissed and England's best troop trainer, Sir John Moore, was sent to counter Napoleon himself, who had come to Spain to clean up the mess. Sir John cleverly upset Napoleon's timetable by advancing into northern Spain, putting his men in an apparent trap and then proving that "a British army retreats with a sting in its tail," by marching his men out of it. Sir John was killed at the embarkation at Corunna, but the poem "The Burial of Sir John Moore" by an Irish schoolboy remains a classic part of English patriotic tradition. Sir John having thus saved the Spanish revolt, Sir Arthur Wellesley returned to the Peninsula. At the same time England's diplomatic efforts saw real success. The army in Spain and negotiations elsewhere in Europe played into each other's hands.

Moore's retreat, for example, having proved that Napoleon could be met on equal terms, Austria renewed the war and thus forced Napoleon to leave Spain. Napoleon did defeat Austria in battle but could not, as in the past, dictate terms. Behind him was an attempted English landing on Walcheren Island that might have captured Antwerp had the two joint commanders not bungled matters. Thereafter, Napoleon was too busy keeping Europe quiet to attend personally to Spain. And there, in Spain, where England could supply an army easily by sea, while French armies starved or robbed because land communications were so bad, constant pressure was kept on the French. Every year Wellesley moved out of winter quarters and taught different French generals the same lesson, that an English line could mow down a French column. Every year the French armies in Spain would be concentrated on Lord Wellington—for at each victory Wellesley moved up in the peerage—and the English army would withdraw into safety. Meanwhile the Spanish would take back from the French control a province or two. The French would swing back against the Spaniards, and Wellington would advance again.

English military history is full of the details of this war, of how the Light Division spearheaded Wellington's attacks, and how the various regiments covered themselves with glory, till the English crossed the Pyrenees into France and Wellington entered Paris as a duke, having put Louis XVIII back on the throne of France. Here were built up the regimental traditions which, to quote the Iron Duke again, made British soldiers "the fine fellows they are." But the wider meaning of the Peninsular campaigns is that they were combined with other pressure to make of Spain the "Spanish ulcer," to use his own words, that drained Napoleon's strength. Just because French armies were pinned down in one corner of

Europe, it was possible for English diplomacy to stir up all the more trouble elsewhere.

Almost everywhere England's diplomacy succeeded. In one case, however, it failed—the United States. At first the American government tried to counter both English and French economic warfare by a "continental system" of its own, Jefferson's Embargo of 1808. When that failed just as did the Continental System and merely aroused internal resentment such as Napoleon was contending with, President Madison tried a variant—an offer to fight whatever country failed to end restrictions. When England was accidentally late in her acceptance of this by a few days, the "War Hawks" of the West pushed America into an invasion of Canada that failed dismally. At sea, American frigates won dramatic single-ship actions, and a stubborn British blockade, finally marred by destructive raids on Washington and New Orleans, vexed America. Finally, when Napoleon was defeated in 1814, it was possible to call it a draw at the peace of Ghent. As news of peace was crossing the Atlantic, the New Orleans raid by Peninsular veterans was defeated crushingly by Andrew Jackson, with great effect on America's pride and national spirit and no effect on peace terms. But important as the War of 1812 was to the new nation of America, it was an interlude to England in her struggle with the Continental System.

The Continental System depended on two things: agreement between Napoleon and Alexander of Russia, and acceptance of its workings by the peoples of Europe. The second was attacked by the merchants of England, aided by their government. Smugglers, traders under supposedly neutral flags, various devious methods of getting goods onto the Continent not only kept England's trade going but furnished constant propaganda against Napoleon's control. In one case, Napoleon's own brother, the nominal King of Holland, planned to revolt to protect his people. And when Napoleon, as he did in the case of Holland, absorbed reluctant satellite states into his French Empire, still independent states became frightened. In particular, Alexander of Russia began wondering where he stood until in 1812 he resisted Napoleon's demands and the French invasion of Russia began.

Here English diplomacy and the British navy did their utmost to help Russia. In Constantinople a young attaché named Stratford Canning persuaded Turkey to make peace with Russia in time to free crucially needed troops. In the Baltic the Navy stepped in, as Sir James Saumarez and his squadron defended the Russian right flank. This time, at last, the gamble was successful. Though Napoleon captured Moscow, he had to evacuate it, in the winter, and his Grand Army was frozen and disrupted in the snows. Napoleon's unwilling ally Prussia then began to change sides, and more serious, the embodiment of the new German national spirit, the Baron vom Stein, gained the confidence of Alexander and urged him to counterattack and invade Germany to liberate it. On the strength of that decision it became possible for English diplomats to enlist Sweden's help by offering the possession of Norway after the war and payment of an army's expenses during the war.

When the Russians, the Swedes, and the Prussians had liberated Prussia, another defection came, and Austria switched sides. Finally, at the Battle of Leipzig, or Battle of the Nations, Napoleon received his first crushing defeat at the hands of man, not weather.

It took time and diplomacy to finish the job. Only the Prussians and the German volunteers really wanted to fight Napoleon to the finish. But the wisdom and determination of Lord Castlereagh, who spent much of his time on the Continent, held this curious team together and kept them loyal to Pitt's peace program. Although Napoleon's genius in warfare shone in defeat as it had in victory, during the winter of 1813–1814 the Fourth Coalition pressed steadily forward until Napoleon was forced to give in and abdicate.

The task before English diplomacy was now to make a lasting peace. It was no easy problem, considering the bitter feelings held against Napoleon. Fortunately, when the negotiators met at Vienna to decide on terms, England had on the spot two Anglo-Irishmen of international reputation, Castlereagh and Wellington. No one could ignore what was said by Castlereagh, who had sat at the Allies' council table and told emperors what armies to put in the field, matching by payments for mercenaries the utmost Russia, Prussia, and Austria could accomplish on their own. No one could ignore his alternate, Wellington, the general who had consistently beaten the supposedly unbeatable French every time he met them, whose brilliant campaigns had drained the strength from the French army. And these men asked surprisingly little for England, except for the idealistic disavowal of the slave trade. All they wanted was a legal fiction that the war had not been against France but against Napoleon. This fortunately fitted the Legitimist ideas of Russia and Prussia, who liked to put the clock back to prerevolutionary 1789, except where they could add to their territories. Therefore a representative of the Bourbon monarch Louis XVIII joined the Congress and helped redraw the map of Europe. There was argument; at one time it was necessary for England, Austria, and royalist France to threaten to fight Russia and Prussia to make those excited victors see sense. But the quality of the statesmanship shown can be judged from results. Most of the boundaries drawn by the Congress in western Europe lasted to the present day, only three changes being made up to 1914, excluding recombinations of units (i.e., the junction of duchies, etc., into the Kingdom of Italy, the German Empire).

In the midst of the Vienna negotiations came the dramatic interlude of Napoleon's "Hundred Days," his short-lived return to power. When Napoleon had abdicated, he had, at the suggestion of the chivalrous Alexander of Russia, been made "Emperor of Elba" and given that tiny Italian island to rule. Soon he tired of such a life. In March, 1815, he landed in the South of France and by sheer personality took the country over. Soon war broke out again. Like the Trafalgar campaign this was a strategic anticlimax, since Napoleon was probably doomed to defeat. But like Trafalgar it added to Britain's prestige. For to the Duke of Wellington was assigned a key command in the allied advance guard in Belgium, which was to hold Napoleon up till Russian and Austrian manpower came to the rescue, and the Duke did more than fight a delaying action. At Waterloo, Blücher and he defeated Napoleon crushingly.

The dramatic story of this final campaign has often been told. Napoleon thought he had split the armies of Wellington and Blücher so far apart that he could crush Wellington. All day on June 18 British squares held off French cavalry, and the "thin red line" smashed back the charges of French columns, in the hopes of holding out till "night or Blücher" came. By forced marches the Prussians rushed to the aid of the Dutch, German, and British troops under Wellington, and so was won the final battle of the war, which the English know as Waterloo, the Germans as *"La Belle Alliance"* (the Beautiful Alliance). Napoleon's reign was ended, and with a dramatic touch the Emperor chose to surrender to the organization that had defeated him, the Royal Navy. His Majesty's government knew what to do with this guest. Napoleon was not allowed to set foot on English soil, though he saw England through a porthole; H.M.S. *Bellerophon* carried him to the East India Company's island of Saint Helena, where he was put under the charge of the former governor of Elba, Sir Hudson Lowe, to drag out his life in captivity and pour out the stream of propaganda reminiscences that was to do so much to make his nephew Emperor Napoleon III.

The Hundred Days and the Waterloo campaign changed the terms of the Treaty of Vienna surprisingly little, but they gave the Duke of Wellington a European reputation. They made it natural to put him in charge of the armies that occupied France and put on him the responsibility of setting the terms on which the French monarchy paid its war indemnity.

So it was that England ended the Napoleonic Wars with tremendous prestige, the command of the seven seas, international disavowal of the slave trade, and a few colonies—Ceylon, Mauritius, Trinidad, British Guiana, and the Cape of Good Hope the chief ones—in short, with the accomplishment of Pitt's aim of a just peace. But the shuffle and redeal of the diplomatic cards that took place at the Congress of Vienna radically altered the game Castlereagh had to play. Balance-of-power methods temporarily were in abeyance, since Napoleonic France, against which the

rest of Europe had been balanced, was defeated and Royalist France
had "rushed to the aid of the victors." In place of the system of balance
of power, a new way of securing peace for Europe was being tried, known
by the names of the Congress system and the Concert of Europe. Annually the five chief powers—Russia, Austria, Prussia, France, and England—held Congresses not unlike the meetings of the Security Council
of the United Nations. Matters that concerned small nations as well, or
special areas where particular small nations had rights, were handled
by the Concert of Europe. This was supposed to mean consent by all
nations concerned. In actual practice it meant that the ambassadors at the
capital nearest the problem worked out the details of its solution. This
was not a formalized system, but in the years immediately after Waterloo
there was a genuine attempt to prolong into peace the wartime cooperation
among allies. It worked not too badly, since no one wanted to be the
first to break up the European unity which had brought peace back to
the Continent.

However, in this state of affairs, England's place in diplomacy became
diametrically changed. The principle of legitimacy, the duty of kings to
rule and subjects to obey, was the keynote of the Vienna settlement. England, as a country in which the king had to obey his people, therefore
found herself at variance with her former allies. This divergence did not
appear at first, since the victors continued to have many interests in
common and since Wellington and Castlereagh were on such terms of
confidence with the leading statesmen of Europe. But gradually double
pressure mounted on them—from European chancellories and foreign
offices, to put down all forms of liberalism; from the opposition in England,
to support liberalism and stop truckling to autocrats.

Among these dilemmas Castlereagh and Wellington steered a realistic
and effective course. They knew well what they could and could not do
with perhaps one exception. A later generation of English statesmen, such
as Lord Palmerston, would have given verbal support to the German
Liberal movement that in the years 1816 to 1820 was being betrayed and
driven underground. Whether such support would have been beneficial,
as Palmerston found in Switzerland and Italy, or useless, as he found it
in Denmark and Germany, must remain a matter of conjecture, though
it is probable that all that England would have accomplished would have
been to weaken her prestige to no avail. Certainly Castlereagh and Wellington, though they had used methods like psychological warfare against
Napoleon, did not use publicity in their postwar diplomacy. But otherwise their policy was marked by wise use of all the powers they possessed.

An example of Castlereagh's wisdom was his realistic treatment of the
United States. He stopped any foolishness of an armament race by agreeing to limit naval forces on the Great Lakes. He stopped any squabble

about who owned the empty land west of the Great Lakes by drawing a line to the Rockies and then agreeing to a "joint occupation" of the Oregon Country, the very Nootka Sound area for which Pitt had threatened to fight Spain. Future generations who accept without a thought "the boundary without a soldier" and the peaceable settlement by Americans of Oregon, by Canadians of British Columbia, might consider what might have been the course of events had not Robert Stewart, Viscount Castlereagh, and John Quincy Adams shown uncommon common sense.

The armies of occupation in France were well handled by Wellington. He bent all his efforts to getting them out as fast as possible, before clashes came. To do this, he had to raise loans in England to enable the French to pay up more quickly the indemnities that the armies were there to secure. His success and the consequent stability of the restored French monarchy increased his already great international reputation.

As for Castlereagh, he had the harder job of being outvoted 4 to 1 at the annual Congresses of the victors and the French monarchy, by which in theory the Continent was kept at peace. He earned opprobrium at home for not coming out against what he could not stop, such as repression of free speech in Germany and interference in such self-government in Naples as had been left over from Lord William Bentinck's career in Sicily. But by thus keeping quiet, he was able to secure, as the price of unanimity, some concessions in action. The strain on him was terrific, such a strain as has caused American secretaries of state who for a shorter time have held such responsibilities to retire. The climax came in 1821 when a French army invaded Spain to restore the autocratic powers of the king and, incidentally, to get for the French monarchy the cheap prestige of having conquered a country that Napoleon had failed to conquer. Since autocracy was popular in Spain, there was nothing Castlereagh could have done had he wanted to. But a stage was approaching when England could act, when the restored Spanish monarchy decided to borrow a Russian fleet wherewith to reconquer its revolted South American colonies. Privately, Castlereagh warned his associates in the Congress that this would not do. Then his iron nerves broke, and from strain and overwork he committed suicide.

That left a place open for his contemporary and rival, George Canning. For Canning's career, Castlereagh's death took place at the right moment. A few days later he would have been on the seas, sailing to India to take up office as Governor-general. Canning's arrival to power brought into use a new form of diplomacy. He did not have Castlereagh's personal contact with the rulers of Europe; he did have a free hand. Here the situation parallels that in which the United States found itself immediately after Franklin Roosevelt's death. Canning began his tenure of office with a dramatic stroke. He told the world publicly what Castlereagh had told the Concert of Europe privately. An attempt to make a joint declaration with the United States failed when United States Secretary of State John Quincy Adams had the courage to get President Monroe to say ahead of Canning what Canning would say anyway, that European intervention in the Americas would be resisted. But in the days of England's utter naval supremacy it was obviously the British Navy that would enforce the Monroe Doctrine. This Canning announced not to Parliament, but to a public meeting of his constituents at Liverpool. There he even drew benefit from having been forestalled by Adams, by declaring he had "called a New World into existence, to redress the balance of the Old."

Here were the germs of a new English foreign policy, or rather a return to certain constant aspects of the foreign policy England had consistently used. For Canning relied on the public declaration of principles as a means of influencing foreign affairs, and on rallying to England's side, by means of those principles, small nations which like England depended on the sea and desired to govern themselves. Under his guidance, England fell out from the Congress system, which soon lost effectiveness since its strength had come from the unanimity of its members. At the same time, of course, England lost what power she had had with the governments of the continent of Europe. As England had not signed Alexander of Russia's Holy Alliance among divine-right kings, it has become customary, though not technically correct, to state that England now stood for parliamentary or some such principles as against the Holy Alliance, the latter term being applied not to all its signatories but only to Austria, Prussia, and Russia. In turn England supported such apparently insignificant states as Portugal and the revolted Greek republic. When the liberal branch of the Portuguese royal family sailed from Brazil to oust the reactionary branch that had first returned to Lisbon, Canning saw to it that the liberals were left alone to defeat the reactionaries. When the Greek revolt began fizzling out and when the Turks called in an Egyptian army to finish the job, Canning lent England's support and England's naval strength to the Concert of Europe, when that otherwise reactionary but consciously Christian body took to backing liberal Christians against reactionary Turks. It was in the midst of the Greek crisis that Canning suddenly died. But he left a legacy—a new, or revived, policy. For he taught the English the lesson that such previous secretaries of state as John Milton and William Pitt the Elder had taught them, that public opinion is a power in diplomacy and that when a statesman has taken an action which changes public opinion, he has affected foreign affairs. Just as John Milton's letters had saved Protestants in the Italian Alps, just as William Pitt's speeches had put courage into the heart of Frederick the Great, so Canning's speeches, even though they dealt with small nations and got them small benefits, impressed the world. His contemporaries felt, and rightly felt, that Canning as Foreign Secretary proved himself a great man. Here Canning was following a policy Britain has often followed, when it has been necessary to create a new balance of power. It has been called—by those who have found it to defeat their aims—the policy of divide and rule. For if powers are to be balanced, they must first be separated, which is just what Canning did. He got the members of the Congress to squabble with one another. And, as long as there was no pairing off into two opposite international organizations, there was no need for England to decide which was weaker. She could help different powers at different times, and benefit by a complete freedom of action.

Two proofs of this exist. One was in the handling of the Greek question after Canning's death. Wellington, his successor as Prime Minister, and Aberdeen, his successor as Foreign Secretary—the Goderich ministry of a few months is here disregarded—had no intention of being liberal. But the forces Canning had unleashed became too much for them. The fleets of the Concert of Europe watched what was going on in Greece and watched so carefully that, when someone fired a gun by mistake in Navarino Bay, there was soon no Egyptian fleet to enable the Turks to reconquer Greece. Nor was there any desire to prevent Greece from being self-governing. On the contrary, the Russians invaded Turkey from the north to force a legitimate government to recognize one founded by revolution. From that flowed, as a natural consequence to those who understand the expansion of empires, a treaty of peace by which a small Greek state gained independence and the Russian ambassador practically ran Turkey.

Another proof of Canning's importance was a speech made by a hitherto retiring member of Parliament, Henry John Temple, Viscount Palmerston, on the Greek question. In putting pressure on the Wellington government to aid Greece get good terms, he showed he had learned how the formation of Parliamentary opinion by a powerful speech, well reported in the press, would mold public opinion too and thus guide foreign affairs. Canning and his methods of open diplomacy rather than Castlereagh and his methods of personal intercourse would set the example for England's future policy.

In 1830, then, this was the situation of England, diplomatically. She had no allies, and the Congress system, the rule by five foreign ministers, had broken down. At the same time, she had as client states Portugal, Greece, and South America—all grateful, all sources of trade. Furthermore, since she was the hope of freedom, the nation which had resisted both Napoleon and the Reaction, she had a tremendous reservoir of friendship on which she might draw, if she but knew how.

28

THE REVIVAL OF THE BRITISH EMPIRE

1783–1830

The significant thing about the so-called Second British Empire is not the area that it covered but the policies which enabled it to grow from the low point to which the First British Empire had fallen in the year 1783. For by the Treaty of Paris of that year England seemed to have lost most of her valuable possessions. Though the naval Battle of the Saints had saved much of the West Indies, after the loss of the Thirteen Colonies all else that remained to her in the Americas were the colonies around the Saint Lawrence valley and gulf, and claims to Honduras and the Falkland Islands. With Gibraltar those made up all the directly held overseas possessions of the King of England. Ireland, Hanover, and the Channel Islands were held by George III, not in virtue of his being King of England but as King of Ireland, Elector of Hanover, and Duke of Normandy. Such African forts as were English were the property of the Company of African Merchants; Saint Helena island and the "factories" in India were the property of the East India Company. No wonder, then, that in the administrative reforms which followed the fall of Lord North's government this truncated Empire was assigned to the part-time attention of a Secretary of State, guided in commercial matters by the advice of a Committee of the Privy Council.

Yet in 1923, the British Empire consisted of six dominions—Canada, New Zealand, Australia, South Africa, Newfoundland, and Ireland; an empire, India; effective control of Palestine, Egypt, and Iraq; a "condominium," the Anglo-Egyptian Sudan; several mandates over former German colonies; and about a hundred Crown colonies. To manage this Empire took the full-time attention of three departments of state—the India Office, the Colonial Office, and the Dominions Office—plus that of the special Egyptian section of the Foreign Office, not to mention the important though part-time attention of the Lords of the Treasury and of the Admiralty, the War and Air Ministries, and the Board of Trade. What were the new policies which explain this phenomenal revival?

To this there may be two general answers. One is that the English in

343

1783 either had or soon acquired a series of "jumping-off-places" from which to expand the Empire again, by consciously or unconsciously practicing what the Germans have called the science of geopolitics. The other, and on the whole the more important one, is that by a series of what might be called laboratory experiments in human relations—particularly in India, at Singapore, and in Canada—the English worked out the principles on which an Empire—or, as they now prefer to call it, a Commonwealth of Nations—can exist in an age of ever-increasing democracy and nationalism.

These two propositions, if they are to be properly examined, require skipping all over the globe, from Newfoundland to New Zealand, from the Falkland Islands to Heligoland. Therefore, at the start, a plan of operations should be laid down. Since the logical course is to move from the simple to the complex, this chapter will first deal with the possessions acquired for strategic reasons. This should throw light on the method of rule by a Governor in Council responsible to London, used to supplant what Colonial Office officials call the "old" or pre-American-Revolution colonial constitutions. Next will come the originally penal settlement of Australia, with a consideration of how population growth broke through the bonds of the original plan. After that will be considered Sierra Leone and West Africa, and then New Zealand, where the humanitarian efforts of the anti-slave-trade movement and of missionaries gave the British Empire much of its policy of dealing with native races. Such a sequence should make it easier to understand South Africa, where missionary influence and population growth worked at cross purposes; India, where strategy, economics, a peculiar background of English rule, and a policy of "indirect government" caused special developments; and the East Indies, where a new economic policy was tested out and found to work. Finally, the West Indies will be taken up, as examples of the "old constitutions" at work and of their limitations, which will lead up to Canada, where Canadians discovered how to surmount those limitations, thus giving the Empire, in later years, a most vital new policy. When all this has been done, the Empire as a whole should be more comprehensible.

POSSESSIONS ACQUIRED FOR STRATEGIC REASONS

Some of the renewed expansion came about when England, after the wars of the French Revolution and Napoleon, kept for strategic or commercial reasons the possessions taken in those wars. To guard the overseas route to India, it had been necessary to take Ascension and Tristan da Cunha Islands, the Cape of Good Hope, Mauritius, the Seychelles Islands, and Ceylon. These were kept, as was the North Sea base of Heligoland. To open up the Mediterranean, advanced bases were secured in the Island of Malta and the Ionian Islands, which extend on the west coast of

Greece from Corfu in the north to Cerigo in the south. In the West Indies, British expeditions captured from the French Dominica and Tobago; from the Spaniards, Trinidad; from the Dutch, what was then the mainland colony of Demerara, now called British Guiana.

These conquered colonies were ruled by military governors who administered local law as they found it and interfered with local institutions only when they had to. After all, it was highly possible that the colony might be returned to its former owner when the war was over. By 1801 so many colonies had been taken that the war secretaryship was made the secretaryship for War and Colonies, and the rest of the colonies were transferred to it from the Home Department. Consequently, when peace came, the tradition of military-type rule by a governor with absolute powers was well established. Some colonies did secure self-government. Tobago did, for it had had an assembly granted it in 1763, and the rights of that assembly had been established by the case of *Campbell v. Hall* in 1774. Dutch Guiana and Malta preserved local rights which existed when they were captured. Since the Ionian Islands were technically independent, they secured a charter that granted them self-government in appearance, but in fact gave the British High Commissioner the real power. But in most cases this new British Empire was ruled as Senegambia and Quebec had been, after 1763, that is, by a governor with very wide powers. He had to act in consultation with a council of the high officials—the exact ones varied from colony to colony—who shared responsibility with him, but if he chose, he might override them as long as he reported his action to London. Thus the government in London, rather than the people in the colony, was sovereign. Here was a side-stepping of the constitutional principles of the "First British Empire," which assumed that Englishmen overseas had similar rights to Englishmen at home.

In the eyes of the law this was perfectly proper, for under the doctrine in *Calvin's case*, the king might do as he pleased with conquered colonies, as long as he respected existing rights, and these were conquered colonies. But constitutionally this set a new pattern for overseas government, which became rather like the government of England under Henry I and Henry II, where a powerful monarch ruled with the advice of his Curia or Council. Furthermore, in London a powerful bureaucracy grew up that had far more effective control than the central government had ever had in the days of the First British Empire. This bureaucracy genuinely tried to rule according to the needs of each colony as it saw them, but inevitably it was paternalistic. There was a measure of parliamentary control, since in 1811 a parliamentary undersecretaryship of the colonies was set up, its first holder being Robert Peel. But in fact, and especially after the permanent undersecretaryship was created in 1825, by sheer weight of experience and long tenure of office the bureaucrats in London became the effective rulers of the colonies that did not have assemblies. Here was a type of government that in the 1840's would become normal for all British acquisitions.

AUSTRALIA

This system was applied not only to "conquered colonies" but to the new settlement in Australia. After the American Revolution the jails of England became overcrowded because it was no longer possible to "transport" convicts to North America. In 1784, humanitarians persuaded Parliament to set up a quasi-military form of government for a convict settlement somewhere in Australia, and in 1788 the "First Fleet" was sent out to New South Wales, under the command of Captain Arthur Phillip, and a settlement was made at Sydney, named after Lord Sydney who, as Home Secretary, was then in charge of both prisons and colonies. Fortunately for the future of Australia, Captain Phillip was a man of vision. He believed that convicts might be redeemed into being good citizens. He gave limited freedom as a reward for good behavior. Whenever a convict was so "emancipated," he was put on a plot of land, which he was to cultivate for himself. This policy worked. From a practical point of view it supplied the colony with food, which no longer had to be shipped all the way around the world. It did more than that; it provided an agricultural surplus, to pay in part for imports. Later the discovery of coal secured another market for the colony. Furthermore, Phillip's trust in the potentialities of the convicts—many of whom, it should be remembered, had been convicted for political offenses or for breaking the game laws, not for faults of character—gave the new land a settled population.

As for the convict basis of the population, that is a sore point with Australians. Were convicts, from the "First Fleet" on, the founding fathers, or did the absence of women in the early shipments mean that it was the apparently fewer free settlers who left descendants and who ultimately filled the inhabitable parts of the continent? Naturally, many Australians prefer to believe the latter, which confuses the information available. However, certain facts do stand out. Some great Australians were emancipists who had served their time and then accepted freedom in a new land, where they made new, honorable, and successful lives for themselves. The period of absolute convict majority over free settlers and emancipists was short. It ended by 1803 in New South Wales, by 1806 in Tasmania. The period of convict background lasted longer. The success of Colonel Lachlan Macquarie's twelve years of dictatorial and largely beneficent rule, from 1809 to 1821, came from the assumption that an exercise of authority was needed to gain a new start for emancipists. As late as 1841, Mrs. Chisholm, the newly arrived wife of an army officer, could find a life's work in building up a future for the time-expired convicts and their families.

This population—convict, emancipist, and free—was not easy to rule, and the supposedly free part of the population was the hardest. Even Phillip could not handle the marines who first were assigned to guard duty, and it was found necessary to replace them with a regiment, the New South Wales Corps. With these, Phillip's successors were less able to deal. Captain Bligh, of the *Bounty* mutiny fame, was locked up by his officers, who in turn lost their commissions in the regiment. Later on these officers were to be known as the "Exclusives" because they made a local aristocracy of themselves. It was this group who grew the famous "Botany Bay" wool from stock sent originally from George III's farms. When the Blue Mountains were crossed, the colony had room to expand. By 1820 Australia was ready for local government.

The sign of this was a struggle with Macquarie, who found himself rewarded for his labors by an investigation, from London, engineered by enemies, and dismissal, at the same time as freedom of the press and a measure of jury trial were given to New South Wales. This was unjust to the man, but a sign that a new era had begun. By this time the English had an inkling of the potentialities of their colony. For whenever French explorers came by, English expeditions hurried out and laid claim to more and more seacoast, so that finally Great Britain asserted she owned the entire continent. Yet another sign came of progress. In 1829, British capitalists who had gained wealth from Canadian lands tried the experiment of buying the southwest corner of Australia—that part of the present state of Western Australia that geographers call Swanland from the presence there of black swans. Phillip's settlement had struck deep roots within forty years, and the seeds of a nation had been sown.

SIERRA LEONE AND WEST AFRICA

So far this picture of the regrowth of the British Empire has suggested that it evolved on lines similar to that of the French colonial empire, which was also administered on centralized lines, and for a long time as part of a military ministry, that of the marine. But that is not the whole story. That omits a feature which gave the British Empire its native policy and helped make it different from other colonial empires, the antislavery and missionary movements.

A salient fact about the late eighteenth century in England, and one often forgotten, is that in all walks of society people went through a moral and ethical transformation. In the aristocracy Charles James Fox went through such a change. He began political life in the footsteps of his venal and dishonest father; he wound up teaching others to follow him in putting principle above place and power. In the middle and lower middle classes the teachings of John Wesley and other evangelicals so struck home as to make, in later years, the words "Nonconformist conscience" stand for rigidly living up to principles, come what may. Just because this wave of moral change was not complete, just because the respect for outward good behavior which it caused led to hypocrisy among self-seekers, one should not be blinded to the extent of this moral and ethical change or to the fact that men of this new moral strength had, because of it, political power. A disinterested lobbyist can achieve miraculous things through his or her single-mindedness—can even achieve them in spite of flaws of character. When people in all walks of society can be united by a moral aim, those so united will prove themselves a political force to be reckoned with.

In the late eighteenth century, along with such moral transformations, there arose a moral aim that united men and women in all walks of life. A few dedicated men gave up their lives to fighting slavery. They won friends in high places, especially Pitt, Fox, and Wilberforce. The publicity they gained by their efforts won them new friends and new supporters who joined with them in working on the many problems that arose from trying to end slavery. First slavery was abolished in England—by a typically English court decision that flew in the face of facts and stated it had never existed in England. Then the freed slaves of England were settled at Sierra Leone. Thus Britain gained a foothold that grew into the present West African possessions of Sierra Leone, the Gold Coast, and Nigeria. The horrors of the slave trade were exposed to the world in a long but finally successful struggle to stop it. The exploration of Africa was begun that more might be known of where the Negroes came from. Missionary organizations sprang up, four important ones being founded in the years 1792 to 1803, to carry the Gospel, first to the Negroes, then to all who had not yet heard it. Thus came into existence the body of opinion that gained the nickname Exeter Hall from the fact that these bodies and similar ones used to hold their annual meetings at Exeter Hall in London. Nor did this movement work from outside the government alone. Almost inevitably some of its leaders gravitated to appointment in the colonial section of the secretaryship of War and Colonies. Finally, when the time was right, antislavery societies were founded, and throughout the Empire, wherever England had direct rule, slavery was abolished. In the process, because of this movement, the Empire gained a native policy and much new territory.

The first step was taken by Granville Sharp, a government clerk who in 1765 had befriended a destitute Negro only to have the Negro's master seize him as property when Sharp had made him once more worth owning. Sharp decided to fight this decision, and in 1772, after much legal warfare, won the Somersett case. In this case Chief Justice Mansfield upset the ruling of 1729 which had allowed the holding of slaves as property when brought into England by their owners, by declaring that slavery had never legally existed in England. Thus, in effect, he freed some 14,000 slaves who had been so imported. This decision created a new problem, since the slaves thus freed in many cases were unable to support themselves. At the urging of Sharp, in 1787 the government gave free transportation to the African coast to such Negroes, where a chartered company endeavored to find a home for them, at Sierra Leone. Pestilence, revolt, capture by a French raid, all combined to hamper the colony, but the wisdom and will power of a former plantation manager from Jamaica, Zachary Macaulay, kept the colony going. In 1807 the charter was surrendered, and Crown colony government established in its stead, which meant that the English government took over the expenses philanthropists until then had borne. To Sierra Leone were, in 1817, added the forts of the dissolved Company of African Merchants, and thus the Gold Coast was brought under direct royal government. By that time, the slave trade had been abolished, and Freetown became the headquarters of the West African Squadron and its anti-slave-trade patrol. At one remove the Somersett case gave England her present territories in West Africa.

The founding of Sierra Leone was not the only activity of Sharp and his associates that affected the Empire. At the same time Sharp, Clarkson, and Wilberforce began the long agitation that eventually made the British Navy a world police to suppress the slave trade, and the Colonial Office a body that thought of itself as a trustee to protect the rights of natives. Their first step was to expose the horrors of the slave trade. Each stage of the grim journey of the slave from Africa to a West India plantation had its special shame. At the start, traders fomented wars with rum and firearms, to gain captives. Among other ill deeds such activities brought the cruel inland tribe of the Ashantis down to the Gold Coast to rob and plunder and enslave. On the "Middle Passage" from Africa to America the unhappy slaves were treated as beasts. It paid to carry large cargoes rather than small, even if the mortality on the voyage were high. Therefore slaves were carried either lying down or kneeling, chained as close together as possible, exercised in batches to keep them alive, and then returned to the foul-smelling cubbyholes from which they had come. At the end of the journey, such as lived—a mortality of only one-third was considered good—were offered for sale, with the inevitable further shame to be seen in a market for human flesh.

The weakest point of all of this was the "Middle Passage." It could be argued that native wars broke out anyway and were nobody's business; it could be pointed out that slaves were often well treated after they had been bought, and that without slaves sugar could not be grown in the West Indies. But it was very hard to say that the English flag should fly over ships engaged in what amounted to the murder of one-third of their passengers. Here it was that an opening wedge could be inserted. Thomas

Clarkson collected evidence about the horrors of slave transportation which in 1788 William Wilberforce presented to the House of Commons. As Wilberforce, a popular young Tory sitting for Yorkshire, was the friend of Pitt, the Commons paid attention to him. His evidence started a movement in Parliament and outside that eventually won the battle against both the slave trade and slavery itself. Two by-products of his agitation were the African Association that sent Mungo Park to explore the Niger River and the little community of reformers who settled in homes around Clapham Common. The Clapham Sect, for such was their popular name, were leaders not only in fighting slavery but also in reviving and practicing evangelicalism in religion. The Sect fought the West India interest by building a humanitarian pressure group in Britain.

For a while, the war with France blocked that humanitarian purpose. The fact that republican France had freed slaves and thereby caused massacres in San Domingo was an argument against it. So, too, was the fear that ending the slave trade would destroy West India wealth during wartime, when wealth was needed to fight France. Such fears prevented Pitt, who as a private member spoke and voted for the abolition of the slave trade, from being able to push the reform through as a Cabinet measure against proslavery associates. But when Fox came in, as the leading spirit of the Ministry of All the Talents, in 1806, the Cabinet could act.

To end the slave trade by a law was not enough. The prohibition had to be enforced. This led to new activities by the English government. English diplomats tried hard to secure real power to stop ships of other nations from conducting the slave trade. Meaningless promises were easy to get; and gradually it became an important bargaining point in diplomacy to allow the English Navy and courts the right of mutual search and seizure, which in effect meant that the English did all the work but the pride of other nations was appeased. More important, there grew up a tradition of interference with self-government in the slave-holding colonies. Tacitly, it was held that the principles for which England fought the American Revolution held good. Protests of such assemblies as that of Jamaica were ignored. When assemblies did not pass the necessary legislation for effective registration of slaves—needed to make sure slaves were not imported—Parliament passed such legislation itself. Because such interference had a moral aim, it was accepted. It is possible to argue that the noble side of England's imperialism, the belief that there was a "white man's burden" of responsibility to assume, stems largely from the work of Sharp, Clarkson, and Wilberforce, and their associates. Certainly, much of England's policy toward native races comes from them.

For this movement did not stop with the effective suppression of the slave trade. In 1821 Wilberforce performed his last great service to the

Negroes. He induced Thomas Fowell Buxton to organize antislavery societies, which continually pressed for the ending of slavery, even at the expense of the British Treasury. This would bear full fruit only after 1830, but before that it kept up pressure on the administration of the colonies.

NEW ZEALAND

Africa and the slave trade were not the only points at which the missionary and humanitarian influence of the age had effect. In New Zealand, in these years, missionaries gained for England a foothold in what would become a dominion and probably gave that dominion some of the characteristics it has to this day. New Zealand had been known to the world ever since Abel Tasman touched there in 1642, but it had remained neglected and unvisited until Captain Cook in the years 1769 to 1779 used it as a forward base for his explorations. Because of this charting of the coasts, the settlement of Australia and the need for new whaling grounds free from privateers during the French wars after 1798 made New Zealand a trading center. Flax was bought from the natives, and so were the pickled human heads that were a by-product of intertribal wars. Far too many of those visiting the islands turned out to be willing to sell firearms, debauch the natives with liquor, and even furnish transportation for raiding parties, if there was money in it. Legislation giving magistrates at Sydney jurisdiction over Englishmen in New Zealand had no effect in curing this situation.

Here missionaries stepped in. Samuel Marsden, the Anglican chaplain of the penal colony in New South Wales, heard of these doings, bought a brig with his own money, and made the 1,200-mile journey to New Zealand to see what he could do. Though his duties forbade his staying, he collected enough information about the Maori language to allow the Professor of Arabic at Cambridge to compile a Maori grammar and thus made possible the translation of the Scriptures into Maori. He also saw to it that both Anglican and Methodist missions were sent out to North Island. These missionaries, especially Henry Williams, a naval officer turned Anglican priest, did noble work. So well did they proselytize North Island that they discovered that their converts had in turn, unknown to them, converted parts of South Island. When, in 1839, settlement began, the English found a partly Christian native population able to keep up its own culture in face of European culture and eventually able to take an important part in the life of the future dominion.

Nor did missionary influence stop at New Zealand. Other missionaries, such as the Methodist John Williams, spread throughout the South Sea islands, preparing the way unconsciously for English control of the South Pacific.

SOUTH AFRICA

In South Africa, too, missionary influence made history. But it was not, as in New Zealand, the only influence at work. The Boers, or Dutch settlers, took their full share in making history. They reacted so sharply against the missionaries that much of the last century and a half of South African history might be written as the struggle between them.

English rule came to South Africa in 1795, when Cape Town was captured by an expeditionary force. This was done simply to prevent the French from again using it as a naval base, as they had in two previous wars, 1757 to 1763 and 1778 to 1783, with disregard for Dutch neutrality. As this was a purely military measure, local institutions were left untouched, and in 1801 the Cape was returned to Holland. This return, not to the commercially minded Dutch East India Company but to the up-and-coming Batavian Republic, brought to the Cape a renewal of Dutch influence, and especially, with legal reforms, a strengthening of the tradition of Romano-Dutch law and of the independence of the judiciary under that law. With the return to war after the Peace of Amiens, a second expedition was sent to the Cape, which was again taken in 1805. This time it was kept, and missionary societies began to send agents to this new field for conversion. As the Dutch had more or less Christianized the Hottentots and Kaffirs near Cape Town, the missionaries went out to the inland frontier of settlement. There they ran head on into the special problems of the Boer frontier.

The South African frontier and frontier life have many parallels with the American frontier, and can well be described as if features from different sections of the American frontier were combined. The climate of 30 degrees south latitude is that of the southwestern plains of Texas or more exactly of northern Mexico, which are at 30 degrees north latitude. On the west are the Damaraland deserts, like the deserts of Arizona and Lower California; on the east the low-lying tropical swamps of Portuguese East Africa, like those around Vera Cruz. In climate and grazing, the High Veldt of the present-day Transvaal and Orange Free State resembles that of the Texas and Mexican plateau. The cattle found on the High Veldt are descended from Portuguese longhorns, much like the Spanish longhorns of Texas. The language of the Boers, and their wagons, resemble the Pennsylvania Dutch and the Conestoga wagons of Pennsylvania frontier days, as is natural, since the Taal comes from the lower Rhine valley, Pennsylvania Dutch from the upper Rhine valley. The religion of the Dutch Reformed Church, like the Presbyterianism the American frontier drew from New York and New Jersey, descends directly from the Synods of the Netherlands which were the founding churches of both denominations. The rifle, which the Pennsylvania Dutch brought to

America, did not reach South Africa till the 1840's, since the heavier shock of a smoothbore bullet suited South African hunting and since there was not a local metal industry to permit much local gunmaking. But the same tradition of marksmanship as necessary for life sprang up.

With such similarities, it was not unnatural for the cattle-driving, Calvinistic, sharpshooting Boer frontiersman to show much the same attitude toward life as the Calvinistic, sharpshooting American frontiersman. In a land where Negroes were both slaves and natives, it was not unnatural for the Boer to have toward them the combined feelings of the Southern frontiersman toward the Negro and the Western frontiersman toward the Indian, with one vital exception. To the Western frontiersman, the best Indian was a dead one; the Boer wanted Negroes to stay alive and work for him. But both knew how to protect themselves. Just as Andrew Jackson and his Tennessee militia went out to fight Indians, so the Boer frontier leaders called out their "commandos" and retaliated on their own initiative for real or fancied outrages by Kaffirs. When at peace, the frontiersmen ruled their homes as would Calvinistic American frontiersmen, with Old Testament patriarchal directness, simplicity, and sternness. A more complete contrast it would be hard to find to the ideas of a Negrophile English missionary. Inevitably there was discord between Boer and missionary.

For when the missionaries came to the frontier they found customary what they considered illegal and outrageous corporal punishment and the waging of native wars without provocation. They demanded that the English governor at Cape Town exercise what they considered proper authority. Having the ear of officials in London, they got their way. The result was just about what it would have been had similar action been taken in Kentucky or Tennessee in pioneer days. The Boers yielded to superior force and burdened their Dutch memories with their version of what had happened. In particular they remembered two events that to their minds were outrages: the Black Circuit of 1812, and the Slagter's Nek hanging of 1816. The Black Circuit was the first set of trials by the new English magistrates, enforcing a new code of treatment of slaves and servants. Slagter's Nek was the hanging twice—the rope broke the first time—of a man named Bezuidenhout who had rebelled and refused to pay taxes. It did not matter, as resentment grew, that the trials had been fair, or that a Boer commando had hunted down and captured Bezuidenhout. Boer frontiersmen, like American frontiersmen, did not like being ordered around by outsiders, especially by Dr. John Phillip and his fellow missionaries.

This resentment was increased by other frontier incidents. In 1820, by a planned emigration scheme, some 5,000 British, the Albany settlers, were planted on the eastern part of Cape Colony. This made the district predominantly British, but did not make the Boers love the British the more. Should something set a spark to the frontier, it might explode. Hitherto the Boers, even though they had come to the Cape in 1652, even though they were as prolific breeders as the American frontiersmen, had moved out from Cape Town only some 300 miles. But they had the techniques, with their wagons, their cattle, their marksmanship, and their commando experience, to bound ahead a thousand miles—the distance to the Zoutpansberg in northern Transvaal, where the Voortrekkers did go in 1834. A mistake in rule would send them forth.

Yet, in the Governor's mansion at Cape Town this was not realized. There all seemed going well. Dutch and British were amalgamating. Dockyard expenditures by the navy sweetened the conquest. The engrafting of jury trial on Dutch law and the respect paid, justifiably, to Dutch lawyers made the transition to English rule easy. The Cape Dutch became bilingual and seemed about to lose their special nationality, as the Guiana Dutch were doing at the same time, as the New Amsterdam Dutch had in the 1670's. No one, even the Boers themselves, realized that the frontiersmen were ready to make a new nation, and, in the process, plenty of problems for the British Empire, which finally had to be turned over to the new nation to solve for itself.

INDIA

Like South Africa, India was a special situation. To understand it, one must remember the position of the English East India Company, and how it changed from a trading monopoly to a means of ruling a subcontinent. In law, that company existed from 1600 to 1874; in fact, it existed from 1600 to 1858, over two and a half centuries. For over one hundred and forty years, that is, over one-half its life-span, say to 1740, it was a business monopoly conducting a special trade. For since in the early days only armed fleets could regularly trade with India, the East India Company had been granted the monopoly rights necessary to pay for such fleets. The Company, once it had settled down to a steady course of business, had established three "Presidencies" in India, Bombay, Madras, and, chief of them, Fort William or Calcutta at the mouth of the Ganges. Based on these Presidencies were its Governors and Writers, who on a commission basis under special privileges from the Mogul Emperor, transacted business with the natives of India. This was a traditional way of organizing overseas trade; in the Middle Ages the German Hanseatic merchants had traded in England under similar special rights, and the French and Danish East India Companies held similar privileges from the Mogul Emperor.

In the 1740's, however, the Mogul Empire lost its grip. Its provincial governors made themselves semi-independent and fought with each other. It became obvious—the French leader Dupleix being the first to see this—

that the European trading companies had to join in these wars out of sheer self-protection. Naturally Dupleix turned his "sepoys," or European-trained native troops, on the English possessions and, but for the bravery and skill of Robert Clive, a young Writer of the Madras Presidency, would have swept English interests out of India. In his turn Clive rose to the top of the Indian officials of the English East India Company. To avenge the "Black Hole of Calcutta," where the Nawab of Bengal had imprisoned the English men, women, and children of that post and allowed them to choke to death in an airless cellar, Clive had deposed the Nawab and replaced him with another. This he did, in 1757, by the Battle of Plassey, where 3,000 English and sepoys defeated 50,000 Bengalese with the help of the British Navy, the bribing of a Bengalese general, and incredible daring. As a reward—for, after all, Writers worked on a commission—Clive took large sums of money for himself, saying afterwards with justice, "I stand astonished at my own moderation," and got for his employers, the East India Company, the presumably lucrative duty of collecting the taxes of Bengal "in farm." That meant that, after remitting a fixed sum to the Mogul Emperor, it was to keep the rest for itself.

But the Court of Directors of the East India Company in London found that this was not such a good bargain after all. By the time the Mogul Emperor had gotten his share, and various Writers and other officials had let stick to their fingers what their consciences would allow them to hold, and an army of sepoys had been kept up to prevent someone else getting possession of Bengal, it was losing money on the deal. Therefore, in 1772, the Company in London applied to Parliament for aid. The first aid it got—a rebate on the tea duty to encourage sales in the North American colonies—led to the Boston Tea Party. At the same time, the Company helped itself, by sending to India an experienced administrator, Warren Hastings, who had already shown his ability by vainly protesting against the mismanagement of the Bengal taxes. It gave him a free hand at Calcutta and general supervision over the other Presidencies, thus, for the first time, uniting British India under a single head. On arrival Hastings set to work. He cut down on payment by commission and to counterbalance this raised nominal salaries to something like the actual cost of living. He made English officials directly rather than indirectly responsible for the collection of taxes, which eliminated one form of graft and made the title Collector a ranking one in the Indian Civil Service as long as Britain ruled India. He also set up a local Indian legal system, here acting as the deputy of the Mogul Emperor. This gave a measure of equal and honest treatment to the Bengalese. He further made a deal with the neighboring province of Oudh, directly, since the Mogul Emperor had no real power, by which the ruler's aunts, the Begums (Princesses) of Oudh, would stop draining its treasury. Thus he built up a buffer state on

Bengal's borders. Having thus started the herculean work of reforming a province of a decaying Empire, Hastings then found that the English Parliament had done its best to undo all he had done.

For in 1774 Lord North, taking time off from losing America, did his best to lose India. He secured the passage of an India Act, which made the governor at Calcutta the executive head of India, and as such subject to control for his political actions to the British Government. This step was long overdue; what was wrong was the means whereby the control was exercised. First of all an English court was set up in Calcutta, to try all cases in which English subjects were concerned. Then a council was appointed to supervise and if need be overrule the Governor, and a majority of the council was sent out from England, of men determined to so overrule Hastings. Sir Philip Francis and his associates set to this work with a will. They gave up the collection system and went back to the graft-producing commission methods of tax gathering. They poured money into the pockets of the Begums of Oudh and thus weakened Bengal's neighbor. They encouraged an Indian named Nuncomar to accuse Hastings of all sorts of crimes, until Hastings succeeded in protecting himself by proving Nuncomar guilty of forgery and then having the death sentence, then usual for that crime, executed as quickly as possible. As for the English judges, they, with the best intentions in the world, upset all business procedure by replacing Indian law, which everyone understood, by English law, which nobody knew how to apply to local transactions.

For a time, about all Hastings could do was adjourn the council the minute it met, to prevent its doing more harm. Then first one councilor died, then another, and Hastings's casting vote in case of a tie allowed him to regain control. Finally, he maneuvered Francis into a duel and so got rid of his opposition. At last he became governor once more in fact as well as in name. He had need of haste, to undo errors of the past. In Madras, for example, things were going so badly that one governor had died in prison, put there by rebellious subordinates. A French fleet, too, was hovering off the coast, and it was only the French general's incompetence that prevented the landing of an army that would have taken India from England.

In this emergency, Hastings took sharp measures. He got back the pensions of the Begums of Oudh, which paid for a rescue expedition to Madras. He stopped the nonsense of applying English law literally in India by appointing Sir Elijah Impey, the English Chief Justice, chief justice as well of the Indian court. Out of this evolved a system whereby English judges checked on Indian justice by hearing appeals. He reappointed the Collectors and straightened out finances. His reward for all this, on his eventual return to England, was to have Sir Philip Francis stir up impeachment proceedings against him under charges of malversion of money, extortion from the Begums, bribery of Sir Elijah Impey, and murder of Nuncomar. It took six years to get rid of the charges, and one of England's greatest men never had due justice done him during his lifetime.

Such, then, was the situation in India, in 1783. Reform had to come, since only a man of genius, who dared violate the law, had been able to make sense of the crazy system of triple government, under which the Governor at Calcutta was responsible at one and the same time to a majority of his own council, to the Court of Directors in London, and to Parliament in Westminster. But how to effect the reform became a matter of party politics. Would Whig or Tory get the advantage of the immense Indian patronage? As has been told elsewhere, Tory beat Whig, and it was Pitt's India Bill, not Fox's, that was enacted into law. There has been much argument as to what difference, if any, there really was between the proposals, except as to who should appoint the controlling body in England, Pitt or Fox. At any rate, a form of government was set up, to last in name until 1858, in fact until 1919 and the Montagu-Chelmsford reforms. In India, rule was to be by the Governor-general in Council. He was, in name, executive, legislature, and judiciary rolled into one, and could be an absolute monarch if he so desired. It was expressly stated that he could overrule his council as long as he gave the reasons for it in writing. Above this potentially absolute monarch was put a Board of Control in England, whose orders he must obey. The head of that Board, after 1793, was called the President of the Board of Control until 1858. In that year his post became Secretary of State for India. In that year, too, the Board became the India Council. But these were changes of name, not power.

As for the East India Company, after this its remaining privileges were to dismiss Governors-general if it dared—as only twice did it venture to do—and to try to mend its broken fortunes through trade and tax collections, as it most successfully did. In name, it kept a private army, collected taxes for the Mogul Emperor, and kept books that showed how those taxes were spent. But in fact India was administered as its Governor-general chose, and he was responsible to the Board of Control, not to the Court of Directors of the Company.

The first Governor-general under this system—excluding an interim officeholder—was Charles, Lord Cornwallis, who in English history books is far more important as the first Governor-general of India and the last Lord Lieutenant of an independent Ireland than as the loser at Yorktown. From Parliament, by Pitt's Act, he had two direct instructions. He was to straighten out the landholding situation in Bengal, and he was not to engage in wars of aggression or political deals with the other subsidiaries of the moribund Mogul Empire. Cornwallis did his job well. He was indeed so ignorant of Indian affairs as to transform minor tax collectors, on whose graft Hastings had been gradually cutting down, into permanent landowners, but at least he gave the ryots, or peasants, the benefits of fixed rents instead of their being charged what the traffic would bear. As for the order not to expand, he interpreted it sensibly, to allow the making of defensive alliances and fighting in accordance with them. Furthermore, he continued Hastings's reforms and put good men into important collectorships, on living salaries. These men showed India what good government could be, something that had almost been forgotten since the death of the Emperor Aurangzeb a century before.

This change in administration was not a transient thing. Pitt's India Act had stressed good administration, and under it the East India Company now recruited a high class of young men and saw to it that they were properly trained for their work. Many were Scotch, in wise deference to the nationality of Dundas, Pitt's President of the Board of Control. Finally a special training college was set up at Haileybury, where lectured such men as the Rev. Thomas Malthus. Even in these early days, the Indian Civil Service was a model of what a civil service should be.

Cornwallis's successor was not of his caliber and took too literally his orders to avoid entangling alliances. As a result, the rest of India threatened to ally itself against the English. Worse than that, Tippoo Sahib, the head of the alliance, got into touch with the French. Here was a great danger, for a few French regulars, and some French officers to train up a sepoy army, could cut a terrible swath through India. Since French regulars did get to Egypt, where in one battle they destroyed the supposedly irresistible Mamelukes, the danger seemed near. That it was averted by Nelson's victory of Aboukir or the Nile did not make it any the less real at the time.

At this new crisis, Pitt and Dundas sent to India a young Irish peer, Lord Mornington—whom they soon made Marquis of Wellesley—and the Thirty-third Regiment of Foot, which since then has had as its motto *Primus in Indis* (First in India). With the Thirty-third they sent Lord Mornington's younger brother, Colonel Arthur Wellesley, the future Duke of Wellington. This team finished Hastings's work and went beyond it. Mornington won his Marquisate of Wellesley by disregarding orders and simply overwhelming native opposition. He soon found that his brother —to whom he showed, if anything, the opposite of favoritism—was his best general. By a series of carefully planned and well-supplied campaigns, the armies of the East India Company made England the paramount power between the Indus and the Ganges and linked up by land as well as by sea the three Presidencies of Calcutta, Madras, and Bombay. As a further precaution Indian troops went to Egypt, there to join with an army from England in capturing the French whom Bonaparte had left behind him when he had sailed back home, in 1799. Ceylon, captured in the years from 1795 to 1798, was handed over to the Colonial Office to administer. This militarily won paramountcy Wellesley made permanent by introducing—or rather, since no Englishman ever seems to introduce a reform but merely to improve something already existing, by extending—the system of "indirect rule." Waving aside the India Act and any contradictory orders from London, Wellesley placed British "Residents" at the courts of the native Princes who had made submission and signed treaties. The Princes continued to rule, in ordinary matters, as they always had. Thanks to British protection, they enjoyed peace and prosperity. But if trouble seemed brewing, the Residents gave hints which were usually quickly taken, for the consequences of not taking them could be dire.

Wellesley was not allowed to complete his work. The Directors in London recalled him, on an occasion when success did not immediately follow his breaking of express orders. That was in 1805. A quiescent period followed. Cornwallis, who was sent to India again as Wellesley's successor, died shortly after landing, and his successors did nothing out of routine. It was only on the arrival of Lord Moira, in 1813, that expansion was resumed. Moira, who was soon promoted to be Marquis of Hastings (unrelated to Warren Hastings), is best known to Americans by an earlier title, for he was the Lord Rawdon who was Cornwallis's subordinate in the Carolina campaigns. This sturdy veteran fought the Gurkhas of Nepal to a standstill and made with them a treaty that held till the end of British direct rule. Under it no European entered Nepal—which has hampered the climbing of Mount Everest—but Gurkhas entered the Indian army and became redoubtable and almost invincible fighters under English training and command.

By now the original purpose of the East India Company, naval protection of trade, had ended. For Trafalgar had given England command of the sea, so that powerfully armed East Indiamen no longer had to sail in convoy and Indian trade no longer had to be a monopoly to support such convoys. Therefore in 1823 an act was passed limiting the monopoly to China, where protection still was needed. In the same year Moira-Hastings's successor became tired of pretending that the East India Company was a vassal of the Mogul Emperor and proclaimed it to be what it in truth was, the sovereign power in India, thus acknowledging that Lord Hastings had finished the work that Warren Hastings had begun. Throughout the lands below the Himalayas, from the Indus to southern Burma, by direct rule, indirect rule, or plain preponderance of power, the East India Company could get its orders obeyed if it wanted to take the trouble. From the nadir of English fortunes, when Warren Hastings had spent his time adjourning a truculent council while matters went from bad to worse, England's power had risen in India till a President of the Board of Control in London could issue orders to a Governor in Council in India much as a colleague Secretary of State could issue orders to a Governor in Council in a colony.

THE EAST INDIES

Just before Moira-Hastings extended English rule to the Himalayas, a trade Empire was being built up in the East Indies and even in the China seas. This began in 1786, when one Francis Light, a "country trader" or independent merchant based on Calcutta, secured rights in the island of Penang on the coast of Malaya. English merchants thus obtained a share in the hitherto almost entirely Dutch trade in the East Indies. At Penang a young writer named Stamford Raffles gained administrative experience and learned not only the Malay language but the essentials of Malay life. He was ready for opportunity, and opportunity came when Lord Minto, Lord Moira's predecessor, ordered the invasion of the Dutch possessions of Java and Sumatra and sent Raffles in as Lieutenant Governor.

Raffles was a product of English Liberal thought in the older and more literal sense of the word liberal. He believed in liberty of trade and liberty of thought, and he practiced his beliefs. He taught the natives of Java and Sumatra new methods of farming and doing business; he freed them from exactions, and unlike many another English ruler, he treated them as humans and equals. His policies were highly successful. Under his governorship, Java and Sumatra were more prosperous and more orderly than before, even though he had to fight the home administration constantly to be allowed to succeed. When, in 1817, against his will most of England's rights in the two islands were given back to Holland, he went back to his superior, Moira-Hastings, with a new project. Why not trade England's remaining scanty rights in Sumatra for a base in Malaya, where there would not be friction over territorial boundaries with the Dutch? What mattered was not territorial possessions but trade. He knew, from old Hindu writings and his own travels, of a vacant site that had once been the great Lion City, Singa-pura, a rich Hindu colony on the Straits of Malacca. Lord Hastings let him make the experiment. In a year Raffles transformed a fishing village into a thriving center; in ten years he made it the greatest seaport of the East. The secret of this success was making Singapore a free port, where all might trade, paying the absolute minimum of port fees. Holland might own the East Indies, but trade would pass through Singapore, where English bankers and merchants and insurers in fair competition would win the profits of handling it that their efficiency deserved.

Singapore was more than the entrepôt of the East Indies; it was a gateway to China. There the Manchu Empire, two centuries behind the Mogul Empire in India, was beginning its process of dissolution. The process had hardly begun. Lord Macartney's mission to China in 1789 failed even to gain audience with the Emperor, who refused to admit that any ruler anywhere in the world was his equal instead of his vassal, even though in arms and in trade the Europeans in Chinese waters had demonstrated their superiority. But the opening of China was obviously on the way, and from Singapore the English would have a position of advantage, to be increased when they later took Hong Kong. When a later generation of Englishmen would carry into effect Raffles's economic policies, England would gain all the more of a monopoly of the China trade because she opened it not as a monopoly but to a free competition in which Englishmen would succeed by merit.

THE WEST INDIES

So far this piece-by-piece analysis of the regrowth of the English Empire has considered colonies, possessions, and trade areas where the forward impulse came from officials who either obeyed orders from the center or succeeded by intelligently disobeying them. The nearest this analysis has come to considering the impulse from a population has been the pointing out that in Australia and South Africa English settlers and Boers were ready to act. But that is not the whole picture. In two regions, the West Indies and Canada, initiative and the future lay with the colonists themselves. There it was that developments took place that would vitally affect the whole Empire.

It is an exaggeration to say that the West Indies held in them the future of the British Empire. Already they were in the process of economic decay. Their wealth came from sugar, raised on slave-cultivated plantations. From a long-term view, the sugar monopoly of the West Indies ended when, to counter the English blockade, French scientists discovered how to get sugar from beets. Profits diminished, even before the abolition of slavery, when the abolition of the slave trade increased the cost of raising sugar cane. But the West Indies, constitutionally, had an important function to perform in the British Empire. The colonies with what Colonial Office officials today call the "Old Constitutions" of tax-levying assemblies took their share in fighting the important battle for self-government, the winning of which had made the Empire the present Commonwealth of Nations. Because of their economic decay, the best they could secure was a draw, and today only the three B's—Bermuda, the Bahamas, and Barbados—preserve the system of government characteristic of all the American colonies before the American Revolution. Jamaica, Tobago, Saint Kitts, and Nevis have fallen by the wayside, and sunk to being Crown colonies. But the reasons for this failure throw light on why Canada was able to succeed and why the Canadian struggle took the form it did.

On the one side were the colonial assemblies, many of them dating from Stuart times. Like the North American assemblies, they were replicas in miniature of the Stuart Parliament at Westminster and were fortified with the power of the purse with which the Stuart Parliaments had eventually won control of administration as well as of legislation. These assemblies could claim that the decision of Lord Mansfield in *Campbell v. Hall* in 1774, and Lord North's Renunciation Act of 1778 freed them from interference in their internal affairs. On the other side were the Governors and Executive Councils appointed from England, attempting to obey orders from the Secretary of State in London. To control the assemblies the Governors employed various devices. They had their social position, which allowed them to gather supporters in the assemblies and which cannot be ignored. They had the argument that theirs was the responsibility for defense and keeping order, which made it the obvious duty of the assemblies to support them for fear of invasion or insurrection. They could draw on independent funds voted by Parliament in England for special purposes. They exercised duties in connection with trade which were clearly outside the province of the Assemblies but within the province of the Imperial Parliament. Above all, they could rely upon the assumed overriding authority that came from representing the King and his Parliament, which could and did legislate for all the King's possessions which he held as King and not by some other title. It was for that last reason that Governors did enforce English legislation about slavery against the will of the West Indian planters.

In the West Indies, which depended on trade for wealth, and which had to accept English funds for defense, these powers upheld the Governors as against the assemblies. But only because of these special conditions was it possible for the Governors in most cases to win in the end. And because the contest so long remained even, the colonial officials in London, as the memory of the American Revolution grew dim in their minds, were forced to keep in mind the essential principle of "No Taxation without Representation" which was the basis from which local self-government could grow. That should serve to make clear the course of events in Canada, in the years 1783 to 1830.

CANADA

At first sight, Canada might seem the most difficult to rule and hold of all the possessions that were left to England in 1783. It had been conquered only in 1760, after three-quarters of a century of bitter warfare between English and French colonists, warfare which had left behind it enduring hatreds. It was next-door neighbor to the Revolutionary United States. In the American Revolution Canada's mother country, France, had intervened on the Revolutionists' side. Yet all this had been counterbalanced by two able men and one wise law. The two men were Sir James

Murray and Sir Guy Carleton, later created Lord Dorchester. The law was the Quebec Act of 1774, drafted on the advice of Murray and Carleton. When Murray and after him Carleton-Dorchester had been the military governors of Canada and had, soldier-fashion, ruled by means of existing local laws, they had earned the respect of the French-Canadian "habitants" and had learned their needs. They were therefore in a position to give advice to Parliament, when that body finally got around to legislating for England's new colony, eleven years after taking possession of it. By their advice Protestant England protected—and even, by legalizing Catholic tithes, financed—the Catholic Church in Quebec, and Common Law England preserved in Canada the Roman Law of France and re-served the cherished Anglo-Saxon jury trial for very special cases, so that to this day a Quebec judge expects to face a jury about twice a year.

To this generosity, the Canadians responded. When, in 1775 in the American Revolution, Generals Montgomery and Arnold invaded Canada, the habitants maintained their new-found allegiance to King George. They helped Carleton hold the fortress of Quebec and thus save the Saint Lawrence valley for England. Similarly the province of Nova Scotia was kept loyal by the presence of naval forces in Halifax and by the Royal Governor's understanding of how to work with and not against a colonial assembly.

At the end of the American Revolution, the wise choice was made of Sir Guy Carleton to command the evacuation of England's last footholds in the United States. Sir Guy had decency and sense. Instead of neglecting the "Loyalists" or "Tories," he did all he could to keep these faithful subjects of King George under the British flag. Some he moved to Nova Scotia as troops to be disbanded and paid off with land instead of money, and some he moved on other pretexts; in one way or another he made the promise of protection to the loyalists a real thing. He was properly backed up in carrying out this promise. The British Government created two new colonies, New Brunswick and New Ireland, to take this new population. Though the latter—comprising eastern Maine—was by the Treaty of Paris eventually relinquished to the United States, the former was filled with "United Empire Loyalists," as was the region southwest of Montreal, then known as Upper Canada in distinction from Lower Canada or Quebec of today.

This rescue of 40,000 loyal subjects of the crown created a batch of new problems, which Carleton had to face when in 1786 he returned to Canada as Governor Lord Dorchester. It was one thing to rule an al-most entirely French colony without jury, assembly, or common law, and with privileges for the Catholic Church, even though England believed the first three to be the essentials of liberty and in those days considered the fourth to be the Church of rebellion and tyranny. But when an English population poured in, deeply imbued with these beliefs, and intermingled with the French, something had to be done to see to it that two very different nationalities were able to live together in peace. Parliament, after its usual delay in facing the problem, this time only of eight years instead of eleven, thought it had the answer. In 1791 it simply divided Canada into two halves, Catholic and French Lower Canada (the present Quebec) and Protestant and English Upper Canada (the present Ontario). Local authorities chose for the dividing line the Ottawa River but assigned Montreal and Jesus Islands at that river's mouth to Lower Canada. Each colony would have an assembly, which would take over and solve local problems.

To Dorchester this made no sense. In Montreal there were English merchants, and in the Eastern Townships of Quebec, on the Vermont border, there was an English population, so that Lower Canada was not purely French. Nor was Upper Canada, through which ranged French trappers, purely English. But Dorchester was overruled, retired, and proved wrong, for once. Both Canadas, as well as New Brunswick and Nova Scotia, got along well enough. The idea of the Canada Act of 1791, that local problems were best solved locally, justified itself. The problems were solved, and both Canadas grew loyal to the English connection. When the Napoleonic Wars crossed the Atlantic and became the War of 1812 with the United States, the militia of Upper Canada, stiffened by a few Regulars and inspired by the genius of General Isaac Brock, successfully drove off invasion after invasion. (This, of course, is not the American version of the War of 1812, but that current in Ontario. However, it is one not unjustified by the facts.) As for Lower Canada, it too took its share in the fighting. Of the battle of Chateaugay—which is also not played up in American history books—a French-Canadian poet could write, "Without *our* aid *your* flag would have ceased to fly." Just as the War of 1812 was for the United States a second war of independence, which gave a fillip to national feeling, so for the Canadas it was a cause of the growth of national pride and a feeling of Canadian nationality.

Loyal to the King the Canadas might be; the King's governors and other local representatives were another matter. Since much of the revenues, in both provinces, either came from England or were controlled from England, the assemblies' rights to vote and withhold taxes were in fact circumscribed, just as they were in the West Indies. This was not merely irritating, it prevented the redress of wrongs. In Upper Canada, since land sales were under control from London, "clergy reserves" of one-seventh of the land were ordered held for Anglican priests, though the new settlers were mostly Presbyterians and Methodists. In Upper Canada, too, there was a local political gang, the "Family Compact." Like the "Exclusives" in New South Wales, this party was of the Governor's social group; unlike the "Exclusives" it cooperated with him and got from him as a reward control of local offices. In Lower Canada, besides language and religious difficulties, there were absentee governors and tactless acts of administration. Consequently, in both provinces there grew up a political movement—led in Upper Canada by the two Baldwins and William Lyon Mackenzie, in Lower Canada by Speaker of the Assembly Louis Papineau—for more effective self-government. As its slogan, the movement had the phrase "responsible government." By this, at first, they merely meant the full power of the purse and the full power to legislate for themselves— in short, the rights that had been held by the American colonies and were held pretty extensively by the West India colonies. But as time went on and the full implications of this demand were realized, the phrase took on fuller meaning.

For in the years from 1791 to 1830, this slow, steady wrangle with the governors and with the Secretary of State for War and Colonies behind the governors secured important results. Gradually, for the record, was built up a set of precedents as to the rights of Canadian assemblies. Gradually, in the minds of officials in England, was developed a habit, not necessarily of conciliation, but of agreeing that these rights were important and should basically be accepted. The same evolution was taking place that, in the years from 1701 to 1767 in New York, in the years from 1679 to 1766 in Jamaica, eventually had led the assemblies of those colonies to assert that they possessed, of right, all the powers held in England by the English Parliament. But, because men in England had at the back of their minds memories of what had happened in America when too stiff a position had been taken against the assertion of such a claim, and because the Law Offices of the Crown felt bound by the Renunciation Act and the decision in *Campbell v. Hall* when the eventual clash came, a different solution would be found to the same problem. This set of precedents, this mental attitude, were to bear important fruit in the year 1839 when John Lambton, Earl of Durham, was to turn his mind to solving this problem and give the Second Empire its Magna Carta, the Durham Report. In Canada, in these years, was worked out the unwritten constitution of that Empire.

So it was, in the years from 1783 to 1830 which this chapter covers, that the evolution of the Second British Empire began. New possessions were taken, by conquest or discovery. By some of them important sea routes were made safe for English trade. Chief among these were the routes through the Mediterranean to the Near East, around the Cape of Good Hope to India, and past Singapore to China. The foundations of three future dominions were begun, with the settlement of Australia, the conversion of some of New Zealand, and the occupation of the Cape of Good Hope. The idealistic colony of Sierra Leone served to save for England the possessions of the Company of African Merchants on the Gold Coast and made a basis for expansion in West Africa.

From the point of view of those in England, new means of administration and new policies were worked out. A system of government by a Governor in Council was worked out, with eventual responsibility to the Secretary of State for War and Colonies. In the Colonial Office in London grew up a body of experts, able to back up or countermand governors with far more wisdom than they were usually credited with. Idealists forced on the government a noble native policy, which the government, in turn, forced on the colonies. In India a similar evolution took place under different names, the responsible minister being the President of the Board of Control and the local authority being the Governor-General in Council. Wellesley's policy of "indirect rule" made England, in the form of the East India Company, in fact and eventually in name, the sovereign power in India. By it a few hundreds of Englishmen held sway over millions of Indians. In the East Indies, the genius of Raffles, and his belief in liberty, gave English merchants a trade empire to be won and held on his principles, with Singapore as its capital.

From the more significant side of the colonists, the balance of power was about to swing to the people from the government. In Australia and in South Africa two peoples as yet hardly conscious of their destiny were about to go on the march. Soon the squatters would go beyond the coastal ranges; soon the Voortrekkers would lead the Great Trek on to the High Veldt. Already in North America a folk migration had taken place, as the United Empire Loyalists had swarmed in to make two new colonies, Upper Canada and New Brunswick. And there even more had happened. Practical legislators were fumbling with the key to the new Empire. They had begun to ask for something they called "responsible government." Just what it was they seem then not to have been sure. But they would ask for it, and get it, and in getting it would transform the Empire and breathe a new life into it.

INTRODUCTION

One of the most universally popular fiction plots is the one that tells of how the poor boy became the rich man. The struggle against odds and the final triumph is ever appealing. One does not have to turn to fiction to discover such a story in the history of England in the years from 1832 to 1870. In every field of social and economic endeavor more changes were made and changes of more far-reaching consequences than in any similar period in English history.

Afterward Britain had to share her leadership in many fields with others. During these years, however, her supremacy in nearly every field was unchallenged, as industry replaced agriculture as the most important means of gaining wealth. Her trade increased so that in these years she became what in the period before she had promised to be, the work-shop of the world. Not only was she supreme in the field of production, but she also led in the fields of social reform and experiment.

Reforms made during these years within the Empire and in the home islands provided a basis for the twentieth-century socialized or collec-tivized state. The outstanding single characteristic, however, was the success and the influence of the idea of *laissez faire* that placed upon the individual the task of making his own life and the lives of others useful and profitable.

The idea that each man should be allowed to seek his own fortune and make his way in the world with a minimum of interference was the dominant philosophy of the period. The industrial classes, now able to share directly in the government, believed in noninterference with their economic activities almost as if the idea were a new commandment. They repealed the protectionist system and ended the Navigation Laws. They encouraged individuals to invest and develop enterprises on their own. All that was asked was that the individual be allowed to make his mistakes in his own way. The laborer should contract for the best wages he could get, and the employer should pay the lowest wages he could. Let the laws of supply and demand operate without undue restraint, and the burst of energy that would—and in this case did—occur would find every man taken care of as he deserved. Men believed in the working out, almost mechanically, of the economic laws proclaimed by Adam Smith and other economists. Let things alone, and ultimately demand and supply would take care of them properly. Laws in restraint of trade or in restraint of the individual were to be repealed or kept at only a necessary minimum.

The Briton who believed in *laissez faire* also believed in removing bad conditions by setting up certain agencies such as poor-law boards and factory inspectors. By passing laws based upon the doctrines worked out by experts, the greatest good for the greatest number could be attained. Thus the industrialist was brought to book for not keeping his factories well lighted or clean. Cities that had allowed slums to grow because of ignorance or greed were investigated and most of the worst areas cleaned up. The practice of injuring life and limb and stunting intellectual and physical growth of children and women who worked in the factories was stopped. These reforms were recognized as necessary and desirable. The nation could not forge ahead with sick workers or mental defectives at the machine. Ill-treatment of workers and bad housing were looked upon as both inhuman and inefficient. In the names of humanity and efficiency the reformers were followed and their schemes applied to the real betterment of conditions, especially in the cities and towns where industries congregated.

The impression one gets of the life of the average Briton in the years between 1832 and 1870 is one of purposeful activity and hard work. People were energetically building or spinning or reforming society. Many writers emphasize this characteristic by saying that this was the era of the iron ship or the iron railway. It was an era of rising real wages for the average worker. After a hard uphill fight for prosperity, accompanied by serious social discontent through the 1840's, the period ended with savings banks crammed with workers' savings and large and splendid profits going to the owners of railways, mines, and factories. Everyone was busy doing something—usually something that was both useful and profitable. The devil found few idle hands after 1850. The road to success had been traveled far, and the nation could look back upon a period of steady growth and progress with the varied emotions of conceit, complacency, and some humility.

The worker, after many struggles, had found himself materially the richest worker in the world. He, and of course all others, could travel in reasonable comfort from one end of the land to the other in cheap railway carriages. Because of the success of the machine, he was taxed less than his father had been and, he could buy more with his money than his father could. More workers could read and write in 1870 than in 1832. The story of how the workingman tried to win decent wages and better working conditions is one of the important chapters of the history of the time. Through trying to get better wages and more food he educated himself in politics. As he became articulate through struggle, he forced upon the aristocracy and middle classes recognition of the political role that he would henceforth play. Of course, the result of the workers' struggle would be to make institutions and government more democratic. Finally, in 1867 the laboring class was to receive the franchise as the middle class had in 1832. This happened because, for the most part, the British workingman was willing to follow a tradition of peaceful persuasion and compromise. Compared to the violent civil strife that distinguished other countries in these years, his is indeed a record testifying to the evenness of his temperament and the high level of his own and upper-class common sense.

However, the middle and upper classes profited most by the triumph of the machine in the industrial age. One serious problem that Great Britain faced after 1832 was that of adjustment between the landed and noble classes and the newly powerful middle classes. Both groups worked together in trying each to understand the problems of the other. The aristocracy admitted the middle class into the government and inner councils of the Empire where they, too, could shape policy as they saw best. The middle classes on their part took into partnership the gentry and aristocracy in industrial and commercial ventures. Cooperation was thus based on the pocketbook and affinity of views that comes from common training and common outlook. By means of the "public schools," which greatly expanded in these years, the coming generations of the aristocracy and the upper middle class were fused together by a common experience. Though insiders could tell the difference, to outsiders the middle-class graduates of Harrow or Rugby and the aristocratic ones were indistinguishable. Consequently, political parties were not divided on class lines. To the Tories, rebaptized Conservatives in 1834, gravitated those of the middle classes who were of a conservative turn of mind and were attracted by the superior financial ability shown by Sir Robert Peel. To the Liberals, as the Whigs increasingly came to be called, though the party as such was not officially founded till 1859, came the aristocrats who felt sympathy for the Liberal program. Thus, while on the continent of Europe the aristocracy lost ground politically, in Great Britain the aristocracy joined the middle class in creating a new elite that applied the experience of the past to the problems of the present and the future.

In dealing with the world and in particular with the Empire, Great Britain in the years from 1832 to 1870 was unquestionably the most important and most detested power because of her strength in the world. A navy that guaranteed British shipping a safe passage to any quarter of the globe was responsible for the confidence with which British statesmen could lead or bully others. Only once, during the years of the Crimean War, 1854 to 1856, did Britain go to war with another European power. She helped Belgium to win her independence from the Netherlands, thus keeping safe the mouth of the Rhine. She also derived satisfaction from conferring upon a little nation the blessings of independence. She helped the states of Italy to unite, and thus put herself behind those favoring national states and liberal constitutional governments. She competed, generally successfully, with France for the balance of power in Spain and elsewhere on the Continent. In the New World she settled her differences with the United States to the surprise of many, for the United States twice nearly came to blows over boundary questions in the 1840's and over British support of the South in the Civil War. As long as no nation threatened the trade routes and as long as the Continent was at peace, the British government acted as friend and mentor to peoples such as the Greeks and the Italians. Those who were adversely critical said that Britain was kinder to the Italians and the Turks than to the Irish.

Within the Empire itself governmental changes of the greatest importance for the future took place. In 1839 the disturbances in Upper and Lower Canada brought about the publication of the Durham Report. This document advised that sufficiently advanced colonies be allowed to govern themselves with responsibility for their internal administrations. In 1867, as a result of a growing Canadian nationalism, Canadian statesmen confederated a group of North American colonies into the Dominion of Canada. This sort of nationalism became evident elsewhere, and in the period following 1870 the Empire developed into the present Commonwealth of Nations. Britain thus kept her Empire by granting to the colonies what she had offered halfheartedly and too late to the Americans in the eighteenth century. The early Victorian English built up their Empire by the process of not wanting to expand it as a governmental unit. When the Boers on the South African frontier migrated into the interior in the Great Trek, they were allowed to set up semi-independent republics. It was the action of a private corporation, the New Zealand Company, that secured that future dominion when French occupation seemed likely. The comparatively large additions made to English rule in India were, in most cases, made reluctantly. It was only the crisis of the Indian Mutiny of 1857 that ended the anomaly of the East India Company being the ruler of the "subcontinent." But though the early Victorians kept their government at home, they themselves had the desire to expand. This was a period of a great folk migration, to the frontiers of Canada, Australia, and New Zealand. Just as the Angles, the Jutes, and the Saxons had poured across the North Sea to make part of Britain into England, so English, Scotch, Welsh, and Irish poured over the oceans to make a "Greater Britain" and widen its frontiers.

In another respect, that of the development of industrial markets, the frontier was also expanded. British merchants in Egypt, South America, the United States, Canada, and the Near East sailed with their goods and exchanged them, usually with profit, for what these lands had to offer. The establishment of British credit and British methods of doing business in these years was to prove invaluable when in the years after 1870 the competition of the Germans and others for markets brought on a race for empire and control of territories. The nation taking more of the British factory production than any other was the United States, where cotton led as the chief article of exchange. Cotton is typical of the international business of Britain, for in a raw stage it was imported and in a finished stage sold at home and abroad to the millions of India, China, and Europe.

The grant of self-government to colonies that were to become dominions was accompanied at home with a gradual shift to a government more democratic in character. The Reform Bill of 1867 gave to the average city worker the right to vote. Thus all but the agricultural workers and the women were able, as the period ends, to make their wants known. The working classes that had become definitely articulate through Chartism, who had steadily pressed for a more democratic franchise, and who had patiently waited for reform were at last rewarded. Strangely enough the Conservative party, which had upheld the theory of representation based on a selective electorate, passed the 1867 Reform Bill. The Liberals, however, were to reap the first fruits of the action, for they had suc-' ceeded in identifying their cause with that of democracy. The government underwent some changes, too. The reforming fervor was applied to making old bureaus more efficient through internal administrative reforms. The Post Office, for example, sent letters through a reorganized service at a penny rate. The Foreign Office was made more efficient. The Home Civil Service was improved by the use of examinations in place of patronage for more and more positions. The reformers were men of method who put away the easygoing ways of the pre-Reform Cabinets and Parliaments.

After 1832 men noticed a change in the conduct and tone of debate in the House of Commons. It was still the greatest debating assembly in the world, but it was no longer a place where oratory and rhetoric were admired above most other accomplishments. After 1832 Parliament and the Cabinet were business institutions which seriously discussed the best and most efficient way of meeting the problems of an empire. Business was the order of the day, and he who would succeed had to be able to talk to men who expected to deal with facts and not fancy flights of oratory. The style of speaking as well as the content of the average speech became that of a businessman persuading fellow directors of the advisability of adopting his recommendations. This does not mean that oratory was unknown or the expression of noble sentiments was not appreciated.

In all parts of public life, as well as in the field of business, the period is characterized by the serious consideration given to the improvement of morals and manners. Cabinet officers, businessmen, and artists were expected to deal with their subjects so that people would be morally improved and enlightened. This was, one must remember, an age that did not laugh at loose morals or gladly tolerate frivolous enterprises, for most Britons took their pleasures seriously and sedately. Propriety was something to be rigidly observed, and an amusement that could improve the mind and character was to be valued over one that merely gave a few moments of pleasure. They were convinced that they had a sufficient moral superiority to entitle them to admonish those not fortunate enough to be subjects of Queen Victoria.

Thus the sobriety and demand for efficiency that was characteristic of the middle class permeated the ideas of all ranks and classes. Benjamin Disraeli, on becoming the head of the Conservative party in the years following the repeal of the Corn Laws, had to abandon lavender gloves, oiled ringlets, and yellow waistcoats. The working classes were proud of being sober and industrious, as the statistics on the lessening consumption of spirituous liquors bears testimony. The middle classes thus were predominant in an era of reform on preconceived principles, great increases of wealth, improvement in the condition of the people, and moral righteousness. The middle class dictated the popular taste as well as the type of government given the nation. It was a class sure of its place and of its rectitude.

Over this empire and all its people ruled a queen whose character and whose place in the scheme of things British made her in many ways the best representative of what her people stood for. Queen Victoria came to the throne in 1837 as a young girl of eighteen. She married, and had a large and attractive family. Her behavior as sovereign, as soon as she had married her excellent consort, Prince Albert, was beyond reproach. The disgrace of immorality that had earned contempt for previous British sovereigns and their courts evaporated under the sunny rays of the Queen's gracious approval of only those things and persons who were good and chaste. Her Majesty was not amused by coarseness, drunkenness, or bad manners. As a hard-working ruler she set an example for her subjects. As a wife and mother she set an example, copied throughout her Empire, of a truly good woman whose tastes in art, the theater, literature, and music were those of most of her subjects. Her ministers found out that she intended to be—and in these years, under the guidance of Prince Albert, was—active in the determination of the policies to be followed by her ministers. This was especially true in the field of foreign affairs, where she and the Prince Consort on one occasion prevented a rupture with the

United States. In an age when the electorate was becoming democratic and the Cabinet and administration, therefore, more responsive to popular will, the Queen was able to make the Crown a well-loved and respected institution. There was never any danger that the people would wish to be rid of a ruler who was herself so magnificent an example of the qualities they held dearest.

29

ECONOMIC AND SOCIAL HISTORY

1832–1870

During the years from 1832 to 1870, greater changes occurred in the economic and social organization of Great Britain than at any other time in the nineteenth century. Industry replaced agriculture as the major economic activity, although farming continued to employ more men than any other single occupation. The town became the place where most people lived and earned their bread, as Great Britain became "the workshop of the world." Naturally, there arose new problems of manufacturing, finance, and social adjustment, which had to be met and solved. To tell of these requires artificially separating what naturally goes together. But as first economic developments, then social reforms are related in this chapter, the reader should remember that they went hand in hand, as mutually interrelated causes and effects.

An example of how industrialization, engineering, science, and wealth can alter the complexion of an economy is found in the development of railways in the years from 1832 to 1870. The demand for faster and cheaper transportation encouraged other major industries and gave employment to thousands. It was estimated that more men were put to work on the railways than had been on the pyramids in ancient Egypt. Production of iron used in rails, carriages, and engines increased about 150 per cent in the years 1830 to 1850. In 1832, railways were just getting their start. Two great spurts to railway building occurred, one in 1837 and the other from 1845 to 1848. The building of main trunk lines was completed by 1850, although construction went on for years after the period under review. At first, only a few lines were opened; and the average length of a single railway moved from 3¼ miles to 112½ miles. Construction authorized in 1846 was 4,538 miles, in 1848, 5,000 miles. In 1858, 8,350 miles were in operation, and in 1870, 13,560 miles. This new industry required the development of new skills and techniques. Engineers had already learned how to supply power and build tracks. By 1835, the experiments of Brunel and Stephenson, showing that locomotives could pull heavy loads up grades and that stationary engines were not

374

needed for this purpose, made possible the rapid expansion described above. This new industry, likewise, required the raising of capital and the clearing up of right-of-way problems. Consequently, the railways afforded an excellent opportunity for making money through the stock exchange. In 1837, and again in the years from 1844 to 1848, thousands made—and lost—money through speculation in railway shares. Many of the lines, of course, were overfinanced and overbuilt, but there was good reason to expect them to pay handsome dividends. Some more solidly established lines in the 1840's, such as the Midland, paid as high as 10 per cent. The trouble with railway financing lay in overconfidence. Thus, in July, 1845, speculation forced shares of the Midland at £100 to £187 and £100 shares of the London and Birmingham to £243. Confidence was lost in 1848 because of the failure of traffic to develop and the fear caused by the revolutions on the Continent. The great bubble burst as always, and thousands of speculators became bankrupt.

Many had trusted to the financial genius of one or two men who seemed to be able to make fortunes for shareholders overnight. Such a railway manipulator was George Hudson of York, the first to conceive a great trunk system stretching from the hub of railways, London, through the Midlands to Scotland. His dream was prophetic and was ultimately carried out. But Hudson went bankrupt when his railways were built at too great a cost and he used capital to pay dividends. His failure and that of his lines took thousands into financial ruin. But while he was building his system, he was the most sought-after man in London. Even the Duke of Wellington consulted him about an investment. Hudson, who sat in the House of Commons as a Conservative, is an example of the political and economic power that came from the new wealth.

Railways in Great Britain were not state enterprises but built by private capital. Parliament refused to control railway dividends and charges, though it did tax the railroads, taxes on passenger traffic alone in 1840 bringing in £112,000. It also regulated the railroads. While at the Board of Trade in 1844, W. E. Gladstone suggested that the government, for public safety, settle disputes about rates and reserve the right of the state ultimately to purchase the lines.

All that was done was to appoint a Railway Department to screen proposals for new lines and set up some general conditions all new railways must accept. The body of officials was, however, abolished the next year. Thereafter Parliament itself decided what new railroads should be built. Evidence was taken on such matters as whether a landlord's coverts might be harmed, or whether the soot and dirt of the engines would cause ill-health in Northampton, and then Parliament did or did not authorize the proposed line. Between 1844 and 1847, the very large sum of £180,-138,901 of new construction was authorized. Not until the Railway and

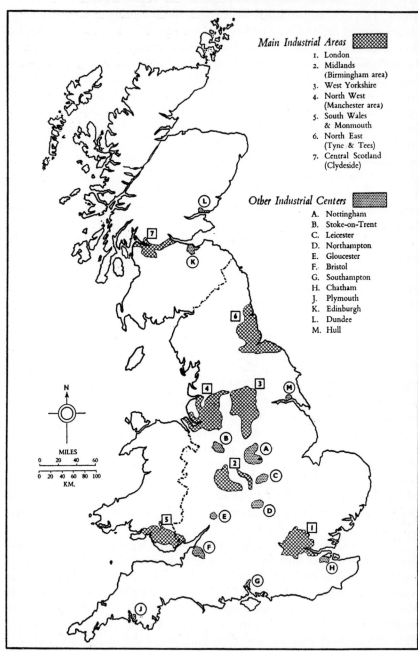

Main Industrial Areas

1. London
2. Midlands
   (Birmingham area)
3. West Yorkshire
4. North West
   (Manchester area)
5. South Wales
   & Monmouth
6. North East
   (Tyne & Tees)
7. Central Scotland
   (Clydeside)

Other Industrial Centers

A. Nottingham
B. Stoke-on-Trent
C. Leicester
D. Northampton
E. Gloucester
F. Bristol
G. Southampton
H. Chatham
J. Plymouth
K. Edinburgh
L. Dundee
M. Hull

N

MILES
0   20   40   60
0   20   40   60   80   100
KM.

*Reproduced by permission of the British
Information Service, Crown Copyright Reserved.*

Canal Commission was set up in 1873 was there a real regulatory government body.

One permanent result this legislation did have—cheap travel for the poor. It required that on all new lines once a day the length of the line there must run a "parliamentary train" with a third-class carriage or carriages, at a fare of no more than a penny a mile.

The railways rapidly captured the traveling public. The fastest stage coaches could average no better than eleven miles per hour; by 1850, express trains were averaging better than fifty miles per hour. In these days it was not the freight but passenger traffic that paid handsome dividends. After 1840 this source of revenue was tapped by vacation and sight-seeing tours arranged by the Rev. Thomas Cook. In 1845, when two-thirds of the railways' income came from passengers, it was obvious that the turnpikes and stage coaches were a thing of the past. One turnpike trust after another went into receivership. Canals also felt the pinch of competition, as railways forced down canal freight rates. For example, the Aire and Calder Canal was forced to reduce rates from 7/ to 2/3 a ton. Gradually, the canals became less important as carriers, although until the present they have continued to carry certain commodities in bulk.

Railways did not exist in a vacuum. Their coming displaced other means of transportation. They ended ways of life that had been created by those ways of transportation, and instead created new ways of life. They substituted the station with its waiting rooms for first-, second-, and third-class passengers for the highway inn or tavern. Thousands of hostlers, innkeepers, drivers, and stableboys lost their employment as the result of the change-over from stage coach to steam train. Some were nostalgic about the loss of an old and picturesque means of travel, but the general public wanted speed and remembered with distaste the freezing journeys on top of, or inside, ill-heated stage coaches. Trains, at first, had no closed carriages for third-class passengers; but by the end of the 1850's, the third class could ride in enclosed carriages on hard wooden benches.

No part of Great Britain was really very far from any other part by rail. Businessmen could travel from London to Manchester and back in a day. London became more than ever the social center of the nation, and gradually replaced English and Welsh provincial capitals as the cultural capital, as well as the financial capital, of the nation. Edinburgh secured a similar position in Scotland. The effect on manners and morals was obvious. People became more sophisticated as the London mode was in a week adopted in Yorkshire or Cornwall.

As the railways were built, new skills were developed such as the arts of laying track and measuring and banking gradients. To run the trains, men had to be taught how to build a steam engine, operate one, and keep it in repair once it had been put to work. Men thrown out of employment through closing of turnpikes or canals could find jobs on the railways. Until the sixties, thousands were needed for construction.

Just as first the canal and then the railway revolutionized land transportation, so first the clipper ship and then the steam ship revolutionized sea transportation. Here free trade led to steam. The first step was taken in 1833 when the China trade was thrown open to competition among British vessels by ending the monopoly of the East India Company. This brought tea to Britain faster. Then in 1848 Britain dared take the final step and end the Navigation Acts. This meant facing the suddenly risen American merchant marine. For American clippers, winging home from the California gold rush, stopped in at Canton and scooped up the best of the tea cargoes. Then the Americans began taking the best cargoes the world over. Though in 1851 American tonnage was but 3,718,640 to Britain's 4,332,085, under differing measurement rules Americans carried an actual ten tons of cargo to the British nine, and because of better ship design an American made five voyages to a Briton's four. The British answer was not to return to the Navigation Acts but to improve their measurement rules by the Merchant Shipping Act of 1854 and meet competition by building better ships. Their clippers, designed for the special conditions of the China trade, recaptured it. For the decade before the opening of the Suez Canal the annual tea race from Pagoda Anchorage to London Docks became a national sporting event, that of 1865 being won by twelve minutes.

But it was business, not romance, that caused the building of such ships; and once steam became reliable, once the Peninsula and Oriental Line could use the Suez Canal, the beautiful *Ariel, Taeping,* and *Fiery Cross* were doomed, just as had been the American *Flying Cloud* and the *Great Republic.* In their places came the typical British tramp, with its double-expansion reciprocating engine. It was this type of vessel that carried to the ends of the earth the "red duster," the union jack on a red background that then was the flag of the merchant marine. Though mechanical problems, such as were caused by the use of paddle wheels, helped keep steam from replacing sail for a long time, the screw propeller, new engines, and the proven efficiency of iron resulted in making seamen prefer steam to sail, often against their aesthetic consciences. In 1840, 69,992 tons were registered in England, Scotland, and Wales, and in 1870, 1,112,-943 tons. The amount of increase of steam vessels is indicated by these figures.

A few statistics may show the nation's progress in those years. The Industrial Revolution ran on coal, for smelters and power looms, as well as locomotives, needed coal. The figures of coal production will tell much.

An output of 44 million tons of coal in 1846 increased to 65 million tons ten years later.

Cotton cloth was Britain's major export. The output of it increased; in 1830, the nation produced 350 million yards; in 1850, 677 million; and in 1870, 1,380 million.

The supremacy of Great Britain in the cotton-textile field came from her early start in manufacturing, the ease with which cotton was transported to her shores, the good damp climate, and the intelligence of her managers and operatives. In spite of the cotton famine of the American Civil War years, Britain was producing in 1866 cotton cloth that in the raw state was estimated at 1,253,800,000 pounds. Most of this cotton came from the United States. In 1861, there were 400,000 looms at work, and 203,000 hands were given employment in the mills producing cotton cloth. Another 248,000 were employed in yarn-spinning sheds. But the average number of workers in a cotton factory had increased in the years 1838 to 1871 from only 138 to 177. It is significant that when the population of Great Britain and Ireland increased from 16,500,000 in 1831 to 31,800,000 in 1871, most of this increase came in urban and industrial areas.

The outstanding characteristic of manufacturing of the period was the steady increase in output and the use of new inventions in small, individually owned factories. Some mass-production enterprises were in existence, of course, but the typical employer was the "little Mester" who hired his men himself and who generally could be found in his office at the plant or mill. The trend toward ownership of manufacturing enterprises by joint stock companies was noticeable only at the end of the period. Most of the woolen industry, for example, was privately owned throughout the whole period. A situation similar to that of the woolen industry is observed in the silk, cutlery, and iron trades and in large portions of the cotton industry. British management was an affair of individuals or a small group of partners, operating on their own capital. It was distrustful of men who evaded responsibility by limited-liability incorporation.

The average factory in the years 1832 and 1870 employed comparatively few men, if judged by today's standard of large-scale mass production, though the average spinning shed was far larger. In the 1850's, it was estimated that the average factory had only ten men working for the employer. Thus, except for textiles, the industries that produced so much and continually increased production were made up of small units. Geographically, industry concentrated during this period in three definite areas, as the trend to put factories where coal and water were available continued. Britain was fortunate in having ports, railways, coal, minerals such as iron, and the working population necessary close together. The Scottish industrial district extended from the west coast and Glasgow to

Edinburgh and the east coast. The English one extended from the north and east section of Durham, south and west to Manchester and Chester, and south to Leeds. In Wales, coal was mined in the southern valleys. The concentration of some industrial activities was intense within these areas. For example, after 1838, 96 per cent of the total English cotton industry was concentrated in Lancashire, Cheshire, Derbyshire, and Yorkshire. The woolen industry was likewise concentrated in certain towns of Yorkshire. This shift of production to many areas was brought about by the proximity to coal and iron. It was also brought about, in the case of cotton, by the climate favorable to spinning and weaving of cloth. Where machines could be made and where the power for them was cheap and distances short, there would be found the factories.

The textile industry was converted largely to power looms before 1850, although in 1840 a parliamentary commission discovered numbers of workers eking out a meager existence through use of hand looms. Only silk was woven profitably on hand looms in this period. However, much of the progress in cotton and woolen manufacture came slowly because of the difficulty of solving problems of weaving with machinery. After 1859, when technical difficulties had been solved, the development of wool-combing machinery helped boost the use of domestic and imported wool from 200 million pounds in 1850 to 416 million pounds in 1870.

The effect of inventions on the increase of production in an industry is perhaps illustrated best by the story of iron and its smelting and refining. Weekly average output by iron furnaces was increased from 64 tons in 1839 to 126 tons in 1860, largely through the adoption of new methods. The use of iron in ships rose from 12,800 tons in 1850 to 255,000 tons in 1870. Most iron firms were small. A change of importance occurred when, in 1859, Bessemer at Sheffield demonstrated how good steel could be made cheaply. Another came in 1869, when Siemens was able to make purer and more malleable steel by using the "open-hearth" method. Bessemer's process demanded the importation of ores from Spain and the employment of thousands of tons of shipping to keep the blast furnaces going. Thomas and Gilchrist were working on the process that in another decade would make it possible to produce excellent steel from cheap ores of high phosphoric content.

The production of minerals kept pace with the demand. New methods of mining, of ventilating the mines, and of hauling coal to the surface were found. Women and children were taken out of mining labor after 1846, so engines and chains had to be used to get coal to the surface. Ventilating devices such as steam jets used to create drafts at mine shaft openings, and power-driven fans were installed to make mining safe and healthy. As steam had been used earlier to pump water from the mines, now it was used to raise coal and ventilate. The story of the successful use of new methods is told in the figures for the increase in coal production in the years 1851 and 1871. In the former year, 57 million tons, with an average of 264 tons per miner, were brought up. In the later year, 117 million tons, or 373 tons per miner, were mined. Tin and copper mining showed an increase too during these years. Only lead production dropped off, owing largely to the exhaustion of the mines.

The production of these goods and services could not be carried out unless some credit and cash were provided. Certainly the average inventor or owner did not possess sufficient cash to build a machine and market it. He had to raise capital somehow and then, for day-to-day operations, had to borrow from a bank. The whole structure of the industrial age was dependent upon the foundations of solidly based credit and a system of banking that could withstand the storm and stress of panics and business depressions. Such a system was created in these years. An interesting part of the story is that the English bankers found that the Scotch, with their system of a central office and branch banks, were better and more successful than they at weathering storms and making profits. As the period under review started, banks operated under the act of 1826, which allowed joint stock banks, sixty-five miles outside London, to issue notes. When the Bank of England was rechartered in 1833, such issue in London itself was permitted. Curiously enough, this, instead of causing the issuance of more paper currency, caused more and more large payments to be made by check. The fact that 91 joint stock banks and 287 private banks each issued its own paper money made the English distrust such money. Another cause of distrust was a wave of bank failures in 1837, stemming from defaults on the bonds of certain American states, overinvestment in railway shares, and a cotton-market crash. Here the Bank of England stood like a tower of strength. By lending money freely in a time of crisis, it allowed its reserves to be drained and thus saved lesser banks from failure. In turn, it replenished its reserves by borrowing across the Channel from the Bank of France. It also made use of a device now classical in central banking—that of raising the rediscount rate. By charging a higher interest on loans secured by promissory notes, the Bank made it less profitable to lend money. This contracted the amount of outstanding loans and stopped overlending.

When, by 1844, it came time to recharter the Bank of England, men desired to give the Bank, by its charter, the duty of supporting the money market in time of crisis. Two theories were advanced as to how this should be done. One was the so-called "banking" theory advanced by Thomas Tooke, the author of the *History of Prices,* and by James Wilson, editor of the *Economist.* These men said that the duty of the Bank of England was to hold enough gold in its coffers to redeem every bank note it issued. The other theory was the "currency" one, proposed by

Samuel Jones Loyd, later Lord Overstone. He and his associates said that all that was required of a bank note was that the bank have enough "quick assets" to allow redeeming it. The difference between the two theories might be put thus: by the "banking" theory, the Bank of England should have a million golden pounds in its coffers if it was allowing a million pounds in notes to circulate; by the "currency" theory, it would be sufficient to have £500,000 in gold and £500,000 in promises to pay that were certain to be redeemed.

It was a serious problem which theory to follow. The Cabinet used a method of solving its problems it had also used with the New Poor Law of 1834. It asked the Political Economy Club, a group of businessmen and theoretical economists, to discuss the question. That group could not resolve the question entirely. Consequently, the Bank Act of 1844, the basic legislation on the Bank of England till it was nationalized, in effect adopted both theories. The Bank was divided into two departments, one for banking and one for note issue. The note department was instructed to have on hand gold to match every bank note, with one exception; it was permitted to issue notes to match the original capital invested in government bonds, back in 1694, and to match a somewhat later investment in bonds, made in the eighteenth century. Thus, in effect, every note of the Bank could be paid off either in gold or, at a terrible crisis, by selling bonds and getting gold for them. As long as the Bank obeyed those conditions, its notes were legal tender. But in the other department, the Bank of England could conduct a central banking business. It could, and did, give credit to other banks, at whatever rate of interest it saw fit. If the Bank felt that business needed encouragement, it could make it easier to borrow money by lowering the rate of interest. This was called the discount rate, since by charter the Bank of England could lend only against promissory notes; and its chief business was giving cash for notes before they were due. But if the Bank felt that business was overextended, it could raise the rediscount rate and thus make it harder to borrow money.

As the reader will realize, in effect this meant that a group of London businessmen supervised lending throughout the nation. It was their task to balance the economy, to make lending easy when business needed stimulus and to make lending hard when business overexpanded. This they did successfully, with three exceptions—the crises of 1847, 1857, and 1866. In each case, the situation became so bad that the Bank did not have enough funds to act as a reserve for hard-pressed banks and also obey the Act of 1844 and hold gold reserve for its notes, since every gold pound it lent out to stop a "run" on a bank meant an equivalent in note issue called in. But in each case, Parliament stopped the crisis by "suspending the act." This allowed the lending of gold, for a limited time, without calling in notes. Within that limit, the raising of the rediscount rate straightened matters out, and business was able to get back on a level keel.

In order to facilitate the transaction of a nation's business, the clearinghouse was enlarged to admit joint stock banks as well as private banks in 1854. In 1864, the Bank of England was admitted to it. Thus, payment by check was possible in all banking institutions.

As savings accumulated, there was a natural desire for new ways to invest them. But to buy a partnership in a business was a risky thing, for even a "sleeping partner" became liable for all the debts of the partnership. Therefore pressure rose for the passage of laws making it easier to form "limited-liability companies." A step in that direction had been taken in 1824, when the restrictions of the Bubble Act of 1824 had been eased. In 1856 a general law was passed, which allowed the formation of a joint stock company without the passage of an expensive special act of Parliament. Now seven or more persons could sign a bill of association and create a company, whose stockholders were liable only for the amount of their subscriptions. This made it possible to raise money on the stock exchange to start a business or to expand it. Not till after 1870 did this practice become general. At first, in the woolen industry for example, limited-liability companies were formed chiefly for poor risks, as is shown by the large number of failures of incorporated woolen companies in these years.

One of the most important of the economic phenomena of the nineteenth and twentieth centuries has been British overseas investment. Widely varied holdings throughout the globe made possible, in great measure, the financing of two world wars. By selling foreign stocks and bonds, Britain was able to find capital and credit to buy goods in times of vital need. The years from 1832 to 1870 set the patterns of investment for the age of imperialistic competition from 1870 to 1914.

In this mid-century period, capital was always to be had for the adventurous who wished to float overseas enterprises. The deposits in banks in 1830 were only 30 million pounds. In 1866, they had risen to 350 million. Before this period, London had been the chief source of investment capital. In these years, provincial bankers, investors, and businessmen came into the market. Minor depressions, such as that of 1837 or 1857, defaults by foreign countries in loan payments, fake companies, and wars only for a short time prevented them. Habitually bad risks such as South American loans did not prevent money from being put out in those countries. Here the British businessman showed courage and optimism in parting with his money. In truth, he may have sometimes lost heavily, but in this period he usually made a profit or established connections that later led him to make a profit. As in other economic and industrial activities, the British investor was often the first in the field; and seldom was his being first disadvantageous. By now appears the phenomenon of the invisible export. In goods, Great Britain is now importing more than she exports, but is keeping her trade accounts balanced by interest earned overseas.

The United States, in the 1830's, received most of the money lent abroad. The great house of Baring's, for example, floated many loans with canal bonds and state bonds as securities. As trade with the United States doubled between 1830 and 1836, so did the amount of money loaned increase. In 1835, the sum of $66,000,000 had been loaned by the British to various states. It represented most of the debts of some of these states. The fall of cotton prices in the United States caused unforeseen calling of notes, and consequent disaster. The failure of the states, particularly in the South, to pay off on their bonds was another cause of loss of money to the British. When, in 1839, Nicholas Biddle and the Bank of the United States went down to final defeat, state securities and the securities sponsored by Biddle collapsed. In 1841, nine states defaulted on payment of their obligations. The British investor had his fingers burned, and for twenty-five years he was wary of the United States as a field for investment. This did not, of course, prevent him from buying shares in the railways in the 1860's or from helping to finance the expansion westward of the nation after the Civil War.

South America had long been the place for the British profit seeker to send his money. Sometimes gold-mining stocks were popular; but until the 1850's, the bonds of various countries were the chief type of investment sought. As in the case of the United States, many government and state bonds were not honored. In the 1840's, over 50 million pounds of state debts were left unpaid by South American countries.

After 1850, it became a practice for the nations of the world to turn to London for floating their loans, among them Piedmont, the Scandinavian countries, Turkey, and Egypt. Later on, it has been said, imperial development followed many of the paths explored by loans at this time to countries like China and Turkey. There was apparently no nation too poor or too remote to receive a loan if it could provide reasonable security and consent to pay sufficiently high interest on the loans. This affability of British bankers and controllers of capital had a marked effect on the trend of business. Men and nations that borrowed pounds sterling had to pay back pounds sterling. Payment usually could be made only in British banks or places of trade. Naturally, exchange of goods and services within the sterling system was easy and convenient. So British loans led to the employment of British engineers, materials, and ideas. The business so well founded continued long beyond the period of any specific loan. Not infrequently business enterprises as a result of one loan led inevitably to more loans and more British business. Between 1866 and 1870, over 320 million pounds were raised in London for foreign issues.

Loans to foreign governments were by no means the only ways by which capital was invested abroad. In the 1830's and 1840's, the preeminence of Britain in industrial techniques led to setting up businesses in other lands. Concessions to build railways came first. In 1840, a British company got a concession for the construction of a railway in France. Thomas Brassey, the great engineer-contractor, had thousands of Englishmen working in the 1840's and 1850's on the Continent building railways. Contractors in these years took with them not only British technique but also British materials. The manufacturer of rails, as well as the engineer-contractor, profited.

As European experts learned their trade, the need for the professional British contractor and engineer passed away. The British businessman then turned to financing and operating, with British engineers and technicians, gas companies, water works, and public utilities in general. The visitor to many towns and cities of the Near East, Africa, and Asia has found reason, time after time, to bless the skill of the British sanitary engineer. The penetration of capital through investment in municipal public works, or other similar enterprises, gave rise both to permanent dividends and expanding opportunities for trade or further investment. Usually, where money had been sunk in some local enterprise, a British bank or branch of a commercial house was at hand to make short-term loans and to promote trade and business. One business, that of note discounting, was so great that one firm, Overend, Gurney and Company, turned over 115 million pounds from 1859 to 1865.

Through foreign investments, the character of the London money market and of British business became cosmopolitan. After 1846, the philosophy of most businessmen and industrialists was that of *laissez faire*. This outlook upon international trade encouraged rather than hindered pouring out money to develop other countries. Britain was, through her use of capital, the great international nation. Wherever one went, some trade or business, governmental or private, was borrowing or paying money to London. But as the European nations learned the skills necessary to carry on their own industrial revolution, Britain lost any privileged position she had won. It was only natural that, as conditions by which money could be invested changed, other markets should be found. It was in keeping with the philosophy of *laissez faire* and the search for new outlets for capital that, in 1860, Richard Cobden should have persuaded the French to sign the Cobden-Chevalier free-trade treaty. This was evidence of the need for opportunities, unhampered by tariff walls and other restrictions, for continental investment and business.

The Empire, too, attracted the investor. Gold had been discovered in Australia in 1851. This discovery had the general effect not only of creating confidence in investment, bolstering prices and credit, but also of making men aware of the possibilities of investment in the colonies. In Australia between 1860 and 1870, £70,510,000 was loaned to the various state governments.

In 1853, the Grand Trunk Railway was financed in Canada and in Britain by a British loan house. The head of the house, George C. Glyn, along with members of the Cabinet from Canada West, was on the board of directors. In India, after 1857, the year of the Mutiny, the Indian government encouraged the building of railways and expansion of communication facilities. From 1858 to 1869, £70,110,000 was put into Indian railroads. The money came from the savings of British investors and was loaned at a guaranteed 5 per cent. The Indian taxpayer bore the cost of the loan and the somewhat inefficient and costly method of operation. He also derived benefit from the increased ease and accessibility of transportation. In the 1850's and 1860's, the jute business, managed by Scotsmen at first, was developed in India by British capital. During the American Civil War, a great deal was spent in encouraging the growth of cotton in India. While Indian cotton did not replace that of the United States, the money spent did encourage Indian business and industry. As trade restrictions, defaults, or competition made investment in private companies in other nations less attractive, the prospect of increasing profits from colonial enterprises under British law and protection became more inviting. In the 1870's, most of the demand for large-scale investment overseas had become imperial in nature.

It is usual to imagine that, in competition for economic leadership, agriculture rapidly declined in the years from 1832 to 1870 and gave way completely to industry. During these years, agriculture in Great Britain, as a way of making a living, continued to be the most important single industry and afforded a livelihood to the largest number of people. The rush to the cities from rural areas stopped in this period. The population of Great Britain increased absolutely, and urban population grew much more rapidly than that of agricultural areas. However, between 1850 and 1870, it has been estimated that the population in rural areas declined only between 1 and 2½ per cent. This slight decline indicates that farmers made a good living. Indeed, many regard the period from 1853 to 1862 as a golden age of agriculture, pointing out that in 1854 there were four million acres of land growing wheat. This would indicate that prices were satisfactory and that demand for agricultural produce was steady. In 1851, it has been estimated there were 24,700,000 acres in farm land in England and Wales, with an average of 111 acres per farm. Scotland, as in the past, showed the largest number of small land holdings. In ten agricultural counties, a general movement toward consolidation of small holdings into large holdings took place, as the figures in the accompanying table indicate.

CONSOLIDATION OF LAND HOLDINGS

Size of holdings, acres	1851	1861
100–299	15,900	14,700
300–499	3,200	3,400
500–999	1,529	1,528
Over 1,000	323	308

The enclosure movement, the chief feature of the agricultural revolution, slowed down between 1845 and 1878. Over 600,000 acres were enclosed after 1845 under the General Enclosure Act of that year. This represented the rounding out in England and Wales of estates or of areas only partially enclosed before and now included in the holdings of some landowner.

In this period, more enclosed land was devoted to pasturage and to the raising of herds of cattle for dairy and meat purposes. Between 1850 and 1870, meat and dairy produce increased 50 per cent. Wool for domestic use did well, and agricultural prices rose rather than fell. The agricultural price index given in the accompanying table shows a steady and profitable return to the farmer.

INDEX OF AGRICULTURAL PRICES
(1892 = 100)

Year	Index number
1837	76
1845	70
1850	70
1855	95
1860	88
1865	90
1870	95

During this period, agricultural production in the British Isles suffered one great disaster. Ireland had become a country of one food crop, potatoes. When in 1845 rains rotted the potatoes in the fields, over a million Irishmen starved to death, other millions suffered terribly, and over a million emigrated to the colonies and to the United States. The Irish, at home and overseas, were understandably bitter about this depopulation of their island and inclined to blame the landlord class for it. Englishmen, perhaps correctly, blamed politics as much as the weather. For the Corn Laws prohibited the importation of grain, and had they not been on the statute books, food might have been brought in much more quickly and thus thousands of people saved from starvation. As a result, however, of the failure of the potato crop in Ireland, the Corn Laws were repealed, and Britain adopted a policy of free trade.

The Conservative party, representing landholders and the traditional landed interest, was deeply affected by the introduction of free trade. Tories claimed that protection ensured a noble way of life that would otherwise be destroyed. They believed that the landed interest of England would be wiped out if free trade were adopted. Lord George Bentinck and Disraeli, leading the gentry, put up a gallant, but useless, battle for protection in the House of Commons. They said, and at least Lord George Bentinck and the squires believed, that free trade would mean the end of agricultural prosperity. The facts prove them wrong. People did not starve under free trade. Englishmen ate more and better food, and farmers did not suffer bankruptcy. For artificial fertilizer increased productivity, in this period, just as enclosure had in the previous period.

Another reason for the success of agriculture was the abolition, in 1836, of the payment of tithes in kind for the support of the Established Church. Also, some laws protecting game and upholding ancient social privileges of landowners were removed, particularly after the end of protection in 1848. A better personal feeling between landlord and tenant, a by-product of the repeal of the Corn Laws, was observed everywhere throughout rural England.

Agriculture advanced because landlords and farmers adopted new and scientific methods. County agricultural societies, by annual fairs and monthly meetings, spread information. In 1838 the Royal Agricultural Society was founded. A royal charter was granted to the Society in 1840, and from that date to her death in 1901 Queen Victoria acted as patroness, thus continuing a traditional interest of her grandfather, George III. The Society published its *Journal,* which, with the *Agricultural Gazette,* reported new developments in farming. These were many, for in 1840 the German scientist Liebig published his great work, and in that same year Sir John Bennet Lawes founded his laboratory farm at Rothamsted, where Liebig's ideas were tested and corrected. As a result, by the 1850's the Scottish drainage systems, or those used in Sussex and Essex, were being copied throughout England. The use of fertilizer became widespread. Guano was first brought from Peru in 1835; after 1850 it was discovered how to use garbage from slaughterhouses. The agricultural societies also encouraged experimentation with types of plows and harrows. It has been said that in the 1830's little or no agricultural machinery was used in tillage and the open-field system had been kept on, but by 1854 Bell's reaper was widely used, and in the 1850's steam was applied to farm machinery. The use of scientific methods of farming, therefore, improved both the amount of agricultural produce and the quality of that produce.

Improvement of the breeds of cattle was shown through the keeping of records in herd books. Agriculture, by the 1870's, was adapting itself to the demands of an industrial and urban community by catering to the need for fresh meat and fruit and dairy products. As the period ends, the meat industry received a very definite check from the cattle plague of 1867. The herds of cattle were decimated. In the years immediately following, the industry did not quite recover its former prosperity. By and large, however, those prophets of doom who had felt that a repeal of the Corn Laws would result in the bankruptcy of British agriculture missed the mark. Agriculture, like other industries, was generally prosperous in the years from 1832 to 1870.

So much was the middle class in the foreground in the years under study that all things good or bad have been attributed to them. Theirs, it is said, was the shame of keeping workers in a miserable condition, wherein they groveled at the feet of the employer for their bread. Theirs, it is said, was the decision that made Great Britain a nation of money-grubbers, whose soul was to be found in the shop and whose ideas of beauty were to be seen engraved on a £10 note. It has also been said that the middle classes gave Britain an era of economic prosperity in which every man and child had more of the world's goods than any man or child had had before in the history. It has been claimed that middle-class Britain did more to stop disease, help the poor, and free slaves in the colonies and in the factories than any other group or class in history. Many, certainly not all, abuses created and inherited through the industrial development of another era were remedied or alleviated. In some respects the middle class sacrificed beauty to efficiency. It preferred the machine to the scythe and the scientific surgeon to the giver of physics to let out the bad humors of the body. The student should expect to find that in some ways the middle-class ascendancy conferred great blessings of an economic and social nature on the Empire; in some respects its way of life was distinctly unsatisfactory.

The best approach to the point of view of the middle class may be found in the earnestness with which it believed in improvement and progress. Essentially, the middle class had faith in itself and the idea that things could be made better by allowing the newly popular ideas of social and economic reform to be applied. Thus, the employing classes believed that the worker received fair wages when he was given what his employer felt was proper. The employer had to make profits, and profits made new factories, and factories produced new commodities that the worker could buy with his wages. The employer was the keystone of the industrial structure because his was the initiative and foresight to make the jobs available for the workers. He did not realize or understand that sometimes his profits, most of which he pocketed, came from the labor of the worker, and that as a customer the worker was denied a chance to increase his purchasing power and standard of living. The employer believed fervently that each man could be left to make his way without interference on the part of society.

The employer looked at his factory or shop and compared the output of previous years with his enlarged operations. This comparison encouraged him, because he had produced more and his products had made living more comfortable for all. He was a believer in the use of machines and the various devices that allowed men to turn out more goods, travel faster, and accumulate more in profits and savings. If a man were industrious and thrifty, he could become a success. The years from 1832 to 1870 were years when men did have more of the useful and practical goods, could travel faster and more cheaply, could live better, and could save some money. The theories of the middle class were confirmed by this experience. It was only natural that a feeling of satisfaction and smugness came to the middle class. They could look upon their handiwork and find that it was pleasing. Diligence, respect for the job, fair dealing, and a belief that to him who works come all the blessings of the world made up the middle-class creed.

The middle class should be judged by the fact that they inherited the industrial world of the eighteenth century and built on and over it. Though to us in the present the terrible slums of the industrial cities stand out as a sore spot on the economic organization of society, the middle-class employers of that time thought otherwise. They believed that living in a slum was a sign of laziness and stupidity. The employer worked twelve hours a day; why could not the mill hand do the same? Then too, the employer was told by the writers of highly learned works on economics that he could not do anything for the poor. Theirs was a bad lot, but it could not be helped because wages represented only a fixed proportion of costs and of income. Who was the employer to contradict economists? It was shown, particularly in the 1840's, that the poor in many towns were living in cellars filled with liquid filth, in alleys where the light of the sun never shone, and where few infants survived their first five years. Crime and disease were accepted as necessary evils arising from slum conditions. Owners of slums pointed out that, even if ten persons were crowded into a room without windows and only four square feet allotted to each individual, the property brought high rent. Clergymen and employers were diligent in urging the inhabitants of a foul courtyard or dank basement—and in Manchester, in 1833, 40,000 such persons were to be found—that God had called them to their humble station and that they should strive as good Christians to bear the burden put thus upon them. High profit and the will of God went hand in hand in the minds of many employers.

The fact of the matter is that the middle class believed that the terrible standard of life and the condition of the poor was not of their making and could not be helped. They were not inhuman, by and large. When the misery and degradation of the industrial worker was pointed out in the findings of parliamentary commission after commission, action was taken by abolishing the impractical system of outdoor poor relief, by building sewers and enforcing sanitary codes, by building new and better houses for workers, and by creating work that allowed the hand to buy more and save. The degraded condition of the mill worker was matched in many places by that of the agricultural laborer. Slowly prosperity filtered down to both. Histories, all founded on fact, have been written taking to task the middle class for lack of feeling and conscience. The historians are, however, apt to forget that, had the conditions they describe been general and as severe as represented, men could not have lived under them. Slums continued to exist, education of an elementary sort was denied to hundreds of thousands, these and the basic problem of the more equitable distribution of goods and wealth were some of the things that the laissez-faire economics of the middle class would not alter. But the worst of the very real abuses were either abolished or reformed through factory acts, commissions' reports, and private charity. No one can deny that the state protected hours of labor and secured better housing and working conditions for the working classes in the years 1832 to 1870. Administrative intervention existed even in this period in the form of the Poor Law Commission and the Factory Inspectors.

As the man of the middle classes changed his way of life, his social and political importance grew. Shortly after this period, any such religious restrictions as may have prevented his son from entering Oxford and Cambridge were removed. He could, and did, send his children to the best of the public schools. The wealthy middle-class man bought estates, and his children assumed the speech and the manners of the landed gentry. Much of this striving to ape his "betters" was caricatured in prints and such magazines as *Punch*. But it went on, and the snobbery it brought about was one of the less pleasant characteristics of the age, as men of wealth tried to enter the select London clubs or the ranks of the aristocracy.

The gentry and nobility did not offer a solid front against these classes. Many a poor gentleman had his fortunes restored by marriage with the daughter of an industrialist. The nobility and gentry had never been absolutely exclusive. Admission to this class depended upon talents and achievements as well as birth.

Indeed, most of the nobility and gentry found that one of their ancestry had at one time been in trade. Thus the middle classes and the upper classes found that, through contact in the House of Commons and through living side by side in town and in the country, much cooperation was possible. Solidly entrenched opinions of the businessman, who was against the Corn Laws and was a Methodist, might conflict with those of the Anglican squire, who was for protection. But they had other interests in common. Both wanted to keep order and preserve property from destruction either by bad theories or by the mob. The upper classes and the middle classes were united in mutual admiration of the British constitution and British institutions in general. After all, they were the people who jointly had been responsible for the reforms of the constitution and of social and civil services.

The middle classes made another contribution to both the immediate and future development of industrial Britain. They perfected the technique of management of industrial enterprises. Shopkeeping and accounting had long since become common skills of the owner. The industrial revolution demanded, too, that men learn how things are made, be able to instruct others in the necessary skills of machine operation, and learn how to apportion costs and work out production schedules. In order to employ even fifty men, to say nothing of five hundred or five thousand, techniques of plant organization and the best way to divide jobs for efficient operation had to be mastered. In a sense the illiterate worker or the poorly educated man could, by learning new procedures, rise in the scale of industrial society. That many rose from the ranks and became directors of corporations and managers of their own large enterprises is a tribute both to their native capacity and to their grit. It should not be forgotten, therefore, that much of the economic prosperity of the Empire depended upon the ability of the businessman to develop and use new skills in sales, production methods, and finance. This was the age that saw the first appearance of that ubiquitous individual, the traveling salesman. It was also an age in which bankers had to become acquainted with production methods and plant finance before they could make loans intelligently.

The change in manners and social habits that occurred in this and the preceding period must largely be ascribed to the influence of the opinions of the middle classes. The outstanding characteristic of this period is the reform in tastes and manners in the general direction of sober and industrious living. The drunkenness so characteristic of the eighteenth century was combated by the continued drive of Wesleyan and other ministers. Thousands of pamphlets told of the evils of drink. Sunday school classes were often schools in which the theories of Bell and Lancaster were applied in teaching children their letters by means of stories of a highly improving nature.

The middle class had no time for frivolous amusements. It devoted itself to good causes, such as the support of societies to abolish slavery in the empire or to found asylums where orphan boys could be taught respect for law and order and a trade. The leaders of middle-class opinion were men whose education was that of the business world. Some of them read widely and well. John Bright, in many ways typical of their tastes, quoted from Milton in the debates of the House of Commons. Perhaps the most successful novel of the 1850's was about a man who rose to the top after many trials and made £10,000 a year. The middle classes read improving works such as the publications of church foundations, the *Quarterly*, and the *Edinburgh Review*. History written by Macaulay or Grote was almost compulsory reading for those pretending to knowledge in ordinary society.

This middle-class sobriety and respect for grave and serious demeanor and habits was not without its effect on the daily conduct of all classes. Thousands of stories and books were read—and believed in by their readers—that had as their purpose the instruction of all classes in the beauty and desirability of living chaste and quietly useful lives. The upper classes, affected by the sober tone of their middle-class neighbors, stopped drinking sherry and took to tea as an afternoon beverage. Dress concealed the female figure, became dark in color, and was thought best when it was sensible and warm. To all respectable people, a proper display of wealth, such as a page boy to carry the prayer book to church, was considered preferable to a more ostentatious show. Attendance at service twice a day on Sundays was expected. Thackeray hit on the spirit of the times when he said that nothing offensive to the sensitive ears of the most delicate female should be printed in the new and comic magazine *Punch*. Perhaps the best example of the outlook of this period was that of the society matron who said that everything she read, or said, or did was done with the end in view of elevating the morals of those in a less fortunate station of life and of giving friendly advice and aid to those in the same station as herself. This era was perfectly sure that its morals were sound, that its habits were approved of by God, and that its endeavor to live with propriety and sober merriment was rewarding.

If the middle classes set the pattern for social conduct, the working classes, who were bound to follow in most respects, had serious problems of living. These had to be improved before they could attain the standard of cleanliness and sobriety thought to be as desirable. Workers had to be taken from mines where they lived and worked in conditions that an owner of animals would not permit his livestock to stay in for a minute. Tenements in slums had to be cleansed and new housing built before crime and viciousness could be controlled. The story of how this was done can be told in two parts: first, the improvements brought about by the workers themselves, helped by charitable societies and philanthropists; and second, the passing of laws that forced reform in city and borough governments, as well as in industries. It was recognized that reform was the only way to raise the morals and the standard of living of the workers.

During the years before 1850, the lot of the worker generally was not too good. Hard times, in the form of unemployment and political uncertainty, as well as economic reform programs, often kept the wage level from rising. After 1850, times were better, and the wage level could rise 48 per cent to the year 1870.

Agricultural wages and what they meant to the farm worker in terms of real income are hard to determine. Often the worker received a cottage or food or other privileges that should be included in real wages. The wages of the farm worker were, however, lower in respect to the average amount of cash received than those of the urban worker, and they reflect the relatively unsatisfactory position of agriculture as compared to industry during these years. Wages for farm workers also differed according to regions, as the accompanying table shows. Sometimes housing would be of the best

WEEKLY AVERAGE WAGES OF FARM WORKERS

Area	1837	1850–1851	1869–1870
East and Northeast	10/4	9/1	11/3
Southeastern and East Midlands	10/	9/5	12/5
West Midlands and Southwest	8/10	7/2	10/10
North and Northwest	12/1	11/10	15/

for the farm hand; sometimes he was expected to live in a hovel. The wealth, generosity, and foresight of the landlord determined much of what the worker would receive in the way of comfort or extra earnings, such as he might make at harvesttime. But it would appear that the days had passed when farm hands made and enjoyed more than the wretch who worked in the towns.

Miners of coal had a hard time in the 1840's and later. The accompanying table indicates their daily wages on an average. They were less well

DAILY AVERAGE WAGES OF MINERS

1831–1840	4/
1841–1850	3/
1851–1860	3/8
1861–1870	3/9

paid than artisans, such as masons and bricklayers. Those skilled trades made, in such cities as London, almost 2s. to 3s. a day more than the miners, though their expenses were also, of course, greater. As to the real income of all these groups, it is possible to say that generally they were better off at the end than at the beginning of the period. After 1840, in spite of the unsettled conditions, there was a fall of 30 per cent in the real cost of living, largely because duties had been taken off such staple commodities as tea and sugar. The accompanying table shows the general gains made.

GAIN IN REAL WAGES
(1850 = 100)

	1850–1854	1860–1864	1870–1874
Average worker in full work	101	107	125
Workers of unchanged grade in full work	101	102	114

One of the most difficult problems to solve in the years 1832 to 1870 was that of urban housing conditions. Various commissions reported on the state of the poor, especially the great Health of Towns Commission of 1844. Sanitary engineering was developed to the point where municipal authorities saw the value of removing the accumulations of human filth allowed to pile up for years. It took time to accomplish these things. The result in healthier people was worth the effort.

In the 1860's, the House of Commons had to suspend sittings because of the uncleansed and malodorous Thames River. In London, and for that matter in most other cities, wells were situated in courtyards where refuse of every description was thrown. The seepings of this refuse were sure to get into the drinking water of the wretches forced, through poverty, to live in the courtyard. Improving one's property did eat into the profits.

After the poor-law guardians had started to work, under central prodding, and the factory inspectors had reported on what they saw, many towns and individuals became aware of the need for cleaner and better-lighted tenements. Especially was this true when Edwin Chadwick campaigned in the 1840's. Then, in 1852, following a terrible cholera epidemic, towns were stirred up to remove manure and garbage for the sake of the public's health. Sewers were laid, and gas companies put through their mains to the slums. In London, for example, progress was made toward the unification of the water-supply companies so that ultimately the metropolitan area would be served by the not too honestly run Metropolitan Board of Works. In the sphere of water supply, the trend was starting in these years toward control and ownership by the town. Services hitherto had been in the hands of private franchise holders. The towns inherited the problems of preceding generations in building and housing. The important fact to remember is that, although this was the era of *laissez faire*, most municipalities and most reformers were willing to admit that state supervision was desirable in some spheres of activity, and real steps toward this end were taken in health and building regulation. New construction in Manchester and London, for example, was pretty carefully supervised in respect to light, heat, and sewers after 1850.

It has been said, and with some degree of truth, that the middle classes of Great Britain were more interested in seeing the savage Africans supplied with Bibles than the poor at home with health and jobs. The remarkable support given by Dissenters as well as members of the Established

Church to the various societies for the abolition of slavery in the Empire perhaps proves this point. The Society for Abolition of Slavery, the missionary organizations with Exeter Hall, London, as headquarters, effectively roused the middle and upper classes. Despite opposition from the "West India Interest," the British taxpayer in 1833 showed his hatred of slavery by putting his hand in his pocket and voting some twenty million pounds to buy out slavery in the Empire by compensating slave owners. Nor did humanitarianism stop there. The work of the antislavery patrol on the West Coast of Africa was continued. Meanwhile, Exeter Hall kept on with its varied work of sending out missionaries and of securing government protection of natives.

The zeal for the slave and the savage was part of the general desire to help the unfortunate that distinguished the men of this era. When abuses of a most glaring nature were found, they were attacked with vigor by philanthropists and private charities. It was in keeping with the doctrines of *laissez faire* that charity and good deeds by individuals should receive the approval of the community and its sympathy. It was not unusual for a merchant to die leaving his wealth to a foundlings' hospital or to a school for the education of orphan or unfortunate boys. One such charity was the "Ragged Schools."

The Ragged Schools were made a cause for the humanitarian rich by Lord Shaftesbury. These schools were often rooms hired for the purpose of teaching children Bible stories and how to read them. Volunteers went into the slums and took the children under their care. They washed, clothed, and fed them, while giving useful information about clean living and religion. Funds were subscribed through the good offices of Shaftesbury and others. It was part of the humanitarian scheme that the soul of the pauper must be uplifted and improved, as well as his physical life. These schools in the slums were an important influence on the community at large. Stories, such as those of Charles Dickens, were also helpful in spreading the story of the need for public support of charities. Such efforts as those of Lord Shaftesbury were never sufficient, however, to remedy the problem of ignorance and crime that caused so much trouble during these years. The state had to clean up the slums and establish schools before the ignorance that makes vice could be combated. This was not finally done in the period under review.

In 1829, three years before the Reform Bill was passed, Sir Robert Peel, as Home Secretary, created a police force in London that became the model and envy of other towns and nations. He substituted, for the old-fashioned town ward and watch and the few Bow Street runners, an efficient force of trained men who could exercise authority and uphold the law. These "bobbies" or "peelers" were made into the best city police of their time. Their record has been one of excellent service ever since.

This reform was widely copied. In 1833, a Lighting and Watching Act allowed separate parishes to set up local constabulary forces. In 1835, boroughs were ordered to set up police forces. In 1839, the inevitable Edwin Chadwick wrote the report of a Constabulary Commission, out of which report evolved the permissive County Constabulary Act of 1839. In turn, this was followed by the compulsory Constabulary Act of 1856. All these police forces were independent. As readers of detective stories know, the chief constable of each county is traditionally jealous of the men from the Scotland Yard office of the Metropolitan Police Force. It is true that the Home Secretary has the power to issue orders to police forces; it is true that by a steadily increasing system of "grants-in-aid" the Home Office does control matters of discipline and equipment. But the effectiveness of the British police stems far more from the British tradition of law-abiding behavior—as evidenced by the fact that no British policeman carries arms—than from such centralization of the police force as is customary, say, in France.

In the field of elementary education at national expense, Great Britain made a poorer showing than any other of the major powers of the nineteenth century. The United States, Germany, and France all had more and better organized schools than Great Britain. Only in Scotland could one find a system of schools that provided elementary instruction for the working classes in anything like a thorough manner. But this system had been developed in centuries previous. It was successful in giving the average Scot a better knowledge of his literature and mathematics, and even a chance to attend a university, than did the English system for the worker south of the border. The sons of the gentry and the middle classes who had money could attend the private establishments known as "public schools." Many were founded by kings and town corporations in centuries gone by. These were the training grounds for the ruling classes. The Duke of Wellington, according to one story, said that the battle of Waterloo was won on the playing fields of Eton. Nearly every man of note in English public life attended such a school as Eton, Harrow, or Winchester. There the discipline of the classics, hazing, and social conformity produced the statesmen of this era. The public school did contribute directly to the social democracy and ease of intercourse within the ruling class that was known in these days. Parliament and the top government offices were filled with men who had been to the same schools, talked the same language, and often had been schoolmates with their party leaders or the gentlemen of the Opposition. Thus one could talk without fear of condescension to a Prime Minister who, as a schoolboy, had blacked one's boots or played football on an opposing team. Sir Robert Peel thought well of Gladstone who, as a young man, came to the Tory party bearing exactly similar Oxford honors that Peel had borne. Both were double firsts;

that is to say, they had won top honors in two subjects. But the child of the laborer had no such opportunities.

Dissenters' schools continued to train the middle-class youth in the classics and mathematics, as did the upper-class public schools. But religious points of view kept the Dissenting academies from being popular and from being noticed. Their work was good, but it was carried on only for a small proportion of the population of school age. Church foundations maintained some schools for the poor. Such societies as the Fishmongers in London looked after the early education and housing of foundlings. But by and large, the child of the worker had no one to teach him his letters. The religious fight over education in these and the years immediately following is largely responsible for the failure of Great Britain to establish a school system worthy of the name.

Elementary education came from voluntary schools, and state aid was looked on askance. Nonconformists feared that the state would force the state Church into the picture; educators of the Church of England feared lest it would not. Therefore such free or cheap elementary education as was available to the poor came from the schools of Bell and Lancaster which have previously been described. But gradually steps were taken, the first being the requirement that Poor Law Unions educate pauper children. As it was then thought unsound policy to give paupers advantages others did not have, this move formed an opening wedge for state aid. Through the Education Committee of the Privy Council—hence in later years the curious title of Vice President of the Council for the Minister in charge of education—grants were made to help schools. At first the sum total of these grants was less than the £20,000 spent on the royal stables, but they had effect. School inspectors, of whom Matthew Arnold was one, used the threat of not providing grants to establish standards.

This reliance on voluntary schools had vast disadvantages. England as contrasted to Scotland, even to the government-supported "National Schools" in Ireland, remained backward in elementary education. On the other hand, the fact that much administrative independence was preserved has today been considered perhaps the outstanding feature of English education in that it preserves education from overcentralization.

So pressing were the demands that something be done that W. E. Forster, with Gladstone's backing, put through the Education Act of 1870, the first large-scale proposal for state aid to education. The Act set up special local authorities, or "school boards," that had the choice of levying local taxes and creating nondenominational schools or merely relying on a central grant and supporting existing denominational schools. Much excitement arose over a clause, which the Dissenters resented, allowing Bible teaching in the school board schools. They feared this as the opening wedge for Anglican proselytizing. This Act led to fiery local electoral battles between members of the Church of England and Nonconformists, the classic being in Birmingham, where a Nonconformist manufacturer, Joseph Chamberlain, built up a smooth-running political machine to capture the local school board from the Anglicans, and then went on to become mayor and enter Parliament for a stormy and dramatic career. But these battles were not for or against state aid to elementary education; they were just over how it would be given. All England agreed with Robert Lowe's remark, after the passage of the Second Reform Bill: "We must educate our masters."

In keeping with the trend toward education for more people and with less religious restraints was the abolition at Oxford and Cambridge of religious requirements for entrance. Along with the admission of Dissenters to the universities, another great revolution took place when courses in biology, chemistry, and the other like sciences were introduced for the first time. Conservative individuals were amazed at how far revolutionary ideas could reach when the classics could be challenged in their preserves on the Cam and Cherwell Rivers.

As the introduction of the sciences typified the pressure of a new reign in the realm of higher education, so did the reforms of Dr. Thomas Arnold of Rugby help bring about the changes in the secondary field that were no less revolutionary. Dr. Arnold wanted his boys to be good students, good athletes, and men of high moral character. He instituted at Rugby a new method of living, of playing games, and of instruction that captured the imagination of the boys and taught them how to cooperate with others, as well as translate or work mathematical problems. His system was almost universally copied in the public schools, and later in the nationally established schools.

Sir Robert Peel, in 1844 and 1845, suggested that the state give aid to the establishment of universities in Ireland and to the Catholic seminary at Maynooth. He was brought up short by the clamor raised by both Dissenters and Church of England men in the House of Commons. Catholics could not be aided by state funds because this would mean that the devil's disciple, the pope, would gradually creep in and overthrow the Protestant religion of Great Britain. The result was that many Catholics were deprived of opportunities, and the cause of extended higher education in Ireland was lost for some time.

The worst feature of the failure to establish an extensive system of schools for the poor was that the workingman and others like him had to get their education piecemeal or not at all. In the race for industrial supremacy, one of the factors that told strongly against Great Britain in the years of the late nineteenth and early twentieth century was the relative ignorance of her working and artisan classes. The race went both to the strong and to the sufficiently educated. The British workingman possessed many virtues, but he could not work at the top of his capability because of his lack of general knowledge. The worker did not receive as much education as he needed or desired. He had, however, the benefit of some teaching. Usually the urban worker somewhere got enough knowledge to read and write or to do simple sums.

The general lot of the workingman was much improved in the years between 1832 and 1870. The Factory Acts of this period and development of trade union movements with the agitation for the People's Charter show that the workingman was helped by the state and his own efforts. He won a better standard of living and a position of greater importance to society. The movement for factory acts was part of a continuing tradition of state interference to protect the young. As early as 1802 the elder Sir Robert Peel had secured an ineffective measure, depending for its enforcement on local justices of the peace. This was somewhat strengthened in 1819. But not until 1833 was an effective act passed. This was done under Conservative auspices, being introduced by the Conservative Lord Ashley, later the seventh Earl of Shaftesbury. Here should be noted the political byplay that surrounded the attempt to regulate factories. Country squires, irked by investigations into the Game Laws, were delighted to counter by investigating factories. Workmen—and Tories seeking their support—advocated a ten-hour day for children with an eye to the fact that in effect that often meant a ten-hour day for adults. Manufacturers, in an age of a twelve-hour day for adults, therefore, looked with suspicion on Conservative zeal for protecting children. That may serve to explain, though not to extenuate, Liberal resistance to factory legislation. It also explains why factory owners might prefer investigation of factories by a royal commission appointed by a Whig government rather than by a House of Commons committee containing Conservatives who would ask embarrassing questions.

The Tory humanitarians Michael Sadler and Richard Oastler had long protested against the long hours that mill hands were forced to work. In 1831 Sadler got a parliamentary committee to investigate factory conditions in industrial England. This was followed by a less sympathetic royal commission.

After the Reform Bill of 1832, Lord Ashley took up where Sadler had left off. The measure he offered would have reduced the working time of those under eighteen to ten hours. As amended by the House of Commons, it provided that children from nine to thirteen should be limited to twelve hours, or a thirteen and one-half hour day if mealtime were included. From thirteen to eighteen years of age, sixty-nine hours a week were allowed. Young people over eighteen were considered to be adults and capable of making their own decisions. In Parliament, the request for ten hours was fought hard by the owners' representatives. High cost of labor, idleness, and unhealthy social life were prophesied for industry and workers, should ten hours of labor a day be adopted as standard. The House of Commons did not, however, kill the most important provision of the bill. This established, in the best Benthamite tradition, a board of factory inspectors, working from a central office in London.

After 1833, the cloth factories were inspected and the owners brought to book should they maintain unhealthy working places and employ children who were under age or improperly worked over the allotted weekly period.

Lord Ashley then turned his attention to the conditions of the mines. In 1842, he secured the the passage of a Mines Act that forbade any employment of boys under the age of ten years. Women were prohibited from working in the mines altogether. Ashley had originally asked that boys under thirteen be prohibited from working, but the Lords felt that this was pampering the young and that labor costs would be too great. They killed a proposal that boys from ten to thirteen years be permitted to work only every other day and amended the bill to read that boys over ten years of age could work every day. Inspection boards for mines were, of course, established.

In 1847, the Ten Hour Bill was passed. Again Lord Ashley helped with this legislation. With the passing of the act, the right of the state to regulate hours and conditions of labor was acknowledged.

It should be noted that at the same time as the middle class was securing the repeal of the Corn Laws and committing the state to an economic policy of *laissez faire*, Parliament was also securing the humanitarianism of the factory acts regulating hours and conditions of labor and committing the state to a policy of control and inspection. No sooner had one philosophy won the day than another, directed toward collectivism, was introduced and adopted. At the time, however, few saw the contradiction between the principles of the repeal of the Corn Laws and the introduction of centralized state-controlled inspection of industry. It should also be noted that economic reformers such as Bright and Cobden were not in favor of protection or inspection of workers' jobs. They were consistent in their support of owners' social, as well as political, philosophies. *Laissez faire*, said these men, was the best of all possible social and economic ideas.

The reform that in the long run had the furthest reaching results was the New Poor Law of 1834. About this important legislation there lie clouds of misrepresentation, for it was passed by propaganda and has since then suffered from detraction by counterpropaganda. Essentially, it was a rural reform in the local-government field that had even more important, and largely unexpected, results in urban areas and central government. The cause of the reform was the existence of a dangerously large number of paupers in rural England, who had been debased by the "allowance" system of relief, ever since that had started at Speenhamland in Berkshire in

1795. This population, in the Last Laborers' Revolt of 1830, had demonstrated what a danger it might be to society at large. But any program of cutting down relief would be political dynamite. Grey's government was faced with a choice of evils. If it did nothing, it got blamed; if it cut down relief, it got blamed. It escaped from the dilemma by a means now classic, referral to a royal commission. The Professor of Political Economy at Oxford, Nassau Senior, was made the active leader of a royal commission of investigation. Senior brought to his task that rare qualification, an open mind. He threw over preconceived notions how to solve the problem, when news came to him of the Nottinghamshire workhouse system. This was part of a moral movement—similar solutions were worked out elsewhere by evangelical clergymen and laymen—to bring back paupers' self-respect. Instead of being asked degrading questions, able-bodied paupers were offered a choice—hard work for subsistence, or going out to find themselves jobs. A workhouse was the key to introducing this system on any large scale, for supervision of outdoor work created many administrative problems.

Here the propaganda aspect of the law comes in. When the Political Economy Club's deliberations had convinced Senior that mere legal changes would not be enough without an enforcing device, when he had convinced his commission that only by building workhouses throughout England could the land be "dispauperized," the next task was to screw up the courage of Cabinet and Parliament to enacting the necessary legislation. To do this required both argument and evidence. To collect the evidence a swarm of assistant commissioners was sent out, of whom the most active was Edwin Chadwick, a former secretary to Jeremy Bentham. The report of the commission, consequently, for all that Senior wrote it, had Benthamite arguments running through it. That report, spread by Lord Brougham all over the land, had a sharp impact. It was meant to make the proposed New Poor Law so obviously sound that Parliament could not but vote for it. The report did what it was intended to do, and Tory joined with Whig in putting the measure through, really on a nonpartisan basis. The act went into effect August 8, 1834, and quite quickly achieved its primary purpose. The able-bodied laborers in rural England were dispauperized, with a resultant raise in the wage level.

But the most important results of the law were not those intended, for rural England, but those unintended, for urban England. Elsewhere, it is explained how local government was revolutionized by being somewhat democratized and put under central control. Here it should be pointed out that the process of clearing the relief rolls of the able-bodied brought out the problems of those not able to earn their living. When children were unable to get jobs because they could not read and write, the central authorities of the Poor Law Commission caused the setting up of what amounted to state-aided elementary schools. Soon this program was being copied by other forms of central state aid. When it was discovered that the cost of medical relief was burdensome, two great reforms were started. The Assistant Commissioner in Essex, Alfred (later Sir Alfred) Power, began to found "clubs," which were really health-insurance societies. Out of these grew the national health insurance of today. The Secretary of the Commission, the indefatigable and largely insufferable Edwin Chadwick, by investigation of health conditions, culminating in the Health of Towns Commission, showed up the need of central enforcement of higher health standards. Out of this grew first the Clauses Acts of 1848, which enabled municipalities to take up special powers if they so chose; and the Board of Health of 1848, as a central enforcing agency, which, after transformation into the Home Office and then the Local Government Board, is now the basis of the Ministry of Health.

Yet another result did the New Poor Law have. For all the words in legislation, enforcement of its provisions depended on the cooperation of local authorities. To get that cooperation, a civil service policy of persuasion was needed. Thus the Assistant Commissioners who "sold" that law to the Poor Law Unions were the first of the deft "Home Civil Servants" who today persuade the English local authorities to do what they ought to do.

Another reforming piece of legislation, not Benthamite in character but drafted by Joseph Parkes of Birmingham, was the passing in 1835 of a Municipal Corporations Act. By this act, and by similar acts of 1833 and 1840 for Scotland and Ireland, the urban government of Britain was reorganized according to a national plan of town administration. Councils were to be more democratically elected. Fancy franchises that put town government in the hands of a select few were abolished. Thus was established a uniform system of local government in the land as far as towns were concerned. This act did a great deal to promote efficiency in government and naturally made easier the ultimate imposition of certain uniform codes of sanitation and public service that were to follow the pattern thus laid down.

The example of Manchester shows what this reform accomplished. In the 1830's this great urban area was still technically a rural manor and paid fees at one time amounting to £80,000 a year to the Moseley family in Derbyshire. Its property-holding inhabitants, voting in a mass as a "police commission," had the right to squabble over sewers, streets, and public order. Then in 1837 a municipal charter was procured, Richard Cobden being a leading petitioner. The "Mayor and Corporation" wrested powers from the police commissioners, and suppressed manorial dues by buying the manor. Then they went ahead to give the citizens first clean streets and properly managed markets, then potable drinking water, and in a later era, tramways, gas and electricity, a profitable sewage-disposal plant, a ship canal, and finally, in the 1930's, more than one model suburban housing project. Thus Manchester has become one of the leading business concerns of England, if one stops to think of it that way.

The combination of private philanthropy and reforming legislation served to secure better treatment for the worker and made Great Britain a leader in social legislation in Europe. The workers were sufficiently intelligent to appreciate what was done for them but felt that they received something short of their due. The social discontent of the 1830's and 1840's was caused partly by bad employment and economic conditions and partly by the appearance on the scene, for the first time in British history, of excellently led, comparatively efficiently organized, and nationally popular movements among workingmen. These movements had as their purpose the achievement of an equal political and economic status with other classes. Thus the Ten Hour movement was political as well as social in its aims. The creation of labor unions was both social and political. The most important movement, Chartism, was sufficiently strong to claim the attention of all classes and cause the upper classes to fear revolution, particularly in 1848.

After the repeal of the Combination Acts in 1825, it was inevitable that workers, when properly stimulated, would form labor unions for the purpose of protecting their jobs and getting better pay and working conditions. The democratic climate of opinion of the Reform Bill years showed the workers, or at least that portion of them who could read and were interested in studying economics, that organization won where individual efforts failed.

The year 1834 also saw much advance in the beginnings of the trade union movement in Great Britain. A builders' union in Birmingham, a cotton spinners' union, Leeds' clothiers, and other workers' lodges from southern Scotland to Kent planned strikes for better wages and shorter hours. Starting in 1832 and 1833, lodges and unions everywhere came out. Organization was the watchword. It was to be expected that someone would try to tie together all labor unions into one bundle. This attempt was made in 1834 by Robert Owen in the Grand National Consolidated Trades Union. The avowed purpose of the Grand National was a nationwide general strike. Disputes and sectionalism among the various types of workers immediately burned so hotly that, in 1835, they had consumed the national union. A nationwide labor organization was not yet feasible. Yet the potentials of labor power had been partially proved. This movement resulted in some hotheaded workers striking and some foolish and fearful constables struggling with them. At Tolpuddle, in Dorsetshire, seven men were sentenced to transportation because the trade union they formed superficially resembled a revolutionary society. This harsh treatment on the part of the Whig administration made the radicals angry. Public opinion, once the facts came out, did secure the repatriation from Australia of the "Tolpuddle Martyrs." The public of middle men and gentry was opposed to any organization of workers that could make its claims stand. The result was that Owen was attacked on all sides. Perhaps the important aspect of Owen's Grand National is that 500,000 workers were temporarily enlisted in the cause of self-help through organization. Some movement or some leader would inevitably catch their fancy, and then would come the mass demonstration for a system in which the worker could speak his piece and receive his just economic and social rewards. The agitation for the People's Charter was such a movement. With Chartism, the working class made its first appearance as a leading character on the stage of national politics.

The objectives of the Chartist movement were political, but its causes were economic. The workers were impressed with the idea, and so were their leaders, that reform of social and economic abuses would inevitably follow the passage of legislation designed to accomplish given aims of the workers. Parliament was thus the goal of the workingman's representatives and leaders. Once in Parliament, the representative of the worker had only to put the good law on the statute book, and everything would go well. It is typical of this era that, in spite of the bad showing made by the reformed Parliaments regarding the demands of workers, both reformers and workers had faith in the ability of a legislature to carry out a program asking for better pay and housing. The working class, therefore, believed that getting their representatives into Parliament was necessary.

The collapse of the Grand National Union left the workers restless and feeling that something else should be done. Bad harvests, the financial panic of 1837, the opposition to the New Poor Law, and the success of the middle classes in winning the reform of 1832 all made the worker ready to follow the lead of those who could organize. The revival of Thomas Attwood's Birmingham Economic and Political Union served as a foundation on which later Chartist organization structures were built. In order to get workers' support for his ideas of currency inflation, Attwood was willing to lend his aid and his organization to the campaign for workers' demands. The Birmingham union was allied with that group of the London Workingmen's Association that first published the People's Charter. William Lovett, a member of the London group, published the Charter in 1838. He had the approval and the help of Francis Place. Place had helped workers in securing repeal of the Combination Acts. A few radical members of Parliament also joined the Chartists.

The Chartist movement caught the workingman's imagination. The organization, especially in the North of England, of hundreds of Chartist meetings and groups was helped by a central committee that met in

London. It directed the activities of hundreds of organizers and propagandists who visited every town and rural area, carrying with them the
inflammatory gospel of the Charter. The answer of the workers to this new
appeal for support and class demonstration was greater than anyone had
anticipated. It seemed as if here was, at last, the cause that would unite
the workers and gain for them the needed laws that would make their
lot better.

The People's Charter contained six articles: (1) manhood suffrage; (2)
vote by secret ballot; (3) annual Parliaments; (4) election districts equal
in numbers of voters; (5) abolition of property qualifications for members
of Parliament; (6) payment of members of Parliament. At the time, conservative opinion was shocked by the radical nature of these demands.
Today, only one of them—annually elected Parliaments—is not part of
the political system. But in 1839, the Six Points seemed to be dangerous.
If they were granted, the country would be faced with an anarchical government of ignorant workers. The Whigs and Tories looked upon the
Chartists as potential revolutionaries. After mass meetings had been held
where inflammatory addresses were made, troops were sent north to be
used in case an attempt to overthrow the government should be made.

The aim of the Chartists was to present the Charter in form of a petition
with the signatures of millions of workers. In 1839, the first petition was
presented with more than 1,200,000 signatures, some forged and some
comic, stating that the people wanted this program. In the House of Commons, the Whigs secured sufficient votes to defeat the handful of radicals
supporting the petition, 235 to 46. The problem that Chartist leaders now
faced was what to do in order to keep alive the interest of the workers and
gain the Charter's acceptance.

A nationally representative convention was chosen to sit in London. The
committee was to direct the work of the Chartists, secure new names, and
keep alive the glorious cause. It called itself a second Parliament and issued
statements to the older Parliament at Westminster that errors made would
be noted and that a day of reckoning would come. Some members, imitat-
ing the older Parliament, put "M.C." after their name. After all, they
said they were more representative of the people than were the M.P.s. It
was suggested that a "sacred month" be set aside when the laboring class
would go on strike and force the aristocracy to its knees. Such strong sentiments, and the even stronger opinion that it would come to physical force,
resulted in splitting the London committee into two groups. One group
wanted the win by peaceful and educational means; the other wanted to
use force.

The physical-force advocates were led by Feargus O'Connor, a fiery
Irishman, who had developed to a fine art the kind of speech that promised
death and destruction to the oppressors of the poor. He became editor of

the *Northern Star,* a Chartist newspaper that in print echoed his threats and stated his program for reform, urging force if persuasion failed. In his advocacy of a militant stand he had the support, at one time or another, of a few reformers such as James Bronterre O'Brien, who believed that his policies would sooner bring the utopia of socialism and reform to the worker than education by gradual processes.

Although O'Connor talked, he would not act or give the signal for an armed uprising. Others not connected with him had felt differently. In 1839, a few hotheads secured the services of some Polish and other continental military exiles. This determined group organized a band of miners in Wales that attacked the courthouse at Newport. One or two were killed. The workers refused to rise. The leaders were punished for this attempt to use force.

After a second petition to Parliament was laughed out of the Commons in 1842, O'Connor led a small remnant of Chartists. He organized schemes for communities of Chartist workers. He took in enough money to buy several tracts of land for the purpose of Chartist settlements. Nothing came of these efforts because, in the early 1840's, everyone was participating in the battle of the repeal of the Corn Laws. The last chance of O'Connor and his group came in 1848. As the result of the continental revolutions and the collapse of the railway boom, the workers momentarily turned to their old physical-force demagogue for leadership.

In May, 1848, the Chartists gathered together and, claiming two million supporters, asked O'Connor, who had been returned to Parliament in 1847, to present the petition of the people to the Commons. It was rumored that the workers were now ready to fight for their rights. Mass meetings in Hyde Park attracted thousands, but not the vast multitudes claimed by the Chartists. But the organization of workers, and the presence in London of hundreds of determined-looking workingmen, threw a panic into the upper classes and the Government. Gentlemen left their clubs and merchants their shops to volunteer for service in a social war. Businessmen and bankers carried sword canes and loaded pistols about with them. Clerks in the Foreign Office were given instructions about saving documents and fighting to the last. The Duke of Wellington, in civilian clothes, surveyed the approaches to the Houses of Parliament and had volunteer companies and regulars posted in strategic spots. The day of the presentation of the petition was one of anticlimax. The mob of Chartists did not materialize. The petition was driven in cabs to the House of Commons. The volunteers returned to their clubs to refresh themselves in an appropriate manner, and nothing at all happened. The House voted down the petition and with that action killed Chartism. O'Connor soon left Parliament and died insane.

In place of Chartism, the trade union movement revived. In the late

1840's, various local "trades clubs" began federating. Their organization was surprisingly like that of the Methodist Church, though there are only a very few cases of Methodist organizers moving into the trade union movement. Of all these unions, the Amalgamated Engineers, founded in 1851, became the leader. Indeed, so successful were these federations as to be, in the 1860's, the cause of employers' associations to combat them. Finally, there appeared the movement that would succeed where Chartism had failed. In Whit-week, 1868, there met at Manchester a Trades Union Conference, out of which grew the present mighty T.U.C., the Trades Union Congress that so largely controls the Labor party.

Thus failed the first movement for social equality and economic reform that came from the working classes. It is not surprising that it should have failed. Leadership was bad and divided. The advocates of physical force frightened away the solid and more reliable elements of the laboring classes. The majority of laborers were drawn into the controversy over the repeal of the Corn Laws and therefore had no time for the Charter. They believed that a repeal of the Corn Laws would bring the blessings that the Reform Bill had not. The resurgence of Chartism in 1848 was the result of excitement and temporary hard times rather than of a universal desire for reform. The importance of the Chartist movement is to be found in the fact that workers could, even if only for a short time, support and organize a social movement and present a logical, considered platform for political reforms. From this time on, the workers were always in the minds of statesmen. Workers' demands were considered, or at least looked at. Certainly they could no longer be ignored. The worker now had a permanent place in politics, and as time went on, a more active role could not be denied him. The masses were, after 1848, articulate; and their demands were for a more democratic franchise and state-aided reforms. That they, unlike their continental counterparts, refused to rebel and use force is a testimony to their common sense and patience.

The year 1850 is the dividing year in the social and economic history of our period. The rioting and the militant mass meetings stopped after this year. In agriculture and industry, peace and general prosperity descended on every class. The symbol of this peace and its accompanying prosperity is to be found in the Crystal Palace Exposition, which opened the next year, 1851. Under the leadership and the driving ability that showed Prince Albert at his best, manufacturers and merchants were persuaded to exhibit their wares to the world in a magnificent glass palace constructed in Hyde Park. So large was the building that whole trees were included in it. It was the construction marvel of the age. Queen Victoria and Prince Albert opened the exhibition and thus gave approval to this unprecedented display of mechanical wonders and goods.

The Exposition showed everything that Great Britain and other lands manufactured. In a small space, one could visit the cotton mill and the woolen mill, see a miniature mine at work, and travel through the bazaars of Egypt and the markets of China. The world's goods were there on display. Everyone was surprised to see how much of the manufactured goods sold on a world-wide basis was made in Britain. It gave the Briton a sense of the power and the supremacy of his industrial system. The surprising fact and chief feature of the exposition was that so many cheap and useful commodities were at the service of the poor and the workers. Here was found concrete proof that in real income the workers of Britain were better off than those of the rest of the world. It was a triumph of the middle classes, whose brains and ability to organize were shown in the results of their industrial activities. The world stood in amazement at the production and skills shown. The British were likewise amazed and overcome with an appropriate feeling of satisfaction.

Although after 1850 the working classes and the rest of England achieved a more satisfactory standard of living and prosperity, some doubts about the Industrial Revolution and what it had done to British civilization were raised. The poet Samuel Taylor Coleridge had, in the 1830's, asked for more state supervision. He disliked the slums and the loss of religious feeling that accompanied the new way of life. On the other hand, the apologists for the Industrial Revolution, such as Richard Cobden, saw nothing but unmixed blessings in the new system. Cobden felt that the Industrial Revolution would change the life not only of England but the world. By free interchange of goods and services, every nation could work with every other nation, and all would become mutually helpful and rich. The workers would have good things in abundance. The industrialists would be happy in leading and in making comfortable profits. War would disappear from the face of the earth. International cooperation in every sphere of human activity would result. All this would come from the application of laissez-faire principles. Truly the new age of the machine would be the best the world had ever seen.

Many writers disapproved of the social results of the Industrial Revolution. Something noble and peaceful had gone out of British life when the farmer moved to the towns. The factories bred hunchedbacked, sickly men with sickly souls. What England needed was a spiritual revival where the underprivileged of the towns would be led back to a better life through a new interest in religion. The Oxford movement, discussed elsewhere, was partly inspired by a desire to reawaken an interest in God, through the activities of the Established Church and a more ritualistic form of worship. Thomas Carlyle wrote against the effects of the Industrial Revolution. While not suggesting concrete reforms, he did attack savagely a system that gave riches to a few and poverty and disease to the many. He poured scorn on the heads of the men who were traditionally the leaders of British society; he excoriated the industrialists who broke the spirit and lives of men in their factories. His proposals were generally for a rejuvenation of the national character through leadership and self-sacrifice of a few able men. The nation could only be saved from moral rot by strong leadership.

The Rev. F. D. Maurice and the Rev. Charles Kingsley preached against the slums and against a system that killed the spiritual life of the man. They, and particularly Kingsley, believed in a cooperative kind of society, where the poor received more of the profits of their work and where healthy bodies could be built to hold clean and healthy spirits.

The novelist, and later Prime Minister, Benjamin Disraeli, saw the solution for England's social ills in a union of hearth and crown. He despised the middle classes and said that English society could be strong and healthy only if the crown and nobles directed, and the cottager and worker happily followed, a sort of gentle parochial way of life. Matthew Arnold, too, regarded the middle classes as defacers not only of character but also of the countryside, with their belching chimneys and dirty slums. He said that the middle classes had no sense of beauty, had no sense of decency in living, and were so busy amassing fortunes that they forgot their Christian duties to their fellow man.

Only two critics demanded that the worker take into his hands the sword and at one blow put an end to the misery of his existence. Friedrich Engels wrote a most factual and revelatory report on the state of the poor in 1844. With Karl Marx, he published the famous and certainly inflammatory Communist Manifesto in 1848. It called upon workers of the world to unite in destroying the chains of slavery by which the middle and upper classes had bound them.

John Stuart Mill wrote in his *Principles of Political Economy* (1848) and in *An Essay on Liberty* (1859) the best defense of the Utilitarian philosophy and the ideas of *laissez faire*. While admitting that some need existed for state regulation of public services and police, he was vigorous and profound in his defense of a system that tested everything by its usefulness. Mill was representative of most of the economic thinking of his day in his advocacy of a system that encouraged men to build and exchange goods without any brakes put upon their activities but those of normal competition. He believed in the sacredness of the individual's personality and right to live as he pleased as long as he did no positive harm to the life or property of his fellows. Evil conditions would be remedied by the operation of economic forces that, if left to work without interference, would bring all to a proper conclusion with every man getting what he justly deserved. The important condition that had to be observed in business and society was to protect the individual in his lawful enterprises. Society should allow him to do as much as he could and realize his potentialities in every way. To Mill and to the majority of middle-class thinkers, freedom meant absence of state interference in the affairs of man. Only freedom could assure a prosperous and progressive society. Mill spoke for the dominant middle classes and, of all the critics of society, he probably said what was in the minds of most men. Freedom and not regulation was the thing wanted most in the Great Britain of the years 1832 to 1870 by men of substance and good will.

30

RELIGION

1832–1870

It is a partial truth, but a useful one, to say that the Victorian era was an age of religious emancipation. For it saw not only Catholic emancipation, but also the freeing of the Nonconformists from disabilities, the Oxford movement that liberated new energies in the Church of England, the breaking away of the Free Kirk from the Church of Scotland, and to twist the words about, a certain amount of emancipation *from* religion. These changes were part and parcel of the times, deeply woven into the warp and woof of English life. As such they deserve separate examination.

Nonconformity, to take it first, was characteristic of Wales and of the working and middle classes of urban regions, especially of the North. As this period began, it had escaped from the nominal control of the Clarendon Code. But the men and women who worshipped in chapel and not in church, *i.e.*, in the Nonconformist Churches and not in the Church of England, were under many other disabilities. They had to pay "church rates" which sometimes meant that a Church of England minority in a parish could assess taxes on the Nonconformist majority. They had to pay tithes in kind. They were kept from the universities. They had to be baptized, married, and buried under the authority of the Church of England. Naturally, they fought back. The Registration Act of 1837 freed conscientious Nonconformists from having to record birth, marriage, and death in an Anglican parish register. Tithe Acts from 1836 to 1860 simplified the collection of tithe and helped to get rid of its weight in many places by allowing commutation, *i.e.*, buying it for a lump sum. But these improvements in status had to be fought for.

The career of the Rev. Edward Miall exemplifies the way the Nonconformists had to struggle. He used the columns of *The Nonconformist or the Dissidence of Dissent* to spread his arguments abroad. He sat in the House of Commons for two Parliaments for the north-country boroughs of Rochdale and Burton. In 1844 he founded a society to attack church rates and university restrictions on Dissenters. In 1853 he helped found the

412

powerful Society for the Liberation of Religion from State Patronage and Control. As the leader of a band of some fifty Nonconformist M.P.s, he made consideration of their claims a condition precedent for their parliamentary support. He did get some results. A Commission on the Universities was set up in 1858, and the universities were thoroughly overhauled and opened to Dissenters—in 1861 for Oxford, in 1862 for Cambridge. In 1868 church rates were made voluntary; in 1869 was secured the disestablishment of the Church in Ireland.

It should not be thought that the Nonconformists were merely political. Far from it. They took their share, more than their share, in the work of Exeter Hall, that meeting ground of evangelicals of all creeds to do what could be done for the aborigines of Africa. To its credit Exeter Hall has the abolition of slavery, which took effect in 1834, and the implementation of that abolition by pressure on the West Indies colonies and South Africa and by the noble work of the antislavery squadrons. Probably a great deal of social disorder and crime was prevented by the propaganda of the Nonconformist sects. Their message was spread abroad through pamphlets and weekly prayer meetings.

Revivals conducted by fiery orators who pictured the hell that awaited the drunkard and the fornicator were given credit for saving many souls from the devil's ways. The Nonconformist clergy lived with their parishioners, and at prayer meetings and twice each Sunday they observed the rectitude of behavior of individuals and groups. The presence of the clergy in the activities of their daily lives helped the poor to bear peacefully the bad as well as the good times. The clergy made the presence of a righteous God real and the fear of his wrath something of a spiritual power in the personal lives of millions. Evangelicalism was reflected in the support given the reforming factory acts and the social legislation of these years. Along with their hostility to paying tithes to the Established Church went their hostility to institutions that spiritually abused their fellow men. Some credit to the effectiveness of the Nonconformist battle against the devil and the pitfalls of industrial society must be given in trying to account for the workers' lack of a desire to use force to fight against bad conditions. A belief in the ultimate reward and of the righteousness of a life ordered by God made people accept the burdens put upon them as partial punishment for sin. Workers believing thus were not revolutionists. They wanted to see fair play and win their just rewards on earth and in heaven in a peaceful manner. The leadership of local preachers in persuading workers to take up a better life cannot be underestimated. They were a strong-minded and vigorous body of men.

In Scotland a religious upheaval of major importance to that country, the Disruption, took place in 1843. In this year about 470 ministers, led by the renowned preacher the Rev. Thomas Chalmers, seceded from the state

Church to establish the Free Kirk. The cause of this was the enforcement by the courts of the law that allowed the incumbent or parson of a parish to be appointed by one man, the patron, instead of being chosen by the parish as a whole. This, according to the secessionists, was an example of the state interfering with God's Church in a matter of vital importance. Therefore, rather than submit to the decisions of the courts, the secessionists "went out," giving up lucrative posts for a matter of conscience. In Scotland, therefore, as in England, men were concerned about the role that the state was playing in control of matters felt by sincere Christians to be out of its proper sphere of activities. Men believing, as did the Scottish secessionists, that the Church was higher than the state and should be independent of it supported the Oxford movement, as they had fought the attempt to disestablish the Established Church in Ireland.

When one speaks of the Established Church in Ireland, terminology may trap one. Technically, from 1801 to 1869 there was no such body, nor a Church of England, but a United Church of England and Ireland. It had been the hope of some Churchmen, when England and Ireland were united, that the position of the state churches there would be as sacrosanct as the Church of Scotland had become in the Union of 1707. This may serve to explain the heat with which certain Tories defended the system—indefensible in other eyes—by which the Established Church in Ireland collected tithes from a Roman Catholic majority in the South and a Presbyterian majority in the North. When the Irish tithes were attacked, in 1834, and when it was proposed to "expropriate" some of the income of the Church in Ireland and apply it to education, Lord Stanley left the Whig party and became a Tory, along with Sir James Graham. Under O'Connell's pressure, the measure was reintroduced and passed in a modified form. Thereafter, as in England, Tithe Commissioners to handle disputes and a policy of commutation, as well as throwing the payment from the Catholic tenant to the usually Protestant landlord, formed a partial solution. Once the wall had been breached, it crumbled. In 1869 Gladstone separated the theoretically inseparable state churches of England and Ireland and disestablished and expropriated the Church of Ireland. To it was given a form of self-government modeled on the Church of England in New Zealand, and thus on the Protestant Episcopal Church of America. Since then the Church of Ireland has been one of the self-governing members of the Canterbury Communion.

Not only did the Nonconformists secure rights against the Church of England, not only did the Free Kirk break away from the Church of Scotland in the Disruption, but also the state Church in England began asserting its independence of the state. This was the Oxford movement. At the time of the Irish Church question, in 1833, the Rev. John Keble preached his Assize Sermon at Oxford, a clarion call to Church regeneration. Too long had the graduates of Oxford and Cambridge, who held a practical though not technically a complete monopoly of the ministry of the Church of England, merely "read divinity" formally, and then acted as a sort of special branch of the national civil service. Keble called men to remember what the Church had been. He revived what had never died but had slept, the claims of certain Churchmen that the Church of England was the true Catholic Church of the land, continuous in doctrine and duty from the landing of St. Augustine. Enthusiastically his followers, such as the Rev. Edward Pusey, the Rev. John Henry Newman, and the Rev. Henry Edward Manning, led a liturgical and theological revival. In their *Tracts for the Times* they preached doctrines that more and more approached those of the Roman Catholics. In their parishes, they adopted old usages of the medieval past. Orders of monks and nuns were founded. Vestments, incense, genuflection came back into the services. Not unnaturally, disputes arose.

There were a series of them. Often appeals were taken to the Judicial Committee of the Privy Council, which had to wrestle with very knotty problems. It handed down a line of decisions which freed clergy and laity from restraint of previous years. Cynical lawyers said of one decision in the *Essays and Reviews* case: "It dismissed Hell with Costs and deprived orthodox members of the Church of England of their last hope of eternal damnation." An earlier case was an attempt to drive from office as a heretic Dr. Hampden, the Professor of Theology at Oxford, a man who certainly did not see eye to eye with the Oxford Movement as to the meaning of the Thirty-nine Articles. Thus the courts lessened state control of the church.

The Oxford Movement had a beneficial effect in awakening the Church, both directly and in the results it had on its opposition. Liturgy improved. The connection with the past became emphasized, even to the point that the self-government of the Church revived, with the revival of the Convocations of both provinces, York and Canterbury, in 1852. Indeed, with the Lambeth Conference of 1867 the Church of England became the center of a world-wide organization partnership. But the other sides of the Church also grew more vigorous. "Low-Churchmen" continued the tradition of Protestant evangelicalism and quietly shortened their services to the legal minimum or beyond. "Broad-Churchmen," like Dr. Hampden, explored the avenues of theology and science. Scoffers might say: "High and crazy, Low and lazy, Broad and hazy." What mattered was that men cared about the Church as they had not cared in the latitudinarian eighteenth century.

The Oxford Movement was also to a slight extent a protest of landed gentlemen against the degrading influence of the Industrial Revolution on the worker. In Manchester, for example, St. Peter's church was built in the slum area to be a center where the Established Church might justify its privileged position in the state by being brought into contact with the needs of the laboring masses.

The Church of England solved the problem of serving the overseas Empire when in 1783 it allowed the consecration at Canterbury of bishops for the American Protestant Episcopal Church without demanding of them an oath of allegiance. By that, and by the consecration of a bishop of Nova Scotia in the next year, it admitted that it would consent to be in religious communion with a church outside its legal jurisdiction and that episcopal sees could be established outside England. Such sees—Montreal, Quebec, Madras, Calcutta, Sydney, Adelaide, and others—were created. Then, in the 1850's, the Synod of New Zealand was organized by Bishop Selwyn, with support from Sir George Grey. This Synod asked and secured what the American Episcopal Church had, the right to its own jurisdiction and more than three bishops, three being the canonical number necessary for the consecration of other bishops on the spot. Just as the grant of self-government drew Canada closer to England, so the grant of self-government ecclesiastically in a sense formed a link of union. Now just because there were no demands for jurisdictional control it became possible to hold, in 1867, a Lambeth Conference that brought churchmen overseas closer to England, and England closer to churchmen overseas.

One English churchman's career may show what was happening generally. Bishop Wilberforce, a son of the humanitarian William Wilberforce, was Bishop of Oxford and later of Winchester. He fought the Tractarians in the Oxford movement controversy, maintaining Low-Church interpretations. He investigated every activity that was carried on in his diocese and made his clergy energetically undertake and perform all required duties. He also helped build up the finances of the diocese through good and prudent management. He fought for and finally won a revival of Convocation of the Established Church so that the representative body of the clergy could meet and make known to the government what the church needed in the way of canonical and other reforms. Bishop Wilberforce was active in combating the growing influence of the Roman Catholic Church. He also fought against the new tendencies to interpret the scriptures in a new way that was displayed by some clergymen in the 1860's. A man like Wilberforce and the work he accomplished are sufficient proof of the renewed vigor that came into the life of the national Church in the years 1832 to 1870 and helped maintain the Church in a new and perilous era in the supreme position it had occupied in earlier days.

Roman Catholicism had a revival. It has been told how the Catholics in 1829 gained seats in Parliament. But more happened to the "Old Faith" than that. It got important new recruits and a new status. For the Oxford movement had gone far, in its *Tracts for the Times*, on the reverse of the trail the Church of England had followed in the days of Elizabeth. Attention had been focused on the intentionally vague words of consecration in the Communion Service, which could be taken in a Protestant or a Catholic sense; *Tract 90* advocated taking them in a Catholic sense. After a while, this became too much for first John Henry Newman and then Henry Edward Manning. Both entered the Roman Church; both studied for, and took, priest's orders in that Church. Later, both rose to the high office of cardinal. This was a profound shock to the devout of the Church of England, for other notable conversions followed. It was also a profound, and perhaps beneficial, shock to the Church of Rome in England. These converts, Manning especially, spurred the Roman Church to activity. This effect was officially recognized by the Pope. It had long been the custom, dating from days when a reconciliation with the Church of England had been hoped for, nominally not to appoint Roman Catholic bishops in England. Instead the bishops who functioned there held titles of extinct bishoprics in Asia Minor. In 1851, this nonsense was stopped. It hurt the English, at first. As *Punch* put it, "Little Lord John chalked up No Popery on the Wall, and then ran away." This refers to the law making it illegal to assert a Roman Catholic title to an English see. As no one dreamed of punishing Cardinal Wiseman, that saintly cleric, for calling himself the Archbishop of Westminster, the law was laughed out of existence and never enforced. Instead, in 1859, the Church of England removed from the Book of Common Prayer the thanksgivings for November 5, the dual anniversary of the discovery of the Gunpowder Plot and the landing of William of Orange in Torbay. Thus, with new blood to join the old, the Roman Catholics rose in position.

In the first half of the nineteenth century scientists such as Lyell and Faraday had, in quietly pursuing their researches, published findings that helped create an intellectual upheaval. Along with German philosophers these men speculated concerning the operation of natural laws. Generally they seemed to say that natural laws operated without divine intervention or that the laws of the universe could be explained without bringing in God. While this idea was not precisely a new one, the fact that so much scientific investigation supported this contention gave it weight. The mere statement with proof of scientific discovery and speculation was sufficient to arouse in the minds of many an eagerness for further questions concerning the composition of the universe and a necessity for restatement of principles of natural laws. In 1859 the most influential book and one certainly that did more to upset the thinking of people about man and his origin was the publication by Charles Darwin of his *Origin of Species.*

Darwin's *Origin of Species,* although not a book that caused too much controversy in the period under review, is an example of the sort of intellectual interest that educated leaders of the nation were displaying in the new world of science. Darwin's book was popular among the upper classes who had time to read such things. Its power over men's imaginations and beliefs was not shown until a later period, but it is significant that it did not hesitate to give an account of mankind that had nothing to do with the Bible stories. Darwin was recording the observations of a scientist, and in so doing he differed somewhat from the recordings of some observations on the same phenomena contained in Scripture. Darwin's book was not, however, the most controversial book of the period. The most controversial book of the time was published in 1860 and was made up of a series of essays and reviews on religious history. It was written by a group of younger clergymen and students of the Anglican faith and called *Essays and Reviews.*

In the eyes of many today nothing very bad was to be found in the *Essays and Reviews* except that it showed a point of view that was unorthodox. The reading and study of many clergymen had brought them to doubt the revelations and the word-for-word accuracy of certain portions of the Bible. They stated their doubts and suggested more logical or scientific interpretations. At once the Church of England and those clergymen and laymen everywhere who believed every word of the Bible to be inspired took up the pen and fought this heretical and dangerous trend of thought. Some of the reviewers were tried in Church courts, found guilty of departing from orthodoxy, and punished. Then the orthodox were shocked to discover that Bishop John Colenso of Natal, South Africa, had expressed many doubts concerning the historical revelation of God. In 1861 Colenso attacked the sacramental system. Of course he was tried and would have been expelled had not the Privy Council, as highest Church court, found that the lower Church courts had erred. The publication of Colenso's writings and the opinions expressed in *Essays and Reviews* furnished clear proof that the Industrial Revolution and the science of such men as Lyell and Darwin in the fields of geology and biology were having an effect upon the minds of educational leaders and thinkers. The most important effect that this criticism was having and would have increasingly was upon the masses of readers who would inevitably hear and read of the new trend in ideas and who might leave the Church or the religious sects of their fathers. In 1870 Great Britain had experienced a spiritual revival, and now was experiencing an attack on religion in the name of new ideas of revealed religion itself.

31

CONSTITUTIONAL HISTORY

1832–1874

The development of popular government through reform of the franchise is the basic constitutional fact of the years from 1832 to 1874. But that is not the whole story. Out of that change in the franchise arose other changes, not only in the relationships of Crown, Parliament, and electorate, but also in the central civil service, in local government, and in the Empire. All these changes fit together, as will be seen by first of all looking at them separately.

The general direction of constitutional growth in Great Britain had been set by the passing of the Reform Bill of 1832. No barrier of principle could withstand the force of fact. If the franchise could be altered to admit the middle classes, it could also be altered to admit other classes, if only these classes knew how to make their demands effective. For a time in the 1830's and the 1840's there was much talk about the extension of 1832 being the last step that would be made toward democracy. This did serve to counteract the demands of the Chartists. But the demands of the Chartists won attention as they were thought over after Chartism had ceased, after 1848, to be dangerous. The way the repeal of the Corn Laws had been obtained by propaganda among the lower middle classes revealed the value of the opinions held by those nonvoters. Then in the 1850's and early 1860's, measures of extension of the franchise were proposed. Four times, from 1852 on, did Lord John Russell, later Earl Russell, introduce into Parliament such measures. In 1859 the Conservatives took their turn. They conflicted with the Liberals in their conception of what made a man fit to vote, for they wanted "fancy franchises," extra votes for the possession of property or education. Neither side, however, could get a measure through to enactment as long as Lord Palmerston was alive. But when he left the scene, the question was merely how and when an extension of the franchise would take place.

The year 1866 saw Russell, now Earl Russell, and W. E. Gladstone proposing to give the vote generally speaking to those who already voted in municipal elections. This roused fears among some Liberals, and the

Conservatives came to office, to face popular demand for the extension of the vote—as shown by mass demonstrations—and parliamentary demand that it be not extended. The Conservative leaders "stole the Whigs' clothes while the Whigs were bathing," "educated their party," and "shot Niagara" by granting in 1867 just about what the Whigs had refused to grant in 1866. Then was passed the Second Reform Bill, which had the following results: In the counties the franchise qualification was lowered from £10 to £5, and for the occupiers of land to £12 annual rental. This increased the county electorate from 540,000 to 790,000. Lodgers in boroughs who occupied tenements of £10 ratable value might vote, and in deference to a custom of "compounding rates" through a landlord, one did not have to be a direct taxpayer to vote. (There was where one fancy franchise fell by the wayside.) In consequence the average voter in municipal elections could vote in parliamentary ones. But this electorate was loaded in two ways. On the one hand the borough franchise was the broader. A man who lived inside a borough could vote, whereas his neighbor outside that line could not, though he had the same property qualification. Secondly, plurality of voting was allowed and even extended. It was not impossible to have four or more votes. A man might have one vote for his university seat (Disraeli added London University and the Scottish universities to Oxford and Cambridge for representation in Parliament), one vote for the City of London, and one vote each for any property qualification he might have throughout England. Only the fact that votes must be given in person prevented a single individual in theory from voting in every constituency in the kingdom. In fact, cases of more than four votes cast are known. This transformed the English parliamentary electorate from a middle-class body to a body that contained the established members of every class, except of the working rural lower class. For while many workers did not vote—and some wealthy men did not vote because of the peculiarities of the way they held property—England now had what might be summed up as head-of-the-household suffrage. A later Reform Bill, the Third, of 1884, would equalize rural and urban rights of voting, but not till 1918 would plural voting end and true universal suffrage exist. At that there would be an age differential between men and women until 1928, since before 1928 men could vote at the age of twenty-one but women had to be twenty-five.

With Reform came Redistribution. Small boroughs that remained "rotten" lost their votes to large towns. Fifty-two seats were thus distributed, twenty-five going to the counties, nineteen to boroughs, one to London University, two to the Scottish universities, and five to Scotland.

With this change in the electorate came a change in the position of the House of Lords. In the eighteenth century the House of Lords had on the whole agreed with the House of Commons, for the simple reason that certain influential members of the House of Lords chose a significant proportion of the members of the House of Commons. But with the filling of the Lords by Pitt's Tory creations, and with the swing to conservatism with a small "c" of the upper classes, the relationships of the two Houses changed. More and more the Lords formed a pro-Conservative check on Commons. At first this was counterbalanced by the fact that the Duke of Wellington used—as it was put—to say, "About face, my Lords," to his followers and give support to government measures whatever the government was. But in the case of Don Pacifico in 1850, life peerages in 1856, the "taxes on knowledge" of 1861, and the abolition of purchase in the Army of 1872, Lords thwarted the will of the people as expressed in Commons. Though in each case except for the life peerages Commons finally had its way— and even did get life peerages for judges—this omened ill for the future. The failure to allow the creation of life peerages prevented a sound solution of the problem of conflicts between the Houses, such as caused the 1911 crisis. For if the party in power could have added to the upper House members who would not have passed on their peerages to their children, it would have been possible to remedy the party balance without mortgaging the future.

The Crown, constitutionally, is part of Parliament. Its relationships with the rest of Parliament changed, too, in this period. At the start William IV inherited some though not all of his brother George IV's unpopularity and also an acknowledged right to dismiss ministers if he so chose. This he did, in November, 1834. When he died, in 1837, and was succeeded by the Princess Victoria, the new Queen became popular. It is true that there was a period, after the death of her husband, the Prince Consort, when she lost popularity from the seclusion in which she lived. But, like her grandfather, George III, she first caught the imagination of her people and then won their affection. Thanks to her the monarchy became a powerful unifying force. On the other hand she lost her power of dismissal. It is true that in 1839 her desire to keep friends in her court, coupled with Sir Robert Peel's fears that such friends might unduly influence her, led to the Bedchamber Crisis, when the Melbourne Government, though defeated over the Jamaica Prisons Bill, stayed in office out of loyalty to the nineteen-year-old girl Queen. It is true that she successfully ordered Lord John Russell to dismiss Lord Palmerston from the Foreign Office, in 1851. It is true that as late as 1894 she successfully preferred Lord Rosebery to Sir William Harcourt as Prime Minister. But this power of choice was residual, steadily diminished as time went on, and became reserved for the emergency breaking of deadlocks. (Such a use, some believe, George V made of his residual powers in 1931, when Ramsay Macdonald went to Buckingham Palace to resign as Prime Minister and came back still in office.) Eventually, as Walter Bagehot's *English Constitution* has put it, the Crown has the right to object, to be consulted, and to be advised about policies, but the policies that are adopted in the Crown's name originate with the Cabinet and the House of Commons.

Internally, Parliament retained some of its eighteenth-century characteristics but was divided into new, nineteenth-century parties. Historically, it is true, the Whigs remained in existence, still centering socially at Brooks's Club, still faithful to the memory of Charles James Fox. But they were no longer in the forefront of change. Technically, the Tory party ceased to exist, being transformed into the Conservative party, though their enemies still call the Conservatives "Tories," for in fact many old Tories continued to sit as Conservatives. But the change of name meant a real change in attitude. The Conservatives were now ready to accept change, even to make changes. This became the party of businessmen as well as of landowners. However, in 1846, loosely speaking, landowners split from businessmen, and the Conservatives were divided into the majority of the party and a Liberal-Conservative or Peelite wing, so called because this wing stayed loyal to Sir Robert Peel. But the balance of power now sometimes fell to three new groups, Liberals, Radicals, and Irish. The Liberals were the middle-class members, usually from urban boroughs, who wanted to go ahead with the removal of government restrictions on business and trade. They were the free-trade group. The Radicals, who got their name because they wanted to get to the root of things—*radix* in Latin—had a program of extending the suffrage and ending special privileges. The Irish wanted to free Ireland from many burdens—landlord control, alien Church, and by repeal of the Union, alien rule. Consequently this was a period, to the very end, of group rule.

From 1832 to 1841, with one short intermission, Whigs, Liberals, Radicals, and Irish in the House of Commons kept a Whig Cabinet in power. From 1841 to the split of 1846, a Conservative majority did rule the House of Commons and support a Conservative Cabinet. But then the repeal of the Corn Laws split Peelite from Conservative. From 1846 right up to 1859, the previous pattern returns—Peelite, Whig, Liberal, Radical, and Irish keep in power Whig Cabinets that hold, for a sop, perhaps a Radical or a Liberal. There intervene two Conservative Cabinets, 1852–1853 and 1858–1859, supported by Peelites and independents, and a coalition Cabinet of Peelites and Whigs, the Aberdeen Cabinet of 1853 to 1855. Only in 1859 is a united Liberal party formed, and it falls apart in 1866, when its right-wing votes it out of office on the Reform issue. The key to Cabinet formation lies in this: Of the four liberal parties, only the Whigs could get support in the House of Lords; therefore Liberals, Irish, and Radicals had to let them take the Cabinet posts. Conversely, only Conservatives could get a majority in the House of Commons; therefore the Tories in the Lords had to let the Cabinets they supported be filled by the most liberally minded of their party.

Seeing these facts and the consequent relationship between Cabinet and Parliament, Walter Bagehot wrote his *English Constitution* which is the classic exposition of the workings of English responsible government. It paints a true picture of the role of Parliament in these years and of the way the Cabinet both led and obeyed the House of Commons. For throughout this period there remained enough independent voters in Parliament to make it necessary for the party leaders to defer to their judgment on certain points. Yet a new era was coming, where the final say would be held not by the independent member of Commons but by the voter at large. More and more political parties acted as units in Parliament in order to appeal to the voter outside. This began when Peel issued his Tamworth Manifesto in hopes that its appeal would persuade voters all over England, not merely in the safe borough of Tamworth, to support the Tory party he had newly christened Conservative. It intensified, when the Anti–Corn Law League outside Parliament gave support to those who in Parliament gave support to the free-trade ideas of Cobden and Bright. Thus this was a transitional age from the special interest groups of the eighteenth century to the cohesive parties of the twentieth century. Already organizations grew up. As the Whigs and Tories had met socially at Brooks's and White's clubs, now the Liberals and Conservatives combined society and political business at the Reform and the Carlton. But there were still "family seats," like Hertford where Whig Cowpers strove with Tory Cecils; it was still possible to buy membership in Commons if one went quietly enough to the right place with enough money. This was an age of transition in parliamentary methods as well as in the franchise.

Part of this transition was the growth of the Cabinet. As Bagehot points out, it became the true executive of the nation. Cabinet traditions crystallized. Eighteenth-century innovations became "constitutional conventions." Documents that its members were supposed to read were sent to it and to the sovereign in the famous "red boxes," and young private secretaries proudly exhibited the "Cabinet key" on their watch chains as they took out and digested the material for their employers. One Prime Minister, Melbourne, legend relates, as a Cabinet meeting broke up, gave the classic example of Cabinet solidarity by asking: "Is it to be lower corn or isn't it? It doesn't matter much which, but we must all say the same thing." Cabinet secrecy remained vital; only the Prime Minister might report to the Crown what was decided, which sometimes led to bitter subsequent arguments with his colleagues. Cohesion was the force which made it possible to keep together a majority in Parliament. "We must say the same thing" became the rule of collective responsibility for Cabinet members.

Cabinet effectiveness increased in Parliament as the Cabinet and the minor ministers guided the debates. "Government business" took up more and more of the House's time. More and more the "Whips," who doubled as "Junior Lords of the Treasury," watched over the voting habits of members. If members did not obey the voting instructions, called "Whips"— especially if they did not obey the vital demand for their votes, the so-called "three-line Whip," the length of which emphasized its seriousness— then disciplinary action was taken. The old forms of discipline of the eighteenth century were over. No longer were pensions and sinecure offices given as bribes. But minor government officials were automatically dismissed for failing to keep ministerial solidarity, and ordinary members found that failing to vote with the party lost the support that could come from central party organizations. That support was not to be neglected. Experts on registration could put favorable voters on the electoral rolls and could challenge unfavorable voters. As voting was still public, everyone knew which was which. More and more the Whips' offices became bases of extra funds and of propaganda material. Thus the party machine grew strong, as in the famous case when a dying and insane Whig, in 1839, was wheeled through the division lobby to gain part of a two-vote majority that kept the Melbourne Government in office. Here are signs of the transition from the semi-independence of members in the early 1800's, 1810's, and 1820's to the strict party voting of today.

As can be seen, the Treasury was the guiding office of the administration. This had been true since Godolphin was Lord Treasurer, from 1701 to 1710, and when Robert Walpole was First Lord of the Treasury from 1721 to 1742. New methods, however, were used. Besides the use of the Junior Lords as party Whips, there was essential control because the Treasury must pass on all expenditures. In the larger detail of administration it gave orders to the other departments. More than that, it controlled appointments. In 1853 Sir George Trevelyan, with Indian experience, and Sir Stafford Northcote wrote the often-referred-to Civil Service Report. They recommended that the policies of competitive examination used in India and by the Poor Law Commission guide all future appointments. Thus, eventually, the permanent Secretary of the Treasury became the Head of the Civil Service. For the Treasury conducted examinations, to ensure qualified men getting office. It is sometimes alleged that the Treasury avoided its own rule that three must compete by having two competitors, the so-called "Treasury idiots," to put its choice at the top of the list. But on the other hand, the cream of the graduates of the universities gravitated to the Home Civil Service competition. The division of the Civil Service into three grades, with immediate responsibility being given to First Division candidates who were successful, gave England, after 1853, a high quality of administration.

In the period under review a whole new structure of government grew up, from top to bottom. Problems were investigated not merely by committees of the Houses of Commons or Lords but by royal commissions. Here is a technique of securing expert advice that began with the Commission on the Poor Law of 1832 and the Commission on Municipal Corporations of 1833 and goes on to the present. Local government bodies sprang up, of two types. First there were the municipal corporations. Many of these, such as Manchester, were entirely new bodies; Manchester was created in 1837 under the terms of the Municipal Corporations Act of 1835. But these boroughs, old or new, had the traditional independence of all outside authority that goes back through the Glorious Revolution to the Middle Ages. They ran their own Watching and Lighting and Sanitation Committees, did their own planning, and, if possible, had their own courts. Their charter form resembled the American city-manager plan, for all executive responsibility went through the City Clerk, the mayor being merely the leading member of the City Council. But besides these independent bodies there were the dependent ones. These were the new feature in English local government.

It was the New Poor Law that created the chief of these bodies, the Poor Law Union. Poor Law Unions sprang up for practical reasons. If parishes had to have workhouses to enforce the New Poor Law, they had to combine to get workhouses economically. So the more than 15,000 parishes of England became the natural rivals of the benches of justices of the peace when new duties were assigned. Registration of births and deaths, vaccinations, road building, correction of tax assessments—all these and many more duties fell to the officials of the Boards of Guardians. But here came the new, or rather the revived, constitutional situation. Those officials were supposed to obey the orders of the Poor Law Commissioners in Somerset House. Thus Somerset House obtained, as its enemies complained, powers resembling those of Star Chamber in the days of the Tudor and early Stuart Privy Council. Here was a case where locally elected bodies did not have the obedience of their servants.

However, whatever the legal theory, the practice was that the Poor Law Guardians were country local government. The assistant poor law commissioners did not have the time to enforce implicit obedience throughout nearly 600 unions. They had to rule by persuasion. Here is the key to the new English local government. More and more of it was responsible to someone at Whitehall; Poor Law Board, Board of Health, Local Government Board, Education Committee of the Privy Council, even occasionally the Home Office. (It would not be truly British for the Home Office to play a major part in home affairs. The Home Office concerns itself with prisons and advice about police.) But the chain of practical command was through the itinerant civil servant: an assistant poor law commissioner, an inspector of prisons or schools or sanitation, a man—or, in a few cases, a woman—chosen after competitive examination for high qualities of mind and personality. The itinerant civil servant suggested, he did not command. Often he did not even suggest; if he was adept at his job, the local government body thought it, not he, had taken the initiative. In a crisis, and only in a crisis, there was an iron hand in the velvet glove and the legal powers of the central government were brought into play. Thus it is not too much to say that the tactful, persuasive Home civil servant in this period became part of the unwritten British constitution. A century later, the same type of man would make the nationalization of industry feasible, by supplying the necessary trustworthy, efficient management group.

Two conflicting tendencies are noted in the years 1832 to 1870 regarding the role of administrative services in the government of the nation. The prevailing political philosophy was one of *laissez faire*. This meant reducing to a minimum the amount of control exercised over the individual by any government office or bureau. This sentiment ran counter to demands that bureaus be established and reforms instituted that would put in the hands of the central government the execution of certain badly needed reforms. Neither the pure freedom demanded by laissez-faire philosophy nor the efficiency desired through centralization was quite achieved in these years. It will be noted, however, that the demands for good government were swinging the practice of administration away from *laissez faire* and into line with the ideas of administrative centralization and therefore of more control by the state of the individual's activities. Constitutional practice was therefore more apt to be that of centralization of power through many executive agencies dependent for their existence on a local or national scale upon the wishes of the voters. Thus the nationalization of service and industries of the twentieth century was foreshadowed.

In another chapter details will be given of the evolution of the Empire. But here one report and four pieces of legislation should be mentioned for their significance in the over-all constitution. The report, obviously, is the Durham Report, which brought back across the Atlantic to the British the Canadian doctrine of "responsible government," the idea that local administration should be responsible to local legislatures. The legislation may be divided into two parts: that increasing freedom overseas, and that decreasing it. Two laws have the first effect: the British North America Act of 1867, which put into legal form the deliberations of the Charlottetown and Quebec Conventions and thus created the Dominion of Canada, and the Colonial Laws Validity Act of 1865, which freed colonial legislation from petty review in English courts. The laws having the opposite tendency are the pair passed in 1843, the British Settlements Act and the Foreign Jurisdiction Act, and the Government of India Act, of 1858. By the first two the Colonial Office or occasionally the Foreign Office or War Office got the power to rule by executive decrees in colonies or in parts of the world where the British government had actual rule though was technically not sovereign. By the last one, the East India Company ceased to rule in India, which became a direct possession of Great Britain— and therefore was managed by a Secretary of State with almost exactly the same powers and duties as his predecessor, the President of the Board of Control.

One of the more obvious characteristics of the British constitution is its perpetual and gradual change as current institutions change. It does not require amendment, because it is not formally written. It requires reinterpretation as courts of law and lawmakers change their ideas. In this period of reform the meaning of the constitution and its institutions such as Parliament, the courts, and the function of the Cabinet underwent important alterations. The theory of the balanced order that had intrigued Blackstone was very definitely replaced by the ideas of Bentham that institutions should change or at least serve society so that they could be useful. After 1832 the task of developing and guiding the Empire fell to those who believed in the reform and growth of the constitution in the direction of making it efficient and subject always to the expressed will of the electorate. One may say that the constitutional theorists were moving in the direction of regarding British institutions as being worthy of preservation only if some good for the people could come of them. The constitution was democratic in this sense.

32

POLITICS

1832–1874

As the bonfires burned out and the bells celebrating the people's victory were hushed, everyone asked the same questions about the new House of Commons of 1832. Years of strain, rioting, and heart searching had convinced the nation of the need for electoral reform. Now that it had been won, what would happen? Three questions were in the public's mind: Would social and economic chaos follow the reform? Would the Whigs lead Great Britain ably and surely along untrod paths? Would the condition of the people really be improved by the reform? The answers were to be determined by the new classes now come into their political maturity through the grant of the suffrage. The next forty-two years, making up our period, gave decided answers: to the first question, "No"; to the second, a rather soft "Yes"; to the third, a decided "Yes." The body that gave those answers was the Reformed Parliament. Therefore it will pay, for a moment, to observe the characteristics of that Parliament as a whole, of the parties and leaders in it, and of the electorate that chose it. To do this will simplify the story which this chapter will relate.

In procedure the new Reformed Parliament, which first met on January 29, 1833, resembled its predecessors. It did take a month or so for the Speaker to teach some new members like Cobbett how to behave. But the old routine was taken up.

It was outside Parliament, more than in Parliament, that the Reform Bill made a change. The new constituencies were of a size favorable to concentration on the merits of individual candidates. They were of a size that made bribery not impossible but far more difficult than before 1832. Yet they were not so large as to prevent candidates being personally known to the electors. This had two results. Nationally organized political agitation became possible. The two great examples of this were the Anti–Corn Law League and the Chartist movement. Here the general public could influence votes. On the other hand, in seats where contests were close, care in the registration of favorable voters and the striking from the rolls of unfavorable ones paid heavy dividends. It was by this "battle of regis-

428

tration" that the Conservative party would so quickly regain importance. With these things in mind, let us turn to the actual political events and see how it was that the Reformed Parliament answered the questions with which this chapter started. It will be found that the Whig Liberals, as the instrument of government of the middle class, deserve credit for much beneficial change and for bringing England through economic crises into prosperity such as had never been known before.

The short period from the summer of 1832 to November, 1834, is a sort of interlude, in which two noble figures, Lord Grey and Lord Althorp, leave the center of the political stage, after seeing to it that the work of Reform is well begun. In 1833 and 1834, the Whig Cabinet over which Grey presided and the overwhelmingly Whig House of Commons which Althorp led passed much beneficial legislation. Slavery was abolished in 1833, the abolition to be effective in 1834. This won general approbation in Great Britain but caused problems overseas, as will be narrated later. In 1833, too, the Bank of England and the East India Company were re-chartered, with improvements in their efficiency, notably in the publication of the Bank's accounts and the introduction of civil service examinations for India. A Factory Act was passed, the first to be enforced by centrally appointed inspectors. The thorny problem of poor relief, highlighted by the "Last Laborers' Revolt of 1830," had already been dealt with by referral to a royal commission in 1832, with instructions to propose a solution. In 1834 the commission's proposal was passed into law, with, as has been related, important social, economic, and constitutional effects. Here was the first outstanding use of a device later frequently employed, sometimes to get expert guidance on a problem, sometimes to shelve a problem to a more suitable time.

But these successes were outbalanced by Irish failure. For any reform of the Irish Church which the Grey Cabinet might propose would certainly be too little for the Irish and the Radicals, and too much for the House of Lords. Furthermore, any struggle would expose the internal weaknesses of that Cabinet. In 1834 that was what happened. Two right-wing Whigs, Lord Stanley and Sir James Graham, left the party and joined the Conservatives because they felt the Cabinet was going too far in redistribution of Church property. In June, the recriminations that ensued caused Lord Grey to resign. He was only too glad to retire from office. He was old, he had fulfilled his pledge to bring about reform, he had taken office only from a sense of a duty to be done. In his place came Lord Melbourne, the Whig with whom, after Lord Grey, King William felt most at home. Then in November, 1834, Lord Althorp's father died, and Lord Althorp had to go to the House of Lords as Lord Spencer, being now a real peer and not merely the bearer of a courtesy title as the heir to an earldom. He, too, was glad to retire from politics. Like Grey, he preferred the role of an elder statesman, giving advice when needed but enjoying the country life that both men loved, far from the political arena.

William IV, it is believed with the sympathy of Melbourne, took the opportunity to dismiss the Whigs. Now came an important electoral reversal, perhaps comparable to that consequent upon the appointment of William Pitt the Younger as Premier half a century before, almost to the month. William IV sent for Sir Robert Peel, then vacationing in Rome. For three weeks, to the country's vast amusement, the Duke of Wellington technically held all the Cabinet offices, while Peel journeyed back. Then Peel formed an administration, dissolved Parliament, and introduced a new political device, the party manifesto. To the electors of the borough of Tamworth, who were going to elect him anyway, he issued an address. This Tamworth Manifesto was intended to win support for Conservative candidates in other constituencies. It did. The vast Whig-Liberal majority was cut down to a little over 100 (273 Conservatives, 380 Whig Liberals). Peel even held office for a while, on sufferance, when the new Parliament met. But soon an arrangement was made, the so-called Lichfield House Compact, by which O'Connell agreed with certain Whig leaders to oust Peel and support them. Russell then became Leader of the House, in a second Melbourne Cabinet.

This Melbourne Government lasted from 1835 to 1841, but it made heavy political weather. It was always on the edge of defeat, for it was always in danger of losing support either from the Radicals and the Irish or from those Whigs who felt that the Radicals and the Irish were pushing it too far. However, the abilities of two men, Melbourne and Russell, pulled it through. Melbourne was truly worldly wise. A roué as well as a sound New Testament scholar, an advanced Whig in early youth, then a Canningite, then a very, very moderate Whig in old age, he might appear a cynic, but he knew how to handle men. Indeed, when a young queen came to the throne, he was to show he even knew how to manage one woman. Lord John Russell was really able and cockily confident. Of him the Rev. Sydney Smith once said that he was ready, at a moment's notice, "to operate for the stone or command the Channel fleet." In the Cabinet and the House of Lords Melbourne smoothed matters over; as Leader of the House of Commons Lord John pushed boldly and effectively ahead. Their accomplishments were notable. They sent to Ireland perhaps her best ruler when under English domination, Thomas Drummond. As undersecretary in Dublin Castle but practical head of the Irish administration, Drummond was able to keep order without that constant curse of Ireland, "Coercion Acts" giving extraordinary powers to the government. Acting on the advice of a royal commission, they gave municipal reform to England, to Scotland, and after a battle with the House of Lords, to Ireland. A tithe commission was set up that began the process of straightening out that vexatious way of paying for the Established Church. Penny Postage, a Registration Act, a County Constabulary Act, an Irish Poor Relief Act all were part of the great business of improving British government. To do this took political skill, for when William IV died in 1837, and for the last time the death of a sovereign caused a general election, the Conservative minority rose to practical equality with the Whigs. Furthermore, as vacancies occurred, more and more Conservatives entered Parliament by by-elections. Indeed, in 1839, over the Jamaica Prisons Bill, when the Whigs un-Whiggishly tried to suspend the Jamaica constitution, they were temporarily put out of office. But they came back because of the loyalty to each other of Lord Melbourne and Queen Victoria. For Sir Robert Peel, fearing that Whig Ladies of the Bedchamber might work against his interests as Abigail Hill Masham had worked against Marlborough's in Queen Anne's court, demanded that Victoria dismiss them and replace them with Conservatives. Constitutionally he was right; humanly he was tactless. Then the Queen begged Melbourne to keep office, and he chivalrously accepted her request. Here we come to Melbourne's great achievement, the education he gave to Queen Victoria by acting as if he were her private secretary.

For when an eighteen-year-old girl was roused in the early morning to find the Archbishop of Canterbury at the door and was told that her uncle had died and she was Queen, it was more than just a sentimentally dramatic event. Melbourne was given a chance to establish sound relations between Crown and Cabinet. The old roué—who twice in recent years had had to defend his name in a divorce trial—showed other sides of his nature, those which made him the patient father of an imbecile son and a keen Biblical scholar. He imbued the Queen with the Whig ideal of correct constitutional conduct, that the Crown must, after explanation and perhaps revision, accept the "constitutional advice" given by the Cabinet, as long as that Cabinet had the support of the House of Commons. Thus, though this ideal was not perfectly lived up to by Queen Victoria, drastic royal action like William IV's dismissal of the Whigs in 1834 was ended. Furthermore, Melbourne, perhaps on the rule that a poacher makes the best gamekeeper, taught the Queen's court decorous behavior. Thus the Crown rose above party. Finally Melbourne arranged a royal marriage that was also a love match. In 1840 Prince Albert of Saxe-Coburg-Gotha married the Queen. On Melbourne's retirement from office in 1841, it was Prince Albert who guided her into less "constitutional" paths. But Melbourne's great work was never undone. Of all British statesmen it is he who most deserves credit for the present unique position of the British monarchy. Under Melbourne, from 1839 to 1841, affairs of state more or less drifted. The Whig-Liberals sent out the Durham Commission to Canada and presented its great report to the Parliament, after *The Times* had forced their hands by publishing it anyway. This is about all of importance that the political situation let them accomplish.

These years saw the growth of two extraparliamentary movements. Chartism and the Anti–Corn Law League, which have been described earlier. Here two political aspects should be noted. Chartism, as a potentially revolutionary force, was quelled by the putting down of the Newport riots, of 1839; as a stimulus to thought it remained, to have later results. The Anti–Corn Law League, founded in 1838, was a great educational movement in the electorate, which would make free trade an article of faith for the majority of Britons until 1931. Here emerge two powerful political figures, Richard Cobden and John Bright. These two men toured the land, Cobden arguing and Bright orating. Their message was simple. If "corn" were not taxed, the poor man's bread would cost less and wages would buy more. If this meant that England must buy her food abroad, what of it? These men were pacifists; they believed that if England manufactured goods and other lands grew food, war would become impossible, because each nation would be too dependent on the other to want to fight. Their attack on the Corn Laws was part of an attack on all trade restrictions. Gradually, this doctrine got attention. Finally, in the spring of 1841, the Whig Liberals took a plunge, since by-elections had cut their majority down to less than ten. They came out for a reduction in the "corn" duties. On this they were defeated and called a general election.

The elections of 1841 were hard fought. In some places they were won by bribery of the crudest sort, both parties buying votes openly. In some ways, the old order died hard. The Conservatives won a majority and, unlike the Whig-Liberals, did not depend upon the Irish or any other group for power.

The Peel Government had conservation as its aim. It made few changes in institutions, except for its skillful reform of the Bank of England in 1844, and spent its time modifying and improving changes which had been made. But it had a weakness that was eventually fatal; its leaders were in advance of their followers. Most of the "backbenchers," as the rank and file in the House of Commons are called from the seats they occupy, were country squires who loved their way of life and believed that it was the Corn Laws that made that life economically possible. A few were idealists. The curious figure of Benjamin Disraeli appeared among them, a faithful Christian proud of his Jewish ancestry, a novelist, and a practical dreamer. He, with Lord John Manners, headed a "Young England movement" which believed that the "old nobility" should lead in social reform. This doctrine Disraeli would preach, in various ways, all his life. Eventually he would imbue the Conservative party with it and thus make it possible for that party to exist in an age of the welfare state. These men would follow where Peel led. The squires dutifully, the Young Englanders gladly, supported the passage of the Mines Act of 1842 that kept women and children above ground and the Factory Act of 1844 that kept them out of the factories at night. But Peel and his team of able administrators went further than their followers realized. For Peel recognized, as had Pitt before him, that the removal of tariff duties can cause an over-all increase in revenue. He therefore took a bold step. He introduced an income tax, as a temporary measure to balance the budget and end the series of Whig deficits, and repealed duties on over 1,000 items. Annually, he had to debate with Cobden and Bright whether this was merely practical administrative improvement or in fact an acceptance of their free-trade theories. These debaters won their argument with an honest man. Finally, so the story goes, in March, 1845, Cobden made a powerful speech. Along the Conservative benches ran a murmur, "Peel, Peel," calling for the Prime Minister to reply. But Peel crumpled the notes for his speech saying, "Those may answer him who can," and a subordinate minister rose instead. That summer Ireland solved the free-trade question for England.

Ireland was suffering from overpopulation and neglect. It had more mouths than it could feed. Drummond had died; his successors at Dublin Castle had not his skill. Agrarian outrage mounted and had to be met with "Coercion Acts." O'Connell was attempting to secure repeal of the Union. His "Repeal Rent" was paying for a great agitation. Behind him loomed the semirevolutionary Young Ireland movement that did not have his distaste for an appeal to force. O'Connell's imprisonment for sedition, though reversed by the House of Lords, merely encouraged extremists to take his place. Though Lord Devon's royal commission in 1845 reported distressing conditions and recommended legal protection to tenants, nothing was done to pass the needed laws. If famine should strike Ireland, the consequences could be terrible. In July, 1845, came "the rains that rained the Corn Laws away." In Ireland potatoes, the staple diet of the country, rotted. In England wheat did not grow. Famine decimated Ireland. By death and emigration population dropped from 8,300,000 to 6,600,000 between 1845 and 1851. To stop famine the Corn Laws had to be suspended and foreign food imported tax free, to feed the starving Irish. Peel determined never to reimpose them.

Politically, the proper step was to resign. This Peel did in December, 1845, telling the Queen to send for Lord John Russell. But "Lord John passed back the poisoned chalice." He well knew that whatever government proposed permanent repeal would earn the undying hatred of the country gentlemen of England, and he preferred that Peel stay in office. He did so, with all his Cabinet except Lord Stanley. Therefore, with Liberal and Irish votes along with those of his ministers, Peel moved to end the Corn Laws. Leaderless, the back-bench protectionists formed a party waiting for a chief to come. Two chiefs did. Lord George Bentinck, hitherto famous for his dramatic efforts to make racing respectable, poured out streams of indignation on Peel. Behind him, advising and coaxing, stood Benjamin Disraeli. These men lost their fight. Peel put the repeal of the Corn Laws through Commons; Wellington ordered the Lords to put it through, and they obeyed. But then Disraeli and Bentinck got revenge. The moment the bill had passed the Lords, they joined with the Whig-Liberals and the Irish to drive Peel from office. Russell came in, to be given a thin majority by the general election of 1847.

An important political and even diplomatic result of the famine was the creation of an Irish overseas community, devoted to redressing what it considered the wrongs of the mother country. Memories of economic and religious oppression mingled with political and patriotic memories to spread doctrines of Irish freedom through the United States and the British colonies, wherever exiled Irishmen and Irishwomen went. Meanwhile, in a short-lived "Union of the North and South," a few Irish M.P.'s after O'Connell's death created an Irish party to work for long overdue land reforms. This broke up in 1854.

Now comes a period of political doldrums, marked by the rise of a new figure, Lord Palmerston. The Russell Cabinet carried on routine. With Irish support—weakened by the death of O'Connell in 1847—and Radical support, it could just hold its own against the Conservatives, whom Disraeli led after Lord George Bentinck's death in 1848. The small band of Peelites or Liberal Conservatives wavered from side to side, often adding undependable votes to Russell's majorities. After Peel died in 1850, this group began slowly to break up, most of them eventually joining the Liberals. Now that Cobden had made free trade popular in the electorate, the remainders of the protective system were swept away. The Navigation Acts were repealed. Other reforms were carried, such as the Clauses Act which enabled boroughs to add to their powers, and the Board of Health Act of 1848, which set up a central supervisory authority for sanitation.

In 1848 the government kept order in London remarkably well at the last Chartist demonstration. A "monster petition" to Parliament was presented without the rioting that many feared might break out and lead to a revolution such as took place on the Continent. But Ireland did see a revolt. The actual fighting took place in "Widow McCormack's cabbage garden" and consisted of policemen's arresting Smith O'Brien, a Protestant landlord. But had not ringleaders of the Young Ireland movement been arrested in time, it could have been more serious.

In 1851 there was a last outburst of "No Popery" when the Pope gave English titles to Catholic bishops, and the foolish Ecclesiastical Titles Bill which forbade this was passed and then never enforced.

Foreign affairs now entered politics with a vengeance. In 1851 came the

Don Pacifico affair, details of which are given in a subsequent chapter. In it Palmerston was called to account for protecting an alleged British subject by a naval intervention in Greece. Till he spoke, the issue was in doubt. When he sat down, he had carried the House with him, in a burst of patriotism. For that the Queen and Prince Albert [1] got revenge in 1852. They ordered Russell to dismiss Palmerston when he had imprudently sent approbation of Louis Napoleon Bonaparte's *coup d'état* in Paris. "Pam" bided his time and had his "tit for tat with Johnny Russell." On a militia bill, the Russell government was defeated. The Queen sent for Stanley, now Lord Derby, as the leader of the largest party. Derby and Disraeli had a hard time finding Cabinet members. Many untried men had to be sworn for the Privy Council. So unknown were they that the deaf Duke of Wellington was heard to ask "Who? Who?" as each name was called.

This "Who, Who" Cabinet tried to hold office by calling a general election. That caused a Conservative gain, but not enough. For Disraeli, as Chancellor of the Exchequer, was not a good financier. However, he settled the free-trade question for many years by announcing that protection was not only dead but damned. A Peelite, William Ewart Gladstone, ripped his Budget up and down. The Derby-Disraeli Ministry went out. In its place came a coalition, the Aberdeen Government, in which a half-Peelite Cabinet ruled with Peelite and Liberal support, Gladstone being Chancellor of the Exchequer and Russell being Leader of the House. This was an able Cabinet, which ruled badly. In 1854 it stumbled into the Crimean War with Russia and bungled it so badly that within a year it was out of office. For when a Radical, J. A. Roebuck, proposed an investigation, Russell deserted his colleagues, resigned, and voted for the investigation. Now Palmerston came into his own. The Queen and the Prince had kept him out of the Foreign Office; now they had to let him be Prime Minister. "Pam" won the war and became immensely popular with the electorate. Then in 1857 he protected the British flag in China in the case of the schooner, or lorcha, *Arrow*. As there were grave and justified doubts about the *Arrow's* rights to fly the Union Jack, Bright and Cobden carried a vote of censure on Palmerston. Palmerston turned round, called a general election, and drove Cobden and Bright from Parliament. But he soon was forced to resign office, in the Orsini bomb case. For proposing a law against plotting in England to cause revolts in foreign countries, "Pam" was defeated, and a second Derby-Disraeli Cabinet formed. This held a general election, gained a few seats, and was driven out. For in 1859 Palmerston called a meeting of Whigs and Liberals, which founded the Liberal party. He returned to power and continued to have Gladstone pass good budgets and himself pass no reforms. Finally, in 1865, aged eighty-

[1] Prince Albert was not made Prince Consort until 1857.

one, the jaunty old gentleman died, and for the second time Russell, now in the Upper House as an Earl, became Prime Minister.

It would be wrong to conclude from this account that the 1850's and early 1860's were years of inactivity. They are marked by one great administrative action and important legislation. To the credit of the Aberdeen Cabinet is the Civil Service Commission of the years 1852 and 1853 and the administrative action which put into effect the new civil service policy. During these years there were many useful pieces of minor remedial legislation and some major ones. In 1855 the Palmerston Government separated the War and Colonial Ministries. In 1858 the second Derby-Disraeli Cabinet passed the Government of India Act. In 1867 the third Derby-Disraeli Cabinet took over a draft from the Liberals and passed the British North America Act. The great Chancellors of the Exchequer of the time, W. E. Gladstone and Sir George Cornewall Lewis, by their skillfully drafted budgets, made the middle-class electorate aware what benefits could come from planning taxation with care and forethought. In 1861 a constitutional device was evolved. When the House of Lords in 1860 refused to repeal the "taxes on knowledge," this repeal was the next year incorporated in an all-inclusive budget and thus pushed through. For the Lords dared not throw out the whole budget, and by constitutional convention they might not amend it.

Perhaps more important than these things is the fact that this was a seedtime of ideas. John Stuart Mill was writing those books which brought the ideas of the age into focus, especially his essay *On Liberty*. In Parliament the few Radicals were proposing specific reforms. Everyone recognized that someday there would be a Second Reform Bill and some sort of extension of the franchise. In the self-governing boroughs, a lowermiddle-class and working-class electorate had gained practice in selfgovernment. Rural Boards of Guardians, too, had been learning their jobs. Only "Pam" with his magic hold on the electorate held back change. With his death, it came with a rush. Russell, as the chapter on Constitutional History has pointed out, had four times tried to extend the parliamentary suffrage. In 1866 he and Gladstone, who had succeeded Palmerston as Leader of the House, tried a fifth time, while outside Parliament John Bright rallied public opinion.

But when Gladstone's proposals came to be debated, it appeared that there were Liberals who honestly feared wider suffrage. Spokesman for them was Robert Lowe. In New South Wales, Lowe had fought to gain the franchise for the "ten-pound householders"; in England he fought to prevent its going beyond them. Bright sneered at him, comparing his following to the discontented who, according to the Bible, rallied against King David in the Cave of Adullam. The speeches of Lowe changed the balance of power. They put Russell and Gladstone out of office, put in in their place Derby and Disraeli. Promptly the people of England took a hand. A huge meeting was called in Hyde Park, England's home of free speech. When the police tried to prevent it, the mob pulled down the park railings and held the meeting. Since no one wanted to engage in repression, this made it clear that there would have to be some sort of Reform Bill.

Here Disraeli saw an opportunity, since to keep office his followers would accept amendments in a Reform Bill that they would reject if they were the Opposition. He introduced a Reform Bill and let Gladstone and the Liberals rewrite it. Steadily, twisting and turning, a measure was hammered out that went further than that which Robert Lowe had defeated. Disraeli truly called it educating his party. The ethics of this may be argued; its efficacy cannot. For not only did Disraeli get his party the credit of passing a popular measure instead of the discredit of fighting against it, he ensured that the House of Lords would not throw the bill out. How could Conservative peers go back on a measure their party had drafted and put through Commons? In vain Lowe thundered about betrayal. In vain one Conservative leader, Lord Robert Cecil—whom we will see later as the Marquis of Salisbury—resigned office in shame at Disraeli's actions. Under Conservative auspices the Second Reform Bill became law. At last Disraeli reached the top of the tree—for Derby had retired from office—and became not only Prime Minister but the man responsible for giving the parliamentary vote to the municipal voter.[1] But Disraeli did not stay in office long. He might outwit the Liberals into doing their work for them over the Second Reform Bill. But Gladstone soon countered. He passed resolutions through Commons favoring the disestablishment of the Church in Ireland. Disraeli had to oppose this, for the Conservatives were the "Church and King" party. Therefore, as soon as the new registers were ready, a general election was called. At these elections of 1868 the people recognized their true benefactor and said, "Thank you, Mr. Gladstone." Disraeli took one more shrewd step. He resigned office without meeting Parliament. Thus he showed that the Conservative party felt that the new electorate was sovereign and bowed to its will.

Though the first Gladstone Cabinet of the years from 1868 to 1874 came after the Second Reform Bill, it forms part of this period of the First Reform Bill because the measures it passed were ones devised in the 1850's and 1860's. First of all, in 1869 the Church was disestablished in Ireland. In 1870 at last something was done about the report of the Devon Commission. Tenants were given credit for improvements they made. A first step was taken at helping them buy their holdings, by government loans. In 1870 also W. E. Forster put through a great Education Act by which

---

[1] Those familiar with the intricacies of English parliamentary franchise will realize that this is an approximation. Municipal and parliamentary registers were separate, but they came close to coinciding.

elective local boards might set up elementary schools. The question of nondenominational religious teaching caused a great furor and made these school boards centers of Nonconformist and therefore Liberal local politics. In 1872 the Army was reformed by Edward Cardwell. Here a constitutional retrogression took place. When the House of Lords blocked legislation abolishing the purchase of commissions, the Queen was induced to cancel the original royal warrant authorizing such purchase. Another great step was the reorganization of the courts. The triple division of the courts of justice into Queen's Bench, Common Pleas, and Exchequer was abolished, as was the special Chancery jurisdiction. In their place was set up one Superior Court. Thus the age-old Statute of Westminster of Edward I was at last brought up to date. By a system of life peerages it was made possible for trained judges to take over the judicial duties of the House of Lords. Religious tests at the universities, too, were abolished.

By setting up a Local Government Board in 1872 a hodgepodge of conflicting central supervisions were unified. By 1873 the country had had enough of reform. As Disraeli put it, the Treasury bench resembled a range of exhausted volcanoes, still potentially dangerous, but smoking and not pouring out lava and laws. At the same time, too, Gladstone's intricate mind got him in trouble. Later on the witty Henry Labouchere would say that he did not mind the "Grand Old Man" having the ace of trumps up his sleeve, but he did mind his saying God had put it there. Gladstone did some pretty queer things. Having passed a law saying that no man could become a law lord, i.e., a judicial peer of Parliament, without holding an inferior judgeship first, he then gave one man a judgeship for a day so that he would be eligible. His Chancellor of the Exchequer, Robert Lowe, got into trouble over a tax on matchboxes. His Postmaster General got into a fix over the conduct of the telegraph lines. He himself violated the letter if not the spirit of the law over a switch of offices, when he took over the chancellorship of the Exchequer from Lowe. This sort of thing was too much for the government, and Gladstone dissolved Parliament. The elections went Conservative. At last, for the first time since the Parliament elected in 1841, the Liberals and their allies were in a minority. With a new electorate, a new political era had begun.

In these years from 1832 to 1874 the middle-class electorate had done much. In two great bursts of reform, from 1832 to 1839 and from 1867 to 1873, Parliament had modernized the United Kingdom. In the 1840's free trade had been brought in by Peel's efficiency, Cobden's reasoning powers, and the Irish famine. By the great budgets of the 1840's, 1850's, and 1860's, the nation's financial structure had been made secure. By a series of quiet administrative improvements the modern state had been made efficient. When the 1870's came, the questions of the 1830's had been given satisfactory answers.

33

THE AGE OF PALMERSTON

1830–1867

Outwardly, in 1830, England's strength lay in the Navy that had won Trafalgar and the Army that had won Waterloo. The first was all-powerful as far as it could reach; the second was not lightly to be disregarded. In the period after the Congress system had broken up and the European powers were no longer able to unite against England, this force was fully adequate for England's needs. But greater than England's visible strength was her invisible strength. Peel's restoration of the gold standard, Huskisson's financial reforms, and the repeal of the Combination and Bubble Acts had released England's enterprise. Her goods circled the globe and made her the uncontested economic leader of the world.

Furthermore, England exported ideas as well as goods and found for them as ready a sale. Important foreign thinkers turned to England for their education. When young Count Cavour decided to become a statesman, his natural action was to go to England and there attend meetings of the Political Economy Club. When Guizot wrote French history as a way of making himself a political figure in France, he got into the swing of it by writing English history as well. As a result of this sort of thing, when an idea became accepted in England, it was the tendency elsewhere to feel that that acceptance established a strong presumption in favor of the soundness of the idea. So it was that from 1830 to 1867 a word of advice from an Englishman, given at the right time and place, could—and often did—change history. Here was a chance for a statesman to put England in a position of power.

As sometimes happens, the times and the man coincided. For twenty-seven of the thirty-seven years from 1830 to 1867, which are covered by this chapter, Henry John Temple, Viscount Palmerston in the Kingdom of Ireland and as such eligible to sit in the House of Commons of the United Kingdom for a non-Irish constituency, was either Secretary of State for Foreign Affairs or First Lord of the Treasury, that is, either Foreign Secretary or Prime Minister. And for two years more, as Home Secretary in the Aberdeen Cabinet, he took an important share in shaping foreign policy. As he embodied, personified, and used the forces that made England strong, it is largely in terms of him, either as principal actor or as agent of forces acting through him, that the story of England's foreign affairs must be told. Using the powers given him by England's Navy and England's ideas, he accomplished much till he met men who could use newer forces and go against the currents that had swept him to success.

Palmerston was not inexperienced in office when, in the autumn of 1830, Lord Grey appointed him Secretary of State for Foreign Affairs. From 1809 to 1827 he had held the office of Secretary at War and had then gained a mastery of office routine and learned the basic facts of international politics by supplying the Army that had liberated Spain, won Waterloo, and occupied France. Then under Lord Grey—who, unlike later Prime Ministers, dominated Palmerston instead of being dominated by him— he had good training. He learned how to handle Russians by negotiating the details of the frontier between Greece and Turkey; he learned how to handle the French and other powers of western Europe by solving the tangle of the separation of Belgium and Holland. This formed a sound apprenticeship for the prime of his career, when relations with Russia and France were England's chief problems.

The Greek negotiations from 1830 to 1834 were largely a cleanup job, finishing the work Canning had begun. The Concert of Europe had agreed that Greece should be free but not how large the free Greece should be. Russia, for reasons not then understood, wanted Greece small; England wanted the opposite. Grey and Palmerston dared put pressure on Russia, got a better boundary than Wellington and Aberdeen had been willing to accept, and thus built up the traditional friendship of Greece for England.

The Belgian negotiations from 1830 to 1839 were more difficult to handle. In 1830 the perennial problem of who should control the Channel coast took a new turn. Both France and Belgium had liberal revolutions. In France the Bourbons were ousted and replaced by Louis Philippe. At the same time the Belgians drove out the pro-British Orange dynasty, split themselves from Holland, and in looking about for a new monarch to head their now independent state, chose Louis Philippe's son. Here was a delicate tightrope to walk. England, who was having her own bloodless revolution, the First Reform Bill, was in thorough sympathy with these comparatively orderly revolutions, that seemed copies of her Glorious Revolution of 1688. But she was not in sympathy with having France own Belgium directly, control Belgium indirectly through a French king, or flout the Concert of Europe by tearing up international agreements about the Franco-Belgian border. Such eventualities would make a cross-Channel invasion easier and would lessen England's chances of getting continental allies in case of a revival of the Napoleonic Wars, a danger that up to 1870 lay in the back of the minds of all statesmen.

Grey and Palmerston managed this well. Though a French army got Louis Philippe prestige by marching into Belgium to keep the Dutch out, English pressure and English joint action with France—always a good way of hampering an overenthusiastic country—persuaded the Belgians not only to withdraw their election of Louis Philippe's son as king but to elect in his stead Leopold of Saxe-Coburg. Since under the Belgian constitution—as became painfully apparent at Dunkirk in 1940—the King had a real share in government, the choice of Leopold made the Channel coast safe for England. He was closely tied to the English royal family, both as widower of Princess Charlotte of Wales and as uncle of Princess Victoria, the heir apparent to the childless William IV. It was easy to get this settlement accepted in fact, but to get it ratified by Holland and the powers took a long time. During that time, Palmerston drew up so many drafts as to win the nickname "Protocol Palmerston." It was not until 1839 that the obstinate Dutch king at last signed a treaty, after eight years of "armistice." Thanks to a suggestion made by the Prussian envoy, the problem of French expansion through Belgium was apparently solved by an international guarantee of Belgian neutrality, and a sore spot in England's foreign relations was salved. During these years, Palmerston—he was consistently in office except for a few months in 1834 and 1835—came to know the diplomats of Europe as well though not as cordially as had Castlereagh.

Here should be noted a change in England's position that occurred so quietly as almost to escape notice, yet had important negative results. When the Princess Victoria became Queen in 1837, England was automatically separated from Hanover, whose throne no woman could inherit. This removed from English political life the blustering, sinister figure of Ernest, Duke of Cumberland, to be King of Hanover; and English statesmen ceased to have to think in terms of holding land in Germany. Here was yet another reason for the evolution of a new English foreign policy, built on a tacit agreement that England and France would cooperate because they were the two liberal, parliamentary great powers. There were too many conflicts of interest for this to be a perfect cooperation, but the fact that it existed gave shape to the international relations of Europe. At the same time there grew up an increasing tension between England and Russia, with Turkey and Central Asia as the points at which their policies conflicted.

The key to the Anglo-Russian difficulties lay in a large part in English ignorance of a change in direction of Russian policy. In 1829 Czar Nicholas decided that the dangers inherent in any breakup of the Turkish empire outweighed any advantages. He therefore took as his aim keeping the

Turkish empire going as a weak state, while Russia expanded into Central Asia. But to do this he interfered in Turkey's affairs in a way that frightened the English. To them it looked as if Russia were planning a double attack on India. One prong would be the taking over of Turkey—that amorphous empire that claimed to extend from Morocco and Tunis to the Danube and thence to Persia. This would block the Mediterranean route to India via Egypt, the route that the steamship and the railway seemed about to make more important than that by the Cape of Good Hope. The other prong would be the seizure of the Central Asian invasion routes into India, the routes the ancestors of the Mogul Emperors had used. In both areas, it became the purpose of English diplomacy to ward off the Russian menace.

In 1833 the Russians gained power in Turkey by protecting the Sultan from a rebellious subject. The Pasha of Egypt, Mehemet Ali, took the opportunity of a war with a fellow pasha to march his armies through Syria to the foot of the Anatolian Plateau and would probably have gone on to overthrow the Sultan had not the Russians sent an army of rescue by sea to Constantinople. In reward the Russians obtained from the Sultan the Treaty of Unkiar-Skelessi, which gave them a preponderant position in Turkey. One clause—a secret one, but it leaked out—was an especial danger to England. It allowed Russian ships to come through the Dardanelles from the Black Sea into the Mediterranean but required the Turks to prevent the British going from the Mediterranean into the Black Sea. In 1838 it looked as if matters might become worse. Mehemet Ali went on the warpath again, and again he overwhelmed resistance. Here Palmerston saved Britain from seeing Turkey either fall to the pro-French Mehemet Ali or be saved at the cost of increased Russian control. First he got the Concert of Europe to compel Russia to give up her special right of egress. Then, scorning French threats to fight, he sent the British fleet to cut Mehemet Ali's supply line and force him back to Egypt, Saint-Jean-d'Acre being one of the Levant ports bombarded in doing this. Thus Palmerston protected the Mediterranean route to India and got great personal prestige for the way he had turned the tables on Russia and France. Now England, not Russia, was the preponderant power in Turkey. In 1841 a new English ambassador, Stratford Canning, used England's position to encourage reforms and thus make Turkey more of a bulwark against Russian expansion.

The United States offered Palmerston slave-trade problems and border problems. America refused to let the British search its ships and justified that refusal by maintaining its own antislavery squadron. This caused constant squabbles. When the Canadian revolt of 1837 broke out, an American attempt to send help caused the incident of the schooner *Caroline*. The Maine militia, two years later, nearly came to blows over the northeastern boundary, in the so-called Potato War; American settlers moved into the

Oregon River valley and tried to block British occupation of the present British Columbia. The right of search problem never was really solved till America abolished slavery, and though Palmerston did keep the peace in 1837, the boundary problems he had to pass on to his successor, Lord Aberdeen.

In Spain Palmerston did much what his model and exemplar Canning had done in Portugal. He "held the ring" in order that the liberal or constitutional branch of the dynasty might win a struggle against the absolutist or legitimist branch. (Throughout this chapter "liberal" is loosely used to qualify parliamentary parties holding ideas similar to those held in England in the same period; it is not used in the strict English party sense, or in the modern American sense, which is equally loose, but loose in a different direction.) In encouraging the Liberals in Spain against the Carlists or followers of the Legitimist claimant Don Carlos, a Foreign Enlistment Act was passed, prohibiting anyone but the Queen of Spain from raising an Army or Navy for foreign service in England. In later years that act would have important effects on America.

In China, too, Palmerston had new-found responsibilities. They came upon him when the East India Company monopoly of the China trade was abolished in 1833 and the duty of negotiating with the hong, or government organization of merchants, at Canton was passed on to a Superintendent of Trade based on the Portuguese island of Macao. Negotiations were hampered by the official stand of the Chinese Emperor. He claimed that all the world was subject to him and that any envoy from England was merely bearing tribute and was not to be dealt with till submission had been admitted and tribute paid. And it took ten months to get reply from Peking to any message important enough to reach the Emperor. Yet negotiations were very necessary since Chinese laws dealing with foreigners were based on an "eye for an eye, tooth for a tooth" system of retaliation, and Chinese officials had an unpleasant habit of killing as many innocent English sailors as Chinese had been killed in seaport brawls. The situation was further complicated by the fact that the Indian opium habit was spreading dangerously in China, that opium selling was forbidden by Chinese edicts, and that the prohibition was not so much enforced as used to extort money from opium smugglers. Palmerston therefore sent out a squadron to enable the Superintendent of Trade to force the Cantonese officials to clear up the situation and stop referring to Peking whenever pushed into a corner. The instructions sent out were to get compensation for the wrongs done England and to take, as such compensation, the island of Hong Kong.

While the China squadron was engaged in backing up demands by capturing, relinquishing, and recapturing forts near Canton, the Whigs were replaced by the Tories in August, 1841, and the only long period began in which Palmerston did not guide England's foreign policy. It is significant of the continuity of foreign policy how little his measures were changed in many parts of the world. In China, after three years of increasing naval pressure, at last a treaty was signed that gave England the island of Hong Kong, the right to have English subjects tried by English judges, and most-favored-nation treatment in the five "Treaty Ports" that were opened to foreign merchants. The treaty also simplified the trade in opium. Hence came the name Opium War for this conflict and the accusation that it had been fought to rivet a pernicious habit on the Chinese people. Here Palmerston's instructions were carried out as if he had been in office.

With the United States Aberdeen dealt ably, in settling boundaries in Maine and Oregon. Here the spirit of the negotiations did not change, though the tone did. In 1842 his special envoy Lord Ashburton compromised with the United States on the Saint John River as the boundary of Maine, thus clearing up an ambiguity in the Treaty of Paris which would either have put American forts within gunshot of the Saint Lawrence or given Canada the potato fields of Aroostook County. In 1846, despite American demands for the Pacific Coast to "54–40," or the Alaskan boundary, he achieved another compromise, which extended the forty-ninth-parallel boundary to the Pacific.

In Turkey, an obstacle to Russian expansion was built up by the efforts of the British ambassador, Strafford Canning, in pushing on legal and administrative reforms. But here Aberdeen's tactful methods were less successful and partly justified Palmerston's accusation that Conservative policy was to gain temporary advantages at the cost of permanent concession. In 1844 Nicholas of Russia reviewed his decision of 1829 to let a weak Turkey continue to exist and act as a buffer state. Now that Turkey was growing stronger, he came to the conclusion that it was "the sick man of Europe." When he visited England that year, he had a long talk with Lord Aberdeen, in which he used that analogy and suggested that the European powers have in mind who should be the heirs should the sick man die, thus preventing a contest over legacies. Such a line of talk was not new to the English. Palmerston had several times in the crisis of 1838 to 1840 made the Turks see reason by suggesting that if they did not, England would abandon them to their fate. Aberdeen therefore politely discussed what must have seemed to him an academic question and left in Nicholas's mind the idea that if Turkey fell apart England would co-operate with him in cleaning up the mess.

In Spain there was a Queen, Isabella, kept on the throne by Palmerston's allowing English volunteers to fight on her side. This "holding the ring" so that liberals might win was typical of the Canning-Palmerston support of liberal movements to gain England friends, the support being not active intervention but a practice of letting a nation settle its own problems for itself. Now the question came up who should be the Queen's husband. To prevent the kind of trouble that had broken out when the Belgians had elected Louis Philippe's son king, Aberdeen and the French foreign minister, Guizot, drew up a list of ineligibles, high on that list being French royalties and Queen Victoria's relatives by marriage, the Belgian Saxe-Coburg-Gotha family. It was by making such cordial gestures to France that Aberdeen was establishing a tradition of cooperation instead of fear across the Channel.

But when Palmerston, far more of a nationalist than Aberdeen, returned to power in 1846, the tone changed back. This was the age of Palmerston's glory, when German legitimist diplomats sadly recited the rhyme, "If the devil has a son, it certainly is Palmerston" (*Hat der Teufel einen Sohn, so ist er sicher Palmerston*). He started off by suggesting that Isabella marry a pro-English ineligible, whereat Guizot capped the trick by getting her to marry a French candidate. Then Palmerston earned more enemies by his deft Swiss intervention of 1847. When the reactionary Sonderbund revolted against the liberal central authority, he offered to join the Concert of Europe in intervention—and then argued about the conditions on which England would intervene so long that the liberals had time to win the civil war and form the present democratic Swiss republic.

It might be thought that this sort of behavior would weaken England's international position. On the contrary, because of the European revolutions of 1848, it tended to strengthen that position. The contrast between the course of events on the two sides of the Channel seemed to show that English ideas of government were the right ones. For in England, despite the Chartist "monster petition," there was peace and quiet. In troublous Ireland, the police were able to keep order without calling for military help. But the capitals of Europe—Paris, Berlin, Rome and Milan, Vienna, Prague, and Budapest—fell into the hands of revolutionaries and were recaptured only by hard fighting and compromise with revolutionary programs. France became a republic, with Louis Napoleon Bonaparte as President; Sardinia-Piedmont became a true constitutional monarchy; Prussia got a parliament. It required the aid of Russian troops to conquer the Hungarian republic and reunite it to the Austrian empire. Though eventually, and with Russian aid, monarchical antiliberal governments were restored in Europe except for France and Sardinia, the restored governments had a different character from those before 1848. They might react against the popular will, but they could not deny the power of the popular will, and they showed that fact in their actions. Some appeased the liberal movement; some relied on naked force. All kept the existence of liberal movements in the forefront of their minds.

Directly England could do little. She had neither reason to intervene nor the power to do so. One action Stratford Canning did take; when the Hungarian republicans fled across the border into Turkish territory, he induced the Turks to take the same stand the English took, that a political exile was not to be surrendered as a murderer would be, but protected— in other words, that political disagreement with a government was not a crime, a doctrine not strictly held within the Turkish empire. Another action England took; she gave shelter, on the same doctrine, to exiles, especially from Italy. England thus became the home of freedom, with the result that expressions of opinion in England were eagerly listened to in Europe. Therefore what Palmerston and other English leaders said had much indirect importance.

Palmerston had much to say in dispatches to foreign governments and in the House of Commons. In one famous case he showed what his words meant. In Greece, one Don Pacifico, who had been born in Gibraltar, got into various forms of trouble ending with the destruction, so he said, of valuable property through the negligence of the Greek government in stopping riots. After the Greek government had continued to neglect his claim for three years, Palmerston sent the Mediterranean fleet to the Piraeus and blockaded it, in the process engaging in more squabbles with the French. The House of Lords, being Tory, censured him; Commons, being balanced between the political parties, seemed about to do so. But in a magnificent speech in which he declared that a British subject, like a citizen of the Roman Empire, would be protected the world over, Palmerston won Commons and public opinion to his side, and he stayed in office.

By now Palmerston seemed almost an independent power by himself in English politics. As a consequence, a constitutional struggle over the conduct of foreign affairs loomed. In custom the Queen, which meant in effect the Prince Consort, had the right to pass on and, if need be, modify all important dispatches. Palmerston, especially after his success in June, 1850, with Don Pacifico, regularly side-stepped this formality, trusting to his hold on Commons and the voters to get him out of any scrape from which his knowledge of official procedure could not extract him. Finally he overstepped when he congratulated President Louis Napoleon Bonaparte of the French Republic on violating that republic's constitution and putting most of his parliament in jail. Here was a situation made to order in which the Queen and the Prince Consort could persuade Prime Minister Lord John Russell to oust Palmerston at a moment when he had un-Palmerstonianly backed reaction. Promptly "Pam" had what he gleefully called his "tit for tat with Johnny Russell." Under Palmerston's leadership the House of Commons voted Russell out of office for not building up the militia as a force to stop a potential French invasion.

Here was, of course, largely a contest of personalities between Palmerston and the Prince Consort, both of them hard-working energetic men who took all the responsibilities handed to them and reached out to get more to do. But out of the contest emerged a working agreement over the position of the Crown in foreign affairs. The queen or king of England still is told what is going on, at a stage in the game where advice can be given. Such advice is valuable; once the Prince Consort stopped a war, and Edward VII and George V took important minor parts in suggesting means of conducting negotiations. But, because of Palmerston's stand, basic responsibility for foreign affairs went to the Foreign Secretary and above him to Cabinet and Parliament. This result "Pam" secured because the Don Pacifico incident and other flag-waving actions got behind him the patriotic emotions of the middle-class voters of the Reform Bill period.

Palmerston was not alone in influencing diplomacy by public opinion. In 1851 occurred a perhaps classic example of the power of private individuals in foreign affairs. Because one man wrote another a letter and published it, a dynasty eventually lost its throne. The Peelite William Ewart Gladstone spent the winter of 1850–1851 in Naples and became horrified at the oppression he saw. On his return he wrote his unvarnished opinion of this to his colleague in Peel's Cabinet, ex-foreign secretary Lord Aberdeen, and then published the letter. This attack on Ferdinand II, known to ill-fame as Bomba from his habit of bombarding his subjects into obedience, let loose a mounting flood of pro-Italian propaganda that, as will be related, nine years later drove Bomba's son from the throne.

As a direct though delayed result of the "tit for tat with Johnny Russell" there came into office the coalition Aberdeen Ministry, it being found that the Tories under Lord Derby could not command a majority, even after gains in a general election, and that Russell could not do so either. In this government Palmerston, without whom it could not have been formed, sat as Home Secretary and Lord Clarendon as Foreign Secretary. It had to face the fact that France was being adventurous in the eastern Mediterranean, at the same time as Russia was reviving her pressure on Turkey. The former President of the French Republic, Louis Napoleon Bonaparte, was at this time endeavoring to copy his uncle's career while avoiding his uncle's mistakes. Like his uncle, he had seized power by a *coup d'état* and had had himself "elected" Emperor. Unlike his uncle, he was trying to make friends with England and to establish a reputation as "the Emperor of Peace." To get this reputation by prestige in foreign affairs, he dug up the fact that in 1740 the Turks had made France the protector of Roman Catholics in Turkey and started to make capital of it. The Russians similarly had rights as protectors of the Greek Orthodox Church. These rights came into conflict in the question of the Holy Places. Which Church, the Roman Catholic or the Greek, should have charge of various churches in Jerusalem, especially as the Greek and Roman calendars were twelve days apart, with consequently varying celebrations of Christmas and Easter?

As can be seen, this was in itself an explosive subject, all the more so since the implications of protection were so vague. Stretched to the limit, they could justify just that sort of outside control that Russia had exercised in Turkey between the Treaty of Unkiar-Skelessi and the replacement of Russian by English influence in 1841.

In 1853 the Russians applied pressure at Constantinople and reminded the Aberdeen Government of the suggestions about the approaching demise of the "sick man of Europe" which had been made in 1844. Then the game of cross-purposes began. The Concert of Europe, in so far as it still was working, agreed that Christians in Turkey deserved more protection than they were getting. The question was, what form of protection could England, France, Russia, Austria and Prussia jointly demand that Turkey should give? On one side, Russia sent her troops into what were then called "the Principalities," the present-day Romania; on the other side, the English and French fleets went to Besika Bay just outside the Dardanelles. The imminence of war brought an apparent agreement, and a joint note, the Vienna Note, was sent to Turkey, stating the reforms that all the powers wanted. But on Stratford Canning's advice—which ran counter to that of his own government—the Turks rejected it, having been shown a flaw in one clause that would make Turkey once more a Russian protectorate. Turkey and Russia then engaged in an undeclared war in which the Russians blew a Turkish fleet out of the water. English and French public opinion decided to get excited about the "Massacre of Sinope," and the joint fleets entered the Black Sea. Russia declined to evacuate the Principalities, and England and France found themselves at war, to defend Turkey from Russia.

Later observers have felt that the Crimean War might have been avoided, if the British government had been either conciliatory, as Aberdeen would have, or bellicose, as Palmerston would have been. But chances to stop it were lost, and the practical question was whether the Trafalgar captains and Waterloo veterans who led the Navy and the Army could defeat Russia, the country that had defeated Napoleon I.

Here the Trafalgar veterans had an advantage. There was practically no Russian navy for them to fight, and something had been done to improve the British Navy. In the early 1830's Sir James Graham, when he was Lord Grey's First Lord of the Admiralty, had reorganized the Admiralty and gotten rid of many abuses. The Sea Lords had gone beyond this and improved the manning and equipment of the Navy. By instituting the rank of cadet below that of midshipman and giving some kind of examination to cadets, they had raised the level of officer recruits. They had begun to use steam propulsion and had early adopted the screw propeller in place of the paddle wheel, an early and tentative sign of the emphasis later put on utilizing new inventions in warfare. Then in 1853, Sir James, back at the Admiralty, had a law passed forbidding impressment, which had, in fact, already ceased to exist. Under the new "continuous service" veteran sailors, instead of being discharged, were transferred to other ships. As a result, the Navy did not do too badly in the war. Though bombardments in the Baltic proved futile, its share in transporting troops to the Crimea was well enough performed.

The Army, on the other hand, had its faults so shown to the world that the Aberdeen Cabinet was driven from office. Strategically, the British troops went to the right spot, because the commander in the field, Lord Raglan, was able to persuade his French colleague that Russia could be hit harder and more effectively by taking the fortress of Sevastopol in the Crimean Peninsula—hence the war's name—than by a landing in the marshes at the mouth of the Danube. But after that sound start, tactically and administratively everything went wrong. A chance to surprise Sevastopol was missed, and the allied armies had to besiege Sevastopol and, at one and the same time, fight off a relieving army. Battlefield blunders were shocking, the most famous but not the only one being the charge of the Light Brigade of cavalry against the wrong Russian battery. Supply blunders were worse. Food and clothing that got to the Crimea never got to the men, who fell sick and died from lack of care. Raglan did what he could, and died. Then outside influences came to help. Miss Florence Nightingale, a nursing enthusiast and a close friend of the Secretary of State for War, Sidney Herbert, took charge of the base hospital at Scutari, near Constantinople, and nursed back to life the men whose health had been ruined by the incompetence of army quartermasters, campmasters, and doctors. Stories of that incompetence and legends of "the lady with the lamp" who had walked the wards of Scutari comforting, encouraging, and saving the sick and dying came back to London to plague the Aberdeen Government. For this was the first war to have been fought with the benefit of correspondents at the front, the best and most powerful of them being Russell of *The Times*. Finally it almost came to the point where the Crimean correspondent of *The Times*, because he knew his business, had more influence with the ministry than the Army command, who did not.

The indignation thus aroused was too much for the Aberdeen Government, which melted away at the threat of parliamentary investigation. In place of it was put a Cabinet headed by Lord Palmerston, who, though as much a veteran of the Peninsular campaigns as anybody, was an effective one. Strength brings allies—in this case, the army of Sardinia, sent by Count Cavour for the purpose of winning a seat for his country at the eventual peace congress. With renewed vigor in direction from London, with hospital casualties cut from a murderous 42 per cent to 2.2 per cent by Miss Nightingale, the English and French finally overcame Todleben's skillful and heroic defense of Sevastopol. Then Austria intervened. When the Russians in 1856 took their troops out of the Principalities because they were needed elsewhere, Austrians marched in. Then in spite of any claims of gratitude Russia might have on Austria for putting down the Hungarian revolt, Austria by threat of war forced Russia to make peace.

With Palmerston at her head, England was now on the crest of the wave. She had rebuffed Russia, the supporter of monarchism. She had proved that publicity, whether turned against her own incompetent generals or against a foreign country, was a powerful weapon. She had shown, in effect, that she could do about as Palmerston pleased. Indeed the only thing that could bring him down from office was publicity, being hoist with his own petard. This happened twice: in 1857 over the lorcha *Arrow* case, and in 1858 over the Orsini bomb affair.

England knew of the lorcha, or Chinese coasting vessel, *Arrow* because news came back from China that, because of wrong done to it, England had gone to war again and occupied once more the forts off Canton. Promptly John Bright accused Palmerston of forcing on war, since the *Arrow* was not a British vessel but a Chinese one, with an expired English license in the coasting trade as its sole justification for claiming the protection of the English government. But though Bright got the House of Commons to censure Palmerston, Palmerston in the ensuing general election got the middle-class voters of England to censure Bright and came back into power apparently more secure than ever.

In China the *Arrow* case had a different aspect. There, ever since the Treaty of Nanking and similar agreements of the 1840's between the European powers and China, trouble had been brewing. The imperial government in Peking had no real control over outlying provinces and indeed was so weak that from 1850 on large parts of southern China, including the former capital Nanking, were in the hands of the Taiping rebels. But this weak imperial government continued to refuse to deal directly with foreign powers. As a result it was almost impossible to do business effectively with local officials who, when pinned down, could always refer to Peking for instructions. So, when the *Arrow* gave an apparently clear-cut excuse for action, European officials on the spot seized the opportunity. Soon, even though the *Arrow* failed them as a reason for demanding a change, plenty of other grievances were piled up. It was agreed by the Chinese that the European envoys—the English one being Lord Elgin, of whom much is said in the following chapter—would be received by the Emperor. But when European squadrons reached the seaport of Tientsin near Peking, advance emissaries were ill-treated and finally held as hostages. The only cure seemed to be to show the Emperor that the Europeans meant business by marching on Peking, and march they did. On arrival a treaty was signed, but only after pressure had been put on the Emperor by burning his Summer Palace. To Elgin and those on the spot that seemed the best way of punishing not the Chinese people who had done no harm, but the Emperor who had. To others the destroying or looting of priceless art treasures has seemed a horrifying way of enforcing one's will on another country.

However, England showed that she was not trying to take China over but build her up. An English officer, "Chinese Gordon," commanding the "Ever-victorious Army," did the largest part of the work in putting down the Taiping rebellion. English officials took over the supervision of the Chinese customs and made it an honest administration. As a result, the Peking government became temporarily stronger—and the China trade became better worth having.

England's Navy and diplomats having thus taught the Chinese empire how to put itself on its feet, as well as how to behave to foreigners, they proceeded to do the same for Japan, which had been opened to foreign trade in 1855 by the Americans. Japan gave foreigners the same rights as China had—travel through the country and diplomatic dealings with the chief of state—but used foreign culture differently when it poured in.

In both countries English policy was complicated by the fact that England's rival, Russia, was on the spot. Russian troops were stationed in the Amur valley on the Chinese border; a Russian port was founded at Vladivostok; Russia had direct contacts with Japan, her troops even for a time holding the island of Tsushima. To support local authorities thus thwarted Russia. Here the lorcha *Arrow* case led to the evolution of a policy of trying to support the Chinese and Japanese empires, much as Nicholas of Russia had tried to support the apparently equally moribund Turkish empire. England would rather see China and Japan ruled by Chinese and Japanese than have to fight over the inheritance if these sick men of the East should die. But in England, as has been pointed out, it led to a general election on the issue of foreign affairs, which returned Palmerston to power with apparently greater support in Commons than before. Yet within a year he was out of office.

The reason for his defeat was his treatment of the Orsini bomb case. In January, 1858, the Italian revolutionary Orsini threw a bomb at Napoleon III to remind that monarch of a pledge made in his youth to free Italy. As the English police might well have stopped the attack by checking on Orsini, the French government made representations to England, and Palmerston introduced legislation to allow the control of foreign plotters. This of course attacked the right of sanctuary for political exiles for which England so stoutly stood, and Parliament defeated Palmerston, who was replaced by Derby and Disraeli.

A further result of this affair was the volunteer movement. Angry speeches by French army officers about how easy it would be to invade

England had a natural reaction. The English clamored to be allowed to prepare to defend themselves. All over England volunteer forces were organized, in which Englishmen trained themselves, largely at their own expense. This served to complicate further an already chaotic army system; however, it also served to create a body of semitrained men, who would prove useful in the Boer War of 1899 to 1902, and, most importantly, to cause a significant part of the British public to think in terms of land war as well as in terms of sea war.

But the results of Orsini's bomb did not stop there. A bomb, for once in history, did what its thrower hoped it would do. It did remind Napoleon III of his promise to free Italy. He got in touch with Count Cavour and planned a French intervention in Italy that would remove Austrian influence from Italy—to be replaced, so Napoleon hoped, by French influence. Here again was the plan for ruling by indirection a divided country, as Nicholas of Russia had Turkey. In the spring of 1859 the war which Napoleon and Cavour had engineered broke out more or less according to schedule—there were some hitches in inducing Austria to fight—and the French veterans of Algeria and the Crimea poured out their blood to free Italy. This campaign was too successful. Napoleon's aim was to free Italy, not unite her, and the people of the small North Italian states took the opportunity to drive out their rulers and join the kingdom of Sardinia-Piedmont. Therefore he stopped the war. But he could not stop the Italian nationalist movement, which now turned to England for aid.

It was natural to look for English help. England felt strongly about Italy. Mazzini, the conspirator, had his headquarters in London. English poets, notably Robert and Elizabeth Barrett Browning, were constantly choosing Italian themes. Gladstone's *Letter to Lord Aberdeen* was still building up indignation against the royal family of Naples. It had been to mobilize such opinion that Count Cavour had sent the Sardinian army to the Crimea, and had accepted as his reward for the blood shed there and the treasure spent there a one-day discussion of Austrian misrule in Italy. Lord Clarendon's blazing unrehearsed words of scorn at that meeting had been payment enough for him, so great was the value then set on an English statesman's public utterances.

The dependence on British aid was justifiable. The Liberal government which came into office in 1859 had the pro-Italians Russell and Palmerston as Foreign Secretary and Prime Minister. Twice did Russell and Palmerston take steps which helped finish the job that Napoleon had laid down. First of all, they were prompt in giving official recognition to the union of Tuscany and Parma and Modena with Piedmont. That forestalled interference by the other less liberal powers. Then came the dramatic subversion of the kingdom of Naples. Underhandedly Cavour provided with arms the international revolutionary Giuseppe Garibaldi, who with a thousand men went to Sicily and conquered that island against odds, then crossed to the mainland and swept through Naples up to the border of the Papal States. At that point Cavour, who until then had been publicly protesting that Piedmont had nothing to do with the affair, sent his army south through the Papal States to join Garibaldi and, by thus hampering him, prevented an attack on the Papal States and all that attacking the pope would have meant in world opinion. For this the Concert of Europe was so grateful to Cavour that they let the people of Naples and of the larger part of the Papal States join the kingdom of Italy. For wherever Garibaldi or the Sardinian army marched the people had risen to join a united Italy.

At every stage in this affair, it was British influence which tipped the scales. Garibaldi's landing was unconsciously aided by the British, for a Neapolitan warship which might have stopped the landing delayed for a crucial hour for fear of a British man-of-war in the offing. Garibaldi's crossing to the mainland was made possible by a secret message from Cavour to Russell—brought up the backstairs to his sickroom—to disregard official Piedmontese willingness to see the crossing blocked by joint naval action of the Concert of Europe. Therefore the British government refused to intervene, and without the Navy which had done its work at Navarino in 1829 and at Acre in 1840, the Concert of Europe could do nothing. As a result, the people of Italy felt more gratitude to England, which had used only words but had let them finish the job, than they did to France, which had poured out blood and treasure but then had tried to stop final unity. Here was the finest triumph of the Canning-Palmerston school of believing in public opinion.

However, a question should be raised here, perhaps by quoting Cavour's own words, "What rascals we should be if we did for ourselves what we have done for Italy!" It is possible that the acceptance of the dishonesty of the means Cavour used, an acceptance made by men of as high standards of integrity as Gladstone, led to an acceptance, later on, of lower standards in international affairs. Bismarck, Rhodes, Mussolini, and Hitler, not to mention Stalin, followed in the Garibaldian tradition; England accepted what they did, at least in the negative sense of doing rather little about it at the time, in part because she had accepted enthusiastically the means Garibaldi and Cavour had used to unite Italy. For if a nation uses its ethical judgments as a means of carrying out foreign policy—and that is what England did here and was to do in other cases later on—it must be careful to keep its ethical standards high. Otherwise it will lose the power it has.

The events of the years immediately following give point to this question. In them England had one more triumph. In 1860, just as these things were happening in South Italy, Richard Cobden, the apostle of free trade, went to France to negotiate a treaty with Napoleon III. Traditionally France was a protectionist country, but Napoleon III had dictatorial powers, and Cobden, in his different way, was as persuasive as Orsini. From Napoleon III this private citizen, temporarily acting as Her Majesty's envoy, secured a free-trade treaty, largely because to him free trade was a belief held not only for economic but for moral reasons.

But this was the last triumph of Palmerstonianism, if indeed anything Cobden did can be called Palmerstonian. The diplomatic successes hitherto recorded had been based on the fact that the policies of the Liberal Tory Lord Palmerston had coincided with those of men all over Europe who had desired change and also with those of the paradoxically liberal dictatorship of the Emperor Napoleon III. The words of Palmerston, Russell, and Gladstone had had great effect because they had told men to do what they were going to do anyway. These words had the greater effect because back of them were not only the British Navy but the French army. But now men would want changes that Palmerston, Russell, and Gladstone did not want, and the French army would meet its master.

One change took place across the Atlantic, when the American Civil War broke out. Here English public opinion, so powerful in Italy when it was united, had less effect because it split into two. To the majority in the English upper classes, this was a war between aristocratic landowners merely asking to govern themselves and political demagogues who wanted to interfere in the lives of others. They therefore sympathized with the Southerners and thought Lincoln and his followers uncouth. But to the cotton spinners of the North of England, to their honor, the Civil War did not have this aspect. Even though the Union blockade of the Confederacy cut off England's cotton supply, the Lancashire mill hands willingly starved if that starvation would aid the American North. Inspired by John Bright, they tightened their belts, endured unemployment, and wished the Union cause well.

It was this split in English opinion that caused a reversal of foreign policy. The first actions of England, when the Civil War broke out, were technically correct but brusquely managed. When the English government recognized the South as belligerents they in effect admitted that the blockade Lincoln had proclaimed of all the South was legal. But Russell never said so in so many words, and he timed his declaration to greet the American minister, Charles Francis Adams, on arrival, an arrival of which he was perfectly aware. With improved transatlantic communications by regular packets, this was not like the accident in 1812 when the United States declared war with the acceptance of American demands crossing the Atlantic at the time. This brusque tone was the outward sign that inside the Cabinet a belief was growing that if the Civil War should continue longer, England and France should intervene jointly to prevent bloodshed and get cotton moving into world trade again. After all, were not French, English and Spanish troops at that moment engaged in re-

storing order in strife-torn Mexico, even though as the year 1862 went on the English and Spanish withdrew?

Inevitably, with England in the unusual position of being a neutral objecting to a blockade rather than a belligerent enforcing one, test questions came up. The first great crisis was the *Trent* affair. In November, 1861, the U.S.S. *San Jacinto* stopped the English mail steamer *Trent* and took from her two Confederate envoys. It is now known that Palmerston, who after all in his younger days had seen the British Navy do many such things in the Napoleonic Wars, was inclined to accept what had been done. To have hauled the *Trent* into an American port and had lawyers argue out the question of whether envoys were contraband would have delayed mails. But the majority of the Cabinet were more Palmerstonian than he and demanded that the envoys be set free. Fortunately, the Prince Consort rewrote the dispatch conveying this demand and softened it enough to make it possible for Lincoln to let the envoys go with a good grace and keep American public opinion satisfied. The envoys so released naturally did all they could to persuade England and France to intervene, and matters came to the stage where the French were ready to act if England took the lead. It seemed as if England would take the lead. Chancellor of the Exchequer William Ewart Gladstone even went so far as to declare publicly, "Jefferson Davis has made an army; he is making, it seems, a navy; what is more, he is making a nation." When the man responsible for setting the tax rate says such things, it sounds like business.

An especial sting of this Newcastle speech lay in the phrase "making a navy." When this was said two things had happened: the U.S.S. *Monitor* had driven the *Merrimac* up the James River and so begun ironclad warfare, and the vessel built at Laird's yard in Birkenhead for an unknown purchaser had been boarded off the Azores by a Confederate crew and renamed the *Alabama*. The first event had proved that the future lay with such men-of-war as the English *Warrior* and the French *La Gloire*, armored iron steam vessels, one of which might be a match for a wooden fleet. The second event had shown that, if the English government winked at it, the Foreign Enlistment Act could be nullified by the technicality of building a ship without guns and putting guns and a crew on it outside English territorial waters. So, if the Confederates wanted a navy and the English government wanted them to have a navy, all that the Confederates needed to do was give the requisite orders to Laird's. This they did. At Laird's were laid down the keels of two ironclad "rams," armored ships that might well have been able to break the Union blockade of the South. Would the British government let them sail?

Gradually, the Cabinet came to realize that intervention would be wrong, thoughts on that subject being provided to them by the speeches of John Bright in the North of England. The mills Bright owned were shut; the mills that employed his listeners were often shut; but he and his audiences wished Lincoln's blockade well, if it were to end slavery. That it was to end slavery the Emancipation Proclamation of January, 1863, made clear. The Cabinet decided at last that indirect intervention by letting the rams sail was wrong and ordered them purchased for the British Navy, as an easy way out. (It should be remembered that the Cabinet came to this decision and acted on it before Charles Francis Adams gave his famous warning to Russell that, if the rams sailed, "it is superfluous for me to point out, my Lord, that this means war." It was merely administrative sloppiness that forced Russell to listen to this fortunately needless lesson on how to do his job.) Then the question of direct intervention was raised when a pro-Southern M.P. moved that England recognize the Southern Confederacy not merely as a belligerent but as a full-fledged nation. On June 30, 1863, John Bright tore that proposal into tatters in the House of Commons. On July 4 General Meade at Gettysburg, General Grant by capturing Vicksburg, proved to the British Cabinet how right they had been to buy the rams. Here, in the handling from the English end of the problems of the American Civil War, was an example of how leaders of public opinion could alter the nation's foreign policy against the will of the Cabinet. A later and less wise example of such an alteration will be seen in the peace ballot of 1935.

Perhaps another proof that the Palmerstonian age was coming to an end was the gesture by which England turned the Ionian Islands over to Greece, just to be consistent. This was done at the insistence of the former High Commissioner, William Ewart Gladstone.

But, in the very years that Palmerstonianism was thus failing because it went against the conscience of England, it also failed because it thought that a conscience unbacked by force was effective outside England. In Prussia in 1862 there broke out a far-reaching constitutional struggle between Crown and parliament, that was eventually to affect many nations besides Prussia. As a last resort before yielding to his parliament, the King appointed as "Minister President" Herr Otto Eduard von Bismarck-Schönhausen, as the most capable of the supposedly extreme reactionaries. Bismarck reacted most effectively to the problems he had to face, telling the Prussian parliament in words that were to ring around the world that liberalism was not enough to solve the German question but that blood and iron were needed. Then he used blood and iron. When in 1863 a revolt against Russia broke out in Poland, and England, France, and Austria intervened by words—which seemingly had done so much in Italy—Bismarck intervened by deeds. He put a cordon of Prussian troops on the border so that the Russians need fear no rebels would escape by that route. The next year when the King of Denmark died and a queer inheritance question came up over whether Schleswig and Holstein should continue to be joined in Denmark or should be separated, Bismarck juggled the legal technicalities in such a way that the Austrians joined him in fighting Denmark to force a separation. Here Palmerston bravely declared that Denmark would not fight alone and then, when Bismarck called his bluff, was obliged to crawl out of it by saying he meant he believed that Sweden would help Denmark. Two years later, 1866, Bismarck engineered another war, this time with Austria, in which Italy was his ally and Hanover (now ruled over by Queen Victoria's first cousin) his enemy. In seven weeks—hence one name for this war—Austria was defeated and Hanover was conquered and ready for annexation. So while England and France sat by and gave unheeded advice, a new nation appeared, a united Germany.

For Bismarck had taken the Prussian army with its highly organized reserves and used it and the emotional forces of nationalism back of it to win both an internal and an external conflict. He had put the King of Prussia above the Prussian parliament by an appeal to patriotism. In doing that, he threw down a challenge to the democratic way of life. At the same time, he put his new united Germany at the center of European diplomatic affairs, in this replacing France as the chief land power. It would not be until 1871 that the French empire would fall and the German empire be officially proclaimed. But everyone realized that the battle of Sadowa, in which Prussia defeated Austria in 1866, was a defeat for Napoleon III. Palmerston did not live to see it, for he had died in 1865, but the diplomatic world which he had known and which he knew how to handle then came to an end. It may be overdramatic to suggest that Bismarck had truly prophesied that liberalism would give way to blood and iron. True as that may have been for a time in Central Europe, it was not true the world over. But certainly after Sadowa the English foreign office could no longer assume that its utterances were enough to change the state of diplomatic affairs. A new era had begun, and England would have to find a new style of diplomacy to fit it.

34

PROCONSULS AND PARLIAMENTS

1830–1867

After 1830 there was a shift in emphasis in the British Empire. Until then what had mattered most was that England had been increasing her overseas possessions; after then, what mattered most was that new nations were being born within that Empire and were kept within the Empire as they reached nationhood. Here history most emphatically did not repeat itself, for although the birth of the United States disrupted the First British Empire, the births of Canada, Austria, New Zealand, and the South African Republics did not disrupt the Second British Empire. Capable statesmen and a changed political philosophy found a new channel in which the history of the Empire could run.

The name "proconsul," by analogy with Roman history, has often been given to the Englishmen, Scotchmen, and Irishmen who thus went out to rule the overseas possessions of the Crown and preserve the Second British Empire. This analogy is apt if it is applied to the more democratic days of the Roman republic rather than to the authoritarian days of the Roman Empire. Just as Rome was a republic, the United Kingdom was a "crowned republic." The proconsuls of Rome were men who had been elected to a series of offices at home before bringing their consular powers to provinces at the uttermost parts of the earth and who looked forward, on their return, to standing for popular election once more. Similarly the mid-century proconsuls of England were in close touch with parliamentary life. Lord William Bentinck of India had sat in the House of Commons and as General in command in Sicily had forced the creation of a parliament there before he became Governor-general of India; after he returned, he again sat in Commons. The Earl of Durham, before he got his title and went to Canada, had been known as "Radical Jack Lambton" for his work for the Great Reform Bill. Sir George Grey, whose career carried him all over the Southern Hemisphere to Australia, New Zealand, and South Africa, wound up that career by serving as Prime Minister of New Zealand and as delegate to the Australian Federal Convention.

Yet these nineteenth-century proconsuls, for all their support of representative government, like the Roman proconsuls fearlessly used all the powers entrusted to them and, when need arose, seized new powers. In India, Lord William Bentinck broke local religious custom to abolish thuggee and suttee. In Canada, Durham shipped prisoners to Bermuda in excess of his legal powers. In New Zealand, Grey suspended the operation of a constitution for which he thought the colony unready. These things were done, and done successfully and beneficially, because they were done with consistent adherence to a political philosophy. These men believed in self-government as the best means of ensuring the supremacy of the law. Only in exceptional cases did they make exceptions to this rule; it just so happened that they were the sort of men who are sent to difficult positions where exceptional methods are needed. They succeeded because it was obvious that they had no intention of extending emergency powers to general use.

On the contrary, they had a program of turning government over to the governed and, until that could be done, of governing in trust for the governed, in such a way as to make them ready for self-rule. This was as true in India as anywhere else, where Bentinck was "the first British statesman who declared and acted upon the policy of governing India in the interests of the people of that country." Most of these men were Whigs, and like many Whigs they believed in accepting the future and cooperating with it. The Whig saying *"Che sara, sara"* (What will be, will be) well reflected their attitude. They wasted no time trying to stop what they felt to be inevitable. On the contrary, they saved their energies for trying to guide the inevitable course of events in what seemed to them the best channels, and in doing so they made the new feelings of nationality, in many cases, a support of the British Empire instead of a cause of resistance to British rule.

For these men Canada in a sense formed a laboratory. When Durham, Buller, and Wakefield met the problems of Papineau's revolt and solved them by the Durham Report as later implemented by Lord Elgin, a model was set up which the British Commonwealth of Nations eventually copied. It took time to find out how and to what extent its principles could be applied to the rest of the Empire. But because John Lambton, Earl of Durham, had had the vision to see what the British Empire might be, that Empire became an association of self-governing nations. And because other men had the wisdom to follow in his footsteps Australia, New Zealand, South Africa, and eventually India followed in Canada's evolution. For convenience, therefore, in this chapter the chief overseas possessions of William IV and Victoria will be considered in the above order.[1]

[1] It is told in the Foreign Affairs chapter, paralleling this, how England added Hong Kong to her possessions and so opened up a trade empire in China. That account need not be repeated here.

CANADA

Durham went to Canada for the summer months of 1838 because in 1837 both Upper Canada (Ontario) and Lower Canada (Quebec) had burst into revolt. In both provinces the majorities in the legislative assemblies had become so disgusted with the constant use of imperial powers to block their desires that certain leaders had lost their heads. No matter how much the legislatures had built up "constitutional" precedents, the governors sent across the Atlantic had continued to find ways and means of obstruction and had continued to make the colonists feel that their legislatures were not truly "responsible." They had relied upon fixed income set aside from legislative control to carry on government when "supply" (i.e., appropriations of money by the legislature) had been withheld, thus going counter to the old English constitutional rule "No supply without redress of grievances." They had made appointments that were vexatious to local opinion. They had used their power of nomination to Upper Councils to create a body that would nullify for them the will of the Assembly, and when that obstacle had been overcome, they used their powers of veto, asserting that in doing so they were either obeying orders from London or referring back to London for fresh orders. Even when, in 1832, the Colonial Office ended many restricted funds and turned over land sales, thus giving the two assemblies pretty full powers of the purse, matters did not mend. The other devices complained of still were used, and gradually it dawned on the Canadian leaders that for a government to be responsible to the people it was not enough for the legislature to be responsible to the people and have full lawmaking powers. True "responsible government" would require that the executive council that carried out the governor's orders must also be responsible to the legislature.

In the summer of 1837 Canadian discontent took an ominous form. "Sons of Liberty" organized. Loyal militia officers were ousted from command. Mass meetings heard threatening oratory. The parallel to 1775 in America came even closer when at St. Charles a mass meeting organized six counties for resistance. Speaker Papineau was ordered arrested, and a revolt flared out. The Governor of Upper Canada sent down troops, which allowed Mackenzie to start a companion revolt in Upper Canada. Both revolts were easily put down, in Lower Canada by Imperial troops, in Upper Canada by loyal militia. But ruling by martial law left the problem unsolved, indeed made it worse. Something had to be done. Therefore, in England, Lord Melbourne's Government solved two problems at once. It got the embarrassingly energetic Lord Durham out of home politics by sending him to Canada, and it transferred the burden in Canada to stronger shoulders by giving him wide and uncertain powers as High Commissioner.

Durham acted sharply and advised wisely. He saw that no French-Canadian jury would convict rebels and that unless rebels were convicted by some form of trial revolt would not be effectively punished or prevented for the future. He therefore summoned the case of the leading rebels before the Executive Council, which he had had filled with his personal associates as a way of securing a nonpartisan interim government. The Council he had thus unintentionally but effectively packed exiled the untriable prisoners to Bermuda, an island over which Durham had no authority. When a similar thing had been done to Massachusetts, in 1774, by act of Parliament, America had eventually revolted and English opinion had been outraged. Certain sections of English opinion therefore chose to be outraged again and urged Durham's recall. But while this storm was brewing in England, Durham was giving great satisfaction in Canada, where he and his assistants, Charles Buller and Edward Gibbon Wakefield, were engaged in drafting a report which has become the Magna Carta of the British Commonwealth of Nations. Like Magna Carta it has this importance because more has subsequently been read into it than the literal meaning of its words. On the face of it the Durham Report merely said that the governors of Canada should be instructed to cooperate with their assemblies by appointing an Executive Council that would not be obnoxious and that they must not look to London for support if they quarreled with an assembly. Expressly that did not give up the powers of veto, referral to London, and patronage that had so vexed English and French Canadians alike. But when adopted as a policy it would end Colonial Office control except for truly imperial matters, and would tend powerfully—indeed, almost inevitably—to make the Canadian government evolve into Cabinet government such as existed in England. So eloquently did the Durham Report argue that Colonial Office control must be ended, and that local legislatures must be allowed to see to the administration of local affairs on the same lines as the English Parliament saw to the administration of local affairs in England, that the rulers of England were permanently convinced.

The outcome of all this was that Durham was recalled—because he had arbitrarily sent prisoners to Bermuda—disavowed, and left to die of a broken heart, while his ideas were silently and effectively adopted. Such acceptance took time; the first governors who presided over Canada, which under Durham's advice had been reunited into one province, followed the letter and not the spirit of the Report. But time gradually proved the wisdom of its spirit, time being aided by the propaganda in England stirred up by Buller and Wakefield, and eventually men came into office who were to finish Durham's work. These were Colonial Secretary Henry George Grey, Third Earl Grey (son of Lord Grey of the Reform Bill), and James Bruce, Eighth Earl of Elgin. Grey fully accepted the Durham

Report and put his present interpretation of it into effect wherever in the Empire assemblies seemed ready for it—or, in at least one case, sooner. Elgin went further, for he better understood its spirit. It was Elgin who, with Grey's loyal backing "at home," gave Canada genuine "responsible government," in the sense of the term which Canadian statesmen thus gave to the world.

In 1847, when Elgin took the governorship of the united provinces of Canada, Durham had become a Canadian national hero, which made Elgin *persona grata*, since he had just married Durham's daughter. Presently he was both beloved and maligned for himself. A general election soon after his arrival returned a majority favorable to some of Papineau's ideas. This majority celebrated its accession to power by voting the "rebellion losses bill" to give compensation to *all*, on whichever side they had been, who had suffered losses in 1837. Naturally there was an outcry from the "loyalist" minority against giving money to rebels. It would have been easy, and no contravention of the words of the Durham Report, for Elgin to have referred the problem to London. Instead, despite mobbings in the street, the burning of the parliament house in Montreal, and attacks in the English Parliament, Elgin made the decision to give assent to the act passed by the representatives of the majority, and he stuck to that decision. By this action he made the Governor of Canada a sort of constitutional monarch and secured to Canada what his father-in-law had explicitly stated he hoped would be allowed there, the same sort of government England had. Be it noted that in so acting he did not make the Governor a figurehead. He took for himself and made for his successors a post like that of the President of the Third Republic in France, that of a permanent and influential nonparty adviser. It was his personally conducted negotiations in Washington that "floated on champagne" an advantageous treaty of commercial reciprocity between Canada and the United States. The social prestige he enjoyed made him and his successors a motive force behind important movements. For example, Lord Minto, in the 1890's and 1900's, did much to foster the development of Canadian military forces, because of a personal interest in such things dating from previous experience with volunteer troops in Scotland. Likewise Elgin made the Governor—and his successors the governors-general of the Dominion—an important link binding Canada with the Crown whose representative he was. By doing all this Elgin established a working relationship within the Empire that did much to implement his father-in-law's vision.

In the wake of Canada, the other provinces of British North America secured "responsible government" despite Earl Grey's attempts to keep some executive decisions in the hands of governors. In the history of each province this advance plays a vital part; but important as it was that different local heroes thus gave life to Durham's ideas, significant as are the names of the men who did this and the means by which they did it, that is more truly part of local histories than of the history of the Empire as a whole. It was Canadians who worked out the slogan of "responsible government," the credit for first using the actual words going to the Baldwins, father and son, in the 1820's in Upper Canada; it was Durham and Elgin who accepted the slogan in the meaning it had acquired after 1832; and thus it was the cooperation of the Canadians and Durham and Elgin which opened the road for others to follow.

One part of Durham's proposal did not work. The union of the two Canadas did not bring assimilation. Canada East and Canada West, as the two halves were called, remained determinedly French and English in language, culture, institutions, and law. This dualism extended into politics, where Cabinets were usually headed by an English and a French leader. Such were the two Baldwin-Lafontaine Ministries which established responsible government and the Macdonald-Cartier Ministry, which in 1858 by the notorious "double-shuffle" became the Cartier-Macdonald Ministry to regain power after a transitory defeat. Thus, when it took the legendary skill of John A. Macdonald to keep a government stable, clearly some form of separation and federation was needed.

During the years that followed, British North America continued to grow, with the growing pains customary to colonies learning how to rule themselves. On the Pacific Coast, Vancouver Island (1849) and British Columbia (1858) secured assemblies. On the Red River, Lord Selkirk's settlement grew slowly into the present city of Winnipeg, in the center of what was then the trapping country and is now wheat fields. To settle the claims of four cities to be the capital of Canada, a fifth, Bytown, on the Ottawa River, received the honor, as the personal choice of Queen Victoria, being at the same time renamed Ottawa. In Canada proper, British and French Canadians grew restive at their enforced union. Among the Maritime Provinces a feeling grew up that the joint problems of New Brunswick, Nova Scotia, and Prince Edward Island should be solved jointly. Statesmen there saw that if they were to prosper they must have unity and command of land communication. Therefore, in 1864 Charles (later Sir Charles) Tupper, Premier of Nova Scotia, called a convention of the Maritime Provinces, to meet at Charlottetown, on Prince Edward Island.

When the Charlottetown Convention met, delegates from Canada asked for admission and proposed widening the scope of the union-to-be. At Charlottetown principles were agreed upon, basic being the division of the Province of Canada into its component halves, to end local strife between French and English. With the blessing of the Liberal Government in England, delegates were elected to the Quebec Convention of October, 1864, to conclude this discussion, thus paralleling at higher speed than in the United States the following up of the preparatory Annapolis Convention by the final Philadelphia Convention of 1787. The Quebec delegates, like our Philadelphia delegates, met in secret and hammered out a bill they would like to see the English Parliament pass into law. This consumed time and required sending representatives to England to thrash out financial details. Probably the delay was fortunate, for in the interim the Liberal Government fell and was replaced by a Conservative one, so that English political parties shared the responsibility for the British North America Act of 1867, which implemented Durham's ideas.

If the Durham Report is the Magna Carta of the British Empire, perhaps the British North America Act is the Empire's equivalent of the Petition of Right and Bill of Rights, for it creates the machinery for giving effect to the principles read into the Durham Report, just as those measures spelled out in 1628 and 1688 the principles men had read into the Magna Carta of 1215. The other great constitutional acts of the Empire have copied it, with variations for local needs. Three things stand out about the British North America Act. First of all, it was basically written in Charlottetown and Quebec, not Westminster, even though it was modified in Westminster before being enacted into law there. That has been true of all later similar constitutional acts, with the possible exception of the Government of New Zealand Act; they have been written on the spot, not in London. And, in actual fact, the Government of New Zealand Act was modified in New Zealand when Sir George Grey rejected the first one and sent it back to be rewritten. Secondly, the last service the British Parliament gave to Canada was to impose from the outside certain constitutional guarantees to prevent a majority from oppressing a minority. In the case of Canada these were financial details that no longer matter, but were very important then, and a minority protection to the French Canadians, which gave the province-to-be of Quebec a guaranteed representation of sixty-five members, which should form the basis, in proportion, of the assignment of representatives to other provinces. In the other Dominions similar guarantees were given, notably the protection of the Cape Colored—or half-breed—vote in the dominion of South Africa which is so much in the news at present writing. Even though later formed dominions have secured the right to rewrite their own constitutions, the fact that their basic legislation had been enacted by the English Parliament has given it permanence.

Thirdly, and perhaps most importantly, the British North America Act provided a general form that other such legislation has followed, a combination of American federal structure and "responsible government." Basic power rested in the House of Commons of the dominion parliament. It passed legislation, subject to alteration by a nominated Senate and to possible overruling by a Supreme Court. The Supreme Court was in itself not supreme, since from it appeal could be had to the Judicial Committee of the Privy Council in Westminster. To that House of Commons the executive privy council of the Dominion was responsible, just as in England the executive part of the Privy Council—the Cabinet—was responsible to the House of Commons of the United Kingdom. The name given this federation was the Dominion of Canada, since at the time it seemed unwise to have a kingdom of Canada next the republic of the United States. Over this Dominion presided in name, but in accordance with Elgin's precedent as constitutional monarch, a Governor-general. In his name executive action was taken, but his chief duty was the rare one of choosing between competing would-be Prime Ministers in cases where no obvious candidate stood out and on similarly rare occasions refusing to call a general election if he felt a majority in Parliament would support such a decision. Here was the constitution adopted, with variants, by New Zealand, Australia, South Africa, Eire, India, and Pakistan. In principle all are governed by variants of the British North America Act.

It was fortunate for the other parts of the Empire that Canada paved the way. Having a successful model to follow greatly eased the situation in Australia and South Africa, and later in Eire.

AUSTRALIA

Australia was left in the last chapter with one chief colony, New South Wales; one subsidiary colony, the island then known as Van Diemen's Land; and one experimental colony, Western Australia. Important developments were brewing in Western Australia and in New South Wales.

The important event in Western Australia was its failure as a business venture, in pounds, shillings, and pence. The investors who founded it discovered that it did not pay to get land cheap, 10,000 miles from England, when any savings on land were counterbalanced by the expensiveness of labor. For why should one, if he were not a convict bound to servitude, work for an employer after he had saved up enough to buy land for himself? That dilemma was the rock on which Western Australia split so quickly that in 1836, within seven years after the initial settlement, the proprietors turned it over to the government. It might pay for capitalists to buy land in Ontario, for resale to a flood of immigrants, because Ontario was a land that was filling up with population. It did not pay in Western Australia, where there was no such flood of immigrants. Furthermore a comparison of what was happening in Ontario with what was happening across the border in the United States seemed to suggest that the American method was the better, for population was streaming south out of Ontario, attracted across the border by the policy of a fixed minimum price for land, along with division into units suitable for individual landowners.

Indeed it was being argued, at the very moment that Western Australia was being founded, that the principles of its founding were wrong and those of the United States Land Office were right. For in 1829, from New-gate Prison, in London, Edward Gibbon Wakefield was issuing his history-making piece of fiction, the *Letter from Sydney*, in which was set forth what was wrong with Australian colonization and what to do about it. Wakefield was an unusual man, as is shown by his reason for being in jail. When offered the choice of fine or imprisonment for abducting an heiress, he had chosen prison as a form of expiation. He had been struck by the desire of his fellow prisoners to be sentenced to transportation to Australia. He had imaginatively, and most accurately, reconstructed the course of events that would naturally take place if a man bought land in New South Wales and tried to farm it, and the moral effect on employer and employed of using either forced convict labor or the only kind of paid labor one could get, incompetent labor. Then, in a final appeal made telling by his vivid prelude, he had asked, in the name of his imaginary migrant, that the price of land be raised, and its proceeds used for the transportation of free immigrants, to make New South Wales a happier land in which to live. This inspired piece of writing fell upon ready ears, for at that moment England's rulers believed she was overpopulated—whether rightly or, as it proved, wrongly is another matter—and that such over-population meant an increasing charge on the poor rates and either national bankruptcy or revolution. At a moment when that belief was at its height, Wakefield suggested a way of reducing the overpopulation and making that reduction pay for itself. Promptly his ideas were taken up both by a Colonization Society which was formed to press his ideas and by the Colonial Office. Lord Howick (later the Third Earl Grey of a few pages back) as Colonial Undersecretary in 1832 ordered an "upset price" of 5s. an acre minimum for all Australian lands. Gradually, Wakefield's principles gained wide acceptance. It became the accepted policy to sell land in small units and use the money to subsidize emigration. Thus was created independent small proprietorship in Australia and the other colonies.

Events played into Wakefield's hands. This was the golden age of Australian land exploration. In the 1820's the hinterland back of the Blue Mountains had been explored, and the upper courses of the Darling and Murrumbidgee Rivers traced. In 1831 these were followed to the Ocean at Spencer Gulf, after their junction with the Murray. Thus the value of the lands around Spencer Gulf became known, as well as their connection with the fruitful inland plains. Here was a place in which to try out Wakefield's ideas. South Australia Commissioners were established who should settle this region, settlers were sent out, and around Adelaide—so named in honor of William IV's Queen—grew up a new colony. It faced many difficulties at first, but by following what were then the American principles of survey before settlement and the payment of a fixed minimum for all land, a society was set up in which small and eventually contented landowners were the rule, rather than large unpopulated estates without the labor to work them. Much of the credit for this goes to Captain George Grey, as he then was, who had been transferred from a post in Western Australia to the governorship of South Australia at a time of crisis and who by sturdy devotion to duty got the colony out of bankruptcy and the colonists to useful work on the land. To the present day, the character of South Australia reflects Wakefield's ideas for founding an agricultural colony quickly and effectively.

Naturally, with such success, the Colonial Office became Wakefieldian in its land policy and tried to apply his ideas to the hinterland of New South Wales. But here was no agricultural society, to be fed by a flow of new immigrants from overpopulated rural England. This was instead sheep country, to be populated from the inhabitants already living in New South Wales. These "squatters," to use the name given them by angered officials in Sydney, at first could not, and later would not, buy the land they grazed. They used unoccupied land for grazing just as the first cattle-men in the American West used the open range a few years later. They drove their flocks from pasture to pasture in search of grass, each man making some one spring his headquarters, and took the gamble that they could keep out of trouble with the authorities until they could market their wool clip at a profit. If they succeeded, they ploughed the profit back into more sheep and rose to wealth. Thus men who in the 1830's began on a shoe-string by the late 1840's formed a "squatter aristocracy." With wealth, they naturally had actual political power, which they equally naturally sought to legalize, the two necessary steps being the wiping off the New South Wales statute books of Wakefieldian land legislation, and the securing of a basically aristocratic constitution for the colony.

The squatters were not the only new element in Australian life. On all sides there was active growth. Capital and consequent expansion were coming to South Australia from copper mines. Van Diemen's Land, tired of its sad reputation as a convict center, was agitating for a change of name to Tasmania, which it achieved first for its Anglican bishopric, then for the colony itself, on attaining self-government in 1852. Sydney was no longer the sole center of population in New South Wales, for to the south at Port Phillip a thriving center was growing up at Melbourne, later to develop into the colony and state of Victoria. Likewise, to the north, graziers had reached the sea from the hinterland of the Darling Downs and were creating a new settlement at Moreton Bay, the present Brisbane, out of which would grow another colony and state, Queensland. But for the moment the squatters were the party of wealth and power, and it was they who took the lead in the political steps that were to lead Australia to her nationhood.

When, in 1842, New South Wales was granted a Legislative Council with members elected on a high property franchise—£20, double that in England—a leader stood forth, William Charles Wentworth. Wentworth's background fitted well the part he was to play. Born in Sydney in 1793, the author while a Cambridge student of the oft-quoted poem "Australia" which prophesied a glowing future for his native continent, a minor explorer in his own right, the ardent champion of "liberty" including liberty for emancipists to live down their convict background, he became in the Legislative Council the voice of the native-born. He pressed for much that was needed—grazing leases to allow the sheep industry to develop without being crippled by purchasing land before using it, the end of transportation of convicts, a university at Sydney—and he got what he demanded, because he had made himself the spokesman of New South Wales when New South Wales badly needed a spokesman. But he also pressed for the continuance of the sort of left-over eighteenth-century aristocracy he had known as a youth. He frankly distrusted democracy, fought the reduction of the franchise to a ten-pound qualification, and when New South Wales was asked to rewrite its own constitution, tried to set up an hereditary peerage.

Wentworth did not have things entirely his own way. Another leader arose, Robert Lowe, an immigrant lawyer from England, who became the voice of the middle classes—as he was to be later in England, when for the middle-class ten-pounders he opposed the Second Reform Bill. In New South Wales Lowe stood for responsible government, as Wentworth did not, since responsible government would have allowed the majority to curtail grazing leases, for the ten-pound franchise, and in general for the needs of Sydney as opposed to those of the back country. Between Lowe and Wentworth there were epic parliamentary battles, worthy of comparison with any at Westminster, and as such establishing an Australian parliamentary tradition.

But those battles never came to a climax; a third party took over. In 1851 two separate events changed the history of the Australian colonies. From England Earl Grey sent out his Government of Australia Act, passed the previous year, which encouraged the colonies to draw up constitutions for submission to Parliament and separated Victoria from New South Wales. Encouraged by this admission of Australian autonomy, Wentworth persuaded the New South Wales Legislative Council to forbid the landing of convicts, who, however, were still sent out, since Western Australia in need of labor asked for them. But as Wentworth was working out the type of constitution he wanted, gold was discovered at Ballarat in Victoria. At once immigrants flowed in from all over the world.

With the influx of the "diggers" Australian society changed. Some diggers were Chartists; all sympathized with Chartist, i.e., democratic, ideals. These men wanted responsible parliamentary government plus universal suffrage. They also had special needs. They disliked Chinese competition and forced a "white Australia" policy on the various colonies. They worked not as individual miners but as employees of mining corporations—the period of individual mining was very short in Australia, because the type of formation in which the gold was found required machinery—and in consequence they early formed unions and demanded government regulation of industry. Furthermore, as workingmen, they favored tariff protection.

Naturally, all this did not spring up overnight, but the course of Australian history was foreshadowed not so much in New South Wales, where the pastoralists still held power and where Wentworth secured not an hereditary upper council but a life-tenure upper council, as in more democratic Victoria. It was in Victoria that the Australian Mounted Police demonstrated their ability to keep order at the diggings, even to suppressing all Sunday work, in distinct contrast to California. It was in Victoria that the process of democratization was speeded up by the easily suppressed miners' revolt of 1853. It was in Victoria that in 1866 David Syme began his campaign for a protective tariff, which after the absurdity of custom-houses the length of the Murray River led to protection becoming a Commonwealth policy after federation. It was from Victoria that the diggers went out to the sheep runs as shearers and, by founding the shearers' union, began the Australian labor movement. And it was the autonomy demanded by Victoria, demonstrated in such matters as variations in railway gauges, that gave the Australian colonies that vigorous particularism that has lasted in the states in federation.

By 1855, after responsible government had reached all the colonies except underpopulated Western Australia, a similar course of events took place in each colony, varying with local circumstances. South Australia, where landownership was more widespread, thanks to Wakefield, led in land legislation. All over the world the Torrens system of registered title has been copied, in one form or another, when ease of land transfer has become a political issue. Pastoralist New South Wales lagged behind in land reform, with the squatters doing all they could to block small owners. With different names for the same thing, the sheepmen played the same legalistic tricks on would-be farmers that American cattlemen played on "nesters." They bought up water holes, made claims under false names, intimidated would-be settlers, and otherwise nullified the Land Occupation Act of 1861. As for Queensland, when that colony was separated from New South Wales in 1859, it too had the special problems of securing labor for its sugar plantations, leading to "blackbirding"—the kidnaping of South Sea Islanders—and eventually to a special variant of the "white Australia" movement, when white labor succeeded in taking over the plantations. But for all these variations, similar causes brought similar effects among like-minded people over the continent. By 1867, the Australian colonies were moving steadily to what they now have, a government largely inspired by Chartist ideals, and were well on the way to shackling the powerful upper houses that had been written into their first constitutions.

NEW ZEALAND

For all that New Zealand is next Australia on the globe, it is over 1,000 miles away. Furthermore, it is markedly different in characteristics and thus in its history. Geographically, it is a counterpart of rural England, for even though North Island lies in subtropical latitudes, its high mountain ranges give it an English climate, favorable to raising sheep. Physiographically, it was well suited to welcome the English, since when the first white settlers reached there there were almost no mammals on the islands, to the degree that such grazing as took place in the lush fields and forests was by grass-eating birds. Here the English farm animals could flourish without competition. However, there was a special problem, for the Maoris were the most advanced race with whom the English have shared a new-found land.

It has been told how the missionaries gained a foothold in New Zealand in the 1810's, 1820's and 1830's, and thus unwillingly prepared the way for white colonization. That colonization came in 1839, when the New Zealand Company's ship *Tory* brought the first settlers. Here again Wakefield appears. He had long been agitating for settlement on his principles in New Zealand, and on his return from Canada, where he had inspired a new land policy, he succeeded in bringing to life the already formed New Zealand Company. In this he was aided by fear of a French occupation of the island—no idle fear, as was later shown by the French preemption of Madagascar from English missionary influence. At first settlement was on the basis of grants from Maori chiefs to the New Zealand Company, under the Treaty of Waitangi. Misunderstandings, to put it mildly, of the meaning of this treaty led to the death of Wakefield's brother and others, at the Massacre of Wairau, and to the first Maori War of 1843 to 1845. This was not a war of all Maoris against the English, for loyalty to the treaty and respect for the missionaries kept many at peace. It was settled by sending from South Australia George Grey, who stopped encroachment by the whites and won the respect of the Maoris, by personal ascendancy over all whom he met.

At this point Grey's namesake Earl Grey shipped out a ready-made constitution, which Grey promptly returned to him as unworkable. Instead Sir George (as he soon became) ran the colony on a direct crown-colony basis, under which effective system settlements were made in the less populated South Island by two new organizations, both semireligious. One was the Otago Association, formed by members of the Scottish Free

Church; the other, the Canterbury Association of the Church of England. Both were strictly Wakefieldian—Wakefield himself came out to the Canterbury settlement, to spend the rest of his life in New Zealand—and both succeeded in building up a population of landowners. Then it was, with an established society in existence, that in 1851 the New Zealand Company was finally dissolved and in 1852 a constitution could be put in force. Under this constitution six provinces were established at once, and later a federal legislature followed, although the Governor kept native affairs in his hands. In 1856, after Grey had left for South Africa, this evolved into responsible government.

Succeeding governors did not have Sir George Grey's ability, and in 1861 it was necessary for him to return and settle another Maori War. This had broken out from similar causes, the encroachment of Paheka, or white, on Maori. It was marked by an attempt to set up a Maori kingdom and a Maori variant of Christianity. Sir George could not settle this war by personal influence, since the Maoris well knew that the central legislature could tie his hands and make his nominal control of native affairs unworkable. But he could and did cooperate with the white New Zealanders. Rather unfairly, he used the fact that his commission as governor made him commander in chief to shoulder aside the English general in charge of regular troops, who was doing the best he could under obstacles put in his way by the settlers. It was New Zealand troops, under Grey, who cracked the last Maori resistance, and it was New Zealand statesmen who eventually made a lasting peace with the Maoris, all the more lasting because it was made by the New Zealanders and not for them.

By the 1860's New Zealand had established its own character, as a highly orderly, self-governing rural England in the antipodes. Here was carried forward the tradition of progressive farming that stems from such Englishmen as Coke of Norfolk and "Turnip" Townshend. Here was carried forward, too, the English tradition—not always so well honored—of respect for a native race, as the New Zealanders themselves, now in charge of native policy, worked out good relations with the Maoris, until in later years the Maoris took to controlling their own destinies. Here, in the establishment of a local Church, self-governing but in religious communion with the Church of England, was taken a most important step in the evolution of the Church of England from a branch of the English government to the world-wide linking of many of a common religious faith in the so-called Canterbury Communion of churches allied to that presided over by the Archbishop of Canterbury. Later generations in New Zealand would have to implement what was here evolving and to build up the special structure of relationship of state to people characteristic of the two islands. The foundations for all this were laid in the days of Grey's two proconsulships.

SOUTH AFRICA

When the British came to South Africa, as has been previously pointed out, they found there a potential national culture about as old as that which the conquerors of Canada had found. The span of time from Champlain, 1608, to the fall of Montreal, 1760, about equals that from Van Riebeeck in 1652 to the two captures of the Cape, in 1795 and 1806. Therefore, as in Canada, the British had to take things as they were; they could not build from emptiness, as they had been able to do in Australia. If they would not accept local customs, they had to do something about it. It will be recalled that, though at Cape Town amalgamation of Dutch and English went smoothly enough, on the frontier matters were different. The frontier Boers had their own way of treating the natives, and it was not the way of the missionaries sent out by "Exeter Hall." English missionaries called to their support the authorities in Cape Town and stopped local "landrosts" and "field cornets" from calling out the Boers "on commando" and taking summary vengeance for real or imaginary provocations. As a result there was on the frontier an explosive situation. Men with the self-reliance and adaptation to their environment of American frontiersmen felt pushed to the limit. And in 1833, the apparent limit came.

The pretext for the boiling over of resentment was the abolition of slavery and the insufficient compensation paid for slaves by the English government, at the very moment that orders from London caused a bungle in a Kaffir War. This was, in fact, a pretext; few frontier Boers held slaves. The reaction was just that determination to have one's own way that led non-slave-holding whites in the Southern states to fight the Civil War. That reaction in this case did not take the form of revolt—the Slagter's Nek affair of 1816 had taught the futility of that—but of mass migration. Boer cattlemen who had been accustomed all their lives to trekking from pastureland to pastureland now set out on the Great Trek across the Orange and Vaal Rivers to find freedom.

An epic story to hand down to the next generation does much to make a nation, and it is the Great Trek that forms much of the Boer epic. Nationality-conscious Boers like to recollect how the Voortrekkers went out to spy out the land and how then whole communities inspanned their oxen, climbed into their wagons, and set out to take over the High Veldt of the interior, the grazing lands so like our far Western plains. Here the Trekkers met the native problem which had been the pretext of the Trek in a new form. The Negroes of the lands near Cape Town were relatively unorganized; the so-called Kaffir Wars were large-scale cattle raids and retributions for them. But in the interior were great fighting tribes which had a powerful and overwhelming charging formation. The "Impis" or regiments of the various chiefs advanced in a semicircle shaped like a bull's two horns that both outflanked and overwhelmed at the same time. With such native forces the Trekkers had to fight for their lives. They would form "lager" with their wagons to make a sort of temporary fort, from which the men would shoot down the attackers while women and children reloaded the muskets. Then when an attack had been repulsed, the men acting as mounted infantry would sally forth to harry the Impis as they re-formed for another assault, and endeavor to rescue the cattle that were being driven off. Here, in the memories of advancing across the High Veldt, was raw material for much pride.[1]

But the clearing of the High Veldt of these tribes was only the first and least dramatic stage in the Trek. To the Trekkers the High Veldt was not as attractive as the fertile plains of Natal on the seacoast. So parties swung south, off the plateau lands, to where there were even fiercer natives, the Zulus, with even better-drilled Impis. At first the Boers tried negotiations, but they were met with treachery. For Dingaan, the Zulu king, summoned the Boer Piet Retief to sign a treaty and slew him and all his party at a place to this day known by the sad name of Weenen or Weeping. Aid was sent for over the mountains, and Pretorius came down, to secure vengeance. On December 16—now the Boer national holiday, Dingaan's Day —the Blood Commando killed Dingaan and found in Retief's wallet the treaty Dingaan had dishonored.

For a moment, the Afrikander (South African Dutch) dream of a Dutch New World with a window to the sea seemed about to come to being, even to the point of negotiating for an alliance with the homeland, Holland. Then English sea power ended it. To preserve the English settlers in Natal from the Zulus, English troops, commanded by a South African, Colonel Cloete, landed. These well-drilled regulars, trained in platoon fire, had as little to fear from Zulu Impis as their predecessors had had from French columns. They cleared the coastal plains of Natal for settlement and offered the Boers the choice of accepting English rule or getting out. Led by Pretorius, they got out, for to them the High Veldt and freedom was preferable to fertile fields and subjugation. Across the Orange and the Vaal, with Bloemfontein and Pretoria as capitals, the frontiersmen who had always, in fact, governed themselves, set up two republics, which gradually acquired the names of the Orange Free State and the Transvaal, or the South African Republic, while Natal became a purely English colony. But even on the High Veldt English pressure on the Trekkers did not

---

[1] South African words have been used purposefully here. Commando, trek, veldt, inspan, lager, and (from the novels of H. Rider Haggard) impi are enough part of the English language for that. The South African flavor they can give may remind students, what some English rulers to their sorrow forgot, that the Afrikander Boers, like the French Canadians, have a true nationality, in the building up of which language has played a great part.

cease. Missionaries pushed inland, too; it was in 1841 that David Livingstone started his career in Bechuanaland and thereafter began the explorations that opened the "Missionary Road" to the north. English regulars continued to keep the natives in check. In particular a Peninsular veteran, Sir Harry Smith, pushed on the borders, in the late 1840's establishing a chain of posts, the two easternmost of which were called Harrismith and Ladysmith for him and his wife. Sir Harry, too, was the first to hold the title of High Commissioner as well as that of Governor, as such being responsible for dealings with native chiefs and the self-governing Boers.

Under him developed a policy of support of two of the three strongest native tribes, the Griquas of the Lower Orange valley and the Basutos of the Caldeon valley and present-day Basutoland, who under their leader Mokesh and with the advice of French Protestant missionaries kept semi-independence and control of their own lands. Here was an origin of a policy in force to this day, of protection of the natives by the Imperial government in London.

Sir Harry therefore wanted to have effective control over the Orange Free State and the Transvaal. Though he intended to allow self-government, he wanted England to have the authority she needed to back the native policies she wished to enforce. But though the Colonial Office wanted to protect the natives and wanted to prevent any outside interference by other countries, such as Holland had threatened in Natal, it was not willing to spend money. Therefore, though Smith got some authority in the Free State, his actions were partially disavowed. Later on, by the Sand River Convention of 1852 and the Bloemfontein Convention of 1854, the Transvaal and the Free State were respectively acknowledged to be self-governing, under British suzerainty, whatever that meant, with British control of their relations with any country beside England. In this confusion of terms lay the seeds of two future Boer Wars.

Earl Grey's ideas of spreading self-government throughout the Empire in due course reached South Africa in the Cape in 1854. Natal became a separate colony in 1856, with representative government only, without executive responsibility to the assemblies. If a further step had been taken, federation would have come in South Africa before it did in Canada. It was no fault of South Africa that it did not. Here Sir George Grey appears on the scene, transferred from New Zealand to see what he could do about the Boer problem. He promptly persuaded the Boers to agree to federation, only to have Lord Carnarvon, the Colonial Secretary in the Derby-Disraeli government of 1858–1859, disavow and recall him. By the time Sir George had reached London and by personal intercession reversed the disavowal, the opportunity had been lost, though what had been lost men did not realize till later.

So South Africa in the 1860's went quietly on, a poor land, where few outsiders cared that the frontiersmen on the High Veldt thought they were independent or on what terms their independence was held. That Sir George Grey could improve the economic life of South Africa by encouraging ostrich farming suggests the meagerness of South Africa's economic life before diamonds and gold, after 1867, changed the picture entirely.

In each future dominion—Canada, Australia, New Zealand, South Africa —full nationality was not reached. Such nationalisms as cropped out were the antagonisms of French and English Canadian, of Boer and English under the mediation of South African Dutch who accepted English rule, and, in a sense, of Maori and Paheka. What did happen was that the granting of responsible government allowed the seeds of local nationalisms to grow to their present fruition in cooperation with English rule rather than opposition to it.

INDIA

Likewise, in India, though in a far more rudimentary way, a national feeling was encouraged, if it be to encourage a national feeling when an outside ruler gives unity, education, and the means of eventual industrial development. In this period when the self-governing Empire progressed, India progressed as well. Great steps were taken—Bentinck's abolition of thuggee and suttee; Macaulay's legal and educational reforms; the Afghan and Sikh wars and the conquest of Sind; Dalhousie's program of public works; and, after the drama of the Mutiny and the nobility of "Clemency Canning," the final transfer of rule from the East India Company to the English government.

Bentinck, a Whig sent out to India in 1829 in the days when the Liberal Tories were coquetting with the Whigs, became, on the renewal of the East India Company's charter in 1833, technically the first Governor-general of India, his predecessors having been in name merely Governors-general of Bengal with extended powers. Bentinck certainly fitted his new title, for he thought for all India. His most dramatic reform was the ending of thuggee and suttee. These were two religious beliefs, one that it was the hereditary duty of one caste, the Thugs, to steal and murder, the other that on the death of a husband his widow should throw herself on the funeral pyre and let herself be burned to ashes. Previous authorities had tolerated such practices, for fear of stirring up a hornet's nest of opposition; Bentinck used his powers, and ended them.

But, more important, Bentinck presided over and made possible great legal and educational reforms. From England was sent out, as the new "legal" member of Council, Thomas Babington Macaulay, to reorganize law and administration. By the time he had left, India had the basis for a new legal code, a freer press, and a system of education. Law became increasingly uniform wherever the East India Company's writ ran. The

English and vernacular press could act as organs of public opinion, though still subject to more restraint than in England. An Indian desirous of gaining an education could gain one, though he had to learn English to get it. For this last Macaulay has been attacked, especially for the vigorous words in which he poured scorn on Indian mythology as a subject of study. But by giving English learning to India, he gave to Indians the chance to gain the knowledge of the Western world which they lacked and needed. Improved knowledge of their own culture could and did come later, and the giving of a common language to all Indians was not without advantage. The first sessions of the Indian Congress in 1885 were conducted in English, which therefore became the language the Indians used to plan to gain their present independence.

Under Bentinck, too, the Indian Civil Service moved forward, for the reformers of England wrote into the renewed East India Charter of 1833 the requirement of selecting future civil servants by competitive examination. A solid basis was thus formed for a strong and expanding English government of India. Here, together with the fostering of trade that came from the final abolition of the East India Company monopoly, even with China, forces were set at work that would give India a unity and a nationality such as she had never known in the past.

Under Bentinck's successor, Auckland, it seemed as if the same peace and quiet would prevail. Auckland's first duty was to show the humanity of using governmental powers to fight famine, something new on that scale in India. But the Eastern Crisis of 1838 to 1841 brought India into world politics and forced expansion. Fear of Russian aggression led to an interference in Afghanistan. An expedition was sent there to replace the pro-Russian Amir with a pro-British one. Kabul and Kandahar were occupied, with apparent success, and English agents were sent to the khanates of Central Asia to combat Russian advance. But when Auckland's successor, Ellenborough, landed in India, he learned that disaster had come. The army in Kabul had been wiped out, only one man returning alive to India. But as reinforcements were hurried across the Indus River, the more heartening news came that the Kandahar army and that at Peshawar had fought their ways into Kabul, to rescue prisoners and restore English prestige somewhat. Ellenborough tried further to bolster that prestige by having the retreating armies—permanent occupation of Kabul was obviously impossible—bring back with them a famous pair of gates that the Afghans had taken from India centuries before. Amid Anglo-Indian derision, the army returned from Kabul with palpable forgeries. Fortunately, the pro-Russian Amir, when left alone, proved wisely neutral, which allayed alarm.

Ellenborough continued to overestimate the value of prestige and plunged into a war with the chiefs of Sind, at the mouth of the Indus.

Again his orders were obeyed. The Peninsular veteran Sir Charles Napier, so a legend relates, sent back the punning one-word Latin report *"Peccavi"* (I have sinned). At this point, the Directors of the East India Company remembered that they had the right to dismiss a Governor-general, and did so. But Ellenborough's legacy, apparently the usual legacy of what Indian officials have called "a forward policy," remained. The warrior Sikhs of the Punjab, who after years of peace were spoiling for a fight, tried to see how much they could insult the English by interfering in Sind. It took two wars to defeat them, and it was only in 1848 that peace returned to India. Thus it was that, in the supposedly peaceful Victorian era, much of India was taken over by force of arms. This came about, not by conscious design, but as a choice of the lesser of two evils; wars broke out only after fair proposals for settling disputes had been rejected, Ellenborough's mistakes being not in fighting but in letting the disputes start.

However, for the Punjab, good came of this. To that newly won province were sent the Lawrence brothers, who gathered around them a team of able young men, outstanding among whom were Herbert Edwardes and the incomparable John Nicholson, the "Nikalseyn" of Sikh ballads. These Punjab civil servants and soldiers gained a reputation for keeping the peace and doing justice that made English and Sikhs friends. So beloved did Nicholson become that a sect grew up that worshipped him, despite his attempt to discourage this by publicly flogging his devotees whenever he came across them.

India now saw an era of comparative peace and progress, under the rule of Lord Dalhousie. Railways were introduced under private management, but with government encouragement. These, along with public works, did much to lessen the curse of famine, for food could now be rushed to areas of starvation and dams irrigated dry but fertile land. Thuggee and suttee were rooted out of the Native States. There was a general impulse to westernization. Here Dalhousie's belief in the beneficence of British government planted the seeds of trouble. Indian princes were frightened by the frequent use of the doctrine of "lapse" under which the East India Company took over heirless states when, in Indian eyes, adopted heirs had valid claims. When the Board of Control in London further ordered the taking over of Oudh because of gross misrule, they were ripe for revolt and needed but a pretext.

In 1857 two pretexts came. Indian tradition had it that the British raj, or rule, would last only a hundred years from its foundation at Plassey, in 1757. That made 1857 the crucial year. In that year, by administrative stupidity, new cartridges greased with a combination of pig's fat and cow's fat were issued to the sepoys, who were told they had to bite them open before inserting them into their muzzle loading muskets. This endangered Moslems who never touched pig's flesh and Hindus to whom the cow was sacred. That summer a flame of mutiny flashed through Bengal. Not only British soldiers but women and children were brutally murdered. The Delhi garrison was wiped out, those in Cawnpore and Lucknow besieged.

The Mutiny was suppressed, by British valor and the loyalty of sepoys who stood firm. The significant thing is that it was checked if not suppressed before reinforcements came, so that the men in India could boast: "Alone we did it." For John Nicholson dashed through the Punjab, disarming mutinous regiments, and then hurried to reinforce the few thousand British and sepoys who were "besieging" 50,000 Indians within the walls of Delhi. Nicholson demanded and led a storm of the city. He died leading a charge, but the job was done and the main center of the Mutiny was broken up. Meanwhile a relief column came up the Ganges, arriving at Cawnpore too late but saving Lucknow. Further reinforcements made possible the complete restoration of British control.

But English valor and initiative accomplished this because it was supported by a general acceptance of English rule. The Mutiny took place chiefly in Bengal, and only where feudal leaders with grievances could capitalize on latent unrest. Madras and Bombay Presidencies hardly were touched, and the newly conquered Sikhs gladly fought against the attempt to revive the Mogul Empire that in years past had persecuted their religion and forced them to become warriors. The pacification of India recognized these facts. "Clemency" Canning, the newly arrived Governor-General, refused to punish any but ringleaders and quietly dropped the doctrine of lapse, after which the Indian Princes became again most loyal supporters of English rule. India returned to normal surprisingly quickly.

The Mutiny had several results. It made the British rely on prestige. They saw what Nicholson had done by sheer personality, and they tended to emphasize their position as a master race. The savagery of the Indians, exemplified by the murders of women and children when Cawnpore had surrendered on terms, led to counterbitterness in the suppression. Thus the old trust between English and Indian lessened. This was hardly true of relations with the fighting races who had supported England; Gurkha and Sikh stayed close to the hearts of their English officers. But elsewhere in India, the precautions taken against another Mutiny, such as the keeping of all artillery in European hands and the building of easily defended cantonments or English quarters outside Indian cities, inevitably created a barrier between English and Indian. Stupid talk about "niggers" flew about till one snobbish club refused admittance to an Indian nobleman whom the King had knighted and whose provable pedigree was older than the history of England. Perforce, the English people became as a race set apart.

The other change was in law rather than in fact. The moribund East

India Company was deprived of all power to rule, which was transferred directly to the Government of England. Eventually, the Company took the hint, if hint it was, and dissolved. But though this meant a change in names, chiefly of the President of the Board of Control to Secretary of State for India, and a saving of circumlocutions in official correspondence, it was largely a change in form, not fact. Powers and duties of councils in England and India, and of the Indian Civil Service, remained the same.

In these years occurred one of the most romantic events of Empire history. A young Englishman in the Indian Civil Service inherited a fortune, went home to England, bought a yacht, cruised in the East Indies, intervened to stop slave running on the coast of Borneo, and wound up as the "white Rajah" of Sarawak. Thus it was that James Brooke became at one and the same time a ruling monarch and a loyal subject of Queen Victoria, who governed his few thousands of subjects in the same spirit as Her Majesty's appointees ruled India, in trust for the governed.

So far, the story of the early Victorian Empire has suggested that self-government, and the government in trust of India, were its keynotes. That is true, but it is not the whole truth. Centralizing tendencies in the Colonial Office were checked for most of the Empire, but not for all. Important in seeing the Empire as a whole is a realization that the antislavery crusade continued and that self-government in the West Indies was curtailed.

ANTISLAVERY

The antislavery movement came to its climax in 1833. As has been recounted, antislavery societies had begun their agitation for abolition in 1823, when Wilberforce passed on his mantle to Thomas Fowell Buxton. Paralleling the movement for parliamentary reform, these societies rose to great political power in the 1830's. A flood of petitions for the abolition of slavery poured in on Parliament from 1830 to 1833, by their very weight helping impress the unreformed House of Commons with the need for Reform. When Reform came and the middle-class "ten-pound householders," the very men who had given the best support to the antislavery movement, elected the Parliament that spent England's monies, it was possible to make the offer to end slavery throughout the Empire by buying the slaves and to ride roughshod over claims of local assemblies by ordering such a purchase and by specifying the terms on which it would be made.

Resistance to this order was useless, and the end having been achieved, antislavery workers either turned to other interests or supported the Navy's suppression of the slave trade and the missionary work that centered in Exeter Hall. But except for securing English contact with Africa, Exeter Hall did little to extend the Empire, in this period. It would only be after Livingstone's explorations that new lands would again be brought into the Empire, in the late-nineteenth-century expansion.

THE WEST INDIES

But the abolition of slavery created special West Indian problems. As a sop to the local assemblies, they were offered a choice of immediate emancipation or a period of apprenticeship. The Bermuda assembly had the wisdom to take the bull by the horns and accept immediate emancipation. In Barbados a hiring system was set up that made the change from slavery to freedom simpler—the Barbadian emancipist got exactly the rights of an agricultural laborer in Hampshire, which may be a reflection on the rights of an agricultural laborer in Hampshire. But elsewhere the assemblies either wrote apprenticeship laws the Colonial Office refused to accept, and thus indirectly chose the type of apprenticeship that had been laid down in England, or else chose it directly. And apprenticeship did not work. How could it, when the West Indies Negroes had been dreaming of the freedom they knew Haiti had gained forty years before? How could it, when the apprenticeship laws would be enforced by local justices of the peace who had formerly themselves held the apprentices as slaves? Parliament had to step in and cut apprenticeship short.

This was a severe blow to the planter oligarchies of the West Indies and their "old-constitution" legislatures. Furthermore, economics struck yet another blow. The power of the old assemblies had been based on the refusal to vote taxes, and to refuse to vote taxes one must first have wealth to tax. That, too, was going. Freed slaves delighted in not working hard. Creditors seized upon the money paid for slaves, so that such payments in effect denuded the West Indies of capital. It had been possible to get extensions of credit, when only by such extensions could loans be repaid, but with available cash to take, creditors took it, and stopped making loans. Things got so bad that many plantations were abandoned and allowed to revert to wilderness.

Jamaica, England's largest and richest West Indian island, may be taken as an exemplar of what happened to a lesser degree elsewhere. In 1839, because of the recalcitrance of her legislature in not passing a Prisons Bill, Parliament threatened to suspend its functions. This brought down the Melbourne Whig Government, because such a treatment of a legislature was so un-Whiggish an action, but Queen Victoria, in the Bedchamber Crisis, put Melbourne back in office, and Jamaica had to come to heel. New governors, Elgin of Canadian fame among them, restored matters somewhat and brought Hindus from India to form a new labor supply. But the end of protection in 1846 hit Jamaica hard, and by 1865 growing taxation and the continued heavy hand of the planter class created a crisis. It took the form of a Negro revolt against oppression, that was put down not by the planter militia but by Governor Eyre. Antislavery emotion had him brought to England for trial—no Jamaica white jury would have convicted him. Nor did an English jury, despite the judge's charge. The victim of the revolt was the Jamaica constitution. It was abrogated, along with it those of Saint Kitts and Nevis, and government by governors and nominated councils replaced constitutions as old as those of the original American colonies, or older. Paid "stipendiary magistrates" responsible to the Colonial Office through the governor replaced the local planter justices of the peace. If the Colonial Office lost authority in Canada, Australia, and New Zealand, here it gained.

This gain in authority was marked in two forms: improved central administration in London, and improved legal position of the central administration. A series of great colonial undersecretaries of state—Stephen, Merivale, and Rogers—"really governed the colonies," as an Australian politician complained. For, despite Charles Buller's gibe at "Mr. Mother Country," these wise and experienced men had the habit of being largely right on individual problems, and in consequence they got their way. As the Colonial Office rose in prestige when it was separated from the War Office in 1854, and as improved means of communication linked the Empire more closely together, centralization and efficiency grew apace.

In 1843 were passed two laws, the Foreign Jurisdiction Act and the British Settlements Act, which tended to increase this central power. Each was passed to meet a specific problem, but each had an extra clause which allowed wider application by an "Order in Council." Ostensibly and in intention, the Foreign Jurisdiction Act merely allowed setting up English courts in Turkey and China, under treaty provisions for special rights for Englishmen. Ostensibly and in intention the British Settlements Act merely allowed the granting of revocable rights of self-government in West Africa. Had not such a restriction been made, a newly created legislature could not, as the law then stood, have its powers taken away except by act of Parliament with all the storm and stress that took place when the Jamaica legislature fought the Melbourne Government in 1839. But since these acts might be applied anywhere by Order in Council it would be possible to have colonial governments made and unmade anywhere in the world by executive action. Such would be the way West Indian and West African constitutions would be made and unmade by officials in Whitehall; after World War I such would be the way that Iraq and Palestine, as mandates, would be put under the Colonial Office. As extended in 1887, 1890, and 1945 these two acts form the basis of the present British colonial Empire. No wonder that two years later—in 1845, so the Oxford Dictionary records —a new phrase entered the English language. This phrase was "Crown colony" to describe a colony under the executive control of the crown. Thus it was that the legal doctrines of the First British Empire were side-stepped, and the Colonial Office, subject to its responsibility to Parliament, became the arbiter of the fate of colonies without parliamentary titles to self-government.

Nor was the Colonial Office the only central institution to grow in power at this time. In 1833 had been passed the Privy Councils Appeals Act. It, too, was primarily intended as an improvement of an existing institution. Hitherto appeals from India had been made to the King in Council, which might mean any three Privy Councilors. Now they were made to a special appeals committee, of certain councilors with judicial office, among whom were retired Indian judges. As at this time a constitutional custom was hardening into law by which appeals to the House of Lords were heard only by legally qualified peers, in fact the Privy Council Committee and the so-called "law lords" became almost interchangeable bodies, except that the Privy Council held in addition judges with Indian—and later colonial—experience. (This description is an oversimplification of the actual situation in law but is close to it in fact.) Thus came into existence a supreme court for the Empire, that tended to unity just as the United States Supreme Court a few decades earlier had done much to strengthen the Federal union. To the Privy Council came appeals from Romano-Dutch law at the Cape and Ceylon, French law from Canada and the Channel Islands, as well as native laws of India, to meet at one center.

These legal forces were not the only ones that helped build up the Empire. As has been explained, the growth of English capital and its migration overseas linked England with her possessions. Without repeating the figures and arguments previously given, a reminder should here be made of that truth. Likewise it should be remembered that population emigrated, along with capital. Missionary zeal should never be forgotten. But, if these truths are kept in mind, it can be seen what sort of a problem Parliament faced. Would there be a collapsing Empire, from which colonies split off into independence? Would there be a centralized Empire, ruled by wise and tactful administrators in London? Parliament would have to decide. In Parliament colonial matters were treated with "a wise and salutary neglect," to use the traditional definition of England's colonial policy of these years. To the free-trade Liberals it was a mistake for England to own colonies. Why should the British taxpayer foot the bill for governments not in England? As John Bright put it, colonial governorships were "a form of outdoor poor relief for the aristocracy," a payment to noblemen for doing nothing useful. The sooner England's overseas dependencies became independent the better, for with world free trade they would continue to afford profitable markets. These ideas the Tories shared. In the 1850's their leader, Benjamin Disraeli, went so far as to write of "those wretched colonies that hang like millstones around our necks." As for the Whigs, they, as believers in self-government at home, naturally tended to believe in self-government across the water.

This unintentionally wise attitude of neglect on the part of the three major political groups had the salutary effect of throwing the active handling of colonial affairs in Parliament into the hands of two relatively small groups: the humanitarians, and the tiny but influential band of Radicals who believed actively in the Empire. Both these groups gave policies to the Empire. Because the humanitarians were willing to spend money in good causes, they made the protection of native races a cardinal point in English colonial administration. This would do much to give England control of Africa. The Radicals did more than this; they foreshadowed the evolution of the Empire into the Commonwealth of Nations. The leader in this work was Charles Buller, who, though he died young, has gone down in history as potentially great. He held toward colonial aspirations for self-government not the negative belief that the colonies were encumbrances to be gotten rid of but the positive belief that freedom shared was a bond of union. Again and again he made himself the advocate of extensions of responsible government and the ending of curbs on the colonies and, by sheer persistence, won his point. He caused colonial statesmen to believe that it was possible to find sympathy in England for their aspirations; he caused some members of the customarily antiexpansionist party to take pride in overseas England. The seeds he so planted later bore fruit.

The record shows that what Buller stood for became policy. It was in the years of his vivid parliamentary career that were passed the great constitutional acts that made Canada truly self-governing. It was shortly after his early death in 1848 that the Australian Constitutions Act and the Government of New Zealand Act gave to the Southern Hemisphere the self-government of North America. But these Acts were not enough. The Empire was still under the sway of the Declaratory Act of 1766, with its assertion of parliamentary supremacy. Here comes the strange tale of that unconscious Empire builder, Mr. Justice Boothby of South Australia. This earnest and meticulous judge, realizing that the laws of England were supreme and that laws repugnant to them were invalid, took to throwing out South Australian laws right and left. Then it became necessary to travel half a world away to rectify matters by appeal to the Privy Council. When Mr. Justice Boothby discovered that the South Australian Constitution was itself repugnant and invalid, it was too much. Parliament passed the Colonial Laws Validity Act, to apply not only in South Australia but throughout the Empire. It declared all colonial laws valid as long as they did not contradict English acts expressly or obviously extended to the colony in question. Thus, quietly and almost by accident, the colonies came of age. Now, where they existed, parliaments could take over from proconsuls, since it had become England's policy to grant to those who had reached political maturity the rights of an adult government. So it might be said that the English Parliament chose neither centralization nor anarchy but the education of its overseas children. Of course that is an idealistic picture of the mid-Victorian Empire. What matters is that it became a guiding ideal.

Part Five THE TRANSITION TO COLLECTIVISM 1870–1914

INTRODUCTION

In the early summer of 1870 Lord Granville, the Secretary of State for Foreign Affairs, confidently predicted a bright future for European peace and tranquillity. Not a cloud appeared on the international horizon. A few weeks later the Franco-Prussian war exploded. The British Empire for the next forty-four years sailed not only on courses not anticipated in 1870, but also into unknown seas that required luck and skillful handling to save the ship of state from sinking.

No one was quite prepared for the speed and direction in which foreign relations were to move. In 1914, Great Britain was to find herself an ally of her hereditary enemy, France, and her newest Asiatic imperial rival, Russia. The German empire that had not existed in June, 1870, in 1914 had taken their places as the enemy. Splendid isolation, seemingly a sure and safe policy in 1870, was to be thrown over for a defensive alliance with little Japan in 1902 and ententes with France in 1904, Russia in 1907. Through unlooked-for chance, Great Britain found herself possessed in 1914 of a new tropical empire in Africa. Therefore, traditional foreign policies were naturally followed less confidently after 1900 than they were in 1870, in part because of the colonial and economic competition that took place among the world's great powers.

While new colonies and islands were added to Britain's Empire, her peoples overseas worked out a new mode of living with themselves and the mother country. In 1870 Canada was a young dominion. The recently completed Confederation was untried and still an experiment. So well did the idea of local self-government and imperial protection in world affairs work out that by 1914 Newfoundland, Australia, New Zealand, and South Africa were also recognized as dominions. A broad concept of a commonwealth of British nations became the foundation for a new and flexible system of imperial government, in which Great Britain was the bulwark of defense, the controller of imperial foreign affairs, yet the leader rather than the ruler. When World War I came, the strength of this system was shown as the self-governing dominions joined the British in battle.

In 1870 British public opinion held that the colonies would someday drop from the trunk of the mother country like overripe fruit. Thirty years later the Empire was regarded not only as an economic necessity but also as a gift of God to the British. Suddenly the British found themselves to be an imperial people blessed with the divine mission of civilizing, ruling, and making profit in lands not before explored or dominated by Western nations. In this happy conceit, the British were at one with France, Russia, Germany, and the United States. These nations discovered also the economic need of overseas empires and their clear duties to civilize barbaric races. It was through imperial competition that the old rivals, Russia and France, were turned into friends and the new German empire into an enemy. At first in Asia, Russia had started her expansion after the Franco-Prussian War. She moved farther into Turkestan, stirred up the Afghans, and with the turn of the century was intriguing in both the Persian Gulf area and Tibet. Her southward drive into China from Manchuria was stopped by the Japanese only in 1905. This check was to lead to the Russian-British understanding of 1907. British statesmen had tried to stop the Russians and had partially succeeded at the Congress of Berlin in 1878. The year 1878 also found Great Britain adding Cyprus to her empire, a cession from Turkey, the nation she was supposed to save from Russian aggression.

Disraeli, always a superb dreamer of Oriental phantasies, had unintentionally arranged for British occupation of Egypt when he bought the Khedive's stock in the Suez Canal in 1875. In 1881 the British found themselves using force to collect the money owed to an international group of European bankers. A brief period of occupation in which debts were to be funded was stretched into years of policing, supervising, and conquering. Not only were the Egyptians brought to heel, but also the Sudan and the strategic Nile Valley had to be brought under British supervision. The occupation of the Nile brought Britain into new conflict. General Gordon lost his life to the fanatical Mahdi. France threatened from 1881 to 1898 to make more trouble in the Nile Valley and Africa. The Germans, now imperialists, had to be met and their African threat to British interests countered. In West Africa and East Africa, boundary lines between French and British, Italian and British, and German and British colonies or protectorates finally were fixed, not without friction and bad feelings all around. Nothing in these areas of Africa caused quite the same trouble as the British had in South Africa.

In South Africa, the Boers, the Bantu, and bullion kept imperial affairs flaming. Diamonds and gold attracted adventurers by the thousands to the Transvaal and the Orange Free State. The Boers continued to dislike the British. Disraeli annexed the Transvaal, then Gladstone almost turned it loose. Ultimately gold, British, and Boers were to cause the war of 1899 to 1901. The Boers, after a valiant fight, were beaten. Reversing most imperial procedures, the British first deprived them of their freedom, then handed back self-government within five years, and in another five years gave dominion status to a united South Africa. Men like Cecil Rhodes were building empires in the hinterland and pushing British imperialism north into "darkest Africa." Here Britain ran head on into German and French, but particularly German, colonial ambitions. Boundaries for German East Africa and Southwest Africa were finally set. Britain found the French agreeable and the Germans obstinate. Britain, in the end, held the key lakes giving her control of the strategic White Nile. Thus, by 1904 the British saw Germany and not France as their African colonial rival. The same held true for the South Pacific area, where Germany in building her empire had run into New Zealand's and Australia's ambitions and hence British claims and plans. In a way, this year of 1904 represents the start of a new era in the history of the empire.

In 1903 the British and the French sat down over the champagne, a natural and inevitable accompaniment of King Edward VII's state visit to France, to settle colonial differences. Before this Britain had reversed her policy of isolation and in 1902 had made her anti-Russian alliance with Japan. Before that in 1898 the Fashoda incident had produced a sensible decision wherein France took herself out of Egypt's affairs and Britain acknowledged French superiority in Morocco. Thus Britain and France were no longer imperial rivals, and a new friendship was sealed in 1904.

In 1907 France helped arrange an understanding about Asiatic rivalry between her ally, Russia, and her new friend, Britain. France had been humiliated by Germany in the Moroccan crisis of 1905 and 1906. Russia had been beaten by Japan in the Far East. Germany was more than ever the target for French attack. Russia had to turn to the Balkans and Turkey, where she still had prestige. She was ready at last to come to an agreement with Great Britain. Iran, then known as Persia, was cut into "spheres of influence" by Britain and Russia. These arguments left only Germany as a rival of the three powers. In the new century, Germany's navy program, her truculent attitude, British nervousness over the North Sea frontier, and the danger to British markets made British distrust very deep. When 1914 came, the British were friendly with Germany's enemies and apprehensive of German good will. Part of this feeling of distrust was born of the Industrial Revolution's rivalries and mass-production methods. Here too, the old rivals, Russia and France, were turned into friends and the new German empire into an enemy.

Mass production and other technological changes in an age of science were to a great degree responsible for the unforeseen complexion of affairs after 1870. Great Britain steadily increased her production of manufactured goods. In doing this she made use of new methods and machines to turn them out. However, the old and sure business-as-usual practices that had built the national economy to unprecedented peaks by 1870 were less effective after that date. Supreme in an age of iron, Great Britain took second and then third place to the United States and Germany in an age of steel. Time after time it was the Americans and the Germans who developed and pushed forward products. Their goods replaced those of Great Britain in many world markets. After 1870, Great Britain lost her place as the undisputed production champion. She remained a leader and even chief producer of some commodities, but she was challenged and surpassed in many new fields of economic enterprise.

Holding to her old economic beliefs, Great Britain tried to make free trade work. After 1870 she nearly did her agriculture to death, since American and Canadian wheat was imported more cheaply than it was grown at home. Foreign high protective tariffs on British goods abroad made an equal exchange of goods and services impossible. Had the United States taken British goods as readily as it sold wheat, all might have been well with free trade. But what the United States did, so did others. Gradually Great Britain learned that colonies and an empire offered markets for goods and investment opportunities when other countries built high tariff walls. The ideal situation of free exchange of goods and services on a world-wide basis dreamed of by economic liberals never came into existence.

Domestic production and distribution did not take place as expected. After 1870 some British workers continued to enjoy high standards of living and income. Depressions lasting from the late 1870's to the early 1890's seriously affected the living standards of the majority and, particularly in agriculture, really hurt. By 1914 the British worker's shilling was buying no more than it had fifteen years before. The worker in 1914 received more in pay than he had in 1870, but he also paid out more in taxes for defense and the support of the new social services. The middle classes and the upper classes also found that the comfortable financial prospects of 1870 were not to be realized. In business a few grew tremendously rich. Small manufacturers and little businesses tended to be gobbled up. Under these new conditions, wealth made on a lavish scale came to a few but not to the many. Capital was controlled and managed by a few able men who directed the domestic and overseas activities of these profitable big enterprises. A nation of shopkeepers was starting to become a nation of big manufacturers served by those who could no longer afford to keep their individual shops.

Immediate calamities were far from the minds of the workers and the shopkeepers. Even farms and farm laborers were doing rather well in

1914, for a few years of bad depression were followed by years of peaceful and steady employment in mills and shops. Politics and foreign affairs therefore held the attention of the British.

Ireland boiled with land wars, Parnellism, and in the end nearly outright armed rebellion in Ulster. Gladstone and the Liberals were trounced in their efforts to give Ireland Home Rule. Political battles were as stimulating as they were bitter. Wars in Africa, climaxing in the Boer War, provided melodrama as well as unexpectedly large casualty lists. The British public accepted these events with joy or anger, as they did the announcement that Disraeli had made Victoria Empress of India or Gordon's death in Khartoum. The extension of suffrage to most males over twenty-one in 1884 was wonderful, but not nearly as stirring as the fight for equal political rights put up by Mrs. Pankhurst and her suffragettes. Pride, faith, and hope were the common intellectual characteristics of the British. They were proud of the Queen's soldiers and of the new Navy that someday might have to sink the German High Seas Fleet. They had faith in the destiny of British white men to rule fairly and honestly over less privileged races. And they had hope that the lag in Britain's world economic leadership would not prove a harmful loss of power or prestige.

Looking backward at these years, it is seen that both power and prestige were shared and, in this sense, diminished. Other nations were able to equal and surpass many British achievements. It is to this that critics call attention when they point out that in this period the British reached and passed their zenith of greatness. Much of this observation, of course, depends upon the critics' definition of greatness. Perhaps it would be more useful to inquire how the British peoples fared at this time. What they did for themselves and how they did it are of greater concern than trying to compare numbers of soldiers or bewailing loss of prestige. In these years the average man, the worker, used the ballot to rule himself and his Empire. His decision and his wishes, in the end, determined what was done. Democratic government of this sort was only anticipated in 1870. By 1914 popular democracy had become a vibrant and irresistible reality.

Lack of age-long familiarity with the operation of political machinery did not prevent the British worker from making known his desires and prejudices. In 1914 most voters could read and write, even if the majority read only newspapers of the more sensational sort. Everything depended on the new master. Gladstone, for example, was the hero of the workers when he led them to condemn the Turks in the 1870's. Disraeli gained their confidence, and lost it for a moment, when he revived imperialism. The twentieth-century Liberals were swept into power in 1906 and kept in because the socialist reforms they proposed were greatly desired by the workers. The House of Lords in 1911 had to bow to the inevitable demand of the average man and surrender its veto power. It retired even more into the political and constitutional shades. This was the will of the common man.

It was beyond belief in 1870 that the common man could organize a real political party of his own. In 1914 nearly a half hundred Labor party representatives sat in the House of Commons. These men were of, by, and for labor. The political and social philosophy of this party called for more and more state supervision, operation, and control over the social and the economic life of the nation. Intellectuals and radical thinkers from Joseph Chamberlain, through the Marxian Socialists of the Social Democrat Federation, to the Fabianism of the Webbs and G. B. Shaw supplied it with ideas and programs. The Independent Labor party and, after 1900, a newly organized Labor parliamentary party became a small and portentous part of the Liberal phalanx. Workingmen, not men of the upper class, represented their fellow workers in the House of Commons. The appearance of a worker's party in Parliament was an important evidence of the effect of industrialization upon British life.

Social ills and their remedies in the new age of industrialization called for new philosophies of reform. *Laissez faire* was found to be inapplicable in practice during the decades after 1870. A new philosophy, one of collectivism or socialism, was found both to fit the facts and to satisfy the intellectual climate of opinion of a working-class democracy.

When it was proved by Charles Booth in the late 1880's that the slums of big cities housed thousands living in diseased poverty, laissez-faire doctrines lost some of their luster. Human misery in industrial areas could be relieved only through laws and agencies that made the local authorities act for the community. Industrial areas, therefore, needed reforms and laws that had at bottom a program of welfare for the group carried out by the state. A remedial legislative and social program was impossible under a broad philosophy of *laissez faire*. The Conservative party, with its new sanitary laws and local government reforms, saw the need for a collectivist approach. But the Liberals, while clinging formally to the spirit of *laissez faire* in the twentieth century, put through most of the socialist legislative program. National health insurance, industrial compensation laws, and death duties that attacked landed wealth were part of the Liberal reforms. Industrial organization of the state demanded popular universal education. Britain had been the most backward of major industrial powers in this respect. An elementary schooling on a nearly universal basis was in existence by 1914. From 1870 to 1914 other reforms placed responsibility for national improvement on state-controlled agencies. An age of the ascendance of the industrial common man was an age when more and more the state provided for the individual those services and benefits that he could no longer secure by his own efforts.

Democracy and the swing toward socialism arrived on the social and political stage together.

Social reforms were the work of both the Conservative and Liberal parties. In the 1870's and 1880's the Conservatives enacted sanitary, building, and local-government codes that made Britain a healthier place to live, and much better administered. Old abuses in municipal and rural government were put away. Some real efficiency in public health administration as well as local government was a Conservative triumph. The Liberals, at the start of the period, carried through some great reforms such as the disestablishment of the Irish Church, introduction of the ballot, introduction of a national state-aided educational system, and reorganization of the Army. But the Liberals were prevented from carrying out a broad plan of reform by Gladstone's devotion to the cause of Irish Home Rule. Nothing was allowed to take precedence over Ireland's woes in Liberal platforms as long as Gladstone led the party. The Liberals, however, did pass the Reform Bill of 1884 that gave the ballot to every male adult. Only in 1906, after long years in opposition, could the Liberals, now under new leadership, carry out their long-deferred program of reforms.

The Liberal reform program was essentially socialist or collectivist. It was therefore adopted by the worker. The state was asked to protect trade unions' collective rights and to provide accident, old-age, and health insurance for the individual trade unionist; and even some unemployment insurance. Wealth, particularly inherited incomes and unearned increment from property, was to bear the costs of the new socialism. Rich men were to pay more as everyone bore "a fair share" of the very large budget increases for the new social services. While the Conservatives fought back at some of these changes, they waited to make a determined fight until the Liberals proposed to remove the House of Lords' veto power. Conservative lords, propertied men sympathetic with the traditions of the landed gentry, had vetoed Lloyd George's Budget of 1909. The nation was convulsed by the constitutional and political fight that followed. In the end, the Lords retained only the right to hold up, but not defeat, bills representing the will of the House of Commons. The House of Commons in this century thus became the instrument of the democratic electorate with its constitutional and political ascendancy unchallenged.

Intellectual dissatisfaction with the *status quo* of 1870 marked the forty-four following years. The first shock given to the moral and intellectual complacency of the Victorians was the rise and spread of the ideas of evolution. Darwin's thesis about descent of man and survival of the fittest was broadcast and absorbed by millions through missionary work of learned men like Professor Huxley.

The revealed religion of the scriptures was mocked, denied, and re-examined by a generation that demanded scientific proofs of biblical texts. Middle-class art and ideals were scorned by men as diverse in talent and points of view as William Morris, Oscar Wilde, and G. B. Shaw. A period that opened with Tennyson as leading literary figure closed with Kipling, H. G. Wells, Arnold Bennett, and John Galsworthy as popular writers. Literary tastes and styles were decidedly mixed when one remembers that the new type of journalism tagged as "yellow" pandered to the popular prejudices at the same time that Pinero, Wilde, and Gilbert and Sullivan were winning highest favor. Change and an expression of new creeds, humor, and ideas were undeniably the intellectual complexion of this time. Motorcars and other new machines revolutionized a familiar pattern of living.

This was an age of electricity and the internal-combustion engine. A few wild-eyed dreamers in 1870 had predicted mechanization of western European society. By 1914 electricity was used to turn the wheels of factories, run streetcars, and illuminate homes and offices. Busses and motorcars were the twentieth century's first revolutionary contribution to the new way of life. Airplanes had flown across the Channel by 1914. The horse and the bicycle, the latter also a newly popular means of transportation, were on the way out when World War I started.

The international catastrophe, World War I, brought to an end forty-four years of unexpected and unlooked-for history. Science, its handmaiden technology, democratic franchises giving control to the masses, and the problems of a new overseas empire made this era something new in British experience. It was all an exciting adventure, even if it did end in the agony of war.

35

ECONOMIC HISTORY

1870-1914

During the last quarter of the nineteenth century and the opening years of the twentieth Great Britain reached the peak of her economic wealth and power. Her goods were used by more British subjects than at any other time. Her foreign trade was at its most profitable, and British subjects invested capital abroad—that is to say, outside the Empire— in a manner unknown at any time. The development of large combinations in producing and carrying goods seemed only the inevitable outcome of the application of large-scale methods of using machinery. More people worked for fewer, but the many seemed to have more or less permanent jobs, and certainly their pay could buy more consumer's goods. This economic well-being made towns expand over more and more of the countryside, so that Britain and parts of Wales and Scotland took on the appearance of great manufacturing districts in which towns were separated only briefly from each other by patches of countryside. Thus the industrialization of British economy was completed in these years, and that meant that the town and the factory at last replaced the farm and the market town. Perhaps the most important thing about this completion of the industrial revolutionary cycle was that Great Britain committed itself to a way of life depending upon the machine, the factory, and the town. Without markets and their demands for the manufactured goods the domestic industries would fail, and the result would be a most terrible loss in wealth and material blessings which the people had come to both depend upon and expect. The displacement of agriculture as a basic industry offers perhaps as good an example of the great change in economic life of the British people as any that can be found.

Some have written that the fall of agriculture in the years from 1870 to 1914 was catastrophic and the cause of most subsequent woes of Great Britain. This assertion is probably the result of someone's belief that a nation can be wealthy only when it has its economic life firmly dug into the soil. That there was a considerable falling off in agricultural wealth and in the number of persons making their living from agriculture is true. In 1851 one in every four workers had been an agricultural worker. In

1881 the ratio had changed to one in ten. In 1911 it had fallen to one in twenty. It is important to remember that in 1881 there were 29,781,000 people in Britain and in 1911 there were 40,830,000. Thus most people were living in urban and industrial areas by 1911.

As to financial prosperity a few simple figures will show that agriculture did not, by and large, hold up. Rents were slow in falling but between 1901 and 1914 they were 30 per cent less than in the year 1879 to 1880. This was disastrous to the farmer or landowner who used his farm to make a steady profit. Of course, not every year throughout the period under study showed as bad a loss as the average of these years, but that the loss was deadly is indicated by the fact that from 1885 to 1913 agricultural holdings of arable land fell in England and Wales from 452,988 in the former year to 435,677 in the latter year. The number of acres planted in that basic grain, wheat, declined from 9,431,000 acres in 1874 to 7,152,000 in 1912. This decline in the area of wheat acreage was accompanied by an increase in the number of acres devoted to pasture. In 1874 pasture was 42.1 per cent of arable land and in 1914 it was 55.2 per cent. Thus grain farming became very much less profitable. But this does not mean that there was a total breakdown in British agriculture.

In the years under study the fortunes of agriculture declined until the opening years of the twentieth century. In 1871, for example, there were 1,366,000 agricultural workers. In 1901 there were 1,208,900. But in 1911 that number had risen to 1,267,300. What attracted workers to the farms after 1900 was the reestablishment of agriculture in certain branches as a prosperous industry. It had been found that beef and mutton paid where grain did not. Many farms that were close to large urban areas and had been abandoned or given up as profitable producers of grain were turned into dairy farms and poultry farms because of the ever-increasing demands of the towns for poultry and milk. Fruit growing was found to be profitable in certain areas, and from 1873 to 1904 there was an increase of 63.9 per cent in the acreage devoted to fruit. Truck, dairy, fruit, and poultry farming were by and large profitable. The farm worker also was better off after 1900 than before. By 1914 his real wages had risen by 40 per cent over 1880. Generally speaking, however, in 1914 rents were a little better, and some measure of prosperity had returned to the farmer.

The Board of Agriculture in the years after 1900 had taken steps to teach the farmer how to use new machinery such as binders and had suggested new methods of using the land. Agricultural colleges were established, and in 1913 agricultural institutes offered instruction to all interested in the scientific aspects of farming. This interest in science and agricultural education on the part of the state, this attention to a faltering industry, and this provision of state aid in the form of advice and agricultural schools showed a very different attitude from that taken by the government in the nineteenth century. Until agriculture had fallen so low the governments, both Liberal and Conservative, took a stand that nothing could be done to save what the economic situation in itself could not save. It was felt that the natural laws of supply and demand should be allowed to determine the fate of agriculture and that artificial respiration in the form of tariffs would only hinder an inevitable trend and only hurt the people. Royal commissions on the state of agriculture sat in 1879 and in 1893. They made reports that described the miserable state of farming but did nothing constructive in the way of offering plans or solutions.

To sum it up, British farming suffered from *laissez faire,* from the weather, and from inventions. For despite increased attention from the government, *laissez faire* remained official policy. Free trade had given the British worker cheap food; then why raise the taxes that fell on the worker, to subsidize high-cost farming? As for the weather, the bad year of 1878–1879 was the worst since the wet year of 1845 had ruined potatoes. Coming on top of a cattle plague which had killed off herds, a practically total loss of grain brought ruin to many an estate. This caused purchasers of grain to desert the home market and buy abroad. For just at this moment came the refrigerated ship, the refrigerated freight car, and the Westinghouse air brake that speeded up long hauls of grain in America and Canada and improved techniques of storing and shipping grain. These are the chief reasons why Britain had plenty of food and ignored home production.

The opening up of the western grass lands in Canada and the United States made possible the farming of millions of acres that produced in their newly cultivated state enough grain to feed the world. Argentina and Australia also, after 1870, produced grain and beef along with Canada and the United States in amounts that no one had dreamed possible a few years previous. For example, Australia and Argentina together sent one-tenth of the food supply for Britain in 1884, and they increased their proportion to one-third by 1908. This meant that Argentine and Australian cattlemen and farmers were doing what the British farmer could no longer do. The United States and Canada found that they could raise, mill, and ship a bushel of grain and deliver it at Liverpool with less cost to the British worker than could the farmer who raised grain a mile outside the corporation limits. They could do this because of the cheapness of the land, the use of new techniques, the fertility of the soil that required no replacement of minerals, and the excellence and cheapness of railroad transportation and of the steam cargo ship. Meat growers throughout the new world and in Australia and New Zealand found that their beef and mutton could be frozen and shipped to London and there sold at a profit for less than the price at which the average British meat grower could deliver at the same place. Speedy trains, refrigerated steel vessels,

cheap and fertile land, and low production costs made it easy for the
foreign farmers to knock out of the market the high-cost produce of the
British farmer. Agricultural economy changed from wheat to meat in this
forty-four-year period.

British agriculture entered the competition with foreign products under
very severe disadvantages. The land was made to support the landlord, the
Established Church, the laborer, and the farmer. Where in Canada or
Australia or the United States an acre was sold for little and taxed very
lightly, each acre of British land was very heavily taxed. Before an acre
could bring in net profit it had to produce enough to pay rent and high
wages. Also the British land was farmed well but at high cost as compared with newer lands that did not need fertilization and constant replacement through chemicals. It was very costly to keep British land producing year after year in quantities that would compare with the rich,
almost virgin, soil of the New World farms. British farming was carried
on in an intelligent but highly traditional manner. Machines were not
found practicable where, as was the case in many areas, the fields were
small. Owners, farmers, and laborers were slow to turn to new methods
and a kind of farming that would deprive men of their jobs. A social
system, centuries old, of living and working was not to be displaced hurriedly. The landlord or the farmer had social obligations to the farm workers. He could not alter their status by clearing them out overnight and
putting machinery in their places, even if machinery would solve the
problems of his production costs. Tradition counted for a great deal when
it came to methods of farming and to the relation of landlord and tenant.

By 1914 the situation in British agriculture had improved very considerably over what it had been at the close of the last century. The British
farmer had lost his grain market. He had lost part but not most of his
meat sales. He had gone through very bad years from 1878 to 1895, but
after that he had done better. The upward trend of prices for all commodities helped the farmer after 1895. Rent rolls had been reduced during the depression years of the 1880's and had not been restored. The
new truck farming and the demand for meat grown in Britain brought
prosperity to many farmers. As indicated by figures given above, there
was a return to agricultural jobs, which indicated that farming could pay.
In 1914 the British farmer was decidedly better off than he had been in
1890. But his was an industry that was no longer the chief resource of
the nation for jobs or productive wealth. The machine had finally forced
the plough to take an inferior place in the national economy.

In her most important industries, in her trade, and in finance Great
Britain suffered serious economic depression in the years 1870 to 1914.
Like agriculture, trade and manufacturing started out with high prices
and in a very prosperous condition, then collapsed, and then in 1914

showed tremendous recovery. The cycle of prosperity and depression is best indicated by the index of wholesale prices, shown in the accompanying table. The fall and rise of prices during these years was irregular. Some-

INDEX OF WHOLESALE PRICES

(1900 = 100)

Year	Index	Year	Index
1871	135	1895	91
1873	152	1896	89
1875	140	1898	94
1879	125	1900	100
1880	129	1902	97
1885	108	1905	97
1887	99	1908	104
1890	108	1910	109
1891	101	1914	118

times the prices rose and then fell sharply; each time a fall occurred the price rise was lower than the previous low point until the years after 1905, rise was lower than the previous low point until the years after 1905, when a definite upswing is noted. The causes of the depression in trade and industry are much the same as the cause of the depression in agriculture but in a way much more important to the economic health of the empire.

By 1870 British trade and industry had come to depend upon the markets and services of the world. Any maladjustment in the world's economic organization was sure to affect the income of the British trader and manufacturer. Tariff walls put up by the United States, as for example the McKinley tariff of 1890, kept Britain's goods from the counters of her best customer and made the British businessman seek new customers in another area. Wars such as the American Civil War and the Franco-Prussian War of 1870 stopped the even flow of goods and always brought about some change in the market price or financial situation. During the American Civil War there had been a serious cotton famine and an attempt to meet it by encouraging Indian cotton growers to send goods taking the place of the American cotton. The Franco-Prussian War temporarily caused a flurry on the stock market and upset the continental market for British goods. Disturbances such as these made selling and making of goods for the overseas customer more of a hazardous business. Natural catastrophes such as the failure of a monsoon in India would reduce the purchasing power of a number of customers and as a result force merchants and manufacturers to readjust too hastily their demands for money and labor at home. The delicate balance upon which economic prosperity depended was in these years very seriously affected by the revolution that took place in the methods of manufacture and organization of business enterprises.

Invention, typified by such new processes as Bessemer's and Gilchrist's in the production of steel, and competition with other countries brought about a revolution in the management of British big business. From 1870 to 1914 British business, like that in every other industrial country, turned to mass-production methods and to concentration of management in the hands of a few large companies. It was found that a ship or a rail or a spool of cotton thread or a box of salt could be produced cheaper by the unit when produced by a large firm half monopolistic or completely monopolistic in character.

The technique of making goods by machinery forced industries into mass-production methods. More and cheaper goods meant larger and costlier plants. The skills of the individual worker, the old traditions of hand craftsmanship, naturally went by the board, as did the small companies that employed ten or a dozen men.

The trend toward bigness in productive enterprises was irresistible. It was easy to find capital for large firms when middle-class investors could be fairly sure of a modest rate of interest on a few pounds spent in the purchase of stocks. In 1884, for example, 1,564 new joint stock companies were floated as compared to only 997 in 1864. The joint stock company offering shares to anyone with money to invest became the typical company for investors to seek out. The result was to put a premium on management activities. As firms grew in size they could turn out more goods as they had money enough to meet competition at home and abroad. Such firms as John Brown & Co. in building ships and the J. & P. Coats, Ltd., in making thread grew so large in the years after 1870 that they almost had a special place in the economy of Britain. Their failure and the failure of those companies like them would have plunged the Empire into economic disorder. As amalgamations took place in industry, so did they take place in banking. By 1914 the nation had to borrow from one of a half dozen or so banking chains such as Barclays, Lloyd's, and the London and Westminster, that had branches in every port and country of the world. The old-style private bank owned by a city or county family had become a thing of the past. Vast sums of money were thus concentrated in the hands of a few managers and suppliers of money for investment.

The development of large-scale business and manufacturing practices in Great Britain was accompanied by similar developments in the rest of the world. In the United States the steel industry followed similar paths, and in Germany the opening of the Lorraine coal and mineral fields helped to bring about in a few years the success of a new steel and iron industry undreamed of in 1870. Great Britain's competitors were as efficient and as active as her own sons. Indeed, Germany and the United States in the field of industrial engineering and management and production techniques surpassed the British producers. New methods were tried more in those countries and new processes were used, while in Britain the usual practice was to hold on to tried and true methods that had emphasized the attainment of the highest output possible by a single worker. In many markets in South America the Germans after careful study of the needs of the local market used newer methods of selling and attracting customers.

In the race to produce new articles and machines under new conditions, the capture of the automobile industry by Americans and Germans shows the falling behind of the British in certain of the new fields of industrial production. The German Rudolf Diesel pioneered in the field of gas engines. Henry Ford, the American production-line genius, showed the world how to produce thousands of cars cheaply and rapidly with the maximum of engineering skill per unit. British automobile makers produced the finest cars such as the Rolls Royce, but where they produced one car the Americans and the Germans produced thousands and hundreds respectively. As for the manufacture and sale of electrical goods, the Germans with the Siemens combine captured the European market. In the United States the new electrical industry grew in a few years to mammoth proportions. Great Britain produced excellent electrical equipment, but in volume and in the number of people served outside the country it fell behind the United States and Germany. British automobile production, however, was sufficient for the domestic market. Motorcar output moved upward from an annual rate of 8,456 in 1904 to 132,005 in 1914.

The extent to which Britain lost her industrial supremacy in world trading as new products and markets were created and opened is indicated best by a few statistics that show both the British increase in production and that of other countries. It should not be forgotten that Britain's production did not necessarily fall off in these years of severe depression and competition. Other nations in many fields met and surpassed her in the production of goods and services, while the world's increasing population demanded more and more of the goods made possible by invention and science. An example both of the loss of a market and of a loss in production is found in the comparison of tin-plate production in Britain and the United States. Tin plate had been produced for generations by Welsh workers. Thousands were brought to West Virginia and there carried on under new conditions their ancient trade. In 1889 American output of tin plate was of little value. But by 1896 it was equal to the amount of tin plate imported from Britain. In 1899 the United States took

64,000 tons of tin plate from Great Britain where in 1889 she had taken 327,000 tons. The difference represents the growth of American tin-plate industry in a decade and a loss to Britain's world trade.

The production figures on pig iron and steel tell a similar story of lost markets and of new and vigorous competition. Here Britain, a pioneer with years of experience, was surpassed both because of the discovery of new ore deposits in the United States and because of technical processes that made possible, as mentioned above, the use of the phosphate iron ores of Lorraine. The figures for pig-iron production and steel production for major nations in the years 1870 to 1874 and in the years 1900 to 1904 are shown in the accompanying tables. It is little wonder, in the light of such

PIG-IRON PRODUCTION
(In tons)

Nation	1870–1874	1900–1904
Great Britain	6,400,000	8,600,000
United States	2,200,000	16,400,000
Germany	1,800,000	8,900,000
France	1,200,000	2,600,000

STEEL PRODUCTION
(In tons)

Nation	1870–1874	1900–1904
Great Britain	500,000	5,000,000
United States	140,000	13,000,000
Germany	300,000	7,000,000
France	130,000	1,700,000

production figures, that British businessmen were thinking kindly of those who preached that Britain should see to it that her colonial empire and her dominions bought British goods. It was the imperialist businessman and merchant who were beginning to command attention with their plea that British possessions and British subjects wherever they were should buy the mother country's goods in preference to those of foreigners. In 1903 the most ardent supporter of protection in Great Britain, Joseph Chamberlain, created a split in the ranks of the Conservative-Unionist party by demanding that Britain follow the example of other countries and adopt a tariff policy that would protect colonies and home markets from competition. That there was some reason for demands of those who said that Britain was losing her grip in international markets is further illustrated by the change in her position as world's leading cotton spinner. In 1881, even after the depression had set in, Great Britain spun 54 per cent of the world's cotton; in 1900, only 43 per cent.

From the foregoing it is clear that British economy suffered from competition and from a change in the way the world bought goods and services. In another respect British industry did not do as well as it had a century earlier in the age of iron. Rubber, electrical products, and internal-combustion engines all represented new products and new industrial areas of development. The field of chemicals, in which the Germans showed particular aptitude, was another where others entered into competition with equal advantage and techniques. Indeed it was a Briton of German descent, Alfred Mond, who in the end organized the British industrial chemical combine, Imperial Chemical Industries, Ltd., that held the British domestic market for some time. However, in 1914 the Germans were able to claim 95 per cent of the world's aniline-dye production. One reason for the success of Britain's rivals was that their own markets were sufficient, aided by protection, to supply an increasing demand, and that government-aided capital was able, as in Germany, to give a strong boost to overseas trade. Every German firm was able to count on government aid directly or indirectly in establishing carrying contracts or sales in new markets. Throughout the years studied the British government held firmly to the belief that free trade was best for both employer and worker and did nothing to assist British merchants and industrialists through financial aid.

One of the chief causes of the economic depression was, therefore, the competition Britain experienced in carrying and making goods. Other vital causes were the agricultural depression noted above, the shortage of gold supply, and the turning of the world to new products that could be supplied as well or better by others. Of these causes the gold shortage has not been discussed.

In the years between 1870 and the early 1890's the mining of gold fell to a very low level. The industrial expansion of European countries and the demands put upon limited gold supplies made gold scarce in relation to other commodities. Prices in terms of gold started to fall. Demands for gold as backing for currency and coinage purposes also went up during these years. Germany and the Scandinavian kingdoms, as well as Holland and the United States, either put their currencies on gold basis or stopped coining silver in favor of gold. The United States, for example, stopped exporting gold in 1878, and the source of the metal was lost to Europe. The resulting fall in prices naturally affected business. After the South African gold fields started to produce in unheard-of amounts, the prices on the world's markets naturally rose. As gold flowed into banks, loans and deposits that made loans possible naturally encouraged business. Between 1894 and 1913 Britain's supply of gold increased 60 per cent.

To the student living in the twentieth century a characteristic of this depression period that appears unusual is the steady appreciation of national wealth and also purchasing power during these years of industrial and economic fluctuation. It has been estimated that national income increased from £1,090,000 in 1880 to £1,400,000 in 1891 to 1895. National wealth increased from an estimated £10,037,000,000 in 1885 to an estimated £13,500,000,000 in 1900. Up to 1900 the output per head in the cotton, steel and iron, and building industries increased and afterwards remained fairly stationary. These figures indicate that during depression years there was a very general upsurge in production as well as in national income and wealth. This condition arose from the work performed by the new amalgamations in industry and commerce to meet competition and new situations and was the result of these efforts. Great Britain worked her way out of a depression by developing trade in her colonies and dominions and at home.

By developing home and imperial markets a stimulus was given to employ workers and create demands through the natural growth of industry. Building iron and steel steam vessels provided employment to thousands who increased British-owned tonnage built in British yards from 519,970 in the year 1896 to 740,810 in 1907. Vessels for foreign owners in the same years increased from 210,840 tons to 296,570 tons. Looked at over a longer period, the British steam vessels increased in the years 1880 to 1906 from 2,732,470 tons registered to 9,612,010 tons registered. The vessels in British registry were sailed largely by British crews and carried goods from home ports to those of the colonies and the world. Copra, for example, from the South Pacific and palm oil from West Africa were new commodities used in Europe and employed more and more men in transportation and manufacture. Whenever a new region such as Queensland in Australia was developed, British men, money, and materials were used to make the undertaking a success. While dominions such as Canada, colonies such as Victoria and Natal, and India each had laws protecting local trade and industry, the British had little or no effective foreign competition in developing trade in other parts of the Empire. The statistics in the accompanying table indicate what a very large part of the total import and export trade with the various parts of the Empire came to play in British economic life. In the case of both exports and imports, percentagewise and in actual value of goods, there was an absolute increase that meant, of course, more income for British workers and em-

EXPORTS

Years	Value, 000,000 omitted	Percentage of total export trade
1870–1874	£ 65	22.5
1890–1894	85	28.8
1900–1904	114	32.5
1910–1913	183	31.5

IMPORTS

Years	Value, 000,000 omitted	Percentage of total imports
1870–1874	£ 76	22
1890–1894	96	22.9
1900–1904	111	20.8
1910–1913	180	25

ployers. Manufacturers of cotton goods tried to get tariffs in India reduced for their benefit. The followers of Joseph Chamberlain saw that the economic benefit to be gained from an imperial tariff system was as great as the moral benefit to be had from having millions in Africa, Asia, and America ruled by the British. Five per cent profit and the bearing of the white man's burden went very nicely together.

Another and very important way out of the depression was to be found through investments in imperial and foreign enterprises. In the years of depression those who were accustomed to receive 20 per cent dividends were discovering that these profits were being cut to 5 or 10 per cent. By investment of huge sums, large corporations could return a regular dividend but usually not more than 5 to 10 per cent on each share of stock. Companies and banks interested in investing the profits made from domestic enterprise found that foreign colonies and foreign undertakings paid a very sure and handsome dividend. British money was to be found, as always, invested in South American ventures. Peruvian and Chilean mines and Argentine railways and waterworks were often built by British loans. In the United States many railways pushed westward to the Pacific because British money was found to buy stocks and bonds. Investments in foreign national and state government securities, mines and railways, iron and steel, and industrial plants were fields where most British money was sent. The heaviest investments were made in mines and railways.

Money was to be found for overseas investment where a likelihood existed for steady returns of dividends, as is indicated by the statistics in the accompanying table. It has been estimated that in the thirty years prior to the start

OVERSEAS INVESTMENTS

Year	Millions of pounds
1870–1874	£ 61
1875–1879	1.7
1885–1889	61.1
1894–1899	26.8
1904–1909	109.5
1909–1913	185

of World War I overseas-investment income increased three or four times. In 1914 it was estimated that £1,780,000 was invested within the British empire in all sorts of enterprises. In Latin America £756,000,000 was invested, and in the United States alone some £754,000,000. In Europe only £218,600,000 had been invested. Thus £983,300,000 was invested abroad, that is, outside the Empire. The grand total of overseas investments of all sorts in 1914 is estimated at £3,763,300,000. Allowing for a rough figure of £4,000,000,000 as total invested abroad, this represented about 25 per cent of the national wealth of Great Britain.

As the demand increased for more goods and services to be sent overseas, the increase in wealth of all sorts at home gradually brought the British into the new era of prosperity. Growth of trade and transportation is indicated somewhat by the increase in the number of miles of traffic-line railways from 15,537 in 1870 to 23,387 in 1910. In tons carried the increase was from 235,300,000 in 1870 to 514,400,000 in 1910. Railways were further regulated, carrying on from the Act of 1854 by establishing in 1873 a commission to hear complaints against overcharges or preferential treatment, and were forced to publish their various rates. Few amalgamations of railways took place after 1870. But working agreements and control through interlocking boards of directors often brought about much the same result that amalgamation would have in the fields of management. Pooling of traffic facilities was common after the turn of the century, and the carrying of goods was thus made easier. Those who had to use the railways were constantly objecting to pooling of rates and facilities because it was claimed that higher rates would result to the user. After 1888, Parliament forced through a revised classification of schedules and rates by law. In these years canal traffic dropped considerably. The locomotive did better work for the public than the canal horse towing a barge. But not all canals ceased to function. As late as 1905, 32,340,264 tons were taken over English and Welsh canals, exclusive of the Manchester Ship Canal.

A revolution in transportation was brought about by the introduction of the electric trolley or street car. As urban areas continued to grow the electric tram was found to be the very thing needed to connect one area with another. British cities were now provided with efficient, rapid, and cheap transportation for workers and others. To this means of transportation was added the motor bus after 1903. By 1913 there were 3,522 motor busses in operation in London alone. While the motor bus was used widely, automobiles for private use numbered 84,840 in 1909. Trucks—or "lorries," as they are called in Great Britain—in that year were 15,181. The day of the automobile was coming on rapidly. Besides carrying passengers within towns, the automobile served to bring the inhabitants of rural areas more easily within reach of urban areas. The natural exchange of ideas, goods, and services was speeded up as a result. After 1910 no part of Great Britain could really be called remote or out of touch with London or the rest of the nation.

A word should be said concerning two of the most stable as well as the oldest of manufactures that had done so much to make Great Britain an industrial leader. Cotton and woolen industrial development went on during these years with increasing consumption and production. At the end of the nineteenth century Great Britain had 42,740,000 cotton spindles at work. In 1908 there were 52,800,000 spindles working. There were 504,000 operatives working to produce 1,530,000,000 pounds at the end of the century and 572,869, excluding outworkers, producing a gross output of 1,970,000,000 pounds in 1908. Work was provided throughout the entire period, with very little loss in employment from 1870 to 1914 when one remembers that in 1870 there were only 463,000 employees in cotton mills. The woolen and worsted trades show similar comfortable production increases in these years. In 1870 there were 2,702,700 woolen spindles and 2,131,400 worsted spindles. By 1904 these had increased in number to 2,901,500 woolen spindles and 3,783,100 worsted spindles. The north-country textile industry held its own throughout the period and maintained its reputation for good business.

The effect upon the people of Great Britain of the rapid changes in methods of manufacture and doing business was most disturbing. Especially was the lot of the worker affected. He who sold his labor in return for wages experienced unemployment or a change in the amount of goods and services his money could buy. Generally the worker's shilling could buy more in the years of depression than in the period before. From 1856 to 1886 his wages increased in money value about 48 per cent and continued to increase modestly up to 1900. After the experiments in social legislation were made where worker's pay checks were assessed for social services and when, after 1905 particularly, prices rose, his shilling bought less and less. From 1870 to 1900, generally speaking, the worker could buy more and had a satisfactory real income because of the products made available through mass production. After 1900 he could still get the cheap products, but rising prices unaccompanied by a similar rise in wages and consequent loss in purchasing power left him with little opportunity for increasing comfort or a better standard of living. At the time it was noted that after 1870 the British worker could clothe himself and his family better than any European worker and could command services and commodities that his father would never have dreamed of possessing. Great numbers of workers sought the job protection offered by trade unions as well as the social services—sick benefits, for example—given by them. Between 1905 and 1914 the worker in Great Britain voted to help support a great national program of social reform that provided him with state-supervised and -granted old-age assistance, health insurance, and unemployment insurance. In this respect he was now better off than any British laborer had ever been.

During the years of depression between 1875 and 1895 many trades were hit by unemployment. In 1886 certain trade unions reported on what was for these times serious unemployment among their members. The ironmongers reported 13.9 per cent unemployed. The blacksmiths reported 14.4 per cent and iron shipbuilders 22 per cent. The average for all trade unions in that year was 9.5 per cent. This was better than the bleak year of 1879, when the unions found an average of 11.4 per cent unemployed. It should also be noted that much of this unemployment was seasonal and very little of it was permanent. Britain's industrial and commercial life depended upon export trade. As export trade increased, unemployment became less and less something to worry about. Workers could be pretty sure of finding employment in a nation that increased exports in value from a depression figure of £298,000,000 in 1880 to 1884 to £581,000,000 in 1910 to 1913.

Undoubtedly one of the greatest and most disruptive results of the use of mass-production techniques and consequent depression was the unsettling effect they had on the personal status of laboring men. The era of unplanned economic organization left the worker without a philosophy of life or the ability to adjust himself to the new conditions. Equally unsettling were the rapid fluctuations in the economic and social structure for the middle and upper classes. The story of how the workers of Great Britain met the demands, both social and economic, of the new industrial era is to be considered first because what they did altered the social, political, and economic policies of the nation. The twentieth-century Briton lives in a society whose main outlines and distinguishing characteristics were drawn in the years from 1870 to 1914.

36

SOCIAL HISTORY

1870–1914

When the Second Reform Bill of 1867 was passed, its great opponent, Robert Lowe, said: "We must educate our masters." He foresaw that this enfranchisement of the urban worker would end the reign of the middle class and would eventually hand Great Britain over to the working class. This would take time, because the Second Reform Bill would need extension by the Third Reform Bill of 1884 that gave the agricultural worker the vote, the Representation of the People Act of 1918, and even the "Flapper Vote" Act of 1928 before there would be true universal male and female suffrage. But the result was inevitable. The working class would become the dominant class of the land.

In Great Britain the rise of the workers followed British precedents. There was little of the strong action or political nonpartisanship of the American labor movement. There was little of the doctrinaire Marxian socialism of the Continent. Except for some strong talk in the late 1880's, there was none of the European revolutionary agitation which flamed out in the Paris Commune of 1871. For a while labor voted Liberal, honored Gladstone, and worked hard in the local Liberal Associations. Then it founded a trade union political party which worked for practical reforms. Labor leaders in England were God-fearing, law-abiding men who intended to make changes constitutionally and gradually. The swift urbanization of England gave them their chance, and they took it.

In 1870 the population of the United Kingdom stood at 31,800,000; in 1911, at 40,800,000. At the same time a flood of emigrants poured out of the land, mostly members of the middle classes, who were able to pay passage. Since most of the increase in population was in urban areas, this meant a great growth in the working class. By 1910 Great Britain had forty-four towns with over 100,000 population, eleven with over 300,000. Vast London had so spread that its diameter was forty miles. For as factories were built, workers' homes sprang up around them, or workers took over middle-class and upper-class homes, while the former owners went outside to a suburb.

Industrial slums, in consequence, became more and more of a problem. The investigations of Charles Booth [1] highlighted the situation. He found that there were cases of two or more families living in one room and that 38 per cent of the people of London were ill-nourished on diets like bread and fish. Private charity seemed inadequate to meet this problem. Public-relief methods of the New Poor Law of 1834 were challenged by the Poor Law Commission of 1905 to 1909 as likewise inadequate. Men began looking for new methods. Booth wished, as did his sponsor, Joseph Chamberlain, for old-age pensions. Others, notably Booth's assistant, Mrs. Sidney Webb, wanted to go much further in state intervention. Here was a task for local and central government. That is why Chamberlain put high in his "Unauthorized Program" a demand that local governments have expropriation powers to clear such slums and that the counties, like the boroughs, be governed by elective councils instead of by benches of justices of the peace of the landlord class. Nor were such demands the demands of radicals. The Conservative Disraeli in 1874 came into office with the slogan, *Sanitas Sanitatum, Omnia Sanitas,* and took his share in pushing matters on. A great program of amelioration was thus carried through, culminating in the Liberal legislation of the 1900's and 1910's, by which the standard of living of the working classes was raised. Here are some of the stages.

In the first Gladstone Ministry, from 1868 to 1874, the central control of local administration was reorganized and unified by setting up the Local Government Board, and a series of sanitary laws were passed. It was the work of Disraeli's Cabinet, from 1874 to 1880, to codify this legislation and add to it. In the late 1880's Chamberlain forced the Conservative Salisbury Government to pass the County Councils Act of 1888 and the London County Council Act of 1889, which gave the voters outside the boroughs the power to vote themselves administrative reforms. The next step was the development of state insurance by Lloyd George and other Liberals, from 1911 on.

This legislation had many results. Inspections multiplied. There was a building code. Ships could not be loaded so as to submerge beyond the "Plimsoll line," named for the reformer who forced Disraeli to protect England's seamen. An Adulteration Act and a Weights and Measures Act protected the consumer. Above all an Old Age Pensions Act took the aged poor out of squalor or dependence on charity, and the National Insurance Act and the Health Insurance Act gave protection from disability or doctors' bills. Many a borough, too, built better housing for the worker, Birmingham here being a leader.

Effectiveness at the local-government level increased, since the councils

---

[1] See Charles Booth, *Labour and Life of the People* (1889) or *Life and Labour of the People in London* (17 vols., 1891–1896).

—borough, county, and district—became schools for politicians. Joseph Chamberlain, like Richard Cobden before him, like Clement Attlee and Herbert Morrison after him, learned his trade locally before entering Parliament. But not all this was governmental. Social insurance was built on mutual societies, going back to the time of the Younger Pitt, and "medical clubs" founded in the 1830's. There, too, was training in practical statesmanship.

But what of technology in this raise in the standard of living? Electricity brought trams earlier than in the United States, electric light later. Here municipal plants, each using a different voltage, prevented the spread of electricity which the United States has seen from the adoption of 110/220-volt 60-cycle alternating current. Refrigeration brought the British workman New Zealand mutton, Argentine beef, Canadian wheat, and some West Indies fruit. In consequence he ate far better, though it would take the planned diets of World War II to cure him of some bad habits. So though the British worker might not be living well by American standards, or by the ideal he set for himself, he was better off in 1914 than in 1870.

Was the improvement in living conditions, however, accompanied by equal progress in standards of thought? Authorities of the time differed on the facts, but they agreed in trying to do something about what they deplored. Matthew Arnold, who coined the name Philistine for the inartistic temperament of the British, was thirty-two years an inspector of schools. John Ruskin, the art critic, lectured at Oxford and caused the movement that led to founding Ruskin College for laboring men. Robert Lowe's services to education as "Vice President of the Council" were such that London University elected him to Parliament as its first representative. These critics of British intellectual life, and others, had faith that what was wrong with it could be cured. But the trouble was that elementary education was scanty. In 1870 the only state support came from annual grants per student, in return for central inspection. In thirty-two years this was changed. By a rather British process of beginning with half measures and then cleaning up the mess, there was set up a national system of compulsory primary education to which was illegally added free secondary education for those qualified. The first step was the Forster Education Act. This permissive act allowed the setting up of local school boards, which might levy "rates," *i.e.*, local taxes, and might compel attendance but must give nondenominational religious education under the controversial Cowper-Temple clause. In 1880, local boards were required to compel attendance. In 1891 they were permitted to remit fees—which actually made elementary education free and created a group of scholarships in fee-charging secondary schools.

During this time education spread widely. Attendance more than doubled, from 2,000,000 to 5,500,000. Nor did this extension of education stop at the elementary level. Certain school boards experimented with higher education, calling it "technical"; certain county and borough councils similarly stretched their powers. Voluntary, *i.e.*, denominational schools went to great efforts to keep up. Then in 1901 came the Cockerton judgment, which declared these extensions of education to the secondary and higher level beyond the powers of the boards and councils. It caused the great Education Act of 1902, drafted largely by that able civil servant Sir Robert Morant. This Act streamlined procedure and transferred local control of both primary and secondary education to local councils. Subsidies to "voluntary schools" were permitted, which enraged Nonconformists then but now are praised for keeping up independence in a state-controlled education system.

Thus the British worker, who in 1870 had to go to a denominational school or not at all, by 1902 had free primary education and a chance to win scholarships at a government secondary school. More than that, universities opened to him. The Cockerton judgment forced the turning over of the London School Board's experiments in higher education to the University of London, in the form of the autonomous Imperial Scientific Institute and the London School of Economics.

To the already existing Durham University and Victoria at Manchester were added Birmingham and Liverpool, while three Welsh universities were federated into one. Thus many young men and women from the working class found careers in education, arts, sciences, and public service within their reach.

What of the effect of the heightened literacy of the working classes? This new market brought into being a new press, the so-called "yellow" journalism, exemplified by two brothers, Alfred and Harold Harmsworth, later Viscount Northcliffe and Viscount Rothermere. They copied the ideas of others, such as the Messrs. Newnes's *Tit-Bits,* a spicy journal of gossip, but went further. The *Evening News,* taken over in 1894, and the *Daily Mail* founded in 1896, transformed the reading of this generation. These papers had women's pages and sporting news, instead of learned discussions and full reports of parliamentary debates. When these papers went up, the older ones went down. In 1908, *The Times,* crippled by the expenses of the Parnell case, fell into Alfred Harmsworth's hands. It was this press that did so much to sponsor imperialism and anti-Boer excitement in the 1890's, just as these two press lords in 1916 did so much to replace Asquith with Lloyd George as Premier.

But such a press was not the only medium by which England's new masters, the working class, got their ideas. Eventually in 1912 they would found their own paper, the *Daily Herald,* as a Labor organ and, thanks to George Lansbury, make a financial success of it. At this time there circulated Winwood Reade's *Martyrdom of Man,* a powerful argument for Darwinism, and Robert Blatchford's *Merrie England,* a picture of a happy, collectivist England of the future. From America Henry George's *Progress and Poverty* would strike home, with its appeal for taxing land values and thus striking at the landlord class. Here would be the ideas that would take lasting root in men's minds.

Darwinism had varied effects on the British. Because Thomas Huxley lectured hard, supported by John Tyndall, the general public met this theory with all its implications. Some were able to reconcile it with revealed religion; others were not. The idea spread widely that there were scientific laws, that society functioned according to those laws, and that wise men, instead of resisting the inevitable, cooperated with it. That left open the questions of just what was inevitable and just what those laws were. The Darwinian idea of the survival of the fitter could justify imperialism and even some unpleasant forms of racialism. It could also lead to a search for better living conditions. Likewise Spencer's ideas of sociology could justify *laissez faire* or cause a belief in collectivism. This was an age when Clerk Maxwell at Cambridge was discovering mathematically rays which Hertz and Curie were to produce actually—thus giving us the radio and the X-ray. It was an age when Einstein, then young, would upset philosophy by the special and the general theories of relativity. Consequently the average man could not remain untouched by scientific thought; he had to react in some way.

One reaction was imperialism, and talk of the "white man's burden." The 1890's were the period when Rudyard Kipling caught the imagination of the intellectuals; in the 1900's his writings, though scorned by the intellectuals, reached a wide general public. Another reaction was atheism. For example, from 1880 to 1886, the House of Commons spent much time debating whether to seat Charles Bradlaugh, who asserted any oath to a God in whom he did not believe was meaningless. It is typical of the trend of men's thinking that eventually the Speaker let him take the oath. Yet a third reaction, as in the Bradlaugh case, was widening tolerance. If Her Majesty, Queen Victoria, Empress of India and Supreme Governor of the Church of England, ruled over more Mohammedans than the Sultan, more pagans than any pagan ruler, just how seriously could one take religious differences?

As a result, religious thinking changed, too. For this there were economic and social reasons. With new careers opening up, the Church of England recruited less talent than in the past, civil service and business more. With new methods of Sunday entertainment, church and chapel alike were deserted, while members of the Established Church and the Dissenting sects amused themselves by bicycling or other outdoor sports. For this, too, in the Established Church there was a theological reason.

The Oxford movement had led to ritualism; ritualism brought some worshippers into the churches and drove others out. It led to the Lincoln case, where Bishop King of that diocese was called to order for his conduct of services and put through a legal ordeal while lawyers decided what latitude a priest of the Established Church might have in interpreting the instructions of the Prayer Book.

It is a mistake to think that religion declined in fervor. This was also the age of home missions. In 1884 Canon Barnett went into the slums of East London and founded Toynbee Hall. Nonconformists and Roman Catholics alike copied this. They learned the problems of the poor whom Charles Booth had studied, and they did what they could to help. In 1889, during the Dock Strike, Toynbee Hall and Cardinal Manning aided the strikers, even though the Archbishop of Canterbury was against them. In this period, too, Nonconformity came ardently into politics. It fought the Cowper-Temple Clause in the Education Act of 1870, as too likely to allow Anglican teaching in the new board schools, and in the Education Act of 1902 fought to retain that clause, as a restraint on Anglicanism. Above all, it fought, and in 1914 finally defeated, the establishment of the Church in Wales. Here David Lloyd George won his political spurs.

In another sense Nonconformity came into politics. Many an English Labor leader learned organization in the Methodist Church and thereby became inspired with that Christian humanitarianism so characteristic of the movement. For Methodism, with its organization so like that of the Amalgamated Engineers, is believed to be the source of much such organization. Nor was Nonconformity alone the cause of Christian socialism. "Uncle George" Lansbury, the grand old man of Labor in the early 1930's, was a devout High Church Anglican, just like W. E. Gladstone, and, just like Gladstone, the more devoted to his political ideals for that reason. This, too, was the time of other Booths than Charles—of "General" William Booth and his family, the founders of the Salvation Army, with its message of spiritual regeneration. Roman Catholicism, too, showed vigor. Cardinal Manning as Archbishop of Westminster and Cardinal Newman from the Oratory at Edgebaston, a suburb of Birmingham, in their separate ways built up a powerful organization and intellectual respect. The monuments were, perhaps, Manning's Westminster Cathedral and Newman's self-defense against Charles Kingsley's sneers, Apologia pro Vita Sua.

Thus Englishmen had many intellectual roads to travel. Typically, Englishmen were eclectic; they picked and chose a bit here, a bit there. Though it is true to say that Darwinism was the outstanding new idea of the times, it should not be forgotten that it was not the only outstanding idea, and that different men received it differently. That may explain the complexity and diversity of thinking of leaders of opinion of the day.

Having thus looked briefly at the conditions under which lived Britain's new masters, the laboring classes, at the educational opportunities they had, and at the ideas that were current around them, let us see what they did for themselves. The great means of their rise was the trade union. As has been told in a previous chapter, in 1868 the T.U.C. was founded. It was guided by a group of practical elderstatesmen of labor, the Junta. Their program may be compared with that of Samuel Gompers. They stayed out of politics, tried to avoid strikes and keep up employment, and negotiated for better wages and conditions. This typical craft-union policy paid dividends. Both parties helped labor. The Liberals passed a basic Trades Disputes Act in 1873; the Conservatives went further, in 1875, and apparently gave unions protection from vexatious lawsuits in their right to strike. This craft unionism differed from American craft unionism in that it also built up social insurance, for which in America the Ladies' Garment Workers are almost unique. Disability, funeral, health, and in a few sturdy unions unemployment insurance, in the decade from 1900 to 1910, took up to 68.5 per cent of union expenses, "strike pay" only 10.7 per cent.

But this craft unionism—again the parallel with America's A.F. of L. and C.I.O. may be instructive—did not reach down. It was the dock workers of London who began the "new unionism" of the 1890's, with their great strike of 1889. From outside, socialists—John Burns, Tom Mann, Ben Tillett—moved in. From Australia came £30,300 of the £48,000 subscribed. From unions elsewhere as well as the general public came support and sympathy. For five weeks the Port of London was tied up. At the end Cardinal Manning negotiated a settlement, and a union of 30,000 members was recognized. Here a militant semisocialist labor movement came to the fore. It was not Marxist. After a few years of notoriety England's "Marxist in a top hat," H. M. Hyndman, faded into the background, though his Social Democratic Federation did start many a future labor leader thinking on non-Marxist lines. It did not stem from the poet William Morris, though Morris's *News from Nowhere* played a part in building up socialist thinking. The key inspiration, outside the ranks of labor itself, came from the Fabian socialists. It was they who, in a British way, guided labor into a British socialism.

Like the Roman general, Fabius Maximus, the Fabians hoped to conquer by caution. Their principle was "the inevitability of gradualness." Darwinianly they hoped to have England evolve into a socialist state by steady slow steps, each advocated as a practical, common-sense reform. A brilliant group of propagandists wrote pamphlets, *The Fabian Essays*, and tirelessly delivered lectures to any who would listen. Outstanding in attracting readers were H. G. Wells and Bernard Shaw. More significant were the great teacher Graham Wallas and the great investigators Sidney and Beatrice Webb. The Fabians got listened to. Men were amused by

Shaw, students were inspired by Wallas, people of influence were "got at" by the Webbs. Just as Morant guided through the Education Act of 1902, the Fabians had their fingers in many a minor pie, as well as the major one of the re-creation of London University as a federation of many institutions, to which was added the London School of Economics under the guidance of Pember Reeves, Seddon's right-hand man from New Zealand. An even greater triumph was the Poor Law Commission of 1905 to 1909, whose *Minority Report*, permeated with Fabian ideas, became a guide to future relief thinking.

These intellectuals succeeded because they worked not merely through other intellectuals but through a rising labor movement. In 1893 was founded the Independent Labor Party, with Keir Hardie as leader; in 1899 was founded the Labor Representation Committee, with J. Ramsay MacDonald as Executive Secretary. This was the decade of the fighting new unionism, somewhat corresponding to our C.I.O. But in the decision to be a party in Parliament, not just a vote-gathering body, the I.L.P. and the L.R.C. took a step Australians had taken but Americans have not. The impetus of this political move increased with the Taff Vale judgment of 1901, when the Amalgamated Society of Railway Servants was made to pay damages for a strike made against its instructions by a Welsh local. Membership increased by leaps and bounds. In the election of 1906 labor played a great part in Liberal victory and was rewarded by the sixth act of the session, a short Trades Disputes Act which made it clear that unions could not be sued. Thus, as the chapter on Constitution and Institutions will tell, labor came of political age.

But before one overestimates the position of organized labor these figures might be set down. In a population of forty-five million there were in 1910 about three million trade-union members. Thirteen million workers were insured before the passage of the National Insurance Act. England's new masters were doing perhaps more to help themselves by insurance than by labor organization.

Thus, by 1914 the British working class, though it had far to go to take over political and economic power, had started on the road. In this period in which the working classes rose, the middle classes seem to have changed in their attitude. The typical member of the mid-Victorian upper middle class had been Carlyle's fictional "Plugson of Undershot," whom for drive and social utility he compared in his *Past and Present* with the medieval Abbot Samson, much as he disliked some of his characteristics. Now the typical member of the upper middle class might be Galsworthy's fictional Forsytes, the number of whose offspring decreased with the drop in the going rate of interest, and who finally married into the aristocratic Monts. More and more the upper middle class stopped fighting the aristocracy, stopped owning their own businesses, and stopped going to Nonconformist chapels; instead, they joined the Conservative party, took civil service posts or posts under others, and went to an Anglican church. Similarly, the lower middle class changed. Its members, instead of ending their lives as proprietors, were apt to retire on a pension as a section chief, chief clerk, or minor executive of a large firm. Small shops decreased and department stores began, though not on an American scale. Even public houses became tied in with great breweries. This loss of drive was not complete. Economically Britain did not see large-scale amalgamations to the extent Germany, France, and America did. Politically and intellectually, Manchester remained a center of vigorous modified Manchesterism, notable for the outstanding Liberal paper, the *Manchester Guardian*. But the decline of the middle class is a social feature of the times.

Besides the economic causes of this, there were social ones. There was much emigration overseas, rates running from 50,000 a year in the 1890's to 237,000 in 1907. This drained to the United States and the dominions from the middle class and the skilled artisans. There was a reduction in size of families and an increase in comfort in the smaller families. The conveniences that favored the worker also favored the middle class. Commuting trains, trams, and bicycles enabled the middle class to live in suburbs and to enjoy sports, like cricket or the newly devised lawn tennis. Such families lived in pleasant homes given prestige by names such as "The Hollyhocks," or "Dahlia Terrace" and sent their children to newly founded "public" schools, modeled on Eton or Rugby. Longer holidays were spent on the Continent. Increased savings were invested in stocks and bonds and brought in a modest dividend. Thus daily living was agreeable, and few thought that their position in the world had worsened.

As in the preceding age, the pattern for middle-class mores and manners was set by the upper classes. Imitation here was sincere. Local clubs were in the image of White's or the Athenaeum. Style in dress was copied by those who could now afford to patronize a local tailor. If the imitation might be criticized as ununderstanding—and poking fun at the middle class was a popular intellectual sport—it brought with it an appreciation of the code of a gentleman. World War I showed that the middle classes continued to deserve the appellation "the backbone of the country."

Did the gentry and nobility deserve similar praise? A music-hall song of the period had the refrain: "It's the rich wot gets the pleasure. . . ." Popular ideas of the romantic and luxurious living of the upper classes were as lush as they were overdrawn. There were those who could support a pack of hounds, a box at the opera, a yacht, and more than one castle. But these increasingly were the exception. Progressive "death duties" struck hard, the classic blow being the crippling of Sir William Harcourt, the Chancellor of the Exchequer who introduced them, through the death of his brother and his nephew in quick succession before he in-

herited Nuneham Harcourt. Lord Salisbury well described the nobility
when he said that he knew many dukes and that as a group they were
poor but honest. Though the Dukes of Bedford and Westminster throve
on ownership of land in Bloomsbury and Westminster, the nobility as a
class was living on capital, selling stocks and land to keep up social appearance. It was the newly rich who were the conspicuous spenders.
The peerage should not be condemned for those to whom the Liberals,
especially, gave titles for reasons suspiciously close to contributions to
party funds. This economic decline of the upper class raises two questions
about the structure of English society: Did private means still enable
leaders to serve their country? Was the upper class still providing the
leadership as it did in the past?

Private means have long given Great Britain statesmen. Thomas Pitt's
doubtful procurement of the Pitt diamond gave her two great leaders.
The elder Peel's mills enabled the second Sir Robert to be premier. His
father's able trading in Liverpool and a few years redeeming the mortgage on his wife's estate allowed Gladstone to devote a life to public
service. Canning married the "rich Miss Scott." It was Labor that mostly
benefited in this period. Sidney Webb and J. Ramsay MacDonald both
married enough money to spare them a struggle to live and permit a
wholehearted dedication to a cause. But Balfour on a trip to New Zealand
made investments that built up his inheritance; Nettlefold and Chamberlain, screw makers, gave their nation three leaders, Joseph, Austen, and
Neville Chamberlain. The British economy, in this period, still contained
a leisure class devoted to public service—or rather an independent class,
for no one could call Sidney Webb and Ramsay MacDonald men of
leisure.

Were the statesmen of the late Victorian Period and early twentieth
century men of lesser stature than their predecessors? Since Tudor times
the upper classes had governed well. Could this be said of the men of
the 1890's and the 1910's? There has been much talk of the "sunset of
Empire" and "the decline and fall of Edwardian England." Is it justified?
Some, of course, is nostalgia for the spacious days of Queen Victoria, a
belief that the high-water marks of British greatness were the Golden
Jubilee of 1887 and the Diamond Jubilee of 1897. But as Dean Inge of
St. Paul's has warned, the immediate past is almost always disregarded
by the men of today. The makers of these charges forget the flaws of their
heroes. Lord John Russell feared the Pope would ruin England by creating bishoprics, Lord Palmerston in the fullness of his wisdom said that
there was nothing wrong about Ireland but the weather, Disraeli stooped
to unbecoming conduct in discussing his sovereign's personal foibles, and
Gladstone's name became bandied about by Englishmen overseas as a
synonym for dangerous blindness to facts. It is also forgotten that the

men of the 1890's and 1900's had to deal with the world which these Victorians made. They did not do badly. Balfour gave Ireland solid institutions, British education its present form, the Cabinet its present organization, and the Commonwealth of Nations its basic policy. Campbell-Bannerman turned two conquered nations into loyal subjects of the Crown as remarkably as ever did Durham. Though Disraeli and Palmerston could pass a law or two and set social problems aside, Asquith and Lloyd George had to, and did, construct a social-welfare system. In foreign affairs, Lord Lansdowne and Sir Edward Grey solved greater problems than their predecessors. Or, to reverse the comparison, could Palmerston or Canning have spoken England's mind as well as Lloyd George did when he checked a trend to war with his Mansion House speech in 1911? Could Peel or Disraeli have handled the constitutional crisis of 1911?

Some differences do stand out. The Victorians were superbly sure of themselves; their juniors were not. The moral authority of Gladstone, the confident maneuvers of Disraeli were replaced by the "philosophic doubt" of Balfour, Asquith's "Wait and See" policy. The court of Edward VII was gayer but less decorous than that of his mother. Such changes were not all to the bad. Making allowance for them, the roll of the Liberal Cabinet of 1914 suggests that England still bred great leaders. In it were middle-class Asquith, of Nonconformist stock; the scion of the Dukedom of Marlborough, Winston Churchill; the Welsh solicitor, David Lloyd George; and the Whig aristocrat, Sir Edward Grey. These were supported by such men as Haldane, the Scottish barrister; Reginald McKenna, the financier; and John Burns, the former Labor agitator. That would seem to prove that from the days of the Tudors to World War I careers had remained open to talent and that talent had come to the top.

Of course this talent looked different—just as the "new men" of the Renaissance looked different to the old medieval nobility. Of course some of the "new men" of this era such as John Burns and Lloyd George outwardly behaved differently, though others such as Asquith had risen through the path of university education and fitted smoothly into the upper-class social pattern. One reason for this is that no clearly defined bundle of ideas marked a man in office from the lower class from a man in office from the upper classes. There was a climate of opinion which distinguished these years, and most men of prominence, as in other ages, lived in the climate of the age and were identified with it.

This was an age of self-criticism. In *Culture and Anarchy* and *Essays in Criticism,* written in the 1860's but effective at this time, Matthew Arnold attacked philistinism. In *News from Nowhere,* by the printing of the Kelmscott Press, by making Morris wallpaper and the Morris chair, William Morris strove to teach ideals of beauty and socialism. From 1870 to 1880 the first Slade Professor of Art at Oxford, John Ruskin, author of

Modern Painters, worked himself into a collapse preaching that art had a mission. It was by talks with Ruskin, while building a road with his hands to learn the nobility of labor, that Arnold Toynbee became inspired with the ideals that led to Toynbee Hall. Two Oxford tutors, T. H. Green and William Bosanquet, took German philosophy and domiciled it in Britain in such a way as to make the British Liberals of the next generation turn from Manchesterism and *laissez faire.* Thomas Huxley conducted his effective crusade for the ideas of evolution. Above all, the Fabians, as has been told, pointed to flaws in British institutions, one of them, the playwright Bernard Shaw, eventually doing very handsomely in the proceeds of his dramas. Oscar Wilde and Kipling, too, were critics of art and of the unimperialness of the British about their Empire.

Britain had all sorts of critics—and honored them. The lengths to which she went may be illustrated by the cases of Wilfrid Scawen Blunt and Sidney Webb. Blunt had two chief windmills to tilt against: Gladstone's imperialism in taking over Egypt, and the vanity of the British in not breeding their horses from contemporary Arab stock. To his estate at Crabbet used to go the great imperialist, George Curzon. The Webbs dissected British institutions and recommended their rebuilding. For this Mr. Webb became Lord Passfield, a member of a body of which he disapproved in principle, and was honored by the nation with burial in Westminster Abbey, an edifice dedicated to a religion of which he did not think highly. Perhaps this self-criticism may explain why one class rose, while two others, relatively, sank, with a good deal of good temper. It is true that in the late 1800's Great Britain saw much bitterness over constitutional issues because they represented an attack on an entrenched class, and much bitterness in strikes, because they represented an attack by a rising class. But characteristic of Great Britain—as opposed to strife-torn Ireland—was a good-humored acceptance of the inevitable.

This chapter began with pointing out the Britishness of the rise of a working-class movement. It should end with the Britishness of the reception of that rise.

37

CONSTITUTIONAL HISTORY

1874–1914

The British constitution proved to be sufficiently flexible to meet the challenges with which a more democratic franchise faced it. The results of the Reform Bill of 1867 appeared in this period. They were augmented by the results of the Ballot Act of 1872, of the Bribery Act of 1884, and of the Reform and Redistribution Acts of 1884. In sum this legislation created a new sort of electorate. Though property qualifications were still required for voting, though plural voting was still possible for the favored few, by 1884 the average English, Scotch, Welsh, and Irish male could vote, once he had settled down and established himself in life. Though the United Kingdom did not yet have universal manhood suffrage, let alone universal suffrage, it did have an approximation to it. Thus at last the laboring classes of England through the exercise of their franchise could freely and unobstructedly make their desires reach fulfillment as far as that is possible by putting them into statutes. This also meant that certain things passed out of political life, certain new things entered into it. Gone was the watching at the polls to see if tenants and tradesmen voted as their landlords and customers wished. The secret ballot ended that. Gone were the tiny close boroughs where a local magnate could usually return almost anyone he chose. Redistribution drove, for example, Lord Randolph Churchill from Woodstock, outside the gates of his father the Duke of Marlborough's Blenheim Palace, to the suburb of South Paddington. Therefore politics became less a matter of local significance, more a matter of national significance.

For in the place of these old ways came the national party machines, which presented a program to the whole nation. A dramatic example of change was Gladstone's Midlothian campaign. When the Grand Old Man came back from political retirement in 1879, to fight a Scottish by-election as a way of dramatizing his concern over the "Bulgarian atrocities," such was the publicity he gained that, willy-nilly, the rest of the Liberals had to follow in his train. Thus this became the age of great political speeches. It became a national joke to ask: "What did Gladstone say in 1882?" so voluminous—and, to his opponents, so contradictory—had been his out-pourings of that year. Since it was the political leaders rather than individual candidates who won votes, the Liberal and Conservative central associations, under the control of the Whips, controlled candidates. Rarely did an Independent buck the machine; the mere threat of withdrawal of support usually was enough to cause the local association to knuckle under. To resist such pressure took titanic efforts, as when Joseph Chamberlain fought and beat his own creation, the Birmingham Caucus, over the Home Rule issue.

Nor did this control by the party stop at the polls. It reached into the House of Commons. In the mid-nineteenth century a man had made his mark by his speeches. Now he made his mark by keeping quiet and voting according to the orders the Whips brought him from the Cabinet. For parliamentary oratory was now not the way of securing votes from one's associates in the House but of securing support from the country outside. In consequence of this the conduct of parliamentary business changed. More and more time was assigned to the Government. The fact that speeches were often made to obstruct business led to new rules. The prime cause for this was the Irish obstruction, notably the three-day continuous session of January, 1881. But though the Irish led, others, notably the Conservatives, followed. Many felt that not only the independence of the individual member but the integrity of Parliament had been compromised by democracy.

Similarly the make-up of Cabinets changed. In the early period both Conservative and Liberal Cabinets were composed of the upper classes. Gladstone surrounded himself with Whig nobles—the Duke of Argyll, the Marquis of Hartington, Earl Spencer. For this there was a practical reason that Liberal Governments were weak in the House of Lords. Conservative Cabinets for that reason were more likely to take in business-men, just because it would be in the House of Commons that the Conservatives would be weak. But gradually the composition of Cabinets changed. Joseph Chamberlain, the Birmingham manufacturer, broke his way first into the Liberal Cabinet and then into the Unionist Cabinet. It proved a source of reproach to the Salisbury Ministry of the early 1900's to have too many members of the Cecil family in it, no matter how individually able they were. By 1914 the Liberal Cabinet contained such leaders as H. H. Asquith, David Lloyd George, and John Burns. A new level of society had come to power and had won representation in the highest offices.

In local government, too, this was an age of increasing democracy. It was in the 1870's that Joseph Chamberlain, first in the Birmingham School Board, then in the Birmingham City Council, built up his great machine, the "Caucus," modeled on American urban political methods. With the control he so gained he fought the Established Church in the School Board, and gave Birmingham "gas and water socialism," in the form of well-run public utilities and trams. Nor was Manchester far behind, with its far-reaching water supply from distant Cumberland and its city-owned Manchester Ship Canal, opened in 1893. Four great legislative steps were taken in advancing this democracy—the County Councils Act of 1888, the London County Councils Act of 1889, the Parish Councils Act of 1893, and the Education Act of 1902. The first ended the age-old power of the justices of the peace. No longer did Quarter Sessions act as an unelected taxing body by ordering public works carried out by parishes or the County Surveyor. Now the electorate chose its own county councils, modeled on city councils. Like city councils, the county councils added to their number aldermen, and elected a presiding officer, the Chairman. Then, in 1889, the corrupt Metropolitan Board of Works was abolished, and replaced by a "London County Council," to rule the area outside the still self-governing medieval city. This body soon built up a great reputation through the deft guidance of its first Chairman, Lord Rosebery. In 1893, the Liberals took a further step, creating parish councils. Finally, in 1902 the Conservatives abolished the school boards and fused their functions with the county councils. Only the poor relief authority, the Boards of Guardians, remained outside Council control. They were attacked by the Poor Law Commission of 1906 to 1908 and would in 1929 find their functions passed on to the county councils. Thus English local government ceased to be a hodgepodge of elected and nominated bodies with special duties and became a hierarchy of elective ones with nearly full control of the area under them.

Politically this created a new way to the top. From Lord Rosebery in the 1890's to Herbert Morrison in the 1940's, the Chairmanship of the London County Council would provide a pathway to the Cabinet. Administratively, this new legislation created a new importance for the Home Civil Service. For with the exception of the still independent boroughs, these councils were the agents to carry out national legislative programs under the guidance of the Local Government Board and the Home Office. Here can be seen the growth in England of the modern state.

The word England has been used instead of Great Britain since, though Scotland and Ireland were given nearly identical institutions, the procedure was to pass separate acts, because of the legacy of a different basic law, dating from before the Unions of 1707 and 1801. But though local rights were respected, vested interests were not. This was an age of legal reform, in which the great Statutes of Westminster of Edward I were at last overhauled. By the Judicature Act, which went into effect in 1875 and was amended by Order in Council in 1880, King's Bench, Common

Pleas, Exchequer, Chancery, and other special jurisdictions were fused into one High Court of Justice which serves throughout the kingdom and has three divisions: Chancery, King's Bench, and Probate, Divorce, and Admiralty. Over this is a Court of Appeal. Over the Court of Appeal is the House of Lords. But, since the reform of 1876, only trained judges may vote in the House of Lords when it is sitting in its judicial capacity. These are "lords of appeal in ordinary," *i.e.*, life peers whose titles cannot be inherited, the Lord Chancellor and any ex-Lord Chancellors, and such judges as happen to have been ennobled. Practically the same body, in virtue of being members of the Judicial Committee of the Privy Council, then turns around and acts as the supreme court of the Empire.

The growth in democracy here described found a constitutional obstacle in the House of Lords. That body blocked, among others, the following measures: the abolition of purchase in the Army in 1870, the Ballot Act of 1872, the Irish land legislation of the 1880's, the Home Rule bills of 1892 and 1912, and Welsh Disestablishment in 1911, as well as the Budget of 1908. Since all these measures were Liberal measures, more and more the House of Lords stood out as an adjunct of the Conservative party. Increasingly the Liberals demanded "to mend it or end it." The crisis came, not with the weak Liberal Government of the years from 1892 to 1895 but with the overwhelmingly strong Liberal Government that held office from 1905 to 1915. When an Education Bill and a Licensing Bill had been rejected, the Liberals laid down a challenge. Into the Budget of 1908, David Lloyd George inserted a land tax guaranteed to irritate landlords. The device succeeded. Lords rejected the Budget. Here was a constitutional conflict of the first order. Not since 1860 had they refused to pass a money bill. In that year they had been brought to heel by Gladstone, who incorporated all taxation into one budget and in effect said to the Lords, "Take it or leave it."

The obvious solution was an appeal to the country. The answer the country gave was to reduce the Liberal party to equality with the Conservatives, but to return over one hundred Irish and Labor members who even more ardently than the Liberals decided to humble the House of Lords. The Liberals accepted this as a mandate to "end it or mend it"; many Conservatives most emphatically did not. Commons passed, and Lords rejected, a proposal to reform the relationships of the Houses. The new King, George V, then called yet another general election. In it the Conservatives gained one seat. The burden of the deadlock fell upon the King. There has been much argument as to the propriety of the "advice" given the King by his Prime Minister, Asquith. For before the election Asquith extracted from the King what seems to have been a secret promise to break a deadlock by the creation of peers. Then a Parliament Bill was passed. This time the House of Lords, when duly warned by the Liberal leader, Lord Morley, gave in. Thereafter the Parliament Act of 1911 became the basic law of the land. Under it, a money bill, certified by the Speaker to be such, goes directly to the King for royal assent without being referred to the Lords. All other bills go to the Lords, for passage, amendment, or rejection. But in case of rejection, if the identical bill is passed three years running, it by-passes the Lords and gets royal assent. Thus the House of Lords sank from being almost equal to the House of Commons to being an advisory and delaying body. And, promptly, Irish Home Rule and Welsh Disestablishment were passed, though World War I, with incalculable results, delayed their being put into effect.

Yet, though the democratization of England lessened the importance of the House of Lords, it increased the importance of the Crown. In the 1870's, Queen Victoria, living in retirement and mourning the Prince Consort, was out of touch with her subjects. But as she emerged from that retirement, especially after the Jubilees of 1887 and 1897, she won their deep affection. She represented something solid and unifying in their lives. Her son, Edward VII, in different ways, won a similar affection. He was more fashionable, less decorous, but in his way a national symbol. Then came George V, unexpectedly the heir to the throne when his brother died in 1893, unexpectedly King when his father suddenly died in 1910. By this time the Crown had lost the administrative functions to which Queen Victoria had so obstinately clung. But as was told in a previous chapter, he found himself, at the outset of his reign, confronted by a new constitutional duty.

In the Parliament Act crisis of 1911, his correct attitude gave England a reservoir of strength. Because he was willing to create peers in 1911, he kept the governmental machinery working. As time went on the nation began to realize how much it owed him for this.

Overseas, a similar evolution took place. There, too, the Crown became the symbol of unity. The feeling aroused by the proclamation of Victoria as Empress of India in 1877 may be a cause why, today, the Republic of India still considers Queen Elizabeth II as Head of the Commonwealth. The Colonial Conferences of 1887 and 1897 were intimately connected with the Jubilees; the world-circling tour of George V, when Duke of Cornwall and York, in 1900, at which he opened the Australian Houses of Parliament, his Durbar in India as Prince of Wales, heightened this connection.

Constitutionally this was an age of democracy first, monarchy second. But it may be considered an age of democratic monarchy because of the emergence of the Crown as a symbol, while it went into abeyance, except in crises, as an organ of government.

38

POLITICS

1874–1914

In this book at times the tightly woven fabric of events has been pulled apart, in order that the threads of imperial and colonial history, economic and social history, and foreign affairs may be examined closely and individually. For the years from 1874 to 1914 perhaps a still clearer understanding may be gained by separating political history into two strands and dealing with the Irish problem after general problems have been discussed. The two cannot be entirely separated, but separate examination should make their connections more comprehensible.

Two characteristics seem to distinguish British political life in the forty-odd years before the outbreak of World War I. First of all the two-party system seemed to work efficiently as Conservatives replaced Liberals and Liberals replaced Conservatives according to the will of the electorate. In round numbers the Conservatives were in office twenty-five years, the Liberals seventeen. This swing of the pendulum between two parties was, however, illusory. Both parties at one time or another were propped up by minority or third parties. Without the help of the Irish Nationalists, the Liberals in 1886 and 1892 would have been in a sorry plight. In 1910 without the Labor and Irish help the Liberals could not have carried on. The Conservatives gladly accepted Parnell's help in 1885, and in 1886 were put into office by the Liberal Unionists. Third-party support, then, was more necessary to the Liberals than to the Conservatives but at times was essential to both.

The second characteristic was the changing importance of men and issues. In 1874 men seemed to come first and the causes they championed second. The personalities of Disraeli and Gladstone stood out over the issues they fought over. Later on Lord Salisbury and Joseph Chamberlain personified the issues of the day. After the opening of a new century somehow the issues were greater than those who spoke on them. Elsewhere it is pointed out that Asquith, Lloyd George, and Balfour were probably not lesser men than some of their predecessors, but that they were dwarfed by the nature of the affairs they tried to handle, when the problems left as political legacies by the giants of the late Victorian decades grew over-whelming in the Edwardian period. It is interesting to speculate how Gladstone would have dealt with the world crisis of July, 1914, or Disraeli of the "fancy franchises" with the socialism of old-age pensions and national insurance.

The Liberal party of this period still gave proof that it had been founded in 1859 by a fusion of Whigs, Liberals, and Radicals. It showed constant tendencies to split apart again into those groups, as the bulk of the party moved away from Whiggery and toward Radicalism. Whigs such as Lord Hartington left the party, to become first allies and then associates of the Conservatives. The average Liberal moved away from laissez-faire thinking toward collectivism. By the 1890's the Liberals were advocating old-age pensions and heavy inheritance taxes; in the 1900's they passed into law the beginnings of a national insurance scheme. In this progress to the left they were led not only by their Radical wing but by the emerging Labor party, which either competed with them for votes or made with them so-called "Lib-Lab" agreements in two-member constituencies. Here is where the Irish question cuts across British politics. It was the Home Rule split of 1885 and 1886 which drove from the party not only the Whig Hartington but the Radical Chamberlain. Another crosscurrent was the fact that traditionally the Liberals were anti-imperialist, yet the party contained an imperialist wing. This caused them trouble in the 1880's and also at the time of the Boer War.

One advantage possessed by the Liberals, and especially by their Radical wing, was that of enthusiastic and smooth-running local associations. Best of all these was Chamberlain's Birmingham Caucus. This political machine, copied from the caucuses of the United States and led by a great ward heeler, Schnadhorst, functioned year in and year out with highly predictable results. The Birmingham free and independent voter was organized and manipulated as well as, or even better than, any other free and independent subject had been. Thus Radicalism personified by Chamberlain showed the world how to regiment, regulate, and control the individual so that he chose the right men to represent him.

Of the Irish party, called Home Rulers or Nationalists, the following chapter will tell. Suffice it to say that after 1880 they formed a solid bloc of some eighty votes, determined to win some form of legislative autonomy for Ireland. When, in 1886, they won the Liberals to their side, they became allies, who were faithful as long as the terms of the alliance were kept.

As for the Labor party, it was a growth of the 1890's, though its origins came earlier. In it two separate movements came together, an intellectual one and a trade union one. There was a Marxist movement in England, the Social Democratic Federation, led by H. M. Hyndman. In itself it petered out, after a few demonstrations in the late 1880's. But it had real educational effect. Many of the Labor leaders of the future were led by it to independent and non-Marxist socialist thinking of their own. More significant was a non-Marxist intellectual movement, the Fabian Society, whose slogan was "the inevitability of gradualness." In it Sidney and Beatrice Webb, Graham Wallas, Bernard Shaw, and H. G. Wells worked to bring in socialism by easy, unnoticed stages. They achieved much by deft suggestions to bureaucrats and politicians. They also did much to recruit support for Labor among intellectuals and to encourage socialist thinking among trade union members. Numerically more significant, furnishing the votes if not the ideas, was the growing interest labor leaders took in local and national politics. First they pressed in local Liberal associations for the choice of candidates favorable to their aims. Then they pressed for actual working-class representation in Parliament. Here appears Keir Hardie, who after entering Parliament in 1892, in 1893 founded the Independent Labor party. Then in 1899 the T.U.C. decided to bring more Labor members into Parliament, and in 1900 set up the Labor Representation Committee, with J. Ramsay MacDonald as secretary. This, after the election of 1906, became the present Labor party. Its function in these years resembled that of the Radicals, of showing the way for the Liberals to follow, and that of the Irish, of insisting on keeping of the terms of an alliance.

Perhaps the new type of leadership which thus was coming to the fore may be symbolized by a matter of costume. The great Radical leader of the 1870's and 1880's had been the Birmingham manufacturer Joseph Chamberlain. Chamberlain's program was so advanced as to win the name "unauthorized." He advocated that the newly enfranchised voter by his vote make the rich "pay ransom," in the form of heavy taxes to subsidize government services for all. But Chamberlain's peculiarity, seized on by cartoonists, was to wear in his buttonhole every day a fresh orchid that had been grown in his own greenhouse. What a difference from the flat workingman's cap that Keir Hardie ostentatiously wore when, under the rules of the House of Commons, his head must be covered if he were to address the Speaker!

While the Liberals were thus a party losing membership by fission, the Conservatives remained close knit, except during the free-trade controversy of the 1900's. Some local Conservative associations were as efficient as the Liberal ones, notably the great Salvidge machine in Liverpool, which survived almost intact the Liberal landslide of 1906. But generally they did not have quite the missionary fervor typical of Liberal and Labor. To the Conservative party, in 1886, came Liberal and Radical support, in order to preserve the Union with Ireland. It was to consolidate that support that the Conservatives for many years adopted the name Unionist.

By so doing, they persuaded many of these recruits, notably Joseph Chamberlain, to fuse with them. However, some Liberal Unionists, like Lord Hartington (later the Duke of Devonshire), sturdily kept up a separate organization.

This emphasis on party machinery was a sign that this was an age in which the electorate was taking the place of Parliament as the body that had the last word. It is the election returns, rather than struggles in Parliament, which decide issues. Once the electorate has made its choice of a party to be in power, in power that party will be, unless internal dissensions bring it down, till the next general election. This is recognized, among other things, by a growing habit of transferring office to the party that has won the election, even before Parliament meets.

Disraeli came into office early in 1874 chosen by the electorate and not by Parliament, when Gladstone followed the precedent set by Disraeli in 1868 and resigned once the result of the elections were known. Indeed the "Grand Old Man," as his followers had come to call him, soon retired from politics, transferring the leadership of the Liberal Opposition to Lord Hartington. This was the first time since 1841 that the electorate had returned a Conservative majority to Commons. It proved Disraeli's contention that widening the franchise would help, not harm, the Conservatives. He brought with him an able Cabinet, though one less progressive than he. Sir Stafford Northcote, a former private secretary to Gladstone, as Chancellor of the Exchequer had his patron's mastery of finance. Lord Salisbury, who when Lord Robert Cecil had opposed the Second Reform Bill, now let bygones be bygones. He would later become Prime Minister. Sir Michael Hicks Beach, though he did not enter the Cabinet till 1876, had a career of success before him, as Irish Secretary, Colonial Secretary, and Chancellor of the Exchequer. But this Cabinet had two weak spots, the Earls of Derby and Carnarvon as Foreign and Colonial Secretaries. The story of this government is of successes where it was strong, failure where it was weak.

Throughout his life Disraeli had claimed that the Conservatives were the party of true social reform. That had been the basis of the romantic Young England movement he had led in the 1840's and of the novels he had written, *Sybil* and *Coningsby*. It had been his slogan in the election of 1874, when he had coined the phrase, *Sanitas Sanitatum, Omnia Sanitas*. In part his government lived up to this tradition. Much was done to codify the legislation passed in previous years. In the codification improvements were made, as in the Trade Disputes Act of 1875, where Conservatives did better than Liberals in protecting the right of unions to strike. But there was much taking of credit for Liberal reforms by rewriting Liberal legislation. In one case, the Merchant Shipping Bill, Disraeli postponed a reform till public opinion drove him to it, after the Liberal Samuel Plimsoll had made a scene on the House of Commons floor. Perhaps the greatest value, therefore, of Disraeli's codification was for the future. It imbued the Conservative party with a belief which it has never lost, that it was a party of social reform. Again and again that belief has eased the path of change. For Disraeli's great service to England was as an educator. He taught ideas to men who were undersupplied with them.

Elsewhere it will be told how Disraeli met the Russo-Turkish War of 1876 and 1877 with such firmness as to fill England with a wave of patriotism and give her new international status. In the process he was able to get rid of Lord Derby and replace him at the Foreign Office by Lord Salisbury. But this left a mark against his record, of having failed to protect the Bulgarians against massacre by the Turks. Then, having taught the English people to hold their heads high in foreign affairs, he preached the Empire to them. By a stroke of propaganda he delighted Queen Victoria and some Englishmen by making her Empress of India. But Carnarvon at the Colonial Office was a weak reed—all his life Disraeli had been hampered by the weakness of the typical second-line Conservative. This was especially true after 1876, when the Conservative leadership in the House of Commons fell into less able hands. In that year Disraeli moved to the House of Lords as Earl of Beaconsfield. This gave the old leader a well-deserved freedom from arduous labors, but left day-to-day management of the Commons to the uninspired Sir Stafford Northcote. As is again told elsewhere, Carnarvon bungled in South Africa. Not enough men were sent to end the Zulu War, not enough skill was shown when the Transvaal or South African Republic was annexed. Carnarvon had to go, replaced by Hicks Beach, and the Conservatives had another black mark against their record.

Their record was what turned the Conservatives out. Indignation burned in Gladstone's breast at the atrocities in Bulgaria. To show that indignation he reentered politics by standing at a by-election in the supposedly hopelessly Conservative Scottish constituency of Midlothian. When he had had his say not only Midlothian but the electorate had been aroused. Then, when Beaconsfield called a general election in 1880, those speeches swept the Liberal candidates into Parliament. Beaconsfield resigned, and no matter how she wished otherwise, Queen Victoria had to see Gladstone as Prime Minister, for Lord Hartington, the nominal Liberal leader, told her it would be impossible for him to form a Cabinet.

Here Benjamin Disraeli, Earl of Beaconsfield, leaves the stage of history. He went into retirement, to die in 1881. His career is a contentious one, for he rose to power by dubious methods. His leadership of the backbenchers in revolt against Peel and his twists and turns in the passage of the Second Reform Bill caused many of his contemporaries to distrust him. On the other hand he had great courage, the skill to impress his bizarre personality on a party of country squires, and, above all, the almost magic power to educate that party. To him should go credit for the fact that the aristocracy still takes an active part in English politics and, unlike the remains of the continental aristocracy, can be a force for progress, not reaction.

From the very start this second Gladstone Cabinet was bedeviled by obstructions of men and events. A ready-made issue came when the atheist Charles Bradlaugh requested to be allowed to affirm instead of taking an oath in the name of a God in whom he did not believe. Four men, Sir Henry Drummond Wolff, Sir John Eldon Gorst, Lord Randolph Churchill, and Arthur James Balfour, almost spontaneously joined forces, even to gravitating to adjoining seats "below the gangway." They used the religious feelings of Gladstone's followers to defeat Gladstone's desire for toleration and so clogged his legislative program at the very start. Following Lord Randolph's injunction, "It is the duty of an opposition to oppose," this "Fourth Party"—as it half-jestingly, half-seriously called itself, the Irish being the "Third Party"—went on to make capital of all Liberal mistakes. The name they gave this was "Tory Democracy." Lord Randolph, who speedily became the leader, even went so far as to capture the Conservative party machinery from the Central Office and, as a compromise, install at its head the most energetic of the former Cabinet, Sir Michael Hicks Beach.

Many a blow did they strike—from the terms of the "Hares and Rabbits" Bill to liberalizing the Reform Bill of 1884. Again and again, it was the "Fourth Party's" urging that pushed the whole Conservative party on toward a stand that would win it votes in the coming election, as they attacked both the Liberal leadership and what they considered the ineptness of Sir Stafford Northcote. These men were nothing compared to Parnell and his Home Rulers. Details of this Irish obstruction will be given later. It appalled many Englishmen and taught the Conservatives the disgraceful methods they used just before World War I. Furthermore, Gladstone had to bear reproaches from imperialists for evacuating the Transvaal after a military defeat, Majuba Hill, even though in Midlothian he had promised such an evacuation, and also from anti-imperialists for sending troops to Egypt to restore order and then not withdrawing them. No wonder extraordinarily little legislation was passed. Finally, in 1884, was passed the Third Reform Bill, which widened the franchise in the counties, thus helping the Liberals and the Irish Nationalists gain votes. However, on the insistence of the House of Lords this was accompanied by a redistribution measure which partially countered that advantage in the Conservatives' favor. This measure has already been described. There were a few other pieces of legislation: the Hares and Rabbits Bill, which allowed farmers to shoot those crop-destroying animals and so lessened the hatreds caused by the Game Laws; permission to Nonconformists to be buried in their own churchyards; the Married Woman's Property Act of 1882; the Bankruptcy and Patent Acts of 1883. But so little was accomplished that it is no wonder that Joseph Chamberlain, in the election of 1885, stepped away from the party and issued his "Unauthorized Program" calling for expropriation power for local government, government housing, graduated taxation, full freedom of elementary education, employers' liability, and a chance for the rural laborer to rent small allotments of land for himself. Pulled one way and another, the second Gladstone Cabinet was about to break up from internal dissension and at the same time lose support in the country and the House of Commons.

The death of General Gordon at Khartoum and the bad showing of the Liberals in the Penjdeh incident were the final blows that brought low Gladstone's second ministry. Frequently Queen Victoria was more than a sovereign; she was the tongue and heart of her people. When news of the disaster at Khartoum was sent her, she in anger reproved Gladstone in a telegram sent straight and without the use of code. Her rebuke was not only her private expression of wrath but also that of a nation feeling that its honor had been besmirched and that Gladstone's neglect had been responsible for the whole fiasco. When Chamberlain broke with his colleagues over an Irish land-devaluation bill and offered to resign, the friction within the Cabinet was apparent to everyone. So when Sir Michael Hicks Beach moved an amendment to the Budget and with Parnell's help carried it against the Liberals, Gladstone resigned promptly on June 9, 1885.

His Cabinet was replaced by the Conservative "Cabinet of Caretakers," to keep the government going till the new voting registers could be drawn up. The events of Lord Salisbury's first administration, June, 1885, to February, 1886, will be told in the chapter on Irish problems. Lord Salisbury brought in some of the wheel horses left from Disraeli's government but bowed to Churchill's "Tory Democracy" by sending Sir Stafford Northcote to the House of Lords as Lord Iddesleigh and making Sir Michael Hicks Beach Chancellor of the Exchequer and Leader of the House. Lord Randolph Churchill went to the India office, where he finished adding Burma to the Empire.

Now all eyes turned toward the judgment of the new electorate to be given in November. Both sides angled for Irish support. In the election Parnell threw his weight—in England—to the Conservative side. This is believed to have helped the Conservatives win borough seats which more than counterbalanced the county gains won by the "Unauthorized Program," and so brought the Liberal membership down to an exact half of the House of Commons. Then came Gladstone's dramatic conversion to Home Rule and the immediate withdrawal of Hartington from the party.

Lord Salisbury decided to give up negotiations with the Irish, "meet Parliament," and force Gladstone to show his hand. These tactics were effective. In February, 1886, Gladstone and Chamberlain did defeat the Government and take office in the third Gladstone Ministry. But the two men then fell out, and Chamberlain left the Cabinet to fight for the preservation of the Union. This was a time when speeches in Parliament did convince waverers as perhaps never since. Sixteen days of debate over the bill found Gladstone at his best. They also saw Hicks Beach, Chamberlain, and Hartington defeat him on point after point. But the sharpest thorn in Liberal flesh was Lord Randolph Churchill, who pricked them until blood ran in the House of Commons and on public platforms outside. The Home Rule Bill was defeated. The Liberals then appealed to the country. In June and July, 1886, came yet another general election, in which party lines were cleared. Conservatives and Liberal Unionists won a majority as long as they were in alliance. However, the Liberal party machine ridded itself of many a Whig. For example, H. H. Asquith took a Scottish constituency back from a Liberal Unionist.

Lord Salisbury took office in August, 1886, after having offered the premiership to Lord Hartington as the man who truly held the balance of power, only to have him decline. Here came the end of Lord Randolph Churchill's meteoric rise. It had been he, in large part, who had won votes in the election. For this Salisbury rewarded him with the posts of Leader of the House and Chancellor of the Exchequer. But before Lord Randolph could introduce a Budget he was gone, after having left a name as one of the great Leaders of the House. For when he tried, in the name of Tory Democracy, to cut expenses on the Army and Navy, and offered his resignation to win his point, that resignation, to his surprise, was accepted. As he ruefully put it, "he forgot Goschen." That eminent Liberal Unionist was put into the Cabinet as Chancellor of the Exchequer; the kindly W. H. Smith of bookstall fame, who was also Sir Joseph Porter of H.M.S. Pinafore, became Leader of the House, and all went surprisingly well without Lord Randolph. For Lord Salisbury well knew that his government could stay in office till the next general election and trusted to being able to win that without Lord Randolph.

Then came steady Conservative rule, till 1892, while Home Rule was shelved and A. J. Balfour gave Ireland "resolute government." But to keep Liberal-Unionist and Radical support, it was necessary to pass the laws that Chamberlain wanted. The sight was seen, again and again, of the best speeches for a Government measure being made by the tall man with the orchid in his buttonhole who rose from the Opposition front bench. The Irish measures, foreign affairs, may have been Conservative. The County Councils Act was the work of Joseph Chamberlain, as were the Technical Education Act of 1889 and the Factory Act of 1891.

In 1891, when the term of the Parliament elected in 1886 was coming to an end, the purged Liberal party held a convention at Newcastle, and gave out its program: Irish Home Rule, Welsh Disestablishment, local option, improved labor legislation such as employers' liability. But the Parnell divorce case worked against them, and in the election they secured fewer votes than the Conservatives, being in office only by the support of eighty Irish Home Rulers, the combined Liberal and Irish Nationalist majority being 40. Lord Salisbury met the new Parliament, only to resign when H. H. Asquith, a coming Liberal junior, moved a vote of no confidence. Then Gladstone, tired, partly deaf and blind, and bent under his eighty-three years, stepped out once more to do battle for Home Rule and the cause of progress. Heads shook over the folly of a man so old and feeble trying to complete so monumental a labor. None was there who did not admire the courage and genius of the greatest parliamentarian of the century. This was to be Gladstone's last battle.

The battle was quickly fought—and lost. Gladstone put Home Rule before any other reform. This meant that Ireland's troubles were more pressing than the Newcastle Program. It also meant that the Liberals would have to get rid of Gladstone if they were to succeed in sponsoring a program of real social reforms. The House of Commons passed a second Home Rule Bill. The House of Lords threw it out on September 8, 1893, with a decisive vote of 419 to 41.

After such a defeat Gladstone stayed on in order to "fill up the cup" of political bitterness for the Conservatives to drink. His party hoped to represent the House of Lords and the Conservatives as impediments in the road toward progress and reform. In the process of putting on the Lords the onus of defeating the Newcastle Program, the useful Parish Councils Act of 1894 was passed. But the defeat of his second Home Rule Bill and the pressure of old age brought Gladstone to end his sixty-one-year career in Parliament. In March, 1894, he retired, to be succeeded as Prime Minister by Lord Rosebery.

On few subjects could Queen Victoria and Gladstone agree at all. On Lord Rosebery they were in partial agreement. Both liked the attractive imperialist Liberal peer, but Gladstone did not allow his personal fondness for a young man of talent to override his political sense. If the Queen had asked his advice, he would have recommended Lord Spencer as Prime Minister. If she had asked the advice of the Liberal party, it would have recommended the Chancellor of the Exchequer, Sir William Vernon Harcourt. But the Queen asked no advice. She sent for Lord Rosebery, as was her constitutional right.

Lord Rosebery was a man of promise. Throughout his life he remained a man of promise. He never quite reached the heights expected of him. This did not prevent him from being a most unusual person. He was

Prime Minister, he won the Derby with his horse "Ladas," and he married an heiress—all three of these being goals he had set for himself in youth. Furthermore, in 1889, he performed great services as the first Chairman of the London County Council. He also was the author of some distinguished studies of statesmen, the best being his appraisal of a predecessor, William Pitt. Unfortunately he was not a good Prime Minister.

Lord Rosebery could not feel the temper of the House of Commons from his place in the House of Lords. He could and did feel the heat generated against him by Sir William Harcourt, the ablest man the Liberals had in the House, whose Budget containing the "death duties" was the only real political triumph of Lord Rosebery's administration.

The death duties, taxing landed inheritances heavily, were the forerunner of the socialist Liberal budgets of the next century. Harcourt and Rosebery fought over policy, indeed over almost every detail of government. On foreign affairs Harcourt was a "little Englander," Rosebery a Liberal imperialist. It was sadly said that the only thing the two men ever agreed to was to resign in 1895, when a "snap division" had put them in a minority.

Yet the Cabinet of 1894 contained some very able men; two future prime ministers were in it. H. H. Asquith showed unusual promise as Home Secretary. Campbell-Bannerman at the War Office was able to secure the removal of the Queen's relative, the Duke of Cambridge, as commander in chief of the Army, and by so doing he made possible badly needed reforms in the organization of staff and command.

The election of 1895 returned 340 Conservatives and 71 Liberal-Unionists, 177 Liberals, and 82 Home Rulers. Lack of harmony among their leaders, the mistaken policy of making the House of Lords and Conservatives squirm with death duties, local liquor veto bills, and the Home Rule Bill caused the Liberal defeat. The majority of Britons wanted the Conservatives, a bigger and better Empire, and very little restriction on their right to drink beer. They were also tired of the Irish question.

The Unionist government which came in in 1895 might be called a triumvirate, since three men shared its leadership. As Prime Minister and Foreign Secretary, Lord Salisbury held the primacy. As Leader of the House and First Lord of the Treasury, Arthur James Balfour was practically deputy premier. But in the Colonial Office was Joseph Chamberlain, who had entered the Cabinet and chosen that post in order to build up the Empire. In Home Affairs this was like the previous Salisbury government, one of sound administration and concentration on keeping order in Ireland. Chamberlain soon overshadowed his colleagues. His was the basic responsibility for the Boer War. His was the plan for Empire preference in trade. It was he who had seized on a minor registration tax on grain and tried to build it up into a revival of the Corn Laws. For Chamberlain through being an imperialist had become converted to protection. He called out the latent protectionism of the Conservatives from the country-squire class along with a new protectionism that had been rising among some manufacturers. In 1900 it was Chamberlain who was largely responsible for the "khaki election," called during the South African War, in which appeals were made to vote Unionist as a patriotic duty. This gave the Unionists a new lease of power, for the divided Liberals could not win seats when the Welsh pro-Boer Lloyd George was making platform speeches so at divergence from those of such Liberal imperialists as R. B. Haldane, Sir Edward Grey, and H. H. Asquith. For after 1895 the Liberal Opposition fell apart. Lord Rosebery grew out of sympathy with his party and resigned the leadership to "plow his lonely furrow." Sir William Harcourt soon followed him into retirement. Leadership devolved upon Sir Henry Campbell-Bannerman. C.-B., as he was nicknamed, had a hard time holding the wings of his party together. Some Liberals attacked the Boer War, some supported it. But he did his best and gradually won the confidence of his followers.

As if to symbolize the start of a new age and the passing of an old one, Queen Victoria died in 1901, having reigned since 1837. In her later years, in spite of openly displayed partisanship in politics, she had become more and more the beloved symbol of the greatness of her age and her people.

King Edward VII was an old man when he was crowned at Westminster Abbey. He was a splendid figurehead, performing with grace and charm the many social and public functions required of a king. He was at his best at the opening of Parliament, reviewing a regiment, at a levee, or paying a state visit to the President of France.

Legend has it that King Edward influenced the course of policy that led to the Anglo-French *rapprochement* in 1904. Probably the only, certainly the greatest, help he gave was to act as a public figure and relieve his ministers from pressure of strenuous social obligations during their stay in Paris. Because he left important decisions to be made by his ministers, he made the Crown more than ever a symbol standing above and beyond the alarms and excursions of party politics. Here, because of his character and lack of ability to follow precisely in his mother's footsteps, Edward VII completed the picture of what an impartial monarch should be and set a precedent for other constitutional sovereigns to follow.

After the Boer War had ended, in 1902, Lord Salisbury retired and turned the premiership over to his nephew, Arthur Balfour. Chamberlain continued to act as an almost independent coleader. His was the plan for Empire preference in trade which would rip the Unionist party into factions. He saw protection as a means of building up the Empire. Already he had, by great colonial loans, done much to bring prosperity. Already by the Commonwealth of Australia Act he had helped weld a continent into one nation. Why not form an economic organization, for the mutual benefit of all? Such was his argument, and there were economists such as Professor Hewins of London who agreed with him. On the other hand, those financiers brought up in the strict Gladstonian tradition would not tolerate desertion of the free-trade dogma. Balfour, like Campbell-Bannerman, found himself at the head of a divided party. However, he did not reconcile its wings as well as did C.-B. Deftly, he secured the resignation of extremists of both sides, Chamberlain and some of those who objected to Chamberlain. He softened the blow by making Chamberlain's son, Austen, Chancellor of the Exchequer.

But this did not bring Balfour peace. Within his Cabinet there were further resignations, chief among them being that of the Duke of Devonshire (Lord Hartington of a few pages earlier). The loss of the Duke was a serious one, for his integrity was widely trusted. Still worse, Joseph Chamberlain stumped the country on a great crusade for tariffs. Up and down the land he went, upsetting men's minds. For to most Britons free trade had become a religion, ever since the Corn Law repeal. Had not even Disraeli said, "Protection is dead and damned"? Therefore the voters became willing converts to the Liberal party, especially when Chamberlain's "shadow," H. H. Asquith, followed him about, attacking his arguments in the same place the next day. A ground swell began away from the Conservatives. This was heightened by four things—the Education Act of 1902, the Licensing Act of the same year, the Taff Vale decision, and "Chinese Slavery."

The Education Act of 1902 was a beneficial reform, in that it put primary and secondary education under the same authority, the County Councils. Its terms brought other vast improvements. But it had two political weaknesses. The abolition of the old school boards cost many a local politician a post of honor. The state subsidization of Church of England schools (the so-called "voluntary schools") roused the combative natures of the Nonconformists. Similarly the Licensing Act of 1902 caused teetotalers to vote against the Conservatives. More serious was the Taff Vale decision. In a railway strike in Wales a member of a union had damaged property. To the surprise of Labor and against previous interpretations of the Trades Disputes Act of 1875, the Union was held responsible for the action of its members and forced to pay a crippling sum. Under this decision unions were set back. For what strike could succeed if a union had to spend funds in legal fees proving itself free from accusations of causing damage? And though a Conservative Government had passed the Trades Disputes Act of 1875, this Unionist Government would not modify it, to bring it to the meaning usually ascribed to it, that a union is immune from lawsuit for damages that occur just because one of its members gets hotheaded. Here was something which would rouse the numbers represented by the Labor

Representation Committee to join the Liberals, who would pass laws protecting the unions.

To cap this, in South Africa, in order to start up the gold mines on the Rand, the Unionist Government had encouraged the importation of Chinese coolies under contracts which gave very large powers to the employers. The revelation of this brought together in opposition to the Government three passions: the old Exeter Hall antislavery feeling, Labor's fear of being undercut by unfair competition, and a racialist dislike of seeing another race brought into a "white man's country." Thus, by 1905 the country was ready for a change.

Balfour did not fully sense this. He did sense that he was having as much trouble holding his party together as C.-B. was having with the Liberals. For at times the only way he could avoid parliamentary defeat was to lead his entire party from the House of Commons, to prevent its splitting wide open on some deftly phrased resolution about free trade. He therefore determined to let C.-B. bear the burden and resigned. C.-B. did have his troubles. For a moment it appeared that the three leading Liberal Imperialists, Asquith, Haldane, and Sir Edward Grey, would not join his Cabinet. But courage and firmness brought them in. Campbell-Bannerman dissolved Parliament and won by a landslide. Into the so-called Mad Parliament went 377 Liberals, 83 Irish Nationalists, and 53 of the Labor party, as against 132 Conservatives and 25 Liberal Unionists.

On the opening of the new Parliament a scene was enacted that revealed the difference in party leadership and the new temper of the House of Commons. Balfour started to quibble and prick the new Prime Minister with nice philosophic distinctions and literary harassments. After putting up with these oratorical flourishes in which Transvaal and Chinese labor problems were mentioned, C.-B. stood up, looked Balfour in the eye, said bluntly, "Enough of this foolery," and turned his attention to the serious business of reforming. This Parliament took its tone from the new Prime Minister. It was a Parliament that would devote itself to reforms of the first importance.

It was also a Parliament with a new party. Labor in these years would chiefly spend its time learning the ways of the House of Commons. In the process it would lean heavily on one skilled member, J. Ramsay MacDonald, Secretary of the Labor Representation Committee. But when it spoke loudly enough, it could have its way. For in many a seat a three-cornered contest—Liberal, Conservative, and Labor—in place of a Lib-Lab alliance would lose the Liberals that seat and give it to the Conservatives. Thus it could drive through a Liberal party full of lawyers and a Conservative House of Lords the repeal of the Taff Vale decision. Here thoughtful men saw the future before them.

The Liberal Ministry that presided over this Parliament was probably as able as ever was gathered. In it were three future premiers, Chancellor of the Exchequer Asquith, President of the Board of Trade Lloyd George, and Undersecretary of the Colonies Winston Churchill (the last a convert for free trade's sake from his father's party), not to mention Haldane, "England's greatest War Minister"; the financier McKenna; and Sir Edward Grey, one of her greatest Foreign Secretaries. This Ministry's difficulty was not in deciding what to do, but in passing legislation to do it. Haldane could get army reform, Lloyd George could set up the Port of London Authority, the model of such bodies as the Port of New York Authority. Labor could force through its Trades Disputes Act. Campbell-Bannerman and Winston Churchill could give responsible self-government to the conquered Orange Free State and Transvaal. But when it came to a matter of the Liberal party program, the House of Lords stood in the way. It rejected an Education Act that would salve the Nonconformists and a Licensing Bill for the teetotalers. In 1907 Campbell-Bannerman warned it against this, by a solemn resolution of the Commons, but it kept on being "Mr. Balfour's pet poodle." The old cry of "end it or mend it" was raised again. Then Campbell-Bannerman died, Asquith became Prime Minister, and Lloyd George Chancellor of the Exchequer. The 1909 Budget contained a provoking proposal to tax land values. At this blow at the great estates that were the economic basis of the House of Lords, that noble body lost its head. It rejected the Budget. This had never happened. Ever since 1668 the House of Lords, by a constitutional convention, had been forbidden to change a money bill but might reject one. Ever since 1861, by a similar convention, the chief money bills had been lumped into one vast Budget, to force through contentious measures.

The Liberals picked up the gage of battle thus thrown down. Asquith secured a dissolution, putting the question to the electorate. The electorate gave a curious answer. They cut down the Liberal majority to equality with the Conservatives and returned about the same number of Nationalists and Laborites as before. Since these two minor parties were hot for the Budget and for Lords reform, this meant that these two would be pushed on with. The Lloyd George Budget was sent up once more, and the Lords were forced to accept it, a year late. (There was a happy moment when the income tax legally expired, but that was soon dealt with.) Then a bill was passed, to restrict the powers of the House of Lords. Commons passed this, and the Lords rejected it. King Edward died, and it was the new king, George V, who had to face the constitutional crisis. As has been related, he chose to promise to break the deadlock, if a second election returned the Liberals to power. The election showed that the people of England were of almost exactly the same mind—only one or two seats changed hands and the changes almost exactly balanced out. Again, amid disgraceful scenes, the Parliament Bill was passed through Commons, clause by clause, word by word, comma by comma, with angry votes on each. Then Lords was faced with it.

There were "last-ditchers" who wanted to fight it out and let Asquith ask the King to create about 500 new peers. But there were also "hedgers" who wanted to save something from the wreck. In a scene of confusion, with strange advice from Cross Bench or nonparty peers, such as Lord Rosebery, the Bill became law. It ended the function of Lords, as a permanent block, on Liberal legislation, but leaving it, as has been explained, power of delay and revision. No longer would the House be Mr. Balfour's poodle. For this Balfour was largely blamed. A crisis arose in the Conservative Party. The *Pall Mall Gazette* took as its slogan "B.M.G.," Balfour Must Go. Finally Balfour went. There was much argument who should succeed him. At last a dark horse, the Canadian-born Andrew Bonar Law, was chosen the Conservative leader, while wits misquoted the Litany: "Have mercy on us, O Lord, and incline our hearts to Bonar Law." Now the Liberals moved toward the Insurance State. Long had friendly societies and trade unions brought forms of social insurance to the working classes. Lloyd George proposed to bring to the aid of this system the taxing power of the state. Thus, as he put it, the worker would get sevenpence for fourpence. An able team, including Sir Robert Morant, Winston Churchill, and Charles Masterman, drafted the measure. Here was a measure that was but a beginning. It offered only old-age and health insurance—unemployment insurance was to come later—with not too wide coverage. But it opened vistas to the future which gave hope to the working classes, roused fears in the wealthy.

This was an era of ill feeling, well described in Daingerfield's *Strange Death of Liberal England.* Suspicious Conservatives charged that Cabinet members had improperly invested in an American subsidiary of the Marconi Company and then given advantages to the parent company. Strikes on the left and ruthless talk on the right made the old-fashioned English tolerance seem a thing of the past. For in 1912, 1913, and 1914 came bitter political battles.

The Parliament Act has been passed to bring about Welsh Disestablishment and Irish Home Rule. These measures were introduced into the House of Commons and met with vituperous opposition. Home Rule, as is elsewhere related, even met with threat of civil war. As a last resort, the King himself entered the picture, calling the Speaker's Conference to see if an accommodation could be reached. It could not. England seemed on the verge of her greatest internal troubles, when external trouble came, the outbreak of World War I.

39

POLITICS, IRELAND

1874–1914

Halfway through the twentieth century the southern and western twenty-six counties of Ireland were flourishing at long last as the Republic of Eire, free from the British and their Empire. Six northern counties were also flourishing, but under a Home Rule Act, as part of Great Britain. In order to reach this divided but possibly happy state of affairs, Ireland had to pass through anarchy, something close to destitution, and civil war, in a series of political, social, and economic conflicts. In the period up to 1914 the story of how this happened is so tied up with the history of the rest of Great Britain as best to be told in terms of the rises and fallings of Liberal and Conservative ministries caused by the Irish question. How difficult that question was will be shown by the position in which we will leave Ireland at the end of this chapter. At that point, 1914, we will find not the traditionally rebellious Catholics of the South but the traditionally loyal Protestants of the North defying law and order with guns in their hands. More than that, Ulster will be backed by the royal and loyal party, the Conservative-Unionists.

All this came about because fate decreed that the Liberals should undertake to right Irish wrongs. For the Liberals in those days were dominated by Gladstone, who in turn was dominated by his convictions. In 1868, when told he had been appointed Prime Minister, his first words were: "My mission is to pacify Ireland." Then, in and out of office he tried to live up to his words till he retired from politics in 1894. He became convinced that the Irish state Church must go—and it was disestablished. He became convinced that Irish land laws needed reforming, and they and the landlord class with them were eventually reformed almost out of existence. But when he felt that the Union of 1801 had been wrong, all his persuasion and force of will failed to achieve his purpose. For in 1886 Whig lords, some Radicals of whom Joseph Chamberlain was the most prominent, and a goodly company of Liberals left him. This split in the Liberal party was never healed. Gladstone held on to his course of helping Ireland first and reforming Britain second. By doing so he kept his party weak and, for most of his remaining political life, on the Opposition side of the House of Commons. For though the Liberals did win an election in 1892, they were unable to pass the Second Home Rule Bill through the House of Lords. Thereafter they remained out of office till 1905, when they secured power, in part by putting social and constitutional reforms first and Irish business last. At that, in 1912, after the House of Lords had finally been curbed by the Parliament Act, Ulster met Home Rule with the threat of armed defiance, so that in 1914 civil war was imminent.

But though Ireland's story in these years can be told in terms of Liberal party political successes and failures, that is but a surface account. Deeper lie the many conflicting aims and fears of different groups, out of which conflicts the Irish question was made. Certain groups desired change. There were would-be rebels, such as the Fenians who in 1867 had invaded Canada and blown up Manchester jail, as the Clan-na-Gael, and as the Invincibles who in 1882 murdered Lord Frederick Cavendish. Their successors, the Irish Republican Brotherhood, would in the Easter Rebellion of 1916 start the movement that finally freed Ireland. There were agrarian reformers, such as Michael Davitt's Land League, whose sturdy pressure would cause the Liberals to reform the land laws and the Conservatives to buy out the landlord class by land purchase. There were cultural nationalists, such as Douglas Hyde's Gaelic League, which had no direct political aims, and Arthur Griffith's Sinn Fein movement, which had first political and then revolutionary aims. Hyde would wind up as President of Eire; Griffith would see his program free Ireland from English rule and would sign a treaty between Ireland and Great Britain. Attempting to find a middle way would be the three great Home Rule leaders, Isaac Butt, Charles Stewart Parnell, and John Redmond, with whom this chapter will deal.

Other groups desired to keep things as they were. Such were the members of the United Church of England and Ireland, if we give that body its legal title as of 1868. Such were the landlords of the "Garrison." Such were the Presbyterian Ulstermen and their South of Ireland leader, the eloquent lawyer Edward Carson. These latter men wanted more than just to protect their property; they feared for their religion. Such were the Irish dramatis personae of this tragedy.

The first step in Irish reform was to disestablish the Church in Ireland. This Gladstone did in 1868. Since then the "Church of Ireland" has been a self-governing part of the Canterbury Communion which now has the same relationship with the Church of England as the Protestant Episcopal Church of the United States. This overdue reform was generally accepted. Then Gladstone took a further step. A curse of Irish life had been the annual leases of land by the tenantry. Regularly, they were "rack-rented," that is, the rent was raised whenever possible. Perhaps the meanest reason for a rent raise was that improvements had been made by the tenant. If the tenant would not pay the increase, out he went. Therefore Gladstone partially extended to the rest of Ireland the "tenant right" which courts had enforced in Ulster as a local custom. By that, tenants got compensation for improvements they made. Then came the Ballot Act of 1872. This requirement of secret voting utterly changed Irish political life. Hitherto landlords had ridden to the polls at the head of their tenants—for who, holding an annual lease, would dare vote in public against his landlord's wishes? Now all was different. Landlords rode to the polls alone; by a mass movement, tenants voted as they pleased. A new Irish party sprang to life, with the first by-election. With the general election of 1874 the Parliament of the United Kingdom saw a third party, the Irish. Isaac Butt, a Protestant landlord, had sat in Parliament and annually proposed that Ireland be given a local legislature, under what he called Home Rule. Thus Ireland would have about the same degree of self-government as a province in the Dominion of Canada. Hitherto he had been politely listened to, and politely and overwhelmingly voted down. Now that he had sixty-odd votes at his back, men began to take him seriously.

Among those who took him seriously was the wise Benjamin Disraeli. When that statesman, now Lord Beaconsfield, dissolved Parliament in 1880, he told the world what it then failed to realize, that Ireland was the paramount political question. For Disraeli had seen a portent, the meteoric rise of Charles Stewart Parnell. On both sides this Protestant landlord inherited hatred of England. His great-grandfather had stoutly voted against Union in the last Irish Parliament. His mother's father, Captain Charles Stewart, U.S.N., had commanded the U.S.S. *Constitution,* "Old Ironsides," in the War of 1812. Parnell shouldered the mild Butt aside as ineffective, caring not that he broke the man's heart as he did so. He took command of the Irish by his personal power and soon forged a new political weapon, obstruction. He used the rules of Parliament to block business till the Irish got what they wanted. Every twist and turn of the rules was utilized, if that would gain an end. "Irish nights" became a horror as Parnell's machine tightened its grip. Behind him, founded in 1879, was Michael Davitt's Land League, formed to force rents down, either by reform of the land laws or by intimidation. Between the Nationalist party and the Land League, by the early 1880's Parnell became "the uncrowned king of Ireland."

It was not until the general election of 1880 had given him a solid parliamentary bloc and Gladstone the premiership that Parnell got into full swing. Then he made his demands clear. They were two things, first the "Three F's"—a land reform—and then Home Rule. The "Three F's" were fixed tenure (no more short leases), fair rent (rent to be fixed by an outside authority), and free sale (the right of a tenant to sell his lease to someone else). The House of Lords rejected the bill which partially granted these. Promptly Parnell gave the Irish tenants advice. "When a man takes a farm from which another has been evicted, you must shun him." This advice was fully taken, in the famous case of Captain Boycott. It was as if he were alone on a desert island. In the end Boycott was rescued by men from Ulster who came to reap his crops. A new weapon was thus added to the armory of the Home Rulers and a new word, boycott, to the English language. Now began the battle by which Parnell drove English politicians to their knees.

An attempt was made to try him for seditious conspiracy—but the Irish jury disagreed. An attempt was made to pass a Coercion Bill practically though not nominally suspending habeas corpus. Here came the greatest feat of obstruction of the Irish. A session lasted from four on Monday afternoon to half past nine Wednesday morning and might be going to this moment had not the Speaker on his own authority suspended the session. Immediately the rules of the House were changed. As a result, an Irish Land Law was passed, but in a form unacceptable to Parnell and Davitt. For inciting to resistance to evictions Parnell was jailed, at Kilmainham. He warned that if he were incarcerated "Captain Moonlight" would rule Ireland instead. His warnings of agrarian disorder proved true, and a deal was made, called by political opponents the Kilmainham Treaty. Parnell was let out of jail, and concessions were planned.

No sooner had this agreement been honored than Home Rule and the Irish were blacked in Englishmen's minds by two brutal murders. A young and attractive Whig nobleman, Lord Frederick Cavendish, had just been made Irish Secretary. He came to Dublin full of good intentions. While walking with Undersecretary Burke, they were stabbed to death in Phoenix Park by a band of extremists, the Invincibles. But though the reaction to this slowed down Parnell's rise to power, it did not check it. There was built up a powerful political, propaganda, and fund-raising machine, which spread all over the world. It was on their travels in New South Wales that the Redmond brothers married sisters. From South Africa, Cecil John Rhodes sent a contribution to Parnell's funds. Above all, Irish Americans helped the Home Rule movement and the Land League. This gave some substance to the Unionist taunt that Parnell was supported by the meager savings of Boston kitchenmaids. But he was also supported by the eloquent pen of John Boyle O'Reilly in the Boston *Pilot,* and it is as significant that world Irishry mobilized public opinion as that it provided funds. A sign of this is that even in 1920 the Republican party in the United States made the freeing of Ireland a platform plank. What this wave of public opinion needed was an opportunity to get results.

In 1884 and in 1885 the opportunity was provided. The Reform Bill of 1884, by greatly increasing the rural vote, enabled the Home Rulers to extend and confirm their sway, so that only in Ulster and the one Protestant constituency of Dublin could they be resisted. Then, in 1885, the Gladstone Government tottered to its fall. In June Parnell, in alliance with Sir Michael Hicks Beach and Lord Randolph Churchill, drove Gladstone from office and put in the Salisbury "Ministry of Caretakers," which was to act as a stopgap until the new election rolls could be made out. This government, by the Ashbourne Land Purchase Act of 1885, found what proved to be the solution to the Irish land problem. The British government lent money to tenants to buy their holdings from their landlords. Terms were so easy that installments often were less than the rents which they superseded. Dickerings began with Parnell. The ill-omened choice for Irish Viceroy was made of "Twitters," the Earl of Carnarvon who had twice botched South African Union—once by blocking Sir George Grey when he had achieved it, and once by mishandling the occupation of the Transvaal. Parnell and he had an interview, which both men reported in different terms, Parnell claiming that Carnarvon had offered what amounted to Home Rule. In return, Parnell publicly asked all Irishmen in England to vote Conservative. Some Liberals at the same time, such as John Morley, became converts to Home Rule. Meanwhile other Liberals, such as the Marquis of Hartington, Lord Frederick Cavendish's brother, determined to leave the party if the Union were endangered. Something had to give.

What gave was Gladstone. In December, 1885, he "flew the Hawarden kite," as it was called. His son made an unauthorized but obviously informed statement that the Liberal leader was converted to Home Rule. At once changes came. Hartington left the Liberals. The Conservatives dropped Carnarvon like a hot brick and prepared to rally to the defense of the Union. Though in a minority, they decided to meet Parliament. Chamberlain and Gladstone prepared to oust the Conservatives.

Thus began the short-lived third Gladstone Ministry. Immediately it came under heavy fire. From the outside speeches poured out against it from Hicks Beach, from Hartington, and above all from Lord Randolph Churchill. Churchill saw the key to the situation, from the Conservative point of view—Ulster. He hurried to Belfast and there gave the slogan that may be said to have created a new nationalism. When he said "Ulster will fight and Ulster will be right," he roused the Protestants of the North of Ireland to a determination to keep separate. The campaign to rouse Ulster succeeded and made Ulster so separatist as today to be apart from the rest of Ireland. Internally, too, the Gladstone Ministry had its troubles. Chamberlain wanted Home Rule as a means of securing greater imperial unity through federation. He could not see eye to eye with Gladstone who saw Home Rule as a just concession to Irish nationalism. Chamberlain walked out, and with him the eloquent John Bright. Still there were waverers; some observers think that, had not Lord Randolph so bedeviled Gladstone in debate as to force him to unnecessary stands, Home Rule might have been carried through Commons. But it was beaten. Gladstone's Ministry fell, and the verdict in the general election was to destroy the Liberal-Irish majority and make it possible for a Conservative Ministry to rule England if it got the support of Hartington's Liberal Unionists and Chamberlain's Radical Unionists.

At this point it may prove simpler to divide the story of Ireland into two parts and tell first of the administrative actions of the twenty years from 1886 to 1906 and then of the political events that made possible a consistent twenty-year program. For Lord Salisbury, in the election of 1886, had given as the Conservative cure for Ireland's ills, "twenty years of resolute government." Another aspect of it was called "killing Home Rule with kindness." These programs were followed consistently from Salisbury's accession as Prime Minister to the fall of the Balfour Government in 1905, with a three-year Liberal interlude from 1892 to 1895.

The Irish leaders struck hard at the Salisbury Government by the "Plan of Campaign." If a landlord refused to take a rent set by the Land League, all rent money was to go to its treasury. This plan produced the time-honored outrages. In reply a Coercion Act was promptly passed, and the struggle started.

Within six months the Irish had broken the health of Sir Michael Hicks Beach, a man of legendary determination, by vituperation and sheer deviltry. Then Lord Salisbury assigned the Irish chief-secretaryship to his nephew Arthur James Balfour, who seemed to be a lackadaisical man about town and who was the author of a book on philosophy. The Nationalists crowed with delight and recited what they had done to the previous Chief Secretaries and what they would do to this victim: "We have killed Forster, blinded Beach, and driven Trevelyan mad—what will we not do to Balfour?" But in Balfour and his evenhanded and steady support of the law-enforcement officials under him they met their match. The Home Rulers cursed him and his Irish assistants, Attorney General Edward Carson and Chief Justice Peter O'Brien, as "Bloody Balfour, Coercion Carson, and Peter the Packer," the last being an accusation that that straightforward and beloved judge had "packed" the juries that came before him. But they had to respect these men's courage and ability and see that in spite of all they could do these three were giving Ireland peace, prosperity, and a chance to make progress.

For Balfour was also trying to end the conflict of landlord and tenant, not by changing the terms of tenancy but by making the tenants owners of the soil. It would save money in the long run if the British treasury lent to the tenant, at uneconomic rates of interest, money with which to purchase his farm. If land ownership by the Irish meant peace in Ireland, peace in Ireland would mean lower taxes. A succession of land acts—the basic Ashbourne Act of 1885, the Balfour Act of 1891, the Gerald Balfour Act of 1896, and above all the Wyndham Act of 1903—gave better and better terms, the Wyndham Act even allowing the government to force landlords to sell. This was not all that the Unionists did for Ireland. By the Congested Districts Act of 1891 a nonpartisan board was empowered to build roads and railways, encourage local industries, and even move population in the grossly overcrowded "rural slums" of western Ireland. The Unionists took local government out of the hands of the gentry and transferred it to the voters. This was done by the Irish Local Government Act of 1897, which abolished the administrative rule of the "grand jury"—the body that in Ireland corresponded to the county justices in England as the means of landlord rule—and replaced it with county councils. Balfour's program worked.

Under the leadership of Sir Horace Plunkett, Catholic and Protestant, Home Ruler and Unionist began to cooperate to improve Irish agriculture. An acre of soil was nonpolitical. Even the most violent could see that. In 1889 Plunkett organized the Irish Agricultural Organization Society to teach the Irish how to apply scientific methods to farming. Soon a Jesuit and a Master of the Orange Lodges sat together in the I.A.O.S. committees. Thus was built up a cooperative dairy economy which brought wealth to landlord and tenant alike. In 1899 an Irish Department of Agricultural and Technical Instruction was created largely because of the success of the I.A.O.S. Ireland by 1905 was well on the way to becoming a prosperous agricultural island, thanks to the ability of all parties to work together for the common economic good.

Two great political events made possible this long-term policy: the Parnell Commission and the Parnell divorce. In 1888 *The Times* struck at Parnell with the publication of letters in which it was alleged that he had approved of the Phoenix Park murders of 1882. The whole cause of Home Rule was put on trial when its champion was attacked. After political pulling and hauling, the dispute was put before a special commission of three judges. The letters were proved to be forgeries by one Richard Pigott, and *The Times* was made to pay damages. This did much to make the Liberals enthusiastic about Home Rule, but left the Conservatives unconvinced. Then in 1890 a divorce action was brought by Captain O'Shea against Mrs. O'Shea and Parnell. This ended the "Chief's" reign, for as co-respondent in the divorce, Parnell could no longer be trusted by Nonconformist Liberals in England and Catholics in Ireland. Deserted by all but a loyal few, Parnell died of a broken heart in 1891. Thereafter the Home Rulers remained divided into Parnellites, led by John Redmond, and anti-Parnellites, not to be reunited until 1902 when Redmond headed a united party.

The official Liberal party continued to stand behind Home Rule. When a reform platform, the Newcastle Program, put Gladstone and the Liberals back into office in 1892, many wanted Home Rule shoved aside for less deadly measures of reform. But Gladstone had dedicated himself to a holy cause. His second Home Rule Bill was introduced in 1893. Unlike the bill of 1886, this Home Rule Bill passed the House of Commons, but the Unionist party killed it in the House of Lords. Then when, full of years and honored everywhere except at Windsor Castle, Gladstone retired in 1894, and when in 1895 the Liberals lost office, Salisbury and Balfour came back to go on with their work. When Balfour resigned in 1905 and the Liberals won a vast majority of reform in the 1906 election, Ireland was largely set aside for collectivist reforms. Some sops were thrown to her, such as the Irish Universities Act and minor land legislation. While these acts were very helpful, political Ireland was growing restless once more. Furthermore under the Liberal Chief Secretary, Augustine Birrell, the level of administration in Ireland sank dangerously below the peak to which Balfour and his successors had raised it.

Consequently Irish nationalism in the years just before World War I took on a new aspect. This change was brought about largely by three organizations at once divergent and similar in character. First there was the Gaelic League. This was a cultural organization founded by Dr. Douglas Hyde, who was to become first president of the Republic of Eire. It existed for the purpose of reviving interest in the folklore, poetry, literature, and history of Celtic Ireland. It insisted upon the restoration of Erse as a language in everyday use. The League made it fashionable to speak Gaelic. By 1914 about one-third of the secondary schools in Ireland taught Erse. This revival of Ireland's Celtic culture helped make the young impatient of British legal control and the Home Rule tactics of fighting it out only on the floor of the House of Commons.

The second of the new organizations was Sinn Fein. The name Sinn Fein, "We Ourselves," was meant to be taken literally. Arthur Griffith, the moving spirit of the new movement, had studied Hungarian history to some purpose. He proposed that Irishmen agree to obey only laws enacted by their own legislature, acknowledge only Irish courts, pay taxes only to Irish collectors. By thus refusing to recognize any legal ties to Great Britain, Irishmen, like the Hungarians of the 1850's and 1860's, might win independence. Tiny and ridiculed though at first it was, Sinn Fein was a growing force that eventually destroyed the Nationalists.

Thirdly there was the Irish Labor party, socialist-syndicalist, revolutionary, and violent, created and led by James Connolly and James Larkin, which gained recruits because workers in Dublin were ill paid, badly housed, and ready material for mass violence. The Irish Labor party in 1913 carried out some very riotous strikes. Later on the shock troops of the Easter Rebellion were to come largely from it. If the Home Rulers failed to gain their ends quickly, these new forces would oust them from political power. As long as the veto of the House of Lords blocked Home Rule, Redmond and the Nationalists could get Ireland behind them to help pass the Parliament Act. But once that had been done, as happened in 1911, Redmond must produce results or see his followers desert him to Sinn Fein.

In the north of Ireland the Protestant minority regarded itself pledged to hold the line against any form of Home Rule for fear of the awful things a Catholic-dominated government would do. These sentiments were largely shared by the Conservative-Unionists. Balfour, for example, talked of the duty of his party and its obligation not to desert the loyal minority. Ulstermen were psychologically ready for extreme measures when the Liberals in 1912 at last introduced the third Home Rule Bill.

Ulster did not tarry for a moment. In 1912 the Orange Lodges drew up a Covenant pledging all true-blue Protestants to resist Home Rule, and 100,000 men volunteered to serve as in the Ulster Defense Force. Sir Edward Carson took over leadership in Ulster. Ulster's arming in defense of minority rights stirred the majority in Southern Ireland to vigorous action. Professor John MacNeill and Patrick H. Pearse, headmaster of a boys' school in the Dublin suburbs where Gaelic was the language of instruction, headed the new Irish Volunteer movement. Soon thousands in Dublin were flocking to the enlistment offices. Here both sides appealed to stirring historic memories. The Ulster Covenant was an intentional copy of the Scotch Covenant of 1638 that had brought Charles I to his knees; the National Volunteers were intentional copies of the Volunteers of 1782 who had forced George III's Parliament to give Ireland parliamentary independence. It was quite probable that with sufficient arms and equipment the two volunteer movements might meet each other on a civil-war battlefield. To make matters worse officers in the regular Army in the so-called "Mutiny at the Curragh" of March, 1914, let it be known that they would not obey orders to fire on Ulster Protestants. Then Ulstermen strained the patience of the government even further by unloading a vessel of arms and ammunition at Larne.

Not to be outdone by their Protestant neighbors to the north, the Irish Volunteers decided it was high time they undertook a little gunrunning themselves. In July, 1914, a shipload of arms and ammunition was smuggled openly at Howth. Such were the circumstances under which an Irish Home Rule Act approved of by Redmond and his group was put on the statute books in September, 1914, after being three times passed by Commons and rejected by Lords. All that was granted were powers of self-government comparable to those of a Canadian province. One concession was given to Ulster: the right to a six-year separation from the rest of

Ireland. This act never became effective because World War I started in August. In order to present a united front of Great Britain and Ireland against the Germans, Liberals and Unionists alike agreed to suspend the Act for the duration of the war. Thus Home Rule was achieved in 1914 and, by a quirk of fate, was denied to Ireland. Because it was thus denied, Sinn Fein took over and eventually won complete freedom.

40

GLADSTONE, SALISBURY, AND GREY

1867–1914

By the 1870's Great Britain's whole position in foreign affairs had changed, because of changes in the basis of power. The iron battleship replaced the wooden one; Germany's universal-service army made England's long-term professional army obsolete; Prince Bismarck's creation of the new German Empire altered the balance of power; the growth of new industrial areas and a change in ways of thought took away England's commercial supremacy and one support for international free trade. Even the English habit of telling others how to mind their own business weakened somewhat, though her moral prestige remained relatively high. It was the feat of her great Foreign Secretary, Robert Gascoyne-Cecil, Third Marquess of Salisbury, that he adapted British policy to this new era, or rather to two new eras—that of Bismarck, and that which came after Bismarck.

In these years British naval power remained high because her naval leaders kept ahead in the race for new weapons. It is a matter of dispute which nation made the first ironclad battleship, France with *La Gloire* in 1859, America with the *Monitor* and the *Merrimac,* or Britain with the *Warrior* which was an answer to and an improvement on *La Gloire.* The dispute is technical and turns on the relative amount of wood and iron used and the way guns were mounted. What matters was that the Royal Navy did not let itself be outdistanced. This was true right through the period. The first self-powered torpedo was used in the Royal Navy, encouraged by Captain A. K. Wilson. At the Whale Island training station Wilson and J. A. Fisher developed long-range gunnery and the use of electrical devices. When the French built torpedo boats, the English countered with torpedo-boat destroyers, one of the first of these, in the 1890's, being commanded by His Royal Highness the Duke of York, later George V. When the range of guns extended, it was Sir Percy Scott who devised director firing even ahead of the Italians and Captain Sims, U.S.N. The culmination of the work of such men as Wilson, Fisher, and Scott came when Fisher became First Sea Lord, on Trafalgar Day, 1902. Nelsonically,

Fisher made all battleships in the world obsolete with his *Dreadnought*, rushed to completion in a year and a day, which could outrun, outshoot, and outendure any ship in existence. While world attention was distracted by this, he planned and built a lightly armored supercruiser, the *Invincible*, which later sank Von Spee's cruiser in two hours without suffering a casualty, and had three of these afloat before the world knew of the type's existence. He also built up a submarine fleet. On retirement from the Admiralty, he found means of gaining British control—at least to 1951— of the Persian oil wells. By means of the work of such men as these, the Royal Navy, to quote Alice, "ran very fast to stay where it was"—at the top. Until 1916 no one doubted that Britannia ruled the waves—that remained a fixed point in all diplomatic thinking—though after 1908 and the German building of dreadnoughts, at the Marinamt in Berlin Admiral von Tirpitz had hopes that someday Germania might take over.

The British Army showed no such steady progress in modernization. It moved ahead by fits and starts, in almost every case being urged ahead not by the bellicose Tories but by the pacific Liberals. As a result the world, which if anything overvalued the Royal Navy, undervalued the British Army. This, too, had diplomatic results. The army of 1870 was obsolete. Officers still bought their commissions, despite what the Crimean War had shown of such methods of selection. Although the Austro-Prussian and Franco-Prussian wars had demonstrated that a short-service army with plentiful reserves could defeat a long-service army without reserves, the British Army clung to twenty-one years' service with the colors. Here stepped in Edward Cardwell, Gladstone's Secretary of State for War, who had been Secretary of State for the Colonies. He concentrated the Army by continuing the withdrawal of colonial garrisons he had begun in the 1860's and making the self-governing colonies responsible for their own defense. He abolished purchase, though it took a constitutional *coup d'état* to break Conservative obstruction. He shortened service to three years with the colors, nine with the reserve. He began localization of regiments. It was a tremendous task, which burned out the energies of the British minister responsible for Canadian Confederation. Cardwell never held office again, after 1874. In 1881 another Liberal, Childers, finished his work, by the linked-battalion system. Individual battalions were joined into pairs in "regiments." [1] This allowed interchange of officers and men between one battalion overseas and another in the recruiting area at home. Periodically, the battalions alternated duty. This gave Britain an army suitable for the small expeditions which enlarged the Victorian Empire. It did not secure good central administration, army training for large-scale operation, or provision for expansion in a major war.

---

[1] In the British Army a regiment is not the unit between a battalion and a brigade but a training organization.

Here it was the Liberal War Secretary, Campbell-Bannerman, of the 1890's, who with infinite tact ended the independence of the Commander in Chief at his office at the Horse Guards—even though the Commander in Chief was the Duke of Cambridge, Queen Victoria's first cousin—and instituted division-scale maneuvers on Salisbury Plain. The fiascos of the Boer War—related in a later chapter, since they are part of imperial history—showed the need for still further reform. Here, for once, the Conservatives did something. The Navy system of coordination at the top, through the Lords of the Admiralty, was copied by setting up the Army Council. Balfour, as Prime Minister, created the nonpartisan Committee on Imperial Defense. This linked up British military thinking with that of the dominions. Later on the Liberal Haldane rounded this out by sending Lord Kitchener to organize the Australian army and creating the post of the Chief of the Imperial General Staff, the C.I.G.S. whose initials appear so often in war histories. Even more important, out of the efficient administrative machinery so set up grew the War Cabinet of 1916 to 1918 and the present Cabinet Secretariat.

Just the same, it required a Liberal government to complete the work. When Richard Burdon Haldane offered to take over the War Ministry in the Campbell-Bannerman Cabinet of 1905, his enemies hoped he had committed political suicide. Instead, by overcoming the problems that had sadly damaged the careers of three Conservative predecessors, he made himself "England's greatest Minister of War," to quote the tribute Douglas Haig paid him after World War I. Haldane fused the complex mass of volunteer and militia organizations into the linked-battalion system, to create a Territorial Army. Each of Britain's fifty infantry regiments would now consist of two regular battalions rotating overseas, under the Cardwell system; a third, depot, or training battalion and a fourth or Territorial battalion, with potential expansion to as many Territorial battalions as could be raised, officered, and trained. The Territorials, like our National Guard, would be for home defense. Thus by interchange of officers, noncoms, and men, a vast expansion could quickly be made. Furthermore, since the Territorials would be ready immediately for home defense, all regular troops in England could be sent out as a British Expeditionary Force, which could be supplemented by the recall of overseas forces and the quick training of new battalions. After this reform an offer of help by the Foreign Secretary meant more than twice as much in speed of mobilization and in the number of rifles to be brought to the front lines. As this reform also meant an actual lessening of expense, it can be seen why Haig praised Haldane as he did and why Foreign Secretary Grey bore increasing weight in Europe, in the troublous years after 1905.

But though the weight of Britain's armed might grew after 1870 that of her wealth did not. She did not lose in absolute wealth, far from it, but her relative position changed sharply. From being practically the only manufacturing nation she became merely a leading manufacturing nation. Foreign competition challenged her. Men's minds changed, consequently, on economic matters, the protectionists in the United States, France, and Germany being part of world-wide rethinking of the advantages of free trade. This had a double effect on British foreign policy. Now other nations, instead of being glad she opened trade routes and carried their goods, would compete with her to secure routes, harbors, and markets. Now her statesmen at home would begin to doubt the value of free trade. First there would be toying with ways of meaning protection without saying it, by slogans such as "fair trade," "imperial preference," "safeguarding retaliation," and the like; then first one party and finally, after 1931, the majority in Parliament would adopt protection.

One good old British quality remained largely unimpaired. The British still knew how to tell others what to do. However, the cheerful unanimity of earlier days had ended. Some said that England should aid the oppressed in the spirit of the old-fashioned self-righteous liberalism of Palmerston's day, or of John Bright's crusades for the Chinese and for the Union cause in America. Others spoke of a duty to civilize the barbarous parts of the world, to "take up the white man's burden." But though Britain now spoke with two or more voices, those voices still had power. For Englishmen did rouse the world against oppression, even when it was the English themselves who seemed to oppress; and compared to others Englishmen did bring good rule to their subjects.

While these changes in Britain's situation took place, the European situation—indeed, the world situation—changed. When under Bismarck's leadership Prussia defeated Austria and France and grew into the German empire, that new empire became the key figure in international politics. When nationalist movements in the Austrian empire weakened that conglomeration of races, Austria-Hungary (as it had become in 1867) alternated between a docile avoiding of international difficulties and a brash search for outside distractions from her internal ferment. When France became, in 1870, a republic, she isolated herself from former friends and was kept so isolated by Bismarck, as a precaution against a war of revenge for the loss of Alsace-Lorraine. When Italy became, instead of a geographical name, the smallest of the great powers, she added complications to diplomacy. When the United States, and after them Japan, became world powers, European diplomacy changed to being world diplomacy. Meanwhile, Russia still remained a threat to India. As Russia advanced into Central Asia and conquered the khanates of Samarkand, Bokhara, and Merv, Englishmen began to see visions of a stream of Cossacks pouring over the Khyber Pass and summoning the restive elements in India to revolt, now that Afghanistan remained the sole barrier.

Furthermore, the direction of foreign affairs changed. The other parts of the Empire began developing their own policies. In 1868 India even invaded Abyssinia—and then amazed the world by evacuating the country. Australian colonies, notably Queensland, Cape Colony, and above all Canada, pressed for policies of their own and obtained power to share in decisions. The Foreign Secretary, too, became less important, the Prime Minister more so. For from the 1870's when Gladstone and Disraeli led foreign policy down to the days when Neville Chamberlain took personal responsibility for Munich and Churchill personally negotiated with Roosevelt and Stalin, the voice with which Her or His Majesty's Government spoke on important occasions became as much that of the Prime Minister as that of the Principal Secretary of State for Foreign Affairs, and the high point in diplomacy in this period came when Robert Cecil, Marquess of Salisbury, was both Prime Minister and Foreign Secretary. Such in part was the more complex world with which Palmerston's successors had to deal.

From December, 1868, until his sudden death in June, 1870, the Earl of Clarendon was British Foreign Secretary. He did much to prevent French infiltration into Belgium and the Rhineland. Bismarck later asserted that had he lived there would have been no Franco-Prussian War. His death gave Gladstone more power in foreign affairs, for when there was no older man like Clarendon to stand up to him, Gladstone's powerful ethical sense and his determined rectitude made him the dominating force in all departments of the Cabinet. And the new Foreign Secretary, Lord Granville, who had the nickname "Pussy," had an undeserved reputation for weakness, gained because much of his political life was spent as Liberal leader in the overwhelmingly Conservative House of Lords. There he had to specialize in diplomatic retreats to gain Liberal ends while conciliating the feelings of his fellow peers. The resultant change in British foreign policy when it was guided by these two men led one annoyed diplomat—in his private letters—to use the first initials of Gladstone and Granville to describe as "Gee-Gee" the double-headed monster which was leading England's foreign affairs out of their accustomed channels.

But in the 1870's, as the record shows, "Gee-Gee" did not do so badly. When the Franco-Prussian war did break out, in July, 1870, the question arose of Britain's guarantee of Belgian neutrality, made in 1839. By signing treaties with each belligerent promising to fight in Belgium should the other be the aggressor, Belgian neutrality was preserved, thus forcing a French army to surrender at Sedan when the only road to safety would have been through Belgium. When, shortly afterward, Russia tried to gain prestige by annulling the "Black Sea" clauses in the Treaty of Paris which had ended the Crimean War, the English ambassador in Berlin (Lord Odo Russell, later Lord Ampthill) won a diplomatic triumph by persuading

Bismarck that such unilateral action would cause war. Bismarck, who did not want the Franco-Prussian War to expand into a European war, then put pressure on Russia to show good manners, and the London Conference annulled the clauses with more dignity. Thus was born a working agreement between the new German empire-to-be and the British Empire —between the most powerful army on the Continent and the lords of the sea. For when the Imperial Army and the Royal Navy spoke together, diplomats listened.

With America "Gee-Gee" had trouble, too, over the *Alabama* claims, the American assertion that England should compensate for damage done by Confederate privateers built and outfitted in England. This served as a constant irritation, for the *Alabama* claims made splendid material for flamboyant speeches by leading Americans, on which it would be hard to back down. Gladstone determined to end this source of potential future trouble. He had passed a new Foreign Enlistment Act that made clear this would never happen again. Then he negotiated an arbitration treaty, which the United States Senate would not ratify. Nothing daunted, "Gee-Gee" tried again. When American, Canadian, and British Commissioners were negotiating the Fisheries Convention the *Alabama* claims were added, including a preposterous American claim to indirect damages for lengthening the war. Gladstone's courage in taking the chance that the Geneva Tribunal might award these damages was justified. Charles Francis Adams, the American member of the Tribunal, moved they be excluded, they were, and the actual damage was assessed at $15,500,000, which England paid.

This negotiation had three results. It gave Britain the prestige of daring to take the blame for mistakes. It gave Britain the advantage that America would be equally bound in case of a future war in which she, rather than Britain, would be neutral. Lastly, it marks the beginning of a Canadian foreign policy. For Canada, taking to heart her feeling that Britain had here put British interests above Canadian, grew determined to conduct her own negotiations—a determination later strengthened when the English member of the Alaskan Boundary Commission, in 1903, voted with the Americans.

The Gladstone-Granville policy of having as little foreign policy as possible was reversed by the election of 1874, which put into power Benjamin Disraeli and the revived Conservative party. This was the imperialist stage of that statesman's career. In 1875 he put through the purchase of the Suez Canal shares, taking delight in buying them through an unusual cash loan from the Rothschilds and then getting Parliamentary sanction for his action. Thus was secured control of the new steamer route to India. In this same year came the Bulgarian Crisis. A revolt in Bulgaria, then a Turkish province, was put down. Soon rumors of massacres reached the outside world. Disraeli did not believe them; Gladstone did. In a series of public addresses Gladstone aroused public opinion and demanded that the Turks be driven out of Europe, "bag and baggage." His pamphlet, *The Bulgarian Horrors and the Question of the East*, seemed likely to dethrone the Sultan, just as his *Letter to Lord Aberdeen* had eventually dethroned the King of Naples. This was especially true as the Russians were anxious to march to the aid of their fellow Christians and the extension of Russian boundaries. Attempts at conciliation conducted at Constantinople by a Conference at which the British delegate was the Marquess of Salisbury were thus hampered by a belief that Britain would not fight. The attempts failed, and Russia, having bought off Austria by letting her take over the Turkish province of Bosnia, went to war with Turkey. It took nine months—April, 1877, to January, 1878—to break a surprisingly sturdy Turkish resistance. During that time British public opinion had swung around to Disraeli's side. When the Russians started forcing the Turks to accept a treaty drafted by army officers just outside Constantinople, the terms of which the Russian Foreign Office refused to divulge, Disraeli was able to act. He broke the resistance inside his Cabinet of Foreign Secretary the Earl of Derby. He sent the Mediterranean fleet to Constantinople, and Indian troops to Malta, and called out the Reserve under the Cardwell system. A song swept the country: "We won't want to fight, but by jingo, if we do, we've got the men, we've got the ships, we've got the money, too." Thus the word "jingo" was added to the English language. Derby resigned, after the ignominy of having a Cabinet committee write his dispatches for him, and Lord Salisbury became Foreign Secretary as Great Britain seemed on the verge of war.

Salisbury cleared up the situation dramatically. In a circular sent to all the great powers, so effective as to gain the name "the Happy Dispatch," he stated unequivocally, almost undiplomatically and yet tactfully, the principles England would insist in seeing incorporated in any treaty between Russia and Turkey. At once it was recognized that a Cecil was managing England's foreign affairs worthy of comparison with the Cecils who had served Elizabeth I. When the Russians knew that they had such a man to deal with, they were willing to come to terms. When Prince Bismarck knew that he had such a man to deal with, he was willing to come forward as an "honest broker" and prevent a European war by calling a Congress at Berlin.

The Congress of Berlin was successful because Salisbury had negotiated beforehand, as Bismarck knew he would, the basic terms of the proposed treaty. It was even then touch and go. Once Disraeli, now the Earl of Beaconsfield, had to adopt the grandstand play of ordering a special train, for leaving the Conference, to get the Russians to come to terms. Again, a Russian delegate blandly redrew a line on a map and got away with the assertion that the altered line had been agreed to. When Russia refused to evacuate Batum, Salisbury and Beaconsfield, in spite of a security leak which caused the passage of the Official Secrets Act, as a countermove "leased" Cyprus from Turkey, that the Royal Navy might have a base near enough to protect Constantinople. Eventually a new treaty was drawn up, which cut down the size and the degree of independence of the new Bulgaria. For Beaconsfield feared that Bulgaria would become a Russian satellite state and did not agree with Gladstone's contention that the best barrier against Russian advance would be "the breasts of free men." Then Beaconsfield proudly returned to London, declaring he had brought back "Peace with Honor."

The Treaty of Berlin marks the first of several changes in the balance of power in Europe, each of which forced Britain to reorient her foreign policy. For it is almost an axiom that when Europe is divided Britain has freedom of action, but that when Europe lines up into two camps Britain loses freedom of action, since she must choose one of the two camps. From 1867 to 1878 the basic fact in European diplomacy was that Bismarck wanted war with nobody but France, and that after the Franco-Prussian war and the consequent creation of the German empire he wanted war with nobody. It was his aim to keep peace. That was why he had helped Gladstone over the Black Sea affair and the London Conference of 1871; that was why he had helped Beaconsfield and Salisbury over the Berlin Conference, once he knew that Salisbury could be trusted. But Bismarck had been able to do this only as long as the only threat to peace was France's impotent desire for revenge and the recovery of Alsace-Lorraine. Now not only did France want to get back the territories lost in 1871 but Russia was smarting under defeat. It was possible that war might break out between England and Russia and that Austria and Germany would have to choose. Austria would have to fight with England or break up. Then Germany would have to choose whether to save Austria or side with Russia and perhaps see Russia dominant on the Continent. Here action was forced on Bismarck by the refusal of the Emperor of Russia to renew the League of Three Emperors which since 1872 had linked Russia, Austria, and Germany.

Bismarck acted. He signed a secret treaty with Austria guaranteeing her against Russian attack and then a secret "reinsurance treaty" guaranteeing Russia against impossible Austrian attack. Meanwhile, Salisbury acted. He did his best to bolster up Turkey against Russian aggression by sending in "military consuls," among them Horatio Herbert Kitchener, to supervise reforms. He did his best to preserve the Suez Canal by inducing the Sultan to depose the extravagant Khedive of Egypt and forcing the new Khedive to accept international bondholder control by the Caisse de la Dette, whose purpose was to keep Egypt solvent. In this Salisbury and Bismarck worked in informal alliance. When Bismarck published some of the terms of the Austrian Alliance and secretly let Salisbury know more, Salisbury publicly welcomed them as "glad tidings of great joy." For it showed that the two great powers of the sea and the land were still cooperating in keeping the peace.

As yet Britain still had freedom of action. But at this very moment she was making a choice that ended her freedom of action. It was no accident that Salisbury had chosen a public platform and the methods of open diplomacy to announce his support of the Austro-German Alliance. For an Englishman was arranging Britain's foreign policy at the bar of public opinion and had to be answered at the same bar. William Ewart Gladstone had come from political retirement to contest Beaconsfield's foreign policy at a by-election in the hitherto steadfastly Conservative constituency of Midlothian. Settling down there as the guest of the young Earl of Rosebery, he poured out a stream of speeches attacking what had been done in Bulgaria, Afghanistan, Zululand, and the Transvaal. These became the Liberal platform in the election of 1880 and swept Gladstone into the premiership. Once more "Gee-Gee" would try his hand at foreign policy.

The international situation in 1880, however, was very different from that in 1870. Bismarck had begun to tie Europe, even the world, together by a spider web of treaties. His purpose was to keep the peace by restraining different nations by making them promises; the result was that whenever "Gee-Gee" acted, surprising counteractions took place. Another change was that Germany was no longer a "satiated power," to use Bismarck's phrase. Though Bismarck did not want colonies, certain Germans did, and he at times had to give in to the "Colonial party" which wanted a "place in the sun." Thirdly, Gladstone had a different program for checking Russian expansion, since he believed that the best barrier was not Turkey but "the breasts of free men." Time seems to have justified him, for later Salisbury confessed that at the Berlin Conference he had been "backing the wrong horse," and today it has been a free Turkey, a free Greece, and a relatively free Yugoslavia which have resisted first Hitler and then Stalin. But the first result of this was utterly to lose English influence in Turkey. These three factors, the system of secret alliances, the growing German demand for colonies, and the reversal of England's Turkish policy, explain the five years of Gladstone's rule.

In the period from April, 1880, to June, 1885, Gladstone had one success —an accidental one—and three failures. The success was in Egypt, where Gladstone's rectitude worked far better than the most Machiavellian statesmanship. In 1881 a nationalist revolt broke out. It was led by Colonel Arabi, the highest-ranking native officer in the Turkish-dominated Egyptian army, and was directed against Turks as well as other foreigners. A vigorous French ministry demanded joint Anglo-French intervention to protect lives and property in Alexandria. Gladstone yielded; then the Gambetta ministry fell and Great Britain intervened alone. This bombardment and occupation of Alexandria broke down such control as the Arabists had of Egypt, and further intervention was necessary. Therefore Sir Garnet Wolseley marched from the Suez Canal to Cairo, winning a battle at Tel-el-Kebir on the way. The British Consul General, Sir Evelyn Baring, was installed as informal but effective chief adviser to the Khedive. Step by step "Gee-Gee" protested that England did not wish to act alone, step by step other nations, for varied reasons, pushed her on to force Gladstone either to eat his words spoken in Midlothian or see Egypt remain in anarchy.

The result of this was that Salisbury's hopes to see Turkey revived by English advisers—as had happened in Native States in India and was happening in part in China through Sir Robert Hart's control of the customs—utterly collapsed. There England lost influence completely, as Salisbury was to discover when he returned to office. But in Egypt the reverse occurred. Baring ran Egypt well. English troops were kept as a basic security for order and the Suez Canal. English officers, including Kitchener, assigned to command duty in the Egyptian army, and English experts in key positions in administration gave Egypt a good army and an effective and honest government. Great financial skill eventually freed Egypt from bondholder control and turned her surplus revenues to public works, like the Assuan Dam and the abolishing of the hated *corvée*, or forced labor.

But this act of unintentional and beneficial imperialism was the downfall of the Gladstone Cabinet. First it was attacked by Liberals for violating the Midlothian pledges. Then came the shame of the Gordon affair. Egypt, ever since the 1830's, had ruled the Sudan, far toward the sources of the Nile. In 1883 a Moslem religious revolt swept away Egyptian rule in the far south. Baring decided to cut the loss and withdraw. In 1884 the chivalrous engineer Major General Charles Gordon, a former Governor-general of the Sudan, was sent to supervise that withdrawal. On arrival at Khartoum, he found that the Egyptians there expected him to stay, and he decided to do his duty as he saw it. The telegraphic battle between him and the Gladstone Cabinet fired public opinion. When Gordon stood siege in Khartoum, two rescue forces were sent. The first, from the Red Sea port of Suakim, was defeated when, as Kipling records, "Fuzzy Wuzzy broke a British square." The second expedition, sent up the Nile and then rushed through the desert, came two days too late. Gordon had died, pistol in hand, in the defense of what he considered England's pledged word. With the news, the Gladstone Government fell, too.

This was the dramatic disaster. There was another set of losses during these years. Baring could get crucial votes in the Caisse de la Dette only by cooperation with the representatives of other nations. German votes could be had, for a price—a large one, in terms of the British and German colonial empires. In spite of protests from the Cape Colony, Germany occupied German South West Africa. In spite of protests from Queensland, which even went so far as to occupy part of New Guinea on her own, a German colony was founded there. Then in 1884 Britain took part of eastern New Guinea, when she might have had all. In spite of protests from missionaries and traders, German influence was allowed to grow paramount in the native island kingdom of Samoa. In spite of protests from missionaries and antislavery groups, German influence was allowed to grow on the African shore opposite the island sultanate of Zanzibar. In spite of protests from consuls on the Niger River assigned to antislavery duty and of merchants trading on the Oil Coast and the Gold Coast of the Gulf of Guinea, German colonies were established at Togoland next the Gold Coast and at Kamerun on the Oil Coast, next the mouth of the Niger.

Yet, just as Gladstone's Government fell the breast of one free man saved it from Russia. Amir Abdur Rahman of Afghanistan, when Russia tried to encroach nearer to India at Penjdeh, bravely stood up in sound reliance on English support and wisely compromised once essentials had been secured. Here the idea of working through a free buffer state, even though it be an autocracy, did succeed.

When Gladstone fell, in June, 1885, Salisbury came in, in the "Ministry of Caretakers," while the electoral lists were being revised, after the Third Reform Bill. He seems to have taken a decisive action. He had the usual confidential interview with the sovereign that all prime ministers have when forming a Cabinet. After World War I the files of the German Foreign Office revealed a letter from Salisbury to Bismarck promising that the latter might in future trust to the stability of British foreign policy. And never again did Earl Granville hold the office of Foreign Secretary. The conclusion seems justified that Queen Victoria agreed to use her royal powers to prevent his doing so, if ever a Liberal Government came into office, and that she kept the agreement. Certainly, Salisbury's promise to Bismarck was kept. When he went out of office, Lord Rosebery, Gladstone's host at Midlothian, came in and continued Salisbury's methods.

Then in August, 1886, Salisbury came in, after the general election, with assurance of long tenure of power. These were years of imperialism, where a positive foreign policy and prestige were needed. Salisbury provided both. In the curious Bulgarian crisis from 1885 to 1887 caused by the Russians kidnaping the Prince of Bulgaria in a way reminiscent of their present-day feats, he successfully stood out for Bulgarian self-government. Then he joined in Bismarck's deftest spider web of treaties, the Mediterranean Agreements of 1887, that kept the peace in the Balkans. Overseas Salisbury followed the same successful policy of guarded alignment with

Germany. He refused to be hurried or pushed. Thus it was possible for the Samoan hurricane to solve the problem of the contest of Germany, the United States, and Great Britain for those islands, after which America and Germany squabbled over joint ownership and Britain took valuable compensation elsewhere. In Africa he gave foreign-office protection to "chartered companies" in Nigeria, Nyasaland, Rhodesia, and East Africa, with the result that for a time more of Africa was ruled by the Foreign Office than by the Colonial Office, and protests from the "men on the spot" ceased. Here his culminating deal with Bismarck was the trade of the tiny island of Heligoland—which could not be fortified without thereby threatening war with Germany—for control of the sources of the Nile and the present-day Kenya, which gave Britain control of the Nile waters so essential to Egypt.

This deal in 1890 was the last made with Bismarck. For in 1890, when it had been made but not concluded, the young Kaiser William II "dropped the Pilot" and dismissed Bismarck. Bismarck had had, to an unusual degree, that "sense of the possible" that makes a great statesman. His most audacious schemes had succeeded because he knew to an inch how far he could go. William II, who had dismissed Bismarck and who took over much of the direction of foreign affairs, did not have this gift. He tried for too much and eventually brought war instead of peace. Two actions largely traceable to him forced yet another reorientation of British policy. He "cut the wire to Saint Petersburg," by giving up the secret agreement with Russia, and thus set Russia free to make the "Dual Alliance" with France in 1893. He kept on pressure to build up a colonial empire, and thus estranged Britain. Thus a triple division of Europe evolved, of Germany, Austria, and with them Italy (the Triple Alliance of 1882), Russia and France (the Dual Alliance), and England.

At first the sufferer was England, against whom the Dual Alliance was directed, as well as Germany and Austria. France in Africa and Indochina and China, Russia in Turkey and Afghanistan and China had anti-British imperial interests. Prime Minister Gladstone and Foreign Secretary Rosebery went through a French war scare over insults to British vessels during the Franco-Siamese war. They also went through a naval scare that speeded up construction. When Rosebery became Prime Minister an act of generosity started an effective counter to this isolation. In 1894 England was the first nation to give up extraterritorial rights in Japan. The contrast of this with the German-inspired prevention of Japan's winning the fruits of victory in her war with China in 1895, in which England did not join Germany, France, and Russia, eventually made Japan her ally.

In June, 1895, Salisbury came back to office, to meet serious problems. He gave up the policy of freedom of action which he had named "splendid isolation," and sought to make some sort of combination that would prevent England, in world affairs, being the underdog as against Germany, France, and Russia. His first attempt was an interview with Kaiser William, in August, at Cowes, when the Emperor was visiting his grandmother, Queen Victoria. The Kaiser misunderstood the overtures and decided on a policy of pressing England for concessions. Then came the sudden flare-up of the Venezuela boundary dispute, when President Cleveland of the United States threatened force to protect Venezuela from fancied British encroachment. Out of the transference of this dispute to arbitration grew up good relations with the United States. But the process of gaining security took time. Great Britain suffered insults when Kaiser William in 1896 publicly congratulated President Kruger of the Transvaal for repelling the Jameson raid. She suffered injuries when she lost influence in Turkey at the time of the Armenian Massacres, the Cretan revolt, and the Greco-Turkish war of 1897 as well as when Germany, France, and Russia seized naval bases in China, forcing her to follow suit. Her international unpopularity was shown by the storm of abuse that fell on her during the Boer War in the years from 1889 to 1902. She ran serious risk of war with France, when Lord Kitchener's forces in the Sudan collided with the French Marchand exploring expedition at Fashoda, in 1898. She ran a risk of losing trade in China, when partition of that country was threatened after the "Boxer War" to rescue the besieged legations in Peking. Here friendship with the United States and Anglo-American advocacy of the policy of the "Open Door" managed to save the day. It would seem little to set against this catalogue of difficulties the signing of a treaty with Portugal, in 1898. Was England reduced to reliance on her "oldest ally"?

She was not. Out of this isolation came renewed strength, for Britain decided to take the risk of permanent linking with another power. This was done not by Salisbury, who from advancing age had retired as Foreign Secretary, but by Lord Lansdowne, the new Foreign Secretary, and by Balfour and Chamberlain. Three overtures were made. First, these two latter tried, but failed, in the Chamberlain-Eckhardstein negotiations, to come to practical terms with Germany. But neither side was willing to pledge enough help in fields where it was not immediately concerned, and the negotiations fell through. Then in 1901 and 1902 Lord Lansdowne negotiated the Anglo-Japanese alliance. This in effect gave England an extra navy in the Pacific in return for a promise that if more than one continental power attacked Japan, England would come to her aid. In 1905 that made it possible for Japan to fight Russia without France aiding Russia. Thirdly, Lord Lansdowne cleared up outstanding difficulties. Neither side wished to be embroiled in the Russo-Japanese War. England had rights in Morocco, the New Hebrides, and Madagascar that were a nuisance to France; France had that vote on the Egyptian Caisse de la Dette and fisheries rights in Newfoundland. These were balanced against each other and wiped out. More than that, the two nations became tacit partners in expansion in Africa. Morally, each would have to support the other, should Moroccan or Egyptian interests be attacked.

A test came soon. In 1905 Kaiser William landed at Tangier and gratuitously announced his desire to protect Morocco. France, militarily, was in a weak position to resist. Japan had just defeated her ally Russia so resoundingly that revolt had broken out in Russia. England might have a Navy that Fisher had just quietly concentrated in the North Sea, but the Boer War had shown how weak her Army was. France had to yield and consent to an International Conference at Algeciras, of all the nations with special rights in Morocco.

By this time Lansdowne was out of office, replaced by Sir Edward Grey, and Great Britain was in the throes of a general election. Grey had to balance matters delicately. He could not promise too little, or France, in desperation, might join Germany and Russia against England. For such a Continental union the Kaiser was still angling; at Björkö he even got temporary Russian consent to it. Yet Grey could not promise too much, for then he could not perform, if a showdown came. With great skill he won through at the Algeciras Conference, got the French the essentials they desired, and got their gratitude, too. With this improvement in Britain's diplomatic position came new strength. In 1905 victorious Japan had renewed her alliance and added to it a pledge to defend India against Russian attack, if England would aid her against any attack. Now weakened Russia agreed to cooperate with England in Persian matters; this entente, like the Anglo-French one, meant general cooperation in wider spheres.

Here again changes in the European situation reoriented British policy. Austria and Russia, both of which feared internal revolt, entered an expansionist phase, their goals being the same—domination of the Balkans. At the same time French and German overseas expansion clashed. Thus Grey was faced with a series of crises, which had to be handled as he had handled the Moroccan crisis. Britain's new partners had to be given enough support to hold them faithful but had, at the same time, to be restrained. Again and again—in the Bosnian Crisis of 1908, the Agadir Crisis of 1911, the First and Second Balkan Wars of 1912—Grey had the same function of mediation to perform. Again and again he succeeded. In the Bosnian affair Russia was persuaded to accept Austrian annexation of that former Turkish province. In the Agadir affair it took a bellicose speech from David Lloyd George, the pacifist Chancellor of the Exchequer, to make the Germans ease their pressure on the French in Morocco. During the Balkan Wars it took two London Conferences to persuade the combative Balkan states and the regenerated Turkey to settle their differences and prevent the wars from expanding. Meanwhile England had her own troubles. Germany took the chance offered by the introduction of the dreadnought to enter into a naval race with England, and caught up so fast that in 1914 she was within two ships of equality. An attempt by Haldane, now Lord Chancellor, to negotiate friendly easing off merely served to discredit Haldane in the eyes of British superpatriots. On the other hand, the conflicts of German and British capitalists over a proposed railway from the Austrian border through the Balkans and Turkey to the Persian Gulf, the so-called Berlin-to-Baghdad railway, were on the point of amicable settlement in July, 1914, thanks to Grey's obvious integrity.

Yet through all these difficulties Grey steered his way with honor and prestige. He prepared for the worst, as the French and British staffs planned for the use of the British Expeditionary Force on the left wing of the French army in war, and as the two navies agreed that England would take responsibility for the Channel, France for the Mediterranean. Here trouble came. Papers concerning these plans were circulated to all the Cabinet, in the well-known "red boxes." But many a leader glanced thoughtlessly at them and initialed them without comprehension of their meaning. Thus Grey took on to the world two aspects. To the French and to the Russians he became the man who would protect them if they did not go to extremes, by bringing Britain into war. To the pacifists among the Liberals he was the man who was stopping war. Then, in 1914, came the crisis where his efforts failed. The murder of the Archduke Francis Ferdinand of Austria by the Serbian "Black Hand" gang gave the Austrian expansionists a chance to make high demands. Russian expansionists, despite Grey's urgings, stood stiffly behind Serbia when she rejected the most outrageous of Austria's claims. Mobilizations began, each causing a countermobilization. Grey tried, but failed, to put out the fuse before it reached the powder barrel. Held back by the natural reluctance of the fellow members of his Cabinet to issue warlike threats, he was unable to make unequivocal statements that Britain would fight till too late for those statements to check the trend to war. At eleven o'clock, August 1, 1914, Grey heard Big Ben strike, knew that the ultimatum sent Germany had gone unanswered, and sadly said: "The lights are going out all over Europe." An era had ended.

During this period, English foreign policy had changed with changing conditions. From 1868 to 1874, Gladstone had applied the methods of Liberalism not without success. Integrity of purpose and a realistic understanding of the limits on England's strength had allowed him to solve the problems of the Franco-Prussian war and of the *Alabama* case. From 1878 to 1892, Salisbury, when in office, in an age of increasing imperialism, had kept a free hand for England, had made her respected in the councils of Europe, and had won for England an African Empire. In 1885 he had imposed on England a tradition of continuity of foreign policy. His successes had been pointed up by the failure of Gladstone's Midlothian program of diplomacy by public indignation and failure to seize opportunities. With the change of Germany from a "satiated" power to an adventurous one, Salisbury's "splendid isolation" had proved too costly and had, in 1900, been given up for a policy of limited commitment. This policy, in the hands of Grey, a man of integrity, had for the years from 1905 to 1914, proved not unsuccessful, despite the policy of adventure that emerged in the unstable Austro-Hungarian monarchy.

In reviewing this period, it seems clear that neither the element of the personality of the foreign secretary, nor the element of the conditions under which he had to work can be called more important. Success or failure must be judged by how well the man met the problem. In a rapidly changing world, methods had to change. However, the *aims* of England's policy remained the same. They were, as ever, to keep trade routes open and to keep the Continent at peace, in order to keep those routes open. Those were Gladstone's and Granville's aims in protecting the neutrality of Belgium and in establishing principles of responsibility in the law of the nations for the restraint of future *Alabamas*. Those were Disraeli's aims in protecting the route to India by buying Suez shares and putting Salisbury in office to protect Turkey from Russia. Those were Gladstone's aims in occupying Egypt. Those were Salisbury's aims in his cooperation with Bismarck, in his attempt to partition Turkey, and in his cooperation with America and Japan in keeping the open door in China. Those were Lansdowne's and Grey's aims in establishing and confirming "ententes" or loose agreements with France and Russia, in solving Balkan problems and in internationalizing the Berlin-Baghdad railway. Viewed thus, England's foreign policy becomes a consistent whole.

41

THE AGE OF IMPERIALISM

1867–1914

In the 1860's and 1870's the existence of the British Empire dawned on its peoples. This was not a partisan discovery—the Empire impressed the Radical Sir Charles Dilke as much as it did the Tory Benjamin Disraeli. Nor was this a discovery made only in the homeland—it was likewise made in Canada by John A. Macdonald and Wilfrid Laurier, in New South Wales by Sir Henry Parkes, and above all, in South Africa by Cecil Rhodes. Furthermore, it was a well-publicized discovery, for Dilke's *Greater Britain,* Sir J. R. Seeley's *Expansion of England,* and Froude's *Oceana* reached wide and influential audiences. Consequently, the imperialism that marked the second half of Queen Victoria's reign was a popular movement. The fact explains its character and its success. Whereas in the past the builders of the Empire had had to struggle against both the home authorities and the people, now they could, if need be, go over the authorities' heads and be sure of the people's support. When, in 1896, Cecil Rhodes had to go back to England to face investigation because of the Jameson Raid, he met that investigation with confidence, saying, "When I went to London all the cab drivers smiled at me, and then I knew I was all right."

But it is not enough to say that men shared a dream of what the Empire might become, and had opportunity to make that dream come true. The dream that they shared was a paradoxical, double, contradictory sort of dream. They saw that the overseas English were proving themselves at one and the same time adept at self-government and at the government of others, so that somehow conquest and the granting of independence did seem to go hand in hand, or at least to be the specialties of the same people. They tried to bring the benefits of the Queen's rule to different parts of the world and obtained very different results. Where one aspect of the dream or the other was dominant, they succeeded well; where the two aspects came into conflict, they met with difficulties. Therefore, to proceed from the simple to the complex, this chapter will consider first of all the self-governing parts of the Empire, Canada, Australia, and

New Zealand, where emigrants were making English nations; secondly, it will consider the externally ruled parts of the Empire, such as India, Malaya, and the West Indies, where a few Englishmen could rule millions of natives, as long as those natives did not want to rule themselves; lastly it will consider the continent of Africa where at each end, in Egypt and in South Africa, the two imperial ideals of self-government and of good government from above came into conflict. Then it will be possible to examine the causes of the Empire's growth, and the new institutions it evolved, in the light of the record.

CANADA

Canada, the first of the dominions, has usually set the precedent for her sisters. This was the case, too, in the years in which she achieved nationhood, from 1867 to 1914. Those years may roughly be divided into two parts, during which different political parties were in power and different types of problems had to be solved. From 1867 to 1891, when for most of the time John A. Macdonald was Premier and the Conservatives were in power, Canada needed to consolidate herself and to absorb the West and Northwest; in the years 1896 to 1914, when for most of the time Sir Wilfrid Laurier was Premier and the Liberals in power, the crucial questions were of Canada's position as a nation within the Empire and of the two nationalities, English and French, within Canada. Like all generalizations this is inadequate, but it offers a working explanation from which to start.

When, on July 1, 1867, Canada became self-governing and thus acquired her national holiday, Dominion Day, the problems of unification had not fully been met. Prince Edward Island, the site of the Charlottetown Convention, had refused to join the Confederation. Strong elements in the Maritime Provinces, led by Joseph Howe, wished to break up the Confederation, and their party, the Liberals, allied itself with the particularists of the newly formed Province of Quebec. Furthermore, expansion to the west of the newly formed province of Ontario found itself blocked by the territories of the Hudson's Bay Company and by the Rocky Mountains which cut off the colony of British Columbia. The first Dominion Premier, John A. Macdonald, set to work to solve these problems. For eastern particularism he had the answer that, under the British North America Act, an intercolonial railway was to be built, connecting Nova Scotia and New Brunswick with Quebec by the shores of the Saint Lawrence. It rarely harms a newly established government to have money to spend, and once communications are secure, they make for unity. Then, in 1869, Macdonald turned to uniting the West as well as the East to the Dominion. He arranged to buy from the Hudson's Bay Company its sovereignty over its lands, reserving to the Company its fur-trading rights and its actual property. He also arranged with British Columbia that it should enter the Confederation if a railway were built across the Rockies to the Coast. The fruits of these actions appeared in the necessary amendments to the British North America Act being made in 1869 and in the admission to the Dominion of the new provinces of Manitoba, British Columbia, and Prince Edward Island, in 1870, 1871, and 1873, respectively.

However, what was easy enough to arrange at Ottawa and Westminster was not so easy to deal with on the spot. The half-breed fur traders of the West did not like the thought of being transferred from the Hudson's Bay Company to a government at Ottawa or at Winnipeg that would favor the farmers. Under the leadership of Louis Riel they threatened trouble, and it was necessary for Colonel Garnet Wolseley to bring troops swiftly to Winnipeg on the Red River expedition to overawe Riel. Riel fled to the United States, to spend his time in and out of insane asylums, and the problem of the West seemed solved, particularly as a special force, the world famous Northwest Mounted Police, kept the Indians at peace and in order, in marked contrast to what was happening across the forty-ninth parallel in the United States.

To build the transcontinental railway needed faith, capital, and political opportunity. Macdonald provided all these. His methods were not above suspicion—once he was ousted for office for a while for them—but he made possible the Canadian Pacific Railway which bound the Dominion together. When frost-resistant wheat was discovered, the C.P.R. made the plains of western Canada one of the granaries of the world.

Success in unifying the Dominion riveted Macdonald in office. It also caused a desire for Canadian manufactures and, in politics, for a Canadian tariff. Here, as in other matters, the Dominion was reaching standing as a nation. Already, pushed to the point by Cardwell's military reforms in England, Canada had undertaken her own defense, under the Minister of Militia. A volunteer force, under professional officers, was built up, that would distinguish itself in the Sudan, South Africa, and two world wars. In international affairs, Canada took its share in the fisheries commission of 1872 that—as has been related—evolved into the *Alabama* arbitration. Then, and in the later fisheries agreement of 1888, Canada made it plain that she intended to have her say in matters that concerned her. Macdonald had presided over the making of a nation.

But in 1885 came a shock it was hard for him to withstand, Riel's Rebellion. For years the métis, or half-breeds, of the West had begged to be granted the lands on which they had long lived; for years nothing was done. In 1885, Louis Riel reappeared and led them in active revolt, rather than in sporadic disorder. With blood having been shed and treason committed, Riel was tried, it being obvious he was guilty and equally obvious that he was unbalanced. Macdonald refused to recommend clemency to the Governor-general and asserted that it was the political function of the Premier to give "constitutional advice" on that matter, which the Governor-general would have to accept unless he dismissed the Macdonald Cabinet. His action brought the issue of French versus English nationality back into politics when, in course of time, the next general election came. This election Macdonald won on his personality, stumping the Dominion to appeal for support for "the old man and the old cause." He then remained Premier till his death.

But when he died in 1891, the Conservatives began their fall from power. For a while different Conservatives were made Premier by the Governor-general, but none could hold their party together, and at last a new Liberal leader, Wilfrid Laurier, won an election for his party. Laurier did not try to undo what Macdonald had done, though he did lower the tariff somewhat. But he grappled with the problem of nationality. In Manitoba, he found it one of cultures, with the English element trying to block French migration by control of the school system. Laurier's policy was to refrain from using powers the Dominion had as against the Province, and by negotiation to get a permanent settlement. At the same time Laurier met the problem caused by Joseph Chamberlain's desire to strengthen the organization of the British Empire; he refused to pledge Canadian aid in advance of a crisis and assured the British that aid given freely when the need for it was seen would be greater than aid given because of previous commitments. How true this was, was soon demonstrated by rousing the Dominion to support the Boer War.

Under Laurier the party situation in Canada became transformed. Because he started a program of state-sponsored railway building that eventually created the Canadian National Railways, the Liberal party became the party of moderate state interference in business. Because, when the new provinces of Alberta and Saskatchewan were admitted to the Dominion provisions were written into their constitutions for denominational schools, to anticipate such a struggle as had occurred in Manitoba, the Liberals supplanted the Conservatives as the party that could carry French Quebec.

Finally, because Laurier held to the old tradition of reciprocity in trade with the United States, he suffered defeat and was replaced in office by the Conservatives. His fall, 1911, was also due to his desire to create a truly Canadian navy, built in Canada, as against the Conservative desire to give Britain ships paid for with Canadian money.

Thus, by 1914, Canada had made herself a nation and had proved that fact to the world. This truth the percipient Rudyard Kipling had recognized as early as 1897, when he wrote of her in "Our Lady of the Snows," as "daughter . . . in her mother's house, but mistress in her own." By then, and even more by 1914, Canada had the institutions needed for unity and nationality—not merely "responsible government" but also national capital, as evidenced in the wealth created by the Canadian Pacific, an export staple in the form of the wheat of the West, means of self-defense, and, at least in connection with the United States, a large share in the negotiation of her own foreign policy. Yet an important part of this sense of nationality was the imperial connection, for it was by appealing to the outside allegiance to the crown that it was possible for two cultures, French and English, to live side by side.

AUSTRALIA

The continent of Australia followed largely in Canada's footsteps, with variations, but the story of how that happened is best told in different terms. Since after Confederation the center of interest in Canadian history is with one government, it is possible to tell of the leading statesmen. In Australia, where up to 1900 six colonies met much the same problems in the same way, the center for attention becomes the problems, not the men. There, it was only in Western Australia and Queensland that special factors entered the picture. Up to federation in 1900 the other four colonies went through much the same evolution. Each, by 1870, had decided upon the same half-Wakefieldian answer to the land problem, that is, at one and the same time encouraging small agricultural farms and tolerating though restricting large-leasehold grazing. Each had a growing local manufacturing industry, treated differently however in free-trade New South Wales from protectionist Victoria. Each had a growing labor movement, which crossed colonial lines. In each colony democracy increased, in the literal sense of the word, as the *demos,* or people, got more and more control of the machinery of government. This took place in three ways: by wider extension of the suffrage, by cutting down the powers of second chambers, and by increasing the powers of state legislatures over against the royal governors and the Colonial Office.

In the various colonies there were epic struggles to increase political democracy, notably in Victoria, where an elective first chamber and an elective second chamber fell into a deadlock and a joint dissolution of both bodies had to be resorted to. Such a joint dissolution, later, was put into the constitution of the Australian Commonwealth. The right to vote was steadily extended, second chambers were steadily weakened, and the rear-guard actions of the royal governors and the Colonial Office were eventually defeated. It took time to do this, because some deadlocks in legislatures could not be resolved by calling an election which everyone knew, in advance, would not change materially the composition of the legislature. In such cases the royal governors stepped into the picture as arbitrators between political parties. They also, more than in Canada, used the powers of "disallowance" by referring to London, powers with which they were vested in the colonial constitutions. Such rear-guard actions may serve to explain, by contrast, the fiery democracy that is to be found in Australia.

So it was that, in the years 1870 to 1900, Australia moved toward democracy. In two colonies, Queensland and Western Australia, special problems arose. North Queensland is sugar country; South Queensland and the "back blocks" are sheep country. Sheep herders early formed unions and believed in a "white Australia"; sugar planters were sure no white man would work in the cane fields and wanted imported native labor. Consequently, in Queensland, which in that respect gave a lead to the rest of the Empire, labor first took on political power and political responsibility. For its own self-interest, it fought "blackbirding" or kidnaping of natives for labor, in the Pacific, and helped enforce the Pacific Islanders' Protection Acts of 1872 and 1875, Labor pushed forward on the economic front, as well, and discovered how white men might work in the cane fields, in competition with native labor, thus making a "white Australia" policy financially possible. Finally, in 1897, for a few days, Queensland saw a Labor Cabinet in power, the first in the Empire. Australia was leading where it would take a quarter of a century for England to follow.

At the opposite end of the continent, it took a feat of engineering to bring Western Australia into line. For many years the northern half of Western Australia had been so costly to administer that the home government had refused to allow responsible government. Then at Coolgardie, far in the interior desert, gold was found. By building a 600-mile conduit to carry water to the mines, Western Australia secured the capital needed for development and the grant of responsible government.

During all these years, the idea of uniting Australia had been present in many minds, but its realization had failed because such a union would have been administratively inefficient. A customs union got no farther than permissive legislation in the Imperial Parliament in 1873. A Federal Council at which to discuss problems of the Pacific was instituted in 1885, but it met seldom and suffered from absenteeism. At last, in 1891, the first Federal Convention fulfilled Sir Henry Parkes's hopes and met at Sydney. At it the problems of federation were thrashed out and the sacrifices needed made plain. At that moment, these were not acceptable, but since the conclusions of the Convention were public property, men's minds began turning on them and agreeing to such ideas as Sir George Grey's insistence on universal manhood suffrage. Then in 1897, 1898, and 1899 a new convention met. With the preliminary haggling already done, it was possible to make a proposal that all except New South Wales and Western Australia immediately accepted, and that New South Wales rejected only for local political causes which were soon overcome. The final problem was to secure passage through the British Parliament, where Colonial Secretary Joseph Chamberlain tried to keep imperial powers and succeeded in keeping a power of appeal to the Privy Council.

With the creation of the Australian Commonwealth came the task of giving it effective unity. One form of unity, the abolition of internal tariff barriers, took immediate effect. Another form, the control of interstate commerce by the Commonwealth, had a somewhat unexpected result. The Commonwealth, during its early years, was ruled by a three-party system. The old Liberals and Conservatives jockeyed for power and found that the new Labor party held the balance, bartering its votes for labor legislation. Indeed, in 1903, 1907, and 1908 Labor though in a minority formed a cabinet. Then, in 1913–1914, a deadlock occurred, which forced a joint dissolution of Senate and House. In this the highly organized Labor machine secured the overwhelming control of the Senate and a working majority in the House and forced the two old parties to coalesce. Thus the Commonwealth became the home of compulsory arbitration, wage fixing by court action, and government ownership. In so doing, and in taking over government of the Northern Territory, with its problems of development and of justice to the fast-disappearing natives, the Commonwealth showed it could manage a continent.

NEW ZEALAND

The history of New Zealand, like that of Australia, was in these years marked by experimentation. As a result, since these experiments either were political or had political results, the story of this dominion can well be told by explaining four nicknames—"Vogel immigrants," the "Greyhounds," the "continuous ministry," and "King Dick." Yet all these manifestations come back to one central theme, the attempt of a people to make the kind of society they thought best in an almost vacant land. For almost vacant New Zealand was, after the Maori wars had ended and the natives had been relegated to reserved areas, largely on the North Island. To Sir Julius Vogel the solution for the immediate problem seemed simple. He filled an empty land and carried the debt of the Maori War by borrowing money in England and using it to pay for immigrants and for public works—among them what was for a few years the longest railway tunnel in the world—to build up the wealth of the colony. This policy gave New Zealand a doubled population, a million immigrants coming in in ten years, the public works necessary for a civilized country, and a burden of debt which caused unemployment to be serious in a newly settled land. Furthermore, as a natural consequence of such central financing, in 1876 were abolished the superintendencies, the local units that originally had formed New Zealand and had been federated and combined by the Government of New Zealand Act. This move, sensible as it was, naturally caused resentment. So did the agrarian problem of the breakdown of the Wakefieldian system, since by evasions of the land law, large estates were being created, which kept would-be settlers off the land. At the election of 1877 this pair of problems caused an upheaval.

For Sir George Grey had come back from England to New Zealand and proclaimed the semi-Chartist views he had always had of the need for universal suffrage. With him as a leader, a group of new men surged into the House of Representatives, following his ideas and calling themselves the "Greyhounds." By their votes the discontented elements secured a narrow and fluctuating majority in Parliament and put in Sir George as Premier. As Premier, Sir George was a failure; the qualities that had made him a successful and dictatorial governor prevented his leading a cabinet. With the return of economic stability, power of sorts returned to its former holders. This was caused, largely, by the deft parliamentary management of Sir Harry Atkinson. During the years from 1876 to 1891, whoever was Premier, Sir Harry was in the Cabinet. As a result, people began to talk of the "continuous ministry" and feel that a change was due.

In the meantime, a change was being prepared, by the discovery of a new economic basis for life in New Zealand. In 1877 the first frozen food was sent to England. In 1882, W. S. Davidson organized a shipment of mutton and butter to England, that proved such foods could arrive fresh. Previously, he had begun the crossing of long-wool merino sheep with the meat-bearing Lincolnshire to make the Corriedale cross. Now it was possible for the small farmer, if he could organize the shipping and marketing side of the wool and meat industries, to outdo the large landholder. Such a form of organization lay at hand, in the locally managed government crop- and lightning-insurance system, and in the locally managed hospital boards. Gradually there built up a demand for encouragement of such institutions, and for enforcement of the Wakefieldian policy that had proved such a success in Otago and Canterbury. In the cities, labor began to organize, and to complain of the "sweating" or overworking characteristic of the garment industry. In 1891, this farmer-labor group took over power in the Liberal party, only to have its measures defeated by the Legislative Council. In 1893, they were swept into office, under a new leader, Richard Seddon. The Council was curbed by swamping it with new members and by making tenure of office in it seven years instead of life. Then began the reign of "King Dick," to last till his death in 1906 and to make New Zealand an example to the world in social legislation.

Two men were leaders in this movement. At its head was Richard Seddon, a big, bluff ex-farm hand, who had been elected superintendent of a district to kill him politically and who had refused to be so smothered. "King Dick" ruled by his sheer ability to get at New Zealanders, physically and emotionally. No one since the great pioneer journeyings of Sir George Grey and Bishop Selwyn had so crisscrossed New Zealand from settlement to settlement. Not even they had gotten on easy terms with everyone so quickly and so completely. Everyone felt he knew "King Dick" and understood what he wanted done; that was what gave Seddon his power. Serving with him as his able lieutenant, to work out the measures Seddon piloted through the House of Representatives, was William Pember Reeves, who may well turn out to have been the intellectual father of the insurance state in the Anglo-Saxon world. For Reeves moved on from Seddon's cabinet to be New Zealand's Agent-general in London and then to be director of the newly founded London School of Economics, where such thinkers as Graham Wallas and Sir William Beveridge formulated the ideas presently to be put into effect in England, ideas surprisingly like those Seddon and Reeves drove past the obstruction of the Legislative Council.

The parallel here is instructive, for it is the most extensive case of a dominion giving a lesson to the mother country. In the 1890's the advanced Liberals in England had a program, the Newcastle Program. It consisted of old-age pensions; varied forms of state-sponsored insurance covering health disability and unemployment; employers' liability for accidents; and a special status for unions. This policy the Liberals failed to push through the House of Lords, though during the fourth Gladstone and Rosebery Ministries they engaged in what they called "ploughing the sands"—passing such measures for the Lords to defeat, in the hopes that those defeats would make a campaign issue. It was not until the "Mad Parliament" of 1906 that it was possible to enact such measures, not until the constitutional crisis of 1911 that the upper chamber was curbed. But in New Zealand the Balance Ministry of 1891 to 1893 created successful campaign issues by sending Reeves's program to the Legislative Council to be defeated, and in 1893 it succeeded in altering the powers of the Legislative Council by increasing its membership and shortening its term and put through measures to be copied in England, except for the unusual Arbitration Act of 1894.

This is not to say that Sir Robert Morant, Sir William Beveridge, Winston Churchill, and Charles Masterman, the civil servants and ministers responsible for the Liberal social security program, copied New Zealand. They did not. They worked out their own program from the facts in front of them. But they were influenced somewhat directly, since the New Zealand results were part of the evidence they used; and they were even more influenced indirectly, by the prestige the London School of Economics early gained.

To return to the history of New Zealand, in 1906 Seddon died, and as happened in Canada after Macdonald's death, his party was weakened without him. Finally, in 1911, the farmer-labor coalition that was the basis of Seddon's success ended. He had gained support by his program for going back to Wakefield and breaking up big estates. With the success of that program, the country vote switched. Distaste at coal and shipping strikes increased the reaction, and for many years after 1911, the Reform party held power, with a program of less government interference.

New Zealand, like Australia and Canada, not only secured nationhood by meeting problems as they arose; she evolved her own foreign policy. With it may be considered Australia's, since the policies were practically identical. Both Australia and New Zealand feared foreign dominance of the Pacific. Phillip's "First Fleet" and the *Tory* had reached respectively Australia and New Zealand just ahead of French expeditions, and ever since the two dominions had tried to establish a cordon of possessions around them. Likewise, from the first influx of Chinese immigrants to their gold diggings Australia and New Zealand had urged a policy of exclusion. A combination of these policies with New Zealand's missionary tradition and the desire of the Queensland Labor party to keep Kanakas out of the sugar plantations led to a humanitarian policy for the Pacific Islands. A desire for protection led to organizing military forces. Here, then, is a brief outline of Australasian foreign affairs, presented in the light of these policies.

In 1872 and 1875 Australia and New Zealand welcomed the passage of the Pacific Islanders' Protection Act, the creation of the post of High Commissioner for the Pacific, and the British protectorate over Fiji. On the other hand, English relations with China were embittered by the passage of Australian exclusion acts directed against the Chinese, and English relations with the Australian colonies were likewise embittered by the suspension and veto of those acts, for diplomatic reasons. Nor were negotiations with Germany made easier by New Zealand's protests against England's inactivity in Samoa, or by Queensland's occupation of New Guinea. Discontent, too, at having French convicts in New Caledonia after Australia had struggled so long to get rid of her convicts was increased by a feeling that the home government was negligent in making adequate representations to the French.

But with the advent of Joseph Chamberlain to power at the Colonial Office cooperation began. Queensland was the first to offer troops for the Boer War, well before it broke out. The prowess shown by Australians and New Zealanders did much for imperial relations during that war. Yet more was done when, in the period of the Entente Cordiale, a European war became probable. Then it was that both Australia and New Zealand adopted universal military training, that the Royal Australian Navy was founded, and that New Zealand gave a present of the battle cruiser *New Zealand* to the Royal Navy. Though the North Pacific was a Japanese lake, sea power in the South Pacific was secured by those two battle cruisers and five cruisers. They fully explained the foreign policy of the two dominions.

So it was that the three chief dominions attained nationhood, in so far as nationhood means ability to handle one's own problems and to deal at least in part with foreign powers. At the same time, self-governing New-foundland obtained "dominion status" in 1907 and then called herself "the oldest of the dominions," having had responsible government before New Zealand and before the formation of the Dominion of Canada. This proved the part of the imperialists' claim that the English knew how to give the substance of independence and keep loyalty.

INDIA

There are many ways of looking at the late Victorian Empire in India. One is to view it as do the diplomatic historians and to see India as yet another part of the British Empire that had a foreign policy of its own, which had to be integrated into a joint Empire policy. Again one can do as the late Victorians did and see the glamour of a few thousand men bringing good government to many millions. That is looking down from above, and it should be done, both in order to see India as many of its rulers saw it and to see how India fitted into the ideals of the Empire of the day. Thirdly, one can see India as the Indians today are inclined to see it, as the growth of two new nations, which eventually, and with their rulers' consent, gained self-government. This is the most important view, for it shows the roots of today's India and Pakistan. Here, in the above order, all three views will be taken, to try to give a well-rounded picture of what happened in those years.

English frontier policy for India—frontier policy being the essence of India's foreign policy—alternated between two schools. One was the "forward school," which needs no explanation. The other was the "Lawrence school," being the method of Sir John Lawrence, Governor-general from 1861 to 1867. He, being a Lawrence of the Punjab and as such immune from aspersions on his courage, could dare to be cowardly. He held Indian rule out of the Afghan foothills and refused to dabble in the dynastic problems of Afghanistan. This was a traditional policy of the old East India Company and a sound one to follow in the days when Persia, Afghanistan, Merv, Samarkand, and Bokhara all formed buffers between English and Russian rule. But in the 1860's and 1870's Russia began expanding in Central Asia as Governor Kaufmann and General Skobelev between them swallowed up the khanates, while the Russian Foreign Office blandly and perhaps with honest ignorance denied the intention of Russian agents.

Benjamin Disraeli, whose ideas of the Empire had vastly changed from the days when he wrote of "those wretched colonies as millstones round our necks," reacted sharply to this. He called upon the reserves of feudal loyalty among the Indian princes by sending the Prince of Wales to India and then by proclaiming Queen Victoria Empress of India. More than that, he sent a viceroy to India, the poet-diplomat Lord Lytton, with instructions to adopt a forward policy. This Lord Lytton did, by intervening in a dispute over the succession to the Afghan throne and sending a British agent, Sir Louis Cavagnari, to reside at Kabul. Cavagnari was murdered while Russian pressure grew—this being in 1878, at the height of the Near Eastern Crisis—and British-Indian armies marched on Kabul and Kandahar. Then it became painfully clear that the problem was not to get armies into Afghanistan but to get them out again. Here "the standing luck of the British Army" got India out of a nasty situation, for it soon became apparent that the English had backed the wrong claimant to the Afghan throne. Fortunately, the ablest of the pretenders, Abdur Rahman, escaped from the custody of the Russians at the moment at which the English garrison at Kandahar had to send for help. Sir Frederick Roberts, V.C., in command at Kabul, was able to evacuate both Kabul and Kandahar by means of a victorious march to Kandahar, aided by Abdur Rahman's political support. That allowed a dignified withdrawal from Afghanistan, the acceptance of Abdur Rahman as Amir, and a return to the Lawrence policy. The Amir, as has been told, repaid this support by preventing war in the Penjdeh crisis of 1885.

The subsequent frontier history of India, by the standards of previous ages, was peaceful. That did not mean the end of romantic border campaigns, such as the Tirah Campaign of 1897, in which Lieutenant Winston Churchill of the fourth Hussars saw action and won literary fame. It did not stop fear of Russian pressure, though that fear was alleviated, just before the Anglo-Russian Entente of 1907, by Sir Francis Younghusband's remarkable march over the Himalayas to Lhasa in Tibet. But after the Afghan War of 1879 India had peace in which she could dwell on her own problems and in which Indian nationalism and a measure of Indian self-government could grow.

By the Empire builder's standards, England did a good job in running India. Services to the population increased immensely from what they had been, tiny as they may seem now compared with present-day needs. A forest service, for instance, was evolved out of the needs of preserving government woodlands. Income from those woodlands was spent in scientific research and scientific management, and so increased itself. Similarly, irrigation canals, which paid for themselves in increased taxes and increased values, also increased the food supply. More important, the encouragement of railways, some privately owned, some government owned, fostered commerce, allowed mass migrations to shrines, and made the defense of India and the keeping of law and order simpler and cheaper.

The railways, too, saved life, for if there had been a railway to Orissa in 1877, the fearful famine of that year could have been checked. By using the railways and Sir Richard Temple's famine code of 1883, the rulers of India successfully met years of potential disaster unexampled for two hundred years, and thus they changed the birth and death rates in India sharply.

In education too, the picture changes. A literate population gradually grew up. Again, it was tiny in proportion to total illiteracy, large in comparison with what had gone before. Under the stimulus of Viceroy Lord Curzon, the direction of education was altered; the learning of English as the road to advancement was discouraged, and the study of native languages for use in India was encouraged.

All this was the result, not of one man's work but of that of a team of men, the Indian Civil Service. It is possible to say that Sir Richard Temple by his leadership of the Famine Commission advanced markedly the solution of that dread problem. It is possible to single out George Nathaniel Curzon from among the viceroys and to characterize his term of service, 1899 to 1905, as the most successful, marked as it was by his soaring imperialist imagination and his profound sense of duty toward the native population he so enjoyed ruling. But those men merely stand out among many men, who worked together. Deputy magistrates, collectors, assistant commissioners, commissioners, and councilors (to ascend the scale in the administrative services); forest officers, judges, political officers, railway and irrigation engineers, and school inspectors (to number a few of the specialists in the Presidencies, the provinces and the nonregulation territories); Residents in the Native States—all these functioned together in a very effective bureaucracy. Its success and its failures can be judged by looking at the India of 1858 and the India of 1914. Population increased, railroads increased, famine markedly decreased, and health improved. Literacy increased—and so, markedly, did the desire to be rid of the English increase. How then to explain this seemingly ungrateful desire for independence?

Part of this was the fault of the English, in their attitude toward those whom they ruled. As more and more English came to staff the government, they developed increasingly into a race apart. Just at the time when a literate group was rising in India who would feel exclusion bitterly, the habit of excluding the Indian became general. The increased ease of communication between England and India, too, meant that Englishmen no longer looked forward to spending a large part of their lives in India but thought in terms of "home leave." The discourtesies and rebuffs caused by this tendency do not explain the desire for independence; they do explain its intenseness and the counterbitterness to be found in it.

What made the subordinate place given to Hindus the more important in this time was the fact that an Indian nationalist movement, the first such in all Indian history, was evolving. The native intellectual leaders of India in the early part of the nineteenth century had turned to England for inspiration, had gladly learned English as a means of tapping the resources of Western culture, and had set to one side their native history and literature. Now a new generation came to the fore, which maintained that India had something unique to give the world. They took those steps which usually lead to national consciousness. They encouraged reading and writing in the native tongues, establishing vernacular schools and a vernacular press. They circulated the holy books of their religion and encouraged native scholarship. Parallel with this there arose a class of Indian businessmen, who ploughed their profits back into manufactures and began to compete with imports from England. Such a group of middle-class capitalists would, in the future, form a fertile field for nationalist propaganda and give support to a nationalist movement. With the unity that peace and good communications gave to India for the first time in her history, here would be leadership that would eventually be able to take over the government of the "subcontinent" from England.

One thing should be noted here, that this movement was more and more Hindu, rather than Moslem. The highest of the Hindu castes was the Brahmin, composed of hereditary priests and scholars. Moslems were fighters, who had come in as conquerors and on the whole looked down on learning. Indian nationalism, for all the truly good intentions of its founders, therefore tended to set Hindu against Moslem.

This nationalist movement rose at the very time that self-government, of a rudimentary but important sort, was being extended to India. That self-government took three forms: increased power and responsibility for the Indian Civil Service, given by various "council acts"; integration of the Native States into the new Indian Empire; and finally a program of Indian participation at various levels.

The importance of the council acts, especially those of 1861 and of 1894, was that power moved from the governor or viceroy as an individual to a council or really a cabinet. This is part of the steady trend the Empire has seen of power moving from the governor alone to the governor in council and then to the council responsible to a legislature. An important part of this step was the appointment of "Indian Members of Council" at all levels, to give from their experience for the formulation of policy.

The second form of increased self-government was the bringing of the Native States into the functioning of India. This was done not only by the Durbar of 1875 but even more by the proclamation of Victoria as Empress of India, "Kaisar-i-Hind," as the successor of Akbar. Now the native Princes were, in spirit if not in law, feudatories, a status that appealed to their imagination. Here was the old Mogul Empire which they understood, come to life again. Durbars, or assemblies of Princes, held in 1875 for the Prince of Wales, in 1902 for the accession of Edward VII, and in 1912 for the visit of George V, dramatized this change. It had a lasting effect in the improved control of the Native States by their Residents, and in the end of fear of war with Native States. On the contrary, the Native States now furnished "imperial service troops" and some Princes gave generously to meet imperial expenses.

These two developments made simpler the task of turning over self-government to the Indians eventually. But the great forward step was made, as it had to be, by the Indians themselves. For when, in 1882, by the Ilbert Bill, an attempt was made from above to give Indian officials power over Englishmen and Englishwomen, it was blocked by what amounted to a strike on the part of the Indian Civil Service, though in later years, by tactful bit-by-bit legislation, Indians were given the power of holding high office. The real beginning came with the First All India Congress of 1885. Though it was ridiculed because its proceedings were conducted in English, the only language shared by all participants, it was most significant as an attempt by Indians to formulate their desires for self-government, in which English sympathizers joined. Therefore, by the time of the Councils Act of 1894, with a minority of elected Indians as members of the legislative councils, some Indians were actively thinking, in practical terms, about what was needed for the progress of their "sub-continent" into a nation. Perhaps the most useful experience was being gained in the city councils of Madras, Calcutta, and Bombay, where English and Indian businessmen met on equality in the solution of day-to-day problems, and learned that they could cooperate.

Minority membership on councils that could be overridden by officials was not enough for the extremists among the Indians. Terrorists arose, especially in Bengal, where the division of that province into Hindu and Moslem halves gave strength to the Hindu nationalist agitation. At this point tension arose again between Hindu and Moslem, the age-old religious conflict being embittered as the Moslems in the Congress movement came to realize that the Hindus would profit more than they by the extension of self-government. Power was tending to go to the educated, and a whole series of social factors—language, the caste system, the fact that the Moslems were country dwellers with a warlike and nonliterary tradition—made the new "elite" of India predominantly Hindu. This tension and terrorism showed itself at the end of Lord Curzon's viceroyalty, in 1905, by assassination and gross disorder in Bengal. Both Indians and the English applied themselves to find a cure. Indian moderates disavowed the extremists. A strict press law stopped incitement to outrage. Strong police action checked the terrorists. Finally, the Morley-Minto reforms, which gave a real measure of power to Indian members of legislative councils, were announced to India at the Durbar of 1909 by the then Prince of Wales, George V. Here, as in South Africa, the traditional Liberal policy of ending disorder by granting an increase in self-government proved efficacious. So did a steady policy of "Indianization" of the civil service and the Army in the lower levels.

Measured by ultimate terms, and by the demands of such leaders as Tilak and Gandhi, the advance was slow. But what was important was that it took place and so enabled further peaceful advance, and that it took place with the consent and at times with the conscious impulsion of top-level British rulers.

MALAYA

The British Empire in India, in the later Victorian era, formed the model for a smaller area of indirect rule in the Malay Peninsula. It has been related how, in 1819, Sir Stamford Raffles made an East India Company settlement at Singapore which gave England trading control of the Eastern Seas. In 1867, the Straits Settlements were transferred from India to the Colonial Office. In 1873 a decision was taken that was so sensible that ever since various people have contested who deserved the credit of making it. That was to open up the country behind the trading settlements of the Straits Settlements by sending in British "Residents." These officials, by sitting on the councils of the Malay chiefs, speedily became the real rulers of Malaya. By bringing in peace, they allowed first Chinese miners to go in and discover the existence of tin and dig it, then British planters to follow, planting rubber. As time went on, and as the individual and frequently individualistic residents met common problems in very different ways, the idea of federation came to the fore. In 1895—these were the days of Joseph Chamberlain at the Colonial Office, when a sound idea got backing—a Federal Council under a Resident General was set up. In structure the Federated Malay States were intricate, since federation built on a foundation of old Malay treaties; in principle it was the same system of indirect rule that Wellesley brought to India, and Cromer had used in Egypt. And it brought from the sultans and rajahs the same emotion of loyalty as from the Indian princes. H.M.S. *Malaya*, the superdreadnought that fought so well in World Wars I and II, was a free gift from them to the Royal Navy. This government might best be described as a "federated bureaucracy." The special conditions of Malaya, where Malays were largely illiterate, and where English and Chinese businessmen were temporary residents, intending to return home when they had made their fortunes, made it difficult to get value out of elective councils. For that reason, the usual evolution from a governor to an elected assembly stopped for a long time at the point where the council shared power with the chief executive.

While dealing with the Empire in Asia, it should be pointed out that the Empire had various fringes. There was the chartered British North Borneo Company, which from 1881 on managed lands northeast of the territories of the Rajah of Sarawak, that independent subject of the Queen whose romantic career has been touched on in a previous chapter. There were the colonies and leased territories of Hong Kong and Weihaiwei, in China. There were special rights in the Persian Gulf, along with a "sphere of influence" in southern Persia. There was the colony of Aden guarding the mouth of the Red Sea. All these represented extensions of the power and wealth of the Empire. Borneo meant mission work among the pagan Malays, and trade. Aden meant the control of the Red Sea at the other end from the Suez Canal. Hong Kong and Weihaiwei meant means of tapping the trade of China. Special rights in the Persian Gulf, clinched by the energy and personal visit of George Nathaniel Curzon, meant English ownership of the Persian oil fields and oil for the Royal Navy, which in turn meant the Empire's concerning itself with the Arab world and the oil fields that underlay that world.

THE WEST INDIES

As for the West Indies, once the richest possessions of the British Crown, they had fallen by the wayside. The three B's—Bermuda, Bahamas, and Barbados—kept their old assemblies and continued the compromise of representative government, neither gaining control of administration nor losing the power to tax and make laws. The same was true of British Guiana. As for the rest of the West Indies, which had lost representative government, their history is a complicated one of many administrative experiments. Councils were set up and put down, federations were formed and dissolved. Economic innovations were tried and often found wanting. One economic change, when tried, succeeded; this was to give the Negro inhabitants the chance to own land. But as this upset the whole social and business system, it was rarely tried. Therefore, the importance of the West Indies to the picture of the Empire as a whole was that they increased the duties of the Colonial Office and continued to be an example of the need of direct administration, a proof that Englishmen were adept at ruling others.

EGYPT

British imperial problems in Africa were different from those of the dominions and India. There government from without came into conflict with already existing self-government, the problems of one possession reacted on other possessions and the expansion into Africa of other European nations added complications. The nature of these problems will be seen by examining first Egypt, then the belt of possessions in East, Central, and West Africa, and finally South Africa.

England came into Egypt, it will be recalled, when Disraeli bought the Khedive's Suez Canal shares in order to control the short route to India. She moved into closer contact in 1879, when the Khedive's bankruptcy was so serious that his deposition was secured and a French and an English minister were imposed on his successor, under the supervision of an international body, the Caisse de la Dette. Then, as has also been recounted, Arabi's nationalist revolt was crushed by Sir Garnet Wolseley at Tel-el-Kebir, and the Gladstone government found itself in fact governing Egypt through the agency of Sir Evelyn Baring, the British Consul General at Cairo. It also found itself faced with a Mohammedan religious revolt in the Sudan of the Mahdi and his dervishes, and with the ignominy of the death of Gordon at Khartoum and the defeat of attempts to rescue him. One of the great epics of the history of the Empire is the story of how Charles Gordon through sheer personality held out against fearsome odds till the dawn attack when he died, revolver in hand. That epic, as followed day by day by the newspaper public, did much to create imperialist feeling, for the telegraphic struggle between Baring and Gordon—the one ordering evacuation, the other holding to those who trusted him—symbolized the difference between a practical man of business cutting his losses and an idealistic Empire builder putting duty above orders.

But that picture—which caused the downfall of the Gladstone Ministry —is unjust to Baring's indirect rule of Egypt. That, too, had its noble side and should be judged in the light of his achievements. In the years 1883 to 1896, Baring transformed Egypt and rightly earned the Earldom of Cromer with which he was rewarded. Egypt remained, technically, a semi-independent province of Turkey, with a foreign commission seeing to it that the interest on the Egyptian debt was paid. But Baring saw to it that able English advisers were in key positions, where nominal Egyptian ministers took their guidance. Those advisers saw to the honest collection of taxes. They created a trustworthy police force. They kept graft out of administration. They saw to the relatively speedy and fair giving of justice in the courts. They built up and trained an army that at Toski defeated an invasion from the Sudan and protected Egypt's borders. They planned irrigation canals and looked forward to fuller use of the Nile by building a dam at Assuan that would revolutionize Egyptian agriculture. Here, therefore, came a connection between the growth of the British Empire in Egypt and in Central Africa.

For if the Nile were to be harnessed, its headwaters must be under secure control. If the Italians could dam the Red Nile or Atbara in Abyssinia, into which they were trying to penetrate, or could dam the Blue

Nile at Lake Tana; if the French could cut in at the swamps of Kordofan; if the Belgians could reach the outlet of Victoria and Albert Nyanza from the Congo; above all, if the Germans from their bases near Zanzibar could control the outlet of those crucial lakes—then they could become the indirect masters of Egypt. The situation became more serious when, in 1886, the Abyssinians overwhelmed the Italians at Aduwa. Soon thereafter, Kitchener began the reconquest of the Sudan. This took two years, from the first move till the final battle of Omdurman. It was a spectacularly efficient war, run on a timetable to days and hours, perhaps the more efficient because Kitchener was not under the War Office but under the Foreign Office. At one point a railway was built, timed to reach the outskirts of a dervish city just as that city was captured; at another point English troops were transferred to the Egyptian budget at a carefully calculated minimum cost, to reach the front only at the exact moment they were needed. At the end, in a spectacular battle on the banks of the Nile, dervish power was overthrown. Then gunboats were rushed up the Nile, just in time to thwart the French Marchand mission in claiming title to the land and perhaps establishing a band of French influence from Senegal in the West through Abyssinia to Jibuti on the Red Sea.

Out of this well-managed campaign evolved the curious "condominium" of the Anglo-Egyptian Sudan, a rule of the land from just above the Assuan Dam to the British protectorate of Uganda. Since England had conquered the land that Egypt nominally still owned, she shared it with Egypt, but in fact English officials governed it until 1953. At present writing self-government is on the way.

But though England thus won many square miles of land, much of which irrigation might make fruitful, Baring's very success in ruling Egypt began to lose England her dominant position there. For Egyptian nationalism continued strong. The Egyptian upper classes resented English control; Egyptian ministers, especially, resented the situation in which they were, in fact, the servants of those nominally under them. At the same time, the relationship of English experts and Egyptian ministers and administrators changed. At first Baring-Cromer and his assistants were few and worked in a framework predominantly Egyptian. They came as advisers, the only honest and effective friends Egypt had. All other advice might be effective but dishonest, as from the French who wanted to regain the position they had had in the days of Mehemet Ali, or honest but ineffective, as from such men as the erratic English horse-breeding squire, Wilfred Blunt. Therefore, when "El Lurd" suggested something it proved wise to accept his advice. It was different in later years. Then, when less help was needed, on the ground was a large English colony to give it, which more and more kept itself apart from Egyptian life. Naturally, a feeling arose that Gladstone's pledge to evacuate Egypt should be honored, now that Baring-Cromer's economies had won Egypt her financial independence.

It was the intention—at least in many quarters—to honor this pledge. Yet at the same time, there were essential English imperial interests in Egypt, chief among them the Suez Canal and the route to India, but also more and more English investment in Egypt. In all honesty, England had to withdraw her influence gradually but not completely. This was a tremendous task, so great a task as probably to have killed the man first entrusted with it, Sir Eldon Gorst. For the moment an Egyptian minister was given actual power, he was tempted to exercise it against English interests just to prove he had it. Gorst had to fight a series of what might be called administrative rear-guard actions and be subject to the attack of both Egyptians demanding more and English calling him a betrayer of the Empire. He achieved much, in doing this earning the affectionate respect of those close to him, and died of the burden he bore, which was too great for his physical strength.

Gorst's problems have been dealt with at this length because he set a pattern other English administrators would later follow, with varying success. The relative respect for England earned during the process of evacuation by Cox in Iraq, by the English administrators in Palestine, and by Lord Mountbatten in India may serve to gauge Gorst's success.

Gorst was followed by the obvious man for the job, Kitchener. "K's" task was made the easier because Gorst had shouldered the blame for the first steps in turning over power to the Egyptians, and because of "K's" prestige and his local knowledge. By here a resumption of power, there a hint to an old friend, Kitchener could in fact continue on Gorst's path and at the same time reassert England's position. As a result, by 1914, Egypt was more nearly controlled by Egyptians than at any time since the bankruptcy of 1873 to 1879. For though Egyptians by no means wielded total power, Baring-Cromer had made what power was handed back to them far more worth having. In Egypt, by 1914, therefore, England had taken steps to give effective self-government to a non-European people. Incomplete those steps might be, but they were a most significant sign for the future.

EAST, CENTRAL, AND WEST AFRICA

The term Central Africa is used here to cover England's widely separated possessions from Sierra Leone in the West to British Somaliland in the East, from Uganda in the North to Nyasaland and Rhodesia in the South, since for the purposes of this account they can be considered together. Here similar causes led to similar results, and English policy of rule over the natives was on the whole the same.

The first cause of expansion was missionary exploration and humanitarian motives. The great explorer was the famous David Livingstone, whose career in many ways epitomized England's expansion into Central Africa. From 1840, when he began looking for a road north from Bechuanaland, to his death on the shores of Lake Tanganyika in 1871, Livingstone opened up the "Dark Continent." His work, and that of those who followed in his footsteps, disclosed the source of the Nile, the chain of Lakes in the center of Africa, and the highlands of the Zambezi that are now called Rhodesia. His saintly life roused enthusiasm for missionary work. The grim news he brought back of the extent of the slave trade conducted by Zanzibari Arabs in Central Africa roused to life the anti-slavery movement. His disappearance, dramatic discovery by Henry M. Stanley, a *New York Herald* reporter—origin of the phrase "Dr. Livingstone, I presume" when two unacquainted Anglo-Saxons met in Central Africa without a mutual friend to make an introduction—and death refusing to leave the natives who trusted him, made Livingstone a national hero. When those natives carried his body to the seacoast, it was brought to be buried in Westminster Abbey, along with England's kings and heroes. With such an appealing figurehead for the movement, it is little wonder that those who wanted England to expand into Africa gained support.

All over Africa, therefore, the English made advances into the interior. At the Gold Coast, in 1873, at last something was done about the Ashanti kingdom in the hinterland, that had hitherto ravaged and pillaged and enslaved with little opposition. In 1873 Sir Garnet Wolseley went out in October, brought out troops in January, 1874, and by February, 1874, had conquered the Ashantis and was sending the troops back, before they could catch fever. In 1879, the traders at the mouth of the Niger organized the United African Company—later the Royal Niger Company—so that traders, missionaries, and the anti-slave-trade consuls were banded together to penetrate that region. In the 1870's, missionaries entered the region of Lakes Nyasa and Tanganyika, subsequently to form the African Lakes Company. Later, the Scotch merchant Stephenson spent £100,000 in building the Stephenson Road along Nyasa, to allow a military force, under Frederick Lugard, to put down the slave trade. In Zanzibar, English influence was gained by a powerful consul general, Sir John Kirk, and a philanthropic and businesslike Bombay merchant, Sir William Mackinnon, sponsored, in 1888, the Imperial British East Africa Company, whose purpose was to open a road and later a railroad from the coast opposite Zanzibar to the Nile valley, and thus to make easier the work of the missionaries and traders in the native kingdom of Uganda.

It will be noticed that the form of occupation was by chartered company, the device used centuries before to enter India, and to found Virginia and Massachusetts, used a short time by the Clapham Sect when it founded Sierra Leone, and used also by the British North Borneo Company to supplement the work of the Brookes at Sarawak. For this there was a good reason. Such companies were freed from the control of the Colonial Office—a real advantage in the heyday of Gladstone—and put under the control of the Foreign Office—a real advantage when Salisbury came in in 1886. It should be remembered that this expansion of England into Africa did not take place in a vacuum; it competed with German, French, Italian, and Portuguese expansion.

It was under the beneficent control of Lord Salisbury that these chartered companies—with which should be included the greatest of them, the British South Africa Company, of which more anon—came to their peak. Salisbury was not an out-and-out Imperialist. Once, when presented with the complaints of an allegedly ill-treated adventurer, he mildly minuted them, "Buccaneers must expect to rough it." He preferred to walk around a quarrel and was willing to pay for peace to those from whom peace could be bought. But as he was not afraid to fight if he had to, and as he drove a good though reasonable bargain, the chartered companies were well protected by him. By the 1890 Heligoland agreement, he gained for the I.B.E.A. (Imperial British East Africa Company) control from the Indian Ocean to the sources of the Nile and undid the work of the great German agent Karl Peters. By his 1898 agreement with Portugal, he cleared the Missionary Road north from Bechuanaland through Rhodesia to Nyasaland. By his 1898 agreement with France he cleared the boundaries of Nigeria and also protected the Nile. As a result of his care in getting a good share of the territory recently opened by exploration, and as a result of the free hand that Foreign Office control gave to the companies, the part of Africa that England got hold of was both suitable for exploitation and managed on a practical basis, without red tape. However, none of the companies could make money, except the British South Africa Company. Only the British South Africa Company and the Royal Niger Company had business as their aim; the I.B.E.A. and the African Lakes Company had philanthropic aims. But, as the Sierra Leone Company had proved, only a government can afford to run a philanthropic colony at a permanent loss. Furthermore, there was a problem of police and defense. If a company did not spend enough on troops, it had expensive small wars. On the other hand, if a company had a private army, as the British South Africa Company was to show, it might misuse it. Finally, once a colony had been settled, it was better run when run by colonial experts, under the Colonial Office. Therefore, as the Colonial Office picked up strength under Joseph Chamberlain in the late 1890's and early 1900's, the personnel of the companies was taken over into the Colonial Civil Service and the company territories were regularized into crown colonies. This brought into the Colonial Civil Service such men as Lugard, who on transfer from Nyasaland to Nigeria most ably put that extensive and complicated colony in order and made these colonies fit the usual crown-colony pattern.

SOUTH AFRICA

South Africa was a far different story from Central Africa, in some ways resembling Egypt. There, in 1870, the land seemed barren, without a source of local wealth that would give capital for expansion. Then matters suddenly changed. A child showed his parents a shiny stone, it got into a geologist's hands, and men began looking for African diamonds. Then a native witch doctor sold his magic charm and the amazing diamond, the Star of Africa, came to join the famous jewels of the world. A swarm of prospectors from all over the world poured in on the farm of the De Beers family, where were to be found the diamond-bearing "pipes" of "blue earth," to which these finds had been traced. At first pits were dug by each prospector. Then, when it was realized that only the blue earth held diamonds and that tunnels had to be dug to follow the pipes, corporations were organized to share individual claims. Here was a chance for young men who knew how to take chances to become millionaires when they were young, and a group of young men such as the world has rarely seen came to vast wealth, earned by themselves, in the prime of manhood. Almost unconsciously they set to work to change South Africa, and they did so.

The first problem to face the original prospectors was that of who ruled the land around the De Beers farm. Both the English and the Orange Free State claimed it, under conflicting agreements with the same native tribe. But the prospectors did not want to be ruled by "Dutchmen," and the Boers saw no value in trying to govern such unruly and unwilling subjects. It was therefore agreed that the diamond fields and surrounding territory should be the English colony of Griqualand West, for which England paid the Free State £200,000 in compensation. As a separate colony Griqualand West lasted but a short time. In 1872 the Cape Colony was granted responsible government, the diamond fields wanted self-government, and the obvious solution was to join Griqualand West to the Cape.

The next problem was that of the conflict of three cultures, English, Boer, and Negro. The diamond fields had evolved their own native policy. Once the diggings had gone deep, it was pleasanter to send Negroes down to dig the blue earth, while white men sorted out the diamonds on the tables where the blue earth was broken up. Therefore, the diamond magnates wanted a large supply of native labor, recruited under fairly decent conditions but definitely kept in its place in compounds. After all, with diamonds so small and so precious, it was necessary to search every native after he had come up from the shafts, lest he smuggle out a jewel, and it was necessary to secure special laws against "illicit diamond buying" and create a special police force to protect what turned out to be the diamond monopoly. As a result, the interests of the greatest amount of capital in South Africa were to have a native policy halfway between the British and the Boer, one with the English ideal of good treatment and the Boer ideal of a lower status. Later, when gold was found in the Transvaal and similar use was made of native labor, an even greater economic value came to be set on this native policy, which is the basic South African policy today.

In 1877, just as this situation had begun to develop, just as the fusion of individual holdings into the great De Beers diamond monopoly had started, the Colonial Office in London began to meddle. Lord Carnarvon, the very man who in 1859 had blocked Sir George Grey's scheme of a South African federation, now sent out James Anthony Froude, later the author of *Oceana,* to urge federation in South Africa. An opportunity then came to put into practice the ideas Froude had tactlessly oversold. The Zulus, under King Cetewayo, began to attack the Boers in the Transvaal. For fear of them, the Boers allowed a British force to march in and assume sovereignty there. Here might have been a real chance to end the conflict between Briton and Boer, had the occupation been well handled. It was not. No one bothered to get confirming votes from the Raad or Congress of the Transvaal, when it would have been easy to do so. Occupying forces were too small. There was not enough Boer participation in government. Consequently, when the Zulus turned on the British, in 1879, seemed for a moment to have smashed them at Isandhlwana, and were only defeated with difficulty at Ulundi, British prestige fell. The way the Zulu menace was ended made the Boers all over South Africa feel they could do the same job better.

All this happened at a crucial time. For an Afrikander culture was coming into existence. In South Africa men were beginning to think not as British subjects and not in a variant of the Dutch language but as Afrikanders in the Afrikaans language. In the Cape Colony Jan Hendrik Hofmeyr had just founded the Afrikander Bond, to create a South African culture and a South African nationalism. The question was, which way would this new-found nationality turn? Did the future hold a South African dominion in the British Empire, or did it hold an independent South African republic stretching from Cape Town to the Limpopo? Leading Boers worked with both purposes in mind. Judge De Villiers, of the Cape, would spend the last years of his life as a member of the House of Lords, despite invitations to serve the Transvaal and the Free State. He presided over the Union Convention, and before that did much to make court decisions uniform throughout South Africa. In the Transvaal lived the old Trekker, Paul Kruger, who despised the English, as his life was to show.

Hofmeyr's Bond, directed as it was to unifying South Africa, might take either course. Now was the moment to be watchful.

This was the time when the English rulers of the Transvaal chose to prosecute for nonpayment of taxes, of all men south of the equator, the grandson of the Bezuidenhout whom they had hanged at Slagter's Nek. Meanwhile Gladstone went through the Scotch county of Midlothian, asking the world what England was doing in attacking nations "rightly struggling to be free," such as the Zulus, the Afghans, and the Boers of the Transvaal. Consequently here was an opportunity, almost an invitation, for an explosion. It came on Dingaan's Day, December 16, 1880. As in the past, the Boers went out on commando, under their elected field cornets, this time to hunt down not Negroes but the "Roineks," the English soldiers with the sunburned necks. Now that they were a people with rifles instead of muskets, at Majuba Hill they surrounded and practically wiped out a British force. Here Gladstone, as Prime Minister, was faced with the question of whether he would avenge British defeat or honor his words in Midlothian. He honored his words, and the Treaty of Pretoria gave the Transvaal back its status of independence under British suzerainty, whatever that word should mean. This would bring later trouble, since the British claimed that suzerainty meant the management of foreign affairs, when in 1882 to 1884 the Germans occupied German Southwest Africa and sought to take advantage of the stresses between Boer and Briton.

For now those stresses grew. Both Boer and Briton wanted the land behind the Transvaal across the Limpopo River. The Boers wanted it because their population had so multiplied that they were—at their scanty scale of population—overrunning the two republics. That was easy to do, for the typical Boer of legend moved away whenever he could see the smoke of another man's chimney. As for the Britons, they had two aims. Exeter Hall, still influential, wanted to save Bechuanaland and the North from Boer ill-treatment of natives. The young magnates at Kimberley began to dream dreams of still more wealth in the unexplored hinterland. Both sides began the kind of pioneer pushing out on the frontiers that has been so typical of Anglo-Saxon nineteenth-century settlement, whether in the American West, in the Canadian West, across the Australian ranges or up into the hills of New Zealand. And, as so often happens, two leaders appeared.

One was the leader of the Transvaal, "Oom Paul" Kruger, one of the last of the Trekkers, now President of the Transvaal, the embodiment of the Boer ideal, who had led the nation in the First Boer War of 1880–1881, and who, in negotiating with the Gladstone Ministry, had shrewdly used the failure of the British to get Boer ratification of the occupation of the Republic to secure better terms. He hoped for a day when the Boers would cross the Limpopo as they had crossed the Vaal. The other leader was the embodiment of English imperialism, Cecil John Rhodes, the still young man who had by sheer force of personality combined the different diamond companies into the great De Beers monopoly. Rhodes had a vision of Boer and Briton as allies under the crown and the union jack, and he had the gift to make almost all who came into contact with him adore him. When in 1886 gold was found in the Rand, just south of Pretoria, and the boom town of Johannesburg gained 100,000 inhabitants in a year, Rhodes moved in to increase his already immense fortune by organizing Consolidated Goldfields, the dominant corporation there. As member of the Cape Parliament for Kimberley, Rhodes was now the other leading figure of South Africa, a colossus whose interests lay throughout the subcontinent. In 1888 he extended his powers. Through an agent—a missionary—he secured from King Lobengula of Matabeleland the exclusive right to all minerals there. Then he organized the British South Africa Company, the greatest of the chartered companies, with Queen Victoria's son-in-law, the Duke of Fife, as Chairman and sent an expedition to find whether there were any such minerals. There were, and a boom began at Salisbury, the capital of the new province of Rhodesia. The next year Rhodes became Premier of the Cape Colony.

Rhodes always "saw big." Even then he was talking of a Cape-to-Cairo railway—and lived to see a Cape-to-Cairo telegraph line. He wanted not only a Union of South Africa but a union of the Anglo-Saxon world; that was why he founded the Rhodes scholarships by his will, in order that the dominions and the United States might draw the benefits from Oxford he had obtained when he had sandwiched in study at Oriel College with making a fortune at Kimberley. He knew that unions to be effective must be voluntary; that was why he set such stock on cooperation with Hofmeyr and the Bond. His political career proved that such unions of minds could be made, for despite all the hatred he later roused among the Boers, his Boer constituency always reelected him to the Cape Parliament. But though he believed in eventual South African federation, the story of the 1890's is that of how he overplayed his hand and delayed federation by about ten years.

As Premier of the Cape and head of the chartered Company he accomplished much. In Rhodesia he took over complete control from Lobengula, after a war in 1894, and built the land up effectively. About why this war broke out there is still contention. Rhodes's enemies assert that an attempt of Lobengula's to negotiate was blocked by trickery. But to balance this possible black mark is Rhodes's sponsorship of the Glen Grey Act to benefit the Negroes. This set up a reserve for natives within the Cape Colony, where they could develop out of the tribal economy to landownership without being the prey of exploitation. But the great problem, wherein he failed, was to settle the conflict of Boer and Briton in the mining settlement at Johannesburg.

Johannesburg and the mining settlement there constituted the key problem in Rhodes's eyes. To the Boers, the wealth of Johannesburg was a means of making others pay the bills for the Transvaal, and they piled on taxes, set up dynamite monopolies, and fixed railroad rates to that end. But to let the "Uitlanders" vote was another matter; such a vote might drive Oom Paul out of office. The "Uitlanders" didn't really want the vote; they had come to Johannesburg to make their fortunes and go. What they wanted was what the vote could give them, protection from exactions. So they talked of revolt to get their rights and planned an outbreak for Christmas, 1895. Rhodes's ideas went further. If the revolt broke out, he intended to send in his private army, the police of Rhodesia, to stop bloodshed. Then he would call a convention of all South Africa and put through federation.

This plan might have worked if tried at any other time of year. But between Christmas and New Year it was the Boer custom to trek to Pretoria for the annual Dutch Reformed Communion service, "Nachtmaal." Suddenly the leaders in Johannesburg realized that with a very large proportion of the population of the Transvaal concentrated nearby, all of the males armed with rifles, a revolt was foolish. Therefore, they called it off. But Dr. Leander Starr Jameson, the Administrator of Rhodesia, who had concentrated his forces at Mafeking on the Transvaal border, felt that if he moved, the revolt would break out, and he went in. The Jameson Raid was a tragic-comic fizzle. Boer commandos easily rounded it up. The leaders were jailed, and the Boers argued whether to shoot them or fine them and turn them over to English justice. Such men as Louis Botha argued for shooting, but Kruger chose the fine and let them go, trusting to English justice.

But the England of 1896 was not the conscientious England of Midlothian. In the June of 1895 a general election had put Salisbury in power again, with Joseph Chamberlain at the Colonial Ministry, to become the apostle of imperialism. Naturally many Liberals were indignant at Rhodes, but their attack was weakened by the gratuitous interference of the Emperor of Germany who sent a public telegram of congratulation to Kruger. As Rhodes later told William, that saved him; it was poaching for a German to interfere. Rhodes's behavior was typical, in the way he handled his Board of Directors, the Cape Parliament, the Imperial Parliament, the Transvaal Boers, and a native rebellion in Rhodesia. He resigned as Premier, paid ransom for friends out of his own pockets, heartened his board to face the storm, and met the challenge of two parliamentary investigations. This took two trips to London in one year, with, sandwiched in between, the singlehanded suppression of a rebellion. It was a triumph of the personality of a kingly man. Whether or not one likes what Rhodes stood for, one can understand why the natives of Matabeland honored him with the royal salute, the *bayete*, hitherto given only to the descendants of King Chaka, and named him "separator of fighting bulls." Likewise, Leander Starr Jameson faced the music and gained such credit that Kipling wrote of him the much-quoted verses, "If." For, like Garibaldi and Cavour in Italy, Rhodes and Jameson had done doubtful deeds for their country, not themselves, and been honest about it. As a result Rhodesia was saved, and these two men, though they lost position, preserved much popularity.

With the Jameson Raid Rhodes's great power in South Africa ended, though to the end of his life he was Rhodesia. He died in 1901, left his fortune to the Rhodes scholarships, and was buried among the Matabele kings, in the Matapos hills. As evidence of his love for the Boers—who steadily after the Raid elected him to the Cape Parliament—is the fact that Jan Hofmeyr is buried at De Groote Schur, Rhodes's house at Cape Town, now the residence of the Premier of the Union of South Africa. It is evidence of Rhodes's faith that federation must come that De Groote Schur was so bequeathed seven years before federation existed.

With Rhodes out of the way, others had to try to solve the problem of the Uitlanders. Chamberlain in England and in South Africa Sir Alfred Milner, formerly Cromer's right-hand man in Egypt, tried to negotiate with Kruger. Perhaps other men that Kruger and Milner could have adjusted the differences between Boer and Briton. Those two dynamic men failed utterly. When negotiations failed, in 1899, the British sent troops to South Africa, and the Boers drew the natural deduction that, if they were going to have to fight anyway, they had better start before the troops landed. Thus the Second Boer War began.

At first the Boer mounted riflemen poured into Natal and around Kimberley, sweeping all before them. Had not three garrisons held out—at Kimberley, Ladysmith, and Mafeking—and had not the then Boer leaders failed to make the most of victories, England would have lost South Africa. For Majuba and the Raid, working on the new nationalism caused by the Bond, were beginning to turn many Cape Colony Dutch against England. Certainly England lost prestige, in the sad defeats of the "Black Week" when the newly landed troops were thrown back in attempts to relieve Kimberley and Ladysmith. Almost the only bright spot was the escape of war correspondent Winston Churchill, whom Louis Botha had personally captured outside Ladysmith, in one of those freakish events which have marked the career of both men. Europe became sure that the English army was incompetent, hoped the British Empire would crack, and revealed an amazing amount of anti-British feeling. Then a team of able men—Roberts of the India Office army in India, Kitchener of the Foreign

Office army in Egypt—was hurried to South Africa, and in a few weeks turned the tide. The troops in Natal at last rescued Ladysmith, named after Sir Harry's bride of the Peninsular War. Sir John French and his cavalry galloped to Kimberley to free Rhodes and his diamond mines, a New South Wales Lancer being the first to enter Kimberley. Sir Herbert Plumer and his Colonials came down from Rhodesia to rescue Sir Robert Baden-Powell and the handful of boys and men with whom he had held Mafeking by bluff, courage, and wits. This final rescue sent London wild, in the celebration that has made Mafeking Night the standard for expression of pent-up emotion. For "B. P." had shown the English when all else went wrong that the spirit of the Elizabethans still lived among them. From Mafeking, too, where boys had done so nobly, grew the Boy Scout movement, to teach boys in peace the virtues the Chief Scout had seen them evidence in war. Then a main Boer army was surrounded and captured, the mines at Johannesburg were freed and reopened, and the two capitals of Pretoria and Bloemfontein taken. It looked as if Roberts might return home with the war over, leaving the cleaning up to Kitchener.

Here the kaleidoscope of the Boer war turned again. When the Boer remnant retreated into the Zoutpansberg mountains, there arose leaders among them, and among those leaders a chief leader, Louis Botha. After a month's recruiting of strength, the Commandos came out of the Zoutpansberg and gave the British Army a lesson in warfare. It took two years, during which Christiaan De Wet captured an English major general and his staff and Jan Christiaan Smuts led his commando to the Atlantic Ocean, before the steady pressure of Kitchener's army forced the more farseeing of the Boers to persuade the bitter-enders to surrender.

Much harm the war did. It acerbated the old hatreds that could go back to Slagter's Nek and Dingaan's Day, the bitter resentment against the English as tyrants and Negro lovers, and added to them new hatreds. If the methods of British concentration camps seemed to the Liberal leader, Campbell-Bannerman, to deserve the name "Methods of Barbarism," no wonder that so many Boers had no love for those who had defeated them. But it had beneficial results too. England learned to respect the rest of the Empire and to be grateful to the "younger nations" for "men who could shoot and ride." Furthermore, a group among the Boers and British learned to respect each other. The self-restraint of the British, the good treatment they gave Boers who had technically broken the "laws of war," the way the racial prejudices were obeyed by keeping it a "white man's war" and not using Indian troops or letting the Basutos loose won the confidence of some of the frontiersmen. The worth of frontier democracy in courage, resourcefulness, and willingness to take counsel together impressed the British. That was why Louis Botha and Jan Smuts were able in the negotiations at Vereeniging to drive a noble bargain with

Milner and Kitchener. For the British promised, in exchange for the Boers becoming the subjects of Edward VII, that they should have not only future self-government but protection for their language and funds for rehabilitation.

Well the English performed their half of the bargain. Milner, as High Commissioner, gathered around him a band of eager, able young men, his "Kindergarten." Among them were John Buchan, later the intelligence officer, novelist and Governor-General of Canada; Dawson, the editor of *The Times;* and Lionel Curtis, who did so much to guide thinking on imperial problems and to offer successful solutions for the Irish and Indian questions. These men gave the conquered republics good government, while Leander Starr Jameson, as Premier, rehabilitated himself by rebuilding the Cape Colony. But one error the "Kindergarten" made. To get a supply of labor to reopen the mines at Johannesburg, while the war was on, they sent to China and India for coolies, thus mixing up the South African racial problem still more. An outcry arose, at the measures taken for isolating the coolies, which greatly contributed to the overwhelming defeat of the Conservatives in the 1906 election in England.

Yet perhaps it might be argued that this had its good side. For the Conservatives and Milner were, not unnaturally, slow to grant self-government to the Transvaal and wanted to move to it through the stage of representative government. But in those days the Boers of the Republics and the Cape looked to one man, Louis Botha. In war years they had learned to lean on his wisdom, and in that intensely individualistic and democratic people the phrase "Louis Botha says" had become the most powerful possible introductory phrase for any political argument. And Louis Botha had said not to accept anything less than complete responsible government.

This the Liberals gave to the Transvaal and the Orange River Colony, the measure being put through Commons by the Undersecretary for Colonies, Botha's former prisoner, Winston Churchill.

For here was Botha's chance. The same facts that had made Grey, Froude, Rhodes, and Chamberlain desire federation made him desire it. And he, having the ability to work with and through both Boer and English, succeeded where they had failed. It took endless negotiating and the stout support of Jameson to put it through. Even when Jameson was told Botha had wanted him shot after the Raid, he merely replied, "Botha is always right," and continued to support him. So strong were particularist feelings that the Constitutional Convention had to migrate from capital to capital and had to give the eventual union three capitals —a parliament house at Cape Town, executive offices at Pretoria, and a supreme court at Bloemfontein. But a united federation was created, the strongest in the Empire, so strong that the party in power appoints administrators for the provinces. In the constitution, too, were special safeguards, especially for the right of the Cape Colored to vote. And excluded from the Union were the native territories of Bechuanaland and Basutoland —Exeter Hall's type of feeling would not trust the Boers with control of them. But Federation ended the problems of railways, dynamite monopolies, Uitlanders, and the like. South Africa, in the Empire as a dominion, found a freedom she had not known before.

Yet one problem, it should be recorded, Botha did not fully solve. Naturally he sent the Chinese back. But with the Indians he met his match. Among them arose a leader, the lawyer Mahatma Gandhi, who successfully resented the Boer attitude to all who were not Boer or Briton. Here began the career of the great advocate of the nonwhite races in the Empire.

THE CHARACTER OF BRITISH IMPERIALISM

In Africa can be seen all sides of British imperialism, bad and good. There were a thirst for profits, and sharp practice to get them—a thirst for power, and sharp practice to get it. There were, on the other hand, missionary zeal, humanitarianism and desire to protect native races, and a belief that freedom willingly granted can be a bond of union. Whatever one may think of imperialism in general, Britain's record in these years is better than, and different from, that of other nations. At the worst she did not equal the German massacres in South West Africa, or the Belgian outrages in the Congo which an Irishman, Roger Casement, revealed to the world and succeeded in stopping. At the best she treated natives well and gave the conquered Boer republics self-government in remarkably short time. This therefore raises the question, what were the qualities which made British imperialism different from other imperialisms?

This is too vast a question to answer in a paragraph. Yet some sort of an answer must be suggested, in order to make sense out of the Empire as a whole. Here, therefore, are some suggestions that may help the student codify his or her thoughts on the subject. First of all, all empires are founded by men of action. A dictionary definition of the word empire usually points out that it is loosely applied, not to a region ruled by an emperor, but to a situation where one people rules one or more other peoples. That does not, as will be noted, exactly apply to the realm of Victoria, but it will do as a start. But, since a rule has to be established by action, it takes energy to make an empire. Energy the Imperialists had —the energy with which Gordon almost singlehanded held Khartoum, with which Cecil Rhodes made South Africa his own, with which Donald Smith drove the C.P.R. across Canada, with which George Curzon made his frail pain-racked body bear the strain of meticulous control of India. But men of action must have faith in what they do; these men and others like them had immense faith. Of course, much of that faith was self-seeking. Rhodes got himself an immense fortune. Mackinnon who made

East Africa was a merchant who hoped, though in vain, for wealth there. England's trade, of course, followed the flag, and paid for the navy that made the Empire secure.

But again and again, as one reads what the Empire builders had to say for themselves, one comes up against the fact that it was not only self-seeking that built the Empire. The men who made Egypt complained how little English merchants took advantage of opportunities—and still went on making those opportunities for German and French traders. To Rhodes his great wealth was but a means to an end; his banker-biographer, Sir Lewis Michell, tells wryly how Rhodes tricked him into handling his affairs and into the task of stemming the tide of his wild generosity. The Empire builders, being men of action, were not good at defining what they thought. But the fragmentary ideas they did form seem to fall into a pattern. They held to a conception which the philosopher Aristotle tried to pass on to his pupil Alexander the Great. Aristotle held that the best form of government was a "mixed government"—neither democracy, oligarchy, nor monarchy but a combination—and that the way such a government was best inspirited was to have all citizens able to rule and also be ruled—"Archein kai archesthai," in the original Greek.

The original Greek has been purposefully quoted, for there is a real connection between English classical public school and university education and the Empire. After all, of these men, two of the greatest were Rhodes of Bishop Stortford Grammar School and Oriel, Oxford, and Curzon of Eton and Balliol, Oxford; the list could be prolonged almost indefinitely, through such men as Milner of Balliol, Buchan of Brasenose, and the like. There was reason for the reliance on the "old school tie" in making the Empire. If as a boy a man had risen from the lower forms of the school to the upper, had first obeyed rules and then shared in making them, he had a feel for government. He had known both sides of the fence. To him it was no paradox that a mixed government—surely the government of Britain was gloriously mixed—should offer at the same time rule from above to some and self-government to others. Both the classical authors he had read and the extracurricular life he had led had shown him not merely that this was possible but that it was probably the natural way to get good government.

The student should note carefully the limitations of this argument. It is not claimed that every English empire builder went to a "public school" modeled after Arnold's methods at Rugby. It is not claimed that every action taken to build the Empire was inspired by pure Aristotelian thought, covered with glory, and pure beyond criticism. It is merely suggested that what made the British Empire different from other empires was that it had back of it, besides the economic and nationalistic motives common to the founding of all the colonial empires of the nineteenth century, an ideal, the clearest expression of which was to be found in the classical education of the public schools, and that because this ideal drew from the ideals of duty of Greece and Rome, it was not unnatural that much of the leadership in building the Empire came from men who could "wear the old school tie."

In conclusion, we may raise the question whether this suggestion fits the facts about the Empire as a whole, during the years from 1870 to 1914. Does it explain the institutions, some formal and some informal, which the later Victorian and Edwardian Empire evolved, which fostered a feeling of common citizenship, and which therefore tended to hold it together?

Of the informal institutions, some were social. Of the world-wide organization of the Anglican Church something has been said in a previous chapter. It remained an international church, with important binding effect. More important than that was the sense of family ties. The constant interconnection between brothers and sisters and cousins in the homeland and the dominions overseas formed close ties of blood relationship to hold the Empire together. To this day, as is recorded in Nevil Shute's novel *The Legacy,* the people of Alice Springs, South Australia, speak of England as "home." A glance at the map, to see that town, in the very center of the Australian continent, may suggest the strength of the ties of blood.

Naturally, economic ties existed. The Empire had been built up, of course, for reasons of trade, which still held valid. London as an insurance center, as a transshipping point for trade, as a market for wool and meat and copper and tin and rubber, above all as a money market for capital, bound the Empire together. It was the Colonial Securities Act, allowing the investment of trust funds in the bonds of the colonies, that paid for the Vogel immigrants to New Zealand and for the Australian and South African railway lines. Equally, language ties were of immense importance, with an Empire-wide press and Empire-wide circulation of books and magazines. Of course to state this is to state the obvious. But it is necessary to remember these obvious things if one is to understand how apparently weak institutional links served to hold an Empire together in bonds of common citizenship.

Of those formal institutional links the chief were the Judicial Committee of the Privy Council, the Colonial Civil Service, the Imperial Conferences, the Committee on Imperial Defense, and above all the Crown.

The Judicial Committee, like the Anglican Church, has been dealt with in a previous chapter. During the years from 1870 to 1914 it increased in importance. By the Judicature Act of 1874 it was amalgamated with the judicial work of the House of Lords, so as to have almost the same membership in fact. As a court of final appeal, compulsory on the colonies and India, permissive for the dominions, it served to hold the Empire together, just as John Marshall's great decisions did much to establish the strength of the American union. Its success as a unifying force has varied with the effectiveness of its decisions, for there have been times when there were earnest and apparently justified attempts to escape its jurisdiction. But it has on the whole tended to unify the Empire, even though the more recent dominion constitutions have made appeal a matter of permission, not of right.

The Colonial Civil Service, by its policy of transfers from colony to colony, has not only prevented stagnation in small colonies but also made for unity. At the higher levels examples of such transfers are those of Frederick Lugard from Nyasaland to Nigeria, and Hugh Clifford from Malaya to succeed him there. Not only did Joseph Chamberlain encourage the building up of this effective bureaucracy, he gave new services to the colonies. Such organizations as the Royal Institution of Tropical Medicine brought modern knowledge where it was most needed, and a willingness to pay some bills from London began that would lead to the Colonial Development Fund of 1940.

But the most important organization to hold the Empire together was a partly accidental creation, the Imperial Conference. In 1887, at the time of Queen Victoria's jubilee, the premiers of the self-governing colonies met in Westminster as part of the celebration, and the opportunity was taken to transact business. From the British side, there was indoctrination in the grandeur of the Empire. From the colonial side, grievances were taken up directly by responsible leaders, instead of, as in the past, by Agents-general who had to send back for instructions. The value of this was great, especially at the extremely frank interchange of views on foreign affairs between Lord Salisbury and the premiers, in the course of which unpublishable truths about the French in the New Hebrides were driven home to Australia and New Zealand, and future interchanges of opinion on that touchy subject greatly eased. In consequence of this, it was agreed to hold such Colonial (or, later, Imperial) Conferences every five years, the next to be at Ottawa in 1892.

The Ottawa Conference was a true intercolonial exchange of opinions at a high technical level. At it postal and cable problems were ironed out and means of facilitating intra-Empire trade were evolved. Then the third Conference, that of 1897, at Victoria's Diamond Jubilee, made Empire history. By then the dynamic Joseph Chamberlain was Colonial Secretary. He had a vision of carrying the Ottawa Program on to intra-Empire tariff preference, the beginning of his evolution into a protectionist. Here, Canada, it seems, taught the Empire how to rule itself. (It should be noted that after most Imperial Conferences most of the delegates take to themselves credit for the successful suggestions. This leads to Empire harmony but confuses the task of the historian afterward.) Sir Wilfrid Laurier, the Canadian Premier, as a French Canadian, well knew the resistance that would be made to any program imposed on French Canada from outside, and insisted that imperial institutions must evolve naturally. He would make no declarations of policy, no sweeping general agreements. He would be most cordial in supporting the Empire, but the support Canada gave must be decided upon by Canadians. This, two years later, he demonstrated by the leadership with which he checked anti-English elements in his party and gave united Canadian support to the Boer War. By this strong stand Laurier checked a probably fruitless attempt to make a tight unit of the Empire, similar in kind but not degree to the failure that caused the American Revolution. For Chamberlain's schemes would have caused the drawing of pro- and anti-imperial party lines throughout the self-governing colonies. On the contrary, the very freedom to disagree has helped bring about cooperation. There has been frank criticism of the homeland such as the protest of Seddon of New Zealand against Chinese labor in South Africa. There has been for that reason frankness in return. After the Imperial Conference of 1911, the dominion premiers found that they had, in fact, secured from Foreign Secretary Sir Edward Grey a fuller appreciation of the diplomatic situation than his own cabinet had received.

This new approach to Empire relationships was given official recognition. In 1907, the Conference agreed upon the name of "dominion" for self-governing colonies in general and acknowledged that in fact Newfoundland and New Zealand were dominions just as much as Canada, even though they did not, like the Australian Commonwealth, have a special title given them by act of Parliament. More than that, the Colonial Office was divided so as to have a dominions side, to deal differently with self-governing colonies. Here, in what became the Dominions Office and now the Office of Commonwealth Relations, was the creation of a new institution.

Out of Laurier's approach to imperial problems evolved yet another institution, the Committee on Imperial Defence. This was created by Arthur James Balfour when Prime Minister in 1904. Intentionally he made it merely an advisory and record-keeping body, although its chief executive officer, the Chief of the Imperial General Staff (C.I.G.S.), has been the unifying technical officer of the Empire in war, as witness the career of Sir John Dill, whom the United States accorded burial in Arlington Cemetery after his death from overwork in World War II. Membership in the Committee was by invitation for specific duties, was nonpartisan, and was truly imperial, Balfour seeing to it that the Canadian Minister of Militia attended one of its earliest sessions. Out of this Committee, which was so nonpartisan that Balfour sat on it during World War I when he was an Opposition member of Parliament, grew up the Imperial War Cabinet, whereon Hughes of Australia, Borden of Canada, and Smuts of South Africa determined England's over-all policies in World War I, along with Milner and Curzon, who might be considered to represent Egypt and India as well as England. Here, in the working of these varied institutions, can be seen what looks like the application of the ideal of Empire citizenship. Subjects of the Crown have a "home," even if they live diametrically across the globe from it in Alice Springs. If they so desire, they can be members of a Church that spreads through and beyond the Empire. There are different levels of political power for different parts, rising from the externally governed Crown colonies to the self-governing dominions that share in top-level decisions, yet that status is flexible. In six years the Transvaal can rise from being conquered territory to being part of a dominion almost equal to the homeland. Inspiring that flexible form of government is a concept that the law can be made universally applicable and that at Westminster are judges who can be trusted to do their best to apply it. Here in this highly "mixed government" is the working out of the idea of ruling and being ruled. As Palmerston put it, in his great Don Pacifico speech of 1850, it is a proud boast to be able to say, "I am a British citizen."

This conception of empire citizenship, of duties as well as rights, turns on one requirement. As Balfour used to put it, the essence of Anglo-Saxon institutions is that there is an intention to make them work. As his godfather, the Duke of Wellington, put it, "The King's government must be carried on." That is why the Crown grew to play such an important part in the workings of the Empire. The king or queen formed the focus of loyalty that inspired this common citizenship, so that the trips of Edward VII as Prince of Wales, the globe-circling tour of his son (later George V) as Duke of Cornwall and York, were essential links in holding the Empire together.

A view of how this conception of the crown grew may be obtained from the changes that took place in the royal title from 1760 to 1902. For when George III came to the throne in 1760, he was "King of Great Britain, France and Ireland, by the Grace of God," and was, outside of England, Elector of Hanover. In other words, he was a European prince who combined in one person three governments and an old claim to a fourth. But when his granddaughter, Victoria, came to the throne as "Queen of the United Kingdom of Great Britain and Ireland," she ruled over a united nation—in theory—and one free from European entanglements. Furthermore, she became, in India, Empress, to mark a special relationship to a special part of her realm. And as for her son Edward, in 1902 he became not only "King of the United Kingdom and Emperor of India," but more than that—"King of the Dominions beyond the Seas." More and more the bonds that held the Empire together had become those of loyalty rather than of sovereignty and force. When World War I broke out, it would be shown how powerful were those new bonds. More than that, after that war the new ideal would take clearer form, till the Crown became the chief link of the Commonwealth of Nations.

INTRODUCTION

World War I was a profound shock to England. At the end of it her place in the world had altered. It is arguable how much England had changed or how much the world had changed. But it can be agreed that certain great military events and certain great political, constitutional, social, and economic events consequent on those military events caused one era to end and another to begin. For an understanding of how this change came about, the best approach seems to be to move from cause to effect. Therefore this section of the book will reverse the order in the previous and the following sections. First the causative military and diplomatic events will be considered, and then the consequent results.

England fought a war of attrition in which much was worn away. Four years' deadlock in France, in the Near East, and on the seas shook England's economy, brought the working class to the fore, and gave the dominions practically equal status with the mother country. Out of it came, too, a split between Ireland and Great Britain and significant change in the position of India.

It would be possible to go into greater detail. It could be pointed out that the English aristocracy was bled white and the middle class pushed down. It could be pointed out also that Ireland and India took the key steps to their present separate status. But to do this would be to state what will soon be repeated more extensively. Therefore let us look at the diplomatic and military events of the years from the declaration of war on August 4, 1914, to the signing of the Armistice on November 11, 1918.

42

FOREIGN POLICY AND MILITARY EVENTS

1914–1918

In after years men have looked back at World War I and have asked themselves whether the British Foreign Secretary, Sir Edward Grey, by some one action or another, could have checked the curious process whereby murder of an Austrian archduke in June, 1914, caused Great Britain to be at war early in August. During that time a quarrel between Austria and Serbia became a quarrel between Austria and Serbia's protector, Russia, and then grew into one between Austria's ally, Germany, and Russia, with Russia's ally, France, and their associate, Great Britain, being dragged in. Was there not somewhere along the line a point at which Sir Edward could have called a halt? The answer seems to be that, throughout the whole drift to war, Sir Edward was faced with a diplomatic dilemma. Much as he wanted to hold back his associates, too great pressure on them might break up the whole structure of agreements for mutual support that he, and Lord Lansdowne before him, had so patiently created. He might urge Serbia to give wide powers to the Austrian police search for the assassins, but he must stop before driving Serbia back to the Austrian alliance from which she had only recently been weaned. He might urge Russia to be moderate in her support of Serbia, but in doing so he must remember the danger of another revolution in Russia worse than that of 1905, or the danger that Russia, too, might return to the German alliance that had held good from 1872 to 1890. German overtures such as had been made in 1904 and 1910 might succeed this time. Nor could France be held back too far. Her national safety turned on the fact that, should she go to war with Germany, Russian troops would march. Her people had, as a patriotic duty, bought Russian bonds to supply these Russian troops. Furthermore, Britain had told France that she might safely withdraw her fleet from the Atlantic. Sir Edward could not remain Foreign Secretary if his country refused to honor this pledge of keeping the Channel safe, and he must urge his Cabinet to remember that if Britain deserted her associates she would never again be trusted.

Furthermore, Sir Edward was held back by the fact that he was a member of a Liberal Cabinet, which drew its support in the House of Commons from Liberals, Labor, and Irish Home Rulers. If any serious split took place in that Cabinet, a political crisis would ensue which might take precious days to resolve. He could make no promises of support and issue no threats of going to war which would not get effective backing. Therefore, it was not until there was danger of war between Germany and France that he could persuade an effective majority in the Cabinet to agree that Britain would protect the Channel coast. It was not until the Germans had violated the Belgian neutrality treaty that he could secure from the Cabinet permission to issue an ultimatum demanding that Germany withdraw from Belgium. It was on that issue of honoring her pledged word that Great Britain went to war.

If Sir Edward failed in keeping the peace, he did succeed in gaining support for the British ultimatum. In Parliament, J. Ramsay MacDonald stood almost alone in speaking against war. Speaking for Ireland, John Redmond gave a deft and noble pledge of support which for a while made the British Isles truly a United Kingdom. At this point the control of events left the hands of the diplomats and went to the Admiralty and the War Office.

The Admiralty and the War Office were ready. Plans had long been laid for this eventuality. Britain's first duty, obviously, was to make sure of the command of the sea. Her battleship strength was barely enough to secure this, for the Germans by hurried building had temporarily come close to equality.[1] First Lord of the Admiralty Winston Churchill had already taken decisive action by using a practice mobilization in July to send the Fleet to its war station at Scapa Flow in the Orkneys. However, when war broke out, there was no great sea battle between the British Grand Fleet and the German High Seas Fleet. German strategy saw the High Seas Fleet as a "fleet in being," by its mere existence pinning down British naval strength and exhausting British resources. And the Germans wanted the British Expeditionary Force to cross the Channel. They felt that an army sunk in the Channel would cause hatred, whereas an army captured on the Continent would be a hostage. Furthermore, they doubted whether they could sink British transports, and they were sure they could capture the British Army. So even a rash raid on Heligoland could not bring the Germans out to fight in the North Sea.

Elsewhere, when the war broke out, German units at large were rounded up. At Coronel, off the Chilean coast, Admiral Graf Von Spee did sink two British cruisers, but speedily two battle cruisers, the *Invincible* and the *Inflexible,* got revenge at the Falkland Islands. The German commerce raider *Emden* gained fame, till she was sunk off Cocos Island by the Royal

[1] In October, 1914, the only way Great Britain kept numerical superiority was by commandeering two battleships under construction for Turkey and Chile.

Australian Navy cruiser *Sydney*. One failure did have serious results. In the Mediterranean the German battle cruiser *Goeben*, by clever evasive action and by steaming so hard that her boilers burst, escaped to Constantinople. Her presence there had weight in bringing Turkey into the war on the German side.

By December, 1914, sea warfare reached a stalemate. England could at her leisure pick up the German colonies, aided by her allies. She took Togoland and the Cameroons in West Africa, thus potentially enlarging the Gold Coast and Nigeria. The dominion of South Africa, after dealing with an internal revolt, in 1915 took over German Southwest Africa. Australia took over New Guinea; New Zealand, Samoa. Japan, with the hampering of a token English cooperation, took Tsingtau in China and, with no hampering, as Americans painfully know, took over the Caroline Islands in the Pacific. It took longer to subdue German East Africa, since the German commander, Von Lettow-Vorbeck, fought most skillfully and valiantly. Actually he kept forces in the field until three days after Germany had surrendered. But except for the fact that South African dominion troops were prevented by the South and East African campaigns from coming to the European front in large numbers, this campaign did not affect the main struggle. Thus, outside the North Sea and the Baltic, Britannia ruled the waves. But there the German navy had important strategic effect. Because the High Seas Fleet remained a fleet in being, Great Britain could not send supplies through the Baltic to Russia. Because of the guns on Heligoland and the German submarine fleet of U-boats, it was impossible to blockade German ports closely. This fact was proved at the battle of Heligoland Bight and at the sinking of three cruisers in one hour by the German submarine U-9. Great Britain was forced to a policy of distant blockade.

However, no one expected World War I to be a long war. That is the easily forgotten fact that explains the military and diplomatic events of the first few months. Both sides looked forward to a quick victory. The French and Russians saw that they outnumbered the Germans and Austrians by more than a million trained men. They wanted the aid of a British Army not for its numbers—Great Britain had fewer trained men than Belgium or Serbia—but for the British Navy and for the effect on morale. They assumed that a simultaneous advance on both sides would crush the Central Powers. It might take time for the slow Russian mobilization to bring to bear the full effect of Russian manpower, but once the Russian "steam roller" began to move, the result—they thought—would be inevitable.

On the other hand, the German General Staff realized that the German army could mobilize quicker than any other. They believed that if Germany attacked instantaneously France could be crushed and the victorious troops rushed back to help the Austrians conquer Russia. This belief explains much of Germany's diplomatic actions before World War I. Since Austrian aid in holding Russia off was essential to this plan, German diplomats went far in backing up Austrian demands on Serbia to make sure of Austrian support. And as France could be conquered quickly only by going around the fortress line that ran from Verdun to Switzerland and through the Belgian plain, the German leaders felt themselves justified in violating Belgian neutrality, as the only means of equalizing French and Russian superiority in numbers.

So it was that World War I, on land, began according to plan and then failed to proceed according to expectation. On the Eastern Front, Austria struck at Russia and was defeated. Russia pushed into East Prussia, from Poland and along the Baltic Coast, and seemed about to "steam roller" her way to Berlin. On the Western Front the French prepared their invasion of Germany while the German right wing smashed its way through Belgium to outflank the French and drive all their forces into Switzerland. Here the small British Expeditionary Force entered the war. During the crucial days of mobilization Lord Haldane took charge of the War Office. According to plans already laid down, he got the B.E.F. to France quickly and efficiently.

Little was expected of the B.E.F., except as a symbol. French authorities did consider the six British divisions would be worth twelve for the morale effect. An incorrect legend had it the Kaiser spoke of the "contemptible" British Army. The German navy was ordered to let the B.E.F. get to France because it was hoped to capture it and hold it as hostage for peace terms. But at Mons the brunt of the German assault through Belgium fell on Sir John French's men, who played a crucial part. Their terrifying platoon fire—reminiscent of the platoon fire of the Napoleonic Wars—so cut down German attacks that captured officers could not be convinced the British were short of machine guns. But the outflanked French and English were forced to retreat hurriedly to avoid encirclement. Traditionally a British Army retreats "with a sting in its tail," and the men who—if they lived— later were to wear the Mons Medal and proudly call themselves "the Old Contemptibles," held together and held off encirclement as they marched south and even east, till they were below the Marne River and Paris. Then came the much-discussed, much-disputed "Miracle of the Marne." Suddenly pressure ceased. The B.E.F. turned about and pushed north again, till it drove retreating Germans to the north bank of the Aisne River. Why this happened is still a matter of argument; that it happened is a vital historical fact. The quick overthrow of France was stopped and the character of the war utterly changed.

This book need not go into detailed discussion of why the German columns wheeled and countermarched with victory apparently within their grasp. But one aspect of this discussion is of importance. Could it be that the Marne was won, not by the merits of French commanders or the demerits of German commanders, but because the British Seventh Division had been landed at Ostend, the British Naval Division at Antwerp? Was Winston Churchill right in pressing his Cabinet colleagues to do this, and should not the entire B.E.F. have been sent there, to act on the German flank? If this is true, the strategic concepts that ruled during World War I—with the exception of the Gallipoli expedition—were wrong, and those that ruled in World War II were right. What should be the function of the British Army? Should it be a "projectile fired by the British Navy" from some such flank as Ostend or Gallipoli in World War I, as Portugal in the Napoleonic Wars, or as Egypt and Africa in World War II? Or should it be, as at Blenheim, Ramillies, and Oudenarde in Marlborough's day and at St. Lo in World War II, an integral part of the main battle line? This question is also part of the history of World War I, for throughout the war there were challenges to the policy of building up the battle line in the Western Front. Civilian leaders—called "frocks" from their frock coats—were the "Easterners" who wanted to strike at German might away from the trench lines of the Western Front in France and Flanders. Soldiers—called "brass" from the brass visors of generals' caps—were "Westerners," who demanded that every effort be made to break through on the Western Front.

Here our story has moved ahead of itself. Why was there need of a Western Front? Why had not the Russian steam roller crushed its way into Berlin? The answer is that at Tannenberg, in East Prussia, there occurred another military miracle. The outnumbered German border guard army first surrounded and annihilated one army larger than itself and then flung another larger army back whence it had come. This victory stabilized the battle lines from the Baltic to the Romanian border. Similarly the Western Front was stabilized. After the Aisne came the "race to the sea" in which the B.E.F. was sent to prevent the Germans reaching the Channel. This the B.E.F. did by linking up with the Seventh Division and the remainder of the Belgian army, after desperate fighting. At one moment the Guards Brigade had to hold off the German Imperial Guard Division; at another, cooks and sutlers seized rifles to mend a breach in the line. But the deed was done. However, by the end of the battle now known as First Ypres, the Old Contemptibles were no more. The organizations remained, but losses and the promotions of experienced veterans to higher posts or their assignment to train and stiffen newly formed units meant that the old British Regular Army was scattered. It was to be a different army that would have to fight the years of mass warfare which followed. This was to be a citizen army that would be poured into the trench fighting and slaughter that took place. The effect on England of such an enlistment of her population was to be incalculable.

The unexpected failure of Germany to conquer France according to the "Schlieffen Plan," and then the equally unexpected failure of Russia to conquer Germany by weight of numbers, led to a military stalemate. In the West a trench line from the Alps to the sea caused such a deadlock; in the East, where warfare was somewhat more mobile, there was a sort of balance between German artillery power and Russian manpower. The struggle to break this deadlock upset the entire life of the combatant nations and caused events Grey rightly described as "steps toward social- ism," as both sides were bled white by losses.

World War I became a siege of the Central Powers by the Entente Allies. The besiegers tried, as do all besiegers, to break down the ramparts, to find new forces for the attack, to find new weapons, and by starvation or propaganda to persuade the besieged to surrender. The besieged, on the other hand, tried by sorties to break out, by obstinacy to wear out the enemy, and by persuasion to gain peace. However, World War I was a sort of double siege. If the Allies cut Germany off, Germany cut Russia off. Furthermore, at one crucial moment, Germany almost succeeded in a submarine blockade of Great Britain. In actual fact, both of the sieges were successful, for Russia fell before Germany did.

The first sortie of the Central Powers was diplomatic. In November, 1914, Turkey entered the war, whereupon Great Britain annexed Cyprus and declared a protectorate over Egypt. The Indian army occupied Basra at the mouth of the Euphrates. British troops and the Australian and New Zealand Army Corps (hence the initials A.N.Z.A.C. and word Anzac) garrisoned Egypt. Then in 1915 came the counterstroke, the British at- tempt to force the Dardanelles. This is one of the "ifs" of history. If the attempt to force the Straits with expendable predreadnought battleships had been renewed, Constantinople would have fallen. If troops had been battle-loaded in England, instead of being reloaded into their transports in Egypt, Constantinople would have fallen. If the attack had been made at the isthmus of Bulair or the attack at Anzac Beach had been pressed home by the British general in command—bitterest of all, if H.M.S. *Queen Elizabeth* had not shelled British troops from the key summit and allowed Mustapha Kemal to retake it, Constantinople would have fallen. In such case supplies would have reached Russia, and the Germans would not have taken Warsaw. On the other hand, had those same troops, which on the evacuation of the Gallipoli peninsula violated Greek neutrality by occupying Salonika, committed the same violation six months earlier, aid could have been brought to Serbia, Bulgaria might have been kept from entering the war, and aid could have been pushed to Russia through the

Balkans. As it was, England lost men, prestige, and for a while the services of Winston Churchill, who was ousted from the Cabinet.

Another recruiting of forces was the enlistment of Italy, technically the ally of Germany and Austria, as an active combatant against them. The price paid for this was high, in promises for future grants of territory; the value was slight, for the Italian army spent itself in constant batterings against the seaport of Trieste and was opposed by Austrian troops of Slavic origin, who would have deserted had they been put on the Russian front. Thus 1915 did the Allies little good in the Mediterranean.

On the Western Front little was accomplished, either. The plan of the French Commander, Joffre, was to win by a break-through or by attrition. But break-throughs failed, and attrition wore down the attacker. Here began the great drain on British manpower. Haldane had not been kept as Minister of War because of a foolish outcry against him as too close to Germany—as if it paid to penalize knowledge of the enemy. In his place was put England's great soldier, Lord Kitchener. "K's" immense prestige was put behind recruiting a vast army. First came "K 1," "the First Hundred Thousand," to be followed by the rest of "the New Army." These men, together with France's conscripts, were to be used in a grand effort on the Western Front. To support them came a great effort in munitions, where the former pacifist Lloyd George made his mark. But the only real success of this year of war was the German discovery that submarines could blockade Great Britain; the only countersuccess was won for the Allies by neutral America, since submarine sinkings without warning outraged the conscience of the American people. President Wilson, by tactful but firm diplomacy, forced the Germans to give up this method, and the submarine blockade of the British Isles was given up, since for a submarine to surface to give warning to merchant shipping would be suicidal.

The year 1916 resembled that of 1915. It was marked by blunders and mishaps. The Irish Easter Rebellion showed that the loyalty which Redmond had inspired was lost. The surrender of British troops at Kut-el-Amara in Mesopotamia was another blow to prestige. In France the Germans attacked Verdun, hoping to smash the French army by pinning it to a fort and shelling the troops so pinned. Six months of battering got no results. But the British agreed to relieve pressure on the French by an offensive on the Somme. It cost 50,000 casualties in one day—more than half the numbers of the original B.E.F.—to prove that it was impossible under circumstances of the time to break through a well-defended trench line. At the end of this offensive was wasted England's secret weapon, the tank.

At sea came the only serious German sortie, the Battle of Jutland. In intention this was an attempt to lure the British Grand Fleet into a submarine trap. The trap proved impossible to set, but the High Seas Fleet came out anyway, for inactivity in harbor had begun to rot morale, and Von Scheer dared not countermand his sailing orders. On May 31, the two navies stumbled into contact. When the advance forces of battle cruisers met, superior damage control kept the German battle cruisers afloat when the British blew up. When the battle fleets met, deft deployment allowed Sir John Jellicoe to cut the Germans from their base, just as night fell. But when dawn came the next day, instead of there being another Glorious First of June of annihilation, surpassing that of 1794, not a German ship was to be seen. They had slipped by night through the British destroyer screen. This battle had two effects: a temporary propaganda one, and a permanent naval one. At first, from the greater losses of British battle cruisers, it was believed that Germany had won a major sea battle. But soon it appeared that Jellicoe had accomplished one of his two purposes. Though he had missed the chance of a resounding victory which would have opened the Baltic, he had forced the Germans to give up hope of naval victory. The blockade would go on.

Here certain changes in leadership should be recorded. In 1915 Conservatives and Labor—but not Home Rulers—were taken into the Asquith Cabinet. In 1916 Lord Kitchener was sent to organize the Russian effort. These changes were part of a slow girding of the nation for war and a slow turn from volunteer enlistment to conscription. En route to Russia, however, Kitchener was drowned.

December, 1916, was the month of decision in World War I. In that month were taken the action that eventually settled its outcome. Let us therefore look at Britain's situation—military, naval, and diplomatic. She had built up an unexpectedly large Army. On the Western Front a brilliant South African Brigade, an Indian Division, the Anzac Army Corps, and what eventually became the Canadian army showed the manpower resources the Empire could add to the homeland. But that Army appeared pinned down, whether in France, or on such other fronts as Salonika, Palestine, Mesopotamia, or German East Africa, where yet more dominion and Indian troops were at work. Her Navy had had only one contact with the enemy's fleet. The enemy's submarines had threatened to starve her and had been stopped by American diplomatic intervention more than by naval countermeasures. Diplomatically, hostages for the future had been given. After having gone to war for a matter of honor, Britain, to keep Russia reassured, had signed secret treaties to get Italy into the war, which would prove hard to implement. Furthermore the naval weapon of blockade was being blunted by American diplomatic intervention. American sympathy was essential, for in America, at the cost of Britain's overseas investments, were being purchased the supplies for the costly trench warfare of the Western Front. Whether he so chose or not, President Wilson of the United States, reelected that November on a "He Kept Us Out of War" platform, held the key to victory.

In December, 1916, there came a clean sweep of the Asquith Cabinet. As is related later, the Lloyd George coalition was put in office, determined to win. To the new Foreign Secretary, Arthur Balfour, came a message from Wilson, demanding to know the aims of both sides, that he might then intervene to secure peace. Already Grey, by sincerity, had won the friendship and aid of the American Ambassador, Walter Hines Page. Now Balfour by deftly stating honorable and suitable terms—the restoration of Belgium, the return of Alsace-Lorraine to France—gained Wilson's confidence. At the same time in Germany the two victors of Tannenberg, Hindenburg and Ludendorff, came to practically dictatorial power. They believed that Russia could be conquered by a new mode of land fighting, "infiltration," and that Britain could be brought to her knees by unrestricted submarine warfare. Germany therefore gave Wilson an unsatisfactory answer as to peace terms. In January, 1917, Wilson therefore issued his famous Fourteen Points, in which he stated terms, rather like Balfour's, on which peace should be made. These points mobilized world opinion, eventually serving to inspirit the Entente Allies, to break up the Austrian empire, and to weaken the will to fight of the German people.

Then, when Wilson's hopes of a "peace without victory" were destroyed, submarine sinkings drove America toward war. As a filibuster in the United States Senate was preventing the arming of American merchantmen, what has been called the German siege of Russia had effect. The first Russian revolution of 1917 made Russia a republic, and Wilson was able to add to his already-drafted war message the statement that this was a war to "save democracy." American aid might now balance the crippling of Russia and the bleeding white of France. To get that aid Balfour was sent to the United States. He persuaded the President and Congress to create a conscript army and to mobilize industry immediately and not delay as Britain had done.

The German submarine offensive came very close to winning the war. Great Britain was down to a dangerous margin of food and to a dangerous margin of shipping with which to carry munitions and food. But reinforcements of American destroyers to the antisubmarine squadrons and the decision to convoy merchant ships saved the day. American naval doctrine holds that this decision to convoy was brought about by Admiral William Sims, U.S.N., who was immediately admitted to the secrets of the Admiralty and practically sat in council as an extra sea lord. British naval doctrine holds that the decision had already been made. Whatever the cause, convoying stopped the submarine menace. Furthermore, now that America was in the war, the Ministry of Economic Warfare could inflict a strangling blockade on Germany.

But though the war was thus saved at sea, on land three disasters occurred, in France, Russia, and Italy. A tremendous French offensive failed so utterly that the French army mutinied. Here the future Marshal Pétain, by his restoration of morale, gained the immense prestige that later in 1940 put him at the head of France. To counterbalance the disaster Sir Douglas Haig, who in 1915 had replaced Sir John French as Commander in Chief in France, mounted heavy attacks at Third Ypres, to put pressure on the Germans and capture submarine bases on the Flanders coast. This move cost Britain many casualties and failed of its objectives.

Two diplomatic events of November, 1917, should be noted here—the Lansdowne letter and the Balfour Declaration. When Lord Lansdowne sent to the *Daily Telegraph* a letter suggesting that Britain state minimum peace terms, it roused a storm of protest. Though, as is now known, this was an officially sponsored attempt to arouse defeatism in Germany, public opinion considered it defeatism on the part of Lord Lansdowne and piled scorn upon him. The Balfour Declaration was a guarded statement pledging that among Britain's war aims would be the creation of a Jewish national home in Palestine. The eventual results of this were a British mandate over Palestine and the foundation of the republic of Israel; the immediate result was to win world Jewry to the side of the Allies.

Meanwhile, in Russia, the Germans struck. They sent in subversives, the Communists Lenin and Trotsky, to undermine the new Russian republic. That sealed train, hurried from Switzerland to Russia, changed world history more than the German High Command realized. Then "infiltration," new tactics for breaking through trenches, finished the job. Despite the valor of her troops, Russia collapsed, and after the October Revolution of 1917, in 1918 Lenin and Trotsky signed the Treaty of Brest Litovsk. Then infiltration and treason were turned on Italy. A German surprise attack from the Alps, at Caporetto, aided by treason at a key post, drove the Italian army from its attacks toward Trieste. Only great valor on the part of certain Italian units, and the sending of French and British aid—the latter under General Plumer—kept Italy in the war, by holding the line of the Piave River.

Out of these disasters came one advance. Unity of allied command was yet to come, but the French general Ferdinand Foch was made a sort of roving chief of staff. Furthermore, the British, after shortening the lines of the Ypres salient, developed their own methods of infiltration, using tanks effectively for the first time at Cambrai. Furthermore, successes in Palestine, where Allenby took Jerusalem, and in Mesopotamia, where Maude took Baghdad, brightened the picture. But now it was a race between American manpower and German infiltration. Could American reinforcements come in time to save France from being overrun as had been Russia and a part of Italy?

In the spring of 1918 came the final thrust. The German attack on the British Fifth Army nearly broke through. There was one moment when —it was later remembered—Marshal Pétain lost hope but yielded to the higher faith of the Frenchmen Clemenceau and Foch, and the Britishers Haig and War Secretary Lord Milner. This was the Doullens interview, to decide whether to let the Germans break through to the Channel or to try to keep the Allied line intact. At this interview Foch was transformed from a coordinator to a real commander in chief. Trusting that American reinforcements would come in time, he threw every man available into the fight.

Doullens marked the end. German infiltration was stopped at Amiens. Other assaults were stopped. The tide turned. French, English, and a growing number of Americans came to the counterattack. Haig, who had always stubbornly held to pressing on, in the slaughters of the Somme and Third Ypres, now stubbornly insisted that victory within the year was possible. He was right. In August, 1918, Ludendorff admitted defeat was inevitable. In September and October, 1918, the English, as their part of a coordinated advance, won a battle not known by the name of a town or the number of times it had been assaulted, such as First, Second, or Third Ypres, but as the Battle of the Rivers, since so many rivers were crossed. That victory and the parallel victories of the French and Americans cracked the will to fight of the German rulers. The winged words Woodrow Wilson had spoken in January, 1918, his Fourteen Points for a just peace—an amplification of the proposals of the British in December, 1916—formed to the mind of the German Reichstag a justification for forcing out the Kaiser. Simultaneous advances of the army pinned for so long in Salonika, the army at Jerusalem, and the Italians driving first Bulgaria, then Turkey, then Austria, to surrender, had made the armistice of November 11, 1918, seem inevitable. "Cease fire" was sounded as the British fought their way back to Mons, where they had started the war on land. Meanwhile a mutiny at Kiel had broken the German navy. At last the siege of the Central Powers had ended.

Such was the military course of World War I, full of effects on Britain, full of lessons for her future conduct in another war. But that was not the only story of the fighting. What have been set down here have been policy decisions. No picture of the war and the effects of the fighting is complete, or anything but unbalanced, without telling of the sacrifice made for victory. England came close to being bled white. A mere look at the battle honors awarded to English regiments, in four years doubling those given from 1685 to 1914, may suggest the amount of fighting. The expansion of regiments may hint at it, too. The King's Royal Rifle Corps grew from four regular battalions to sixteen that saw combat. The Guards Brigade had added to it a new regiment, the Welsh Guards, and expanded into an army corps. The Colonel of the Manchester regiment could estimate he had had 50,000 men under his nominal command. These men had suffered heavily, the highest casualty rates, except for the incredible rate of the twice-wiped-out South African Brigade, being those of the English county regiments. Nor were these casualties spread out over a long time; when they came they came horribly fast, so that it was estimated that the length of life of a subaltern officer of infantry in the Battle of the Somme was three days. In quality of sacrifice, too, England paid bitterly. Her Army was a volunteer one at first, and her best died that others might learn how to fight. Since men of the upper classes had had a chance to demonstrate their merits early in life, something of what England lost in leadership is known. Killed in action was Raymond Asquith, who promised to be of a stature fully worthy of his Prime Minister father. In hospital Julian Grenfell died of wounds. In one and the same week Grenfell had written the inspiring poem "Into Battle" and had outboxed and knocked out the heavyweight champion of the British Army. What might not such a man have done in the years to come? Wasted on a useless local attack was Gilbert Talbot, whose religious movement, Toc H, lives after him, trying to do in peacetime in the Church of England what his Talbot House did as religious inspiration to the men who were under fire. The list of the might-have-beens can stretch out long. In it would be Mark Hovell, the historian, whose insight opened out understanding of Chartism and what it meant; Rupert Brooke, the poet; and Auberon Herbert, Lord Lucas, who had become president of the Board of Agriculture before he joined the Royal Flying Corps. In this list, too, should be Captain William Redmond, John Redmond's brother, dying in the arms of an Ulsterman, as the Ulster and Irish divisions charged side by side. Here was a man who might have kept Ireland united.

And if there was such known ability lost, what of the unknown ability, the men who would have come to the top in less fortunate classes, equally poured out in this sacrifice of the best? Would England recover from the loss of her best stock? Those were questions the English began to ask as the bugles blew "cease fire" on November 11, 1918, and the answers they gave to those questions showed in their World War II policy.

43

POLITICS, ECONOMICS, AND SOCIETY

1914–1918

POLITICS, CONSTITUTION, AND DOMINIONS, 1914–1918

During World War I political events, constitutional changes, and happenings in India and the dominions were closely linked. Political events, especially the formation of the Lloyd George coalition Cabinet, led to two great constitutional changes: a new organization for the Cabinet, and the decay of the once powerful Liberal party. Dominion events led to two more constitutional changes: the creation of an Empire executive, and the new status of the dominions as the equals of independent nations. Therefore it seems natural to consider these things together, rather than separately.

In constitutional theory, the entire Empire—not only the United Kingdom of Great Britain and Ireland but "the dominions thereunto belonging"—went to war on August 4, 1914, by the single executive action of King George V, for which his British ministers were responsible. In actual fact this was largely true. In the Parliament at Westminster John Redmond deftly and nobly pledged that the Irish Volunteers would defend Ireland's coast and free British troops for overseas service. He added that he expected the Ulster Defense Force to act the same way. This offer of help from the illegal Irish forces that had been threatening to fight each other in civil war was tantamount to a recruiting appeal and was treated as such. Carson himself led the Ulster Defense Force to the Belfast recruiting station. Ireland, North and South, except for a few extremists like the Sinn Feiner Arthur Griffith, was back of the war. Similarly in England only such Liberals as Lord Morley and John Burns and such Labor extremists as Ramsay MacDonald protested against the war. Later on, Griffith and MacDonald would gain prestige and power from their consistency. At the time what stood out was national union. Similarly overseas, with one exception, support was quick and enthusiastic. Princes and people of India in a surge of enthusiasm offered help, which should have been accepted as a matter of morale. Canada, Australia, and New Zealand mobilized forces and sent them to war. Only in South Africa, where hatreds of the Boer War had not been fully assuaged and where the German colony of Southwest Africa formed a danger point, was there trouble. There Maritz and General De Wet rebelled. But the rebellion was speedily put down by the wisdom of Premier Louis Botha, who called out Boer commandos to deal with what he kept a family affair and who used the mobility of the automobile to catch mounted riflemen. The colonies, too, offered their share of help. There appeared, gloriously, the same sort of voluntary cooperation whose emergence in 1756 had made Pitt's name famous, but it was manifested to a far greater degree.

Then, when war settled down, rifts began to appear. First was a piece of parliamentary business. If Home Rule and Welsh Disestablishment were to get onto the statute books over the Lords' veto, Commons had to pass them a third time. This was done in September, 1914, amid violent expressions of anger from the Conservatives, even though suspensory acts were passed at the same time, making these two measures ineffective till the war should end and for six months thereafter. But this was a temporary storm. The great political and constitutional changes came not in 1914 but in 1915 and especially in 1916. In 1915 the Dardanelles failure and the explosive resignation of First Sea Lord Lord Fisher caused a Cabinet shuffle. Some Liberals went out, including Lord Chancellor Lord Haldane; some Conservatives came in, including their leader Bonar Law and Balfour. Now the Committee of Imperial Defense rose in importance. It had been set up in 1904 by Balfour as an informal advisory body, whose very power would come from its being advisory with a flexible membership. From the start of the war the existence of the Committee made it possible to take Opposition leaders, notably Balfour, into the heart of affairs. The fact that the Committee kept full records meant that in its hands lay the information needed to get results. Three sets of results were urgently needed—more shells, more men, and a strategic plan. The shells and men were the demands of the commander in chief in France, Field Marshal French. The plan was the demand of the men at home who did not trust French. The leader of those providing the shells and demanding the plan was David Lloyd George, who had in the May, 1915, crisis moved from the Exchequer to the newly created Ministry of Munitions. He and Asquith were of opposite tendencies and personalities. An observer said of them what is much quoted: "Asquith has all the qualities of a great prime minister except resolution; Lloyd George none of them, except resolution." Constant struggles took place, Asquith standing for cohesion in the government and Lloyd George for getting on with the war. First Lloyd George secured what all sadly wanted, the replacement of French as Commander in Chief. But in his place went not a man of Lloyd George's temperament but the simple Douglas Haig. Then came the two crises of April, 1916: the coal strike, and the Easter Rebellion in Ireland.

The coal strike of Clyde and South Wales was a disaster that did not happen, but a rehearsal for future trouble. In April a strike was threatened. Asquith seemed flabby in his plans for it, both to Lloyd George and to Bonar Law. Law took the extreme step of entering into communication with King George V, to plan for eventualities if a parliamentary vote should drive Asquith from office. However, Lloyd George settled the strike by simple direct appeals.

The Easter Rebellion in Ireland was another matter. Irish extremists, the Irish Republican Army which had been left over from the Fenians of the 1860's and the Invincibles of the 1880's, tried to seize Dublin in concert with the landing of arms from Germany. The revolt was put down, with outrages on both sides. Then the situation was bungled. Asquith took responsibility by going over to Ireland, interviewed the prisoners, and showed by his behavior that he intended to be lenient. That was no way to treat single-hearted, realistic, idealist revolutionaries. They saw he could be pushed, which gave them confidence. He offered immediate Home Rule and then sent Lloyd George over to quibble about how it would come. The conclusion the Irish drew was natural; only the forceful methods of Ulster would get results. This conclusion doomed Redmond's Nationalist party. Two years later, in 1918, in Great Britain's greatest peril, Ireland was ripe for revolt and had to be under martial law. So the Easter Rebellion, which might have been treated as a misguided and rather shameful aid to Prussianism, became the rallying point of Irish national pride.

To carry further the story of what happened in Ireland, all that need be done is to list English mistakes. Lloyd George's offer in 1916 of immediate Home Rule fell through because he made what were interpreted as contradictory promises to Ulster and to the Home Rulers. One was to exclude Ulster permanently; the other was to force Ulster to join the rest of Ireland after a temporary delay. In 1917 an Irish Convention was summoned. It failed because of more contradictory promises, which led the Ulster members to refuse assent to the Convention's proposals. Meanwhile the men of the Easter Rebellion captured the imagination of the land. Above all Eamon De Valera stood out, as the personification of the movement for Irish independence. This became evident when John Redmond's brother, William, was killed in battle and De Valera stood for the vacancy to Parliament and won it. Redmond died early in 1918, before England's last bungle, which was to apply conscription to Ireland and then withdraw it before united Irish opposition. Now was the time for Sinn Fein to take over, according to Griffith's plans, and Griffith reissued his program of action and built up the organization that, within three years, was to gain most of Ireland not Home Rule but dominion status.

Bungling did not take place in Ireland alone. The attempt to have conscription and yet not have it, by a national registration, failed. In 1916, when some Liberals—notably Sir John Simon, the Home Secretary—left the Cabinet the Conscription Act was passed. Yet this was not enough. Mutterings in and out of Parliament mounted.

In November defections appeared in House of Commons votes. The "press lords" took a hand. Lord Northcliffe, owner of *The Times,* and Sir Max Aitken (later Lord Beaverbrook), owner of the *Daily Mail,* brought together Bonar Law and Lloyd George. Finally Lloyd George struck. He demanded that Asquith turn over to him the chairmanship of a war committee in the Cabinet, which should get things done. Asquith at first tended to believe something could be worked out but then stood on his primacy as Prime Minister. Then the fat was in the fire. All agreed that Lloyd George with his driving energy was essential. The King therefore called a conference at Buckingham Palace, to concert measures. The Conference decided that if Bonar Law could not form a Cabinet in which Asquith would serve under him, Lloyd George would try. Asquith and his friends refused. Then Lloyd George got a group together, mostly of Conservatives but with a large minority of Liberals who were not so closely tied to Asquith.

This coalition Government acted speedily and effectively. As has been related, it brought a new tempo to the war. More than that, it accomplished two things: it reformed the Cabinet, and it gave the Liberal party a blow from which it has never recovered. The reform in the Cabinet was first of all to take over the machinery of the Committee of Imperial Defense, even to the services of Sir Maurice Hankey, its Secretary. A small War Cabinet ran the war, much as Pitt had done as Secretary of State in the 1750's, much as Churchill would do as Minister of Defense—with the same machinery, even to Hankey's services—in the 1940's. To this new small Cabinet, Lloyd George made a significant addition. Theoretically it is not necessary for a Cabinet member to belong to either House of Parliament; all that is necessary is that he be a Privy Councilor. There have been occasions, either when a man is seeking election to Commons or when he is about to receive a peerage, when he has remained in the Cabinet outside Parliament. Now Lloyd George gave a new twist to this. Dominions Ministers when in London were summoned to the War Cabinet, which thus became a central Empire Executive, the Imperial Cabinet. Borden of Canada, Hughes of Australia, and Botha and Smuts of South Africa were thus kept in touch with things from the center. Indeed, Smuts proved himself so useful that he stayed in England as part of the War Cabinet. Here was a constitutional development that would be abused and discredited in the early 1920's and of great value in the 1940's when, for example, Fraser of New Zealand would for months join in the work of the Churchill Cabinet.

At roughly the same time as these developments in England, in Australia and Canada there were Cabinet upheavals. In Australia Labor, though willing to fight, refused to grant conscription. From this there arose a curious political situation. Prime Minister W. M. Hughes left his party and formed a coalition government. But though his government could carry on, it could not get the Australian voters, to whom the issue was submitted in two referenda, to grant conscription. Here was Australia showing, in the midst of valiant support of the war effort, a new nationalism.

A somewhat similar situation arose in Canada. There, too, a coalition government was formed. This time the objection to conscription came from the French Canadians, harder hit by it than would be the city dwellers or the large-scale farmers of the West. A complex of motives caused this resistance. Some were economic, for conscription would hit the peasant life hard, calling needed young men from tiny farms. Some were social, for fear this would disrupt their way of life. Much was part of the particularism of Quebec, that central feature in Canadian life. But conscription was put through.

In India, at first there was a burst of loyalty. Almost all groups, from the Princes to the Nationalists, supported the war. But as time wore on, opposition mounted. Finally Lloyd George determined to win Indian support by granting a large measure of self-government. The War Cabinet issued a promise of "eventual dominion status." The unusual step was taken of sending the new Indian Secretary, Edwin Montagu, to India. As will be told in a later chapter, he brought into being, by the Montagu-Chelmsford reforms, an Indian electorate with real political power and thus started the Indian Empire on the road it took to become the Dominion of Pakistan and the Republic of India.

Throughout the Empire, the war had one result; it increased bureaucratic powers. Particularly was this true in England, where the Defense of the Realm Act, which gave the effect of law to "Orders in Council," allowed the government to regulate life in many ways. "Dora"—the initials D.O.R.A. suggested the thought—became conceived of as a meddling aunt, who took the fun out of life. For that lady gave a blow to traditional English liberty from state interference from which it has never recovered. She did much to bring in the welfare state, too, with its highly arguable advantages and disadvantages.

Vigorous as the Lloyd George Government might be, it was not immune to criticisms. In 1918 the Lloyd George–Haig feud came to the point at which Lloyd George made what many thought a misstatement of fact as to the number of troops in France. He was challenged to a vote of confidence, the so-called Maurice motion. Against him were 106 Liberals. Lloyd George stayed in office and marked his foes for destruction.

Then, when the war ended, Lloyd George called an immediate election, against George V's protests, and issued a list of the members of Parliament who had been faithful to him. That doomed his opponents, even Asquith being driven from the House of Commons. It also made Lloyd George the prisoner of the Conservatives.

To attempt a summary, then, these appear to have been the political and constitutional results of World War I: It made the Cabinet more effective through Lloyd George's reforms. It highlighted the residual power of the Crown to solve deadlocks in Cabinet making. It gave the bureaucrats great power. It showed the possibility of executive cooperation in the Empire. And it imbued the dominions with a feeling of their position as equal nations rather than dependencies. In short, the war marks the transition from nineteenth-century Great Britain and her dependencies to twentieth-century Great Britain as part of the Commonwealth of Nations.

ECONOMICS, 1914–1919

Failure of men, of plans, and of material and misdirections of both men and weapons make the battle chaos called "the fog of war." Once World War I had failed to come to a speedy end, an economic "fog of war" settled down over Great Britain. Men had no practical experience to go by. For a century minor wars had been paid for out of revenue or by relatively small loan issues. Great Britain had to go back to the Napoleonic Wars for an example of going into debt for national survival. Though modern weapons had come into existence, they had never been used on the scale which became customary. On an average the artillery in France shot in four days more shells than had been used in the entire Boer War. Trench warfare required the use of sandbags at the rate of six million a month. Never before had the British Isles been subjected to blockade as they were under the German submarine campaigns. Here were problems where new solutions had to be found, where grit and imagination must be the guide rather than traditional wisdom.

The first economic problem was the dislocation of currency and exchange. This was met by a short debt moratorium and the issuance of pound notes bearing the name of Sir John Bradbury, Secretary to the Treasury, hence the nickname of a "Bradbury" for a pound. This in fact ended the use of gold coinage in Great Britain, but preserved London's vital position as a world money market. The greater economic problem was to find means of payment for war costs. With this, three Chancellors of the Exchequer wrestled: Lloyd George until 1915, when he became Minister of Munitions; Reginald McKenna from then till he stuck by

Asquith when the Lloyd George Coalition was formed in December, 1916; and thereafter, Bonar Law. Each followed the same general policy of trying to raise enough by taxation to meet ordinary expenses and the interest on the fast-mounting national debt. All found that estimates of expenses always fell short of actual disbursements and that taxation must be piled higher and higher. Of the three, McKenna was the most revolutionary, for it was his McKenna duties, imposed to conserve exchange by preventing imports, which breached the traditional free-trade policy to which his Liberal party pinned its faith.

Figures may show the extent of this financial problem. Total war costs were £9,593,000,000, of which only 28 per cent or 2,733 million was raised by taxes, the remaining 72 per cent being raised by loans and bond issues. Lloyd George's budget for 1914 and Bonar Law's for 1918 are shown for comparison in the accompanying table. By the end of the war the average outlay per day was 8 million pounds. Taxes on spirits and wine went up to 50 per cent. The income tax of 3s. in the pound of August, 1914, reached 6s. by November, 1918, and reached down to lower income levels in the hitherto untouched working class. Corporations paid an excess-profits tax of 80 per cent. By the time McKenna had finished his work, indirect taxes hit not only luxury items like furs and motorcars, but also sugar, flour, and tobacco.

BUDGETS

(In millions of pounds)

1914, November

Ordinary expenditures	£207	Revenue	£211
War expenditures	328	Borrowed	324
	£535		£535

1918, April

Ordinary expenditures	£422	Revenue	£842
War expenditures	2,550	Borrowed	2,130
	£2,972		£2,972

This heavy financial burden affected Britain's world position. British overseas investments were sold to obtain exchange wherewith to pay for munitions. Thus ownership of certain American railways passed from foreign to native capitalists. Indeed, when, in 1917, the United States entered the war, Britain was dangerously close to the end of her financial resources. It was American money that, in July, 1917, saved the day by preventing "a financial disaster that would be worse than defeat in the field," to quote Balfour. The sums asked were provided, and the flow of munitions was kept steady.

Here a word should be said of interallied loans, from America to Great

Britain and from Great Britain to other allies. Great Britain did borrow 4,600 million dollars from the United States. On the other hand, she lent £1,500,000 to her allies; no matter how low the pound sank, that was a larger sum than she borrowed. She did not expect repayment in full. Money had been advanced as loans, not subsidies, to enable her to control expenditure, for in past centuries she had had unhappy results with the direct-subsidy policy. What she borrowed from the United States was largely spent in the United States and caused prosperity there. Furthermore her leaders believed that if war debts were largely remitted, it would be money well spent in reviving the European market. These facts may serve to explain the postwar British attitude to war debts.

It is true that there was a bright side to the effect of the war on overseas investments. Some, such as Anglo-Iranian oil, did become more profitable because of war orders. On the balance, however, because of World War I Britain lost her position of world predominance, though she remained the leader in insurance, shipping, and the handling of exchange. To survive as a nation she had to take a different and lower place in the world economy.

Internally, Britain's war burdens altered her social and economic structure. There was a redistribution of income throughout the nation. Those living on fixed incomes were struck by increased taxation, in the form of the doubled income tax and the addition to it of the progressive supertax on incomes in any degree larger than the taxable minimum. They were also hit by the increased cost of living, which rose to 220 on the base of 1914 as 100. On the other hand, war needs created full employment, and wages rose along with—though behind—the cost of living, so that real wages remained at about 89 or 91 per cent of the 1914 level. Though there were war profiteers, the result of the war was a social leveling down of the upper classes, up of the lower.

Furthermore, there was a reorganization of the economy, caused by the fact that the British Isles were blockaded. More food had to be raised. It was. Pressure was put to increase the farm labor force and the area under cultivation. Thus the Ministry of Agriculture gained increased power. Munitions had to be produced more efficiently. That need led to the creation of an unhappy Ministry of National Service, where the Mayor of Birmingham, Neville Chamberlain, found himself squeezed among political pressures as he tried to sort out those who would be most useful at the front from those who could serve best at home. Above all, when shipping became precious, central control was essential. Here was the great part played by Sir Arthur Salter and the Allied Shipping Control. During the existence of the convoy system this body, by the allocation of tonnage, became the economic master of Britain and accomplished much in the correct choice of economic effort toward victory. Then, the moment its power of allocation ended, its powers ceased. But its results remained, as a lesson of what intelligent central control could achieve.

To sum up the economic history of Britain, there is perhaps no more telling sentence than the one Grey spoke on August 4, 1914. "This," said he, "is the greatest single step towards Socialism ever taken." For to win the war, the state had to intervene—and it got the habit.

SOCIETY, 1914–1918

On August 4, 1914, the people of Great Britain and the Empire were totally unprepared for war. They were thinking about cricket, as the German embassy had recently reported back to Berlin, and about the Irish problem. When war came, in spite of the issuance of a spate of regulations, "Business as usual" was the cry. It took the shock of the Marne to make the public realize that "there was a war on." At that, at first there was much wishful thinking about how soon it would be over. An exemplification of this was the wild rumor that Russian troops were passing secretly through Britain. Then, too, there was hysteria over allegations of German atrocities in Belgium, most of which were unfounded. The only man to expect a long war was Lord Kitchener. Probably only his immense prestige and authority could have persuaded the English people to accept his plans for such a war. For the average Briton not until 1915 did the truth of "K's" warning fully sink in. But then it struck home in many ways.

In spite of the fact that strikes and higher wages that were granted as a result of the strikes might hold up production of war material, workers used the war, not only to improve their political and economic position, but also to press forward their political platform of socialism. At one time 120,000 Welsh miners were out on strike. The T.U.C. in 1916 used the war and the government regulation of railways as an argument for the nationalization of railways and government seizure of basic industries, thereby abolishing unemployment. From the report of the Whitley Commission of 1917 came a recommendation for the conduct of business in a more democratic manner. From problems faced by workers in factories, as well as management, under the high tension of long hours and the extreme conditions of war manufacture, both labor and management had to give in and adjust to new policies of dealing with each other. The Whitley Report recommended that each factory be run by a council representing management and labor. The workers were to be consulted and were to cooperate with management rather than resort to strikes and lockouts, as had been the case before the war started. It is generally agreed that long hours and nervous and physical fatigue were what brought about a widespread strike in the engineering industries in 1917. The most important outcomes of this strike, that was quickly settled after the strike had relieved pressure caused by pent-up emotions, was the appearance of shop stewards. These shop stewards were new to the industrial scene, and they became a permanent feature of postwar labor-management relations. Many of them were Communists who had no regard for preserving industrial democracy or for helping workers and management reach an amicable agreement. The mass of workers in England supported the war first in a rather nervous and emotional manner. Later on they carried on with emotion and the grim determination that had always seen the British peoples through the most intense struggles.

When it became obvious in 1915 that the war would be unprecedented in the cost of lives and money, all classes had to take a new view of their condition. Rich man and poor man served side by side in the ranks. The country gentleman and his tenant shared a common grave in Flanders or at the bottom of the Atlantic. At home people, regardless of their privileged or unprivileged social status, who could do things necessary to promote the war were given place and position. What caste lines had previously existed were now thrown down, and a united effort temporarily was made with one goal, that of sudden victory, replacing other personal or class goals.

The women, who had previously played little part in public life, now in hundreds of thousands came out of the home and went into shop, factory, and management. In uniform women were to be found in the WAAC's, WRN's, and WRAF's. Women as clerks, managers of shops, and workers in positions heretofore reserved for men distinguished themselves by their devotion, capacity, and downright enthusiasm. Obviously the social pattern of British life had been shattered. Women had proved their right not only to be given the ballot but also to occupy a much larger and more important position in the economic world.

The support of women for the war effort played another important and vital role. Hundreds of men found that they could receive the social approval of their girls only if they were in uniform. Women at home poured scorn on men who were at home and not in uniform. Not only for the sake of proper utilization of manpower, but also to save face, arm bands and deferment cards had to be issued to those men who were not in uniform.

Only 2 per cent of the working force was unemployed in the spring of 1914. Before the end of 1915 there was no unemployment in England. As everyone had expected, the rising costs of war were accompanied by rising salaries. When the nation was fighting for its life, the government did not quibble about salaries paid to the individual. As the women came from their homes to the shops and factories, they demanded and received a higher wage than those working in similar occupations had received in 1913. The increased war cost, due to demand, brought in higher profits to the manufacturer. As has been seen above, many of those profits were taken back by the state in the form of excess-profits taxes. But throughout the war the rising cost of living was met by increased wages. Thus, the working class came out of the war with higher wages and an increased standard of living that came from these wages. To the surprise of everyone, during the first two and a half years of war there was a vast amount of consumers' goods available on the open market. As workers made more money, they could invest in interest-bearing bonds and could purchase consumers' goods even when these goods had increased in price. Therefore, with no unemployment and with good wages that kept pace with rise of living costs, the years of the war were far from uncomfortable for the working class.

Austere critics observed testily that the workingman had forsaken his traditional tipple, beer, and used his increased wages to buy more gin, whiskey, and champagne than he had previously been accustomed to purchase. During the war attendance at theaters and cinemas became a feature of the new and high-pressure way of living. Soldiers home on leave wanted to see musical comedies and dance. The popular musical *Chu Chin Chow* played to packed houses in London for years. Charlie Chaplin, the great Anglo-American movie comedian, was as well known as Lloyd George. Everywhere people of all classes, with money to spend in their pockets, turned from the more sober pleasures to those that provided quick and cheap thrills. With the appearance of women in industry and in the shops, there was a great opportunity for freer social conduct. It was said that morals became much looser than they had been before the war, simply because soldiers, girls, and workers were bent upon living a full life in a very few days or hours. This increase of nervous gaiety on the part of the British people was one of the most notable changes in the social scene of the twentieth century. Certainly the peace, order, and deliberateness of prewar days disappeared almost completely.

The extent to which the population of Great Britain was upset by the war may be illustrated by the statistics in the accompanying table. It will be noted that an extremely high percentage of men and women of employment and military age groups were used for military purposes.

When the Armistice was signed on November 11, 1918, the people of the Empire gave way to a hysterical and emotional outburst of celebration. No similar celebration expressed such pent-up emotion and downright happiness at the end of any other period of hostilities. The masses, however, in 1918 had become embittered, tired, and disillusioned with war and everything about it. A hatred had been born in their minds of their enemies, and although they had displayed great courage and determination in winning, their fatigue, hatred, and skepticism were to constitute one of the determining factors in the new world—and a world presumably made safe for democracy.

MOBILIZATION OF MANPOWER IN 1918
(Men 16–64; women 14–59)

	Men		Women		Total	
	Millions	Per cent	Millions	Per cent	Millions	Per cent
Armed forces and civil defense	4.60	34.1	0.10	0.7	4.70	16.9
Group I industries *	2.12	15.7	0.91	6.3	3.03	10.9
Group II industries †	3.05	22.6	0.70	4.9	3.75	13.5
Group III industries and nonindustrial population ‡	3.72	27.6	12.64	88.1	16.36	58.7
Total	13.49	100.0	14.35	100.0	27.84	100.0

* Group I covers metal manufacture, engineering, motors, aircraft and other vehicles, shipbuilding and ship repairing, metal-goods manufacture, chemicals, explosives, oils, etc.

† Group II covers agriculture, mining, national and local government services, gas, water and electricity supply, transport and shipping.

‡ Group III covers food, drink and tobacco, textiles, clothing and other manufactures, building and distribution trades, commerce, banking, etc.

SOURCE: Ministry of Labor.

INTRODUCTION

Few there were who did not expect that mankind was about to enter upon a period of peace and good will when the news of the November 11, 1918, Armistice was flashed around the world. After all, the Allies had fought to make the world safe for democracy. Surely the sacrifices made by the Allies and the subjects of King George V in blood and treasure had not been made in vain. Time and the turn of world's events were to disillusion the hopeful. Twenty years after the Versailles Conference, a war even more terrible than that of 1914 to 1918 nearly shattered what was left of civilization. Instead of peace and reorganization, the post–World War I period was twenty years of chaos, disorganization, and disappointment, relieved occasionally by the bright promise of good will or noble achievements. For the British Empire it was a time of reorganization and adjustment to new ways of life.

Politicians promised the returning veteran that the grateful nation would give him a job and a home fit for a hero such as he was. In order to fulfill this promise, the economic health of the Empire had to be as good as—in fact, much better than—it had been in 1914. National burdens of debt had shot up into the stratosphere. Taxes were high, and costs were out of reason, if comparison with prewar "normal" times was made. The whole question of resumption of "normal" ways of life depended upon the ability of Great Britain and the empire to exchange goods and services with other nations. It had to be done in such a way that war-incurred burdens could be shouldered without breaking down the economic framework that had been strained for four years.

Twenty years' struggle to gain prewar prosperity ended in failure. The British kept their chins up, worked hard, and tried to meet unprecedented economic conditions sensibly and turn out profits. But the world situation did not permit too much success. Before 1914 Great Britain had been a trading and manufacturing power, sending her goods and services to the whole world. It was impossible to do this in the two decades following the Versailles conference. In Europe former markets were closed either by high tariffs, imposed by nations that wanted to develop their own industries, or by lack of goods and money to exchange and buy where previously there had been British markets. In the New World, the United States built new tariff walls that kept British goods from the best potential market of the postwar world. In the dominions nationalist policies, as in Canada and South Africa, favored local industries or trading with rival nations that had goods that the dominion wanted. Italian locomotives were taken in exchange for South African beef. Japanese cotton goods were cheaper in India than Lancashire-spun cotton and were much preferred to it. Markets in East Asia and the Near East were invaded by Italians, Japanese, and Americans who sometimes could beat the British at their game of cheap production and distribution. Without the trade and profits of world business, the old system of manufacturing and trading broke down in Great Britain.

The major profit-making industries of cotton, shipping, coal, and iron became depressed and money-losing activities after 1919. When these big businesses fell, millions were unemployed through no fault of their own or even of their employers. World business depression hit rich and poor, laborer and employer alike. The answer of Great Britain to the economic catastrophe, particularly after the severe slump of 1929 to 1931, was to reduce expenses, turn to the development of new industries and enterprises, and pay more taxes. By meeting the economic blizzard of the late twenties and early thirties head on, the British were able to recover from the shock of the depression before other major industrial powers. To do this, Great Britain abandoned the economic policy of *laissez faire* for one of protection. She paid dearly through the pockets of the middle and upper classes for survival. In the end, a new industrial and economic system was in the process of completion when World War II stopped it.

At the council tables of Versailles the dominions and India were seated as states with equal privileges and rights with those of the mother country. As it was said, they were "daughters in their mother's house, but mistresses in their own." Each dominion, and later the Irish Free State, was recognized to be free to speak and act for itself. With the Irish exception, the dominions cooperated by and large through the twenty years whenever it was possible. Their status was defined in a formula written by Lord Balfour in 1926 and made part of the British constitution in the Statute of Westminster, 1931. India was the scene of the struggle of the nationalist Congress party, personified by Gandhi, to win virtual independence. Attempts at dual government in India were not successful. World War II found India strong enough to stand apart from the fight almost as long as nationalist leaders wished. At the same time the Irish Free State, or Eire, remained neutral under guarantee of treaties recognizing her fundamental right to stand apart from the fight for survival of Western civilization. New conditions, therefore, led to new relations between dominion and mother country. But the real test of unity was given on the field of battle when for the second time the British overseas made the King's cause their own.

In Great Britain the turmoil in the twenty years of disruption and depression was reflected in the powerful upsurges of economic and social unrest. A symbol of a new age coming on the political world was the decline of the Liberal party and the rise of the Labor party. The Liberals had been preeminently the party of business, *laissez faire,* and progress. Its platform had only recently turned toward socialization as the way to get progress and reform. It was the middle-class strength that upheld the Liberals in alliance with the politically undeveloped Labor party. After the war the leadership of the party split in Parliament, and the party organization split with it. Then, too, the Liberals ceased to talk a language that meant much to the average voter. The Labor party started to talk such a language.

Coming out of the war with little or no war-caused stigmas such as were attached to the older parties, the Labor party could put forth its platform of domestic reforms that, in the main, emphasized the protection of job, home, and health by the state. Socialism—thorough socialism, not the piecemeal prewar Liberal kind—was the source of the Labor party's success with the voters. Women were enfranchised—the wives of the workers in 1918, and the shop girls in 1928. Labor platforms seemed to make sense to the laborer and the middle-class man of small means who felt the need for job security and extended state protection of health and life. The first Labor Ministry, that of J. Ramsay MacDonald, sat briefly in 1924. A second Labor Government 1929 to 1931 turned itself into a "National" government in alliance with Conservatives and Liberals when the pressure of the economic crisis was too great for it to carry alone. Depression and fear robbed Labor of much popular support between 1929 and 1939. The end of the period found Labor a weak opposition party in a Parliament dominated by the Conservatives.

If the "National" government of MacDonald from 1931 to 1935 and the postwar coalition of Lloyd George are counted as Conservative-controlled governments, the Conservatives were in power seventeen of the twenty years between two wars. It was Baldwin and Chamberlain who made the errors in judgment or the shrewd decisions that carried the nation through to promises of stable domestic economic and social security. The General Strike of 1926 and the abdication of King Edward VIII, each in its own way, were crises of first magnitude that were met and handled well. Facing facts turned the Conservatives into socialists; for example, their record in building homes for workers is good. They were able to persuade the upper classes and the commercial world to tighten belts when lean times came to business. They rode over the schemes of the fascist and the communist parties, and even the Labor party, by trying to hold changes to those that the laboring and middle classes would accept. Their greatest failure was in the area of foreign relations. Even there the failures were not all due to British bad judgment or ignorance.

After the Versailles conference Great Britain pledged herself to the general support of collective security as embodied in the idea of the League of Nations. Throughout the twenties support of the League, particularly when Ramsay MacDonald or his henchman Arthur Henderson was at the Foreign Office, all seemed to go well with the idea of collective security. The Locarno pacts, negotiated by the Conservative Austen Chamberlain, were guarantees of the system. Then the depression, the rise of Nazi Germany, public disgust with military costs, and distrust of France acted as checks on policies that would have called forth the air, land, and sea forces in the empire to do battle. In fact, the mother country was not sure that the dominions would supply her with the needed material and men should she go to war without their consent. All these reasons and forces added up to weakness and indecision on the part of a government faced with fascist aggression in Africa and Europe. Appeasement is the name given the policy of Neville Chamberlain, who spoke for the majority of Britons in the later and crucial years of this period. In his dislike for the use of force that would cost heavily in men, money, and material, Chamberlain did not offend the majority. He spoke for middle-class, working-class, and upper-class lovers of peace.

In 1783 the landed gentry and upper classes were definitely in the saddle. Theirs was the prevailing will of the land. From 1832 to 1870 the middle classes shared power with the upper classes, then replaced them. From 1870 to 1914 the middle classes were still supreme but in turn shared their place as spokesmen and directors with the workingmen, whose numbers told heavily in their favor. After World War I the labor policy of collectivism or socialism was the one forced upon all classes by circumstances of depression. The upper-class politicians and statesmen as individuals were still powerful, but their policies were those of the socialist-inclined masses. This was the era of the laboring man. His interests and what he suffered were decisive factors in the directions given national affairs. In the final analysis the laboring man determined what should be done.

The most vital question concerning the future of Great Britain, and one that World War II did not answer completely, is that of the working class's fitness to rule. Was this class, now possessing power and place, up to the job? The landed gentry guided Great Britain through the centuries from the fifteenth to the twentieth with success. Can the workingmen produce leaders and policies that will do as well in the twentieth century? Are the new labor leaders as able and as skillful as those of the gentry in the past? Are they inept and visionless in matters of great policy because of narrow devotion to socialist cant and ritual? Or is a new elite coming to the top, fitter than its predecessors? Has the loss of wealth and economic advantage destroyed the remnants of the older ruling classes to such an extent that they cannot cooperate with the working-class leaders in carrying the burden of government? Only the future can answer these questions.

44

ECONOMICS

1919–1939

The miseries of peace are often harder to bear than the horrors of war. In battle the enemy is visible and tangible. Nations can meet an enemy on the battlefield more easily than they can fight the subtle, invisible, and gradual batterings of depressions and unemployment. When a firm loses its market or an individual his job, somehow the loss appears to affect only the corporation or the man. When thousands of corporations and millions of men lose their incomes and means of livelihood, it becomes a catastrophe as serious as full-scale war. Depressions call for courage, perhaps slightly different from the military kind, and willingness to sacrifice for the sake of economic well-being, with want and depression as the antagonist.

In the hour of victory in November, 1918, the British, joined by their allies and even by the vanquished, looked toward the dawn of a new era of peace and plenty, with "Homes Fit for Heroes," jobs for all, and markets ready and waiting for the energetic. World-wide need of peacetime goods was expected to start this era of plenty. In their haste to get on with profit making, the British forgot that it had taken more than thirty years for Europe to recover economically from the Napoleonic Wars, when in comparison the loss, political, personal and economic, was insignificant. The empires of Russia, Germany, and Turkey had disappeared and with them an established European economic order. No one should have believed that in the postwar years men and their needs, to say nothing of their ability to meet their needs, could be as they were before the war. Yet the millions and their leaders confidently expected that business could be resumed under "normal" conditions.

During the twenty years between world wars Great Britain, as a leading member of the family of industrial states, found it impossible to go back to the good old days of 1914. She was not alone in making this discovery. Her economic position and history were like those of other nations trying to get back on their feet.

The Industrial Revolution had turned Great Britain into a principal

634

producer of the world's goods and services. Her prosperity depended upon her ability to sell and carry her goods to other nations. Their prosperity, in part, depended upon their ability to exchange their goods and services with her. World war and politics destroyed this free and easy intercourse. Loss of markets through loss of customers and change of political orientation in postwar years shut off Britain's easiest road to economic recovery.

Postwar markets did not open as rapidly as hoped. Profits did not roll in. New conditions called for new measures to meet them. World-wide depression, part of the consequences of the war, put an end to what was left of the prewar international system of business. Great Britain's problem became one not of modifying an old order but of building a new one. World War II came upon her before the new organization could be completed. Thus the history of twenty troubled years between wars is of the fall of an old economic structure and the valiant attempt to create a new one under most unfavorable conditions.

The story of Britain's recovery of lost fortunes after 1919 falls into two periods. First came the immediate postwar boom and bust. Partial recovery was made by following, whenever possible, principles of international cooperation and free trade. Some moderate success rewarded these efforts until the depression of 1929 put an end to this period and ushered in the second. From 1929 until the start of World War II, Great Britain abandoned free trade in principle and restored a system of protection for domestic industry. This step was necessary if Britain were to live under a system based upon facts of life. Recovery from the depression seemed to be rapid and reasonably satisfactory until international conditions put an end to straightforward recovery programs by vast purchases of arms and materials of war after 1936.

In the twenty years separating the wars, certain hard conditions prevailed that affected the course of prosperity regardless of temporary ups and downs of business. For one thing the coal and textile industries were never as prosperous as they had been before 1914. Unemployment remained high in these industries regardless of the prosperity of other industries. One singular feature of British economy was the great number of steadily unemployed. Besides the slump in major industries there was the problem of investment and currency regulation under new conditions that helped to impose hardships.

Discussion here of the various industries and problems of the years 1919 to 1939 will proceed as follows: First a general and brief account of over-all economic trends will be given, ending with an analysis of how Great Britain got out of her depression. Next follow more detailed accounts of the coal, iron and steel, engineering, transport, and agricultural industries. A brief description of financial policy and investment trends is next. Last of all is a discussion of unemployment.

In mid-1919 everyone was pleased with the way business and industry were supplying world markets starved for materials denied by four years of war. It looked as if the world could not get enough of British goods. However, during the last half of 1919 and the year 1920 markets tumbled, prices fell, and profits ceased to be made for a time. Serious slumps everywhere in 1921, especially in Europe and the United States, hit hard. A national coal strike in June, 1921, made it hard to get fuel for industry. In meeting this first crisis of the period, the banks helped out with loans, the strike was settled, and widespread use of laborsaving devices and cost cutting in factories brought back production to a place where British industry could compete fairly in overseas markets. Had Central Europe been able to recover in some measure, 1922 would have been a good year. But it was not until 1923 that Europe got even part way on its economic feet. Through 1924 and 1925 business abroad and at home was good, so good that the government decided to restore the pound sterling to the gold standard, which had been abandoned as a wartime measure. This decision meant that in the opinion of the financial leaders things were pretty nearly "normal." Business should have been excellent in 1926. Unfortunately domestic economy was disrupted from top to bottom by the General Strike, the first in British history, and the continuance of the strike by coal miners after the ten days of General Strike was over. In spite of the setbacks of 1926, major industries pulled ahead, while the most noticeable advance in the year 1927 was that of the lesser trades. Through 1928 and into 1929 increased quantities of goods were produced with a fixed labor force until many industries put forth more in quantity than they had before 1914. But British prosperity in 1929 depended upon the world's ability to buy her products, and because of the great depression and the closing down of world markets British prosperity came to an end.

The general collapse of export trade and business in the years 1929 to 1932 left Britain in a very bad plight. The fall in prices shows how bad things were. With 1929 as a base of 100, the British price index fell from 104 in February, 1929, to 91 in February, 1930, and to its lowest point of 64 in June, 1932.

The fall in prices was mirrored by the fall in production. Coal, shipbuilding, textiles, and iron—the old mainstays of the British economy—were hardest hit. Such durable-goods industries as steel castings turned from making profits to unprecedented losses. Production fell, on the base of 100 for 1928, from 111 in October, 1929, to 50 in September, 1931. Unemployment in durable-goods industries went to 28 per cent, though in other industries it averaged only 8 per cent.

The normal course of the business cycle would have brought Great Britain part way out of the depths of depression. Clothing would have worn out, ships would have had to be replaced, and automobiles could not last forever. Demand for new goods would have pumped life into industry, and in fact it did so. No economy could afford to wait for the upswing of demand and production without very serious social and political setbacks. Each nation had to take steps to revive and protect its standards of living and industrial equipment. For our purposes it is interesting to compare some of the steps taken by Great Britain to get out of the depression with those taken by the United States. Great Britain embarked on her fight for prosperity with some advantages in existing organizations and laws that the United States did not have. But only a general description of what Great Britain did and how she did it is possible here.

In ending her depression, Great Britain revived some of her flagging industries part way and emphasized the profitable nature of others. For example, the very depressed industry of coal mining was given protection and the benefits of reorganization, while newer engineering industries, such as automobile production, forged ahead as profit-making enterprises in a new economy. In 1930, two years before the United States showed a trend toward prosperity in durable-goods industries, British durable goods were working their way out of the bad position of the depression. The accompanying table tells the story of British and American recovery in these

INDEX LEVELS OF ECONOMIC ACTIVITY
(1929 = 100)

	1932	1937
Employment:		
United States	61.0	95.0
Great Britain	91.0	113.0
Production of pig iron and steel:		
United States	25.6	91.2
Great Britain	94.1	208.5
Industrial production:		
United States	54.0	92.0
Great Britain	83.5	124.5

crucial depression years. Just how did the British do these things, and what laws and institutions did they have that gave them a head start over the Americans?

A fundamental reason for Great Britain's rapid recovery was the fact that, unlike the United States, she was not obliged to experiment with new schemes for social adjustment in a time of economic rehabilitation. This does not mean that no laws were passed to protect or undertake economic reforms; but it does mean that experiments in social readjustment, such as the New Deal, were not needed. Since 1911 a national insurance law under which workers, the state, and employers contributed took care of much of the support of the unemployed. In the relatively good years from 1911 to 1929, the coverage of the national insurance was extended and the reserves in money grew to the point that unemployment payments were enough to meet the first blows of the depression. Company insurance, generally adopted, covered the needs of salaried employees. By 1920 most industries were covered by national insurance. Between 1919 and 1929 certain industries were the subjects of legislation providing for minimum wages. In 1921 an act established a British Railway Wages Board, and in 1924 an act set up a similar wage board for agricultural workers. These laws helped stabilize workers' income and wage rates. The Poor Law Acts were amended in 1927 and again in 1930 in such a way that administration of relief became more efficient.

British recovery was further made easy by the existence of a central bank, the Bank of England, that stood behind national credit and gave a conservative and sound lead to financing of business. During the depression, unlike the United States, Great Britain had no bank failures. Credit was available whenever sound investment and expansion were possible. Although British stocks fell an average of £6 in response to the debacle of the New York stock market in 1929, they never lost in value as much as in the United States. Confidence and credit were maintained throughout the depression because of the conservative approach of financiers to the problems of business. Encouragement was given by the government and by banks to new investment and new industry whenever it seemed wise. This cautious approach to recovery helped keep up land values, which slumped very little as compared with those in the United States.

In the crisis the National Government of Ramsay MacDonald took Great Britain off the gold standard of 1931, because of the bad position of British business throughout the world and the need to protect the pound sterling in domestic as well as foreign markets. The Bank of England had lent on short terms to several European nations that proved to be bad risks. Then by the Exchange Stabilization Act of 1931, there was set aside an emergency reserve of 375 million pounds in gold, to counteract bad influences of short-term speculation and fluctuation in the securities market.

In 1932 the government took a daring and practical step to save money. It converted the interest on national debt from 5 per cent to 3.5 per cent and provided that there would be no specific date for interest payment. Millions of pounds were thus saved. Another decision that helped recovery was the refusal to undertake expensive public-works programs. There the Labor party declared in favor of a public-works program like that of the United States, but neither MacDonald's National coalition nor Chamberlain's administration would consider it for a moment.

In order to stop what were called "abnormal imports" the government after 1930 passed a series of laws that gave protection to certain home industries, particularly agriculture. This was the first general abandonment of free trade since 1846. Protection for coal mining was part of this program. In 1930 was passed a Coal Mines Act that established a licensing system for the mining of coal in various areas, under which each area was allowed a fixed share of the domestic and foreign market. This step had been foreshadowed by a trend toward consolidation or "rationalization" of certain industries. "Rationalization" helped reduce operating costs and made management of big enterprises more efficient. For example, in 1921 a law permitted the consolidation of all railways in Great Britain into four major systems. In 1926, the Central Electrical Board was created to build and operate a national grid with main generating and booster stations at strategic points. Employment in this industry remained steady. Electrical power for domestic and commercial consumption was sold at amazingly cheap rates, to both the home owners and the industrial users. Thus through laws encouraging reorganization and consolidation the governments before 1929 had laid aside a store of economic weapons to fight the depression that were added to and refurbished in the troubled years.

Statistics will serve to indicate the way in which policies of industrialists and of the government succeeded in creating a new economy for Great Britain while bringing some measure of prosperity. By May, 1935, the general production index, though not the wholesale index, had reached the monthly average of 1929. By 1937 the profit position of British industry generally was thirteen points higher than it had been in 1935. The Bank of England had increased its gold reserve from £145,000,000 in 1929 to £326,400,000 in 1937. The basic health and power of recovery of British business had been proved. The accompanying table illustrates this fact.

BRITISH BUSINESS RECOVERY
(1929 = 100)

Year	Index
1932	83.5
1935	106.2
1937	124.5

Included in the figures for 1935 and 1937 are the expenditure and business coming from the rearmament program.

Recovery in Great Britain was due to good management, the natural operation of the laws of demand and supply, and the attention given to building a new economy for the domestic market. Exports played their role in recovery, but they were not as vital as the building of new markets at home. Out of ninety-nine industries, twenty showed that more people were employed during the depression than before. Consumers'-goods industries, for example, did not fall off from the levels of production in the 1920's.

The building industry saw little or no depression throughout the postwar years. From 1923 to 1938 over 3,666,000 new houses were built in England and Wales alone. Of these, 1,011,000 were built by local authorities using state funds. The rest were built by private enterprise. Throughout the 1920's at various times funds were made available by the national government for the development of housing projects, to clear out slums, and to assist individuals to build new homes. The unemployment in this industry was 2.2 per cent, much less than the average for workers in industry. Another domestic industry that developed was that of food processing; cereals packaged attractively competed with traditional bacon and eggs on the British breakfast table. When World War II started, Great Britain was a nation that depended less on foreign trade and markets than she had at the start of World War I. A more detailed account of what happened in certain of the more important trades and industries follows.[1]

No understanding of the changes in British economy between 1919 and 1939 can be obtained without specific reference to changes in some of the major industries. The production of coal, iron and steel, engineering, and textiles present the best examples of these changes. With overseas trade added to these examples, a reasonably good picture of the economic gains, losses, and changes is seen. Coal mining and processing is first on our list of examples because British industry and transportation made use of this commodity so extensively during the nineteenth and twentieth centuries. It was one of the basic industries of such great importance that any alteration of its place in the economy could mean the difference between economic well-being and disaster. In the twenty years under review, the coal industry was one of the major industries where depression was steady, unemployment high, and its situation constantly a danger to the welfare of the nation.

Though British coal reserves were sufficient for three hundred years, coal production depended on domestic and foreign markets. Where in 1913 287,300,000 tons were mined where the postwar average had been 250,-000,000 tons, in 1933 the minimum of 207,100,000 tons was reached, and recovery in 1937 attained only 240,400,000 tons. Overseas markets were disastrously lost. In 1913, 32.9 per cent of the output had been purchased abroad; in 1937, only 21.6 per cent.

Domestic use of coal did not decline, but on the contrary, changed

---

[1] This chapter omits discussion of the General Strike of 1926 and of the various government reports such as those of the Macmillan Commission of 1931. It is believed that, since so much of this is political as well as economic, it would be better to discuss these reports and events in the chapter on politics.

little. In 1913 gas works consumed 16.7 million tons. In 1932 they consumed 19.4 million tons; and in the good year 1937, 18.2 million tons. In 1913, 107.9 million tons were used for domestic industrial and domestic purposes; in 1937, 107.7 million tons.

Loss of foreign markets and depressed trade at home were, therefore, the reasons why less coal was mined or called for. The level of home consumption varied about 15 per cent in the postwar years. This variation reflects the actions of the trade cycle. The continued bad picture for the coal industry as a whole was caused by the catastrophic fall in foreign-market demands.

When the loss of foreign markets was severely felt, those areas that had hitherto catered to the foreigners tried to sell coal at home in competition with areas that had previously supplied the home market. These coal-producing areas were in South Wales, in Scotland, and on the northeast coast of England. Since the home markets were not quite as large as they had been, competition from new mining areas harmed the whole industry.

So serious was the competition for the home market that the Coal Mines Act of 1930 regulated the amount to be mined in each district in order to maintain even employment. By the adoption of protection some antiquated high-cost mines were kept going and the labor force in South Wales was assured of jobs. In many cases loss of profits prevented the installation of machinery, but enough mechanization took place to raise the level of production per worker from the low after World War I. The amount of machine-cut production rose from 8 per cent in 1913 to 59 per cent in 1938. This, however, led to unemployment, since mine workers traditionally were hard to shift to other industries.

The number of men employed in mining declined steadily in the postwar years. The percentage of employed as compared with those employed in 1913 is evidence of this fact. In 1929 only 87.8 per cent were employed as compared to 1913; in 1932, only 72.5 per cent; and in 1937—a comparatively good business year—only 72.6 per cent. This drop from 1913 to 1937 of 27.4 per cent in employment of miners shows the decline in the coal industry to have been markedly injurious to the national economy. It meant that very large numbers of permanently unemployed would have to be taken care of by the state in one way or another.

Fields that had become exhausted or expensive to operate were closed down, while new fields were worked intensively. Also, when industry moved south or to another part of the nation, the coal fields nearest to them were made efficiently productive. Thus Yorkshire and Derbyshire fields produced much more coal than the South Wales fields in the depression years.

Along with coal, the production of iron and steel represented a basic commodity upon which British wealth and prosperity had been established in the nineteenth century. In the years following World War I, the manufacturing of iron and steel was greatly affected by the exhaustion of certain areas that had been producing iron ore, by the development of other areas, and by the new market demands respectively for iron and steel. In the period from 1870 to 1914 it was pointed out that the world market expanded and that, while British production expanded with it, Britain did not make as high a percentage of the world's iron and steel as she had made in 1855.

The exhaustion of certain producing districts is the first fact that should be noticed when observing the change in the production pattern of iron. For example, in 1855 South Wales and the Forest of Dean produced 16 per cent of the domestic iron ore, but in 1913 they were producing 0.4 per cent. In the period under review, the East Midlands that had produced 0.8 per cent in 1913 were producing 38.9 per cent in 1938. Scotland in 1913 had produced 13.3 per cent of the pig iron but in 1937 was only producing 5.9 per cent. North Lincolnshire, on the other hand, had produced only 4.4 per cent of the pig iron in 1913 but had increased its percentage to 12.3 in 1937. The northeastern coast section, a highly industrialized area, had produced 37.7 per cent in 1913 but in 1937 was reduced to 28.6 per cent. These figures indicate that increased cost of production and depletion of the ore reserves led to a geographic change in places where cheaper pig iron could be produced.

Another factor of importance was the increase in the importation of ore for the making of pig iron. In 1913, for example, the northeastern-coast iron manufacturers had used 60 per cent native Cleveland ironstone. In 1932 they used only 54 per cent and in 1937 only 37 per cent. Imported iron ore for the same area was 33.5 per cent in 1913, 35 per cent in 1932, and 52 per cent in 1937. This meant that old established firms in certain areas either suffered financial losses or had to be amalgamated with other firms in order to continue production at all.

Pig-iron production in England generally fell off. In rough figures the output of pig iron and alloys decreased from 10,260,000 tons in 1913 to 7,590,000 tons in 1929, and during the depression year of 1932 it was 3,570,000 tons. Following the general pattern of British recovery, the year 1937 saw an output of 8,490,000 tons. While this recovery shows that in 1937 more pig iron was being produced than in 1929, a peak year in postwar production, nevertheless it does not represent the high level of production of 1913.

By the introduction of new processes in rolling mills, and through the development of techniques of production, the production of steel represents a picture different from that of the pig-iron industry. British steelmakers, unlike their fellow workers in pig iron, showed a satisfactory increase in production during this period. In the case of steel production, as in that of pig iron, the world's total output and consumption increased, and the percentage of the world's production that Great Britain had was much less than it had been during the middle of the nineteenth century. However, by using native pig iron and importing when necessary, steel showed a very satisfactory enlargement of output and an improvement in general profit conditions. Open-hearth steel furnaces were to be found on the northeastern coast and in the North Midlands. It was profitable to operate the hearths close to the mines that produced suitable ores. For example, the East Midlands, Lancashire, and Yorkshire in percentage produced 6.7 per cent of the steel of Great Britain in 1913, 8 per cent in 1929, 7 per cent in 1931, and 11.6 per cent in 1937. The Sheffield area, long known for its production of steel, produced 11.5 per cent in 1913, 12.6 per cent in 1929, 14.9 per cent in 1931, and 13.4 per cent in 1937. A decline is observed in the case of Scotland, where production was 18.7 per cent in 1913, 16.4 per cent in 1929, 13 per cent in 1931, and 14.6 per cent in 1937.

In quantities, the total production of steel in the United Kingdom showed, as indicated above, a gratifying increase. In 1913, 7,660,000 tons had been produced. In 1929, 9,640,000 tons were produced. During the depression year of 1931, 5,200,000 tons were produced, but in 1937, 12,-980,000 tons were turned out. While England lost her market and capacity for pig-iron ore, her capacity and market for the output of steel increased during the postwar years. Steel and its by-products were being used to a greater extent in the making of ships and in fabricating the thousand and one parts and machines necessary to carry on the most basic of industrial activities. It would seem that England was able to keep her steel industry alive and competitive during the postwar years. The figures for 1937 undoubtedly represent demands made upon the steel industry in the rearmament program that was carried forward at this time.

British steel and iron production followed, and indeed helped establish, the general pattern of depression and recovery. From the good year 1929 there was a terrible decline during the next three or four years of depression, followed by a rise in production and consumption. This was a true picture in the case of pig iron and steel. Only in the case of steel did Great Britain show a greater output than had been characteristic of the prosperous prewar year of 1913.

Another excellent thermometer of the economic health of nineteenth-century industrial Britain is found in the production figures in the textile trades. In the manufacturing of woolen and cotton cloth, Great Britain took the lead through the development of vast markets in Asia, as well as in Europe and the Americas. It is safe to say that in this field Great Britain was preeminent. She maintained her relative position in manufacturing and exporting woolen goods, since other nations lacked the proper climate, the experience, and the equipment for making fine worsteds and woolens in which she had led for so long. During the years under review, the woolen industry followed to some extent the trend of British trade both for home and export markets. Generally speaking, however, the woolen industry maintained a more favorable position.

The cotton industry, because of climate, had originally been set up in northern England. In the nineteenth century, it became one of the most profitable of all British industries. It sold millions of yards of goods to the rest of the world. However, competition with the Japanese, with the United States, and with other nations, as well as with the dominions and India, put this basic industry into chronic ill-health. The accompanying table is a fever chart showing the serious illness of the industry.

PRODUCTION, EXPORT, IMPORT, AND HOME CONSUMPTION OF COTTON PIECE GOODS
(In millions of linear yards)

	Production	Export	Production less export	Import	Available for home consumption
1912	8,044	6,913	1,131	98	1,229
1924	5,590	4,649	941	31	972
1930	3,179	2,530	649	70	719
1933	3,183	2,117	1,066	18	1,084
1935	3,081	2,013	1,068	22	1,080

In certain fields of cotton manufacturing the depression was not felt as severely as in others. Cotton goods for home consumption were more plentiful, and therefore the consumption of cotton at home would have ensured a profitable trade position had the most vital part of the industry, namely exports, held their own. The second table briefly tells the story of the decline of piece-goods exports for cotton. One of the interesting

DISTRIBUTION OF COTTON-PIECE-GOODS EXPORT
(In percentages of total export of each year)

	1913	1929	1935	1935 as percentage of 1913 (1913 = 100)
Europe	7.3	11.9	14.9	40.9
Asia	66.5	50.9	22.7	6.9
Africa	10.0	15.7	21.9	44.5
Americas	12.7	15.2	25.9	40.9
Australasia	3.0	5.6	14.1	94.5
British Empire	56.4	53.2	58.4	20.9
Dominions	5.5	8.4	29.5	108.3
India	43.2	33.9	12.5	5.8
Crown Colonies	7.7	10.9	16.4	43.0

aspects of this table is the increased consumption of British goods by the dominions and crown colonies. The great decline, of course, is to be noticed in the consumption of goods by India. Thus the cause of the depression in the cotton industry was not so much the lack of markets, raw materials, or efficiency as it was a fundamental change in international competition, to which should be added the increased use of such materials as nylon and rayon in the postwar years, for the factor of fashion and perhaps that of better clothing design seriously affected the amount of cotton used.

When industries are declining, a question is always raised concerning their relative efficiency. It has been mentioned above that wage rates were set for the cotton industry by legislation following World War I. It should also be noted that the amalgamations of many firms were undertaken in the interest of operating efficiency. Technical improvements as, for example, those that allowed one operator to look after more looms, each producing more goods, resulted in Lancashire in a general wage saving of from 20 to 30 per cent in total cost of cloth. At the same time there was a general overhauling of plant and equipment to improve operations and to reduce unit costs to the lowest levels. On the whole, most of the attempts to save were effective. An example of these tendencies was the organization of the Lancashire Cotton Corporation formed in 1929. This corporation acquired mills and sheds that were either not in production or held in bankruptcy by banks. By control of credit and central purchasing, it was possible to perform efficiently under one corporation the activities of many firms that had been forced out of business.

While the unsatisfactory status of the cotton industry gives us an excellent example of a change in the twentieth century in the economic organization of the British Empire, a different picture is to be found upon looking at the development of what in Great Britain are called the engineering industries—the making of machines and engines, the construction of vehicles, and what in the United States are called the machine-tool industries. Two important aspects of the engineering industry from 1919 to 1939 will be noted: the shift in their geographical location, which was partly responsible for the movement of industrial population in the postwar years, and the increase in the production of machines and machine tools to the great profit of British trade and industry.

The engineering trades in England were naturally situated close to the basic industries, such as textiles, that they would be required to serve. As new industries, such as automobile production, developed, it was found that the central and southern portions of England were better areas. In the period following World War I the general movement of industry was toward the East Midlands, the Southeast, and the Greater London area. Employment in the engineering trades increased 45 per cent in the London area between 1924 and 1935. In 1935, 25.3 per cent of those employed in engineering trades were in the Greater London area. In these trades many who were employed in other activities could find jobs because operation of automobile machinery required less skilled labor. Skilled labor in the engineering industry fell from 60 per cent in 1913 to 32 per cent in 1933, while the proportion of unskilled workers was 20 per cent in 1913 and rose to 57 per cent in 1933. Thus, many who were unemployed or who had received only basic training in the operation of machinery found new positions in the expanding engineering industries.

An example of the shift in employment from an old to a new industry may be found by comparing shipbuilding and electrical engineering. The accompanying table tells a story of decline and shift in employment patterns. While, of course, not all those engaged in shipbuilding found employ-

NUMBER EMPLOYED

	1924	1930	1935
Shipbuilding	141,867	133,453	82,020
Electrical engineering	150,884	191,970	247,948

ment in electrical engineering, these figures are an example of how the development of new industries served to relieve unemployment.

It is interesting to observe how the changes in demand affected the output of one of the nineteenth-century basic industries during the postwar years. In the building of ships for nonmilitary purposes there had been a decline from the years 1914 to 1938 of 36 per cent in the total output of English and Scotch shipbuilding firms. This output represents a decline caused by a general falling off of world trade and competition by other countries such as Italy, Japan, and the United States for what carrying trade there was. The figures in the accompanying table give the picture.

BRITISH NONMILITARY SHIPBUILDING

	Gross tons
1913	1,930,000
1929	1,520,000
1937	920,000

Thus the decline in output of shipbuilding was severe, and another major industry of nineteenth-century England suffered a lasting depression in the twentieth century.

However, the engineering industry in the production and sale for home and private consumption of automobiles shows a most gratifying increase. In 1913, for example, there were 106,000 automobiles in use in Great Britain. In 1929 there were 998,000, and in 1939, 1,984,000. The vast majority of these private cars were built and engineered in England.

In Coventry and Cowley, a suburb of Oxford, cars were assembled and put together, bringing to these areas thousands of pounds in profit and payrolls, and new workers by the thousands, as well.

The increase in the production and use of automobiles for private or family use was paralleled by the increased use of trucks. These trucks became carriers of every commodity and, with the private cars, established and maintained repair and manufacture-of-parts businesses that brought both profit and prosperity to those engaged in them. So important did the automobile industry become that it has been estimated that in 1935 there were thirty-two private cars and ten trucks per 1,000 people. Like the United States, England had taken to the road. Of the cities manufacturing automobiles and commercial vehicles in 1938, Birmingham made 25.9 per cent of the output of both categories, with Greater London in second place making 20.1 per cent.

Another source of income of British engineering trades and industry was to be found in the development of the aircraft industry that distributed its production not only to the defense services of Great Britain and the Empire, but also to private owners for commercial aviation. Greater London in 1935 had over 37.2 per cent of the total employment in the aircraft manufacturing business. Greater London and adjacent areas in the same year had 54.6 per cent of the total of the nation. Thus, the development of this industry has with the automobile manufacture tended to pull population from the north to the south and south central regions.

A similar picture of the electrical trades is also given when one notes that the total number of workers employed in the electrical trades increased from 150,610 in 1924 to 247,948 in 1935. Of the total employed in Great Britain in the electrical trades, 46.1 per cent in electrical engineering found employment in Greater London in 1935.

A word should be said concerning the value to the Empire market of the exports of some of these products. As other countries either set up high tariff barriers or were able to compete successfully for British automobiles, the British Empire continued to buy British. Much of the profit of the automobile industry, to name but one, was made through export to the British Empire. In 1924 the Empire took 86.9 per cent of the automobiles exported. In 1929 it took 86.4 per cent, and in 1938, 81.2 per cent.

One effect of the development of the automobile industry upon the British economy was to increase greatly the amount of freight traffic handled by road. The twentieth century saw a return to the use of highways because of the automobile. Competition with the railways for the carriage of freight was immediate and severe. Networks of highways, such as the Great West Road, connected various rural and urban areas of thickly populated sections and made possible the development of community transportation by bus, with the result that much of the railroad traffic that had hitherto been devoted to transportation of passengers and freight evaporated. However, because of the railroad reorganization after 1921 and also because of the transportation competition, the railroads improved their general condition. In the late 1920's and throughout the 1930's railroads could haul goods and passengers more efficiently when the distance involved was over seventy-five miles. Under seventy-five miles, trucks could definitely do better than the railways. Everywhere in England one saw carriage of goods by trucks, both by private individuals who, in the outlying sections of the country, would carry both goods and passengers, and also by well-organized truck lines. In 1933 over 5,418,000 passenger journeys were taken in omnibusses and motor coaches. In the postwar period, therefore, for short distances both freight and passengers deserted the railroads and took to the more convenient and cheaper motorcar. The network of concrete highways made possible also the growth of the "petrol" (gasoline) selling industry and the roadside restaurant or tea shop.

The railroads did not suffer as badly during this period as one might imagine, however. In 1938 there were 20,007 miles of rail open to traffic in Great Britain. After the Railway Act of 1921, railroads were amalgamated into four systems, the Southern, Great Western, London Middle and Scottish, and London and Northeastern. Of these four railroads, the Southern derived a very high percentage of its traffic receipts (78 per cent in 1938) from passenger fares because it served the metropolitan area of London and of the South. In the same year 46 per cent of the national total receipts of British railways came from passenger fares. The London Midland and Scottish, the Great Western, and the London and Northeastern served as long-distance carriers both of passengers and of goods. The quantity of goods varied, of course, within the area served. For example, the London Midland and Scottish penetrates largely the industrial section of central and northwestern England. The Great Western and the London and Northeastern serve not only industrial areas but also rural ones.

Generally speaking, the amalgamation of 1921 resulted in better service at less cost than had been the case in 1913. It also resulted in keeping open the arteries of traffic when, during the depression and the years immediately following, it was necessary that every branch of British economy be operated at the greatest efficiency possible. Railroad rates during the postwar years were adjusted to meet the demands of industry within each area, and it was calculated that in 1925 coal that was exported paid in its charges 9.2 per cent of its export value in rail rates. That year, 1.8 per cent of export value was paid by steel and 0.9 per cent for machinery. This estimate is only rough, but it gives some idea of the burden that rail rates put upon exports in a time of high international competition.

Some comparison of the passengers carried by motor busses and by railways may be obtained by comparing the number of passenger journeys on public road vehicles and by railroads. In 1937 approximately 108,-000,000 journeys were made on public road vehicles and 1,259,000,000 journeys were made on railroads. One of the interesting characteristics of British economy in the nineteenth century was the excellent communication system afforded by both railways and roads. Few countries of the world in the twentieth century could compare either in service or in accessibility with Great Britain in respect to passenger and freight accommodations. England, therefore, continued to retain after World War I much of the advantage that she had previously had in respect to her rail and road communication.

Coal, iron, engineering, and transportation were very largely dependent for profits on export trade. It is well to look at the condition of export trade now. When Great Britain cannot trade abroad, her economic life stands still. In a period when the economy of every single nation of the globe underwent radical changes, it could not be expected that the export and import trade of Great Britain would in these years resemble that preceding the war. In the international field, European countries built up tariff walls and in many cases entered into competition with Great Britain in export trade. The United States ceased to export raw materials and in the postwar years tended to export finished products that in innumerable instances competed with British goods.

In general, Great Britain retained more imports in 1937 than in 1913 and exported slightly less. In 1913, 55.7 per cent of imports was retained, and 94.7 per cent in 1937. In 1913, 44.3 per cent of produce and manufacture was exported, but only 35.3 per cent in 1937. Actually, the excesses of imports over exports is perhaps the most notable feature of the change. Whereas textiles had formerly been a great portion of British exports, now we find its place taken by machinery and electrical appliances; exports of this kind exceeded imports. This is true also of such durable goods as motorcars and aircraft.

Another interesting feature of British foreign trade was the increase in trade with the dominions and colonies as compared with that with foreign countries. The table on page 650 shows conclusively that trade with British countries increased absolutely, while trade with foreign countries declined considerably in the years 1913 to 1937. For example, of the total trade of Great Britain, Australia and New Zealand together took 8.3 per cent of the total exports in 1913 but were taking 11.7 per cent in 1937. The United States, which took 5.6 per cent in 1913, was taking 6.4 per cent in 1937. Industrial continental Europe, which had taken 22.0 per

GEOGRAPHICAL DISTRIBUTION OF BRITISH FOREIGN TRADE WITH
EMPIRE AND FOREIGN COUNTRIES, 1913–1937

(Excluding Eire)

	1913		1929		1937	
	(1) °	(2)	(1)	(2)	(1)	(2)
A. Values in million pounds						
British countries	£ 135.4	£ 195.3	£ 255.0	£ 288.4	£ 344.6	£ 230.3
Foreign countries	523.9	329.9	812.3	404.9	588.0	269.5
B. Percentages						
British countries	20.5	37.2	23.9	41.6	36.9	46.1
Foreign countries	79.5	62.8	76.1	58.4	63.1	53.9
C. Percentages of total trade of each year						
British countries	11.4	16.5	14.5	16.4	24.1	16.1
Foreign countries	44.2	27.9	46.1	23.0	41.0	18.8

° (1) Retained imports, (2) exports of British produce and manufacture.

cent in 1913, was taking only 18.6 per cent in 1937. Likewise, Mediterranean Europe, which had taken 5.8 per cent in 1913, was taking only 3.2 per cent in 1937. Thus, economic dependence of Great Britain upon her empire for markets was greatly increasing in the postwar years. In certain of her well-established markets, specifically South America, the percentage of imports increased, whereas British exports fell. But trade with British South America and tropical Africa expanded steadily. The trade with India, of course, is in a separate category, and in this one trade area, Japan was able to compete against Great Britain and the rising and fast-developing local Indian industry. Another good example of the change in foreign trade was with Japan. In 1913 exports from Britain to Japan had exceeded imports. But after the war, as a result of the industrialization of Japan, exports to this country declined, whereas imports from there greatly increased.

The tables above show the rise and decline of imports and exports in foreign trade. It will be noted that in 1913 and in 1937 retained imports exceeded in value the exports of British produce and manufacture. Retained imports, for example, in 1913 were 659 million pounds and in 1937 were 953 million pounds. The exports for 1913 were 525 million pounds and were 521 million pounds in 1937. In the postwar period England retained more imports and exported less than she had in 1913. In 1913, 55.7 per cent of the imports were retained of the total trade, and in 1937 64.7 per cent. Exports of 44.3 per cent in 1913 fell off to only 35.3 per cent in 1937.

These figures should not be taken as a simple token that Britain was economically less well off in 1937 than she was in 1913. She usually had a satisfactory balance in payments in respect to income from shipping, overseas investment, and business commissions. This, when added to the excess of imports over exports, usually was able to account for a balance on the credit side that made the difference between prosperity and unfortunate conditions. The favorable position of British business for so long after 1919 was the result of the world-wide services of discount, carriage, insurance, and brokerage. As the accompanying table demonstrates, these services were of first importance.

BRITAIN'S BALANCE OF PAYMENTS
(In millions of pounds)

	1913	1929	1931	1933	1937
Visible trade: *					
Net excess of imports of merchandise	£145	£381	£408	£263	£442
Estimated net income from services:					
Shipping	94	130	80	65	130
Overseas investment	210	250	170	160	210
Commissions	25	65	30	30	40
Other sources †	10	39	24	8	6
Total	£339	£484	£304	£263	£386
Estimated credit or debit balance	+149	+103	−104	. . .	−56

* Includes movement of silver, but excludes movement of gold bullion.

† Includes (a) net balance of Government receipts and payments overseas, and (b) balance of tourists' expenditure of British nationals abroad (debit) and foreign nationals in Britain (credit).

There was a credit balance in 1913; a considerable loss, but still a credit balance, by 1929; an almost total reversal of the favorable situation in 1931; then, as an indication of rapid recovery, an almost exact balance in 1933; and then, because of an unusual amount of imports in 1937, the credit balance was unfavorable once more. The amount of imports in 1937 that threw off the favorable balance came from the importation of raw and other materials used for the rearmament program. Undoubtedly the rapid recovery in 1933, as compared to the terrible losses of 1931, is accounted for by the effects of the import duties act that adjusted the balance of trade in favor of British industry, thereby cutting the necessity for much of the imports.

Although Great Britain suffered a most severe depression along with the rest of the industrial Western nations, she had a remarkable record of recovery and prosperity when compared to the United States or any other nation.

In order to round out our review of economic changes we must review briefly the position of Britain's largest single industry, agriculture, and the manner in which successive administrations dealt with the economics of foreign exchanges and credit. The importance of agriculture in British life had been greatly changed since 1783. In the period from 1870 to 1914 we saw agriculture ceasing to be attractive and population moving from the farm to the town. In 1911, it has been estimated, there were 1,497,000 farmers and helpers working on the land. In 1921 there were 1,318,000, and in 1931 a steady decline was beyond question when 1,198,-000 were to be found on the land. During World War I, Great Britain imported four-fifths of her wheat and two-fifths of her meat. She increased the production of her milk and vegetables so that these two items were largely taken care of by domestic production.

During the war years a central Agricultural Wages Board had been established in order to secure decent wages and establish some over-all control of labor. A philosophy favoring state aid or partial control over agriculture was followed in the Agricultural Act of 1921. In return for a guarantee of basic cereal prices, farmers were expected to utilize their land as efficiently as possible, under government inspection. It was provided that the Ministry of Agriculture could, under certain specified conditions, see to it that the land was efficiently utilized. At the same time, a Tenant Right Law was passed that allowed a tenant to sue his landlord for unusual or unnecessary disturbance in the course of his tenancy, thus allowing him to feel more secure and to look forward to a greater use of land. However, so attached were the majority of Britons to the philosophy of *laissez faire* that the coalition government in 1921 rescinded the agricultural act of the previous year. Prices were thus allowed to fluctuate under the general belief that *laissez faire* secured prosperity and low-priced bread for city workers.

Agricultural prices fluctuated until in the depression they reached their lowest point in 1933. From 1933 to 1939 they made a slow recovery, assisted not only by government protection but also by an improvement in the whole price structure. Agricultural prices generally fell less sharply than other prices. So, even in 1933 with prices at their lowest point, actually the purchasing power of agricultural commodities was relatively favorable as compared with the purchasing power of other commodities and better than their purchasing power had been in 1913. However, agriculture was in such an unfortunate situation that no government, Labor or Conservative, could neglect the necessity for ensuring agricultural labor some security. In 1924 an Agricultural Wages Act was passed that provided for a guaranteed minimum wage set by local boards. The agricultural wages were not, of course, as high as those of industrial workers. However, the real wage of the agricultural laborer compared favorably to that of the employed semiskilled or unskilled laborer in the cities. Another feature of agriculture was a steadily declining demand for labor in agriculture. From 1925 to 1934 the number of farm workers declined

14 per cent. Because of the introduction of machinery and improved techniques during the same year, the productivity of farms in Great Britain increased by 18.5 per cent. Until the introduction of the protective regulations after 1931, crop production in cereals remained about the same. With government assistance some new crops were introduced and production greatly increased. For example, the government wished to encourage the growth of sugar beets. Acreage devoted to the development of this crop increased from 22,000 in 1924 to 404,000 in 1935. In the latter year, sugar beets accounted for one-fourth of the total consumption of sugar in Great Britain.

Certain sections of the agricultural industry were greatly aided by a change in dietary habits following World War I. Particularly was this true in regard to meat. In the comparatively prosperous years 1909 to 1913, Great Britain consumed 46,700,000 hundredweight of meat. But during the unfavorable years of 1929 to 1931, the consumption of meat had increased to 54,700,000 hundredweight. Thus the domestic meat industry, and with it the dairy industry, produced more for domestic use. It should be noticed, however, that in certain portions of the meat-producing industry a large percentage was imported; thus imports of bacon and pork in the early 1930's were 90 per cent of all the bacon consumed.

One of the problems during the depression was that of keeping alive this industry which was so important for the nation's health and which, in time of international crisis, might be asked to prevent a starvation of the people. Not only for the purposes of protecting domestic markets, but also to pump new vigor into a portion of the economic system during the depression, the Coalition Government of 1931 and the Conservative Government of 1933, following the Conservative commitment to measures of protection, passed two acts that reversed completely the philosophy that had regulated British economic activity since 1846. In 1931 a clear break was made with the philosophy and system of *laissez faire,* and a partial return to protection was provided by the passing of the Agriculture Marketing Act. This Act provided that if two-thirds of the farmers producing two-thirds of the total domestic production of a single agricultural commodity agreed to the government control of prices and production, the government would then step in and, with the aid of farmers' councils, put that commodity under protection and regulation. The hops industry was the first to take advantage of this Act. Farmers were somewhat skeptical about the success of such controls because the amount of grain and other produce was not regulated by the Act. A second Agricultural Marketing Act, of 1933, protected the home market by prohibiting the importation of most agricultural produce. In the end milk, pigs, bacon, and potatoes were thus barred. Because of the special place that wheat occupied in the agricultural economy of Britain, a wheat subsidy was granted in 1932. This had the effect of increasing wheat acreage 47 per cent from 1931 to 1937. Thus, with Protection coming at the end of the period, those engaged in agriculture, whether workers or managers and owners, could look forward to protection from outside competition and, in the dairy, meat, and cereal production, a reasonably satisfactory price and profit for their produce.

From 1919 to 1939 there was a general trend to increase the number of landowners who, as small farmers, occupied and lived on the land. Death duties, high taxes, and the unprofitable position of the great landlords were responsible in part for the movement. Also governmental legislation at the beginning of the period in the shape of public works in 1933 gave state assistance to war veterans and others who wanted to return to the land. In 1928 under an Agricultural Mortgage Act the Bank of England and private banks provided capital for farm mortgages. This made it possible for a farm owner to increase his holdings and find the necessary credit with comparative ease. In this respect the government was willing to help guarantee prosperity of agriculture. As in the Agricultural Act of 1920 and the Agricultural Wages Act of 1924, the Government of the day, by requiring the Bank of England to assist in the establishment of credit, showed definitely that *laissez faire* was becoming less and less attractive.

In many countries, the Scandinavian, for example, marketing societies for the cooperative sale and production of farm produce accounted for the largest share of the total business. This was not true, however, in Great Britain. In 1936 there were 514 societies with 138,541 members that cooperated in the sale of farm produce. Milk marketing and hop marketing represented two sections of agriculture where cooperatives in the sale of produce were extensive. However, the British farmer seemed to dislike the idea of cooperative marketing. It did not affect greatly the majority of British producers, who welcomed state aid in protection and in finance but were not in favor of aid from marketing cooperatives.

Great Britain was not only the creditor of the world in 1914 but also the center for international financial activity. In the postwar years she lost her place as world's creditor to the United States but continued her role as carrier, broker, and general insurer of the world's goods. Also, the ties that had bound British finances to those of Asia and Africa were not destroyed by the war. The excellence of British banking overseas was not impaired, from the point of view either of service or of efficiency, by the war. In rebuilding trade and commerce it was found that the British possessed, through their overseas banks and commercial agents, the most efficient system for discount, insurance, and carrying of goods. Therefore, it was easiest to trade with and buy from British firms because of the accessibility of these financial services. The pound sterling was, more than the American dollar or the French franc, an international medium of exchange. What happened to the British pound in value obviously affected financial transactions of many countries. So central in international business was the pound sterling that when in 1931 Great Britain went off the gold standard she took some forty countries with her.

In 1919 the declared policy of the Bank of England and of British business in general was one of restoration of prewar conditions at home and overseas. In spite of the recession of 1921, business improved so much that in 1925 the Conservative Government put the pound back on the gold standard, to the accompaniment of patriotic cheers from the City of London when at last the pound could stand "shoulder to shoulder" with the gold dollar of the United States. President Harding of the United States had proclaimed that his country was back to "normalcy," whatever that might be, and the British wanted to be there, too. This policy meant that the pound on the international market in terms of gold would remain stable and other nations could count on its value remaining steady. It was the hope of those who restored the gold standard that the pound's stability would encourage trade and commerce, to the profit not only of the British empire but also of the world. However, the gold standard imposed a burden because it often made exported British goods costlier and therefore put them out of the reach of purchasers who did not have funds to buy in a market based on a gold standard pound.

The return to gold was also the result of a mistaken belief that free trade of some sort would be possible throughout the world. In truth, tariff barriers in these years were made even higher than they had been in 1914, and the philosophy of relatively free international trade did not conform to the facts. British financiers were forced to change their policies and adopt a philosophy of economic nationalism, of protection of domestic industry through tariffs and preemption in dominion and colonial trade. It was pointed out that the dominions had long since adopted protection, and the mother country was urged to follow this course, in the hope that concessions would then be made by the dominions to give favored trade position to Great Britain. The economic blizzard of 1929 led Great Britain to adopt this policy of trying to build up business within the British family of nations. When in 1931 she went off the gold standard, exchange control and the fact that London was the financial center for dominions and colonies were purposefully used to foster this "imperial preference." Agriculture, likewise, was built up by protection, under the persuasive leadership of Walter Elliot, the Minister of Agriculture.

All this had an effect on overseas investment. The wave of investment in the Empire, so marked from 1870 to 1900, resumed after World War I. Though of the 4 billion pounds of overseas investment held in Great

Britain in 1914, 600 million had been taken to pay for munitions and 150 million more had been lost in enemy countries by 1939, the sum had been built up again by 375 million. The source of this new investment was largely the British carrying trade and the profitable overseas investment of maturing overseas loans. However, because of the depression and the adoption of protection, the tendency was now for the Briton to invest his money at home.

A great deal has been written about the unsatisfactory social and economic position of the British workingman during depression years. Because the misery and poverty of unemployment ceased to be a phase of the turn of the business cycle, it became a fixed and disagreeable part of British economy. After 1921 unemployment in Great Britain was never less than one million, and for the seventeen years between 1921 and 1937, the national average of unemployment among industrial workers was 14 per cent. Before World War I, unemployment had never been more than 10 to 11 per cent in the worst years, and only 1 to 2 per cent in the better years. Thus, the presence of a million or more workers without jobs was a totally unexpected and completely new pattern in the economic picture. The unemployment occurred in certain depressed industries such as textiles, shipping, mining, iron, and steel, and reflected throughout these years the unfavorable economic picture. Not only because of bad business conditions but also because of technical achievements, the unemployed presented a problem to successive administrations which they were incapable of solving. The accompanying table gives a brief but graphic statement of the numbers of unemployed. It will be noted that the figures in the table are based upon those workers that were insured under the National Insurance Act of 1911 and amendments to that act.

UNEMPLOYMENT

	July, 1923	July, 1929	July, 1932	July, 1937	July, 1938
Number insured	11,503,000	12,092,400	12,808,000	13,697,800	14,210,000
Number unemployed	1,324,000	1,777,000	2,921,000	1,389,600	1,819,000
Percentage unemployed	11.5	9.7	22.8	10.1	13.3

An insurance act was passed in 1920 for practically every worker, with the exception of those engaged in agricultural occupations, who made less than £250 a year. This meant that the unemployed could collect benefits on their insurance. General provisions of the act gave insurance at first to those who would be employed for a specific number of months, but before the depression was over, the legislation was modified to include practically anyone who had worked or who was willing to work. The unemployment throughout these years was concentrated in what was to be known as depressed areas, Northeast, North, and Central England;

South Wales; and Scotland. Where there had been extensive steel, iron, coal, textile, and shipping industries, the unemployed were found in greatest numbers.

In order to take care of daily needs of the unemployed, the state provided certain specified sums, called the dole, that were paid up to 1924. After that date the dole ceased and the unemployment insurance was saddled with the great burden of providing for the subsistence of the unemployed. The savings from the national insurance fund were of course wiped out, and the state had to shoulder the responsibility of meeting the unprecedented demand of relieving the unemployed. The state not only assisted by subsidies through the national insurance scheme, but also voted certain other subsidies; the Ministry of Transportation provided subsidies for the building of local public works and for road and bridge construction. The Ministry of Labor between 1921 and 1937 helped assist the migration of 650,000 workers from depressed areas. These workers in some instances were taught new trades, and the Ministry of Labor assisted in establishing these individuals in new jobs. However, unemployment was finally reduced only by the gradual recovery of trade and industry and what might be called natural processes of economic rehabilitation. Thus, the percentage of unemployed, which had been 22.8 per cent of those insured in 1932, was reduced to 10.1 per cent in 1937. The presence of a million or more unemployed, however, was never regarded by any of the administrations as desirable, and the policy of every government was directed toward the wiping out of all but a very small proportion of the unemployment. This desirable goal was never achieved, and everyone admitted, no matter how reluctantly, that unemployment seemed to be a permanent disease of the economic body of Great Britain.

45

SOCIAL HISTORY

1919–1939

In the course of the changes that followed World War I, the most important study is that of what happened to the British people. Did the heroes get homes fit to live in? Did the British people lose their moral courage and strength of character? Did the war raise, relatively speaking, one class over another? These questions cannot, of course, be definitely answered. To raise them requires discussion of the fundamental problems of life in a period of rapid transition when all comparisons are partly false and all statistics partly inaccurate. In support of nearly any point of view ample evidence can be found to demonstrate its truth— or that of the opposite contention. Since the previous sections of this study have discussed the social and other changes of a given period as they affected the working, middle, and upper classes, the same scheme will be followed here.

The average man in Great Britain after 1919 was the workingman living in an urban community. Sharp class lines dividing the less skilled of the middle classes and the semiskilled of the laboring classes were pretty well obliterated during World War I. There were more lower-middle-class and laboring-class people in Britain because of the similarity of wage levels and circumstances in which people of these groups lived. It is difficult to indicate precisely how the standard of life was improved or was lowered after the war. For those who were continuously employed in a new industry, such as automobile engine manufacture, conditions as compared to those of 1914 were good. For the miner in South Wales or the shipwright on the Clydeside, they probably were bad, for coal mining and shipbuilding were (more or less) permanently depressed industries. The relative position of workers after 1919 can be known by an inspection of the cost of living and the wage scales prevalent at various times.

Wages in general rose faster than costs. Even in the depression, the employed workingman fared better in the matter of real wages than he had in the normal mid-twenties. By 1937 figures show his wages had actually doubled since the prewar year, 1914, whereas his cost of living had increased by only 55 per cent. Thus at the start of World War II in 1939 he was better off than he had been at the start of World War I.

With an advantageous economic position in respect to income and living costs, the British worker possessed another asset of real value. Through use of machinery, public policy, and the pressure of labor unions the worker had to spend less time on the job to earn more than he had in 1914.

Industrial engineers had proved that long working days made men less fit to carry on and products more expensive. The virtues of the nine-hour day were shown to be, in many industries, nonexistent. Shorter hours and better working places encouraged men to produce more. After the war, workers in industry generally used their unions to demand and get the forty-eight-hour week. In the Coal Mines Act of 1930 the working day was set at seven and one-half hours. Railway workers in 1919 were reduced from sixty to forty-eight hours per week. The average industrial worker was asked to work only eight hours for a day's pay. The reduction of hours in a day's work was supposed to give the worker needed rest and relaxation. Some critics bewailed the reduction in working hours and the raises in pay as tending to undermine the character of the sturdy Briton. No longer would the worker feel that he had to turn in a good day's work for honest pay. He could ask his union to get it for him through a strike or other forms of pressure. He could sit back and cultivate lazy habits or visit the public house and there drink away his increase in wages. Other critics pointed out that since machines now did so much of the work, it was better to pay workers enough to improve their standard of living, while giving them time to enjoy the new life made possible. Why wear out men, they said, when machines could be scrapped at so little comparative cost?

Some conception of the relative position of the working classes in British economy is given in the table on page 660, which shows the distribution of national income during the postwar years and compares it with that of a representative prewar year. It will be referred to again when discussing the relative changes in social conditions of the middle and upper classes.

The workers benefited from the fact that services of the state and increased costs arising from the depression were paid for by others and not themselves. The increased burden of unemployment costs and state administration following World War I was borne largely by the middle and upper classes. The workers too paid an increased share, but it was smaller in amount and percentage than that paid by other classes. The organization of the tax system was partly responsible for this. Also, the workers could not, as individuals, be expected to pay in the same propor-

DISTRIBUTION OF NATIONAL INCOME
(In millions of pounds)

	1911	1924	1929	1932	1935
Home-produced income	£1,842	£3,320	£3,553	£3,138	£3,745
Income from overseas	220	280	315	175	215
Total income	£2,062	£3,600	£3,868	£3,313	£3,960
Distribution of total income:					
Wages	£728	1,399	1,486	1,333	1,520
Percentage of total	35.3	38.9	38.4	40.2	38.4
Salaries	£288	841	944	890	937
Percentage of total	14.0	23.4	24.4	26.9	23.7
Profits and interest	£843	1,114	1,136	765	1,164
Percentage of total	40.9	30.9	29.4	23.1	29.4
Rents	£203	246	302	325	339
Percentage of total	9.8	6.8	7.8	9.8	8.5

SOURCE: Colin Clark, *National Income and Outlay*, p. 94.

tion as individual millionaires and shop managers. However, there was transference of income from the richer to the poorer classes after 1919. Economists call it a redistribution of income. It has been estimated that in 1913–1914 the working class paid about 34.3 per cent of central and local taxes; in 1925–1926, only 28.7 per cent. Under protection the costs of taxes had increased so that the working classes paid about 33 per cent of central and local taxes. For social services from which the workingmen benefited most directly, the workers gained by having the cost increased for other classes but not themselves. Thus in 1913 the workers paid in taxes about what they received in the shape of special benefits. In 1925 special benefits such as insurance, were 310 million pounds, but only 265 million came from labor. The rest came from the taxes of the wealthier upper classes. In 1935–1936 the upper classes paid 90 million pounds for benefits enjoyed almost completely by unemployed, recipients of social insurance, and those receiving general state aid.

WORKING CLASSES

In a period of socialism, social and economic forces that had been at work shifting political balances between classes were equally effective in changing the visible and invisible lines that had marked one class from another. For a century each generation of British workingmen had been able to look backward and note that the state and their own efforts allowed them to live in more ease and comfort than had their fathers or grandfathers. Generally speaking, in Great Britain the workingman improved his living conditions after 1919. Exceptions, of course, occurred in depressed areas. There was probably a decline in the standard of living for the unemployed miners in South Wales, shipyard workers on the Clydeside, or miners or steelworkers in Durham. Outside of these depressed areas, however, the conditions of the urban and agricultural worker could not be called unsatisfactory.

A social survey undertaken during the depression indicated that less than 10 per cent of the workers in London were living on a margin of poverty and want. In 1880 it will be remembered that Charles Booth had discovered that almost one-third of London's population was below the line of starvation and want. There is no question that the general living conditions had greatly improved. The semiskilled and skilled working man could, with his lower-middle-class colleague, buy a home for a small down payment and continue through monthly payments to enjoy his own house and garden and make of it a castle for himself and his family. He could live in the suburbs or in blocks of apartments landscaped and built so that he could look with pleasure upon grass and flowers and trees. The garden cities in such places as Birmingham and Manchester were constructed with an eye to preserving picturesqueness and the beauty of the countryside. The military-block type of worker's dwelling, dreary row after dreary row, was not popular.

The worker and his wife had, owing to the blessings of mass production, the use of more mechanical improvements than their fathers. This had been the case, of course, for over a century. As far as communication was concerned, the worker could ride in an electric trolley bus or a motor bus to and from his plant with comparative comfort and a maximum of speed. It was not unusual to find workers living twenty to thirty miles away from their jobs and thus able to return each night to the comparative peace and quiet of suburban districts and escape the noise and dirt of the city. In the postwar period the urban worker, by dint of saving and scraping, could acquire a motor bicycle, a motorcycle, or (if he belonged to the upper part of his class) a small and inexpensive automobile. Transportation improvements thus made the worker for the first time the peer of the lord of the manor and the man of the middle classes.

Motor, automobile, bus, and train opened new forms of recreation to the worker and thus changed the social life of Britain. Families went to the seashore in increasing numbers, or as "trippers" traveled en masse throughout England, Scotland, and Wales and onto the Continent. Nor was the gasoline engine the only invention to change the worker's life. The moving picture projector brought in the "flicks" and thus drove out the traveling theatrical company and lessened the custom at the local public house. High taxes on wine, spirits, and beer conduced to sobriety, and in consequence less was heard of "local option" to enforce local prohibition.

In food, the working man fared better. Imports of fruit and increase of home production of fruit replaced starches to some extent and helped balance his diet. The candy consumption in England, always tremendous, increased because of mass production, new methods of marketing, and more working-class wealth wherewith to buy "sweets" for the children. In other respects the worker got better consumer's goods and more of them. Chains of stores made money out of bringing him and his wife what had been luxuries. Those same stores gave employment to the women of his family and, by increasing purchasing power, increased their own markets.

Socially, there was a degree of leveling up, as mass production of clothes enabled the workingman's wife to follow the fashion and dress as did the lady of rank. Improved purchasing power and mass production also allowed the workingman to buy tailor-made suits. Perhaps the radio set led to a mental leveling up, for the worker could listen as well as the lord to the programs of the British Broadcasting Corporation, the state monopoly that provided amusement and edification for all. It is impossible, of course, to prove or to disprove this assertion.

It is possible, however, to note the effect of public education upon working classes. Sons of workers in increasing numbers were to be found as scholars and as students in Oxford, Cambridge, London, Wales, the Scottish, and other universities. No longer after 1919 could it be said that British universities were reserved for the sons of the middle and upper classes. Scholarships and ability brought the industrious and intelligent young people of the working classes into the universities. From the universities they went into the professions and their lives' work, carrying with them not only the point of view of educated people but also the memories of their early life. In this way it was possible for them to bring to public life and service not only their personal viewpoint but an intelligent and understanding representation of how the working class felt.

Those who had been educated in the public-supported schools since the opening of the century were of course avid readers of racing forms and of the women's pages that were part of popular journalism. The great newspapers, catering to the taste of the working classes, continued as they had before World War I to reduce news to rather simple levels. However, the more intelligent and sober of the working class had made available for them through the efforts of various societies and trade unions cheaply printed editions of serious and intelligent works on economics, social problems, and authors of literary merit. The works of people like G. B. Shaw, the Fabians, Harold Laski, and Graham Wallas were made available to industrious workers through membership in the Left Book Club. This club was kept alive by the subscriptions of small groups who purchased books and passed them from hand to hand.

MIDDLE CLASSES

Winds of depression and social reorientation may have blown good for the employed working class; they blew ill for the middle classes, who in a previous century had put their mark on the social fabric of the culture.

The relative position as to personal well-being and resumption of life interrupted by the war would be somewhat different for the British middle classes. Certainly this class whose thought, manners, and position were dominant in the last half of the nineteenth century and first part of the twentieth century could not have been expected under postwar conditions to remain precisely the same as before. We have observed a general social and economic improvement in the ranks of laborers and those of the lower middle class who found employment. The majority of the middle classes, particularly those in the professions, did not fare in the postwar years nearly as well as they had in the prewar years.

The middle classes in England had been accustomed to maintain a standard of living that could be observed easily not only in their position and display of material wealth but also in the type of income that had come to distinguish their activities. A position of responsibility, bringing as a reward a comfortable salary, the possession of a house or flat in town, a place in the country, and above all the employment of one or more domestic servants, was a badge of social distinction of the middle classes, particularly of the upper groups. In the nineteenth century and first part of the twentieth century ownership of horses, membership in clubs in town or country, whether one of the great clubs or often membership in one of the well-known political and social clubs in London, gave to the middle classes a general sense of well-being and security. The salaries or first earnings in professions were augmented either by income inherited from sources such as ownership of land and collection of rents, or by dividends from stocks and bonds and speculation in securities on the stock exchange.

The middle class, of course, included a range from those who were on small salaries and had no inherited income to those who had very large salaries and income apart from these. The dividing line between the more wealthy members of the middle and upper classes was merely one of amount of wealth and membership in clubs. An upper-middle-class man might belong to a political club such as the Reform or the Carlton but would not be invited to join one of the more celebrated and socially prominent ones. The standard of living of the upper middle class included sending sons to schools such as Eton and Harrow. This was possible for the more wealthy of the middle class, but entrance was still somewhat difficult for them to secure. However, there were many good schools which the sons of doctors, lawyers, and shop managers, as well as merchants, could attend and there receive the rigorous training in manners and thinking that had come to distinguish the British gentleman. Through dress and possession of material wealth, therefore, as well as manners, one could observe the effects of a sudden falling off of income.

Most of the middle classes in the years after 1920 experienced a very sudden depression. The lower middle class on salaries, such as the stenographers and clerks in public offices, as well as those on low salaries in business offices, finally were given some assistance through the unemployment-insurance scheme. The state displayed no such tender consideration, however, for the middle class in general. In the disastrous year of 1921 thousands of assistant managers, managers, and junior writers lost their jobs. When they did not lose their jobs, their income was cut drastically. They had to give up membership in the cricket club, dispense with one servant, or employ a servant only for part time. The income that had allowed for a continental holiday or the purchase of an automobile now had to be revised downward; the holiday plans had to be forgotten, and the automobile became merely a memory. Children who had been promised that they could attend a public school now had to either go to one that was state-supported, attend the public school as scholars, or not go at all.

Although during the middle and late 1920's the earning power of the middle class improved, as trade and business improved, nevertheless the heavy taxes on excess profits, incomes, and amusements had the effect of wiping out the cash reserves of the middle class as well as forcing them to reduce their standard of living. They could still live, of course, in some comfort and with the lower classes share in the luxury and delights to be found in the cinema, in the purchase of cheaper goods, and in modest excursions for holidays. The ladies could still wear evening dresses, although the same garment might be used until it had become slightly unfashionable, because the business cycle did not keep pace with the cycle of fashions. The reduction of interest paid to holders of the national debt after 1932 affected seriously the stable income of many widows and people about ready to retire, who had up to this time received 5 per cent and after the refunding of the debt had to take 3½ per cent. Many of the middle class had received small but steady incomes from stocks and bonds in textile, shipping, and steel companies. Very often they were asked to take much lower dividends or no dividends at all when the companies failed to make a profit or were liquidated.

Thus, the comfortable nest egg that had come to distinguish the middle class disappeared entirely or became pitifully small. The result naturally was the creation of a great deal of bitterness in that class. The government was blamed for extravagance or the working classes for their demands for state-provided security. The tradition of personal independence that had become an intellectual characteristic of this class, as a personal philosophy as well as a class philosophy, seemed false and illusory. Regardless of a man's efficiency and his determination to work, rewards in the form of bonus or increased salary simply did not materialize. The middle class that had allied itself to big business and management had ample time to discover that salaried rewards were not forthcoming. This does not mean necessarily that the middle class was discontented with big business or the effects of production upon the national economy. It means that the middle class had to readjust its habits of life to a lower standard of living, and quite naturally those who were forced into a new and less satisfactory social and economic position did not look with universal approval upon the advantages won by labor. Some critics believed that this dissatisfaction was caused by conditions beyond their control, and dislike of labor's over-all improvement is a reason the Conservative party won the support of so many of the middle classes that had previously been Liberal. The Liberal philosophy of *laissez faire* simply did not conform to the stark realities of the postwar years.

As a whole the middle class grumbled, but paid its ever-increasing taxes courageously. Its members were able to comprehend some of the causes for the economic disasters that had occurred in the more important of the prewar industries. As managers, clerical workers, and salaried employees, they adjusted very well to the new industrial opportunities and to the economic shift that occurred in British business. They continued to be reasonably level-headed and aggressive, and they displayed their usual efficiency. It was not their fault if management and continued world economic crises did not bring them as individuals increased revenue. On the whole the upper half of the middle groups were able to maintain the outward appearances of middle-class comfort and ease. They could still dress for dinner and perhaps afterwards partake, although in greatly reduced quantities, of the luxuries to which they had become accustomed in prewar years.

Most noticeable, of course, was the trend of working-class women to move from domestic service into factories and offices where these young ladies assumed at once the manners and dress of the middle class. The young lawyer's wife had to do a greater share of her domestic work than a young lawyer's wife had been required to do before the war. When holidays were taken on the Continent, not as much money was spent stopping at first-class hotels and dining at the best restaurants as had been spent in prewar years. The American tourist in this respect replaced the British after 1920.

Some critics observe that the loss in salary and in stocks and bonds of income had an improving effect upon the middle class. As a group the middle class started to think, read, and vote in a way that their fathers would not have dreamed possible. Since the natural curiosity of this group as to why a change was brought about in their standard of living made them more thoughtful, the result was that this class took a greater interest in social problems and in politics than it had displayed for some time.

The middle class was forced to think about socialization of the national economy, and in successive elections it cast its vote for one or another of the programs for socialism. The Liberal party in 1929 put forth a reform program calculated to appeal to middle-class votes. It suggested a way out of the depression. But even then this party, that had been the standard bearer for the middle class in politics, resorted to the temporary expedient of state aid. Thus, the middle classes, formerly wedded to a broad philosophy of personal freedom and social and economic *laissez faire,* seemed to be now forced to support a philosophy of state control or management of certain social services and activities. The choice presented was one of the extent to which socialization should be permitted to go, and whether socialization should be permanent or merely a temporary phenomenon which was caused by unfortunate domestic and world conditions.

In the years after World War I the middle classes suffered severely because of the economic revolution. No longer did the economic balance lie with the middle class; above it were greater accumulations of wealth, below it was a working class with greater purchasing power. No longer did the political balance lie with the middle class; universal suffrage had ended that. No longer was the middle class financially secure. As a result there was an intellectual and moral revolution.

This revolution, by which "the Bright Young People" took over leadership, was outwardly shown in dress and deportment. Women's dresses were no longer designed to conceal feminine charms. Petticoats and ankle-length dresses gave way to filmy undergarments and skirts at the knee. Smart young men wore "Oxford bags"—shapeless and balloonlike trousers, which covered the entire shoe—or golf knickerbockers. In the evening gentlemen wore white waistcoats with dinner jackets, to the horror of an older generation. Though ladies of rank before the war had shunned mention in the newspapers save for the court circular, they now accepted money for indorsements, under their photographs of lotions, perfume, and even cooking utensils. Gossip columns flourished. There was public exhibitionism in the type of dance, as the Charleston replaced the waltz, that in its day had been considered daring, and in the type of party hostesses gave. This same revolution appeared in the writings of the time. Aldous Huxley's *Brave New World,* and Evelyn Waugh's *Vile Bodies* suggest that those who gave tone to social life cared little about the future, were disillusioned about the present, and were contemptuous of the past.

UPPER CLASSES

If the middle class had suffered severe reversals in its social, moral, and economic positions, what could be said of the upper classes? As compared with the situation of a century earlier, one might say that the outward symbols of power, prestige, and privilege were much the same. But it could also be said that these were symbols of the power and prestige of a former advantage and social order. The evidence of the postwar change in the status of the upper classes could be seen in every daily paper advertising the sale of estates and, if they had been made public, in the tax bills presented to great property holders.

The death duties originally imposed by Sir William Harcourt had been merely portents of what the state might do to the wealthy. In the years following 1914 what the death duties could accomplish was observed when noblemen and other members of upper classes tried to avoid inheriting estates because the death duties often wiped out the entire value. In order to pay them the inheritor might have to borrow money and jeopardize the present financial stability of his family, to say nothing of that of his descendants. Manors and large estates that had been regarded as the homes of the gentry had to be sold before the period was over. It was not uncommon to find the lord of the manor living in a cottage formerly belonging to the gamekeeper. The manor house was left in the possession of wealthy American tourists or rented to a charitable organization. Estates of noblemen became country clubs or rest homes, or were cut up and sold to tenants, because the taxes were so very heavy. However, an enterprising businessman, a new man who was making his way in a difficult world, was often able to marry into an older family and revive its family prestige by the addition of his wealth. This was of course no departure from a well-established and ancient tradition. It was to be expected also that old estates would fall into the hands of men who were successful in the conduct of business.

One of the problems connected with the changing fortunes of the upper class as landholders was whether or not they would continue to give prestige and social and political leadership that had been theirs in country areas up to World War I. Many specific instances can be found where the upper classes, because of their changing financial status, could no longer provide for local charities and carry their political and social obligations that had become customary. By and large, however, the rural areas continued to remain under the social and political leadership of the prominent landlord who as justice of the peace or chairman of the county council continued the honorable and ancient function of giving a lead in local affairs. Naturally, because of the altered relationship between landlord and the tenant, the shop and the manor house, the upper classes could command respect but could not demand recognition in a political sense. The position of prestige could be won only through strength of character, although respect naturally was paid to those who by custom had represented social leadership in the past. Nevertheless, the political power of the gentry, or at least the similarity of point of view between landed gentry and their neighbors, was demonstrated by the more or less solid support given in postwar years to the Conservative party. Where collectivists' influences were not great, it would seem that individuals living in rural communities supported the Conservative party and its philosophies. The sons of gentlemen continued to do well in the civil service and the professions, although their achievement was personal and was owed on a decreasing scale to an inherited title or the reputation of their ancestors. Of course, if a boy wanted an introduction to the great world of politics or business, it was not harmful for him to have a parent who was a bank director or a member of the House of Lords. It was best, however, if the young man received a high score on civil service examinations and had family connections among leaders of the political parties.

Because of the tremendous tax burden borne by the upper classes and because, like the middle classes, the reserves that had been built up in the shape of bonds and stocks declined increasingly throughout the period, the habits of life and the pattern of social conduct were very definitely modified. For when the money necessary for the maintenance of large estates and large retinues of servants was lost, the maintenance of luxury and dignity that had been a distinguishing characteristic of the British gentry and upper classes in former times was also lost. Indeed, it might be said that the social wheel turned full circle, because during this period it no longer became a source of amusement to discover that instead of idly wasting time in the pursuit of scared foxes, rabbits, or chorus girls, the titled sons of the gentry were becoming business managers, automobile mechanics, and newspaper reporters working for wages and salaries. They worked not only because of personal preference but also because a title no longer was an indication of wealth. Naturally, some of the nobility had so much wealth in one form or another that their standard of living was comparatively little affected by the economic misfortunes of the war and high taxes. However, the cost of social services and the cost of upkeep of government were taken from the pockets of the property owners, and those who had achieved wealth and position had to pay heavily for the retention of their privileges. Most of the upper classes reduced their standards of living to some extent, in conformity with the requirements of the postwar generation.

Thus the gap that separated the lower from the upper classes was closed somewhat, and the tremendous disparity in class levels was not quite as noticeable after 1919 as it had been in the earlier years of the century. To this extent the war brought about a closer connection between the upper, middle, and lower classes. Often pride of family and birth, the background of a public-school education, but not finances separated the middle from the upper classes and the upper classes from the lower classes. Migrants into the upper classes from the middle and lower classes after 1919 were as they had always been—vigorous, ambitious, and keen men who in the face of appalling odds and competition were able to claim and achieve respect because of their personal achievements, either in public or private enterprise. It should be remembered that the war brought about a change in the classes to the extent that a socialist public servant such as Sidney Webb, who had married into the upper classes, should end his days as Baron Passfield, and a former trade-union leader should end his political career as Viscount Snowden.

In the postwar years, therefore, success in England was still patterned upon the formula of careers open to talents, and with the lowering of the financial barrier and the economic depression, the upper classes and the lower classes were brought closer together in their sharing of common misfortune. England, it might be said, was approaching for perhaps different reasons the socialist goal of a classless society. Certainly she had not reached that goal in 1939, but there was little denying that class differences based upon wealth, educational opportunities, and tradition were much less important in social life than they had been before World War I.

RELIGION

In a period of social change and spiritual unrest it is impossible to judge the effectiveness of the churches and clergymen of various denominations. Statistics merely say this: England and Wales, in 1937, had some 4,835,440 members reported for twelve Protestant denominations. In the same year there were 2,345,504 Roman Catholics in England and Wales. The four largest Protestant denominations in England and Wales reported membership as follows: Church of England, 2,294,000; Methodist, 1,250,-589; Congregational, 494,119; Baptist, 392,535.

A new law, the Church of England Assembly (Powers) Act of 1919, reorganized the machinery of the established church. This Act provides for a Church Assembly consisting of a House of Bishops, a House of Clergy, and a House of Laity that has power to frame legislation on Church affairs. When passed by the Church Assembly the measures then are referred to two committees of fifteen members of the House of Lords nominated by the Lord Chancellor and fifteen of the House of Commons nominated by the Speaker. When the committees approve, Parliament may or may not pass the measures as resolutions that are then engrossed on the statute books.

The new machinery, however, did not operate smoothly in the matter of adaption of a revised Prayer Book. Lord St. Aldwyn's commission of 1905 had given clergy and laity much spiritual food to chew. At last in 1927 a revised Book of Common Prayer was presented for Parliament's approval. It was turned down in 1928 after argument and controversy that often generated considerable heat. The position of the Church of England and of other churches in England and Wales was not greatly changed in this period from what it had been in the years before World War I. Forces working for and against the churches were much the same.

The nineteenth-century breach in the Presbyterian Church in Scotland was healed on October 2, 1929. The Church of Scotland and the United Free Church of Scotland were, after nearly a century's disunion, reunited under the name of the Church of Scotland. The united church in 1937 had 1,284,450 members distributed throughout some 2,565 congregations. The church of Calvin and John Knox was once more able to present a united front to the 414,021 Roman Catholics and some 57,000 Scotch Episcopalians. There was, of course, no question of the increased power and prestige that arose from the healing of the schism in the two branches of the Kirk.

46

CONSTITUTIONAL HISTORY

1919–1953

Just before he died, the late Professor Laski delivered lectures at Manchester, later published as *Reflections on the Constitution*. One point in this suggestive book deserves examination. He asserted that there was an eighteenth-century constitution no longer valid in the twentieth century. Is this assertion correct? To what extent has the twentieth century outgrown the system of government it inherited? Evidence here points two ways, whether in administration and the party system, which were both revamped; in the Cabinet, which was greatly strengthened; or in the Crown, which was given a new importance. For many claim that, despite superficial alterations, these institutions remain essentially what they had been in the past.

In administration, centralization has continued. With the abolition of the Poor Law Guardians in 1929, local administration was unified into one hierarchy of elective councils. The reorganization of the Ministry of Health in 1929 made one Cabinet member dominant over local government. With the removal of friendly societies and similar bodies from the picture, the National Insurance Act of 1946 made Great Britain a government-insurance state. This may all seem new. Yet Lord Chief Justice Hewart, in an angry book, *The New Despotism,* attacked this as a reversion to the old Tudor and Stuart centralization under the Privy Council. This change could, therefore, seem a revival of the old, as much as a new development.

The party system saw two great changes: the decadence of the old Liberal machine, and the emergence of the new Labor machine. The Liberal party split into two. Lloyd George kept the funds; Asquith and his successors, the machine. The fund eventually was spent. The machine, staffed by loyal enthusiasts, kept alive. It poured out propaganda. Its Liberal Summer School and other agencies recruited new followers. Persistently a large though dwindling minority voted Liberal, running up a large popular vote and winning sadly few seats, as a later chapter will show. In place of the Liberal party the Labor party rose. In 1918 it formed its constitution. This gave powers of guidance to two bodies, the T.U.C. and the Party Convention. Each represented a different phase of Labor. The T.U.C. gave the basic funds, the core of votes. The Party Convention represented the workers who went out and got the nonunion, frequently middle-class, votes by which a union minority could become a voting majority in a constituency. Thus the party history of Labor is of the growth of this machine, its surge in 1923, its first real success in 1929, its crash in 1931, and its struggle back to power, by way of winning and holding the London County Council in the 1930's. Here may seem something definitely twentieth-century. Yet this is but an expansion of the democratization of parties which was the inevitable result of the Reform Bill of 1867. Parties still remain basically what they were when Shaftesbury founded the Whig party in 1678.

The Cabinet took on the new efficiency given it by World War I. It kept records. It dominated Parliament and controlled the business of Parliament. This is in itself a continuance, however, of past tendencies. The basic idea of one "prime" minister who shall connect Cabinet and Crown remains the same as it was when Walpole got that position and the Pelhams defended it, in the eighteenth century. Here a World War I tendency, perhaps a nineteenth-century tendency, strengthens itself, that of cooperation on an equal base with the dominions. Summoning to the British Cabinet those dominions leaders, usually Premiers, who were British Privy Councilors proved a successful wartime device, though a failure, as will later be shown, in peace. Here appears a constitutional convention, again Canadian-created. The decisions of such a Cabinet meeting are binding on the dominion in question only if made by the Dominion Premier and answered for by him to his Parliament. On this Borden in the Versailles Conference, King in World War II, successfully insisted, backed by Menzies of Australia.

This cooperation of equals, however, is a close one. Typical of it is the exchange of information and support at foreign capitals, where the King's or Queen's minor representatives regularly meet together for consultation. Typical is the exchange of technical information, made often but not always at Westminster. Typical are the frequent Conferences, no longer Colonial, no longer Imperial, but Commonwealth, now held the world over, the most significant being the Colombo Conference on Asiatic problems, held in the new-founded dominion of Ceylon in 1949. As the phrase goes, the Commonwealth is now a "club" of mutual help as well as mutual independence. But is this not of the eighteenth century, the ideal of the first Pitt, which he carried out as in the 1750's and, as Earl of Chatham, vainly advocated as the necessary means of stopping the American Revolution? Has the position of the Crown changed? Or is it a matter of residual powers being exercised? During this period four ancient powers of the Crown have been called out of abeyance: the power to dismiss ministers, the power to choose among contestants for Prime Minister, the power to refuse to dissolve Parliament, and the power to abdicate. Dismissal has taken place once, in New South Wales, when the Crown's representative, the Lieutenant Governor, dismissed the Lang government (which was acting illegally in relation to the Australian Commonwealth), put in a successor, called a general election, and thus secured popular ratification of this unusual action. This incident is significant for the use of the Crown's power by the Crown's overseas representative and for the reliance on popular ratification. A similar use, in Canada, of the power not to dissolve, the so-called King-Byng affair of 1926, is significant because popular ratification did not come. Lord Byng refused to let Mackenzie King call an election to break a parliamentary deadlock; gave power to his opponent, Arthur Meighen; and then gave Meighen the dissolution he had refused King. But King won the election. The power to choose was taken by George V, when in the emergency of Bonar Law's dying of cancer of the throat, it fell to him, not Bonar Law, to choose between Baldwin and Curzon as Law's successor. The power not to dissolve, in 1931, was used by George V, on the advice of Sir Herbert Samuel, as a means of meeting the crisis of that year. Later on a dissolution and general election ratified this. In 1936, Edward VIII, in a very different crisis—and this time proceeding by acts of Parliament for ratification—abdicated, with the consent of all the dominions. Here are eighteenth- or even seventeenth-century actions still taking place. Yet be it noticed that in every case it was an emergency action, ratified by the people except for the power to choose, and tacitly ratified by Parliament. One can contest, as in the King-Byng affair, whether the action was sound; to this day Labor contests the action of 1931, as will be told. What matters is the final reference to the people. Here one may say that certain residual powers do reappear and form contestable emergency devices, but that these continue to exist only because they are now subject to popular review.

There remains to be examined one function of the Crown, that of the link that united the Commonwealth of Nations. In 1926 executive action of the Committee of Premiers of the Imperial Conference proclaimed the British Empire to be the British Commonwealth of Nations, a free association of equals. In 1931 the Parliaments of the Commonwealth ratified this proclamation by jointly passing the act known as the Statute of Westminster, to clear up the legal tangles caused by this new status. No longer would the Colonial Laws Validity Act force a dominion to go hat in hand to the British Parliament to secure the repeal of an antiquated law, applicable to it in colonial times but now outdated. Now such dominions as accepted the Statute could make what laws they chose, could even, unless the Statute prevented it by express wording, amend their own constitutions. But such independence had its penalties as well as its pleasures.

Some such penalties were avoided by special clauses that reserved to the British Parliament control over Province-Confederation relations in Canada and Commonwealth-State relations in Australia, and by one clause that permitted the British Parliament to legislate for dominions by request. Even then the new status, though immediately taken by Canada, Eire, and South Africa, was not attractive enough for Australia until 1942, or for New Zealand until 1947. As for Newfoundland, it backhandedly accepted the Statute in 1949 by becoming a province of Canada.

But the Statute has a more important effect. It made the Crown and the Crown alone the legal connection between Britain and her sister realms. Thus was created a league of nations, inside the usual international interconnections. Each member of the Commonwealth treats with the others through "High Commissioners" who rank as ambassadors. Thus comes the executive cooperation at all levels which is the distinguishing mark of the Commonwealth. The Crown, directly or through its representatives, functions in the same way in each realm. That is why the question of succession and titles has importance and why the Statute of Westminster requires them to be the unanimous action of all the Dominions. The question of succession came in 1936, during the abdication, when South Africa acted one day early, Eire one day late, in proclaiming the new reign of George VI, but all members acted concurrently. The question of title is more significant. In 1927, to ease Irish susceptibilities, the royal title was changed from King of Great Britain and Ireland and the Dominions beyond the Seas, which thus made Ireland part of Great Britain, to King of Great Britain, Ireland, and the Dominions beyond the Seas, which made Ireland a separate kingdom. This was repealed in 1953, after Ireland had left the Commonwealth in 1949. In 1947, the title of Emperor of India was dropped when India became first a dominion, then a republic, within the Commonwealth. In 1949, at a Conference of Commonwealth Premiers, plans were laid for a new approach to the royal title, which plans were passed into law in 1953 in time for the coronation of Elizabeth II. Her Majesty no longer has the same title throughout the Commonwealth. In each member her title differs, except that in each she is Head of the Commonwealth, though she is monarch in all parts save India. This was shown at the coronation, when eight premiers marched together in the procession but the Queen swore to rule only seven realms. Basically, the monarchical title follows with local variants this form: "Queen of this realm and all her other realms and territories." Thus today the Crown rules in seven realms under seven different titles, "heads" one republic, and holds sway, besides, over many varied territories that may eventually aspire to equality.

Here a new term may have entered constitutional law, that of "realm." It solves the problem of having one name for the dominions of Canada,

Ceylon, and Pakistan; the Commonwealth of Australia; the Union of South Africa; and New Zealand, which has no particular legal appellation. Furthermore this name suggests, as "dominion" does not, independent monarchical sovereignty. Yet is this an innovation? Was not George III in the eighteenth century, at one and the same time, King of Great Britain, King of Ireland, King of Corsica, and Elector of Hanover? On the other hand, Her present Majesty has a new title, Head of the Commonwealth.

Thus in matters of title, as in others, it may be said that Professor Laski's point is both false and true. Were he alive, he would probably be the first to admit it. For as ever the essential point about the British constitution seems to remain this: the more it changes, the more it remains the same. Indeed one might add that in this time of increased democratization, which is the change Professor Laski was driving at, the other significant change is internationalization. For it is the same "unwritten constitution" that now guides all Queen Elizabeth II's realms.

47

POLITICS

1919–1939

When World War I ended, peacetime political life opened with a dream. Since Great Britain now had manhood suffrage and her women, too, could vote, was it not time for a truly National Government, which would win the peace in the same spirit as it had won the war? So Lloyd George, who had long dreamed this dream, even before World War I, forced George V to let him dissolve Parliament and appeal to the people. But this dream turned out a nightmare. Labor would not accept a peacetime coalition. In Ireland, rebellion was the campaign issue that won candidates for Sinn Fein. As for those Liberals who had voted against Lloyd George on the Maurice motion, they were barred from his backing. Mordantly, Asquith sneered at the "coupons" Lloyd George issued to the Conservatives and the Coalition Liberals. Shamefully, during the election, wartime bitternesses were kept up, with demands by the press supporting the Coalition to "hang the Kaiser" and, in demand for reparations, to "squeeze the orange till the pips squeak." These drowned out the nobler appeal for "Homes Fit for Heroes." The result was the ill-fated "Parliament of Hard-faced Men." In it Lloyd George had an apparently overwhelming majority. Behind him were 470 Coalitionists. On the Opposition benches —for Sinn Fein refused to sit—were 60 Laborites and a meager 28 Asquithian Liberals without Asquith.

The program which Lloyd George had campaigned on was this: make peace, incidentally collecting 100 million pounds from Germany, and go forward with social legislation. Lloyd George then went to Paris to make peace—and the program was not carried out. Peace was a failure; reparations proved impossible to assess. In Ireland rebellion broke out and could not be quenched. The returning soldiers—who had almost mutinied at the methods of release from service, forcing Winston Churchill to be hurried to the War Office in Milner's place—got "the dole," not "homes fit for heroes." For jobs were not to be found, and instead the government handed out weekly the equivalent of the unemployment insurance it was genuinely giving to workers in some industries. Failure in Ireland culminated—after much big talk—in giving twenty-six counties of Ireland not Home Rule but dominion status, while the six counties of Ulster got Home Rule in separation from the rest of Ireland. The failure of reparations conferences discredited Lloyd George. His Near Eastern policy broke down. Finally, when at the Chanak incident war with Turkey was narrowly averted, the rank and file of the Conservative party had had enough. The Conservative party met at the Carlton Club and, despite the loyal pleadings of those in the Cabinet, voted 187 to 87 to withdraw support from Lloyd George and form a purely Conservative administration. The leader here was the comparatively unknown Stanley Baldwin. Then there came into office the Bonar Law Government, of minor party members, while such experienced Conservatives as Austen Chamberlain—who resigned the party leadership—and Lord Birkenhead went into exile.

During this time the political picture changed, and new issues came to the fore. The Opposition Liberals pulled themselves together a bit, kept hold of the party machinery, and did one very important thing. They taught the new Labor party the "tricks of the trade" in the House of Commons. Labor thus in these years gained invaluable experience in parliamentary responsibility, which would pay dividends when they should become the party in power. At the same time two issues rose. The burden of taxation was heavy. A debt of seven billion pounds by its interest terms alone was crushing and prohibited social legislation. Here would be one major problem. Another would be the depressed industries. Chief among these was coal. English methods were outmoded and uneconomical. Both labor and management rejected proposals for change. An investigating commission was appointed, under Mr. Justice Sankey. It so completely failed to agree that it made three reports, one by labor, one by management, one by public representatives. Thus a double industrial problem arose. On the one hand, protectionists demanded an end to free trade. On the other, Labor demanded action. This was an era of strikes, the most notable ones being the railway strikes of 1919 and 1921 and the coal strikes of 1920 and 1921. Certain Labor leaders began to believe that they could tie up the nation's economy; some on the other side became frightened by their talk. Such was a background to the election of 1922, in which Bonar Law, to make his ousting of Lloyd George the main issue, pledged he would not give up free trade and introduce protection.

The Parliament returned by that election of 1922 held 344 Conservatives, 55 Lloyd George Liberals, 60 Asquithian Liberals, and 138 members of the Labor party, which therefore remained the official Opposition, with the responsibility that that entails. The Bonar Law Cabinet was a crippled body. Its head was mortally ill. As all who had supported Lloyd George were exiled from office, such men of ability as Churchill, Balfour, Austen Chamberlain, and Birkenhead were not in it. The chief leaders in it were

Lord Curzon, who decided after vacillation to leave Lloyd George and join Bonar Law, and Stanley Baldwin, the leader of the rebellion against Lloyd George. The chief accomplishment of the Bonar Law Cabinet was to negotiate a debt settlement with America. Here Chancellor of the Exchequer Baldwin committed his country to pay a total of eleven billion pounds in principal and interest in return for a loan of less than four billion. He got an interest rate eight times larger than Italy's, six times larger than France's. Later, the Americans who negotiated with Baldwin stated that he offered them more than they would have asked, let alone accepted.

Just the same, Baldwin held the loyalty of his followers. When Bonar Law died it was he, not Curzon, for whom the King sent to head the Ministry. For Baldwin had definite political virtues. A businessman, he knew industrial problems. He had filled his wartime post at the Board of Trade efficiently. The story leaked out that he had given one-tenth of his property to the nation every year of the war, and men respected him for this quiet proof of patriotism which he had tried to conceal. He had a sense of what the average Englishman wanted which made him one of the most efficient political leaders in modern history. Above all, he was a sort of artist at being an Englishman. With a literary gift like that of his first cousin, Rudyard Kipling, he painted for the voters a picture of himself as an up-to-date John Bull. A man who had done what he had done, who was Prime Minister, and who smoked an underslung pipe and looked over fences at pigs won popular confidence in his philosophy of trust and tranquillity. It is probably not inaccurate to compare him in ability, statesmanship, and learning with Presidents Harding, Coolidge, and Hoover who in America stood for much the same thing.

But the year 1923 was not one in which Baldwin could sit quietly. Unemployment shot up to over a million, and depression continued. Baldwin therefore decided to use the cures he believed in, protection and imperial preference. If tariffs protected British industry and if reciprocal agreements with the dominions got Britain markets, recovery might be attained. But in the election the Conservatives had pledged themselves not to give up free trade, and Baldwin felt himself honor bound to call an election. In defense of free trade the Lloyd George and Asquithian Liberals temporarily joined in acrimonious harmony and in the election of 1923 presented a united front that was in reality neither a front nor united. The electorate chose 259 Conservatives, 191 Laborites, and 158 Liberals. Thus the decision as to who would rule lay in the hands of the Liberals. Asquith refused to support Baldwin or to take office with Conservative support and announced the Liberals would keep Labor in office. His Majesty thereupon sent for J. Ramsay MacDonald to be Prime Minister.

Administratively, philosophically, and politically, the first Labor Cabinet in the homeland—Queensland had had one twenty-seven years before—had many difficulties to face. Had not Lord Haldane been willing to join as Lord Chancellor, it would not have contained a single member with Cabinet experience until Arthur Henderson finally got into Parliament in a by-election. MacDonald felt, with some justice, that he must bear the triple burden of the premiership, leading the House, and the Foreign Office, and was in consequence harried and at times hurried in his decisions. As the Cabinet could stay in office only with Liberal support, and as the Labor party was divided into a trade union wing and a socialist wing, its policies were largely a matter of compromise. Indeed, of seventy bills introduced to Parliament, sixty-five were Liberal-sponsored and not according to the official Labor party program. Yet to counterbalance this there were assets. MacDonald had very real personal prestige. His arduous work in building up the Labor party in the early 1900's as Secretary of the Labor Representation Committee and his clear-cut and brave record as an antiwar pacifist in World War I gained him respect. His behavior as a typical British statesman in Parliament and social functions disarmed criticism. As for the Labor party itself, it was brimful of vigor and the thrill of being His Majesty's Government. In consequence a good deal was achieved.

As part of good socialist doctrine, Communist Russia was recognized. As part of the internationalism of the Labor movement MacDonald helped negotiate the abortive Geneva Protocol of 1924 with its program of collective defense of peace by an international army. When Campbell, the editor of the Communist newspaper in London, advocated the overthrow of the government, the Labor Attorney General, to preserve freedom of speech, quashed the indictment. As a matter of parliamentary tactics, MacDonald refused to resign even when defeated on what he considered nonessentials. Finally the time came when the Cabinet felt it must go to the country, choosing, technically, a question of a mild degree of protection as a defense of the living standard of the workers. But this election was not fought, as MacDonald had hoped, on the record of his Government. There appeared in the press—though its original has never been found— a letter of the Russian Foreign Commissar Zinoviev giving instructions as to how to conduct a workers' revolution in Great Britain. This struck a heavy blow at the party which had recognized Russia and had done its best to bring about close relations. On such a confused set of issues a new Parliament was elected containing 400 Conservatives, 150 Laborites, and 40 Liberals, mostly followers of Asquith, who himself was defeated and went to the House of Lords, by the personal action of George V.

Now it was Baldwin's turn to meet the problems of postwar Britain. This time he had a stronger party, for the political breach had been healed; Balfour, Birkenhead, and Austen Chamberlain were brought back into the Cabinet. As Chancellor of the Exchequer was chosen Winston Churchill, who after electoral vicissitudes had found a safe parliamentary seat and was on his way to rejoining the Conservative party he had left in 1904. The first action of the Baldwin government was to restore the gold standard, though the pound was pegged at a lower level than in the past. Gold coins were not issued, but the Bank of England dealt with other central banks in gold bullion. This, it was hoped, would restore Britain's position in world trade, even though it did raise costs at home. But Baldwin's chief problem was coal, the most grievously hit of all British industries.

As a temporary expedient, Baldwin subsidized coal, to keep wages up even though the industry was being run at a loss. Then he appointed an investigating commission, headed by the Liberal statesman, Sir Herbert Samuel, to devise a long-term cure. The Commission reported that either high-cost mines should be shut or wages cut. The operators refused to shut mines; the unions refused to take a wage cut, claiming that what was received was barely enough for subsistence as it was. Yet something had to be done, for the subsidy could not go on forever. The miners threatened to strike, and to achieve a settlement, the T.U.C. threatened to back them up with labor's most powerful weapon, the general strike. Negotiations with the government fell through, and on May 3, 1926, came Britain's first and only General Strike.

For nine days the struggle went on. All services were shut off. The only newspaper circulating in the country was the *Gazette* that Winston Churchill and some volunteers brought out. Trains and other forms of transportation were run by volunteers, many recruited by the government-controlled British Broadcasting Corporation. Peace was kept remarkably well, and after nine days the General Strike was called off, though the miners stayed out for seven months till their union funds were exhausted. The defeat of the General Strike gained Baldwin much prestige, but also caused long-standing resentment in the working class. This resentment was intensified by the Trade Disputes Act of 1926, which not only made a general strike illegal but restricted the labor movement, by forbidding intimidation of strikebreakers and the joining by government employees of organizations that were likely to go out on strike.

Ending the strike did not end the problems it was designed to settle. Baldwin hoped to cure them by increasing the prosperity of the nation through tax reduction. Despite adventurous and imaginative fiscal policies, Chancellor of the Exchequer Churchill could not cut costs beyond the low of 791 million pounds the Laborite Snowden had reached. For three years, 1925–1926, 1926–1927, and 1929–1930, Churchill had deficits, respectively of fourteen million, thirty-seven million, and fourteen million pounds. But in 1927–1928 and 1928–1929 he achieved the miracle of surpluses of four million and eighteen million. Churchill also used a device, derating, that went back to Disraeli's day. By this the national exchequer took over certain expenses from local bodies, and therefore removed an immediate financial burden of rates or local taxes from individuals and industry. To balance this the gasoline tax was raised. As is told elsewhere, this government, by the Balfour Report, solved a serious imperial crisis and pursued a quiet foreign policy.

As the 1929 elections approached, the Liberals and the Laborites rallied, each in their own way, to win the election. The three parties entered the campaign in three very different moods: the Conservatives in one of vague confidence in their accomplishments; the Liberals, of cautious reunion; the Laborites, of a crusade for peace. The Conservatives had confidence in their political machine and a hope that the people would continue to want normalcy. The Liberals, having superficially patched up their quarrels and brought together the Asquithian machine and the Lloyd George party fund of over a million pounds, hoped that a great program of new ideas would catch men's minds. But Labor came into the election in a crusading mood, determined to make peace truly secure and have "socialism in our time." It was Labor that caught the voters' imaginations in May, 1929. Constituency after constituency that had never voted that way before fell to their candidates. As a result, Ramsay MacDonald's followers held a plurality, 258 as against 255 Conservatives and 57 Liberals. Now it was not, as in 1924, necessary for them to have Liberal votes to carry their measures, but merely for the Liberals to abstain from voting and let them defeat the Conservatives.

Ramsay MacDonald, therefore, assumed office after the election. People quickly learned that though in domestic affairs the Labor party might express sympathy with the condition of the unemployed and might even advocate socialism, in practice it would depart in no important way from the policies of previous administrations. Snowden at the Exchequer made budget proposals more ironbound and traditional than those suggested by the more flexible Winston Churchill. He committed the Cabinet to gradual amelioration of conditions, sound finance, and the rejection of a public-works program. Conservative-minded trade-union Labor M.P.'s backed Snowden and MacDonald in this, but it irked the Independent Labor party, an organization founded in 1893 to lead the voters toward socialism. The "Wild Men of the Clyde," the Scottish M.P.'s, who now composed the majority of that body, threatened a left-wing revolt. Promptly MacDonald, always at his best when his moral position was attacked, resigned from the I.L.P., to which he had belonged since 1894, stating that it had outlived its usefulness. This action brought upon him criticism. It was felt that he was deserting old comrades, that from association with the aristocracy he had ceased to be a Socialist, that he was a Laborite only in name, and that in private life he preferred to think, act, and talk like a Conservative.

From 1929 to 1931 a committee under the chairmanship of Lord Macmillan had considered the problems of depressed Britain. In June, 1931, it reported, asking for tighter international control of money through central banks and warning that tighter control over interest rates and over business in general would be necessary to defeat the depression. Later on, protectionists were to draw arguments from this to justify a change in Britain's economic policy.

In 1931 came a crisis that gave point to this charge. As depression was deepening in America and Europe, the national credit of Great Britain was being used to fight it by means of loans from the Bank of England to the central banks of Central Europe. The ability to give this help apparently depended on the British gold standard, which could be kept only by a balanced budget. Snowden contrived as best he could to meet deficits by the means made classical in the nineteenth century. But in February, 1931, he had to admit that Britain's credit was in grievous danger. The May Economy Committee was therefore set up. It reported on July 31, 1931, that only drastic cuts in expenses could save the gold standard. The consensus of banking opinion backed the May Committee up. Here the Labor Cabinet split. To most of its members the existing rate of relief and of unemployment insurance were sacrosanct. They refused to make reductions. Instead they urged abandoning the gold standard. As this policy would lose Liberal support, MacDonald left the Cabinet meeting to present his resignation to George V. To the Cabinet's surprise MacDonald came back to announce that he had not resigned office, but was forming a coalition all-party Cabinet to save the nation's credit, which he invited them to join. Of his colleagues only a handful, chief among them Snowden, accepted his offer. What had happened at Buckingham Palace? This is a question still asked, but it is now known that George V, in the light of the crisis, summoned to him a Liberal and a Conservative leader. The Liberal, Sir Herbert Samuel, arrived first, and urged compellingly the formation of the all-party Government. Baldwin, the Conservative, accepted the suggestion and pledged support. The King took Samuel's "constitutional advice" and kept MacDonald in office.

The new National Government was made as nonpartisan as possible. Many offices were held by elder statesmen come out of retirement. It tried to tread the path of economy that would save the gold standard and Britain's credit. On September 10, Snowden introduced a second budget which proposed to gain a surplus of £360,000 by drastic cuts on salaries, pensions, and expenses and by a heavy increase in income tax. Murmurings met this, though most people accepted it in good part. On September

15 came the shocking news that the fleet at Invergordon in protest had, at an unfair allocation of cuts, refused to obey orders. The allocation was remedied, the fleet went back to duty, and morale was restored. But the damage was done. Despite Snowden's cuts, England went off gold on September 21. Then the National Government called an election to gain a mandate from the people.

A mandate it got, an overwhelming one. Bitterly Labor fought what it called a "bankers' ramp," or trick; bitterly it vilified its lost leader. In return MacDonald pointed to the dangers of inflation. Before audiences he waved depreciated German money as a warning to the British public of what would happen if the National Government were not kept in office. Fearful of the postwar horrors that had swept Germany, the people returned 470 Conservatives and with them 70 "National Liberals" and "National Laborites." In opposition were the four members of the Lloyd George group and 52 Laborites. On the Labor side every former Cabinet minister except George Lansbury lost his seat. Thus was put in overwhelming power a government now predominantly Conservative, though it still tried to be all-party. MacDonald was Prime Minister. Baldwin as Lord President was more and more the actual leader. Since Snowden from age and ill-health retired to the House of Lords, Neville Chamberlain became Chancellor of the Exchequer, for Winston Churchill was too contentious a figure to be rewarded with office. Yet, by keeping the Liberals Samuel and Simon as Home and Foreign Secretaries, the Laborite Thomas as Dominions Secretary, and similar Liberals and Laborites in other offices, the idea of a National Government was kept alive.

The National Government turned to the task at hand. A rigid reexamination of all relief cases caused real savings. Debt interest to the United States was no longer paid, the Hoover moratorium thus becoming permanent. Then the vast Conservative majority demanded that their economic remedy of protection and imperial preference be tried. In order to maintain the "all-party" nature of the Government, an "agreement to differ" kept the Liberals and Snowden in the Cabinet while the Ottawa Conference was called to hammer out details. Those details became unacceptable, and Snowden and the Samuelite Liberals resigned, while the Simonite Liberals became, as had their Liberal Unionist predecessors, less and less distinguishable from Conservatives. Tariffs and other protective legislation discussed earlier were then enacted. Although budget deficits appeared in 1934 and 1935, some semblance of balance and prosperity was brought about by the resumption of industrial production. After 1936 it became possible to borrow from the United States and France, and the country was back on reasonably stable footing.

As the worst of the economic blizzard passed, the National Government held on to its political prestige. No one liked the loss of salaries or the lowness of dividends, but President Roosevelt, who had called the London Economic Conference of 1933 and then "torpedoed" it, was a convenient villain to curse for the failure of international cooperation for recovery. Attention turned to India and to foreign affairs. Then in 1935 foreign affairs invaded the field of home politics, in the overwhelming success of the Peace Ballot circulated by Lord Cecil's League of Nations Union. About four million Britons were asked if they would fight again and under what conditions. Most answered, in effect, that they would do almost anything to keep the peace. Pacifism became a popular mood. At Oxford and Cambridge and other universities the youth of the nation loudly refused to fight for King and Country. These young men later observed these pledges by dying at Dunkirk and by shooting down German planes in the Battle of Britain with commendable accuracy. It was in such an atmosphere that the term of the 1931 Parliament drew to its end.

In June, 1935, MacDonald, under the increasing handicaps of ill-health and sharp decline in prestige, resigned as Prime Minister and turned that office over to Baldwin. In November came the general election. Mac-Donald gamely contested his old seat of Seaham. He was defeated and forced to take refuge in the safe Conservative seat of the Scottish universities. But his campaign in defense of his record did much to hold the National majority high. Thus MacDonald leaves the stage of history, rarely attending the House of Commons any more, and dying in 1937 on a trip to the West Indies. He has been vilified as a traitor to his party. He has been scorned as a vaporer—Winston Churchill called him "the boneless wonder" after one vague and gaseous speech. But to his credit stand two great achievements: in the 1900's he trained Labor to be a parliamentary party, and in the 1920's he proved that Labor could govern England. The man who advised the rising young men of his ministry not to spoil their careers by joining his National Government deserves honor for service to his party and his country that posterity will eventually give him, whatever his manifest faults. Even though Labor picked up over a hundred seats, the Conservatives alone had a comfortable membership of 387 and needed National Liberals and National Labor support not for votes but for preserving the remnants of the all-party aspect of the Government.

To turn to the situation of the Labor opposition, when MacDonald and Snowden were read out of the party for desertion in 1931, the older leadership of the Laborites fell into quarrels and sad party splits. The left-wing Independent Labor party led by James Maxton was thrown out in 1934 because it was too Marxist and rebellious. Sir Oswald Mosley, who at first had been a promising young socialist recruit from the nobility, cut away and organized his British Fascist party, an annoying lunatic-fringe group that tried unsuccessfully to turn British workers into imitation storm troopers. Since other older leaders had lost their seats in Parliament, George Lansbury, the best-loved of the old guard of Labor leaders, led the party in the House of Commons, with Attlee and Sir Stafford Cripps as his aides. Sidney Webb, who had written the new party constitution in 1918, led in the Lords, as Lord Passfield. Lansbury's total pacifism, however, was too much for the T.U.C. in a period when fascism was on the rise and rearmament obviously necessary. In 1935, the Transport Workers' chief, Ernest Bevin, led a revolt that drove Lansbury from political leadership, to be replaced by Major Clement Attlee, a convert to socialism. Once a solicitor, Attlee had managed a settlement house he had founded and paid for, become socialist mayor of a London borough, and entered the House of Commons. In support was Herbert Morrison, who as Secretary of the London Labor party had swept the London County Council elections in 1934 and made that body a labor stronghold, and the able lawyer Sir Stafford Cripps.

When safely in office, Baldwin had to meet the abdication crisis of 1936. George V died early that year. He had been a beloved monarch, as the demonstrations of the Silver Jubilee of 1935 had shown the world. The accession of his bachelor son, the popular Prince of Wales, had been looked forward to, for the Prince seemed to have the winning charm of his grandfather, Edward VII. Suddenly a crisis came. The new Edward VIII wanted to marry. That he intended to marry outside of royalty was no bar. Had not his brother, the Duke of York, married Lady Elizabeth Bowes-Lyon? But that he intended to marry a divorcée was another matter. The bishops of the Church here taking a lead, it was intimated to the King that this was impossible. In this situation Baldwin was at his skillful best. The crisis was long kept private, so that Great Britain heard of it first through the American press. The attitude of the dominions was shown the King and underscored. When the King's determination to stick by the "woman he loved" proved inflexible, Baldwin deftly managed the constitutional problems of abdication. There was no precedent, since previous "abdications" have in fact been oustings from the throne, as in the cases of James II and earlier of Edward II and Richard II. Thus 1936 became "the year of three kings" when on December 11—curiously enough, the anniversary of James II's flight—the Duke of York succeeded to the throne as George VI. The former Edward VIII, after a stirring address to the world—in the introduction to which he was correctly entitled "Prince Edward"—was made Duke of Windsor by his brother. Then, in 1937, Their new Majesties were crowned in Westminster Abbey.

The new reign opened with industry and business on the upsurge, stimulated partly because of the rearmament program. The Italian adventures of Mussolini in Africa, the Spanish Civil War, and the menace growing hourly more terrible that came from Hitler's Germany had at last convinced most of the pacifist Laborites and the money-saving Conservatives that the expense of defense could no longer be avoided. Britain was faced with the breakdown of collective agreements, collective security, and the whole international framework of the League of Nations. But the new organization of defense and the political fortunes of the nation were placed in the hands of a new Prime Minister. The weight of years and the cares of office were too much for Baldwin, once he had seen Edward VIII safely off the throne. He retired to the House of Lords as Earl Baldwin.

The choice of his successor was inevitable and easy. Neville Chamberlain, the Chancellor of the Exchequer, was the only man with sufficient experience and prestige for the position. The younger son of the great Joseph Chamberlain had been tempered by years in business and administrative posts in local government. After managing some of the Chamberlain family's business ventures, he had followed the family tradition and had been elected Mayor of Birmingham. As mayor he helped build houses for the workers and make of that city a model industrial center for others to envy and copy. During the first war he served for a time as Director of National Service. Under the coalition government of Lloyd George he was Postmaster General, Minister of Health, and Paymaster General. In Baldwin's first government he was Chancellor of the Exchequer but drew up no budget. From 1924 to 1929 he performed nobly as Minister of Health. This was the old Local Government Board turned into a ministry. From 1929 to 1931 he directed the reorganization of the Conservative central offices. A proven administrator, a sound man of business, and a good speaker, he seemed to fill the Conservative bill. In the conduct of his Cabinet and the routine of Parliament he was firmly in control every minute.

Chamberlain's conduct of foreign policy was the great trial of his ability and foresight and the most important aspect of the years from 1937 to 1939. The menace of totalitarian world aggression and how he met it are properly told in the chapter on foreign affairs. Convinced of the purity of his motives, his abilities, his knowledge gained from hard experience, Chamberlain led Britain down what he felt sure was the right road. Never once did he falter in doing what he thought was the right thing for King and Country. Fate and Adolf Hitler blew up his plans for security and peace. The coming of World War II in 1939 was due neither to his lack of a pacific policy nor to his desire for conflict. He met the crisis of the years 1938 and 1939 with the clear vision and will to win of a typical industrialist who was sure he was sane and practical. The vision of the industrialist who saw things in terms of board meetings and balanced ledgers was, unfortunately, at best myopic in the light of terrible facts.

As the war started two questions were in the minds of the British people.

First, were they prepared to withstand the attack of Germany? Second, if the attack could be stopped, was there enough courage and strength in the Empire to attack in turn and knock out the attempt of Germany to dominate Europe, and the world, for the second time in the twentieth century? Six grinding and terrible years were to be lived through before both these questions were answered. A vastly changed Britain and British Empire were to be found at the end in 1945. This, however, is the story of another chapter.

48

INTERWAR DIPLOMACY

1919–1939

During the years between 1919 and 1939, many observers thought that the old established rules for managing England's foreign affairs had ceased to apply. With no powers that would balance each other, balance-of-power diplomacy was pointless. Since command of the seas or lack of it seemed to have little to do with world trade and planned economic control seemed to have much, it appeared that free trade should be abandoned. Since, contrary to previous experience, ethical issues in international affairs appeared to work at cross purposes with England's interests, what was right now countered what was expedient instead of corresponding with it. Finally, a new, though still weak superstate, the League of Nations, claimed men's allegiance above their homeland. With men's minds confused by some or all of these reversals of thoughts, England's diplomacy reached a low point, equaled perhaps only when in the early 1600's James I threw away the prestige Elizabeth I had gained. For, most unfortunately, when about 1933 the cobwebs were blown away and the validity of the old rules became again apparent, England's rulers dared not act. While a few outspoken men won themselves reputations by their brave words of warning, England as a nation lost prestige, not to win it back till war broke out and those men were called upon to rule her.

But before England's leaders of this era are too severely blamed one should examine the tools with which they had to work—Navy, Army, Air Force, economic power, and national reputation. The Royal Navy, first of all, no longer commanded the seas. One after another, important areas had been abandoned to others. In 1902 much of the Far East had been surrendered to Japan by the Anglo-Japanese Alliance. By 1907 with the building of the U.S.S. *Michigan*—the counterpart of the *Dreadnought* in American naval history and actually designed before the *Dreadnought* —the western Atlantic was taken over by the United States. The Anglo-French agreements of 1912, in conjunction with Franco-Italian agreements, gave up control of the Mediterranean. When the German navy was built to be a rival to the Royal Navy, there was automatically lost to the latter not only the Baltic but also parts of the North Sea. It is true that for a time, after the 1918 surrender of the German navy, the North Sea and Baltic were won back, but they were lost again by the Anglo-German Naval Agreement of 1935. And not only did England lose command of the seas here mentioned, but by the Washington Disarmament Conference of 1921 she admitted that fact. Such a sharing with friendly powers—in theory all powers were friendly from 1918 to 1939—did not restrict British trade, but it did weaken British diplomatic power, as was evidenced at Corfu in 1923 and during the Spanish Civil War of 1936 to 1939.

This reduction of the Royal Navy was compelled by finances. England's armed forces were cut to the bone by Sir Eric Geddes, who held office in Army, Navy, and Air Force at the same time and wielded the "Geddes ax" to balance the budget. But though the Navy was reduced in size, it was not reduced in quality. The competitive struggle to keep on full pay caused great energy in the commissioned ranks of the Senior Service, with results to be shown in World War II at Narvik, the River Plate, and the miracles in the Mediterranean. Leadership was so fine as to overcome the effects of the unnecessary and shameful peacetime Invergordon Mutiny of 1931, and inventiveness was such as to give England new weapons such as asdic, the English equivalent in submarine detection by underwater acoustics of the American sonar.

The Army, too, suffered from the Geddes ax. It did not advance by spectacular reforms. The Haldane Territorial system, having proved its worth, was revived, refurbished, and retained. A degree of mechanization was introduced, many of the age-old cavalry regiments being turned into light-tank regiments. In consequence of the economy wave, the Army shrank in size, so that in 1939, England had fewer divisions to send to France than in 1914, even though in that year she sent a larger proportion of her whole army. At the very end, in 1939, conscription was introduced, and the energetic Leslie Hore-Belisha did what he could to increase efficiency and put the right men in the right posts. Fortunately, through all this period Army morale remained high, onerous police duties were well performed, and the officer corps planned for modern warfare.

The new third arm of the service, the Royal Air Force, likewise stayed efficient, by the same narrow margin that was to mean England's survival in September, 1940. It, also, was drastically cut down, but thanks to a spirit of loyal opposition in the country it kept up its technical advance. The eccentric Tory tax dodger Lucy, Lady Houston, gave from the sums she saved in income tax by living in the Channel Islands to pay for the research needed to start the Spitfire fighter that in 1940 saved England. Valiant men such as Lord Knebworth, who died in experiments with dive bombing, learned new flying techniques. Pressure by scientific boards inspired first by Lord Balfour, then by Winston Churchill, led to the development of radar. This, by the time of Munich in 1938 and all through 1939, guarded the coasts of England. By a terribly narrow margin, England was ready, not to put pressure on others, but at least to fight for her life.

In this same period from 1919 to 1939 England's economic power decreased and changed. All over the world she lost markets, whether because of new competition, as when the Japanese and the Indians themselves cut her out in textile sales in India, or because of tariff walls, which rose inside the Commonwealth as well as out. Though she did go back on the gold standard, the value of the pound became shaky. In consequence, much of her diplomacy was directed to preserving international stability. Her bankers fought for her a rear-guard action that did give her diplomats cards to play. In matters of reputation Britain remained the home of free speech, where the oppressed of the world did turn for a forum to air their grievances. But because she no longer backed her words with deeds the old trust in her slackened and became dormant, not to revive till a leader came who believed in deeds and could make capital out of England's old reputation. Thus, as can be seen, British diplomats had weaker hands to play than in the past, and should be judged accordingly.

This was true from the start of this period. Comparison has often been made, and rightly made, between what Castlereagh and Wellington accomplished at Vienna and after in the years from 1814 to 1823 and what Lloyd George, Balfour, and Curzon accomplished at Versailles and afterwards, in the years from 1918 to 1923. To be fair, this comparison must take account of the greater difficulties that had to be met after World War I. Castlereagh and Wellington, in Pitt's proposals of 1805, in the Treaty of Chaumont, and in the doctrine of legitimacy, had a clear-cut program for peace to which their allies had already agreed. The reparations they demanded from defeated France were not beyond the ability of private bankers to finance. But Lloyd George, Balfour, and Curzon had a conflicting set of peace proposals to iron out in the form of Wilson's Fourteen Points and the secret treaties to both of which they were pledged, and a demand for excessive reparations that it seemed politically impossible to resist. Castlereagh and Wellington had plenty of force behind them to enforce their decisions. Their successors had to obtain results with an army that was clamoring to be disbanded. Castlereagh was secure in office till he died; Lloyd George and Balfour had behind them a truculent Parliament that finally did oust them from office. Nowadays it is the fashion to do Castlereagh belated justice for his successful diplomacy at and after Vienna. Perhaps similar justice is due Lloyd George.

The story of the Versailles Conference has often been told. Here what concerns us is the part of Great Britain and the dominions. The problem before the "British Empire Delegation" was to iron out at the conference table many conflicting interests. At first it seemed possible that President Wilson of the United States would successfully insist on scrapping the secret treaties and using the Fourteen Points as the basis for peace, as Castlereagh had used the Treaty of Chaumont. This did not happen, and it became necessary to wrangle over each discrepancy between the Fourteen Points and special demands by one ally or another. Fortunately Lloyd George succeeded in postponing the explosive reparations issue. Fortunately Balfour was able to seize a moment when both Lloyd George and President Wilson were absent to rush to completion detailed drafting of the treaties. Gladly the idealists on the British Empire Delegation took up Woodrow Wilson's proposal of a League of Nations. Quite firmly, the dominions pointed out that they were equal partners in negotiations. Just in time, as communism was spreading from Russia into Hungary and Germany, the five treaties of Versailles, Saint Germain, Neuilly, the Trianon, and Sèvres were signed with Germany, Austria, Bulgaria, Hungary, and Turkey, respectively. These treaties made the world with which British diplomats would have to deal until World War II.

The following were the effects, though not the precise terms, of these treaties: the Treaty of Versailles had written into it the League of Nations; that was why the United States Senate would not ratify it without amendments which Woodrow Wilson would not accept. It gave Alsace-Lorraine back to France and acknowledged an independent Poland, cut out of the former empires of Germany, Austria, and Russia. Germany was demilitarized. Allied troops were to occupy the Rhineland till reparations were paid. German colonies were transferred to the League, to be handed out by the League as mandates. The Treaty of Saint Germain recognized an Austrian Republic, from which Czechoslovakia had been cut away, and forbade this now entirely German land to join Germany. The Treaty of Neuilly reduced the size of Bulgaria. That of Trianon cut Hungary down to two-thirds of its former size. The Treaty of Sèvres split Palestine and Iraq off from Turkey as British mandates and Syria as a French mandate, and it attempted to make Constantinople an international city.

All these treaties created problems. The amount of reparations to be collected from Germany had to be decided upon. That led to constant friction, as will be told. The creation of a series of new states in eastern Europe made a new balance of power. France was delighted to see a "Cordon Sanitaire" run from the Arctic to the Black Sea and the Adriatic. Finland, Estonia, Latvia, Lithuania, Poland, Czechoslovakia, Romania, and Yugoslavia in French eyes had a double value. All of them sealed off Communist Russia. Poland, Czechoslovakia, Romania, and Yugoslavia encircled defeated Germany, Austria, and Hungary. France therefore encouraged all these states and allied herself with them. But with France now supreme unless challenged by Russia, Great Britain naturally fell away from her. Great Britain did join in the postwar attempts to drive communism out of Russia, but not enthusiastically. Once it was clear that anit-Communist forces were doomed but that communism could not swamp eastern Europe, Britain left to France the task of holding off Russia through aid to Poland.

The creation of mandates led to imperial problems in the Near East, as will be told in the relevant chapter. Elsewhere Great Britain gained a doubtful reward, for to her were assigned most of the former German East Africa (now Tanganyika), a strip of Togoland to rule from the Gold Coast, and a strip of the Cameroons to rule from Nigeria. More significantly, three dominions—South Africa, with the award of German South-West Africa; Australia, with the award of German New Guinea and the Bismarck Archipelago; and New Zealand, with the award of Samoa—became recognized as members of the family of nations.

To counterbalance these problems in part, there was an instrument of international cooperation. The League of Nations offered a meeting place for solving international problems, which was supported by world-wide public opinion. Here was the situation Lloyd George, Balfour, and Curzon must meet.

In these times, foreign affairs were managed curiously. Lloyd George had a passion for controlling them and for gaining his information about them from independent sources. As a result, he went for technical advice not to the Foreign Office experts but to a group of men and women who worked in temporary buildings in the garden of 10 Downing Street and were naturally nicknamed the Garden Suburb. As long as Balfour had been Foreign Secretary this had done comparatively little harm. As an ex-Prime Minister Balfour had sympathy with any Prime Minister who wanted full information, and as a creator of the Second Coalition he believed in giving "the little man" a chance to get results in the way he understood. As Balfour stood no nonsense about not being informed of what he should know, the two men succeeded in collaborating. But when he retired in October, 1919, to the sinecure office of Lord President of the Council and was replaced by Lord Curzon, matters worsened. The pompous side of Curzon's character was a standing temptation to the impish side of Lloyd George, who took to interfering not only when he felt it the Prime Minister's job to interfere but apparently in order to tease. As a result, Lord President Balfour found himself occasionally interceding for Curzon with Lloyd George and, more importantly, engaged in superintending special negotiations. Thus English foreign policy was split into three, in effect. As Prime Minister, Lloyd George handled the unfinished business of the German and Turkish peace treaties; Balfour conducted special errands, notably to America and the League; and Curzon took charge of routine.

The work Balfour did lasted. At a moment when he was substituting for Curzon at the Foreign Office he suggested to the powers which owed England money that England would give up her demands for repayments and reparations from them if America would do the same to her. The "Balfour Note" had the eventual effect of lining Europe up behind England against the United States in all multilateral dealings about war debts. Then, when United States President Warren G. Harding called the Washington Disarmament Conference of 1921, Balfour, as head of the British Delegation, made the best of England's abandonment of the rule of the seas. When the American delegation offered great sacrifices of battleship strength, Balfour willingly matched those sacrifices for England. This was making a virtue out of necessity, since neither England nor Japan could afford to continue an armaments race with America. Then, with the good will he had won by this concession, he secured the supplementary Nine Power and Five Power Pacts to keep conditions in the Pacific and the Far East the same as if England still held mastery of those waters. To do this, it was necessary, under pressure from the dominions and from the United States, to abrogate the Anglo-Japanese Alliance, which was done by the polite fiction that it was expanded into these pacts. By this realistic acceptance of the fact that the elements of sea power had changed, Balfour "cut England's losses" to a marked degree. Furthermore, he established a foreign policy that worked for about ten years, in preserving the "Open Door" in China and thus allowing Chiang Kai-shek to unite South and North China in 1925, free from outside interference.

Balfour took yet another important step, this time in Europe. It fell to him to be the Cabinet member to attend the first sessions of the League of Nations, and there to take the action which led to the League's settling the struggle between Germans and Poles over the Upper Silesian boundary. Here, and with the handling of other boundary problems through League machinery, he did much to build a faith on the part of many Englishmen that the League could keep the peace. Particularly did Balfour's cousin, Lord Robert Cecil—at one time the South African representative at Geneva—lead in spreading this faith. Here there is a suggestive comparison with a century before and the work of Castlereagh and Canning. Balfour, like Castlereagh, engaged in international cooperation; like Canning, he used public opinion as a means of reaching diplomatic agreements. His successes did not last, unless one counts as a success the ultimate failure of the United States to collect from any nation save Finland, for the League and the Nine and Five Power Pacts were swept away by World War II, but he made the imaginative best of what lay at hand.

On the contrary, reparations and the problems of Germany, Russia, and Turkey were beyond the abilities of Lloyd George, which probably means that they were beyond the abilities of any English statesman of the time. During the years 1920 to 1923 no less than eight conferences were held, Lloyd George and various French premiers attending all of them, to try to settle reparations. During them the money asked for was reduced from 100 billion dollars to a few billions, in the process a German offer of ten times what was eventually agreed to being refused. Lloyd George found himself trapped by Geddes's election speeches about squeezing the German orange till the pips squeaked, by a natural intransigence of the French, and by the fact that no German government could have stayed in power if it had conceded all that was demanded. Before any terms were agreed to, three things had happened. A French occupation of the Ruhr had caused long-time hatreds. A willful inflation of German currency by the German government had destroyed the German middle classes and thus not only much of Germany's capacity to pay any reparations but also her capacity to become a democracy. Finally Soviet Russia and Germany had come to an agreement, by the Treaty of Rapallo, that was to foreshadow Russo-German agreements. This was all the harder blow as the treaty was signed while Lloyd George and the French minister, Briand, were playing golf at nearby Cannes with apparently not a care in the world. The net result of these eight publicized and apparently unsuccessful conferences, for all Lloyd George's deft attempts to get sense into people's heads, was to lose him his immense prestige in Parliament. To the rank and file of Conservatives behind him he ceased to be the indispensable leader who won the war, and became again the treacherous "little man," whom they so hated.

The problems of Russia and of Soviet attempts at world revolution the Lloyd George Government did not solve. Here, again, they retreated. From attempts, in 1919, to help anti-Soviet forces in Russia the British drew back to a mere refusal to admit Soviet Russia existed, while letting the "Cordon Sanitaire" of new states on Russia's borders contain communism. There was a moment when it looked as if France's ally, Poland, would fall, and an English proposal for a boundary, the so-called Curzon Line—with which Lord Curzon had little or nothing to do, except to hold the office of Foreign Secretary when it was suggested—was discussed and then ignored when the Poles finally succeeded in defeating the Russians and winning themselves a more easterly boundary. Otherwise, England's Russian policy was neither a resolute anticommunism, as in France, nor attempted friendship, but one of neglect.

The unfinished Turkish business also fell to Lloyd George. There the problem was an unexpected resurgence of Turkey. Once the Turks had no subject nationalities to exploit, they turned their energies to making a modern nation of themselves. Under the leadership of Mustapha Kemal —whom we have seen save Gallipoli from England—the Turkish National Assembly repudiated the Treaty of Sèvres and drove from Asia Minor the forces occupying the Aegean and Mediterranean coasts. Italians and French left quickly, the French even making a virtue of necessity and setting up a working agreement with Mustapha Kemal. The Greeks, who were not trying to make a colony but to extend Greek rule over a Greek population, fought back, urged on by a belief that Lloyd George would support them. Finally the Turks won. They not only drove the Greeks into the sea but threatened the international control of Constantinople that English troops were trying to enforce. Suddenly, a few English soldiers at Chanak—across the Dardanelles from Gallipoli—were in danger of a defeat that might humiliate the whole Empire. The Cabinet, at the impulse of Colonial Secretary Churchill, announced it would fight and sent for aid from the dominions. As will be related later, this led to a crisis in Empire relations, when New Zealand and Australia promised aid and Canada refused it. Fortunately, the asking was enough, and the man on the spot, General "Tim" Harington, with the wholehearted backing of his old chief, Lord Plumer, then Governor of Malta, was able to withdraw with some dignity.

That, however, was the end of the "Welsh Wizard." Though most of his Cabinet stuck loyally to him, Bonar Law and Baldwin pulled away the Conservative support that had kept him in office, by the Carlton Club meeting, and Lloyd George remained politically ostracized for the rest of his life. Then, when Lloyd George fell, Curzon came into his own and turned to the task of cleaning up the Turkish mess. In spite of the knowledge that Bonar Law and Baldwin would not back him up if his bluffs were called, he dominated the Conference of Lausanne, which had been called to sign a treaty with the Turks and put a legal end to war. There he tied the interests of France, Italy, and England together so deftly that those three powers which had formerly had divergent policies in Asia Minor made a common front against Turkey. By doing this, he got for England's new client state, Iraq, the Mosul oil fields, which thus became available to England. He had further the courage, when the Turks refused to sign, to abide by their refusal and let the conference dissolve, secure in the knowledge that the agreement on terms he had created would last and that the Turks would eventually accept just about what had been offered.

Curzon met yet another crisis when Mussolini, the new dictator of Italy, tried to gain cheap prestige by seizing the Greek island of Corfu in defiance of the League of Nations. Again he showed courage by intimating to Mussolini that the British Navy would back up League orders. Here, however, Curzon has been blamed for allowing the matter to be turned over to a council of ambassadors for settlement as a way of saving Italian pride. For this move tended to weaken the prestige of the League, which Balfour had been so carefully building up. These events were not in themselves earth-shaking, but they were such improvements on previous failures that England gained in reputation.

Curzon's full tenure of the foreign office was short. Bonar Law died, and, as has been recounted, Curzon failed in his life's ambition to be the only Viceroy of India to become Prime Minister, seeing Baldwin preferred to him. Baldwin, in an access of honesty and hope, called for a general election to ratify his protectionist program and was defeated. Thus Curzon, Lloyd George, and Balfour all passed from the stage of diplomacy, opening the way for a new era. In comparison with Castlereagh and Wellington, these men had not done badly. Though they failed to solve a vastly greater reparations problem than had faced the victors over Napoleon, they apparently had created, in the League of Nations, a working tool for keeping the peace that was better than the old Congress system because it made use of the people's wills instead of contradicting them. It now remained to be seen whether their successors could solve reparations and make full use of the League.

Throughout Europe the year 1924 marked a great change in public opinion. Democratic statesmen in Germany seemed to be making headway with their policy of international cooperation as a means of gaining admission to the League. In England the idealists led by Lord Robert Cecil fostered belief in the League. In France the voters put in men willing to work with and through the League. Could Britain's leaders make good use of the expressed will of the people to cooperate with others in executing a foreign policy?

The short-lived first Ramsay MacDonald Government, 1923–1924, in which MacDonald bore the triple burdens of the premiership, the leadership of the House, and the Foreign Office, had a triple program. One part was good treatment of Germany. By summoning a conference in London in the summer of 1924, and letting General Charles Gates Dawes of Chicago take direction of it, a "Dawes Plan" was worked out to help reestablish German finances and make possible some reparations payments. Another part was trying to set up effective machinery by which the League could enforce peace. A "Geneva protocol" was drafted by which an actual League army would be created, with assigned national contingents. This plan MacDonald was unable to put through. President Millerand's reactionary and unconstitutional direction of the French government blocked it. The dominions not unnaturally refused to get into a position where they would have to fight a European war for European reasons; a League majority of European nations would force them against their will into a European war. And when the French constitutional upheaval of 1924 occurred, it was too late for successful arrangements to be made before MacDonald himself fell. For the third part of MacDonald's program— good relations with Russia—broke down from Russian bad faith and broke his government down. The Russians repaid the recognition of their government and the signing of a commercial treaty by using their commercial organization in England as an espionage system. On the publication of the Zinoviev letter, which revealed Russian espionage, Liberal support was withdrawn from the MacDonald Government, and it floundered to defeat in the general election. In its place came the second Baldwin Government, in which Austen Chamberlain, Joseph Chamberlain's elder son, was Foreign Secretary.

The Baldwin-Chamberlain foreign policy did not, like the MacDonald one, take account of public opinion and lead it. On the contrary, it followed. It was, in 1925, German suggestion and French leadership that brought into being the Locarno Pact, by which England, France, Germany, Belgium, and Italy guaranteed the Rhine frontier from attack by either Germany or France. The "Locarno spirit" of amity, a glowing cordiality that helped relax international tensions, was the creation not of any Englishman but of the Frenchman Aristide Briand. On the contrary, England increased those tensions in 1927, by denouncing her commercial treaty with Russia, after Russia had joined the League of Nations.

The Baldwin-Austen Chamberlain system of semi-isolation did, under the then circumstances in Europe, make sense. France, in a short-term view, was the strongest power in Europe, and use of League machinery was, on the whole, the best way to counterbalance her, even though the partial dominion veto on the use of the League and the skepticism as to the League's true strength made English support of the League half-hearted. But the basis of that policy was that England's financial strength —increased apparently by her resumption of the gold standard—was the chief counterforce in diplomacy. Already new forces were appearing. In Germany a book, *Mein Kampf,* was circulating, that would give increasing power to its author, Adolf Hitler. Mussolini's successes in Italy were causing men all over Europe to think of a nationalist corporate state. In 1928, in England's oldest ally, Portugal, Dr. Salazar came to power as the key man in a beneficent authoritarian government. A growing undercurrent was beginning to sap the prestige of the democracies that were carrying out the international policies of fulfillment and the "Locarno spirit." Some crisis could bring the new forces to power.

Signs of crisis appeared. When Germany could not keep going under the Dawes Plan's arrangements, another American plan was tried. Owen

D. Young intervened with a scheme for easier payments. Had the Young Plan gone through, all would have been well. But the 1929 stock-market crash on Wall Street and the 1931 crash in London and in Central Europe killed all chance for setting up a stable international economy. In Britain the Bank of England tried, in cooperation with the Federal Reserve Bank of New York, to work out some solution. These attempts failed, and in the end President Hoover had to announce a moratorium in debt payments. British foreign policy from 1929 and 1931 was one of trying to save Germany, scrapping cruisers through international naval treaties, and restoring confidence in England's ability to carry on.

The diplomatic history of the years 1929 to 1933 was largely financial, with negotiations as much between the Bank of England and the Federal Reserve Bank of New York as between foreign offices. It also consisted in attempts to raise German morale by evacuating the Rhineland and to keep up the savings on naval expenses by a further naval disarmament program, this time keeping cruisers below 10,000 tons in size. Financially, the program failed. President Hoover of the United States, in 1931, in effect though not in form, acknowledged the principles of the Balfour Note by giving a moratorium or stay of payments on war debts to create a similar stay of reparations. The moratorium became permanent. From failure to balance the budget, the MacDonald Labor Government fell, being replaced by the MacDonald National Government, in August, 1931.

It might well be said that for the eight and one-half years between the collapse of the MacDonald Labor Government in August, 1931, and the premiership of Winston Churchill in May, 1940, England had no foreign policy. Certainly, in those years England lost the initiative, and decisions in diplomatic matters were made, as perhaps never before, outside London. This happened because the governments of those years—the MacDonald National Government of 1931 to 1935, the Baldwin Government of 1935 to 1937, and the Neville Chamberlain Government of 1937 to 1940 —all had plenty to do at home, successfully fighting the depression that had destroyed the MacDonald Labor Government. What spare energies they had went to wrestling with the Indian problem. Therefore, they were willing to pay a high price for peace—and did. Four general stages appear in the decline of England's world position. First, there was the period from 1931 to 1933, when the methods of the twenties still seemed feasible, and when there was still a democratic Germany with which to cooperate. Then there was the period from 1933 to 1935, when Mussolini offered himself as a mercenary to keep Hitler under control, but asked a price the people of England would not pay, even if her rulers were willing. After that came the period from 1935 to 1938, when the German-Italian Axis was formed, which was also the period of the Spanish Civil War. Lastly, there was the period of large-scale Nazi aggression, 1938 and 1939, that drove England to war without any allies but France and Poland. The facts of these periods may explain why England fell so low.

Immediately after the formation of the National Government came a prophetic warning of the dangers that any collapse, economic or otherwise, might bring to England—the so-called Invergordon Mutiny in the Navy. When the outside world believed that discipline had broken down in the Royal Navy in peacetime, Japanese army units tore up the Five Power and Nine Power Pacts by invading Manchuria, and a "flight from the pound" drove England off the gold standard. It did not matter that the so-called Mutiny was, like the 1797 Mutiny at Spithead, a respectful protest against injustices in pay cuts and was settled as soon as the nature of the injustices had become clear. What mattered was that the Trotskyite Communists who had fostered the movement had achieved their aim of moving one step nearer world revolution, because the forces that wanted to upset Versailles settlements and the League took confidence.

As yet those forces were not in the ascendant. The militarists had not seized power in Japan; that was why Manchuria was invaded against orders from Tokyo, by a "spontaneous" movement designed to discredit the home authorities. As yet the Nazis were a minority party in Germany, though they were growing in power. Mussolini, as he was to show, still remembered the lesson of Corfu and believed that Italy with her defenseless coastline had to be England's ally. In Russia the Stalinite Communists, still concentrated on internal problems, exiled the Trotskyites who were working directly for a world revolution, and still made promises of "coexistence" on peaceful terms with any nation that would give something in exchange for such a promise. But now fascism and communism saw troubled waters in which to fish, and hindsight shows that action by England at this time might have saved much trouble. But the attention of the MacDonald Government was concentrated on recovery at home and on what Empire trade might do to replace the world trade it was feared might be lost.

It was others who tried to save the situation. In cooperation with other central banks, the Bank of England did try to prop up the European economy while yet there was time and to repeat the interventions that in the early 1920's had almost miraculously saved Austria and Hungary. Now the problem was greater and the resources less. The preoccupation of political leaders led to postponing till too late plans that might have worked, and the downward economic spiral was not halted. In the Far East, where diplomatic and military rather than economic intervention was needed, Great Britain failed to back up American protests about the Japanese invasion of Manchuria. Consequently the democratic governments in Germany, Austria, and China grew weaker and turned to using undemocratic emergency powers.

In Germany this had a dangerous result. In 1933 Hitler's Nazis were able to obtain power legally, by joining a coalition government, and then by the excitement caused by the trumped-up Reichstag fire secured a grant of the emergency powers that others had created to hold him and his party in check. Even then men had hopes that the type of economic and financial cooperation that had evolved the Dawes and Young plans might save the day. Hitler was stressing the idealistic and socialistic side of his National Socialism. When, even after going off the gold standard, the new President of the United States, Franklin Roosevelt, called a London Economic Conference, it seemed as if world recovery could be obtained by world cooperation and the peace thus kept. These hopes were in vain, for Roosevelt broke up the conference he had summoned by withdrawing American delegates, and a period of American isolation began, ending the economic support to Europe that had been given by the Coolidge and Hoover administrations.

Still there was a deceptive peace in the world. England's economic situation grew slowly better, thanks to the measures of economy of the Mac-Donald National Government and thanks to the devaluation of the pound, though that of France grew worse. Though tales of outrages came from Hitler's Germany, it was still largely believed that his bombast was for home consumption and that in fact he was willing to cooperate. In the summer of 1934 it was demonstrated how untrue this belief was, but not, unfortunately, so as to convince the rulers of England. At the end of June by the "blood purge" Hitler both killed off the leaders of his Brown Shirts and, as it turned out, enlisted the rank and file in the rapidly growing German army. In July a Nazi rebellion in Austria nearly led to German conquest of the tiny remainder of the once great Empire. What stopped it was Mussolini's prompt movement of Italian troops to the German border. By this time it was clear that Hitler was doing just what he had said he would, in *Mein Kampf*—build up the forces of theoretically disarmed Germany so as to tear up the treaty of Versailles. A new English policy was needed to meet this threat.

No conscious policy seems to have been adopted, but the day-to-day actions of the English Government amounted to a policy. It was to let someone else do the threatening against Hitler, preferably France and Italy, while England took credit for all concessions, thus carrying water on both shoulders. First of all it was the French who took the initiative, as they tried to revive the Little Entente, the protective eastern cordon against Germany, in the guise of an eastern "Locarno" agreement, guaranteeing the boundaries mutually against aggressors. In this pact Russia would be included, and for this purpose Russia was brought into the League of Nations. But the whole program depended on the will of one man, Louis Barthou, the French Foreign Minister, who was murdered, along with King Alexander of Yugoslavia, in Marseilles that autumn. In his place Pierre Laval directed French foreign policy, without Barthou's courage. His policy was to let Mussolini do the work. This policy was, in effect, agreed to by the Stresa Conference of early 1935 of England, France, and Italy. England's contribution to all this was not entirely relished by her two associates. She urged France not to irritate Germany by enlarging her army. When Barthou wanted to delay a plebiscite in the Saar region, she forced it on so that after Barthou's death the Saar went to Hitler. And right after the "Stresa Front" Sir John Simon, the Foreign Secretary, signed a naval agreement with Germany that did three things: it tore up the Versailles Treaty without reference to the League, it surrendered to Germany the control of the Baltic, and it served notice on Mussolini that the "Stresa Front" could be broken.

During this time, England's force grew relatively weaker. Navally, she kept to technical restrictions as to ship size laid down by the Washington Conference. Her Army was smaller than it had been in 1914. New airplanes the government refused to build, as being provocative. While this was happening, the Germans were less and less secretly building a small but effective navy, were laying plans for recruiting a large-scale army, and had an air force in the blueprint stage that would soon outmatch England's. Furthermore, England's will to fight was doubtful. A strong League of Nations sentiment was afloat that had all the practical effects of a pacifist movement. It was believed that the surest way to peace was to disarm, and that one should not fight until after the League had exhausted all possible means of conciliation. To drive this home Lord Robert Cecil and others circulated a "Peace Ballot" in which voters were asked to state whether or not they backed this policy. Eleven million stated that they did, a result which materially affected England's future, for not only was a general election in the offing, but Mussolini was engaged in his conquest of Ethiopia. The election was won by Stanley Baldwin—who in June replaced the aging and tired MacDonald as Premier—on a program of peace through the League, which program he then applied. He made Anthony Eden Cabinet Minister for League of Nations Affairs and in effect let Eden at Geneva and Sir Samuel Hoare, his Foreign Secretary, in London handle the Ethiopian question in two ways at once.

First of all, Eden roused the League to action when the smoldering Italo-Ethiopian question broke into war in October, 1935. By a vote of 50 to 1 the League resolved to use "sanctions," that is, to use first economic and then perhaps military pressure in Italy. Mussolini retorted that sanctions would mean war. He held a trump card, since, as force in Europe was distributed, he held the balance of power. If they joined each other, militant Italy and rearming Germany might well be the equivalents in force of pacific England and economically unstable France. If he were given due consideration, however, he would gladly continue to supply the troops with which Hitler was kept in order, as he had in 1934. What would have happened if sanctions had fully been applied is one of the "ifs" of history. They were not. Premier Laval of France and Sir Samuel Hoare got quietly together and proposed to give Mussolini a large slice of Ethiopia. When this proposal was made public a storm of indignation drove Sir Samuel from office, to be replaced by Eden. But nothing more was done, and Mussolini went on with the conquest of Ethiopia. Only the most trivial sanctions were applied, and the world was thus shown that England could be ignored with impunity. Ignored with a vengeance England was, from then on, for four years leading to World War II.

Perhaps the loss of Italy could have been balanced, at a higher price, by the use of Russia as a mercenary to keep peace. The year 1936 was one in which Russia began to come close to the democracies in Europe. In March the French ratified their defensive alliance with Russia. A month after that, the French election put in power a "Popular Front" government that had Communist support, and a similar election in Spain set up a similar Popular Front government with even stronger ties with Communism. But this possibility was swiftly checked by Hitler. The Franco-Russian alliance triggered off his perhaps most audacious move, the occupation of the Rhineland. A few days later he sent troops into the zone that had been "demilitárized" under the provisions of the Treaty of Versailles and the Locarno Pact. This was bluff; it is now known that his troops had orders to withdraw if the French acted. But the French dared not act unless the English gave them promises of support, and the English did not give those promises. Thus it was that Hitler was able to begin the Siegfried Line of forts on the Rhine, which would nullify the superiority in numbers that the French army then possessed and so leave him able to adventure elsewhere. From then on, the whole series of interconnecting agreements that were preserving European peace fell apart with alarming speed. The mere listing of these diplomatic disasters makes sad reading.

The first was the Spanish civil war. In Spain, after a series of government-sponsored murders in June, 1936, a bitter struggle broke out, which soon through the welter of murders on both sides appeared as a war of conservatives aided by Fascists on one side against liberals aided by Communists on the other, with the extremists in each case gaining control. England, with her command of the seas, might have ended this struggle swiftly. If in the first few weeks she had prevented rebel army units crossing from Morocco and the Canary Islands it is possible that the legitimate Spanish republic might have been able to reassert its control. If she had allowed the friendly Popular Front French government to send munitions to its Popular Front counterpart in Spain the war, though bloody, could have been won by the republicans.

But England did none of these things. Acting in the belief that arms manufacturers caused wars, she used what powers she had to see to it that no arms went to Spain. The result merely was that no English or French arms went there, while the Communists and Fascists more and more openly used Spain as a bull ring in which to kill each other off and a testing ground in which to try out their new weapons. In Loyalist Madrid the Russian ambassador sat in the Cabinet. Under the Rebel leader Franco appeared "volunteer" organizations that bore a surprising resemblance to units of the German and Italian armies. Meanwhile all that the two democracies of England and France could contribute was a neutrality patrol by the navies of England, France, Germany, and Italy, that was meant to stop arms from reaching either side and that did stop arms reaching the Loyalists. Only when it came to the point of "pirate" submarines appearing was it possible for Eden to put his foot down. Once he persuaded the Baldwin Cabinet to let him announce that the Royal Navy would stop "piracy," it was possible to hold a conference at Nyon where for once England was listened to. Otherwise all that England did was watch Spaniards slaughter each other for three years, till in March, 1939, the Loyalist government finally collapsed.

In the meanwhile, the list of diplomatic losses lengthened. In October, 1936, Mussolini finally chose sides and joined with Hitler in what came to be known as the Berlin-Rome Axis, around which they intended European affairs to revolve. In November another anti-Russian and antidemocratic power was added to the Axis, when Japan joined in what was known as the anti-Comintern pact, the Comintern being short for the Communist International. In March, 1937, the Little Entente of states supporting France was broken, when Yugoslavia sold herself to the highest bidder. England's answer was to do much the same, by sending Lord Halifax, the former Viceroy of India, to deal with Hitler. Then when Neville Chamberlain, the Premier who had just succeeded Baldwin, got settled in the saddle, he proposed to go further and acknowledge Italian control of Ethiopia. Chamberlain combined this project with the rejection of a secret offer of diplomatic support from President Roosevelt of the United States. This was too much for Eden, who in February, 1938, resigned, Halifax taking his place.

The year 1938 was a worse year yet. In March Hitler took advantage of a French Cabinet crisis of unusual virulence to summon the Chancellor of Austria to Berchtesgaden, his Bavarian home, there to bully him into giving a Nazi control of all police in Austria. That meant that, in a matter of days, Nazi armies marched in unopposed. And all England did in answer was to recognize Mussolini's conquest of Ethiopia, in return for which Mussolini would withdraw a few troops from Spain! This expansion was not enough for Hitler. He at once discovered new "oppressed" Germans to deliver, this time in Czechoslovakia. Steadily, through the summer, matters were worked up to a crisis. At last England and France were doing some arming, though not enough even to hold their relative position behind Germany. But Hitler continued to use his most effective technique, the continued belief in England that there was merit in his claims. By playing on this suspicion he was able to persuade Prime Minister Neville Chamberlain to send Lord Runciman to mediate between the Czech government and its own subjects. Then when the harvest had been gathered and the Siegfried-line forts seemed strong enough to prevent French aid reaching Czechoslovakia by land, Hitler raised his demands, and German troops were mobilized.

For a moment, it looked as if England would at last act. But though the fleet went to Scapa Flow, Chamberlain tried personal intercession. He flew to Berchtesgaden—his plane being screened, as it set off, by the first English radar to operate—and made a deal with Hitler. On Chamberlain's return, Hitler repudiated that deal as insufficient. At a second visit, this time to Godesberg, Chamberlain rejected Hitler's new proposals, only to accept them at yet a third conference, that of Munich, where Italy and France were represented, but Czechoslovakia was not. For a moment, though this final settlement entailed German annexation of the fortress line that guarded Czechoslovakia and destroyed that country as an effective ally of France and England, it was enthusiastically received by all but a few. It was genuinely believed that peace had been secured. Chamberlain's umbrella, which he had gaily waved on starting off on his flights, became a symbol of peace. Those who suffered from that delusion soon were cured. In March, 1939, almost simultaneously, the last Spanish republicans were forced to surrender and Hitler took over what was left of Czechoslovakia. At last England and France woke up and rearmed feverishly. They also looked feverishly for allies. But there were few to be had.

In a desperate scramble, in the summer of 1939, all England and France could secure was the acceptance by three countries—Poland, Romania, and Turkey—of a one-sided promise that if Germany invaded them they would accept English and French support. Russia refused to join unless she could conquer Latvia, Estonia, and Lithuania as a reward. This could not be stomached. All that Hitler needed now was a pretext for war.

This he found in the existence of the Danzig Free State and the Polish corridor, which gave Poland access to the Baltic. But this time when he offered a choice of war or the strangling of England's ally, at last England chose war. On September 3, Great Britain went to war with Germany, to be followed by India and all the dominions except Eire. England had failed to keep the peace she had made in 1919, and two decades later had to fight because of that failure.

The question now arises, how did this all happen? Why did England fall so low? To this there are several answers. One is very plain, and can be given in the words of warning that Lord Lloyd spoke to Neville Chamberlain in the summer of 1935 as the Italian crisis broke out: "Strength comes before policy, that is what the Cabinet has forgotten." Comparisons of the relative forces of England, France, Italy, and Germany in 1920, 1930, 1935, and 1939 tell much, especially when those figures are considered in the light of how modern was the equipment of each nation. But illuminating as those figures are, they do not tell the whole story. For they point to a mystery—why did not the democracies act in 1935, or even March, 1936, when they still had the preponderance of force and saw that they might lose it? The answer lies deeper than in mere lists of men, planes, ships, and guns; it lies in the field of attitude and will.

First of all, no one in England wanted war. All parties, all walks of life so hated and feared a repetition of the carnage of 1914 to 1918 that they would take great risks to avoid it. Some went beyond this hatred of war to a positive pacifism, a belief that force was wrong, a belief in the power of "nonresistance." So strong was this sort of thing that those who did not share this belief had to take it into consideration in their thinking. Indeed active pacifism or a noble sympathy with it reached high into the councils of both parties. George Lansbury, the leader of the Labor Opposition from 1931 to 1935, stood firmly by this conscientious belief—and won by-elections by his fervor. Lord Halifax, from the sympathy he had with "nonresistance," as Viceroy of India won the confidence of the great non-resister, Gandhi. Such things made it hard for England to build up her forces and hard for her to threaten to use them.

Secondly, England largely and genuinely sympathized with Germany. In part this was the legacy of the policy of "fulfillment" of the Weimar republic. Because the democratic German politicians had been trusted, Hitler inherited the trust they had won. That made it easy for him to reoccupy the Rhineland with the claim that Germans should protect their own boundaries. As late as 1938 men could honestly believe that he was really intervening in Czechoslovakia and Austria to unite Germans with Germany. In part this was sympathy with the state socialist aims that were avowed—and, at times, carried out—by the National Socialist party. The economic and social recovery that appeared in Germany after Hitler impressed and bewildered many Englishmen. They admired the results while they hated many of the methods used. Such a belief was chiefly found among Tories, for Labor hated the antiunion side of Nazism. Yet again, it was hard for the tolerant Englishman to believe that anyone could be as intolerant as the Nazis said they were. This blindness to the intensity of nationalist feelings has its highly creditable side, but in foreign affairs, as in Empire affairs, it did much to weaken England's policy. Finally, there is the point that England has been a traditionally unreliable ally for the victors. It has long been a cardinal point in England's policy to obstruct her allies when she thought they needed blocking. Such had been Lloyd George's eventually successful attempts to make the French see reason about reparations, such had been the whole policy of building up a democratic Germany in the 1920's in the justified hopes it would enter the League of Nations. This policy had worked well in the 1920's. It was natural for it to be used in the 1930's.

Perhaps the whole situation may be summed up in the point Lord Vansittart has made in his *Lessons of My Life*. There he insisted that the British people were slow to distrust German intentions and slow to see coming dangers. For a democracy has certain practical weaknesses in carrying on diplomacy, as the latter part of this chapter has painfully shown, and from 1924 on the foreign affairs of England were ultimately managed by the people of England, at least by their veto on certain policies. But there is another side to this. Since England was a democracy, "His Majesty's Loyal Opposition" had its chance to say what it would recommend. When the workings of Opposition are considered, it is clear that a "foreign affairs Opposition" existed that cut across parties and that eventually formed an alternative Government, in May, 1940.

In the highly pacifist Labor party, this opposition was headed outside Parliament by the trade union leader, Ernest Bevin. Twice he was to strike, and strike hard, against pacifism. In the autumn of 1935 he complained, at a Labor party conference, that he was tired of seeing George Lansbury's conscience carted around. Thus he drove the pacifist from leadership and replaced him with Major Clement Attlee, at the same time making resistance of sorts to fascism a cardinal plank in the Labor platform. Then, as will be related, in 1940 his speeches drove out the Chamberlain Government. But the key opposition was not Labor but Tory. Five men symbolize it, and in so doing show how day-to-day loyal opposition works in England, at varied levels. These were Winston Churchill, George, Lord Lloyd of Dolobran, Anthony Eden, Sir Robert Vansittart, and Professor Lindemann. These men stood for the old English program—make England strong, gain allies, and preach the gospel of liberty.

Each of these men contributed in different ways. Lord Lloyd spoke from his permanent seat in the House of Lords and in confidential communications with members of the Government. Anthony Eden, first as Undersecretary for Foreign Affairs, then as Minister for League Affairs, as Foreign Secretary until he resigned, and thereafter as a supporting critic of the Government, pressed for details of daily conduct of diplomacy. Churchill, from his position as independent member of the House of Commons for Epping Forest, pressed hard for rearmament. In the civil service Sir Robert Vansittart, as he then was, saw to it that the facts of diplomacy reached the ears of the authorities, deaf though those authorities proved themselves.

Professor Lindemann, as adviser to Churchill and as technical member of the Imperial Committee on Air Defense, provided the knowledge that led to the development of radar. The first task these men set themselves to was that of getting some sort of armament program going. In this and in this alone were they truly successful. The vital point is that their prodding did get results. By a terribly narrow margin, England was ready. In 1939 she did have radar; she did have a Navy that commanded all nearby seas except the Baltic; she did have fighter planes that were the best in quality; she did have conscription which was put into effect in the summer of 1939. She was ready to fight for her life and save it. More than that, she had an alternative government that knew what to do when the Chamberlain government should fall, as it did in May, 1940, and did it. Then, when Churchill came to power she could have Lloyd and Eden in his Cabinet, along with Bevin and the ex-soldier, Attlee, whom Bevin had put in place of Lansbury at the head of the Labor party.

Thus, when these two decades of 1919 and 1939 are summed up, three things stand out. One is that the team of Lloyd George, Balfour, and Curzon, who made the peace after World War I, did leave behind them machinery that might have preserved the peace. Through the League and a policy of economic assistance with reparations and of frontier guarantees to allow disarmament, they had done much of what Castlereagh and Wellington did with the Congress system, guarantees, and clearing up reparations. More than that, they had done this so as to enlist the support of the peoples of Europe, instead of, as had Castlereagh, siding with rulers against ruled. It is not they but their successors who should bear the blame for failure. The next thing that stands out is the failure of the National Governments of 1931 to 1939 to meet changing conditions. When the methods of the twenties still might have worked, they were not used, till fascism became triumphant. Then, when new methods or rather a return to old methods became necessary, they did not make the change. They wasted force when they had it, and they lost allies through weakness and through dealing behind those allies' backs. For this the English people's hatred of war bears its responsibility along with the leaders. The fact remains that, as Churchill said, they did too little, too late. But one other fact remains. Because they did not muzzle opposition, it was possible for Churchill, Bevin, Lloyd, and Eden in public, Vansittart and Lindemann in private—to name but the outstanding ones—to have the right program ready. When in 1940 England called for a new deal, she had leaders to hand.

49

THE COMMONWEALTH OF NATIONS

1919–1953

In recent years a great deal has happened to the British Empire. By 1921 it had expanded to its greatest size. Then its area was about 13,600,000 square miles, its population about 448,000,000. This computation is made by totaling the homeland of the United Kingdom, the dominions, the Crown colonies, the Empire of India, and enemy-occupied territory about to become mandates. The roll since then of its peaceful losses is almost equally impressive: the dominions of Eire and Burma have become republics; the mandates of Iraq and Jordan, kingdoms; the mandate of Palestine, the republic of Israel; the protectorate of Egypt, a republic. Yet at the same time a new economic linkage has grown up, of imperial preference, along with other forms of cooperation, which binds with unsuspected strength. Above all, the Empire has changed in name and nature. It has dropped the adjective British and become simply and plainly the Commonwealth of Nations. Superficially, therefore, it seems difficult to tell the story of this evolution.

But as one looks under the surface, a pattern appears. As is suggested by the Empire's new name, nationalism affords an explanation of these changes. Throughout the Empire similar forces have arisen, similar mistakes in handling those forces have led to similar failures, similar acts of foresight to similar successes. Therefore the way to tell the story of the Commonwealth seems plain: find the completest and clearest example of the pattern, examine that series of events for its general significance, and then test the validity of that examination by applying that pattern elsewhere. The example to use is obvious. Perhaps the most striking change in the Empire occurred when twenty-six Irish counties of the United Kingdom broke away to become, in due course, the independent Republic of Eire. Furthermore, this was perhaps the best-commented-on change of them all. In 1904 Arthur Griffith prophesied the course of action that could make of Ireland a recognized nation, and he died in 1921 the acknowledged leader of that nation. On the other hand, able proconsuls have met the problem of incipient nationalism, come to terms with it, and enabled new nationalisms to stay within the Commonwealth. Therefore this chapter will begin with the Irish example of how to break up the Empire and will then contrast it with the clear-cut example in Malta of what a proconsul could do to hold the Empire together. These examples will be tested against events in the Near East and in India, in the Crown colonies, and in the original dominions. Then it will be possible to end by considering the present nature of the Commonwealth. Here the story will be taken down to the time of writing, since World War II did not alter Commonwealth history but merely speeded up a process already at work.

Griffith succeeded in Ireland because he had a clear idea of the Irish nation he wanted to see made and how to make it. He intended to use the methods by which the Magyar leaders of Hungary between 1849 and 1866 had gained equal national status within the Austrian empire. This he set down in articles in his paper *The United Irishman,* which were later published as a book, *The Resurrection of Hungary, a Parallel for Ireland.* He made three main proposals with a fourth held in reserve for emergencies— cultural, economic, governmental, and, if need be, military. He intended to create a truly Irish national spirit by reviving the Erse language, just as the Hungarians had revived the Magyar. This would give him as conscious or unconscious allies such organizations as the Gaelic League and even the Abbey Theatre. He proposed to create an Irish economy by encouraging better farming and building up home industries. This would make every agricultural society a recruiting agency, every manufacturer a potential supporter. Then he proposed to set up an alternative government. Just as the Hungarians had insisted that the union of Austria and Hungary in 1849 was "unconstitutional," he proposed to assert that the union of England and Ireland in 1800 was "unconstitutional." Instead of the Union Parliament at Westminster, he proposed to constitute a governing body in Dublin. By the power of election he hoped to gain control of local governmental bodies which would then obey Dublin rather than Westminster. If possible, he hoped to win the majority of the parliamentary seats in Ireland and send those so elected to Dublin to form his Irish Parliament. In so far as these three steps went, his motto would be "nonresistance." Consequently, those who might be horrified at violence would join his party. Just the same he was realistic, as the Hungarians had been. He remembered the old saying, "England's extremity is Ireland's opportunity." If the English did not listen to popular demand, and if a crisis came, then he would threaten. Similarly had the Hungarians threatened, in the Austro-Prussian War of 1866. Then the Austrians had given peacefully what they would have otherwise lost by war, because they knew that the Hungarians would fight. Griffith, too, was ready to fight, after he had exhausted other means.

This clear-cut program worked. Indeed, at its last stages the British

Commander in Chief in Ireland kept a copy of *The Resurrection of Hungary* on his desk, as a guide to what to expect next. The story of the years 1904 to 1921 is the story of how it worked. Similarly, the stories of the nationalist movements in Iraq, Egypt, Israel, India, Pakistan, and Burma are those of similar programs, independently evolved for the most part, gaining similar success. But the program worked only when the time was ripe, and only when the force that could check it—what Griffith attacked as "Lion and Unicorn loyalty"—had been dissipated. In Ireland in December, 1918, the time was ripe. British bungles, as has been related, had destroyed the loyalty John Redmond had created in 1914. Irish scholars, Irish farmers, and Irish industry were more ready than they knew for a change. Ireland had heroes, the men of the Easter Rebellion, and shock troops, the young men "on the run" from police for political reasons. Therefore Griffith took the next to last step on his program. The successful Sinn Fein candidates in the parliamentary elections of 1918 met as an Irish Parliament at Dublin, under the Irish name of Dail Eireann. The Dail, filled with Rebellion heroes, took the final step on Griffith's program. It proclaimed the Irish Republic, with the eloquent New York-born Eamon de Valera as President, the lovable and efficient London clerk Michael Collins as Minister of Finance, and Arthur Griffith as Minister of Home Affairs. De Valera went to America to raise funds, Collins went underground to command the resistance, and Griffith guided. This was the "Invisible Republic" that meant to rule Ireland despite the Cabinet at Westminster and the Viceroy and Chief Secretary at Dublin Castle.

The British government failed to meet the challenge. It knew that Ulster, or at least six counties of Ulster, would resist just as bitterly if Home Rule, let alone anything more, were applied so as to unite it with South Ireland even though the Third Home Rule Bill had become law in September, 1914. The government temporized, holding up the application of Home Rule under the pretext that the war had not legally ended. While yet there was time, it failed to repress Sinn Fein. As a compromise it passed a Government of Ireland Act, separating Ireland into two parts, Ulster and the rest. This merely had the result that Ulster adopted the form of self-government with representation at Westminster which it now has and the elections allowed Sinn Fein to demonstrate strength by electing a new Dail. The South Ireland Parliament met formally just long enough for its four loyal members to advertise the success of Sinn Fein at the polls. Now broke out the curious Civil War which the Irish call "the Troubles."

Here appears a pattern sometimes to reappear, notably in Palestine, of the British police authorities fighting what they consider terrorism, only to find it is, to those on the other side, patriotism. Subsequently both sides have accused each other, with too much justice, of excesses. The "Irish Republican Army" cracked the Royal Irish Constabulary by terrorizing their families and forced the British to enlist auxiliary police, the ill-famed Black and Tans, veterans marked out by khaki uniforms and black caps. The Black and Tans too often yielded to the temptation to meet excess by counterexcess. It was possible to shut the Sinn Fein courts, which over much of western and southern Ireland had taken over legal control—and done, it appears, a pretty good job. But the propaganda battle was won by Sinn Fein. The Lloyd George government, which had announced it would not treat with murderers, began to notice the reception given to Asquith's demand that Ireland have dominion status. Meanwhile, Balfour spoke some home truths about ruling justly or getting out completely. In August, 1921, a truce was made, for though the British authorities had regained sway over most of Ireland, they were ruling it as a conquered country.

Terms were hard to reach. Lloyd George demanded two things, recognition of the King as ruler—loyalism mattered much emotionally, especially to a Coalition government made up largely of Unionists—and the use of Irish naval bases for England's protection. De Valera would not yield on the first, demanding almost exactly the same connection between the Crown and the Irish Republic that now exists between the Crown and the Indian Republic. Griffith and Collins therefore took over, and they made terms when they had found the point at which Lloyd George was willing to resume the use of force. The terms—all since torn up—were these: The King of Great Britain and the Irish Republic would make a treaty by which the whole of Ireland would become a dominion like Canada, in which officials would take an oath to the King. Certain naval bases would remain British. The Irish would pay to the Crown the sums advanced for land purchase. The six counties of Ulster might leave the dominion. If they did, the boundary would be rectified.

The treaty was signed and was ratified by the British Parliament and, after an intense struggle, by a thin majority in the Dail. Then the process of tearing up went on. It took Ulster only twenty-four hours to leave the Irish Free State, the new dominion. The boundary never was rectified; the boundary commission split wide open, and it was agreed to keep the illogical county boundaries, though that gave to "North Ireland" a South Irish population large enough to send two members to Westminster and kept a few Ulstermen out of Ulster. Thus partition, which Carson, recent documents reveal, had suggested as a steppingstone to make Home Rule palatable to Ulster, became the creation of a sort of Ulster local nationalism, determined to stick to Great Britain as a way of keeping separate from the rest of Ireland.

In the Irish Free State—as it was from 1922 to 1937—the process of tearing up took longer. Collins and Griffith wanted to make a loyal trial of dominion status. Griffith died just after the Dail ratified the treaty.

Collins was murdered in a second civil war. But their successors, President Cosgrave and Home Affairs Minister Kevin Higgins, put down opposition. After all, Irishmen would accept police methods from fellow Irishmen they would reject from the English. De Valera refused to take the oath and thus exiled himself from politics. But Irish Free State politics were, from the imperial point of view, struggles between two nationalist parties. The Cosgrave government secured a change in the royal title, recognizing that Ireland was separate from Great Britain and calling King George V "King of Ireland"—a title that was dropped in 1953. Then, after the murder of Higgins, the Irish intransigents changed their minds. De Valera took the oath—George V is said to have hoped De Valera would not make so many promises because he was sure to break them—denied its validity as he took it, won the election of 1930, and proceeded to take over control. For seventeen years he ruled, tearing up the treaty bit by bit. The governorship-general was abolished, land-purchase repayments were impounded, the Free State became Eire, a tariff war persuaded the British to abandon the naval bases, and Eire stayed neutral in World War II. Then the Costello government came into office in 1947, and destroyed the last two remaining links with Britain—the oath consuls abroad took, to gain the benefits of British cooperation, and the failure to declare absolute independence.

Would history have been changed had De Valera been allowed, in 1921, the oath that he asked for—and that India received? It is a suggestive speculation, for this pattern of Nationalist success has a counterpart—the story of Malta, where British rule was preserved and perhaps fortified by wise firmness and wise cooperation with local nationalism. Here British naval needs were saved and loyalty secured. Yet in 1919, when Lord Plumer of Messines was sent to be governor, the situation was serious. A local nationalism, feeding on the cultural connection with Italian nationalism and local economic desires, including a postwar depression, met him with a hostile demonstration as he landed. In twenty minutes he had dispersed the demonstration by waving aside both his heavy armed guard and the wreaths that had been laid to insult him. In two years he had restored prosperity and order. Yet this was not paternalism. Not for nothing had the army loved him for his motto "Be fair." When, in 1921, Undersecretary of the Colonies Leopold Amery came to Malta to consult him about the introduction of self-government, he found Plumer in the great proconsular tradition of Durham and Elgin eager to transfer control to the Maltese. A system of dual government was worked out, with a Maltese Cabinet responsible to the Assembly for local matters, while the Governor and his council took charge of defense of the naval base and all that that required.

Until 1929 dual government worked. Then Italian Fascism, a local nationalism, and a quarrel over the status of religion made "responsible government" impossible. With the wisdom of the serpent—rarely employed in imperial matters—not only was the Malta Patent canceled by act of Parliament but Maltese rather than Italian was made the second language of the island. Gradually there grew up a generation that was Maltese and not pro-Italian. This was proven by the valiant loyalty of that much-bombed island during World War II. After the war, the dual government was restored, and it still appears to work. Malta is proud of the Cross of St. George given the Island by the King, and "Lion and Unicorn loyalty" has won out because at the crisis the firm hand was applied by a man who meant it when he said: "Be fair."

Palestine affords a curious confirmation of these patterns. Here rule went well when Plumer was there. But it is not as simple as that. Palestine —now divided into Israel and Jordan—had a curious problem of two nationalisms: one native, weak, and upper-class; the other immigrant, aggressive, and popular. Great Britain had the Palestine mandate for varied reasons. She genuinely wanted a national homeland for the Jews, and in honor was bound to repay the support given in World War I by world Jewry when she had made that promise, by the Balfour Declaration of 1917. Also she needed to protect the route to India and to Near Eastern oil. Furthermore she had duties to the Arabs, and there were those who had hopes of seeing "Brown Dominions," eventually self-governing and united to the Crown. British rule of the mandate broke down at the start when the Jews and Arabs boycotted a representative council. Thus was missing the organ through which self-government could be built up. Instead Jew immigrant and Arab native built up tension and also built up their organizations, the Jewish Council and, later, the Arab Higher Committee. Complicating the whole situation was one plain social and economic fact—thousands of Jewish immigrants could live, with the modern methods they employed, where hundreds of Arabs were starving, but to use those methods they must oust the Arabs. If a Jewish agriculture, a Jewish economy, a Jewish culture, and a Jewish self-government should grow up through immigration, keeping the peace would be a great problem.

In such a quandary, the solution for the Colonial Office was plain. Plumer, who wanted to retire from Malta to be President of the Marylebone Cricket Club and thus the honored head of the British national sport, from a sense of duty took the Palestine post. There, while he ruled, sights were seen that have not been seen since. The Grand Mufti of Jerusalem, the leading Arab troublemaker, minded as he was told. Though 30,000 French could not keep order in Syria, all Plumer needed was a guard of honor and local police. At the same time, Palestine paid its way; Jewish immigrants founded cities and a university and expanded their farms. But when Plumer retired, matters changed. Arab and Jew rioted over the Arab-owned Jewish

Holy Place, the Wailing Wall in Jerusalem. Troops were flown in, the first great example of such use of air power. Plumer's precious heritage of order was lost, never to be regained. As was ruefully admitted in Parliament, his presence was worth a battalion of troops. Thereafter, as Durham reported of Canada, two nations quarreled in one bosom.

There is a grim, sad story of British failure to keep order. Lord Pass-field (Sidney Webb of earlier) as Colonial Secretary tried to reduce tension by putting a quota on immigration. This created new tension. A sad cycle of disorder, investigating commission, new proposal, and new disorder seemed to show that Palestine could not be politically united and yet economically ought not to be divided. Meanwhile, Jew and Arab, who would not cooperate, showed increasing ability in self-government as they organized to quarrel with each other and with the British holders of the mandate.

What made the quarrel worse was the outside pressure. The Moslem world, acting through the nearby Arab states, urged the cause of the native-born dispossessed. World Jewry, especially after the Nazi persecutions had begun, urged the cause of the European dispossessed. Because there was no safety valve of representative institutions, the British authorities had to bear the brunt. For example, when they set immigration quotas, great publicity was given to the unfortunates who were turned back or were punished for attempting to enter. Investigations showed what was wrong, but their proposals led to no results. World War II brought an end to some of the difficulties, since Jew and English joined against Nazi. After the war had ended, the British could endure no more. They wisely gave up the mandate in 1948, part of the great practical wisdom shown by the Attlee Government. In consequence Palestine was divided into the Republic of Israel and the Kingdom of Jordan, for by then the Jewish immigrants could found Israel, May 14, 1948, and defend its independence. Unfortunately, however, British troops had to march out of Jerusalem and the Union Jack be hauled down, as had happened in Dublin. Though, as in Ireland, Britons had enabled the building of institutions, as in Ireland they were evicted.

In Egypt, Jordan, and Iraq, nationalism took a different form. Where in Ireland, Malta, and Israel it was democratic, here it was oligarchical. There was an age-old Moslem culture, a new industry, and forms of local self-government through which nationalism could express itself according to Griffith's formula, but aside from some students the chief expressers of nationalism would be landlords, for these are countries still held in great estates. Consequently, there was a seventeenth- and eighteenth-century flavor to political events, for a king could make headway against a group of landlords—as had Charles II and George III—as a king could not against a popular movement. The story of the growth of national freedom would be that of a small ruling class winning it, with popular support, rather than the people themselves.

In Egypt a minor discourtesy triggered off the inevitable. Saad Zaghlul Pasha, former Minister of Education, wished to lead an Egyptian delegation to the Versailles Peace Conference. This was a device taken likewise by Irish and South African nationalists and received a similar treatment. Passports were held up. At once there was a grievance—the Egyptian delegation (Wafd el Misri, in Arabic) had been denied its rights. A political party, the Wafd, was founded with this grievance of nonrecognition as its basic platform and was almost inevitably successful in any election. Egypt burst into disorder, for the fellahin, the peasantry, had been grossly ill-treated by the enlistment of labor battalions during World War I. Through bureaucratic error, the ill-famed *corvée* or forced labor, abolished by Cromer, had been thus backhandedly reintroduced. Disorder was all the more serious since the chief body of troops in the land, Australians, were eager to get home and struck back very hard at those who had killed their comrades.

The Lloyd George Cabinet, notable in these years for its mishandling of the Empire, tried its usual solution, of a combination of force and yielding. It sent for a strong general, Lord Allenby, nicknamed the "Bull," and then sent the Milner Commission to negotiate with Egyptian leaders. Fortunately, Allenby was strong enough to restrain himself. He finished the very able police work by which order had been quietly restored, and he refused to be stampeded. While the Milner Commission showed it knew how to yield and therefore caused the various Egyptian leaders to raise their demands, Allenby made his plan. In 1921 he went to London and enforced it. Someday his maneuvers may be a classic of the constitution. He used his right of direct access to the Crown as a Privy Councilor and his seat in the House of Lords to give circulation to his demands and to threaten publicity for them. Thus he forced the Cabinet to back his program. It was simple and in the proconsular tradition as this book has used the term. The Egyptian government was told that the protectorate would be ended if indemnity were given the British for all past actions of an occupying force and the British garrison were allowed to remain, as the ultimate guardian of the Suez Canal and general order. Then Egypt, as an independent kingdom, would freely negotiate with Great Britain in regard to their future relationships. This—as Allenby's biographer, Lord Wavell, has revealed—was part of a conscious policy. Allenby believed that only by giving the Egyptians responsibility for governing themselves could an Egyptian government be created with which it would be possible to deal. This comment is of interest, for Lord Wavell penned his volume while Viceroy of India and facing a similar problem of evacuation there.

It took time for this to work, and a tragedy to clinch it. For the King of

Egypt entered into an eighteenth- or even seventeenth-century wrangle with his Wafd-dominated Parliament lasting till 1924, when at last Zaghlul and the Wafd had power. Then came great popular excitement, culminating in the murder of Sir Lee Stack, the Governor-general of the Sudan. At that point Allenby struck, and struck far harder than London would have done. He presented an ultimatum to Egypt. As atonement for this outrage certain obvious points must be agreed to: pensions for English civil servants, a twenty-year garrison at Suez, punishment of the offenders, and control of the Nile waters—or British occupation of the land. He got his demands and soon remitted the intentionally excessive Nile demand.

But the newly appointed Baldwin Government did not see eye to eye with Allenby. Shortly after his success, he was brutally dismissed. In his place was put George, Lord Lloyd. Lloyd's program was the exact opposite. He believed that the British High Commissioner would take an active share in the direction of affairs. This he did, with great ability and good practical results. It can be argued which was the right policy, for, as Wavell has suggested, this prevented the educative results of responsibility reaching the Egyptians. The Wafd continued to be the one party that could win elections that were not rigged; the King and his ministers continued to use seventeenth-century methods to carry out anti-Wafd but advisable policies. Then, in 1929, the newly appointed MacDonald Government dismissed Lloyd with, if possible, more peremptoriness than Allenby had received.

Now began a period when Allenby's policy was partially tried. Gradually, something approaching a two-party system grew up. At length, in 1937, a treaty was signed, making Egypt practically independent and finishing the work Allenby had begun. A fruit of the delay was Egypt's neutrality during World War II and the later troubles, culminating with the ousting of the King, in 1952, and self determination for the Anglo-Egyptian Sudan in 1953.

Jordan has had a peculiar relationship with Great Britain. The nation began as a military accident. At the time of the Cairo Conference, of which more anon, the late King Abdullah was on his way to lead an Arab invasion of Syria. Winston Churchill and the Conference offered him a choice —R.A.F. bombing if he went on, or a kingdom where he was. He made the obvious decision, founded a kingdom under British mandate, cooperated by allowing British training of his Arab Legion, and eventually, in the war with Israel, obtained for Jordan the Arab part of Palestine. Here, perhaps because Major Glubb of the Arab Legion was left alone to work with Abdullah, a formless land was turned into an effective locally governed small nation. The quick giving of both freedom and aid made Jordan a friend, not an enemy.

Iraq is a more complex story. Mesopotamia, the land between the Tigris and the Euphrates, was invaded in 1914 by troops of the Indian army, conquered in 1916 and 1917, and then governed by officials led by the brilliant Arnold Wilson and imbued with the Indian Civil Service tradition. They did a good, though expensive, job; Wilson got the ardent devotion of his subordinates, the respect of the general population, and the hatred of the local nationalists. These nationalists and upper-class landlord and official group were divided from the general population by the fact that they were Sunnite Moslems, while Mesopotamia was the center of Shiite Moslemism. But nationalism can conquer such barriers. A sharp revolt made it clear that, as in Ireland, the British had the choice of ruling as conquerors or making terms. Sir Percy Cox came down from Persia and made terms. To appease religious discontent Sir Percy procured the choice of Emir Feisal of Mecca as king, a constitution was issued, and Great Britain took the mandate of Iraq, with British advisers in key posts.

For this decision Churchill was responsible. He had been made Colonial Secretary to clean up the mess, had summoned to advise him the great philo-Arabs, St. John Philby and T. E. Lawrence, and at the Cairo Conference of 1921 had come to two conclusions. One, which proved itself sound, was that Great Britain could ensure her defense by air power and could cheaply keep order in Iraq by that means. The other, which proved itself unsound, seems to have been that there might yet be "Brown Dominions," Arab states which shared a partnership similar to that of Canada with Great Britain. Iraq worked not ineffectively with Britain, since Britain was wise enough to gain for her the Mosul oil fields and to release her from mandate ahead of schedule. But it was a practical relationship, not an emotional one. Internally Iraq has been governed by an inner ring, with no more of a two-party system than England saw under Robert Walpole. Civil rights have not been so highly regarded as by Walpole, and twice, in 1936 and 1942, there have been *coups d'état,* the one in 1942 being put down by the air-force base at Habbaniya. It does take a generation or two for the practice of responsible government to be learned; that Iraq has been well managed during this period of education is to its credit. Meanwhile those institutions on which Griffith insisted have developed, local agricultural, industrial, and cultural bodies, out of which effective nationalism grows and on which it can feed.

In India, Burma, and Ceylon, the institutions of nationalism already existed. Locally owned industry and age-old cultural institutions had political guidance from the All India Congress and Gandhi. On the other hand, those local political institutions which could be seized by the nationalists might also foster "Lion and Unicorn loyalty." The story here is of a race narrowly won in Ceylon, Pakistan, and even in India and lost in Burma, but still only narrowly. In 1916 Lloyd George realized that India was a great problem. He therefore issued a promise of eventual dominion status and gave Edwin S. Montagu the post of Indian Secretary and the duty of seeing to it that this promise got carried out. Montagu took the unusual step of going to India. There, after a preliminary period of suspicion, he worked in cooperation with Viceroy Lord Chelmsford in the practical drafting of the Montagu-Chelmsford reforms. These, the first basic change in Indian government since Pitt's Act of 1784, at the provincial level offered dual government—here named dyarchy—much as in Malta. An elected council would control a responsible Cabinet, in certain fields. The Governor and his nominated Council would control in other fields. More fields might be transferred; on the other hand, the Viceroy held emergency powers. Centrally, the Viceroy ruled, as before, through his council but had a consultative assembly. This program was to last ten years and be reviewed.

But when the Government of India Act was passing through Parliament, it seemed as if it might last only ten minutes. The Montagu-Chelmsford reforms were not conceived of in a vacuum but were hurried through to be effective before the ground swell of rising Indian nationalism broke down British government in India. That movement had just found its great leader, Mohandas K. Gandhi, whom the Indian people and the world soon would call Mahatma, or the "great-souled." In South Africa he had been the only man ever to get the better of Botha and Smuts. Now he had a program that caught Indian imaginations. It was *Satyagraha,* or "peaceful noncooperation," based on the ideas of the Hindu religion. Tied in with this was admiration for Indian village life, emphasis on village industries, and a "hartal" or boycott of British goods. The purpose of this movement was swaraj, or self-rule. Thus it was the Sinn Fein program, even to the alternative offered to the British, self-government in the Empire or independence. This program, though based on Hindu culture, worked through the Indian National Congress and secured Moslem support. For this was the time of the short-lived anti-British Khalifat movement, when Indian Moslems feared that the British peace terms to Turkey were oppressing the Sultan in his capacity of Caliph or religious head of Islam.

The clash came in the spring of 1919, when discontent had caused Lord Chelmsford to issue the much-derided and never-enforced Rowlatt Acts against incendiary agitation. Finally, at the time of a key debate in the House of Commons a day of "noncooperation" in Amritsar in the Punjab led to rioting. This General Dyer put down with dramatic harshness. There are two sides to Amritsar. It was, like the sharp police action in Ireland and Palestine, a propaganda victory for the nationalists, a victory sealed by a House of Commons investigating committee reporting against Dyer's methods. But Dyer, as a House of Lords Committee showed, had a better case than is recognized. He did stop what might have been rebellion, in time—by hours—to hurry troops to the border and meet the invasion which began the Third Afghan War.

After Amritsar came a period of quiet, in which the "dyarchy" of the Montagu-Chelmsford reforms might be tried out. In 1921 Lloyd George sent to India as Viceroy Lord Chief Justice Lord Reading, who had some success. He got a measure of Indian confidence by his manifestations of genuine regret for Amritsar, by his repeal of the Rowlatt Acts, and by his policy of Indianization of the army and the civil service. This last was partial, tiny, and most significant. It was a step in grappling with the problem of setting up self-government in a desperately divided land. Having shown good faith, Reading also showed strength and deftness. He had Gandhi tried for sedition and jailed. When Indian Moslems were perturbed at seeing the British government aid Greeks against the Turks, Montagu and he publicly protested in the name of India. As a result of this policy, dyarchy began to work. From the start the "National Liberal Federation" had been willing to enter the legislative councils. Now Moslem parties gladly protected themselves in the same way. Finally the Indian National Congress voted to accept dyarchy, though with the avowed purpose of obstruction. This purpose was not achieved. In Bombay especially, under the leadership of Lord Lloyd, British administrators and Indian legislators worked out practical cooperation.

But this was a temporary thing. Reading urged on the home government that concessions be made quickly, before they were demanded. He considered the Montagu-Chelmsford program of revision in ten years too slow. But though his advice was taken by sending the Simon Commission to India in 1926, it took till 1935 to get a true revision. During that time the disorder Reading had feared took place. This delay occurred because the British did not understand the intensity of Indian nationalism, nor did the Indians understand the difficulty of governing India. The Simon Commission—which went to India in 1926 but did not report till 1930—failed to gain acceptance because the Indians would not let any outside body, even a nonpartisan commission from both houses of the British Parliament, tell them how to rule themselves. Though the defections from the Indian National Congress of the Liberal Federation and some Moslems had presaged the growth of genuine political parties, these groups now combined against British rule in the All Party Conference and demanded action. British political opinion was moving toward concession. The Conservatives Baldwin and Amery and the Labor leader MacDonald were working together, against the opposition of Churchill and Lloyd, but not until 1931 was it possible to call in London a Round Table Conference. By this time Gandhi had gone to extremes. In 1929 he started "civil disobedience" again and in 1930 made his "march to the sea," there ceremonially to break the government salt monopoly by drying a few grains of salt from the sea water. Into jail he went, having refused to attend the first Round Table Conference; out of jail he came, to attend the second Round Table Conference. By then, in 1932, it may be said that the British had learned their lesson, that India could not permanently be held. Now it became India's task to meet her special problems. Independent Indian Princes did not want to surrender sovereignty; Moslems feared for their religion. It was hard for Hindus to realize that their caste system must be changed— Gandhi in 1932 had to start a boycott and "fast unto death" to gain some rights for the "untouchables." Moslems, led by Mohammed Ali Jinnah, split apart into a Moslem League which refused to agree to any dominion status without special minority rights for Moslems. Rather than that, Moslem extremists began to say, they would split off from the Indian empire the lands west of the Indus and east of Calcutta, into a separate land, Pakistan, a name one young enthusiast invented.

To solve these legislative problems was set up a Joint Select Committee on Indian Constitutional Reform, under the chairmanship of the Marquis of Linlithgow. Gradually, a solution was hammered out, using the perennial device of federation to get Moslems, Native States, and the Hindu majority under one central government. This was the basis of the Government of India Act of 1935, to take effect in 1937. By it dyarchy was ended, but a state of tutelage remained. Though the Indian Parliament and the provincial councils could rule through cabinets, the powers that were transferred might in emergency be recalled. Again India went through the same process of growing acceptance of a forward step. First the Congress party boycotted the new legislatures, and then increasing cooperation came.

By now the picture in India had changed. "Indianization" of army and civil service had begun to take effect. Fed by the Indian universities, there was a reservoir of trained men who could administer the land and defend it. Indian industry progressed rapidly; much support to Gandhi came from men of wealth. The argument that India was not ready for self-government was no longer plausible. Had not World War II come, perhaps the Government of India Act of 1935 might have proved effective. Credit for this should go, among others, to a series of effective viceroys. Lord Irwin— now Lord Halifax—did much to gain the partial confidence of Gandhi and reach a *modus vivendi* with him. Lord Willingdon ruled well in the troublous period when the Act of 1935 was being hammered out. Lord Linlithgow, as Chairman of the Committee that drafted that Act and as Viceroy who enforced it, also formed part of the proconsular tradition. Perhaps he had the hardest task, for he had to face rule during World War II.

For India, now technically self-governing, refused to join in the war. Gandhi demanded the free right to choose war or peace, and full dominion status, before he would cooperate. That made it necessary for Lord Linlithgow to declare war by his emergency powers. Consequently India's very real contribution to World War II was through viceregal action. A large volunteer army was raised. Much military equipment manufactured, with consequent benefit to Indian industry. In fact, Great Britain became a debtor nation to India. As long as the war was with Germany and Italy, this did not matter. But when Japan struck, in December, 1941, Great Britain was in dire need of willing Indian cooperation. Therefore, in 1942 a mission was sent to India, headed by the Labor statesman Sir Stafford Cripps, to offer immediate dominion status, with the exception that British command of the army would continue to the end of the war. This was rejected. The war ended, even after an actual invasion of India from Burma, as it had begun, with rule by viceregal action, the Viceroy now being Lord Wavell, who after serving as Commander in Chief in India from 1942 became Viceroy in 1943.

In 1945 the Attlee Labor Government came into power. It had three great qualifications for handling India. Major Attlee had been a member of the Simon Commission from 1926 to 1930 and knew the problem. The Labor party was on record as always having stood for self-government for India. Perhaps most significant, the Attlee Government was determined to give freedom before it was compelled to, as it later showed in Palestine. India was told it would have dominion status in 1947 and had better get ready. All actions needed to obtain this result were taken. Lord Wavell was replaced as Viceroy by another former Commander in Chief, Lord Mountbatten. The princes of India were in effect told to make the best terms they could. When the Moslems and the Hindus quarreled over minority rights and the Moslems began talking seriously of a separate Pakistan, a separate Pakistan was given. When boundaries were argued about, general lines were drawn, and the two future dominions were told to settle details.

This solution worked. In 1947 the title of Emperor of India was dropped, and ahead of schedule, on August 15, 1947, government was transferred to the elected members of the Indian Parliament, as divided into the Parliaments of India and Pakistan.

The same thing happened that had happened in Ireland and in Palestine. Stern solutions were accepted because it was no longer the British who were stern. Just as Collins was killed in civil war, so a Hindu extremist killed Gandhi and a Moslem killed Ali Khan, the Pakistani Prime Minister. Just as Arab and Jew fought over boundaries, so Indian and Pakistani fought—not over boundaries but over population exchange. In bitter massacres the Hindus and the Moslems sorted themselves out. At present writing there is still contention over which shall take over the Hindu-ruled and largely Moslem state of Kashmir. More significant, both Pakistan and India remained dominions, and when India became a republic, she agreed to remain a member of the Commonwealth, having the same relationship De Valera had asked for in 1921.

Today India and Pakistan are respected and effective members of the United Nations, with independent foreign policies, which at the same time work together with other members of the Commonwealth in Commonwealth Conferences. Pragmatically, the Government of India Act of 1947 has worked. In Ceylon, too, dominion status has met the challenge of nationalism. There, in a land of Buddhists, Hindus, and even a significant population of Dutch descent, there was the same problem of internal division as on the Indian mainland. To meet this problem the Donoughmore Commission in 1928 recommended copying the committee system of the London County Council rather than the party system of the British Parliament. This device for education in political responsibility carried Ceylon through to dominion status, in 1948. Therefore it is Burma alone which the Commonwealth has lost. Burma, long uneasy in being ruled with India, was separated in 1935. But there nationalism reached the extreme of aiding the Japanese invasion of 1942. When, with Nationalist Chinese aid, that invasion was driven out by General Slim's forces in 1945, Burma was offered the choice of independence or dominion status, took the former—and has attended Commonwealth Conferences since then. Thus, though in the Near East the British Empire lost territory in India, it suffered only one loss and otherwise changed in nature.

This process of self-realization under the Union Jack has also gone on in the Crown colonies, the mandates, and the condominium of the Sudan, where political institutions and nationalism have not been so far advanced. Constitutionally the familiar pattern has been followed: single governor, governor with council, elected membership in council, representative government by a wholly elected council, and finally responsible government. But now the pattern is a conscious one. Ever since in 1948 eventual dominion status was promised to Nigeria it has been the policy in London to aid this evolution. Consequently, the historian can put his finger on colony, mandate, or condominium and say that here the normal course of events has taken place, and there some important local situation has disturbed that course of events.

In Rhodesia, for example, the course of events seemed altered by the fact that the ruling body was the British South Africa Company. But in fact an advisory council assisted the governor until 1923. Then the Company surrendered its charter, and the whites and a few educated Negroes of Southern Rhodesia became a "self-governing colony" under what was then the Dominions Office. Southern Rhodesia differs from a dominion only in having, like the dominion of Ceylon, no control over foreign policy, and in being supervised in its native policy. Northern Rhodesia has become a Crown colony, not having as yet full self-government. In

Kenya, on the other hand, a vigorous white minority wants to create a "white man's country" and has been held in check by the Colonial Office, while an Indian minority had demanded recognition. Consequently, the Colonial Office, which under the British Settlements Act regulated forms of local government, has not been willing to put the governor any more at the mercy of his council, by introducing any more elected members. In the Gold Coast and Nigeria, social evolution has brought out groups capable of bearing political responsibility, notably the village headmen and tribal councils inland in the Gold Coast, the coastal city councils of both colonies, and the local Emirs of the Nigerian states. At the time of writing attempts are being made to find transitional forms of government where, as in India, emergency powers can be retained by the governor while normal powers are increasingly transferred to elected bodies. Similarly, a Sudanese Parliament has come into being, which in fact and perhaps soon in name will take basic responsibility. In Cyprus a block has come, which for two decades has prevented progress. There a Greek-Christian majority of the elected members of the council has split on religious and racial lines with a Turkish-Moslem minority. Consequently, though there are technically more elected members than nominated ones, in fact, the Governor retains control because he can command control of a combination of nominated and Turkish members.

To extend our review further, in Malaya the problem has been to find politically responsible groups. The Malays are not interested in voting; the Chinese, until recently, have been temporary immigrants intending to return to China. Thus, though an administrative federation of Malaya came in the 1890's, Malayan government is, for all practical purposes, still an administrative federation. This has not prevented the rise of the problems of industrialization, from Chinese-run tin mines and British-run rubber plantations. As was the case in Palestine it has merely removed the safety valve of representative institutions, as the present trouble with Communist guerrillas demonstrates. Finally in the West Indies, the age-old home of representative institutions, the same problem remains, the legacy of the nineteenth century—the absence of taxable wealth. There is a vigorous movement for local self-government, for education has reached the masses. There are frequent plans for federation. But the fact that the West Indies must rely on the Colonial Development Fund and the fact that then those in London who pay the piper must call the tune has formed an obstacle that is as yet unsurmounted.

As this review shows, the nature of the Empire has changed. There is still the ideal, going back to Joseph Chamberlain and beyond him to the great humanitarian administrators of the nineteenth century, of aid from London. It now takes the form of the Colonial Development Fund rather than of the antislavery patrol, but the two have much in common. Here is the concept of "trusteeship" of the United Nations seemingly functioning. But a belief is steadily gaining more adherents that all colonies will eventually become self-governing, that this trusteeship is temporary, and that dominion status is the eventual end. That raises the question, what has been the history of the dominions which had gained that status before World War I? What trends do they show?

One of the dominions is no more. After an economic collapse in the 1930's, Newfoundland surrendered herself to rule by a commission sent out from England. Commissioners changed too fast for permanence of administration, and at long last Newfoundland became a province of the Dominion of Canada. The other dominions have progressed fairly uneventfully. Political power in them has alternated between two parties. In Canada these have been Liberal and Conservative, with Liberal predominating. In Australia and in New Zealand, Labor has come to the top, gaining power in the 1930's from variously named coalitions—in New Zealand the National or Reform party, in Australia a coalition of Liberal and Country parties. In each, the pendulum has swung back from Labor. In South Africa the struggle has been three-sided, among General Smuts's Commonwealth or South African party, the Nationalists (once led by General Hertzog, now by Dr. Malan) and Labor. When the Nationalists have been in power, it has, however, been Labor that has put them in. In war and in depression, there have been coalition governments.

In the internal history of these four dominions a pair of patterns, one economic and one nationalist, seem to have emerged. In Australia and New Zealand there has been an alternation between Farmer-Liberal and Labor-Socialist parties. Circumstances differed here. In Australia the Labor party was the politically outstanding party at the outset of this period. It was kept down by a coalition among its opponents, the old Liberal party, the new farmers' Country party, and the few Laborites who with W. M. Hughes left the Labor party during World War I over conscription. For most of the two decades between 1919 and 1939 Labor was kept out of office. During World War II it came in, proceeded with a nationalization program, and was ousted in 1950. In New Zealand, on the other hand, Labor was a young party, and the struggle was between Reform and Liberal. Here there was a progression to the left; Liberal, under the name United, came back to power in 1928 for the first time since the Seddon machine had broken up, but in coalition with Labor, which in turn took over in 1935. Labor then held office until 1950.

In Canada and South Africa the story has been different, one of nationalism. In Canada nationalism has been a key issue but not the key issue. The solid political fact is that the Province of Quebec returns Liberal members to Ottawa. The Liberal party has won handsomely outside Quebec, as well, but it has been those votes which have ensured its staying in office for all but six of the years since 1921. (It is said the late W. Mackenzie King postponed his retirement from politics till he could claim to have held office as First Minister of the Crown longer than even Sir Robert Walpole.) Quebec nationalism has shown itself in the curious form of a Nationalist party—the Union Nationale—which carries Quebec provincial elections overwhelmingly against the Liberals, but lets them hold the Quebec seats in the Dominion Parliament. But though French nationalism in Canada, for all its obviousness, has apparently reached a *modus vivendi*, matters are otherwise in South Africa. There Boer nationalism has been complicated with racialism. The political history of the Union has reflected this fact from the very outset. For when General Hertzog resigned from the pre–World War I Cabinet of Louis Botha to keep his freedom to express Boer nationalist sentiments, he started an alternation of Boer-British coalitions which emphasized loyalty to the Commonwealth and Nationalist or Nationalist-Labor governments which emphasized Afrikanderdom and racialism. For herein lies the difference between French-Canadian and Boer nationalisms. French-Canadian nationalism benefits from the British connection—it is the inviolability of the British North American Act which protects French culture. But the British South Africa Act blocks racialism. Therein lies the problem that has faced Boer leadership. Some leaders, like Botha and Smuts, have thrown their whole weight on the side of the British connection. That kept Smuts in office until 1926, and returned him to office in coalition with Hertzog in 1931, to stay there till his death. Others—here Hertzog is the great example—have been torn two ways. It was Hertzog who led a Boer deputation to Versailles to plead for South African independence; it was Hertzog who secured the drafting of the Balfour Report of 1926 and declared it satisfied him completely. It was Hertzog who passed the Flag Act of 1927, and it was Hertzog who fused his party with Smuts's in 1934. Yet others have been intransigent. Such has been the record of D. F. Malan, the present premier. It was he who secured the recognition of Afrikaans, the local tongue, rather than Dutch, a European language, as the second legal language of the Union. It is he, in power since 1948, who today is preaching "apartheit"—in American usage, "segregation"—practicing what he preaches, and in doing so striking at the British connection.

The recent history of the overseas possessions of the British Crown is not merely that of a series of parallel events in different parts of the world. These possessions have a common history, for they have created a constitutional law and what amounts to a loose-knit common executive in the course of working out together that new institution, the Commonwealth of Nations. After the attempt at creating an Imperial Cabinet had failed but had shown what course not to follow, the Conference of Premiers of 1926 steered men's thinking to the point at which the Statute of Westminster could be passed in 1931 and economic cooperation be established.

The story of the Imperial Cabinet is soon told. At the Paris Peace Conference, Empire cooperation was facilitated by meetings of the British War Cabinet plus dominion premiers. This got speedy joint action. Then after the Treaties of Paris were signed the Lloyd George Cabinet held annual Imperial Cabinets. These became viewed with more and more suspicion. Somehow they seemed to come at just the right time to commit dominion premiers to policies they might not have adopted. The crisis came when, just before a scheduled Imperial Cabinet of 1922, the Chanak affair broke out. Though Australia and New Zealand offered to fight for England, India, as has been told, protested, and Canada bluntly refused help. Here was created a definite piece of the "unwritten imperial constitution." The dominions felt that executive action could only be taken by the King's "constitutional advisers" in that dominion. They were willing that their premiers should be members of the British privy council as well as of their own dominion executive councils and "offer advice" as individuals. It has long been a useful safety valve in the British constitution that in an emergency a Privy Councilor who is not in either house of the British parliament or in the Cabinet may "offer advice." Such was Allenby's action in submitting a report as a Privy Councilor directly to George V, such seems to have been Canadian Premier Mackenzie King's action in giving direct advice to Edward VIII at the time of the abdication. But after Chanak the dominions barred regular meetings of dominion members of the Privy Council with the English Cabinet.

With the failure of the Imperial Cabinet, with the repudiation of imperial economic cooperation by England's preferring free trade in the election of 1923, and with a growing nationalism in Ireland and in South Africa, imperial relations came to a parlous state by the time of the Imperial Conference of 1926. Conservative Premier Stanley Baldwin and Colonial and Dominions Secretary Leopold Amery there met this problem. To a committee of dominion premiers, presided over by Lord Balfour, himself an ex-premier, was handed over the question of intra-Empire relations. After much discussion the committee came out with the so-called and much-quoted "Balfour Report," which defined the dominions as "autonomous communities within the British Empire, equal in status, in no way subordinate one to another in any aspect of their domestic or external affairs, though united by a common allegiance to the crown and freely associated as members of the British Commonwealth of Nations." This was a realistic document made by responsible executives. Later on it pointed out the obvious truth that though the dominions and England were equal in status they were not equal in function, so that, for example, they would rely on England's Navy and diplomatic service to carry the major part of the burden. Because it was a realistic document, it became a constitutional landmark. It established what might be called—indeed, later was called—constitutional usage for the Commonwealth.

The Balfour Report did what it was intended to do; it relieved tensions. General Hertzog of South Africa, who had been largely responsible for the choice of certain key words in it, publicly declared on his return to Cape Town that it had ended his lifelong antagonism to the Empire. It was followed up by other actions that relieved tension. Irish feelings were relieved by the Royal Titles Act of 1927, which admitted that the Irish treaty of 1921 had ended the existence of a United Kingdom of Great Britain and Ireland. Despite Dr. Malan's campaign on the subject, the South Africans relieved their own tensions on the tricky question of a South African flag by putting the English Union Jack in the middle of it. Above all a new constitutional usage came into being. No longer did the Dominions Office in London communicate with a dominion government through the Governor-general, as if to say that orders were coming through the King's representative. Now in dominion after dominion, till at last conservative New Zealand was the only exception, the Governor-general became the King's representative, while a High Commissioner dealt with the government in the name of the British government, as between equals. Thus it might be said that the Commonwealth operated more and more as if it were seven independent Kingdoms—Great Britain, Newfoundland, New Zealand, Canada, Australia, South Africa, and the Irish Free State, in respective order of reaching true dominion status—joined by sharing the same king and the same law of succession.

True though this might be, there remained the problem of bringing the law into line with constitutional usage. As the previous chapter on the constitution has pointed out, this raised very real legal problems, to solve which required the efforts of the technical Conference on the Operation of Dominion Legislation, which reported in 1929, and of yet another Imperial Conference. Then at last an identical measure was passed through all the parliaments of the Empire and in December, 1931, became the Statute of Westminster. It should be stressed that this was a permissive act and one written by the dominions. To each dominion it gave only what that dominion asked. This was a wide measure of freedom for the Irish Free State and South Africa, and a straightening out of tangles for Canada, Australia, New Zealand, and Newfoundland. At that, Australia and New Zealand did not accept the act till, respectively, 1942 and 1947, and Newfoundland accepted it only by joining Canada. But, when that is kept in mind, it is then safe to say that the Statute of Westminster altered the nature of Britain's overseas rule.

For the essence of the Statute is not in the clauses that clarify old legislation and undo legal tangles. It is in the preamble that recognizes as "established constitutional position" that all changes in "the Succession to the Throne or the Royal Style and Titles shall hereafter require the Assent as well of the Parliaments of all the Dominions as of the Parliament of the United Kingdom" and that "no law hereafter made by the Parliament of the United Kingdom shall extend to any of the said Dominions as part of the law of that Dominion otherwise than at the request and with the consent of that Dominion." This was shown at Edward VIII's abdication, when indeed, by a constitutional freak the Commonwealth had two kings for three days, the abdication being recognized a day early by South Africa, a day late by the Irish Free State.

Herein lies the importance of the Statute of Westminster. When it received the Royal Assent in December, 1931, it was put on record for all to see that the dominions had equal status. It might be said that that date —unless one prefers the date of the Balfour Report—marks the change of the Empire into the Commonwealth. This does not mean that imperial feeling has ceased. The "Church of England in Canada" has recently issued a Prayer Book so new as to have prayers for the Duke of Edinburgh as the Princess Elizabeth's husband, which yet has prayers for "the Legislatures of the Empire." This is not to say that the breed of "Empire builders" is dead. A glance at the files of *Blackwoods Magazine* will show that such men still live, still valiantly fill the ranks of "the Legion of Frontiersmen." The attitude satirized by the "Colonel Blimp" of Low's cartoons is still to be found expressed, in nobler forms worthy of Curzon. But after 1926 or 1931, as one chooses, it is possible and correct to speak of the Commonwealth in distinction to the Empire, the one as the free association of equal and independently acting nations, the other as the steadily lessening lands under the jurisdiction of the "Parliament of the United Kingdom." Such is the usage apart from direct quotations followed in this chapter.

After the Statute had been passed, cooperation within the Commonwealth became easier. The next year, 1932, there met at Ottawa an Imperial Economic Conference, where, amid horse trading, a system of imperial preference was set up. As yet it is impossible to measure the exact result of setting up this system. There has been backsliding, for not all the Ottawa Agreements were renewed. On the other hand, the habit of agreement has built up. Two forms of imperial cooperation already existed, in the diplomatic and financial fields.

All over the world the British diplomats and consuls lent a hand to those of the dominions, whenever a dominion legation or consulate should be opened, or served for the dominions where they had no legation or consulate. Even the Irish Free State clung to this form of cooperation until 1948. Then central banks worked together, forming the Sterling Bloc. Here was a day-to-day cooperation of great cohesive force. A measure of that cohesion is the wartime cooperation of the Commonwealth. Here the idea of an Imperial Cabinet revived, but with safeguards. It was made very clear to Churchill that the dominions were coequal with Britain and knew how to say "No" to her. Specific cases were General MacNaughton's refusal to send the Canadian Corps to France, in 1940, the Australian refusal to leave troops in Tobruk. But as equals cooperation was hearty, and dominion prime ministers sat in the War Cabinet in one case for over a month, to coordinate action. Since World War II this cooperation has, if anything, intensified. Commonwealth Conferences are held regularly; at the time that these words are being written a Conference of Commonwealth Premiers is sitting in London. During the three decades since Chanak the cooperation that there broke down has been made real, now that the dominions are no longer followers, but fully equal partners in the Commonwealth.

What then is this Commonwealth into which the Empire has in part evolved? The first significant use of the name appears to have taken place in 1883 in a speech at Adelaide, South Australia, by Lord Rosebery. It was taken up in 1917 by General Smuts and attracted such favorable notice that the formal credentials of the Empire delegation to the Paris peace conference of 1919 used that title. So did the wording of the Irish Peace Treaty of 1921. Both the names, Empire and Commonwealth, appear in the Balfour Report of 1926. By the time India had become a republic, in 1947, the name Commonwealth without an adjective had become official, even to the existence of a separate Ministry of Commonwealth Relations in the Cabinet. As this shows, there is a growing tendency to consider the realms of Elizabeth II a free association of equal nations. This is marked even in the part of those realms which might still be called Empire, those regions ruled over by the Colonial Office. For, as has been pointed out, there is a progression toward responsible government. Here a dramatic example is Rhodesia, which in 1923 was taken from the British South Africa Company, given responsible government in its southern half, and put under the Dominions Office. Thus it seems safe to say that the Commonwealth is the stage to which the Empire will, it is hoped, evolve.

If this conjecture is cautiously used, the nature of the Empire seems apparent. It should be remembered that there are many who still think consciously or unconsciously in the old-fashioned terms of the English ruling over lesser races. Some who do this are "leftovers" from the past; others are bureaucrats who see so intensely the trees of particular problems that particular colonies cannot master without help that they cannot understand the changing nature of the whole wood and so fail to see that the Empire is evolving into a free association of equal and self-governing peoples. Not to remember this would be to give a false picture.

But once that warning has been given it is possible to turn to the prophetic few who have proved themselves able to see into the future, and from their ideas gain some insight into the nature of the Commonwealth.

Such a prophet was Arthur James Balfour. In the course of a long life he did three things that demonstrate his understanding of the nature of the Commonwealth. He gave Ireland good firm rule, in the "twenty years of resolute government" of 1886 to 1905. He drafted the Balfour Report that created the Commonwealth. Finally, like Arthur Griffith, he prophesied his creation before he made it. Therefore he can be considered as an embodiment of this special concept. To take his Irish career first, it should be noted how just was his claim in 1929 that he had made the Irish Free State. By solving the tenancy problem through land purchase, by giving Ireland county councils, by bringing up the economically weak West through his Congested Districts Board, he transformed Ireland. If this part of his career is compared with that of the other men who have made future dominions and nations, it can be seen how he deserves the title proconsul. Just as Hastings and Bentinck made India, for others to build on, just as Sir George Grey made New Zealand, the great early residents made Malaya, just as Cromer made Egypt, just as Arnold Wilson did much to make Iraq, so Balfour can be said to have made Ireland. But it should also be stressed that though like these men he freely used autocratic emergency powers to accomplish this, he, like all of them save Arnold Wilson, kept in mind that these powers were to be relinquished. This is well documented, for in 1913, once he was free of the leadership of the Conservative party, he spoke his mind about Irish Home Rule. He took the stand that Home Rule was either too much or too little, that there was no stopping point between union of Ireland with England and a status far in advance of any advocated at that time by any other statesman. If Ireland would not stay with England, he advocated "requiring her to manage her own finances, pay her own bills, borrow on her own credit, control her own rebels, settle her own constitution, remaining, if she desire it, a self-governing colony within the limits of the Empire." This is more than dominion status; it is the free choice of independence, with its penalties along with its pleasures. Here, in 1913, is the former leader of the Unionist party advocating the very relationship that Eire, Burma, and to a degree India, had reached in the late 1940's. To him the Empire cannot be lasting as the Commonwealth can be.

A noteworthy thing about this way of looking at the Commonwealth is that it is consistent with past history. When the Guild of St. Thomas of Canterbury, later the Merchant Adventurers, took to governing itself overseas some time before 1266, when in the 1600's the early colonies of Virginia, Massachusetts, Barbados, and Bermuda took to ruling themselves according to the rights of Englishmen, when at the time of the

American Revolution the Elder Pitt stood out for the same rights of self-government, above all when Durham and his fellow proconsuls of the Victorian age pushed ahead with grants of responsible government, they all shared a similar ideal, of the right of peoples to govern themselves. Similarly, when dominion leaders—MacDonald and Laurier of Canada, Botha and Smuts of South Africa, Hughes and Fraser of Australia and New Zealand—gave loyalty to the Commonwealth, they showed a similar ideal, that freedom could unite, not separate. Such would seem to be the ideal of the Commonwealth, an ideal of course imperfectly lived up to, but for all its flaws the essence of the Commonwealth: the age-old belief that England's rule should bring eventual freedom and could hope for permanence only through giving freedom.

50

CONFLICTS WITH THE FUTURE

Enemies of Great Britain should learn from modern history how wrong it is to predict her early downfall. In 1588 Philip of Spain was sure his Armada was invincible; it was shattered. From 1672 to 1706 Louis XIV had high hopes of world domination; thanks to England, it eluded his grasp. In 1805 Napoleon Bonaparte struck medals in anticipation of his entry into London; in 1815 he was a prisoner at Saint Helena. In his turn, Kaiser William found that British arms were not contemptible. The latest prophet to foresee Britain's end was Adolf Hitler, whose soldiers sang "Wir Fahren gegen England" but never got across the Channel. Throughout history the British have had the annoying characteristic when they go to war—annoying to their foes, that is—of winning the last battle no matter how badly they start.

They are a people used to meeting conflicts, too, off the battlefield. In modern times they have waged wars against poverty, distress, and bad markets. In these conflicts they have managed to survive. So, while it is impossible to tell what the future will bring, such guidance as the past affords points to conflict and survival. That is why this chapter is entitled "Conflicts with the Future." In 1939 it would have been appropriate to name a similar concluding chapter, "The Newest Conflict—Will England Carry On?" She did, but at a cost which affects her prospects today. Therefore, to understand the story of the years after World War II we must deal briefly with World War II and what it did to Great Britain.

The direct cause of hostilities was the fact that, on September 1, 1939, the German army flooded over the Polish frontiers. Bound by treaty to come to Poland's aid, Great Britain and France declared war on Germany, on September 3. The basic cause of the war was that, at last and almost too late, the democracies had decided to face up to Nazism and Fascism. The margin of safety to which "the years of the locust" had reduced them was thin, thinner than they realized. Allies had been lost. Czechoslovakia had fallen. The Little Entente had been broken up. Russia, rejected when she offered help, flirted with when too late, was now Hitler's ally and soon joined him in the attack on Poland. Yet, even though Poland fell with astonishing speed, during the winter of 1939–1940, the period of so-called "phony war," Britain and France showed a complacent optimism. For this there were two sets of reasons, psychological and material. The governments of both countries were still composed of the men who had been blind to danger; they remained blind. Then the situation looked good. Germany was hemmed in by a ring of neutrals and the splendid French Maginot forts. British blockade had crushed her the last time, backed as it was by the dominions. All the dominions but Eire had joined the west, although South Africa came in by the narrow margin of 80 parliamentary votes to 67. Why not this time again?

This view very largely neglected the facts of modern war, as the spring of 1940 was grimly to prove. Almost alone the French prophet-soldier Charles de Gaulle had a full vision of what would come, though there were others, notably what has been called the "foreign affairs opposition" in England, who had a great measure of foresight. Therefore, from the historian's comfortable seat of hindsight, let us look at some of those facts of modern war.

In the first place this was a total war. Air power would make England not a safe refuge but "an aircraft carrier anchored off Europe." Her population would have to live the life of a destroyer crew on the Okinawa "picket line." German bombs would hit every conceivable target from munitions factories to cathedrals and at times would be intentionally directed at working-class homes. Science would be called upon for new weapons. In 1940 it would be because radar had been devised just in time that England would be saved from air conquest. In 1944 it would be because guided missiles would be devised a few months too late that counterinvasion of the Continent would remain possible. Constantly new devices would be created, such as "mulberries," or artificial harbors, and sonar submarine detectors; long lists of such inventions can be made. On land, tanks would revolutionize the battlefield. This would make the manufacture of munitions as important as the use of munitions. Thus the whole population would be not only the target of enemy fire but, in one way or another, those who struck back. The distinction between civilian and soldier would lessen. A grim pair of figures for Great Britain shows this: civilian casualties, 297,710; military, 305,000.

Secondly, this would be a war of ideas. That in itself was not new, and here old methods would prove true when tried again. But this would explain sudden defeats and sudden victories. The fact that Nazi faith defeated French cynicism but was met by Frenchmen of equal faith explains both the sudden fall of France and the brave revival, resistance, and redemption led by De Gaulle. The basic idealism of the British explains their steadfastness. Irish and Indian nationalism explain the legal neutrality of Eire and the practical neutrality of Indian leaders. The discouraging effect of racialism and colonialism will explain the minor and defensive role played by the Commonwealth in India and the Far East. Irish defection was serious, for in 1935 Eire had been given the naval bases formerly held by Great Britain. As a result of Irish neutrality, England "had to breathe with only one lung." Once German submarines could be based on Brest, only the North of Ireland route remained open, greatly reducing the shipping which could reach England. However, though Eire stayed neutral, to their credit 300,000 of her citizens did not.

For here England had an answer. In fighting for her own interests—safety, freedom from invasion, and independence—Great Britain also identified herself with great ideals and issues. As in previous contests against world domination by one state, England was fighting the world's battles as well as her own. If freedom for European nations and freedom of expression are desirable, then England's stand was correct both in a selfish and an altruistic sense. Others realized this, and it won her allies. Churchill's rolling periods made a stout and effective answer to Goebbels's propaganda.

Thirdly, in this war England's enemy had a carefully thought out strategy. A student of geopolitics, Hitler had his plan for outwitting sea power. It was simple—to stay away from the sea. If the land mass of Eurasia could be conquered, Britain would be isolated. In effect this would be Napoleon's Continental System all over again. Hitler therefore planned to march around the oceans, crossing only the narrow seas such as the Baltic and the Mediterranean, and take over Europe, Asia, and Africa, out of range of the British Navy.

England's counterstrategy to this, as finally evolved, was triple. As in the past, she relied on blockade to starve her enemy and deprive him of munitions. As in the past, she struck at her enemy where his land supply lines were long and more easily counterbalanced by her sea supply lines, in this case the base being in the Near East with Egypt as the center. Furthermore, now that the long-range bomber allowed direct attack, she struck at the source of enemy supplies, in the heart of Germany. Along with this struggle was a subsidiary but vital one, on the part of the Germans to blockade Britain by submarine and airplane, on the part of the English and Canadians to keep the sea lanes open. Such was the general pattern of the war, till counterinvasion could be mounted.

But in 1939 this was in the future. Then Britain used her old methods of blockade and sent an expeditionary force to France. A mark of her unpreparedness was that this body of troops, though smaller than the B.E.F. of 1914, formed a larger proportion of her total army.

During the winter of "phony war" the chief events were at sea. There a German submarine sank the *Royal Oak*, and Commodore Harwood, with three cruisers firing from different sides and protecting each other by smoke screens, defeated the pocket battleship *Admiral Graf Spee* and forced her to scuttle herself at Montevideo.

Suddenly the character of the war changed. On April 9, 1940, the Nazis struck north. As the saying went, they "conquered Denmark by surprise, Norway by treachery, and Sweden by telephone." They quickly overran Denmark, landed in Norway through collaboration by Norwegian Nazis, and by threats forced Sweden to stay neutral and sell munitions. The Anglo-French counter was ineffective. A landing at Namsos was bombed out; the landing at Narvik was too far from the center to matter. This blow had an important political effect. After the evacuation of Namsos the House of Commons came to life as it had not done since 1886, threw over party discipline, and sternly indicated to Chamberlain that a new government should be formed. Outside Parliament Ernest Bevin, speaking the mind of the trade unions, demanded a change. It came. Winston Churchill, who had been called to office as First Lord of the Admiralty the day war broke out, became Prime Minister, First Lord of the Treasury, and Minister of Defense. Though some former members of the Cabinet stayed in office, notably Neville Chamberlain until his death, the core of the Cabinet was what has been called the "foreign affairs Opposition"— Churchill, Bevin (now given a seat in Parliament), Eden, and Lloyd. To demonstrate the union of all parties Major Clement Attlee, leader of the Labor opposition, was made Deputy Premier. This brought a new life into Britain's government.

It was high time for this to happen. Belgium, Luxembourg, and Holland were next on Hitler's timetable. Invasion began on May 10, 1940. First came terrifying bombing of unarmed cities; then masses of men swarmed across the boundaries; finally an armored spearhead struck through the Ardennes forests, found a weak spot in the French lines, and drove through to the Channel. By May 27 the Dutch and the Belgian governments had joined the Poles in London as a "government in exile." The main Dutch and Belgian armies had surrendered, along with King Leopold of Belgium. Lord Gort's B.E.F. was thus almost encircled—the Forty-fourth Division, in fact, facing south in trenches it had dug facing north. This looked like one of the greatest defeats of all time.

Here high drama enters the picture. As the German spearhead turned north along the Channel coast to finish the B.E.F. off, heroically the Guards held Boulogne till the last possible moment before evacuation, heroically the Rifles died almost to a man at Calais. In the precious time so bought, the British and the valiant French Twentieth Corps fought their way to the beaches of Dunkirk. And to the beaches of Dunkirk went the seamen of England. In bureaucratic circles it was believed that a "small-craft pool" had been called on for rescue work. True though that may have been, the English people sensed it differently. In their eyes private citizens had just quietly dropped other concerns and crossed the Channel to do the job, in the same calm spirit in which Francis Drake and some other private citizens had crossed the Channel to deal with the Armada. While they worked the carefully hoarded Spitfires and the newly released Hurricanes and Defiants of the Royal Air Force gave cover from the *Luftwaffe*. So it was that the Dunkirk legend was born. To another nation this would have been a disastrous and humiliating defeat. But though their armed forces had lost almost all their equipment, so that the newly arrived Canadian Corps remained the only large organized body of troops in the island to meet invasion, the English had conquered their indecision.

This new spirit came in the nick of time. Soon Britain had an added enemy and lost her ally. The same break-through which almost annihilated the British Army gave the Germans the French manufacturing districts. Pétain, now the French Premier, was faced with the choice of fighting in desperation or making terms while yet there was time. At the same time Mussolini saw his chance and entered the war. Pétain surrendered, despite a last-minute appeal by Churchill to fuse the Parliaments of the two nations. Out of the wreck was retrieved—by kidnaping —one French leader, General Charles de Gaulle. That was much, for De Gaulle had vision. His radio addresses persuaded certain key French colonies—notably the Negro governor Éboué of the Congo—to stand firm and roused the beginnings of the Resistance in France. For De Gaulle dared proclaim a truth no one else voiced—that if only the democracies held out the war must reach the United States, and that the United States' entry would bring victory.

De Gaulle's prophecy serves well as a guide to the events of 1940 and 1941. Thanks to the way the British held out, it was possible to rally almost all the free world to fight Germany and to add Russia as well. The first duty of the British was to preserve their island from invasion. The Churchill Government therefore reminded French naval units of the treaty obligation not to make a peace separately and offered those units three choices: joining the British, internment, or sinking. Many units joined De Gaulle, a few were interned, and at Oran, where the British could strike, the French Mediterranean forces were sunk or driven to Toulon. Then came the grim job, once command of the sea had been secured, of preserving local command of the air. For in August, 1940, once the occupation of half of France had been completed, German air attacks began.

Now came what Churchill has well called "England's finest hour." He promised the English people nothing but "blood, sweat, and tears," and nobly the English responded, with a morale perhaps never equaled since Francis Drake "singed the King of Spain's beard." What of the odds—as the song went, "There'll always be an England." Stoutly and skillfully the Royal Air Force met the attacks of the *Luftwaffe* with the Spitfire plane and tracking by radar. To quote Churchill again, "Never has so much been owed by so many to so few." The margin of success was narrow. At one moment the last reserve airplane had left the ground, so that Britain was without a relief plane to guard the airfields, when those fighting came to refuel. But Minister of Defense Churchill and Air Marshal Park, who watched that plane take off, also saw the skies clear of enemy, and knew that England had been saved. From that point on, the air war of the Battle of Britain changed from a German attempt to gain command of the skies to an attempt to wear down by attrition. All through the lengthening winter nights came Goering's bombers to saturate London. To control the damage, air raid wardens and fire fighters—that is, the British civilian population—strove to the utmost. They won. That winter saw the worst over, though there were repeated attempts to crush Britain, notably the horror raid on Coventry. But even this last failed of its aim; the Coventry factories were at work the next day. Gradually, counterblows were struck in the air. Until 1944, however, there was still danger of invasion, and every summer the troops of England "went to the seaside," just to make sure.

But now the center of historic interest must turn to the advance made from the Commonwealth center in Egypt. At the worst moment in England's fortunes, Prime Minister Churchill and War Secretary Eden took the step that Lord Moran, the doctor holder of the Victoria Cross, in his *Anatomy of Courage,* has called the bravest act of statesmanship. From England, disarmed by the matériel losses of Dunkirk, these two sent tanks to Egypt. Even in England's greatest moment of peril they had faith in ultimate victory and planned for it. Good use was made of these precious weapons, for in Egypt were two able commanders, General Wavell and Admiral Cunningham.

A mere listing of the feats of arms of the Commonwealth base in Egypt may seem amazing. Here it should be made clear that these were Commonwealth feats, that Australia, New Zealand, South Africa, and the Indian government bore their share in making key decisions. Though London was a center of authority, that authority was moral and a matter of convenience. Indeed, when the Egyptian base was in full swing, it was an Australian, Richard Casey, also a member of the British Privy Council, who was "Minister in Residence," and the link through whom political decisions were made on the spot. Counting the Ethiopian fronts as two and the sea as another, this base fought on a total of eight fronts and eventually won on all. Britain had one ally, brought in in October, 1940, when Italy attacked Greece on the Albanian front. By mutual consent, Britain did not intervene directly with land forces but sent planes and above all, by the daring Taranto torpedo-plane attack, crippled the

Italian fleet. Then in December, 1940, Wavell on his own initiative unleashed a land attack in Libya, drove to the Gulf of Tripoli, and captured 100,000 prisoners. Promptly troops were switched to Ethiopia, while South Africans, drilling wells as they went, pushed up with amazing speed from Kenya. This move forced Hitler to take a hand. He decided to crush Greece by moving through an intimidated Yugoslavia. But the people of Yugoslavia were braver than their leaders. They ousted the Regent and fought. At the same time Hitler detailed General Rommel and the highly trained Afrika Corps to Tripoli. Valiantly, the Commonwealth—Menzies of Australia was a member of the War Cabinet that made the decision, New Zealand and South Africa concurred by cable—took the course of honor and ultimate success. Troops were withdrawn from Tripoli, and sent to Greece, while the daring sea action of Cape Matapan kept the sea lanes clear. The attempt failed. Within three weeks Greece had fallen— and so had Tripoli, save for the Australian garrison holding out in Tobruk.

Now came more hammer blows. The German paratroop corps with desperate fighting took Crete from the Commonwealth and the Greeks, for all Sir Bernard Freyberg, V.C., the New Zealand commander, could do. A Nazi-inspired coup in Baghdad was met by the courage of the R.A.F. base at Habbaniya even before Indian troops and a flying column from Syria could be concentrated for aid. When Crete fell, Syria, with a Vichy French garrison, became a danger spot. A tiny force of Commonwealth troops, Free French, and Poles attacked and saved the day. Then, bravely, "Operation Crusader" attempted, but failed, to relieve Tobruk. Against odds, just the same, a miracle had been achieved like that other miracle that, in the summer of 1704, had "saved old England."

Then, June 22, 1941, the value of this miracle was dramatically proved. Thieves fell out; the Nazis attacked their Russian allies. Despite British warnings, the Russians were unprepared, but thanks to British resistance, the attack came a month late and was deprived of the paratroops who had been decimated in Crete. Now a new stage of the war began, in which Britain would have powerful allies—first Russia, then the United States— and the problems of handling those allies.

To make this part of the story clear requires going back a bit, for American support of Britain long antedated actual American entry into war. In September, 1939, the repeal of the American Neutrality Act and its replacement by "cash and carry" legislation in effect aided Britain, who alone had the cash and could carry munitions across the seas. An Atlantic neutrality patrol, nominally to prevent the war reaching the shores of either America, in fact reduced the area the Royal Navy and the Royal Canadian Navy would have to cover. The stationing of the bulk of the American fleet at Pearl Harbor in effect guaranteed that the British, Australian, and New Zealand navies and the Royal Indian Marine would be supported in keeping command of the Pacific if Japan became adventurous. Above all, in 1940, at the height of the presidential election, badly needed destroyers, forty of them, were transferred to England by the United States, in return for the privilege of garrisoning a number of naval bases in British possessions. Not only was this a sound insurance against the loss of the bases should England fall to Hitler, it also released English garrisons to fight overseas. Finally, in the winter of 1940, after the election had been won by President Roosevelt, the lend-lease act was passed. By this law American military material might be lent to countries obviously fighting the United States' battles for her. As at that time the Soviet-Nazi pact was still in force and the danger of joint world domination by that partnership was in the offing, England was obviously the potential recipient of such aid. This system of aid to England, carefully graduated to the temper of American public opinion, was facilitated by the exchange of messages between Churchill and President Roosevelt, which Churchill had initiated when he was First Sea Lord in 1939, even before he became Premier. But though these two men at times went just as far as public opinion and their intimacy would let them, and though by their actions they guided public opinion, they took care to have the peoples of their countries with them. That was why it was possible for them to take one further step, in August, 1941. Then the two leaders met, and on August 12 issued a declaration of personal opinions that has taken the name of the Atlantic Charter and has formed a declaration of world policy many have shared in all lands. Thus, should any event bring America into war, she would come ready prepared to fight immediately at England's side.

With Russia matters were otherwise. England and Russia viewed each other with suspicion. However, it was clearly to the interest of both to defeat the common enemy, and it was clear what the means of cooperation should be. England, especially after lend-lease, had the supplies; Russia had the men. What was needed was a means of getting the supplies to the men. This was done in two ways. Convoys were sent around Nazi-held Norway, by the Murmansk route. The other route was by way of Iran. This was opened against Nazi-inspired interference by a joint Anglo-Russian show of force, in late August, 1941. Thus in Russia's extremity aid was brought to her that helped in slowing to a stop, in the dead of winter, the Nazi invasion.

In December, 1941, as all Americans painfully know, the whole scope of the war widened. American Pacific policy and Japanese Pacific policy had for some time been at loggerheads. On December 7, 1941, the Japanese broke the diplomatic deadlock with their attack on Pearl Harbor. Soon thereafter, Hitler and Mussolini declared war on America. And now England had two great allies, given her perhaps by the follies of her enemies, but ready to provide the preponderance of force she had hitherto lacked, when struggling alone. What, then, was the situation of England at this moment?

Here, again, it is necessary to retrace our steps and tell how England was preparing to strike across the Channel when the time came, how she kept going at home, and how the Atlantic supply line was preserved. In order to win, and to get the means whereby to win, men had to be trained and material produced. Men and women were put under a national-service law that gave the government the right to determine where and at what each person should work. The cities became factories where work was carried on among the ruins without letup despite constant air raids. Typical of the efforts made and use of space was the conversion of an unused subway tube in London into a mile-long factory. The land was plowed up and planted according to a grand over-all plan for supplying food. Women and children were taken out of the cities and boarded in the country where they were less likely to be hit by bombs. No man able to work or fight was permitted to shirk his appointed task. Food, clothing, and other necessities were put under price control and a rationing system. Families who lost their homes and merchants who lost their shops through air raids were supplied with funds to meet necessary costs. New ministries with complete control over production, such as the Ministry of Aircraft Production, swiftly organized the capacities of labor and management. Soon planes, tanks, and the million essential parts of a modern attack force were being rushed from the assembly lines. Weapons new to warfare—such as the mulberries, or artificial harbors—were devised. Meanwhile troops were being trained for eventual invasion. In August, 1942, the Canadians made the practice raid at Dieppe.

But since England cannot today feed her population or provide raw materials, once more the success of Great Britain depended upon her ability to import. The Navy and supporting air power provided cover for the ships that brought in the raw materials for the factories and supplies and food for the people. The German navy and air force did all in their power to stop the flow of goods that came over the bridge of ships. Here the British merchant marine was joined by the tankers and freighters of the Dutch, the Norwegians, and the other nations who fell victims to Axis attacks. Submarines attacking alone or in wolf packs harried this Allied shipping with punishing results, as did long-range aircraft. During the war 23,351 British and American vessels were sunk. In 1942 the Allies lost 6,250,000 tons to submarines, which unlike the surface vessels that they could bottle up could slip in and out of captured French and Norwegian ports.

In 1941 the war between the U-boats and the destroyer escorts and convoy guards was carried on relentlessly and without stopping. In May, 1941, the German capital ship *Bismarck*, supposed to be invincible, was sunk by aircraft after a chase from Greenland nearly to Cherbourg before it could damage the supply lines. Gradually the efficiency of the U-boat was more than mastered by the science of the British and their allies. While the American navy took chief responsibility for the Pacific theater, the Royal Navy and the Royal Canadian Navy undertook in the Atlantic the most severe convoy duty of history. The Canadians added 700 corvettes to the hound packs of destroyer escorts and destroyers that hunted the Nazi submarine wolves or escorted huge convoys, each vessel with antiaircraft guns and an armed guard. Observation planes and bombers patrolled the sea lanes and kept the U-boats at a distance. Improved detection equipment and depth charges increased the accuracy of surface attack on the submarines. As the German Admiral Doenitz later admitted, by 1943 the war on the sea had been lost by the Germans. Before V-E Day in May, 1945, some 782 German submarines were destroyed.

But England had another nation besides herself to supply by sea—Russia. On the bleak road to Murmansk the ships of the Allied navies were put to the hardest of tests. Though the larger units of the German navy were either sunk or demobilized, raiders in the air and under the sea had to be driven off when convoys or single ships tried to get through. Wherever they were, in the mid-Atlantic or the Arctic, the fighting demanded the utmost endeavor and courage. The enemy was brave, daring, and well trained.

Here the tradition and superior equipment of the British sea services told. Long centuries of experience and a tradition of how to fight on the sea gave the Royal Navy strategic insight. Officers and men knew seamanship as well as how to use their weapons. The Royal Naval Reserve and Royal Naval Volunteer Reserve—called the "wavy Navy" from the wavy stripes their officers wore—became the equals of the Royal Navy in seamanship and fighting ability. The chain of supply ships to the islands and to Russia never was snapped. This is the final proof of the Navy's ability to do its duty.

Yet another sort of struggle went on that should not be forgotten. German bombing of England did not stop in 1940. It continued steadily, with the dread V-1 and V-2 rockets taking over when the balance of air power in 1944 went against the Luftwaffe. It was countered by civilian defense, including air-raid wardens, fire brigades, rescue squads—in other words, the whole English people. When one thinks of heroism at sea, in the air, or on desert battlefields, one should also think of heroism in the streets and houses of the homeland, against destruction raining from above.

These digressions on the special subject of alliances and of sea warfare have branched off from the main story of the war, as England and the Commonwealth saw it, at June, 1941, the invasion of Russia. It now remains to tell first of the struggle to the finish with Germany and then, separately, of the struggle to the finish with Japan.

For some time, the Near East remained the sole land contact point between the Commonwealth and the Axis, as the Russians again and again commented as they pressed for a "Second Front" in Europe. Here there was a new commander. Wavell had been worn out by his tremendous labors and was replaced by General Auchinleck. Auchinleck bided his time till November, 1941, and then struck hard at Rommel. Like Wavell in 1940 he was able to advance far, he relieved the garrison of Tobruk, but meeting an abler antagonist, he was checked sooner. In May, 1942, just as disaster fell in the East, as will be recorded, Rommel struck back. He smashed ahead, took Tobruk which had been held by sea power, and came within an ace of capturing Cairo. He even had had the temerity—since Egypt was technically neutral—to reserve rooms at Shepheard's Hotel by radio. But at the very last possible defense line, El Alamein, the British held.

Now, with American force to add to British and with the Russian front engaging the bulk of the Nazi troops, it was possible to take the offensive. A plan for a cross-Channel offensive was rejected as requiring strength the Allies did not have. Instead, it was agreed to land American and British troops in French North Africa, the Americans to land first and the commander over all to be American, so that the Vichy French might have every excuse to surrender. At the same time, a new commander was given to the Eighth Army; General Montgomery, hitherto the quiet commander of the counterinvasion forces, was rushed to Egypt. He saw the character of the men he was about to command, their need of cockiness after years of desperate struggle against odds, and created for them the idol they needed. A Royal Tank Regiment beret to show he commanded from a tank in the field, a drama of headquarters in tents in the desert—and meticulously careful preparations for assault by tanks and overwhelming artillery strength —and he was ready. First at El Alamein in August the "Desert Rats" struck forward. Then in November American forces under General Eisenhower landed in Morocco. Rommel's veterans fought like veterans, but relentlessly and skillfully the Eighth Army marched ahead to clear Africa of the Axis, till at Tunis in May, 1943, it could join hands with the Americans and the British First Army. One piece of pageantry the British allowed themselves at this. Ever since June, 1940, England's church bells had been stilled, to be rung as a signal of Nazi invasion. Now, for the victory of El Alamein, they rang out in joy.

From Tunis it is a short trip as the crow flies to Sicily. Although the Allied army did not fly as the crow, its air power in short order reduced the Italian fortified island of Pantelleria and then went on to bomb Sicily. On

July 10, 1943, this was followed by American, Canadian, and British, Australian and New Zealand invasion of Sicily. They jumped from there over the straits of Messina to enter Naples on October 1. The Italians, tired of Mussolini and burning to hit out at their allies the Germans, decided to make the best of their bad bargain. King Victor Emmanuel ordered Mussolini's arrest and a surrender to the Allies. His government declared war on Germany—while Hitler had Mussolini kidnaped and set up an "Italian Republic" to fight on. The year ended with the Allied armies moving slowly uphill in the mud and cold toward Rome. For now the striking base was to change from Egypt to England.

In the British Isles in these years a vast invasion force was being prepared. While it was training and arming for the desperate amphibious task ahead of it, air power was striking hard at Germany. By night the British bombed; by day from high altitudes, the Americans. Fighters swept over France to drive the *Luftwaffe* from the skies. Germany's transport and munitions supplies were crippled, in the greatest air assault in history, repaying for all she had done in the blitz. Finally, on June 6, 1944, two years of build-up and planning were put to the test. This was D Day. British troops commanded by Montgomery, Americans commanded by Eisenhower, went back to France that had been left in 1940.

Now it was the turn of the Germans to meet defeat. As Churchill has said: "Before Alamein we never had a victory. After Alamein we never had a defeat." The Normandy landing was successful. As the British on the left wing pinned the Germans, the Americans pivoted around them, freed Cherbourg as a supply port, and then broke through into open country at Saint-Lo. This was made possible by the bulldog way the British drove ahead through the *bocage* country near Caen, battering their way from hedgerow to hedgerow to pin down the German main body. At one time in this drive regimental commanders were upbraiding their junior officers for bringing their companies to the appointed assembly point—through opposition—ten minutes late. How could the Germans overcome dash and spirit like this, heartened as it was by the news that Rome had fallen to General Alexander in Italy?

Now, in two tremendous bounds, interleaved by a deft, vigorous German counterattack, World War II went on to the winning by the English of "the last battle." On August 23, Free French forces under General Leclerc entered Paris, the same day that another Allied invasion force occupied Marseilles on the Mediterranean. In September and October the Allies drove north and east across the northern part of France and north up the Rhone valley. It was good for the British that the Calais and Boulogne area was taken in September, because it was from there that the Germans had been sending over their huge V-1 and V-2 rockets. Few weapons were as hard on civilian morale as these rockets that plunged down without warning and were aimed at no specific target. The Germans were suffering from the effects of round-the-clock bombing and steady defeats handed them on all fronts from the Schelde to the Carpathians. However, they still had enough courage and might to make a final desperate drive. In the Ardennes region, where they had in 1940 broken through to the Channel, they made a surprise attack that bit deep into the American lines before being repulsed with fearful losses in men and in equipment. It was not, thereafter, a question of how or where but of how soon Germany would collapse after the British and Canadians opened their offensive on the Maas and Rhine, in February, 1945. The combined forces of the Allies were over the Rhine by April 1 and were meeting the Russians on the Elbe on April 26, as the British received the surrender of Bremen. Nazi Germany died in Berlin with its great hero, Adolf Hitler, who chose to become a bridegroom and a corpse on the same day. Mussolini was executed by Italian partisan soldiers a few days before the Fuehrer's suicide. Thus death rung down the curtain on the modern tragedy of the Reich that was to last 1,000 years and on the "New Roman Empire."

Now to turn back the story and tell how the Commonwealth struggled with Japan. Here it played a subsidiary role, because of the problems of distance and supplies, and the United States bore the brunt. When war broke out in December, 1941, Japan achieved much by surprise and by the fact that it was second-line troops and generals who had been sent to the apparently quiet East. Just as the Japanese overran the Philippines till they came upon the hard core of resistance of the Filipino and American forces on Bataan, so they overran Hong Kong, Malaya, and Burma. At Hong Kong, a hopeless post, the Quebec Rifles showed themselves a worthy sister battalion of the Royal Rifles at Calais. But Hong Kong had been written off from the start. In the Malayan Peninsula, so it was hoped, the island fortress of Singapore would be impregnable, defended as it was by the great capital ships the *Prince of Wales* and the *Repulse*, and by inland jungles. But the two ships, caught without air cover in trying to prevent Japanese troops landing, were sunk by torpedo planes, and the jungle proved no barrier to the Japanese. Singapore fell, creating a crisis in Commonwealth relations. For Australia had sent all her three trained divisions to Egypt and refused to let them stay locked up in Tobruk. Out they came, just before Auchinleck relieved that fortress, to be replaced by Poles and British. For Australia had to face the danger of attack. Just as the Japanese were pushing through the jungles of Malaya and even Burma, so they were advancing by leaps and bounds through the Pacific islands and New Guinea. At the utmost point of their advance, their bombers were attacking the Australian port of Darwin, giving the Australians furiously to think about defending their own continent and its pure-white racial policy.

Americans well know how this Japanese thrust was turned back: how

General MacArthur was summoned from Bataan to provide experienced command in Australia and New Guinea, how the United States Navy at victories for which its carriers are named—Coral Sea, Midway, Savo, the Philippine Sea—reversed the tide, how landings were made against fiery opposition till MacArthur could keep his promise and "return," till Okinawa fell, and till Hiroshima and Nagasaki proved the terrors of the atom bomb. It would be well to remember the share the Commonwealth took: how Australian divisions fought in New Guinea, how scouts from the Pacific islands and Maoris from New Zealand seemed to take more than ordinary pleasure in reverting to premissionary head-hunting and paying the Japanese back in their own coin. And it might be well to remember the risks that Australia and New Zealand took. Their armies in the African and European theaters were so vast in proportion to their population that at one time it was necessary to call men back to fill empty factory benches. It took courage and confidence in what the United States could offer in protection so to divide the labors of the war and send every man possible to a distant war.

In one vital characteristic the war against Japan, as waged by the Commonwealth, differed from the war against Germany. The Commonwealth was fighting for the freedom of Europe; it could not in the same way lay claim to fighting for the freedom of Asia. Australia was fighting to keep the traditional "white Australia." Even though today a noble immigration program for displaced persons from Europe is at work, even though discourtesies of the Australian immigration laws were ended, the Asiatic peoples are still not welcome in Australia. As for India and its neighbor Burma, England's attitude was entirely clear. Dominion status might come—but only after the fighting was over. That will serve to explain the course of events in the C.B.I., China-Burma-India sector. When the Japanese came to Burma, the Burmese welcomed them and helped them overrun the land. In India, the nationalist movement showed the same intransigence it always had. The details of the eventual settlement have already been told, in another chapter. Here it should be pointed out that during the war India was in a stalemate. Sir Stafford Cripps's offer of dominion status, except for army command, was rejected. The Nationalists just sat on their hands and watched. The English, by a great recruiting effort, got an army built up that achieved much in Africa, in Egypt, and in Syria, and that saved Iraq. Eventually, with assistance from American-commanded Nationalist Chinese, they stopped a 1944 attempt of the Japanese to invade India and under General Slim made a creditable counterstroke into Burma. Then the atom bomb and the unexpected American advance in the Pacific gained Singapore without firing a shot. England had been ready to fight further. Her soldiers in Europe joked of the shoulder insignia they wore--B.L.A., or British Liberation Army—and said it meant "Burma Looms Ahead." So it was that an unstable propaganda position prevented the British from doing, from the India base, the great feats they had accomplished from their Egyptian and homeland bases.

To sum up the part played in the two phases of World War II, before and after El Alamein, it is necessary to draw a sharp distinction. From June, 1940, to June, 1941, England really fought alone. Her resources and her leadership made head against the Nazis. Even up to December, 1941, or to December, 1942, that is, to El Alamein and the stopping of the German advance into Russia, England still played a leading part. But thereafter as the American and Russian forces came into the field, she became one of the many United Nations. Churchill, because of his immense prestige, continued to make policy, but he now did this in partnership with President Roosevelt and Premier Stalin. Therefore a process began that has been frequent at the end of wars of alliances conducted by Great Britain. Great Britain, which follows consistent principles in foreign policy, veers away from her allies as they veer away from her principles. Here are the steps by which this took place. In August, 1941, the Atlantic Charter represented a meeting of minds. The idea of the four freedoms in Europe was one to which both Great Britain and the United States could subscribe. But when the United Nations was organized, first as the name for the alliance of anti-Axis states and later as the machinery for keeping world peace, problems arose. One appeared at the Casablanca Conference of 1943, when Roosevelt used the words "unconditional surrender," to Churchill's surprise. That was not according to the English idea of waging war, that he has summed up thus: "In war, resolution; in defeat, defiance; in victory, magnanimity; in peace, good will." Nor did the English believe that Russia could become a true partner in the United Nations or that Nationalist China was a "good risk." As a result, when at last Roosevelt, Churchill, and Stalin finally met at Teheran and Yalta, it was Roosevelt who urged cooperation with Russia and Churchill who warily tried to get guarantees that the eastern European states that had been submerged by Nazism should not in turn be submerged by communism. As the record shows, it was his swift intervention that saved Greece from the fate to which Yugoslavia, Hungary, Poland, and after a hopeful beginning, Czechoslovakia were subjected.

Thus England emerged from World War II with a foreign policy very similar to those that were applied after the Napoleonic Wars and World War I. When at the Potsdam Conference Attlee superseded Churchill, he and his foreign minister, Ernest Bevin, did what Castlereagh and Wellington, Lloyd George and Balfour, had done. Once again England behaved as the "loyal Opposition" in a world-wide international organization, taking

her part in resisting the extreme actions of the victors. As at the start of
the war, so at the finish, she showed a consistency admirable to those who
agreed with her, annoying to those who differed from her.

When World War II ended, it left a harvest of problems. Before their
destruction the totalitarian states wreaked havoc with their enemies and
with the world in general, so great that no man can see the end or predict
what reconstruction of the world will look like, when, if ever, it is completed. Losses and destruction suffered by Great Britain should be here
discussed. A small part of the tangible loss and its weight of misery and
pain can be described. What bombing, or death of loved ones, or financial
setbacks meant to the survivors of such a holocaust cannot be measured by
statistics. What can be set down in figures is sufficiently staggering.

Over all, Great Britain suffered physical and financial losses totaling
some thirty billion dollars or about one-fourth of her total estimated
wealth.[1] When itemized, some of these losses come under the following
headings: Shipping losses, for example, were one-half, or nine million tons

1. Loss of physical resources in Great Britain	$6 billion
2. Cargo and shipping losses	3 billion
3. "Disinvestment" or loss to industrial plant	3.5 billion
4. Loss abroad through property damage, sale of assets and building new liabilities	7 billion

of a total of eighteen million under British registry. Destruction of one-
third, or four million out of twelve million, homes is another part of the
bill of expense. One estimate has it that it would take seven years at the
prewar rate to create sufficient capital to make good the physical damage
in Great Britain. Investments overseas such as stocks and bonds in foreign
corporations and losses in gold amounted to one-third to one-half of the
total estimated value. To these losses coming directly from enemy action
or war expenditure should be added the new burden of public debt that
now absorbs one-sixth of the national income. On top of this should be
piled a postwar defense program that in 1947 ate up another 11 per cent
of the national income. Could any nation survive these shocks and be asked
for a second time in a century to undertake readjustment and rehabilitation of the lives of millions of her citizens? The answer to the question lies
in the ability of the British to draw on their store of psychic and economic
capital.

For in losing so much wealth and so many lives, the British recovered
their souls. Faced with the choice of slavery or sacrifice, they resolutely
and with courage never equaled in their history fought off the vicious
attacks of the best-prepared of modern predatory powers. The toughness
and courage that their ancestors had shown at the time of the Armada, in

[1] *Labor and Industry in Britain*, Vol. IX, No. 1, March, 1951, p. 29.

the wars against Napoleon, and later in Flanders during World War I was matched and surpassed. No similar effort had ever been made calling for the will and determination to win that this war did. Gone by 1940 was the timidity and hesitation of the years of appeasement. Gone was the feeling of "business as usual" or that someone else would do the job. From the crucible of war's suffering and sacrifice emerged a united people possessed of a great determination to enter into the conflicts of the future and come out victorious as it had in the past.

It should be remembered that England has an asset to be balanced against the liabilities here listed—the richness and fulness of her national heritage. Fused together in that heritage one finds what has been handed down from the distant past effectively and usefully combined with a creation of the present. A glance at the heritage, as it stands today, may therefore serve to show what else lies on the credit side of the ledger.

England's most ancient and most central institution is the Crown. The lineage of Her present Majesty, Queen Elizabeth II, goes back to William the Conquerer, in 1066; her office, to the first Bretwalda, Aella of the South Saxons, in 477. Her full royal title is reminiscent of the distant past, including as it does claims such as that to be Defender of the Faith that go back to Henry VIII. Yet at the same time the Crown is a very up-to-date thing in the life of the Commonwealth, as is shown by the emphasis on it as the binding link, in the Statute of Westminster of 1931. The royal title, too, is modern, its most recent change dating to 1946. The power of the monarch, too, is of today. Though in the eyes of the law, by a useful fiction, Her Majesty is absolute, this is but a means to personify the power of the state. Now the Queen is not a ruler but a uniter. The House of Windsor is powerful from the force it has on the minds of men, a force created by recent monarchs. Here it should be noted that the late King was respected and loved not only because his great-grandmother was a symbol of the Victorian age; not only because his grandfather was a genial *bon vivant* who embodied all that was attractive in the Edwardian age; not only because his sailor father by his very simplicity gave strength and courage to the complex people over whom he reigned; but also because to the faith that had been handed down from the past he added his own very personal contribution of valor, kindness, and simplicity. In what he stood for, England's past contributed directly to her present.

Similarly does the past serve and contribute to the present in England's sovereign body, Parliament. It is ancient yet constantly adapting its form and functions to new needs. Its privileges remain the keystone of the structure of British democracy. Today its upper house, that of Lords, has as members some barons whose titles go back to Runnymede and others who started life as schoolteachers and workingmen. Though it has been shorn of its privileges—indeed, so some think, just because it has so been shorn—it performs a highly useful function, that of debating in a non-partisan manner measures that need a critical examination such as the House of Commons cannot give. For in Lords, where today new members come by merit, there is sure to be an expert on almost every subject—the Queen's physician on medical matters; an industrial magnate on questions of production; an ex-governor of the Bank of England on finance; a great social worker; a colonial administrator; a winner of a Nobel prize in science; a trade union executive. Today no one would intentionally create such an undemocratic body as the House of Lords, but now that its power of blocking has been ended, no one would lightly discard such a useful institution.

In Commons, too, the distant and the nearby past combine to serve the needs of the present. The pageantry of the opening of a session goes back to days not long after Runnymede, when kings were truly powerful. The awesome summons by "Black Rod" to Her Majesty's presence, the submission to Her Majesty of the name of him who will speak for the faithful Commons that Her Majesty may approve, are relics of a highly undemocratic age; yet they still have value, for they may serve to remind members of Parliament that they have a duty to serve and hold their power in trust. Any evil this may do is more than counterbalanced by other reminders of another stage in the past of the Commons. When ceremonially the door of the House of Commons is shut in the face of Black Rod, this custom going back to the days of Edward III bears memories of the fact that the monarch cannot enter the place of their debates without their consent and that one king, Charles I, started a civil war by bringing soldiers with him to arrest the Five Members. There is a lesson in civility in the row of hooks in the outer hall where members must hang their swords lest they use them to give point to their debates. A Prime Minister and his Cabinet may take their duties more seriously because they recall they sit where of old Hyde and Falkland sat when they were the chief advisers of Charles I. Symbolic of the dignity of the proceedings of the House is the impressive wig devised for himself and his successors by the eighteenth-century Speaker Onslow, who created the great tradition of the Speaker's impartiality. A mark of the efficiency of the proceedings of the House is the methods of getting rid of petty detail and obstructive stalling that go back no further than Parnell and the Parliament Act of 1911 and still have the nicknames of those days—the "kangaroo" and the "guillotine." Again, though no one would today devise the ceremonial of Parliament, it remains a valuable heritage because it creates the right sort of atmosphere in which to transact democracy's business.

All through England's governmental structure one finds this same use made of the legacy of the past. The chief courts of the land no longer sit in Westminster Hall that was built by William Rufus, because they have moved elsewhere, to the new law courts nearer the legal centers of the "Inns of Court." But the old ways of those courts remain. The Queen's judges still take royal honors, such as Henry II granted to them, and combine with the juries of Norman institution and the shire reeves that go back to Anglo-Saxon times to give justice, in which the people share, just as they did when Angles, Jutes, and Saxons crossed the North Sea. Law enforcement has the same feeling of confidence in it that comes from being age-old. An English policeman is the heritor of a long series of trustworthy predecessors. His powers as a constable go back to Edward I's Statute of Winchester. His reputation for kindliness, along with his nickname "Bobby," goes back to Sir Robert Peel and the Metropolitan Police Act of 1829. The efficiency and discretion of the forces of crime detection, based on Scotland Yard, hark back to blind Sir John Fielding and his Bow Street runners of the 1740's, whose office was moved to Scotland Yard in 1829.

It is tempting to trace other vestiges of the past—to point out how the dress uniform of Her Majesty's Guards, which gives drama to the "trooping of the colors," is, paradoxically, the red coats given them by Oliver Cromwell; to recount how the officers of Her Majesty's Navy on at least one ship are served on silver given them by Lord High Admiral James, Duke of York, and how officers on all Her Majesty's ships drink Her Majesty's health sitting, because one monarch, William IV, so often bumped his head when, as a midshipman, he stood to drink to his father. But the point that is being made here is not that what is quaint remains for tourists to admire but that what is useful is kept and utilized—and is the more useful because it is time-tried. What English men and English women, English boys and English girls, do from habit, they do in many cases unconsciously, as part of a long process of trial and error and discovery of the best way to do it, inherited from their forebears. For example, English boys get their schooling from varied institutions. The late Sir Stafford Cripps, Labor trouble shooter, attended what its graduates know as "the College of St. Mary apud Winton," others as Winchester, founded over five hundred years ago, before going on to the comparatively young University of London. Gladstone attended a slightly younger but still flourishing institution, Eton, founded by King Henry VI. Churchill attended the school on Harrow Hill established by sturdy John Lyon in the days of Good Queen Bess, before going on with that process of self-education he has so engagingly described in *A Roving Commission*. Major Attlee attended Haileybury, whose history is typical of the way the English use what they have. Its buildings were put up by the East India Company, for a college for training civil servants before going to India. In the 1860's, there being no need for it for that use, a school modeled on Rugby was established there. These and other "public schools," called public because they are dedicated to and managed for public service, coexist with yet younger ones, founded in a sense in the 1870's by that dangerous radical, Joseph Chamberlain, for rich and poor alike. Two of the universities of England are so old that jestingly they claim to have been founded by King Alfred and Pythagoras. One that is not at all the youngest was given its inspiration by a scholar-statesman from New Zealand, Pember Reeves. These and many other institutions fuse together into one national system, each contributing its special quality.

All through English life one finds what is good in the old still being asked to contribute. At Laxton, in Nottinghamshire, until very recently it was possible to see in use the old three-field system of narrow strips, each covering an acre, that were laid out by the Angles when first they landed. In nearby Lincolnshire, combines and machines cultivate and harvest perhaps the most fertile and at times the most up-to-date farms in the world. When into the local offices of the Ministry of Labor come wage and salary earners to buy stamps and put them into books, they are buying what in one way or another Englishmen and Englishwomen have bought for a century and a quarter—insurance against insecurity. They buy—as some have, since Sir Alfred Power instituted "medical clubs" in the days of the New Poor Law—protection against the doctor's bills. They buy— as some have, since such unions as the Amalgamated Society of Engineers first gave its members such services—protection against losing their jobs. For social insurance is just as much part of the English heritage as any of the proud titles of the nobility. Social planning is even older. It today is carried out in borough and county halls, by councilor and alderman. Those powers were democratized at the inspiration of Joseph Chamberlain, in 1888, but they go back, through the establishment of the county bench of justices of the peace in the reign of Edward III, as the name "alderman" suggests, to the hundred courts and wapentakes of the Angles and Saxons. Even the act of buying a stamp at the post office carries more meaning to it than one might think. For that same penny and a half that carries a letter across the street might carry it to the heart of Australia, and that is true because the Victorian Sir Rowland Hill gave England a cheap and efficient postage and because the Earl of Durham and Earl Balfour first gave England a self-governing Empire and then made that Empire into a Commonwealth of Nations. Nor should the ladies feel neglected. Today an English girl can go to a public school that is as good as her brother's. She can go to a college at the ancient universities and compete there on an equal footing with her brothers. Ever since Cambridge University opened its degrees as well as its doors to women, attainment at all universities has been equally recognized for both sexes. Almost the only door shut to a woman is that of the House of Lords. But in rejoicing in this equality of opportunity, the women of England might stop for a moment to recognize what they owe to the militant and sometimes tactful pioneers who in the last hundred years won them this equality.

So it is that, when one attempts to add up the balance sheet of Great Britain, one should put in some sort of item covering the value of being a long-established "going concern." In meeting conflicts with the future the English have that to build on. Long ago Alfred the Great asked what value a famous father was if one did not live up to him. England's fathers have at least passed down an example and knowledge to their sons and daughters.

Upon leaving school or college the young man or woman faces a world not unlike that which his father faced after World War I. Jobs in the civil services, the mines, the shops, and the mills are still open. After World War II, however, the state is more likely to be his direct or indirect employer than was the case with his father. He can join the Army or Navy; he is likely to be required by law now to serve in uniform for some time. Then, perhaps, he can sail the seven seas hunting for cargoes or do business in foreign markets as his father did. Where the young man or woman of today must find work, it will be harder to make a living, but it will not be impossible as long as Great Britain can hold something like her place of old in the world economy.

Since Great Britain is a democracy, the decision as to how the future would be met was a decision to be made by the people. The people so decided. On July 26, 1945, the papers carried the announcement of a political and social upheaval of the first magnitude. The Conservative party that had held sway for so long found it had lost 181 seats in the national elections. Labor, with 395 seats, was swept into office with a majority of 148 over all other parties or groups. This came as a shock not only to foreigners but also to leading members of the Conservative party, who had expected the voters to show love and appreciation for Conservative leadership during the greatest war in British history. Why did this sweeping change happen and what did it mean for postwar Britain? It was obvious that the Labor party had worked hard in the election campaign, launched with the publication of the pamphlet *Let Us Face the Future* early in the year. As a piece of campaign literature this pamphlet was most effective in presenting to a people tired of war and anxious for peace a reasoned and logical program. The Conservatives failed to put their case in a similarly effective way. They believed that the magnificent reputation of Churchill and vague promises of the "trust us" variety of slogans like "Carry through and win with Winnie" were sufficient. But any appeal to Churchill's reputation as a war leader fell flat because everyone in England had served in the war and could show his or her medals and wound stripes. While admiring Churchill both as a great war leader and as a man, the people of

Great Britain failed to admire him as a peacetime leader when he was the head of a party that was out of touch with their hopes and desires for the future.

What did the British want? What did they feel was the best use to be made of their social and political and economic heritage? The best answer that can be found is in the platform of the Labor party that won the election and was summarized in *Let Us Face the Future*. For that was built on the hopes and desires of members of the Labor party and on the change of mind that had taken place among the middle and lower-middle classes concerning relationships between the individual and the state. It was obvious to everyone that the country could not return to the social *status quo ante* of before World War II. The economic position of most voters as well as their social aspirations were certainly not those of 1938. War—and the opportunities given by five years of assignment of services according to merit—caused the middle class and the working class to make up their minds about the sort of new world in which they wanted to live. Here are the seven points offered in *Let Us Face the Future*:

1. Jobs for all. This was a program demanding full employment.

2. Industry and finance to be managed in the service of the people. This meant the creation of a National Investment Board; nationalization, or public ownership, of the Bank of England, fuel and power, iron and steel, and domestic transport; and public supervision of cartels and monopolies.

3. Substantial aids and over-all national planning for agriculture.

4. Town and country planning with a new houses and buildings program undertaken by the state.

5. Expansion of educational and recreational facilities.

6. A social security program expanded to mean government guarantee of decent standards of living, decent housing, state provision of medical services from "the cradle to the coffin."

7. Aid and planning for the social and economic development of the overseas possessions of England, along with intra-Commonwealth and international cooperation in the maintenance of peace.

By their votes the people of Britain put their stamp of approval on this program of state socialism.

It is most significant how much Labor's proposals resembled the general philosophy of the Conservative party, which in principle was not opposed to a single one of them. Actually, Labor had stolen the Conservatives' clothes in that portion of its program which recommended social security and the nationalization of the coal industry, the fuel and power industry, and the Bank of England. Practically every step looking toward national control and ownership was to be found in the recommendations that a special committee had already made to a Conservative Parliament. Industrialists who might be expected to support the Conservatives, such as the directors of the Cable and Wireless Corporation, actually advised that nationalization take place. Why, then, did the English people not continue to vote Conservative when there was so little difference between the parties in what they planned for postwar England? Again *Let Us Face the Future* affords an answer. As it points out, the Conservatives talked about socialism and broad programs of social welfare but did nothing; Labor meant what it said and would act. That, as their votes showed, was what the people believed.

This was not the only reason for their choice of Labor. In 1936 Labor leaders had come to the conclusion that it would take them a long time to win an election as a national party. Their defeat at the polls in 1935 had made them feel a program of mass education was needed if the middle classes were to be won over. Book clubs such as the Left Book Club put into the hands of thousands of workers and shopkeepers well-written arguments for the socialist point of view, the ideas of such prominent socialists as Professor Harold Laski of the London School of Economics. Behind this was the efficiency of the Labor political machine and a measure of dry rot in the superb machine that in 1925 Alderman Salvidge had given Stanley Baldwin and the Conservatives. Finally, it must be remembered that events for some years had been preaching socialism. The Conservatives, though not Churchill, had appeasement and Munich to live down, whereas thanks to Bevin the whole Labor party had a good antifascist record since Ethiopia. Churchill, and some Conservatives, obviously hankered after an adventurous foreign policy that England at the moment could not afford. More than that, for five years the youth of England had been living under socialism and having to like it, for what is an army, a navy, or an air force, but socialism at work? And for those five years, thanks to a careful orientation policy in the armed services, they had been encouraged to think democratically and to discuss Britain's war aims freely. On leave, too, they had seen government controls work, in rationing and the apportioning of goods and foods. They had seen the average level of nutrition, for example, rise in England under rationing. The reasons for this might lie in the curing of bad eating habits as much as in the virtues of socialism; the telling fact remained. Therefore, since the Labor platform said just what the masses were thinking, it got their support.

With the election of 1945 Parliament came back to its most efficient organization, that of the two-party system. Between the two world wars this had not been the way things were done; only during the years 1923 and 1925 to 1929 did the governing party form the majority in Commons. The ministries of MacDonald, 1923 and 1929 to 1931, were minorities; those of Lloyd George, 1919 to 1923, and of the National Governments of 1931 to 1939 were coalitions, even though at the end very few Liberals and National Laborites coalesced with very many Conservatives. Neither minorities nor coalitions have governed well in England. Likewise with Attlee the Cabinet returned to normal. War Cabinets, for reasons of executive decision, have tended to be small; Churchill had five to nine fellow members and told the dominion premiers he wished they were less. Attlee could and did use seventeen to twenty-one, and he therefore could have a group large enough to work out a legislative program.

In the years 1945 to 1950, the Attlee Cabinet carried out the party platform, while the Conservative opposition, as oppositions should, criticized. Thus some measures, on which there was general consent, went through smoothly, while others, where opinion was truly divided, caused contention. Especially did the proposal to nationalize the iron and steel industry, which the Conservatives considered to be healthy and in no need of government interference, draw fire. So did the plan to make the dental and medical professions a semistate service.

The arguments in the medical controversy deserve examination. Against the Labor program was the argument that medical care was already being given, that the already existing but noncompulsory Health Insurance Panels reached the classes not able to pay high prices, and that to force all to join these panels would destroy the intimate relationship between doctor and patient. On the other side it was argued that in fact medical care reached chiefly those who could pay for it, the upper class and the upper middle class, and that the health of the nation was more important than the selected private practice of the physician. Terrifying statistics were adduced. Of miners called to the colors in war, 68 per cent had been found unfit; of the volunteers in the general population, 52 per cent had been. In one area of the city of Bristol lived some 35,000 without either a hospital or a private practicing physician. Something had to be done. As for the arguments about the value of private practice, they did not persuade Labor M.P.s. Large portions of England's population, in the classes from which these members came, had never seen private practice. In England health insurance was widespread long before even the Insurance Act of 1909. So Labor ignored Opposition arguments and went ahead.

The most generally accepted of Labor's proposals for a new world was the unification and refurbishing of the social security system. Here the heritage of the English past had not provided a tradition of success, merely one of good intentions. Four different conceptions had guided legislation: poor relief dating back to 1601, state aid dating back to the supposedly laissez-faire Victorians, private insurance dating back to the definitely self-helping Victorians, and the program of state guidance of insurance started by Lloyd George. In the years since World War I much thought had been given to this, and especially by Sir William Beveridge. He prepared a government-sponsored report in 1942, and his own personal report in 1944. Liberal, Conservative, and Labor parties alike took these as a starting point.

The result was the National Insurance Act of 1946, as supplemented by an act of 1948 ending the poor-law system. In place of the old hodgepodge of various authorities having various powers came one basic idea. When possible all forms of security would be based on insurance to which the insured contributed, and which the state—no longer would there be private bodies to tangle the system—would manage. In such cases where there was exceptional and uninsurable need, there would be direct state aid, as in the case of family allowance for those with two or more children of school age. Approved societies for insurance, relief committees of county and borough councils, all such vestiges of the past would be swept away, and the insurance state would guarantee the basic decencies of food, clothing, shelter, and medical care from the cradle to the grave.

Finance and industry met nationalization, too. The Bank of England was taken from its 17,000 stockholders—who were duly compensated—and put into the hands of a Board of Governors appointed by the Government. Coal, gas, communications overseas, wireless, and air transport were similarly brought under state control. An over-all plan for the rebuilding of cities and the proper utilization of land for towns was made and began to be put into effect. The agricultural marketing acts of the 1930's were carried further, as were over-all controls over agricultural methods. The location of new factories was made subject to control. Not their owners but government officials would decide where, in the light of labor supply, raw materials, and the danger of air raids, it would be best to place them.

Overseas, too, there was socialism, here continuing the Colonial Development Fund of 1940. It is the continuation of the old Labor policy—indeed, the old British policy—of municipal trading and planning. Just as Birmingham might decide it was wiser to own its own gas plant or water supply, or build its own markets and rental stalls there, so the Empire as a whole, acting through an appropriate agency, might plan a hydroelectric plant like Victoria Nyanza or take over the planting of peanuts—"groundnuts" to the English—on a large scale, as the only body that could have the capital wherewith to do it. Indeed, the link to Birmingham is direct. It was the "gas-and-water socialist" mayor of Birmingham, Joseph Chamberlain, who was the first Colonial Secretary to spend important central funds on colonial development. The Uganda groundnuts scheme has been so widely publicized, especially by those who used its failure as an antisocialist argument, that it is easy to forget two essential things: that both political parties share the same aim, and that a long list of projects can be added, in British Honduras, British Guiana, Nigeria, the Gold Coast. If one failure and the consequent burden on the taxpayer of paying for a bureaucrat's mistakes stands out here, so also should stand out the willingness of government to do economic as well as humanitarian good to the less well placed in other lands.

Overseas, too, socialism had its program, politically. It has been told previously how the Attlee Government gave independence to Burma, republican status to India, and dominion status of different sorts to Pakistan and Ceylon. In doing this and in daring to do it quickly, the Labor Government got amazing good will from previously hard-to-rule regions, as well as exemplifying its good faith.

However, all that the Labor Government did succeeded or failed according to the answer they gave to the problem of whether the British could manufacture, sell, and carry goods with some margin of profit. It makes little difference whether the goods and services are taken by the colonial Empire, by the Commonwealth, or by South American, European, Asiatic, or North American states—Great Britain can adjust her trade to meet the needs of nearly any market—but a market, an open market, must be there. If war, high tariffs, lack of exchange or credit or gold, or iron curtains bar trade, then Great Britain can look forward to bankruptcy and even starvation. To this problem the Labor Government had to find an answer. One was in socialization—perhaps "insurancization" might here be coined —of the homeland, to put basic services under national control. Secondly, a financial and trade struggle had to be waged and won. Credit had to be gained from abroad, in the forms of loans from the United States, Canada, and curiously enough India, to allow a start. Then, when the situation had become clear, the financial structure, complicated as it was by a world diplomatic struggle, had to be reorganized. Here, in outline, is the story of what happened.

At first England had to live on capital, simply to get the money needed for replacements. At all levels five years of war had worn England out. Factories needed new tools, people needed new clothes. Unfortunately, she had to live, as far as an essential margin went, on capital borrowed from abroad. This took the form of direct borrowing, $3,750,000 from the United States, $1,250,000 from Canada, and an ingenious deferring of claims from Indian private creditors. This did not fill the bill at all. Credits that should have lasted for years were liquidated speedily in 1946. A plan to restore ease in trade by ending exchange controls and making the pound readily convertible in 1946 had to be given up. It looked as if the end were in sight. Meanwhile, a grim specter appeared in Eastern Europe. All the fond hopes of a democratic set of East European states fostered by the words of the Yalta Agreement were proved vain as in "satellite" after "satellite" governments took over, right up to the line of occupation by English, French, and American troops. Here history repeated itself, for the party in power was divided in its views and the Opposition, from its seat of advantage for criticism, was united. Just as some of the National Government leaders between 1933 and 1939 had tried in vain to "do business with Hitler," so confiding left-wing Laborites felt that it would be possible, if only patience were shown, to reach an understanding with Communist Russia. Meanwhile, Churchill, in an address in the United States, coined the phrase "iron curtain," that today is the acknowledged description of the political, economic, social, and even intellectual barrier that cuts Europe in two.

But adversity has its advantages. It became to the self-interest of the United States to keep democratic Europe going. This truth was stated publicly by United States Secretary of State Marshall, in an address at Harvard College. The idea fell on willing ears on both sides of the Atlantic. After much dickering with those nations too near Russia for comfort, at last the idea was put into effect. Cooperation was to be the key to the Marshall Plan, to be managed by an Organization for European Economic Cooperation. While under the American Foreign Assistance Act of 1948 there would be American money to start things going, aid would go only to those who would help themselves and also help others. Help herself and others Great Britain did. She produced 50 per cent of the coal, 30 per cent of the cotton yarn, 55 per cent of the trucks, 35 per cent of the automobiles, and 59 per cent of the merchant shipping of the sixteen Marshall Plan countries. Not only in production was Great Britain's recovery significant, but in international business and finance as well, because the trade within the Commonwealth and Empire, or Sterling Bloc, adds up to about one-fourth of the total for the world.

Marshall Plan dollars helped close the gap between expenditures for necessary imports and receipts from exports. It was beyond hope that exports would exceed imports so soon after the end of the war, or that the receipts from profits on investments and from services would be large enough to make up the difference between import payments and export receipts, by "invisible exports." Thus dollar credits made available allowed Great Britain to undertake a program of reconstruction and production that went a long way to recover the worst of the war losses. The accompanying table shows British recovery in imports and exports and in industrial production. During the later part of 1949 and the year 1950 general

BRITISH RECOVERY
(In millions of dollars; index base, 1938 = 100)

Year	Imports	Exports	Production index
1947	$7,224	$4,824	114
1948	8,376	6,636	128
1949	8,484	6,828	137

conditions improved in Great Britain so much that Marshall Plan aid was suspended from January 1, 1951. Obstacles in the path such as the low coal stocks and winter of snow and floods of 1946 to 1947 had been over-

come. Her economy had achieved sufficient balance and regained its
strength to the point at which she could now go it alone.

In order to dispense with Marshall Plan aid the average Briton had to
tighten his belt considerably. During the war rationing had been imposed
to the point where few luxuries were left. Meat, eggs, and ordinary staples
were rationed. "The bold British breakfast of bacon and eggs," of which
sings the poet A. P. Herbert, had become a memory. V-J Day did not see
the end of this rationing. Shoes and clothing were made available, but in
limited quantities. Meat, butter, eggs, and other rationed items continued
in short supply for the housewife, who had to stand in queues for her small
allotment. This "austerity" was imposed so that Great Britain might again
find independence—in this case, economic. By practicing such self-denial
precious dollars could be obtained and exports balanced against imports
the more quickly. Exports did shoot up. The major commodities that were
sold overseas under the 1938 level were coal, steel, cotton cloth, rayon,
automobiles, and trucks. Taking 1947 as a base for 100, exports in these
commodities were 92 in 1938, 127 in 1948, 139 in 1949, and 162 in 1950. Rationing was, under these circumstances, worth the sacrifice of comfort and
luxury.

The Labor party, which accomplished this program, in its operation and
in its general philosophy held true to custom and tradition. No government led by Major Clement Attlee could be extremist. He, himself a member of the middle class, came up through Labor party ranks. After public
school and University College, Oxford, he put in years of social work in
the slums of London and administrative responsibility in the boroughs of
London. An officer in World War I, he was a regular party official who
worked his way to the top. He is in the tradition of F. D. Maurice, Charles
Kingsley, and those others who in the nineteenth century objected to the
way the bad effects of the industrial revolution had degraded the laboring
classes. Party officials such as Herbert Morrison and the late Ernest Bevin
are British socialists in the trade union tradition, interested in immediate
specific programs. Rather than talk about oppression on the part of capitalists they spent their time in trying to provide jobs, setting up social security, and pulling the nation's economy out of its postwar slump. Such
party leaders expelled Communist sympathizers from Labor party ranks
in 1948 with a ruthlessness which surprised Moscow. Their socialism and
the philosophy of their administration was taken, in so far as it had roots
outside practical day-to-day experience, from Jeremy Bentham and John
Stuart Mill, and even has a slight flavor of Herbert Spencer. Therefore
much of the success of their sweeping program of nationalization came
because it was in line with long-established British tradition and an accepted British point of view.

Another reason for the success of Labor's program lay in the support that was given it by the actual governing classes. After World War II there was little gap between rich and poor; it is said that by then less than two dozen individuals had a private income greater than $25,000 a year. Few had the privileges of wealth. Noble families, in order to keep up their estates, had to admit tourists on alternate Wednesdays and charge a fee for viewing the great hall and the stables. It was not unusual to find the former lord of the manor deeding his castle to the National Trust that preserves historic homes and living in the house once occupied by his gatekeeper. Many of the middle classes who had once had a servant or two, a flat in town, and a house in the country, came down to the flat alone. But this did not mean the end of the privileges of social station. A lord remained a lord and was treated as such. It still was natural for Englishmen and Englishwomen to enter domestic service as a life work, almost a half million being so employed in 1946. As the catechism in the Book of Common Prayer phrases it, the English still are satisfied with the station in life to which they are called. But rank, in this view of life, has its duties, and the university graduates and public-school men at the top of the tree, in the Home Civil Service's first or administrative division, and the leaders of the nationalized industries naturally did their best in the station in life to which they found themselves called. The good will and sense of duty of these people, regardless of personal political connections, provided England with the necessary staff of experts and public servants to accomplish the great changes of the Labor program.

Two points should be made here. One is that there are those of the upper classes who support socialism. Such was Sir Stafford Cripps, of a noble family of the barony of Parmoor. Perhaps equally significant, if not more so, there is a new elite. England has throughout the ages been a land in which new paths to the top have opened up. First of all its aristocracy was of the landowners who were armed knights. Then came the new men of the Elizabethan age, merchants and lawyers who bought landed estates and came to the top. The nineteenth century saw the industrialists take the same road. But the twentieth century has seen a new phenomenon. For the first time it has been possible to reach the top without allying oneself with the landed classes. Now a clever young man or young woman can win scholarships to the universities—and not at all necessarily to Oxford or Cambridge, but to a new one—and from there can enter the first division of the Civil Service, thus forming a new aristocracy of government of the ablest without joining the old one. These new men of the twentieth century deserve credit, too, for making the Labor program work.

Five years brought the customary election under the Parliament Act of 1911. In 1950 the Labor Government went to the polls to get ratification for its actions and authority, in particular, to push the nationalization of iron and steel through the House of Lords. Barely did it get that mandate.

Reasons for this seem to be these. There is a natural pendulum effect in British politics which brings in the outs, puts out the ins. There was, naturally, an almost inevitable psychological reaction against "austerity" and the sacrifices demanded of the people, instead of restoring prewar living conditions. And there was some dislike of controls as controls, and of the taking of iron and steel out of the hands of people who were doing the job well. The result was a curiously divided Parliament. Labor got back into power, but by a scant margin of a half dozen more seats than Conservative and Liberal combined. Had the comparatively big Liberal vote been added to Conservative, or had the total popular vote been reflected in seats in Commons, Labor would have been in a minority. For some time there was a chance that a "snap vote" would drive Attlee from office. But a sense of fair play in the opposition parties, possibly reinforced by a suspicion that an immediate general election would help rather than hinder Labor, as by-elections hinted, worked for a while for the Attlee Government. The people of England, in spite of the fact that many of the middle class had changed their minds about certain aspects of Labor's program, seem to have ratified its principles and made them permanent.

For the great change in England is not that it has become a country of nationalized industry, with insurance protecting the standard of living of all. That change began with the Insurance Act of 1909 and the growing assumption of state control in the 1920's and 1930's. What the 1940's have seen is a new way of securing leadership. As was pointed out, World War I had decimated the old ruling class, those who would normally have been expected to inherit posts of responsibility assigned them by education and by tradition. The general question was whether a democratic society could produce men fit to rule who did not have, as individuals or as a class, the old tradition of special opportunity. And subsidiary but vital to it, as was pointed out on the previous page, came the question whether the new widespread education that goes back to the Education Act of 1870 could provide from all society the experts needed in modern society whom earlier generations had drawn from one class.

Throughout their history the British have opened the doors to those who could tackle the job and get it done. No change in this tradition came after World Wars I and II. When Major Attlee presented to the King his Cabinet list in 1945, it is said that George VI asked him who his best man was and told him to put that man, Ernest Bevin, at the key post of Secretary of State for Foreign Affairs. It mattered not that he had started as a day laborer; he had earned his place in the cabinet. He was not the first so to rise. J. Ramsay MacDonald and Viscount Snowden had similarly come to the top. What is significant is that this has ceased to seem exceptional. In World War II, under the leadership of Churchill, the best had been called to power from all ranks of society. Now one feels a new sense that all ranks can take leadership. Where once the assumption of political power meant the joining of a leadership class, that is no longer true in the same way. Labor used to assert that MacDonald had become too much of a country gentleman by being Premier. That sort of thing seems gone. England seems no longer to have a ruling caste.

With the turn of the new year of 1950 the help coming from Marshall Plan funds would cease, as no longer needed, and Great Britain hoped to be able to stand alone on the rapidly developing trade with the empire and the world. Freedom from American dollar domination was, in the economic sense, something that had to be won or the threat of bankruptcy would be more than a threat. The outbreak of the Korean war, its expense as well as the drying up of trade with Communist China, did not foretell a happy future for British business. During the next two years business continued to be unsatisfactory. Nothing that the Labor Government could do, and nothing that the Churchill Government could do after November, 1951, could reverse the trend toward bankruptcy. The markets in the world and in the empire that had to absorb the speeded-up production of goods and services did not open. European and African markets, as well as those in Asia, did not grow as had been anticipated. Some increases were, of course, welcome, as was that of a year's increase of 433 million pounds in exports to the colonies for the year ending March 1, 1951. But no single upsurge in exports or in business or all of them together were sufficient to do more than hold back momentarily a steady loss in trade. In 1950, as an example of the unsatisfactory trend, imports into Great Britain were £2,602,945,000 and exports only £2,255,048,000. Had these figures been reversed, everyone in the kingdom would have breathed a sigh of relief. It was the unrelieved gloom of the economic picture and the pressure of the austerity program that contributed so greatly to the defeat of the Labor party in the second general election since 1945.

Labor's shiny new socialist policy of nationalizing industry and providing for every subject from cradle to grave basic social services did not make actual living conditions much better. The British housewife continued to stand in queues and her husband to see his whiskey sent to the United States. The Conservatives protested against the extent to which nationalization was taking place. Particularly did they protest against making the steel industry public property. They were not opposed to the social-benefit part of the Labor program. They made it their own and, like the Republicans in recent elections in the United States, said they would do a better job of administration of social benefits than the present government was doing. In most vote-catching parts of their party platform the Conservatives were "me tooers." However, they did not claim as loudly as did the Labor party that all the virtue and good sense of their platform was as sacred as the Ten Commandments.

In a time of great stress the Conservatives proved to be the party with a more flexible program and a less rigid attitude toward reforms. Labor committed itself to a golden rule of socialism that had to be followed strictly as the laws of the Medes and the Persians. The Conservatives were more ready to admit a margin for error and to change as the times decreed. The Labor party, even in the face of its disastrous experiment in growing peanuts in Africa, announced that its policies were absolutely right because of their justness. The Conservatives disliked the rapidity with which socialism was applied to basic industries and tore into the government as unrepresentative of the real wishes of the people. At last came the general election of October, 1951.

That election replaced the Labor party with the Conservative. It did not give the Conservatives a mandate so clear that they dared reverse any fundamental reform or turn toward a new nationalization policy. They did denationalize the steel and transportation industries as far as normal management and operation were concerned. But the state continued to supervise the general economic organization and the activities of all enterprise, as it had under the Laborites. The change was from state-managed corporations to state-supervised ones. In fact a very few voters, probably the body of independent voters who swing one way or another each election and are without formal party ties, determined the course of this election. Many Liberals gave up their party as lost in this election. After it, only six Liberals answered the party Whip. The Conservatives and Laborites almost reversed themselves from their 1950 positions. The Conservatives in 1951 had 321, the Labor party 295. With a probable majority of 26 and an absolute majority of only 18, Churchill, just as he celebrated his seventy-seventh birthday in November, 1951, became Prime Minister for the second time.

The most important political and economic fact bearing down on Great Britain is that there continued to be fewer customers for her amply produced goods and services than are needed to operate at a profit. Shoes for workers' children, meat on the table three times a day, and complete removal of austerity restrictions were both impossible and improbable in 1952. The Conservatives might stem, for a time, the downward path of the nation's business, but they could not turn it about and make it go upward. World conditions bore hardly upon a patient, valorous, and very tired people. Britain's world position and world trade suffered when she lost Iranian oil in 1952 and cut the Sudan free in 1953. The Mau-Mau's in Kenya weakened her prestige. But a wise granting of much responsible government to the Gold Coast gave hopes of progress to true self-government in Africa, and her Conservative Government did get a budget surplus, cut taxes, and keep its pledge to denationalize steel.

George VI had been in bad health for some time. His death in February,

1952, was not a surprise to his people. Like his father the King had won, with his Queen, Elizabeth, a solid place in the affections of his people. During the air blitz of World War II he had stayed in London and had taken his chances with his subjects. His courtesy and good humor set an example for his people, and one that was followed with a will. His daughter Elizabeth succeeded him, with the hopes and good wishes that always go to a charming, young, and conscientious queen.

It is too soon after the world disorder that has followed World War II to judge fairly or accurately the position of Great Britain in a new world order. Two very rich and very strong powers, strong in every sense of the word, seem to have surpassed her in influence and prestige. These are the United States and Soviet Russia. But it would be a mistake for this reason to rate Great Britain as a second- or third-rate power. She came out of the war with her colonies and her dominions ready to cooperate for the advancement of mutual interests. By an agreement made in 1950 the mother country is pledged to help those colonies not enjoying self-government to attain it, and to give most-favored-nation treatment politically and economically to the dominions. Even more than before 1939, the Commonwealth is a league of states bound by ties of affection, commercial interest, and common tradition. Because it is such ties that are used to bind, the Republic of India has remained connected with the Commonwealth. By pledging help to such colonies as Nigeria to attain the same status, Great Britain has shown she has taken to heart the lessons she has learned from past reactions to overseas rule, dating back past the Durham Report to the American Revolution, and that she see it as a privilege —and also a solution of difficulties—to help peoples hitherto dependent to stand on their own feet. The way that such an attitude benefits her is shown by the settlement of such troublemaking nationalist problems as the independence of Eire and the division of India into Pakistan and India.

Without doubt the most severe loss, a loss of vital importance, is that of productive facilities, foreign trade and investment capital. These are the basic necessities for power and prosperity in the twentieth century. But if willingness to sacrifice, to work, and to take chances are qualities that will help recover these losses, then Great Britain has demonstrated remarkable powers of recuperation. Thanks to sister members of the Commonwealth and to the United States, the financial and economic aid needed to give her a start on the road back came in time. New and greater costs for armament in face of Communist aggression in Korea and threat of it in Europe may hold back a swift or steady recovery, but she is moving in the right direction, uncertain as the future is.

Britain's foreign policy remains consistent—and as consistently puzzling, it seems, to those who do not take into consideration its basic starting points. Since the days of the first Elizabeth the British have worked through allies. They consequently are willing to bow to the prejudices of their friends or of those whom they hope to make friends. Parliamentary Britain, in the eighteenth century, allied itself with absolutist Prussia. Protestant Britain, in the early nineteenth century, cooperated with Catholic Spain. Likewise, today, British policy will embrace allies perhaps repugnant to other nations. Again, Britain believes that trade brings peace. That was Richard Cobden's belief. That was the device by which she brought the first Napoleon low. Thus, though Britain is the nation which first brought blockade to a fine art, she also pins her faith to trade as an economic and psychological weapon. This may explain why, in a period of "Cold War," she is more willing to trade across the Iron Curtain and why her nationals are under fewer restrictions. Whether or not she is right in these policies, she is certainly here using the experience of the past to meet the problems of the present.

England's greatest asset in the postwar world is her democratic constitution, with its flexible and effective structure of government. Here is a governmental system that can get things done. Here, too, is a social and political system that can meet change and make use both of the best of ancient institutions and of what is new. When other nations are groping for internal order and peace, too high a value can hardly be set on this.

No one can attempt to answer the question, "Will there always be an England?" If history counts for anything, however, there can be little doubt that in spite of wars and catastrophes Great Britain will remain a world power of major importance, taking her rightful place among the mighty of the earth. But one of the privileges of the historian is that of withholding predictions about the future. Predictions of things to come he leaves to those exact social scientists the sociologist, the economist, and the theologian.

BIBLIOGRAPHY

This bibliography has two purposes: to provide a basic list of books for further reading, and to offer critical commentary where such commentary may seem useful to some readers. More extensive critical commentary and more listing may be obtained in George Dutcher *et al.*, *Guide to Historical Literature* (1931), and in the *English Historical Review*, the *American Historical Review*, and the *Journal of Modern History*. Further listings may be found in Charles Gross, *Sources and Literature of English History to 1485* (1915); Conyers Read, *Bibliography of British History, Tudor Period, 1485–1603* (1933); Godfrey Davies, *Bibliography of British History, Stuart Period, 1603–1714* (1928); and Stanley Pargellis and D. J. Medley, *Bibliography of British History, the Eighteenth Century, 1714–1789* (1951); as well as in Royal Historical Society (A. T. Milne, ed.), *Writings on British History, 1934–1938* (v.d.), and in various specialized bibliographies. The listing below is in the following order: general histories, periods of history in chronological order, books on special subjects, and works of reference. At the end are suggested some fiction and other writings which seem to a high degree to combine historical information and readability. Inevitably this is a selective bibliography. The mass of writings on British history force selection. However, an attempt has been made to include not only basic authorities but new publications not listed in the sources named above and such material as seems especially helpful in connection with the presentation made in this book. Material is listed by author and title, as sufficient indication for securing a book from a library, but dates of publication (in parentheses) are frequently given when dating seems useful for evaluating a work or when it indicates a preferred edition.

GENERAL HISTORIES

There are many good one-volume histories of England. Sharing the title *History of England* are those by G. M. Trevelyan, Keith Feiling, Walter P. Hall and Robert G. Albion, W. E. Lunt, F. O. Marcham, and Arthur L. Cross. John Richard Green's *Short History of the English People* is also

767

still worth consulting, though first written in 1874. In more detail is the eight-volume series edited by Sir Charles Oman: Sir Charles Oman, *England before the Norman Conquest;* H. W. C. Davies, *England under the Normans and Angevins, 1066–1272;* Kenneth Vickers, *England in the Later Middle Ages, 1272–1485;* Arthur D. Innes, *England under the Tudors, 1485–1603;* G. M. Trevelyan, *England under the Stuarts, 1603–1714;* Sir Charles Grant Robertson, *England under the Hanoverians, 1714–1815;* and Sir John A. R. Marriott, *England since Waterloo, 1815–1885,* and *Modern England, 1885–1932.* Of the fourteen-volume *Oxford History,* the following have been completed: R. G. Collingwood and J. N. L. Myres, *Roman Britain and the English Settlements* (1937); Sir Frank Stenton, *Anglo-Saxon England, c. 550–1087* (1947); Austen L. Poole, *From Domesday Book to Magna Carta, 1087–1216;* J. D. Mackie, *The Earlier Tudors, 1485–1558* (1952); J. B. Black, *The Reign of Elizabeth, 1558–1603* (1936); Godfrey Davies, *The Early Stuarts, 1603–1660* (1937); G. N. Clark, *The Later Stuarts, 1660–1714* (1934); Basil Williams, *The Whig Supremacy, 1714–1760* (1939); Sir Ernest Woodward, *The Age of Reform, 1815–1870* (1938); and R. C. K. Ensor, *England, 1870–1914* (1936). Earlier, somewhat restricted, but more detailed is the *Political History of England,* edited by William Hunt and Reginald Lane Poole. This includes Thomas Hodgkin, *The Political History of England from the Earliest Times to the Norman Conquest;* George B. Adams, . . . *From the Norman Conquest to the Death of John, 1066–1216;* T. F. Tout, . . . *From the Accession of Henry III to the Death of Edward III, 1216–1377;* Sir Charles Oman, . . . *From the Accession of Richard II to the Death of Richard III, 1377–1485;* H. A. L. Fisher, . . . *From the Accession of Henry VII to the Death of Henry VIII, 1485–1547;* A. F. Pollard, . . . *From the Accession of Edward VI to the Death of Elizabeth, 1547–1603;* F. C. Montague, . . . *From the Accession of James I to the Restoration, 1603–1660;* Sir Richard Lodge, . . . *From the Restoration to the Death of William III, 1660–1702;* I. S. Leadam, . . . *From the Accession of Anne to the Death of George II, 1702–1760;* Rev. William Hunt, . . . *From the Accession of George III to the Close of Pitt's First Administration, 1760–1801;* Hon. G. C. Broderick, . . . *From the Addington Administration to the Close of William IV's Reign, 1801–1837;* and Sir Sidney Low, *The Reign of Queen Victoria, 1837–1901.*

The relevant chapters of the *Cambridge Modern History, Cambridge Medieval History, Cambridge Ancient History, Cambridge History of the British Empire* (two volumes sometimes found separate as the *Cambridge History of India*), *Cambridge History of British Foreign Policy,* and perhaps the *Cambridge History of British Literature* should prove useful. Lord Acton planned these volumes to provide students doing honors work with full basic information on a subject, for which purpose they are excellent.

Attention should here be called to the *Home University* series, containing such works as G. M. Trevelyan's *The English Revolution, 1688–89;* to the *British Empire* series, edited by the late Sir Reginald Coupland; and to the series of biographies edited by A. L. Rowse. These form highly useful and time-saving insights into periods and subjects.

WORKS ON PERIODS

For prehistory and the Roman period are suggested V. G. Childe, *The Bronze Age* (1930); H. J. Fleure, *Races of England and Wales* (1923); J. J. Haverfield, *Roman Occupation of Britain* (1924) and *Romanization of Roman Britain* (1912); T. D. Kendrick and C. F. Hawke, *Archaeology of England and Wales* (1932). H. J. Mackinder's *Britain and the British Seas* (1914) might well be included here. For the Anglo-Saxon period are suggested H. M. Chadwick, *Studies on Anglo-Saxon Institutions* (1905); R. W. Chambers, *England before the Norman Conquest* (1926); B. A. Lees, *Alfred the Great* (1915); C. Plummer, *The Life and Times of Alfred the Great* (1902); J. R. Green, *The Making of England* (1882); R. H. Hodgkin, *A History of the Anglo-Saxons* (2 vols., 1935); E. R. Hull, *The Northmen in Britain* (1913); and T. D. Kendrick, *A History of the Vikings* (1930).

The Middle Ages in general are well covered in Sir Maurice Powicke's *Medieval England, 1066–1485* (1931). Feudalism is perhaps best discussed in Sir Frank Stenton's *First Century of English Feudalism* (1932), though J. H. Round's *Feudal England* (1895) cannot be ignored. In chronological order then would come, perhaps, E. A. Freeman, *History of the Norman Conquest* (5 vols., 1867–1870); C. H. Haskins, *The Normans in European History* (1915); Alice Stopford Green, *Henry the Second* (1889); Kate Norgate, *England under the Angevin Kings* (1887); Ann Kelly, *Eleanor of Aquitaine* (1949); A. L. Poole, *The Twelfth Century* (1951); Kate Norgate, *Richard the Lion Heart* (1924) and *John Lackland* (1902); Sir F. M. Powicke, *Stephen Langton;* Sidney Painter, *The Reign of King John* (1949); Kate Norgate, *The Minority of Henry III* (1912); Sir F. M. Powicke, *King Henry III and the Lord Edward* (1947); E. P. Cheney, *The Dawn of a New Era, 1250–1453* (1936); G. M. Trevelyan, *England in the Age of Wycliffe* (1904); Sir Charles Oman, *The Great Revolt of 1381* (1906); J. H. Wylie, *History of England under Henry V* (1884–1898) and *Reign of Henry V* (1924–1929); C. L. Kingsford, *Henry V* (1923) and *Prejudice and Promise in Fifteenth Century England* (1925); R. B. Mowat, *The Wars of the Roses* (1914); C. L. Scofield, *The Life and Reign of Edward IV* (1923); and J. Gairdner, *History of the Life and Reign of Richard III* (1898).

For the Tudor period in general, there are Conyers Read, *The Tudors* (1936), and L. F. Salzman, *England in Tudor Times.* There are also the following specific studies: J. Gairdner, *Henry VII* (1899); A. F. Pollard,

Henry VIII (1913), *Wolsey* (1929), and *Cranmer* (1925); J. E. Neale, *Queen Elizabeth* (1934); A. L. Rowse, *The England of Elizabeth* (1951); Conyers Read, *Walsingham* (1929); and T. F. Henderson, *Mary Queen of Scots* (2 vols., 1905). These titles bring out the biographical approach so common in British history and suggest the father of all such biographies, Francis Bacon's *History of Henry the Seventh* (1622), at least as an exercise in historiography. On the verge of religious history are Cardinal F. A. Gasquet's *Henry VIII and the English Monasteries* (1895); J. Gairdner's *The English Church in the Sixteenth Century* (1904), and James Anthony Froude's *History of England from the Fall of Wolsey to the Defeat of the Spanish Armada* (new ed., 12 vols., 1899). Sir Julian Corbett's *Drake and the Tudor Navy* (2 vols., 1898) and J. A. Williamson's *The Age of Drake* perhaps belong here, though they are also naval history.

Besides the works already listed as part of a general series, the Stuart period is briefly dealt with by David Mathew's *The Jacobean Age* (1938) and *The Age of Charles I* (1951), as well as by Arthur Bryant's *King Charles II* (1946). The classic long work is Samuel Rawson Gardiner's *History of England,* each volume variously titled for the years it covers between 1603 and 1656, best used in the new edition of 1901–1903. To this, at Gardiner's request, Sir Charles Firth added his *Last Years of the Protectorate, 1656–1658,* which came out in 1909. The story was taken up in 1685 by T. B. Macaulay's *History of England,* which goes to the death of William of Orange in 1702. It is, in a sense, finished by his great-nephew, G. M. Trevelyan, in his *England under Queen Anne* (1930–1934). Among other biographies may be suggested John Buchan's *Cromwell* (1934), Sir Charles Firth's *Cromwell* (1909), Arthur Bryant's *Samuel Pepys,* Sir John Marriott's *Falkland,* and Winston Churchill's *Marlborough, His Life and Times. The Life of Colonel Hutchinson,* written by his widow, Lucy Hutchinson, between 1664 and 1671 but first published in 1806, deserves reading for its vivid, sympathetic presentation of a Puritan leader. This but scratches the surface of special studies, such as *The Reign of King Pym* by J. A. Hexter and Lady Burghclere's *Thomas Wentworth, Earl of Strafford.*

The historical problem of the eighteenth century is that of the political and constitutional evolution of England. Perhaps the classic over-all picture is still Lecky's *History of England in the Eighteenth Century,* of which a new edition came out in 1943. Sir Lewis Namier's *Structure of Politics at the Accession of George III* (2 vols., 1929) and his *England in the Age of the American Revolution* (1930), D. A. Winstanley's *Personal and Party Government, 1760–1766* (1910) and his *Lord Chatham and the Whig Opposition,* Herbert Butterfield's *George III, Lord North, and the People* (1949), and Richard Pares's *King George III and the Politicians* (1953) are all books that deal ably with the great crisis of this period. Sir

George Otto Trevelyan's *American Revolution* (variously titled for separate volumes) from the Whig point of view treats of English and American affairs in parallel, giving the interpretation that Namier and Butterfield attack. For the formative period before that covered in the works, W. T. Laprade's *Public Opinion and Politics in Eighteenth Century England to the Fall of Walpole* (1932) and, in a different vein, F. S. Oliver's *The Endless Adventure* (1931) give the story of how the office of Prime Minister was created. Biographies of the first William Pitt, Earl of Chatham, abound. That by Basil Williams is perhaps the most serviceable, though the recent *Die Pitt und Die Fox*, now translated as *Pitt versus Fox*, by Erich Eyck, has the advantage of giving an outside interpretation and of showing the two generations of Foxes and Pitts in struggle.

Some authorities consider December, 1783, and the accession of William Pitt the Younger as Prime Minister the turning point in British history. Such is the starting point of G. M. Trevelyan's *British History in the Nineteenth Century* (1922), as opposed to G. D. H. Cole and Raymond Postgate's *The British Common People*, which begins in 1746. With these events deal W. T. Laprade's *Public Opinion and Party Politics in 1784* (1934) and also Donald Grove Barnes's *George III and William Pitt* (1939). For the Napoleonic Wars, see J. Holland Rose's *William Pitt and National Revival* and *William Pitt and the Great War* (both 1911). Some authorities, on the other hand, take 1815 as the turning point of modern times. This is the start of the late Elie Halévy's *History of the English People*, which has now been posthumously completed with a volume quickly covering the period from 1841 to 1895. Few general studies deal with this period, except for the volumes in continued series. Spencer Walpole's *History of England from the Conclusion of the Great War in 1815* (6 vols., 1878–1886) and his *History of Twenty-five Years, 1856–1880* (4 vols., 1904), are outdated. H. W. C. Davis's *Age of Grey and Peel* is a brilliant fragment. But this, and the post-1900 period, are well covered by biographies. Outstanding, besides the classic *Gladstone* by John Morley and *Beaconsfield* by Monnypenny and Buckle, are Philip Guadella, *Wellington;* G. M. Trevelyan, *Lord Grey of the Reform Bill* and *John Bright;* Lady Gwendolen Cecil, *The Life of Robert, Marquis of Salisbury;* Blanche Dugdale, *Arthur James Balfour;* J. A. Garvin, *Joseph Chamberlain;* J. A. Spender, *The Life of Lord Oxford and Asquith;* Thomas Jones, *David Lloyd George;* Raymond Postgate, *George Lansbury* (especially valuable for its picture of a Labor leader in the Christian tradition); and Keith Feiling, *Neville Chamberlain.* Sir Harold Nicolson's *George V* contains valuable new information. Two histories of World War I, one by C. R. M. F. Crutwell and one by Captain Basil Liddell Hart, are both entitled *History of the Great War.* One gives a balanced picture; the other, suggestive criticisms. Sir Winston Churchill's *World Crisis*, his *Second World*

War (in progress), and, on the opposite side of the fence, Francis Williams's *Socialist Britain* (1949) perhaps offer the most useful starting point for the history of recent times. Beyond that, advice would probably be out of date by the time this book is published.

CONSTITUTIONAL HISTORY

The classics on the British constitution remain F. W. Maitland's *Constitutional History of England* (1908, with many reissues) and Walter Bagehot's *The English Constitution* (1872, with the 1928 edition containing Balfour's introduction perhaps the best). The first is a clear-cut and surprisingly detailed account of the evolution of institutions; the latter, a lucid exposition of the workings of the constitution today. F. Pollock and F. W. Maitland, *History of English Law,* is equally a classic source. For local institutions, Sidney and Beatrice Webb, *English Local Government* (6 vols., 1906–1929), should be corrected by Rudolph Gneist, *Englische Verfassungsrecht* (1885); Joseph Redlich and F. W. Hirst, *English Local Government* (1902); and Edwin Canaan, *Local Rates* (1901). Special studies in chronological order are J. E. A. Jolliffe, *The Constitutional History of Medieval England* (1937); C. H. McIlwain, *The High Court of Parliament* (1910); W. A. Morris, *The Constitutional History of England to 1215* (1930); A. F. Pollard, *The Evolution of Parliament* (1920); S. B. Chrimes, *Constitutional Ideas in the Fifteenth Century* (1936); D. L. Keir, *Constitutional History of Modern Britain 1485–1937;* K. Pickthorne, *Early Tudor Government* (1934); S. R. Gardiner, *Constitutional Documents of the Puritan Revolution* (1906); W. R. Anson, *The Law and Custom of the Constitution* (1906); F. G. M. Evans, *The Principal Secretary of State* (1923); E. Porritt, *The Unreformed House of Commons* (1921); C. C. Brinton, *English Political Thought in the Nineteenth Century* (1933); Harold Laski, *Political Thought in England from Locke to Bentham* (1920), and *Reflections on the Constitution* (1950).

EMPIRE, COLONIES, AND COMMONWEALTH

On these subjects there is a plethora of writings, and the problem is one of selection. The compiler's personal preferences would be Arthur Berridale Keith, *Constitutional History of the First British Empire* (1930), and Martin Wight, *The Development of the Legislative Council, 1606–1945,* as the clearest exposition of British thinking; C. H. McIlwain, *The American Revolution* (1923), and R. L. Schuyler, *Parliament and the British Empire* (1929), for the basic constitutional argument; Sir Reginald Coupland, *The American Revolution and the British Empire* (1930), for a summary of why the British Empire did revive; H. T. Manning, *British Colonial Government after the American Revolution* (1933), for how it revived; Arthur Griffith, *The Resurrection of Hungary, a Parallel for Ire-*

land (1918 ed.), for instructions on how to overthrow the Empire; and a little-known pair, T. Harrington, *Plumer of Messines* (1935), and H. F. Prevost Battersby, *Richard Corfield of Somaliland* (1914), along with Lord Wavell, *Allenby*, Vol. II, for descriptions of modern proconsuls in action. This signifies that the compiler disagrees with the line of thought in such writings as the voluminous ones of Lionel Curtis, A. F. Zimmern's *The Third British Empire*, and, to a lesser degree, with W. P. Hall, *Empire into Commonwealth*—which are therefore and in consequence recommended.

For further information are suggested Paul Knaplund's works, especially his *History of the British Empire since 1815;* C. Mullett's *The British Empire;* and S. L. Beer's *The Origins of the British Colonial System.*

Canada, of all the dominions, has the most available material. Histories of Canada are those of George M. Wrong, P. Glazebrook, and Gerald Graham. Sir Reginald Coupland's *Quebec Act,* J. B. Brebner's *North Atlantic Triangle,* Sir Joseph Pope's *Memoirs of Sir John Alexander Macdonald,* and John S. Willison's *Sir Wilfrid Laurier* all are valuable. Ernest Scott's *Short History of Australia* has steadily been brought up to date. Eric Walker's *History of South Africa* and that by Cornelius de Keweit, along with Jan Hofmeyr's *South Africa* and lives of Rhodes by Sir Lewis Michell and Basil Williams might be supplemented by Stuart Cloete's *Against These Three* (a trilogy on Rhodes, Kruger, and Lobenguela, King of the Matabele). Edmund Curtis's *History of Ireland* now has two competitors for the palm: J. C. Beckett's *Short History of Ireland* (1952), by an Ulsterman, and Patrick O'Hegarty's *History of Ireland under the Union* (1952), in which the point of view is that of a Republican. Philip L. Soljack's *New Zealand, Pacific Pioneer* (1946) affords a good balance between two schools of New Zealand history, the heavily factual and the highly interpretative. No one-volume history of India gives fully both the British and the Indian side. Perhaps the most useful short account of recent times can be gleaned from Lord Mersey's *Viceroys . . . of India, 1757–1947* (1949), which gains in impartiality by being critical of its subjects.

If a reader wishes to go further, books abound. Among many which deserve recommendation are Philip Ireland's *Iraq* (1938); Sir Hubert Young's *The Independent Arab* (1933); *New Zealand and the Statute of Westminster,* edited by J. C. Beaglehole (1947), which is valuable in explaining the problems the statute was devised to face; Norman Bentwich's *Palestine* (1951); M. Abbas's *The Sudan Question* (1952); Sir Arnold Wilson's classic two volumes, *Loyalties;* as well as Chester New's *Lord Durham* (1929). But it would be more helpful to advise such a reader that most books on the Empire and the Commonwealth are in some way or other partisan than to list many books without comment. This criticism, however, cannot be made of two important studies now in progress: Lawrence Gipson's *The First British Empire* and Vincent Harlow's *The Founding of the Second British Empire*.

ECONOMIC AND SOCIAL

Two good short economic histories are F. C. Dietz, *The Economic History of England* (1942), and E. Lipson, *The Growth of English Society* (1950). A useful pair would be Sir John Clapham's *Concise Economic History of Britain,* which goes to 1750, and T. S. Ashton's *Industrial Revolution* (1948), which goes from 1760 to 1830. Clapham's three-volume *Economic History of Modern Britain* covers from about 1820 to 1929. The chief social history of England is that of G. M. Trevelyan, *The Social History of England* (now appearing in an illustrated edition), which supersedes the many volumes of H. R. Traill and J. S. Mann's *Social England* (1909). In chronological order are suggested E. Lipson, *Economic History of England* (1929–1931); L. F. Salzman, *English Industries in the Middle Ages* (1923); F. A. Gasquet, *The Black Death of 1348 and 1349* (1908); A. Abram, *English Life and Manners in the Later Middle Ages* (1913); C. R. Fay, *Great Britain from Adam Smith to the Present Day* (1928); D. G. Barnes, *A History of the English Corn Laws, 1660–1846* (1930); S. E. Finer, *The Life and Times of Sir Edwin Chadwick* (1952), which differs from the interpretation of Chadwick and the Poor Law made in Marian Bowley's *Nassau Senior and Classical Economics* (and there documented) and followed in this book; Lionel Robbins, *The Classical Economists* (1952); Lord Ernle, *English Farming, Past and Present* (1913); Chester Kirby, *The English Country Gentleman* (1938); Max Beer, *History of British Socialism* (1923); Sidney and Beatrice Webb, *History of English Trade Unionism* (1920); Leland Jenks, *Migration of British Capital to 1875* (1927); G. D. H. Cole, *Short History of the Working Class Movement* (1927); F. W. Hirst, *The Consequences of the War to Great Britain* (1934); U. K. Hicks, *The Finances of the British Government, 1920–1936* (1938); Herbert Heaton, *The British Way to Recovery* (1934); C. F. Brand, *Labor's Rise to Power* (1941); W. K. Hancock, *British War Economy* (1949); and Wilfrid Smith, *An Economic Geography of Great Britain* (1949).

RELIGION

The standard history of the Church of England is the nine-volume *History of the Church of England,* edited by William R. W. Stephens and William Hunt (1899–1910). To this might be added Norman Sykes's *Church and State in England in the Eighteenth Century* (1935), M. D. Knowles's *The Monastic Order in England* (1940), R. G. Usher's *The Rise and Fall of High Commission* (1913), and W. K. Jordan's four-volume *Development of Religious Toleration in England* (1932–1940). For the

Church of Scotland the brief *The Kirk in Scotland, 1558–1929* (1930) will be found useful. For dissent see H. S. Skeats's *History of the Free Churches* (1868). For the question of the founding or not of the Church of England the two best accounts seem to be those in the *Catholic Encyclopedia*, article "Anglican Orders," and W. Nes, *The Breach with Rome*. C. Stephenson and F. G. Marcham, *Sources of English Church History* (1937), can provide source documents. Robert F. Wearmouth's *Methodism and the Working Class Movements* (1937) throws light on an important aspect of British history. Into the more polemical parts of British religious history the compiler does not tread, except to suggest that those convinced by Cardinal Gasquet's arguments should read Professor Coulton and vice versa, remembering that Coulton had the argumentative advantage of the last word.

FOREIGN AFFAIRS

With the exception of general diplomatic histories, such as W. L. Langer's *Diplomacy of Imperialism*, and such special studies as Elaine Windrich's *British Labor's Foreign Policy* (1952), the *Cambridge History of British Foreign Policy*, and Algernon Cecil's *British Foreign Secretaries*, the approach has been biographical. Conyers Read's *Walsingham*, Sir Charles Webster's *Foreign Policy of Castlereagh* and *Foreign Policy of Palmerston*, Lady Gwendolen Cecil's *Salisbury*, and G. M. Trevelyan's *Grey of Falloden* together with Harold Temperley's *Foreign Policy of Canning* cover a long range.

MILITARY AND NAVAL HISTORY

The great source for the British Army up to Cardwell's reforms is Sir John Fortescue's *History of the British Army*, to be supplemented by Firth's *Cromwell's Army* and Oman's *Peninsular War*. For naval history, Callandar's *Naval Side of British History* is an excellent compendium, to be supplemented by David Hannay, *Short History of the British Navy*, in two volumes, and A. T. Mahan's three classics: *The Influence of Sea Power upon History, 1660–1783* (1928), *The Influence of Sea Power upon the French Revolution and Empire* (1898), and *Nelson, the Embodiment of Sea Power* (1900).

BOOKS OF REFERENCE

England is a land of books of reference, where it is easy to "look people up." Burke's *Peerage*, Debrett's *Peerage*, Kelley's *Handbook to the Landed, Titled, and Official Classes*, the *Army List*, the *Navy List*, *Crockford* for the clergy, all contain a surprising amount of incidental information, when used with discretion. Above all, the *Dictionary of National Biography*, written to cover up to the end of the nineteenth century, with supplements now to 1940, is a mine of concise and usually reliable information. A naval biography signed with the initials J. K. L. for Sir John Knox Laughton, for instance, will probably be based on more careful research than many a formal biography. Not all biographies come up to this standard, but most can be trusted.

READING FOR PLEASURE

Both authors of this book have, like many another person, had the experience of picking up a book to read it for pleasure and then finding their historical understanding had been improved as well. Many a student of British history may find this approach beneficial. Below, therefore, are listed a few books the authors know to have worked with them, and to combine in a high degree readability and information. These are not guaranteed to work in every case. The list is not in the least exclusive. But it is hoped that such a list may help to more insight, either through these books or through others.

Much can be learned of Nelson's Royal Navy from C. S. Forrester's "Hornblower" series; of Wellington's Army from his *Gun* and *Rifleman Dodd* (English title, *Death to the French*) and from Georgette Heyer's *Spanish Bride*, the tale of Sir Harry Smith and the Lady for whom Ladysmith was later named. The paradoxes of Ireland are to be found in Lord Dunsany's *Curse of the Wise Woman*. The classic of the Australian Bush is Rolf Bolderwood's *Robbery under Arms*. To see "Empire building" as the "Empire builders" saw it, look at a back file of *Blackwoods*, or take from the shelf a volume of Kipling's later short stories. To know England's fear of Germany in 1913, read Erskine Childers' *Riddle of the Sands*, or Saki's (H. H. Munro's) *When William Came*. Talbot Mundy's *King of the Khyber Rifles* gives the spirit of the Punjab Independent Frontier Force. Dennys Reitz's *Commando* deserves the praise Field Marshall Smuts gave it as the description of the young Boer's attitude to the Briton. Though the list could go on and on, it must close. The idea is worth trying.

The reader will note that these books are light, and that pictures of the British social scene are not included. Many will find profit from such books as Victoria Sackville-West's *The Edwardians*, from the writings of Arnold Bennett, H. G. Wells, Jane Austen, and Charles Dickens, to name at random. Those to whom the Middle Ages are unfamiliar could bring them to life by Charles Kingsley's *Hereward the Wake*, Maurice Hewlett's *Richard Yea and Nay*, Sir Arthur Conan Doyle's *The White Company*, or Robert Louis Stevenson's *Black Arrow*, and then correct any misapprehensions by reading with an aroused interest works on the period. Or they could side-step into this by Laetitia Lyell's *Medieval Post Bag*. But it is the method that is useful, not the particular book used.

INDEX

In order to make this index more useful for reference purposes, certain devices and abbreviations have been used.

Dates of events, lives, reigns, and prime-ministerships have been added in parentheses. Reigns are given in boldface numerals.

Even though peers up to the rank of duke are customarily called Lord, and even though barons are always called Lord except in the most official circumstances, the official titles of nobility are here given; so are family names, needed when referring to the *Dictionary of National Biography,* and numbers in inheritance, needed when referring to *Burke's Peerage* and to *Webster's Biographical Dictionary.*

B. = Battle

court. = peer's son holding courtesy title and eligible for membership in House of Commons

cr. = title of peerage created during holder's life

d. = died

k. = king

PM = Prime Minister

q. = queen

A

Aberdeen, George Hamilton Gordon, 4th Earl of (1794–1860, PM 1852–1855), 435, 436, 443–445, 447–449

Abukir or Nile (B. 1798), 252, 319, 329, 332, 358

Acre or St. Jean d'Acre, sieges of (1191), 50; (1799), 329; (1840), 442

Addington, Henry, *cr.* Visct. Sidmouth (1757–1844, PM 1801–1804), 252, 298, 301, 331

African Company (various names), 120–122, 236, 343, 349

Agriculture, 5, 14, 34, 95, 188, 195, 264–267, 386–389, 493–496, 651–655; experimentation in, 265, 388; government policy for, 495. 653–654 (*see also* Corn Laws); in Ireland, 387, 545; in New Zealand, 471, 572

Agricultural Revolution, 5, 187–188, 193, 195, 256, 263–267

Albany Congress (1754), 243, 247

Albert, Prince of Saxe-Coburg-Gotha (1819–1861, Prince Consort after 1857), 372, 408, 431, 435, 446–447, 455

Alfred (849, **871–899**), 13, 22–24

Allenby, Edmund, *cr.* Visct. (1861–1936), 613, 715–716, 726

Althorp, John Charles Spencer *court.* Visct., later 3rd Earl Spencer (1782–1845), 214, 287, 307–308, 429

Ambrosius Aurelianus (*ca.* 440), 10–11, 67

American Revolution, 124, 190–191, 232–233

Amery, Leopold (1873–), 712, 719, 726

Amiens, Mise of (1264), 57

Angles, 1, 11–12, 16

Anglican Liberties, 38, 48, 94

Anjou, 44–45, 50, 52

Anne (1665, **1702–1714**), 159, 168–169, 171, 179–181, 183, 185, 204–211, 227, 229

Anti-Corn Law League, 423, 432

MEMBERS OF THE COMMONWEALTH OF NATIONS
(Dates at which they secured responsible government)

Great Britain – 1721
New Zealand – 1855
Canada (Dominion) – 1867
Australia (Commonwealth) – 1901
South Africa (Union) – 1909
Eire, Dominion in 1921, left
  Commonwealth in 1949

Pakistan – 1947
India – 1947 (Republic but still
  member of Commonwealth)
Ceylon – 1948
Southern Rhodesia – 1923
Newfoundland – 1851, became
  Province of Canada 1949

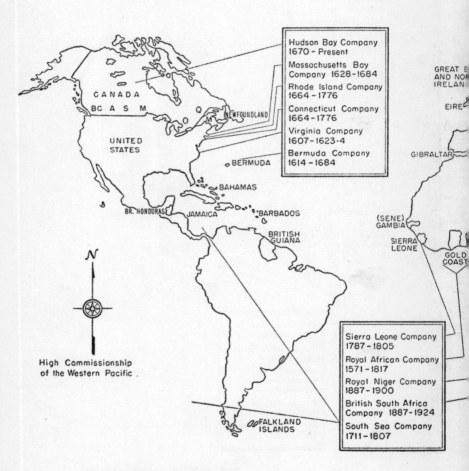

Hudson Bay Company 1670 – Present
Massachusetts Bay Company 1628 – 1684
Rhode Island Company 1664 – 1776
Connecticut Company 1664 – 1776
Virginia Company 1607 – 1623-4
Bermuda Company 1614 – 1684

Sierra Leone Company 1787 – 1805
Royal African Company 1571 – 1817
Royal Niger Company 1887 – 1900
British South Africa Company 1887 – 1924
South Sea Company 1711 – 1807

High Commissionship of the Western Pacific

PROVINCES OF CANADA

BC – British Columbia
A – Alberta
S – Saskatchewan
M – Manitoba
Q – Quebec

M – The Maritimes (Prince
  Edward Island, New
  Brunswick, Nova Scotia)
O – Ontario